About the author

JAMES HALLIDAY is Australia's most respected wine writer. Over the past 30-plus years he has worn many hats: lawyer, winemaker and grapegrower, wine judge, wine consultant, journalist and author. He has discarded his legal hat, but actively continues in his other roles, incessantly travelling, researching and tasting wines in all the major wine-producing countries. He judges regularly at wine shows in Australia, Europe, the US, South Africa and New Zealand.

James Halliday has written or contributed to more than 50 books on wine since he began writing in 1979 (notable contributions include those to the *Oxford Companion to Wine* and the *Larousse Encyclopedia of Wine*). His books have been translated into Japanese, French, German, Danish and Icelandic, and have been published in the UK and the US as well as Australia.

His works include *Varietal Wines*, *Classic Wines of Australia and New Zealand* (3rd edition) and *Wine Odyssey: A Year of Wine, Food and Travel*.

James Halliday

AUSTRALIAN WINE COMPANION

2006

BESTSELLING GUIDE TO AUSTRALIAN WINES

COMPLETELY REVISED & UPDATED

Collins

Collins

An imprint of HarperCollins*Publishers*

First published as Australia and New Zealand Wine Companion in Australia in 1997
This edition first published in Australia in 2005
by HarperCollinsPublishers Australia Pty Limited
ABN 36 009 913 517
www.harpercollins.com.au

Published in the United Kingdom in 2005
by Collins
Collins is a registered trademark of HarperCollinsPublishers Ltd
The Collins website address is www.collins.co.uk

HarperCollins*Publishers*

25 Ryde Road, Pymble, Sydney, NSW 2073, Australia
31 View Road, Glenfield, Auckland 10, New Zealand
77–85 Fulham Palace Road, London W6 8JB, United Kingdom
2 Bloor Street East, 20th floor, Toronto, Ontario M4W 1A8, Canada
10 East 53rd Street, New York NY 10022, USA

ISBN 0 7322 8072 9 (Australia)
ISBN 0 00 721702 1 (UK)
ISSN 1448-3564

A catalogue record for this book is available from the British Library.

Cover design by Jenny Grigg
Internal design by de Luxe & Associates
Preliminary pages typeset by Katy Wright, HarperCollins Design Studio
Body text typeset by Kirby Jones in Miller Text 9/10
Printed and bound in Australia by Griffin Press on 60gsm Bulky Paperback White

6 5 4 3   06

Contents

INTRODUCTION — 6

WINE REGIONS OF AUSTRALIA — 8

AUSTRALIA'S GEOGRAPHICAL INDICATIONS — 10

GRAPE VARIETY PLANTINGS — 13

AUSTRALIAN VINTAGE 2005: A SNAPSHOT — 16

AUSTRALIAN VINTAGE CHART — 20

BEST OF THE BEST OF AUSTRALIAN WINE 2006 — 23

   Best of the best by variety — 24

   Special value wines — 35

   Ten of the best new wineries — 37

   Best wineries of the regions — 39

   Ten dark horses — 41

WINE AND FOOD OR FOOD AND WINE? — 43

ON CORKS AND SCREWCAPS — 46

HOW TO USE THE *COMPANION* — 49

A NOTE ON TASTING TERMS — 53

AUSTRALIAN WINERIES AND WINES 2005 — 57

ACKNOWLEDGMENTS — 659

INDEX OF WINERIES (BY REGION) — 661

Introduction

For the first time, there are more than 2000 wineries in this book, and there are almost 1000 more wines rated than in last year's edition. Necessity has kept the increase in the number of pages to a minimum; space has been saved in a number of ways, most significantly the deletion of the 'product range' in each winery entry.

The apparent slowdown in the birth rate of new wineries (down from 377 last year to 172 this year) has to be put in context. First, the number of Australian wineries in the 2000 edition of the *Companion* was only 1000, give or take a few. So the total growth achieved over 175 years of wine growing between 1825 and 2000 was equalled in the following 6 years.

Second, a reality check strongly suggested it would be counterproductive to go chasing the details of several hundred additional wineries I know are out there. Paperback books of this size must have a finite page number if they are to stand up to repeated reading.

Thus the day is fast approaching when there will be some criterion for entry, even if it is as basic as whether or not a winery responds to the annual survey form which I send to every new, existing or suspected winery. The number of tasting notes and ratings may also have to be circumscribed.

On the good news side is the inclusion of website addresses for the first time; some will be under construction, others outdated, but the majority contain valuable additional information which – for obvious reasons – cannot be included in a book such as this.

In the bigger picture, the industry continues to grow. Updated figures from the Australian Bureau of Statistics show the following plantings since 1997:

	1997	1998	1999	2000	2001	2002	2003	2004
Hectares	89,797	98,612	122,915	139,861	148,257	158,594	157,492	164,181
Tonnes	707,992	975,669	1,125,840	1,342,814	1,423,950	1,605,846	1,398,528	1,816,556
Production (million L)	580.8	695.2	811.4	824.4	1052.9	1195.2	1059.4	1424.2
Domestic Sales ($m)					1830.9	1946.3	2097.9	1970.9
Exports ($m)	603.2	873.7	1068.0	1372.7	1751.8	2105.2	2423.5	2591.1
Exports (million L)	154.4	192.4	200.9	284.9	338.3	418.4	518.6	584.4

(Figures for domestic sales in dollar terms for the years 1997 to 2000 are not available.)

This statistical snapshot shows an industry increasingly – and so far very successfully – dependent on exports. But it does have an agricultural base, with long lead times juxtaposed against fickle seasonal growing conditions and a currency which has strengthened ominously against the US dollar. Thus the oversupply of some grapes, notably cabernet sauvignon, in the 2005 vintage, and falling grape prices across the board, is hardly surprising. But while the size of the 2004 and 2005 vintages may not please everyone, the overall quality from these two years is well above average across most of the multitude of regions and varieties. By rights, many lovely wines at mouthwatering prices should come your way over the next year.

Wine regions of Australia

Key to regions

1 Lower Hunter Valley
2 Upper Hunter Valley
3 Hastings River
4 Mudgee
5 Orange
6 Cowra
7 Swan Hill
8 Murray Darling
9 Riverina
10 Perricoota
11 Hilltops
12 Canberra District
13 Gundagai
14 Tumbarumba
15 Shoalhaven
16 Henty
17 Grampians
18 Pyrenees
19 Ballarat
20 Bendigo
21 Heathcote
22 Goulburn Valley
23 Nagambie lakes
24 Upper Goulburn
25 Rutherglen and Glenrowan
26 King Valley
27 Alpine Valleys and Beechworth
28 Gippsland
29 Mornington Peninsula
30 Yarra Valley
31 Geelong
32 Sunbury
33 Macedon Ranges
34 Northern Tasmania
35 Southern Tasmania
36 Mount Gambier
37 Coonawarra
38 Wrattonbully
39 Mount Benson
40 Padthaway
41 Langhorne Creek
42 McLaren Vale
43 Kangaroo Island
44 Southern Fleurieu Peninsula
45 Adelaide Hills
46 Eden Valley
47 Adelaide Plains

48 Barossa Valley
49 Riverland
50 Clare Valley
51 Southern Eyre Peninsula
52 Great Southern
53 Pemberton and Manjimup
54 Blackwood Valley
55 Margaret River
56 Geographe
57 Peel
58 Perth Hills
59 Swan District
60 South Burnett
61 Queensland Coastal
62 Granite Belt

WA

59 **Perth**
58
57
56
55 54
53 52

NT

QLD

SA

NSW

60
61
Brisbane ●
61
62
61

3
2
4
1
5
6
Sydney ●

50
48
46
47 45
51
Adelaide ●
42
43 44 41
49
8
7
9
13
11
12
ACT

40
38
39
37
36
16
10
18 20
17   21
24
19 33
22
25
23 26
32
27
30
14
15

31
Melbourne ●
29
28

VIC

34
TAS
35
● **Hobart**

0   250   500 km

N

Australia's geographical indications

The process of formally mapping Australia's wine regions continues to ever-so-slowly inch forward. The division into zones, regions and subregions follows; those regions or subregions marked with an asterisk are variously in an early or late stage of determination. In two instances I have gone beyond the likely finalisation: it makes no sense to me that the Hunter Valley should be a zone, the region Hunter, and then subregions which are all in the Lower Hunter Valley. I have elected to stick with the traditional division between the Upper Hunter Valley on the one hand, and the Lower on the other.

I am also in front of the game with Tasmania, dividing it into Northern, Southern and East Coast and, to a lesser degree, have anticipated that the Coastal Hinterland Region of Queensland will seek recognition under this or some similar name. Those regions and subregions marked with an asterisk have taken, or are likely to take, steps to secure registration; they may or may not persevere.

Zone	Region	Subregion
VICTORIA		
Central Victoria	Bendigo Goulburn Valley Heathcote Strathbogie Ranges Upper Goulburn	Nagambie Lakes
Gippsland		
North East Victoria	Alpine Valleys	Kiewa Valley* Ovens Valley*
	Beechworth Glenrowan King Valley* Rutherglen	Myrrhee* Whitlands* Wahgunyah*
North West Victoria	Murray Darling Swan Hill	
Port Phillip	Geelong Macedon Ranges Mornington Peninsula Sunbury Yarra Valley	
Western Victoria	Grampians Henty Pyrenees	

Zone	Region	Subregion
NEW SOUTH WALES		
Big Rivers	Murray Darling Perricoota Riverina Swan Hill	
Central Ranges	Cowra Mudgee Orange	
Hunter Valley	Hunter	Allandale* Belford* Broke Fordwich Dalwood* Pokolbin* Rothbury*
Northern Rivers	Hastings River	
Northern Slopes		
South Coast	Shoalhaven Coast Southern Highlands New England*	
Southern NSW	Canberra District Gundagai Hilltops Tumbarumba	
Western Plains		
WESTERN AUSTRALIA		
Central Western Australia		
Eastern Plains, Inland and North of WA		
Greater Perth	Peel Perth Hills Swan District	Swan Valley
South West Australia	Blackwood Valley Geographe Great Southern	Albany Denmark Frankland River Mount Barker Porongurup
	Manjimup* Margaret River Pemberton*	
WA South East Coastal	Esperance	

Zone	Region	Subregion
SOUTH AUSTRALIA		
Adelaide (Super Zone, above Mount Lofty Ranges, Fleurieu and Barossa)		
Barossa	Barossa Valley	
	Eden Valley	High Eden
		Springton*
Far North	Southern Flinders Ranges	
Fleurieu	Currency Creek	
	Kangaroo Island	
	Langhorne Creek	
	McLaren Vale	Clarendon*
	Southern Fleurieu Peninsula	
Limestone Coast	Coonawarra	
	Mount Benson	
	Penola*	
	Padthaway	
	Wrattonbully*	
Lower Murray	Riverland	
Mount Lofty Ranges	Adelaide Hills	Gumeracha*
		Lenswood
		Piccadilly Valley
	Adelaide Plains	
	Clare Valley	Auburn*
		Clare*
		Hill River*
		Polish Hill River*
		Sevenhill*
		Watervale*
The Peninsulas	Southern Eyre Peninsula*	
QUEENSLAND		
Queensland	Granite Belt	
	Coastal Hinterland*	
	South Burnett	
TASMANIA		
Tasmania	Northern Tasmania*	
	Southern Tasmania*	
	East Coast Tasmania*	
AUSTRALIAN CAPTIAL TERRITORY		
NORTHERN TERRITORY		

Grape variety plantings

The 2004 vintage of 1.81 million tonnes was by far the largest in Australia's history, the increase of well over 35 per cent above the 2003 vintage magnified by the lower than normal yields in 2003. At the time of going to print, it seemed likely the 2005 crush would be of similar size, and cause all involved in the growing, making and marketing of wine continuing pain until stocks of bulk and bottled wine come back to normal levels.

The increase in plantings, while in one sense surprising, is of insufficient size to cause problems, given the lag time before the vines come into production. The medium-term outlook, indeed, is for grape shortages to reappear as exports continue to grow notwithstanding the much weaker US dollar.

The foregoing apart, it seems the 40 per cent white, 60 per cent red mix of plantings (the reverse of the split as recently as 1999) is in balance with medium-term, and perhaps longer-term, demand.

	1997	1998	1999
CHARDONNAY hectares tonnes	13,713 119,678	14,662 148,515	16,855 210,770
RIESLING hectares tonnes	3,423 32,907	3,345 33,811	3,347 30,144
SAUVIGNON BLANC hectares tonnes	1,725 13,328	1,904 18,405	2,413 22,834
SEMILLON hectares tonnes	4,803 52,829	5,287 57,112	6,044 80,191
OTHER WHITE hectares tonnes	27,047 265,288	25,566 271,620	26,331 282,459
TOTAL WHITE **hectares** **tonnes**	**50,711** **484,030**	**50,764** **529,463**	**54,990** **626,398**
CABERNET SAUVIGNON hectares tonnes	11,219 67,015	14,695 91,876	21,169 127,494
GRENACHE hectares tonnes	2,014 24,198	1,988 23,842	2,255 24,196
MOURVEDRE hectares tonnes	614 7,629	696 8,238	866 9,217
MERLOT hectares tonnes	2,461 10,331	3,802 13,881	6,387 31,801
PINOT NOIR hectares tonnes	1,896 13,924	2,192 19,123	2,996 19,668
SHIRAZ hectares tonnes	13,410 94,848	17,930 131,427	25,596 192,330
OTHER RED hectares tonnes	6,149 34,503	6,372 38,224	8,656 45,103
TOTAL RED **hectares** **tonnes**	**37,763** **252,448**	**47,675** **326,611**	**67,925** **449,809**
TOTAL GRAPES **hectares** **tonnes**	**88,474** **736,478**	**98,439** **856,074**	**122,915** **1,076,207**
PERCENTAGE (TONNES) **White** **Red**	**65.73%** **34.27%**	**61.85%** **38.15%**	**59.21%** **41.79%**

2000	2001	2002	2003	2004
18,526	18,434	21,724	24,138	28,008
201,248	245,199	256,328	233,747	311,273
3,658	3,558	3,962	3,987	4,255
26,800	26,980	27,838	28,994	36,404
2,706	2,766	2,914	2,953	3,425
21,487	25,326	28,567	21,028	39,774
6,832	6,803	6,610	6,283	6,278
77,506	88,427	100,785	77,096	99,237
27,873	25,781	26,215	24,700	23,925
265,196	232,334	255,253	196,209	266,794
59,595	**57,342**	**61,425**	**62,051**	**65,891**
592,237	**618,266**	**666,771**	**557,074**	**753,482**
26,674	28,609	29,573	28,171	29,313
159,358	249,288	257,223	225,723	319,955
2,756	2,427	2,528	2,322	2,292
23,998	22,563	26,260	19,866	24,987
1,147	1,128	1,238	1,092	1,040
10,496	11,624	12,452	11,822	13,992
8,575	9,330	10,101	10,352	10,804
51,269	80,142	104,423	92,865	123,944
3,756	4,142	4,414	4,270	4,424
19,578	29,514	21,341	27,949	41,690
32,327	33,676	37,031	37,106	39,182
224,394	311,045	326,564	309,000	436,691
11,347	11,621	12,284	12,268	11,235
57,255	68,640	99,467	85,297	101,816
86,582	**90,933**	**97,169**	**95,491**	**98,290**
546,348	**772,816**	**847,730**	**772,522**	**1,063,075**
146,177	**148,275**	**158,594**	**157,492**	**164,181**
1,138,585	**1,391,082**	**1,514,501**	**1,329,596**	**1,816,556**
52.02%	**44.45%**	**44.02%**	**41.90%**	**41.48%**
47.98%	**55.55%**	**55.98%**	**58.10%**	**58.52%**

Australian vintage 2005: a snapshot

The last forecast for the 2005 vintage made prior to its commencement was 1,820,000 tonnes, an increase on the November 2004 estimate of 1,730,000 tonnes. If the final forecast proves correct, it will result in a crush equal to that of 2004, and keep downwards pressure on grape and wine prices, good news for the consumer. Equally good news is the overall quality in most regions following adequate winter rain and generally favourable growing conditions through summer.

New South Wales

Both the **LOWER HUNTER** and **UPPER HUNTER** beat the odds by having most rain when needed (in the winter months) with only 70mm in late February causing concern for those who had not finished picking. Lower-yielding vineyards will produce very good whites from the main three varieties (semillon, chardonnay and verdelho), Shiraz being more variable – some good, some not so good.

MUDGEE set the scene for much of the western slopes of the Great Dividing Range, with a generally cool growing season promoting even ripening. Intermittent rainfall during harvest presented problems, but the quality of Chardonnay, Shiraz and Cabernet Sauvignon will be well above average. As it did last year, **ORANGE** went even better, with good crops and high quality. The **SOUTHERN HIGHLANDS** also experienced even ripening conditions producing disease-free grapes with good flavour intensity and length.

Further south, the **HILLTOPS** had to contend with some rain, but it was **COWRA** which struggled most with an unhappy combination of big crops, rain and hail causing disease and ripening problems in some vineyards. Further south still, **TUMBARUMBA** had an excellent vintage, low-yielding chardonnay the standout.

At the opposite end of the state the nascent **NEW ENGLAND** (Northern Slopes Zone) region experienced very good weather conditions leading up to and through harvest; the reds will be excellent, the whites very good.

Finally, the important **RIVERINA** region had problems with rainfall and above-average crops with some varieties; this was largely offset by the benefit of a cooler than normal growing season.

Victoria

Overall, the state looks set to have one of its very best years. In Central Victoria, **GRAMPIANS**, **PYRENEES**, **BENDIGO** and **HEATHCOTE** finally got the winter rain to back up 2004 and end the drought sequence, followed by ideal growing and ripening conditions through to the autumn harvest – which took place on average two weeks earlier than 2004. In a pattern repeated throughout Victoria and much of South Australia, natural acidity was so high that acid adjustment (even at high baume levels) was seldom required. All these regions are confident that the outcome will be elegant wines, with great finesse. If it were possible, **HENTY**, in the far southwest, had an even better vintage: sheer perfection.

In southern Victoria, the **YARRA VALLEY**, **MORNINGTON PENINSULA**, **SUNBURY**, the **MACEDON RANGES** and **GEELONG** all shared good winter rains, with follow-up rainfall during spring through to January, sometimes heavy, with the result that irrigation was barely necessary. Ideal weather through the second half of February until well into April meant an early vintage, the low to moderate crops of chardonnay and pinot noir a welcome change from 2004, and boding well for quality. If there is a question about the vintage, it is that chemical ripening outran flavour ripening; high acidity and high baume did not necessarily mean the best outcome.

Finally, **RUTHERGLEN** had every reason to be pleased with its table wines; it was a mixed bag for the fortifieds, Tokay suffering from rot, the Muscat, by contrast, very good. **BEECHWORTH** had a late but high-quality vintage, which may prove to be even better than 2002.

South Australia

The **BAROSSA VALLEY** had a much cooler than normal vintage, with rainfall in mid to late January and February boosting the yields of the white varieties. However, the absence of any stress in the vines meant full ripening with excellent acidity levels; all are agreed it is a top white vintage, and good to very good for the mainstream red varieties, with the likelihood of elegant, medium-bodied wines, not up to 2004. The **CLARE VALLEY** reversed the Barossa pattern for red wines, being better than 2004, with strong varietal character and full fruit flavour. The cool nights and moderate, even daytime temperatures have resulted in outstanding Riesling, particularly from Watervale and Polish Hill River. The **EDEN VALLEY** looks set to make wines close to the 2002 vintage in quality, with perfect natural acidity and intense fruit flavour. The only question for the **ADELAIDE HILLS** is whether chemical ripening outpaced flavour development; it was a compressed vintage with all varieties ripening more or less at the same time. This to one side, the prospects are very good indeed.

MCLAREN VALE had a relatively late vintage due to the cool, stress-free ripening conditions. For the white wines the only question is whether 2004 or 2005 will prove to be the superior year. The reds – Shiraz, Grenache and Cabernet Sauvignon – hung on at low fruit ripeness before suddenly surging to high sugar levels; the fleet of foot will produce the best outcomes. A similar pattern was experienced in the SOUTHERN FLEURIEU and LANGHORNE CREEK regions, with high natural acidity giving vibrant fruit flavours across the range.

The Limestone Coast regions of COONAWARRA, PADTHAWAY, MOUNT BENSON and ROBE had ideal weather from January through to April, with average daily maximums of 25°C and almost no rain to contend with (40 per cent down on the long-term average). Average yields after the excesses of 2004 were another cause for comfort, and the earlier than usual vintage was an almost inevitable outcome. The only question is: just how good will the vintage be?

The RIVERLAND had an unusually cool December and January (after earlier rainfall and hail); low vine stress led to an early start to vintage. Chardonnay, with very good acid balance, was the pick of the whites; Semillon and Sauvignon Blanc were not up to expectations. The red wines, with exceptional colour, did not achieve flavour ripeness until high baume levels were reached, acidity once again delaying ripening.

Western Australia

MARGARET RIVER had a warm, mild and humid growing season, but without any significant rainfall until the end of March, when an unusual burst of 75mm of rain fell. Most of the white varieties had been harvested prior to the rain, and the overall quality is significantly better than 2004 in the vineyards which did not overcrop. Chardonnay will be the star (no surprise), but Sauvignon Blanc has the vibrancy and punch lacking in 2004, and Semillon is reliably good. The disappointment is Merlot, upset by the rain and struggling for maturity; spicy Shiraz and strong Cabernet Sauvignon fared much better.

GREAT SOUTHERN is a vast region, strongly maritime in ALBANY and DENMARK (two of its subregions), but much more continental in PORONGURUP, FRANKLAND RIVER and MOUNT BARKER. But there was a common pattern, with a warm and very dry lead-up to vintage leaving the fruit in impeccable condition. All continued without a hitch until an unprecedented storm hit the region in early April, dumping between 150mm and 300mm of rain following three abnormally hot days. Prior to this, all the white varieties had been harvested; they will produce excellent wine. Many growers, knowing the storm was approaching (satellite forecasts five days out have changed many things), raced to pick as much red grape as winery fermentation capacity could handle. The blocks left unpicked will have little hope of making wine equal to that made before the storm.

Tasmania

In some years Tasmania breaks step with the southern mainland, but not in 2005. Here, too, the summer was very cool and dry in both **NORTHERN** and **SOUTHERN TASMANIA**, but paradoxically did not delay the start of harvest nor lead to excessively high acidity. Pinot Noir is outstanding, looking every bit as good as the benchmark 2000 vintage, perhaps even better for some makers. Chardonnay and Riesling are not far behind; this will be a year to remember.

Queensland

One vigneron in the **GRANITE BELT** summed up the vintage by observing, 'Global Warming has been good for us.' After a good start to the season, with average rainfall through to the end of November building on rain earlier in the year, the **GRANITE BELT** entered its driest February in 130 years, and conditions remained good through to the end of harvest in April. While Shiraz and Cabernet Sauvignon are the standouts, with sugars up to 14.5° baume, white wine quality is also very promising, helped by the absence of any extreme heat at any stage during the summer.

SOUTH BURNETT also had 'a dream run for a viticultural region which expects at least one harvest interruption from a monsoonal downpour'. After a warm, dry spring, the first rain in early December was welcome, the only significant fall of 100mm following in mid-January. February was quite hot (30°C to 33°C) and dry, pushing up Merlot, Shiraz and Cabernet Sauvignon to full ripeness in early March, when vintage concluded in ideal conditions.

Australian vintage chart

Each number represents a mark out of ten for the quality
of vintages in each region; '-' denotes no rating.

■ RED   ▨ WHITE

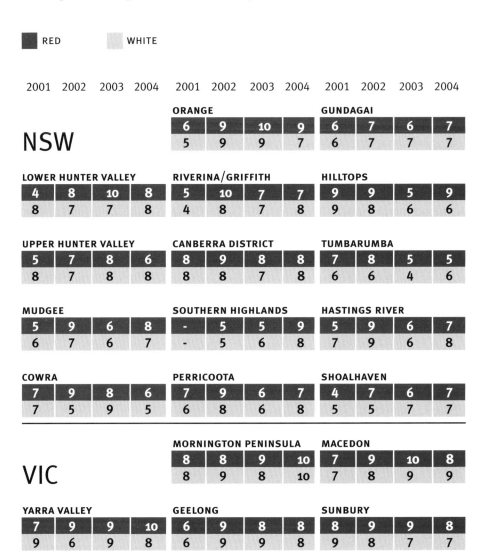

NSW

Region	2001	2002	2003	2004
ORANGE (Red)	6	9	10	9
ORANGE (White)	5	9	9	7
GUNDAGAI (Red)	6	7	6	7
GUNDAGAI (White)	6	7	7	7
LOWER HUNTER VALLEY (Red)	4	8	10	8
LOWER HUNTER VALLEY (White)	8	7	7	8
RIVERINA/GRIFFITH (Red)	5	10	7	7
RIVERINA/GRIFFITH (White)	4	8	7	8
HILLTOPS (Red)	9	9	5	9
HILLTOPS (White)	9	8	6	6
UPPER HUNTER VALLEY (Red)	5	7	8	6
UPPER HUNTER VALLEY (White)	8	7	8	8
CANBERRA DISTRICT (Red)	8	9	8	8
CANBERRA DISTRICT (White)	8	8	7	8
TUMBARUMBA (Red)	7	8	5	5
TUMBARUMBA (White)	6	6	4	6
MUDGEE (Red)	5	9	6	8
MUDGEE (White)	6	7	6	7
SOUTHERN HIGHLANDS (Red)	-	5	5	9
SOUTHERN HIGHLANDS (White)	-	5	6	8
HASTINGS RIVER (Red)	5	9	6	7
HASTINGS RIVER (White)	7	9	6	8
COWRA (Red)	7	9	8	6
COWRA (White)	7	5	9	5
PERRICOOTA (Red)	7	9	6	7
PERRICOOTA (White)	6	8	6	8
SHOALHAVEN (Red)	4	7	6	7
SHOALHAVEN (White)	5	5	7	7

VIC

Region	2001	2002	2003	2004
MORNINGTON PENINSULA (Red)	8	8	9	10
MORNINGTON PENINSULA (White)	8	9	8	10
MACEDON (Red)	7	9	10	8
MACEDON (White)	7	8	9	9
YARRA VALLEY (Red)	7	9	9	10
YARRA VALLEY (White)	9	6	9	8
GEELONG (Red)	6	9	8	8
GEELONG (White)	6	9	9	8
SUNBURY (Red)	8	9	9	8
SUNBURY (White)	9	8	7	7

	2001	2002	2003	2004
GRAMPIANS				
	8	7	9	10
	7	7	8	6
PYRENEES				
	9	8	8	10
	7	8	6	9
HENTY				
	6	8	7	9
	5	8	10	9
BENDIGO				
	9	9	7	9
	6	7	6	9
HEATHCOTE				
	8	9	8	10
	7	8	6	9

	2001	2002	2003	2004
GOULBURN VALLEY				
	8	9	8	9
	7	8	6	7
UPPER GOULBURN				
	7	9	7	7
	7	7	6	7
STRATHBOGIE RANGES				
	-	8	8	8
	-	8	7	8
GLENROWAN & RUTHERGLEN				
	7	10	9	9
	6	9	7	6
KING VALLEY				
	6	10	7	8
	7	9	8	9

	2001	2002	2003	2004
ALPINE VALLEYS				
	6	9	4	9
	8	8	4	9
BEECHWORTH				
	-	8	8	10
	-	7	6	8
GIPPSLAND				
	8	5	7	10
	7	5	6	9
MURRAY DARLING				
	5	9	7	7
	5	8	6	7

SA

	2001	2002	2003	2004
CLARE VALLEY				
	7	10	8	9
	9	10	10	8
BAROSSA VALLEY				
	8	10	7	8
	5	8	7	7
EDEN VALLEY				
	9	9	7	8
	8	10	9	9

	2001	2002	2003	2004
COONAWARRA				
	8	9	9	7
	7	8	8	6
ADELAIDE HILLS				
	8	9	8	8
	8	9	8	7
PADTHAWAY				
	8	9	8	7
	7	9	9	7

	2001	2002	2003	2004
ADELAIDE PLAINS				
	8	9	6	8
	7	8	7	7
MOUNT BENSON & ROBE				
	5	9	8	7
	7	9	9	8

	2001	2002	2003	2004		2001	2002	2003	2004		2001	2002	2003	2004
WRATTONBULLY	6	8	7	4	**SOUTHERN FLEURIEU**	7	8	7	7	**KANGAROO ISLAND**	7	7	7	8
	6	7	8	7		6	8	7	8		6	6	7	7
McLAREN VALE	7	9	8	8	**LANGHORNE CREEK**	7	9	8	8	**RIVERLAND**	5	10	8	8
	5	8	7	7		8	7	7	7		6	9	9	8

WA

	2001	2002	2003	2004		2001	2002	2003	2004
MANJIMUP	9	7	6	9	**SWAN DISTRICT**	9	10	7	9
	8	8	6	5		6	9	6	7
MARGARET RIVER	8	8	8	9	**PEMBERTON**	8	7	6	8	**PEEL**	-	8	8	8
	8	8	8	8		8	8	7	8		-	9	8	7
GREAT SOUTHERN	9	8	7	7	**GEOGRAPHE**	6	7	8	9	**PERTH HILLS**	6	9	7	9
	8	8	6	8		9	9	8	9		8	8	8	7

QLD

	2001	2002	2003	2004		2001	2002	2003	2004
GRANITE BELT	8	9	8	7	**SOUTH BURNETT**	7	8	8	6
	7	8	7	9		6	8	8	6

TAS

	2001	2002	2003	2004		2001	2002	2003	2004
NORTHERN TASMANIA	8	9	7	6	**SOUTHERN TASMANIA**	8	9	8	7
	8	9	7	8		8	9	7	8

Best of the best of Australian wine 2006

I make my usual disclaimer: while there were two periods of intense tasting activity in the 12 months during which the tasting notes for this edition were made, and while some wines were tasted more than once, an over-arching comparative tasting of all the best wines was and is simply not possible, however desirable it might be.

So the points for the individual wines scoring 94 or above stand uncorrected by the wisdom of hindsight. Nonetheless, the link between variety and region (or, if you prefer, between variety and terroir) is in most instances strikingly evident. It is for this reason that I have shown the region for each of the best wines. Those critics – particularly in the United Kingdom – who wish to consign Australian wine to the industrial waste bin might care to think again.

Best of the best by variety

Riesling

The 2004 vintage was not in the same overall class for Clare Valley and Eden Valley as 2003 and 2002, but many of the best makers came through regardless. On the other hand, it opened up the field for the other classic riesling regions, most notably Great Southern, Tasmania and Henty.

96	**2004 Grosset Polish Hill Riesling** (Clare Valley)
96	**1997 Paulett Polish Hill River Aged Release Riesling** (Clare Valley)
96	**2000 Pewsey Vale Museum Release Contours Riesling** (Eden Valley)
96	**2004 Crawford River Riesling** (Henty)
96	**2004 Seppelt Drumborg Riesling** (Henty)
96	**1998 Moorilla Estate Riesling** (Tasmania)
95	**2004 Leasingham Bin 7 Riesling** (Clare Valley)
95	**2004 McWilliam's Clare Valley Riesling** (Clare Valley)
95	**2004 Stringy Brae Riesling** (Clare Valley)
95	**2000 Taylors St Andrews Riesling** (Clare Valley)
95	**2004 Wilson Vineyard Polish Hill River Riesling** (Clare Valley)
95	**2004 Howard Park Riesling** (Denmark)
95	**2004 MadFish Riesling** (Great Southern)
95	**2004 Bay of Fires Tigress Riesling** (Tasmania)
95	**2004 Wellington Riesling** (Tasmania)
94	**2003 Annie's Lane Copper Trail Riesling, 2004 Barretts Riesling, 2000 Byrne & Smith Ardent Estates Eden Valley Riesling, 2004 Domain Day Riesling, 2004 Frankland Estate Isolation Ridge Riesling, 2004 Freycinet Riesling, 2004 Gibraltar Rock Porongurup Riesling, 2004 Gilberts Mount Barker Riesling, 2004 Granite Hills Knight Riesling, 2004 Grosset Watervale Riesling, 2004 Harewood Estate Mount Barker Riesling, 2004 Humbug Reach Vineyard Riesling, 2004 Kilikanoon Mort's Block Reserve Riesling, 2004 Knappstein Ackland Vineyard Watervale Riesling, 2004 Knappstein Hand Picked Riesling, 2004 Leo Buring Leonay Riesling, 2004 Moores Hill Estate Riesling, 2004 Neagles Rock Vineyards Frisky Filly Reserve Clare Valley Riesling, 2004 O'Leary Walker Watervale Riesling, 2003 Patrick T The Caves Vineyard Riesling, 2004 Petaluma Hanlin Hill Riesling, 2000 Peter Lehmann Eden Valley Reserve Riesling, 2002 Pewsey Vale The Contours Eden Valley Riesling, 2004 Pikes The Merle Reserve Riesling, 2002 Pooley Coal River Riesling, 2004 Riddells Creek Amee Alyce Riesling, 2001 Rockford Eden Valley Riesling, 2004 Sevenhill Cellars Riesling, 2004 Shaw & Smith Riesling, 2004 Trevelen Farm Riesling, 2004 Wilson Vineyard DJW Riesling.**

Semillon

A select list, as ever, dominated by the Hunter Valley; the Margaret River and Adelaide Hills are the only other regions with more than one wine. A pointer to the future may be Peter Lehmann's Reserve Eden Valley joining the three aged-release specialists, of Brokenwood ILR Reserve, McWilliam's Lovedale and Tyrrell's.

96	2000 **Brokenwood ILR Reserve Semillon** (Hunter Valley)
96	1999 **McWilliam's Mount Pleasant Lovedale Semillon** (Hunter Valley)
95	2000 **Penfolds Reserve Bin Semillon** (Adelaide Hills)
95	1999 **Peter Lehmann Reserve Semillon** (Eden Valley)
95	2004 **Keith Tulloch Semillon** (Hunter Valley)
95	2004 **Rockfield Estate Semillon** (Margaret River)
95	2004 **Vasse Felix Semillon** (Margaret River)
94	2004 **Braydon Estate Home Paddock Hunter Valley Semillon**, 2002 **Burge Family Olive Hill Semillon**, 1999 **Capercaillie Hunter Valley Semillon**, 2004 **Chain of Ponds The Red Semi Semillon**, 2004 **Colvin De Beyers Vineyard Hunter Valley Semillon**, 2004 **Kulkunbulla The Glandore Semillon**, 2004 **Lowe Family Hunter Valley Semillon**, 2004 **Merum Pemberton Semillon**, 2004 **Mountview Reserve Semillon**, 2003 **Palandri Baldivis Estate Semillon**, 2004 **Pothana Belford Hunter Valley Semillon**, 2004 **Somerset Hill Semillon**, 2004 **Tatler Nigel's Hunter Valley Semillon**, 2004 **Tower Estate Hunter Valley Semillon**, 1998 **Tyrrell's Belford Semillon**, 2000 **Tyrrell's Stevens Reserve Semillon**.

Sauvignon Blanc and blends — and a few others

Once again, cool regions dominate proceedings for Sauvignon Blanc and Sauvignon Blanc blends. It is only with the handful of Marsannes, Pinot Gris and Viogniers that warmer regions make a guest appearance. To the extent that oak plays any role in this group, its impact is subtle.

95	2004 **Limbic Sauvignon Blanc** (Port Phillip Zone)
94	2004 **Old Kent River Sauvignon Blanc** (Frankland River)
94	2004 **Hackersley Ferguson Valley Sauvignon Blanc** (Geographe)
94	2004 **Willow Bridge Estate Reserve Sauvignon Blanc** (Geographe)
94	2004 **Phillip Island Vineyard Sauvignon Blanc** (Gippsland)
94	2004 **Hanging Rock The Jim Jim Sauvignon Blanc** (Macedon Ranges)
94	2004 **Deep Woods Estate Sauvignon Blanc** (Margaret River)
94	2004 **Port Phillip Estate Sauvignon Blanc** (Mornington Peninsula)
94	2004 **Prince of Orange Sauvignon Blanc** (Orange)

94   **2004 Browns of Padthaway Sauvignon Blanc** (Padthaway)
94   **2004 Wellington Sauvignon Blanc** (Tasmania)
94   **2003 Gembrook Hill Sauvignon Blanc** (Yarra Valley)

95   **2002 Cape Mentelle Walcliffe Sauvignon Blanc Semillon** (Margaret River)
94   **2004 Annvers Semillon Sauvignon Blanc** (Adelaide Hills)
94   **2004 Grosset Semillon Sauvignon Blanc** (Clare Valley)
94   **2004 Harewood Estate Sauvignon Blanc Semillon** (Denmark)
94   **2004 Cullen Semillon Sauvignon Blanc** (Margaret River)
94   **2004 Hay Shed Hill Sauvignon Blanc Semillon** (Margaret River)
94   **2004 Stella Bella Semillon Sauvignon Blanc** (Margaret River)
94   **2001 Voyager Estate Reserve Semillon Sauvignon Blanc** (Margaret River)

95   **2002 Turkey Flat The Last Straw Marsanne** (Barossa Valley)
94   **2003 Petaluma Viognier** (Adelaide Hills)
94   **2004 Tollana Viognier** (Barossa Valley)
94   **2003 Heggies Vineyard Viognier** (Eden Valley)
94   **2004 Irvine Eden Crest Pinot Gris** (Eden Valley)
94   **2004 Seppelt Coborra Drumborg Vineyard Pinot Gris** (Henty)
94   **2003 All Saints Estate Family Cellar Marsanne** (Rutherglen)

Chardonnay

An eclectic selection of Australia's best Chardonnays, embracing both elegant fruit-driven styles and wines of great complexity where the winemaker has pushed the envelope to the maximum extent, consistent, however, with the underlying varietal fruit expression. All but Lake's Folly come from cool regions, led by Margaret River.

97   **2002 Ashbrook Estate Chardonnay** (Margaret River)
96   **2002 Penfolds Yattarna Chardonnay** (Adelaide Hills)
96   **2002 Hardys Eileen Hardy Chardonnay** (Cool climate blend)
96   **2002 Phillip Island Vineyard Chardonnay** (Gippsland)
96   **2003 by Farr Chardonnay by Farr** (Geelong)
96   **2003 Lake's Folly Chardonnay** (Lower Hunter Valley)
96   **2002 Lake's Folly Chardonnay** (Lower Hunter Valley)
96   **2003 Bindi Wine Growers Quartz Chardonnay** (Macedon Ranges)
96   **2003 Howard Park Chardonnay** (Margaret River)
96   **2002 Leeuwin Estate Art Series Chardonnay** (Margaret River)
96   **2003 Voyager Estate Chardonnay** (Margaret River)
96   **2003 The Moorooduc Chardonnay** (Mornington Peninsula)
96   **2001 Canobolas-Smith Orange Chardonnay** (Orange)
96   **2003 Hoddles Creek Estate Chardonnay** (Yarra Valley)
95   **2003 Cape Mentelle Chardonnay, 2002 Capel Vale Frederick Chardonnay, 2003**

De Bortoli Reserve Yarra Valley Chardonnay, 2002 Dromana Estate Reserve Chardonnay, 2003 Eldridge Estate Chardonnay, 2002 Evans & Tate Redbrook Chardonnay, 2003 Smiths Vineyard Flamsteed Beechworth Chardonnay, 2003 Grosset Piccadilly Chardonnay, 2003 Hamelin Bay Five Ashes Reserve Chardonnay, 2002 Hardys Tintara Cellars Chardonnay, 2003 Wellington Chardonnay, 2003 Main Ridge Estate Chardonnay, 2002 Metier Tarraford Vineyard Yarra Valley Chardonnay, 2003 Montalto Vineyards Chardonnay, 2000 No Regrets Vineyard Chardonnay, 2003 Oakridge Chardonnay, 2003 Penfolds Reserve Bin Chardonnay, 2001 Penfolds Yattarna Chardonnay, 2002 Petaluma Tiers Chardonnay, 2003 Pierro Chardonnay, 2002 Scotchmans Hill Sutton Vineyard Chardonnay, 2003 Seppelt Jaluka Drumborg Vineyard Chardonnay, 2003 Shadowfax Chardonnay, 2003 Shaw & Smith M3 Vineyard Chardonnay, 2000 Stonehaven Limited Vineyard Release Padthaway Chardonnay, 2003 Toolangi Vineyards Estate Chardonnay, 2003 Willow Creek Tulum Chardonnay, 2003 Wise Wine Single Vineyard Pemberton Reserve Chardonnay, 2002 Yabby Lake Vineyard Mornington Peninsula Chardonnay.

Sparkling, Sweet and Rose

Tasmania is the new millennium powerhouse for conventional (as opposed to red) sparkling wines, although the coolest mainland regions are represented, and will continue to be so.

96	1999 Hardys Arras (Tasmania)
95	1998 Freycinet Radenti (East Coast Tasmania)
95	1998 Norfolk Rise Vineyard Vintage Brut (Mount Benson)
95	1998 Lake Barrington Estate Alexandra Methode Champenoise (Northern Tasmania)
95	2002 Yarrabank Cuvee (Yarra Valley)
94	2002 Petaluma Croser (Adelaide Hills)
94	2000 Old Kent River Diamontina (Frankland River)
94	2003 Silver Wings Winemaking Grand Reserve Brut XO (Macedon Ranges)
94	2000 Clover Hill (Northern Tasmania)
94	2000 Jansz Premium (Northern Tasmania)
94	2000 Domaine Chandon Z*D (Yarra Valley)

The three best red sparkling wines stand out from a depressing number of failed red table wines made from inappropriate varieties.

95	1994 Seppelt Great Western Show Sparkling Shiraz (Grampians)
94	NV Primo Estate Joseph Sparkling Red (Adelaide Plains)
94	NV Rockford Black Shiraz (Barossa Valley)

Something happened with the sweet table wines this year, with botrytis Semillons missing in action. However, the two late-harvest Rieslings point a way to the future: they are made in a Mosel Kabinett style, perceptibly off-dry, but with freshness and balance.

96   **2002 Brown Brothers Patricia Noble Riesling** (King Valley)
95   **2000 Brown Brothers Patricia Noble Riesling** (King Valley)
94   **2004 Poacher's Ridge Vineyard Late Harvest Riesling** (Great Southern)
94   **2004 Delatite Late Picked Riesling** (Upper Goulburn)

Only two Roses, but with many well-made wines behind them; perhaps my overall points were too parsimonious.

95   **2004 Yering Station Pinot Noir ED Rose** (Yarra Valley)
94   **2004 Charles Melton Rose Of Virginia** (Barossa Valley)

Pinot Noir

The last year in which Pinot Noirs from the great 2002 vintage will make their mark, although hopefully many remain in private hands to be enjoyed over the next 5–10 years. It is obvious that the 2003 vintage was kinder to the Mornington Peninsula than the other pinot regions, including the Yarra Valley.

97   **2003 Paringa Estate Reserve Special Barrel Selection Pinot Noir** (Mornington Peninsula)
96   **2002 Ashton Hills Pinot Noir** (Adelaide Hills)
96   **2003 Bannockburn Vineyards Pinot Noir** (Geelong)
96   **2003 Paringa Estate Pinot Noir** (Mornington Peninsula)
96   **2002 Paringa Estate Pinot Noir** (Mornington Peninsula)
95   **2002 Tomboy Hill Nintinbool Vineyard Pinot Noir** (Ballarat)
95   **2002 Tomboy Hill Rebellion Pinot Noir** (Ballarat)
95   **2002 Clyde Park Vineyard Reserve Pinot Noir** (Geelong)
95   **2003 Caledonia Australis Reserve Pinot Noir** (Gippsland)
95   **2002 Dromana Estate Reserve Pinot Noir** (Mornington Peninsula)
95   **2002 Eldridge Estate Clonal Selection Pinot Noir** (Mornington Peninsula)
95   **2003 Kooyong Pinot Noir** (Mornington Peninsula)
95   **2003 The Moorooduc Pinot Noir** (Mornington Peninsula)
95   **2002 Moorooduc Estate Pinot Noir** (Mornington Peninsula)
95   **2003 Stonier Reserve Pinot Noir** (Mornington Peninsula)
95   **2003 Yabby Lake Vineyard Pinot Noir** (Mornington Peninsula)
95   **2003 Dalrymple Special Bin Pinot Noir** (Northern Tasmania)
95   **2002 Dalrymple Pinot Noir** (Northern Tasmania)
95   **2003 Kelvedon Pinot Noir** (Southern Tasmania)
95   **2002 Stefano Lubiana Estate Pinot Noir** (Southern Tasmania)

95   2002 **Winstead Reserve Pinot Noir** (Southern Tasmania)
95   2003 **Yering Station Reserve Pinot Noir** (Yarra Valley)
94   2003 **Balgownie Estate Yarra Valley Pinot Noir**, 2003 **Barratt Piccadilly Valley Pinot Noir**, 2003 **Barringwood Park Pinot Noir**, 2003 **Caledonia Australis Pinot Noir**, 2002 **Curlewis Geelong Pinot Noir**, 2003 **Domaine Epis Macedon Ranges Pinot Noir**, 2002 **Dromana Estate Pinot Noir**, 2003 **Farr Rising Mornington Peninsula Pinot Noir**, 2003 **Freycinet Pinot Noir**, 2003 **Grosset Pinot Noir**, 2003 **Hillcrest Vineyard Yarra Valley Pinot Noir**, 2003 **Main Ridge Estate Half Acre Pinot Noir**, 2002 **Main Ridge Estate Half Acre Pinot Noir**, 2003 **Merricks Creek Nick Farr Pinot Noir**, 2003 **Montalto Vineyards Pinot Noir**, 2003 **Moores Hill Estate Pinot Noir**, 2003 **Moorooduc Estate Wild Yeast Pinot Noir**, 2003 **Pankhurst Pinot Noir**, 2003 **Paringa Estate Peninsula Pinot Noir**, 2002 **Patrick's Vineyard Pinot Noir**, 2003 **Phillip Island Vineyard Pinot Noir**, 2001 **Red Hill Estate Classic Release Pinot Noir**, 2003 **Rochford Macedon Ranges Reserve Pinot Noir**, 2002 **Tarrawarra Estate Pinot Noir**, 2003 **Ten Minutes by Tractor Wine Co Wallis Vineyard Pinot Noir**, 2003 **Three Wise Men Pinot Noir**, 2003 **Tokar Estate The Reserve Pinot Noir**, 2003 **Tower Estate Yarra Valley Pinot Noir**, 2002 **Whisson Lake Piccadilly Valley Pinot Noir**, 2003 **Willow Creek Tulum Pinot Noir**, 2002 **Willow Creek Tulum Pinot Noir**, 2002 **Winstead Pinot Noir**, 2002 **Yabby Lake Vineyard Mornington Peninsula Pinot Noir**.

Shiraz

Shiraz is the quintessential Australian varietal wine, mainly because it has adapted so well to so many different regions, and partly because it has been grown for over 150 years in many of those regions, giving rise to generational experience. Thus 10 regions have produced wines scoring 96 points or above, the number doubling with wines pointed at 95 or above. The list is especially long this year as the flood peak of releases from the superb 2002 vintage makes its mark.

97   2002 **Wirra Wirra RSW Shiraz** (McLaren Vale)
96   2002 **Petaluma Shiraz** (Adelaide Hills)
96   2002 **Charles Melton Shiraz** (Barossa Valley)
96   2002 **Kaesler Old Bastard Shiraz** (Barossa Valley)
96   2000 **Penfolds Grange** (Barossa Valley)
96   2001 **Peter Lehmann The 1885 Shiraz** (Barossa Valley)
96   1999 **Peter Lehmann Stonewell Shiraz** (Barossa Valley)
96   2003 **Torbreck The Descendant** (Barossa Valley)
96   2002 **Torbreck The Factor** (Barossa Valley)
96   2002 **Turkey Flat Shiraz** (Barossa Valley)
96   2002 **Wolf Blass Platinum Label Barossa Shiraz** (Barossa Valley)
96   2003 **Pondalowie Vineyards Special Release Shiraz** (Bendigo)
96   2002 **Kilikanoon Oracle Shiraz** (Clare Valley)
96   2001 **Hardys Eileen Hardy Shiraz** (Cool-climate blend)

96 **2002 Punters Corner Spartacus Reserve Shiraz** (Coonawarra)
96 **2003 Bannockburn Vineyards Shiraz** (Geelong)
96 **2001 Seppelt St Peters Shiraz** (Grampians)
96 **2000 Seppelt St Peters Shiraz** (Grampians)
96 **2003 Westgate Vineyard Endurance Shiraz Viognier** (Grampians)
96 **2003 Bress Unfiltered Heathcote Shiraz** (Heathcote)
96 **2003 Domaines Tatiarra Cambrian Shiraz** (Heathcote)
96 **2003 Cobaw Ridge Shiraz Viognier** (Macedon Ranges)
96 **2002 Journeys End Vineyards Arrival Shiraz** (Southeast Australia)
96 **2002 Mt Billy Antiquity Shiraz** (Southern Fleurieu Peninsula)
96 **2001 Punt Road MVN Shiraz** (Yarra Valley)
95 **2002 Amietta Vineyard Geelong Shiraz, 2003 Arakoon Blewitt Springs Shiraz, 2002 Balnaves of Coonawarra Shiraz, 2003 Barrgowan Vineyard Shiraz, 2002 Brini Estate Blewitt Springs Shiraz, 2002 Brokenwood Wade Block 2 McLaren Vale Shiraz, 2002 Brown Brothers Patricia Shiraz, 2003 By Farr Shiraz by Farr, 2003 Cape Mentelle Walcliffe Shiraz, 2002 Claymore Nirvarna Clare Valley Reserve Shiraz, 2004 Clonakilla Hilltops Shiraz, 2003 Clonakilla Canberra District Shiraz Viognier, 2002 Coriole Lloyd Reserve Shiraz, 2002 De Bortoli Yarra Valley Shiraz, 2003 Domaines Tatiarra Caravan of Dreams Heathcote Shiraz Pressings, 2002 Eldredge Blue Chip Shiraz, 2002 Foggo Hubertus Reserve Shiraz, 2001 Grant Burge Meshach Shiraz, 2002 Happs Three Hills Shiraz, 2002 Heritage Rossco's Shiraz, 2001 Houghton Gladstones Shiraz, 2001 Houghton Frankland River Justin Vineyard Shiraz, 2002 Kabminye Hubert Shiraz, 2002 Kaesler Old Vine Shiraz, 2003 Mitolo Savitar McLaren Vale Shiraz, 1999 Orlando Lawson's Padthaway Shiraz, 2003 Paringa Estate Reserve Shiraz, 2002 Penny's Hill Footprint McLaren Vale Shiraz, 2002 Pertaringa Over The Top Shiraz, 2002 Pikes The EWP Reserve Shiraz, 2002 Pirramimma McLaren Vale Shiraz, 2002 RockBare Barossa Valley Shiraz, 2001 Saltram No. 1 Reserve Shiraz, 2001 Seppelt Great Western Chalambar Bendigo Grampians Shiraz, 2003 Seville Estate Old Vine Reserve Shiraz, 2002 Summerfield Reserve Shiraz, 1999 Tahbilk Reserve Shiraz, 2003 Torbreck Vintners The Struie, 2002 Torbreck Vintners The RunRig, 2003 Two Hands Lily's Garden Shiraz, 2002 Two Hands Ares Barossa Valley Shiraz, 2004 Warrabilla Parola's Limited Release Shiraz, 2002 Westgate Vineyard Endurance Shiraz, 2002 Wirra Wirra McLaren Vale Shiraz, 2002 Wonga Estate Heathcote Shiraz, 2003 Wynns Coonawarra Estate Michael Shiraz, 2003 Yering Station Reserve Yarra Valley Shiraz Viognier, 2002 Yering Station Yarra Valley Shiraz Viognier.**

Australian and Rhône blends and varietals

A group reflecting the fact that until the latter part of the 1960s, Australia's red wines were overwhelmingly made from only three varieties: shiraz, grenache and mourvedre (or mataro, as the latter was then called). Cabernet sauvignon then entered the scene in growing, but still limited, quantities; shortage of the variety was the principal reason for the then uniquely Australian blend of Cabernet sauvignon and shiraz. Partly in deference to history I have elected to group these blends under a dual umbrella. Finally, it is no accident that many of these wines come from warmer regions, with the Barossa Valley the epicentre. The two Durifs are cuckoos in this nest.

95   2001 **Wolf Blass Black Label Shiraz Cabernet** (South Australia blend)
94   2002 **Barossa Ridge Wine Estate Litterini** (Barossa Valley)
94   2002 **Kaesler W.O.M.S. Shiraz Cabernet** (Barossa Valley)
94   2003 **McLean's Farm Reserve Shiraz Cabernet** (Barossa Valley)
94   2002 **McLean's Farm Reserve Barossa** (Barossa Valley)
94   2002 **Taltarni Cephas** (Pyrenees)

95   2002 **Charles Melton Nine Popes** (Barossa Valley)
95   2002 **Penfolds Cellar Reserve Grenache** (Barossa Valley)
94   2003 **Hewitson Old Garden Mourvedre** (Barossa Valley)
94   2002 **Murray Street Vineyard Benno Shiraz Mataro** (Barossa Valley)
94   2003 **Penfolds Old Vine Bin 138 Grenache Shiraz Mourvedre** (Barossa Valley)
94   2003 **Two Hands Brave Faces Shiraz Grenache** (Barossa Valley)
94   2002 **Hewitson Private Cellar Shiraz Mourvedre** (McLaren Vale)

95   2004 **Warrabilla Parola's Limited Release Durif** (Rutherglen)
94   2002 **Stanton & Killeen Durif** (Rutherglen)

Cabernet Sauvignon

Cabernet sauvignon is a notoriously robust grape, its thick skin helping protect it against weather conditions (seasonal or regional) which ought to debilitate it. When conditions are as favourable as they were in 2002, it simply exceeds expectations in those regions which ought to be too warm for it (such as the Barossa Valley). But in the bigger picture, it does best in cooler regions, with Coonawarra, Margaret River, Great Southern and the Yarra Valley at the forefront.

96   1998 **Hardys Reynell Basket Pressed Cabernet Sauvignon** (McLaren Vale)
96   2001 **Howard Park Cabernet Sauvignon** (Margaret River)
96   2001 **Moss Wood Cabernet Sauvignon** (Margaret River)
96   2002 **Suckfizzle Cabernet Sauvignon** (Margaret River)
96   2001 **Houghton Gladstones Cabernet Sauvignon** (Swan Valley)
96   2002 **The Yarra Yarra** (Yarra Valley)
96   2001 **The Yarra Yarra** (Yarra Valley)
95   2002 **Charles Melton Cabernet Sauvignon** (Barossa Valley)

95   **1999 Orlando Jacaranda Ridge Cabernet Sauvignon** (Coonawarra)

95   **2002 Penfolds Bin 707 Cabernet Sauvignon** (Barossa Valley)

95   **2002 Turkey Flat Cabernet Sauvignon** (Barossa Valley)

95   **2002 Hollick Cabernet Sauvignon** (Coonawarra)

95   **2002 Penley Estate Reserve Cabernet Sauvignon** (Coonawarra)

95   **2000 Stonehaven Limited Release Cabernet Sauvignon** (Coonawarra/Padthaway)

95   **2001 Bremerton Cabernet Sauvignon** (Langhorne Creek)

95   **2002 Wirra Wirra The Angelus Cabernet Sauvignon** (McLaren Vale/Coonawarra)

95   **2002 Howard Park Cabernet Sauvignon** (Margaret River)

95   **2001 Juniper Estate Cabernet Sauvignon** (Margaret River)

94   **2002 Alkoomi Frankland River Cabernet Sauvignon, 1997 Amberley Estate Cabernet Sauvignon, 2002 Annvers Langhorne Creek Cabernet Sauvignon, 2002 Blue Pyrenees Estate Richardson Cabernet Sauvignon, 2001 Brookland Valley Reserve Cabernet Sauvignon, 2001 Cape Mentelle Cabernet Sauvignon, 2002 Cardinham Estate Smith Family Vineyards Clare Valley Cabernet Sauvignon, 2002 Cellarmasters Black Wattle Vineyard Mount Benson Cabernet Sauvignon, 2003 Chalkers Crossing Hilltops Cabernet Sauvignon, 2002 Crane Cabernet Sauvignon, 2002 d'Arenberg The Coppermine Road Cabernet Sauvignon, 2002 Devil's Lair Margaret River, 2000 Domaine A Cabernet Sauvignon, 2002 Dominic Versace Reserve McLaren Vale Cabernet Sauvignon, 2002 Eden Hall Cabernet Sauvignon, 2002 Elderton Barossa Cabernet Sauvignon, 2003 Faber Vineyard Frankland River Cabernet Sauvignon, 2003 Ferngrove Vineyards Majestic Cabernet Sauvignon, 2002 Foggo Cabernet Sauvignon, 2001 Gralaine Vineyard Cabernet Sauvignon, 2003 Gralyn Estate Cabernet Sauvignon, 2000 Hardys Reynella Thomas Hardy Cabernet Sauvignon, 2001 Houghton Margaret River Cabernet Sauvignon, 2002 House of Certain Views Coonabarabran Cabernet Sauvignon, 2002 Huntington Estate Special Reserve Cabernet Sauvignon, 2002 Kabminye HWG Cabernet Sauvignon, 2000 Katnook Estate Odyssey Cabernet Sauvignon, 2002 Knappstein Single Vineyard Clare Valley Cabernet Sauvignon, 2002 Langmeil Jackaman's Cabernet Sauvignon, 2002 Majella Cabernet Sauvignon, 2002 Petersons Glenesk Mudgee Cabernet Sauvignon, 2002 Pikes Clare Valley Cabernet Sauvignon, 2002 Pirramimma McLaren Vale Cabernet Sauvignon, 2002 Punters Corner Cabernet Sauvignon, 2002 Richard Hamilton Hut Block Cabernet Sauvignon, 2003 Sandalford Margaret River Cabernet Sauvignon, 2003 Setanta Black Sanglain Cabernet Sauvignon, 2002 Shelmerdine Vineyards Heathcote Cabernet Sauvignon, 2003 Sinclair Giovanni Manjimup Cabernet Sauvignon, 2002 Stone Coast Cabernet Sauvignon, 1999 Tahbilk Reserve Cabernet Sauvignon, 2001 Tatachilla 1901 McLaren Vale Cabernet Sauvignon, 1999 Taylors St Andrews Cabernet Sauvignon, 2001 Turkey Flat Cabernet Sauvignon, 2003 Wolf Blass Grey Label Cabernet Sauvignon.**

Bordeaux blends, and other Bordeaux varieties

It has taken longer than I expected in the late 1980s for Bordeaux blends – usually those with a centrepiece of Cabernet Sauvignon or Merlot – to gain the full attention of winemakers and consumers alike. Indeed, it has been as much to do with the runaway Merlot express train as a single varietal wine as to the synergies of blending. In turn, other lesser Bordeaux varietals (lesser in volume) have clambered on board. The cooler regions of Western Australia are handsomely represented by this group, but not to the exclusion of South Australia.

96	2002 **Vasse Felix Heytesbury** (Margaret River)	
96	2001 **Houghton Jack Mann** (Great Southern)	
95	2002 **Primo Estate Joseph Moda Cabernet Merlot** (Adelaide Plains)	
95	2002 **Haan Wilhelmus** (Barossa Valley)	
95	2002 **d'Arenberg The Galvo Garage** (McLaren Vale)	
95	2001 **Brookland Valley Cabernet Sauvignon Merlot** (Margaret River)	
95	2003 **Woodlands Margaret Cabernet Merlot** (Margaret River)	
95	2001 **McWilliam's 1877 Cabernet Sauvignon Shiraz** (Southeast Australia)	
95	2002 **Yarra Yarra Cabernets** (Yarra Valley)	
95	2003 **Howard Park Best Barrels Merlot** (Margaret River)	
94	2003 **Robert Johnson Vineyards Alan & Veitch Merlot** (Adelaide Hills)	
94	2002 **Haan Merlot Prestige** (Barossa Valley)	
94	2002 **Linfield Road Limited Release Merlot** (Barossa Valley)	
94	2003 **Capel Vale Howecroft Merlot** (Geographe)	
94	2002 **Phillip Island Vineyard Merlot** (Gippsland)	
94	2003 **Mount View Estate Flagship Merlot** (Lower Hunter Valley)	
94	2003 **Stefano Lubiana Merlot** (Southern Tasmania)	
94	2003 **Ferngrove Vineyards King Malbec** (Frankland River)	
94	2002 **Bungawarra Malbec** (Granite Belt)	
94	2002 **Pirramimma Petit Verdot** (McLaren Vale)	
94	2003 **Woodlands Reserve du Cave Cabernet Franc** (Margaret River)	
94	2003 **Anderson Cellar Block Petit Verdot** (Rutherglen)	

94   2001 **Alkoomi Blackbutt**, 2002 **Ballandean Estate Cabernet Shiraz**, 2002 **Ben Potts Jenny's Block Cabernet Malbec**, 2000 **Geoff Merrill Pimpala Vineyard Cabernet Merlot**, 2002 **Grosset Gaia**, 2003 **Lake's Folly Cabernets**, 2002 **Majella The Malleea**, 2002 **Mount Horrocks Cabernet Merlot**, 2002 **Neagles Rock Vineyards One Black Dog Reserve Cabernet Shiraz**, 2002 **Penfolds Bin 389 Cabernet Shiraz**, 2002 **Petaluma Coonawarra**, 2002 **Redbank Sally's Paddock**, 2002 **Stringy Brae of Sevenhill Cabernet Shiraz**, 2002 **Summit Estate Cabernet**

Merlot, 2001 Temple Bruer Reserve Organically Grown Cabernet Sauvignon Petit Verdot, 2001 TK The Palatine, 2002 Yalumba Smith & Hooper Wrattonbully Cabernet Sauvignon Merlot.

Fortified wines

A priceless group of wines which have no equal in any other part of the world.

97   NV All Saints Estate Rare Rutherglen Tokay Museum Release (Rutherglen)
97   NV All Saints Estate Rare Rutherglen Muscat Museum Release (Rutherglen)
97   NV Campbells Isabella Rare Rutherglen Tokay (Rutherglen)
97   NV Chambers Rosewood Rare Rutherglen Muscat (Rutherglen)
97   NV Morris Old Premium Liqueur Rare Muscat (Rutherglen)
97   NV Morris Old Premium Rare Rutherglen Muscat (Rutherglen)
97   NV Morris Old Premium Rare Rutherglen Tokay (Rutherglen)
96   **NV All Saints Estate Rare Rutherglen Tokay** (Rutherglen)
96   **NV All Saints Estate Rare Rutherglen Muscat** (Rutherglen)
96   **NV Stanton & Killeen Rare Rutherglen Muscat** (Rutherglen)
95   **NV Bullers Calliope Rare Rutherglen Liqueur Muscat** (Rutherglen)
95   **NV Campbells Merchant Prince Rare Rutherglen Muscat** (Rutherglen)
95   **NV Campbells Grand Rutherglen Tokay** (Rutherglen)
95   **NV Morris Grand Rutherglen Tokay** (Rutherglen)
95   **NV Baileys of Glenrowan Winemaker's Selection Old Muscat** (Glenrowan)

Special value wines

As always, these are lists of ten of the best value wines, not the ten best wines in each price category. There are literally dozens of wines with similar points and prices, and the choice is necessarily an arbitrary one. I have, however, attempted to give as much varietal and style choice as the limited numbers allow.

Ten of the best value whites under $10

86	2004 De Bortoli Sacred Hill Semillon Chardonnay $5.50
87	2004 Hardys Voyage Colombard Semillon Sauvignon Blanc $6
86	2004 Angove's Butterfly Ridge Riesling $6.99
89	2004 Yalumba Oxford Landing Sauvignon Blanc $8
90	2004 Dominion Vinus Sauvignon Blanc Semillon $8.95
89	2004 Grant Burge Barossa Vines Riesling $9.95
90	2004 Angove's Long Row Sauvignon Blanc $9.99
87	2004 Orlando Jacob's Creek Chardonnay $9.99
90	2004 Zilzie Buloke Reserve Chardonnay $9.99
87	2004 Penfolds Rawson's Retreat Chardonnay $9.99

Ten of the best value reds under $10

87	2004 De Bortoli Sacred Hill Cabernet Merlot $5.50
87	2003 Hardys Voyage Cabernet Sauvignon Petit Verdot Merlot $6
87	2003 Angove's Stonegate Limited Release Petit Verdot $8.99
88	2003 Lindemans Bin 50 Shiraz $8.99
87	2001 Clarence Hill Martins Road Shiraz Cabernet Sauvignon $9
86	2003 Jindalee Estate Shiraz $9
92	2002 Casella yellow tail Cabernet Sauvignon $9.95
86	2003 Poet's Corner Shiraz Cabernet Sauvignon $9.99
92	2003 The Long Flat Wine Co Yarra Valley Pinot Noir $9.99
86	2002 The Long Flat Wine Co Coonawarra Cabernet Sauvignon $9.99

Ten of the best value whites $10–$15

93   **2003 Allison Valley Semillon Sauvignon Blanc** $10
91   **2004 Yalumba Y Series Viognier** $11.95
92   **2002 Byrne & Smith Ardent Estates Margaret River Chardonnay** $12
94   **2004 Braydon Estate Home Paddock Hunter Valley Semillon** $12.50
93   **2004 Willow Bridge Estate Sauvignon Blanc Semillon** $14.50
93   **2004 Mount Trio Vineyard Great Southern Sauvignon Blanc** $14.90
93   **2004 Sticks Chardonnay** $14.99
94   **2002 Cleveland Macedon Chardonnay** $15
93   **2004 Marribrook Frankland River Semillon Sauvignon Blanc** $15
94   **2003 Patrick T The Caves Vineyard Riesling** $15

Ten of the best value reds $10–$15

90   **2003 Water Wheel Memsie Shiraz Cabernet Malbec** $12
92   **2003 Hardys Oomoo McLaren Vale Shiraz** $13
91   **2001 Moondah Brook Cabernet Sauvignon** $13
91   **2004 Yarra Brook Estate Yarra Valley Shiraz** $13.75
90   **2003 Red Hill Estate Bimaris Pinot Noir** $14
90   **2002 Trentham Estate Merlot** $14.50
90   **2003 Rouge Homme Cabernet Sauvignon** $14.99
91   **2003 Cuttaway Hill Estate Southern Highlands Merlot** $15
90   **2003 Judds Warby Range Estate Durif** $15
91   **2003 McCrae Mist Mornington Peninsula Shiraz** $15

Ten of the best new wineries

The challenge facing the 172 new wineries in this edition in finding appropriate ways to the market is a formidable one. However, these ten wineries have easily satisfied the most important requirement of the best possible wine quality.

Aramis Vineyards McLAREN VALE page 72

Owner Lee Flourentzou has brought together a highly experienced team to manage this estate-based operation, viticulturist David Mills being a third-generation McLaren Vale resident, and Scott Rawlinson a winemaker with Mildara Blass for 8 years. It draws on 18 ha of shiraz and 8 ha of cabernet sauvignon, already producing wine of top quality.

Brini Estate Wines McLAREN VALE page 121

The Brini family has been growing grapes in McLaren Vale for over 50 years, but it was not until 2000 that brothers John and Marcello Brini decided to have part of the production from the oldest vines vinified under the Brini Estate Wines label. District veteran Brian Light has made a series of quite wonderful wines.

Eden Hall EDEN VALLEY page 211

David and Mardi Hall have established 32 ha of vines on the historic 120-ha Avon Brae property in the Eden Valley, selling most of the grapes, holding back 10 per cent to be vinified by James and Joanne Irvine for the Eden Hall label, with suitably gratifying results.

Foggo Wines McLAREN VALE page 231

Herb and Sandie Van De Wiel have been McLaren Vale grapegrowers for 16 years, and in the Riverland before that. They have three vineyards, the oldest (on Foggos Road) with 9 ha of shiraz dating back to 1915; 80-year-old grenache and 45-year-old cinsaut add to the mix. In a familiar pattern, most grapes are sold, with the best retained for the Foggo Wines label.

Heathcote Estate HEATHCOTE page 277

This 40-ha vineyard has been planted to 85 per cent shiraz and (unusually for the region) 15 per cent grenache; it is a joint venture between Louis Bialkower, founder of Yarra Ridge, and Robert Kirby, who also features with Yabby Lake Vineyards. Only one wine will be produced, the percentage of grenache varying from year to year, but always matured in French oak.

Humbug Reach Vineyard NORTHERN TASMANIA page 296

Paul and Sally McShane purchased the Humbug Reach Vineyard in 1999, with plantings of pinot noir, riesling and chardonnay dating back to the late 1980s. Skilled contract winemaking by Julian Alcorso has brought out the best of the grapes in distinctively elegant and intense Tasmanian style.

Limbic PORT PHILLIP ZONE page 352

Limbic is the word for a network of neural pathways in the brain that link smell, taste and emotion, and was chosen by Jennifer and Michael Pullar as the name for their 6.2-ha organic vineyard which sits on the hills between the Yarra Valley and Gippsland. It is tempting to say the beautifully balanced and structured wines take the best features of their neighbours.

Tomboy Hill BALLARAT page 588

The result of a patient 20-year building process by former schoolteacher Ian Watson, who has brought together a series of small grower vineyards clustered around the town of Ballarat, solely planted to chardonnay and pinot noir. A labour of love for all concerned, wine quality being exemplary.

Wonga Estate YARRA VALLEY page 637

Greg and Jady Roberts began the development of their 1.8-ha vineyard in the Yarra Valley in 1997, and since 2002 have made a second wine with shiraz grown in the Colbinabbin area of Heathcote, introducing an entirely different perspective. With help from consultant winemaker Sergio Carlei, they have made some wines of great style and quality, which have found their way onto some of the best wine lists in Melbourne.

Yabby Lake Vineyard MORNINGTON PENINSULA page 644

Together with Tomboy Hill, the most outstanding new vineyard in this edition. Robert and wife Mem Kirby (of Village Roadshow) have secured the services of Tod Dexter (ex Stonier) and Larry McKenna (ex Martinborough Vineyards, New Zealand) as the winemaking team for the 40 ha of estate plantings, pinot noir and chardonnay being the main wines.

Best wineries of the regions

As I have already observed, I made four sequential attempts to come up with this year's winery ratings. For obvious reasons, deciding on the 5-star wineries was especially difficult. On the one hand, I didn't want to altogether ignore prior 5-star ratings, but on the other, I wanted the rating to reflect the wines tasted for this edition. Doubtless some of the inclusions will surprise, and some of the exclusions will cause heartache. Simply remember that these are ratings for this year, not for life; next year there will be many changes. For the record, 8.5% of the wineries in this edition received 5 stars.

ADELAIDE HILLS
Annvers Wines
Barratt
Chain of Ponds
Petaluma
Setanta Wines
Shaw & Smith

ADELAIDE PLAINS
Primo Estate

ALBANY
Montgomery's Hill

BALLARAT
Tomboy Hill

BAROSSA VALLEY
Charles Melton
Haan Wines
Hamilton's Ewell Vineyards
Kabminye Wines
Kaesler Wines
Kalleske
Langmeil Winery
McLean's Farm Wines
Orlando
Penfolds
Peter Lehmann
Rockford
Schubert Estate
Seppelt
Torbreck Vintners
Turkey Flat
Wolf Blass

BEECHWORTH
Castagna Vineyard
Giaconda

BENDIGO
BlackJack Vineyards
Bress
Laanecoorie
Pondalowie Vineyards

CANBERRA DISTRICT
Clonakilla

CLARE VALLEY
Grosset
Kilikanoon
Knappstein Wines
Mount Horrocks
Neagles Rock Vineyards
O'Leary Walker Wines
Pikes
Stringy Brae of Sevenhill
Taylors
Wendouree
Wilson Vineyard

COONAWARRA
Balnaves of Coonawarra
Majella
Punters Corner

DENMARK
Harewood Estate
Howard Park

EAST COAST TASMANIA
Freycinet

EDEN VALLEY
Eden Hall
Henschke
Pewsey Vale

FRANKLAND RIVER
Alkoomi
Ferngrove Vineyards
Old Kent River

GEELONG
Bannockburn Vineyards
Barrgowan Vineyard
by Farr
Curlewis Winery
Scotchmans Hill
Shadowfax

GEOGRAPHE
Capel Vale

GIPPSLAND
Bass Phillip
Caledonia Australis
Phillip Island Vineyard

GLENROWAN
Baileys of Glenrowan

GRAMPIANS
Best's Wines
Grampians Estate
Mount Langi Ghiran
   Vineyards
Seppelt Great Western
Westgate Vineyard

HEATHCOTE
Domaines Tatiarra
Heathcote Estate
Jasper Hill
Shelmerdine Vineyards

HENTY
Crawford River Wines

HILLTOPS
Chalkers Crossing

LOWER HUNTER VALLEY
Brokenwood
Capercaillie
Chateau Pâto
Chatto Wines
Keith Tulloch Wine
Lake's Folly
McWilliam's
    Mount Pleasant
Tower Estate
Tyrrell's

MACEDON RANGES
Bindi Wine Growers
Metcalfe Valley

MARGARET RIVER
Ashbrook Estate
Brookland Valley
Broomstick Estate
Cape Mentelle
Cullen Wines
Devil's Lair
Hamelin Bay
Happs
Howard Park
Leeuwin Estate
Moss Wood
Suckfizzle & Stella Bella
Vasse Felix
Voyager Estate
Wise Wine
Woodlands

McLAREN VALE
Brini Estate Wines
d'Arenberg
Foggo Wines
Gemtree Vineyards
Geoff Merrill

Mitolo Wines
Pirramimma
Richard Hamilton
Wirra Wirra

MORNINGTON PENINSULA
Dromana Estate
Main Ridge Estate
Montalto Vineyards
Moorooduc Estate
Paringa Estate
Port Phillip Estate
Stonier Wines
Ten Minutes by Tractor
    Wine Co
Willow Creek
Yabby Lake Vineyard

MOUNT BENSON
Norfolk Rise Vineyard

MUDGEE
Huntington Estate

NAGAMBIE LAKES
Tahbilk

NORTHERN TASMANIA
Clover Hill
Dalrymple
Humbug Reach Vineyard
Jansz
Moores Hill Estate

ORANGE
Canobolas-Smith

PADTHAWAY
Stonehaven

PEMBERTON
Merum
Picardy

PORONGORUP
Gibraltar Rock

PORT PHILLIP ZONE
Limbic
Three Wise Men

PYRENEES
Dalwhinnie
Summerfield

RIVERINA
McWilliam's

RUTHERGLEN
All Saints Estate
Bullers Calliope
Campbells
Chambers Rosewood
Morris
Stanton & Killeen Wines
Warrabilla

SOUTHWEST AUSTRALIA
WJ Walker Wines

SOUTHEAST AUSTRALIA
Hewitson
Two Hands Wines

SOUTHERN TASMANIA
Hood Wines/Wellington
Kelvedon
Moorilla Estate
Stefano Lubiana

SUNBURY
Craiglee

SWAN VALLEY
Faber Vineyard
Houghton

YARRA VALLEY
De Bortoli
Gembrook Hill
Hillcrest Vineyard
Metier Wines
Mount Mary
Seville Estate
Tarrawarra Estate
Toolangi Vineyards
Wonga Estate
Yarra Yarra
Yarra Yering
Yarrabank
Yering Station
Yeringberg

Ten dark horses

A highly subjective list of wineries that have excelled themselves over the past 12 months, ranging in size from very small to very large.

Annvers Wines ADELAIDE HILLS page 70
In no small measure a beneficiary of the 2002 vintage, but has made every post a winner across all wine styles.

Capercaillie LOWER HUNTER VALLEY page 142
Like many Hunter Valley wineries these days, does not hesitate to take grapes from other regions, the common denominator being a wide range of beautifully made wines.

Dalrymple NORTHERN TASMANIA page 185
Once known chiefly for its Sauvignon Blanc, but now up with the very best with its Pinot Noir and Chardonnay.

De Iuliis LOWER HUNTER VALLEY page 194
Three generations of the De Iuliis family have been involved, third-generation winemaker Michael taking the label to new heights.

Dromana Estate MORNINGTON PENINSULA page 207
Winemaker Rollo Crittenden has ignored the external distractions surrounding the corporate owners of Dromana Estate, and produced a string of top-flight wines.

Faber Vineyard SWAN VALLEY page 222
Former Houghton winemaker John Griffiths, in partnership with wife Jane Micallef, makes no apology for being a great fan of traditional warm-area Australian wine styles, but is not afraid to also craft lovely cool-climate Cabernet Sauvignon.

Gibraltar Rock PORONGURUP page 246
Perth orthopaedic surgeon Dr Peter Honey intends to gradually increase the proportion of the wine made from the 26 ha of vineyards. Selling wines of this quality should not present any problem.

Peter Lehmann BAROSSA VALLEY page 455

Peter Lehmann, admittedly with the help of a talented team headed by chief winemaker Andrew Wigan, just gets better and better; the wines are great value at every price point, with five superb wines at the top of the tree.

Pikes CLARE VALLEY page 462

The current releases from Pikes are, without doubt, the best yet, the red wines showing all the quality one expects from 2002, and the white wines defying the odds in 2004.

Willow Creek MORNINGTON PENINSULA page 626

Always a strong performer, but has excelled itself with its Chardonnays and Pinots from 2002 and 2003.

Wine and food or food and wine?

It all depends on your starting point: there are conventional matches for overseas classics such as caviar (Champagne), fresh foie gras (Sauternes, Riesling or Rose), and new-season Italian white truffles (any medium-bodied red). Here the food flavour is all important, the wine merely incidental.

At the other extreme come 50-year-old classic red wines: Grange, Grand Cru Burgundy, First Growth Bordeaux, or a Maurice O'Shea Mount Pleasant Shiraz. Here the food is, or should be, merely a low-key foil, but at the same time must be of high quality.

In the Australian context I believe not enough attention is paid to the time of year, which – particularly in the southern states – is or should be a major determinant in the choice of both food and wine. And so I shall present my suggestions in this way, always bearing in mind how many ways there are to skin a cat.

Spring

SPARKLING
Oysters, cold crustacea, tapas, any cold hors d'oeuvres

YOUNG RIESLING
Cold salads, sashimi

GEWURZTRAMINER
Asian

YOUNG SEMILLON
Antipasto, vegetable terrine

PINOT GRIS, COLOMBARD
Crab cakes, whitebait

VERDELHO, CHENIN BLANC
Cold smoked chicken, gravlax

MATURE CHARDONNAY
Grilled chicken, chicken pasta, turkey, pheasant

ROSE
Caesar salad, trout mousse

YOUNG PINOT NOIR
Seared kangaroo fillet, grilled quail

MERLOT
Pastrami, warm smoked chicken

YOUNG MEDIUM-BODIED CABERNET SAUVIGNON
Rack of baby lamb

LIGHT TO MEDIUM-BODIED COOL CLIMATE SHIRAZ
Rare eye fillet of beef

YOUNG BOTRYTISED WINES
Fresh fruits, cake

Summer

CHILLED FINO
Cold consommé

2–3-YEAR-OLD SEMILLON
Gazpacho

2–3-YEAR-OLD RIESLING
Seared tuna

YOUNG BARREL-FERMENTED SEMILLON SAUVIGNON BLANC
Seafood or vegetable tempura

YOUNG OFF-DRY RIESLING
Prosciutto and melon/pear

COOL-CLIMATE CHARDONNAY
Abalone, lobster, Chinese-style prawns

10-YEAR-OLD SEMILLON OR RIESLING
Braised pork neck

MATURE CHARDONNAY
Smoked eel, smoked roe

OFF-DRY ROSE
Chilled fresh fruit

YOUNG LIGHT-BODIED PINOT NOIR
Grilled salmon

AGED PINOT NOIR (5+ YEARS)
Coq au vin, wild duck

YOUNG GRENACHE/SANGIOVESE
Osso bucco

MATURE CHARDONNAY (5+ YEARS)
Braised rabbit

HUNTER VALLEY SHIRAZ (5–10 YEARS)
Beef spare ribs

MERLOT
Saltimbocca, roast pheasant

MEDIUM-BODIED CABERNET SAUVIGNON (5 YEARS)
Barbequed butterfly leg of lamb

ALL WINES
Parmigiana

Autumn

AMONTILLADO
Warm consommé

BARREL-FERMENTED MATURE WHITES
Smoked roe, bouillabaisse

COMPLEX MATURE CHARDONNAY
Sweetbreads, brains

FULLY AGED RIESLING
Char-grilled eggplant, stuffed capsicum

AGED MARSANNE
Seafood risotto, Lebanese

AGED PINOT NOIR
Grilled calf's liver, roast kid, lamb or pig's kidneys

MATURE MARGARET RIVER CABERNET MERLOT
Lamb fillet, roast leg of lamb with garlic and herbs

SOUTHERN VICTORIAN PINOT NOIR
Peking duck

COOL-CLIMATE MERLOT
Lamb loin chops

MATURE GRENACHE/RHONE BLENDS
Moroccan lamb

RICH, FULL-BODIED HEATHCOTE SHIRAZ
Beef casserole

YOUNG MUSCAT
Plum pudding

Winter

DRY OLOROSO SHERRY
Full-flavoured hors d'oeuvres

SPARKLING BURGUNDY
Borscht

VIOGNIER
Pea and ham soup

AGED (10+ YEARS) SEMILLON
Vichyssoise (hot)

SAUVIGNON BLANC
Coquilles St Jacques, pan-fried scallops

MATURE CHARDONNAY
Quiche Lorraine

CHARDONNAY (10+ YEARS)
Cassoulet

MATURE SEMILLON SAUVIGNON BLANC
Seafood pasta

YOUNG TASMANIAN PINOT NOIR
Squab, duck breast

MATURE PINOT NOIR
Mushroom ragout, ravioli

MATURE MERLOT
Pot au feu

10-YEAR-OLD HEATHCOTE SHIRAZ
Char-grilled rump steak

15–20-YEAR-OLD FULL-BODIED BAROSSA SHIRAZ
Venison, kangaroo fillet

COONAWARRA CABERNET SAUVIGNON
Braised lamb shanks/shoulder

MUSCAT (OLD)
Chocolate-based desserts

TOKAY (OLD)
Crème brûlée

VINTAGE PORT
Dried fruits, salty cheese

On corks and screwcaps

Thirty or so years ago a wine writer acquaintance used to give a detailed description of the quality and appearance of each cork extracted from each wine he tasted. My reaction was simple: what a twerp. But he was absolutely right and I was equally wrong. What has changed so dramatically in the interim?

Back then only a few visionaries were looking beyond corks to alternative closures. The shortcomings of cork were either suffered (notably cork taint) or not sufficiently recognised (insidious random bottle oxidation). The first was usually caused by a mould called trichloranisole, or TCA for short; the second was caused by partial failure of the cork to prevent the ingress of air (and hence oxygen) into the bottle.

Ultimately, leaking corks (as they can for convenience be called) would allow so much air into the bottle that the level would fall down the neck, and thereafter down the shoulder of the bottle. At this point, the mechanical performance of the cork has ceased to function, and the wine is destroyed.

Screwcaps have been embraced by a majority of Australasian winemakers, and they have not lost their minds. Provided the wine has been properly prepared for bottling, and the screwcap properly applied, there is no downside, only upside, from the screwcap. This has been accepted by third party Doubting Thomases for white wines, but not always for red wines. Yet research by Professor Emile Peynaud 30 years ago, and in 2005 by Allen Hart, Research and Development Winemaker for Southcorp, shows that the maturation of red wine can and does proceed anaerobically – in other words, that it does not require oxygen. The flipside is that the more oxygen is available, the faster the maturation process will be.

Coming back to cork, I have paid far more attention to the quality and condition of each cork. Cork suppliers rightly recommend that the bottles should be left in a vertical position for 24 hours after the cork has been inserted to allow it to expand evenly and create as perfect a seal as possible within the constraints of cork and bottle quality.

Even a few hours will be a major advantage, but if the bottle is laid on its side in storage bins or cartons immediately after it comes off the line, wine will seep along the sides of the cork, compromising its longer-term effectiveness.

Then there is the inherent quality of the cork, which can come in three so-called reference (or quality) grades, determined by the number of dark blemishes (or minor cavities) in its sides. Next is the question of size: most commonly 44mm (length) by 24mm (circumference), although much larger (54mm by 24 or 25mm) or 'Chateau length' are used by some.

Even though sorting procedures (primarily electronic) have improved, there is still significant variation unless hand-sorted reference 1 corks (costing $1.50, or 3–4 times as much as the cheapest one-piece corks) are used. So comments such as 'dodgy cork', 'stained cork', 'heavily stained cork', or 'dreadful cork' may not apply to every bottle, or conceivably to the majority. Conversely, 'high-quality cork' refers to a largely blemish-free cork with no wine-staining along its sides, just a purple disc (in the case of red wines) on the end in contact with the wine.

In terms of sealing capacity over 10 to 20 years, high-quality, properly inserted corks will have a far greater chance of survival. Even here there are three variables: TCA has no respect for cork quality; the irregularity of the internal bore of the neck of the bottle may cause problems; and poor storage or transport conditions may likewise create havoc. Finally, and most disturbingly, there is the inherently variable permeability of each and every cork.

The research by Allen Hart showed that the permeability of 35 randomly selected 44 x 24mm reference 2 corks varied from <0.001 to >1.0 cc of O_2 per day, a differential of 1000 times. He commented that while this 'should not be considered typical, it is certainly not unusual for natural cork'.

I also refer to other types of closures. Twin Tops are corks with a body of agglomerated particles and two discs of one-piece cork glued at either end, making it irrelevant which way up they are inserted. The air/oxygen barrier capacity seems good; the longer-term viability is yet to be demonstrated, with most concern about the wine extracting glue taint (colloquially goût de glue) as it can do with sparkling wine corks, which are constructed in the same way.

More recent alternative corks are Diamant and ProCork. Diam (as it is known for short) has been on the market for some time, and so far performs well on all counts (it is in fact a second-generation descendant of Altec). Super-fine cork granules are treated to remove all TCA or similar taint by vacuum extraction, and compressed under high pressure. Stained Diams are very rare, as are tainted examples. Once again, long-term performance is unknown.

ProCork (www.procork.com.au) is an Australian invention, and had a long-term development. It involves a condom-like sheath covering each end and part of the sides of the cork. While very thin, the sheath is a multiple membrane, the outer side with an abrasive quality, which grips the glass and thus minimises air passage. The membrane should also contain any TCA in the body of the cork. It can be applied to any type or quality of cork, including Twin Tops. They are yet to pass into general use.

Next, there are synthetic corks. While there is a measure of disagreement as to whether or not these impart a plastic taint, experience shows they progressively lose elasticity, and even from the outset cannot deal with irregularities in the inside bore of the bottle. After 12 months or so, oxidation will commence on a largely uniform and time-progressive path.

Finally, there is a curious and inherently ugly device called a Zork (www.zork.com.au), made from black polymer and a metallic sheet entombed somewhere in its insides. It is linked to McLaren Vale's Cadenzia wines, all with grenache as a component. One of its sales pitches is that it makes a pop like a cork when it is removed. It is an exceedingly complex way to achieve an end of doubtful worth, even if it does make a popping noise when extracted (by hand; like screwcap, no corkscrew is involved). Its longer-term oxygen barrier capacity is unknown.

In the future, glass stoppers with a silicone O-ring applied to specifically made bottles with a corresponding circular groove in their necks to accommodate the O-ring may appear in Australia. In sharp contrast to the Zork, they look elegant and appear expensive; on the other hand, like the Zork, their longer-term seal capacity is unknown.

How to use the *Companion*

The *Australian Wine Companion* is arranged with wineries in alphabetical order; the index at the back lists the wineries by region, which adds a search facility. The entries should be self-explanatory, but here I will briefly take you through the information for each entry, using Henschke as an example.

Winery entries

Henschke ★★★★★

Henschke Road, Keyneton, SA 5353 **REGION** Eden Valley
T (08) 8564 8223 **F** (08) 8564 8294 **WEB** www.henschke.com.au **OPEN** Mon–Fri 9–4.30, Sat 9–12, public hols 10–3
WINEMAKER Stephen Henschke **EST.** 1868 **CASES** 40 000
SUMMARY Regarded as the best medium-sized red wine producer in Australia, and has gone from strength to strength over the past two decades under the guidance of Stephen and Prue Henschke. The red wines fully capitalise on the very old, low-yielding, high-quality vines and are superbly made with sensitive but positive use of new small oak: Hill of Grace is second only to Penfolds Grange as Australia's red wine icon. Exports to all major markets.

WINERY NAME Henschke

Although it might seem that stating the winery name is straightforward, this is not necessarily so. To avoid confusion, wherever possible I use the name that appears most prominently on the wine label, and do not refer to any associated trading name.

RATINGS ★★★★★

The winery star system may be interpreted as follows:

★★★★★ Outstanding winery capable of producing wines of the highest calibre.
★★★★☆ Excellent producer of very high quality wines.
★★★★ Very good producer of wines with class and character.
★★★☆ A solid, usually reliable, maker of good to very good wines.
★★★ A typically good winery, but may have some lesser wines.
★★☆ Adequate; usually aspires to improve.
NR Normally ascribed where I have not tasted any current release wines.

I have subtly tweaked the application of the star rating system this year, deliberately focusing more on the best wines from the producer than on the least. Putting to one side the 30 per cent of wineries falling in the ★★☆ to NR group, the most numerous are the ★ ★ ★ ★ to ★ ★ ★ ☆ wineries representing 35 per cent. Roughly 11 per cent of wineries receive ★ ★ ★ , and 8 per cent ★ ★ ★ ★ ★ .

This may seem a high number falling in the top bracket, but I am comfortable with the way the numbers have fallen. It is not a precise science, any more than points (or glasses) given to individual wines, and there are bound to be discrepancies here and there.

Moreover, the dividing line between each of the winery star ratings is often very fine, particularly where there are numerous tasting notes for a given winery.

That said, I am all too conscious of the importance each producer attaches to the rating given, and I have made a particular effort this year to rationalise the ratings, with no less than four sweeps through the book, to focus on this issue. Even then, the question arises whether past performance should be taken into account, and, if so, how much. Human nature being what it is, everyone is happy if their rating rises, unhappy if it falls.

CONTACT DETAILS Henschke Road, Keyneton, SA 5353 T (08) 8564 8223 F (08) 8564 8294

The details are usually those of the winery and cellar door but in a few instances may simply be of the winery; this occurs when the wine is made under contract at another winery and is sold only through retail.

REGION Eden Valley

The mapping of Australia into Zones and Regions with legally defined boundaries is now well underway. This edition sees radical changes (and additions) to the regional names and boundaries. Wherever possible the official 'Geographic Indication' name has been adopted, and where the registration process is incomplete, I have used the most likely name. Occasionally you will see 'Warehouse' as the region. This means the wine is made from purchased grapes, in someone else's winery. In other words, it does not have a vineyard or winery in the ordinary way.

WEB www.henschke.com.au

A new feature which I have commented on in the Introduction.

OPEN Mon–Fri 9–4.30, Sat 9–12, public hols 10–3

Although a winery might be listed as not open or only open on weekends, some may in fact be prepared to open by appointment. Many will, some won't; a telephone call will establish whether it is possible or not. Also, virtually every winery that is shown as being open only for weekends is in fact open on public holidays as well. Once again, a telephone call will confirm this.

WINEMAKER Stephen Henschke

In the large companies the winemaker is simply the head of a team; there may be many executive winemakers actually responsible for specific wines.

EST. 1868

A more or less self-explanatory item, but keep in mind that some makers consider the year in which they purchased the land to be the year of establishment, others the year in which they first planted grapes, others the year they first made wine, others the year they first offered wine for sale, and so on. There may also be minor complications where there has been a change of ownership or a break in production.

CASES 40 000

This figure (representing the number of cases produced each year) is merely an indication of the size of the operation. Some winery entries do not feature a production figure; this is either because the winery (principally but not exclusively the large companies) regard this information as confidential or because the information was not available at the time of going to press.

SUMMARY Regarded as the best medium-sized red wine producer in Australia, and has gone from strength to strength over the past two decades under the guidance of Stephen and Prue Henschke. The red wines fully capitalise on the very old, low-yielding, high-quality vines and are superbly made with sensitive but positive use of new small oak: Hill of Grace is second only to Penfolds Grange as Australia's red wine icon. Exports to all major markets.

My summary of the winery. Little needs to be said, except that I have tried to vary the subjects I discuss in this part of the winery entry.

The vine leaf symbol indicates the 172 wineries that are new entries in this year's listing.

Tasting notes

RATINGS

94–100	♈♈♈♈♈	Outstanding. Wines of the highest quality, usually with a distinguished pedigree.
90–93	♈♈♈♈♈	Highly recommended. Wines of great quality, style and character, worthy of a place in any cellar.
87–89	♈♈♈♈	Recommended. Wines of above average quality, fault-free, and with clear varietal expression.
84–86	♈♈♈♈	Fair to good. Wines with plenty of flavour (usually varietal) and good balance; free of technical faults.
80–83	♈♈♈	Everyday wines: price is particularly relevant; under $10 will represent good value.
75–79	♈♈♈	Also tasted: usually wines with some deficiency, technical or otherwise.

I should emphasise that the ratings are for the vintage(s) specified in the notes. Thus in outstanding vintages such as 2002 many of the red wines in particular have higher points than normal. I also freely acknowledge that the 100-point scale is effectively a 20-point scale, with 0.1 increments if viewed as being out of 20. In international usage the same holds true.

> ♈♈♈♈♈ **Joseph Hill Gewurztraminer 2004** Delicate but bell-clear rose petal and spice varietal fruit; a dry but very long and fine palate; one of the very best examples of the variety. **RATING** 94 **DRINK** 2010 $ 27.80

The tasting note opens with the vintage of the wine tasted. With the exception of a very occasional classic wine, this tasting note will have been made within the 12 months prior to publication. Even that is a long time, and during the life of this book the wine will almost certainly change. More than this, remember that tasting is a highly subjective and imperfect art. NV = non-vintage. The price of the wine is listed where information is available. Another innovation is the frequent comment, at the end of the tasting note, on the closure used. I discuss this issue at some length on page 47.

DRINK 2010

Rather than give a span of drinking years, I have simply provided a (conservative) 'best by' date. Modern winemaking is such that, even if a wine has 10 or 20 years' future during which it will gain much greater complexity, it can be enjoyed at any time over the intervening months and years.

A note on tasting terms

I have used a few tasting terms in this *Companion* that are not as widely encountered as others, although I do not claim to have invented them. They are related to texture and structure rather than flavour; the latter terms tend to be self-defining, and will either strike a bell with the reader or not. Some writers decry the use of any flavour mnemonics, but most use them to a lesser or greater degree. If not used, and the variety or colour of the wine isn't disclosed by its name, an isolated reading of the tasting note may give no clue as to whether the wine is a dry white or dry red. But as I say, any further explanation brings one around in a very quick circle.

Three terms, falling under the general concept of mouthfeel (hopefully itself self-explanatory) are:

LINE So far as I know, Len Evans is the author of this word, which operates alongside terms such as length, finish and aftertaste. It connotes a wine, white or red, which delivers its flavour and character in a seamless flow from the time it first enters the mouth to its finish and aftertaste. The impression may rise and fall to a degree, but will never fracture; each new sensation will be linked to that which preceded it. Wines with line are always harmonious.

CRUNCHY ACIDITY Becoming more commonly used, and most usually describes the flinty, minerally acidity of a young, dry, unwooded white wine which will be relatively low in alcohol, and leaves the mouth fresh, asking for more of the wine.

SQUEAKY ACIDITY Normally, but not always, found in white wine, and is very nearly the obverse of crunchy. It feels as if there is a thin (tasteless) sheath of rubber between the side of the tongue and the teeth as the wine is rolled around inside the mouth; although it doesn't make an audible squeaky sound, it feels as if it might or should.

Australian Wineries and Wines 2006

Abbey Creek Vineyard ★★★☆

1091 Porongurup Road, Porongurup, WA 6324 **REGION** Porongurup
T (08) 9853 1044 **F** (08) 9853 1040 **OPEN** By appointment
WINEMAKER Robert Diletti (Contract) **EST.** 1990 **CASES** 900
SUMMARY This is the family business of Mike and Mary Dilworth, the name coming from a winter creek running alongside the vineyard, and a view of The Abbey in the Stirling Range. The vineyard is only 1.5 ha, roughly split between riesling, pinot noir, cabernet sauvignon and a little merlot, the pinot noir and riesling planted in 1990, the remainder in 1993. Another 0.5 ha of riesling may follow in the near future. The Rieslings, in particular, have had significant show success.

♥♥♥♥♡ **Porongurup Riesling 2003** A faint hint of reduction on the bouquet; light-bodied; apple, mineral, slate and spice; good length, dry finish. Screwcap. **RATING** 90 **DRINK** 2010 $17

♥♥♥♡ **Porongurup Pinot Noir 2003 RATING** 86 **DRINK** 2007 $22

Abbey Rock NR

67 Payneham Road, College Park, SA 5069 (postal) **REGION** Murray Darling
T (08) 8362 0677 **F** (08) 8362 9218 **WEB** www.abbeyrock.com.au **OPEN** Not
WINEMAKER Les Sampson **EST.** 2001 **CASES** NA
SUMMARY A recent but expanding business with wines sourced from a number of regions spread across South Australia. The premium wines will be made from pinot noir (2.2 ha) and chardonnay (3.5 ha) near Hahndorf in the Adelaide Hills, and from chardonnay (2 ha), semillon (6.5 ha), shiraz (8 ha) and grenache (2 ha) in the Clare Valley. Plans are afoot to increase both the Adelaide Hills and the Clare Valley plantings.

AbbeyVale NR

392 Wildwood Road, Yallingup, WA 6282 **REGION** Margaret River
T (08) 9755 2121 **F** (08) 9755 2121 **WEB** www.abbeyvale.com.au **OPEN** 7 days 10–5
WINEMAKER Philip May **EST.** 1986 **CASES** 10 000
SUMMARY The new AbbeyVale is a completely different business from that which operated prior to May 2003, when a 19-member grower group contributed $1.25 million for start-up capital, coupled with grape supply agreements. Well-known and highly-skilled vigneron Philip May heads the operation (indeed he is the only director) and the services of two equally skilled and experienced winemaking consultants, Richard Rowe and Bruce Dukes, have been secured.

Abercorn ★★★★

Cassilis Road, Mudgee, NSW 2850 **REGION** Mudgee
T 1800 000 959 **F** (02) 6373 3108 **WEB** www.abercornwine.com.au **OPEN** Thurs–Mon 10.30–4.30
WINEMAKER Tim Stevens **EST.** 1996 **CASES** 8000
SUMMARY Tim and Connie Stevens acquired the 25-year-old Abercorn Vineyard in 1996. The quality of the red wines has improved over the years to the point where two-thirds of the production is released under the 'A Reserve' banner, led by A Reserve Shiraz and A Reserve Shiraz Cabernet Merlot. These now rank among the best of the region, selling out prior to the next release. A few hundred cases of white wines continue to be made for cellar door release only.

♥♥♥♥♡ **A Reserve Shiraz 2003** Rich blackberry, plum, chocolate and spice aromas; medium to full-bodied; excellent mouthfeel and balance. Stained and deformed cork a travesty. **RATING** 93 **DRINK** 2008 $50
A Reserve Shiraz Cabernet Merlot 2002 Rich, full and focused array of black fruits; ripe tannins and balanced oak; altogether stylish. **RATING** 93 **DRINK** 2017 $49.95
A Reserve Shiraz 2001 Interesting, almost Italian, tannins run through the length of the savoury palate; a wine of considerable style and class. **RATING** 91 **DRINK** 2016 $49.95

♥♥♥♥ **Mudgee Cabernet Merlot 2003** Fresh, vibrant blackcurrant and cassis mix; light to medium-bodied; supple mouthfeel, minimal oak and tannins. Screwcap. **RATING** 89 **DRINK** 2008 $20

🌿 Acacia Ridge

NR

169 Gulf Road, Yarra Glen, Vic 3775 **REGION** Yarra Valley
T (03) 9730 1492 **F** (03) 9730 2292 **WEB** www.acaciaridgeyarravalley.com **OPEN** By appointment
WINEMAKER Various (Contract) **EST.** 1996 **CASES** 500
SUMMARY Tricia and Gavan Oakley began the establishment of 4 ha each of pinot noir, shiraz and
cabernet sauvignon in 1996. Most of the grapes are sold to three other Yarra Valley winemakers, and
when the Oakleys decided to have part of the production vinified for them under the Acacia Ridge
label, they and some other small vignerons set up a marketing and grape-sharing cooperative known
as Yarra Valley Micromasters. It was through this structure that the Oakleys obtained their
Chardonnay, which complements the Cabernet Merlot and Shiraz made from their own plantings.
Visitors to the property (by appointment or invitation only) will find an 1850 miner's hut, originally
built near Castlemaine, and which found its way to the Acacia Ridge property by a circuitous route.
The three wines sell for $20 a bottle, or $220 per case.

🌿 Across the Lake

 ★★★☆

Box 66, Lake Grace, WA 6353 **REGION** Central Western Australia Zone
T (08) 9864 9026 **F** (08) 9864 9126 **OPEN** Not
WINEMAKER Diane Miller (Contract) **EST.** 1999 **CASES** 220
SUMMARY The Taylor family has been farming (wheat and sheep) for over 40 years at Lake Grace; a
small diversification into grapegrowing started as a hobby, but has developed into a little more than
that with 1.6 ha of shiraz. They were also motivated to support their friend Bill (WJ) Walker, who had
started growing shiraz 3 years previously, and has since produced a gold medal-winning wine.
Having learnt the hard way which soils are suitable, and which are not, the Taylors intend to increase
their plantings.

🍷🍷🍷🍷   **Shiraz 2003** Sweet plum and blackberry fruit; vanillan oak evident but not
overwhelming. Confirms the potential of the region. **RATING** 88 **DRINK** 2009

Ada River

 ★★★★☆

2330 Main Road, Neerim South, Vic 3831 **REGION** Gippsland
T (03) 5628 1661 **F** (03) 5628 1661 **OPEN** Weekends & public hols 10–6
WINEMAKER Peter Kelliher **EST.** 1983 **CASES** 1500
SUMMARY The Kelliher family first planted vines on their dairy farm at Neerim South in 1983,
extending the original Millstream Vineyard in 1989 and increasing plantings further by establishing
the nearby Manilla Vineyard in 1994. Until 2000, Ada River leased a Yarra Valley vineyard; it has
relinquished that lease and in its place established a vineyard at Heathcote in conjunction with a
local grower.

🍷🍷🍷🍷🍷   **Heathcote Reserve Shiraz 2003** Deep colour; dense, rich and gently sweet plum,
blackberry, licorice and spice mix; velvety mouthfeel; carries its alcohol (just). Cork.
RATING 94 **DRINK** 2018 $ 32

🍷🍷🍷🍷🍸   **Heathcote Cabernet Sauvignon 2003** Saturated with sweet blackcurrant and chocolate
fruit; soft tannins, minimal oak. Cork. **RATING** 90 **DRINK** 2013 $ 24

🍷🍷🍷🍷   **Gippsland Chardonnay 2003** Light to medium-bodied; slightly funky barrel ferment
aromas; delicate but long palate; citrussy fruit. Value. Cork. **RATING** 89 **DRINK** 2007 $ 16
Gippsland Pinot Noir 2003 Light to medium-bodied, but quite complex ripe plum and
spice; balanced finish. Cork. **RATING** 88 **DRINK** 2007 $ 18
Gippsland Pinot Gris 2003 Lively and fresh; an attractive twist of lemon adds interest
and flavour; no alcohol heat. Cork. **RATING** 87 **DRINK** Now $ 16

🍷🍷🍷🍸   **Gippsland Cabernet Merlot 2003** **RATING** 86 **DRINK** 2008 $ 17

🌿 Adelina Wines

NR

PO Box 75, Sevenhill, SA 5453 **REGION** Clare Valley
T (08) 8842 1549 **F** (08) 8842 2909 **WEB** www.adelina.com.au **OPEN** Not
WINEMAKER Colin McBryde, Jennie Gardner **EST.** 2000 **CASES** 400

SUMMARY The Gardner family has owned and managed Spring Farm Estate, on which the Adelina Wines vineyard is situated, since 1986. When the family acquired the property, it had 0.5 ha of shiraz and 0.3 ha of grenache planted around 1910, and a further 0.3 ha of cabernet sauvignon and pinot noir planted in 1970. For a number of years the small production was sold to Tim Adams, but in 2000 parents Elaine and Will, and children Jennie and Andrew, decided to cease selling the grapes and establish Adelina Wines. Winemakers Jennie Gardner and Colin McBryde have a broad background, from winemaking and cellar experience to medical research and hospitality, both having worked in numerous regions in New and Old World wineries over the past 10 years. Both are currently completing their doctorates in oenological science at the University of Adelaide (Waite Campus), studying yeast metabolism.

Adinfern ★★★☆

Bussell Highway, Cowaramup, WA 6284 **REGION** Margaret River
T (08) 9755 5272 **F** (08) 9755 5206 **WEB** www.adinfern.com **OPEN** 7 days 11–5.30
WINEMAKER Merv Smith, Kevin McKay (Contract) **EST.** 1996 **CASES** 2500
SUMMARY Merv and Jan Smith have farmed their property as a fine wool and lamb producer for over 30 years, but in 1996 diversified by the development of a 25-ha vineyard planted to sauvignon blanc, semillon, chardonnay, pinot noir, merlot, shiraz, cabernet sauvignon and malbec. One hundred tonnes of grapes are sold to other makers, 25 retained for Adinfern Estate. They also built two self-contained rammed earth cottages. The wines (which have had show success) are sold through the cellar door, by mail order and website. Exports to the UK and Singapore.

▼▼▼▼ **Margaret River Cabernet Sauvignon 2002** Light to medium-bodied; a mix of blackcurrant, cassis and more earthy/savoury notes; fine tannins, faint bitterness. **RATING** 88 **DRINK** 2010 $ 23
Margaret River Sauvignon Blanc 2004 Fractionally reduced; light-bodied; at the crisp, slate/mineral/herbaceous end of the spectrum; clean finish. **RATING** 87 **DRINK** 2007 $ 18

▼▼▼ **Musterers Magic Pinot Noir 2003** **RATING** 83 $ 20

Affleck NR

154 Millynn Road (off Bungendore Road), Bungendore, NSW 2621 **REGION** Canberra District
T (02) 6236 9276 **F** (02) 6236 9090 **WEB** www.affleck.com.au **OPEN** Fri–Wed 9–5
WINEMAKER Ian Hendry **EST.** 1976 **CASES** 500
SUMMARY The cellar door and mail order price list says that the wines are 'grown, produced and bottled on the estate by Ian and Susie Hendry with much dedicated help from family and friends'. The original 2.5-ha vineyard has been expanded to 7 ha, and a tasting room (offering light lunches) opened in 1999.

🍇 Agincourt Partners NR

Playford Highway, Parndana, SA 5220 **REGION** Kangaroo Island
T (08) 8559 6031 **OPEN** Not
WINEMAKER Contract **EST.** 1986 **CASES** NA
SUMMARY The Denis family moved to their sheep-farming property, Agincourt, west of Parndana, in 1986. Like many others, the downturn in the wool industry caused them to look to diversify their farming activities, and this led to the planting of shiraz and cabernet sauvignon, and to the subsequent release of their Wollombi brand wines. The wines are available by mail order.

🍇 Ainsworth & Snelson NR

22 Gourlay Street, St Kilda East, Vic 3183 **REGION** Warehouse
T (03) 9530 3333 **F** (03) 9530 3446 **WEB** www.ainsworthandsnelson.com **OPEN** Not
WINEMAKER Brett Snelson **EST.** 2002 **CASES** 4500
SUMMARY Brett Snelson, Gregg Ainsworth, Paul Finch and Robert McDowell bring varied and interesting backgrounds to the business. After 12 years with the Victorian Institute of Sport and the Victorian cricket team, Brett Snelson's other interest, wine, took him to work at Domaine de la Pertusiane in Rousillon, an annual pilgrimage he still makes. Gregg Ainsworth had 12 years' marketing experience in international drinks trade companies, including LVMH and Allied

Domecq. They and their partners have sourced grapes from various parts of Australia, having the red wines made in McLaren Vale by Boar's Rock, and the white wines made at YarraHill in the Yarra Valley. The stated style aspiration is low intervention.

Ainsworth Estate ★★★★

110 Ducks Lane, Seville, Vic 3139 **REGION** Yarra Valley
T (03) 5964 4711 **F** (03) 5964 4311 **WEB** www.ainsworth-estate.com.au **OPEN** Thurs–Mon 10.30–5
WINEMAKER Denis Craig **EST.** 1994 **CASES** 3000
SUMMARY Denis Craig and wife Kerri planted their first 2 ha of chardonnay and shiraz near Healesville in 1994, establishing a second vineyard at Ducks Lane, Seville, with another 2 ha of vines, planted to shiraz and pinot noir. They have also turned from selling to purchasing chardonnay, shiraz and cabernet sauvignon. For the time being, at least, Denis Craig and Al Fencaros make the wines at Fencaros' Allinda Winery in Dixons Creek. Three executive apartments overlooking the vineyard are available.

ΨΨΨΨΨ **Yarra Valley Chardonnay 2003** Funky Burgundian barrel ferment aromas; powerful, complex and long palate; nectarine fruit holds its own with the oak. Screwcap. **RATING** 93 **DRINK** 2010 $ 23

ΨΨΨΨ **Yarra Valley Cabernet Sauvignon 2003** Light-bodied; fresh, linear cassis and blackcurrant fruit; minimal tannins and oak; well enough made. Screwcap. **RATING** 87 **DRINK** 2008 $ 35

ΨΨΨΨ **Yarra Valley Pinot Noir 2003** Quite complex, spicy, savoury, smoky aromas; drying tannins unbalance the palate. A pity. Screwcap. **RATING** 86 **DRINK** 2007 $ 25
Yarra Valley Shiraz 2003 **RATING** 86 **DRINK** 2008 $ 20

Albert River Wines ★★★☆

1–117 Mundoolun Connection Road, Tamborine, Qld 4270 **REGION** Queensland Coastal
T (07) 5543 6622 **F** (07) 5543 6627 **WEB** www.albertriverwines.com.au **OPEN** 7 days 10–4
WINEMAKER Peter Scudamore-Smith MW (Consultant) **EST.** 1998 **CASES** 6000
SUMMARY Albert River is one of the high-profile wineries on the Gold Coast hinterland. All of its distribution is through cellar door, mail order and local restaurants. The proprietors are David and Janette Bladin, with a combined 30 years' experience in tourism and hospitality, who have acquired and relocated two of Queensland's most historic buildings, Tamborine House and Auchenflower House. The winery itself is housed in a newly constructed annex to Auchenflower House; the Bladins have established 10 ha of vineyards on the property, and have another 50 ha under contract. Exports to Japan.

ΨΨΨΨΨ **Merlot 2002** A very well-made mix of sweet red and blackcurrant fruit, neatly off-set by fine tannins. **RATING** 91 **DRINK** 2010 $ 24

ΨΨΨΨ **Estate Viognier 2004** A very powerful, quirky wine, barrel-fermented in old oak; some honey and a suggestion of botrytis. Cork. **RATING** 86 **DRINK** Now $ 26

ΨΨΨ **Unwooded Chardonnay 2004** **RATING** 83 $ 18

Aldgate Ridge ★★★☆

23 Nation Ridge Road, Aldgate, SA 5154 **REGION** Adelaide Hills
T (08) 8388 5225 **F** (08) 8388 5856 **WEB** www.aldgateridge.com.au **OPEN** By appointment
WINEMAKER David Powell (Contract) **EST.** 1992 **CASES** 400
SUMMARY Jill and Chris Whisson acquired their vineyard property in 1988, when the land was still being used as a market garden. The 2.5 ha of pinot noir now established were planted in 1992 and 1997, the first block with some of the first of the new Burgundian clones to be propagated in Australia. Further plantings of pinot noir and a small block of sauvignon blanc have been added. The vineyard is typical of the Adelaide Hills region, on a rolling to steep southeast-facing hillside at the 440-m altitude line. The wine is contract-made by the celebrated David Powell of Torbreck in the Barossa Valley, and apart from mail order, has limited fine wine retail distribution.

ΨΨΨΨ **Sauvignon Blanc 2004** Asparagus, grass and gooseberry; ever so faintly smoky; lively finish. **RATING** 89 **DRINK** Now $ 19

ΨΨΨΨ **Pinot Noir 2002** **RATING** 84 **DRINK** Now $ 33

Aldinga Bay Winery ★★★

Main South Road, Aldinga, SA 5173 **REGION** McLaren Vale
T (08) 8556 3179 **F** (08) 8556 3350 **OPEN** 7 days 10–5
WINEMAKER Nick Girolamo **EST.** 1979 **CASES** 8000
SUMMARY The former Donolga Winery has had a name and image change since Nick Girolamo, the son of founders Don and Olga Girolamo, returned from Roseworthy College with a degree in oenology. Nick has taken over both the winemaking and marketing; prices remain modest, though not as low as they once were, reflecting an increase in the quality and an upgrade in packaging. Aldinga Bay also has some very interesting varietal plantings, 16 varieties in all, including petit verdot, nebbiolo, barbera and sangiovese.

Alexandra Bridge Wines ★★★☆

101 Brockman Highway, Karridale, WA 6288 **REGION** Margaret River
T (08) 9758 5999 **F** (08) 9758 5988 **WEB** www.alexandrabridgewines.com.au **OPEN** 7 days 10–4.30
WINEMAKER Vanessa Carson, Virginia Willcock **EST.** 1999 **CASES** 3500
SUMMARY Alexandra Bridge has become the operating arm of Australian Wine Holdings. The 800-tonne winery, commissioned in February 2000, was the first built in the Karridale area at the southern end of the Margaret River. The Brockman Vineyard, planted in three stages commencing in 1995, is estate-owned and has a total of 30 ha of semillon, sauvignon blanc, chardonnay, shiraz and cabernet sauvignon. The grapes coming from the Brockman Vineyard are supplemented by long-term supply agreements with other Margaret River growers. Tastings have been hampered by a number of corked wines. Exports to Europe and South-East Asia.

 101 Chardonnay 2001 Glowing gold; medium to full-bodied; rich, toasty overlay to soft, peachy fruit; acidity helps the finish. Cork. **RATING** 89 **DRINK** Now $ 37.70
Margaret River Chardonnay 2003 Soft melon and fig fruit; minimal oak; easy access style. Screwcap. **RATING** 87 **DRINK** Now $ 18.85

 Margaret River Cabernet Merlot 2002 RATING 85 **DRINK** 2007 $ 18.85

Alkoomi ★★★★★

Wingebellup Road, Frankland, WA 6396 **REGION** Frankland River
T (08) 9855 2229 **F** (08) 9855 2284 **WEB** www.alkoomiwines.com.au **OPEN** 7 days 10.30–5
WINEMAKER Michael Staniford, Merv Lange, Darren Burke **EST.** 1971 **CASES** 80 000
SUMMARY For those who see the wineries of Western Australia as suffering from the tyranny of distance, this most remote of all wineries shows there is no tyranny after all. It is a story of unqualified success due to sheer hard work, and no doubt to Merv and Judy Lange's aversion to borrowing a single dollar from the bank. The substantial production is entirely drawn from the ever-expanding estate vineyards – now over 100 ha. Wine quality across the range is impeccable, always with precisely defined varietal character. Exports to all major markets.

Frankland River Cabernet Sauvignon 2002 Strong colour; a potent mix of blackcurrant and blackberry; persistent but ripe tannins give great texture and structure. **RATING** 94 **DRINK** 2017 $ 22
Blackbutt 2001 Medium red-purple; classically framed and built medium-bodied wine; blackcurrant and olive; fine tannins. **RATING** 94 **DRINK** 2011 $ 59

Frankland River Riesling 2004 Ultra-fragrant apple blossom and citrus aromas, then citrus and passionfruit flavours with plenty of length. **RATING** 93 **DRINK** 2012 $ 19
Frankland River Sauvignon Blanc 2004 Clean, fresh, no reduction; long palate; gooseberry, citrus and mineral; fresh aftertaste. **RATING** 93 **DRINK** Now $ 19
Frankland River Shiraz Viognier 2003 Fragrant blackberry and warm spices; good structure; fine ripe tannins and subtle oak. **RATING** 93 **DRINK** 2013 $ 22
Southlands Semillon Sauvignon Blanc 2004 Lively and crisp lemon, lime and tropical mix; sustained fruit on the finish. **RATING** 92 **DRINK** Now $ 15

Southlands Unwooded Chardonnay 2004 Pleasant melon and stone fruit; balanced, easy style. **RATING** 87 **DRINK** Now $ 15
Southlands Cabernet Merlot 2003 Abundant, bright, fresh red fruits do the talking; simple but enjoyable. **RATING** 87 **DRINK** Now $ 15

Allandale ★★★★

132 Lovedale Road, Lovedale, NSW 2321 **REGION** Lower Hunter Valley
T (02) 4990 4526 **F** (02) 4990 1714 **WEB** www.allandalewinery.com.au **OPEN** Mon–Sat 9–5, Sun 10–5
WINEMAKER Bill Sneddon, Rod Russell **EST.** 1978 **CASES** 18 000
SUMMARY Owners Wally and Judith Atallah have overseen the growth of Allandale from a small, cellar door operation to a business with sales in all the eastern states, and export markets in five countries. Allandale has developed a reputation for its Chardonnay, but offers a broad range of wines of consistently good quality, including red wines variously sourced from the Hilltops, Orange and Mudgee regions. Exports to the UK, the US and other major markets.

ΨΨΨΨΨ **Matthew Shiraz 2003** Very good colour; medium-bodied; ripe, not jammy, blackberry and blood plum fruit; good balance and length; oak and acidity likewise. Quality cork. **RATING** 91 **DRINK** 2015 $ 22
Hunter Valley Semillon 2003 Still in its absolute infancy; lemongrass and hints of spicy minerality; good focus and length. Screwcap. **RATING** 90 **DRINK** 2012 $ 17

ΨΨΨΨ **Hunter Valley Chardonnay 2003** Gentle, smooth peachy fruit; matching gently sweet oak; easily accessible. Screwcap. **RATING** 88 **DRINK** 2007 $ 18

Allinda NR

119 Lorimers Lane, Dixons Creek, Vic 3775 **REGION** Yarra Valley
T (03) 5965 2450 **F** (03) 5965 2467 **OPEN** Weekends & public hols 11–5
WINEMAKER Al Fencaros **EST.** 1991 **CASES** 2500
SUMMARY Winemaker Al Fencaros has a Bachelor of Wine Science (Charles Sturt University) and was formerly employed by De Bortoli in the Yarra Valley. All of the Allinda wines are produced onsite; all except the Shiraz (from Heathcote) are estate-grown from a little over 3 ha of vineyards. Limited retail distribution in Melbourne and Sydney.

Allison Valley Wines ★★★☆

RSM 457 North Jindong Road, Busselton, WA 6280 (postal) **REGION** Margaret River
T (08) 9755 4873 **F** (08) 9474 1804 **WEB** www.allisonvalley.com.au **OPEN** Not
WINEMAKER Paul Green (Contract) **EST.** 1997 **CASES** 5000
SUMMARY The Porter family planted 10 ha of semillon, sauvignon blanc, shiraz and cabernet sauvignon with the sole intention of selling the grapes to other winemakers in the region. However, as has been the case with hundreds of other such ventures, the family has decided to have some of the production vinified under the Allison Valley Wines label. There is no cellar door; the value-packed wines are sold via mail order and website.

ΨΨΨΨΨ **Semillon Sauvignon Blanc 2003** Spotlessly clean; striking mouthfeel, flavour and intensity; an exceptionally rich food style. Screwcap. **RATING** 93 **DRINK** 2010 $ 10
Sauvignon Blanc 2003 Potent, powerful varietal aromas; a long palate with a mix of gooseberry, kiwifruit and herbaceous notes. **RATING** 90 **DRINK** 2007 $ 10

ΨΨΨΨ **Cabernet Sauvignon 2002** **RATING** 86 **DRINK** 2008 $ 10
Shiraz 2002 **RATING** 85 **DRINK** 2007 $ 10

All Saints Estate

All Saints Road, Wahgunyah, Vic 3687 **REGION** Rutherglen
T (02) 6035 2222 **F** (02) 6035 2200 **WEB** www.allsaintswine.com.au **OPEN** Mon–Sat 9–5.30, Sun 10–5.30
WINEMAKER Dan Crane **EST.** 1864 **CASES** 35 000
SUMMARY The winery rating reflects the fortified wines, but the table wines are more than adequate. The Terrace restaurant (open 7 days for lunch and Saturday night for dinner) makes this a most enjoyable stop for any visitor to the northeast. All Saints and St Leonards are now wholly owned by Peter Brown; the vast majority of the wines are sold through the cellar door and by mailing list. The faux castle, modelled on a Scottish castle beloved of the founder, is now classified by the Historic Buildings Council. Exports to the US.

ŸŸŸŸŸ **Rare Rutherglen Tokay Museum Release NV** Dark olive-brown; the extreme age shows most clearly in the incredible length, finish and aftertaste of the wine; not a trace of staleness. RATING 97 DRINK Now $434.50

Rare Rutherglen Muscat Museum Release NV An exceedingly complex wine, yet retains elegance; like the Museum Tokay, no hint of staleness. The description of flavours is endless, as is the lingering finish. RATING 97 DRINK Now $434.50

Rare Rutherglen Tokay NV Far, far deeper colour than the Grand; layer upon layer of lusciously rich varietal fruit, moving beyond tea leaf into the Christmas cake/Christmas pudding spectrum. RATING 96 DRINK Now $107.50

Rare Rutherglen Muscat NV Deep, dark brown, dark olive rim; very complex, with a balance of aged raisiny material and a touch of youthful freshness; the equally complex, powerful palate has a strong nutty, rancio framework but great balance and suppleness, then a cleansing, dry finish. RATING 96 DRINK Now $107.50

Family Cellar Marsanne 2003 A truly attractive wine; lots of character; superbly subtle oak handling as background support; rich mouthfeel; classic honeysuckle notes. RATING 94 DRINK 2008 $26.50

Grand Rutherglen Tokay (375 ml) NV Lusciously rich and complex, with Christmas cake and dried fruit flavours, along with the hallmark echoes of tea leaf and butterscotch, and a lovely skein of sweet fruit running through the mid-palate, the structure fine and intense. RATING 94 DRINK Now $55

Grand Rutherglen Muscat (375 ml) NV Deep, olive-rimmed brown; a very complex, extremely rich bouquet with intense rancio and some volatile lift; an ultra-rich and dense palate with abundant raisin and plum pudding flavours, the twist of volatility on the finish well within bounds. RATING 94 DRINK Now $55

ŸŸŸŸ̉ **Classic Rutherglen Tokay (500 ml) NV** Tea leaf, smoke, toffee and butterscotch aromas lead into an intense, long and lingering palate with abundant weight. Future releases might well see a little more fresh, younger material in the blend. RATING 91 DRINK Now $30.50

Riesling 2004 Highly aromatic lemon blossom bouquet; crisp; lots of lemon and passionfruit; skilled winemaking defies region. RATING 90 DRINK 2012 $17.50

Classic Rutherglen Muscat (500 ml) NV Distinct olive hints to the full tawny colour; the bouquet and palate show considerable rancio, complexity and depth. Just a suggestion of the pendulum swinging a little too far towards aged material. RATING 90 DRINK Now $30.50

ŸŸŸŸ **Family Cellar Chardonnay 2003** Gently complex; controlled barrel ferment/lees inputs to cashew/creamy notes over stone fruit; medium-bodied, well made. RATING 89 DRINK 2008 $26.50

Allusion Wines   NR

Smith Hill Road, Yankalilla, SA 5203 REGION Southern Fleurieu
T (08) 8558 3333 F (08) 8558 3333 OPEN Thurs–Sun 11–5
WINEMAKER Contract EST. 1996 CASES 750
SUMMARY Steve and Wendy Taylor purchased the property on which Allusion Wines is established in 1980, since planting 4 ha of vines and 35 000 trees. Steve Taylor's 20 years as a chef has strongly influenced both the varietal plantings and the wine styles made: not altogether surprisingly, they are designed to be consumed with good food. The wine is fermented offsite, then matured onsite before being contract-bottled.

Allyn River Wines   NR

Torryburn Road, East Gresford, NSW 2311 REGION Upper Hunter Valley
T (02) 4938 9279 F (02) 4938 9279 OPEN Fri–Mon & public hols 9–5, or by appointment
WINEMAKER David Hook (Contract) EST. 1996 CASES 650
SUMMARY Allyn River is situated on the alluvial soils on the banks of the stream which has given the vineyard its name. The plantings of 1.5 ha each of semillon and chambourcin were in part inspired by the knowledge that Dr Henry Lindeman had established his famous Cawarra Vineyard in the locality; since Allyn River's foundation in 1996, others have moved to the area to establish vineyards totalling more than 20 ha within a 10-km radius of Allyn River. As well as a winetasting room and picnic facilities, self-contained cottage accommodation (the Maples Cottage) is available.

Amarillo Vines

27 Marlock Place, Karnup, WA 6176 **REGION** Peel
T (08) 9537 1800 **F** (08) 9537 1800 **OPEN** 7 days 10–5
WINEMAKER Phil Franzone (Contract) **EST.** 1995 **CASES** 700
SUMMARY The Ashby family have market garden and landscaping backgrounds, and the establishment of a small vineyard on the block of land in which their house sits seemed a natural thing to do. What is unusual is the density of the planting, the utilisation of a lyre trellis, and the permanent netting erected around the vineyard – this means they do not speak of acres or ha, but of the 2500 vines planted, and of the production as 8400 bottles.

TTT **Shiraz 2002** **RATING** 80 **$** 16

Amarok Estate

Lot 547 Caves Road, Wilyabrup, WA 6284 (postal) **REGION** Margaret River
T (08) 9756 6888 **F** (08) 9756 6555 **OPEN** Not
WINEMAKER Kevin McKay (Contract) **EST.** 1999 **CASES** 1500
SUMMARY John and Libby Staley, with their youngest daughter Megan, her husband Shane (and youngest grandson Lewis) have all had hands-on involvement in the establishment of 20 ha of vineyards, clearing bushland, ripping, rock picking, stick picking and planting, etc. The soils are gravelly loam over a clay granite base; the vineyard has a western aspect and is 5 km from the Indian Ocean. The Staleys senior have built a home on the property, and Shane and Megan carry out all of the viticultural tasks. Production will increase significantly as the vines come into full bearing.

TTTT **Merlot 2003** Medium-bodied; good structure and texture; gently savoury edges to red fruit; balanced oak. **RATING** 88 **DRINK** 2010 **$** 17

Amberley Estate ★★★★

Thornton Road, Yallingup, WA 6282 **REGION** Margaret River
T (08) 9755 2288 **F** (08) 9755 2171 **WEB** www1.amberleyestate.com.au **OPEN** 7 days 10–4.30
WINEMAKER Paul Dunnewyk **EST.** 1986 **CASES** 120 000
SUMMARY Based its initial growth on its ultra-commercial, fairly sweet Chenin Blanc, which continues to provide the volume for the brand, selling out well before the following release. However, the quality of all the other wines has risen markedly over recent years as the 31 ha of estate plantings have become fully mature. Purchased by Canadian company Vincor in early 2004. Exports to the UK and the US.

TTTTT **Cabernet Sauvignon 1997** Stylish, savoury, spicy bottle-developed wine; excellent length, structure and balance; will go on from here. Cork. **RATING** 94 **DRINK** 2015 **$** 70

TTTTT **First Selection Shiraz 2002** Medium-bodied; fragrant blackberry aromas; flows across the tongue, with fruit, oak and tannins well balanced. Very stained cork a worry. **RATING** 90 **DRINK** 2010 **$** 36.85
Cabernet Merlot 2001 Ripe, dark berry fruit in abundance; blackcurrant and some cassis; good structure and length. Cork. **RATING** 90 **DRINK** 2012 **$** 22

TTTT **First Selection Semillon 2002** Still very youthful; complex aromas and flavours with slightly edgy oak inputs; firm mouthfeel and acidity; needs more time to resolve its aggression. High-quality cork. **RATING** 89 **DRINK** 2012 **$** 36.85
Sauvignon Blanc 2004 Clean; more weight than many from 2004, though the varietal character is slightly muted; good balance and mouthfeel; not sweet. **RATING** 89 **DRINK** Now **$** 18
Semillon Sauvignon Blanc 2004 Fresh, crisp and lively; light to medium-bodied; good length and pleasingly bone-dry finish. **RATING** 89 **DRINK** 2008 **$** 18

TTTY **Chardonnay 2004** **RATING** 86 **DRINK** Now **$** 17.50
Charlotte Street Merlot 2002 **RATING** 84 **DRINK** Now **$** 15

TTT **Chenin Blanc 2004** **RATING** 83 **$** 15
Shiraz 2003 **RATING** 80 **$** 14

Ambrook Wines

NR

114 George Street, West Swan, WA 6055 **REGION** Swan Valley
T (08) 9274 1003 **F** (08) 9379 0334 **WEB** www.ambrookwines.2ya.com **OPEN** Wed–Fri 12–5,
weekends & public hols 10–5
WINEMAKER Rob Marshal **EST.** 1990 **CASES** 1200
SUMMARY Michele Amonini has established 4 ha of chenin blanc, semillon, verdelho, shiraz, cabernet
sauvignon and merlot and quietly gone about producing a solid range of varietal, estate-based wines
which have had their fair share of success at the various West Australian regional wine shows.
Modest pricing increases the appeal.

Amherst Winery

 ★★★★☆

Talbot–Avoca Road, Amherst, Vic 3371 **REGION** Pyrenees
T (03) 5463 2105 **F** (03) 5463 2091 **WEB** www.amherstwinery.com **OPEN** Weekends & public hols
10–5
WINEMAKER Graham Jukes (Red), Paul Lesock (White) **EST.** 1991 **CASES** 880
SUMMARY Norman and Elizabeth Jones have planted 4 ha of vines on a property with an
extraordinarily rich history, a shorthand reflection of which is seen in the name Dunn's Paddock
Shiraz. This variety dominates the planting, with 3.4 ha; the rest is cabernet sauvignon and
chardonnay. Samuel Knowles was a convict who arrived in Van Diemen's Land in 1838. He endured
continuous punishment before fleeing to South Australia in 1846 and changing his name to Dunn.
When, at the end of 1851, he married 18-year-old Mary Therese Taaffe in Adelaide, they walked from
Adelaide to Amherst pushing a wheelbarrow carrying their belongings. They had 14 children, and
Samuel Dunn died in 1898, a highly respected citizen; his widow lived until 1923.

▼▼▼▼▼ **Dunn's Paddock Pyrenees Shiraz 2002** Fragrant, complex, black fruit and vanilla
aromas; an elegant but intense palate; long finish, fine-grained tannins; 14° alcohol.
RATING 94 **DRINK** 2015 $ 25

▼▼▼▼▽ **Reserve Pyrenees Shiraz 2002** Dense colour; full-bodied; powerful, complex blackberry,
bitter chocolate and vanilla; strong tannins in support role; big-impact style; 14.5° alcohol.
RATING 93 **DRINK** 2015 $ 36

▼▼▼▼ **Chinese Garden Pyrenees Cabernet Sauvignon 2003** Distinctly austere, savoury
tannins are the framework; blackcurrant and cassis fill in the centre. Needs time. High-
quality cork. **RATING** 89 **DRINK** 2013 $ 25

▼▼▼▽ **Lachlan's Pyrenees Chardonnay 2004** **RATING** 84 **DRINK** Now $ 15

Amietta Vineyard

 ★★★★☆

30 Steddy Road, Lethbridge, Vic 3332 **REGION** Geelong
T (03) 5281 7407 **F** (03) 5281 7427 **OPEN** By appointment
WINEMAKER Nicholas Clark, Janet Cockbill **EST.** 1995 **CASES** 450
SUMMARY Janet Cockbill and Nicholas Clark are multitalented. Both are archaeologists, but Janet
manages to combine part-time archaeology, part-time radiography at Geelong Hospital and part-
time organic viticulture. Nicholas Clark has nearly completed a viticulture degree at Charles Sturt
University, and both he and Janet worked vintage in France at Michel Chapoutier's biodynamic
Domaine de Beates in Provence in 2001. Production is tiny, because they are unwilling to release
wines which they consider not up to standard. Part of the small production comes from locally
grown, purchased grapes. Amietta is producing cameo wines of some beauty.

▼▼▼▼▼ **Geelong Shiraz 2002** Intense, spicy blackberry fruit with touches of leather and anise;
very good balance and length; top-class wine. **RATING** 95 **DRINK** 2012 $ 30

▼▼▼▼▽ **Geelong Riesling 2004** Herb, nettle, mineral and a touch of lime; tingling, lemony
acidity, achieved without adjustment, and with a soupçon of sweetness. Screwcap.
RATING 91 **DRINK** 2007 $ 20

▼▼▼▽ **Geelong Rose 2004** **RATING** 86 **DRINK** Now $ 18

Amulet Vineyard ★★★★

Wangaratta Road, Beechworth, Vic 3747 **REGION** Beechworth
T (03) 5727 0420 **F** (03) 5727 0421 **OPEN** Fri–Mon, public & school hols 10–5, or by appointment
WINEMAKER Sue Thornton, Ben Clifton **EST.** 1998 **CASES** 2000
SUMMARY Sue and Eric Thornton have planted a patchwork quilt 4-ha vineyard, with sangiovese taking 1 ha, the other varieties 0.5 ha or less, and in descending order of magnitude are barbera, shiraz, cabernet sauvignon, merlot, nebbiolo, orange muscat, pinot gris and pinot blanc. The vineyard (and cellar door) is 11 km west of Beechworth on the road to Wangaratta, the vines planted on gentle slopes at an elevation of 350m. Co-winemaker and son Ben Clifton is studying wine science at Charles Sturt University. The cellar door enjoys panoramic views, and wine sales are both by the glass and by the bottle.

ŶŶŶŶŶ **Beechworth Sangiovese 2002** Fragrant; positive varietal character on both bouquet and palate; a mix of savoury and cherry fruit; fine tannins. **RATING** 90 **DRINK** 2007 $ 25

ŶŶŶŶ **Beechworth Sangiovese Fuso 2003** Very attractive light to medium-bodied wine; sweet spicy notes to gentle cherry and blackberry fruit; fine tannins. Sangiovese/Cabernet/Nebbiolo. Quality cork. **RATING** 88 **DRINK** 2009 $ 18
Beechworth Chardonnay Orange Muscat 2004 Highly charged, scented, grapey orange blossom aromas; the flavours go down the same track; good length and balance. Cork. **RATING** 87 **DRINK** Now $ 16
Beechworth Shiraz 2002 Slightly dull, blackish colour; leathery, spicy overtones to blackberry fruit; soft tannins. **RATING** 87 **DRINK** Now $ 28

ŶŶŶŶ **Beechworth Rosato 2004** **RATING** 86 **DRINK** Now $ 16

ŶŶŶ **Beechworth Rosato 2003** **RATING** 83 $ 16

Anderson ★★★★☆

Lot 12 Chiltern Road, Rutherglen, Vic 3685 **REGION** Rutherglen
T (02) 6032 8111 **F** (02) 6032 9028 **WEB** www.andersonwinery.com.au **OPEN** 7 days 10–5
WINEMAKER Howard Anderson **EST.** 1992 **CASES** 1700
SUMMARY Having notched up a winemaking career spanning over 30 years, including a stint at Seppelt Great Western, Howard Anderson and family started their own winery, initially with a particular focus on sparkling wine but now extending across all table wine styles. There are 4 ha of estate shiraz, and 1 ha each of durif and petit verdot, with yields controlled at a very low 2.5 tonnes per hectare (or, in the old money, 1 tonne per acre).

ŶŶŶŶŶ **Cellar Block Petit Verdot 2003** Powerful but civilised, and very varietal black fruits, clean earth; persistent but controlled tannins; underlying ripeness simply adds to the quality. **RATING** 94 **DRINK** 2018 $ 26

ŶŶŶŶŶ **Cellar Block Durif 2003** Impenetrable purple colour; absolutely massive black fruits, licorice, chocolate and vanilla; tannins big but in balance. Overall, remarkably soft. **RATING** 93 **DRINK** 2023 $ 29.50
Cellar Block Shiraz Viognier 2003 Deep purple; that lift in aroma and flavour from Viognier works in warm climates too; dark fruits, lingering tannins; patience. Slightly creased cork. **RATING** 91 **DRINK** 2013 $ 26

Andraos Bros NR

Winilba Vineyard, 150 Vineyard Road, Sunbury, Vic 3429 **REGION** Sunbury
T (03) 9740 9703 **F** (03) 9740 9795 **OPEN** Fri–Sun & public hols 11–5, or by appointment
WINEMAKER Fred Andraos, Mario Marson (Consultant) **EST.** 1989 **CASES** 2500
SUMMARY The original Winilba Vineyard was first planted in 1863, and remained in production until 1889. Exactly 100 years later the Andraos brothers began replanting the vineyard on the property they had purchased 5 years earlier. Over the following years they built a winery from the ruins of the original bluestone cellar, making the inaugural vintage in 1996. They have also established Estelle's Cellar Restaurant on the second floor of the building (open for dinner from Tues–Sun and for lunch on Fri–Sun and public holidays).

Andrew Garrett ★★★

Ingoldby Road, McLaren Flat, SA 5171 **REGION** McLaren Vale
T (08) 8383 0005 **F** (08) 8383 0790 **WEB** www.andrewgarrett.com.au **OPEN** 7 days 10–4
WINEMAKER Charles Hargrave **EST.** 1983 **CASES** 170 000
SUMMARY Andrew Garrett has long been owned by the Beringer Blass wine group, with many of the wines now not having a sole McLaren Vale source but instead being drawn from regions across southeastern Australia. Over the years, winemaker Charles Hargrave has produced some excellent wines which provide great value for money; this crop is atypical.

ΨΨΨΥ **Cabernet Merlot 2003** **RATING** 85 **DRINK** 2008 $14.99
Chardonnay 2004 **RATING** 84 **DRINK** 2007 $13
Shiraz 2003 **RATING** 84 **DRINK** 2008 $14.99

Andrew Harris Vineyards ★★★☆

Sydney Road, Mudgee, NSW 2850 **REGION** Mudgee
T (02) 6373 1213 **F** (02) 6373 1296 **WEB** www.andrewharris.com.au **OPEN** 7 days 9–5
WINEMAKER Damian Grindley **EST.** 1991 **CASES** 65 000
SUMMARY Andrew and Deb Harris lost no time after purchasing a 300-ha sheep station southeast of Mudgee in 1991. The first 6 ha of vineyard were planted that year; 106 ha are now planted. A portion of the production is sold to others, but production has risen significantly in recent years. Exports to the US, Canada, Malaysia, Japan and New Zealand.

ΨΨΨΨ **Highfields Mudgee Merlot 2003** Light to medium-bodied; appropriate savoury, spicy, tangy edges to the core of sweet, red fruits. Cork. **RATING** 88 **DRINK** 2010 $14.95
Highfields Mudgee Semillon 2004 Clean; solid structure and flavour possibly from some skin contact. Screwcap. **RATING** 87 **DRINK** 2008 $14.95
Highfields Mudgee Verdelho 2004 Aromatic and plenty of varietal fruit salad; nicely balanced. Screwcap. **RATING** 87 **DRINK** 2008 $14.95
Highfields Mudgee Shiraz 2002 Savoury, earthy, spicy fruit; medium-bodied; some vanilla oak. **RATING** 87 **DRINK** 2008 $14.95

ΨΨΨΥ **Mudgee Cabernet Sauvignon 2001** **RATING** 86 **DRINK** 2009 $24.95
Harvest Road Cabernet Merlot 2003 **RATING** 85 **DRINK** 2007 $9.95
Harvest Road Shiraz Cabernet 2002 **RATING** 84 **DRINK** Now $9.95

Andrew Peace Wines ★★★

Murray Valley Highway, Piangil, Vic 3597 **REGION** Swan Hill
T (03) 5030 5291 **F** (03) 5030 5605 **WEB** www.apwines.com **OPEN** Mon–Fri 8–5, Sat 10–4, Sun by appointment
WINEMAKER Andrew Peace, Nina Viergutz **EST.** 1995 **CASES** 300 000
SUMMARY The Peace family has been a major Swan Hill grapegrower since 1980, with 100 ha of vineyards. They moved into winemaking with the opening of a $3 million winery in 1996. The modestly priced wines are aimed at supermarket-type outlets in Australia and exports to all major markets.

ΨΨΨΨ **Master Peace Estate Malbec 2003** Good colour; abundant, supple varietal fruit, with notes of raspberry jam; soft tannins. **RATING** 89 **DRINK** 2008 $19

ΨΨΨΥ **Chardonnay 2003** **RATING** 85 **DRINK** Now $14

Andrew Pirie NR

17 High Street, Launceston, Tas 7250 (postal) **REGION** Northern Tasmania
T (03) 6334 7772 **F** (03) 6334 7773 **WEB** www.andrewpirie.com **OPEN** Not
WINEMAKER Andrew Pirie **EST.** 2004 **CASES** 8000
SUMMARY After a relatively short break, Andrew Pirie has re-established his winemaking activities in Tasmania, while retaining his chief executive management role for Parker Estate in Coonawarra. He has leased the Rosevears Winery, where he will produce the wines for the Rosevears Group, for his own brands, and for others on a contract basis. For the foreseeable future he will rely on contract-grown fruit of the highest possible quality.

Angas Plains Estate   ★★★☆

PO Box 283, Strathalbyn, SA 5255 **REGION** Langhorne Creek
T (08) 8537 3159 **F** (08) 8537 3353 **WEB** www.angasplainswines.com.au **OPEN** At Bremer Place,
Langhorne Creek
WINEMAKER Judy Cross (Contract) **EST.** 2000 **CASES** 2500
SUMMARY A family-operated business, with 14 ha of shiraz, 10 ha of cabernet sauvignon and 1 ha of
chardonnay; it is situated 10 minutes' drive south from the historic town of Strathalbyn, on the banks
of the Angas River. The wines are available through the Bremer Restaurant, which offers tastings of a
number of wines from local wineries.

ΥΥΥΥ **PJ's Shiraz 2003** Predominantly red fruits with some lift; medium-bodied, controlled oak.
RATING 88 **DRINK** 2012 $ 18
PJ's Cabernet Sauvignon 2003 Light to medium-bodied; supple, smooth cassis and
blackcurrant; nice flavour; early drinking. **RATING** 88 **DRINK** 2010 $ 18
PJ's Unwooded Chardonnay 2004 Clean, fresh, very tangy/citrussy; cool-grown
crossover with Sauvignon Blanc flavour; long finish. **RATING** 87 **DRINK** Now $ 15

Angas Vineyards   NR

PO Box 53, Langhorne Creek, SA 5255 **REGION** Langhorne Creek
T (08) 8537 3337 **F** (08) 8537 3231 **OPEN** Not
WINEMAKER Ben Glaetzer (Contract) **EST.** 1997 **CASES** NA
SUMMARY Angas Vineyards is the umbrella organisation for a number of separately marketed brands.
Its principal viticultural resource is 222 ha of vineyards, with multiple examples of ultra-trendy
varietals: verdelho, viognier, pinot gris, grenache, cabernet sauvignon, merlot, malbec, shiraz,
mataro, petit verdot, sangiovese, barbera, dolcetto, lagrein and tempranillo. Most of the wine is
exported under either the Angas Vineyards or Bushy Road Vineyard brands.

Angove's   ★★★★

Bookmark Avenue, Renmark, SA 5341 **REGION** Riverland
T (08) 8580 3100 **F** (08) 8580 3155 **WEB** www.angoves.com.au **OPEN** Mon–Fri 9–5
WINEMAKER Warrick Billings, Shane Clohesy, Tony Ingle **EST.** 1886 **CASES** 1.8 million
SUMMARY Exemplifies the economies of scale achievable in the Australian Riverland without
compromising potential quality. Very good technology provides wines which are never poor and
which sometimes exceed their theoretical station in life; the white varietals are best. Angove's
expansion into Padthaway has resulted in estate-grown premium wines at the top of the range.
Angove's also acts as a distributor for several small Australian wineries. Exports to all major markets.

ΥΥΥΥΥ **Long Row Sauvignon Blanc 2004** Remarkable varietal character; fresh, lively, tangy
minerally aromas; herb and passionfruit flavours. Outstanding value. **RATING** 90
DRINK Now $ 9.99
Red Knot McLaren Vale Shiraz 2003 Rich, full, ripe and concentrated plum and black
fruits; nice ripe tannins; subtle oak, good finish. **RATING** 90 **DRINK** 2013 $ 16.99
Vineyard Select McLaren Vale Shiraz 2002 Medium-bodied; classic regional mix of
blackberry and dark chocolate; fine, ripe tannins; good length. **RATING** 90 **DRINK** 2010
$ 16.99
Vineyard Select Coonawarra Cabernet Sauvignon 2002 Herb, spice and mint aromas;
medium-bodied; blackcurrant plus the characters of the bouquet; gentle, savoury tannins.
RATING 90 **DRINK** Now $ 23

ΥΥΥΥ **Vineyard Select Adelaide Hills Sauvignon Blanc 2004** Spice, apple and pear aromas;
the palate opens well with mineral, apple and lime but falters slightly towards the finish.
RATING 88 **DRINK** 2009 $ 16
Red Knot Fleurieu Cabernet Sauvignon 2003 Medium-bodied; attractive red and
blackcurrant fruit; fine tannins; unforced style. All three 'Knot' wines use a Zork closure.
RATING 88 **DRINK** 2009 $ 16.99
Stonegate Limited Release Petit Verdot 2003 Vivid red-purple; highly aromatic but
paradoxically slightly reduced; bright, black fruits; low tannins. **RATING** 87 **DRINK** Now
$ 8.99

YYYY **Butterfly Ridge Riesling 2004** Remarkable varietal aromas; tangy mineral and lime; nice flavour, though fractionally short. Screwcap. Outstanding value. **RATING** 86 **DRINK** Now $6.99

Butterfly Ridge Merlot Cabernet 2004 Very nice wine at the price; has a surprising well of blackcurrant and cassis fruit. Great value. Twin Top. **RATING** 86 **DRINK** 2007 $7

Long Row Chardonnay 2003 **RATING** 85 **DRINK** Now $10

White Knot McLaren Vale Chardonnay 2004 **RATING** 84 **DRINK** Now $16.99

Sarnia Farm Shiraz 2002 **RATING** 84 $14.99

Butterfly Ridge Shiraz Cabernet 2004 **RATING** 84 **DRINK** 2007 $7

Butterfly Ridge Shiraz Cabernet 2003 **RATING** 84 **DRINK** Now $6.99

Bear Crossing Cabernet Merlot 2003 **RATING** 84 **DRINK** Now $8.99

YYY **Bear Crossing Chardonnay 2004** **RATING** 83 $8.99

Bear Crossing Chardonnay 2003 **RATING** 83 $8.99

Sarnia Farm Chardonnay 2003 **RATING** 83 $14.99

Stonegate Verdelho 2004 **RATING** 83 $8.99

Butterfly Ridge Colombard Chardonnay 2004 **RATING** 83 $7

Nine Vines Grenache Shiraz Rose 2004 **RATING** 83 $14

Butterfly Ridge Spatlese Lexia 2004 **RATING** 82 $6.99

Butterfly Ridge Colombard Chardonnay 2003 **RATING** 81 $6.99

Angullong Wines
★★★☆

Four Mile Creek Road, Orange, NSW 2800 (postal) **REGION** Orange
T (02) 6366 4300 **F** (02) 6466 4399 **WEB** www.angullong.com.au **OPEN** Not
WINEMAKER Contract **EST.** 1998 **CASES** 2000
SUMMARY The Crossing family (Bill and Hatty Crossing, and third generation James and Ben Crossing) have owned a 2000 ha sheep and cattle station for over half a century. Located 40 km south of Orange on the lower slopes of the Orange region, overlooking the Belubula Valley, 217 ha of vines have been planted since 1998. In all, there are 13 varieties, with shiraz, cabernet sauvignon and merlot leading the way. Most of the production is sold to Hunter Valley wineries, but it is intended to increase the range under the Angullong brand from 2005.

YYYY **Orange Pinot Gris 2004** Pale bronze-pink; pear, spice, musk and stone fruit; soft rather than alcoholic. Screwcap. **RATING** 88 **DRINK** 2007 $19

Orange Sangiovese 2003 Light to medium-bodied; savoury, spicy, sour cherry aromas and flavours; varietal, but needs food in best Italian tradition. **RATING** 87 **DRINK** 2008 $19

Angus the Bull
★★★☆

PO Box 237, Woollahra, NSW 2025 **REGION** Southeast Australia
T (02) 9363 0173 **F** (02) 9363 0173 **WEB** www.angusthebull.com **OPEN** Not
WINEMAKER Hamish McGowan **EST.** 2002 **CASES** NFP
SUMMARY Hamish McGowan, who describes himself as 'a young Australian wine industry professional', has taken the virtual winery idea to its ultimate conclusion, with a single wine (Cabernet Sauvignon) designed to be drunk with premium red meat, or, more particularly, a perfectly cooked steak. The source of the wine varies from year to year, typically with a major component from either the Barossa Valley or McLaren Vale.

YYYY **Cabernet Sauvignon 2003** Medium-bodied; black fruits and blackcurrant set against balanced but evident tannins; best yet under this label. **RATING** 88 **DRINK** 2009 $20

Angus Wines
★★★★☆

Captain Sturt Road, Hindmarsh Island, SA 5214 **REGION** Southern Fleurieu
T (08) 8555 2320 **F** (08) 8555 2323 **WEB** www.anguswines.com.au **OPEN** Weekends & public hols 11–5
WINEMAKER Mike Farmilo **EST.** 1995 **CASES** 3000
SUMMARY Susan and Alistair Angus are the pioneer viticulturists on Hindmarsh Island, an island which has never been far from the headlines, but for reasons entirely divorced from viticulture. If the Bridge has had problems to contend with, so have the Anguses as they have progressed from a test plot of vines planted in 1992 through to the first commercial crop in 1998. They have established 3.75 ha of shiraz, and 1.25 ha of semillon; the wine is contract-made. Part is bottled under the Angus

Wines label, some is sold in bulk to other wineries. Every aspect of packaging and marketing the wine has a sophisticated touch. Exports to the UK and Malaysia.

ŶŶŶŶŶ Sturt Ridge Shiraz 2002 Classic temperate climate characters; fine, medium-bodied; blackberry and savoury edges; good length and extract; fine tannins, no oak frills. **RATING** 92 **DRINK** 2017 $ 24

Sturt Ridge Semillon 2004 Spotlessly clean; pristine, youthful herb, lemon and lanolin varietal character; good mouthfeel and flow. **RATING** 91 **DRINK** 2014 $ 17

Annapurna Wines ★★★★

Simmonds Creek Road, Mt Beauty, Vic 3698 **REGION** Alpine Valleys
T (03) 5754 4517 **F** (03) 5754 4517 **WEB** www.annapurnawines.com.au **OPEN** Wed–Sun 10–5
WINEMAKER Ezio Minutello **EST.** 1989 **CASES** 25 000
SUMMARY Ezio and Wendy Minutello began the establishment of the 21-ha vineyard at 550m on Mt Beauty in 1989, planted to pinot noir, chardonnay, pinot gris and merlot. The decision to produce some wine under the Annapurna label was taken in 1995, and the following year Annapurna was named the Victorian Wines Show Vineyard of the Year (assessed purely on the viticulture, not the wines). Finally, in 1999, the first wines were released. Annapurna, the second highest mountain after Mt Everest, is Nepalese for 'goddess of bountiful harvest and fertility'.

ŶŶŶŶŶ Mt Beauty Vineyards Pinot Noir Reserve 2004 Aromatic, elegant, light-bodied style; clear strawberry and cherry fruit; good balance and length; unforced. Screwcap. **RATING** 90 **DRINK** 2008 $ 20

ŶŶŶŶ Mt Beauty Vineyards Pinot Gris 2004 Aromatic pear and grass bouquet; crisp, fresh pear and green apple; doesn't show its 13.5° alcohol. Screwcap. **RATING** 89 **DRINK** 2007 $ 18

Mt Beauty Vineyards Merlot 2004 Medium-bodied; clean, fresh redcurrant and raspberry fruit aromas and flavours; fine, sweet tannins; no obvious oak. Screwcap. **RATING** 89 **DRINK** 2008 $ 20

Mt Beauty Vineyards Chardonnay 2004 Delicate, fine and fresh; melon and grapefruit; gentle acidity; good unwooded style, has length. Screwcap. **RATING** 88 **DRINK** 2007 $ 18

ŶŶŶŶ Mt Beauty Vineyards Pinot Gris 2002 RATING 86 **DRINK** Now $ 15

Annie's Lane ★★★★☆

Quelltaler Road, Watervale, SA 5452 **REGION** Clare Valley
T (08) 8843 0003 **F** (08) 8843 0096 **WEB** www.annieslane.com.au **OPEN** Mon–Fri 8.30–5, weekends 11–4
WINEMAKER Mark Robertson **EST.** 1851 **CASES** 120 000
SUMMARY The Clare Valley portfolio of Beringer Blass, formerly made at the historic Quelltaler winery, is sold under the Annie's Lane label, the name coming from Annie Weyman, a turn-of-the-19th century local identity. Since 1996, a series of outstanding wines have appeared under the Annie's Lane label; Copper Trail is the flagship release.

ŶŶŶŶŶ Copper Trail Riesling 2003 A complex web of lime, apple, spice and mineral running through to a long, bone-dry finish. **RATING** 94 **DRINK** 2015 $ 38

ŶŶŶŶŶ Semillon 2003 Very attractive early developing style; medium to full-bodied; ripe lemon and tropical fruit mix; rich, but not phenolic. **RATING** 91 **DRINK** 2008 $ 18

Riesling 2004 Deep, rich, ripe lime juice runs right through both bouquet and palate. **RATING** 90 **DRINK** 2010 $ 19

ŶŶŶŶ Shiraz 2002 Medium-bodied; attractive blackberry fruit, but slightly simple and off the pace for 2002. **RATING** 88 **DRINK** 2009 $ 20

Chardonnay 2004 Soft stone fruit and peach; plenty of flavour, above average for the region. **RATING** 87 **DRINK** Now $ 19

Annvers Wines ★★★★★

Lot 11 Main Road, McLaren Vale, SA 5171 **REGION** Adelaide Hills
T (08) 8323 9603 **F** (08) 8323 9502 **WEB** www.annvers.com.au **OPEN** 7 days 10–5
WINEMAKER Duane Coates **EST.** 1998 **CASES** 7000

SUMMARY Myriam and Wayne Keoghan established Annvers Wines with the emphasis on quality rather than quantity. The first Cabernet Sauvignon was made in 1998, and volume increased markedly since then. The quality of the wines is exemplary, no doubt underwriting the increase in production and expansion of markets both across Australia and in most major export markets other than the UK. Work in progress will see a change in the spelling of the name 'Annvers' to 'Anvers', said to be the original spelling.

ŸŸŸŸŸ **Adelaide Hills Semillon Sauvignon Blanc 2004** Clean, aromatic, lemon zest/lemongrass and spice aromas; lovely palate, adding passionfruit to the mix; near-invisible oak; first-class finish. Screwcap. **RATING** 94 **DRINK** 2007 $16
Reserve Shiraz 2002 Medium to full-bodied; smooth, sultry black fruits and spices; a long palate disguises 15° alcohol; oak and tannins a pure support role. Adelaide Hills/McLaren Vale/Langhorne Creek. Cork. **RATING** 94 **DRINK** 2017 $38
Langhorne Creek Cabernet Sauvignon 2002 Smooth, supple, sweet cassis and blackcurrant fruit; medium to full-bodied; round, soft tannins and sympathetic oak. Seductive wine. Cork. **RATING** 94 **DRINK** 2015 $28

ŸŸŸŸŸ **McLaren Vale Shiraz 2002** Medium-bodied; black fruits, earth, chocolate and vanilla; the balanced palate carries 14.9° alcohol with ease. Cork. **RATING** 91 **DRINK** 2012 $28
Reserve Aged Tawny Port NV Obvious age; pale tawny colour, no red hues; good rancio; relatively elegant spicy biscuit flavours, clean finish. **RATING** 90 **DRINK** Now $42

ŸŸŸŸ **Adelaide Hills Chardonnay 2003** Medium-bodied; a gently complex fusion of nectarine and nutty/creamy oak and malolactic influences; 50% barrel-fermented in new French oak. Cork. **RATING** 89 **DRINK** 2008 $20
Shiraz Cabernet Rose 2004 Bright fuchsia; attractive raspberry and cherry aromas and flavours; has length, dry finish. Adelaide Hills. **RATING** 88 **DRINK** Now $16

Antcliff's Chase ★★★☆

RMB 4510, Caveat via Seymour, Vic 3660 **REGION** Strathbogie Ranges
T (03) 5790 4333 **F** (03) 5790 4333 **OPEN** Weekends 10–5
WINEMAKER Chris Bennett, Ian Leamon **EST.** 1982 **CASES** 800
SUMMARY A small family enterprise which began planting at an elevation of 600m in the Strathbogie Ranges in 1982; wine production from the 4-ha vineyard began in the early 1990s. After an uncertain start, wine quality has picked up considerably.

Apsley Gorge Vineyard NR

The Gulch, Bicheno, Tas 7215 **REGION** East Coast Tasmania
T (03) 6375 1221 **F** (03) 6375 1589 **OPEN** By appointment
WINEMAKER Brian Franklin **EST.** 1988 **CASES** 3000
SUMMARY While nominally situated at Bicheno on the east coast, Apsley Gorge is in fact some distance inland, taking its name from a mountain pass. Clearly, it shares with the other east coast wineries the capacity to produce Chardonnay and Pinot Noir of excellent quality.

Apthorpe Estate NR

Lot 1073 Lovedale Road, Lovedale, NSW 2321 **REGION** Lower Hunter Valley
T (02) 4930 9177 **F** (02) 4930 9188 **WEB** www.apthorpe.com.au **OPEN** Fri & Mon 10–4, weekends 10–5
WINEMAKER Mark Apthorpe, Jim Chatto (Contract) **EST.** 1996 **CASES** 1200
SUMMARY Samuel Apthorpe was given 14 years' imprisonment as a convict in Australia for stealing a few teaspoons. In the mid-1850s, after he had completed his sentence, he established a vineyard in the Hunter Valley at Bishops Bridge. In 1996 his great-great-great-grandson Mark Apthorpe continued the tradition when he planted 2.5 ha of cabernet franc and 2.5 ha of chambourcin at nearby Lovedale. The wines are made at Monarch under the direction of Jim Chatto, with input from Mark Apthorpe, and it can be safely assumed the quality is good.

Arakoon

★★★★☆

229 Main Road, McLaren Vale, SA 5171 **REGION** McLaren Vale
T (08) 8323 7339 **F** (02) 6566 6288 **OPEN** Fri–Sun 10–5, or by appointment
WINEMAKER Patrik Jones, Raymond Jones **EST.** 1999 **CASES** 2500
SUMMARY Ray and Patrik (sic) Jones' first venture into wine came to nothing: a 1990 proposal for a film about the Australian wine industry with myself as anchorman. Five years too early, say the Joneses. In 1991 they opened an agency for Australian wine in Stockholm, and they started exporting wine to that country, the UK, Germany and Switzerland in 1994. In 1999 they took the plunge into making their own wine, and exporting it as well as the wines of others. Patrik is the winemaker, having completed a degree at the Waite Campus of the University of Adelaide. New label and packaging designs are totally appropriate for wines of this quality. Exports to Denmark, Belgium and Sweden.

ΤΤΤΤΤ **Blewitt Springs Shiraz 2003** Dense, deep colour; massively rich and complex; blackberry, dark chocolate and spice; 15° alcohol, but not jammy. **RATING** 95 **DRINK** 2018 $ 32

ΤΤΤΤΥ **Doyen Willunga Shiraz 2003** Powerful, intense, rich spice, licorice and bitter chocolate; persistent but balanced tannins and oak; amazing (16.5°) alcohol does not unduly heat the finish. **RATING** 93 **DRINK** 2018 $ 50
Sellicks Beach Shiraz 2003 Complex, powerful wine with saturated black fruits; tannins run through the length of the palate and dominate the finish. Patience needed. **RATING** 90 **DRINK** 2015 $ 20
The Lighthouse McLaren Vale Cabernet Sauvignon 2003 An ultra-regional dark chocolate coating wraps around the black fruits, perhaps helped by oak; soft tannins. **RATING** 90 **DRINK** 2013 $ 20

Aramis Vineyards

★★★★☆

PO Box 208, Marleston, SA 5033 **REGION** McLaren Vale
T (08) 8238 0000 **F** (08) 8234 0485 **WEB** www.aramisvineyards.com **OPEN** Not
WINEMAKER Scott Rawlinson **EST.** 1998 **CASES** 4000
SUMMARY The estate vineyards have been planted to just two varieties: shiraz, with 18 ha, and cabernet sauvignon, with 8 ha. With the possible exception of old vine grenache, these are the red varieties which have made McLaren Vale so well known. Viticulturist David Mills is a third-generation McLaren Vale resident, and has been involved in the establishment of the vineyards from the very beginning. Winemaker Scott Rawlinson was with Mildara Blass for 8 years before joining the Aramis team under the direction of owner Lee Flourentzou. Exports to the UK, the US, Canada, Singapore and Hong Kong.

ΤΤΤΤΤ **The Governor Shiraz 2002** Rich, potent juicy blackberry fruit and a touch of bitter chocolate; fine, lingering tannins; line and length. Cork. **RATING** 94 **DRINK** 2015 $ 38

ΤΤΤΤΥ **Black Label Shiraz 2003** Dense, opaque purple; strong, spicy, peppery wild herb aromas; powerful, dense blackberry and bitter chocolate fruit; a slight hole in the mid-palate, still resolving itself. Slightly stained cork. **RATING** 93 **DRINK** 2015 $ 25

ΤΤΤΤ **Black Label Cabernet Sauvignon 2003** Smooth, medium-bodied blackcurrant/ blackberry fruit; needs a touch more on the back palate. Cork. **RATING** 89 **DRINK** 2012 $ 25

Archer Falls Vineyard & Winery

NR

1253 Newrum Road, Kilcoy via Woodford, Qld 4514 **REGION** Queensland Coastal
T (07) 5496 3507 **F** (07) 5496 3507 **OPEN** Weekends & public hols 10–5
WINEMAKER Contract **EST.** 1995 **CASES** NA
SUMMARY Ronald Field has a small vineyard of chardonnay and shiraz. The wine is sold through the cellar door and by mail order; there are the usual cellar door facilities, including barbecue and picnics.

Arlewood Estate

Harmans Road South, Wilyabrup, WA 6284 **REGION** Margaret River
T (08) 9755 6267 **F** (08) 9755 6267 **WEB** www.arlewood.com.au **OPEN** Weekends 11–5
WINEMAKER Juniper Estate (Contract) **EST.** 1988 **CASES** 6000
SUMMARY The Heydon and Gosatti families acquired Arlewood Estate in October 1999, having previously established a small vineyard in Cowaramup in 1995. George Heydon is a Perth dentist whose passion for wine has led him to study viticulture at the University of Western Australia; Garry Gosatti has been involved in the boutique brewing and hospitality industries for many years. The area under vine has been expanded to 15 ha. The quality and consistency of the wines is now impeccable. Retail distribution in most states and exports to the US and the UK.

TTTTT **Reserve Chardonnay 2002** Toasty barrel ferment inputs obvious on the bouquet; an intense, powerful, rich and long palate; ripe stone fruit, good balancing acidity. **RATING** 94 **DRINK** 2010 $ 32

TTTTT **Cabernet Sauvignon 2001** Aromatic cassis/blackcurrant aromas; powerful, complex, focused black fruits; balanced tannins, subtle oak. **RATING** 93 **DRINK** 2014 $ 32
Single Vineyard Semillon Sauvignon Blanc 2002 Very complex and powerful; a rich tapestry of fruit and oak, the latter just a little overdone. Needs time to show its best. **RATING** 90 **DRINK** 2012 $ 27
Cabernet Merlot 2002 Fragrant, spicy, minty berry aromas; medium-bodied; fine, ripe, savoury tannins. **RATING** 90 **DRINK** 2009 $ 27

TTTT **Shiraz 2002** Aromatic, spicy, savoury bouquet; supple black fruits, again with savoury, spicy notes; frugal oak. **RATING** 89 **DRINK** 2008 $ 22

Armstrong Vineyards

Lot 1 Military Road, Armstrong, Vic 3381 (postal) **REGION** Grampians
T (08) 8277 6073 **F** (08) 8277 6035 **OPEN** Not
WINEMAKER Tony Royal **EST.** 1989 **CASES** 2000
SUMMARY Armstrong Vineyards is the brain- or love-child of Tony Royal, former Seppelt Great Western winemaker who now runs the Australian business of Seguin Moreau, the largest of the French coopers. Armstrong Vineyards has 5 ha of shiraz, the first 2 ha planted in 1989, the remainder in 1995–96. Low yields (4.5 to 5.5 tonnes per hectare) mean the wine will always be produced in limited quantities. Exports to the UK.

TTTTT **Great Western Shiraz Viognier 2003** Very good colour; clean; excellent focus and definition; blackberry fruit; fine, savoury tannins; Viognier contribution subtle; drink now or later. **RATING** 92 **DRINK** 2013 $ 33

Arranmore Vineyard

Rangeview Road, Carey Gully, SA 5144 **REGION** Adelaide Hills
T (08) 8390 3034 **F** (08) 8390 0005 **WEB** www.arranmore.com.au **OPEN** By appointment
WINEMAKER John Venus **EST.** 1998 **CASES** 600
SUMMARY One of the tiny operations which are appearing all over the beautiful Adelaide Hills. At an altitude of around 550m, the 2-ha vineyard is planted to clonally selected pinot noir, chardonnay and sauvignon blanc. The wines are distributed by Australian Premium Boutique Wines, and sold by mail order. Exports to the UK.

Arrowfield

Denman Road, Jerrys Plains, NSW 2330 **REGION** Upper Hunter Valley
T (02) 6576 4041 **F** (02) 6576 4144 **WEB** www.arrowfieldwines.com.au **OPEN** 7 days 10–5
WINEMAKER Tim Pearce **EST.** 1968 **CASES** 70 000
SUMMARY Arrowfield continues in the ownership of the Inagaki family, which has been involved in the Japanese liquor industry for over a century. It has boosted its management team under the direction of new managing director Michael Goundrey, supported by veteran Chris Anstee and Caroline Duke on the marketing and distribution side. Arrowfield has at last emerged from the

vinous wilderness, with a series of well-made, well-priced wines under the Sophie's Bridge label and super-premium wines in the Show Reserve range. Exports to all major markets.

ΥΥΥΥΥ **Show Reserve Riesling 2004** Fragrant and floral; very pure, delicate but beautifully balanced Riesling. From Great Southern. RATING 93 DRINK 2014 $19.95
Show Reserve Shiraz 2003 Medium-bodied; fresh red and black fruits; vanilla oak also sits in the front seat; fine tannins. Barossa/McLaren Vale/Hunter. RATING 90 DRINK 2012 $19.95
Show Reserve Cabernet Sauvignon 2003 Medium-bodied; fresh cassis and blackberry; fine tannins, some length; subtle oak. RATING 90 DRINK 2012 $19.95

ΥΥΥΥ **Show Reserve Chardonnay 2004** Well-crafted and balanced; gentle melon and stone fruit, subtle oak. From estate plantings in the Hunter Valley. RATING 89 DRINK 2008 $19.95
Sophie's Bridge Sauvignon Blanc 2003 Light to medium-bodied; clean, fresh, light varietal fruit, then authentic, crisp dry finish. Well priced. RATING 87 DRINK Now $12.95
Sophie's Bridge Verdelho 2003 Fragrant fruit salad aromas; good flavour and balance; well above average. Hunter Valley. RATING 87 DRINK 2007 $12.95
Sophie's Bridge Rose 2003 Well made; good balance and length; raspberry and lemon fruit; relatively dry finish. Hunter Cabernet. RATING 87 DRINK Now $12.95
Sophie's Bridge Cabernet Merlot 2003 Light to medium-bodied; good balance and structure; some dark fruits, then savoury tannins. Hunter, Alpine and King Valleys. RATING 87 DRINK 2008 $12.95

ΥΥΥΥ **Sophie's Bridge Chardonnay 2003** RATING 85 DRINK Now $12.95
Sophie's Bridge Shiraz 2003 RATING 84 DRINK Now $12.95

Artamus ★★★★

PO Box 489, Margaret River, WA 6285 REGION Margaret River
T (08) 9757 8131 F (08) 9757 8131 WEB www.artamus.com.au OPEN Not
WINEMAKER Michael Gadd EST. 1994 CASES 280
SUMMARY Ann Dewar and Ian Parmenter (the celebrated television food presenter) planted 1 ha of chardonnay cuttings (from Cape Mentelle) at their property on the north bank of the Margaret River. Their first wine was produced in 1998, made for them by Michael Gadd, and the style of each succeeding vintage has been remarkably consistent.

Arthurs Creek Estate ★★★★

Strathewen Road, Arthurs Creek, Vic 3099 (postal) REGION Yarra Valley
T (03) 9714 8202 F (03) 9824 0252 WEB www.arthurscreekestate.com OPEN Not
WINEMAKER Tom Carson (Contract), Gary Baldwin (Consultant) EST. 1975 CASES 1500
SUMMARY A latter-day folly of leading Melbourne QC SEK Hulme. He began the planting of 3 ha of chardonnay, 4.3 ha of cabernet sauvignon and 0.7 ha of merlot at Arthurs Creek in the mid-1970s, and had wine made by various people for 15 years before deciding to sell any of it. The back vintages, sadly, are long since gone. Exports to the UK, the US, Denmark and Japan.

Arundel ★★★☆

Arundel Farm Estate, PO Box 136, Keilor, Vic 3036 REGION Sunbury
T (03) 9335 3422 F (03) 9335 4912 OPEN Not
WINEMAKER Bianca Hayes EST. 1995 CASES 600
SUMMARY Arundel was built around an acre of cabernet and shiraz that was planted in the 1970s, but abandoned. When the Conwell family purchased the property in the early 1990s, the vineyard was resurrected, the first vintage being made by Rick Kinzbrunner in 1995. Thereafter the cabernet was grafted over to shiraz, the block being slowly increased to 1.6 ha. After 1999, Bianca Hayes took over the responsibility for winemaking onsite. An additional 4 ha of shiraz and 1.6 ha of viognier and marsanne have been planted.

ΥΥΥΥΥ **Shiraz 2003** Vivid purple-red; medium-bodied plum, blackberry and spice; good length and intensity. Cork. RATING 93 DRINK 2013 $28

▼▼▼♀ **Marsanne 2004** Wild herb and grass, chalk and mineral; dry, austere finish. Quality cork. **RATING** 86 **DRINK** 2009 $ 20
Viognier 2004 RATING 86 **DRINK** 2008 $ 28

Ashbrook Estate ★★★★★

Harmans Road South, Wilyabrup via Cowaramup, WA 6284 **REGION** Margaret River
T (08) 9755 6262 **F** (08) 9755 6290 **OPEN** 7 days 11–5
WINEMAKER Tony Devitt, Brian Devitt **EST.** 1975 **CASES** 8000
SUMMARY A fastidious maker of consistently excellent estate-grown table wines which shuns publicity and the wine show system alike and is less well-known than it deserves to be, selling much of its wine through the cellar door and by an understandably very loyal mailing list clientele. All of the white wines are of the highest quality, year in, year out. Exports to the UK, Canada, Japan, Singapore and Hong Kong.

▼▼▼▼▼ **Margaret River Chardonnay 2002** Glowing light green-yellow; very complex aromas and intense flavours; exceptional mouthfeel and weight; smoky barrel ferment on luscious nectarine and white peach fruit; long finish. Best Wine of Show '04 Margaret River Wine Show. Cork. **RATING** 97 **DRINK** 2015 $ 29
Margaret River Shiraz 2002 Elegant, medium-bodied; delicious satsuma plum, raspberry and cherry fruit; fine, ripe tannins; subtle oak. Quality cork. **RATING** 94 **DRINK** 2015 $ 29

▼▼▼▼♀ **Margaret River Semillon 2004** In inimitable Margaret River style: powerful, tight and focused, carrying its 14° alcohol with ease. Enough flavour now or later. **RATING** 92 **DRINK** 2010 $ 16
Margaret River Sauvignon Blanc 2004 Clean; light mineral, herb and gooseberry aromas; more attack and presence run through to a long finish on the palate. **RATING** 92 **DRINK** 2008 $ 18

Ashley Estate NR

284 Aldersyde Road, Bickley, WA 6076 **REGION** Perth Hills
T (08) 9257 2313 **F** (08) 9257 3403 **OPEN** Sunday & public hols by appointment
WINEMAKER John Griffiths (Contract) **EST.** 1988 **CASES** NA
SUMMARY Ashley Estate (formerly Ashley Park) has 8 ha of vines planted exclusively to pinot noir by proprietor John Ashley. Highly experienced winemaker John Griffiths is responsible for winemaking, and the wine is sold through the cellar door.

Ashton Hills ★★★★☆

Tregarthen Road, Ashton, SA 5137 **REGION** Adelaide Hills
T (08) 8390 1243 **F** (08) 8390 1243 **OPEN** Weekends 11–5.30
WINEMAKER Stephen George **EST.** 1982 **CASES** 1500
SUMMARY Stephen George wears three winemaker hats: one for Ashton Hills, drawing upon a 3.5-ha estate vineyard high in the Adelaide Hills; one for Galah Wines; and one for Wendouree. It would be hard to imagine three wineries with more diverse styles, from the elegance and finesse of Ashton Hills to the awesome power of Wendouree. The Riesling, Chardonnay and Pinot Noir have moved into the highest echelon. Exports to the UK and the US.

▼▼▼▼▼ **Pinot Noir 2002** Intensely savoury and very Burgundian, spicy and stylish; on a strong upwards trajectory. **RATING** 96 **DRINK** 2012 $ 30

▼▼▼▼♀ **Riesling 2004** Herbs, flowers and apple blossom aromas; delicate, crisp apple and lime fruit; balanced acidity and length. **RATING** 93 **DRINK** 2014 $ 24
Pinot Noir 2003 Complex savoury, spicy, foresty, brambly aromas; discreet plum and spice fruit; lingering tannins. Screwcap. **RATING** 91 **DRINK** 2009 $ 42
Chardonnay 2003 Elegant, fresh and youthful; still almost painfully delicate and shy; will deliver in the longer term. Screwcap. **RATING** 90 **DRINK** 2010 $ 27.50

▼▼▼▼ **Three 2004** Gently aromatic; a crisp, restrained palate; improbably, Pinot Gris seems to have gagged the other two varieties; nice, clean finish. Gewurztraminer/Pinot Gris/Riesling. Screwcap. **RATING** 88 **DRINK** 2009 $ 20

Piccadilly Valley Pinot Noir 2003 Light to medium-bodied; bright, fresh cherry, plum and spice fruit; clean and direct; slightly stemmy notes on the finish. Screwcap. **RATING** 88 **DRINK** 2007 $ 22

Audrey Wilkinson Vineyard ★★★☆

Oakdale, De Beyers Road, Pokolbin, NSW 2320 **REGION** Lower Hunter Valley
T (02) 4998 7411 **F** (02) 4998 7824 **WEB** www.audreywilkinson.com.au **OPEN** Mon–Fri 9–5, weekends & public hols 9.30–5
WINEMAKER Mark Woods **EST.** 1999 **CASES** 12 500
SUMMARY One of the most historic properties in the Hunter Valley, set in a particularly beautiful location, and with a very attractive cellar door. In 2004 it was acquired by Brian Agnew and family, and hence is no longer part of the Pepper Tree/James Fairfax wine group. The wines are made from estate-grown grapes; the vines were planted between the 1970s and 1990s.

ΥΥΥΥ **Reserve Hunter Valley Semillon 2001** Ultra-fresh, early-picked (10° alcohol) style; crisp and racy; spicy lemon zest; still needs more time. Cork. **RATING** 89 **DRINK** 2011 $ 22

ΥΥΥΥ **Reserve Hunter Valley Shiraz 2001 RATING** 86 **DRINK** 2008 $ 30

Auldstone ★★★☆

Booths Road, Taminick via Glenrowan, Vic 3675 **REGION** Glenrowan
T (03) 5766 2237 **F** (03) 5766 2131 **WEB** www.auldstone.com.au **OPEN** Thurs–Sat & school hols 9–5, Sun 10–5
WINEMAKER Michael Reid **EST.** 1987 **CASES** 2000
SUMMARY Michael and Nancy Reid have restored a century-old stone winery and have replanted the largely abandoned 26-ha vineyard around it. All the Auldstone varietal and fortified wines have won medals (usually bronze) in Australian wine shows. Gourmet lunches are available on weekends.

ΥΥΥΥ **Shiraz 2001** Fully ripe fruit; elements of blackberry jam; also savoury/spicy characters; medium-bodied; good overall mouthfeel. Gold medal Concours des Vins du Victoria 2003. **RATING** 89 **DRINK** 2009 $ 20
Liqueur Muscat NV Good young raisined varietal character; fresh and lively; good balance and length. **RATING** 88 **DRINK** Now $ 25

ΥΥΥΥ **Merlot 2001 RATING** 86 **DRINK** 2009 $ 20
Chardonnay 2002 RATING 85 **DRINK** Now $ 19

ΥΥΥ **Riesling 2003 RATING** 83 $ 17

Austin's Barrabool ★★★★

870 Steiglitz Road, Sutherlands Creek, Vic 3331 **REGION** Geelong
T (03) 5281 1799 **F** (03) 5281 1673 **WEB** www.abwines.com.au **OPEN** By appointment
WINEMAKER Scott Ireland, Richard Austin **EST.** 1982 **CASES** 25 000
SUMMARY Pamela and Richard Austin have quietly built their business from a tiny base, and it has flourished. The vineyard has been progressively extended to 56 ha, and production has soared from 700 cases in 1998 to 25 000 cases in 2005. Scott Ireland is now full-time resident winemaker in the new and capacious onsite winery, and the quality of the wines is admirable.

ΥΥΥΥ **Pinot Noir 2003** Generous, ripe plum and black cherry fruit; soft and long; good balance and mouthfeel. Avoids going over the top. **RATING** 93 **DRINK** 2012 $ 25
Shiraz 2002 Complex herb, jam and black fruits in striking mode; strongly reminiscent of the southern Rhône. **RATING** 92 **DRINK** 2011 $ 25
Six Foot Six Pinot Noir 2003 Aromas of underbrush, herbs and spices, then intense black cherry, plum and spice flavours; good depth; very good value. **RATING** 90 **DRINK** 2007 $ 16.95
Merlot 2003 Clean; good varietal character; a core of red fruits with touches of olive and a hint of lemon; very fine tannins; good length. **RATING** 90 **DRINK** 2010 $ 25

ΥΥΥΥ **Six Foot Six Pinot Noir 2004** Light purple-red; clean, light to medium-bodied; plum and spice; good length, though not especially complex. **RATING** 88 **DRINK** 2007 $ 16

Riesling 2004 Shows a touch of reduction (likely ex screwcap); rich, full-bodied and and spicy; early-drinking style. **RATING** 87 **DRINK** Now $ 20

Chardonnay 2003 Moderate varietal character, intensity and weight; melon, stone fruit and cashew. **RATING** 87 **DRINK** Now $ 25

Rose 2004 Cherry/strawberry flavours, with some sweetness; very good cellar door style. **RATING** 87 **DRINK** Now $ 12

ỲỲỲỲ **Cabernet Sauvignon 2002 RATING** 86 **DRINK** 2007 $ 25

Sauvignon Blanc 2004 RATING 85 **DRINK** Now $ 20

Ellyse Chardonnay 2003 RATING 85 **DRINK** Now $ 28

Reserve Pinot Noir 2003 RATING 85 **DRINK** 2008 $ 45

Australian Domaine Wines   NR

95a Walkerville Terrace, Walkerville, SA 5081 **REGION** Clare Valley
T (08) 8342 3395 **F** (08) 8269 4008 **OPEN** By appointment
WINEMAKER Neil Pike (Polish Hill River Winery) **EST.** 1993 **CASES** 3000
SUMMARY Australian Domaine Wines is the reincarnation of Barletta Bros, who started their own brand business for the leading Adelaide retailer, Walkerville Cellars, which they then owned. The wines are made at Pike's Polish Hill River Winery using tanks and barrels owned by the Barlettas. Retail distribution in South Australia and Melbourne; exports to the UK, the US and other major markets.

Australian Old Vine Wine   ★★☆

Farm 271, Rossetto Road, Beelbangera, NSW 2680 **REGION** Riverina
T (02) 6963 5239 **F** (02) 6963 5239 **OPEN** 7 days 10–4
WINEMAKER Brian Currie, Dom Piromalli (Contract) **EST.** 2002 **CASES** 1570
SUMMARY Elio and Marie Alban have registered the name Australian Old Vine Wine Pty Ltd for their business. It is designed to draw attention to their 7.6 ha of 50-year-old shiraz and 2.4 ha of 40-year-old cabernet sauvignon. The younger wines, coming from chardonnay, colombard, semillon, merlot and chambourcin plantings, are released under the Australian Sovereign label. The plan is ultimately to buy grapes from old vines in the Barossa Valley and McLaren Vale for an Old Vine blend. The 2003 Australian Old Vine Shiraz, with its extraordinary label, has been selected for service in the NSW Parliament.

ỲỲỲỲ **Shiraz 2002 RATING** 84 **DRINK** 2007 $ 12

ỲỲỲ **Chambourcin 2003 RATING** 83 $ 12

Avalon Vineyard   ★★★☆

RMB 9556 Whitfield Road, Wangaratta, Vic 3678 **REGION** King Valley
T (03) 5729 3629 **F** (03) 5729 3635 **WEB** www.avalonwines.com.au **OPEN** 7 days 10–5
WINEMAKER Doug Groom **EST.** 1981 **CASES** 1000
SUMMARY Roseworthy graduate Doug Groom, and wife Rosa, have established a 10-ha vineyard, selling part of the grapes, but making Chardonnay (described as French-inspired), Pinot Noir and highly rated Shiraz. Non-interventionist winemaking is reflected in the use of indigenous yeasts and unfiltered wines.

ỲỲỲỲ **Shiraz 2002** Light to medium-bodied; a complex mix of herbs, spices, black fruits, licorice and cedar; fine tannins. Cork. **RATING** 88 **DRINK** 2010 $ 20

ỲỲỲỲ **Rosado 2004** Spicy; nice texture and mouthfeel; exemplary dry finish. Shiraz/ Pinot Noir/Tempranillo. Screwcap. **RATING** 86 **DRINK** Now $ 16

Sangiovese 2003 Unusually deep colour; powerful, slightly extractive; unusual play for Sangiovese; could age well. Cork. **RATING** 86 **DRINK** 2010 $ 18

Avalon Wines   ★★★☆

1605 Bailey Road, Glen Forrest, WA 6071 **REGION** Perth Hills
T (08) 9298 8049 **F** (08) 9298 8049 **WEB** www.avalonvineyard.com.au **OPEN** By appointment
WINEMAKER Rob Marshall (Contract) **EST.** 1986 **CASES** 700
SUMMARY One of the smaller wineries in the Perth Hills, drawing upon 0.75 ha each of chardonnay, semillon and cabernet sauvignon. Plans to open a cellar door sales and tasting area in 2006/07.

Avenel Park/Hart Wines ★★★

24/25 Ewings Road, Avenel, Vic 3664 **REGION** Goulburn Valley
T (03) 9347 5444 **F** (03) 9349 3278 **WEB** www.avenelpark.com.au **OPEN** Sunday 11–4, or by appointment
WINEMAKER David Traeger, Sam Plunkett (Contract) **EST.** 1994 **CASES** 1000
SUMMARY Jed and Sue Hart have, in their words, 'turned the rocky, ironstone soils of Lovers Hill into a 22-acre vineyard over some back-breaking years'. Seven of the 10 ha are planted to shiraz and cabernet sauvignon, with a small amount each of merlot, semillon and chardonnay. Most of the grapes have been and will continue to be sold to Southcorp, but since 2000 the equivalent of 1000 cases of wine have been retained and contract-made by David Traeger. Nonetheless, the Harts' main viticultural business (Jed Hart is in aviation) will be grapegrowing.

Aventine Wines NR

86 Watters Road, Ballandean, Qld 4382 **REGION** Granite Belt
T 0409 270 389 **F** (07) 3001 9299 **WEB** www.aventinewines.com.au **OPEN** Weekends & public hols 9–6
WINEMAKER Jim Barnes **EST.** 1995 **CASES** 25 000
SUMMARY The 9-ha Aventine vineyard is situated at an elevation of 1000m, on a north-facing hill high above the Ballandean Valley. The highest portions of the site are planted to nebbiolo and sangiovese, the soils shallow, weathered granite; shiraz, cabernet sauvignon and muscat are also planted. All wines are estate-grown.

Avonbrook Wines NR

7 Benrua Road, Clackline, WA 6564 **REGION** Central Western Australia Zone
T (08) 9574 1276 **F** (08) 9574 1070 **OPEN** Weekends & public hols 10–5
WINEMAKER Peter Murfit **EST.** 1993 **CASES** NA
SUMMARY Avonbrook Wines is loosely based on 2.3 ha of vineyards planted to chenin blanc, chardonnay, verdelho, merlot and shiraz by winemaker/viticulturist Peter Murfit. The wines are exported to the UK and the US under various brands.

Avonmore Estate ★★★★

Mayreef–Avonmore Road, Avonmore, Vic 3558 **REGION** Bendigo
T (03) 5432 6291 **F** (03) 5432 6291 **WEB** www.avonmoreestatewine.com **OPEN** Wed–Sun & public hols 11–5, or by appointment
WINEMAKER Shaun Bryans, Rob Bryans **EST.** 1996 **CASES** 1500
SUMMARY Rob and Pauline Bryans own and operate a certified Grade A biodynamic farm, producing and selling beef, lamb and cereals as well as establishing 9 ha of viognier, sangiovese, cabernet sauvignon, cabernet franc and shiraz which produced its first crop in 2000. Most of the wine is contract-made, but a small amount is made on the property, and are marketed in Australia with the worldwide Demeter logo. Exports to Canada and Thailand.

ŸŸŸŸŸ **Bendigo Shiraz 2002** Powerful, savoury black fruits, dark chocolate and spice; medium to full-bodied; good texture, length and mouthfeel; good oak, modest 14° alcohol another plus. Grapes and wine Demeter-certified. Quality cork. **RATING** 93 **DRINK** 2012 $ 22.50

Baarrooka Vineyard NR

Coach Road, Strathbogie, Vic 3666 **REGION** Strathbogie Ranges
T (03) 5790 5288 **F** (03) 5790 5205 **WEB** www.baarrooka.com.au **OPEN** Weekends & public hols 11–5 Sept–May, or by appointment
WINEMAKER Paul Evans, Travis Bush, Russell Synnot **EST.** 1996 **CASES** 1200
SUMMARY The establishment of the 32-ha Baarrooka Vineyard began in 1995, on a north-facing slope at an elevation of 550m. Plantings consist of riesling, sauvignon blanc, chardonnay, pinot noir, cabernet sauvignon, shiraz, merlot, zinfandel and small blocks of petit verdot, cabernet franc and malbec. The majority of the grapes are sold under contract into the Yarra Valley, but a small quantity is released under the Baarrooka label, the quantities and varieties varying according to the vintage.

Bacchanalia Estate   NR

160 Taverner Street, Bacchus Marsh, Vic 3340 **REGION** Sunbury
T (03) 5367 6416 **F** (03) 5367 6416 **OPEN** Most weekends & public hols
WINEMAKER John Reid, Peter Dredge (Contract) **EST.** 1994 **CASES** 1000
SUMMARY Noted ABC broadcaster and journalist John Reid, and wife Val, established Bacchanalia
Estate in 1994 on the fertile black soils of Bacchus Marsh, adjacent to the Werribee River.
Consultancy viticultural advice from Dr Richard Smart pointed to the inevitably vigorous growth to
be expected from the rich, black soil, so a Geneva Double Curtain (GDC) trellis and canopy was
utilised from the outset. The 3.2-ha vineyard is planted to shiraz, semillon, cabernet sauvignon and
viognier. Apart from local distribution through Geelong and Ballarat, the wine is available at Nick's
Wine Merchants throughout Melbourne.

Bacchus Hill   NR

100 O'Connell Road, Bacchus Marsh, Vic 3340 **REGION** Sunbury
T 0412 124 166 **OPEN** Weekends 10–5
WINEMAKER Bruno Tassone **EST.** 2000 **CASES** 3500
SUMMARY Lawyer Bruno Tassone migrated from Italy when he was 8 years old, and watched his
father carry on the Italian tradition of making wine for home consumption. Tassone followed the
same path before purchasing a 35-ha property at Bacchus Marsh with his wife Jennifer. Here they
have planted 2 ha each of riesling, semillon, sauvignon blanc, chardonnay, pinot noir, merlot, shiraz
and cabernet sauvignon, plus 1 ha each of chenin blanc and nebbiolo. It was known locally as the Hill
Property, so Bacchus Hill Winery became the obvious name. The plan is to sell most of the wine
through local outlets and the newly opened cellar door. The property prominently situated just off
the Western Highway, less than 50 km from Melbourne.

Badger's Brook   ★★★☆

874 Maroondah Highway, Coldstream, Vic 3770 **REGION** Yarra Valley
T (03) 5962 4130 **F** (03) 5962 4238 **WEB** www.badgersbrook.com.au **OPEN** Wed–Mon 11–5
WINEMAKER Contract **EST.** 1993 **CASES** 5000
SUMMARY Situated next door to the well-known Rochford. It has a total of 10 ha of vineyard, mainly
planted to chardonnay, sauvignon blanc, pinot noir, shiraz and cabernet sauvignon, and a few rows
each of viognier, roussanne, marsanne and tempranillo. All of the wines, under both the second
Storm Ridge label and the primary Badger's Brook label, are Yarra Valley-sourced. Now houses a
smart brasserie restaurant with well-known chef Gary Cooper in charge. Domestic distribution
through The Wine Company; exports to Asia.

ᵀᵀᵀᵀ **Storm Ridge Sauvignon Blanc 2004** Positive varietal character throughout; gooseberry,
mineral, grass and green pea aromas and flavours; crisp and bright palate; well made.
Screwcap. **RATING** 90 **DRINK** 2007 $ 17

ᵀᵀᵀᵀ **Shiraz Viognier 2002** Medium-bodied; fresh, showing the fruit intensity of the
vintage, but has diminished tannin structure, possibly due to the Viognier component.
High-quality cork. **RATING** 89 **DRINK** 2010 $ 25
Storm Ridge Pinot Noir 2003 Clean, fresh, light to medium-bodied; spice, cherry and
plum; not forced, fair length. Screwcap. **RATING** 88 **DRINK** 2007 $ 17

ᵀᵀᵀ **Storm Ridge Rose 2004** **RATING** 86 **DRINK** Now $ 17

Bago Vineyards   ★★★

Milligans Road (off Bago Road), Wauchope, NSW 2446 **REGION** Hastings River
T (02) 6585 7099 **F** (02) 6585 7099 **WEB** www.bagovineyards.com.au **OPEN** 7 days 11–5
WINEMAKER Jim Mobbs, John Cassegrain (Consultant) **EST.** 1985 **CASES** 6000
SUMMARY Jim and Kay Mobs began planting the Broken Bago Vineyards in 1985 with 1 ha of
chardonnay, with total plantings now 12.5 ha. Regional specialist John Cassegrain is consultant
winemaker.

Baileys of Glenrowan ★★★★★

Cnr Taminick Gap Road and Upper Taminick Road, Glenrowan, Vic 3675 **REGION** Glenrowan
T (03) 5766 2392 **F** (03) 5766 2596 **WEB** www.baileysofglenrowan.com.au **OPEN** Mon–Fri 9–5,
weekends 10–5
WINEMAKER Paul Dahlenburg **EST.** 1870 **CASES** 15 000
SUMMARY Just when it seemed that Baileys would remain one of the forgotten outposts of the Bering
Blass empire, the reverse has occurred. Since 1998 Paul Dahlenburg has been in charge of Baileys. He
has overseen an expansion in the vineyard to 143 ha and the construction of a totally new 2000-
tonne winery. The cellar door has a heritage museum, winery viewing deck, contemporary art gallery
and landscaped grounds; much of the heritage value of Baileys has been preserved. Baileys has also
picked up the pace with its Muscat and Tokay, reintroducing the Winemaker's Selection at the top of
the tree, while continuing the larger-volume Founder series.

ℽℽℽℽℽ **Winemaker's Selection Old Muscat (375 ml) NV** Very rich, very complex dried raisin
and plum pudding; viscous and luscious; quite fresh despite its age. **RATING** 95 **DRINK** Now
$ 30
Winemaker's Selection Old Liqueur Tokay NV Excellent balance between older and
younger material; tea leaf, Christmas cake and butterscotch; complexity without a hint of
staleness. **RATING** 94 **DRINK** Now $ 30

ℽℽℽℽℽ **Founder Liqueur Tokay NV** Moderate age showing in the colour; very good varietal
character ranging through tea leaf, malt, butterscotch and Christmas cake; good balance;
clean finish. **RATING** 92 **DRINK** Now $ 17
Founder Liqueur Muscat (375 ml) NV Rich, intense, dried raisin, Christmas pudding and
spice; varietal character again bell-clear; good balance, moderate age. **RATING** 92
DRINK Now $ 17
Founder Tawny Port NV Tawny as it is made in northeast Victoria: more luscious and
raisined than classic South Australian Tawnys. Clean, modern packaging a feature for the
fortified range. **RATING** 90 **DRINK** Now $ 17

ℽℽℽℽ **Classic Style Shiraz 2003** Powerful wine; clean, blackberry and plum fruit; slightly
grippy tannins need to soften. Quality cork. **RATING** 89 **DRINK** 2011 $ 17
1920's Block Shiraz 2001 Earthy black fruits, cedar and vanilla; medium-bodied; well
balanced, but all in the savoury end of the spectrum; fine tannins. Quality cork. **RATING** 89
DRINK 2012 $ 25
Cabernet Sauvignon 2003 Powerful blackcurrant fruit; heroic, old-style Baileys; lots of
tannins to soften. Cork. **RATING** 88 **DRINK** 2013 $ 17

ℽℽℽℽ **Frontignac 2004** Pink blush; gently grapey, strawberry mix; delicate, and not as sweet as
feared. Alternative Rose. Screwcap. **RATING** 86 **DRINK** Now $ 16

Bainton Family Wines ★★★☆

390 Milbrodale Road, Bulga, NSW 2330 (postal) **REGION** Lower Hunter Valley
T (02) 9968 1764 **F** (02) 9960 3454 **WEB** www.bainton.com.au **OPEN** Not
WINEMAKER Tony Bainton **EST.** 1998 **CASES** 3500
SUMMARY The Bainton family, headed by eminent Sydney QC Russell Bainton, has 48 ha of vineyard,
with the oldest semillon planted over 80 years ago (1923), most in 1940. The major part of the shiraz,
too, dates back to plantings of 1950 and 1955.

Bald Mountain ★★★★

Hickling Lane, Wallangarra, Qld 4383 **REGION** Granite Belt
T (07) 4684 3186 **F** (07) 4684 3433 **OPEN** 7 days 10–5
WINEMAKER Simon Gilbert (Contract) **EST.** 1985 **CASES** 5000
SUMMARY Denis Parsons is a self-taught but exceptionally competent vigneron who has turned Bald
Mountain into one of the viticultural showpieces of the Granite Belt. The two Sauvignon Blanc-based
wines, Classic Queenslander and Late Harvest Sauvignon Blanc, are interesting alternatives to the
mainstream wines. Future production will also see grapes coming from new vineyards near
Tenterfield just across the border in New South Wales. Significant exports to The Netherlands.

ΥΥΥΥΥ **Shiraz 2000** Rich, complex and quite luscious; excellent texture and structure. Museum class, Queensland Wine Awards 2004. **RATING** 94 **DRINK** 2007

ΥΥΥΥ♈ **Shiraz Cabernet 2000** Strong wine; slightly sinewy but plenty of flavour, and good texture on the finish. **RATING** 93 **DRINK** 2010

ΥΥΥΥ **Late Harvest Sauvignon Blanc NV** Golden brown; complex cumquat-accented flavours; does shorten slightly. **RATING** 87 **DRINK** Now

Balgownie Estate ★★★★☆

Hermitage Road, Maiden Gully, Vic 3551 **REGION** Bendigo
T (03) 5449 6222 **F** (03) 5449 6506 **WEB** www.balgownieestate.com.au **OPEN** 7 days 11–5
WINEMAKER Tobias Ansted **EST.** 1969 **CASES** 5000
SUMMARY Balgownie Estate continues to grow in the wake of its acquisition by the Forrester family. A $3 million upgrade of the winery coincided with a doubling of the size of the vineyard to 35 ha, and in 2003 Balgownie Estate opened a separate cellar door in the Yarra Valley (see separate entry). Exports to the UK, the US and other major markets.

ΥΥΥΥΥ **Bendigo Shiraz 2003** Dense, opaque purple-red; full-bodied, velvety, rich, blackberry, plum and dark chocolate; ripe tannins. Screwcap. **RATING** 94 **DRINK** 2023 $ 34

ΥΥΥΥ♈ **Bendigo Cabernet Sauvignon 2003** Medium-bodied; attractive spicy, savoury blackcurrant fruit; lingering ripe tannins and a hint of chocolate; good oak and tannins. Screwcap. **RATING** 92 **DRINK** 2018 $ 34

🍇 Balgownie Estate (Yarra Valley) ★★★★☆

Cnr Melba Highway and Gulf Road, Yarra Glen, Vic 3775 **REGION** Yarra Valley
T (03) 9730 2669 **F** (03) 9730 2647 **WEB** www.balgownieestate.com.au **OPEN** 7 days 10–5
WINEMAKER Tobias Ansted **EST.** 2004 **CASES** NA
SUMMARY Balgownie Estate opened a very attractive rammed-earth cellar door in 2004, offering the full range of Balgownie wines. The Yarra Valley range of Chardonnay, Pinot Noir, Shiraz and Cabernet Sauvignon are 100% Yarra Valley, using contract-grown grapes from several vineyards. The café is open daily 11–4. A resort and conference centre is scheduled to open in late 2005 (further details from www.ariaproperty.com.au).

ΥΥΥΥΥ **Pinot Noir 2003** Concentrated, complex and powerful; savoury, spicy edges to rich plum fruit; good texture and length. Screwcap. **RATING** 94 **DRINK** 2010 $ 25

ΥΥΥΥ♈ **Chardonnay 2003** Quite rich, ripe stone fruit, fig and cashew; malolactic and barrel ferment influences well judged; subtle oak, good texture. Screwcap. **RATING** 91 **DRINK** 2009 $ 25

ΥΥΥΥ **Pinot Noir 2002** Very good colour, still purple-red; firm and fresh, slightly hard, low pH style; may or may not evolve, but does need time. **RATING** 87 **DRINK** 2009 $ 25

🍇 Balhannah Vineyards ★★★

Lot 100, Johnson Road, Balhannah, SA 5242 **REGION** Adelaide Hills
T (08) 8398 0698 **F** (08) 8398 0698 **OPEN** By appointment
WINEMAKER Rod Short, Rachel Short **EST.** 1997 **CASES** 500
SUMMARY Rod and Rachel Short began the planting of 3 ha of shiraz, 2 ha of chardonnay, 1.5 ha of merlot and 1 ha of pinot noir in 1997. 2002 was the first vintage, made from 100% estate-grown grapes. Yields are limited to 1.5 to 2 tonnes per acre for the red wines, and 2 to 3 tonnes for the chardonnay. Most of the grapes are sold; the limited production is sold by mail order.

ΥΥΥΥ **Shiraz 2002** At the other extreme to the ultra-ripe Pinot Noir; spicy herbal notes intermingle with restrained American oak to add a touch of sweetness. **RATING** 87 **DRINK** 2009 $ 22

ΥΥΥ♈ **Pinot Noir 2002** **RATING** 86 **DRINK** 2008 $ 45

Ballabourneen Wines ★★★☆

Talga Road, Rothbury, NSW 2320 **REGION** Lower Hunter Valley
T (02) 4930 7027 **F** (02) 4930 9180 **WEB** www.ballabourneenwines.com.au **OPEN** Thurs–Sun 10–5, or by appointment
WINEMAKER Alasdair Sutherland, Andrew Thomas **EST.** 1994 **CASES** 900
SUMMARY Between 1994 and 1998 Alex and Di Stuart established 2 ha of chardonnay, 1.5 ha of verdelho and 1 ha of shiraz. The viticulture uses natural sprays, fertilisers, mulches and compost, with a permanent sward maintained between the rows. Competent contract winemaking by Alasdair Sutherland has bought show success for the Verdelho, the high point being a trophy at the 1999 Hunter Valley Wine Show.

ΥΥΥΥΥ **Shiraz 2003** Incredibly dense and deep for the region, but only 12.6° alcohol; as yet, powerful structure imprisons blackberry fruit; low pH style, watch development. **RATING** 90 **DRINK** 2013 $ 20

Ballandean Estate ★★★★

Sundown Road, Ballandean, Qld 4382 **REGION** Granite Belt
T (07) 4684 1226 **F** (07) 4684 1288 **WEB** www.ballandeanestate.com **OPEN** 7 days 9–5
WINEMAKER Dylan Rhymer, Angelo Puglisi **EST.** 1970 **CASES** 12 000
SUMMARY The senior winery of the Granite Belt and by far the largest. The white wines are of diverse but interesting styles, the red wines smooth and usually well made. The estate specialty, Sylvaner Late Harvest, is a particularly interesting wine of great character and flavour if given 10 years bottle age, but it isn't made every year.

ΥΥΥΥΥ **Cabernet Shiraz 2002** Full flavoured, with plenty of depth to the black fruits and spice; manages to retain elegance and length. **RATING** 94 **DRINK** 2012 $ 29.50

ΥΥΥΥΥ **Shiraz 2002** A powerful, robust wine with plenty of blackberry fruit; slightly gritty tannins. **RATING** 90 **DRINK** 2010 $ 16.50

ΥΥΥΥ **Chardonnay 2002** **RATING** 86 **DRINK** 2007 $ 20
Sylvaner 2004 **RATING** 86 **DRINK** 2007 $ 16

ΥΥΥ **Cabernet Sauvignon Merlot 2002** **RATING** 82 $ 20

Ballast Stone Estate Wines ★★★

Myrtle Grove Road, Currency Creek, SA 5214 **REGION** Currency Creek
T (08) 8555 4215 **F** (08) 8555 4216 **WEB** www.ballaststone.com.au **OPEN** 7 days 10.30–4.30
WINEMAKER John Loxton **EST.** 2001 **CASES** 15 000
SUMMARY The Shaw family had been grapegrowers in McLaren Vale for 25 years before deciding to establish a large vineyard (250 ha) in Currency Creek in 1994. The vineyard is planted mainly to cabernet sauvignon and shiraz, with much smaller quantities of other trendy varieties. A large onsite winery has been built, managed by Philip Shaw (no relation to Rosemount's Philip Shaw), and John Loxton (formerly senior winemaker at Maglieri). Only a small part of the production will be sold under the Ballast Stone Estate label; most will be sold in bulk. A cellar door is to be established on the main Strathalbyn-Victor Harbour Road, tapping into the tourism trade of the Southern Fleurieu Peninsula. Exports to the UK and Germany.

ΥΥΥΥ **Stonemason Cabernet Sauvignon 2002** Fine, very savoury, earthy, briary; does have good length and balance. Twin Top. **RATING** 87 **DRINK** Now $ 15

ΥΥΥΥ **Stonemason Semillon Sauvignon Blanc 2004** **RATING** 86 **DRINK** 2007 $ 13
Stonemason Chardonnay 2003 **RATING** 86 **DRINK** Now $ 13
Petit Verdot 2002 **RATING** 86 **DRINK** 2012

ΥΥΥ **Stonemason Shiraz 2003** **RATING** 83

Balnaves of Coonawarra ★★★★★

Main Road, Coonawarra, SA 5263 **REGION** Coonawarra
T (08) 8737 2946 **F** (08) 8737 2945 **WEB** www.balnaves.com.au **OPEN** Mon–Fri 9–5, weekends 12–5
WINEMAKER Peter Bissell **EST.** 1975 **CASES** 9500

SUMMARY Grapegrower, viticultural consultant and vigneron Doug Balnaves has 52 ha of high quality estate vineyards. The pick of the crop is made by the immensely talented Pete Bissell in the winery built in 1996. The wines are invariably excellent, often outstanding. The wines are notable for their supple mouthfeel, varietal integrity, balance and length. The tannins are always fine and ripe, the oak subtle and perfectly integrated. Coonawarra at its best. Exports to the UK, Switzerland, Denmark, the US, Canada, Uruguay, Hong Kong and Japan.

ᵀᵀᵀᵀᵀ **Shiraz 2002** Full, rich and sweet blackberry and plum mid-palate fruit; good structure and oak management; long finish. Trophy winner 2004 Limestone Coast Wine Show. **RATING** 95 **DRINK** 2013

Chardonnay 2003 Fresh nectarine and citrus fruit, with a neat touch of malolactic fermentation and subtle oak; good balance and, above all else, great length. Trophy winner 2004 Limestone Coast Wine Show. **RATING** 94 **DRINK** 2009 $ 28

ᵀᵀᵀᵀᵧ **The Blend 2002** Elegant, light to medium-bodied wine; attractive mix of red and black fruits; good length. **RATING** 91 **DRINK** 2012 $ 19

ᵀᵀᵀᵀ **Cabernet Sauvignon 2002** A powerful wine, with some austere elements; good length. **RATING** 88 **DRINK** 2010 $ 31

ᵀᵀᵀᵧ **Cabernet Merlot 2002 RATING** 86 **DRINK** 2009 $ 24

Balthazar of the Barossa ★★★★

Lot 10 Stonewell Road, Marananga, SA 5355 (postal) **REGION** Barossa Valley
T (08) 8562 2949 **F** (08) 8562 2949 **WEB** www.balthazarbarossa.com **OPEN** At the Small Winemakers Centre, Chateau Tanunda
WINEMAKER Anita Bowen **EST.** 1999 **CASES** 1000
SUMMARY Anita Bowen announces her occupation as 'a 40-something sex therapist with a 17-year involvement in the wine industry': she is also the wife of experienced winemaker Randall Bowen. She undertook her first vintage at Mudgee, then McLaren Vale, and ultimately the Barossa; she worked at St Hallet while studying at Roseworthy College. As to her wine, she says, 'Anyway, prepare a feast, pour yourself a glass (no chalices, please) of Balthazar and share it with your concubines. Who knows? It may help to lubricate thoughts, firm up ideas and get the creative juices flowing!' Exports to all major markets.

Bamajura NR

775 Woodbridge Hill Road, Gardners Bay, Tas 7112 **REGION** Southern Tasmania
T (03) 6295 0294 **F** (03) 6295 0294 **OPEN** By appointment
WINEMAKER Scott Polley **EST.** 1987 **CASES** NA
SUMMARY Bamajura's name is derived from the first two letters of the names of the late Ray Polley and his sisters Barbara, Margaret and Judy. The vineyard was planted by Ray Polley, and son Scott took over in the early 1990s; having undertaken the TAFE Tasmania viticulture course, he converted the vineyard to the Scott Henry trellis. In 2002 he took over the winemaking mantle from Michael Vishacki.

Banks Road ★★★☆

600 Banks Road, Marcus Hill, Vic 3222 **REGION** Geelong
T (03) 9822 6587 **F** (03) 9822 5077 **WEB** www.banksroadwine.com.au **OPEN** By appointment
WINEMAKER Justyn Baker, William Derham **EST.** 2001 **CASES** 1500
SUMMARY Banks Road, owned and operated by William Derham, has 2 vineyards: the first, of 2.5 ha, is on the Bellarine Peninsula at Marcus Hill, planted to pinot noir and chardonnay; the second is at Harcourt in the Bendigo region, planted to 3 ha of shiraz and cabernet sauvignon, the vines ranging from 8 to 12 years of age. Winemaker Justyn Baker has dual degrees from Charles Sturt University, and has worked in the Hunter Valley, France and the Mornington Peninsula. The Bellarine vineyard is newly planted, with the first wines to be released in 2005/06.

ᵀᵀᵀᵀ **Bendigo Cabernet Sauvignon 2002** Clear, bright and clean; light to medium-bodied; fresh cassis and blackberry fruit; fractionally dusty tannins. Screwcap. **RATING** 89 **DRINK** 2009 $ 26

Banks Thargo Wines ★★★★

Racecourse Road, Penola, SA 5277 (postal) **REGION** Coonawarra
T (08) 8737 2338 **F** (08) 8737 3369 **OPEN** Not
WINEMAKER Banks Kidman, Jonathon Kidman **EST.** 1980 **CASES** 900
SUMMARY The unusual name comes directly from family history. One branch of the Kidman family
moved to the Mt Gambier district in 1858, but Thomas Kidman (who had been in the foster care of
the Banks family from the age of 2 to 13) moved to the Broken Hill/southwest Queensland region to
work for the famous Kidman Bros pastoral interests. When he 'retired' from the outback, he bought
this property, in 1919. His second son was named Banks Thargomindah Kidman, and it is he and wife
Jenny who decided to diversify their grazing activities by planting vines in the 1980s: 16.5 ha are
under contract, leaving 1.3 ha each of merlot and cabernet sauvignon for the Banks Thargo brand.

ΨΨΨΨΨ **Coonawarra Merlot 2003** Good colour; medium to full-bodied; considerable ripe fruit
weight; soft tannins; more depth than length. **RATING** 90 **DRINK** 2012

ΨΨΨΨ **Coonawarra Cabernet Sauvignon 2002** **RATING** 84 **DRINK** 2009

Bannockburn Vineyards ★★★★★

Midland Highway, Bannockburn, Vic 3331 (postal) **REGION** Geelong
T (03) 5281 1363 **F** (03) 5281 1349 **WEB** www.bannockburnvineyards.com **OPEN** Not
WINEMAKER Gary Farr (former) **EST.** 1974 **CASES** 10 000
SUMMARY With the qualified exception of the Cabernet Merlot, which can be a little leafy and gamey,
produces outstanding wines across the range, all with individuality, style, great complexity and depth
of flavour. The low-yielding estate vineyards play their role, but so did the French-influenced
winemaking of former winemaker Gary Farr. The Serre Pinot Noir, from a close-planted block, is
absolutely outstanding. Whoever follows Farr will have massive shoes to fill. Export markets have
been established in the UK, Denmark, the US, Hong Kong, Singapore, New Zealand and Malaysia.

ΨΨΨΨΨ **Pinot Noir 2003** Ultra-complex and powerful spiced plum aromas; beguiling palate, with
again plum and exotic spices; intense, yet not heavy or alcoholic. Cork. **RATING** 96
DRINK 2012 $ 50
Shiraz 2003 Fragrant, spicy black cherry fruits; beautifully silky and supple mouthfeel;
lovely wine. Cork. **RATING** 96 **DRINK** 2015 $ 50
Chardonnay 2003 Ultra-complex, slightly feral barrel ferment aromas and flavours; a
surprisingly elegant, light, Chablis-like palate. High-quality cork. **RATING** 94 **DRINK** 2012
$ 50

ΨΨΨΨΨ **Geelong Sauvignon Blanc 2004** As usual, restrained and tight; citrus and redcurrant
fruit flavours; clean finish. Cork. **RATING** 91 **DRINK** 2008 $ 25

ΨΨΨΨ **Geelong Saignee Rose 2004** Subtle style; textural complexity; gentle spice and some
strawberry. Cork. **RATING** 89 **DRINK** Now $ 25

Banrock Station ★★★

Holmes Road (off Sturt Highway), Kingston-on-Murray, SA 5331 **REGION** Riverland
T (08) 8583 0299 **F** (08) 8583 0288 **WEB** www.banrockstation.com **OPEN** 7 days 10–5,
except public hols
WINEMAKER Mark Zeppel, Paul Kassebaum **EST.** 1994 **CASES** 1.9 million
SUMMARY The $1 million visitors' centre at Banrock Station was opened in February 1999. Owned by
Hardys, the Banrock Station property covers over 1700 ha, with 240 ha of vineyard and the
remainder being a major wildlife and wetland preservation area. The wines have consistently offered
excellent value for money.

ΨΨΨΨ **The Reserve Petit Verdot 2003** Tending hard in the mouth, but does have abundant
black fruit and chocolate flavours; strongly varietal. **RATING** 87 **DRINK** 2010 $ 12

ΨΨΨΨ **The Reserve Chardonnay 2003** **RATING** 86 **DRINK** 2008 $ 12
Semillon Chardonnay 2004 Nicely balanced fresh and crisp; juicy lemony fruit; excellent
value. **RATING** 86 **DRINK** Now $ 8
White Shiraz 2004 **RATING** 85 **DRINK** Now $ 7

Baptista

c/- David Traeger, 139 High Street, Nagambie, Vic 3608 **REGION** Heathcote
T (03) 5794 2514 **F** (03) 5794 1776 **WEB** www.baptista.com.au **OPEN** 7 days 10–5
WINEMAKER David Traeger **EST.** 1993 **CASES** 500
SUMMARY In 1993 David Traeger acquired a vineyard he had coveted for many years, and which had been planted by Baptista Governa in 1891. He has been buying grapes from the vineyard since 1988, but it was in a run-down condition, and required a number of years' rehabilitation before he felt the quality of the grapes was sufficient for a single-vineyard release. Ownership of the business did not pass to Dromana Estate when that company acquired the David Traeger brand; it is jointly owned by David Traeger and the Wine Investment Fund, the latter a majority shareholder in Dromana Estate. Exports to the UK, Singapore and Japan.

♆♆♆♆♆ Heathcote Shiraz 1999 Still very good colour; very complex and powerful wine; black fruits and tannins duel with each other, but end up in balance; smoky, briary, plummy fruit; definitely shows old vine strength and length. Vines planted 1891. High-quality cork. **RATING** 93 **DRINK** 2019 $120

Barak Estate

NR

Barak Road, Moorooduc, Vic 3933 **REGION** Mornington Peninsula
T (03) 5978 8439 **F** (03) 5978 8439 **OPEN** Weekends & public hols 11–5
WINEMAKER James Williamson **EST.** 1996 **CASES** 500
SUMMARY When James Williamson decided to plant vines on his 4-ha Moorooduc property and establish a micro-winery, he already knew it was far cheaper to buy wine by the bottle than to make it. Undeterred, he ventured into grapegrowing and winemaking, picking the first grapes in 1993 and opening Barak Estate in 1996. Old telegraph poles, railway sleepers, old palings and timber shingles have all been used in the construction of the picturesque winery.

Barambah Ridge

79 Goschnicks Road, Redgate via Murgon, Qld 4605 **REGION** South Burnett
T (07) 4168 4766 **F** (07) 4168 4770 **WEB** www.barambahridge.com.au **OPEN** 7 days 10–5
WINEMAKER Stuart Pierce **EST.** 1995 **CASES** 10 000
SUMMARY Barambah Ridge is owned by Tambarambah Limited, an unlisted public company, and since its inception in 1995 has quickly established itself as one of the major players in the Queensland wine scene. Its estate plantings at Redgate include chardonnay, semillon, shiraz, verdelho and cabernet sauvignon, producing the first vintage in 1997. A modern winery was built in 1998, and in 2003 crushed 500 tonnes of grapes, much of it as contract winemaker for many other Queensland wineries. Full details of its three retail outlets are on the website.

♆♆♆♆♆ Chardonnay 2004 Bright green-yellow; aromatic, elegant and fresh; light-bodied but poised. **RATING** 92 **DRINK** 2007 $15.90

♆♆♆ Verdelho 2004 RATING 82 $17.90

Baratto's

NR

Farm 678, Hanwood, NSW 2680 **REGION** Riverina
T (02) 6963 0171 **F** (02) 6963 0171 **OPEN** 7 days 10–5
WINEMAKER Peter Baratto **EST.** 1975 **CASES** 6250
SUMMARY Baratto's is in many ways a throwback to the old days. Peter Baratto has 15 ha of vineyards and sells the wine in bulk or in 10 and 20 litre casks from the cellar door at old-time prices, from as little as a few dollars per litre.

🐛 Bare Rooted

NR

101 Broome Street, Cottesloe, WA 6011 (postal) **REGION** Margaret River
T (08) 9384 9764 **F** (08) 9385 3120 **OPEN** Not
WINEMAKER Contract **EST.** 1996 **CASES** 200

SUMMARY Ross and Jeannine Ashton planted 1 ha of sauvignon blanc in 1996, located on their 8-ha property surrounded by groves and avenues of poplars, cork oaks, deciduous trees, conifers, olives and eucalypts; a small frog-filled dam overlooks the vineyard. The quirky name comes from the fact that when vine rootlings are planted, they are devoid of any soil around their roots and are in a dormant phase. The one wine, Semillon Sauvignon Blanc, sells for the mouthwatering price of $84 a carton (the semillon comes from purchased grapes). Sales are by mail order and word of mouth.

Barfold Estate ★★★★☆

57 School Road, Barfold, Vic 3444 REGION Heathcote
T (03) 5423 4225 F (03) 5423 4225 WEB www.barfoldestate.com.au OPEN 7 days 10–5
WINEMAKER Craig Aitken EST. 1998 CASES 450
SUMMARY Craig and Sandra Aitken acquired their farm property in the southwestern corner of the Heathcote wine region with the specific intention of growing premium grapes. They inspected more than 70 properties over the 18 months prior to purchasing Barfold, and are in fact only the second family to own the property since the 1850s. So far they have planted 3.4 ha of shiraz, and 0.6 ha of cabernet sauvignon; a small planting of viognier is planned for the future.

ŸŸŸŸŸ **Heathcote Shiraz 2003** Dense colour; extremely dense and concentrated, but not jammy; masses of dark plum; spicy balanced tannins. Concentrated by drought. Ten years, who knows? Quality cork. RATING 93 DRINK 2023 $ 25

Barnadown Run ★★★★

390 Cornella Road, Toolleen, Vic 3551 REGION Heathcote
T (03) 5433 6376 F (03) 5433 6386 WEB www.barnadownrun.com.au OPEN 7 days 10–5
WINEMAKER Andrew Millis EST. 1995 CASES 1700
SUMMARY Named after the original pastoral lease of which the vineyard forms part, established on rich terra rossa soil for which Heathcote vineyards are famous. Owner Andrew Millis carries out both the viticulture and winemaking at the 5-ha vineyard. Exports to the US and the UK.

ŸŸŸŸŸ **Cabernet Sauvignon 2002** Fully ripe, luscious, sweet blackcurrant fruit; fine, ripe tannins; oak a purely support role. High-quality cork. RATING 91 DRINK 2015 $ 29.95
Henry Bennett's Voluptuary 2002 Big, powerful and concentrated with lots of fruit and tannins; slightly rustic edges need to settle. RATING 90 DRINK 2014 $ 45

ŸŸŸŸ **Shiraz 2002** Earthy/spicy/herbal edges to medium-bodied, black fruit flavours; fine tannins; slightly hot alcohol finish (15°). RATING 89 DRINK 2012 $ 35

ŸŸŸŸ **Merlot 2002** RATING 85 DRINK 2008 $ 29.95

Barokes Wines ★★★

75 Cecil Street, South Melbourne, Vic 3205 (postal) REGION Warehouse
T (03) 9684 7121 F (03) 9690 8114 WEB www.wineinacan.com OPEN Not
WINEMAKER Steve Barics EST. 1997 CASES 60 000
SUMMARY Barokes Wines provides a comprehensive answer to those who believe that wine bottled with screwcap closures cannot age. Barokes takes the process a whole lot further, packaging its wines in aluminium cans. The filling process is patented, and has been in commercial production since 1997. The wines show normal maturation development, and none of the cans used since startup shows signs of corrosion. The wines are supplied in bulk by 7 large wineries in southeast Australia, with Peter Scudamore-Smith MW acting as consultant. Exports to northern Europe, Canada, Hong Kong, Taiwan and Singapore.

ŸŸŸŸ **Bin 241 Chardonnay Semillon NV** Bright, light colour; fresh, clean, light-bodied; well balanced; no hint of taint or reduction. Points largely irrelevant. RATING 84 DRINK Now $ 4.50
Bin 121 Cabernet Shiraz Merlot NV Slightly jammy, porty fruit, due to the base wine, not to the container. RATING 84 DRINK Now $ 4.50
Bubbly Wine Bin 242 Chardonnay Semillon NV Interesting; obviously, has kept its mousse well; respectable, balanced and surprisingly (pleasingly) dry, RATING 84 DRINK Now $ 4.50

Bubbly Wine Bin 171 Cabernet Shiraz Merlot NV Plenty of flavour, and not too sweet. **RATING** 84 **DRINK** Now $4.50

Barossa Cottage Wines

NR

Nuriootpa–Angaston Road, Angaston, SA 5353 **REGION** Eden Valley
T (08) 8562 3212 **F** (08) 8562 3243 **WEB** www.barossawines.com.au **OPEN** Mon–Sat & public hols 10–4.30
WINEMAKER Rod Chapman **EST.** 1990 **CASES** NA
SUMMARY Heather and Ray Bartsch have been grapegrowers for over 20 years; they are descendants of Gottfried Harwig who settled in the Eden Valley in 1860, and have 26 ha of vines in the Eden Valley, and 12 ha at Angaston. Most of the 300 tonnes of annual grape production is sold to others, but a small percentage is made into a modestly priced but wide range of wines.

Barossa Ridge Wine Estate

Light Pass Road, Tanunda, SA 5352 **REGION** Barossa Valley
T (08) 8563 2811 **F** (08) 8563 2811 **OPEN** By appointment
WINEMAKER Marco Litterini **EST.** 1987 **CASES** 2000
SUMMARY A grapegrower turned winemaker with a small list of interesting red varietals, including the Valley of Vines blend of Merlot, Cabernet Franc, Cabernet Sauvignon and Petit Verdot. All of its wines are built in an impressively heroic style. Increasing retail distribution in Australia, exports to Switzerland, Germany, Malaysia and Thailand.

ᵀᵀᵀᵀᵀ **Litterini 2002** Potent, brooding savoury/tarry/spicy aromas; long and intense black fruits and bitter chocolate; fine, savoury tannins; good oak; 67% Shiraz, 33% Cabernet Sauvignon. **RATING** 94 **DRINK** 2015 $35

ᵀᵀᵀᵀᵧ **Old Creek Shiraz 2002** Notes of smoke, tar, spice and black fruits on the bouquet; savoury blackberry fruits and some dark chocolate; ripe tannins. **RATING** 92 **DRINK** 2015 $28

ᵀᵀᵀᵀ **Old Creek Limited Release Shiraz 2000** A mix of spice and ripe, slightly jammy/confection fruit; holding well, but shows the lesser vintage. **RATING** 88 **DRINK** 2009 $30

ᵀᵀᵀᵀᵧ **Litterini 2001** Clean and quite fragrant; very different from the 2002; much riper, sweeter fruit aromas and flavours; good mouthfeel. Cabernet Sauvignon 67%, Shiraz 33%. **RATING** 90 **DRINK** 2011 $35

Barossa Settlers

Trial Hill Road, Lyndoch, SA 5351 **REGION** Barossa Valley
T (08) 8524 4017 **F** (08) 8524 4519 **OPEN** 7 days 11–3
WINEMAKER Jane Haese **EST.** 1983 **CASES** 500
SUMMARY A superbly located cellar door (dating back to 1860) is the only outlet (other than mail order) for the wines from this excellent vineyard owned by the Haese family; the shiraz was planted in 1887. Most of the grapes from the 31-ha vineyard are sold to others.

Barossa Valley Estate

Seppeltsfield Road, Marananga, SA 5355 **REGION** Barossa Valley
T (08) 8562 3599 **F** (08) 8562 4255 **WEB** www.bve.com.au **OPEN** 7 days 10–4.30
WINEMAKER Stuart Bourne **EST.** 1984 **CASES** 100 000
SUMMARY Barossa Valley Estate is owned by Hardys, marking the end of a period during which it was one of the last significant co-operative owned wineries in Australia. Across the board, the wines are full flavoured and honest. E&E Black Pepper Shiraz is an upmarket label with a strong reputation and following; the Ebenezer range likewise. Over-enthusiastic use of American oak (particularly with the red wines) has been the Achilles heel in the past.

ᵀᵀᵀᵀ **E&E Black Pepper Shiraz 2001** Clean; medium-bodied, no-frills style; straightforward red and black fruits; gentle tannins. Expensive. **RATING** 89 **DRINK** 2011 $60

ᵀᵀᵀᵧ **Spires Chardonnay 2003** **RATING** 86 **DRINK** 2008 $11
Ebenezer Shiraz 2001 **RATING** 84 **DRINK** Now $33

Barratt ★★★★★

Uley Vineyard, Cornish Road, Summertown, SA 5141 **REGION** Adelaide Hills
T (08) 8390 1788 **F** (08) 8390 1788 **OPEN** Weekends & public hols 11.30–5, or by appointment
WINEMAKER Lindsay Barratt, Jeffrey Grosset (Contract) **EST.** 1993 **CASES** 1500
SUMMARY Lindsay and Carolyn Barratt own 2 vineyards at Summertown: the Uley Vineyard, purchased from the late Ian Wilson in August 1990, and the Bonython Vineyard. They have 8.4 ha of vines; sauvignon blanc and merlot were added to the wine range from 2002. Part of the production from the vineyards is sold to other makers, with Jeffrey Grosset the maker of the Chardonnay and Reserve Pinot Noir. Arrangements were finalised for a winery facility at the Adelaide Hills Business and Tourism Centre at Lobethal in time for the 2003 vintage. Limited quantities are sold in the UK, Canada and Asia.

▼▼▼▼▼ **Piccadilly Valley Chardonnay 2003** Very elegant and highly focused style; seamless stone fruit, citrus and gently spicy French oak; faultless balance; 20-year-old vines. Screwcap. **RATING** 94 **DRINK** 2010 **$** 26
Piccadilly Valley Pinot Noir 2003 Lively, fresh, intense, tangy, spicy plum; elegant and beautifully balanced; sensitive handling of oak and extract throughout. High-quality cork. **RATING** 94 **DRINK** 2009 **$** 28

▼▼▼▼ **Piccadilly Valley Sauvignon Blanc 2004** Water white; minerally aromas with a faint touch of reduction; better palate; lemon, capsicum and herb. **RATING** 89 **DRINK** 2008 **$** 19
Piccadilly Sunrise Rose 2004 Clean and fresh; no reduction. A long palate; bright red fruits; clever juxtaposition of sugar and acidity. Pinot noir base. **RATING** 89 **DRINK** Now **$** 18

Barrecas ★★★★

South West Highway, Donnybrook, WA 6239 **REGION** Geographe
T (08) 9731 1716 **F** (08) 9731 1716 **OPEN** Sun–Mon 10–5, or by appointment
WINEMAKER Iolanda Ratcliffe **EST.** 1994 **CASES** NA
SUMMARY Three generations of the Barreca family have been involved in winemaking, first in Italy and ultimately in Donnybrook. Third-generation Tony Barreca sold his orchard in 1994, using the proceeds to buy the site upon which he has since established 33 ha planted to a Joseph's Coat of 26 different varieties. Most of the grapes are sold under contract, but a small, modern winery onsite produces a limited amount of wine.

▼▼▼▼▽ **Shiraz 2003** Elegant, intense cool-climate style; sweet cherry fruit and lovely spice. **RATING** 90 **DRINK** 2008 **$** 13.50

Barretts Wines ★★★★☆

Portland–Nelson Highway, Portland, Vic 3305 **REGION** Henty
T (03) 5526 5251 **OPEN** 7 days 11–5
WINEMAKER Rod Barrett **EST.** 1983 **CASES** 1000
SUMMARY Has a low profile, selling its wines locally, but deserves a far wider audience. The initial releases were made at Best's, but since 1992 all wines have been made (with increasing skill) on the property by Rod Barrett, emulating John Thomson at Crawford River Wines. The 5.5-ha vineyard is planted to riesling, pinot noir and cabernet sauvignon.

▼▼▼▼▼ **Riesling 2004** Highly aromatic and flowery; lime blossom and passionfruit; great balance and line. Screwcap. **RATING** 94 **DRINK** 2014 **$** 18

▼▼▼▼▽ **Pinot Noir 2003** Firm, fresh, savoury/sous bois aromas and flavours, but not green or thin; has length and presence. Screwcap. **RATING** 90 **DRINK** 2008 **$** 20

🍇 Barrgowan Vineyard ★★★★★

30 Pax Parade, Curlewis, Vic 3222 **REGION** Geelong
T (03) 5250 3861 **F** (03) 5250 3840 **OPEN** By appointment
WINEMAKER Dick Simonsen **EST.** 1998 **CASES** 150
SUMMARY Dick and Deb (Elizabeth) Simonsen began the planting of their 0.5 ha of shiraz (with five clones) in 1994, intending to simply make wine for their own consumption. All five clones will come into full production by 2006, and the Simonsens expect a maximum production of 200 cases; they have accordingly released small quantities of Shiraz, which sell out very quickly. The vines are hand-

pruned, the grapes hand-picked, the must basket-pressed, and all wine movements are by gravity. This attention to detail, coupled with the excellent vineyard site, has seen the 2002 and 2003 Shiraz winning gold medals at the 2003 and 2004 Geelong Wine Shows, and being the Public Choice on each occasion. Until sold out, the wine is available by mail order at $33 a bottle plus freight.

ΨΨΨΨΨ **Shiraz 2003** Complex licorice, blackberry and boot polish aromas and flavours; tight structure and nervy acidity; flavour and elegance. **RATING** 95 **DRINK** 2018 $ 33

Barringwood Park ★★★★☆

60 Gillams Road, Lower Barrington, Tas 7306 **REGION** Northern Tasmania
T (03) 6492 3140 **F** (03) 6492 3360 **OPEN** Wed–Sun & public hols 10–5
WINEMAKER Tamar Ridge (Contract) **EST.** 1993 **CASES** 1700
SUMMARY Judy and Ian Robinson operate a sawmill at Lower Barrington, 15 minutes south of Devonport on the main tourist trail to Cradle Mountain, and when they planted 500 vines in 1993 the aim was to do a bit of home winemaking. In a thoroughly familiar story, the urge to expand the vineyard and make wine on a commercial scale came almost immediately, and they embarked on a 6 year plan, planting 1 ha a year for the first 4 years (doing all the work themselves while also running their sawmill), and then built the cellar and tasting rooms during the following 2 years.

ΨΨΨΨΨ **Pinot Noir 2003** Elegant, well-balanced wine; gentle red fruits; silky ripe tannins. **RATING** 94 **DRINK** 2010 $ 25

ΨΨΨΨ **Mill Block Pinot Noir 2002** Intense, sappy palate, with substantial oak inputs; long finish. **RATING** 92 **DRINK** 2009 $ 27

ΨΨΨΨ **Schonburger 2004** Quite aromatic; lively, fresh and crisp; lemony fruit; not particularly sweet. **RATING** 88 **DRINK** 2009 $ 22
Chardonnay 2003 Solid wine; plenty of fruit; nutty oak nuances. **RATING** 87 **DRINK** 2008 $ 21

ΨΨΨ **Pinot Grigio 2004** **RATING** 86 **DRINK** 2007 $ 22

ΨΨΨ **Pinot Meunier 2003** **RATING** 83 $ 19

Barrymore Estate ★★★☆

76 Tuerong Road, Tuerong, Vic 3933 **REGION** Mornington Peninsula
T (03) 5974 8999 **F** (03) 9789 0821 **WEB** www.barrymore.com.au **OPEN** Weekends 11–5, or by appointment
WINEMAKER Peter J Cotter **EST.** 1998 **CASES** 1500
SUMMARY Barrymore Estate is part of a much larger property first settled in the 1840s; the abundance of water and wetlands, with the confluence of the Devil Bend and Balcombe Creeks nearby, has sustained grazing and farming since the first settlement. Peter Cotter has planted 8.5 ha of pinot noir, 1 ha each of chardonnay and sauvignon blanc, and 0.5 ha of pinot gris, selling part of the grapes and making part under the Barrymore label.

🐌 Bartagunyah Estate NR

7 Survey Road, Melrose, SA 5483 **REGION** Southern Flinders Ranges
T (08) 8666 2136 **F** (08) 8666 2136 **WEB** www.smartaqua.com.au/bartagunyah **OPEN** By appointment
WINEMAKER Charles Melton, O'Leary Walker (Contract) **EST.** 2000 **CASES** 2000
SUMMARY Rob and Christine Smart have established 3 ha of shiraz, 2 ha of cabernet sauvignon and 1 ha of viognier on a property adjoining the southern ridge of the beautiful and rugged Mt Remarkable. It is hidden away in a valley in the hills about 5 km south of Melrose along the historic Survey Road. It is a hop, step and jump into the Flinders Ranges, and the Smarts offer 4-wheel drive tours and mountain bike tours to take in both the scenery and the abundant wildlife.

Barwang Vineyard ★★★★☆

Barwang Road, Young, NSW 2594 (postal) **REGION** Hilltops
T (02) 6382 3594 **F** (02) 6382 2594 **WEB** www.mcwilliams.com.au **OPEN** Not
WINEMAKER Jim Brayne, Martin Cooper, Russell Cody, Stephen Cook **EST.** 1969 **CASES** NFP

SUMMARY Peter Robertson pioneered viticulture in the Young region when he planted his first vines in 1969 as part of a diversification program for his 400-ha grazing property. When McWilliam's acquired Barwang in 1989, the vineyard amounted to 13 ha; today the plantings exceed 100 ha. Wine quality has been exemplary from the word go: always elegant, restrained and deliberately understated, repaying extended cellaring.

ΥΥΥΥΥ Shiraz 2002 Potent, intense and long black fruit flavours run through to a lingering finish, supported by excellent tannins. Richly deserved its gold medal at the National Wine Show 2004. **RATING** 94 **DRINK** 2017

ΥΥΥΥΥ Chardonnay 2004 Elegant stone fruit, melon and citrus; subtle oak; good acidity. **RATING** 90 **DRINK** 2009 $ 18

Barwick Wines ★★★

Yelverton North Road, Dunsborough, WA 6281 **REGION** Margaret River
T (08) 9765 1216 **F** (08) 9765 1836 **WEB** www.barwickwines.com **OPEN** Wed–Sun & public hols 10.30–5
WINEMAKER John Griffiths, Flying Fish Cove (Contract) **EST.** 1997 **CASES** 120 000
SUMMARY The production gives some guide to the size of the operation. Since 1997 Barwick Wines has been supplying grapes and bulk wine to some of the best-known names in Western Australia and the eastern states from three very large vineyards. The first is the 83-ha Dwalganup Vineyard in the Blackwood Valley region, the second the 38-ha St John's Brook Vineyard in the Margaret River, and the third the 73-ha Treenbrook Vineyard in Pemberton. The wines are contract-made at two locations, and sell for thoroughly old-fashioned prices. Local sales come from what the owners describe as 'friends of Barwick'.

ΥΥΥΥ The Collectables Sauvignon Blanc Semillon 2004 No reduction; a complex wine with some barrel ferment inputs; overall richness and slight sweetness. Screwcap. **RATING** 89 **DRINK** 2007 $ 21
The Collectables Viognier 2004 Fresh, clean pastille and apricot aromas; light to medium-bodied; good balance and length; not phenolic. Screwcap. **RATING** 88 **DRINK** 2009 $ 21
St Johns Brook Chardonnay 2004 Light-bodied; sweet peachy fruit, butterscotch and vanilla, finishing with good acidity; a strange contrast. Screwcap. **RATING** 87 **DRINK** 2007 $ 13.99

ΥΥΥΥ St Johns Brook Sauvignon Blanc Semillon 2004 RATING 86 **DRINK** Now $ 13.99
St Johns Brook Margaret River Cabernet Sauvignon 2001 RATING 86 **DRINK** 2008 $ 13.99
Rock Wallaby Red 2004 RATING 86 **DRINK** 2007 $ 10.99
The Collectables Chardonnay 2004 RATING 85 **DRINK** 2007 $ 21

ΥΥΥ Rock Wallaby White 2004 RATING 83 $ 10.99
Crush 2004 RATING 83 $ 10
St Johns Brook Pinot Noir 2003 RATING 83 $ 10.99
St Johns Brook Margaret River Shiraz Cabernet 2000 RATING 82 $ 13.99

🐦 Barwite Vineyards ★★★☆

PO Box 542, Mansfield, Vic 3724 **REGION** Upper Goulburn
T 0408 525 135 **F** (03) 5776 9800 **WEB** www.barwitevineyards.com.au **OPEN** Not
WINEMAKER Contract **EST.** 1997 **CASES** 2500
SUMMARY David Ritchie and a group of fellow grape and wine enthusiasts established their substantial vineyard in 1997 on a slope facing the mouth of the Broken River and thereon to Mt Stirling. A little under 28 ha of pinot noir and 9.4 ha of chardonnay were planted for Orlando, to be used in sparkling wine. Given the reputation of the region for the production of aromatic white wines, 4.5 ha of riesling were also planted; the intention again was to sell the grapes. However, since 2003 some of the best parcels have been kept aside and vinified at King Valley Wines by Wayne Proft. The wine is distributed in Victoria, New South Wales and Queensland by QED Australia Pty Ltd and is available by mail order.

ΥΥΥΥ Riesling 2004 Tangy, minerally, citrussy aromas; tight minerally structure off-set by a flick of sweetness on the finish. **RATING** 87 **DRINK** 2008 $ 9.20 (ML)

Riesling 2003 Light-bodied, crisp, minerally; fresh finish. **RATING** 87 **DRINK** 2007 $ 9.20 (ML)

ʒʒʒʒ **Chardonnay 2004** **RATING** 85 **DRINK** Now $ 9.20 (ML)

Barwon Plains ★★★★

61 Trebeck Court, Winchelsea, Vic 3241 **REGION** Geelong
T (03) 5267 2792 **F** (03) 5267 2792 **OPEN** By appointment
WINEMAKER Phil Kelly **EST.** 1995 **CASES** 300
SUMMARY Phil and Merridee Kelly planted 1.5 ha of pinot noir, 1 ha of chardonnay and 0.5 ha of shiraz between 1995 and 1998. The Kellys personally carry out all of the vineyard and winery operations, selling most of the grape production to Shadowfax Winery. The first commercial wine release under the Barwon Plains label was in 2000, and the wines have been consistent medal winners at the Geelong Wine Show.

ʒʒʒʒʒ **Pinot Noir 2003** Good colour; medium-bodied cherry, berry and plum; good balance and elegance. **RATING** 92 **DRINK** 2010 $ 15

ʒʒʒʒ **Shiraz 2003** Light to medium-bodied; ripe blackberry and plum fruit; soft, sweet oak and tannins background. **RATING** 88 **DRINK** 2008 $ 15

Chardonnay 2003 Tight, reserved style; citrus and melon fruit; scores for its length more than anything else. **RATING** 87 **DRINK** Now $ 12

Basedow ★★★☆

c/- James Estate, 951 Bylong Valley Way, Baerami via Denman, NSW 2333 (postal) **REGION** Barossa Valley
T 1300 887 966 **F** (02) 6574 5164 **WEB** www.basedow.com.au **OPEN** Not
WINEMAKER Peter Orr **EST.** 1896 **CASES** 50 000
SUMMARY An old and proud label, once particularly well known for its oak-matured Semillon, but which has changed hands on a number of occasions before passing into the ownership of James Estate in 2003. Continues making ultra-traditional styles, particularly the American-oaked Semillon which, while in no way reflecting the future direction for the variety in the valley, is a true-to-itself rock of ages. Exports to the UK and the US.

ʒʒʒʒ **Eden Valley Riesling 2000** Gold-green; long, lingering lime juice fruit; very good balance and mouthfeel. **RATING** 92 **DRINK** 2010 $ 20

ʒʒʒʒ **Semillon 2000** While unashamedly full-blown, full-bodied and in an old-fashioned White Burgundy style, still has some varietal freshness to tighten the finish. **RATING** 87 **DRINK** Now $ 14.99

Barossa Shiraz 2001 Medium-bodied; clean, gently sweet black and red fruits; air brush of American oak; soft tannins. Cork. **RATING** 87 **DRINK** 2009 $ 25

Basket Range Wines NR

PO Box 65, Basket Range, SA 5138 **REGION** Adelaide Hills
T (08) 8390 1515 **F** (08) 8390 1515 **OPEN** Not
WINEMAKER Phillip Broderick **EST.** 1980 **CASES** 500
SUMMARY A tiny operation known to very few, run by civil and Aboriginal rights lawyer Phillip Broderick, a most engaging man with a disarmingly laid-back manner.

Bass Fine Wines ★★★★

1337 Pipers River Road/4238 Bridport Road, Pipers Brook, Tas 7254 (postal) **REGION** Northern Tasmania
T (03) 6331 0136 **F** (03) 6331 0136 **OPEN** Not
WINEMAKER Guy Wagner **EST.** 1999 **CASES** 27500
SUMMARY Bass Fine Wines runs entirely counter to the usual Tasmanian pattern of tiny, estate-based businesses. Guy Wagner has set up Bass as a classic negociant operation, working backwards from the marketplace. He has completed a wine marketing degree at the University of Adelaide and intends to continue studies in oenology. The wines have been purchased from various vineyards in

bottle and in barrel, but from the 2000 vintage were also purchased as grapes. The winery has been set up to focus on Pinot Noir, with three levels of Pinot in the business plan, commencing with Strait Pinot in the fighting varietal sector of the market, then Bass as a premium brand, and ultimately a super-premium Pinot, possibly to come from 30-year-old plantings which have been contracted.

ŸŸŸŸ♈ **Strait Pinot Noir 2003** Abundant, spicy black plum and cherry fruit; deep and solid.
RATING 90 **DRINK** 2008 $18

ŸŸŸŸ **Strait Riesling 2004** Long, powerful and quite intense; good focus and balance.
RATING 88 **DRINK** 2009 $19
Strait Pinot Gris 2003 Still water white; tight, minerally, more in grigio style than gris; dry finish is a plus. **RATING** 87 **DRINK** Now $17

ŸŸŸ♈ **Strait Chardonnay 2004 RATING** 84 **DRINK** Now $21

Bass Phillip ★★★★★

Tosch's Road, Leongatha South, Vic 3953 **REGION** Gippsland
T (03) 5664 3341 **F** (03) 5664 3209 **OPEN** By appointment
WINEMAKER Phillip Jones **EST.** 1979 **CASES** 1500
SUMMARY Phillip Jones has retired from the Melbourne rat-race to handcraft tiny quantities of superlative Pinot Noir which, at its best, has no equal in Australia. Painstaking site selection, ultra-close vine spacing and the very, very cool climate of South Gippsland are the keys to the magic of Bass Phillip and its eerily Burgundian Pinots.

Bass Valley Estate Wines NR

175 Nyora–St Helier Road, Loch, Vic 3945 **REGION** Gippsland
T (03) 5659 6321 **F** (03) 5659 0256 **OPEN** 7 days 10–6
WINEMAKER Robert Cutler, Roger Cutler **EST.** 1991 **CASES** NA
SUMMARY The Cutler family has established 3 ha of riesling, pinot noir, cabernet sauvignon and shiraz on the eastern slopes of the Bass River Valley. The cellar door has barbecue and picnic facilities which take full advantage of the expansive views over the Valley.

Batista NR

Franklin Road, Middlesex, WA 6258 **REGION** Manjimup
T (08) 9772 3530 **F** (08) 9772 3530 **OPEN** By appointment
WINEMAKER Bob Peruch **EST.** 1993 **CASES** 1200
SUMMARY Batista is in fact the baptismal name of owner Bob Peruch, a Pinot Noir devotee whose father planted 1 ha of vines back in the 1950s; these have since gone. The estate has 2 vineyards, one for pinot noir and chardonnay, and the other, 2 km away, for shiraz, cabernet sauvignon, cabernet franc and merlot. The well-drained soils are of quartz and ironstone gravel; yields are restricted to around 7 tonnes per hectare.

battely wines ★★★★

1375 Beechworth–Wangaratta Road, Beechworth, Vic 3747 **REGION** Beechworth
T (03) 5727 0505 **F** (03) 5727 0506 **WEB** www.battelywines.com.au **OPEN** By appointment
WINEMAKER Russell Bourne **EST.** 1998 **CASES** 450
SUMMARY Dr Russell Bourne is an anaesthetist and former GP at Mt Beauty, who has always loved the food, wine and skiing of northeast Victoria. He completed his oenology degree at Charles Sturt University in 2002 following his acquisition of the former Brown Brothers Everton Hills vineyard. A few years ago I shared in a bottle of 1964 Everton Hills Cabernet Shiraz which had been entombed at Brown Brothers for over 35 years. The vineyard was sold by Brown Brothers many years ago (low yields made it uneconomic) and was overgrown and abandoned when Dr Bourne purchased it in 1998. In that year he planted 1.6 ha of shiraz and viognier in the spring of 2001, with further Rhône Valley varietal plantings planned, including counoise. While battely wines owns the former Everton Vineyard, Brown Brothers retained the brand name, and has recently released a range of wines under the Everton label. Since 2001 all wines made under the battely label have come from the estate vineyards, which have increased to 2.3 ha. Exports to the US and Singapore.

Battle of Bosworth ★★★★☆

Edgehill Vineyards, Gaffney Road, Willunga, SA 5172 **REGION** McLaren Vale
T (08) 8556 2441 **F** (08) 8556 4881 **OPEN** By appointment
WINEMAKER Ben Riggs (Consultant) **EST.** 1996 **CASES** 1500
SUMMARY The 75-ha Edgehill Vineyard, established many years ago by Peter and Anthea Bosworth, was taken over by son Joch Bosworth in 1996. He set about converting 10 ha of shiraz, cabernet sauvignon and chardonnay to fully certified A-grade organic viticulture, and is now in the process of converting the chardonnay (which takes 4 years). The regime prohibits the use of herbicides and pesticides; the weeds are controlled by soursob, the pretty yellow flower considered a weed by many, which carpets the vineyards in winter, but dies off in early spring as surface moisture dries, forming a natural weed mat. But organic viticulture is never easy, and when Joch Bosworth moved to make the first wines from the vines, the Battle of Bosworth name was a neat take. Joch's partner, Louise Hemsley-Smith, runs the marketing and promotion side of the business in her spare time: her day job is with Penny's Hill. Exports to the UK and the US.

 McLaren Vale Shiraz 2002 Clean; ultra-classic McLaren Vale blackberry and dark chocolate; silky mouthfeel (14.5° alcohol), fine tannins, real elegance. Cork. **RATING** 94 **DRINK** 2015 **$** 25

 McLaren Vale Cabernet Sauvignon 2002 Bright, clear colour; medium-bodied; fresh blackcurrant fruit; supple, silky, fine tannins; good oak. Quality cork. **RATING** 93 **DRINK** 2013 **$** 24

Battunga Vineyards NR

RSD 25A Tynan Road, Meadows, SA 5201 (postal) **REGION** Adelaide Hills
T (08) 8388 3866 **F** (08) 8388 3877 **OPEN** Not
WINEMAKER Robert Mann, Simon White **EST.** 1997 **CASES** A few
SUMMARY The development of this substantial vineyard venture began in 1997 under the direction of David Eckert. The plantings extend to pinot noir (7 ha), merlot (3.6 ha), sauvignon blanc (3.4 ha), chardonnay (2.3 ha), shiraz (2 ha), pinot gris (1.8 ha) and viognier (1.8 ha), but only a limited amount of wine is made and released under the Battunga Vineyards brand.

Baudin Rock Wines NR

RSD 109, Kingston SE, SA 5275 (postal) **REGION** Mount Benson
T (08) 8768 6217 **F** (08) 8768 6217 **OPEN** Not
WINEMAKER Contract **EST.** 1997 **CASES** NA
SUMMARY The Ling family, headed by Robin Ling, began the development of Baudin Rock Wines in 1997, and now has 40 ha planted to sauvignon blanc, cabernet sauvignon, merlot and shiraz. The wines are made under contract, but with assistance from James Ling; the viticulturist is Paul Ling, and the production manager Robin Ling. Only a small amount of the wine is made under the Baudin Rock label, with most of the production sold.

Baxter Stokes Wines NR

65 Memorial Avenue, Baskerville, WA 6065 **REGION** Swan Valley
T (08) 9296 4831 **F** (08) 9296 4831 **OPEN** 9.30–5 weekends & public hols
WINEMAKER Greg Stokes **EST.** 1988 **CASES** 750
SUMMARY A weekend and holiday operation for Greg and Lucy Stokes, with the production sold by mail order and through the cellar door.

Bay of Fires ★★★★☆

40 Baxters Road, Pipers River, Tas 7252 **REGION** Northern Tasmania
T (03) 6382 7622 **F** (03) 6382 7225 **WEB** www.bayoffireswines.com.au **OPEN** 7 days 10–5
WINEMAKER Fran Austin **EST.** 2001 **CASES** 3000
SUMMARY In 1994 Hardys purchased its first grapes from Tasmania, with the aim of further developing and refining its sparkling wines, a process which quickly gave birth to Arras. The next stage was the inclusion of various parcels of chardonnay from Tasmania in the 1998 Eileen Hardy,

then the development in 2001 of the Bay of Fires brand, offering wines sourced from various parts of Tasmania. As one would expect, there is great potential for the brand. The winery was originally that of Rochecombe, then Ninth Island, and now, of course, Bay of Fires.

ŢŢŢŢŢ **Tigress Riesling 2004** Fresh, clean and crisp; lively, pure lime juice; good length and balance; great drive. **RATING** 95 **DRINK** 2014 $ 21.50

ŢŢŢŢŢ **Pinot Chardonnay 2001** Tight, bright, racy style; pear and apple fruit; fresh, bright acidity. **RATING** 92 **DRINK** 2007 $ 28
Pinot Chardonnay 1999 Very delicate, fresh, crisp and fine aperitif style; citrussy flavours; good balance and length. **RATING** 92 **DRINK** Now $ 27.50
Tigress Chardonnay 2003 Elegant and stylish; nice malolactic and barrel ferment inputs; a hint of sweetness detracts slightly. **RATING** 91 **DRINK** 2009 $ 21.50
Tigress Pinot Chardonnay NV Abundant, quite ripe and rich fruit, but avoids heaviness. **RATING** 91 **DRINK** 2007 $ 21.50
Chardonnay 2003 Tangy grapefruit and melon; subtle oak and perfectly balanced acidity; lively and stylish. **RATING** 90 **DRINK** 2008 $ 29

ŢŢŢŢ **Tigress Rose 2004** Spicy strawberry aromas; racy, citrussy edges to the palate; nice crisp finish. Screwcap. **RATING** 88 **DRINK** Now $ 24
Pinot Noir 2003 Fresh red fruits; controlled oak; quite good length. **RATING** 88 **DRINK** 2008 $ 34
Tigress Pinot Noir 2003 Light, fresh cherry and plum fruits; slightly simple. **RATING** 87 **DRINK** 2008 $ 21.50

ŢŢŢŢ **Gewurztraminer 2004** **RATING** 86 **DRINK** 2009 $ 27
Tigress Sauvignon Blanc 2004 **RATING** 86 **DRINK** 2008 $ 24
Tigress Pinot Gris 2004 **RATING** 86 **DRINK** 2007 $ 21.50

Bay of Shoals ★★★☆

19 Flinders Avenue, Kingscote, Kangaroo Island, SA 5223 (postal) **REGION** Kangaroo Island
T (08) 8553 2229 **F** (08) 8553 2229 **OPEN** Not
WINEMAKER Bethany Wines (Contract) **EST.** 1994 **CASES** 1000
SUMMARY John Willoughby's vineyard overlooks the Bay of Shoals, which is the northern boundary of Kingscote, Kangaroo Island's main town. Planting of the vineyard began in 1994, and has now reached 10 ha of riesling, chardonnay, sauvignon blanc, cabernet sauvignon and shiraz. In addition, 460 olive trees have been planted to produce table olives.

ŢŢŢŢ **Riesling 2004** Attractive lime, citrus and a hint of herb; good length, though slightly on the broad side. **RATING** 87 **DRINK** 2008 $ 18.50

ŢŢŢ **Cabernet Sauvignon 2001** Medium-bodied; blackcurrant; hints of spice and cedar; savoury, fine tannins lengthen the finish; interesting acid profile. **RATING** 90 **DRINK** 2011 $ 23

Bayview Estate NR

365 Purves Road, Main Ridge, Vic 3928 **REGION** Mornington Peninsula
T (03) 5989 6130 **F** (03) 5989 6373 **WEB** www.bayviewestate.com.au **OPEN** 7 days 11–7
WINEMAKER Dean Burford **EST.** 1980 **CASES** 10 000
SUMMARY Few enterprises have cast such a broad net over the tourist traffic in the Mornington Peninsula. The estate has The Pig and Whistle Tavern and cellar door, the 5-star Views Restaurant (which also serves 70 local and imported beers), an 80-seat beer garden, a produce store, fly fishing, antiques, and rose and lavender gardens. Almost incidental are the 7 ha of pinot gris, pinot noir and pinot grigio which produce wine that is sold through the cellar door, the Hilton Hotel and Crown Casino and several Mornington Peninsula restaurants.

B'darra Estate ★★★

1415 Stumpy Gully Road, Moorooduc, Vic 3933 **REGION** Mornington Peninsula
T 0418 310 638 **OPEN** Weekends 10–5
WINEMAKER Gavin Perry **EST.** 1998 **CASES** 2000

SUMMARY Gavin and Linda Perry fell in love with Bedarra Island (off the north Queensland coast) when they stayed there, hence the name of their property, which they acquired in 1998. They planted just under 5 ha of vines in 1999, and are progressively developing the 21-ha holding. A revegetation and wetland, of which a lake and two big dams form part, are planned. Gavin Perry made his first wine in 1993 from grapes grown in the Peninsula while completing a Winery Supplies course. He won numerous trophies and gold medals, including Most Successful Exhibitor in 1997, 1999 and 2000 in the amateur section of the Victorian Wines Show.

ŸŸŸŸ **Reserve Shiraz 2003** Plenty of fruit flavour; tending to raspberry and plum jam; fine tannins. Cork. **RATING** 89 **DRINK** 2008 $ 45
Chardonnay 2003 Light-bodied; clean, fresh, stone fruit and a hint of citrus; minimal oak; nice balance. Screwcap. **RATING** 87 **DRINK** 2008 $ 18

ŸŸŸŸ **Sauvignon Blanc 2004 RATING** 86 **DRINK** 2007 $ 15
Pinot Noir 2003 RATING 84 **DRINK** 2007 $ 20

ŸŸŸ **Heckles Red NV RATING** 83 $ 12

Beattie Wines   NR

53 Andrew Street, Windsor, Vic 3181 (postal) **REGION** Upper Goulburn
T 0411 187 871 **F** (03) 9682 3630 **OPEN** Not
WINEMAKER Brendon Beattie **EST.** 1998 **CASES** NA
SUMMARY Brendon Beattie has planted chardonnay, cabernet sauvignon and merlot at his Kanumbra vineyard. The small production is sold by mail order.

Beaumont Estate   ★★★★

Lot 20, 155 Milbrodale Road, Broke, NSW 2330 **REGION** Lower Hunter Valley
T 0419 616 461 **F** (07) 5474 3722 **OPEN** Not
WINEMAKER Contract **EST.** 1998 **CASES** 2750
SUMMARY The estate vineyards were planted in September 1999 on the river flats of Parson Creek, nestled between the Yengo and Wollemi National Parks. The soils were enhanced with organic preparations; after 17 months the 2.2 ha of semillon and 1.3 ha of merlot produced a substantial crop, the vine growth, it is said, equivalent to 3 years under normal conditions. The intention is to continue the organic farming approach, and to eventually become certified biodynamic. Currently the wines are sold by phone, mail order and email; there are plans for a cellar door. Profits from wine sales will support a respite and natural therapies centre for limited life children that is currently being constructed on the property.

ŸŸŸŸ **Hunter Valley Semillon 2004** Attractive lemon and citrus peel aromas; crisp; good line and length. Screwcap. **RATING** 91 **DRINK** 2012 $ 21

Beckett's Flat   ★★★★

Beckett Road, Metricup, WA 6280 **REGION** Margaret River
T (08) 9755 7402 **F** (08) 9755 7344 **WEB** www.beckettsflat.com.au **OPEN** 7 days 10–6
WINEMAKER Belizar Ilic **EST.** 1992 **CASES** 8000
SUMMARY Bill and Noni Ilic opened Beckett's Flat in September 1997. Situated just off the Bussell Highway, midway between Busselton and the Margaret River, it draws upon 14 ha of estate vineyards, first planted in 1992. Since 1998 the wines have been made at the onsite winery. Accommodation is available. Exports to the UK, Singapore and Canada.

ŸŸŸŸ **Belizar's Reserve Chardonnay 2003** Strong barrel ferment aromas with a nice touch of funk; elegant nectarine fruit; good length. Screwcap. **RATING** 91 **DRINK** 2010 $ 25
Belizar's Sauvignon Blanc 2004 Water white; spotlessly clean spice and mineral aromas; more to herbaceous than tropical flavours; good length and finish. Screwcap. **RATING** 90 **DRINK** 2007 $ 16

ŸŸŸŸ **Belizar's Cabernet Merlot 2003** Soft, spicy fruit with an overall impression of sweetness, part ex fruit, part ex oak; fine tannins, user-friendly. Screwcap. **RATING** 89 **DRINK** 2009 $ 23
Belizar's Shiraz 2003 Spicy, leafy berry aromas and flavours; light to medium-bodied; not overmuch depth. Screwcap. **RATING** 88 **DRINK** 2010 $ 23

ŸŸŸŸ **Belizar's Verdelho 2004 RATING** 86 **DRINK** 2007 $ 16

Beckingham Wines

6-7/477 Warrigal Road, Moorabbin, Vic 3189 **REGION** Mornington Peninsula/Goulburn Valley
T (03) 9258 7352 **F** (03) 9360 0713 **WEB** www.beckinghamwines.com.au **OPEN** Weekends 10-5
WINEMAKER Peter Beckingham **EST.** 1998 **CASES** 1700
SUMMARY Peter Beckingham is a chemical engineer who has turned a hobby into a part-time business, moving operations from the driveway of his house to a warehouse in Moorabbin. The situation of the winery may not be romantic, but it is eminently practical, and more than a few winemakers in California have adopted the same solution. His friends grow the grapes, and he makes the wine, with the Mornington Peninsula, Echuca and the Strathbogie Ranges the prime source of grapes, and other regions (such as the Yarra Valley) contributing from time to time.

ＹＹＹＹＹ **Cornelia Creek Shiraz 2003** Good colour; clean, medium-bodied; attractive, fresh blackberry and spice fruits; subtle oak, good length. Cork. **RATING** 90 **DRINK** 2010 $18

ＹＹＹＹ **Cornelia Creek Merlot 2002** Very developed colour; surprising varietal character with appropriate texture and weight, though falls away on the finish. Cork. **RATING** 86 **DRINK** 2007 $18
Edgehill White 2004 RATING 85 **DRINK** 2007 $15

Beechwood Wines NR

PO Box 869, Echuca, Vic 3564 **REGION** Goulburn Valley
T (03) 5482 4276 **F** (03) 5482 1185 **OPEN** Not
WINEMAKER Gavin Beech **EST.** 1995 **CASES** NA
SUMMARY The Beech family (headed by Gavin and Keith) have planted 4.5 ha of verdelho, shiraz and cabernet sauvignon. There are no cellar door facilities; the wine is distributed by Brian Downie.

Beelgara Estate

Farm 576, Beelbangera, NSW 2686 **REGION** Riverina
T (02) 6966 0200 **F** (02) 6966 0298 **WEB** www.beelgara.com.au **OPEN** Mon–Sat 10-5, Sun 11-3
WINEMAKER Belinda Morandin, Andrew Schulz, Danny Toaldo **EST.** 1930 **CASES** 600 000
SUMMARY Beelgara Estate was formed in 2001 after the purchase of the 60-year-old Rossetto family winery by a group of growers, distributors and investors. The name Beelgara is a contraction of Beelbangera. The new management is placing far greater emphasis on bottled table wine (albeit at low prices), but continues to supply bulk, cleanskin and fully packaged product for both domestic and export markets. Spreading its wings to premium regions, but still maintaining excellent value for money.

ＹＹＹＹＹ **Woorowa Coonawarra Adelaide Hills Sauvignon Blanc 2004** Spotlessly clean aromas; lively, fresh palate; excellent line and length; very good balance and dry finish. A bargain. **RATING** 90 **DRINK** Now $11.99

ＹＹＹＹ **The Gun Shearer Adelaide Hills Sauvignon Blanc 2004** Light to medium-bodied; crisp, clean kiwifruit and spice aromas; good line and flow; just the vintage dilution factor. Screwcap. **RATING** 89 **DRINK** 2007 $20
Sun Dried Shiraz 2003 Deep colour; very powerful, concentrated and dense; ultimate dead fruit through partial desiccation on mats; doesn't quite come off. High-quality cork. **RATING** 89 **DRINK** 2013 $28
Black Shiraz 2003 Strong colour; abundant sweet plum and black cherry; subtle oak; a hint of sweetness; will outlive the ratty cork. **RATING** 88 **DRINK** 2010 $15.99
Rascal's Prayer Sauvignon Blanc 2004 Clean; plenty of tropical gooseberry fruit; slightly fuzzy finish with a hint of sweetness; good value nonetheless. Screwcap. **RATING** 87 **DRINK** Now $12
Reserve Margaret River Chardonnay 2003 Light-bodied; nectarine and citrus fruit; nice mouthfeel; suitably restrained oak. Cork. **RATING** 87 **DRINK** 2008 $15
Rascal's Prayer Cabernet Merlot 2003 Good colour; medium-bodied; plenty of blackcurrant fruit on the mid-palate; ripe tannins; excellent value. Cork. **RATING** 87 **DRINK** 2008 $12
The Gun Shearer Coonawarra Cabernet Sauvignon 2002 A somewhat austere and savoury expression of the cool vintage; has length and persistence, but also a few green elements. **RATING** 87 **DRINK** 2012 $20

▼▼▼▼ **Riverina Chardonnay 2003** Quite lively and fresh tangy fruit; a whisper of oak; very good for the region. Twin Top. **RATING** 86 **DRINK** 2007 $9.99
Vineyards Shiraz 2003 **RATING** 86 **DRINK** 2007 $9.99
Sun Dried Shiraz 2002 **RATING** 86 **DRINK** 2008 $35
Rascal's Prayer Verdelho 2004 **RATING** 85 **DRINK** Now $12
Cabernet Merlot 2003 **RATING** 85 **DRINK** 2007 $9.99
11–04 Pinot Grigio 2004 **RATING** 84 **DRINK** Now $15.99
Woorowa Riverina Verdelho 2004 **RATING** 84 **DRINK** Now $11.99
Black Shiraz 2002 **RATING** 84 **DRINK** Now $15

▼▼▼ **White Shiraz 2004** **RATING** 83 $9.99
V.O.T.P. NV **RATING** 83 $18

Beer Brothers
NR

Pheasant Farm Road, Nuriootpa, SA 5355 **REGION** Barossa Valley
T (08) 8562 4477 **F** (08) 8562 4757 **WEB** www.maggiebeer.com.au **OPEN** 7 days 10–5
WINEMAKER Contract **EST.** 1997 **CASES** 500
SUMMARY Yes, they really are Beer brothers, and, yes, they grow grapes and make wine, not beer. The brothers in question are Colin Beer (brother of famed chef and author Maggie Beer) and Bruce, who became a partner in the grapegrowing venture in 1987. Ten years later they decided to venture into winemaking, using the team at Yalumba (to whom they sell the lion's share of the grape production); after selling some of the 40-year-old Barossa shiraz to Rockford for inclusion in the Basket Press Red, they persuaded Dave Powell (of Torbreck) to make Old Vine Barossa Shiraz. The brothers' second vineyard is at Cobdogla, on the Murray River. Visitors to the cellar door won't have the food which Maggie Beer made famous at the Pheasant Farm, but light meals are provided, plus local produce; no guesses required to work out what that might be.

Belgenny Vineyard
★★★☆

92 De Beyers Road, Pokolbin, NSW 2320 (postal) **REGION** Lower Hunter Valley
T (02) 9247 5300 **F** (02) 9247 7273 **WEB** www.belgenny.com.au **OPEN** Not
WINEMAKER Monarch Winemaking Services (Contract) **EST.** 1990 **CASES** 7000
SUMMARY In 1999 partners Norman Seckold and Dudley Leitch realised a long-held ambition to establish a vineyard in the Hunter Valley with the acquisition of their 17-ha site. Plantings have steadily increased and are presently chardonnay (5.7 ha), shiraz (4.9 ha), merlot (2 ha), semillon (1.2) and a carefully thought out marketing strategy has been put in place. A cellar door and restaurant are planned. Exports to Hong Kong and Singapore.

Belgravia Vineyards
★★★★

Belgravia Road, Orange, NSW 2800 **REGION** Orange
T (02) 6365 0633 **F** (02) 6365 0646 **WEB** www.belgravia.com.au **OPEN** By appointment
WINEMAKER David Lowe, Jane Wilson (Contract) **EST.** 2003 **CASES** 6000
SUMMARY Belgravia is an 1800-ha mixed farming property (sheep, cattle and vineyards) 20 km north of Orange. The first plantings took place in 1996, and there are now 180 ha contracted to Southcorp, and 10 ha for the Belgravia wine brand. Owner Richard Hattersley has assembled an impressive team under the direction of general manager Alan Hardy, and the seriousness of the venture is also evidenced by exports to the UK and Denmark; and thereafter releases onto the domestic market. The property also has a B&B cottage, and is presently restoring 300 ha of grassy whitebox woodland.

▼▼▼▼▼ **Woodland 2002** Medium-bodied; delicious mouthfeel and texture; spicy, velvety plum and black cherry fruit; fine, ripe tannins; nice oak. Shiraz/Merlot/Cabernet Sauvignon. Twin Top. **RATING** 93 **DRINK** 2012 $23
Reserve Cabernet Sauvignon 2002 Medium-bodied; a mix of black fruits, earth and dark chocolate; fine, savoury tannins; good length. Stained cork. **RATING** 90 **DRINK** 2013 $23

▼▼▼▼ **Viognier 2004** Positive varietal character to both bouquet and palate; rich apricot, pear and fruit pastille; weight without heat. Very poor cork. **RATING** 89 **DRINK** 2008 $23
Late Harvest Semillon 2003 Complex honey, cumquat, citrus and vanilla; moderately luscious mouthfeel; good balance. **RATING** 88 **DRINK** 2007 $15

Reserve Shiraz 2002 A strange contrast between 15° alcohol and spicy herbal notes; licorice/anise and earth; possibly shrivelled/dead fruit. Stained cork. **RATING** 87 **DRINK** 2010 $ 23

Bellarine Estate ★★★★

2270 Portarlington Road, Bellarine, Vic 3222 **REGION** Geelong
T (03) 5259 3310 **F** (03) 5259 3393 **WEB** www.bellarineestate.com.au **OPEN** 7 days 10–4
WINEMAKER Robin Brockett **EST.** 1995 **CASES** 7000
SUMMARY A substantial business, with 4 ha each of chardonnay and pinot noir, 3 ha of shiraz (producing an excellent wine with a dash of viognier), 1 ha of merlot and 0.5 ha each of pinot gris and viognier. The wines are made by Robin Brockett at Scotchmans Hill. Bella's restaurant is open for lunch 7 days and dinner on Friday and Saturday evenings.

ΨΨΨΨΫ Two Wives Shiraz 2003 Deep colour; rich, dense, ripe fruit with strong, milky tannins. **RATING** 92 **DRINK** 2013 $ 28
Phil's Fetish Pinot Noir 2003 Complex and rich plum/dark berry fruit; good texture and length. **RATING** 91 **DRINK** 2009 $ 26.50
Sauvignon Blanc 2004 Clean, crisp, minerally aromas; passionfruit and lemon flavours, then cleansing acidity. Screwcap. **RATING** 90 **DRINK** 2007 $ 24

ΨΨΨΨ Julian's Merlot 2003 Light-bodied; supple cedar, leaf, spice and berry; super-fine tannins, gentle oak. **RATING** 88 **DRINK** 2007 $ 28
James' Paddock Chardonnay 2003 Light, fresh melon and a touch of creamy malolactic influence; fair length and acidity. **RATING** 87 **DRINK** 2008 $ 26.50

🐌 Bellarmine Wines ★★★★

PO Box 1450, Manjimup, WA 6258 **REGION** Pemberton
T (08) 9776 0667 **F** (08) 9776 0657 **WEB** www.bellarmine.com.au **OPEN** Not
WINEMAKER Mike Bewsher, Tam Bewsher, Robert Paul (Consultant) **EST.** 2000 **CASES** 5000
SUMMARY This substantial operation is owned by German residents Dr Willi and Gudrun Schumacher. Long-term wine lovers, with a large personal wine cellar, the Schumachers decided to take the next step by establishing a vineyard and winery of their own, using Australia partly because of its stable political climate. The venture is managed by Mike and Tam Bewsher, both of whom have extensive knowledge of the wine industry in both Pemberton and Mudgee. There is 25 ha of chardonnay, riesling, sauvignon blanc, pinot noir, shiraz, merlot and petit verdot.

ΨΨΨΨΫ Pemberton Pinot Noir 2004 Soft, mouthfilling plum; some spice; good texture with fine, silky tannins; impressive for the region. **RATING** 90 **DRINK** 2009 $ 15

ΨΨΨΨ Pemberton Riesling 2004 Pale, and light-bodied; has a lot of similarities with German rieslings, particularly those of the Mosel region; delicate limey fruit, and obvious sweetness balanced by acidity in a Kabinett style; outside the square. **RATING** 89 **DRINK** 2007 $ 15
Pemberton Sauvignon Blanc 2004 Faintly smoky/sweaty reduction to the aromas; cleans up on the gooseberry, capsicum and citrus palate; good length. **RATING** 87 **DRINK** 2007 $ 15

ΨΨΨΫ Pemberton Chardonnay 2004 RATING 85 **DRINK** 2008 $ 15
ΨΨΨ Bellarmino Chardonnay Pinot 2004 RATING 83 $ 15

Bell River Estate NR

Mitchell Highway, Neurea, NSW 2820 **REGION** Central Ranges Zone
T (02) 6846 7277 **F** (02) 6846 7277 **WEB** www.bellriverestate.com.au **OPEN** 7 days 9–6
WINEMAKER Sandra Banks **EST.** 1974 **CASES** 500
SUMMARY Situated 15 km south of Wellington, Bell River Estate was formerly known as Markeita Cellars, the name change due to its purchase by Michael and Sandra Banks. They have 2.5 ha of grenache, cabernet sauvignon, shiraz and muscat, and as well as producing Bell River Estate wines, offer bottling, contract winemaking and viticultural services. The wines can be ordered through the website.

Bell's Lane Wines   NR

Mangoola Road, Denman, NSW 2328 **REGION** Upper Hunter Valley
T (02) 6547 1191 **F** (02) 6547 1191 **OPEN** Weekends 10–5, or by appointment
WINEMAKER John Hordern **EST.** 1998 **CASES** NA
SUMMARY In the words of Paul and Megan Melville, 'we were a typical hardworking Sydney couple, but we were tired of the daily slog of city life and conversations about real estate prices, so we uprooted the kids, sold the house, cleared the land and started planting the vines – 30 000 in all'. Thus was born Bell's Lane Vineyard, 3 km from Denman, in 1998. A dilapidated dairy on the property has been converted to a cellar door, which serves light lunches on weekends. The wines are also sold through selected bottle shops and by mail order.

Bellvale Wines   ★★★★

Forresters Lane, Berrys Creek, Vic 3953 **REGION** Gippsland
T (03) 5668 8230 **F** (03) 5668 8230 **OPEN** By appointment
WINEMAKER John Ellis **EST.** 1998 **CASES** 2000
SUMMARY John Ellis, of Bellvale Wines, is the third under this name to be actively involved in the wine industry. His background as a former 747 pilot, and the knowledge he gained of Burgundy over many visits, sets him apart from the others. In 1998 he established 10 ha of pinot noir and 3 ha of chardonnay on the red soils of a north-facing slope on the property. He chose a density of 7150 vines per hectare, following as far as possible the precepts of Burgundy, but limited (as are so many) by tractor size, which precludes narrower row spacing and thus even higher plant density.

♥♥♥♥♡ **Gippsland Pinot Noir 2003** Deep colour; very rich, powerful and concentrated; lashings of dark plum fruit, almost Central Otago in style; certainly New World. **RATING** 93 **DRINK** 2009 $ 30

Belubula Valley Vineyards   NR

Golden Gully, Mandurama, NSW 2798 (postal) **REGION** Orange
T (02) 6367 5236 **F** (02) 6362 4726 **OPEN** Not
WINEMAKER David Somervaille **EST.** 1986 **CASES** 650
SUMMARY Belubula Valley is a foundation member of the Central Highlands Grapegrowers Association (now ORVA), centred on Orange; the vineyard is on the Belubula River, near Carcoar, and the small amounts of wine made to date have not yet been commercially released. David Somervaille was the chairman of partners of the national law firm Blake Dawson Waldron. Like myself, he is a self-taught winemaker, his early experience with wine coming through his participation in a partnership which operated the Oakdale Vineyard in the Hunter Valley; it was sold in 1980.

Benarra Vineyards   ★★★☆

PO Box 1081, Mt Gambier, SA 5290 **REGION** Mount Gambier
T (08) 8738 9355 **F** (08) 8738 9355 **OPEN** Not
WINEMAKER Martin Slocombe **EST.** 1998 **CASES** 150
SUMMARY Lisle Pudney has planted a substantial vineyard with the help of investors. In all there are over 26 ha of pinot noir and 4 ha each of sauvignon blanc and chardonnay, with another 40 ha to be planted over the next 3 years. The vineyard is 20 km from the Southern Ocean on ancient flint beds; a million-year-old mollusc found on the property is depicted on the label of the Pinot Noir. Most of the grapes are sold; a small portion is contract-made for the Benarra label, and is of good quality and varietal character.

Bendigo Wine Estate   NR

682 Axedale–Goornong Road, Axedale, Vic 3551 **REGION** Bendigo
T (03) 5439 7444 **F** (03) 5439 7433 **OPEN** 7 days
WINEMAKER Contract **EST.** 2000 **CASES** NA
SUMMARY A quite substantial operation, with plantings of riesling, chardonnay, verdelho, pinot noir, cabernet sauvignon, merlot, malbec, shiraz and mourvedre, producing both table and sparkling wines. The wines are chiefly sold by mail order and through the cellar door, which has barbecue and picnic facilities, and periodically stages events.

Ben Potts Wines

★★★★☆

Step Road, Langhorne Creek, SA 5255 (postal) **REGION** Langhorne Creek
T (08) 8537 3029 **F** (08) 8537 3284 **WEB** www.benpottswines.com.au **OPEN** Not
WINEMAKER Ben Potts **EST.** 2002 **CASES** NA
SUMMARY Ben Potts is the sixth generation to be involved in grapegrowing and winemaking in Langhorne Creek, the first being Frank Potts, founder of Bleasdale Vineyards. Ben completed the oenology degree at Charles Sturt University, and (aged 25) ventured into winemaking on a commercial scale in 2002. Fiddle's Block Shiraz is named after great-grandfather Fiddle; Lenny's Block Cabernet Sauvignon Malbec after grandfather Len; and Bill's Block Malbec after father Bill. The wines are available by mail order.

ŸŸŸŸŸ **Lenny's Block Cabernet Malbec 2002** Very good colour; blackcurrant, cassis and plum; medium-bodied; smooth, supple texture; ripe tannins, very good oak. Quality cork. **RATING** 94 **DRINK** 2015 $ 32

ŸŸŸŸŸ **Fiddle's Block Shiraz 2002** Light to medium-bodied; supple, rounded and smooth texture; aromas and flavours more complex; smoky, spicy, slightly peppery black fruits; fine, ripe tannins. Quality cork. **RATING** 91 **DRINK** 2012 $ 32

ŸŸŸŸ **Bill's Block Malbec 2002** Substantial wine; lots of dark plum, chocolate and black fruits; tannins on the finish; does dip slightly on the mid-palate. Quality cork. **RATING** 89 **DRINK** 2010 $ 28

Ben's Run

★★★☆

PO Box 127, Broke, NSW 2330 **REGION** Lower Hunter Valley
T (02) 6579 1310 **F** (02) 6579 1370 **OPEN** Not
WINEMAKER Contract **EST.** 1997 **CASES** 850
SUMMARY Ben's Run, say the owners, 'is named for our kelpie dog for graciously allowing part of his retirement run to be converted into a showpiece shiraz-only vineyard'. Patriarch Norman Marran was one of the pioneers of the Australian cotton industry. He has had a long and distinguished career as a director of both the Australian Wheat Board and the Grains Research Corporation, and is currently chairman of a leading food research company. The decision has been taken to produce only 500 cases of wine a year from the 3-ha vineyard; the remainder is sold to Andrew Margan.

ŸŸŸŸ **Single Vineyard Shiraz 2003** Medium-bodied; quite rich, ripe blackberry and plum fruit; good acidity. Will improve further from here. **RATING** 89 **DRINK** 2012 $ 22

Bent Creek Vineyards

★★★★

Lot 10 Blewitt Springs Road, McLaren Flat, SA 5171 **REGION** McLaren Vale
T (08) 8383 0414 **F** (08) 8239 1538 **WEB** www.bentcreekvineyards.com.au **OPEN** Sundays & public hols 11–5
WINEMAKER Michael Scarpantoni, Peter Polson **EST.** 2001 **CASES** 5000
SUMMARY Loretta and Peter Polson became wine drinkers and collectors a decade before they acquired a small patch of 40-year-old dry-grown chardonnay and shiraz at McLaren Flat. This was followed by the purchase of another small property at McLaren Vale, planted to grenache, cabernet franc and chardonnay. Say the Polsons, 'Land barons? Hardly: 10 acres in all, but you will appreciate that it is enough for one man to look after and hand-prune.' Until recently, all the grapes were sold to d'Arenberg, but now an increasing proportion is kept for the Bent Creek Vineyards. Exports to Canada and Belgium.

ŸŸŸŸŸ **The Black Dog McLaren Vale Shiraz 2003** Oozes with ripe blackberry, plum, chocolate and spice fruit; has eaten 13 months of new American oak. Good cork. **RATING** 93 **DRINK** 2013 $ 21

ŸŸŸŸ **Adelaide Hills Sauvignon Blanc 2004** Green apple and mineral aromas; more to lime and passionfruit on the palate; good length. Screwcap. **RATING** 89 **DRINK** 2008 $ 17

ŸŸŸ **McLaren Vale Unwooded Chardonnay 2004** **RATING** 83 $ 17

Beresford Wines ★★★

26 Kangarilla Road, McLaren Vale, SA 5171 **REGION** McLaren Vale
T (08) 8323 8899 **F** (08) 8323 7911 **WEB** www.beresfordwines.com.au **OPEN** Mon–Fri 9–5,
weekends 10–5
WINEMAKER Scott McIntosh, Rob Dundon **EST.** 1985 **CASES** 130 000
SUMMARY The Beresford brand sits at the top of a range of labels primarily and successfully aimed at
export markets in the UK, the US, Hong Kong and China. The intention is that ultimately most, if
not all, the wines will be sourced from grapes grown in McLaren Vale. A new cellar door and
boutique winery recently opened, as planned. Incidentally, it is run as an entirely separate operation
to its sister winery, Step Road in Langhorne Creek.

ŸŸŸŸ **McLaren Vale Shiraz 2002** medium-bodied; red and black fruits; fair structure and
extract; balanced oak and tannins. **RATING** 87 **DRINK** 2007 **$** 25

ŸŸŸŸ **McLaren Vale Chardonnay 2004** **RATING** 86 **DRINK** 2007 **$** 18
Reserve Shiraz 2001 **RATING** 86 **DRINK** 2008 **$** 45

Berrys Bridge ★★★★☆

633 Carapooee Road, Carapooee, Vic 3478 **REGION** Pyrenees
T (03) 5496 3220 **F** (03) 5496 3322 **WEB** www.berrysbridge.com.au **OPEN** Weekends 10.30–4.30, or
by appointment
WINEMAKER Jane Holt **EST.** 1990 **CASES** 1500
SUMMARY While the date of establishment is 1990, Roger Milner purchased the property in 1975,
intending to plant a vineyard; he had worked for 3 years at Hardys Reynell winery in South Australia.
In the mid-1980s he returned with Jane Holt, and together they began the construction of the stone
house-cum-winery. Planting of the existing 7 ha of vineyard commenced in 1990, around the time
that Jane began viticultural studies at Charles Sturt University (completed in 1993, and followed by a
wine science degree course in 2000). Until 1997 the grapes were sold to others; the first vintage
(from 1997) was released in November 1998. The wines are distributed in Victoria through
Winestock to a number of well-known retailers. Exports to the US, Germany and Switzerland.

ŸŸŸŸŸ **Shiraz 2002** Deep, dense colour; extremely powerful, dense black fruits; ultra-powerful
tannins; needs 20 years minimum. Cork. **RATING** 93 **DRINK** 2025 **$** 64
Cabernet Sauvignon 2002 Potent, brooding, powerful black fruits; hallmark slightly dry
tannins needing infinite patience. **RATING** 91 **DRINK** 2022 **$** 64

Best's Wines ★★★★★

111 Best's Road, Great Western, Vic 3377 **REGION** Grampians
T (03) 5356 2250 **F** (03) 5356 2430 **WEB** www.bestswines.com **OPEN** Mon–Sat 10–5, Sun 11–4
WINEMAKER Viv Thomson, Hamish Seabrook **EST.** 1866 **CASES** 30 000
SUMMARY Best's Great Western winery and vineyards are among the best-kept secrets of Australia.
Indeed the vineyards, with vines dating back to 1867, have secrets which may never be revealed: for
example, certain vines planted in the Nursery Block have defied identification and are thought to
exist nowhere else in the world. The cellars, too, go back to the same era, constructed by butcher-
turned-winemaker Joseph Best and his family. Since 1920, the Thomson family has owned the
property, with father Viv and sons Ben, Bart and Marcus representing the fourth and fifth
generations. Consistently producing elegant, supple wines which deserve far greater recognition
than they receive. The Shiraz is a classic; the Thomson Family Shiraz magnificent. Exports to all
major markets.

Bethany Wines ★★★★☆

Bethany Road, Bethany via Tanunda, SA 5352 **REGION** Barossa Valley
T (08) 8563 2086 **F** (08) 8563 0046 **WEB** www.bethany.com.au **OPEN** Mon–Sat 10–5, Sun 1–5
WINEMAKER Geoff Schrapel, Robert Schrapel **EST.** 1977 **CASES** 25 000
SUMMARY The Schrapel family has been growing grapes in the Barossa Valley for over 140 years, but
the winery has only been in operation since 1977. Nestling high on a hillside in the site of an old
quarry, it is run by Geoff and Rob Schrapel, who produce a range of consistently well-made and
attractively packaged wines. They have 36 ha of vineyards in the Barossa Valley, 8 ha in the Eden

Valley and (recently and interestingly) 2 ha each of chardonnay and cabernet sauvignon on Kangaroo Island. The wines enjoy national distribution in Australia, and are exported to the UK, Germany, Sweden, Switzerland, Denmark, Holland, New Zealand, Japan and Singapore.

ΥΥΥΥΥ **GR7 Shiraz 1999** Lush, ripe, but not jammy, plum and blackberry fruit; smooth and supple mouthfeel; ageing convincingly. **RATING** 94 **DRINK** 2014 $ 68

ΥΥΥΥ **Shiraz 2002** A super-abundance of plush plum and small berry black fruits; relatively restrained alcohol; balanced oak and tannins. Cork. **RATING** 92 **DRINK** 2012 $ 28.50

ΥΥΥΥ **Riesling 2004** A highly aromatic, tropical pineapple bouquet; subsides a little on the palate. Screwcap. **RATING** 88 **DRINK** 2009 $ 16
Select Late Harvest Riesling 2004 Old-fashioned, perhaps, but has the acidity and structure to improve for as long as the cork holds in the 500 ml bottle. **RATING** 88 **DRINK** 2019 $ 18

ΥΥΥΥ **Barossa Chardonnay 2002 RATING** 86 **DRINK** 2007 $ 18
Grenache 2003 RATING 86 **DRINK** 2007 $ 17.90
Barossa Cabernet Merlot 2002 RATING 86 **DRINK** 2008 $ 23.50
Barossa Semillon 2003 RATING 85 **DRINK** 2007 $ 16.50

Bettenay's   ★★★

Cnr Harmans South Road/Miamup Road, Wilyabrup, WA 6284 **REGION** Margaret River
T (08) 9755 5539 **F** (08) 9755 5539 **WEB** www.bettenaysmargaretriver.com.au **OPEN** 7 days 10–5
WINEMAKER Greg Bettenay, Peter Stanlake (Consultant) **EST.** 1989 **CASES** 1500
SUMMARY Greg Bettenay began the development of 10 ha of vineyards in 1989, planted to sauvignon blanc, semillon, chardonnay, cabernet sauvignon, merlot and shiraz. The development now extends to two farm vineyard cottages and a luxury tree-top spa apartment known as The Leafy Loft.

ΥΥΥΥ **Chardonnay 2003** Light and citrussy; delicate style; lingering acidity helps length. **RATING** 87 **DRINK** 2009 $ 32

Bettio Wines   ★★☆

RMB 9329 Whitfield Road, King Valley, Vic 3678 **REGION** King Valley
T (03) 5727 9308 **F** (03) 5727 9344 **OPEN** By appointment
WINEMAKER Daniel Bettio **EST.** 1995 **CASES** 2000
SUMMARY The Bettio family, with Paul and Daniel at the helm, have established 20 ha of vines in the King Valley and 5 ha at Cheshunt. The plantings are of sauvignon blanc, chardonnay, merlot and cabernet sauvignon, and the wines, including a range of back vintages, are chiefly sold through the cellar door and by mail order.

ΥΥΥΥ **Chardonnay 2004 RATING** 85 **DRINK** 2007

Beyond Broke Vineyard   NR

Cobcroft Road, Broke, NSW 2330 **REGION** Lower Hunter Valley
T (02) 6026 2043 **F** (02) 6026 2043 **WEB** www.wine2go.com.au **OPEN** At Broke Village Store 10–4
WINEMAKER Pete Howland (Contract) **EST.** 1996 **CASES** 4000
SUMMARY Beyond Broke Vineyard is the reincarnation of a former Lindemans vineyard, purchased by Bob and Terry Kennedy in 1996. In a more than slightly ironic twist, the 1997 Beyond Broke Semillon won two trophies at the Hunter Valley Wine Show of that year, the first for the Best Current Vintage Semillon and the second, the Henry John Lindeman Memorial Trophy for the Best Current Vintage Dry White Wine. Subsequent shows have been less spectacularly kind, but there is nothing surprising in that; its turn will come again when vintage conditions permit.

Bianchet   ★★★☆

187 Victoria Road, Lilydale, Vic 3140 **REGION** Yarra Valley
T (03) 9739 1779 **F** (03) 9739 1277 **OPEN** Thurs–Fri 10–4, weekends 10–5
WINEMAKER Contract **EST.** 1976 **CASES** 2500

SUMMARY Owned by a small Melbourne-based syndicate which acquired the business from the founding Bianchet family. One of the most unusual wines from the winery is Verduzzo Gold, a late-harvest sweet white wine made from the Italian grape variety. The wines are still basically sold through the cellar door.

Bidgeebong Wines ★★★★☆

352 Byrnes Road, Wagga Wagga, NSW 2650 REGION Gundagai
T (02) 6931 9955 F (02) 6931 9966 WEB www.bidgeebong.com OPEN Mon–Fri 9–4
WINEMAKER Andrew Birks, Keiran Spencer EST. 2000 CASES 12 000
SUMMARY Encompasses what the founders refer to as the Bidgeebong triangle – between Young, Wagga Wagga, Tumbarumba and Gundagai – which provides grapes for the Bidgeebong brand. Two of the partners are Andrew Birks, with a 30 year career as a lecturer and educator at Charles Sturt University, and Simon Robertson, who studied viticulture and wine science at Charles Sturt University, and after working in Europe and the Barwang Vineyard established by his father Peter in 1969, built a substantial viticultural management business in the area. A winery was completed for the 2002 vintage, and will eventually be capable of handling 2000 tonnes of grapes: for Bidgeebong's own needs, and those of other local growers and larger producers who purchase grapes from the region. Exports to the UK and the US.

▼▼▼▼▼ **The Alabama Shiraz 2002** Blackberry, black cherry and spice; excellent texture and structure; fine, silky tannins; medium-bodied, long finish. RATING 94 DRINK 2012 $ 29.95

▼▼▼▼▽ **Tumbarumba Chardonnay 2003** Aromatic and fresh bouquet; grapefruit and melon flavours; bright mouthfeel, subliminal oak. RATING 90 DRINK 2009 $ 20

▼▼▼▼ **Tumbarumba Sauvignon Blanc 2004** Fresh, clean, light-bodied; grass, herb and gooseberry. RATING 88 DRINK Now $ 17
Triangle Chardonnay 2004 Melon and citrus fruit aromas and flavours; the faintest touch of oak adds to texture. Gundagai/Hilltops/Tumbarumba. Screwcap. RATING 88 DRINK 2007 $ 14

▼▼▼▽ **Gundagai Shiraz 2003** RATING 86 DRINK 2008 $ 21.95
Triangle Shiraz 2003 RATING 86 DRINK 2013 $ 12.95
Tumbarumba Merlot 2003 RATING 86 DRINK 2008 $ 24
Tumbarumba Tempranillo 2003 RATING 86 DRINK 2007 $ 24

Big Barrel Vineyard and Winery NR

787 Landsborough Road, Maleny, Qld 4551 REGION Queensland Coastal
T (07) 5429 6300 F (07) 5429 6331 OPEN 7 days 10–5
WINEMAKER Stuart Pierce EST. 2000 CASES 1280
SUMMARY The Pagano family's forebears made wine on the foothills of Mt Etna for many generations, and the family has been involved in the Australian wine industry for over 40 years. But it was not until 12 years ago that father Sebastian and wife Maria Pagano saw the Maleny area with its Glasshouse Mountain and surrounding Blackall Range, reminiscent of a scaled-down Mt Etna. They have now planted 4 ha of chambourcin, and opened a tasting room (in the shape of a giant barrel) which sells a wide range of wines sourced from elsewhere in Australia. In best Queensland tradition, there are plenty of attractions for tourists, including vineyard tours, light foccacia lunches Mon–Sat, and a continental buffet lunch on Sunday.

Big Hill Vineyard

Cnr Calder Highway/Belvoir Park Road, Big Hill, Bendigo, Vic 3550 REGION Bendigo
T (03) 5435 3366 F (03) 5435 3311 WEB www.bighillvineyard.com OPEN 7 days 10–5
WINEMAKER Stuart Auld (Contract) EST. 1998 CASES 1200
SUMMARY A partnership headed by Nick Cugura began the re-establishment of Big Hill Vineyard on a site which was first planted to grapes almost 150 years ago. That was in the height of the gold rush, and there was even a long-disappeared pub, the Granite Rock Hotel. The wheel has come full circle, for Big Hill Vineyard now has a café-restaurant overlooking the vineyard, and plans for B&B cottages. The restaurant specialises in wedding receptions, and provides limited conference facilities. The modern-day plantings began with 2 ha of shiraz in 1998, followed by 1 ha each of merlot and cabernet sauvignon.

big shed wines ★★★☆

1289 Malmsbury Road, Glenlyon, Vic 3461 **REGION** Macedon Ranges
T (03) 5348 7825 **F** (03) 5348 7825 **WEB** www.bigshedwines.com.au **OPEN** 7 days, winter 10–6, summer 10–7
WINEMAKER Ken Jones **EST.** 1999 **CASES** 1400
SUMMARY Founder and winemaker Ken Jones was formerly a geneticist and molecular biologist at Edinburgh University, and the chemistry of winemaking comes easily. The estate-based wine comes from the 2 ha of pinot noir; the other wines are made from purchased grapes grown in various parts of Central Victoria.

🍷🍷🍷🍷 **Shiraz Cabernet 2003** Generous, ripe blackberry, prune and plum fruit; ripe tannins; a twitch of alcohol heat on the finish. Ominously stained cork. **RATING** 89 **DRINK** 2013 $27
Pinot Noir 2003 Good colour; savoury, foresty, spicy plum aromas and flavours; fine tannins. **RATING** 88 **DRINK** 2008 $25

🍷🍷🍷🍷 **Moonstruck Chardonnay 2004** **RATING** 86 **DRINK** 2008 $22
Field of Dreams Chardonnay 2004 **RATING** 84 **DRINK** 2007 $20

Bimbadgen Estate

790 McDonalds Road, Pokolbin, NSW 2321 **REGION** Lower Hunter Valley
T (02) 4998 7585 **F** (02) 4998 7732 **WEB** www.bimbadgen.com.au **OPEN** 7 days 9.30–5
WINEMAKER Simon Thistlewood, Jane Turner **EST.** 1968 **CASES** 60 000
SUMMARY Established as McPherson Wines, then successively Tamalee, then Sobels, then Parker Wines and now Bimbadgen, this substantial winery has had what might be politely termed a turbulent history. It has the great advantage of having 109 ha of estate plantings, mostly with now relatively old vines, supplemented by a separate estate vineyard at Yenda for the lower-priced Ridge series, and purchased grapes from various premium regions. The restaurant is open 7 days for lunch and Wed–Sat for dinner. Exports to the UK, Hong Kong and Japan.

🍷🍷🍷🍷🍷 **Signature Individual Vineyard Shiraz 2003** Very deep, dark colour; remarkable concentration ex drought year; powerful tannins. Pity a cork, rather than a screwcap. **RATING** 94 **DRINK** 2013 $48

🍷🍷🍷🍷🍷 **Myall Road Botrytis Semillon (375 ml) 2004** Considerable intensity and length of flavour; well made and well balanced; luscious fruit off-set by crisp acid. From Griffith. **RATING** 93 **DRINK** 2009 $18.50
Shiraz 2003 Deeply coloured; very powerful and concentrated black fruits and dark chocolate; ripe tannins, long finish. Pokolbin/McLaren Vale. Screwcap. **RATING** 92 **DRINK** 2018 $19.50
Signature Semillon 2002 Fresh, intense, lemon zest; bordering on sharp acidity; clean finish, needing more time. Cork. **RATING** 90 **DRINK** 2012 $25
Merlot 2003 Strong colour; lashings of spicy redcurrant fruit; fine tannins; balanced acidity. Hunter Valley/Orange. Screwcap. **RATING** 90 **DRINK** 2013 $19.50
Signature Sangiovese Merlot 2003 Interesting wine; sour cherry and olive fruit flavours; fine, persistent tannins run throughout. Orange/Hunter Valley. Cork. **RATING** 90 **DRINK** 2015 $32

🍷🍷🍷🍷 **Art Series Semillon Sauvignon Blanc 2004** A harmonious blend, quasi-Margaret River style; spine of Semillon, gentle tropical fruit ex Sauvignon Blanc from Orange. Good length. Screwcap. **RATING** 88 **DRINK** 2009 $20
Art Series Sangiovese 2004 An attractive, light to medium-bodied wine; well structured around a core of bright cherry/sour cherry/spice fruit. Orange/Mudgee. Screwcap. **RATING** 88 **DRINK** 2009 $20

🍷🍷🍷🍷 **Ridge Chardonnay 2004** **RATING** 86 **DRINK** 2007 $12.50
Pinot Grigio 2004 Light to medium-bodied; pear, spice, mineral and slate aromas and flavours; fair length and balance. Mount Benson/Orange. Screwcap. **RATING** 86 **DRINK** 2009 $17.50
Ridge Shiraz Cabernet Merlot 2003 **RATING** 86 **DRINK** 2008 $12.50
Ridge Semillon Chardonnay Verdelho 2004 **RATING** 85 **DRINK** 2007 $12.50

Bindaree Estate

NR

Fish Fossil Drive, Canowindra, NSW 2804 **REGION** Cowra
T (02) 6344 1214 **F** (02) 6344 3217 **WEB** www.bindareeestate.com.au **OPEN** Wed–Fri 11–5, weekends
10–5
WINEMAKER Contract **EST.** 1998 **CASES** 2000
SUMMARY The Workman family have established their property in the foothills of the Belubula River
Valley, near Canowindra. They have planted 1 ha of chardonnay, and 3 ha each of cabernet sauvignon
and shiraz. The first vintage (2001) was successful in the 2002 Cowra Wine Show, the Reserve
Chardonnay winning silver and the Unwooded Chardonnay bronze.

Bindi Wine Growers

343 Melton Road, Gisborne, Vic 3437 (postal) **REGION** Macedon Ranges
T (03) 5428 2564 **F** (03) 5428 2564 **OPEN** Not
WINEMAKER Michael Dhillon, Stuart Anderson (Consultant) **EST.** 1988 **CASES** 1500
SUMMARY One of the icons of Macedon, indeed Victoria. The Chardonnay is top-shelf, the Pinot Noir
as remarkable (albeit in a very different idiom) as Bass Phillip, Giaconda or any of the other tiny-
production, icon wines. The addition of the Heathcote-sourced Shiraz under the Bundaleer label
simply confirms Bindi as one of the greatest small producers in Australia. Notwithstanding the tiny
production, the wines are exported (in small quantities, of course) to the UK, the US and other major
markets.

Quartz Chardonnay 2003 Distinctly tighter, more minerally and more intense than its
brother; very long and fine, headed towards Aloxe-Corton or Chablis; marvellous wine.
From the heaviest, quartz-laden silt stone soils. Cork. **RATING** 96 **DRINK** 2012 $ 65
Chardonnay 2003 Rich and full; layers of complexity to both texture and flavour; cashew,
fig, melon and stone fruit, malolactic and barrel ferment inputs integrated; very good
balance; 1 tonne per acre. Cork. **RATING** 94 **DRINK** 2010 $ 37.50

Bundaleer Shiraz 2003 Iconoclastic Heathcote style; medium-bodied, smooth and
supple black cherry, blackberry and spice; fine, sweet tannins; only 13.5° alcohol.
RATING 93 **DRINK** 2018 $ 36
Block 5 Pinot Noir 2003 Much more structure than the Original Vineyard; more savoury
aspects; texture, feel and flavours all very different; spice, black cherry and red cherry
fruit. Terroir at work. Cork. **RATING** 92 **DRINK** 2009 $ 80
Original Vineyard Pinot Noir 2003 Light to medium-bodied; bright red cherry and plum;
fine and unforced; doesn't really show the tiny crop (less than 1 tonne to the acre), subtle
and smooth, but needs a touch more horsepower. Cork. **RATING** 90 **DRINK** 2009 $ 55

Bird in Hand

★★★★

Bird in Hand Road, Woodside, SA 5244 **REGION** Adelaide Hills
T (08) 8232 9033 **F** (08) 8232 9066 **WEB** www.birdinhand.com.au **OPEN** Not
WINEMAKER Andrew Nugent, Kym Milne **EST.** 1997 **CASES** 15 000
SUMMARY This substantial wine and olive oil-making property is situated on the Bird in Hand Road
at Woodside, which in turn took its name from a 19th century gold mine called Bird in Hand. It is the
venture of the Nugent family, headed by Dr Michael Nugent, who was formerly an owner and
director of Tatachilla, and who acquired the property in 1997. Son Andrew Nugent is a Roseworthy
graduate, and has had a successful career in managing vineyards in various parts of South Australia.
(Andrew's wife Susie manages the olive oil side of the business.) The family also has properties on the
Fleurieu Peninsula and in the Clare Valley, the latter providing both riesling and shiraz (and olives
from 100-year-old wild olive trees). National distribution and exports to the UK, the US and other
major markets.

Adelaide Hills Merlot 2003 Clean; good varietal expression; olive and spice notes to red
and black fruits; supple tannins and mouthfeel. **RATING** 91 **DRINK** 2009 $ 30

Nest Egg Cabernet Sauvignon 2003 Opens with blackcurrant and blackberry fruit, but
persistent tannins cut in early on the palate and need to soften. **RATING** 87 **DRINK** 2010
$ 60

Birdwood Estate ★★★☆

Mannum Road, Birdwood, SA 5234 (postal) **REGION** Adelaide Hills
T (08) 8263 0986 **F** (08) 8263 0986 **OPEN** Not
WINEMAKER Oli Cucchiarelli **EST.** 1990 **CASES** 700
SUMMARY Birdwood Estate draws upon 7 ha of estate vineyards progressively established since 1990.
The quality of the white wines, and in particular the Chardonnay, has generally been good. The tiny
production is principally sold through retail in Adelaide, with limited distribution in Sydney and
Melbourne.

Birnam Wood Wines NR

Turanville Road, Scone, NSW 2337 **REGION** Upper Hunter Valley
T (02) 6545 3286 **F** (02) 6545 3431 **OPEN** Weekends & public hols 11–4
WINEMAKER Monarch Winemaking Services (Contract) **EST.** 1994 **CASES** 8000
SUMMARY Former Sydney car dealer Mike Eagan and wife Min moved to Scone to establish a horse
stud; the vineyard came later (in 1994) but is now a major part of the business, with 32 ha of vines.
Most of the grapes are sold; part only is vinified for Birnam Wood. Son Matthew has now joined the
business after working for 5 years for Tyrrell's in its export department. Exports to Switzerland,
Canada and China.

Bishop Grove Wines NR

Lot 136 Old Maitland Road, Bishops Bridge, NSW 2326 **REGION** Lower Hunter Valley
T (02) 4930 4698 **F** (02) 4930 4698 **WEB** www.bishopgrove.com.au **OPEN** By appointment
WINEMAKER Greg Silkman (Contract) **EST.** 1990 **CASES** NA
SUMMARY Retired engineer Harry Wells began planting the vineyard in 1990, choosing chardonnay,
verdelho and shiraz. Initially the grapes were sold, but then Harry's daughter Beth and son-in-law
Peter Parkinson began producing wines under the Bishop Grove Label. Thanks to skilled contract-
winemaking and mature vines Bishop Grove has had significant show success, including the top gold
and trophy for Best 2002 Chardonnay at the NSW Boutique Winemakers Show of that year. A large
house is available for rent; the wines are sold by mail order.

Black George ★★★

Black Georges Road, Manjimup, WA 6258 **REGION** Manjimup
T (08) 9772 3569 **F** (08) 9772 3102 **WEB** www.blackgeorge.com **OPEN** 7 days 10.30–4.45
WINEMAKER Gregory Chinery **EST.** 1991 **CASES** 3750
SUMMARY Black George arrived with aspirations to make high-quality Pinot Noir. As with so much of
the Manjimup region, it remains to be seen whether the combination of soil and climate will permit
this; the quality of the Black George Merlot Cabernet Franc once again points in a different direction.
Retail distribution in New South Wales, Victoria, Western Australia and Queensland; exports to the
UK and The Netherlands.

 Pinot Noir 2003 Very savoury, foresty style; lingering, persistent tannins. Slightly dry
aftertaste. **RATING** 86 **DRINK** Now $ 26.50

Blackgum Estate NR

166 Malmsbury Road, Metcalfe, Vic 3448 (postal) **REGION** Macedon Ranges
T (03) 5423 2933 **F** (03) 5423 2944 **WEB** www.macedonranges.com/blackgum estate **OPEN** Not
WINEMAKER Simonette Sherman **EST.** 1990 **CASES** 400
SUMMARY Simonette Sherman is the sole proprietor, executive winemaker and marketing manager of
Blackgum Estate. It is situated 9 km northeast of the historic village of Malmsbury, and 1.6 km from
the town of Metcalfe. The 4.5-ha 10-year-old vineyard is planted to riesling, chardonnay, shiraz and
cabernet sauvignon, with a planting of sagrantino (which sent me scuttling to Jancis Robinson's
Oxford Companion to Wine) planned. It is a red variety grown strictly around the Italian university
town of Perugia, and is said to produce wines of great concentration and liveliness with deep ruby
colour and some bitterness. So there; the varietal atlas of Australia continues to expand.

BlackJack Vineyards ★★★★★

Cnr Blackjack Road/Calder Highway, Harcourt, Vic 3453 **REGION** Bendigo
T (03) 5474 2355 **F** (03) 5474 2355 **WEB** www.blackjackwines.com.au **OPEN** Weekends & public hols 11–5, when stock available
WINEMAKER Ian McKenzie, Ken Pollock **EST.** 1987 **CASES** 2500
SUMMARY Established by the McKenzie and Pollock families on the site of an old apple and pear orchard in the Harcourt Valley, best known for some very good Shirazs. Ian McKenzie, incidentally, is not to be confused with Ian McKenzie formerly of Seppelt Great Western. Exports to New Zealand.

YYYYY **Shiraz 2002** Supple, smooth, fine blackberry and plum fruit; good oak handling; stylish. **RATING** 94 **DRINK** 2012 $ 30
Block 6 Shiraz 2002 Medium-bodied; black fruits, chocolate and spice supported by fine tannins; excellent structure and length. **RATING** 94 **DRINK** 2015 $ 30

YYYY **Cabernet Merlot 2002** **RATING** 86 **DRINK** 2009 $ 25

Blackwood Crest Wines NR

RMB 404A, Boyup Brook, WA 6244 **REGION** Blackwood Valley
T (08) 9767 3029 **F** (08) 9767 3029 **OPEN** 7 days 10–6
WINEMAKER Max Fairbrass **EST.** 1976 **CASES** 1500
SUMMARY A remote and small winery which has produced one or two notable red wines full of flavour and character; however, quality does fluctuate somewhat.

Blackwood Wines ★★★

Kearney Street, Nannup, WA 6275 **REGION** Blackwood Valley
T (08) 9756 0088 **F** (08) 9756 0089 **WEB** www.blackwoodwines.com.au **OPEN** 7 days 10–4
WINEMAKER Peter Nicholas **EST.** 1998 **CASES** 10 000
SUMMARY Blackwood Wines draws upon 1 ha each of chardonnay, merlot and chenin blanc and 0.5 ha of pinot noir, supplemented by contract-grown fruit which significantly broadens the product range. It also operates a Cellar Club with discounted prices for members, and a restaurant is open Thur–Tues. Exports to Ireland, Singapore and The Netherlands.

YYYY **Fishbone Cabernet Shiraz 2003** Clean; fresh blackcurrant, plum and blackberry; fruit-driven, though tannins are there in support. Screwcap. **RATING** 87 **DRINK** 2008 $ 15

YYYY **Fishbone Semillon Chenin Blanc 2004** **RATING** 86 **DRINK** 2007 $ 15
Shiraz 2002 **RATING** 84 **DRINK** 2007 $ 15

YYY **Fishbone Unwooded Chardonnay 2004** **RATING** 83 $ 15

Blanche Barkly Wines ★★★★☆

14 Kingower–Brenanah Road, Kingower, Vic 3517 **REGION** Bendigo
T (03) 5438 8223 **F** (03) 5438 8223 **OPEN** Weekends & public hols 10–5, or by appointment
WINEMAKER David Reimers, Arleen Reimers **EST.** 1972 **CASES** 1200
SUMMARY The Reimers are happy with their relatively low profile; yields from the 30+-year-old, dry-grown vines are low, and the quality of the wines is reward in itself. Limited availability makes the mailing list the best way of securing the wines.

YYYYY **Charlotte Elise Shiraz 2002** Good colour; full bodied, concentrated and intense, but not jammy; has soaked up 2 years in French oak; very good length and balance. Quality cork. **RATING** 94 **DRINK** 2017 $ 48

YYYY **George Henry Cabernet Sauvignon 2002** Deep colour; dense, rich and ripe; a cascade of blackcurrant fruit and persistent, fine tannins. Distorted, stained cork. **RATING** 93 **DRINK** 2015
Mary Eileen Shiraz 2002 Medium-bodied; elegant, savoury, spicy style; long palate, lingering, fine tannins. Quality cork. **RATING** 90 **DRINK** 2012 $ 32

YYYY **Johann Cabernet Sauvignon 2002** Medium-bodied; a mix of savoury, earthy, spicy notes along with blackcurrant; moderate tannins. **RATING** 88 **DRINK** 2010 $ 32

YYYY **Alexander Cabernet Sauvignon 2002** **RATING** 86 **DRINK** 2010 $ 25

Bleasdale Vineyards ★★★★

Wellington Road, Langhorne Creek, SA 5255 **REGION** Langhorne Creek
T (08) 8537 3001 **F** (08) 8537 3224 **WEB** www.bleasdale.com.au **OPEN** Mon–Sun 10–5
WINEMAKER Michael Potts, Renae Hirsch **EST.** 1850 **CASES** 100 000
SUMMARY One of the most historic wineries in Australia, drawing upon vineyards that are flooded every winter by diversion of the Bremer River, which provides moisture throughout the dry, cool, growing season. The wines offer excellent value for money, all showing that particular softness which is the hallmark of the Langhorne Creek region. Production has soared; export markets established in the UK, the US, New Zealand, Switzerland and Germany.

ŶŶŶŶŶ **Mulberry Tree Cabernet Sauvignon 2002** Elegant medium-bodied wine, with gently sweet fruit; pleasing structure and tannins. **RATING** 91 **DRINK** 2012 $ 16.50

Blind Man's Bluff Vineyard ★★☆

Lot 15 Bluff Road, Kenilworth, Qld 4574 **REGION** Queensland Coastal
T (07) 5472 3168 **F** (07) 5472 3168 **OPEN** Weekends & school hols 10–5
WINEMAKER Peter Scudamore-Smith (Contract) **EST.** 2001 **CASES** 450
SUMMARY Noel Evans and Tricia Toussaint have planted 1 ha of chardonnay and 1.3 ha of shiraz on their property. Wines are available both by the glass and bottle, and can be purchased with a local cheese platter.

ŶŶŶŶ **Sophist Red 2004 RATING** 84 **DRINK** Now $ 17

ŶŶŶ **Chardonnay 2004 RATING** 82 $ 20

Bloodwood ★★★★☆

4 Griffin Road, Orange, NSW 2800 **REGION** Orange
T (02) 6362 5631 **F** (02) 6361 1173 **WEB** www.bloodwood.com.au **OPEN** By appointment
WINEMAKER Stephen Doyle **EST.** 1983 **CASES** 4000
SUMMARY Rhonda and Stephen Doyle are two of the pioneers of the burgeoning Orange district. The wines are sold mainly through the cellar door and by an energetically and informatively run mailing list; the principal retail outlet is Ian Cook's Fiveways Cellar, Paddington, Sydney. Bloodwood has done best with elegant but intense Chardonnay and the intermittent releases of super-late-harvest Ice Riesling. Exports to the UK.

ŶŶŶŶŶ **Schubert 2002** Soft, nutty, creamy overtones to medium-bodied nectarine fruit; very good mouthfeel and length. **RATING** 92 **DRINK** 2008 $ 25
Chardonnay 2003 Ripe peach and stone fruit aromas and flavours; subtle oak, good length. **RATING** 91 **DRINK** 2009 $ 22
Riesling 2004 Clean; light to medium-bodied with mineral, herb and touches of citrus; minerally finish. **RATING** 90 **DRINK** 2010 $ 18

ŶŶŶŶ **Pinot Noir 2003** High-toned strawberry/red fruit aromas; light-bodied; fresh fruit; lacks persistence. **RATING** 87 **DRINK** 2007 $ 30

ŶŶŶŶ **Big Men in Tights 2004** Vivid, pale red-purple; light rose petal and strawberry fruit flavours; dry finish. **RATING** 86 **DRINK** Now $ 14
Shiraz 2002 RATING 85 **DRINK** 2008 $ 24

Blown Away ★★★★

PO Box 108, Willunga, SA 5172 **REGION** McLaren Vale
T (08) 8557 4554 **F** (08) 8557 4554 **OPEN** Not
WINEMAKER Trevor Tucker (Contract) **EST.** 2001 **CASES** 500
SUMMARY Dave and Sue Watson purchased their property, situated on the corner of Plains Road Rogers Road at the base of Sellicks Hill, in 1993. It had 0.8 ha of old shiraz, cabernet sauvignon, a few rows of grenache, and a little over 3 ha of almond trees. In 1995 they removed the trees and planted the area to shiraz and grenache. Between 1995 and 1999 they planted an additional 3 ha; the grapes from the new plantings are sold, the production for Blown Away coming entirely from the old block.

Blueberry Hill Vineyard   NR

Cnr McDonalds Road/Coulson Road, Pokolbin, NSW 2320 **REGION** Lower Hunter Valley
T (02) 4998 7295 **F** (02) 4998 7296 **WEB** www.blueberryhill.com.au **OPEN** 7 days 10–5, until 6.30
Fri–Sat in summer
WINEMAKER Greg Silkman (Contract) **EST.** 1973 **CASES** 2000
SUMMARY Blueberry Hill Vineyard is part of the old McPherson Estate, with fully mature plantings of
chardonnay, sauvignon blanc, shiraz, pinot noir, merlot and cabernet sauvignon. Until 2000 the
grapes were sold to other winemakers, but since that year part of the crush goes towards the
extensive Blueberry Hill range.

Bluebush Estate   NR

Wilderness Road, Cessnock, NSW 2325 (postal) **REGION** Lower Hunter Valley
T (02) 4930 7177 **F** (02) 4930 7666 **WEB** www.bluebush.com.au **OPEN** Not
WINEMAKER Contract **EST.** 1991 **CASES** 200
SUMMARY 2 ha of vineyards (half chardonnay, half shiraz) have been established by Robyn and David
McGain; the wines are contract-made and sold by mail order, and B&B and self-contained
accommodation (Bluebush Cottage and Bridstowe Barn) overlooks the vineyard.

Blue Metal Vineyard   ★★★☆

Lot 18 Compton Park Road, Berrima, NSW 2025 **REGION** Southern Highlands
T 0438 377 727 **F** (02) 9327 2753 **WEB** www.bluemetalvineyard.com **OPEN** Not
WINEMAKER Kim Moginie, Joe Duncan **EST.** 2002 **CASES** NA
SUMMARY The 10.5-ha Blue Metal Vineyard is situated on part of a cattle station, and at an elevation
of 790m; the name comes from the rich red soil that overlies the cap of basalt rock. A wide range of
grape varieties are planted, including sauvignon blanc, pinot gris, merlot, cabernet sauvignon,
sangiovese and petit verdot. The wines have been very competently made: Kim Moginie has long
experience in the region (dating back to 1983), and assistant winemaker Joe Duncan has cool-
climate winemaking experience in Alsace and Chablis. Exports to the UK.

???? **Southern Highlands Pinot Gris 2004** Pale salmon-pink; interesting wine; strawberry
and subliminal spice; good length and balance; crisp finish. Screwcap. **RATING** 89
DRINK 2007 **$** 24
Southern Highlands Sauvignon Blanc 2004 Soft, ripe bordering on sweet tropical,
fleshy fruit; surprising given the altitude. Screwcap. **RATING** 87 **DRINK** Now **$** 19
Southern Highlands Cabernet Merlot Petit Verdot 2003 Fresh, clear and bright; light to
medium-bodied; well made and nice mouthfeel; simply lacks fruit depth. Screwcap.
RATING 87 **DRINK** 208 **$** 24

Blue Pyrenees Estate   ★★★★☆

Vinoca Road, Avoca, Vic 3467 **REGION** Pyrenees
T (03) 5465 3202 **F** (03) 5465 3529 **WEB** www.bluepyrenees.com.au **OPEN** Mon–Fri 10–4.30,
weekends & public hols 10–5
WINEMAKER Andrew Koerner **EST.** 1963 **CASES** 100 000
SUMMARY Forty years after Remy Cointreau established Blue Pyrenees Estate (then known as
Chateau Remy), it sold the business to a small group of Sydney businessmen led by John Ellis (no
relation to the John Ellis of Hanging Rock). The winemaking and marketing teams remain in place,
although John Ellis has become involved in all areas of the business. The core of the business is the
180-ha estate vineyard, much of it fully mature. Exports to all major markets.

????? **Richardson Cabernet Sauvignon 2002** Medium to full-bodied; ripe, supple
blackcurrant, cedar and earth; quality French oak, ripe tannins, good length and balance.
Quality cork. **RATING** 94 **DRINK** 2016

????? **Shiraz 2002** Deep colour; dense blackberry fruit; abundant but ripe and fine tannins.
Best for years; very good value. **RATING** 90 **DRINK** 2012 **$** 18
Shiraz Viognier 2002 Some lift, but overall distinctly savoury, spicy; light to medium-
bodied; good length. Cork. **RATING** 90 **DRINK** 2012

Cuvee Riche 2000 Fruity strawberry aroma and mid-palate flavour; long, lemony finish; not too obviously sweet; clever making. Why so expensive? RATING 90 DRINK Now $33
Midnight Cuvee 2000 Fine and elegant; lingering citrussy/lemony flavours; dry finish. Blanc de Blanc. RATING 90 DRINK 2010 $32

ΥΥΥΥ **Richardson Shiraz 2002** Medium-bodied; distinctly earthy, savoury, spicy edges to black fruits; fine tannins; needs a touch more sweetness. Cork. RATING 89 DRINK 2015
Estate Reserve Red 2000 Medium-bodied; earthy/briary style, with a certain austerity, but good structure and length. RATING 89 DRINK 2010 $32
Pyrenees Sauvignon Blanc 2004 Quite complex aroma and texture. Ripe, but not flabby, tropical fruit flavours give personality. RATING 88 DRINK 2009 $18
Pyrenees Chardonnay 2003 Well made; nicely balanced and integrated oak with soft melon fruit. RATING 88 DRINK Now $18
Blanc de Noir 2000 Pale pink, no straw; fine, crisp, elegant; tight acidity; largely unevolved. RATING 88 DRINK 2007 $23
Fiddlers Creek Shiraz Cabernet 2002 Attractive juicy plummy fruit on entry; thins out a little on the finish, but not bad, and well priced. RATING 87 DRINK 2008 $12
Pyrenees Merlot 2002 Light to medium-bodied; not intense, but has a nice core of small red fruits. RATING 87 DRINK 2008 $18
Sparkling Shiraz 2001 Plenty of red berry flavour; a trifle tannic, but not too sweet. RATING 87 DRINK 2010

ΥΥΥΨ **Fiddlers Creek Chardonnay 2003** RATING 85 DRINK Now

Blue Wren ★★★☆

433 Cassilis Road, Mudgee, NSW 2850 REGION Mudgee
T (02) 6372 6205 F (02) 6372 6206 WEB www.bluewrenwines.com.au OPEN 7 days 10.30–4.30
WINEMAKER Various contract EST. 1985 CASES 2000
SUMMARY James and Diana Anderson have 2 vineyards. The first is Stoney Creek, which was planted in 1985 and acquired from the Britten family in early 1999. It has 2 ha each of chardonnay and semillon, 1.5 ha of cabernet and 0.5 ha of merlot. It is 20 km north of Mudgee, and the vines are dry-grown. The second vineyard has been planted to 3.8 ha of shiraz and verdelho, leaving more than 20 ha unplanted. The Bombira Vineyard, as it is known, is adjacent to the old Augustine vineyards. The onsite restaurant is recommended – as are the wines.

ΥΥΥΥ **Mudgee Rose 2004** Plenty of fruity strawberry/raspberry flavour; sweetness is integrated with the fruit. Screwcap. RATING 87 DRINK Now $18

ΥΥΥΨ **Mudgee Verdelho 2004** RATING 86 DRINK 2007 $17

🍎 Boat O'Craigo ★★★★☆

458 Maroondah Highway, Healesville, Vic 3777 REGION Yarra Valley
T (03) 9899 9986 F (03) 9987 1442 WEB www.boatocraigo.com.au OPEN Thurs–Sun 10–5
WINEMAKER Rob Dolan, Kate Goodman, Al Fencaros (Contract) EST. 1998 CASES 7000
SUMMARY The 13.6-ha hillside vineyard is one of the highest sites in the Yarra Valley, bounded on the south by the Little Grace Burn River. It was acquired by Steve Graham in October 2003, who changed the name to Boat O'Craigo, a tiny place in a Scottish valley where his ancestors lived. Plans are afoot to graft the 4.6 ha of cabernet sauvignon and shiraz to chardonnay and sauvignon blanc, a sensible move given the very cool site.

ΥΥΥΥΥ **Black Cameron Shiraz 2003** Deep colour; rich, round, velvety black fruits; nice touch of spice, good oak; excellent structure, depth and mouthfeel. From the Healesville and Kangaroo Ground vineyards. RATING 94 DRINK 2015 $24

ΥΥΥΥΨ **Yarra Valley Shiraz Viognier 2004** Bright, full purple-red; generous, rich, blackberry fruit; soft and supple mid-palate; firms on the finish. Only 4% Viognier; Kangaroo Ground. Quality cork. RATING 92 DRINK 2012 $22
Black Spur Sauvignon Blanc 2004 Clean, fresh, crisp, bright and minerally; long and lingering finish. Screwcap. RATING 90 DRINK 2007 $19

Boatshed Vineyard ★★★

703 Milbrodale Road, Broke, NSW 2330 (postal) **REGION** Lower Hunter Valley
T (02) 9876 5761 **F** (02) 9876 5761 **OPEN** Not
WINEMAKER Tamburlaine (Contract) **EST.** 1989 **CASES** 3500
SUMMARY Mark and wife Helen Hill acquired the property in June 1998. At that time it had 5 ha of chardonnay, and in the spring of 1999 the plantings were extended with 2 ha each of verdelho, merlot, chambourcin, shiraz and cabernet sauvignon. As Mark Hill says, the name of the vineyard has much more to do with his lifetime involvement with rowing, first as a schoolboy competitor and thereafter as a coach of his school's senior IVs. Sustainable viticultural practices are used, and no insecticides have been applied for the past 15 years. The wines are made under contract at Tamburlaine, with approximately 25% of the wine made and bottled for Boatshed, the remainder being taken by Tamburlaine. There is no cellar door, and all sales are mail order or ex the vineyard on a wholesale basis to Sydney restaurants.

Bochara Wines

1099 Glenelg Highway, Hamilton, Vic 3300 **REGION** Henty
T (03) 5571 9309 **F** (03) 5570 8334 **WEB** www.bocharawine.com.au **OPEN** Fri–Sun 11–5, or by appointment
WINEMAKER Martin Slocombe **EST.** 1998 **CASES** 1500
SUMMARY This is the small husband and wife business of experienced winemaker Martin Slocombe and former Yalumba viticulturist Kylie McIntyre. They have established 1 ha each of pinot noir and sauvignon blanc, together with 1.6 ha of shiraz and cabernet sauvignon, and 0.5 ha of pinot meunier, supplemented by grapes purchased from local grapegrowers. The modestly priced, but well-made wines are principally sold through the cellar door sales cottage on the property, which has been transformed from a decrepit weatherboard shanty with one cold tap to a fully functional 2 room tasting area, and through a number of local restaurants and bottle shops. The label design, incidentally, comes from a 1901 poster advertising the subdivision of the original Bochara property into smaller farms.

▼▼▼▼▼ **Pinot Noir 2002** Deep colour for the variety; ultra-complex, ultra-powerful, brooding plum, briar, smoke, forest, herb and mint; will be very long-lived. Outstanding value. Slightly stained-quality cork. **RATING** 93 **DRINK** 2011 $ 20

Boggy Creek Vineyards ★★★☆

1657 Boggy Creek Road, Myrrhee, Vic 3732 **REGION** King Valley
T (03) 5729 7587 **F** (03) 5729 7600 **WEB** www.boggycreek.com.au **OPEN** Weekends (Nov–Apr), or by appointment
WINEMAKER Contract **EST.** 1978 **CASES** 8000
SUMMARY Graeme and Maggie Ray started their vineyard in 1978, planting small quantities of riesling and chardonnay. Since then the vineyard has grown to over 40 ha with the addition of cabernet sauvignon, shiraz, barbera, pinot gris and other experimental lots. It is situated on northeast-facing slopes at an altitude of 350m, with warm summer days and cool nights. Exports to the US, Malaysia and Hong Kong.

▼▼▼▼▼ **King Valley Riesling 2003** Aromatic spice and green herb aromas; lively and quite intense; sweet apple and lime flavours, good length. **RATING** 90 **DRINK** 2010 $ 16
King Valley Shiraz 2003 Substantial wine; medium to full-bodied; sweet plum and blackberry fruit. **RATING** 90 **DRINK** 2012 $ 20

▼▼▼▼ **King Valley Shiraz Cabernet Sauvignon 2002** Quite powerful red and black fruits, but needed more barrel work; brisk finish. **RATING** 86 **DRINK** 2008 $ 20

▼▼▼ **King Valley Sauvignon Blanc 2004** **RATING** 83 $ 25
King Valley Unwooded Chardonnay 2003 **RATING** 83 $ 16

🐚 Bogie Man Wines

160 Gum Road, Caveat, Vic 3660 (postal) **REGION** Strathbogie Ranges
T (03) 5790 4024 **F** (03) 5790 4025 **WEB** www.bogiemanwines.com **OPEN** Not
WINEMAKER Sam Plunkett (Contract) **EST.** 2001 **CASES** 600

SUMMARY Andrew Smythe and family have planted a little under 4 ha of chardonnay, and 0.7 ha of the rare Italian grape lagrein. Plantings did not begin until 2001, and until they come into bearing, the chardonnay comes from 18-year-old vines on a nearby vineyard, the shiraz from 25-year-old vines near Murchison in the Goulburn Valley. Plans are in place to expand the vineyard to 18 ha, with varieties including tempranillo and prosecco as well as more mainstream grapes being considered. For the time being, the wines are sold by mail order; a website is under construction.

ŸŸŸŸ **Watson's Strathbogie Ranges Chardonnay 2004** Unwooded style with lots of punchy, citrussy fruit; length and intensity impressive. **RATING** 89 **DRINK** 2007 $ 22
Watson's Goulburn Valley Shiraz 2002 Medium-bodied; an array of spice, mint, berry and leaf aromas and flavours; fine tannins. **RATING** 88 **DRINK** 2010 $ 35
Watson's Strathbogie Ranges Chardonnay 2003 Similar style to the '04; good presence and length; slightly less intense. **RATING** 87 **DRINK** Now $ 22

Bogong Estate   NR

Cnr Mountain Creek Road/Damms Road, Mt Beauty, Vic 3699 **REGION** Alpine Valleys
T 0419 567 588 **F** (03) 5754 4946 **WEB** www.pinotnoir.com.au **OPEN** 7 days 10–5
WINEMAKER Bill Tynan **EST.** 1997 **CASES** 2500
SUMMARY In the flesh, Bill Tynan looks exactly as a tax partner for a large accounting firm should look: slim, quietly spoken and self-deprecating. His business card, featuring the imprint in vivid pink of an impression of Marilyn Monroe's lips, tells you all is not what it seems. He has in fact given up accounting practice, and planted 10 ha of pinot noir in the upper reaches of Kiewa River Valley, with no near neighbours to keep him company. Winemaking is all about fermenting pinot noir in large plastic bags with gas valves, a system developed by the Hickinbotham family. Marketing the wine is no less lateral: Pinotnoir.com.au 2002 Pinot Noir is aimed at the younger, fast movers of Melbourne and Sydney. The estate wine is directed to the serious, probably older, market.

Boireann   ★★★★☆

Donnellys Castle Road, The Summit, Qld 4377 **REGION** Granite Belt
T (07) 4683 2194 **OPEN** 7 days 10–4.30
WINEMAKER Peter Stark **EST.** 1998 **CASES** 600
SUMMARY Peter and Therese Stark have a 10-ha property set amongst the great granite boulders and trees which are so much part of the Granite Belt. They have established 1.5 ha of vines planted to no less than 11 varieties, including the four Bordeaux varieties which go to make a Bordeaux-blend; Shiraz and Viognier; Grenache and Mourvedre provide a Rhône blend, and there will also be a straight Merlot. Tannat (French) and barbera and nebbiolo (Italian) make up the viticultural League of Nations. Peter Stark is a winemaker of exceptional talent, making cameo amounts of red wines which are quite beautifully made and of a quality equal to Australia's best.

ŸŸŸŸŸ **Shiraz Viognier 2003** Very good colour; high-toned aromatics ex the Viognier; medium-bodied plum and spice fruit; fine, lingering tannins. Beautifully made. **RATING** 93 **DRINK** 2013 $ 35
Grenache Mourvedre Shiraz 2003 Excellent texture and structure; an array of red fruits, raspberry and redcurrant; fine tannins; lovely wine. **RATING** 92 **DRINK** 2009 $ 24
Granite Belt Cabernet Sauvignon 2003 Very good colour; medium-bodied; blackcurrant fruit; fine, silky tannins; subtle oak. **RATING** 90 **DRINK** 2010 $ 20

ŸŸŸŸ **Cabernet Merlot 2003** Medium-bodied; bright red fruits with touches of leaf and mint; subtle oak. **RATING** 89 **DRINK** 2008 $ 17

Boneo Plains   NR

RMB 1400, Browns Road, South Rosebud, Vic 3939 **REGION** Mornington Peninsula
T (03) 5988 6208 **F** (03) 5988 6208 **OPEN** By appointment
WINEMAKER R D Tallarida **EST.** 1988 **CASES** 2500
SUMMARY A 9-ha vineyard and winery established by the Tallarida family, well known as manufacturers and suppliers of winemaking equipment to the industry. The Chardonnay is the best of the wines so far released.

Bonneyview

NR

Sturt Highway, Barmera, SA 5345 **REGION** Riverland
T(08) 8588 2279 **OPEN** 7 days 9–5.30
WINEMAKER Robert Minns **EST.** 1975 **CASES** 2500
SUMMARY The smallest Riverland winery selling exclusively cellar door, with an ex-Kent cricketer and Oxford University graduate as its owner/winemaker. The Shiraz Petit Verdot (unique to Bonneyview) and Cabernet Petit Verdot add a particular dimension of interest to the wine portfolio.

Boora Estate

NR

'Boora', Warrie Road, Dubbo, NSW 2830 **REGION** Western Plains Zone
T(02) 6884 2600 **F**(02) 6884 2600 **WEB** www.boora-estate.com **OPEN** 7 days 2–5
WINEMAKER Frank Ramsay **EST.** 1984 **CASES** 500
SUMMARY The wheel comes full circle with Boora Estate, where Frank Ramsay has established approximately 0.5 ha each of chardonnay, semillon, cabernet franc, cabernet sauvignon, merlot, tempranillo and shiraz. In the 1870s and 1880s Dubbo supported a significant winemaking industry, with Eumalga Estate (owned and run by French-born JE Serisier) said (by the local newspaper of the time) to have the second-largest winery in Australia (which I doubt). Another highly successful winery was established by German-born Frederick Kurtz; Mount Olive won a number of awards in international exhibitions in the 1880s. That achievement was matched 120 years later by Boora Estate winning a silver medal at the 2001 Brisbane Wine Show with its 2000 Shiraz, competing against wines from all parts of Australia.

Borambola Wines

★★★

Sturt Highway, Wagga Wagga, NSW 2650 **REGION** Gundagai
T(02) 6928 4210 **F**(02) 6928 4210 **WEB** www.borambola.com **OPEN** 7 days 11–4
WINEMAKER Andrew Birks **EST.** 1995 **CASES** 6000
SUMMARY Borambola Homestead was built in the 1880s, and in the latter part of that century was the centre of a pastoral empire of 1.4 million ha, ownership of which passed to the McMullen family in 1992. It is situated in rolling foothills 25 km east of Wagga Wagga in the newly declared Gundagai region. Just under 10 ha of vines surround the homestead (4 ha shiraz, 3.5 ha cabernet sauvignon, 2.2. ha chardonnay) and the wines are made for Borambola at Charles Sturt University by the Charles Sturt winemaker Andrew Birks.

♥♥♥♥   **Shiraz 2003** Rich, full-bodied, blackberry, prune and plum; substantial tannins needing to soften; plenty of potential. **RATING** 88 **DRINK** 2010 $18

♥♥♥♡   **Gundagai Chardonnay 2003** **RATING** 85 **DRINK** Now $14

Borrodell on the Mount

★★★★☆

Lake Canobolas Road, Orange, NSW 2800 **REGION** Orange
T(02) 6365 3425 **F**(02) 6365 3588 **WEB** www.borrodell.com.au **OPEN** 7 days 10–5
WINEMAKER Chris Durrez **EST.** 1998 **CASES** 1300
SUMMARY Borry Gartrell and Gaye Stuart-Williams have planted 4 ha of pinot noir, sauvignon blanc, pinot meunier, traminer and chardonnay adjacent to a cherry, plum and heritage apple orchard and trufferie. It is 10 minutes' drive from Orange, and adjacent to Lake Canobolas, at an altitude of 1000m. The wines have been consistent medal winners at regional and small winemaker shows, and are served in the two modern, self-contained 3 bedroom homes on the property.

♥♥♥♥♥   **Winemaker's Daughter Gewurztraminer 2004** Fragrant and flowery; delicious sweet citrus, passionfruit, apple and lychee; the lightest hint of sweetness; no phenolics. Screwcap. **RATING** 94 **DRINK** 2008 $16

♥♥♥♥♡   **Sauvignon Blanc 2004** Light to medium-bodied; clean, fresh grass, mineral and hints of kiwifruit; not particularly intense, but certainly correct. Screwcap. **RATING** 90 **DRINK** 2007 $18

Boston Bay Wines ★★★

Lincoln Highway, Port Lincoln, SA 5606 **REGION** Southern Eyre Peninsula
T(08) 8684 3600 **F**(08) 8684 3637 **WEB** www.bostonbaywines.com.au **OPEN** Weekends,
school/public hols 11.30–4.30
WINEMAKER David O'Leary, Nick Walker **EST.** 1984 **CASES** 3000
SUMMARY A strongly tourist-oriented operation which has extended the viticultural map in South
Australia. It is situated at the same latitude as Adelaide, overlooking the Spencer Gulf at the southern
tip of the Eyre Peninsula. Say proprietors Graham and Mary Ford, 'It is the only vineyard in the world
to offer frequent sightings of whales at play in the waters at its foot.'

Botobolar ★★★☆

89 Botobolar Road, Mudgee, NSW 2850 **REGION** Mudgee
T(02) 6373 3840 **F**(02) 6373 3789 **OPEN** Mon–Sat 10–5, Sun 10–3
WINEMAKER Kevin Karstrom **EST.** 1971 **CASES** 4000
SUMMARY One of the first organic vineyards in Australia, with present owner Kevin Karstrom
continuing the practices established by founder Gil Wahlquist. Preservative Free Dry White and Dry
Red extend the organic practice of the vineyard to the winery. Shiraz is consistently the best wine to
appear under the Botobolar label. Exports to the UK, Denmark and Germany.

♟♟♟♟ **Organically Grown Mudgee Shiraz 2001** Spice, cedar, earth, herb, leaf and blackberry
mix; light to medium-bodied; tannins exemplary. Cork. **RATING** 88 **DRINK** 2011 $13.95
Mudgee Cabernet Sauvignon 2001 Medium-bodied; spicy, earthy, secondary black fruit
aromas; nicely balanced, fruit-driven palate; unpretentious but enjoyable style. Cork.
RATING 88 **DRINK** 2011 $19
Organically Grown Mudgee Shiraz 2002 Blackberry, herb, mocha and spice; powerful
wine; tannins needed more fining. Stained-quality cork. **RATING** 87 **DRINK** 2010 $13.95

♟♟♟♟ **The King Cabernet Sauvignon Shiraz 2001** **RATING** 86 **DRINK** 2009 $24
Preservative Free Dry Red 2004 **RATING** 84 **DRINK** Now $16

Bowen Estate ★★★★

Riddoch Highway, Coonawarra, SA 5263 **REGION** Coonawarra
T(08) 8737 2229 **F**(08) 8737 2173 **OPEN** 7 days 10–5
WINEMAKER Doug Bowen, Emma Bowen **EST.** 1972 **CASES** 12 000
SUMMARY Bluff-faced regional veteran Doug Bowen, now with daughter Emma at his side in the
winery, presides over one of the Coonawarra landmarks. A token Chardonnay accompanies a range
of full-bodied reds, which rather resemble their maker (Doug, that is).

♟♟♟♟ **Shiraz 2002** **RATING** 85 **DRINK** Now $26.20
Cabernet Sauvignon 2002 **RATING** 85 **DRINK** 2009 $27.10

Box Stallion ★★★★

64 Turrarubba Road, Merricks North, Vic 3926 **REGION** Mornington Peninsula
T(03) 5989 7444 **F**(03) 5989 7688 **WEB** www.boxstallion.com.au **OPEN** 7 days 11–5
WINEMAKER Alex White **EST.** 2001 **CASES** 9000
SUMMARY Box Stallion is the joint venture of Stephen Wharton, John Gillies and Garry Zerbe, who
have linked 2 vineyards, one at Bittern and one at Merricks North, with 20 ha of vines planted
between 1997 and 2003. What once was a thoroughbred stud has now become a vineyard, with the
Red Barn (in their words) 'now home to a stable of fine wines'. Those wines are made at the jointly
owned winery with Alex White as winemaker, and won two trophies (Shiraz and Pinot Noir) at the
2003 Concours des Vins du Victoria. The café is open daily from 11 am to 5 pm. Exports to the US
and Canada.

♟♟♟♟♟ **Arneis 2003** Fragrant, flowery aromas of citrus blossom; considerable drive to the palate;
one of the best yet from this variety. **RATING** 90 **DRINK** 2007 $27
Shiraz 2003 Spicy black pepper and black cherry; lively cool-grown style; light to
medium-bodied, has length. Cork. **RATING** 90 **DRINK** 2010 $27

TTTT **Red Barn Chardonnay 2003** Rounded aromas and mouthfeel with ripe stone fruit and melon, unencumbered by oak; good length. **RATING** 89 **DRINK** 2008 $19

The Enclosure Pinot Noir 2003 Very powerful, briary, stemmy style; spiced plum fruit, then a fairly firm finish. Approach with caution, or with food at hand. Cork. **RATING** 88 **DRINK** 2009 $35

Dolcetto 2003 Attractive colour; lots of black cherry fruit; considerable tannin structure. **RATING** 88 **DRINK** 2013 $22

Sauvignon Blanc 2003 Gooseberry, kiwifruit aromas; light-bodied, and lacks penetration/crispness, but is clean and balanced. **RATING** 87 **DRINK** Now $19

Moscato 2003 Lively, fresh, delicate grapey aromas and flavours; a touch of passionfruit; perfect balance. **RATING** 87 **DRINK** Now $19

Blaze Rose 2003 Even with screwcap, showing some development; musky edges to light red fruits. **RATING** 87 **DRINK** Now $16

TTTY **Sweet Harmony 2002** **RATING** 86 **DRINK** 2009 $19

TTT **The Enclosure Chardonnay 2003** **RATING** 83 $27

Boynton's ★★★☆

Great Alpine Road, Porepunkah, Vic 3741 **REGION** Alpine Valleys
T (03) 5756 2356 **F** (03) 5756 2610 **OPEN** 7 days 10–5
WINEMAKER Kel Boynton, Eleana Anderson **EST.** 1987 **CASES** 11 000
SUMMARY Kel Boynton has a beautiful 16-ha vineyard, framed by Mt Buffalo rising into the skies above it. Overall, the red wines have always outshone the whites. The initial very strong American oak input has been softened in more recent vintages to give a better fruit/oak balance. The Paiko label is for wines grown near Mildura by business partner and famed nurseryman Bruce Chalmers. The wines have distribution through the east coast of Australia; exports to Germany, Austria and the US.

Bracken Hill NR

81 Tinderbox Road, Tinderbox, Tas 7052 **REGION** Southern Tasmania
T (03) 6229 6475 **OPEN** Annual open weekends in March & October
WINEMAKER Contract **EST.** 1993 **CASES** 120
SUMMARY Max Thalmann came from Switzerland in 1961, retiring 30 years later, and took the decision to plant his 0.4-ha vineyard entirely to gewurztraminer. As Tasmanian writer Phil Laing has pointed out, it is probably the only specialist gewurztraminer producer in the southern hemisphere, making Thalmann's decision all the more curious, because he prefers red wine to white wine. His logic, however, was impeccable: he could sell the grapes and/or the wine from his vineyard and use the money to buy red wines of his choice. Bracken Hill has its open weekend in October, and participates in the annual Tasmanian cellar door open weekend in March. The label, incidentally, comes from a painting by Max Thalmann, which proves he is a man of many talents.

Braewattie ★★★☆

351 Rochford Road, Rochford, Vic 3442 **REGION** Macedon Ranges
T (03) 9818 5742 **F** (03) 9818 8361 **OPEN** By appointment
WINEMAKER Jillian Ryan, John Ellis **EST.** 1993 **CASES** 300
SUMMARY Des and Maggi Ryan bought Braewattie in 1990; Maggi's great-grandfather, James McCarthy, had acquired the property in the 1880s, and it remained in the family until 1971. When the property came back on the market the Ryans seized the opportunity to reclaim it, complete with a small existing planting of 300 pinot noir and chardonnay vines. Those plantings now extend to 5.5 ha; part of the production is sold as grapes, and a small amount is contract-made. The Macedon Brut is a particularly good wine.

TTTTY **Macedon Brut Pinot Noir Chardonnay 2000** Bright gold; very tight citrussy, lemony acidity; long finish. **RATING** 90 **DRINK** 2010 $29

TTTT **Macedon Brut Pinot Noir Chardonnay NV** Complex wine; very long palate; slightly twitchy acidity. **RATING** 87 **DRINK** 2008 $29

TTTY **Macedon Chardonnay 2003** **RATING** 85 **DRINK** 2008 $20
Macedon Pinot Noir 2003 **RATING** 85 **DRINK** 2007 $25

Brahams Creek Winery

NR

Woods Point Road, East Warburton, Vic 3799 **REGION** Yarra Valley
T (03) 9566 2802 **F** (03) 9566 2802 **OPEN** Weekends & public hols 11–5
WINEMAKER Geoff Richardson, Chris Young **EST.** 1990 **CASES** 1200
SUMMARY Owner Geoffrey Richardson did not start marketing his wines until 1994; a string of older vintages are available for sale at the cellar door at an enticing price. Part of the grape production is sold to other Yarra Valley winemakers.

Bramley Wood

NR

RMB 205 Rosa Brook Road, Margaret River, WA 6285 (postal) **REGION** Margaret River
T (08) 9757 9291 **F** (08) 9757 9291 **OPEN** Not
WINEMAKER Cliff Royle, Mike Edwards (Voyager Estate) **EST.** 1994 **CASES** 200
SUMMARY David and Rebecca McInerney planted 2 ha of cabernet sauvignon in 1994, with an inaugural vintage in 1998, released in December 2000. Encouraged by the quality of that wine and, in particular, the 1999 which followed it, the McInerneys plan to one day expand their plantings. For the time being, the tiny production is sold by mail order and through the two self-contained chalets on the property, each capable of hosting 4–6 adults.

Brand's of Coonawarra

Riddoch Highway, Coonawarra, SA 5263 **REGION** Coonawarra
T (08) 8736 3260 **F** (08) 8736 3208 **WEB** www.mcwilliams.com.au **OPEN** Mon–Fri 8–5, weekends 10–4
WINEMAKER Jim Brayne, Peter Weinberg **EST.** 1966 **CASES** NFP
SUMMARY Part of a very substantial investment in Coonawarra by McWilliam's, which first acquired a 50% interest from the founding Brand family then moved to 100%, and followed this with the purchase of 100 ha of additional vineyard land. Significantly increased production of the smooth wines for which Brand's is known has followed.

TTTTY **Special Release Merlot 2002** Varietal precision; medium-bodied; long, intense and savoury, with olive, red fruits and black fruits all intermingling; long finish. **RATING** 92 **DRINK** 2012 $ 31.50

Cabernet Sauvignon 2002 Surprisingly sweet cassis/blackcurrant mid-palate, switching to a more savoury finish; lingering aftertaste. **RATING** 90 **DRINK** 2012 $ 24

Patron's Reserve 2002 Medium-bodied; smooth and rounded, with a mix of savoury, mint and berry flavours. **RATING** 90 **DRINK** 2012

Brangayne of Orange

★★★★☆

49 Pinnacle Road, Orange, NSW 2800 **REGION** Orange
T (02) 6365 3229 **F** (02) 6365 3170 **WEB** www.brangayne.com **OPEN** By appointment
WINEMAKER Simon Gilbert (Contract), Richard Bateman **EST.** 1994 **CASES** 3000
SUMMARY Orchardists Don and Pamela Hoskins decided to diversify into grapegrowing in 1994 and have progressively established 25 ha of high quality vineyards. With consultancy advice from Dr Richard Smart and skilled contract-winemaking, Brangayne made an auspicious debut, underlining the potential of the Orange region. Pamela has now taken over responsibility for the day-to-day management of the business and marketing. Exports to the UK, Canada and Singapore.

TTTTY **Tristan 2002** Elegant, fruit-driven style; light to medium-bodied; supple blackcurrant and cassis; integrated and balanced oak; fine tannins. Quality cork. **RATING** 92 **DRINK** 2013 $ 29

Isolde Reserve Chardonnay 2002 Subtle and restrained; complex barrel ferment, malolactic ferment and fruit aromas and flavours; long finish, long future. Screwcap. **RATING** 91 **DRINK** 2010 $ 22.50

Sauvignon Blanc 2004 Spotlessly clean; fresh passionfruit, gooseberry and herb/grass mix; quite intense. Screwcap. **RATING** 90 **DRINK** 2007 $ 22

Pinot Noir 2002 Firm, fresh black cherry fruit; good balance and structure; some spicy notes; has length. Screwcap. **RATING** 90 **DRINK** 2010 $ 26 ᵀᵀᵀᵀ **Chardonnay 2004** Elegant grapefruit and nectarine aromas and flavours; fruit-driven; has length and balance; no oak evident. Screwcap. **RATING** 89 **DRINK** 2008 $ 16.50

🦢 Brave Goose Vineyard NR

PO Box 633, Seymour, Vic 3660 **REGION** Goulburn Valley
T (03) 9593 9421 **F** (03) 9493 9431 **OPEN** By appointment
WINEMAKER John Stocker **EST.** 1988 **CASES** 500
SUMMARY Dr John Stocker and wife Nina must be among the most highly qualified boutique vineyard and winery operators in Australia. John Stocker is the former chief executive of CSIRO and chairman of the Grape and Wine Research and Development Corporation for the past 7 years, and wife Nina is completing the Roseworthy postgraduate oenology course. Moreover, they established their first vineyard (while living in Switzerland) on the French/Swiss border in the village of Flueh, working in conjunction with friends. On returning to Australia in 1987 they finally found a property on the inside of the Great Dividing Range with north-facing slopes and shallow, weathered ironstone soils. Here they have established 2.5 ha each of shiraz and cabernet sauvignon, and 0.5 ha each of merlot and gamay, selling the majority of grapes from the 17-year-old vines, but making small quantities of Cabernet Merlot, Merlot and Gamay, principally sold through the mailing list.

🦢 Braydon Estate ★★★★☆

40 Londons Road, Lovedale, NSW 2325 (postal) **REGION** Lower Hunter Valley
T (02) 4990 9122 **F** (02) 4990 9133 **OPEN** Not
WINEMAKER David Hook (Contract) **EST.** 1998 **CASES** 500
SUMMARY Peter and Lesley Giles have established 1.25 ha of vines, split equally between semillon and shiraz. The vine count is 1500 of each variety, which the Giles' describe as 'truly boutique'. The vineyard is looked after by Keith Holder of Pokolbin Viticultural Services, who has a 35-year track record, and the winemaking is carried out by the highly skilled David Hook.

ᵀᵀᵀᵀᵀ **Home Paddock Hunter Valley Semillon 2004** Top-quality young Semillon; intense fruit; lemon, almost tropical; remarkable mid to back-palate. **RATING** 94 **DRINK** 2014 $ 12.50

ᵀᵀᵀᵀᵞ **Home Paddock Hunter Valley Shiraz 2003** Deep colour; a clean, powerful array of black fruits; fine but firm tannins; still a baby. **RATING** 91 **DRINK** 2013 $ 15

Bream Creek ★★★★

Marion Bay Road, Bream Creek, Tas 7175 **REGION** Southern Tasmania
T (03) 6231 4646 **F** (03) 6231 4646 **OPEN** At Potters Croft, Dunally, tel (03) 6253 5469
WINEMAKER Julian Alcorso (Contract) **EST.** 1975 **CASES** 3500
SUMMARY Until 1990 the Bream Creek fruit was sold to Moorilla Estate, but since then the winery has been independently owned and managed under the control of Fred Peacock, legendary for the care he bestows on the vines under his direction. Peacock's skills have seen both an increase in production and also a vast lift in wine quality across the range, headed by the Pinot Noir. The 1996 acquisition of a second vineyard in the Tamar Valley has significantly strengthened the business base of the venture.

ᵀᵀᵀᵀᵀ **Chardonnay 2003** Very good colour; smoky/charry oak; tight nectarine fruit; a long, piercing and intense palate. Has come into its own with bottle age. **RATING** 94 **DRINK** 2013 $ 19

ᵀᵀᵀᵀᵞ **Pinot Noir 2003** Medium-bodied; very neatly balanced and weighted; gently ripe plum fruit. **RATING** 92 **DRINK** 2009 $ 25

ᵀᵀᵀᵀ **Pinot Noir 2002** Quite fresh red fruits, but not a lot of richness. **RATING** 87 **DRINK** 2007 $ 25

ᵀᵀᵀᵞ **Riesling 2004** **RATING** 86 **DRINK** 2008 $ 18
Sauvignon Blanc 2004 **RATING** 86 **DRINK** Now $ 19
Late Picked Schonburger 2004 **RATING** 86 **DRINK** 2007 $ 22
Gewurztraminer 2004 **RATING** 85 **DRINK** Now $ 19

Bremerton Wines ★★★★☆

Strathalbyn Road, Langhorne Creek, SA 5255 **REGION** Langhorne Creek
T (08) 8537 3093 **F** (08) 8537 3109 **WEB** www.bremerton.com.au **OPEN** 7 days 10–5
WINEMAKER Rebecca Willson **EST.** 1988 **CASES** 25 000
SUMMARY The Willsons have been grapegrowers in the Langhorne Creek region for some considerable time but their dual business as grapegrowers and winemakers has expanded significantly over the past few years. Their vineyards have more than doubled to over 100 ha (predominantly cabernet sauvignon, shiraz and merlot), as has their production of wine under the Bremerton label, no doubt in recognition of the quality of the wines. In February 2004 sisters Rebecca and Lucy (marketing) took control of the business, marking the event with (guess what) revamped label designs. Exports to the UK, the US and other major markets.

🍷🍷🍷🍷🍷 **Cabernet Sauvignon 2001** Lovely wine; excellent fruit and oak balance and integration; fine, sweet blackcurrant; supple, silky mouthfeel; good length. **RATING** 95 **DRINK** 2016 **$** 40

🍷🍷🍷🍷½ **Old Adam Shiraz 2002** Medium to full-bodied; powerful, concentrated and focused; blackberry, a touch of anise; balanced but lingering tannins. **RATING** 93 **DRINK** 2015 **$** 35
Selkirk Shiraz 2002 Medium-bodied; excellent structure through fine, lingering tannins, the blackberry fruit with a savoury twist. **RATING** 90 **DRINK** 2012 **$** 20

🍷🍷🍷🍷 **Rebecca Wilson Sauvignon Blanc 2004** Spotlessly clean (screwcap); lively, tangy palate; quite juicy; good balance and length, very good value. **RATING** 89 **DRINK** Now **$** 15
Tamblyn 2002 Fresh, fruit-forward style; an array of red and black fruits; subtle oak inputs and fine tannins; very good value. Cabernet/Shiraz/Malbec/Merlot. **RATING** 89 **DRINK** 2009 **$** 16
Wiggy Sparkling Chardonnay 2001 Elegant, flavoursome nectarine and stone fruit; good balance and mouthfeel. **RATING** 87 **DRINK** 2007 **$** 25

🍷🍷🍷½ **Langhorne Creek Racy Rose 2004** **RATING** 85 **DRINK** Now **$** 15
Verdelho 2004 **RATING** 84 **DRINK** Now **$** 17.50

Bress ★★★★★

Mt Alexander Vineyard, 3894 Calder Highway, Harcourt, Vic 3453 **REGION** Bendigo
T (03) 5474 2262 **F** (03) 5474 2553 **OPEN** Weekends & public hols 11–5, or by appointment
WINEMAKER Adam Marks **EST.** 2001 **CASES** 4000
SUMMARY Adam Marks won the Ron Potter Scholarship in 1991 to work as assistant winemaker to Rodney Hooper at Charles Sturt University. Since then he has made wine in all parts of the world, worked as winemaker at Dominion Wines for 2 years, then taken the brave decision (during his honeymoon in 2000) to start his own business. He has selected Margaret River semillon and sauvignon blanc as the best source of white Bordeaux-style wine in Australia; Yarra Valley as the best pinot noir region; and shiraz from Heathcote for precisely the same reason. In early 2005 the Marks family acquired the former Mt Alexander Vineyard and cellar door, expanding the distribution base: New South Wales (Vinous Solutions) and WA (Liquid Library). Exports to Indonesia.

🍷🍷🍷🍷🍷 **Unfiltered Heathcote Shiraz 2003** Very good colour; lovely wine right from the outset; blackberry, plum and spice flavours; outstanding tannin structure woven through the palate. **RATING** 96 **DRINK** 2016 **$** 31.99
Yarra Valley Chardonnay 2002 Very complex; strong barrel ferment inputs on the bouquet; very intense, concentrated and focused; ripe stone fruit and melon power through on the finish. **RATING** 94 **DRINK** 2012 **$** 25.99

🍷🍷🍷🍷½ **Margaret River Semillon Sauvignon Blanc 2004** Clean (screwcap); medium-bodied; rich, smooth mouthfeel with tropical passionfruit, gooseberry and grass. **RATING** 90 **DRINK** 2008 **$** 17.50

🍷🍷🍷🍷 **Yarra Valley Pinot Noir 2004** Opens quietly with plum and cherry fruit; gains strength on the finish and aftertaste; classic peacock's tail. **RATING** 89 **DRINK** 2008 **$** 17.99

🍷🍷🍷½ **Harcourt Valley OD Riesling 2004** **RATING** 86 **DRINK** 2007 **$** 17.99

Briagolong Estate ★★★★

Valencia–Briagolong Road, Briagolong, Vic 3860 **REGION** Gippsland
T (03) 5147 2322 **F** (03) 5147 2400 **OPEN** By appointment
WINEMAKER Gordon McIntosh **EST.** 1979 **CASES** 400
SUMMARY This is very much a weekend hobby for medical practitioner Gordon McIntosh, who tries hard to invest his wines with Burgundian complexity. Six years of continuous drought, with one break in 2002 when hail destroyed the crop, has meant no Chardonnay in 2000, 2001 or 2002, nor Pinot for 2001 and 2002. Given the quality of the 2000 Pinot, the loss is all the keener. The one ray of sunshine comes in the form of micro-releases of prior vintages (back to 1996) for mailing list customers, and a last offering of 2000 Pinot Noir.

Brian Barry Wines ★★★☆

PO Box 23, Fullarton, SA 5063 **REGION** Clare Valley
T (08) 8363 6211 **F** (08) 8838 3205 **OPEN** Not
WINEMAKER Brian Barry, Judson Barry **EST.** 1977 **CASES** 6000
SUMMARY Brian Barry is an industry veteran with a wealth of winemaking and show-judging experience. His is nonetheless in reality a vineyard-only operation, with a substantial part of the output sold as grapes to other wineries and the wines made under contract at various wineries, albeit under his supervision. As one would expect, the quality is reliably good. Retail distribution through all states, and exports to the UK and the US.

 TTTTY **Jud's Hill Handpicked Riesling 2004** Developed yellow-green; generous, fairly soft tropical and citrus aromas and flavours. **RATING** 90 **DRINK** 2008 $ 18

TTTT **Judd's Hill Merlot Cabernet Sauvignon 2004** Light to medium-bodied; overall, quite elegant; fine, savoury tannins; dry, briary style. **RATING** 87 **DRINK** 2009 $ 20

Briarose Estate ★★★★

Bussell Highway, Augusta, WA 6290 **REGION** Margaret River
T (08) 9758 4160 **F** (08) 9758 4161 **WEB** www.briarose.com.au **OPEN** 7 days 10–4.30
WINEMAKER Cath Oates **EST.** 1998 **CASES** 12 000
SUMMARY Brian and Rosemary Webster began the development of the estate plantings in 1998, which now comprise sauvignon blanc (2.33 ha), semillon (1.33 ha), cabernet sauvignon (6.6 ha), merlot (2.2 ha) and cabernet franc (1.1 ha). The winery is situated at the southern end of the Margaret River region, 6 km north of Augusta, where the climate is distinctly cooler than that of northern Margaret River.

TTTTY **Margaret River Cabernet Merlot 2003** Ripe but not jammy blackcurrant and cassis; medium-bodied, smooth and supple; subtle oak, fresh finish. Screwcap. **RATING** 91 **DRINK** 2012
Margaret River Sauvignon Blanc Semillon 2004 Glowing yellow-green; a complex wine with an array of flavours from tropical to gooseberry; a faint hint of oak; good acidity. Screwcap. **RATING** 90 **DRINK** 2008 $ 17

TTTT **Margaret River Sauvignon Blanc 2004** Light to medium-bodied; grass and gooseberry aromas; some passionfruit joins in on the palate; fraction broad. Screwcap. **RATING** 88 **DRINK** 2007 $ 19
Margaret River Rose 2004 Carefully balanced and made; gently sweet strawberry, raspberry fruit; spot on the market. Screwcap. **RATING** 87 **DRINK** Now $ 15.60

Briar Ridge ★★★★

Mount View Road, Mount View, NSW 2325 **REGION** Lower Hunter Valley
T (02) 4990 3670 **F** (02) 4990 7802 **WEB** www.briarridge.com.au **OPEN** 7 days 10–5
WINEMAKER Karl Stockhausen, Mark Woods **EST.** 1972 **CASES** 25 000
SUMMARY Semillon and Shiraz, each in various guises, have been the most consistent performers, underlying the suitability of these varieties to the Hunter Valley. The Semillon, in particular, invariably shows intense fruit and cellars well. Briar Ridge has been a model of stability with the winemaking duo of Karl Stockhausen and Steven Dodd, and also has the comfort of over 48 ha of estate vineyards, from which it is able to select the best grapes. Exports to the US and Canada.

🐦 Brick Kiln ★★★★☆

13 Blyth Street, Glen Osmond, SA 5064 (postal) **REGION** McLaren Vale
T (08) 8379 9314 **WEB** www.brickiln.com.au **OPEN** Not
WINEMAKER Contract **EST.** 2001 **CASES** 1000
SUMMARY This is the venture of Malcolm and Alison Mackinnon, Garry and Nancy Watson, and Ian and Pene Davey. They purchased the 8-ha Nine Gums Vineyard, which had been planted in 1995/96, in January 2001. The majority of the grapes are sold with a lesser portion contract-made for the partners under the Brick Kiln label, which takes its name from the Brick Kiln Bridge adjacent to the vineyard.

🍷🍷🍷🍷🍷 **Shiraz 2003** Excellent colour; perfect balance and integration of plummy fruit and oak on the bouquet; massively rich and highly flavoured; does show its alcohol (14.7°) but is not over-extracted; time needed. **RATING** 93 **DRINK** 2018 $ 22

Bridgeman Downs ★★★

Barambah Road, Moffatdale via Murgon, Qld 4605 **REGION** South Burnett
T (07) 4168 4784 **F** (07) 4168 4767 **OPEN** Thurs–Mon 10–4
WINEMAKER Bruce Humphery-Smith **EST.** NA **CASES** NA
SUMMARY A substantial, albeit new, vineyard with 4 ha of vines, the major plantings being of verdelho, chardonnay and shiraz and lesser amounts of merlot and cabernet sauvignon.

🍷🍷🍷🍷 **Chardonnay 2004** Quite intense and attractive entry, then slightly hard acidity on the finish; nonetheless, has good overall flavour. **RATING** 89 **DRINK** 2007

🍷🍷🍷 **Verdelho 2004 RATING** 82
Shiraz 2003 RATING 82

Briery Estate NR

Lot 16 Briar Lane, Bindoon, WA 6502 **REGION** Perth Hills
T (08) 9576 1417 **F** (08) 9576 1417 **WEB** www.brieryestatewines.com **OPEN** Wed–Mon 10–6, Tuesday by appointment
WINEMAKER Ron Waterhouse **EST.** 1994 **CASES** 500
SUMMARY Ron Waterhouse and Christine Smart run Briery Estate (formerly Jacaranda Homestead) in the hills of Bindoon. There they have 9 ha of verdelho, pinot noir, grenache, shiraz, cabernet sauvignon, muscat, furmint and harslevelu, although they steer away from varietal naming of their wines. The wines are chiefly sold by mail order and through the cellar door, which has barbecue and picnic facilities, and crafts.

Brindabella Hills ★★★★☆

Woodgrove Close, via Hall, ACT 2618 **REGION** Canberra District
T (02) 6230 2583 **F** (02) 6230 2023 **OPEN** Weekends, public hols 10–5
WINEMAKER Dr Roger Harris **EST.** 1986 **CASES** 2000
SUMMARY Distinguished research scientist Dr Roger Harris presides over Brindabella Hills, which increasingly relies on estate-produced grapes, with small plantings of cabernet sauvignon, cabernet franc, merlot, shiraz, chardonnay, sauvignon blanc, semillon and riesling, and a new planting of sangiovese and brunello. Wine quality has been consistently impressive. Limited retail distribution in New South Wales and the ACT.

🍷🍷🍷🍷🍷 **Canberra District Riesling 2004** Fragrant lime blossom and passionfruit aromas; lingering palate; fine finish. Screwcap. **RATING** 93 **DRINK** 2014 $ 20
Canberra District Shiraz 2003 Clean, focused black cherry and blackberry fruit; medium-bodied, good mouthfeel; fine tannins and well-handled oak. Cork. **RATING** 91 **DRINK** 2013 $ 25
Canberra District Merlot 2003 Light to medium-bodied; appropriate texture and structure for the variety; olive, blackcurrant and spice; good mouthfeel. Quality cork. **RATING** 90 **DRINK** 2010 $ 18

▼▼▼▼ **Canberra District Cabernets 2003** Medium-bodied; a mix of initially sweet and then more savoury blackcurrant fruit; slightly austere finish. Quality cork. **RATING** 87 **DRINK** 2010 $ 20

🍇 Brini Estate Wines ★★★★★

RSD 600 Blewitt Springs Road, McLaren Vale, SA 5171 (postal) **REGION** McLaren Vale
T (08) 8383 0080 **F** (08) 8383 0104 **OPEN** Not
WINEMAKER Brian Light (Contract) **EST.** 2000 **CASES** 3000
SUMMARY The Brini family has been growing grapes in the Blewitt Springs area of McLaren Vale since 1953. In 2000 brothers John and Marcello Brini established Brini Estate Wines to vinify a portion of the grape production; up to that time it had been exclusively sold to companies such as Penfolds, Rosemount Estate and d'Arenberg. The flagship Sebastian Shiraz is produced from dry-grown vines planted in 1947, the Shiraz Grenache from dry-grown vines planted in 1964. Skilled contract winemaking, coupled with impeccable fruit sources, has resulted in a new star in the McLaren Vale firmament.

▼▼▼▼▼ **Blewitt Springs Shiraz 2002** Deep colour; complex, intense, lingering; whispers of dark chocolate to the core of plum fruit; slightly savoury tannins; 15 months in American oak swallowed up. **RATING** 95 **DRINK** 2012 $ 18
Sebastian McLaren Vale Shiraz 2003 Rich, ripe (not over-ripe) black fruits and spices and a touch of chocolate; fine tannins; very good balance and length; carries its 14.5° alcohol with ease. **RATING** 94 **DRINK** 2013 $ 28

▼▼▼▼▽ **Sebastian McLaren Vale Shiraz 2001** Typical chocolate, savoury, blackberry regional mix; medium-bodied; fine tannins, good length. **RATING** 93 **DRINK** 2011 $ 28
McLaren Vale Shiraz Grenache 2002 A fragrant bouquet with hints of spice; elegant, light to medium-bodied, fine, long palate; silky tannins. **RATING** 93 **DRINK** 2009 $ 18
McLaren Vale Shiraz Grenache 2003 Sweet fruit aromas, with the Grenache obvious; medium-bodied; very fine, soft, tannins. **RATING** 92 **DRINK** 2008 $ 18

Brischetto Wines NR

106 Hughes Road, Bargara, Qld 4670 **REGION** Queensland Coastal
T (07) 4159 0862 **F** (07) 4159 0860 **OPEN** 7 days 8–5
WINEMAKER Joe Brischetto, Angelo Puglisi (Contract) **EST.** 1996 **CASES** NA
SUMMARY Joe and Elizabeth Brischetto planted the first vines in 1996, expanding the vineyard to its present size of 12 000 vines (around 8 ha) the following year. The winery is at the coastal town of Bargara, 12 km from Bundaberg, and offers views of the sea and vineyards from the outdoor tasting area.

Bristol Farm ★★★★

59 Bellingham Road, Main Ridge, Vic 3928 **REGION** Mornington Peninsula
T (03) 9830 1453 **F** (03) 9888 6794 **WEB** www.bristolfarm.com.au **OPEN** By appointment
WINEMAKER Contract **EST.** 1997 **CASES** 250
SUMMARY Bristol Farm is a pinot noir specialist; Wayne Condon has established slightly over 1 ha of multiple clones of the variety and, for good measure, has not used irrigation in their establishment or ongoing grapegrowing. Monty's Paddock is the premium release, made only in the best vintages; Lionheart is the normal label. The tiny production is sold by mail order.

Britannia Creek Wines NR

75 Britannia Creek Road, Wesburn, Vic 3799 **REGION** Yarra Valley
T (03) 5967 1006 **F** (03) 5780 1426 **OPEN** Weekends 10–6
WINEMAKER Charlie Brydon **EST.** 1982 **CASES** 1600
SUMMARY The wines are made under the Britannia Falls label from 4 ha of estate-grown grapes. A range of vintages are available from the cellar door, with some interesting, full-flavoured Semillon.

Broadview Estate ★★★☆

Rowbottoms Road, Granton, Tas 7030 **REGION** Southern Tasmania
T (03) 6263 6882 **F** (03) 6263 6840 **OPEN** Tues–Sun 10–5
WINEMAKER Andrew Hood (Contract) **EST.** 1996 **CASES** 250
SUMMARY David and Kaye O'Neil planted 0.5 ha of chardonnay and a 0.25 ha each of riesling and pinot noir in the spring of 1996, and produce limited quantities of normally very good Riesling and Chardonnay.

Brockville Wines ★★★

15th Street Ext, Irymple South, Vic 3498 **REGION** Murray Darling
T (03) 5024 5143 **WEB** www.brockvillewines.com.au **OPEN** 7 days 10–4
WINEMAKER Contract **EST.** 1999 **CASES** 800
SUMMARY Mark Bowring, a great-grandson of WB Chaffey (responsible for the design and implementation of the irrigation scheme in the Sunraysia district in the 1880s), and wife Leigh have been growing grapes since 1975. They have 10 ha of chardonnay, 4.4 ha of cabernet sauvignon and 1 ha of shiraz. Most of the grapes are sold to local wineries, but in 1999 the Bowrings decided to have a small portion of cabernet sauvignon vinified for their own label. They chose Brockville as the name, as it is (or was) the Canadian hometown of WB Chaffey. More recently (in 2003) they acquired an additional 23 ha of vineyard directly across the road from their original plantings, and have opened a cellar door.

Broke Estate/Ryan Family Wines ★★★☆

Wollombi Road, Broke, NSW 2330 **REGION** Lower Hunter Valley
T (02) 9664 3000 **F** (02) 9665 3303 **WEB** www.ryanwines.com.au **OPEN** Weekends & public hols 10–5
WINEMAKER Matthew Ryan **EST.** 1988 **CASES** 18 000
SUMMARY This is the flagship operation of the Ryan Family, with 25 ha of largely mature vineyards, the lion's share to chardonnay, but also including meaningful plantings of semillon, sauvignon blanc, shiraz, merlot, barbera, tempranillo, cabernet sauvignon and cabernet franc.

TTTTY **Broke Estate On Monkey Place Creek Semillon 2000** Great, glowing green-yellow; soft honey and lemon fruit; hints of toast; if only it had a screwcap. Cork. **RATING** 90 **DRINK** Now $ 22

TTTT **Ryan Free Run Chardonnay 2001** Ripe yellow peach; flavoursome though not complex; good example of warm-grown Unwooded Chardonnay with some maturity. Cork. **RATING** 87 **DRINK** Now $ 14
Ryan Single Vineyard Cabernets 2001 Still quite lively and fresh; spicy components; tobacco and blackcurrant; good oak. Cabernet Sauvignon/Cabernet Franc. Cork. **RATING** 87 **DRINK** 2009 $ 15

TTTY **Broke Estate On Monkey Place Creek Cabernet Sauvignon 1999** **RATING** 86 **DRINK** Now $ 33

Broken Gate Wines ★★★★

101 Munster Terrace, North Melbourne, Vic 3051 (postal) **REGION** Southeast Australia
T (03) 9348 9333 **F** (03) 9348 9688 **OPEN** Not
WINEMAKER Contract **EST.** 2001 **CASES** 4000
SUMMARY Broken Gate is a partnership between Brendan Chapman and Joseph Orbach. Chapman has an extensive liquor retailing background, and is presently bulk wine buyer for Swords Wines, responsible for the purchase of 160 000 litres of wine across Australia. It is he who doubtless provides the entree cards for the wines released under the Broken Gate label. Joseph Orbach lived and worked in the Clare Valley from 1994 to 1998 at Leasingham Wines, while also leading the restoration of the Clarevale Winery Co-op building. If this were not enough, he was the head chef and team lead in Tasting Australia, representing the Clare Valley, and the designer and creator of a prism-shaped wine cask, selling at Sainsbury wine stores in the UK (full of Chilean Chardonnay and Merlot).

ΨΨΨΨ **Heathcote Shiraz 2003** Rich blackberry, spice, plum, mocha and vanilla mix; good structure; no drought stripping; good length. Poor, stained cork. **RATING** 92 **DRINK** 2013 $19.95

Clare Valley Riesling 2004 Powerful mineral, talc, slate and herb aromas; long, flinty/lemony, lancing palate. Screwcap. **RATING** 90 **DRINK** 2012 $18.95

ΨΨΨΨ **Adelaide Hills Chardonnay 2003 RATING** 86 **DRINK** 2013 $19.95

Heathcote Cabernet Sauvignon 2002 RATING 85 **DRINK** 2007 $19.95

Brokenwood ★★★★★

McDonalds Road, Pokolbin, NSW 2321 **REGION** Lower Hunter Valley
T (02) 4998 7559 **F** (02) 4998 7893 **WEB** www.brokenwood.com.au **OPEN** 7 days 10–5
WINEMAKER Iain Riggs **EST.** 1970 **CASES** 110 000
SUMMARY Deservedly fashionable winery producing consistently excellent wines. Has kept Graveyard Shiraz as its ultimate flagship wine, while extending its reach through many of the best eastern regions for its broad selection of varietal wine styles. Its big-selling Hunter Semillon remains alongside Graveyard, and there is then a range of wines coming from regions including Orange, central NSW ranges, Beechworth, McLaren Vale, Cowra and elsewhere. Exports to the UK, the US, Canada, Hong Kong and New Zealand.

ΨΨΨΨΨ **ILR Reserve Semillon 2000** Brilliant green-yellow, spotlessly clean and still youthful, with lemon and lanolin aromas, and touches of toast and honey lurking in the shadows. **RATING** 96 **DRINK** 2012 $35

Wade Block 2 McLaren Vale Shiraz 2002 Intense aromas provide a strong regional counterpoint; dark chocolate edges to the black fruit core of the Hunter; excellent tannin and oak management. **RATING** 95 **DRINK** 2015 $35

Mistress Block Shiraz 2002 Controlled power; dark fruits with some regional savoury touches to lengthen the palate and finish. From a 30-year-old vineyard. **RATING** 94 **DRINK** 2017 $50

ΨΨΨΨ **Mt Panorama Chardonnay 2004** Very complex yet subtle wine; medium-bodied; wild yeast barrel ferment inputs to melon and cashew flavour; excellent in-built acidity. Screwcap. **RATING** 93 **DRINK** 2010 $30

Graveyard Chardonnay 2002 Surprisingly developed colour given the screwcap; complex barrel ferment inputs to white peach fruit; good acidity and length. **RATING** 93 **DRINK** 2008 $40

Mt Panorama Chardonnay 2001 Complex; plenty of mouthfeel and texture; ripe stone fruit developing at an impressively leisurely pace. **RATING** 92 **DRINK** 2008 $30

Rayner Vineyard Shiraz 2002 A complex array of spice, licorice and leather aromas; full-bodied, rich McLaren Vale style; shows alcohol sweetness. A polar opposite to the '02 Graveyard. **RATING** 92 **DRINK** 2017 $65

McLaren Vale/Padthaway Shiraz 2001 Excellent structure and texture; blackberry, bitter chocolate and touches of vanilla oak; fine, ripe tannins. **RATING** 92 **DRINK** 2015 $25

Indigo Vineyard Beechworth Viognier 2004 Soft, round and mouthfilling; ripe pear and apricot, soft acidity; no alcohol heat at all. Screwcap. **RATING** 90 **DRINK** 2008 $35

Indigo Vineyard Beechworth Viognier 2003 Masses of rich pastille and musk fruit aromas and flavours; good wine; sweetness from alcohol; has attitude. **RATING** 90 **DRINK** 2007 $28

Indigo Vineyard Pinot Noir 2003 Plenty of varietal plum and cherry; from the big end of town, but should develop well; good structure, length and finish. **RATING** 90 **DRINK** 2008 $30

Shiraz 2003 Well balanced, medium-bodied; blackberry, plum and a lick of vanilla oak; fine tannins; simply needs time. **RATING** 90 **DRINK** 2013 $35

Graveyard Shiraz 2002 Medium-bodied; strongly regional, earthy/leathery overtones to the black fruits; fine tannins; integrated oak. **RATING** 90 **DRINK** 2012 $90

Cabernet Sauvignon Merlot 2002 Medium to full-bodied; clean blackcurrant and redcurrant fruit; neatly balanced, relatively long finish. **RATING** 90 **DRINK** 2009 $28

Jelka Vineyard McLaren Vale Riesling 2004 Very rich, concentrated and luscious; lime, mandarin and cumquat; just a fraction short. From raisined and botrytised grapes. Screwcap. **RATING** 90 **DRINK** 2008 $21.50

ΨΨΨΨ **Cricket Pitch Red 2002** Light to medium-bodied; tangy, savoury/spicy with a touch of oak sweetness; easy style. **RATING** 89 **DRINK** Now $19

Rayner Vineyard McLaren Vale Sangiovese 2003 Spicy morello and sour cherry; fruit-forward style; despite 15° alcohol, a quite silky finish. Screwcap. RATING 89 DRINK 2008 $30

ŸŸŸŸ **Unwooded Chardonnay 2004** RATING 86 DRINK Now $17

Broke's Promise Wines ★★★☆

725 Milbrodale Road, Broke, NSW 2330 REGION Lower Hunter Valley
T (02) 6579 1165 F (02) 9438 4985 WEB www.brokespromise.com.au OPEN By appointment
WINEMAKER Andrew Margan (Contract) EST. 1996 CASES 2000
SUMMARY Jane Marquard and Dennis Karp (and their young children) have established Broke's Promise on the banks of the Wollombi Brook adjacent to the Yengo National Park. They have followed tradition in planting shiraz, chardonnay and semillon, and broken with it by planting barbera and olive trees – the latter two inspired by a long stay in Italy. Exports to the UK and Asia.

Brook Eden Vineyard ★★★★

Adams Road, Lebrina, Tas 7254 REGION Northern Tasmania
T (03) 6395 6244 F (03) 6395 6211 WEB www.brookeden.com.au OPEN 7 days 10–5
WINEMAKER Mike Fogarty (Contract) EST. 1988 CASES 800
SUMMARY Sheila and the late Jan Bezemer established a 2.2-ha vineyard on the 60-ha Angus beef property which they purchased in 1987. The vineyard site is beautiful, with viticultural advice from the noted Fred Peacock.

ŸŸŸŸŸ **Riesling 2003** A closed bouquet, but a fine, tight minerally and racy palate interwoven with lime juice; has improved out of sight over the past 12 months. RATING 92 DRINK 2009 $21

Brookhampton Estate NR

South West Highway, Donnybrook, WA 6239 REGION Geographe
T (08) 9731 0400 F (08) 9731 0500 WEB www.brookhamptonestate.com.au OPEN Wed–Sun 10–4
WINEMAKER Contract EST. 1998 CASES 4000
SUMMARY Brookhampton Estate, situated 3 km south of Donnybrook, has wasted no time since its establishment in 1998: 127 ha of vines have been established with three fashionable red varietals to the fore – cabernet sauvignon (34 ha), shiraz (29 ha) and merlot (22 ha). One hectare of tempranillo and 3 ha of grenache can safely be classed as experimental. The three white varieties planted are chardonnay, sauvignon blanc and semillon. The first contract-made vintage was in 2001.

Brookland Valley ★★★★★

Caves Road, Wilyabrup, WA 6280 REGION Margaret River
T (08) 9755 6042 F (08) 9755 6214 WEB www.brooklandvalley.com.au OPEN 7 days 10–5
WINEMAKER Robert Bowen EST. 1984 CASES 2800
SUMMARY Brookland Valley has an idyllic setting, plus its much enlarged Flutes Café (one of the best winery restaurants in the Margaret River region) and its Gallery of Wine Arts, which houses an eclectic collection of wine and food-related art and wine accessories. After acquiring a 50% share of Brookland Valley in 1997, Hardys moved to full ownership in September 2004. Exports to the UK, Germany, Switzerland, Japan and Hong Kong.

ŸŸŸŸŸ **Cabernet Sauvignon Merlot 2001** Medium purple-red; elegant, medium-bodied and spotlessly clean wine; cassis, redcurrant and blackcurrant; soft, fine tannins. RATING 95 DRINK 2016 $39.50
Chardonnay 2002 Light but bright and intense green-yellow; fine, tight citrus/grapefruit/nectarine; entirely fruit-driven; long finish and good acidity. RATING 94 DRINK 2010 $35
Reserve Cabernet Sauvignon 2001 Abundant cassis and blackcurrant fruit bouquet and palate; good oak; soft, ripe, lingering tannins. RATING 94 DRINK 2016 $58

ŸŸŸŸ **Sauvignon Blanc 2004** RATING 86 DRINK Now $26.50
Verse 1 Semillon Sauvignon Blanc 2004 RATING 86 DRINK Now $15.90
Cabernet Sauvignon Merlot Cabernet Franc 2001 RATING 86 DRINK 2011 $35

Brookside Vineyard

NR

5 Loaring Road, Bickley Valley, WA 6076 **REGION** Perth Hills
T (08) 9291 8705 **F** (08) 9291 5316 **WEB** www.geocities.com/brooksidevineyard **OPEN** Weekends &
public hols 11–5
WINEMAKER Darlington Estate (Contract) **EST.** 1984 **CASES** 400
SUMMARY Brookside is one of the many doll's house-scale vineyard operations which dot the Perth Hills.
It has a 0.25 ha each of chardonnay and cabernet sauvignon, and sells the wine through a mailing list. It
also offers B&B accommodation at the house, which has attractive views of the Bickley Valley.

Brookwood Estate

★★★

Treeton Road, Cowaramup, WA 6284 **REGION** Margaret River
T (08) 9755 5604 **F** (08) 9755 5870 **WEB** www.brookwood.com.au **OPEN** 7 days 10–5
WINEMAKER Trevor Mann, Lyn Mann **EST.** 1999 **CASES** 2000
SUMMARY Trevor and Lyn Mann began the development of their 50-ha property in 1996, and now
have 1.3 ha each of shiraz, cabernet sauvignon, semillon, sauvignon blanc and chenin blanc planted.
An onsite winery was constructed in 1999 to accommodate the first vintage. Viticultural consultants
advise on management in the vineyard; the Manns are aiming to establish export markets.

Broomstick Estate

★★★★★

4 Frances Street, Mt Lawley, WA 6050 (postal) **REGION** Margaret River
T (08) 9271 9594 **F** (08) 9271 9741 **WEB** www.broomstick.com.au **OPEN** Not
WINEMAKER Andrew Gaman (Contract) **EST.** 1997 **CASES** 500
SUMMARY Robert Holloway and family purchased the property on which the vineyard is now
established in 1993 as an operating dairy farm. In 1997, 6 ha of shiraz was planted. Over the following
years 5.5 ha of merlot, and then (in 2004) 5.2 ha of chardonnay and 2 ha of sauvignon blanc were
added. The picturesque winery, situated alongside a large dam, is the first wine grape vineyard in
Western Australia to be awarded the SQF 2000 Quality Assurance Certification. The Holloways see
themselves as grapegrowers first and foremost, but have kept back enough shiraz to make 500 cases a
year, offered by the case freight-free anywhere in Australia.

 Margaret River Shiraz 2003 Complex, medium to full-bodied; lovely spicy overtones to
blackberry/blackcurrant fruit; good oak handling; excellent balance and length.
RATING 94 **DRINK** 2013 $ 16.50

Brothers in Arms

★★★★

PO Box 840, Langhorne Creek, SA 5255 **REGION** Langhorne Creek
T (08) 8537 3070 **F** (08) 8537 3415 **WEB** www.brothersinarms.com.au **OPEN** Not
WINEMAKER David Freschi **EST.** 1998 **CASES** 18 000
SUMMARY The Adams family has been growing grapes at Langhorne Creek since 1891, when the first
vines at the famed Metala vineyards were planted. Tom and Guy Adams are the fifth generation to
own and work the vineyard, and over the past 20 years have both improved the viticulture and
expanded the plantings to the present 40 ha (shiraz and cabernet sauvignon). It was not until 1998
that they decided to hold back a small proportion of the production for vinification under the
Brothers in Arms brand. Exports to the US (The Grateful Palate), Canada, the UK and Singapore.

 No. 6 Shiraz Cabernet 2002 Flooded with ripe, sweet, spicy raspberry, redcurrant and
blackcurrant fruit; off-setting tannins. **RATING** 89 **DRINK** 2012 $ 20

Brown Brothers

★★★★☆

Snow Road, Milawa, Vic 3678 **REGION** King Valley
T (03) 5720 5500 **F** (03) 5720 5511 **WEB** www.brownbrothers.com.au **OPEN** 7 days 9–5
WINEMAKER Wendy Cameron, Marc Scalzo, Trina Smith, Joel Tilbrook **EST.** 1885 **CASES** 1 million
SUMMARY Brown Brothers draws upon a considerable number of vineyards spread throughout a
range of site climates, ranging from very warm to very cool. It is also known for the diversity of
varieties with which it works, and the wines represent good value for money. Deservedly one of the
most successful family wineries in Australia. Exports to all major markets.

ŦŦŦŦŦ **Patricia Noble Riesling 2002** Glowing gold; intensely aromatic and flavoured; lime juice, orange peel and cumquat; integrated and balanced oak; very good acidity. Cork. RATING 96 DRINK 2012 $ 26
Patricia Shiraz 2002 Spicy, charry oak off-set by sweet plum and blackberry fruit; good mouthfeel and texture. RATING 95 DRINK 2012 $ 44.95
Patricia Noble Riesling 2000 Golden yellow; an immensely complex yet vibrant mix of cumquat, apricot and crystallised citrus. Perfect acidity. RATING 95 DRINK 2009 $ 26

ŦŦŦŦŸ **Very Old Tokay NV** Classy aged Tokay; great rancio; intense tea leaf, Christmas cake and spice; like the Very Old Muscat, not stale. RATING 93 DRINK Now $ 27.90
Very Old Muscat NV Age and complexity very obvious, a light year from the Reserve Muscat; Christmas pudding fruit; clean rancio cut; good length and acidity. RATING 93 DRINK Now $ 27.90
Patricia Pinot Noir Chardonnay Brut 1998 Complex nutty, bready autolysis aromas; sweet, creamy stone fruit flavours, then crisp acidity. RATING 92 DRINK 2007 $ 39
Patricia Cabernet Sauvignon 2002 Medium-bodied; black fruits, chocolate, spice and vanilla; supple, smooth tannins; good oak. Quality cork. RATING 91 DRINK 2012 $ 44.95
Aged Release Cabernet Shiraz 1999 Full-bodied; huge, inky wine; lots of dark, black fruits, licorice and blackcurrant; tannins in balance, though certainly there. Cork. RATING 91 DRINK 2014 $ 25
Whitlands Sauvignon Blanc 2004 Faintly smoky grass and gooseberry aromas and flavours; crisp, crunchy finish; good balance. RATING 90 DRINK Now $ 17.40
Cellar Door Release Heathcote Durif 2003 Dense colour; massively rich, dense and concentrated; black fruits and bitter chocolate; powerful tannins in balance. RATING 90 DRINK 2013 $ 18.90

ŦŦŦŦ **Victoria Pinot Grigio 2004** Expressive floral, spice and musk aromas; lively, fresh and vibrant fruit; crisp finish. RATING 89 DRINK 2007 $ 15.90
Whitlands Blanc de Blanc 1999 Fresh, clean, crisp and lively lemon citrus through good line, length and balance. Will age well on cork. RATING 89 DRINK 2008 $ 31
Victoria Riesling 2004 Strong tropical lime and herb aromas; solid palate, with slightly more herbal fruit; flavoursome. RATING 88 DRINK 2007 $ 14.40
Reserve Muscat NV Attractive, fresh varietal character; essence of raisins; good balance; could be served slightly chilled. RATING 88 DRINK Now $ 18.40
Aged Release Chardonnay 2000 Soft, developed peachy fruit; holding nicely; indifferent oak quality is the underbelly. Cork. RATING 87 DRINK Now $ 21
Moscato 2004 As ever, brimming with grapey fruit and fully sweet; excellent example of genre; 6° alcohol. RATING 87 DRINK Now $ 13.90
Milawa Graciano 2002 Light to medium-bodied; fresh, sweet, juicy red fruits, raspberry and cherry; minimal tannins. Cellar door release. RATING 87 DRINK 2008 $ 18.90

ŦŦŦŸ **Victoria Chardonnay 2003** RATING 86 DRINK 2007 $ 18.40
Victoria Dry Muscat 2004 RATING 86 DRINK Now $ 11.90
Cellar Door Release Roussanne 2002 RATING 86 DRINK Now $ 15.40
Everton Chardonnay Sauvignon Blanc Pinot Grigio 2004 RATING 86 DRINK Now $ 13
Victoria Cabernet Sauvignon 2002 RATING 86 DRINK 2008 $ 18.60
King Valley Barbera 2002 RATING 86 DRINK 2007 $ 15.90
Cellar Door Release Tempranillo 2003 RATING 86 DRINK 2008 $ 18.90
Victoria Tarrango 2004 RATING 86 DRINK Now $ 12
Orange Muscat & Flora 2004 RATING 86 DRINK Now $ 9.90
Aged Release Shiraz Mondeuse Cabernet 1998 RATING 85 DRINK 2018 $ 27
Victoria Merlot 2002 RATING 85 DRINK 2007 $ 17.20
Everton Cabernet Sauvignon Shiraz Malbec 2002 RATING 85 DRINK 2007 $ 13
Heathcote Sangiovese 2003 RATING 85 DRINK Now $ 18.90

ŦŦŦ **Dolcetto Syrah 2004** RATING 83 $ 13.90

Brown Hill Estate ★★★★

Cnr Rosa Brook Road/Barrett Road, Rosa Brook, WA 6285 REGION Margaret River
T (08) 9757 4003 F (08) 9757 4004 WEB www.brownhillestate.com.au OPEN 7 days 10–5
WINEMAKER Nathan Bailey EST. 1995 CASES 3000
SUMMARY The Bailey family's stated aim is to produce top-quality wines at affordable prices, via uncompromising viticultural practices emphasising low yields per hectare, in conjunction with the

family being involved in all stages of production with minimum outside help. They have established 7 ha each of shiraz and cabernet sauvignon, 4 ha of semillon, and 2 ha each of sauvignon blanc and merlot, and by the standards of the Margaret River, the prices are indeed affordable.

ҮҮҮҮ **Finniston Reserve Shiraz 2003** Powerful, sinewy wine; black cherry, earth and blackberry; savoury tannins; handles higher alcohol (14.5°) better; simply needs time. Cork. **RATING** 90 **DRINK** 2013 $ 25

ҮҮҮҮ **Ivanhoe Reserve Cabernet Sauvignon 2003** Light to medium-bodied; a gentle mix of cassis, blackcurrant, earth and spice belies its 14.8° alcohol; fine tannins, subtle oak. Cork. **RATING** 89 **DRINK** 2012 $ 25
Lakeview Semillon Sauvignon Blanc 2004 Slightly reduced bouquet; lots of ripe tropical, passionfruit and gooseberry; nearly, but not quite, there. Screwcap. **RATING** 87 **DRINK** 2007 $ 13
Chaffers Shiraz 2003 Shows elevated alcohol (14.5°) in slightly jammy fruit and grippy tannins, but ample presence. Cork. **RATING** 87 **DRINK** 2009 $ 16

ҮҮҮҮ **Hannans Cabernet Sauvignon 2003** **RATING** 86 **DRINK** 2009 $ 16

🦅 Brown Magpie Wines ★★★★

125 Larcombes Road, Moriac, Vic 3249 **REGION** Geelong
T (03) 5261 3875 **F** (03) 5261 3875 **WEB** www.brownmagpiewines.com **OPEN** 7 days 12–3
WINEMAKER Loretta Breheny, Shane Breheny, Karen Coulston (Consultant) **EST.** 2000 **CASES** 3000
SUMMARY Shane and Loretta Breheny began the planning for Brown Magpie Wines in 1998, purchasing a 20-ha property predominantly situated on a gentle, north-facing slope, with cypress trees on the western and southern borders providing protection against the wind. Over 2001 and 2002, 9 ha of vines were planted, with pinot noir (5 ha) taking the lion's share, followed by pinot gris (2 ha), shiraz (1.5 ha) and 0.25 ha each of chardonnay and sauvignon blanc. The wine is made onsite under the direction of Karen Coulston, who has over 10 years' experience in cool-climate viticulture and winemaking. Viticulture is Loretta Breheny's love; winemaking (and wine) is Shane's.

ҮҮҮҮ **Shiraz 2003** Blackberry, herb, thyme and spice; good mouthfeel and balance; fine tannins. **RATING** 93 **DRINK** 2013 $ 22

ҮҮҮҮ **Pinot Noir 2003** Big frame, with distinctly savoury edges, possibly from some whole bunch fermentation; has considerable length. **RATING** 89 **DRINK** 2010 $ 24

🦅 Brown's Farm Winery ★★★

3675 Great North Road, Laguna, NSW 2325 (postal) **REGION** Lower Hunter Valley
T (02) 4998 8273 **F** (02) 4998 8273 **OPEN** Not
WINEMAKER Frank Geisler, Jarmila Geisler **EST.** 1998 **CASES** 250
SUMMARY Frank and Jarmila Geisler established their 1-ha vineyard with the simple belief that 'the best wine is made in the smallest vineyard'. It is principally planted to cabernet sauvignon and merlot, with a small quantity of chardonnay and pinot gris. It is managed on quasi-organic principles, and both the viticulture and winemaking are carried out by the Geislers 'without too much outside help'. There is no cellar door; the Cabernet Sauvignon and Merlot are sold by mail order and word of mouth at $144 a case.

ҮҮҮҮ **Merlot 2003** **RATING** 85 **DRINK** 2008 $ 12
Cabernet Sauvignon 2003 **RATING** 84 **DRINK** 2007 $ 12

Browns of Padthaway ★★★★☆

Keith Road, Padthaway, SA 5271 **REGION** Padthaway
T (08) 8765 6063 **F** (08) 8765 6083 **WEB** www.browns-of-padthaway.com **OPEN** At Padthaway Estate
WINEMAKER Contract **EST.** 1993 **CASES** 35 000
SUMMARY The Brown family has for many years been the largest independent grapegrower in Padthaway, a district in which most of the vineyards were established and owned by Wynns, Seppelt, Lindemans and Hardys, respectively. After a slow start, has produced excellent wines since 1998, and wine production has increased accordingly.

ŸŸŸŸŸ **Sauvignon Blanc 2004** Complex, slightly flinty aromas; accelerates through the palate to the finish and aftertaste. Trophy 2004 Limestone Coast Wine Show. **RATING** 94 **DRINK** Now

ŸŸŸŸŸ **T-Trellis Shiraz 2003** Elegant, medium-bodied; spicy licorice edges to blackberry fruit; good balance and subtle oak. **RATING** 93 **DRINK** 2015

The Brigstock 2002 A ripe and powerful wine, with the malbec component helping considerably; generous and round in the mouth. **RATING** 93 **DRINK** 2017

Riesling 2004 Clean, quite fragrant apple/apple blossom aromas; apple and lime flavours, minerally finish; good length. **RATING** 91 **DRINK** 2010

Ernest Family Reserve Shiraz 2002 A chewy and rich wine, with ripe blackcurrant and dark chocolate fruit; lots of depth. **RATING** 91 **DRINK** 2012

Chardonnay 2004 Elegant stone fruit and citrus; good balance and length; minimal oak. **RATING** 90 **DRINK** 2007

Edward Family Reserve Malbec 2002 Ultra-typical of variety, with a juicy, jammy mid-palate, then surprising tannins. **RATING** 90 **DRINK** 2012

ŸŸŸŸ **Verdelho 2004** Quite aromatic; lively fruit salad with a touch of lemon; way better than most wines from this variety. **RATING** 89 **DRINK** Now

ŸŸŸŸ **Unwooded Chardonnay 2004** **RATING** 86 **DRINK** 2007

Brumby Wines

Sandyanna, 24 Cannon Lane, Wood Wood, Vic 3596 **REGION** Swan Hill
T 0438 305 364 **F** (03) 5030 5366 **WEB** www.brumbywines.com.au **OPEN** Mon–Fri 9–5
WINEMAKER Neil Robb, John Ellis, Glen Olsen (Contract) **EST.** 2001 **CASES** 3500
SUMMARY The derivation of the name is even more direct and simple than you might imagine: the owners are Stuart and Liz Brumby, who decided to plant grapes for supply to others before moving to having an increasing portion of their production from the 15 ha of chardonnay, cabernet sauvignon, shiraz and durif vinified under their own label. For the time being sales are through the cellar door, mailing list and website, but the plan is to establish retail sales and exports.

Brunswick Hill Wines   NR

34 Breese Street, Brunswick, Vic 3056 **REGION** Port Phillip Zone
T (03) 9383 4681 **OPEN** By appointment
WINEMAKER Peter Atkins **EST.** 1999 **CASES** NA
SUMMARY Peter Atkins owns the Brunswick Hill Wines venture, which is claimed to be Melbourne's only urban winery, situated in the heart of urban Brunswick, 15 minutes from the CBD. Studley Park Vineyard is even closer, but its grapes are sent to Granite Hills for winemaking. The ability to open the winery where it is doubtless reflects Peter Atkins' background as an environmental and urban planner, and his present position as a senior manager in the Department of Natural Resources and the Environment. A member of the Eltham and District Winemakers Guild, Atkins moved to commercial winemaking after 10 years as an amateur. Brunswick Hill Wines takes grapes from a number of Victorian regions, ranging from cool to warm. 1999 was the first fully fledged commercial vintage; a number of vintages are available by mail order and cellar door.

Brush Box Vineyard   NR

c/- 6 Grandview Parade, Mona Vale, NSW 2103 (postal) **REGION** Lower Hunter Valley
T (02) 9979 4468 **F** (02) 9999 5303 **OPEN** Not
WINEMAKER Contract **EST.** 1997 **CASES** 1000
SUMMARY Paul and Suzanne Mackay have established their 6.5-ha Brushbox Vineyard at Broke. It is situated in a secluded part of the Fordwich Hills, with views across the Wollombi Valley to the northern perimeter of Yengo National Park. It is planted to chardonnay, verdelho, cabernet sauvignon and merlot, and so far sold by mail order only.

Bulga Wine Estates   NR

Bulga Road, Swan Hill, Vic 3585 **REGION** Swan Hill
T (03) 5037 6685 **F** (03) 5037 6992 **OPEN** By appointment
WINEMAKER Rod Bouchier **EST.** 1999 **CASES** NA

SUMMARY Bulga Wine Estates draws on a little over 50 ha altogether: chardonnay (10 ha), cabernet sauvignon (10 ha), the remainder shiraz and a little colombard. Only part of the wine is vinified under the Bulga Wine Estates label, and handsomely so.

Bullers Beverford ★★☆

Murray Valley Highway, Beverford, Vic 3590 **REGION** Swan Hill
T (03) 5037 6305 **F** (03) 5037 6803 **WEB** www.buller.com.au **OPEN** Mon–Sat 9–5
WINEMAKER Richard Buller (Jnr) **EST.** 1951 **CASES** 120 000
SUMMARY This is a parallel operation to the Calliope winery at Rutherglen, similarly owned and operated by third-generation Richard and Andrew Buller. It offers traditional wines which in the final analysis reflect both their Riverland origin and a fairly low-key approach to style in the winery. It is, however, one of the few remaining sources of reasonable quality bulk fortified wine available to the public: 22-litre Valorex barrels at appealingly low prices.

▼▼▼▽ **Caspia Victoria Riesling 2004** RATING 86 DRINK 2007 $9
　　　 Caspia Victoria Chardonnay 2004 RATING 85 DRINK 2007 $10
　　　 Caspia Victoria Shiraz 2002 RATING 85 DRINK Now $10
　　　 Victoria Rose 2004 RATING 84 DRINK Now $12

Bullers Calliope ★★★★★

Three Chain Road, Rutherglen, Vic 3685 **REGION** Rutherglen
T (02) 6032 9660 **F** (02) 6032 8005 **WEB** www.buller.com.au **OPEN** Mon–Sat 9–5, Sun 10–5
WINEMAKER Andrew Buller **EST.** 1921 **CASES** 4000
SUMMARY The Buller family is very well known and highly regarded in northeast Victoria, and the business benefits from vines that are now 80 years old. The rating is for the superb releases of Museum fortified wines. Limited releases of Calliope Shiraz and Shiraz Mondeuse can also be very good. Exports to the UK and the US.

▼▼▼▼▼ **Rare Rutherglen Liqueur Muscat NV** Deep brown with a touch of olive on the rim; full and deep, almost into chocolate, with intense raisined fruit; richly textured, with great structure to the raisined/plum pudding fruit flavours, and obvious rancio age. Clean finish and aftertaste. RATING 95 DRINK Now $60
　　　 Rare Rutherglen Liqueur Tokay NV Medium deep golden-brown; a mix of sweet tea leaf and Christmas cake is a highly aromatic entry point for the bouquet; the palate has a sweet core of muscadelle fruit, and rancio, tea leaf, nutty and cake elements surrounding the core. RATING 94 DRINK Now $60

▼▼▼▼▽ **Fine Old Classic Rutherglen Muscat NV** The deepest coloured of the Classic Muscats, full tawny, olive on the rim; rich and generous, with grapey/raisiny fruit off-set by an airbrush of wood-aged rancio; the palate is still fruit-forward, but with a compelling skein of complexity. RATING 92 DRINK Now $18
　　　 Durif 2002 Complex, rich, spicy licorice, blackberry, chocolate and prune aromas and flavours; fine tannins; unexpectedly aspires to elegance. RATING 91 DRINK 2015 $35
　　　 Shiraz 2002 Rich, ripe blood plums and black fruits; hint of vanilla oak and ripe tannins; does show its 16° alcohol, simply part of the wine style. RATING 90 DRINK 2017 $40

▼▼▼▼ **Fine Old Classic Rutherglen Tokay NV** A mix of tea leaf and dried muscadelle aromas, the palate following the same track, with distilled muscadelle fruit stemming directly (in flavour terms) from the fruit base. Good balance and richness. RATING 89 DRINK Now $18

▼▼▼▽ **Limited Release Indigo Valley Marsanne 2003** RATING 84 DRINK Now $14

Bulong Estate ★★★☆

70 Summerhill Road, Yarra Junction, Vic 3797 (postal) **REGION** Yarra Valley
T (03) 5967 2487 **F** (03) 5967 2487 **WEB** www.bulongestate.com **OPEN** Not
WINEMAKER Contract **EST.** 1994 **CASES** 2000
SUMMARY Judy and Howard Carter purchased their beautifully situated 45-ha property in 1994, looking down into the valley below and across to the nearby ranges with Mt Donna Buang at their peak. Most of the grapes from the immaculately tended vineyard are sold, with limited quantities made for the Bulong Estate label. Exports to the UK.

🍷🍷🍷🍷🍷 **Merlot 2003** Good colour; medium-bodied; round, silky and supple; attractive array of blackcurrant and redcurrant fruit; fine tannins and oak. Cork. **RATING** 90 **DRINK** 2012 $ 21

🍷🍷🍷🍷 **Pinot Gris 2004** Flowery blossom aromas; crisp, clean; light to medium-bodied, has some length. Cork. **RATING** 87 **DRINK** Now $ 18

🍷🍷🍷🍷 **Pinot Noir 2003** **RATING** 86 **DRINK** 2007 $ 21

Bundaleera Vineyard   ★★★☆

449 Glenwood Road, Relbia, Tas 7258 **REGION** Northern Tasmania
T (03) 6343 1231 **F** (03) 6343 1250 **OPEN** Weekends 10–5
WINEMAKER Andrew Pirie (Contract) **EST.** 1996 **CASES** 1000
SUMMARY David (a consultant metallurgist in the mining industry) and Jan Jenkinson have established 2.5 ha of vines on a sunny, sheltered north to northeast slope in the North Esk Valley. The 12-ha property on which their house and vineyard are established give them some protection from the urban sprawl of Launceston; Jan is the full-time viticulturist and gardener for the immaculately tended property.

🍷🍷🍷🍷 **Chardonnay 2002** **RATING** 86 **DRINK** 2007 $ 19.50
   Chardonnay 2003 **RATING** 84 **DRINK** 2007 $ 19.50
   Pinot Noir 2003 **RATING** 84 **DRINK** 2007 $ 22

Bundaleer Wines   NR

41 King Street, Brighton, SA 5048 (postal) **REGION** Southern Flinders Ranges
T (08) 8296 1231 **F** (08) 8296 2484 **WEB** www.bundaleerwines.com.au **OPEN** Not
WINEMAKER Angela Meaney (Contract) **EST.** 1998 **CASES** 600
SUMMARY Bundaleer is a joint venture between third-generation farmer Des Meaney and manufacturing industry executive Graham Spurling (whose family originally came from the Southern Flinders). Planting of the 8-ha vineyard began in 1998, the first vintage coming in 2001. It is situated in a region known as the Bundaleer Gardens, on the edge of the Bundaleer Forest, 200 km north of Adelaide, at an altitude of 500 m. Bundaleer Wines is one of 5 growers with their own labels in the newly declared Southern Flinders Ranges region. The wines are made under the care of industry veteran Angela Meaney at Paulett Winery in the Clare Valley. This should not be confused with the Bundaleer Shiraz brand made by Bindi.

Bungawarra   ★★★★☆

Bents Road, Ballandean, Qld 4382 **REGION** Granite Belt
T (07) 4684 1128 **F** (07) 4684 1128 **OPEN** 7 days 10–4.30
WINEMAKER Jeff Harden **EST.** 1975 **CASES** 2000
SUMMARY Now owned by Jeff Harden. It draws upon 5 ha of mature vineyards which over the years have shown themselves capable of producing red wines of considerable character.

🍷🍷🍷🍷🍷 **Paragon 2002** Good colour; rich and ripe, with excellent fruit weight and mouthfeel; superior oak handling. **RATING** 94 **DRINK** 2012

🍷🍷🍷🍷 **Foundation Unwooded Chardonnay 2004** Lively, fresh stone fruit flavours; good length and balance; has more fruit than most wines of the vintage. **RATING** 92 **DRINK** 2008 $ 14

Bunnamagoo Estate   ★★★★

Bunnamagoo, Rockley, NSW 2795 (postal) **REGION** Central Ranges Zone
T 1300 304 707 **F** (02) 6377 5231 **WEB** www.bunnamagoowines.com.au **OPEN** Not
WINEMAKER Robert Black (Contract) **EST.** 1995 **CASES** 2500
SUMMARY Bunnamagoo Estate (on one of the first land grants in the region) is situated near the historic town of Rockley, itself equidistant south of Bathurst and west of Oberon. Here a 6-ha vineyard planted to chardonnay, merlot and cabernet sauvignon has been established by Paspaley Pearls, a famous name in the pearl industry. The wines are contract-made and sold by mail order.

🍷🍷🍷🍷 **Chardonnay 2002** Bright yellow-green; light to medium-bodied, elegant; good balance and fruit and oak integration; developing at a leisurely pace. **RATING** 90 **DRINK** 2008 $ 18.99

ΥΥΥΥ   **Cabernet Sauvignon 2002** Blackcurrant, earth, spice and herb; medium-bodied; fine tannins. Likethe Chardonnay, well-priced. **RATING** 89 **DRINK** 2009 $18.99

Burge Family Winemakers ★★★★☆

Barossa Way, Lyndoch, SA 5351 **REGION** Barossa Valley
T (08) 8524 4644 **F** (08) 8524 4444 **WEB** www.burgefamily.com.au **OPEN** Thurs–Mon 10–5
WINEMAKER Rick Burge **EST.** 1928 **CASES** 3300
SUMMARY Rick Burge and Burge Family Winemakers (not to be confused with Grant Burge, although the families are related) has established itself as an icon producer of exceptionally rich, lush and concentrated Barossa red wines. Rick Burge's sense of humour is evident with the Nice Red (a Merlot Cabernet blend made for those who come to cellar door and ask 'Do you have a nice red?').

ΥΥΥΥΥ   **Olive Hill Semillon 2002** Developed but bright yellow-green; complex flavours; ripe citrus with subtle spicy/nutty oak; considerable length and flavour. Top gold Winewise Small Vigneron Awards 2004. **RATING** 94 **DRINK** 2007 $24

ΥΥΥΥΥ   **Olive Hill Semillon 2004** Brilliant, glowing green-yellow; very powerful, very intense, very long; lemon, spice and slate; no oak evident. **RATING** 93 **DRINK** 2010 $20
     G3 Grenache Shiraz Mourvedre 2002 Clean, dark berries; quite powerful texture and structure; savoury/earthy/chocolatey edges to the fruit core; lots of character; long finish. **RATING** 93 **DRINK** 2012 $50
     Draycott Shiraz 2003 Powerful and complex; black fruits, blackberries; ripe, lingering tannins, good oak; 10% Grenache. **RATING** 92 **DRINK** 2013 $42

Burgi Hill Vineyard ★★★☆

290 Victoria Road, Wandin North, Vic 3139 **REGION** Yarra Valley
T (03) 5964 3568 **F** (03) 5964 3568 **WEB** www.burgihill.com.au **OPEN** By appointment
WINEMAKER Christopher Sargeant **EST.** 1974 **CASES** 300
SUMMARY The 4.5-ha vineyard now operated by Christopher Sargeant and family was established 30 years ago. For many years the grapes were sold, but now some are vinified for the Burgi Hill label. The varieties planted are chardonnay, sauvignon blanc, pinot noir, merlot and cabernet sauvignon.

ΥΥΥΥ   **Yarra Valley Pinot Noir 2001** Light-bodied; nicely developed spicy plum fruit; fine tannins; good balance and length. Cork. **RATING** 89 **DRINK** 2008 $20
     Yarra Valley Chardonnay 2001 Good colour; light-bodied melon, fig and a touch of citrus; controlled oak, ageing quite well. Cork. **RATING** 88 **DRINK** 2007 $18

Burke & Hills ★★★★

Cargo Road, Lidster, NSW 2800 **REGION** Orange
T (02) 6365 3456 **F** (02) 6365 3456 **OPEN** Fri–Mon 11–5 at Lakeside Café, Lake Canobolas
WINEMAKER Christophe Derrez, Lucy Maddox **EST.** 1999 **CASES** 3500
SUMMARY In response to my standard request for insight into motives and goals, founder Doug Burke wrote, 'I guess you would scream if you heard another new small vineyard/winery prattling on about small volumes, low yields, best practice ... in a quest for great quality, subtlety and complexity.' Very likely, but here the facts speak for themselves: the selection of a steeply sloping, frost-free, north-facing slope rising to an altitude of 940 m on Mt Lidster; the planting of 10 ha of classic varieties, but including a mix of the best clones of pinot noir; the appointment of Brett Wilkins as viticulturist (with consultant Di Davidson in the background) and former Gevrey Chambertin-cum-Flying Winemaker Christophe Derrez; the erection of a 200 tonne capacity winery to supplement cash flow by undertaking contract winemaking; and the running of the Lakeside Café at Lake Canobolas, 2 km from the winery ... All of these things point to a business plan with one objective: in Burke's words, 'Don't go broke.'

ΥΥΥΥ☆   **Orange Chardonnay 2003** Elegant, melon, stone fruit; light to medium-bodied with touches of cashew; excellent length and texture. Cork. **RATING** 90 **DRINK** 2009 $27
     O'Hara 2002 Clean, sweet cassis, raspberry and blackcurrant fruit; light to medium-bodied; supple, nicely relaxed tannins. Questionable cork. **RATING** 90 **DRINK** 2012 $36

ΥΥΥΥ   **Orange Rose 2004** Vivid colour; fresh strawberry and citrus flavours; has length; balanced, dry finish. Pinot Saignee. Cork. **RATING** 87 **DRINK** Now $22

ŸŸŸ♀ **Orange Sauvignon Blanc 2004** Clean but subdued; no technical fault, simply diminished varietal character. Possibly scalped by the cork. **RATING** 86 **DRINK** 2007 $ 22

Burke & Wills Winery   ★★★☆

3155 Burke & Wills Track, Mia Mia, Vic 3444 **REGION** Heathcote
T (03) 5425 5400 **F** (03) 5425 5401 **WEB** www.wineandmusic.net **OPEN** By appointment
WINEMAKER Andrew Pattison **EST.** 2003 **CASES** 1500
SUMMARY Andrew Pattison established Burke & Wills Winery in 2003, after selling Lancefield Winery. He is in the course of establishing 1 ha of shiraz, 0.5 ha of gewurztraminer, and has 1 ha each of chardonnay and cabernets at Malmsbury, plus 0.5 ha of pinot noir, supplemented by contract-grown grapes from a Macedon Ranges vineyard supplying chardonnay, pinot noir and cabernets. Not to be confused with Burke & Hills.

ŸŸŸŸ **Heathcote Shiraz 2003** Fresh, medium-bodied; the lighter side of Heathcote with some young vine characters to the blackberry and black cherry fruit. **RATING** 89 **DRINK** 2013 $ 24
Pattison Cabernet Sauvignon Merlot 2003 Light to medium-bodied; pleasant spicy red berry fruits and riper elements come together well. Macedon Ranges/Bendigo blend. **RATING** 88 **DRINK** 2009 $ 19.50
Dig Tree Merlot 2003 Attractive, if slightly simple, red fruit-driven wine; good balance, clean finish. **RATING** 87 **DRINK** 2008 $ 17

ŸŸŸ♀ **Dig Tree Cabernet Sauvignon 2003 RATING** 86 **DRINK** 2007 $ 17
Dig Tree Unwooded Chardonnay 2003 RATING 84 **DRINK** Now $ 14

Burnbrae   ★★★☆

Hill End Road, Erudgere via Mudgee, NSW 2850 **REGION** Mudgee
T (02) 6373 3504 **F** (02) 6373 3601 **OPEN** Wed–Mon 9–5
WINEMAKER Alan Cox **EST.** 1976 **CASES** NFP
SUMMARY The founding Mace family sold Burnbrae to Alan Cox in 1996. It continues as an estate-based operation with 23 ha of vineyards. Since that time the Burnbrae wines have gone from strength to strength, improving beyond all recognition, attesting to the value of the old, dry-grown vines and the accumulation of winemaking experience by Alan Cox.

Burramurra   NR

Barwood Park, High Street, Nagambie, Vic 3608 **REGION** Nagambie Lakes
T (03) 5794 2181 **F** (03) 5794 2755 **OPEN** Fri–Sun & public hols 10–5, or by appointment
WINEMAKER Mitchelton (Contract) **EST.** 1988 **CASES** 1000
SUMMARY Burramurra is the relatively low-profile vineyard operation of the Honourable Pat McNamara. Most of the grapes are sold to Mitchelton; a small amount is contract-made for the Burramurra label.

Burrundulla Vineyards   ★★★☆

Sydney Road, Mudgee, NSW 2850 **REGION** Mudgee
T (02) 6372 1620 **F** (02) 6372 4058 **WEB** www.burrundulla.com **OPEN** 7 days 10–4
WINEMAKER Contract **EST.** 1996 **CASES** 3000
SUMMARY A substantial venture; the Cox family (Chris, Michael and Ted) have established 60 ha of shiraz, cabernet sauvignon, chardonnay, merlot and semillon, selling much of the production, and having part made in two ranges: Heritage at the top, then GX.

ŸŸŸŸ **Heritage Mudgee Semillon 2004** Clear-cut, intense herb, spice and lemon varietal aromas; crisp, crunchy acidity, but does back off on the mid-palate. Cork. **RATING** 89 **DRINK** 2010 $ 15.50
Heritage Mudgee Shiraz 2003 Polished black cherry fruit; quite firm; should develop well. Cork. **RATING** 88 **DRINK** 2013 $ 19.50
Mudgee Merlot 2004 Bright, fresh, juicy cassis and cherry fruits; minimal tannins. Cork. **RATING** 88 **DRINK** 2010 $ 13.50

TTTY **GX Mudgee Chardonnay 2004** RATING 86 DRINK 2007 $13.50
GX Mudgee Cabernet Sauvignon 2004 RATING 85 DRINK 2007 $13.50

TTT **GX Mudgee Merlot Cabernet 2003** RATING 83 $14.50

Burton Premium Wines ★★★

PO Box 242 Killara, NSW 2071 REGION Southeast Australia
T (02) 9416 6631 F (02) 9416 6681 WEB www.burtonpremiumwines.com OPEN Not
WINEMAKER Mike Farmilo, Pat Tocacui (Contract) EST. 1998 CASES 5000
SUMMARY Burton Premium Wines has neither vineyards nor winery, purchasing its grapes from the
Limestone Coast (including Coonawarra) and McLaren Vale, and having the wines made in various
locations by contract winemakers. It brings together the marketing and financial skills of managing
director Nigel Burton, and the extensive wine industry experience (as a senior judge) of Dr Ray
Healy, who is director in charge of all aspects of winemaking. Exports to the UK, the US, Canada,
Finland, Sweden, Taiwan and Japan.

TTTY **Mclaren Vale Chardonnay 2003** RATING 85 DRINK 2007 $20
Coonawarra Cabernet Sauvignon 2002 RATING 84 DRINK 2008 $30

Bush Piper Vineyard NR

Badenoch, Horspool Way via Molong Road, Orange, NSW 2800 REGION Orange
T (02) 6361 8280 F (02) 6361 8432 WEB www.orangewines.com.au/wineries.cfm OPEN By
appointment
WINEMAKER Mark Davidson (Tamburlaine) EST. 1996 CASES 3000
SUMMARY Shortly after Jo and Richard Cummins moved to Orange, they realised their property was
ideal viticultural land. Planting began in 1996 with cabernet sauvignon, followed the next year by
further blocks of cabernet and shiraz. The wines are sold by mail order and through select
restaurants.

by Farr ★★★★★

PO Box 72, Bannockburn, Vic 3331 REGION Geelong
T (03) 5281 1979 F (03) 5281 1979 OPEN Not
WINEMAKER Gary Farr EST. 1999 CASES 3000
SUMMARY In 1994 Gary Farr and family planted 11 ha of clonally-selected viognier, chardonnay, pinot
noir and shiraz, at a density of 7000 per hectare, on a north-facing hill which is directly opposite the
Bannockburn Winery, having acquired the land from the late Stuart Hooper (Bannockburn's then
owner). For a multiplicity of reasons, in 1999 Farr decided to establish his own label for part of the
grapes coming from the vineyard; the remainder went to Bannockburn. The quality of the wines is
exemplary, their character subtly different from those of Bannockburn itself – due, in Farr's view, to
the interaction of the terroir of the hill and the clonal selection. Exports to the UK, Russia, the US,
Canada, Singapore and Japan.

TTTTT **Chardonnay by Farr 2003** Fabulously rich, tapestried stone fruit and nutty/creamy
texture and flavour make a wine of great distinction. RATING 96 DRINK 2012 $50
Shiraz by Farr 2003 Typically rich, textured and complex; black fruits, spices and licorice
in a warm swathe of oak and tannins. RATING 95 DRINK 2018 $50

TTTTY **Viognier by Farr 2003** Superior wine; very good balance and mouthfeel; flavours of
preserved apple; dry finish. RATING 93 DRINK 2008 $50
Sangreal 2003 Stylish, but far from overwhelmed by fruit; fine, long, savoury tannins.
Pinot Noir. RATING 90 DRINK 2008 $55

Byramgou Park NR

Wade Road, Brookhampton, WA 6239 REGION Geographe
T (08) 9731 8248 F (08) 9731 8248 WEB www.byramgou.com.au OPEN 7 days 10–6
WINEMAKER Siobhan Lynch EST. 1997 CASES 700
SUMMARY The unusual name comes courtesy of the great-great-grandfather of Richard Knox, who is,
with Geraldine Knox, the proprietor of the business. It was the name of the ship which his forebear

sailed to Arabia in 1821; he received a gold cup, depicted on the label, for his deeds. These details to one side, there are 5 ha of chardonnay, grenache, shiraz and cabernet sauvignon, and the wine is made by Siobhan Lynch, a district veteran. It hardly need be said that the wines meet their aim of representing value for money.

Byrne & Smith Wines ★★★★

PO Box 640, Unley, SA 5061 REGION Southeast Australia
T (08) 8272 1900 F (08) 8272 1944 OPEN Not
WINEMAKER Roger Harbord (Contract) EST. 1999 CASES 20 000
SUMMARY This is the reincarnation of a producer first known as St Francis, then Brewery Hill, and now Byrne & Smith. It is a substantial business with 2 vineyards totalling 53 ha at Stanley Flat in the northern Clare Valley, and a third vineyard of 106 ha near Waikerie in the Riverland. The major part of the grapes are sold, and the wines being marketed also use purchased grapes from regions as far away as the Margaret River. The low prices are not reflected in wine quality; the Ardent Estates and Artisan brands in particular have had substantial show success.

ŦŦŦŦŦ **Ardent Estates Eden Valley Riesling 2000** Excellent bottle-developed complexity; rich lime and honey flavours; round and mouthfilling but with balancing acidity. Screwcap. RATING 94 DRINK 2009 $ 11.99

ŦŦŦŦŸ **Ardent Estates Margaret River Chardonnay 2002** Well-made melon, fig and peach mix; nice touch of barrel ferment; medium-bodied, good mouthfeel and finish. Cork. RATING 92 DRINK 2007 $ 12
Ardent Estates Artisan Chardonnay 2002 Elegant, fresh, light to medium-bodied; stone fruit, citrus and hints of spice and cashew; good line and flow. Cork. RATING 90 DRINK 2008 $ 8.50

ŦŦŦŦ **Ardent Estates Clare Valley Merlot 2003** Light to medium-bodied; sweet blackcurrant and cassis; round and supple, fine tannins. Cork. RATING 89 DRINK 2008 $ 13.99
Ardent Estates McLaren Vale Cabernet Franc 2001 Spicy, cedary tobacco and berry; clear varietal character; attractive wine, and a major surprise. Cork. RATING 88 DRINK 2007 $ 13.99

ŦŦŦŸ **Ardent Estates McLaren Vale Shiraz 2001** RATING 86 DRINK 2007 $ 15
Ardent Estates Limestone Coast Cabernet Merlot 2001 RATING 85 DRINK 2007 $ 12
Ardent Estates Artisan Shiraz Cabernet Sauvignon 2001 RATING 84 DRINK Now $ 9.99

ŦŦŦ **Ardent Estates Sparkling Cabernet Sauvignon NV** RATING 83 $ 9.99

Calais Estate NR

Palmers Lane, Pokolbin, NSW 2321 REGION Lower Hunter Valley
T (02) 4998 7654 F (02) 4998 7813 WEB www.calaiswines.com.au OPEN 7 days 9–5
WINEMAKER Adrian Sheridan EST. 1987 CASES 11 000
SUMMARY Richard and Susan Bradley purchased the substantial Calais Estate winery in April 2000. Long-serving winemaker Adrian Sheridan continues his role, and the estate offers a wide range of facilities for visitors, ranging from private function rooms to picnic spots to an undercover outdoor entertaining area.

Caledonia Australis ★★★★★

PO Box 54, Abbotsford, Vic 3067 REGION Gippsland
T (03) 9416 4156 F (03) 9416 4157 WEB www.caledoniaaustralis.com OPEN Not
WINEMAKER MasterWineMakers (Contract) EST. NA CASES 6000
SUMMARY The reclusive Caledonia Australis is a Pinot Noir and Chardonnay specialist, with a total of 18 ha planted to chardonnay and pinot noir in three separate vineyard locations. All of the vineyards are in the Leongatha area, on red, free-draining, high-ironstone soils, on a limestone or marl base, and the slopes are east to northeast-facing. Small-batch winemaking by Martin Williams MW (MasterWineMakers) has resulted in consistently high-quality wines.

ŦŦŦŦŦ **Reserve Pinot Noir 2003** Deeper colour; excellent structure, length and mouthfeel to the dark cherry and spice fruit; very stylish. RATING 95 DRINK 2010 $ 46

Chardonnay 2002 Bright green-gold; elegant stone fruit and citrus with a gentle creamy, malolactic overlay and subtle oak. **RATING** 94 **DRINK** 2009 $ 36

Pinot Noir 2003 Fine, elegant and silky mouthfeel; pristine varietal character of spice, cherry and a hint of forest; good length and aftertaste. **RATING** 94 **DRINK** 2008 $ 30

ΥΥΥΥ **Reserve Chardonnay 2002** Gold-yellow; more complex and more nutty than the varietal; the screwcap of the varietal has done a better job than the cork of this wine. **RATING** 93 **DRINK** 2007 $ 48

ΥΥΥΥ **Mount Macleod Pinot Noir 2003** Fresh, light-bodied cherry and spice; subtle oak; simple. **RATING** 87 **DRINK** Now $ 17

Calem Blue/Shelton Wines NR

PO Box 4132, Wembley, WA 6913 **REGION** Margaret River
T (08) 6380 1511 **F** (08) 6380 1522 **WEB** www.sheltonwines.com **OPEN** Not
WINEMAKER Flying Fish Cove, Bill Crappsley (Contract) **EST.** 1996 **CASES** NA
SUMMARY David and Nicky Shelton are vineyard holders within the 80-ha Margaret River Vineyards Estate in Clews Road, Cowaramup. The Estate is a relatively rare example of so-called *clos* farming being an unqualified success, with a generally high level of viticulture throughout. The viticulture is under the control of Ian Davies. The name Calem is a combination of the Sheltons' children's names, Cal and Emma. The vineyard was planted in 1996, and the first vintage was 2000. The show success of the wines comes as no surprise, and the wines have secured wholesale distribution throughout Queensland, South Australia and the Northern Territory. Bin 168 Cabernet Sauvignon, has been specifically developed for the Asian market, and is available only by mail order.

Callipari Wine NR

Cureton Avenue, Nichols Point, Vic 3501 **REGION** Murray Darling
T (03) 5023 4477 **F** (03) 5021 0988 **WEB** www.callipari.com **OPEN** Weekends & public hols 10–4
WINEMAKER Michael Callipari **EST.** 1999 **CASES** 3000
SUMMARY Michael Callipari is among the third generation of the Callipari family, the first members of which left Calabria, Sicily in May 1951. Various members of the family have developed vineyards over the years, with over 23 ha of vines on two properties. Mother Giuseppa Callipari makes the food products (from produce grown on the family farm) that are sold through the cellar door and at tourism outlets and shops in the district. Ned's Red, incidentally, is described as a 'premium red wine with a dash of orange and lemon'.

Calyla Vines Estate NR

PO Box 523, Brighton, SA 5048 **REGION** Southeast Australia
T (08) 8298 8877 **F** (08) 8298 8878 **OPEN** Not
WINEMAKER Contract **EST.** 1999 **CASES** NA
SUMMARY This is a virtual winery run by Gerald Lopez, with chardonnay and cabernet sauvignon contract-grown and contract-made; there are no local sales, only exports to the US, France and Japan.

Cambewarra Estate

520 Illaroo Road, Cambewarra, NSW 2540 **REGION** Shoalhaven Coast
T (02) 4446 0170 **F** (02) 4446 0170 **WEB** www.cambewarraestate.com.au **OPEN** Thurs–Sun 10–5 & public & school hols
WINEMAKER Tamburlaine (Contract) **EST.** 1991 **CASES** 3500
SUMMARY Louise Cole owns and runs Cambewarra Estate, near the Shoalhaven River on the central southern coast of New South Wales, with contract winemaking competently carried out at Tamburlaine Winery in the Hunter Valley. Cambewarra continues to produce attractive wines which have had significant success in wine shows.

ΥΥΥΥ **Anniversary Verdelho 2004** Fresh, tangy and lively; citrussy flavours; clean, dry finish. Screwcap. **RATING** 87 **DRINK** 2008

Anniversary Late Harvest Chardonnay 2004 Lively citrussy flavours intermingle with more tropical characters; excellent acidity drives the palate. Screwcap. **RATING** 87 **DRINK** Now

ΥΥΥΥ **Anniversary Chardonnay 2004** Ripe stone fruit; subtle oak influence; fraction sweet. Cellar door special. Screwcap. **RATING** 86 **DRINK** 2007

Anniversary Petit Rouge 2004 RATING 84 **DRINK** Now

Camden Estate Vineyards   NR

172 Macarthur Road, Spring Farm, NSW 2570 (postal) **REGION** Sydney Basin
T 0414 913 089 **F** (02) 4568 0110 **OPEN** Not
WINEMAKER Evans Wine Company **EST.** 1975 **CASES** 800
SUMMARY Camden Estate Vineyards was originally known as Bridge Farm Wines when it was established by Norman Hanckel. The 17 ha of chardonnay he planted was one of the largest single plantings in Australia at the time, if not the largest. Over the years, most of the grapes were sold to other producers, various estate labels appearing and then disappearing in relatively short order. The grapes are now sold to the Evans Wine Company and the brand is exclusively sold in the US.

Campbells

Murray Valley Highway, Rutherglen, Vic 3685 **REGION** Rutherglen
T (02) 6032 9458 **F** (02) 6032 9870 **WEB** www.campbellswines.com.au **OPEN** Mon–Sat 9–5, Sun 10–5
WINEMAKER Colin Campbell **EST.** 1870 **CASES** 60 000
SUMMARY A wide range of table and fortified wines of ascending quality and price, which are always honest; as so often happens in this part of the world, the fortified wines are the best, with the extremely elegant Isabella Rare Tokay and Merchant Prince Rare Muscat at the top of the tree; the winery rating is for the fortified wines. A feature of the cellar door is an extensive range of back vintage releases of small parcels of wine not available through any other outlet. National distribution through Red+White; exports to the UK, the US, Canada and New Zealand.

ΥΥΥΥΥ **Isabella Rare Rutherglen Tokay NV** Very deep olive-brown; broodingly complex, deep and concentrated aromas, then layer upon layer of flavour in the mouth. Incredibly intense and complex, with varietal tea leaf/muscadelle fruit continuity. **RATING** 97 **DRINK** Now $94

Grand Rutherglen Tokay NV Deep mahogany, olive rim. An intensely complex bouquet, with hints of smoke, abundant rancio. Glorious malty, tea leaf flavours linger long in the mouth; great style and balance. **RATING** 95 **DRINK** Now $94

Merchant Prince Rare Rutherglen Muscat NV Dark brown, with olive-green on the rim; particularly fragrant, with essencey, raisiny fruit; supple, smooth and intense wine floods every corner of the mouth, yet retains elegance, and continues the house style to perfection. **RATING** 95 **DRINK** Now $94

ΥΥΥΥΥ **Classic Rutherglen Tokay NV** Medium brown; a complex bouquet with dried muscadelle fruit; deliciously idiosyncratic. The faintly smoky palate has power and depth, again with dried muscadelle grapes reflecting the bouquet. **RATING** 93 **DRINK** Now $34.60

Grand Rutherglen Muscat NV Full olive-brown; highly aromatic; a rich and complex palate is silky smooth, supple and long, the raisiny fruit perfectly balanced by the clean, lingering acid (and spirit) cut on the finish. **RATING** 93 **DRINK** Now $94

Classic Rutherglen Muscat NV Spicy/raisiny complexity starting to build; in typical Campbells style, lively, clearly articulated, with good balance and length. **RATING** 92 **DRINK** Now $34.60

Rutherglen Tokay NV Bright, light golden-brown; classic mix of tea leaf and butterscotch aromas lead into an elegant wine which dances in the mouth; has balance and length. **RATING** 92 **DRINK** Now $16.70

Rutherglen Muscat NV Bright, clear tawny-gold; a highly aromatic bouquet, spicy and grapey, is mirrored precisely on the palate, which has nigh on perfect balance. **RATING** 90 **DRINK** Now $16.70

ΥΥΥ **Shiraz Durif Cabernet Sauvignon 2002 RATING** 80 $15.50

Camyr Allyn Wines ★★★

Camyr Allyn North, Allynbrook Road, East Gresford, NSW 2311 **REGION** Upper Hunter Valley
T (02) 4938 9576 **F** (02) 4938 9576 **WEB** www.camyrallynwines.com.au **OPEN** 7 days 10–5
WINEMAKER James Evers **EST.** 1999 **CASES** 3000
SUMMARY John and Judy Evers purchased the property known as Camyr Allyn North in 1997, and immediately set about planting 1.7 ha of verdelho, 1.4 ha of merlot and 1.3 ha of shiraz. The wines are made at the new Northern Hunter winery at East Gresford by James Evers, who worked for Mildara Blass in Coonawarra for some time. The promotion and packaging of the wines is innovative and stylish.

ŸŸŸŸ **Hunter Valley Verdelho 2004** Tangy but light; has length, not sweet; preferable to many. High-quality cork. **RATING** 86 **DRINK** 2007 $ 18
Hunter Valley Rose 2004 Spicy aromas; cherry and raspberry fruit; good balance; not too sweet. Merlot Saignee. Cork. **RATING** 86 **DRINK** Now $ 16
Hunter Valley Shiraz 2003 Light to medium-bodied; savoury, earthy, spicy, leathery; very regional; needs more sweet fruit. Stained cork. **RATING** 86 **DRINK** 2007 $ 18.50
Hunter Valley Merlot 2003 RATING 85 **DRINK** 2007 $ 18.50

Candlebark Hill ★★★★

Fordes Lane, Kyneton, Vic 3444 **REGION** Macedon Ranges
T (03) 9836 2712 **F** (03) 9836 2712 **WEB** www.users.bigpond.com/candlebarkhillwines.htm **OPEN** By appointment
WINEMAKER David Forster, Vincent Lakey, Llew Knight (Consultant) **EST.** 1987 **CASES** 600
SUMMARY Candlebark Hill has been established by David Forster at the northern end of the Macedon Ranges, and has magnificent views over the central Victorian countryside north of the Great Dividing Range. The 3.5-ha vineyard is planted to pinot noir (1.5 ha), 1 ha each of chardonnay and the three main Bordeaux varieties, and 0.5 ha of shiraz and malbec. The Reserve Pinot Noir is especially meritorious.

ŸŸŸŸ **Cabernet Sauvignon 2001** An elegant mix of redcurrant and blackcurrant fruit; fine tannins, good balance. **RATING** 89 **DRINK** 2010 $ 25

ŸŸŸ **Wooded Chardonnay 2003 RATING** 83 $ 19

Cannibal Creek Vineyard ★★★★

260 Tynong North Road, Tynong North, Vic 3813 **REGION** Gippsland
T (03) 5942 8380 **F** (03) 5942 8202 **WEB** www.cannibalcreek.com.au **OPEN** 7 days 11–5
WINEMAKER Patrick Hardiker **EST.** 1997 **CASES** 1800
SUMMARY The Hardiker family moved to Tynong North in 1988, initially only grazing beef cattle, but aware of the viticultural potential of the sandy clay loam and bleached sub-surface soils weathered from the granite foothills of Tynong North. Plantings began in 1997, using organically based cultivation methods. The family decided to make their own wine, and a heritage-style shed built from locally milled timber has been converted into a winery and small cellar door facility. Exports to the UK.

ŸŸŸŸŸ **Chardonnay 2003** Elegant, creamy melon and fig; very good barrel ferment inputs; supple, smooth mouthfeel; good balance. Cork. **RATING** 93 **DRINK** 2009 $ 20
Pinot Noir 2002 Savoury but intense; a long, finely structured palate; wild strawberries and spice flavours. **RATING** 90 **DRINK** 2008 $ 28

ŸŸŸŸ **Sauvignon Blanc 2004** Super intense; faintly sweaty, with aromas and flavours at the tropical end of the range; a love it or hate it style. Cork. **RATING** 89 **DRINK** 2007 $ 18
Pinot Noir 2003 Ripe black cherry and plum, some spice; medium-bodied; balancing acidity helps. Quality cork. **RATING** 88 **DRINK** 2008 $ 28

ŸŸŸŸ **Merlot 2003 RATING** 85 **DRINK** 2007 $ 28

Canobolas-Smith ★★★★★

Boree Lane, off Cargo Road, Lidster via Orange, NSW 2800 **REGION** Orange
T (02) 6365 6113 **F** (02) 6365 6113 **OPEN** Weekends & public hols 11–5
WINEMAKER Murray Smith **EST.** 1986 **CASES** 2000

SUMMARY Canobolas-Smith has established itself as one of the leading Orange district wineries, and has distinctive blue wraparound labels. Much of the wine is sold from the cellar door, which is well worth a visit. Exports to the US and Asia.

🍷🍷🍷🍷🍷 **Orange Chardonnay 2001** Pale, bright straw-green; beautifully balanced fruit and barrel ferment inputs; exceptionally good nectarine fruit, developing with absolute surety. Acidity spot on. Screwcap. **RATING** 96 **DRINK** 2011 **$** 28

Shine Reserve Chardonnay 2002 Excellent tight, fresh citrus and melon fruit in layer upon layer; good barrel ferment and spicy French oak; developing slowly, time to go yet. **RATING** 94 **DRINK** 2010 **$** 35

🍷🍷🍷🍷 **Orange Pinot Noir 2002** Savoury, spicy, stemmy style; good length; another wine to point to the suitability of the variety for the region in cool vintages. **RATING** 88 **DRINK** 2009 **$** 28

Alchemy 2001 Light to medium-bodied; lively, savoury/lemony edges to red and black fruits; fresh; minimal tannins. **RATING** 87 **DRINK** 2008 **$** 33

Canonbah Bridge ★★★★

Merryanbone Station, Warren, NSW 2824 (postal) **REGION** Western Plains Zone
T (02) 6833 9966 **F** (02) 6833 9980 **WEB** www.canonbahbridge.com **OPEN** Not
WINEMAKER John Hordern (Contract) **EST.** 1999 **CASES** 17 000

SUMMARY The 29-ha vineyard has been established by Shane McLaughlin on the very large Merryanbone Station, a Merino sheep stud which has been in the family for four generations. If you head out of Dubbo towards Bourke, you will pass Warren, northwest of Dubbo. The wines are at three price points: at the bottom is Bottle Treen, from Southeast Australia, then Ram's Leap, specific regional blends, and at the top, Canonbah Bridge, either estate or estate/regional blends. The wines are available by mail order and in select Sydney restaurants and wine shops; the majority is exported to the US, the UK, Canada, Malaysia and Hong Kong.

🍷🍷🍷🍷½ **Ram's Leap Western Plains Shiraz 2003** A rich array of black fruits, dark chocolate and ripe tannins; particularly good control of extract and oak. Cork. **RATING** 92 **DRINK** 2012 **$** 15

Shiraz Grenache Mourvedre 2002 Attractive Southern Rhône-style blend; sweet berry fruit and fine tannins. **RATING** 91 **DRINK** 2010 **$** 20

🍷🍷🍷🍷 **Ram's Leap Semillon Sauvignon Blanc 2004** Nicely composed and balanced; clean, gently tropical fruit; a hint of sweetness well judged. Western Plains/Orange. Screwcap. **RATING** 89 **DRINK** 2007 **$** 15

🍷🍷🍷½ **Bottle Tree Cabernet Merlot 2003** **RATING** 85 **DRINK** 2008 **$** 10

🍷🍷🍷 **Bottle Tree Semillon Chardonnay 2004** **RATING** 83 **$** 10

Bottle Tree Shiraz Cabernet 2003 **RATING** 83 **$** 10

Canungra Valley Vineyards ★★★½

Lamington National Park Road, Canungra Valley, Qld 4275 **REGION** Queensland Coastal
T (07) 5543 4011 **F** (07) 5543 4162 **WEB** www.canungravineyards.com.au **OPEN** 7 days 10–5
WINEMAKER John Hislop, Mark Davidson (Contract) **EST.** 1997 **CASES** 5000

SUMMARY Canungra Valley Vineyards has been established in the hinterland of the Gold Coast with a clear focus on broad-based tourism. The vines (8 ha) have been established around the 19th century homestead (relocated to the site from its original location in Warwick), but these provide only a small part of the wine offered for sale. In deference to the climate, 70% of the estate planting is chambourcin, the rain and mildew-resistant hybrid; the remainder is semillon.

🍷🍷🍷🍷 **Platypus Play Unwooded Chardonnay 2004** Light-bodied; elegant citrussy/tangy fruit flavours; fairly high acidity. **RATING** 88 **DRINK** 2007 **$** 18

Cape Barren Wines ★★★★½

Lot 20, Little Road, Willunga, SA 5172 **REGION** McLaren Vale
T (08) 8556 4374 **F** (08) 8556 4364 **OPEN** By appointment
WINEMAKER Brian Light (Contract) **EST.** 1999 **CASES** 3000

SUMMARY Lifelong friends and vignerons Peter Matthews and Brian Ledgard joined forces in 1999 to create Cape Barren Wines. In all they have 62 ha of vineyards throughout the McLaren Vale region, the jewel in the crown being 4 ha of 70-year-old shiraz at Blewitt Springs, which provides the grapes for the Old Vine Shiraz. The McLaren Vale Grenache Shiraz Mourvedre and McLaren Vale Shiraz come from their other vineyards; most of the grapes are sold. Exports to New Zealand, Switzerland, the US and Canada.

YYYYY McLaren Vale Old Vine Shiraz 2003 Good colour; rich, ripe blackberry, plum, prune and chocolate flavours; controlled oak, firm tannins. **RATING** 91 **DRINK** 2018 $ 32.95

Cape Bouvard NR

Mount John Road, Mandurah, WA 6210 **REGION** Peel
T (08) 9739 1360 **F** (08) 9739 1360 **OPEN** 7 days 10–5
WINEMAKER NA **EST.** 1990 **CASES** 2000
SUMMARY While it continues in operation after its sale in 2003, there have been recent changes, the details of which are still unavailable.

Cape d'Estaing

PO Box 214, Kingscote, Kangaroo Island, SA 5223 **REGION** Kangaroo Island
T (08) 8383 6299 **F** (08) 8383 6299 **WEB** www.capedestaingwines.com **OPEN** Not
WINEMAKER Mike Farmilo (Contract), Robin Moody **EST.** 1994 **CASES** 4000
SUMMARY Graham and Jude Allison, Alan and Ann Byers, Marg and Wayne Conaghty and Robin and Heather Moody have established 10 ha of cabernet sauvignon and shiraz near Wisanger on Kangaroo Island. Robin Moody was a long-serving senior employee of Southcorp, and has a broad knowledge of all aspects of grapegrowing and winemaking. Limited retail distribution in Adelaide, and exports to US. The wines are also available by mail order.

YYYYY Shiraz 2001 Deep colour; rich, blackberry and licorice; lots of mouthfeel; subtle oak, fine tannins. Perhaps some hint of bacterial activity. Serious wine. **RATING** 91 **DRINK** 2001

YYYY Cabernet Sauvignon 2001 Quite ripe; medium-bodied cassis/black fruits; clear varietal character; slightly spiky acidity, but tannins and oak neatly controlled. **RATING** 89 **DRINK** 2010 $ 43

Cape Grace ★★★★

Fifty One Road, Cowaramup, WA 6284 **REGION** Margaret River
T (08) 9755 5669 **F** (08) 9755 5668 **WEB** www.capegracewines.com.au **OPEN** 7 days 10–5
WINEMAKER Robert Karri-Davies, Mark Messenger (Consultant) **EST.** 1996 **CASES** 2000
SUMMARY Cape Grace Wines can trace its history back to 1875, when timber baron MC Davies settled at Karridale, building the Leeuwin lighthouse and founding the township of Margaret River; 120 years later, Robert and Karen Karri-Davies planted just under 6 ha of vineyard to chardonnay, shiraz and cabernet sauvignon, with smaller amounts of merlot, semillon and chenin blanc. Robert is a self-taught viticulturist; Karen has over 15 years of international sales and marketing experience in the hospitality industry. Winemaking is carried out on the property; consultant Mark Messenger, a veteran of the Margaret River region, has over 9 years' experience at Cape Mentelle and 3 at Juniper Estate. Exports to Singapore.

YYYYY Margaret River Chardonnay 2003 Focused and intense melon and nectarine fruit; classy but subtle oak; very good mouthfeel. **RATING** 92 **DRINK** 2010 $ 29

YYYY Margaret River Shiraz 2003 Bright and fresh black cherry and plum in fruit-forward style; somewhat underworked. **RATING** 87 **DRINK** 2010 $ 29.50
Margaret River Cabernet Sauvignon 2003 Medium-bodied; earthy/spicy/savoury aromas and flavours; overall, rather tight and needs more work, like the Shiraz. **RATING** 87 **DRINK** 2010 $ 38.50

Cape Horn Vineyard

Echuca–Picola Road, Kanyapella, Vic 3564 **REGION** Goulburn Valley
T (03) 5480 6013 **F** (03) 5480 6013 **WEB** www.capehornvineyard.com.au **OPEN** 7 days 11–5

WINEMAKER John Ellis (Contract) **EST.** 1993 **CASES** 1800

SUMMARY The unusual name comes from a bend in the Murray River which was considered by riverboat owners of the 19th century to resemble Cape Horn: this is now on the wine label. The property was acquired by Echuca GP Dr Sue Harrison and her schoolteacher husband Ian in 1993. Ian Harrison has progressively planted their 9-ha vineyard to chardonnay, shiraz, zinfandel, cabernet sauvignon, marsanne and durif.

TTTT **Echuca Marsanne 2004** Very well made; honeysuckle and lemon braced by squeaky acidity; good length, should develop. Screwcap. **RATING** 87 **DRINK** 2008 $ 18
Echuca Shiraz 2003 Excellent colour; plenty of black cherry and plum fruit; not overmuch structure; enjoy while young. Diam. **RATING** 87 **DRINK** 2007 $ 22

TTTY **Echuca Chardonnay 2003** Clean, light to medium-bodied; well-handled touch of French oak; creamy cashew palate. High-quality cork. **RATING** 86 **DRINK** 2007 $ 19
Shiraz Cabernet Durif 2004 **RATING** 86 **DRINK** 2007 $ 15
Echuca Durif 2003 Deep colour; powerful black fruits; spare-framed, but still impressive value. Diam. **RATING** 86 **DRINK** 2008 $ 23
Echuca Cabernet Sauvignon 2003 **RATING** 85 **DRINK** 2007 $ 21

TTT **Echuca Rose 2004** **RATING** 83 $ 15

Cape Jaffa Wines ★★★★

Limestone Coast Road, Cape Jaffa, SA 5276 **REGION** Mount Benson
T (08) 8768 5053 **F** (08) 8768 5040 **WEB** www.capejaffawines.com.au **OPEN** 7 days 10–5
WINEMAKER Derek Hooper **EST.** 1993 **CASES** 30 000
SUMMARY Cape Jaffa is the first of the Mount Benson wineries, and all of the production now comes from the substantial estate plantings of 16.4 ha, which include the four major Bordeaux red varieties, plus shiraz, chardonnay, sauvignon blanc and semillon. The winery (built of local paddock rock) has been designed to allow eventual expansion to 1000 tonnes, or 70 000 cases. Exports to the UK, The Philippines, Hong Kong, Singapore and China.

TTTTY **Brocks Reef Semillon Sauvignon Blanc 2004** Spotlessly clean, no reduction, unlike the Sauvignon Blanc; very lively, fresh and intense; lemon zest, asparagus, grass and gooseberry; bright finish. Screwcap. **RATING** 93 **DRINK** 2008 $ 15
Mount Benson Shiraz 2002 Luscious, ripe black fruits; excellent balance and structure; good tannins. **RATING** 93 **DRINK** 2012 $ 23
Siberia Shiraz 2002 Mega-style; huge black fruits and tannins; needs decades. **RATING** 90 **DRINK** 2022 $ 34.95
Brocks Reef Cabernet Merlot 2002 Unusually ripe for the vintage, with masses of blackcurrant fruit, verging on overripe. **RATING** 90 **DRINK** 2010 $ 17

TTTT **Semillon Sauvignon Blanc 2004** Solid; not particularly aromatic, but has fair depth of flavour. **RATING** 87 **DRINK** Now $ 19
Brocks Reef Chardonnay 2004 Light-bodied; some elegance; sweet nectarine and peach fruit; subliminal oak. Screwcap. **RATING** 87 **DRINK** Now $ 15
Chardonnay 2003 Light to medium-bodied, with fractionally simple fruit, but nice length. **RATING** 87 **DRINK** Now $ 21
Jaffa Juice Semillon Botrytis 2004 Moderately complex botrytis and oak aromas; good acidity tightens and lengthens the palate. **RATING** 87 **DRINK** 2008 $ 19

TTTY **Sauvignon Blanc 2004** **RATING** 86 **DRINK** 2008 $ 19
Mount Benson Cabernet Sauvignon 2002 **RATING** 86 **DRINK** 2010 $ 23

TTT **Unwooded Chardonnay 2004** **RATING** 83 $ 19
Siberia Shiraz 2001 **RATING** 81 $ 34.95

🌿 Cape Lavender ★★★★

4 Carter Road, Metricup, WA 6280 **REGION** Margaret River
T (08) 9755 7552 **F** (08) 9755 7556 **WEB** www.capelavender.com.au **OPEN** 7 days 10–5
WINEMAKER Peter Stanlake, Eion Lindsay **EST.** 1999 **CASES** 3500
SUMMARY With 11.5 ha of vines, a much-awarded winery restaurant, and lavender fields which help make unique wines, this is a business with something extra. There are seven Lavender Range wines, moving from sparkling through table to port, which have been infused with *Lavandula angustifolia*;

the impact isn't overwhelming, but is nonetheless evident, and far from unpleasant. Whether it is a legal additive to wine, I do not know. There is also a conventional estate range of Semillon, Sauvignon Blanc, Chardonnay, Merlot, Shiraz and Cabernet Sauvignon, made without lavender.

ŸŸŸŸŸ **Margaret River Shiraz 2003** Medium-bodied; complex texture and structure; spicy berry fruits, integrated oak, lingering tannins. RATING 92 DRINK 2013 $ 22.50
Lavender Shiraz 2003 Definite inclusion of a left-field note ex the lavender. Medium-bodied; fine tannins, good length. RATING 90 DRINK 2012 $ 25

ŸŸŸŸ **Margaret River Semillon Sauvignon Blanc 2003** Clean; medium-bodied; a collage of ripe, tropical fruits; abundant flavour; slightly cluttered finish. RATING 87 DRINK Now $ 21

ŸŸŸŸ **Margaret River Merlot 2003** RATING 86 DRINK 2008 $ 25
Margaret River Cabernet Sauvignon 2002 RATING 86 DRINK 2009 $ 26
Margaret River Sparkling Lavender 2003 RATING 86 DRINK Now $ 27.50
Margaret River Sparkling Shiraz 2003 RATING 86 DRINK Now $ 28.50
Margaret River Chardonnay 2003 RATING 85 DRINK 2007 $ 25

Capel Vale ★★★★★

Lot 5 Stirling Estate, Mallokup Road, Capel, WA 6271 REGION Geographe
T (08) 9727 1986 F (08) 9727 1904 WEB www.capelvale.com OPEN Cellar door & restaurant 7 days 10–4
WINEMAKER Nicole Esdaile (former), Rebecca Catlin EST. 1979 CASES 100 000
SUMMARY Capel Vale has expanded its viticultural empire to the point where it is entirely an estate-run business, with 220 ha of vineyards spread through Mount Barker, Pemberton, Margaret River and Geographe. Its wines cross every price point and style from fighting varietal to ultra-premium; always known for its Riesling, powerful red wines are now very much part of the portfolio. Exports to all major markets.

ŸŸŸŸŸ **Frederick Chardonnay 2002** Light green-yellow; intense, tangy aromas; a touch of French feral adds to the appeal; very good weight and mouthfeel; long, complete palate. Screwcap. RATING 95 DRINK 2010 $ 38
Kinnaird Shiraz 2003 Fragrant spice and black cherry aromas and flavours; medium-bodied; fine, silky tannins; elegant, and convincing cool-climate style. Quality cork. RATING 94 DRINK 2018 $ 50
Howecroft Merlot 2003 Supple, smooth, rich and satiny blackcurrant and black olive fruit; fine support tannins; long finish. Subtle French oak. Deserves a better cork. RATING 94 DRINK 2015 $ 50

ŸŸŸŸŸ **CV Sauvignon Blanc 2004** Talc, slate and spice aromas; good focus, grip and length; grass and asparagus; excellent finish, long and crisp. RATING 91 DRINK Now $ 16
Semillon Sauvignon Blanc 2003 Round and supple; appealing fruit salad, gooseberry and lemon juice flavours; balanced finish. RATING 91 DRINK 2008 $ 17
Whispering Hill Vineyard Riesling 2004 Spotlessly clean; light passionfruit and apple; lingering, squeaky acidity; fresh finish. Screwcap. RATING 90 DRINK 2014 $ 24

ŸŸŸŸ **Riesling 2004** Crisp, minerally, yet to build aromas; fine, long palate but low in varietal fruit. RATING 89 DRINK 2007 $ 17
Riesling 2003 Tangy herb, spice, lemon and apple blossom aromas; complex flavours in early-drinking style. RATING 89 DRINK 2007 $ 17
CV Unwooded Chardonnay 2004 Fresh, lively citrus and melon; good length; crisp finish. RATING 89 DRINK 2007 $ 16
CV Shiraz 2002 Clean; medium-bodied, fruit-focused; cool-grown, spicy red fruits. RATING 89 DRINK 2009 $ 16
Shiraz 2001 Spicy berry cool-climate fruit, with a hint of leaf; lingering tannins. RATING 89 DRINK 2010 $ 21
Merlot 2002 Spicy, gently savoury and elegant; nice olive and redcurrant varietal fruit; subtle oak. Cork. RATING 89 DRINK 2012 $ 21
Cabernet Shiraz Merlot 2002 Light to medium-bodied; a nice display of spicy black fruits and gentle tannins; lick of vanilla oak. Cork. RATING 88 DRINK 2009 $ 17
Sauvignon Blanc Semillon 2004 Spotlessly clean; light and fresh mix of herbaceous and passionfruit aromas and flavours; crisp acidity. Screwcap. RATING 87 DRINK Now $ 17
Duck! Rose 2004 Bright colour; fresh red cherry and plum fruit; a hint of spice; good balance. Pemberton Shiraz base. RATING 87 DRINK Now $ 16

CV Pinot Noir 2003 Savoury, spicy, foresty notes to light-bodied plum and cherry fruit; very presentable varietal character. Screwcap. **RATING** 87 **DRINK** 2008 $15
Shiraz 2000 Light to medium-bodied; bright spice and red fruit flavours; light, slightly savoury tannins. Cork. **RATING** 87 **DRINK** 2009 $21

ŦŦŦŸ **Chardonnay 2002 RATING** 86 **DRINK** 2008 $21
CV Cabernet Merlot 2003 RATING 86 **DRINK** 2008 $15
CV Cabernet Merlot 2002 RATING 86 **DRINK** 2007 $16
Verdelho 2004 RATING 85 **DRINK** Now $17

ŦŦŦ **Shiraz 2002 RATING** 83 $16

Cape Mentelle ★★★★★

Wallcliffe Road, Margaret River, WA 6285 **REGION** Margaret River
T (08) 9757 0888 **F** (08) 9757 3233 **WEB** www.capementelle.com.au **OPEN** 7 days 10–4.30
WINEMAKER John Durham, Eloise Jervis, Simon Burnell **EST.** 1970 **CASES** 55 000
SUMMARY Part of the LVMH (Louis Vuitton Möet Hennessy) group. Since the advent of Dr Tony Jordan as Australasian CEO there has been a concerted and successful campaign to rid the winery of the brettanomyces infection which particularly affected the Cabernet Sauvignon. The Chardonnay and Semillon Sauvignon Blanc are among Australia's best, the potent Shiraz usually superb, and the berry/spicy Zinfandel makes one wonder why this grape is not as widespread in Australia as it is in California. Exports to all the major markets.

ŦŦŦŦŦ **Wallcliffe Sauvignon Blanc Semillon 2002** Very complex, powerful wine; citrus, herb and gooseberry with cashew, malolactic and barrel ferment complexity; excellent squeaky acidity provides length and structure. Quality cork. **RATING** 95 **DRINK** 2009 $32.50
Chardonnay 2003 Aromatic; excellent fruit and oak balance to the bouquet; medium-bodied; long, elegant melon, cashew, fig and stone fruit; impeccable oak. **RATING** 95 **DRINK** 2015 $38
Wallcliffe Shiraz 2003 Powerful, layered and complex, with some similarities to Heathcote Shiraz; blackberry, plum and a touch of licorice; compelling wine. Screwcap. **RATING** 95 **DRINK** 2018 $55
Cabernet Sauvignon 2001 Rich, gently savoury blackcurrant, earth and dark chocolate; medium to full-bodied; excellent tannin structure, good oak. No brett; lovely wine. High-quality cork. **RATING** 94 **DRINK** 2015 $66

ŦŦŦŦŸ **Sauvignon Semillon 2004** Clean and bright; the barrel ferment portion adds more to texture than to flavour; a nice mix of citrus, gooseberry and mineral. **RATING** 92 **DRINK** 2008 $23.99
Trinders Cabernet Merlot 2003 Deep colour, good hue; powerful and complex; masses of blackcurrant and spice; abundant, ripe tannins. Screwcap. **RATING** 92 **DRINK** 2013 $29
Zinfandel 2003 Deep red-purple; rich multi-spice black fruits; sumptuous and supple, though 16° alcohol does heat the finish. Screwcap. **RATING** 92 **DRINK** 2012 $47
Marmaduke 2003 Rich, quite luscious, yet not heavy or jammy; bright redcurrant, raspberry and cherry fruit; full of life. Shiraz/Grenache/Mataro. Screwcap. **RATING** 90 **DRINK** 2008 $17

ŦŦŦ **Georgiana 2004 RATING** 83 $15

Capercaillie ★★★★★

Londons Road, Lovedale, NSW 2325 **REGION** Lower Hunter Valley
T (02) 4990 2904 **F** (02) 4991 1886 **WEB** www.capercailliewine.com.au **OPEN** Mon–Sat 9–5, Sun 10–5
WINEMAKER Alasdair Sutherland, Daniel Binet **EST.** 1995 **CASES** 6000
SUMMARY The former Dawson Estate, now run by Hunter Valley veteran Alasdair Sutherland. The Capercaillie wines are particularly well made, with generous flavour. Following the example of Brokenwood, its fruit sources are spread across southeastern Australia. Exports to the UK, New Zealand, Japan and Singapore.

ŦŦŦŦŦ **Hunter Valley Semillon 1999** Still very fresh, tight and youthful; herb and grass flavours; good length and acidity. A fine wine, still evolving. Good cork. **RATING** 94 **DRINK** 2014 $37.50

Hunter Valley Chardonnay 2004 Light-bodied; attractive citrus edge to white peach and nectarine fruit with a nice touch of integrated French oak; has length. Screwcap. **RATING** 94 **DRINK** 2014 $ 21

The Ghillie Shiraz 2003 Spotlessly clean and pure; lovely ripe plum and blackberry fruit; medium-bodied, with perfect control of tannins and extract; minimal 20 years. Screwcap. **RATING** 94 **DRINK** 2023 $ 45

TTTT **Orange Highlands Merlot 2003** Intense, sweet dark fruits but in an appropriate medium-bodied frame; fine finish; lovely Merlot. Screwcap. **RATING** 92 **DRINK** 2013 $ 27

Ceilidh Shiraz 2002 Elegant medium-bodied wine, with both the flavour and structure of McLaren Vale (65%) doing most of the work. Supple, smooth red and black fruits; fine, ripe tannins. Screwcap. **RATING** 91 **DRINK** 2015 $ 28

The Clan 2002 A certain Bordeaux-like austerity and flavour; cedary, earthy, spicy blackberry mix; particularly good tannins, finish and aftertaste. Multi-region, multi-varietal blend. Screwcap. **RATING** 90 **DRINK** 2012 $ 28

Dessert Style Gewurztraminer 2004 Very intense and quite luscious; spice and lime aromas; long lime juice palate; good acidity. Cork. **RATING** 90 **DRINK** 2008 $ 18

TTTT **Slàinte Red 2002** Clean, fresh, well balanced; lots of red fruits; soft tannins, spot-on early-drinking style. Screwcap. **RATING** 87 **DRINK** 2007 $ 15

TTTT **Hunter Valley Gewurztraminer 2004** Very well made; simply the wrong region for the variety; not too sweet, and delicious lemony flavours if you don't miss varietal typicity. Screwcap. **RATING** 86 **DRINK** 2008 $ 19

Hunter Valley Chambourcin 2004 **RATING** 86 **DRINK** 2007 $ 21

Capogreco Winery Estate NR

3078 Riverside Avenue, South Mildura, Vic 3500 **REGION** Murray Darling
T (03) 5022 1431 **F** (03) 5022 1431 **OPEN** Mon–Sat 10–5
WINEMAKER Bruno Capogreco, Domenico Capogreco **EST.** 1976 **CASES** NFP
SUMMARY Italian-owned and run, the wines are a blend of Italian and Australian Riverland influences. The estate has 13 ha of chardonnay, 14 ha of shiraz and 6 ha of cabernet sauvignon, but also purchases other varieties.

Captains Creek Organic Wines NR

160 Mays Road, Blampied, Vic 3364 **REGION** Ballarat
T (03) 5345 7408 **F** (03) 5345 7408 **WEB** www.captainscreek.com **OPEN** By appointment
WINEMAKER Alan Cooper, Norman Latta, David Cowburn **EST.** 1994 **CASES** 1000
SUMMARY Doug and Carolyn May are the third generation of farmers at the Captains Creek property, and have been conducting the business for over 20 years without using any chemicals. When they began establishing the vineyard in 1994, with 1 ha each of chardonnay and pinot noir, they resolved to go down the same path: they use preventive spray programs of copper and sulphur, thermal flame weeding, and beneficial predatory insects to control weeds and mites.

Captain's Paddock

18 Millers Road, Kingaroy, Qld 4610 **REGION** South Burnett
T (07) 4162 4534 **F** (07) 4162 4502 **WEB** www.captainspaddock.com.au **OPEN** 7 days 10–5
WINEMAKER Luke Fitzpatrick **EST.** 1995 **CASES** 1000
SUMMARY Don and Judy McCallum planted the first hectare of vineyard in 1995, followed by a further 3 ha in 1996, focusing on shiraz and chardonnay. It is a family affair; the mudbrick cellar door building was made with bricks crafted by Don McCallum and Judy's screen printing adorns the tables and chairs and printed linen that are for sale. Their 2 children are both sculptors, with works on display at the winery. Captain's Paddock is fully licensed, offering either light platters or full dishes incorporating local produce. Meals are served either inside or alfresco in the courtyard, with views over the Booie Ranges.

TTTT **Rosetta Chardonay Cabernet Sauvignon 2003** Sweet cellar door style, but nicely handled. **RATING** 87 **DRINK** Now $ 12

TTT **Merlot Cabernet 2003** **RATING** 82 $ 19.50

Carabooda Estate   NR

297 Carabooda Road, Carabooda, WA 6033 **REGION** Swan District
T (08) 9407 5283 **F** (08) 9407 5283 **WEB** caraboodaestatewines.com.au **OPEN** 7 days 10–6
WINEMAKER Terry Ord **EST.** 1989 **CASES** 1500
SUMMARY 1989 is the year of establishment given by Terry Ord, but it might as well have been 1979 (when he made his first wine) or 1981 (when he and wife Simonne planted their first vines). It has been a slowly, slowly exercise, with production from the 3 ha of estate plantings now supplemented by purchased grapes. The first public release was in mid-1994, and production has risen significantly since.

Carbunup Crest Vineyard   ★★★☆

PO Box 235, Busselton, WA 6280 **REGION** Margaret River
T (08) 9754 2618 **F** (08) 9754 2618 **OPEN** Not
WINEMAKER Flying Fish Cove (Contract) **EST.** 1998 **CASES** 2000
SUMMARY Carbunup Crest is operated by three local families, with Kris Meares managing the business. Initially it operated as a grapevine rootling nursery, but it has gradually converted to grapegrowing and winemaking. There are 6 ha of vineyard, all of which are all now in production, and plans to extend the plantings to 20 ha (the property is 53 ha in total). The contract-made wines are great value.

TTTT **Shiraz 2003** Voluminous blackberry and plum fruit; chippy oak catches a little on the finish. **RATING** 89 **DRINK** 2008 $12.92
Margaret River Merlot 2003 Sophisticated winemaking has produced a full-flavoured palate with red and black fruits, a twist of olive, fine tannins and a hint of sweetness. Ready to go right now. **RATING** 89 **DRINK** 2007 $12.50

TTTY **Unwooded Chardonnay 2004** **RATING** 86 **DRINK** Now $12.90

Cardinham Estate   ★★★★☆

Main North Road, Stanley Flat, SA 5453 **REGION** Clare Valley
T (08) 8842 1944 **F** (08) 8842 1955 **WEB** www.cardinham.com **OPEN** 7 days 10–5
WINEMAKER Scott Smith, Emma Bowley **EST.** 1980 **CASES** 4500
SUMMARY The Smith family has progressively increased the vineyard size up to its present level of 60 ha, the largest plantings being of cabernet sauvignon, shiraz and riesling. It entered into a grape supply contract with Wolf Blass, which led to an association with then Quelltaler winemaker Stephen John. The joint venture then formed has now terminated, and Cardinham is locating its 500-tonne winery on its Emerald Vineyard, and using only estate-grown grapes. This has seen production rise, with the three staples of Riesling, Cabernet Merlot and Stradbroke Shiraz available from the winery and through retail distribution, and additional wines made in small volume available only at the cellar door and by mail order. Exports to Singapore.

TTTTT **Smith Family Vineyards Clare Valley Cabernet Sauvignon 2002** Medium-bodied; elegant; a nice blend of blackcurrant, sweet leather, earth and spice; fine, ripe tannins; long finish. Cork. **RATING** 94 **DRINK** 2017 $30

TTTTY **Smith Family Vineyards Clare Valley Riesling 2004** Lemon blossom, apple and spice, spotlessly clean; full-flavoured, rich, early-drinking style. Screwcap. **RATING** 91 **DRINK** 2007 $18
Smith Family Vineyards Stradbrooke Clare Valley Shiraz 2003 Dark colour; powerful savoury, blackberry, licorice and plum; substantial tannins; needs time. Distorted cork. **RATING** 90 **DRINK** 2013 $20
Smith Family Vineyards Clare Valley Cabernet Merlot 2003 Medium to full-bodied; ripe cassis and blackcurrant, round and mouthfilling, but not jammy; balanced tannins. Cork. **RATING** 90 **DRINK** 2015 $20

TTTT **Smith Family Vineyards Clare Valley Sangiovese 2004** Attractive spice and red cherry fruit, with gently ripe tannins; more substance than many. **RATING** 89 **DRINK** 2009 $18

TTTY **Smith Family Vineyards Clare Valley Unwooded Chardonnay 2004** **RATING** 86 **DRINK** 2007 $18

Cargo Road Wines ★★★★

Cargo Road, Orange, NSW 2800 **REGION** Orange
T (02) 6365 6100 **F** (02) 6365 6001 **WEB** www.cargoroadwines.com.au **OPEN** Weekends & public hols 11–5, or by appointment
WINEMAKER James Sweetapple **EST.** 1983 **CASES** 3000
SUMMARY Originally called The Midas Tree, the vineyard was planted in 1984 by Roseworthy graduate John Swanson. He established a 2.5-ha vineyard that included zinfandel: he was 15 years ahead of his time. The property was acquired in 1997 by a Charles Lane, James Sweetapple and Brian Walters. Since then they have rejuvenated the original vineyard, and planted more zinfandel, sauvignon blanc and cabernet. They are all actively involved in the Orange region community, and have opened the Pippin Bistro.

ŸŸŸŸŸ **Orange Riesling 2004** Well made; lime blossom aromas; lime/citrus flavour; good balance, length and aftertaste. Screwcap. **RATING** 90 **DRINK** 2010 $16
Orange Sauvignon Blanc 2004 Clean, no reduction; a delicate mix of tropical, gooseberry and green apple fruit; crisp, flinty acidity; long finish and aftertaste. Screwcap. **RATING** 90 **DRINK** 2008 $16

ŸŸŸŸ **Orange Merlot 2003** Good colour; clean, fresh red and blackcurrant fruit; gently savoury tannins, good length. **RATING** 88 **DRINK** 2010 $19
Orange Cabernet Sauvignon 2003 Fairly lean and savoury overall, but has considerable length. **RATING** 87 **DRINK** 2008 $19
Orange Zinfandel 2002 Light, tangy, spicy bouquet; light-bodied varietal style; has length and slippery acidity. **RATING** 87 **DRINK** 2009 $25

ŸŸŸŸ **Orange Gewurztraminer 2004** **RATING** 86 **DRINK** Now $16
Orange Cabernet Merlot 2000 Light red, quite developed; light to medium-bodied, but ageing nicely; good length. Drink soon. **RATING** 86 **DRINK** Now $22

Carilley Estate NR

Lot 23 Hyem Road, Herne Hill, WA 6056 **REGION** Swan Valley
T (08) 9296 6190 **F** (08) 9296 6190 **WEB** www.carilleyestate.com.au **OPEN** 7 days 10.30–5
WINEMAKER Rob Marshall **EST.** 1985 **CASES** 2000
SUMMARY Doctors Laura and Isavel Carija have 8 ha of vineyard planted to shiraz, chardonnay, viognier and merlot. Most of the grapes are sold, with only a small proportion made under the Carilley Estate label; very limited retail or mail order distribution. The winery café supplies light Mediterranean food.

Carindale Wines ★★★☆

Palmers Lane, Pokolbin, NSW 2321 **REGION** Lower Hunter Valley
T (02) 4998 7665 **F** (02) 4998 7065 **WEB** www.carindalewines.com.au **OPEN** Fri–Mon 10–5
WINEMAKER Brian Walsh (Contract) **EST.** 1996 **CASES** 1500
SUMMARY Carindale draws upon 2 ha of chardonnay, 1.2 ha of cabernet franc and 0.2 ha of merlot (together with few muscat vines). Exports to the US, Canada, Singapore China.

Carlei Estate & Green Vineyards ★★★★☆

1 Albert Road, Upper Beaconsfield, Vic 3808 **REGION** Yarra Valley
T (03) 5944 4599 **F** (03) 5944 4599 **WEB** www.carlei.com.au **OPEN** Weekends by appointment
WINEMAKER Sergio Carlei **EST.** 1994 **CASES** 10 000
SUMMARY The Green Vineyards and Carlei Estate has come a long way in a little time, with Sergio Carlei graduating from home winemaking in a suburban garage to his own (real) winery in Upper Beaconsfield, which happens to fall just within the boundaries of the Yarra Valley. Along the way Carlei acquired a Bachelor of Wine Science from Charles Sturt University. He also established a 2.25-ha vineyard with organic and biodynamic accreditation adjacent to the Upper Beaconsfield winery. As each vintage has passed, more and more irresistible parcels of quality wine from here, there and everywhere have led to a bewildering but usually excellent array of wines made in quantities as small as 50 cases.

ŸŸŸŸŸ **Carlei Estate Yarra Valley Chardonnay 2003** Showing some bottle development; full-on sweet peachy/stone fruit flavours have absorbed all the French oak. Opulently complex. **RATING** 93 **DRINK** 2008 $ 39

Green Vineyards Yarra Valley Chardonnay 2003 Complex ripe, sweet melon and stone fruit have swallowed up the oak; long, dry finish. **RATING** 93 **DRINK** 2009 $ 32

Carlei Estate Yarra Valley Pinot Noir 2002 Complex, savoury, foresty, sappy style; long finish. **RATING** 90 **DRINK** 2007 $ 49.95

Carn Estate   NR

Eleventh Street, Nichols Point, Vic 3501 **REGION** Murray Darling
T (03) 5024 7393 **F** (03) 5021 2929 **OPEN** 7 days
WINEMAKER Contract **EST.** 1997 **CASES** NA
SUMMARY Richard Carn has established 9 ha of colombard, cabernet sauvignon, merlot and shiraz on two vineyard sites, and has the wine contract-made. In a relatively short time, exports to England have been established, and the cellar door offers light meals, barbecue and picnic facilities.

Carosa   NR

310 Houston Street, Mt Helena, WA 6082 **REGION** Perth Hills
T (08) 9572 1603 **F** (08) 9572 1604 **WEB** www.perthhills.iinet.net.au/carosa **OPEN** Weekends & hols 11–5, or by appointment
WINEMAKER James Elson **EST.** 1984 **CASES** 800
SUMMARY Very limited production and small-scale winemaking result in wines which sell readily enough into the local market. Winemaker Jim Elson has extensive eastern Australia winemaking experience (with Seppelt). The wines are sold through the cellar door and by mailing list.

Carpinteri Vineyards   NR

PO Box 61, Nyah, Vic 3594 **REGION** Swan Hill
T (03) 5030 2569 **F** (03) 5030 2680 **OPEN** Not
WINEMAKER Michael Kyberd (Contract) **EST.** 1945 **CASES** 900
SUMMARY Vince and Con Carpinteri are primarily grapegrowers, with 30 ha planted to chardonnay, grenache, malbec, shiraz, mourvedre, black muscat and sultana. A small amount of wine is made under contract by Michael Kyberd at Red Hill Estate in the Mornington Peninsula, and the wines are sold by mail order for between $50 and $111 per dozen, and also through East Melbourne Cellars.

Casa Freschi   ★★★★

PO Box 45, Summertown, SA 5141 **REGION** Langhorne Creek
T 0409 364 569 **F** (08) 8536 4569 **WEB** www.casafreschi.com.au **OPEN** Not
WINEMAKER David Freschi **EST.** 1998 **CASES** 1000
SUMMARY David Freschi graduated with a degree in Oenology from Roseworthy College in 1991, and spent most of the decade working overseas in California, Italy and New Zealand, finishing with a senior winemaking position with Corbans in New Zealand in 1997. In 1998 he and his wife decided to trade in the corporate world for a small family-owned winemaking business, with a core of 2.5 ha of vines established by David Freschi's parents in 1972; an additional 2 ha of nebbiolo have now been planted adjacent to the original vineyard. Says David Freschi, 'the names of the wines were chosen to best express the personality of the wines grown in our vineyard, as well as to express our heritage'. The establishment of a 3-ha vineyard in the Adelaide Hills began in 2004, with further plantings in 2005. Exports to the US and Canada.

ŸŸŸŸŸ **Profondo Grand 2002** Very powerful, deep black fruits; pervasive tannins should soften; needs a decade. Cabernet Sauvignon/Shiraz/Malbec. **RATING** 91 **DRINK** 2022 $ 58

ŸŸŸŸ **La Signora 2002** Deceptively light colour; fragrant red fruit aromas; the palate gains impact progressively; fine but persistent tannins. Nebbiolo blend. **RATING** 89 **DRINK** 2017 $ 38

Casas Wines ★★★★

RMB 236D Rosa Brook Road, Margaret River, WA 6285 **REGION** Margaret River
T (08) 9757 4542 **F** (08) 9757 4006 **WEB** www.casas.com.au **OPEN** By appointment
WINEMAKER Janice MacDonald **EST.** 1992 **CASES** 2000
SUMMARY John Casas has established 5 ha of shiraz, 4 ha of cabernet sauvignon and 1 ha each of
chardonnay and sauvignon blanc. The vineyard is managed to produce low yields of 1–2 tonnes per
acre, with the aim of making a wine of sufficient power and density to merit barrel maturation of
1½–2½ years. Domestic distribution by the quirkily named Medicinal Purposes Wine Co (0438 250
372) supplements website sales. Exports to the UK and the US.

ΥΥΥΥΥ **LBE Reserve Shiraz 2001** Medium-bodied; smooth and supple plum and blackberry
fruit; fine, ripe tannins; good line and length. **RATING** 91 **DRINK** 2011 $ 55

ΥΥΥΥ **Shiraz 2002** Light to medium-bodied; spicy red and black cherry fruit; has length rather
than depth. **RATING** 88 **DRINK** 2009 $ 26

Cascabel ★★★★☆

Rogers Road, Willunga, SA 5172 (postal) **REGION** McLaren Vale
T (08) 8557 4434 **F** (08) 8557 4435 **OPEN** Not
WINEMAKER Susana Fernandez, Duncan Ferguson **EST.** 1997 **CASES** 2500
SUMMARY Cascabel's proprietors, Duncan Ferguson and Susana Fernandez, established Cascabel,
planting it to a mosaic of 9 southern Rhône and Spanish varieties, amounting to 5 ha in all. The
choice of grapes reflects the winemaking experience of the proprietors in Australia, the Rhône Valley,
Bordeaux, Italy, Germany and New Zealand – and also Susana Fernandez's birthplace, Spain. Both
are fully qualified and have moved the production steadily towards the style of the Rhône Valley,
Rioja and other parts of Spain. The wines have consistently impressed. Exports to the UK, the US,
Switzerland, Japan and Spain.

ΥΥΥΥΥ **Eden Valley Riesling 2004** Clean, floral spice, apple and mineral aromas; light to
medium-bodied; good line and length, persistent finish. **RATING** 93 **DRINK** 2014 $ 25
Fleurieu Shiraz 2003 Clean and aromatic; a supple array of blackberry, licorice, chocolate
and spice aromas and flavours; fine, savoury tannins. Screwcap. **RATING** 93 **DRINK** 2018
$ 30
Tempranillo Graciano 2003 Unexpectedly rich, dense and powerful black fruits; twists of
spice, earth and bitter chocolate; should age very well. Cork. **RATING** 90 **DRINK** 2015 $ 38

ΥΥΥΥ **Tipico Grenache Monastrell Shiraz 2003** Light to medium-bodied; spicy, fine tannins
run through the palate; a mix of sweet jam ex the Grenache, and more savoury flavours.
(Monastrell is Mourvedre.) Screwcap. **RATING** 89 **DRINK** 2009 $ 23
Joven McLaren Vale Tempranillo 2004 A touch of reduction; redcurrant, raspberry
fruits; fine tannins; not especially complex. Screwcap. **RATING** 87 **DRINK** Now $ 20
Monastrell 2003 Developed colour; jammy, biscuity, spicy fruit flavours; fine tannins;
slightly hot alcohol. **RATING** 87 **DRINK** 2008 $ 38

Casella Wines ★★★☆

Wakely Road, Yenda, NSW 2681 **REGION** Riverina
T (02) 6961 3000 **F** (02) 6961 3099 **WEB** www.casellawines.com.au **OPEN** Not
WINEMAKER Alan Kennett, Con Simos, John Quarisa **EST.** 1969 **CASES** 5 million
SUMMARY One of the modern-day fairytale success stories, transformed overnight from a substantial,
successful but non-charismatic business shown as making 650 000 cases in 2000. Its opportunity
came when the American distribution of Lindemans Bin 65 Chardonnay was taken away from WJ
Deutsch & Sons, leaving a massive gap in its portfolio, which was filled by yellow tail. It has built its US
presence at a faster rate than any other wine or brand in history. The only problem is the weakening
US dollar; all the financial and marketing skills of Casella and WJ Deutsch will be needed to keep sales
growing. A major plus in 2004 was Casella's capture of two most important trophies in Australia,
Brisbane's Stoddart and Melbourne's Jimmy Watson (both with unbottled wines, however).

ΥΥΥΥΥ **yellow tail Cabernet Sauvignon 2002** Slightly sweet, but very good texture and
structure; nice tannins. Sweetness apparent at National Wine Show 2004, but accepted.
RATING 92 **DRINK** 2008 $ 9.95

Yenda Vale Tempranillo 2003 Deep colour; far more depth than most Tempranillos tasted to date; abundant soft raspberry and cherry fruits; hints of spice and chocolate. RATING 90 DRINK Now $ 18

 TTTT **yellow tail Reserve Chardonnay 2003** Quite complex; nice nectarine fruit; long and slightly sweet finish. RATING 89 DRINK 2007 $ 14.99
Yenda Vale Limited Release Sangiovese 2003 Good colour; savoury tannins are legitimately assertive and slightly sandy; cedar and cherry flavours. RATING 88 DRINK Now $ 18

TTTY **yellow tail Shiraz 2004** Full flavoured, round and soft; distinct sweetness, but not unpleasantly so. Synthetic cork. RATING 86 DRINK Now $ 9.95
Black Stump Durif Shiraz 2003 RATING 86 DRINK 2008 Export only
Yenda Vale Limited Release Petit Verdot 2001 RATING 86 DRINK Now $ 18
Family Reserve Limited Release Vat 011 Tempranillo 2003 RATING 85 DRINK 2009 $ 16.99
Family Reserve Limited Release Vat 010 Durif 2000 RATING 84 DRINK 2007 $ 16.99

TTT **yellow tail Cabernet Sauvignon 2003** RATING 81 $ 9.99
Family Reserve Limited Release Vat 008 Petit Verdot 2001 RATING 80 $ 16.99

Casley Mount Hutton Winery ★★★

'Mount Hutton', Texas Road, via Stanthorpe, Qld 4380 REGION Granite Belt
T (07) 4683 6316 F (07) 4683 6345 OPEN Fri–Sun 10–5
WINEMAKER Grant Casley EST. 1999 CASES NA
SUMMARY Grant and Sonya Casley have established 9 ha of sauvignon blanc, chenin blanc, semillon, chardonnay, cabernet sauvignon, merlot and shiraz, making the wine onsite. The chief wine sales are by mail order and through the cellar door, which offers all the usual facilities, and meals by prior arrangement.

TTTY **Chardonnay 2004** RATING 84 DRINK Now

Cassegrain ★★★★

764, Fernbank Creek Road, Port Macquarie, NSW 2444 REGION Hastings River
T (02) 6583 7777 F (02) 6584 0354 WEB www.cassegrainwines.com.au OPEN 7 days 9–5
WINEMAKER John Cassegrain EST. 1980 CASES 60 000
SUMMARY A very substantial operation based in the Hastings Valley on the north coast of New South Wales, purchasing fruit from regions across Australia according to the variety and price point needed, supplementing the substantial estate plantings at Port Macquarie. Exports to all major markets.

TTTTY **Hastings River Semillon 2004** Classic, restrained delicacy, bright fresh and crisp; quite minerally. Hunter/Hastings Valley blend. RATING 90 DRINK 2007 $ 17.95

TTTT **Cassae NV** Golden colour; very complex aromas and flavours; raisins, dried apple, honey and pear; a Pineau des Charentes, fortified style. Serve chilled. RATING 89 DRINK Now $ 16.95

TTTY **Stone Circle Semillon Sauvignon Blanc 2004** RATING 86 DRINK Now $ 12.95
Verdelho 2004 RATING 86 DRINK Now $ 16.95

Castagna Vineyard ★★★★★

Ressom Lane, Beechworth, Vic 3747 REGION Beechworth
T (03) 5728 2888 F (03) 5728 2898 WEB www.castagna.com.au OPEN By appointment
WINEMAKER Julian Castagna EST. 1997 CASES 2000
SUMMARY The elegantly labelled wines of Castagna will ultimately come from 4 ha of biodynamically managed estate shiraz and viognier being established (the latter making up 15% of the total). Winemaker Julian Castagna is intent on making wines which reflect the terroir as closely as possible, and declines to use cultured yeast or filtration. Genesis Syrah deserves its icon status.

TTTTT **Genesis Beechworth Syrah 2002** Light to medium-bodied; a finely strung mix of spice and black fruits; fine, savoury tannins on a long finish; supremely elegant. RATING 94 DRINK 2013 $ 55

YYYYY La Chiave Sangiovese 2002 Complex savoury edges to black cherry and spice fruit; persistent tannins; demands food. **RATING** 92 **DRINK** 2010 $ 75

Castle Glen Vineyard NR

Amiens Road, The Summit, Qld 4377 **REGION** Granite Belt
T (07) 4683 2363 **F** (07) 4683 2169 **OPEN** 7 days 10–5
WINEMAKER Cedric Millar **EST.** 1990 **CASES** NA
SUMMARY Unashamedly caters for the general tourist, with a large castle boasting an open fire set in 40 ha, and specialising in 27 liqueur-style fruit wines, but with Chardonnay, Shiraz, Merlot, Cabernet Sauvignon, Semillon and White Muscat also available.

Castle Rock Estate

Porongurup Road, Porongurup, WA 6324 **REGION** Porongurup
T (08) 9853 1035 **F** (08) 9853 1010 **WEB** www.castlerockestate.com.au **OPEN** Mon–Fri 10-4, weekends & public hols 10–5
WINEMAKER Robert Diletti **EST.** 1983 **CASES** 5000
SUMMARY An exceptionally beautifully sited vineyard, winery and cellar door sales area on a 55-ha property with sweeping vistas from the Porongurups, operated by the Diletti family. The standard of viticulture is very high, and the site itself ideally situated (quite apart from its beauty). The 2-level winery, set on the natural slope, maximises gravity flow, in particular for crushed must feeding into the press. The Rieslings have always been elegant, and have handsomely repaid time in bottle; the Pinot Noir is the most consistent performer in the region.

YYYYY Chardonnay 2000 Glowing yellow-green; cool-grown style with a gently toasty entry, then stone fruit, cashew and grapefruit; long, lingering finish. **RATING** 89 **DRINK** Now $ 17

YYYYY Riesling 2004 Considerable texture, power and weight; deep mid and back palate lime juice; will develop more quickly than some from this Estate. **RATING** 92 **DRINK** 2010 $ 18
Pinot Noir 2003 Light-bodied; cherry, spice and forest; well balanced, good texture. **RATING** 90 **DRINK** 2008 $ 23
Shiraz 2003 Very good colour; clean; supple cherry and plum; fruit-driven; medium-bodied, but has length. **RATING** 90 **DRINK** 2013 $ 19

YYYY Shiraz 2002 Light to medium-bodied; well balanced; harmonious black fruits, spice and oak. **RATING** 89 **DRINK** 2012 $ 19

Cathcart Ridge Estate ★★★★

Moyston Road, Cathcart via Ararat, Vic 3377 **REGION** Grampians
T (03) 5352 1997 **F** (03) 5352 1558 **WEB** www.cathcartwines.com.au **OPEN** 7 days 10–5
WINEMAKER David Farnhill **EST.** 1977 **CASES** 10 000
SUMMARY In recent years has raised capital to fund a significant expansion program of both vineyards and the winery, but is still little known in the wider retail trade. Mount Ararat Estate is a parallel operation to Cathcart Ridge, David Farnhill being the Chief Executive of both. There are 2.5 ha of vineyard in the Grampians region, and another 7.5 ha at Mildura, providing riesling, chardonnay, colombard, grenache and shiraz. Exports to Ireland. The 2001 Grampian Shiraz was made Shiraz of the Year in 2004 by *Winestate* magazine.

YYYYY The Grampian Shiraz 2001 Dense red-purple; full-bodied; rich, ripe, concentrated blackberry and satsuma plum; round, soft tannins; good oak. Stained cork. **RATING** 92 **DRINK** 2014 $ 80
The Grampian Shiraz 2000 Holding hue well; spicy notes to the bouquet lead into a medium-bodied, lusciously sweet plum and dark berry fruit palate; fine tannins. Cork. Winner of *Winestate* magazine's Wine of the Year trophy in 2004. **RATING** 92 **DRINK** 2010 $ 80

YYYY Cabernet Sauvignon 1999 Light to medium-bodied; cedary, earthy, spicy, blackberry fruit; not much concentration or structure. **RATING** 87 **DRINK** 2007 $ 38

YYYY Cabernet Sauvignon 2000 RATING 86 **DRINK** 2007 $ 38

Cathedral Lane Wines ★★★★

228 Cathedral Lane, Taggerty, Vic 3714 **REGION** Upper Goulburn
T (03) 5774 7305 **F** (03) 5774 7696 **WEB** www.cathedrallanewines.com **OPEN** By appointment
WINEMAKER MasterWineMakers (Contract) **EST.** 1997 **CASES** 450
SUMMARY Rod Needham and Heather Campbell formed the Acheron Valley Wine Company, which
makes the Cathedral Lane wines, in 1997. The 3.2-ha vineyard is on the lower slopes of Mt Cathedral,
at a height of 280 m. A variant of the Scott Henry trellis system, with high-density 1 m spacing
between the vines, alternately trained up or down, has been used. The vineyard planning was
supervised by former Coldstream Hills viticulturist Bill Christophersen.

Catherine's Ridge NR

Fish Fossil Drive, Canowindra, NSW 2804 **REGION** Cowra
T (02) 6344 3212 **F** (02) 6344 3242 **OPEN** By appointment
WINEMAKER Contract **EST.** 1999 **CASES** NFP
SUMMARY Kay and David Warren have 18 ha of chardonnay, verdelho, shiraz and cabernet sauvignon.
The wine is made under contract from part of the annual grape production.

Catherine Vale Vineyard ★★★★

656 Milbrodale Road, Bulga, NSW 2330 **REGION** Lower Hunter Valley
T (02) 6579 1334 **F** (02) 6579 1299 **WEB** www.catherinevale.com.au **OPEN** Weekends & public hols
10–5, or by appointment
WINEMAKER John Hordern (Contract) **EST.** 1994 **CASES** 1200
SUMMARY Former schoolteachers Bill and Wendy Lawson have established Catherine Vale as a not-
so-idle retirement venture. Both were involved in school athletics and sports programs, handy
training for do-it-yourself viticulturists. Part of the production from the 5.8-ha vineyard is sold to
contract winemaker John Hordern; the remainder is vinified for the Catherine Vale label. A new
cellar door opened in May 2004. Exports to Germany.

ⓉⓉⓉⓉⓎ **Semillon 2003** Clean, clear-cut semillon aromas; still very fresh, and finishing with
minerally acidity, with an array of fruit flavours on the way through. **RATING** 90
DRINK 2013 $14
Chardonnay 2003 Nicely made; well-balanced and integrated oak into peachy stone fruit
flavours. Plenty of substance. **RATING** 90 **DRINK** 2009 $16

ⓉⓉⓉⓉ **Verdelho Semillon 2003** Cleverly conceived and made; Semillon to tighten the structure,
Verdelho the tropical fruit, American oak a background shadow. **RATING** 88 **DRINK** 2007
$12

ⓉⓉⓉⓎ **Winifred Barbera 2003** **RATING** 85 **DRINK** 2009 $16

Catspaw Farm NR

Texas Road, Stanthorpe, Qld 4380 **REGION** Granite Belt
T (07) 4683 6229 **F** (07) 4683 6386 **WEB** www.catspaw.cjb.net **OPEN** Thurs–Sun & public hols 10–5,
7 days Easter, June & September school hols
WINEMAKER Christopher Whitfort **EST.** 1989 **CASES** 300
SUMMARY The foundations for Catspaw Farm were laid back in 1989 when planting of the vineyard
began with chardonnay, riesling, cabernet franc, cabernet sauvignon, merlot, chambourcin and
shiraz, totalling 4.6 ha. More recently, Catspaw has planted roussanne, semillon, barbera and
sangiovese, lifting total plantings to just under 8 ha. The newer plantings are yet to come into bearing
and the wines are some time away from release. In the meantime a mixed bag of wines are available,
some dating back to 1998. Catspaw also offers on-farm accommodation in a self-contained
farmhouse (with disabled access) and picnic facilities.

🍇 Cavalier Crest ★★★★

Davis Road, Rosa Glen, WA 6285 **REGION** Margaret River
T (08) 9757 5091 **F** (08) 9757 5091 **OPEN** 7 days 10–5 by appointment
WINEMAKER Andrew Gamon (Contract) **EST.** 1978 **CASES** 2500

SUMMARY The Halcyon Vineyard, as it is known locally, was established in 1978 with the planting of little under 5 ha of cabernet sauvignon, merlot, pinot noir, chardonnay and semillon. When Graham and Sue Connell purchased the property in 1991, they increased the plantings to 8 ha, planting more pinot noir, cabernet sauvignon and merlot. Until 2003 they were content to sell all the grapes to other winemakers in the region, but in that year small batches of Cabernet Sauvignon, Merlot, Pinot Noir and Semillon were contract-made by Andrew Gamon. Trademark difficulties meant the Halcyon Vineyard name could not be used. The Connells live on the property, hence the 7 day cellar door sales, but would prefer a phone call in advance.

TTTTY **Margaret River Merlot 2003** An attractive mix of small red fruits, olives and spices; fine, silky, ripe tannins; subtle oak. Screwcap. **RATING** 90 **DRINK** 2011 $28

TTTT **Margaret River Semillon 2003** Quite rich; some citrus and stone fruit flavours; powerful back palate; 200 cases made. Screwcap. **RATING** 89 **DRINK** 2008 $18
Margaret River Semillon 2004 Light-bodied and crisp; a touch of French barrel ferment adds solely to texture; fairly dry, flinty style; will evolve. Screwcap. **RATING** 88 **DRINK** 2009 $18
Margaret River Cabernet Sauvignon 2003 Powerful blackcurrant, earth and bitter chocolate; assertive tannins need to soften. Screwcap. **RATING** 87 **DRINK** 2009 $24

TTTY **Margaret River Pinot Noir 2003** **RATING** 84 **DRINK** 2009 $20

Cawdor Wines NR

Old Mount Barker Road, Echunga, SA 5153 **REGION** Adelaide Hills
T (08) 8388 8456 **F** (08) 8388 8807 **WEB** www.cawdorwines.com.au **OPEN** By appointment
WINEMAKER Contract **EST.** 1999 **CASES** 350
SUMMARY Jock Calder and his family began the establishment of Cawdor Wines with the purchase of 22 ha near the township of Echunga; 5 ha of sauvignon blanc were planted that year, with a further 2.6 ha of sauvignon blanc, 7.9 ha of shiraz and 2.7 ha of riesling the following year. The major part of the production is sold to Nepenthe Wines, but Cawdor nominates how much it wishes to have vinified under its own label each year. It has followed a softly, softly approach, with only small amounts being made. There is no cellar door; nor is one planned. The wine is sold via fax, email, phone, etc, with limited wholesale distribution.

Ceccanti Kiewa Valley Wines NR

Bay Creek Lane, Mongans Bridge, Vic 3691 **REGION** Alpine Valleys
T (03) 5754 5236 **F** (03) 5754 5353 **WEB** www.ceccanti.com.au **OPEN** 7 days 11–5
WINEMAKER Angelo Ceccanti, Moya Ceccanti, Danny Ceccanti **EST.** 1988 **CASES** NA
SUMMARY Parents Angelo and Moya Ceccanti, with son Danny, have established 16 ha of vines, and now use all the production for their wines, which are made onsite by the family. Angelo, raised in Tuscany, had extensive exposure to viticulture and winemaking, but it is Moya and Danny who have the technical knowledge.

Cedar Creek Estate ★★☆

104–144 Hartley Road, Mount Tamborine, Qld 4272 **REGION** Queensland Coastal
T (07) 5545 1666 **F** (07) 5545 4762 **WEB** www.cedarcreekestate.com.au **OPEN** 7 days 10–5
WINEMAKER Contract **EST.** 2000 **CASES** 1500
SUMMARY Opened in November 2000, Cedar Creek Estate takes its name from the creek which flows through the property at an altitude of 550 m on Tamborine Mountain. A 3.7-ha vineyard has been planted to chambourcin and verdelho, and is supplemented by grapes grown elsewhere. The focus will always be on general tourism, with a host of facilities, including a restaurant, for visitors; it also offers wines from Ballandean Estate.

TTT **Unwooded Chardonnay 2003** **RATING** 82 $17.50

Cellarmasters ★★★★

Dorrien Estate, Cnr Barossa Valley Way/Siegersdorf Road, Tanunda, SA 5352 **REGION** Barossa Valley
T (08) 8561 2200 **F** (08) 8561 2299 **WEB** www.cellarmasters.com.au **OPEN** Not

WINEMAKER Simon Adams, Steve Chapman, Nick Badrice, John Schwartzkopff, Sally Blackwell, Neil Doddridge **EST.** 1982 **CASES** 800 000
SUMMARY The Cellarmaster Group was acquired by Beringer Blass in 1997. Dorrien Estate is the physical base of the vast Cellarmaster network which, wearing its retailer's hat, is by far the largest direct-sale outlet in Australia. It buys substantial quantities of wine from other makers either in bulk or as cleanskin (unlabelled bottles), or with recognisable but subtly different labels of the producers concerned. It is also making increasing quantities of wine on its own account at Dorrien Estate, many of which are quite excellent, and of trophy quality. The labelling of these wines is becoming increasingly sophisticated, giving little or no clue to the Cellarmaster link. Chateau Dorrien is an entirely unrelated business.

ŸŸŸŸŸ **Black Wattle Vineyard Mount Benson Cabernet Sauvignon 2002** Strong varietal character; highly focused and tight blackcurrant fruit; fine tannins. **RATING** 94 **DRINK** 2017 $ 35.99

ŸŸŸŸŸ **Heemskerk Pinot Noir 2003** Attractive plum, raspberry and cherry fruits; fine, ripe tannins; nice balance. **RATING** 92 **DRINK** 2009 $ 25
Heemskerk Riesling 2004 Flinty/minerally; lively, tingling, sherbet acidity; only Tasmania does this; intense and striking. **RATING** 90 **DRINK** 2012 $ 23.99
Heemskerk Chardonnay 2002 Mouthfilling, ripe stone fruit and peach; good supporting oak. **RATING** 90 **DRINK** 2008 $ 25.99
Black Wattle Vineyard Mount Benson Shiraz 2002 Firm, powerful, long and focused blackcurrant fruit; typical of vintage. **RATING** 90 **DRINK** 2012 $ 35.99

ŸŸŸŸ **Black Wattle Vineyard Mount Benson Shiraz 2001** Fresh, light to medium-bodied with attractive red fruit aromas; lingering, juicy, fruit-driven finish. **RATING** 89 **DRINK** 2011 $ 31.99
Amberton Shiraz 2003 Sweet berry fruit with a dash of chocolate; ripe tannins. **RATING** 88 **DRINK** 2010 $ 18
Addison Section 49 Mount Benson Cabernet Sauvignon 2001 Light to medium-bodied; neatly balanced fruit, oak and tannins, but not a lot of weight. **RATING** 88 **DRINK** 2007 $ 22.50
Heemskerk Tasmania Pinot Chardonnay 2002 Very fine, very delicate, very crisp; has length, but not complexity; bottle age will help. **RATING** 88 **DRINK** 2009 $ 27.99
Lysander Mount Benson Chardonnay 2004 Generous, soft, peachy stone fruit flavours. **RATING** 87 **DRINK** 2007 $ 14.50
Black Wattle Vineyard Mount Benson Chardonnay 2003 Soft nectarine and citrus fruit; gently honeyed finish. **RATING** 87 **DRINK** Now $ 20.99
Langhorne Creek Area Red Blend 2001 Quite fragrant; elegant, light to medium-bodied red fruits and slightly savoury edges. **RATING** 87 **DRINK** 2009 $ 33.99
Riddoch Coonawarra Cabernet Sauvignon 2002 Light to medium-bodied; nicely balanced with some red and blackcurrant fruit. **RATING** 87 **DRINK** 2007 $ 22.99

ŸŸŸŸ **Woolshed Coonawarra Chardonnay 2003** **RATING** 86 **DRINK** Now $ 13.50
Alexanders Coonawarra Shiraz 2003 **RATING** 86 **DRINK** 2009 $ 19
Riddoch Coonawarra Shiraz 2002 **RATING** 86 **DRINK** 2008 $ 20
Lysander Cabernet Sauvignon Merlot 2002 **RATING** 86 **DRINK** 2009 $ 16.99
The Ridge Coonawarra Cabernet Sauvignon 2002 **RATING** 86 **DRINK** 2009 $ 19.50
Black Wattle Vineyard Mount Benson Cabernet Sauvignon 2001 **RATING** 86 **DRINK** Now $ 32.99
McGuigan Gold Label Mount Benson Classic Dry White 2004 **RATING** 84 **DRINK** Now $ 13
Addison Section 49 Mount Benson Cabernet Sauvignon 2002 **RATING** 84 $ 22.50

ŸŸŸ **Magill Cellars Limestone Coast Chardonnay 2004** **RATING** 83 $ 19.50
Wrights Bay Mount Benson Chardonnay Verdelho 2003 **RATING** 83 $ 15.50
Addison Section 49 Mount Benson Shiraz 2003 **RATING** 82 $ 22.50

Celtic Farm

NR

39 Sweyn Street, North Balwyn, Vic 3104 (postal) **REGION** Southeast Australia
T (03) 9857 3600 **F** (03) 9857 3601 **OPEN** Not
WINEMAKER Gerry Taggert **EST.** 1997 **CASES** 4000

SUMMARY Yet another warehouse winery, these days owned and run by co-founder Gerry Taggert, joined by long-time friends Mark McNeill and Mike Shields – all fine Celts, according to Taggert. Taggert says, 'Celtic Farm is produced from classic varieties selected from Australia's premium wine regions and made with a total commitment to quality. While we have a desire to pay homage to our Celtic (drinking) heritage we are also acutely aware that wine should be about enjoyment, fun and not taking yourself too seriously.' Unsurprisingly, the team is negotiating with importers in Ireland, and in conjunction with the Celtic Farm brand, may develop an exclusive export label in addition to Celtic Farm.

Centennial Vineyards ★★★★☆

'Woodside' Centennial Road, Bowral, NSW 2576 **REGION** Southern Highlands
T (02) 4861 8700 **F** (02) 4681 8777 **WEB** www.centennial.net.au **OPEN** 7 days 10–5
WINEMAKER Tony Cosgriff **EST.** 2002 **CASES** 10 000
SUMMARY Centennial Vineyards is a substantial development jointly owned by wine professional John Large and investor Mark Dowling, covering 133 ha of beautiful grazing land, with over 30 ha planted to sauvignon blanc, riesling, verdelho, chardonnay, merlot, pinot noir, cabernet sauvignon and tempranillo. Production from the estate vineyards (the vines of which age from 4–7 years) is supplemented by purchases of grapes from other regions, including Orange. The new onsite winery has a 120-tonne capacity, and worked close to this capacity in 2003. A substantial and very popular restaurant is open 7 days. Sales are mainly through local distribution, cellar door, mailing list and some exports.

TTTTT Reserve Chardonnay 2003 Complex and intense; classy barrel ferment inputs; a long palate with citrus, nectarine and cashew; clean, long finish. Orange. Screwcap. **RATING** 94 **DRINK** 2010 $ 25

TTTTT Reserve Merlot 2003 Medium-bodied; red and blackcurrant aromas and flavours; supple, smooth and long; controlled extract and tannins. Orange. Cork. **RATING** 92 **DRINK** 2013 $ 27
Reserve Shiraz 2003 Bright, fresh red and black fruit mix; fine-grained tannins, subtle oak; long finish. Hilltops. Cork. **RATING** 91 **DRINK** 2012 $ 26
Reserve Cabernet Sauvignon 2003 Medium-bodied; distinctive supple texture and structure; blackcurrant and some cassis; excellent oak and tannin management. Orange. Cork. **RATING** 91 **DRINK** 2013 $ 24

TTTT Woodside Southern Highlands Chardonnay 2003 Elegant, light to medium-bodied; smoky/peaty aromas; citrus and stone fruit; crisp finish. Screwcap. **RATING** 89 **DRINK** 2009 $ 25
Bong Bong White 2004 Crisp, tangy, lively, juicy lemony; fresh as a daisy, clever label. Sauvignon Blanc/Chardonnay from Bowral. Screwcap. **RATING** 87 **DRINK** Now $ 17
Rose 2004 Clean, red cherry; fresh and lively; nice balance, not sweet. Bowral and Hilltops. Screwcap. **RATING** 87 **DRINK** Now $ 17

TTTT Sauvignon Blanc 2004 RATING 86 **DRINK** 2007 $ 20
Verdelho 2004 RATING 85 **DRINK** Now $ 19
Bong Bong Red 2003 RATING 84 **DRINK** Now $ 17

Ceravolo Wines ★★★★

Suite 16, 172 Glynburn Road, Tranmere, SA 5073 (postal) **REGION** Adelaide Plains
T (08) 8336 4522 **F** (08) 8365 0538 **WEB** www.ceravolo.com.au **OPEN** Not
WINEMAKER Colin Glaetzer, Ben Glaetzer (Contract) **EST.** 1985 **CASES** 15 000
SUMMARY Joe Ceravolo, dental surgeon-turned-vigneron, and wife Heather have been producing single-vineyard wines from their family-owned estate since 1999, centred around Shiraz, but with Chardonnay and Merlot in support. Conspicuous success at the London International Wine Challenge led both to exports and the registration of the Adelaide Plains region under the GI legislation. Wines are released under the Ceravolo, St Andrews Estate and Red Earth labels. Exports to the UK, Denmark and Asia.

TTTTT Adelaide Hills Pinot Gris 2004 Clean, crisp bouquet; attractive citrus overlay to pear and apple palate; 12.5° alcohol spot on. Screwcap. **RATING** 90 **DRINK** 2007 $ 17.99

ɫɫɫɫ **Adelaide Plains Shiraz 2002** Medium-bodied; has elegance combined with length and persistence. RATING 89 DRINK 2009 $ 19.99

Adelaide Plains Petit Verdot 2003 Typically good colour; a quite rich and smooth mix of black fruits and dark chocolate; ripe tannins; carries 15.5° alcohol well. Screwcap. RATING 88 DRINK 2010 $ 22.99

Adelaide Hills Sauvignon Blanc 2004 Very light; fresh apple and mineral, hints of citrus; well made; simple lack of fruit intensity. Screwcap. RATING 87 DRINK 2007 $ 14.99

Adelaide Plains Chardonnay 2004 Light, fresh, clean and crisp; squeaky acidity; shows the benefit of the cool vintage and early picking (11.5° alcohol). Screwcap. RATING 87 DRINK 2008 $ 14.99

Adelaide Plains Sangiovese 2004 Light-bodied; fresh red cherry; lacks density and structure, but does have length and quite good fruit balance. Screwcap. RATING 87 DRINK 2008 $ 14.99

ɫɫɫɰ **Red Earth Cabernet Sauvignon 2004** RATING 85 DRINK 2007 $ 9.99

Red Earth Shiraz 2003 RATING 84 DRINK Now $ 9.99

ɫɫɰ **Unwooded Chardonnay 2004** RATING 79 $ 14.99

Chain of Ponds ★★★★★

Adelaide Road, Gumeracha, SA 5233 REGION Adelaide Hills
T (08) 8389 1415 F (08) 8389 1877 WEB www.chainofponds.com.au OPEN Mon–Fri 11–4, weekends & public hols 10.30–4.30
WINEMAKER Neville Falkenberg EST. 1993 CASES 17 500
SUMMARY Chain of Ponds is the largest grower in the Adelaide Hills, with 100 ha of vines at Gumeracha and 120 ha at Kersbrook, and producing 1000 tonnes of grapes a year. Almost all are sold to other wineries, but a small amount of wine is made under the Chain of Ponds label; these enjoy consistent show success. The Vineyard Balcony Restaurant is open for lunch on weekends and public holidays. Exports to the UK, the US and Singapore.

ɫɫɫɫɫ **The Red Semi Semillon 2004** Clean, crisp; touches of lemon and herb; bright, fresh mouthfeel with plenty of flavour and development potential. RATING 94 DRINK 2010 $ 19

The Morning Star Chardonnay 2001 Elegant and youthful, and developing slowly but impressively; melon, stone fruit; finely structured; subtle oak. RATING 94 DRINK 2011 $ 55

ɫɫɫɫɰ **Corkscrew Road Chardonnay 2002** Elegant, slow-developing style; some Chablis-like notes; nectarine, melon fruit, subtle oak. RATING 93 DRINK 2009 $ 24.95

Purple Patch Adelaide Hills Riesling 2004 Spotlessly clean apple blossom, herb and spice aromas; the first signs of development add weight and complexity to the passionfruit flavour. Screwcap. RATING 91 DRINK 2009 $ 18

Adelaide Hills Pinot Grigio 2004 Spotlessly clean; perfect focus, balance and length; gentle citrus, spice and pear fruit; bright finish. Screwcap. RATING 90 DRINK 2008 $ 18

ɫɫɫɫ **Black Thursday Sauvignon Blanc 2004** Clean, crisp and correct; good balance and line; simply lacks positive varietal character. RATING 89 DRINK 2007 $ 19

Adelaide Hills Viognier 2004 A relatively quiet bouquet, then intense, tangy tropical/pastille fruit races through to the finish of the palate; striking. Screwcap. RATING 89 DRINK 2010 $ 20

Jupiter's Blood Adelaide Hills Sangiovese 2003 Good colour and hue; gently sweet spice and sour cherry fruit; fine, savoury tannins. Has attitude. RATING 89 DRINK 2010 $ 20

Chalice Bridge Estate ★★★★☆

Rosa Glen Road, Margaret River, WA 6285 REGION Margaret River
T (08) 9388 6088 F (08) 9382 1887 WEB www.chalicebridge.com.au OPEN By appointment
WINEMAKER Janice McDonald EST. 1998 CASES 14 000
SUMMARY Chalice Bridge Estate is a recent arrival in wine terms, but has a history dating back to 1924, when it was densely forested with jarrah and marri trees; a group of English settlers arrived with the aim of converting the forest to grazing land. Most gave up, but the Titterton family persevered, eventually selling the property in 1977. Planting of the vineyard began in 1998; there are now 28 ha of cabernet sauvignon and shiraz, 27 ha of chardonnay, 12.5 ha of semillon, 18 ha sauvignon blanc, 7 ha merlot, with lesser plantings of viognier and muscat making up the total

plantings of 122 ha; it is the second-largest single vineyard in the Margaret River region. Exports to the US, Singapore, Switzerland, The Netherlands and Malaysia.

TTTTY **Shiraz 2003** Excellent depth and structure; raspberry and blackberry fruit, subtle oak and good tannins. RATING 93 DRINK 2015 $20

Sauvignon Blanc 2004 Fragrant and aromatic; delicate gooseberry and passionfruit flavours; cleansing acidity. RATING 92 DRINK Now $19.95

Unwooded Chardonnay 2004 Attractive mix of melon and stone fruit; balanced acidity and good length; good example of the style. RATING 91 DRINK Now $18

Semillon Sauvignon Blanc 2004 Herbs and spice; tight, crisp mineral and citrus flavours; good length. RATING 90 DRINK 2007 $18

Shiraz Cabernet Sauvignon 2003 Fragrant; hints of leaf and mint; fresh and fruit-driven blackberry and raspberry flavours; very typical Chalice Bridge style; fine tannins, subtle oak. RATING 90 DRINK 2012 $23

Merlot 2003 Vivid red-purple; bright red fruits; good structure ex fine tannins; authentic varietal character. RATING 90 DRINK 2008 $19.95

TTTT **Margaret River Cabernet Sauvignon 2003** Light to medium-bodied; juicy cassis and blackcurrant; clean, fruit-driven; some spice. Screwcap. RATING 89 DRINK 2010 $19.95

Chalkers Crossing ★★★★★

387 Grenfell Road, Young, NSW 2594 REGION Hilltops
T (02) 6382 6900 F (02) 6382 5068 WEB www.chalkerscrossing.com.au OPEN 7 days 10–4
WINEMAKER Celine Rousseau EST. 2000 CASES 10 000
SUMMARY Owned and operated by Ted and Wendy Ambler, Chalkers Crossing is based near Young, where the first vines were planted at the Rockleigh vineyard in late 1997, with follow-up plantings in 1998 lifting the total to 10 ha. It also purchases grapes from Tumbarumba and Gundagai. A winery was opened for the 2000 vintage, with Celine Rousseau as winemaker. Born in France's Loire Valley and trained in Bordeaux, Celine has worked in Bordeaux, Champagne, Languedoc, Margaret River and the Perth Hills, an eclectic mix of climates if ever there was one. This French Flying Winemaker (now an Australian citizen) has exceptional skills and dedication. Exports to France, Hong Kong and the UK.

TTTTT **Hilltops Shiraz 2003** Vibrant red-purple; plush blackberry and blood plum aromas and flavours; perfect tannin and oak balance. RATING 94 DRINK 2013 $25

Hilltops Cabernet Sauvignon 2003 Dark red-purple, it has intense varietal blackcurrant and cassis with a cool-climate twist of herb and olive, which add to rather than detract from this Bordeaux-style bargain. RATING 94 DRINK 2013 $25

TTTTY **Hilltops Semillon 2003** Glowing yellow-green; excellent bottle development and sophisticated French oak barrel ferment inputs; harmonious mix of citrus, honey and a touch of oak spice. RATING 92 DRINK 2010 $16.50

Hilltops Semillon 2004 Particularly good mouthfeel from 4 months on lees; silky, lemony fruit; good length and finish. Screwcap. RATING 91 DRINK 2014 $16.50

Tumbarumba Chardonnay 2003 Super-refined and delicate despite 14° alcohol; grapefruit and melon have absorbed the 9 months in French oak. Twin Top. RATING 91 DRINK 2010 $18

Tumbarumba Sauvignon Blanc 2004 Delicate passionfruit and gooseberry aromas and flavours; tight focus and structure; long finish. Screwcap. RATING 90 DRINK 2008 $16.50

TTTT **Hilltops Riesling 2004** Subdued bouquet; tight, mineral-framed palate; limey fruit comes on the finish; time needed. Screwcap. RATING 89 DRINK 2010 $16.50

Chalk Hill ★★★★

PO Box 205, McLaren Vale, SA 5171 REGION McLaren Vale
T (08) 8556 2121 F (08) 8556 2221 WEB www.chalkhill.com.au OPEN Not
WINEMAKER Emma Bekkers EST. 1973 CASES 5000
SUMMARY Chalk Hill is in full flight again, drawing upon 3 vineyards (Slate Creek, Wits End and Chalk Hill) of grapegrowing owners John and Di Harvey, who acquired Chalk Hill in 1995. There has been considerable work on the Chalk Hill home vineyard since its acquisition: part has been retrellised, and riesling has been replaced by new plantings of shiraz and cabernet sauvignon, plus small amounts of barbera and sangiovese. Domestic distribution is solely by mail order; a small portion is exported to the US, Canada and Holland (under the Wits End label).

𝖸𝖸𝖸𝖸𝖸 **McLaren Vale Cabernet Sauvignon 2002** Attractive mix of cedar, earth, bitter chocolate and blackcurrant aromas and flavours; good use of oak; ripe tannins. Cork. **RATING** 91 **DRINK** 2015 $25
McLaren Vale Shiraz 2002 Medium-bodied; quite elegant, strongly regional dark chocolate substrate; ripe, soft tannins. Modest 14.5° alcohol. Cork. **RATING** 90 **DRINK** 2012 $25

𝖸𝖸𝖸𝖸 **McLaren Vale The Procrastinator 2004** Plenty of spice, tobacco and cedar under the red fruit coat; not much structure, but is great value; 95% Cabernet Franc, 5% Shiraz. Screwcap. **RATING** 86 **DRINK** 2007 $11

Chambers Rosewood ★★★★★

Barkly Street, Rutherglen, Vic 3685 **REGION** Rutherglen
T (02) 6032 8641 **F** (02) 6032 8101 **OPEN** Mon–Sat 9–5, Sun 11–5
WINEMAKER Bill Chambers, Stephen Chambers **EST.** 1858 **CASES** 20 000
SUMMARY The winery rating is given for the Grand Muscat and Tokay and the Rare wines, which are on a level all their own, somewhere higher than five stars. The chief virtue of the table wines is that they are cheap. Exports to the US, the UK, Belgium, Singapore and New Zealand.

𝖸𝖸𝖸𝖸𝖸 **Rare Rutherglen Muscat NV** Very deep mahogany-brown, olive rim; the bouquet comes on like a blitzkrieg, so powerful and complex it very nearly imprisons the senses. The palate is a magical combination of extreme rancio driving the length and finish, but seamlessly filled out by essence-like raisin fruit. **RATING** 97 **DRINK** Now
Grand Rutherglen Muscat NV Full olive-brown; ultra-complex aromas, with a piercing strand of rancio; layer upon layer of flavour, balanced and integrated, with no one flavour dominant. **RATING** 94 **DRINK** Now $50

𝖸𝖸𝖸𝖸 **Anton Ruche Shiraz Mondeuse 2001** Ripe, juicy blackberry, plum and a hint of prune; supple and fleshy. Cork. **RATING** 88 **DRINK** 2011 $15
Rutherglen Tokay NV Glowing orange-gold; very young, strongly varietal in tea leaf and malt biscuit primary phase. No bottle development possible, of course. **RATING** 87 **DRINK** Now $15

𝖸𝖸𝖸𝖸 **Rutherglen Cabernet Sauvignon 2001 RATING** 86 **DRINK** 2009 $12
Rutherglen Muscat NV RATING 86 **DRINK** Now $15
Rutherglen Shiraz 2001 RATING 85 **DRINK** 2011 $10
Blue Imperial Cinsaut 2002 RATING 85 **DRINK** 2008 $12
Gouais 2001 RATING 85 **DRINK** Now $12
Rutherglen Fino Sherry NV RATING 85 **DRINK** Now $10
Ruby 1998 RATING 84 **DRINK** Now $15
Old Cellar Vintage Port 2002 RATING 84 **DRINK** 2010 $15

𝖸𝖸𝖸 **Rutherglen Riesling 2000 RATING** 83 $8

Channybearup Vineyard ★★★★

Lot 4 Channybearup Road, Pemberton, WA 6260 (postal) **REGION** Pemberton
T (08) 9776 0042 **F** (08) 9776 0043 **WEB** www.channybearup.com.au **OPEN** Not
WINEMAKER Larry Cherubino (Contract) **EST.** 1999 **CASES** 13 500
SUMMARY Channybearup has been established by a small group of Perth businessmen who have been responsible for the establishment of 62 ha of vineyards (the majority planted in 1999 and 2000). The leading varieties are chardonnay, pinot noir, merlot, shiraz, cabernet sauvignon and pinot noir, with lesser amounts of verdelho and sauvignon blanc. While principally established as a grape supplier to other makers, the amount of wine being vinified for Channybearup has increased significantly. Exports to the US.

Chanters Ridge ★★★★

440 Chanters Lane, Tylden, Vic 3444 **REGION** Macedon Ranges
T 0427 511 341 **F** (03) 9509 8046 **WEB** www.chantersridge.com.au **OPEN** Weekends 10–4 by appointment
WINEMAKER John Ellis **EST.** 1995 **CASES** 600

SUMMARY Orthopaedic surgeon Barry Elliott, as well as running the surgery unit at Melbourne's Alfred Hospital, became involved with the Kyneton Hospital 5 years ago. Through a convoluted series of events, he and his wife acquired the 24-ha property without any clear idea of what they might do with it; later his lifelong interest in wine steered him towards the idea of establishing a vineyard. He retained local overlord John Ellis as his consultant, and this led to the planting of 2 ha of pinot noir, and the first tiny make in 2000. Barry Elliott intends to retire from surgery and devote himself full-time to the challenge of making Pinot Noir in one of the more difficult parts of Australia, but one which will richly reward success.

ㅜㅜㅜㅜ♀ **Pinot Noir 2001** Powerful wine; lots of depth to the array of red and black fruits; lingering balanced acidity. **RATING** 93 **DRINK** 2007 $ 25

ㅜㅜㅜㅜ **Back Paddock Pinot Noir 2003** Attractive small red fruit and a hint of plum; noticeable acidity. **RATING** 88 **DRINK** 2007 $ 15

ㅜㅜㅜ♀ **Pinot Noir 2003** **RATING** 86 **DRINK** 2007 $ 25

Chapel Hill ★★★★

Chapel Hill Road, McLaren Vale, SA 5171 **REGION** McLaren Vale
T (08) 8323 8429 **F** (08) 8323 9245 **WEB** www.chapelhillwine.com.au **OPEN** 7 days 12–5
WINEMAKER Angela Meaney, Michael Fragos **EST.** 1979 **CASES** 50 000
SUMMARY A leading medium-sized winery in the region; in the second half of 2000 Chapel Hill was sold to the diversified Swiss Thomas Schmidheiny group, which owns the respected Cuvaison winery in California as well as vineyards in Switzerland and Argentina. Wine quality is as good, if not better, than ever. Exports to the UK, the US, Canada, Switzerland, Germany, Belgium, New Zealand and Hong Kong.

ㅜㅜㅜㅜ♀ **McLaren Vale Shiraz 2001** Medium-bodied; elegant black plum and black cherry fruit; good acidity and mouthfeel, fine tannins and a sweet touch of totally integrated oak. **RATING** 93 **DRINK** 2011 $ 28
McLaren Vale/Coonawarra Cabernet Sauvignon 2002 Finely balanced and structured; blackcurrant, earth and chocolate; ripe tannins, good oak. **RATING** 92 **DRINK** 2012 $ 25
McLaren Vale Shiraz 2002 Pleasant red and black fruits; smooth, medium-bodied; fine tannins. **RATING** 90 **DRINK** 2010 $ 28

ㅜㅜㅜㅜ **Reserve Chardonnay 2003** Light to medium-bodied; neatly balanced fruit and oak, melon and cashew, and a nice cut of acidity. **RATING** 89 **DRINK** 2008 $ 23
Il Vescovo 2002 Aromatic, tangy and spicy; persistent tannins; genuine Italian style. Sangiovese 70%, Cabernet Sauvignon 30%. **RATING** 88 **DRINK** Now $ 20
Verdelho 2004 Nice fruit salad with some length and life; clean finish and aftertaste. **RATING** 87 **DRINK** Now $ 16

ㅜㅜㅜ♀ **Unwooded Chardonnay 2004** **RATING** 84 **DRINK** Now $ 15

Chapman's Creek Vineyard NR

RMS 447 Yelverton Road, Wilyabrup, WA 6280 **REGION** Margaret River
T (08) 9755 7545 **F** (08) 9755 7571 **OPEN** 7 days 10.30–4.30
WINEMAKER Various Contract **EST.** 1989 **CASES** 5000
SUMMARY Chapman's Creek was founded by the late Tony Lord, an extremely experienced wine journalist who for many years was editor and part-owner of *Decanter* magazine of the UK, one of the leaders in the field. Notwithstanding this, he was always reticent about seeking any publicity for Chapman's Creek; why, I do not know. Regrettably, it is now too late to find out, as he died in February 2002. Chapman's Creek will continue to be managed by his long-term pal, Chris Leach, who was one of those who kept an eye on him throughout his prolonged illness.

Chapman Valley Wines NR

Lot 14 Howatharra Road, Nanson, Chapman Valley via Geraldton, WA 6530 **REGION** Central Western Australia Zone
T (08) 9920 5148 **F** (08) 9920 5206 **WEB** www.chapmanvalleywines.com.au **OPEN** 7 days 10–5
WINEMAKER Stephen Murfit (Contract) **EST.** 1995 **CASES** 5500

SUMMARY Chapman Valley Wines is Western Australia's most northern winery, situated 30 km northeast of Geraldton in the picturesque valley which gives the business its name. A hobby on a nearby property led to the establishment of 5 ha of vines in 1995, followed by a further 3 ha in 1999. The varieties are varied but strictly mainstream: semillon, chenin blanc, chardonnay, verdelho, sauvignon blanc, shiraz, merlot, cabernet sauvignon and (somewhat rarer) zinfandel. The wines are made by Steve Murfit at Lilac Hill Estate in the Swan Valley, and are chiefly sold by mail order and through the cellar door, which is complemented by a restaurant with a full food selection, offering inside or outdoor seating under gazebos. It also caters for evening functions by arrangement.

Charles Cimicky ★★★★☆

Gomersal Road, Lyndoch, SA 5351 **REGION** Barossa Valley
T (08) 8524 4025 **F** (08) 8524 4772 **OPEN** Tues–Sat 10.30–4.30
WINEMAKER Charles Cimicky **EST.** 1972 **CASES** 15 000
SUMMARY These wines are of very good quality, thanks to the lavish (but sophisticated) use of new French oak in tandem with high-quality grapes. The intense, long-flavoured Sauvignon Blanc has been a particularly consistent performer, as has the rich, voluptuous American-oaked Signature Shiraz. Limited retail distribution in South Australia, Victoria, New South Wales and Western Australia, with exports to the UK, the US, Switzerland, Canada, Malaysia and Hong Kong.

ΨΨΨΨΨ **Trumps Shiraz 2003** Densely coloured, the wine has lush blackberry, plum, prune and spice aromas and flavours, with echoes of bitter chocolate on the finish, and well-handled oak. **RATING** 93 **DRINK** 2013 $16
The Autograph Shiraz 2003 Stylish wine; abundant, gently ripe plum and black fruits on the mid-palate; long, gently savoury, dry finish; fine tannins. **RATING** 92 **DRINK** 2015 $35
Reserve Shiraz 2002 Big, powerful blackberry fruit; persistent tannins. **RATING** 90 **DRINK** 2017 $60

ΨΨΨΨ **Allegro Rosso Cabernet Sauvignon Rose 2004** **RATING** 86 **DRINK** Now $16

Charles Melton ★★★★★

Krondorf Road, Tanunda, SA 5352 **REGION** Barossa Valley
T (08) 8563 3606 **F** (08) 8563 3422 **WEB** www.charlesmeltonwines.com.au **OPEN** 7 days 11–5
WINEMAKER Charlie Melton, Nicola Ormond **EST.** 1984 **CASES** 18 000
SUMMARY Charlie Melton, one of the Barossa Valley's great characters, with wife Virginia by his side, makes some of the most eagerly sought à la mode wines in Australia. Inevitably, the Melton empire grew in response to the insatiable demand, with a doubling of estate vineyards to 13 ha (and the exclusive management and offtake of a further 10 ha) and the erection of a new barrel store in 1996. The expanded volume has had no adverse effect on the wonderfully rich, sweet and well-made wines. Exports to all major markets.

ΨΨΨΨΨ **Shiraz 2002** Elegant, medium-bodied; excellent texture and structure; fine, intense black fruits, no hint of alcohol heat; integrated oak, long, lingering finish. **RATING** 96 **DRINK** 2017 $41.90
Nine Popes 2002 Fragrant, spicy aromas; has far more structure than many such blends, but not over the top; a delicious compote of black fruits, red fruits and a variety of spices. **RATING** 95 **DRINK** 2012 $43.90
Cabernet Sauvignon 2002 Voluptuous cassis and blackcurrant aromas and flavours drive the wine; ripe tannins, perfectly integrated oak. **RATING** 95 **DRINK** 2017 $43
Rose of Virginia 2004 Vivid red-purple; as ever, bursting with strawberry and raspberry aroma and flavour, yet retains delicacy. **RATING** 94 **DRINK** Now $18.90

Charles Reuben Estate ★★☆

777 Middle Tea Tree Road, Tea Tree, Tas 7017 **REGION** Southern Tasmania
T (03) 6268 1702 **F** (03) 6231 3571 **OPEN** Wed–Sun 10–5
WINEMAKER Tim Krushka **EST.** 1990 **CASES** 350
SUMMARY Charles Reuben Estate has 1.5 ha of pinot noir, 0.5 ha of chardonnay and a few rows of riesling in production. It has also planted 1.2 ha of the four Bordeaux varieties, headed by cabernet sauvignon, with a little cabernet franc, merlot and petit verdot, and 0.6 ha of sauvignon blanc plus a few rows of semillon.

ŸŸŸ⍩ **Pinot Noir 2002** RATING 85 DRINK 2007

ŸŸŸ **Unwooded Chardonnay 2004** RATING 83
Chardonnay 2002 RATING 82

Charles Sturt University Winery ★★★☆

McKeown Drive (off Coolamon Road) Wagga Wagga, NSW 2650 REGION Big Rivers Zone
T (02) 6933 2435 F (02) 6933 4072 WEB www.csu.edu.au/winery/ OPEN Mon–Fri 11–5,
weekends 11–4
WINEMAKER Andrew Drumm EST. 1977 CASES 15 000
SUMMARY A totally new $2.5 million commercial winery (replacing the 1977 winery) was opened in
2002, complementing the $1 million experimental winery opened in June 2001. The commercial
winery has been funded through the sale of wines produced under the Charles Sturt University
brand; these always offer the consumer good value. Interestingly, this teaching facility is using
screwcaps for all its wines, white and red.

ŸŸŸŸ **Shiraz 2003** Powerful, robust wine with black fruits and plum; plenty of tannins and
structure; considerable ageing potential; very good price. Big Rivers/Gundagai. Screwcap.
RATING 89 DRINK 2012 $13.20
Sauvignon Blanc 2004 Clean, fresh, ripe tropical/gooseberry aromas and flavours;
balanced finish. Cowra/Gundagai/Wagga/Yarra. Screwcap. RATING 88 DRINK 2007
$13.20

ŸŸŸ⍩ **Cabernet Sauvignon Merlot 2003** RATING 86 DRINK 2009 $13.20
Limited Release Chardonnay Pinot Noir 2000 RATING 86 DRINK 2008 $19.80

Charlotte Plains NR

RMB 3180, Dooleys Road, Maryborough, Vic 3465 REGION Bendigo
T (03) 5361 3137 OPEN By appointment
WINEMAKER Roland Kaval EST. 1990 CASES 80
SUMMARY Charlotte Plains is a classic example of miniaturism. Production comes from a close-
planted vineyard which is only 1.6 ha, part being shiraz, the remainder sauvignon blanc. The
minuscule production is sold solely through the mailing list and by phone.

Charlotte's Vineyard NR

Kentucky Road, Merricks North, Vic 3926 REGION Mornington Peninsula
T (03) 5989 7266 F (03) 5989 7500 OPEN 7 days 11–5
WINEMAKER Michael Wyles EST. 1987 CASES NFP
SUMMARY Susan Wyles has purchased the former 3-ha Hanns Creek Vineyard and renamed it
Charlotte's Vineyard. The quality of the first releases was impeccable.

Chartley Estate ★★★

38 Blackwood Hills Road, Rowella, Tas 7270 REGION Northern Tasmania
T (03) 6394 7198 F (03) 6394 7598 OPEN 7 days 10–5
WINEMAKER Julian Alcorso, Leigh Clarnette (Contract) EST. 2000 CASES 180
SUMMARY The Kossman family began the establishment of 2 ha each of riesling, sauvignon blanc and
pinot noir, and 1 ha of pinot gris, in 2000. Some appealing Pinot Gris has been made.

ŸŸŸŸ **Pinot Gris 2004** Very pale coloured; lively apple, citrus and pear mix; clean finish.
RATING 87 DRINK 2008 $24.95

ŸŸŸ **Riesling 2004** RATING 82 $21

Chateau Champsaur NR

Wandang Lane, Forbes, NSW 2871 REGION Central Ranges Zone
T (02) 6852 3908 F (02) 6852 3902 OPEN Saturday 10–5, or by appointment
WINEMAKER Pierre Dalle, Andrew McEwin EST. 1866 CASES 200

SUMMARY Yes, the establishment date of 1866 is correct. In that year Frenchmen Joseph Bernard Raymond and Auguste Nicolas took up a 130-ha selection and erected a large wooden winery and cellar, with production ranging up to 360,000 litres in a year in its heyday. They named it Champsaur after Raymond's native valley in France, and it is said to be the oldest French winery in the southern hemisphere. In recent years it traded as Lachlan Valley Wines, but under the ownership of Pierre Dalle it has reverted to its traditional name and French ownership.

Chateau Dore NR

303 Mandurang Road, Mandurang near Bendigo, Vic 3551 **REGION** Bendigo
T (03) 5439 5278 **OPEN** 7 days 10–5
WINEMAKER Ivan Grose **EST.** 1860 **CASES** 1000
SUMMARY Has been in the ownership of the Grose family since 1860, with the winery buildings dating back to 1860 and 1893. All wine is sold through the cellar door and function centre.

Chateau Dorrien

Cnr Seppeltsfield Road/Barossa Valley Way, Dorrien, SA 5352 **REGION** Barossa Valley
T (08) 8562 2850 **F** (08) 8562 1416 **OPEN** 7 days 10–5
WINEMAKER Fernando Martin, Ramon Martin **EST.** 1985 **CASES** 2000
SUMMARY The Martin family, headed by Fernando and Jeanette, purchased the old Dorrien winery from the Seppelt family in 1984, officially opening it as Chateau Dorrien on 13 January 1985. In 1990 the family purchased Twin Valley Estate, and moved the winemaking operations of Chateau Dorrien to the Twin Valley site. All the Chateau Dorrien group wines are sold at Chateau Dorrien; Twin Valley is simply a production facility. Exports to Singapore and the US.

Chateau Francois

Broke Road, Pokolbin, NSW 2321 **REGION** Lower Hunter Valley
T (02) 4998 7548 **F** (02) 4998 7805 **OPEN** Weekends 9–5, or by appointment
WINEMAKER Don Francois **EST.** 1969 **CASES** 300
SUMMARY The retirement hobby of former NSW Director of Fisheries, Don Francois. He makes soft-flavoured and structured wines which frequently show regional characters but which are modestly priced and are all sold through the cellar door and by the mailing list to a loyal following. The tasting room is available for private dinners for 12–16 people. Don Francois sailed through a quadruple bypass followed by a mild stroke with his sense of humour intact, if not enhanced. A subsequent newsletter said (inter alia) '... my brush with destiny has changed my grizzly personality and I am now sweetness and light ... Can you believe? Well, almost!' He even promises comfortable tasting facilities. The 1997 Semillon won top gold in its class at the 2004 Hunter Valley Wine Show; a most beautiful, mature wine.

Chateau Leamon

5528 Calder Highway, Bendigo, Vic 3550 **REGION** Bendigo
T (03) 5447 7995 **F** (03) 5447 0855 **WEB** www.chateauleamon.com.au **OPEN** Wed–Mon 10–5
WINEMAKER Ian Leamon **EST.** 1973 **CASES** 2500
SUMMARY One of the longest-established wineries in the region, with estate and locally grown shiraz and cabernet family grapes providing the excellent red wines. Limited retail distribution in Victoria, New South Wales and Queensland; exports to the UK, Asia and Canada.

▼▼▼▼▽ **Reserve Shiraz 2003** Medium-bodied; slightly more intensity than the varietal Shiraz; notes of dark chocolate and good vanilla oak; supple tannins. Quality cork. **RATING** 93 **DRINK** 2013 $ 38
Reserve Cabernet Sauvignon 2003 Fragrant blackcurrant and cassis with a whisper of chocolate; medium-bodied, supple and smooth; silky tannins, controlled oak. Cork. **RATING** 93 **DRINK** 2015 $ 38
Bendigo Shiraz 2003 Medium-bodied; has some elegance despite 15° alcohol; intense, savoury, spicy black fruits; fine-grained tannins. Screwcap. **RATING** 91 **DRINK** 2013 $ 22

▼▼▼▼ **Bendigo Cabernet Sauvignon Cabernet Franc Merlot 2003** Very much at the savoury, earthy, leafy, briary end of the spectrum. Cork. **RATING** 87 **DRINK** 2008 $ 22

Chateau Pâto ★★★★★

Thompson's Road, Pokolbin, NSW 2321 **REGION** Lower Hunter Valley
T (02) 4998 7634 **F** (02) 4998 7860 **OPEN** By appointment
WINEMAKER Nicholas Paterson **EST.** 1980 **CASES** 300
SUMMARY Nicholas Paterson took over responsibility for this tiny winery following the death of father David Paterson during the 1993 vintage. The winery has 2.5 ha of shiraz, 1 ha of chardonnay and 0.5 ha of pinot noir; most of the grapes are sold, with a tiny quantity of shiraz being made into a marvellous wine. David Paterson's inheritance is being handsomely guarded.

ŶŶŶŶŶ Shiraz 2003 Very good colour; shows the great vintage to full advantage; lovely blackberry, plum fruit with spicy/earthy/licorice nuances; long finish. Screwcap. **RATING** 94 **DRINK** 2018 $ 38

Chateau Tanunda ★★★★

9 Basedow Road, Tanunda, SA 5352 **REGION** Barossa Valley
T (08) 8563 3888 **F** (08) 8563 1422 **WEB** www.chateautanunda.com **OPEN** 7 days 10–5
WINEMAKER Ralph Fowler **EST.** 1890 **CASES** 12 000
SUMMARY This is one of the most imposing winery buildings in the Barossa Valley, built from stone quarried at nearby Bethany in the late 1880s. It started life as a winery, then became a specialist brandy distillery until the death of the Australian brandy industry, whereafter it was simply used as storage cellars. It has now been completely restored, and converted to a major convention facility catering for groups of up to 400. The large complex also houses a cellar door where the Chateau Tanunda wines are sold; Chateau Bistro, gardens and a croquet lawn; the Barossa Small Winemakers Centre, offering wines made by small independent winemakers in the region; and, finally, specialist support services for tour operators. It is a sister winery to Cowra Estate, as both are owned by the Geber family. Prior to the 2005 vintage Ralph Fowler joined the business as full-time chief winemaker, leaving Ralph Fowler Wines in the care of his daughter, Sarah Squires.

ŶŶŶŶŶ Grand Barossa Shiraz 2002 Powerful blackberry, plum and prune mix; plenty of structure and tannins; balanced oak. **RATING** 90 **DRINK** 2012 $ 33
The Chateau Cabernet Sauvignon 2002 Good colour; medium-bodied; nice counterbalance between earthy blackberry fruit and gently sweet vanilla oak; quality tannins, long finish. Cork. **RATING** 90 **DRINK** 2012 $ 28

ŶŶŶŶ Barossa Tower Shiraz 2002 RATING 85 **DRINK** 2008 $ 18

Chatsfield ★★★★☆

O'Neil Road, Mount Barker, WA 6324 **REGION** Mount Barker
T (08) 9851 1704 **F** (08) 9851 2660 **WEB** www.chatsfield.com.au **OPEN** By appointment
WINEMAKER Dionne Miller **EST.** 1976 **CASES** 4000
SUMMARY Irish-born medical practitioner Ken Lynch can be proud of his achievements at Chatsfield, as can most of the various contract winemakers who have taken the high-quality estate-grown material and made some impressive wines, notably the Riesling and spicy licorice Shiraz. Exports to the US, Ireland and Japan.

ŶŶŶŶŶ Reserve Shiraz 2003 Vigorous spicy black cherry, blackberry, plum and licorice; quality French oak supports the fruit and long finish; 160 cases made. Diam. **RATING** 94 **DRINK** 2016 $ 25

ŶŶŶŶŶ Mount Barker Chardonnay 2004 Piercing, lively nectarine and citrus fruit; subtle, integrated French oak; long finish. Screwcap. **RATING** 93 **DRINK** 2012 $ 17.50

ŶŶŶŶ Mount Barker Riesling 2004 Very pale; light, crisp mineral and lime blossom aromas and flavours; clean finish; will develop. Screwcap. **RATING** 89 **DRINK** 2010 $ 15
Sweet White 2004 Crisp, clean, minerally; light touch of lime blossom; barely off-dry. Time please. Screwcap. **RATING** 87 **DRINK** 2010 $ 12

ŶŶŶŶ Cabernet Franc 2004 RATING 86 **DRINK** Now $ 17.50

Chatto Wines ★★★★★

McDonalds Road, Pokolbin, NSW 2325 **REGION** Lower Hunter Valley
T 0417 109 794 **F** (02) 4998 7294 **WEB** www.chattowines.com.au **OPEN** 7 days 9–5
WINEMAKER Jim Chatto **EST.** 2000 **CASES** 5000
SUMMARY Jim Chatto spent several years in Tasmania as the first winemaker at Rosevears Estate, and indeed helped design the Rosevears winery. He has since moved to the Hunter Valley to work for Monarch Winemaking Services, but has used his Tasmanian contacts to buy small parcels of riesling and pinot noir. Possessed of a particularly good palate, he has made wines of excellent quality under the Chatto label. He was a star Len Evans Tutorial scholar and is an up-and-coming wine show judge. Exports to Canada and Denmark.

TTTTT **Hunter Valley Shiraz 2003** Medium-bodied; smooth but tight texture; pure blackberry and cherry fruit; balanced oak and extract; very fine tannins; long haul. Screwcap.
RATING 94 **DRINK** 2018 $ 35

TTTTY **Tamar Valley Pinot Noir 2003** Highly aromatic, spicy, charry plum and black cherry bouquet; elegant, medium-bodied palate tightens up nicely. Quality cork. **RATING** 93
DRINK 2010 $ 35
Canberra District Riesling 2004 Bone-dry, minerally and crisp; herb and lemon, almost into Semillon; will grow in bottle. Screwcap. **RATING** 90 **DRINK** 2009 $ 17.50

Chepstowe Vineyard NR

178 Fitzpatricks Lane, Carngham, Vic 3351 **REGION** Ballarat
T (03) 5344 9412 **WEB** www.chepstowevineyard.com **OPEN** Weekends 10–5, or by appointment
WINEMAKER Matt Thain, Sally Thain **EST.** 1994 **CASES** 1500
SUMMARY Way back in 1983 Bill Wallace asked the then Yellowglen winemaker Dominique Landragin what he thought about the suitability of a block of steeply sloping grazing land on the side of the Chepstowe Hill, looking northeast across to the Grampians and its various mountains, including Mt Misery. Landragin replied, 'it might be possible to grow grapes there', and Wallace subsequently acquired the property. It was not until November 1994 that 1 ha each of pinot noir and chardonnay was planted, followed by an additional hectare of pinot noir in 1996. In the warmest of vintages it is possible to obtain full ripeness for table wines, but in normal years I suspect sparkling wine (of potentially high quality) might be the best option.

Chestnut Grove ★★★★

Chestnut Grove Road, Manjimup, WA 6258 **REGION** Manjimup
T (08) 9772 4255 **F** (08) 9772 4543 **WEB** www.chestnutgrove.com.au **OPEN** By appointment
WINEMAKER Mark Aitken, Virginia Willcock **EST.** 1988 **CASES** 12 000
SUMMARY A substantial vineyard (18 ha) which is now mature, and the erection of an onsite winery are the most obvious signs of change, but ownership, too, has been passed on by the late founder Vic Kordic to his sons Paul (a Perth lawyer) and Mark (the general manager of the wine business) and thence (in 2002) to Mike Calneggia's Australian Wine Holdings Limited group. Exports to Canada, Denmark, Germany, Hong Kong, Singapore and the UK.

TTTTY **Tall Timber Sauvignon Blanc Semillon 2004** Medium-bodied; generous, well balanced, driven by ripe passionfruit and gooseberry, then tangy acidity to close. Screwcap.
RATING 93 **DRINK** 2008 $ 16
Estate Chardonnay 2003 Elegant stone fruit and citrus; subtle, spicy barrel ferment inputs; good length and acidity. Cork. **RATING** 90 **DRINK** 2008 $ 32

TTTT **Tall Timber Shiraz Cabernet 2003** Medium-bodied, but quite firm and fresh; red and black fruits, fine tannins. **RATING** 89 **DRINK** 2010 $ 16
Cabernet Merlot 2001 Medium-bodied; savoury black fruits and spices; earth and bitter chocolate overtones. Cork. **RATING** 89 **DRINK** 2010 $ 20

TTTY **Verdelho 2004** **RATING** 84 **DRINK** Now $ 20

Chestnut Hill Vineyard ★★★★

1280 Pakenham Road, Mount Burnett, Vic 3781 **REGION** Gippsland
T (03) 5942 7314 **F** (03) 5942 7314 **WEB** www.chestnuthillvineyard.com.au **OPEN** Weekends & public
hols 10.30–5.30, or by appointment
WINEMAKER Charlie Javor **EST.** 1995 **CASES** 1200
SUMMARY Charlie and Ivka Javor started Chestnut Hill with small plantings of chardonnay,
sauvignon blanc and pinot noir in 1985 and have slowly increased the vineyards to their present total
of a little over 3 ha. The first wines were made in 1995, and all distribution is through the cellar door
and direct to a few restaurants. Less than one hour's drive from Melbourne, the picturesque vineyard
is situated among the rolling hills in the southeast of the Dandenongs near Mt Burnett. The label
explains, 'Liberty is a gift we had never experienced in our homeland', which was Croatia, from which
they emigrated in the late 1960s.

TTTTT **Mount Burnett Sauvignon Blanc 2004** Minerally, grassy green pea aromas; picks up the
pace on the back palate and long finish. Cork. **RATING** 90 **DRINK** 2007 $ 24

TTTT **Mount Burnett Pinot Noir 2003** Light to medium-bodied; distinctly savoury, spicy, briary
aromas and flavours, though within the Pinot Noir spectrum; some red cherry fruit.
Quality cork. **RATING** 88 **DRINK** 2007 $ 27.50

TTTT **Mount Burnett Chardonnay 2003 RATING** 86 **DRINK** Now $ 27.50

Cheviot Bridge/Long Flat ★★★★

10/499 St Kilda Road, Melbourne, Vic 3004 (postal) **REGION** Upper Goulburn
T (03) 9820 9080 **F** (03) 9820 9070 **WEB** www.cheviotbridge.com.au **OPEN** Not
WINEMAKER Hugh Cuthbertson **EST.** 1998 **CASES** NFP
SUMMARY Cheviot Bridge/Long Flat brings together a highly experienced team of wine industry
professionals and investors who provided the $10 million-plus required to purchase the Long Flat
range of wines from Tyrrell's; the purchase took place in the second half of 2003. In November 2004
the group acquired the listed vehicle Winepros Limited, changing its name to Cheviot Bridge
Limited, and also acquiring the Terrace Vale brand, with an option to acquire its assets. The bulk of
the business activity in the future will be that of virtual winery, acquiring bulk and/or bottled wine
from various third party suppliers. The brands (other than those of Terrace Vale) include Cheviot
Bridge Yea Valley, Cheviot Bridge CB, Kissing Bridge, Thirsty Lizard, Long Flat and the The Long
Flat Wine Co. The wines all represent outstanding value. Exports to all major markets.

TTTTT **Cheviot Bridge Yea Valley Shiraz 2003** A complex array of plum, blackberry and
blueberry fruits; very good structure and mouthfeel; oak in restraint. A bargain.
RATING 94 **DRINK** 2013 $ 18

TTTTT **The Long Flat Wine Co. Yarra Valley Pinot Noir 2003** Abundant varietal plum and spice
aromas and flavours, off-set by a pleasingly savoury finish sustaining the length and
aftertaste. **RATING** 92 **DRINK** Now $ 9.99

TTTT **The Long Flat Wine Co. Adelaide Hills Sauvignon Blanc 2004** Clean; tropical
gooseberry palate; good length; crisp finish. Utterly remarkable value. **RATING** 89
DRINK Now $ 11
Cheviot Bridge Yea Valley Riesling 2004 Quite rich overall; substantial palate with
tropical-accented fruit. **RATING** 88 **DRINK** 2008 $ 18
Cheviot Bridge CB Adelaide Hills Chardonnay 2004 Bright green-yellow; light-bodied,
elegant and well balanced; a hint of oak (probably chips) well handled; nectarine and
stone fruit flavours; value plus. **RATING** 88 **DRINK** 2007 $ 17
Cheviot Bridge Heathcote Shiraz 2004 Bright purple-red; fresh, simple, fruit-forward
style; bright cherry and plum; minimal tannins. Highly likely mico-oxygenation used.
Synthetic. **RATING** 87 **DRINK** 2008 $ 12.50

TTTT **Cheviot Bridge CB Yarra Valley Cabernet Merlot 2003 RATING** 86 **DRINK** 2007 $ 12
The Long Flat Wine Co. Coonawarra Cabernet Sauvignon 2002 RATING 86 **DRINK** Now
$ 9.99
Cheviot Bridge CB Classic Dry White 2004 RATING 84 **DRINK** Now $ 12

Chidlow's Well Estate NR

PO Box 84, Chidlow, WA 6556 **REGION** Perth Hills
T (08) 9572 3770 **F** (08) 9572 3750 **OPEN** By appointment
WINEMAKER Rob Marshall **EST.** 2002 **CASES** 500
SUMMARY Chidlow is around 60 km east of Perth, and was originally known as Chidlows Well; its railway station was a hub for train services to the interior of the state. While within the Perth Hills region, it is some way distant from the majority of the wineries in the region. Rod and Marilyn Lange have 3 ha of chardonnay, chenin blanc and shiraz, using the experience and skill of Rob Marshall as contract winemaker. The sales are by word-of-mouth, mail order and through the cellar door (by appointment).

Chittering Valley Winery/Nesci Estate Wines NR

Lot 12 Great Northern Highway, Chittering, WA 6084 **REGION** Perth Hills
T (08) 9571 4102 **F** (08) 9571 4288 **OPEN** Not
WINEMAKER Kevin Nesci **EST.** 1948 **CASES** NA
SUMMARY The roots of this business go back well over 50 years. Kevin Nesci has 25 ha of sauvignon blanc, chenin blanc, semillon, chardonnay, pinot noir, grenache, merlot, shiraz, cabernet sauvignon, zinfandel and pedro ximinez. Most of the grape production is sold; a lesser amount is made onsite, and sold by mail order.

Chiverton NR

605 Mid Western Highway, Cowra, NSW 2794 **REGION** Cowra
T (02) 6342 9308 **F** (02) 6342 9314 **OPEN** Weekends & public hols 10–4
WINEMAKER Simon Gilbert (Contract) **EST.** 1994 **CASES** NA
SUMMARY Greg Thompson began the development of Chiverton in 1994; in 1998 a cellar door and small tasting room attached to the Chiverton Homestead were opened. The wines are sold under the Chiverton, Billygoat Hill and Nude Estate labels, with exports to England. Much of the production from the 107 ha of semillon, chardonnay, verdelho, cabernet sauvignon, merlot and shiraz is sold to other wineries.

Chrismont Wines ★★★☆

Upper King Valley Road, Cheshunt, Vic 3678 **REGION** King Valley
T (03) 5729 8220 **F** (03) 5729 8253 **WEB** www.chrismontwines.com.au **OPEN** 7 days 11–5
WINEMAKER Warren Proft **EST.** 1980 **CASES** NA
SUMMARY Arnold (Arnie) and Jo Pizzini have established 80 ha of vineyards in the Whitfield area of the Upper King Valley. They have planted riesling, sauvignon blanc, chardonnay, pinot gris, cabernet sauvignon, merlot, shiraz, barbera, marzemino and arneis. The La Zona range ties in the Italian parentage of the Pizzinis, and is part of the intense interest in all things Italian.

Christmas Hill ★★★★

RSD 25C, Meadows, SA 5201 (postal) **REGION** Adelaide Hills
T (08) 8388 3779 **F** (08) 8388 3759 **OPEN** Not
WINEMAKER Peter Leske (Contract) **EST.** 2000 **CASES** 1000
SUMMARY Christmas Hill is primarily a grapegrower, selling all but a small part of its production from the 12.5 ha of chardonnay, sauvignon blanc, shiraz, cabernet sauvignon and pinot noir, but keeping back the equivalent of around 100 cases of Sauvignon Blanc, which is made for Christmas Hill by Peter Leske at Nepenthe Wines. It is primarily sold to two leading Adelaide clubs, a restaurant and through Christmas Hill's mailing list, with a dribble finding its way onto the Adelaide retail market. It is offered only by the case to mailing list customers.

ΥΥΥΥΥ Kuitpo Adelaide Hills Sauvignon Blanc 2004 Spotlessly clean; lots of herbaceous varietal fruit expression on the bouquet; tangy, herbal mineral mouth; crisp, lemony acidity. Screwcap. **RATING** 92 **DRINK** 2007 $ 14

Churchview Estate ★★★☆

Cnr Bussell Highway/Gale Road, Metricup, WA 6280 **REGION** Margaret River
T (08) 9755 7200 **F** (08) 9755 7300 **WEB** www.churchview.com.au **OPEN** Mon–Sat 9.30–5.30
WINEMAKER Bill Crappsley (Contract) **EST.** 1998 **CASES** 18 000
SUMMARY The Fokkema family, headed by Spike Fokkema, immigrated from The Netherlands in the 1950s. Their business success in the following decades led to the acquisition of the 100-ha Churchview Estate property in 1997, and to the progressive establishment of 56 ha of vineyards, with another 14 ha scheduled for planting by 2007. This will result in production rising from the present 18 000 cases to 60 000 cases, sustained by exports to Asia and The Netherlands. The family lives onsite, and carries out much of the viticultural work, with the vineyard canopy managed on the Smart Dyson model. Yields are controlled to 10 tonnes per hectare, and veteran West Australian winemaker Bill Crappsley is in charge, producing consistently good wines.

Ciavarella ★★★☆

Evans Lane, Oxley, Vic 3678 **REGION** King Valley
T (03) 5727 3384 **F** (03) 5727 3384 **OPEN** Mon–Sat 9–6, Sun 10–6
WINEMAKER Cyril Ciavarella, Tony Ciavarella **EST.** 1978 **CASES** 3000
SUMMARY Cyril and Jan Ciavarella both entered the wine industry from other professions; they have been producing wine since 1992. The vineyard was planted in 1978, with plantings and varieties being extended over the years. One variety, aucerot (first released in 375 ml bottles late 2001) was first produced by Maurice O'Shea of McWilliam's Mount Pleasant in the Hunter Valley 50 or more years ago; the Ciavarella vines have been grown from cuttings collected from an old Glenrowan vineyard before the parent plants were removed in the mid-1980s. A purpose-built tasting room has been added to the winery. Tony Ciavarella left a career in agricultural research in mid-2003 to join his parents at Ciavarella.

TTTT **Oxley Estate Chardonnay 2003** Honeyed, nutty aromas; peach and stone fruit, subtle oak; good acid balance. **RATING** 87 **DRINK** 2008 $ 19
Oxley Estate Chenin Blanc 2004 Fresh, elegant fruit salad; good varietal presence; not sweet. **RATING** 87 **DRINK** Now $ 18
Oxley Estate Shiraz Viognier 2002 Spicy, savoury aromas, with some lifted fruit characters ex the Viognier; light to medium-bodied, minimal tannins. **RATING** 87 **DRINK** 2010 $ 22
Oxley Estate Durif 2001 Much lighter and more savoury than most examples of the variety; quite tangy and earthy, plus a touch of chocolate; bottle development obvious. **RATING** 87 **DRINK** Now $ 28

TTTY **Oxley Estate Verdelho 2004** **RATING** 86 **DRINK** 2007 $ 18
Oxley Estate Cabernet Merlot 2002 **RATING** 84 **DRINK** 2007 $ 20

Clairault ★★★★☆

Caves Road, Wilyabrup, WA 6280 **REGION** Margaret River
T (08) 9755 6225 **F** (08) 9755 6229 **WEB** www.clairaultwines.com.au **OPEN** 7 days 10–5
WINEMAKER Will Shields **EST.** 1976 **CASES** 35 000
SUMMARY Bill and Ena Martin, with sons Conor, Brian and Shane, acquired Clairault several years ago. This has led to a major expansion of the vineyards on the 120-ha property. The 12 ha of vines established by the Lewises (these are up to 30 years old) are being supplemented by another 70 ha of vines on the property, with an end-point ratio of 70% red varieties to 30% white varieties. The restaurant is open for lunch 7 days. Domestic distribution throughout all states; exports to the UK, the US and other major markets.

TTTTY **Sauvignon Blanc 2004** Spotlessly clean, highly aromatic and flavoured passionfruit/tropical fruit mix, balanced by lingering acidity. Cork. **RATING** 93 **DRINK** 2007 $ 19.50
Estate Semillon 2004 A complex wine, highlighted by squeaky acidity balancing the rich fruit and a touch of toasty, spicy oak; works well; long finish. Cork. **RATING** 92 **DRINK** 2008 $ 23
Estate Cabernet Sauvignon 2002 Medium to full-bodied; clean and intense blackcurrant fruit supported by ripe tannins and quality French oak. Cork. **RATING** 92 **DRINK** 2015 $ 19.50

Margaret River Chardonnay 2003 Subtly complex amalgam of French barrel ferment and malolactic ferment inputs on melon fruit; understated but satisfying. Quality cork. **RATING** 91 **DRINK** 2009 $ 19.50

Margaret River Chardonnay 2004 Light to medium-bodied, fresh and lively; tangy citrus and stone fruit; subtle oak, long finish. Cork. **RATING** 90 **DRINK** 2007 $ 19.50

Cabernet Sauvignon 2002 A mix of ripe and more earthy savoury blackcurrant fruit; balanced tannins and oak. Cork. **RATING** 90 **DRINK** 2012 $ 30

ŤŤŤŤ **Swagman's Sauvignon Blanc Semillon 2004** Lively and fresh, the Semillon component (one-third) adding herbal notes to the bouquet; good length and balance. **RATING** 89 **DRINK** 2007 $ 14.99

Estate Cabernet Merlot 2002 Strong regional notes to the earthy tannins; the black fruits, too, tend to the austere, dry side of the spectrum. Cork. **RATING** 89 **DRINK** 2012 $ 28

Swagman's Cabernet Merlot 2002 Medium-bodied, with quite firm, dark berry fruits and integrated tannins; long finish; needs time. **RATING** 88 **DRINK** 2012 $ 14.99

Clancy's of Conargo

NR

Killone Park, Conargo Road, Deniliquin, NSW 2710 **REGION** Riverina
T (03) 5884 6684 **F** (03) 5884 6779 **OPEN** 7 days 10–6
WINEMAKER Bernard Clancy, Jason Clancy **EST.** 1999 **CASES** 1000
SUMMARY The Clancy family has been carrying on a mixed farming enterprise (lucerne growing, cropping and sheep production) on their property north of Deniliquin for over 25 years. A tiny planting of taminga was made in 1988, but it was not until 6 ha were planted in 1997 that the Clancys ventured into commercial grapegrowing and winemaking. The predominant varieties are shiraz and semillon, and all of the production is sold locally and through the cellar door.

Clarence Hill

★★★

PO Box 530, McLaren Vale, SA 5171 **REGION** McLaren Vale
T (08) 8323 8946 **F** (08) 8323 9644 **WEB** www.clarencehillwines.com.au **OPEN** Not
WINEMAKER Claudio Curtis, Brian Light (Contract) **EST.** 1990 **CASES** 50 000
SUMMARY In 1956 the Curtis family emigrated from Italy to Australia, and purchased its first vineyard land from one Clarence William Torrens Rivers. They renamed it Clarence Hill. Further land was acquired in the 1980s and 1990s, establishing the Landcross Farm and California Rise vineyards, which, together with Clarence Hill, now have over 100 ha in production. In 1990 Claudio Curtis, having acquired a science degree from the University of Adelaide, formed the Tiers Wine Co to undertake wine production and sales. A new winery adjacent to the company's vineyards is called Landcross Estate Winery, to complicate matters. Numerous additional, lower-rated wines tasted under the Landcross Estate label. Exports to the UK, the US and other major markets.

ŤŤŤŤ **Martins Road Shiraz Cabernet Sauvignon 2001** Medium-bodied; rich, ripe plum, blackberry, vanilla plus a dash of mocha and chocolate. Diam. **RATING** 87 **DRINK** 2009 $ 9

ŤŤŤŤ **Riesling 2003 RATING** 86 **DRINK** 2007 $ 12
McLaren Vale Chardonnay 2003 RATING 86 **DRINK** 2007 $ 14
McLaren Vale Shiraz 2001 RATING 86 **DRINK** 2008 $ 20
McLaren Vale Grenache Shiraz 2002 RATING 86 **DRINK** 2007 $ 15
Rose 2004 RATING 85 **DRINK** Now $ 14
McLaren Vale Shiraz 2002 RATING 85 **DRINK** 2007 $ 20
McLaren Vale Cabernet Sauvignon 2003 RATING 85 **DRINK** Now $ 20
McLaren Vale Sauvignon Blanc 2004 RATING 84 **DRINK** Now $ 14
McLaren Vale Cabernet Sauvignon Merlot 2002 RATING 84 $ 20

ŤŤŤ **Landcross Estate Chardonnay 2003 RATING** 83 $ 12
Landcross Estate Sauvignon Blanc 2004 RATING 82 $ 12
Martins Road Semillon Chardonnay 2004 RATING 82 $ 9

Clarendon Hills

★★★★☆

Brookmans Road, Blewitt Springs, SA 5171 **REGION** McLaren Vale
T (08) 8364 1484 **F** (08) 8364 1484 **OPEN** By appointment
WINEMAKER Roman Bratasiuk **EST.** 1989 **CASES** 12 000

SUMMARY Age and experience, it would seem, have mellowed Roman Bratasiuk – and the style of his wines. Once formidable and often rustic, they are now far more sculpted and smooth, at times bordering on downright elegance. Exports to the UK, the US and other major markets.

Classic McLaren Wines ★★★★

Lot B Coppermine Road, McLaren Vale, SA 5171 **REGION** McLaren Vale
T (08) 8323 9551 **F** (08) 8323 9551 **WEB** www.classicmclarenwines.com **OPEN** By appointment
WINEMAKER Tony De Lisio **EST.** 1996 **CASES** 7100
SUMMARY Tony and Krystina De Lisio have established a substantial business in a relatively short time. They have established vineyard plantings of shiraz (20.47 ha), merlot (11.34 ha), cabernet sauvignon (9.29 ha), semillon (3.9 ha) and chardonnay (0.41 ha), and are building a new winery and underground cellar storage for wine in barrel and packaged wine. When the new buildings are completed, there will be facilities for tastings, promotions and the possibility of limited cellar door sales. The wines are distributed in Sydney and Melbourne by Ultimo Wine Centre; Adelaide is serviced direct from the winery. Exports to the UK, the US, Thailand, Germany, Belgium, Switzerland and New Zealand have been established at impressively high prices.

ŸŸŸŸŸ **Cabernet Merlot 2001** Lashings of sweet blackcurrant, cassis and chocolate; smooth tannins, long finish, nice oak. Cork. **RATING** 92 **DRINK** 2011 $ 18
La Testa Shiraz 2001 Spicy black fruits, a dash of chocolate, and clever oak handling are the feature of a supple and smooth wine. **RATING** 90 **DRINK** 2013 $ 99
Shiraz 2001 Medium-bodied; supple, smooth, velvety and ripe; chocolate, vanilla and black fruit mix; soft tannins; subtle oak. Cork. **RATING** 90 **DRINK** 2010 $ 22
La Testa Cabernet Sauvignon 2001 Sweet black fruits; soft, supple tannins; spicy, sweet choc-malt vanilla oak. Cork. **RATING** 90 **DRINK** 2011 $ 45

ŸŸŸŸ **La Testa Merlot 2001** Ripe, rich black fruit typical of McLaren Vale; good balance and mouthfeel; fine tannins. Very stained cork. **RATING** 89 **DRINK** 2010 $ 39
Semillon Sauvignon Blanc 2003 Solidly structured, medium to full-bodied; a mix of herbaceous and gooseberry fruit; good balance. Screwcap. **RATING** 87 **DRINK** 2008 $ 12

ŸŸŸŸ **Grenache 2001 RATING** 86 **DRINK** Now $ 16
La Testa Grenache 2001 RATING 86 **DRINK** 207 $ 32

Clayfield Wines ★★★★☆

Wilde Lane, Moyston, Vic 3377 **REGION** Grampians
T (03) 5354 2689 **WEB** www.clayfieldwines.com **OPEN** Mon–Sat 10–5, Sun 11–4
WINEMAKER Simon Clayfield **EST.** 1997 **CASES** 500
SUMMARY Former long-serving Best's winemaker Simon Clayfield and wife Kaye are now doing their own thing. They have planted 2 ha of shiraz between 1997 and 1999, and after early vintages from 1999 to 2001, would have produced a substantial crop in 2002 were it not for a grass fire a month before vintage. The volumes so far made are tiny, and the Clayfields expect to be producing more than 750 cases of Shiraz by 2005. The splendid Black Label Shiraz sold for $45 at the cellar door and is distributed through Woods Wines Pty Ltd (03) 9381 2263, and at Armadale Cellars, High Street, Prahran. Currently one-third of the production is exported to the US.

ŸŸŸŸŸ **Grampians Shiraz 2002** Very ripe, essency blackberry and blackcurrant aromas; similar jammy fruit; no alcohol heat (only 14.5°); perhaps grape shrivel. High-quality cork.
RATING 91 **DRINK** 2015 $ 48
Massif Shiraz 2002 Elegant, light to medium-bodied wine; spicy and peppery, at the other end of the spectrum to Grampians; brisk finish. Screwcap. **RATING** 90 **DRINK** 2010 $ 24

Claymore Wines ★★★★☆

Leasingham Road, Leasingham, SA 5452 **REGION** Clare Valley
T (08) 8351 7963 **F** (08) 8125 7963 **WEB** www.claymorewines.com.au **OPEN** Weekends & public hols 10–5
WINEMAKER David Mavor **EST.** 1998 **CASES** 5000
SUMMARY Claymore Wines draws on various vineyards, some situated in the Clare Valley, others in McLaren Vale. The Kupu-Kupu Vineyard at Penwortham has 9 ha of shiraz and 2 ha of merlot

planted in 1997; the Nocturne series of Wines come from the Wilpena and Moray Park vineyards owned by the Trott family; the Joshua Tree Watervale Riesling comes from old vines on the Leasingham-Mintaro Road which are not estate-owned (although the story is, I must admit, somewhat complex). It is the Joshua Tree Rieslings which have attracted high ratings from magazines and at the Clare Valley Wine Show. Exports to Denmark, Sweden and The Philippines.

ŸŸŸŸŸ **Nirvarna Clare Valley Reserve Shiraz 2002** Medium-bodied; elegant but super-intense black fruits/blackberries; long, lingering, finely balanced tannins. Stained cork. **RATING** 95 **DRINK** 2015 $ 35

ŸŸŸŸŸ **Joshua Tree Clare Valley Riesling 2004** Clean but subdued bouquet; long palate; very precise lime zest and mineral brings the wine into its own. **RATING** 92 **DRINK** 2014 $ 18
Dark Side of the Moon Clare Valley Shiraz 2002 Elegant, medium-bodied mix of dark fruits and spices; fine, lingering tannins. Da Vinci Code label. Stained cork. **RATING** 92 **DRINK** 2012 $ 25

Clearview Estate Mudgee ★★★

Cnr Sydney Road/Rocky Water Hole Road, Mudgee, NSW 2850 **REGION** Mudgee
T (02) 6372 4546 **F** (02) 6372 7577 **OPEN** Fri–Mon 10–4, or by appointment
WINEMAKER Letitia (Tish) Cecchini **EST.** 1995 **CASES** 1500
SUMMARY No relationship with the famous Hawke's Bay winery, but doubtless John E Hickey and family would be delighted to achieve the same quality. They have progressively planted 4.23 ha of shiraz, 2.27 ha each of chardonnay and cabernet sauvignon, 1.2 ha of merlot, and small amounts of cabernet franc, semillon, pinot grigio, barbera and sangiovese (yet to come into bearing) since 1995, and send the grapes to the Hunter Valley for contract-making. An 'Aussie Farm'-style cellar door, with a timber deck looking out over the vineyard and surrounding vista was opened in September 2000. Exports to the US.

ŸŸŸŸ **Rocky Waterhole Cabernet Sauvignon 2002** **RATING** 86 **DRINK** 2007 $ 18
Liqueur Chardonnay NV **RATING** 86 **DRINK** 2008 $ 25

Cleggett Wines ★★★☆

'Shalistin', Langhorne Creek, SA 5255 (postal) **REGION** Langhorne Creek
T (08) 8537 3133 **F** (08) 8537 3102 **WEB** www.cleggettwines.com.au **OPEN** At Bremer Place,
Langhorne Creek
WINEMAKER Contract **EST.** 2000 **CASES** 2000
SUMMARY The Cleggett family first planted grape vines at Langhorne Creek in 1911. In 1977 a sport (a natural mutation) of cabernet sauvignon produced bronze-coloured grapes; cuttings were taken and increasing quantities of the vine were gradually established, and called malian. Ten years later one of the malian vines itself mutated to yield golden-white bunches, and this in turn was propagated with the name shalistin. There are now 4 ha of shalistin and 2 ha of malian in bearing. Shalistin is made as a full-bodied but unoaked white wine; malian produces both an early and a late harvest wine, the former in a rose style, the latter with significant residual sugar, but again in a rose style. These wines are available, along with Cabernet Sauvignon, at the cellar door, in selected liquor outlets and restaurants, or direct from Cleggett Wines. Exports to the UK.

ŸŸŸŸ **Cabernet Sauvignon 2001** Blackcurrant, spice and earth aromas; medium-bodied; fine tannins; long, silky finish. Quality cork. **RATING** 89 **DRINK** 2011 $ 20

ŸŸŸŸ **Shalistin 2003** **RATING** 85 **DRINK** Now $ 14

Clemens Hill ★★★★

686 Richmond Road, Cambridge, Tas 7170 **REGION** Southern Tasmania
T (03) 6248 5985 **F** (03) 6248 5985 **OPEN** By appointment
WINEMAKER Julian Alcorso (Contract) **EST.** 1994 **CASES** 650
SUMMARY The Shepherd family acquired Clemens Hill in June 2001 after selling their Rosabrook winery in the Margaret River to Palandri Wines. They also have a shareholding in Winemaking Tasmania, the newly established contract winemaking facility run by Julian Alcorso, who makes the Clemens Hill wines. The estate vineyards have now been increased to 2.1 ha.

ΨΨΨΨ♀ **Chardonnay 2003** Smooth, supple nectarine and melon fruit; very good mouthfeel and balance; subtle oak. RATING 92 DRINK 2009 $17.50

Pinot Noir 2003 Medium to full-bodied; rich, ripe plum and black cherry fruit; controlled oak. RATING 92 DRINK 2011 $27.50

ΨΨΨ♀ **Sauvignon Blanc 2004** RATING 86 DRINK 2007 $17.50

Cleveland ★★★★

Shannons Road, Lancefield, Vic 3435 REGION Macedon Ranges
T (03) 5429 9000 F (03) 5429 2143 WEB www.clevelandwinery.com.au OPEN 7 days 9–5
WINEMAKER David Cowburn, Kilchurn Wines (Contract) EST. 1985 CASES 2500
SUMMARY The Cleveland homestead was built in 1889 in the style of a Gothic Revival manor house, but had been abandoned for 40 years when purchased by the Briens in 1983. It has since been painstakingly restored, and 3.8 ha of surrounding vineyard established. In January 2002 new owner Grange Group of Conference Centres initiated fast-track development of The Grange at Cleveland Winery, with 22 suites, plus a large conference room and facilities alongside a new winery and warehouse.

ΨΨΨΨΨ **Macedon Chardonnay 2002** Complex, intense and lively; very good oak balance and integration; plenty of mouthfeel, long finish. RATING 94 DRINK 2010 $15

ΨΨΨ♀ **Pinot Noir 2001** RATING 84 DRINK 2007 $26

Cliff House NR

57 Camms Road, Kayena, Tas 7270 REGION Northern Tasmania
T (03) 6394 7454 F (03) 6394 7454 OPEN By appointment
WINEMAKER Julian Alcorso (Contract) EST. 1983 CASES 2500
SUMMARY Cliff House has undergone a metamorphosis. In 1999 Geoff and Cheryl Hewitt sold the 4-ha vineyard they established in the Tamar Valley area in 1983. They have now turned a 2-hole golf course around their house into a second, new vineyard, planted to riesling and pinot noir.

Clonakilla ★★★★★

Crisps Lane, Murrumbateman, NSW 2582 REGION Canberra District
T (02) 6227 5877 F (02) 6227 5871 WEB www.clonakilla.com.au OPEN 7 days 11–5
WINEMAKER Tim Kirk EST. 1971 CASES 6000
SUMMARY The indefatigable Tim Kirk is the winemaker and manager of this family winery founded by father, scientist Dr John Kirk. Tim Kirk's thirst for knowledge is inexhaustible. It is not at all surprising that the quality of the wines is excellent, especially the highly regarded Shiraz Viognier, which sells out quickly every year. Exports to all major markets.

ΨΨΨΨΨ **Hilltops Shiraz 2004** Beautifully made, balanced and modulated; cool-grown spicy, peppery, licorice and blackberry shiraz fruit; smooth and supple; fine, ripe tannins; very good length. High-quality cork. RATING 95 DRINK 2016 $25

Canberra District Shiraz Viognier 2003 Vibrantly fragrant and spicy; elegant, medium-bodied black cherry fruit; long and balanced. RATING 95 DRINK 2013 $70

ΨΨΨΨ♀ **Canberra District Viognier 2004** Powerful, intense and focused; honeysuckle, pear, apricot and apple all intermingle, none dominant; long finish; likely development very interesting. Screwcap. RATING 93 DRINK 2010 $45

Canberra District Riesling 2004 Solid, lime/tropical fruit; some CO_2 spritz helps a lively palate, but needs to subside. RATING 92 DRINK 2014 $24

Clos Clare NR

Old Road, Watervale, SA 5452 REGION Clare Valley
T (08) 8843 0161 F (08) 8843 0161 OPEN Weekends & public hols 10–5
WINEMAKER Various Contract EST. 1993 CASES 1200
SUMMARY Clos Clare is based on a small (2 ha), unirrigated section of the original Florita Vineyard once owned by Leo Buring; it produces Riesling of extraordinary concentration and power. Exports to the US, Singapore and Ireland.

Clovely Estate ★★★★

Steinhardts Road, Moffatdale via Murgon, Qld 4605 **REGION** South Burnett
T(07) 3216 1088 **F**(07) 3216 1050 **WEB** www.clovely.com.au **OPEN** Fri–Sun 10–5
WINEMAKER Luke Fitzpatrick **EST.** 1998 **CASES** 120 000
SUMMARY Although new-born, Clovely Estate has the largest vineyards in Queensland, having established 173 ha of immaculately maintained vines at two locations just to the east of Murgon in the Burnett Valley. There are 127 ha of red grapes (including 74 ha of shiraz) and 47 ha of white grapes. The attractively packaged wines are sold in four tiers: Clovely Estate at the top end (it will not be produced every year); Left Field, strongly fruity and designed to age; Fifth Row, for early drinking; and Queensland, primarily designed for the export market. Clovely Estate now claims to be twice as large as the next-biggest Queensland winery.

♥♥♥♥♡ **Queensland Chardonnay 2003** Light to medium-bodied; elegant style; nice touch to oak handling. **RATING** 90 **DRINK** Now $ 11

♥♥♥♥ **Left Field Chardonnay 2003** Quite fragrant; light to medium-bodied; pleasant mouthfeel and balance; entirely fruit-driven. **RATING** 89 **DRINK** 2008 $ 15
South Burnett Shiraz 2002 Fresh and aromatic; lively, light to medium-bodied red and black fruits; fine, savoury tannins; subtle oak, unforced; well made. Quality cork. **RATING** 88 **DRINK** 2010 $ 24
Queensland Verdelho 2004 Lifted, lemony, tangy/citrussy overlay to the fruit giving interest. **RATING** 87 **DRINK** Now $ 11

♥♥♥♡ **Left Field Verdelho 2004 RATING** 86 **DRINK** Now $ 15
South Burnett Merlot 2003 Light to medium-bodied; very savoury, fractionally green olive/tannins; a tad more ripeness needed. Quality cork. **RATING** 86 **DRINK** 2009 $ 24
Left Field Rose 2004 RATING 85 **DRINK** Now $ 15
Queensland Shiraz Merlot Cabernet Sauvignon 2002 RATING 85 **DRINK** 2008 $ 11
Left Field Verdelho 2003 RATING 84 **DRINK** Now $ 15

♥♥♥ **Angel Fish Semillon Chardonnay 2003 RATING** 83 $ 11
Reserve Merlot 2003 RATING 83 $ 24
Southern Orange-Eyed Tree Frog Chardonnay 2003 RATING 82 $ 11
Black Cockatoo Shiraz 2002 RATING 82 $ 11
Scarlet Honeyeater Shiraz Merlot Cabernet 2002 RATING 80 $ 11

♥♥♡ **Left Field Shiraz 2001 RATING** 77 $ 15

Clover Hill ★★★★★

60 Clover Hill Road, Lebrina, Tas 7254 **REGION** Northern Tasmania
T(03) 6395 6114 **F**(03) 6395 6257 **WEB** www.taltarni.com.au **OPEN** 7 days 10–5, by appointment in winter
WINEMAKER Leigh Clarnette, Loic Le Calvez, Louella McPhan **EST.** 1986 **CASES** 6000
SUMMARY Clover Hill was established by Taltarni in 1986 with the sole purpose of making a premium sparkling wine. Its 21 ha of vineyards, comprising 12 ha of chardonnay, 6.5 of pinot noir and 1.5 of pinot meunier, are now all in bearing, although extensive retrellising took place in 2002. The sparkling wine quality is excellent, combining finesse with power and length.

♥♥♥♥♥ **2000** Bright green-yellow; silky smooth ripe apple, citrus and touches of brioche; voluminous mouthfeel and length. **RATING** 94 **DRINK** 2007 $ 35

Clyde Park Vineyard ★★★★☆

2490 Midland Highway, Bannockburn, Vic 3331 **REGION** Geelong
T(03) 5281 7274 **F**(03) 5281 7274 **WEB** www.clydepark.com.au **OPEN** Weekends & public hols 11–4
WINEMAKER Simon Black **EST.** 1979 **CASES** 5000
SUMMARY Clyde Park Vineyard was established by Gary Farr, but sold by him many years ago, and then passed through several changes of ownership. It is now owned by Terry Jongebloed and Sue Jongebloed-Dixon. It has significant mature plantings of pinot noir (3.4 ha), chardonnay (3.1 ha), sauvignon blanc (1.5 ha), shiraz (1.2 ha) and pinot gris (0.9 ha). Wine quality is excellent, no doubt aided by the mature vineyard.

♥♥♥♥♥ **Reserve Pinot Noir 2002** Stacked with rich, ripe, plummy fruit moving through to a stylishly savoury and lingering finish. **RATING** 95 **DRINK** 2015 $ 29

ŸŸŸŸ♀ **Shiraz 2003** Soft, supple blackberry and cherry fruit supported by fine tannins and well-handled oak. **RATING** 92 **DRINK** 2013 $ 27
Sauvignon Blanc 2003 Complex texture and structure, dense though fruit-driven; grass, gooseberry and asparagus flavours. Cork. **RATING** 90 **DRINK** Now $ 22
Chardonnay 2003 Smooth, melon and stone fruit; subtle oak and well balanced; will develop. **RATING** 90 **DRINK** 2009 $ 24

ŸŸŸŸ **Pinot Gris 2004 RATING** 86 **DRINK** Now $ 22
Pinot Noir 2003 RATING 86 **DRINK** 2009 $ 27

Coal Valley Vineyard ★★★☆

257 Richmond Road, Cambridge, Tas 7170 **REGION** Southern Tasmania
T (03) 6248 5367 **F** (03) 6248 4175 **WEB** www.coalvalley.com.au **OPEN** Wed–Mon 10–4
WINEMAKER Andrew Hood (Contract) **EST.** 1991 **CASES** 600
SUMMARY Coal Valley Vineyard is the new name for Treehouse Vineyard & Wine Centre, the change brought about by the fact that Treehouse had been trademarked by the Pemberton winery, Salitage. The vineyard was purchased by Todd Goebel and wife Gillian Christian in 1999. They have set about doubling the size of the riesling vineyard, and establishing 1.5 ha of another vineyard planted to pinot noir, with a few vines of cabernet. The Wine Centre now incorporates a full commercial kitchen and overlooks the existing vineyard and the Coal River Valley.

ŸŸŸŸ **Chardonnay 2004** Light but long melon and citrus aromas and flavours; regional acidity; will develop. Screwcap. **RATING** 89 **DRINK** 2010 $ 20
Cabernet Merlot 2003 Good colour; light to medium-bodied; well balanced, with nice red fruits and touches of herb and leek. **RATING** 88 **DRINK** 2010 $ 30

ŸŸŸŸ **Riesling 2004 RATING** 86 **DRINK** 2010 $ 21
Pinot Noir 2003 RATING 85 **DRINK** 2008 $ 25

ŸŸŸ **Cabernet Merlot 2003 RATING** 83 $ 30

Coalville Vineyard NR

RMB 4750 Moe South Road, Moe South, Vic 3825 **REGION** Gippsland
T (03) 5127 4229 **F** (03) 5127 2148 **OPEN** 7 days 10–5
WINEMAKER Peter Beasley **EST.** 1985 **CASES** 3000
SUMMARY This is the new name for Mair's Coalville, following the sale of the property by Dr Stewart Mair to Peter Beasley, who has significantly increased not only the volume but the range of wines available.

Cobaw Ridge ★★★★☆

31 Perc Boyer's Lane, East Pastoria via Kyneton, Vic 3444 **REGION** Macedon Ranges
T (03) 5423 5227 **F** (03) 5423 5227 **WEB** www.cobawridge.com.au **OPEN** 7 days 10–5
WINEMAKER Alan Cooper **EST.** 1985 **CASES** 1500
SUMMARY Nelly and Alan Cooper established Cobaw Ridge's 6-ha vineyard at an altitude of 610m in the hills above Kyneton, complete with pole-framed mudbrick house and winery. The plantings of cabernet sauvignon have been removed and partially replaced by lagrein, a variety which sent me scuttling to Jancis Robinson's seminal book on grape varieties: it is a northeast Italian variety typically used to make delicate Rose, but at Cobaw Ridge it is made into an impressive full-bodied dry red. Exports to the UK.

ŸŸŸŸŸ **Shiraz Viognier 2003** Vivid purple-red; gloriously scented example; vibrant black cherry, raspberry and spice; lively and long; oak eaten by fruit. Cork. **RATING** 96 **DRINK** 2017 $ 42

ŸŸŸŸ♀ **Chardonnay 2003** Elegant, medium-bodied; ripe stone fruit supported by barrel ferment French oak inputs; good flavour and mouthfeel, and acidity to close. Cork. **RATING** 90
DRINK 2008 $ 32
Pinot Noir 2003 Light to medium-bodied; wild strawberries, black cherries and spice; good balance and structure. Cork. **RATING** 90 **DRINK** 2007 $ 38

ŸŸŸŸ **Lagrein 2003** Bright red-purple; light to medium-bodied; supple, smooth red fruits; minimal tannins. Cork. **RATING** 88 **DRINK** 2009 $ 60

Cobbitty Wines   NR

Cobbitty Road, Cobbitty, NSW 2570 **REGION** South Coast Zone
T (02) 4651 2281 **F** (02) 4651 2671 **OPEN** Mon–Sat 9.30–5.30, Sun 11–5.30
WINEMAKER Giovanni Cogno **EST.** 1964 **CASES** 5000
SUMMARY Draws upon 10 ha of estate plantings of muscat, barbera, grenache and trebbiano, relying
very much on local and ethnic custom.

Cobb's Hill   ★★★☆

Oakwood Road, Oakbank, SA 5243 **REGION** Adelaide Hills
T (08) 8388 4054 **F** (08) 8388 4820 **WEB** www.cobbshillwine.com.au **OPEN** Not
WINEMAKER Shaw & Smith (Contract) **EST.** 1997 **CASES** 400
SUMMARY Sally and Roger Cook have a 140-ha property in the Adelaide Hills that takes its name from
Cobb and Co., which used it as a staging post and resting place for 1000 horses. The Cooks now use
the property to raise Angus cattle, grow cherries and, more recently, grow grapes. Three different
sites on the property, amounting to just over 10 ha, were planted to selected clones of sauvignon
blanc, chardonnay, semillon, riesling and merlot. Part of the production is sold to Shaw & Smith, who
vinify the remainder for Cobb's Hill. The Sauvignon Blanc has been most successful.

Cockatoo Ridge   NR

PO Box 855, Nuriootpa, SA 5355 **REGION** Riverland
T (08) 8563 6400 **F** (08) 8563 1117 **WEB** www.cockatooridge.com.au **OPEN** Not
WINEMAKER Stephen Obst **EST.** 1990 **CASES** NFP
SUMMARY Cockatoo Ridge was established by Geoff Merrill, and rapidly built volume by sales
through the large retail chains, the extremely colourful label standing out on the shelf. The business
was already a large one when it was acquired by a company headed by ex-Orlando winemaker Ivan
Limb, and is now distributed by Tucker Seabrook through a wide range of outlets; also, exports to all
Australia's major export destinations. The large production is based on estate plantings of 98 ha at
Waikerie on the Murray River, supplemented by grapes grown under contract in the Barossa Valley.

Cockfighter's Ghost   ★★★☆

Lot 251 Milbrodale Road, Broke, NSW 2330 **REGION** Lower Hunter Valley
T (02) 9563 2500 **F** (02) 9563 2555 **WEB** www.poolesrock.com.au **OPEN** At Poole's Rock
WINEMAKER Patrick Auld **EST.** 1994 **CASES** 30 000
SUMMARY Like Poole's Rock Vineyard, part of a rapidly expanding wine empire owned by Sydney
merchant banker David Clarke, has been housed at the former Tulloch winery since 2003.
Accommodation is, however, available at the Milbrodale property. The wine has retail distribution
throughout Australia and is exported to the UK, the US and other major markets.

ŸŸŸŸ **Semillon 2004** High-toned style with some spritz; lemon zest flavours dance on the
tongue; particular style. **RATING** 89 **DRINK** 2009 $17

ŸŸŸŸ **Chardonnay 2004** Very subtle barrel ferment inputs; light to medium-bodied; has some
length and yellow peach fruit; soft finish. **RATING** 86 **DRINK** Now $11.29
Verdelho 2004 **RATING** 86 **DRINK** Now $17
Chardonnay 2003 **RATING** 85 **DRINK** 2007 $18

ŸŸŸ **Unwooded Chardonnay 2004** **RATING** 83 $12.04

Cody's   NR

New England Highway, Ballandean, Qld 4382 **REGION** Granite Belt
T (07) 4684 1309 **F** (07) 5572 6500 **OPEN** 7 days 10–5
WINEMAKER Adam Chapman (Contract) **EST.** 1995 **CASES** 500
SUMMARY John Cody has established 2.5 ha of cabernet sauvignon, merlot and shiraz at his
Ballandean vineyard. The wines are contract-made by Adam Chapman at Sirromet, and are sold by
mail order and through the cellar door, which offers the usual facilities.

Cofield Wines

Distillery Road, Wahgunyah, Vic 3687 **REGION** Rutherglen
T (02) 6033 3798 **F** (02) 6033 0798 **OPEN** Mon–Sat 9–5, Sun 10–5
WINEMAKER Max Cofield, Damien Cofield **EST.** 1990 **CASES** 11 000
SUMMARY District veteran Max Cofield, together with wife Karen and sons Damien (winery) and Andrew (vineyard), is developing a strong cellar door sales base, and also providing a large barbecue and picnic area. The Pickled Sisters Café is open for lunch Wed–Mon; telephone (02) 6033 2377. The influence of Damien Cofield in developing an impressively broad-based product range is quite evident. Limited retail distribution through Prime Wines in Melbourne; exports to the US.

ΨΨΨΨ **Late Harvest Muscadelle 2002** Stylish wine; tangy complex aromas (botrytis?); excellent balance and length; moderately sweet peachy fruit and residual sugar off-set by crisp acidity. Cork. **RATING** 90 **DRINK** 2008 $ 18

ΨΨΨΨ **Sauvignon Blanc 2004** Clean, crisp and minerally; excellent length and structure; lemony fruit; exceptional achievement from Rutherglen. Screwcap. **RATING** 88 **DRINK** 2007 $ 15
Quartz Vein Malbec 2001 Sweet, juicy, slightly jammy berry fruit utterly typical of the variety; soft tannins, but big flavour impact. Good cork. **RATING** 88 **DRINK** 2009 $ 28
Sparkling Shiraz NV T XIII. Light to medium-bodied; has some restraint and elegance, and is not too sugar-sweet; well-balanced acidity and length. **RATING** 88 **DRINK** 2010 $ 28
Reserve Muscat NV Relatively young but good quality; Christmas cake, raisin and spice mix; fresh finish. Cork. **RATING** 88 **DRINK** Now $ 23
Cabernet Sauvignon 2002 Light to medium-bodied; nicely balanced savoury, briary style; not forced; tannin and oak controlled. Good cork. **RATING** 87 **DRINK** 2008 $ 18
Pinot Noir Chardonnay NV Spicy nutmeg and strawberry aromas quite unexpected; nicely balanced, if on the light side. **RATING** 87 **DRINK** 2007 $ 22
Sparkling Shiraz 2000 Light to medium-bodied raspberry and cherry fruit; excellent dry finish; again, some clever thinking and winemaking. **RATING** 87 **DRINK** Now $ 28

ΨΨΨΨ **Quartz Vein Shiraz 2001** Very ripe fruit flavours, though alcohol (14.7°) is relatively controlled; soft tannins. Good cork. **RATING** 86 **DRINK** 2009 $ 28
Rutherglen Merlot 2002 **RATING** 86 **DRINK** 2008 $ 18
QVP Shiraz Vintage Port 2004 **RATING** 86 **DRINK** 2015 $ 23
Chenin Blanc 2004 **RATING** 84 **DRINK** 2007 $ 15

Coldstream Hills

NR

31 Maddens Lane, Coldstream, Vic 3770 **REGION** Yarra Valley
T (03) 5964 9410 **F** (03) 5964 9389 **WEB** www.coldstreamhills.com.au **OPEN** 7 days 10–5
WINEMAKER Andrew Fleming, Greg Jarratt, James Halliday (Consultant) **EST.** 1985 **CASES** 55 000
SUMMARY Founded by the author, who continues to be involved with the winemaking, but acquired by Southcorp in mid-1996. Expansion plans already then underway have been maintained, with well in excess of 100 ha of owned or managed estate vineyards as the base. Chardonnay and Pinot Noir continue to be the principal focus; Merlot came on-stream from the 1997 vintage. Vintage conditions permitting, these three wines are made in both varietal and Reserve form, the latter in restricted quantities. Tasting notes are written by James Halliday and Andrew Fleming.

Sauvignon Blanc 2004 A vibrant nose of lifted tropical fruit with notes of lantana and gooseberry; sweet tropical fruit flavours and good length; soft acidity adds to a refreshing, crisp finish. **NR** **DRINK** Now $ 26.50
Chardonnay 2003 Attractive white peach, melon and quince fruit; subtle cashew barrel fermentation overtones and toasty integrated oak. **NR** **DRINK** 2008 $ 26.50
Reserve Chardonnay 2003 Attractive white peach, quince and nectarine aromas with underlying cashew barrel ferment characters; a seamless palate with elegance and length; mouthwatering stone fruit and grapefruit/citrus characters, complexed by a hint of fruit-derived minerality. **NR** **DRINK** 2015 $ 48
Pinot Noir 2002 Intense and tight spicy/savoury plum flavours; long, lingering finish and excellent acidity. **NR** **DRINK** 2010 $ 26.50
Reserve Pinot Noir 2002 Savoury, spicy dark fruit aromas, with perfectly balanced and integrated oak; another dimension of richness and complexity on the palate, still showing the very cool vintage and low yields, yet supple and silky. The slightly stalky undertone will soften as the wine ages. **NR** **DRINK** 2012 $ 65

Limited Release Shiraz 2003 Ripe shiraz fruit characters of plum and cherries, with attractive rose petal and cracked pepper spice aromas, dance across the bouquet. Toasty charry oak adds further complexity, without dominating the wine's varietal characters. **NR DRINK** 2010 $ 35

Cabernet Sauvignon 2003 Medium-bodied; fine and seamless tannin structure; attractive, ripe, fine and seamless tannin structure; cassis and dark cherry fruit is complemented by toasty, charry French oak. **NR DRINK** 2010 $ 27

Reserve Cabernet Sauvignon 2001 Dark berry fruits combine with secondary aromas of mocha and chocolate, following onto a flavoursome palate with subtle French oak spice and cedar notes adding complexity and structure. The finish is long and elegant, supported by firm, yet fine-grained, tannins. **NR DRINK** 2014 $ 52

Chardonnay Pinot Noir 1999 Rich, complex, bready and berry fruit aromas. Well-balanced; fruit flavours ranging from ripe pear to citrus. **NR DRINK** Now $ 24.95

Coliban Valley Wines ★★★☆

Metcalfe–Redesdale Road, Metcalfe, Vic 3448 **REGION** Heathcote
T (03) 9813 3895 **F** (03) 9813 3895 **WEB** www.heathcotewinegrowers.com.au **OPEN** Weekends 10–5
WINEMAKER Helen Miles **EST.** 1997 **CASES** 100
SUMMARY Helen Miles (with a degree in science) and partner Greg Miles have planted 3.5 ha of shiraz, 0.75 ha of cabernet and 0.25 ha of merlot near Metcalfe, at the southern end of the Heathcote wine region. The granitic soils, with a band of clay, minimise the need for irrigation; the vines are mulched with material from the surrounding paddocks. The climate also means minimal spraying, predominantly copper and sulphur, with some biological sprays. Most of the production is sold as grapes to others at the moment, but it is intended to increase the amount made under the Coliban Valley label, and also to evaluate a small trial planting of sangiovese as a possible blend mate with cabernet sauvignon.

YYYY Heathcote Cabernet Sauvignon 2002 Light to medium-bodied; elegant, savoury, spicy style (13° alcohol), needing greater fruit density, particularly given the region. **RATING** 87 **DRINK** 2009 $ 20

YYYY Heathcote Cabernet Merlot 2003 RATING 84 **DRINK** 2007

Colmaur NR

447 Native Corners Road, Campania, Tas 7026 **REGION** Southern Tasmania
T (03) 6260 4312 **F** (03) 6260 4580 **OPEN** By appointment
WINEMAKER Michael Vishacki (Contract) **EST.** 1994 **CASES** 120
SUMMARY Colmaur is sufficiently small for the vines to be counted: presently 1100 chardonnay and 1700 pinot noir are in production. In 2000/2001 a further 600 chardonnay, 1350 pinot noir and 250 cabernet sauvignon were planted, and that will be the total extent of the vineyard. Likewise, production will be limited to the 5 new French oak barrels purchased in 2000, producing 100 to 120 cases of wine per year; any surplus grapes will be sold. There are 700 olive trees in production, and Colmaur has its own oil press.

Colvin Wines ★★★★☆

19 Boyle Street, Mosman, NSW 2088 (postal) **REGION** Lower Hunter Valley
T (02) 9908 7886 **F** (02) 9908 7885 **WEB** www.colvinwines.com.au **OPEN** Not
WINEMAKER Andrew Spinaze, Trevor Drayton (Contract) **EST.** 1999 **CASES** 500
SUMMARY Sydney lawyer John Colvin and wife and Robyn purchased the De Beyers Vineyard in 1990; its history goes back to the second half of the 19th century. By 1967, when a syndicate headed by Douglas McGregor purchased 35 ha of the original vineyard site, no vines remained. The syndicate planted semillon on the alluvial soil of the creek flats, and shiraz on the red clay hillsides. When the Colvins acquired the property the vineyard was in need of attention. Up to 1998 all the grapes were sold to Tyrrell's, but since 1999 quantities have been made for distribution under the Colvin Wines label. These include Sangiovese, from a little over 1 ha of the variety planted by John Colvin in 1996 because of his love of the wines of Tuscany.

YYYYY De Beyers Vineyard Hunter Valley Semillon 2004 Bright, crisp and powerful lemon zest and herb; lively, tangy finish; good length. Screwcap. **RATING** 94 **DRINK** 2014 $ 26.25

ΥΥΥΥ **De Beyers Vineyard Hunter Valley Shiraz 2003** Aromatic, spicy, earthy blackberry fruit; strongly regional; light to medium-bodied, elegant and fresh, barely showing its 13.5° alcohol; 50 cases made from 30-year-old vines. Quality cork. **RATING** 93 **DRINK** 2013 $ 33.30

ΥΥΥ **De Beyers Vineyard Ragamuffin Red 2002 RATING** 83 $ 19.20

Connor Park Winery
NR

59 Connors Road, Leichardt, Vic 3516 **REGION** Bendigo
T (03) 5437 5234 **F** (03) 5437 5204 **WEB** www.connorparkwinery.com.au **OPEN** 7 days 10–6
WINEMAKER Ross Lougoon **EST.** 1994 **CASES** 7000
SUMMARY The original planting of 2 ha of vineyard dates back to the mid-1960s and to the uncle of the present owners, who had plans for designing an automatic grape harvester. The plans came to nothing, and when the present owners purchased the property in 1985 the vineyard had run wild. They resuscitated the vineyard (which formed part of a much larger mixed farming operation) and until 1994 were content to sell the grapes to other winemakers. Since then the vineyard has been expanded to 10 ha. Production has risen from 2000 to 10 000 cases, with exports to the US, Canada and Singapore and retail distribution in Melbourne supplementing cellar door and mailing list sales.

Constable & Hershon

205 Gillards Road, Pokolbin, NSW 2320 **REGION** Lower Hunter Valley
T (02) 4998 7887 **F** (02) 4998 6555 **WEB** www.constablehershon.com.au **OPEN** 7 days 10–5
WINEMAKER Neil McGuigan (Contract) **EST.** 1981 **CASES** 3000
SUMMARY Features four spectacular formal gardens, the Rose, Knot and Herb, Secret and Sculpture; a free 30 minute garden tour is conducted every Monday to Friday at 10.30 am. The 12-ha vineyard is spectacularly situated under the backdrop of the Brokenback Range. Offers a range of several vintages of each variety ex cellar door or by mailing list.

ΥΥΥΥ **Merlot 2003** A pretty wine; bright, fresh, small red berry fruits, but lacks structure. Cork. **RATING** 86 **DRINK** 2008 $ 26
Cabernet Merlot 2003 RATING 84 **DRINK** 2008 $ 26

Coolangatta Estate

1335 Bolong Road, Shoalhaven Heads, NSW 2535 **REGION** Shoalhaven Coast
T (02) 4448 7131 **F** (02) 4448 7997 **WEB** www.coolangattaestate.com.au **OPEN** 7 days 10–5
WINEMAKER Tyrrell's (Contract) **EST.** 1988 **CASES** 5000
SUMMARY Coolangatta Estate is part of a 150-ha resort with accommodation, restaurants, golf course, etc; some of the oldest buildings were convict-built in 1822. It might be thought that the wines are tailored purely for the tourist market, but in fact the standard of viticulture is exceptionally high (immaculate Scott-Henry trellising), and the contract winemaking is wholly professional. Has a habit of bobbing up with gold medals at Sydney and Canberra wine shows.

ΥΥΥΥΥ **Semillon 2004** Very lively and fresh tangy, lemony fruit; lingering, clean finish. **RATING** 91 **DRINK** 2012 $ 18

ΥΥΥΥ **Verdelho 2004** Clean, fresh fruit salad with a twist of lemon; good extension; not sweet. **RATING** 87 **DRINK** Now $ 18
Sauvignon Blanc Verdelho 2004 Lively and fresh, similar to the Verdelho except even more lively and tangy; very well made. **RATING** 87 **DRINK** Now $ 16

Coombe Farm Vineyard

11 St Huberts Road, Coldstream, Vic 3770 **REGION** Yarra Valley
T (03) 9739 1136 **F** (03) 9739 1136 **WEB** www.coombefarm.com.au **OPEN** Not
WINEMAKER Wine Network (Contract) **EST.** 1999 **CASES** 2000
SUMMARY Coombe Farm Vineyard is owned by Pamela, Lady Vestey, Lord Samuel Vestey and The Right Honourable Mark Vestey. Lady Vestey is Dame Nellie Melba's grand-daughter. After a small initial planting, the decision was taken in 1999 to very significantly extend the vineyard: there are now 25 ha of pinot noir, 18 ha of chardonnay, 7.4 ha of merlot, 5.4 ha of cabernet sauvignon, 1.9 ha of

marsanne and 0.7 ha of arneis. The vast majority of the fruit is sold; a small amount is made for the Coombe Farm Vineyard label.

ΨΨΨΨ **Chardonnay 2003** Light straw-green; complex, with some funky barrel ferment aromas; a rich palate, but does shorten somewhat. Screwcap. **RATING** 88 **DRINK** 2007 $ 27.95

ΨΨΨΨ **Pinot Noir 2003** **RATING** 86 **DRINK** 2007 $ 27.95

Coombend Estate ★★★☆

Coombend via Swansea, Tas 7190 **REGION** East Coast Tasmania
T (03) 6257 8881 **F** (03) 6257 8484 **OPEN** 7 days 9–6
WINEMAKER Andrew Hood (Contract) **EST.** 1985 **CASES** 4000
SUMMARY John Fenn Smith originally established 1.75 ha of cabernet sauvignon, 2.25 ha of sauvignon blanc, 0.5 ha of pinot noir and 0.3 ha of riesling (together with a little cabernet franc) on his 2000-ha sheep station, choosing the part of his property immediately adjacent to Freycinet. This slightly quixotic choice of variety has been justified by the success of the wine in limited show entries. In December 1998 Coombend opened a purpose-built cellar door sales area. It has also significantly expanded its plantings to include riesling and sauvignon blanc. Exports to Hong Kong and the UK.

ΨΨΨΨ **Sauvignon Blanc 2004** Well-controlled oak, but needs more fruit for higher points. **RATING** 87 **DRINK** 2008 $ 20

ΨΨΨΨ **Riesling 2004** **RATING** 86 **DRINK** 2007 $ 17

ΨΨΨ **Cabernet Sauvignon 2003** **RATING** 83 $ 25

Cooperage Estate NR

15 Markovitch Lane, Junortoun, Vic 3551 **REGION** Bendigo
T 0418 544 743 **OPEN** Not
WINEMAKER Graham Gregurek **EST.** 1995 **CASES** NA
SUMMARY The Gregurek family has established 2.2. ha of shiraz and cabernet sauvignon at their vineyard on the southern outskirts of Bendigo. As the name suggests, there is also a cooperage onsite.

Cooper Wines ★★☆

Lovedale Road, Lovedale, NSW 2321 **REGION** Lower Hunter Valley
T (02) 4930 7387 **F** (02) 4930 7900 **OPEN** Mon–Fri 10–5, Weekends 9.30–5
WINEMAKER Greg Silkman (Contract) **EST.** 2001 **CASES** 2000
SUMMARY Max Cooper is a Qantas pilot who purchased the former Allanmere Winery & Vineyard, leasing the winery back to Allanmere but retaining the vineyards. The chardonnay is estate-grown; the other wines are made from grapes purchased by growers in the region.

Coorinja ★★☆

Toodyay Road, Toodyay, WA 6566 **REGION** Greater Perth Zone
T (08) 9574 2280 **OPEN** Mon–Sat 10–5
WINEMAKER Michael Wood **EST.** 1870 **CASES** 3200
SUMMARY An evocative and historic winery nestling in a small gully which seems to be in a time warp, begging to be used as a set for a film. A revamp of the packaging accompanied a more than respectable 'Hermitage', with lots of dark chocolate and sweet berry flavour, finishing with soft tannins.

Cooyal Grove ★★★★

Lot 9 Stoney Creek Road, Mudgee, NSW 2850 **REGION** Mudgee
T (02) 6373 5337 **F** (02) 6373 5337 **OPEN** 7 days by appointment
WINEMAKER Moore Haszard (Contract) **EST.** 1990 **CASES** 1000
SUMMARY In late 2002 the 10-ha Cooyal Grove property of vines, pistachio nut trees and olives was purchased by Sydney publican John Lenard, and Paul and Lydele Walker, a local Mudgee vigneron and wife. The partners say, 'We have worked almost every weekend in the vineyard and grove, undertaking

every task from planting new blocks, pruning, training, harvesting, bottling and labelling. Given that all of the partners are only 30 years old and not yet financially able to employ outside labour, we seem to call on every friend, relative and friend's relatives to assist in the production of the crops. This has made for a feeling of building something from scratch which we are proud of.' The vineyards are now 4.5 ha in total, with chardonnay, semillon, sauvignon blanc, merlot, shiraz and cabernet sauvignon. The wines are principally sold by mail order and through selected NSW and Queensland outlets.

▼▼▼▼Y **Mudgee Merlot 2003** Strongly savoury, earthy, olive edges to blackcurrant fruit, all entirely varietal; good tannins. Cork. RATING 90 DRINK 2013 $18

▼▼▼▼ **Mudgee Shiraz 2003** Powerful blackberry, plum and dark chocolate mix; good tannin structure; great value. Stained cork. RATING 89 DRINK 2012 $15
Mudgee Semillon Sauvignon Blanc 2004 Clean, crisp, correct; lemon and citrus; crisp acidity. Screwcap. RATING 87 DRINK 2007 $15
Mudgee Chardonnay 2004 Nectarine and melon; smooth and supple; some creamy notes. Screwcap. RATING 87 DRINK 2008 $15

▼▼▼Y **Mudgee Cabernet Sauvignon 2003** RATING 85 DRINK 2009 $15

Cope-Williams ★★★★

Glenfern Road, Romsey, Vic 3434 REGION Macedon Ranges
T (03) 5429 5428 F (03) 5429 5655 OPEN 7 days 11–5
WINEMAKER David Cowburn EST. 1977 CASES 7000
SUMMARY One of the high country Macedon pioneers, specialising in sparkling wines which are full flavoured but also producing excellent Chardonnay and Pinot Noir table wines in the warmer vintages. A traditional 'English Green'-type cricket ground is available for hire and booked out most days of the week from spring through till autumn.

▼▼▼▼Y **R.OM.S.E.Y. Rose 1999** Full-on rose style; excellent balance and a touch of strawberry. RATING 90 DRINK 2007

▼▼▼Y **Chardonnay 2001** RATING 86 DRINK 2007

Copper Bull Wines NR

19 Uplands Road, Chirnside Park, Vic 3116 REGION Yarra Valley
T (03) 9726 7111 OPEN Wed–Sun 11–6
WINEMAKER David Schliefert EST. 1982 CASES 800
SUMMARY Copper Bull is the reincarnation of Halcyon Daze. The Rackleys, having gone into semi-retirement, have leased the vineyard, winery and cellar door to David and Janie Schliefert, who produced the first wines under the Copper Bull label in 2003. David Schliefert spent 19 years at Lindemans Karadoc winery, becoming a cellar supervisor in the process, while wife Janie worked in quality management at Lindemans. The small production is sold from the cellar door.

Copper Country NR

Lot 6 Kingaroy Road, Nanango, Qld 4615 REGION South Burnett
T (07) 4163 1011 F (07) 4163 1122 OPEN 7 days 9–5
WINEMAKER Contract EST. 1995 CASES 1000
SUMMARY The Winter family (Derek, Helena, Stephen and Justyne) were restaurateurs before venturing into grapegrowing and winemaking. The name of the vineyard and the restaurant recognises that copper was the first mineral mined in the region. The Winters also make cheese; the principal outlet for their products is their restaurant and cellar door.

Coriole ★★★★☆

Chaffeys Road, McLaren Vale, SA 5171 REGION McLaren Vale
T (08) 8323 8305 F (08) 8323 9136 WEB www.coriole.com OPEN Mon–Fri 10–5, weekends & public hols 11–5
WINEMAKER Grant Harrison EST. 1967 CASES 34 000
SUMMARY Justifiably best known for its Shiraz, which – in both the rare Lloyd Reserve and the standard forms – is extremely impressive. One of the first wineries to catch on to the Italian fashion

with its Sangiovese, but its white varietal wines lose nothing by comparison. It is also a producer of high-quality olive oil distributed commercially through all states. The wines are exported to the UK, the US and other major markets.

▼▼▼▼▼ **Lloyd Reserve Shiraz 2002** Beautifully structured wine, an exercise in restraint; smooth, supple blackberry, chocolate and tannin mix; clean finish. Wine-stained and creased cork a worry. RATING 95 DRINK 2017 $ 65

▼▼▼▼♀ **Mary Kathleen Reserve Cabernet Merlot 2002** Ultra-smooth medium-bodied wine; aromatic, sweet berry fruits; silky tannins; subtle oak; all in harmony. RATING 93 DRINK 2015 $ 39
Lalla Rookh Grenache Shiraz 2002 Engaging mix of spice, raspberry, redcurrant, plum and chocolate; fine tannins, good length. RATING 92 DRINK 2009 $ 22
Redstone 2002 Elegant savoury, spicy style; excellent structure and length; fine tannins. Shiraz Cabernet Merlot. RATING 90 DRINK 2010 $ 18.50

▼▼▼▼ **Semillon Sauvignon Blanc 2004** Substantial wine; solid, firm structure; herbal/grassy semillon dominates the palate. RATING 89 DRINK 2007 $ 18
Old Barn Cabernet Shiraz 2002 Elegant, light to medium-bodied; sweet fruit, cassis and mulberry; touches of savoury mint; fine tannins. RATING 89 DRINK 2007 $ 30
Fortified Shiraz 2003 Relatively speaking, a lighter style, but still abundant spice/pepper overlay to blackberry fruits; pleasingly dry finish. Will evolve. RATING 89 DRINK 2013 $ 17.50
Chenin Blanc 2004 As ever with Coriole, has that little extra zip and bite, reminiscent of Primo Estate La Biondina; fresh finish. RATING 88 DRINK Now $ 14.50
Contour 4 Sangiovese Shiraz 2002 Savoury, spicy red cherry fruits; good structure and style; fine tannins. Vines planted 1985. RATING 88 DRINK 2009 $ 14.50
McLaren Vale Sangiovese 2003 Light colour; undoubtedly varietal, with savoury rose petal aromas, but really needs more flesh and conviction to persuade me. RATING 87 DRINK 2008 $ 17

▼▼▼♀ **Racked Chenin Blanc 2003** RATING 84 DRINK Now $ 13

Cosham ★★★

101 Union Road, Carmel via Kalamunda, WA 6076 REGION Perth Hills
T (08) 9293 5424 F (08) 9293 5062 WEB www.coshamwines.com.au OPEN Weekends & public hols 10–5
WINEMAKER Julie White (Contract) EST. 1989 CASES 1000
SUMMARY Has grown significantly over recent years, though admittedly from a small base. The vineyard is planted on an old orchard, and consists of 2 ha of cabernet sauvignon, merlot, shiraz, pinot noir, cabernet franc, chardonnay and petit verdot, established between 1990 and 1995. They grow in gravelly loam with some clay, but overall in a well-drained soil with good rainfall. Depending on the grape variety, vintage ranges from late February to early April.

▼▼▼♀ **Bickley Valley Chardonnay 2003** A restrained mix of mineral and light melon fruit; given the screwcap, will develop more. RATING 86 DRINK 2007 $ 15
Bickley Valley Cabernet Merlot 2001 RATING 85 DRINK 2007 $ 18

🐌 County View Vineyard/Moothi Mud ★★★

85 Rocky Waterhole Road, Mudgee, NSW 2850 (postal) REGION Mudgee
T (02) 9868 6014 F (02) 9868 6017 WEB www.countyview.net OPEN Not
WINEMAKER Drew Tuckwell EST. 1995 CASES 1000
SUMMARY Phil and Susan Moore purchased a property on the northwest-facing slopes of Mt Frome, at an elevation of 550m in 1995. The site has reddish-brown clay with limestone, quartz and ironstone gibber soil, well suited to the chardonnay, shiraz, merlot and cabernet sauvignon established on the property, amounting to 24 ha in all. The rather odd names for the wines are derived from the Koori name for Mudgee, which is Moothi; Moothi Mud is said to be local slang for Mudgee's full-bodied reds. Wines can be purchased from the website.

▼▼▼▼ **Moothi Mud Shiraz 2002** Fresh; light to medium-bodied red and black fruits; smooth drinking, easy style. RATING 87 DRINK 2010 $ 25

▼▼▼♀ **Moothi Mud Cabernet Sauvignon 2002** RATING 86 DRINK 2007 $ 25

Cow Hill NR

PO Box 533, Beechworth, Vic 3747 **REGION** Beechworth
T 0411 249 704 **OPEN** Not
WINEMAKER Andrew Doyle **EST.** 2001 **CASES** NA
SUMMARY Andrew Doyle began the development of Cow Hill with the planting of 1.5 ha each of viognier and nebbiolo on very steep mudstone, slate and shale soils. Tempranillo and muscat, and possibly shiraz, are to follow, taking the plantings to a total of 10 ha. In the meantime, Doyle purchases grapes from other vineyards in the Beechworth region to produce his wines.

Cowra Estate ★★★☆

Boorowa Road, Cowra, NSW 2794 **REGION** Cowra
T (02) 9907 7735 **F** (02) 9907 7734 **OPEN** At The Quarry Restaurant, Tues–Sun 10–4
WINEMAKER Ralph Fowler, Simon Gilbert (Contract) **EST.** 1973 **CASES** 6000
SUMMARY Cowra Estate was purchased from the family of founder Tony Gray by South African-born food and beverage entrepreneur John Geber in 1995. A vigorous promotional campaign has gained a higher domestic profile for the once export-oriented brand. John Geber is actively involved in the promotional effort and rightly proud of the wines. The Quarry Wine Cellars and Restaurant offer visitors a full range of Cowra Estate's wines, plus wines from other producers in the region. The Geber family, incidentally, also owns Chateau Tanunda in the Barossa Valley.

🍷🍷🍷🍷 **Cabernets Rose 2004** Bright pale pink; light-bodied; raspberry and cassis; balanced residual sugar and acidity. Screwcap. **RATING** 86 **DRINK** Now **$** 15
Chardonnay 2002 **RATING** 85 **DRINK** Now **$** 15

Crabtree of Watervale ★★★★

North Terrace, Watervale SA 5452 **REGION** Clare Valley
T (08) 8843 0069 **F** (08) 8843 0144 **OPEN** Mon–Sat 11–5
WINEMAKER Robert Crabtree **EST.** 1979 **CASES** 5000
SUMMARY Robert Crabtree and wife Elizabeth are the drivers of the business, making full-flavoured, classic Clare Valley styles with great success in some recent vintages. Exports to Canada and Malaysia.

🍷🍷🍷🍷🍷 **Riesling 2004** A complex, tangy mix of mineral, lime and herb; excellent length and structure. **RATING** 93 **DRINK** 2014 **$** 20

🍷🍷🍷🍷 **Bay of Biscay Rose 2004** **RATING** 86 **DRINK** Now **$** 20
Zibibbo 2004 **RATING** 84 **DRINK** Now **$** 20

Craig Avon Vineyard ★★★

Craig Avon Lane, Merricks North, Vic 3926 **REGION** Mornington Peninsula
T (03) 5989 7465 **F** (03) 5989 7615 **OPEN** By appointment
WINEMAKER Ken Lang **EST.** 1986 **CASES** 1000
SUMMARY The estate-grown wines are produced from 0.9 ha of chardonnay, 0.5 ha of pinot noir and 0.4 ha of cabernet sauvignon. They are competently made, clean, and with pleasant fruit flavour. All the wines are sold through the cellar door and by mailing list.

Craigie Knowe NR

80 Glen Gala Road, Cranbrook, Tas 7190 **REGION** East Coast Tasmania
T (03) 6259 8252 **F** (03) 6259 8252 **OPEN** 7 days by appointment
WINEMAKER Dr John Austwick **EST.** 1979 **CASES** 500
SUMMARY John Austwick makes a small quantity of full-flavoured, robust Cabernet Sauvignon in a tiny winery as a labour of love on weekends and holidays. The Pinot Noir is made in a style which will appeal to confirmed Cabernet Sauvignon drinkers.

Craiglee ★★★★★

Sunbury Road, Sunbury, Vic 3429 **REGION** Sunbury
T (03) 9744 4489 **F** (03) 9744 4489 **WEB** www.craiglee.com.au **OPEN** Sun, public hols 10–5, or by appointment
WINEMAKER Patrick Carmody **EST.** 1976 **CASES** 3000
SUMMARY A winery with a proud 19th-century record which recommenced winemaking in 1976 after a prolonged hiatus. Produces one of the finest cool-climate Shirazs in Australia, redolent of cherry, licorice and spice in the better (warmer) vintages, lighter-bodied in the cooler ones. Maturing vines and improved viticulture have made the wines more consistent (and even better) over the past 10 years or so. Exports to the UK, the US and New Zealand.

Craigow ★★★★

528 Richmond Road, Cambridge, Tas 7170 **REGION** Southern Tasmania
T (03) 6248 5379 **F** (03) 6248 5482 **WEB** www.craigow.com.au **OPEN** 7 days Christmas to Easter (except public hols), or by appointment
WINEMAKER Julian Alcorso (Contract) **EST.** 1989 **CASES** 1500
SUMMARY Craigow has substantial vineyards, with 5 ha of pinot noir and another 5 ha (in total) of riesling, chardonnay and gewurztraminer. Barry and Cathy Edwards have moved from being grapegrowers with only one wine made for sale to a portfolio of 5 wines, while continuing to sell most of their grapes. Craigow has an impressive museum release program; the best are outstanding, others show the ravages of bottle oxidation, which affects some bottles and not others. Exports to the UK.

ŸŸŸŸŸ **Chardonnay 1999** Glowing yellow-green; tangy nectarine and grapefruit; rich and long; balanced Tasmanian acidity. **RATING** 93 **DRINK** Now **$** 32
Riesling 1999 Glowing yellow-green; has flowered in its secondary phase; rich lime juice off-set by acidity. Cork. **RATING** 91 **DRINK** 2008 **$** 28

ŸŸŸŸ **Pinot Noir 2003** Intense but very tannic; certainly has length. **RATING** 89 **DRINK** 2010 **$** 28
Sauvignon Blanc 2004 Long, quite intense; apple and gooseberry; crunchy acidity. **RATING** 87 **DRINK** 2007 **$** 18.95

ŸŸŸŸ **Gewurztraminer 2004** **RATING** 86 **DRINK** Now **$** 24
Chardonnay 2003 **RATING** 86 **DRINK** 2007 **$** 22.50
Chardonnay 2004 **RATING** 84 **DRINK** Now **$** 22.50

Craneford NR

Moorundie Street, Truro, SA 5356 **REGION** Barossa Valley
T (08) 8564 0003 **F** (08) 8564 0008 **WEB** www.cranefordwines.com **OPEN** 7 days 10–5
WINEMAKER John Zilm, Colin Forbes (Consultant) **EST.** 1978 **CASES** 25 000
SUMMARY The purchase of Craneford by owner/winemaker John Zilm wrought many changes. It has moved to a new winery (and café) and is supported by contract-grown grapes, with the purchase price paid per hectare, not per tonne, giving Craneford total control over yield and (hopefully) quality. Retail distribution in Sydney and Melbourne, and exports to Japan through Australian Prestige Wines.

Crane Winery ★★★★

Haydens Road, Kingaroy, Qld 4610 **REGION** South Burnett
T (07) 4162 7647 **F** (07) 4162 8381 **WEB** www.cranewines.com.au **OPEN** 7 days 10–4
WINEMAKER John Crane **EST.** 1996 **CASES** 4000
SUMMARY Established by John and Sue Crane, Crane Winery is one of several in the burgeoning Kingaroy (or South Burnett) region in Queensland, drawing upon 8 ha of estate plantings but also purchasing grapes from 20 other growers in the region.

ŸŸŸŸŸ **Cabernet Sauvignon 2002** A complex and very powerful wine; abundant black fruits, and ripe tannins. **RATING** 94 **DRINK** 2012 **$** NA Sold out

ŸŸŸŸ **Merlot 2002** Clean; ripe fruit in the blackcurrant spectrum; a sweet lick of vanilla oak and dark chocolate; ripe tannins. **RATING** 88 **DRINK** 2010 **$** NA Sold out

ŸŸŸ **Barrel-Fermented Chardonnay 2001** **RATING** 82 **$** 19

Crawford River Wines

741 Hotspur Upper Road, Condah, Vic 3303 **REGION** Henty
T (03) 5578 2267 **F** (03) 5578 2240 **OPEN** By appointment
WINEMAKER John Thomson **EST.** 1975 **CASES** 4000
SUMMARY Time flies, and it seems incredible that Crawford River has celebrated its 30th birthday. Once a tiny outpost in a little-known wine region, Crawford River has now established itself as one of the foremost producers of Riesling (and other excellent wines) thanks to the unremitting attention to detail and skill of its founder and winemaker, John Thomson. Exports to the UK and Denmark.

ŸŸŸŸŸ **Riesling 2004** Very fine and intense lime blossom aromas; a mix of lime, apple, spice and mineral on the perfectly balanced and very long palate; lemony acidity. Screwcap.
RATING 96 **DRINK** 2014 $ 27

ŸŸŸŸŸ **Sauvignon Blanc Semillon 2004** Fragrant and flowery passionfruit aromas; generous, ripe mid-palate tightens nicely on the finish with balanced acidity and the spine of Semillon. Screwcap. **RATING** 93 **DRINK** 2009 $ 22

ŸŸŸŸ **Cabernet Merlot 2003 RATING** 86 **DRINK** 2009 $ 27

🐛 Creeks Edge Wines NR

Creeks Edge Vineyard, Lue Road, Mudgee, NSW 2850 **REGION** Mudgee
T (02) 6372 6186 **F** (02) 6372 6182 **WEB** www.creeksedge.com.au **OPEN** Thurs–Mon 9.30–5
WINEMAKER Simon Gilbert, Damian Grindley (Contract) **EST.** 2003 **CASES** 5000
SUMMARY Creeks Edge Wines is a redevelopment of an old 43-ha vineyard purchased from Orlando Wyndham by a partnership of American and Australian wine enthusiasts. The oldest vines were planted in 1976, with follow-on plantings in 1988 and a final block of semillon in 1994. To date the wines have been contract-made in part at Simon Gilbert Wines and in part at Andrew Harris Wines and are available through the cellar door (and through the website) pending the appointment of distributors. The red wines are brought to the onsite barrel store for maturation, and the intention is to make small quantities of super-premium Shiraz and Cabernet onsite in the 2005 vintage.

Crisford Winery NR

556 Hermitage Road, Pokolbin, NSW 2321 **REGION** Lower Hunter Valley
T (02) 9387 1100 **F** (02) 9387 6688 **OPEN** Not
WINEMAKER Steve Dodd **EST.** 1990 **CASES** 340
SUMMARY Carol and Neal Crisford have established 2.6 ha of merlot and cabernet franc which go to produce Synergy. Neal Crisford produces educational videos on wine used in TAFE colleges and by the Australian Society of Wine Education. The wine is sold through the Hunter Valley Wine Society.

Crittenden at Dromana ★★★☆

25 Harrisons Road, Dromana, Vic 3936 **REGION** Mornington Peninsula
T (03) 5981 8322 **F** (03) 5981 8366 **OPEN** 7 days 11–5
WINEMAKER Garry Crittenden **EST.** 2003 **CASES** NA
SUMMARY Like a phoenix from the ashes, Garry Crittenden has risen again, soon after his formal ties with Dromana Estate were severed (son Rollo remains chief winemaker at Dromana Estate). He took with him the Schinus range; has Sangiovese and Arneis due for progressive release under the Pinocchio label; and, under the premium Crittenden at Dromana label, wines made from the 22-year-old 5-ha vineyard surrounding the family house and cellar door. The wines are distributed by Red+White.

ŸŸŸŸ **Schinus Sauvignon Blanc 2004** Nice wine, well made; clean, light to medium-bodied gooseberry and sweet redcurrant fruit. Strangely, cork-finished. **RATING** 87 **DRINK** Now $ 15

Melon 2004 Lively and fresh; interesting wine; has real mid to back-palate flavour, then good minerally acidity. The grape of Muscadet, France. First in Australia. **RATING** 87 **DRINK** 2007 $ 25

ŸŸŸŸ **Schinus Chardonnay 2004 RATING** 86 **DRINK** Now $ 15

Crooked River Wines

NR

11 Willow Vale Road, Gerringong, NSW 2534 **REGION** Shoalhaven Coast
T (02) 4234 0975 **F** (02) 4234 4477 **WEB** www.crookedriverwines.com **OPEN** 7 days 10.30–4.30
WINEMAKER Bevan Wilson **EST.** 1998 **CASES** 6500
SUMMARY With 14 ha of vineyard planted to chardonnay, verdelho, arneis, shiraz, cabernet
sauvignon, merlot, ruby cabernet, sangiovese and chambourcin, Crooked River Wines has the largest
vineyard on the south coast. Production is expected to increase to 10 000 cases through an onsite
winery. Cellar door sales, craft shop and café opened in December 2001.

Cross Rivulet

NR

334 Richmond Road, Cambridge, Tas 7170 **REGION** Southern Tasmania
T (03) 6228 5406 **OPEN** First weekend in March, or by appointment
WINEMAKER Lloyd Mathews **EST.** 1980 **CASES** 350
SUMMARY Geologist Lloyd Mathews is a self-taught viticulturist and winemaker, readily confessing
that his main experience is learning from mistakes, a short adult education course on winemaking
notwithstanding.

Crosswinds Vineyard

10 Vineyard Drive, Tea Tree, Tas 7017 **REGION** Southern Tasmania
T (03) 6268 1091 **F** (03) 6268 1091 **OPEN** Mon–Fri 10–5
WINEMAKER Andrew Vasiljuk **EST.** 1990 **CASES** 650
SUMMARY Crosswinds has 2 vineyards: the 1-ha Tea Tree Vineyard and the 2-ha Margate Vineyard.
As well as cellar door sales, has retail distribution in Melbourne and small exports to the UK and
South-East Asia. Both Chardonnay and Pinot Noir have excelled in recent years.

Cruickshank Callatoota Estate

2656 Wybong Road, Wybong, NSW 2333 **REGION** Upper Hunter Valley
T (02) 6547 8149 **F** (02) 6547 8144 **WEB** www.cruickshank.com.au **OPEN** 7 days 9–5
WINEMAKER John Cruickshank, David Main, Andrew Thomas (Consultant) **EST.** 1973 **CASES** 5000
SUMMARY Owned by Sydney management consultant John Cruickshank and family. There is
continued improvement in wine quality and style, presumably reflecting the input of Andrew
Thomas. The Rose continues its good form, but it is with the younger Cabernet Franc and Cabernet
Sauvignon wines that the greatest show success is being achieved (mainly in the Hunter Valley
Boutique Winemakers Show).

ŸŸŸŸŸ **Shiraz 2003** Deep colour; solid black fruits; touches of regional leather and earth in the
background; good balance and length. Gold Hunter Valley Wine Show '04. Cork.
RATING 91 **DRINK** 2012 $ 25

ŸŸŸŸ **Rose 2004** Lots of spicy red fruits; plenty of flavour, but not sweet; borders Light-bodied
Dry Red. Cork. **RATING** 87 **DRINK** Now $ 15

ŸŸŸŸ **Cabernet Franc 2002 RATING** 86 **DRINK** 2007 $ 20
Cabernet Franc 2000 RATING 86 **DRINK** Now $ 20

ŸŸŸ **Cabernet Sauvignon Pressings 2001 RATING** 83 $ 18

Cullen Wines

Caves Road, Cowaramup, WA 6284 **REGION** Margaret River
T (08) 9755 5277 **F** (08) 9755 5550 **WEB** www.cullenwines.com.au **OPEN** 7 days 10–4
WINEMAKER Vanya Cullen, Trevor Kent **EST.** 1971 **CASES** 20 000
SUMMARY One of the pioneers of Margaret River which has always produced long-lived wines of
highly individual style from the substantial and mature estate vineyards. Since the 2003 vintage, the
vineyard has received 'A grade' certification from the Biological Farmers Association, and received
the award as runner-up for best organic producer (all crops) with less than 5 years' certification.
Winemaking is now in the hands of Vanya Cullen, daughter of the founders; she is possessed of an
extraordinarily good palate. It is impossible to single out any particular wine from the top echelon;

all three are superb. The wines are distributed throughout Australia and also make their way to significant export markets in the UK, the US, Europe and Asia.

ŸŸŸŸŸ **Semillon Sauvignon Blanc 2004** Spotless mineral and thyme aromas; immaculately made; intensely focused and structured; very good balance and length. **RATING** 94 **DRINK** 2012 $29

ŸŸŸŸŸ **Ellen Bussell White 2004** Fragrant and tangy herb and spice aromas; good length and balance. **RATING** 90 **DRINK** 2007 $23
Ellen Bussell Red 2003 A bright and fresh array of predominantly red fruits; minimal tannins, balanced acidity. **RATING** 90 **DRINK** 2007 $23

Cumulus Wines ★★★☆

PO Box 41, Cudal, NSW 2864 **REGION** Orange
T (02) 6390 7900 **F** (02) 6364 2388 **WEB** www.cumuluswines.com.au **OPEN** Not
WINEMAKER Philip Shaw, Phillip Dowell, Nic Millichip **EST.** 1995 **CASES** 550 000
SUMMARY Cumulus Wines is the reborn Reynolds Wines, purchased by Assetinsure (a specialist insurance underwriter and partly owned by Babcock & Brown, international providers of venture capital) in 2003. Philip Shaw, previously head of winemaking for Rosemount and Southcorp, is the Chief Executive Officer, and Phillip Dowell (for 10 years winemaker at Coldstream Hills) is winery manager and winemaker. This is an asset-rich business, with over 500 ha of vineyards planted to all the mainstream varieties, the lion's share going to shiraz, cabernet sauvignon, chardonnay and merlot. The wines are released under three brands: Rolling, with a Central Ranges region of origin, coming in under $15; Climbing, solely from Orange fruit, at $18–20; and a third, yet to be named, super-premium from the best of the estate vineyard blocks. The quirky, striking labels will undoubtedly attract attention on the retail shelves of the world; principal exports to the UK and the US.

ŸŸŸŸŸ **Climbing Merlot 2003** Pretty wine, with attractive red fruits; good varietal character; nice oak and fine tannins. **RATING** 90 **DRINK** 2008 $19.99

ŸŸŸŸ **Climbing Cabernet Sauvignon 2003** Light to medium-bodied; savoury blackcurrant fruit; fine, ripe tannins; a touch of oak sweetening. **RATING** 87 **DRINK** 2008 $19.99

ŸŸŸŸ **Climbing Shiraz 2003** **RATING** 86 **DRINK** 2008 $19.99
Climbing Chardonnay 2004 **RATING** 84 **DRINK** 2007 $19.99

Curlewis Winery ★★★★★

55 Navarre Road, Curlewis, Vic 3222 **REGION** Geelong
T (03) 5250 4567 **F** (03) 5250 4567 **WEB** www.curlewiswinery.com.au **OPEN** By appointment
WINEMAKER Rainer Breit **EST.** 1998 **CASES** 1500
SUMMARY Rainer Breit and partner Wendy Oliver have achieved a great deal in a remarkably short period of time. In 1996 they purchased their property at Curlewis with 1.6 ha of what were then 11-year-old pinot noir vines; previously, and until 1998, the grapes had been sold to Scotchmans Hill. They set to and established an onsite winery; Rainer Breit is a self-taught winemaker, but the full bag of pinot noir winemaking tricks is used: cold-soaking, hot-fermentation, post-ferment maceration, part inoculated and partly wild yeast use, prolonged lees contact, and bottling the wine neither fined nor filtered. While Breit and Oliver are self-confessed 'pinotphiles', they have planted a little chardonnay and buy a little locally grown shiraz and chardonnay. The wines are sold into top restaurants or by mail order. Exports to Asia.

ŸŸŸŸŸ **Geelong Pinot Noir 2002** Intense, high-toned savoury, spicy, foresty aromas and flavours; fine and long; has finesse. Quality cork. **RATING** 94 **DRINK** 2010 $42.50

ŸŸŸŸŸ **Geelong Chardonnay 2003** Very complex, powerful wine; rich, luscious stone fruit balanced by quality French oak and acidity; long finish. Quality cork. **RATING** 93 **DRINK** 2010 $42.50

Curly Flat ★★★★☆

Collivers Road, Lancefield, Vic 3435 **REGION** Macedon Ranges
T (03) 5429 1956 **F** (03) 5429 2256 **WEB** www.curlyflat.com **OPEN** Sun, or by appointment
WINEMAKER Phillip Moraghan, Jillian Ryan **EST.** 1991 **CASES** 5000

184 | James Halliday

SUMMARY Phillip and Jeni Moraghan began the development of Curly Flat in 1992, drawing in part upon Phillip's working experience in Switzerland in the late 1980s, and with a passing nod to Michael Leunig. With ceaseless help and guidance from the late Laurie Williams the Moraghans have painstakingly established 8.5 ha of pinot noir, 3.4 ha of chardonnay and 0.6 ha of pinot gris, and a multilevel, gravity-flow winery. Exports to the UK.

ŸŸŸŸŸ **Chardonnay 2003** A powerful wine, with good intensity, line and length. Will develop further. **RATING** 93 **DRINK** 2009 $ 35
Pinot Noir 2003 Has complexity and power, but is not heavy; plum and spice fruit; excellent structure and balance; long finish. **RATING** 93 **DRINK** 2010 $ 44
Pinot Gris 2004 Faint pink blush; fragrant and aromatic wild flowers; elegant, light-bodied; long and graceful finish. **RATING** 90 **DRINK** 2007 $ 20

ŸŸŸŸ **Rose 2004** Bright, light red; strawberry and raspberry fruit; good length, not sweet. **RATING** 87 **DRINK** Now $ 18

🐦 Currans Family Wines ★★★☆

PO Box 271 SM, Mildura South, Vic 3501 **REGION** Murray Darling
T (03) 5025 7154 **F** (03) 5025 7154 **WEB** www.curransfamilywines.com.au **OPEN** Not
WINEMAKER Glen Olsen **EST.** 1997 **CASES** 1500
SUMMARY The Currans' story is a familiar one. In 1997 Chris and Sue Curran planted 4 ha of shiraz for sale to large wineries, but after 2 years of production (2000 and 2001) their grapes were suddenly no longer required, notwithstanding the great vintage. The only solution was to find a winemaker who was in tune with their organic approach to viticulture; they duly retained Oakleigh, Victoria, winemaker Glen Olsen. The story has a happy ending, with the 2002 Reserve Shiraz winning a bronze medal at the prestigious Great Australian Shiraz Challenge and a trophy at the Australian Inland Wine Show for Best Grapegrowers Wine (in the under 5000 litre section). The wines are made with deliberately low sulphur levels. The success has encouraged the Currans to plant an additional 0.25 ha of durif and 1 ha of viognier. The wines are available by mail order, with limited exports to the US.

ŸŸŸŸ **Minimum Preservatives Reserve Shiraz 2002** Shows cooler growing season; longer, less over-the-top ripe fruit, but still plenty of concentration. **RATING** 89 **DRINK** 2007 $ 20
Low Sulphur Shiraz 2003 Dense colour; extremely ripe prune, dark chocolate and raisin aromas and flavours; soft tannins, mega style. **RATING** 87 **DRINK** Now $ 15

ŸŸŸ **Saragina 2003 RATING** 79 $ 15

Currency Creek Estate ★★★☆

Winery Road, Currency Creek, SA 5214 **REGION** Currency Creek
T (08) 8555 4069 **F** (08) 8555 4100 **WEB** www.currencycreekwines.com.au **OPEN** 7 days 10–5
WINEMAKER John Loxton **EST.** 1969 **CASES** 9000
SUMMARY For over 30 years this relatively low-profile winery has produced some outstanding wood-matured whites and pleasant, soft reds selling at attractive prices. Exports to the US and Canada.

ŸŸŸŸŸ **The Black Swan Cabernet Sauvignon 2002** Medium-bodied; good structure and substance; attractive ripe blackcurrant, cassis mix; fine tannins, subtle oak. **RATING** 90 **DRINK** 2012

ŸŸŸŸ **Ostrich Hill Shiraz 2002** medium-bodied; good balance and length; red fruits, subtle oak. **RATING** 89 **DRINK** 2012 $ 20
Carabid Merlot 2002 Light-bodied; tangy, savoury, olive varietal character, aroma and flavour; needs more substance, however. **RATING** 87 **DRINK** 2008

Cuttaway Hill Estate ★★★★☆

PO Box 2034, Bowral, NSW 2576 **REGION** Southern Highlands
T (02) 4862 4551 **F** (02) 4862 2326 **WEB** www.cuttawayhillwines.com.au **OPEN** Not
WINEMAKER Jim Chatto, Mark Bourne (Contract) **EST.** 1998 **CASES** 10 000
SUMMARY Owned by the O'Neil family, Cuttaway Hill Estate is one of the largest vineyard properties in the Southern Highlands, with a total of 38 ha on three vineyard sites. The original Cuttaway Hill vineyard at Mittagong has 17 ha of chardonnay, merlot, cabernet sauvignon and shiraz. The Allambie

vineyard of 6.9 ha, on the light sandy loam soils of Ninety Acre Hill, is planted to sauvignon blanc, pinot gris and pinot noir. The third and newest vineyard is 14.2 ha at Maytree, west of Moss Vale in a relatively drier and warmer meso-climate. Here cabernet sauvignon, merlot and pinot noir (and a small amount of chardonnay) have been planted. The standard of both viticulture and contract winemaking under the direction of Jim Chatto at Monarch Winemaking Services is evident in the quality of the wines, not to mention the growth in production and sales.

ΤΤΤΤΥ **Southern Highlands Chardonnay 2002** Glowing yellow-green; toasty barrel ferment aromas; intense nectarine and white peach drives through to the finish. **RATING** 92 **DRINK** 2008 $ 20

Southern Highlands Semillon Sauvignon Blanc 2004 Again, very well made; tangy, intense and focused citrus, gooseberry and grassy fruit flavours. **RATING** 91 **DRINK** 2007 $ 15

Southern Highlands Merlot 2003 Light to medium-bodied; clean, fresh red berry fruit; elegant fine tannins and nice oak; harmonious. **RATING** 91 **DRINK** 2010 $ 15

Southern Highlands Sauvignon Blanc 2004 Spotlessly clean; very well made; ripe citrus edges to gooseberry fruit; good length. **RATING** 90 **DRINK** Now $ 15

Southern Highlands Chardonnay 2003 Developed yellow-green; toasty, nutty barrel ferment aromas; ripe peachy fruit balanced by acidity. Oak integrated. **RATING** 90 **DRINK** 2007 $ 20

Southern Highlands Pinot Gris 2004 Bronze colour; considerable fruit aromas and flavours; ripe pear and musk; good length; subliminal oak; impressive. **RATING** 90 **DRINK** 2007 $ 20

ΤΤΤΥ **Southern Highlands Cabernet Sauvignon 2003** **RATING** 86 **DRINK** 2008 $ 15

Dalfarras ★★★☆

PO Box 123, Nagambie, Vic 3608 **REGION** Nagambie Lakes
T (03) 5794 2637 **F** (03) 5794 2360 **OPEN** Not
WINEMAKER Alister Purbrick, Alan George **EST.** 1991 **CASES** 15 000
SUMMARY The personal project of Alister Purbrick and artist wife Rosa (née) Dalfarra, whose paintings adorn the labels of the wines. Alister, of course, is best known as winemaker at Tahbilk, the family winery and home, but this range of wines is intended to (in Alister's words) 'allow me to expand my winemaking horizons and mould wines in styles different from Tahbilk'. It now draws upon 23 ha of its own plantings in the Goulburn Valley.

ΤΤΤΥ **Shiraz 2001** **RATING** 86 **DRINK** 2009 $ 14.95

Dalrymple ★★★★★

1337 Pipers Brook Road, Pipers Brook, Tas 7254 **REGION** Northern Tasmania
T (03) 6382 7222 **F** (03) 6382 7222 **WEB** www.dalrymplevineyards.com.au **OPEN** 7 days 10–5
WINEMAKER Bertel Sundstrup **EST.** 1987 **CASES** 6000
SUMMARY A partnership between Jill Mitchell and her sister and brother-in-law, Anne and Bertel Sundstrup, inspired by father Bill Mitchell's establishment of the Tamarway Vineyard in the late 1960s. In 1991 Tamarway reverted to the Sundstrup and Mitchell families and it, too, will be producing wine in the future, probably under its own label but sold ex the Dalrymple cellar door. As production has grown (significantly), so has wine quality across the board, often led by its Sauvignon Blanc, and (more recently) Pinot Noir.

ΤΤΤΤΤ **Special Bin Pinot Noir 2003** Dense colour; big, rich, ripe plummy fruit; good use of oak; seductive and voluptuous. Top Gold Tasmanian Wines Show 2005. **RATING** 95 **DRINK** 2011 $ 30

Pinot Noir 2002 Complex leathery/savoury aromas with a background of violets; good length, fine tannins and supporting acidity. Multiple trophies Tasmanian Wines Show 2005. **RATING** 95 **DRINK** 2010 $ 30

Chardonnay 2002 Powerful, still with the same strong barrel ferment characters of youth, but with the intense nectarine and grapefruit now carrying the day. **RATING** 94 **DRINK** 2009 $ 20

ΤΤΤΤΥ **Chardonnay 2003** Clean, fresh, lively and crisp; nectarine and grapefruit; sensitive oak. Has developed excellently. **RATING** 90 **DRINK** 2008 $ 20

ŸŸŸŸ **Sauvignon Blanc 2004** Fine, crisp; quite punchy/crunchy apple; good length and persistence. **RATING** 88 **DRINK** 2007 $ 25
Unwooded Chardonnay 2003 Although unoaked, skilful use of lees contact and malolactic fermentation, and quite possibly wild yeast, results in a complex wine. **RATING** 88 **DRINK** 2008 $ 20
Chardonnay 2001 Very citrussy, Sauvignon Blanc crossover; lively and zippy in typical Tasmanian style. **RATING** 88 **DRINK** 2008 $ 20

ŸŸŸ **Unwooded Chardonnay 2004 RATING** 83 $ 20

Dalwhinnie ★★★★★

448 Taltarni Road, Moonambel, Vic 3478 **REGION** Pyrenees
T (03) 5467 2388 **F** (03) 5467 2237 **WEB** www.dalwhinnie.com.au **OPEN** 7 days 10–5
WINEMAKER David Jones, Gary Baldwin (Consultant) **EST.** 1976 **CASES** 4500
SUMMARY David and Jenny Jones are making outstanding wines right across the board. The wines all show tremendous depth of fruit flavour, reflecting the relatively low-yielding but very well-maintained vineyards. It is hard to say whether the Chardonnay, the Cabernet Sauvignon or the Shiraz is the more distinguished; the Pinot Noir is a startling arrival from out of nowhere. A further 8 ha of shiraz (with a little viognier) were planted in the spring of 1999 on a newly acquired block on Taltarni Road, permitting the further development of exports to the UK, Sweden, Switzerland, the US, Canada, New Zealand and Hong Kong. A 50-tonne contemporary high-tech winery now allows the Eagle Series Shiraz and Pinot Noir to be made onsite.

ŸŸŸŸŸ **Eagle Series Pyrenees Shiraz 2001** Complex, ripe, spice, cedar and mocha; high-toned, vibrant follow-through; ripples of spice and juicy berry fruit; fine, silky tannins. Slightly stained high-quality cork. **RATING** 94 **DRINK** 2016 $ 148

ŸŸŸŸ♡ **Moonambel Shiraz 2003** Very ripe, juicy, jammy fruit aromas and fore-palate; 13.5° alcohol less than expected; slight hole before the tannins on the finish. High-quality cork. **RATING** 92 **DRINK** 2013 $ 48
Pinot Noir 2003 Ripe, rich, plum varietal fruit; medium-bodied; good flow, texture and length; the usual conundrum of region and variety. High-quality cork. **RATING** 91 **DRINK** 2009 $ 38

ŸŸŸŸ **Moonambel Cabernet Sauvignon 2003** Medium red-purple, clear and bright; crisp, taut style proclaiming its low (12.5°) alcohol; out of style for Dalwhinnie. Another drought stress manifestation. **RATING** 88 **DRINK** 2010 $ 44

Dalyup River Estate ★★★★☆

Murrays Road, Esperance, WA 6450 **REGION** Western Australia South East Coastal Zone
T (08) 9076 5027 **F** (08) 9076 5027 **OPEN** Weekends 10–4 Oct–May
WINEMAKER Tom Murray **EST.** 1987 **CASES** 1000
SUMMARY Arguably the most remote winery in Australia other than Chateau Hornsby in Alice Springs, drawing upon 2.5 ha of estate vineyards. The quantities are as small as the cellar door prices are modest; this apart, the light but fragrant wines show the cool climate of this ocean-side vineyard. Came from out of the clouds to win the trophy for Best Wine of Show at the West Australian Show in 1999 with its Shiraz, but hasn't repeated that success.

ŸŸŸŸŸ **Esperance Shiraz 2002** Ageing wonderfully well; very elegant and stylish; long, medium-bodied. Shows its prior success was not an aberration on the part of the judges. Terrific tannins and finesse. **RATING** 94 **DRINK** 2012 $ 19

Dal Zotto Estate ★★★★

1944 Edi Road, Cheshunt, Vic 3678 **REGION** King Valley
T (03) 5729 8321 **F** (03) 5729 8490 **WEB** www.dalzottoestatewines.com.au **OPEN** 7 days 11–5
WINEMAKER Otto Dal Zotto, Michael Dal Zotto **EST.** 1987 **CASES** 15 000
SUMMARY Dal Zotto Wines remains primarily a contract grapegrower, with 48 ha of vineyards (predominantly chardonnay, cabernet sauvignon and merlot, with smaller plantings of riesling, pinot gris, shiraz, sangiovese, barbera, marzemino and prosecco). Increasing amounts are made under the Dal Zotto label, with retail distribution in New South Wales and Victoria; exports to the UK, Canada, Hong Kong and China.

ᵀᵀᵀᵀ♀ **King Valley Riesling 2004** Spicy, minerally aromas; moving to sweet apple and citrus on the palate; long, cleansing acidity. Screwcap. **RATING** 92 **DRINK** 2014 $15

ᵀᵀᵀᵀ **King Valley Arneis 2004** Faintly flinty, smoky, spicy aromas; bursts into life on the palate with white peach, ripe apple and lemon juice; crisp finish. Screwcap. **RATING** 89 **DRINK** 2007 $22

King Valley Merlot 2001 Light to medium-bodied; supple mouthfeel; gently earthy, savoury notes, but sweet red fruits as well. Stained cork. **RATING** 89 **DRINK** 2008 $19

King Valley Pinot Grigio 2004 Pear, spice and talc aromas; tangy palate; citrus and pear; good length. Screwcap. **RATING** 88 **DRINK** Now $19

King Valley Family Reserve Shiraz 2002 Abundant plum, blackberry and black cherry fruit; some spice; soft tannins and oak. Quality cork. **RATING** 88 **DRINK** 2010 $29

King Valley Sangiovese 2003 Fine, light to medium-bodied; attractive, spicy black cherries/red cherries; supple, easy access. **RATING** 87 **DRINK** 2008 $22

King Valley Barbera 2002 Warm, ripe, spicy/jammy aromas; a central core of fruit, but no structure to support it. An odd mixture. Cork. **RATING** 87 **DRINK** Now $22

ᵀᵀᵀᵀ♀ **King Valley Rose 2004** **RATING** 86 **DRINK** Now $16
King Valley Cabernet Merlot 2001 **RATING** 86 **DRINK** 2007 $19
King Valley Cabernet Sauvignon 2001 **RATING** 85 **DRINK** 2008 $19
King Valley Chardonnay 2003 **RATING** 84 **DRINK** Now $22

Danbury Estate

NR

Billimari, NSW 2794 (PO Box 605, Cowra, NSW 2794) **REGION** Cowra
T (02) 6341 2204 **F** (02) 6341 4690 **OPEN** Tues–Sun 10–4
WINEMAKER Hope Estate (Contract) **EST.** 1996 **CASES** 6000
SUMMARY A specialist Chardonnay producer established by Jonathon Middleton, with 22 ha in production. The Quarry Restaurant at the winery is open Tuesday to Sunday 10–4.

d'Arenberg

★★★★★

Osborn Road, McLaren Vale, SA 5171 **REGION** McLaren Vale
T (08) 8323 8206 **F** (08) 8323 8423 **WEB** www.darenberg.com.au **OPEN** 7 days 10–5
WINEMAKER Chester Osborn, Phillip Dean **EST.** 1912 **CASES** 250 000
SUMMARY Originally a conservative, traditional business (albeit successful), d'Arenberg adopted a much higher profile in the second half of the 1990s, with a cascade of volubly worded labels and the opening of a spectacularly situated and high-quality restaurant, d'Arry's Verandah. Happily, wine quality has more than kept pace with the label uplifts. The winery has over 100 ha of estate vineyards dating back to the 1890s, 1920 and 1950s, and a Joseph's Coat of trendy new varieties planted in the 1990s. Exports to all major markets.

ᵀᵀᵀᵀᵀ **The Galvo Garage 2002** A scented and spicy bouquet with touches of leaf and mint leads into a supple palate with rich, sweet fruits. **RATING** 95 **DRINK** 2011 $30

The Dead Arm Shiraz 2002 Clean and quite fragrant; abundant blackberry and dark chocolate fruit; controlled extract and good balance. Poor-quality cork. **RATING** 94 **DRINK** 2015 $60

The Coppermine Road Cabernet Sauvignon 2002 Pungent, powerful, raunchy style; intense blackcurrant fruit; nice French oak. **RATING** 94 **DRINK** 2017 $60

ᵀᵀᵀᵀ♀ **The Broken Fishplate Sauvignon Blanc 2004** Clean and fresh; no reduction; passionfruit and blossom; good length and drive to the palate; fresh finish. **RATING** 93 **DRINK** Now $19.95

d'Arry's Original Shiraz Grenache 2002 Complex savoury/spicy/earthy flavours with a red fruit core; spicy echoes; fine structure and tannins. **RATING** 93 **DRINK** 2009 $19.95

The Custodian Grenache 2002 Plush, luscious raspberry/blackberry fruit in archetypal varietal style; good weight, subtle oak. **RATING** 93 **DRINK** 2007 $19.95

The Bonsai Vine Grenache Shiraz Mourvedre 2001 Nicely balanced and constructed; savoury, spicy elements; notable elegance and finesse; 70/25/5 blend. **RATING** 92 **DRINK** 2012 $30

The Footbolt Old Vine Shiraz 2002 Well-balanced and framed blackberry and redcurrant fruit; surprisingly elegant given its substantial alcohol. **RATING** 91 **DRINK** 2009 $19.95

Twenty Eight Road Mourvedre 2001 Medium to full-bodied; spice, earth and bitter chocolate; varietal tannins; controlled oak. **RATING** 91 **DRINK** 2010 $ 35

The Laughing Magpie Shiraz Viognier 2003 Fragrant, fresh, raspberry and redcurrant, almost into sarsaparilla; minty touches too. **RATING** 90 **DRINK** 2007 $ 30

Fortified Shiraz 2002 Good balance; dark blackberry, black fruits and spice; dry but potent; deserves at least 5 years. **RATING** 90 **DRINK** 2017 $ 34.95

ΤΤΤΤ   **The Lucky Lizard Chardonnay 2003** Lots of winemaking footprints; barrel ferment and malolactic inputs obvious; the use of a basket press is decidedly quixotic. **RATING** 89 **DRINK** 2007 $ 25

The High Trellis Cabernet Sauvignon 2002 Bramble, spice, herb and blackcurrant aromas; dark fruits, black chocolate and savoury flavours. **RATING** 89 **DRINK** 2008 $ 32

The Hermit Crab Marsanne Viognier 2003 Big, rich, full flavoured; ripe tropical fruit; carries 14.5° alcohol surprisingly well. **RATING** 88 **DRINK** 2007 $ 16.95

The Last Ditch Viognier 2003 French oak barrel fermentation and maturation very obvious; some musk and fig varietal fruit to balance. **RATING** 87 **DRINK** 2007 $ 19.95

The Cadenzia Grenache Shiraz Mourvedre 2003 Light to medium-bodied; spicy, jammy, juicy style; minimal tannins and oak; the dreaded Zork. **RATING** 87 **DRINK** 2008 $ 25

ΤΤΤΤ   **The Dry Dam Riesling 2004** **RATING** 86 **DRINK** Now $ 16.95

The Olive Grove Chardonnay 2003 **RATING** 86 **DRINK** Now $ 16.95

The Money Spider Roussanne 2004 **RATING** 86 **DRINK** Now $ 19.95

The Money Spider Roussanne 2003 **RATING** 86 **DRINK** 2007 $ 19.95

The Stump Jump Riesling Sauvignon Blanc Marsanne 2004 **RATING** 86 **DRINK** Now $ 11.95

The Feral Fox Pinot Noir 2003 **RATING** 86 **DRINK** Now $ 30

The Noble Blend 2003 **RATING** 86 **DRINK** Now $ 25

The Stump Jump Riesling Sauvignon Blanc Marsanne 2003 **RATING** 84 **DRINK** Now $ 11.95

Dargo Valley Winery   NR

Lower Dargo Road, Dargo, Vic 3682 **REGION** Gippsland
T (03) 5140 1228 **F** (03) 5140 1388 **OPEN** Mon–Thurs 12–8, weekends & hols 10–8 (closed Fridays)
WINEMAKER Hermann Bila **EST.** 1985 **CASES** 500
SUMMARY The winery's 2.5 ha are situated in mountain country north of Maffra and looking towards the Bogong National Park. Hermann Bila comes from a family of European winemakers; there is an onsite restaurant, and Devonshire teas and ploughman's lunches are served – very useful given the remote locality. The white wines tend to be rustic, the sappy/earthy/cherry Pinot Noir the pick of the red wines. B&B accommodation is available.

Darling Estate   ★★☆

Whitfield Road, Cheshunt, Vic 3678 **REGION** King Valley
T (03) 5729 8396 **F** (03) 5729 8396 **OPEN** By appointment
WINEMAKER Guy Darling **EST.** 1990 **CASES** 500
SUMMARY Guy Darling was one of the pioneers of the King Valley when he planted his first vines in 1970. For many years the entire production was purchased by Brown Brothers, for their well-known Koombahla Estate label. Much of the production from the 23 ha is still sold to Brown Brothers (and others), but since 1991 Guy Darling has had a fully functional winery established on the vineyard, making a small portion of the production into wine – which was, in fact, his original aim. All the wines on sale have considerable bottle age.

Darling Park   ★★★★

232 Red Hill Road, Red Hill, Vic 3937 **REGION** Mornington Peninsula
T (03) 5989 2324 **F** (03) 5989 2324 **WEB** www.darlingparkwinery.com **OPEN** First weekend in month 11–5
WINEMAKER Robert Paul (Winenet) **EST.** 1986 **CASES** 3000

SUMMARY Josh and Karen Liberman and David Coe purchased Darling Park before the 2002 vintage. The Winenet consultancy group is providing advice on both the viticultural and winemaking side, and the product range has been revamped.

ΥΥΥΥ **Masters Collection Chardonnay 2004** Aromatic grapefruit and stone fruit with subtle barrel ferment oak inputs; considerable length and intensity. Screwcap. **RATING** 92 **DRINK** 2010 $ 24
Masters Collection Basket Pressed Syrah 2003 Very good colour; black cherry, plum, spice and pepper; medium-bodied; fine, silky tannins; fresh finish. Cork. **RATING** 92 **DRINK** 2013 $ 33
Masters Collection Te Quiero Pinot Noir Shiraz Merlot 2003 Strong colour; the Pinot Noir swamped by black cherry and plum Shiraz and Merlot; lots of ripe fruits; successful design by committee. Screwcap. **RATING** 90 **DRINK** 2010 $ 18

ΥΥΥΥ **Limited Release Pinot Noir 2004** Light to medium-bodied; small red fruits and plums; good tannin structure and length. Screwcap. **RATING** 89 **DRINK** 2008 $ 28
Querida Rose 2004 Fresh, lively strawberry, cherry and spice aromas and flavours; has length, good balance, and is not sweet. Screwcap. **RATING** 88 **DRINK** Now $ 17

ΥΥΥΥ **Griognier 2004** A blend of Pinot Gris and Viognier; aromatic, but fails to convince on the palate. Screwcap. **RATING** 86 **DRINK** 2007 $ 24
Limited Release Pinot Noir 2003 **RATING** 85 **DRINK** 2007 $ 28
Estate Merlot 2001 **RATING** 84 **DRINK** 2008 $ 22

Darlington Estate ★★☆

Lot 39 Nelson Road, Darlington, WA 6070 **REGION** Perth Hills
T (08) 9299 6268 **F** (08) 9299 7107 **WEB** www.darlingtonestate.com.au **OPEN** Thurs–Sun & hols 12–5
WINEMAKER Caspar van der Meer **EST.** 1983 **CASES** 1500
SUMMARY Established by the van der Meer family, it is one of the oldest – and was once the largest – wineries in the Perth Hills, for a while setting the standard. After an intermission, Caspar van der Meer has returned to the winemaking role.

Darlington Vineyard ★★★

Holkam Court, Orford, Tas 7190 **REGION** Southern Tasmania
T (03) 6257 1630 **F** (03) 6257 1630 **OPEN** Thurs–Mon 10–5
WINEMAKER Andrew Hood (Contract) **EST.** 1993 **CASES** 450
SUMMARY Peter and Margaret Hyland planted a little under 2 ha of vineyard in 1993. The first wines were made from the 1999 vintage, forcing retired builder Peter Hyland to complete their home so that the small building in which they had been living could be converted into a cellar door. The vineyard looks out over the settlement of Darlington on Maria Island, the site of Diego Bernacci's attempt to establish a vineyard and lure investors by attaching artificial bunches of grapes to his vines.

ΥΥΥΥ **Pinot Noir 2003** Light to medium-bodied; good structure; spicy fruit, fine tannins; has length. **RATING** 88 **DRINK** 2008 $ 22

ΥΥΥΥ **Riesling 2004** **RATING** 84 **DRINK** 2007 $ 17

ΥΥΥΥ **Sweet Riesling 2004** **RATING** 85 **DRINK** 2007 $ 17

David Traeger ★★★☆

139 High Street, Nagambie, Vic 3608 **REGION** Nagambie Lakes
T (03) 5794 2514 **F** (03) 5794 1776 **OPEN** Mon–Fri 10–5, weekends & public hols 11–5
WINEMAKER David Traeger **EST.** 1986 **CASES** 10 000
SUMMARY David Traeger learned much during his years as assistant winemaker at Mitchelton, and knows central Victoria well. The red wines are solidly crafted, the Verdelho interesting and surprisingly long-lived. In late 2002 the business was acquired by the Dromana Estate group, but David Traeger has stayed on as winemaker. See also Baptista entry. Exports to the UK, Japan, Italy and Canada.

ŸŸŸŸ **Verdelho 2004** Fresh, lively fruit salad; above-average intensity and length; cool vintage helps. Screwcap. **RATING** 88 **DRINK** 2007 $ 17.50
Verdelho 2003 More texture and mouthfeel than many; fruit salad with a twist of lemon. **RATING** 87 **DRINK** Now $ 17.50

ŸŸŸŸ **Shiraz 2001 RATING** 84 **DRINK** 2009 $ 29.50

Dawson Estate ★★★★

Cnr Old Naracoorte Road/Kangaroo Hill Road, Robe, SA 5276 **REGION** Mount Benson
T (08) 8768 2427 **F** (08) 8768 2987 **OPEN** Not
WINEMAKER Derek Hooper (Contract) **EST.** 1998 **CASES** 500
SUMMARY Anthony Paul and Marian Dawson are busy people. In addition to establishing over 20 ha of chardonnay, pinot noir, shiraz and cabernet sauvignon, they are in the process of opening a wine bar/restaurant in Robe, and intend to continue extending the vineyard on a further 16 ha of plantable land. All of this is largely financed by the crayfishing boat which Anthony runs in the crayfish season.

ŸŸŸŸŸ **Shiraz 2003** Round, medium-bodied; juicy blackberry fruit, balanced oak and soft tannins. **RATING** 90 **DRINK** 2013

ŸŸŸŸ **Shiraz 2002** Very ripe licorice, prune and plum fruit on a concentrated palate. Slight dead fruit characters. **RATING** 87 **DRINK** 2009

ŸŸŸŸ **Cabernet Sauvignon 2002 RATING** 86 **DRINK** 2009

Dawson's Patch ★★★★

71 Kallista–Emerald Road, The Patch, Vic 3792 (postal) **REGION** Yarra Valley
T 0419 521 080 **OPEN** Not
WINEMAKER Paul Evans (Contract) **EST.** 2000 **CASES** 500
SUMMARY In 1996 James and Jody Dawson planted 1.2 ha of chardonnay on their vineyard at the southern end of the Yarra Valley. The climate here is particularly cool, and the grapes do not normally ripen until late April. Jody Dawson manages the vineyards, and is completing a degree in viticulture through Charles Sturt University. The tiny production is sold through local restaurants and cellars in the Olinda/Emerald/Belgrave area. So far only a barrel-fermented (French oak) wine has been produced, but it may be that an unoaked version will join the roster sometime in the future.

ŸŸŸŸ **Yarra Valley Chardonnay 2003** Rich, ripe nectarine, peach and melon fruit; integrated and balanced French oak. Cork. **RATING** 89 **DRINK** 2008 $ 31

Dead Horse Hill ★★★

Myola East Road, Toolleen, Vic 3551 **REGION** Heathcote
T (03) 9578 4962 **F** (03) 9578 4962 **OPEN** By appointment
WINEMAKER Jencie McRobert **EST.** 1994 **CASES** 500
SUMMARY Jencie McRobert (and husband Russell) 'did a deal with Dad' for approximately 65 ha of her parents' large sheep and wheat farm at Toolleen, 20 km north of Heathcote. It took a number of years for the 4-ha dry-grown vines to achieve reasonable yields, but (drought notwithstanding) they are now yielding between 3.7 and 5 tonnes per hectare of high-quality fruit. Jencie's introduction to wine came partly through the family dining table (she was introduced to Barossa Shiraz from a very young age) and partly from meeting Steve Webber, then working for Lindemans at Karadoc, and Tony Royal, working for Mildara at Merbein, when she was working in soil conservation and salinity management in the Mallee. She subsequently completed a course at Charles Sturt University, and makes the wine at De Bortoli in the Yarra Valley with the odd bit of assistance from Webber. The wine is distributed by Jencie; a distinguished list of Melbourne restaurants stock the wine.

ŸŸŸŸ **Shiraz 2003** Very savoury style; black fruits and fine but persistent tannins across the palate. **RATING** 86 **DRINK** 2010 $ 30

Deakin Estate ★★★

Kulkyne Way, via Red Cliffs, Vic 3496 **REGION** Murray Darling
T (03) 5029 1666 **F** (03) 5024 3316 **WEB** www.deakinestate.com.au **OPEN** Not

WINEMAKER Phil Spillman **EST.** 1980 **CASES** 500 000
SUMMARY Effectively replaces the Sunnycliff label in the Katnook Estate, Riddoch and (now) Deakin Estate triumvirate, which constitutes the Wingara Wine Group, now 60% owned by Freixenet of Spain. Sunnycliff is still used for export purposes but does not appear on the domestic market any more. Deakin Estate draws on over 300 ha of its own vineyards, making it largely self-sufficient, and produces competitively priced wines of consistent quality and impressive value. Exports to the UK, the US, Canada, New Zealand and Asia.

TTTT **DE Rose 2004** Spotlessly clean, fresh red fruits; very good balance; subliminal sweetness. Good value. **RATING** 87 **DRINK** Now $ 9.99
Select Shiraz 2002 Elegant, light to medium-bodied; lifted cherry and spice fruit. **RATING** 87 **DRINK** 2007 $ 15

TTTY **Sauvignon Blanc 2004** **RATING** 85 **DRINK** Now $ 10

TTT **DE Chardonnay 2004** **RATING** 83 $ 9.99
Brut NV **RATING** 83 **DRINK** Now $ 10

De Bortoli ★★★★

De Bortoli Road, Bilbul, NSW 2680 **REGION** Riverina
T (02) 6966 0100 **F** (02) 6966 0199 **WEB** www.debortoli.com.au **OPEN** Mon–Sat 9–5, Sun 9–4
WINEMAKER Julie Mortlock, Helen Foggo, Ralph Graham **EST.** 1928 **CASES** 3 million
SUMMARY Famous among the cognoscenti for its superb Botrytis Semillon, which in fact accounts for only a minute part of its total production, this winery turns around low-priced varietal and generic wines which are invariably competently made and equally invariably provide value for money. These come in part from 250 ha of estate vineyards, but mostly from contract-grown grapes. The death of founder Deen De Bortoli in 2003 was widely mourned by the wine industry. Exports to all major markets.

TTTTY **Vat 5 Botrytis Semillon 2002** Rich, honeyed peach, vanilla and spice; smooth and supple, good acidity. Cork. **RATING** 90 **DRINK** 2008 $ 10

TTTT **Deen Vat 4 Petit Verdot 2002** Still holding dense colour; very aromatic black fruits; lots of mid-palate plum and blackcurrant flavour; minimal tannins. **RATING** 88 **DRINK** 2007 $ 10
Deen Vat 1 Durif 2002 Bright red-purple; plenty of red and black fruits; long palate, persistent tannins. Value plus. **RATING** 88 **DRINK** Now $ 10
Deen Vat 2 Sauvignon Blanc 2004 Delicate fragrance, no reduction; gooseberry fruit and a touch of spritz. Excellent value. **RATING** 87 **DRINK** Now $ 11
Sacred Hill Cabernet Merlot 2004 Attractive sweet, juicy redcurrant fruit, bright and fresh; very good value. **RATING** 87 **DRINK** Now $ 5.50
Montage Cabernet Merlot 2004 Impressive young wine; sweet red berry fruit; supple and flavoursome; fruit-driven. Twin Top. **RATING** 87 **DRINK** 2007 $ 7.90
Sero King Valley Cabernet Merlot 2003 Light to medium-bodied; a fresh, entirely fruit-driven palate; gently ripe red and black berry mix; minimal tannins. **RATING** 87 **DRINK** 2007 $ 11

TTTY **Sero King Valley Unwooded Chardonnay 2004** **RATING** 86 **DRINK** Now $ 11
Deen Vat 7 Chardonnay 2004 Tangy, citrus edges to melon and nectarine aromas; slight sweetness on the palate in deference to the market; yellow tail style, but a good one. Cork. **RATING** 86 **DRINK** Now $ 10
Sacred Hill Semillon Chardonnay 2004 Lively and fresh; gentle lemony nectarine mix; subliminal oak; inevitably a touch short. Twin Top. **RATING** 86 **DRINK** Now $ 5.50
Sacred Hill Cabernet Merlot 2004 Similar winemaking skills; mouthfilling and balanced; some tannins; a hint of oak. Twin Top. **RATING** 86 **DRINK** 2007 $ 5.50
Sacred Hill Rhine Riesling 2004 **RATING** 85 **DRINK** Now $ 6
Sacred Hill Traminer Riesling 2004 **RATING** 84 **DRINK** Now $ 6
Sacred Hill Colombard Chardonnay 2004 **RATING** 84 **DRINK** Now $ 5.50
Sacred Hill Shiraz Cabernet 2004 **RATING** 84 $ 5.50

TTT **Montage Semillon Sauvignon Blanc 2004** **RATING** 83 $ 7.90
Wild Vine Chardonnay 2004 **RATING** 83 $ 7.50
Deen Vat 7 Chardonnay 2003 **RATING** 83 $ 11
Montage Chardonnay Semillon 2004 **RATING** 83 $ 9
Wild Vine White Zinfandel 2004 **RATING** 83 $ 7.50
Montage Cabernet Merlot 2003 **RATING** 82 $ 9

De Bortoli (Hunter Valley) ★★★☆

532 Wine Country Drive, Pokolbin, NSW 2320 **REGION** Lower Hunter Valley
T (02) 4993 8800 **F** (02) 4993 8899 **WEB** www.debortoli.com.au **OPEN** 7 days 10–5
WINEMAKER Scott Stephens, Sarah Fagan **EST.** 2002 **CASES** 35 000
SUMMARY De Bortoli extended its wine empire in 2002 with the purchase of the former Wilderness Estate, giving it an immediate and substantial presence in the Hunter Valley courtesy of the 26 ha of established vineyards; this was expanded significantly by the subsequent purchase of an adjoining 40-ha property.

ΨΨΨΨ **Black Creek Verdelho 2004** Quite tangy; good balance and varietal character; attractive lemony acidity; dry finish. Screwcap. **RATING** 87 **DRINK** Now $ 14

ΨΨΨΨ **Black Creek Hunter Valley Semillon 2004 RATING** 85 **DRINK** 2008 $ 12
Black Creek Semillon Sauvignon Blanc 2004 RATING 85 **DRINK** Now $ 14

De Bortoli (Victoria) ★★★★★

Pinnacle Lane, Dixons Creek, Vic 3775 **REGION** Yarra Valley
T (03) 5965 2271 **F** (03) 5965 2464 **WEB** www.debortoli.com.au **OPEN** 7 days 10–5
WINEMAKER Stephen Webber, David Slingsby-Smith, Ben Cane, Paul Bridgeman **EST.** 1987 **CASES** 400 000
SUMMARY The quality arm of the bustling De Bortoli group, run by Leanne De Bortoli and husband Stephen Webber, ex-Lindeman winemaker. The top label (De Bortoli), the second (Gulf Station) and the third label (Windy Peak) offer wines of consistently good quality and excellent value – the complex Chardonnay and the Pinot Noirs are usually of outstanding quality. The volume of production, by many times the largest in the Yarra Valley, simply underlines the quality/value for money ratio of the wines. Exports to all major markets.

ΨΨΨΨΨ **Reserve Yarra Valley Chardonnay 2003** Intense but elegant; complex barrel ferment notes with a touch of funk; nectarine and melon; great mouthfeel, long finish. **RATING** 95 **DRINK** 2010 $ 40
Yarra Valley Shiraz 2002 Good colour; supremely intense and focused; spicy, cool vintage style; black fruits; long, savoury/spicy tannins; firm profile. Northern Rhône lookalike. High-quality cork. **RATING** 95 **DRINK** 2017 $ 32

ΨΨΨΨΨ **Yarra Valley Shiraz Viognier 2003** Complex aromas; spice, berry, animal, apricot and licorice come together on an intense, long and powerful palate. Stained cork. **RATING** 92 **DRINK** 2010 $ 32
Yarra Valley Chardonnay 2003 The typical elegant, restrained style of De Bortoli; melon fruit with gentle fig and cashew malolactic and oak inputs. **RATING** 91 **DRINK** 2009 $ 26
Yarra Valley Shiraz 2003 Complex, spicy cool-climate fruit; good structure and texture. **RATING** 91 **DRINK** 2013 $ 29
Gulf Station Shiraz 2003 A powerful and rich mix of black fruits and spices; plenty of tannins for the long haul; subtle oak. Cork. **RATING** 90 **DRINK** 2013 $ 17

ΨΨΨΨ **Gulf Station Riesling 2004** Plenty of lemony flavours tinged with passionfruit; overall, quite generous. **RATING** 89 **DRINK** 2008 $ 17
Windy Peak Riesling 2004 Quite elegant; fine mineral, lime and herb; good length and balance. **RATING** 89 **DRINK** 2008 $ 12
Gulf Station Semillon Sauvignon Blanc 2004 Spotlessly clean and well balanced; delicate tropical/gooseberry fruit, then lingering acidity to close. **RATING** 89 **DRINK** 2007 $ 16
Windy Peak King Valley Sangiovese 2003 Above-average colour presages a palate with supple red and black cherry fruit, the tannins fine and gently spicy; an enticing fruit-foremost style. **RATING** 89 **DRINK** 2007 $ 12
Windy Peak Sauvignon Blanc Semillon 2004 Fragrant light passionfruit and tropical mix, plus hints of grass and mineral; clean finish. **RATING** 88 **DRINK** Now $ 12
Gulf Station Cabernet Sauvignon 2003 Leafy/minty edges to redcurrant/blackcurrant mix; light to medium-bodied; fine tannins. **RATING** 87 **DRINK** 2007 $ 16

ΨΨΨΨ **Windy Peak Chardonnay 2004 RATING** 86 **DRINK** 2007 $ 12
Windy Peak Cabernet Rose 2004 Very pale purple-red; crisp, clean but very light; not sweet; food style. Good value. **RATING** 86 **DRINK** Now $ 12

Sero King Valley Cabernet Merlot 2003 RATING 86 DRINK 2007 $ 10
Windy Peak Cabernet Shiraz Merlot 2002 RATING 86 DRINK 2007 $ 12
Sero King Valley Unwooded Chardonnay 2004 RATING 85 DRINK Now $ 10
Windy Peak Spaetlese Riesling 2004 RATING 84 DRINK 2009 $ 12

Deep Dene Vineyard   NR

36 Glenisla Road, Bickley, WA 6076 REGION Perth Hills
T (08) 9293 0077 F (08) 9293 0077 OPEN By appointment
WINEMAKER Contract EST. 1994 CASES 4000
SUMMARY Improbably, was once one of the largest Perth Hills vineyards, but no more. It has 4 ha of
pinot noir and 0.5 ha of shiraz, continuing the near obsession of the Perth Hills vignerons with pinot
noir in a climate which, to put it mildly, is difficult for the variety, other than in sparkling wine.

Deep Water Estate   NR

12 Morpeth Street, Mount Barker, WA 6324 REGION Mount Barker
T (08) 9851 1435 F (08) 9851 1435 OPEN Wed–Mon 10–5
WINEMAKER Keith McPake EST. 2001 CASES 1000
SUMMARY Keith and Rebecca McPake are newcomers to the wine industry, but have big plans. Keith
wants to make his own wine, cutting out the winemaker/wholesaler/retailer margins, but realised
'after all, we can only drink so much ourselves'. He started by leasing the 6-ha Kincora Vineyard on
the northern slopes of Mt Barker, planted to pinot noir, cabernet sauvignon and semillon, between
1991 and 1995. They have now begun the development of an estate vineyard, with 4 ha of cabernet
franc, merlot, riesling and chardonnay planted in 2003. Construction of a cellar door area looms in
the near future. In the meantime there is a substantial range of wines available at two price levels:
Aviators at the lower end and Deep Water Estate (headed by Reserve wines), at the higher end.

Deep Woods Estate

Lot 10 Commonage Road, Yallingup, WA 6282 REGION Margaret River
T (08) 9756 6066 F (08) 9756 6366 WEB www.deepwoods.com.au OPEN Tues–Sun 11–5, 7 days
during hols
WINEMAKER Ben Gould EST. 1987 CASES 20 000
SUMMARY The Gould family acquired Deep Woods Estate in 1991, 4 years after the commencement of
the estate plantings. There are 15 ha of estate vines planted to nine varieties, with the intake
supplemented by extended family-grown grapes for the Ebony and Ivory wines. At the top of the tree
are the occasional and tiny releases under the Boneyard label. These wines are only available to
mailing list customers, and are likely to be pre-sold to those on a waiting list, but overall production
continues to steadily increase. A second vineyard at Cowaramup is being established: 7 ha of
sauvignon blanc and 7 ha of semillon have been planted and another 32 ha of various varieties will
follow. Exports to Switzerland. In 2005 the business was acquired by Peter Fogarty (owner of
Millbrook and Lake's Folly) but Ben Gould is being retained as winemaking and (now) general
manager.

TTTTT Margaret River Sauvignon Blanc 2004 Spotlessly clean; vibrant gooseberry and
        kiwifruit; almost sweet acidity; long finish. Screwcap. RATING 94 DRINK 2007 $ 18

TTTTT Boneyard Chardonnay 2004 Medium-bodied; sweet nectarine, peach and melon fruit,
        with malolactic and barrel ferment inputs woven throughout; good length and finish.
        Screwcap. RATING 92 DRINK 2009 $ 38
        Margaret River Cabernet Merlot 2003 Very attractive supple, smooth blackberry, cherry
        and raspberry mix; medium-bodied; soft tannins, good oak. Screwcap. RATING 91
        DRINK 2013 $ 19.50
        Block 7 Margaret River Shiraz 2003 Medium-bodied; firm blackberry and plum fruit;
        fine tannins; good French oak handling. Diam. RATING 90 DRINK 2013 $ 25
        Cabernet Sauvignon 2003 Rich, with layers of juicy blackcurrant fruit and plenty of ripe
        tannins; subtle oak. RATING 90 DRINK Now $ 22

TTTT Block 8 Verdelho 2004 RATING 86 DRINK 2007 $ 18
        Margaret River Ivory 2004 RATING 84 DRINK Now $ 14

De Iuliis

★★★★☆

21 Broke Road, Pokolbin, NSW 2320 **REGION** Lower Hunter Valley
T (02) 4993 8000 **F** (02) 4998 7168 **WEB** www.dewine.com.au **OPEN** 7 days 10–5
WINEMAKER Michael De Iuliis **EST.** 1990 **CASES** 10 000
SUMMARY Three generations of the De Iuliis family have been involved in the establishment of their 45-ha vineyard. The family acquired the property in 1986 and planted the first vines in 1990, selling the grapes from the first few vintages to Tyrrell's but retaining small amounts of grapes for release under the De Iuliis label. Winemaker Michael De Iuliis has completed postgraduate studies in oenology at the Roseworthy Campus of Adelaide University and was a Len Evans Tutorial scholar. The overall quality of the wines is good; they are available through the cellar door and at select restaurants in the Hunter and Sydney, with small amounts coming to Melbourne.

▼▼▼▼▼ **Limited Release Shiraz 2003** Shares many characters with the Show Reserve; slightly finer structure and more length; excellent use of French oak. Screwcap. **RATING** 94 **DRINK** 2017 $ 32

▼▼▼▼▽ **Limited Release Chardonnay 2004** Complex, strong French funk on bouquet and palate; the fruit does carry it; will likely polarise opinions. Slightly sweet finish. Wild yeast fermentation in new French oak. Screwcap. **RATING** 93 **DRINK** 2009 $ 25

Semillon 2004 Pale straw-green; light-bodied, but quite intense; lemony, minerally aromas and flavours; good balance, long finish. Screwcap. **RATING** 92 **DRINK** 2014 $ 14

Show Reserve Shiraz 2003 Attractively rich, gently sweet blackberry fruit; medium-bodied fine, ripe tannins, subtle oak. Shows top vintage. Screwcap. **RATING** 92 **DRINK** 2013 $ 20

Late Picked Semillon 2004 Luscious apricot, peach, cumquat and vanilla; nice squeaky acidity. Screwcap. **RATING** 90 **DRINK** 2010 $ 16

▼▼▼▼ **Show Reserve Merlot 2003** Light to medium-bodied; juicy red and black berry fruits; light, slightly green, tannins. Twin Top. **RATING** 88 **DRINK** 2008 $ 27

Delacolline Estate

NR

Whillas Road, Port Lincoln, SA 5606 **REGION** Southern Eyre Peninsula
T (08) 8682 5277 **F** (08) 8682 4455 **OPEN** Weekends 9–5
WINEMAKER Andrew Mitchell (Contract) **EST.** 1984 **CASES** 650
SUMMARY Joins Boston Bay as the second Port Lincoln producer; the white wines are made in the Clare Valley. The 3-ha vineyard, run under the direction of Tony Bassett, reflects the cool maritime influence, with ocean currents that sweep up from the Antarctic.

Delamere

★★★

Bridport Road, Pipers Brook, Tas 7254 **REGION** Northern Tasmania
T (03) 6382 7190 **F** (03) 6382 7250 **OPEN** 7 days 10–5
WINEMAKER Richard Richardson **EST.** 1983 **CASES** 2000
SUMMARY Richie Richardson produces elegant, rather light-bodied wines that have a strong following. The Chardonnay has been most successful, with a textured, complex, malolactic-influenced wine with great, creamy feel in the mouth. The Pinots typically show pleasant varietal fruit, but seem to suffer from handling problems. Retail distribution in Victoria through Prime Wines, in Tasmania via Red+White.

▼▼▼▽ **Cuvee 2001** **RATING** 84 **DRINK** Now $ 28

▼▼▼ **Reserve Pinot Noir 2004** **RATING** 83 $ 32

Delaney's Creek Winery

NR

70 Hennessey Road, Delaneys Creek, Qld 4514 **REGION** Queensland Coastal
T (07) 5496 4925 **F** (07) 5496 4926 **OPEN** Wed–Fri 11–4, weekends & public hols 10–5
WINEMAKER Stuart Pearce (Contract) **EST.** 1997 **CASES** 3000
SUMMARY Barry and Judy Leverett established Delaney's Creek Winery in 1997 and thus expanded the vineyard map of Queensland yet further. Delaney's Creek is near the town of Woodford, not far northwest of Caboolture. In 1998 they planted an exotic mix of 1 ha each of shiraz, chardonnay,

sangiovese, touriga nacional and verdelho. In the meantime they are obtaining their grapes from 4 ha of contract-grown fruit, including cabernet sauvignon, cabernet franc, merlot, shiraz, chardonnay, marsanne and verdelho.

Delatite
★★★★☆

Stoneys Road, Mansfield, Vic 3722 **REGION** Upper Goulburn
T (03) 5775 2922 **F** (03) 5775 2911 **WEB** www.delatitewinery.com.au **OPEN** 7 days 10–5
WINEMAKER Rosalind Ritchie **EST.** 1982 **CASES** 16 000
SUMMARY With its sweeping views across to the snow-clad Alps, this is uncompromising cool-climate viticulture, and the wines naturally reflect that. Light but intense Riesling and spicy Traminer flower with a year or two in bottle, and in the warmer vintages the red wines achieve flavour and mouthfeel. In spring 2002 David Ritchie (the viticulturist in the family) embarked on a program to adopt biodynamics, commencing with the sauvignon blanc and gewurztraminer. He says, 'It will take time for us to convert the vineyard and change our mindset and practices, but I am fully convinced it will lead to healthier soil and vines.' Exports to Japan and Malaysia.

ŸŸŸŸŸ **Late Picked Riesling 2004** Fragrant, flowery lime and apple blossom aromas; crisp, crunchy acidity beautifully counterbalanced by sweetness; 10° alcohol; brilliant example of a Mosel lookalike. Screwcap. **RATING** 94 **DRINK** 2015 $ 20

ŸŸŸŸŸ **V.S. Limited Edition Riesling 2004** Attractive wine, balancing sweet, limey/tropical fruit with distinct minerally notes to the acidity; curious packaging in a non-Riesling bottle. Quality cork. **RATING** 93 **DRINK** 2010 $ 23
Dead Man's Hill Gewurztraminer 2004 Gentle rose petal aromas; ample richness and varietal character; quite full in the mouth. Screwcap. **RATING** 91 **DRINK** 2010 $ 19.97
Sauvignon Blanc 2004 Pale, bright green; harmonious aromas and flavours; gentle passionfruit, herb and mineral; long, fresh finish and aftertaste. Screwcap. **RATING** 91 **DRINK** 2007 $ 18
Riesling 2004 Flint, mineral and apple aromas and flavours; clean; good line; gentle-impact style. Screwcap. **RATING** 90 **DRINK** 2010 $ 19.97

ŸŸŸŸ **Devil's River 2002** Light to medium-bodied; attractive blackcurrant, cassis and spice; fine tannins, subtle oak. Cabernet Sauvignon/Merlot. Cork. **RATING** 89 **DRINK** 2009 $ 23
Limited Release Cabernet Sauvignon 2002 Supple cassis, blackcurrant, spice and leaf; faint touch of mint; flows nicely across the tongue. Screwcap. **RATING** 89 **DRINK** 2012 $ 25
Demelza Pinot Noir Chardonnay 2001 Elegant, fresh and crisp; citrussy minerally palate; bright, dry finish. **RATING** 89 **DRINK** 2008 $ 29.50
Pinot Gris 2004 Typical Pinot Gris; fleeting pear, apple, musk and spice nuances; scores on mouthfeel. **RATING** 87 **DRINK** 2007 $ 19.97
Limited Release Merlot 2002 Light to medium-bodied; savoury, earthy, bramble and berry fruit; not minty, simply spicy. Nice balance. Screwcap. **RATING** 87 **DRINK** 2008 $ 25

ŸŸŸŸ **Rose 2004 RATING** 86 **DRINK** Now $ 18
Limited Release Malbec 2002 RATING 86 **DRINK** 2009 $ 25

del Rios
★★★★

2320 Ballan Road, Anakie, Vic 3221 **REGION** Geelong
T (03) 9497 4644 **F** (03) 9497 4644 **WEB** www.delrios.com.au **OPEN** Weekends 10–4, bus tours by appointment
WINEMAKER Keith Salter, Ray Nadeson (Contract) **EST.** 1996 **CASES** 5000
SUMMARY German del Rio was born in northern Spain (in 1920) where his family owned vineyards. After three generations in Australia, his family has established 15 ha of vines on their 104-ha property on the slopes of Mt Anakie, the principal focus being chardonnay, pinot noir and cabernet sauvignon (4 ha each) then marsanne, sauvignon blanc, merlot and shiraz (1 ha each). Planting commenced in 1996, and vintage 2000 was the first commercial release; winemaking moved onsite in 2004.

ŸŸŸŸŸ **Chardonnay 2003** Elegant melon, stone fruit and citrus provides excellent mouthfeel. **RATING** 92 **DRINK** 2009 $ 19
Marsanne 2003 Very interesting wine; plenty of presence and impact; floral notes; slightly questionable oak. **RATING** 92 **DRINK** Now $ 19

ᵀᵀᵀᵀ **Sauvignon Blanc 2004** Clean, soft gooseberry fruit; not phenolic, but does shorten off on the finish. **RATING** 87 **DRINK** Now $ 18

ᵀᵀᵀ♀ **Andres Brut 2004 RATING** 86 **DRINK** 2009 $ 25
Rose 2004 RATING 84 **DRINK** Now $ 16

Demondrille Vineyards ★★★

RMB 97, Prunevale Road, Prunevale via Harden, NSW 2587 **REGION** Hilltops
T (02) 6384 4272 **F** (02) 6384 4292 **OPEN** Weekends 10.30–5, or by appointment
WINEMAKER George Makkas **EST.** 1979 **CASES** 1500
SUMMARY Planted in 1979, and a totally dryland vineyard, Demondrille is set on a ridge between the towns of Harden and Young in NSW. In the past most of the wines were made under contract, but from the 2002 vintage all wines have been made onsite. Greek-born and Australian-raised winemaker George Makkas completed his degree in wine science at Charles Sturt University in 2003. Rob Provan runs the vineyard and cellar door. The Raven (Shiraz) has received several awards.

Dennis ★★★★

Kangarilla Road, McLaren Vale, SA 5171 **REGION** McLaren Vale
T (08) 8323 8665 **F** (08) 8323 9121 **OPEN** Mon–Fri 10–5, weekends & hols 11–5
WINEMAKER Peter Dennis **EST.** 1970 **CASES** 5000
SUMMARY Egerton (Ege) was well-known in McLaren Vale, starting his vineyard at McLaren Flat in 1947 after serving in the RAAF during the war. Wine production under the Dennis Wines label in 1971, and in 1979 winemaking and management passed to son Peter. The 36-ha vineyard is planted to cabernet sauvignon, shiraz, merlot, chardonnay and sauvignon blanc, most now fully mature. Exports to the UK, New Zealand and Canada.

ᵀᵀᵀᵀ♀ **McLaren Vale Shiraz 2002** Complex, savoury blackberry fruits; has the intensity the '03 lacks; long palate; sweet, ripe tannins, subtle oak. Cork. **RATING** 91 **DRINK** 2015 $ 20
McLaren Vale Sauvignon Blanc 2004 Aromatic tropical passionfruit bouquet flows into the palate with similar fruit flavours; lots of expression, but not over the top. Screwcap.
RATING 90 **DRINK** 2007 $ 18
McLaren Vale Cabernet Sauvignon 2002 Savoury, powerful blackberry and earth fruit; a replay of the Shiraz; fine, persistent tannins. Cork. **RATING** 90 **DRINK** 2012 $ 20

ᵀᵀᵀ♀ **McLaren Vale Shiraz 2003 RATING** 85 **DRINK** 2007 $ 20
McLaren Vale Merlot 2003 RATING 85 **DRINK** 2007 $ 20
McLaren Vale Cabernet Sauvignon 2003 RATING 85 **DRINK** 2008 $ 20
McLaren Vale Unwooded Chardonnay 2004 RATING 84 **DRINK** Now $ 14

Derwent Estate ★★★★

329 Lyell Highway, Granton, Tas 7070 **REGION** Southern Tasmania
T (03) 6263 5802 **F** (03) 6263 5802 **WEB** www.derwentestate.com.au **OPEN** Wed–Sun 10–4 (closed winter)
WINEMAKER Julian Alcorso (Contract) **EST.** 1993 **CASES** 1000
SUMMARY The Hanigan family has established Derwent Estate as part of a diversification program for their 400-ha mixed farming property: 10 ha of vineyard have been planted, since 1993, to riesling, pinot noir, chardonnay, cabernet sauvignon and pinot gris.

ᵀᵀᵀᵀ♀ **Pinot Noir 2003** Powerful, ripe and sweet plum fruit; good tannins, controlled oak.
RATING 92 **DRINK** 2010 $ 25
Riesling 2004 An attractive mix of lime, tropical and mineral fruit; good balance, focus and length. **RATING** 90 **DRINK** 2011 $ 20

ᵀᵀᵀᵀ **Chardonnay 2003** Strong lemony accents surround the apple and melon fruit; excellent mouthfeel and acid balance; typical Tasmanian. Screwcap. **RATING** 89 **DRINK** 2008 $ 20
Pinot Noir 2003 Good colour; solid, ripe, plum and black cherry; some length, still to unfold. Screwcap. **RATING** 89 **DRINK** 2010 $ 25

ᵀᵀᵀ **Chardonnay 2004 RATING** 82 $ 20

Devil's Lair ★★★★★

Rocky Road, Forest Grove via Margaret River, WA 6285 **REGION** Margaret River
T (08) 9757 7573 **F** (08) 9757 7533 **WEB** www.devils-lair.com **OPEN** Not
WINEMAKER Stuart Pym **EST.** 1985 **CASES** 40 000
SUMMARY Having rapidly carved out a high reputation for itself through a combination of clever packaging and marketing and impressive wine quality, Devil's Lair was acquired by Southcorp Wines (Penfolds, etc) in December 1996. The estate vineyards have been substantially increased since then.

ΨΨΨΨΨ **Chardonnay 2002** Ultra-complex bouquet, quasi-Burgundian; voluptuous peach and stone fruit flavours; balanced oak. **RATING** 94 **DRINK** 2012 $ 39.95
Margaret River 2002 Some savoury edges to the bouquet; medium to full-bodied; powerful, concentrated blackcurrant and dark chocolate; very good ripe tannins and oak management. **RATING** 94 **DRINK** 2017 $ 57.95

ΨΨΨΨΨ **Chardonnay 2003** Light to medium green; refined style; nectarine, melon and citrus fruit; long, silky mouthfeel. **RATING** 93 **DRINK** 2008 $ 39.95
Fifth Leg Dry Red 2003 Clean and vibrant array of fresh fruit aromas and flavours; supple fine tannins and gentle oak. **RATING** 91 **DRINK** 2010 $ 18.99

ΨΨΨΨ **Fifth Leg White 2004** Crisply balanced citrus, lemon and mineral; clean and non-phenolic. **RATING** 89 **DRINK** Now $ 18.99

ΨΨΨΨ **Fifth Leg Rose 2004** **RATING** 86 **DRINK** Now $ 18.95

Diamond Valley Vineyards ★★★★

PO Box 4255, Croydon Hills, Vic 3136 **REGION** Yarra Valley
T (03) 9710 1484 **F** (03) 9710 1369 **WEB** www.diamondvalley.com.au **OPEN** Not
WINEMAKER James Lance **EST.** 1976 **CASES** 7000
SUMMARY One of the Yarra Valley's finest producers of Pinot Noir and an early pacesetter for the variety, making wines of tremendous style and crystal-clear varietal character. They are not Cabernet Sauvignon lookalikes but true Pinot Noir, fragrant and intense. The Chardonnays show the same marriage of finesse and intensity, and the Cabernet family wines shine in the warmer vintages. In early 2005 the brand and wine stocks were acquired by Graeme Rathbone (of SpringLane); the Lances continuing to own the vineyard and winery, and to make the wine.

ΨΨΨΨΨ **Yarra Valley Pinot Noir 2003** Highly aromatic and rich aromas redolent with plum and spice, which flow through to the palate. **RATING** 92 **DRINK** 2008 $ 23

ΨΨΨΨ **Yarra Valley Sauvignon Blanc 2004** Very crisp and fresh; minerally, grassy, spicy; needs a touch more sweet fruit. Screwcap. **RATING** 89 **DRINK** 2007 $ 19
Yarra Valley Chardonnay 2003 Ripe stone fruit/yellow peach and fig; some cashew; subtle oak. **RATING** 89 **DRINK** 2007 $ 19.95

Diggers Rest NR

205 Old Vineyard Road, Sunbury, Vic 3429 **REGION** Sunbury
T (03) 9740 1660 **F** (03) 9740 1660 **OPEN** By appointment
WINEMAKER Peter Dredge **EST.** 1987 **CASES** 1000
SUMMARY Diggers Rest was purchased from the founders Frank and Judith Hogan in July 1998; the new owners, Elias and Joseph Obeid, intend to expand the vineyard resources and, by that means, significantly increase production.

DiGiorgio Family Wines

Riddoch Highway, Coonawarra, SA 5263 **REGION** Coonawarra
T (08) 8736 3222 **F** (08) 8736 3233 **WEB** www.digiorgio.com.au **OPEN** 7 days 10–5
WINEMAKER Pat Tocaciu **EST.** 1998 **CASES** 10 000
SUMMARY Stefano DiGiorgio emigrated from Abruzzi, Italy, arriving in Australia in July 1952. Over the years, he and his family gradually expanded their holdings at Lucindale. In 1989 he began planting cabernet sauvignon (99 ha), chardonnay (10 ha), merlot (9 ha), shiraz (6 ha) and pinot noir (2 ha). In 2002 the family purchased the historic Rouge Homme winery, capable of crushing 10 000

tonnes of grapes a year, and its surrounding 13.5 ha of vines, from Southcorp. The Lucindale plantings are outside any existing region, and are simply part of the Limestone Coast Zone. The enterprise is offering full winemaking services to vignerons in the Limestone Coast Zone. Exports to Germany and The Netherlands.

ΥΥΥΥ **Lucindale Chardonnay 2002** Light to medium-bodied; gently sweet peach, nectarine and citrus fruit; a subtle whisk of French oak. Screwcap. **RATING** 89 **DRINK** 2008 $18
Lucindale Merlot 2002 Medium-bodied; quite sweet fruit on the mid-palate is followed by slightly sharp acidity on the finish. **RATING** 87 **DRINK** 2010 $22.50

ΥΥΥΥ **Lucindale Sparkling Merlot 2002** **RATING** 86 **DRINK** 2009 $19

Diloreto Wines   NR

45 Wilpena Terrace, Kilkenny, SA 5009 (postal) **REGION** Adelaide Plains
T (08) 8345 0123 **OPEN** Not
WINEMAKER Tony Diloreto **EST.** 2001 **CASES** 250
SUMMARY The Diloreto family have been growing grapes since the 1960s, with 8 ha of shiraz, cabernet sauvignon, mourvedre and grenache. The vineyard was founded by father Gesue Diloreto and, like so many Adelaide Plains grapegrowers, the family sold the grapes to South Australian winemakers. However, at the end of the 1990s, son Tony and wife Gabriell (herself with a winemaking background from the Rhine Valley in Germany) decided they would jointly undertake a short winemaking course. In 2001 Tony Diloreto entered two wines in the Australian Amateur Wine Show, competing against 700 vignerons from around Australia. Both were Shiraz from the 2001 vintage, one with new oak, the other not. Both won gold medals, and the judges strongly recommended that the wines be made and sold commercially. Great oaks from little acorns indeed.

di Lusso Wines   ★★★★

Eurunderee Lane, Mudgee, NSW 2850 **REGION** Mudgee
T (02) 6373 3125 **F** (02) 6373 3128 **WEB** www.dilusso.com.au **OPEN** 7 days 10–5
WINEMAKER Drew Tuckwell (Contract) **EST.** 1998 **CASES** 2700
SUMMARY Rob Fairall and partner Luanne Hill have at last been able bring to fruition the vision they have had for some years to establish an Italian 'enoteca' operation, offering Italian varietal wines and foods. The plantings of 2 ha each of barbera and sangiovese, 1 ha of nebbiolo and 0.5 ha of picolit, supplemented by the purchase of aleatico and sangiovese from the Mudgee region, and pinot grigio from Orange, set the tone for the wine, which is made by Drew Tuckwell, a specialist in Italian varieties. The estate also produces olives for olive oil and table olives, and it is expected that the range of both wine and food will increase over the years. An onsite winery came on-stream in early 2003, and the full cellar door has opened. The decision to focus on Italian varieties has been a major success.

Dindima Wines   NR

Lot 22 Cargo Road, Orange, NSW 2800 **REGION** Orange
T (02) 6365 3388 **F** (02) 6365 3096 **WEB** www.dindima.com.au **OPEN** Weekends & public hols 10–5, or by appointment
WINEMAKER James Bell **EST.** 2002 **CASES** 440
SUMMARY David Bell and family acquired the property known as Osmond Wines in 2002, renaming it Dindima Wines, with the first vintage under the new ownership made in 2003 from the 4.5 ha plantings. It is a retirement occupation for Dave Bell and his wife, but both sons are becoming involved with grapegrowing and winemaking.

Dingo Creek Vineyard   NR

265 Tandur–Traveston Road, Traveston, Qld 4570 **REGION** Queensland Coastal
T (07) 5485 1731 **F** (07) 5485 0041 **WEB** www.dingocreek.com.au **OPEN** Weekends 10–4, or by appointment
WINEMAKER Bruce Humphery-Smith **EST.** 1997 **CASES** NA
SUMMARY Marg and David Gillespie both had agricultural or viticultural backgrounds before moving to Queensland. Marg worked in the wine industry, with Bullers Wines. In 1994 they began a search

for agriculturally viable land with permanent water to start their own vineyard, and the property at Traveston provided the answer. Planting began in 1997 with chardonnay and cabernet sauvignon, followed a year later by merlot and sauvignon blanc; a total of 2 ha is now under vine. The cellar door offers a full range of tourist facilities, one feature being a 6m x 18m aviary, and live jazz on the first Sunday of each month.

Dionysus Winery ★★★

1 Patemans Lane, Murrumbateman, NSW 2582 **REGION** Canberra District
T (02) 6227 0208 **F** (02) 6227 0209 **WEB** www.dionysus-winery.com.au **OPEN** Weekends & public hols 10–5, or by appointment
WINEMAKER Michael O'Dea **EST.** 1998 **CASES** 1000
SUMMARY Michael and Wendy O'Dea are both public servants in Canberra seeking weekend and holiday relief from their everyday life at work. In 1996 they purchased their property at Murrumbateman, and planted 4 ha of chardonnay, sauvignon blanc riesling, pinot noir, cabernet sauvignon and shiraz between 1998 and 2001. A small winery was constructed in 2002, and handled the 2003 vintage. Michael has completed an associate degree in winemaking at Charles Sturt University, and is responsible for viticulture and winemaking; Wendy has completed various courses at the Canberra TAFE and is responsible for wine marketing and (in their words) 'nagging Michael and being a general slushie'.

 Our John's Shiraz 2002 RATING 85 **DRINK** 2007 $18
Cabernet Sauvignon 2002 RATING 85 **DRINK** 2008 $18

Di Stasio NR

Range Road, Coldstream, Vic 3770 **REGION** Yarra Valley
T (03) 9525 3999 **F** (03) 9525 3815 **OPEN** By appointment, or at Café Di Stasio, 31 Fitzroy Street, St Kilda
WINEMAKER Rob Dolan, Kate Goodman (Contract) **EST.** 1995 **CASES** 900
SUMMARY Famous Melbourne restaurateur Rinaldo (Ronnie) Di Stasio bought a virgin bushland 32-ha hillside block in the Yarra Valley, adjacent to the Warramate Flora and Fauna Reserve, in 1994. He has since established 2.8 ha of vineyards, equally split between pinot noir and chardonnay, put in roads and dams, built a substantial house, and also an Allan Powell Monastery, complete with art gallery and tree-filled courtyard sitting like a church on top of the hill. Production has never been large, but did commence in 1999, the wines of that and subsequent vintages being initially sold through Café Di Stasio in St Kilda, a Melbourne icon. In 2003 he took the plunge and appointed Domaine Wine Shippers as his distributor, and the wines are now spread through the smartest restaurants in Melbourne and Sydney. The less said about the scrawled, handwritten labels, the better. Exports to the UK.

Divers Luck Wines ★★★

'Hellenvale', Nelson Bay Road, Bobs Farm, Port Stephens, NSW 2316 **REGION** Northern Rivers Zone
T (02) 4982 2471 **F** (02) 4982 2726 **OPEN** 7 days 10–5
WINEMAKER Anthony Adams **EST.** 2000 **CASES** 2000
SUMMARY Anthony Adams and wife Hellen purchased the property now known as Hellenvale in June 2000, after Anthony Adams had spent 10 years as an abalone diver on the far south coast of New South Wales. He was struck down with a severe case of the bends in 1999, and after spending 4 days in the re-compression chamber at the Prince of Wales Hospital in Sydney, he wisely decided on a change of career. The Adams and their son Damien have a 3-ha vineyard planted to chambourcin, merlot, shiraz, verdelho and chardonnay, and built the onsite boutique winery. The wines are sold by mail order and through the cellar door.

Dixons Run ★★★☆

5 Carrick St, Mont Albert, Vic 3127 (postal) **REGION** Yarra Valley
T (08) 9898 7476 **F** (03) 9349 2434 **WEB** www.dixonsrun.com **OPEN** Not
WINEMAKER Contract **EST.** 2002 **CASES** 2000
SUMMARY Named after a Mr Dixon who grazed cattle on a squatter's run in the 1840s. The area became known as Dixons Run, and is now home to a number of vineyards and wineries in the Dixons

Creek subregion of the Yarra Valley. The 18.5-ha vineyard is planted to chardonnay, sauvignon blanc, pinot noir and cabernet sauvignon, heralding further increases in production.

ŦŦŦŦ **Chardonnay 2003** Very similar to the '04; light-bodied, some elegance, and subtle complexity; has length. Cork. RATING 89 DRINK 2008 $22.99
Sauvignon Blanc 2004 Tangy; faintly smoky/sweaty, but good length and varietal presence. RATING 88 DRINK Now $19.90
Chardonnay 2004 Subtle interplay of barrel and malolactic ferment; melon fruit; light-bodied, but has textural complexity. Screwcap. RATING 88 DRINK 2009 $22.99

ŦŦŦŦ **Cabernet Sauvignon 2003** RATING 86 DRINK 2008 $24.90

Djinta Djinta Winery ★★★

10 Stevens Road, Kardella South, Vic 3951 REGION Gippsland
T (03) 5658 1163 F (03) 5658 1163 WEB www.winesofgippsland.com/Wineries/DjintaDjinta/ OPEN 7 days 10–6
WINEMAKER Peter Harley EST. 1991 CASES 600
SUMMARY One of a group of wineries situated between Leongatha and Korumburra, the most famous being Bass Phillip. Vines were first planted in 1986 but were largely neglected until Peter and Helen Harley acquired the property in 1991, set about reviving the 2 ha of sauvignon blanc and a little cabernet sauvignon, and planting an additional 3 ha (in total) of merlot, cabernet franc, cabernet sauvignon, semillon, marsanne, roussanne and viognier. The first vintage was 1995, while Peter Harley was completing a Bachelor of Applied Science (Wine Science) at Charles Sturt University. They are deliberately adopting a low-technology approach to both vineyard and winery practices, using organic methods wherever possible.

ŦŦŦŦ **Rutherglen Muscat NV** Rich Christmas pudding, toffee and raisin flavours; well looked after; not stale. RATING 89 DRINK Now
Semillon 1999 Glowing yellow-green; powerful wine; still lots of minerally, herbal grip; good style. RATING 87 DRINK 2008 $17.50

ŦŦŦŦ **Sauvignon Blanc 1999** RATING 84 DRINK Now $20

ŦŦŦ **Merlot Cabernets 2001** RATING 82 $25

DogRidge Vineyard ★★★★

RSD 195, Bagshaws Road, McLaren Flat, SA 5171 REGION McLaren Vale
T (08) 8383 0140 F (08) 8383 0430 WEB www.dogridge.com.au OPEN By appointment
WINEMAKER Dave Wright, Jen Wright, Fred Howard, Mike Brown (Consultant) EST. 1993 CASES 2500
SUMMARY Dave and Jen Wright had a combined background of dentistry, art and a Charles Sturt University viticultural degree when they moved from Adelaide to McLaren Flat to become vignerons. They inherited vines planted in the early 1940s as a source for Chateau Reynella fortified wines, and their viticultural empire now has 56 ha of vineyards, ranging from 2001 plantings to some of the oldest vines remaining in the immediate region today. At the McLaren Flat vineyards, DogRidge has 60+-year-old shiraz in the 1-ha DV3 block, as well as 60-year-old grenache. Only part of the grape production is retained; most is sold to other leading wineries. Exports to the UK, the US, Canada, Singapore and New Zealand.

ŦŦŦŦŦ **DV3 McLaren Vale Cabernet Sauvignon 2002** Oak a tad assertive on the bouquet, but the palate is rich and supple, with sweet blackcurrant, chocolate, vanilla and spice. Screwcap. RATING 92 DRINK 2017 $28
DV7 McLaren Vale Shiraz 2002 Deep colour; dense black plum, dark chocolate and prune; tannins and oak well controlled, though 15° alcohol nips a little. Screwcap. RATING 91 DRINK 2022 $30

ŦŦŦŦ **DV2 McLaren Vale Merlot 2002** More regional than varietal; black fruits, bitter chocolate, mocha and vanilla; balanced tannins. Screwcap. RATING 89 DRINK 2012 $22
DV6 McLaren Vale Cabernet Sauvignon 2001 Savoury, earthy blackcurrant, leaf and spice; gentle, ripe tannins; 20-year-old vines. Cork. RATING 89 DRINK 2011 $30
Cadenzia Grenache Petit Verdot 2002 Good colour; very different from DV2 Grenache, seemingly not just from the 5% Petit Verdot component; a deeper, darker fruit register. Zork. RATING 87 DRINK 2008 $22

ŦŦŦŦ **DV2 McLaren Vale Grenache 2002** RATING 85 DRINK 2007 $22

Domain Day

24 Queen Street, Williamstown, SA 5351 **REGION** Barossa Valley
T (08) 8524 6224 **F** (08) 8524 6229 **WEB** www.domaindaywines.com **OPEN** By appointment
WINEMAKER Robin Day **EST.** 2000 **CASES** NA
SUMMARY This is a classic case of an old dog learning new tricks, and doing so with panache. Robin Day had a long and distinguished career as winemaker, then chief winemaker, then technical director of Orlando; participated in the management buy-out; and profited substantially from the on-sale to Pernod Ricard. After the sale he remained as a director, but became a globe-trotting adviser, consultant and observer. He has hastened slowly with the establishment of Domain Day, but there is nothing conservative about his approach in establishing his 15-ha vineyard at Mt Crawford, high in the hills (at 450m) of the southeastern extremity of Australia's Barossa Valley wine region, bordering (on two sides of the vineyard) the Eden Valley. While the mainstream varieties are merlot, pinot noir and riesling, he has trawled Italy, France and Georgia for the other varieties: viognier, sangiovese, saperavi, lagrein, garganega and sagrantino.

ŸŸŸŸŸ **Riesling 2004** Crisp, minerally, floral apple blossom and wild herb aromas; an elegant, fresh, lively and intense palate; classy wine. **RATING** 94 **DRINK** 2014 $ 20

ŸŸŸŸŸ **Viognier 2003** Clearly expressed varietal character; an attractive range of ripe and dried fruit flavours; good balance; not too phenolic. **RATING** 91 **DRINK** 2007 $ 25
Lagrein 2003 Attractive mouthfeel and balance; spicy red fruits; a hint of cedary oak, and supple tannins. **RATING** 91 **DRINK** 2008 $ 28
One Serious Merlot 2003 Olive, spice and cedar aromas; considerable depth and structure; fine but persistent tannins; be patient. **RATING** 90 **DRINK** 2013 $ 28
Sangiovese 2003 Not serious, perhaps, but not bad either; cherry, rose petal and spice flavours on the light to medium-bodied palate; fine tannins and particularly good length. **RATING** 90 **DRINK** 2010 $ 28

ŸŸŸŸ **One Serious Pinot Noir 2003** Solidly structured plummy fruit; good length and aftertaste; hovers between Pinot and dry red style. **RATING** 89 **DRINK** 2008 $ 28
Saperavi 2002 Full but not death-defying colour; gently savoury/earthy/leathery spectrum of aromas and flavours. **RATING** 88 **DRINK** 2007 Sold out
One Serious Rose 2004 Fresh, light to medium-bodied; direct, no-frills style; good balance, dry finish; small red fruits, and some texture. **RATING** 87 **DRINK** Now $ 16

Domaine A

Campania, Tas 7026 **REGION** Southern Tasmania
T (03) 6260 4174 **F** (03) 6260 4390 **WEB** www.domaine-a.com.au **OPEN** Mon–Fri 9–4, weekends by appointment
WINEMAKER Peter Althaus, Vetten Tiemann **EST.** 1973 **CASES** 5000
SUMMARY The striking black label of the premium Domaine A wine, dominated by the single, multicoloured 'A', signified the change of ownership from George Park to Swiss businessman Peter Althaus many years ago. The wines are made without compromise, and reflect the low yields from the immaculately tended vineyards. They represent aspects of both Old World and New World philosophies, techniques and styles. Exports to the UK, Denmark, Switzerland, Germany, France, China and Singapore.

ŸŸŸŸŸ **Cabernet Sauvignon 2000** Spotlessly clean; very powerful and long; ripe blackcurrant fruit with tannins running through the length of the palate. Very much like young Bordeaux red. **RATING** 94 **DRINK** 2015 $ 60

ŸŸŸŸŸ **Lady A Fume Blanc 2002** Complex, potent and powerful; oak 100% integrated; definitely towards white Bordeaux in style, but has varietal character. **RATING** 93 **DRINK** 2008 $ 50

Domaine Chandon

Green Point, Maroondah Highway, Coldstream, Vic 3770 **REGION** Yarra Valley
T (03) 9739 1110 **F** (03) 9739 1095 **WEB** www.yarra-valley.net.au/domaine_chandon/ **OPEN** 7 days 10.30–4.30
WINEMAKER Dr Tony Jordan, Neville Rowe, James Gosper, John Harris **EST.** 1986 **CASES** 150 000

SUMMARY Wholly owned by Möet et Chandon, and one of the two most important wine facilities in the Yarra Valley, the Green Point tasting room having a national and international reputation and having won a number of major tourism awards in recent years. The sparkling wine product range has evolved, and there has been increasing emphasis placed on the table wines. The return of Dr Tony Jordan, the first CEO of Domaine Chandon, has further strengthened both the focus and quality of the brand. Exports to the UK, Asia and Japan.

🍷🍷🍷🍷🍷 **Z*D 2000** Gently complex aromas; springs to life on the palate; fresh and lively fruit intensified by the absence of dosage (rather than the reverse). **RATING** 94 **DRINK** 2007 $ 33.95

🍷🍷🍷🍷🍷 **Sparkling Pinot Shiraz NV** Well balanced; starting to settle down with longer bottle age; neither phenolic nor the least bit sweet; excellent, if unusual, example of the style. **RATING** 93 **DRINK** 2012 $ 24.95

Blanc de Blanc 2000 Complex bready autolysis aromas; a vibrant mix of stone fruit, citrus and an appealing hint of creaminess on the palate. **RATING** 92 **DRINK** 2007 $ 33.95

Cuvee Riche NV Cunningly balanced and made; no-holds-barred sweetness, but neatly off-set by acidity. **RATING** 92 **DRINK** Now $ 33.95

Green Point Vineyards Chardonnay 2003 Spotlessly clean and fresh; elegant, light-bodied nectarine and melon fruit; restrained oak. Screwcap. **RATING** 90 **DRINK** 2008 $ 23.95

Green Point Reserve Pinot Noir 2002 An array of strawberry, cherry, plum and spice aromas and flavours; has finesse; slightly sweet oak. **RATING** 90 **DRINK** 2007 $ 42

NV NV Much lighter and fresher than prior releases; fine melon and citrus fruit; clean, crisp finish. **RATING** 90 **DRINK** Now $ 23.95

Domaine Epis ★★★★☆

812 Black Forest Drive, Woodend, Vic 3442 **REGION** Macedon Ranges
T (03) 5427 1204 **F** (03) 5427 1204 **OPEN** By appointment
WINEMAKER Stuart Anderson **EST.** 1990 **CASES** 900
SUMMARY Three legends are involved in the Epis and Epis & Williams wines, two of them in their own lifetime. They are long-term Essendon guru and former player Alec Epis, who owns the two quite separate vineyards and brands; Stuart Anderson, who makes the wines, with Alec Epis doing all the hard work; and the late Laurie Williams, the father of viticulture in the Macedon region and the man who established the Flynn and Williams vineyard in 1976. Alec Epis purchased that vineyard from Laurie Williams in 1999, and as a mark of respect (and with Laurie Williams' approval) continued to use his name in conjunction with his own. The Cabernet Sauvignon comes from this vineyard, the Chardonnay and Pinot Noir from the vineyard at Woodend, where a small winery was completed prior to the 2002 vintage.

🍷🍷🍷🍷🍷 **Macedon Ranges Pinot Noir 2003** Fresh, lively and focused cherry and plum fruit; long palate, excellent acidity; will flower. Good cork. **RATING** 94 **DRINK** 2013 $ 45

🍷🍷🍷🍷🍷 **Macedon Ranges Chardonnay 2003** Subtle but intense, driven by long citrussy/lemony acidity; nectarine and melon fruit; an airbrush of oak. Good cork. **RATING** 92 **DRINK** 2010 $ 35

🍷🍷🍷🍷 **Epis & Williams Cabernet Sauvignon Merlot 2003** Light to medium-bodied; overall savoury and a touch green, but does have a core of gentle red fruits. **RATING** 87 **DRINK** 2010 $ 35

Domaines Tatiarra ★★★★★

2/102 Barkers Road, Hawthorn, Vic 3124 (postal) **REGION** Heathcote
T 0411 240 815 **F** (03) 9822 4108 **WEB** www.cambrianshiraz.com **OPEN** Not
WINEMAKER Ben Riggs (Contract) **EST.** 1991 **CASES** 2000
SUMMARY Domaines Tatiarra Limited is an unlisted public company, its core asset being a 60-ha property of Cambrian earth first identified and developed by Bill Hepburn, who sold the project to the company in 1991. It is intended to produce only one varietal wine: Shiraz. The majority of the wine will come from the Tatiarra (Aboriginal word meaning beautiful country) property, but the Trademark Shiraz is an equal blend of McLaren Vale and Heathcote wine. The wines are made at the Pettavel Winery in Geelong, with Ben Riggs commuting between McLaren Vale and the winery as required.

♥♥♥♥♥ Cambrian Shiraz 2003 Strong colour; archetypal Heathcote layered, sweet blackberry and plum fruit off-set by velvety, fine tannins. Excellent oak handling. **RATING** 96 **DRINK** 2018 $40

Caravan of Dreams Heathcote Shiraz Pressings 2003 Opaque colour; full-bodied, dense, rich and chewy, laden with blackberry, spice and abundant, but ripe, tannins. Miraculously keeps balance with 15.5° alcohol. Quality cork. **RATING** 95 **DRINK** 2023 $50

Trademark Heathcote McLaren Vale Shiraz 2003 Strong colour; medium to full-bodied; good structure and texture; a mix of blackberry, earth, spice, chocolate and a touch of oak; lingering tannins. Quality cork. **RATING** 94 **DRINK** 2018 $60

Dominic Versace Wines

Lot 258 Heaslip Road, MacDonald Park, SA 5121 **REGION** Adelaide Plains
T (08) 8379 7132 **F** (08) 8338 0979 **WEB** www.versacewines.com.au **OPEN** By appointment
WINEMAKER Dominic Versace, Armando Verdiglione **EST.** 2000 **CASES** 1500
SUMMARY Dominic Versace and brother-in-law Armando Verdiglione have a long association with wine, through their families in Italy, and in Australia since 1980. In that year Dominic Versace planted 4.5 ha of shiraz, grenache and sangiovese (one of the earliest such plantings in Australia), selling the grapes to Joe Grilli of Primo Estate until 1999. Armando Verdiglione, with Caj Amadio and Michael von Berg, had in the meantime helped create the first commercial vineyard on Kangaroo Island. In 2000 the pair decided to pool their experience and resources, using the near-organically grown grapes from the Versace vineyard, and deliberately rustic winemaking techniques, including open fermenters, a basket press, no filtration, no pumping and old barrels.

♥♥♥♥♥ Reserve McLaren Vale Cabernet Sauvignon 2002 Medium-bodied; elegant black fruits and bitter chocolate; good mouthfeel and line; 15° alcohol; ripe tannins, exceptional finish. Quality cork. **RATING** 94 **DRINK** 2017 $55

♥♥♥♥♡ Reserve McLaren Vale Shiraz 2002 Classic McLaren Vale mix of blackberry, dark chocolate and spice; long, fine savoury palate with restrained 15° alcohol a real plus. Fine tannins. Quality cork. **RATING** 93 **DRINK** 2012 $31

Dominion Wines

Upton Road, Strathbogie Ranges via Avenel, Vic 3664 **REGION** Strathbogie Ranges
T (03) 5796 2718 **F** (03) 5796 2719 **WEB** www.dominionwines.com **OPEN** By appointment
WINEMAKER Travis Bush, Michael Clayden **EST.** 1999 **CASES** 140 000
SUMMARY Dominion is a major player in the Victorian wine industry. Between December 1996 and September 1999, 91 ha of vines were planted at Alexander Park with sauvignon blanc, chardonnay, pinot noir, shiraz and cabernet sauvignon the principal varieties, and smaller amounts of riesling, verdelho and merlot. Prior to the 2000 vintage a winery designed by award-winning architect Scott Shelton was erected at Alexander Park; at full capacity it will be able to process up to 7500 tonnes of fruit. It has two functions: the production of the company's own brands of Dominion Estate, Alexander Park, Vinus and Saddle Mountain, and contract winemaking for other major Australian wine companies.

♥♥♥♥♡ Alexander Park Shiraz 2003 Medium-bodied; elegant, fine blackberry and plum; silky, smooth mouthfeel; good oak and extract. Gold medal and trophy winner. Cork **RATING** 93 **DRINK** 2012 $15.95

Vinus Sauvignon Blanc Semillon 2004 Bright green-yellow; light to medium-bodied; attractive pure, clean, fresh sweet lemon, passionfruit and apple flavours; good structure. Screwcap. **RATING** 90 **DRINK** 2008 $8.95

♥♥♥♥ Alexander Park Chardonnay 2003 Very good green-yellow; gentle stone fruit, cashew and melon; nicely rounded and balanced; subtle oak. Quality cork. **RATING** 89 **DRINK** 2008 $15.95

Alexander Park Riesling 2004 Floral lime blossom and herb aromas; firm and tight, moderately fruity; good balance. Screwcap. **RATING** 88 **DRINK** 2009 $15.95

♥♥♥♡ Alexander Park Verdelho 2004 RATING 86 **DRINK** 2007 $15.95

Vinus Chardonnay 2004 RATING 85 **DRINK** 2007 $8.95

Alexander Park Cabernet Sauvignon 2001 RATING 85 **DRINK** 2007 $16

Vinus Shiraz Cabernet 2004 RATING 84 **DRINK** 2007 $8.95

Dominique Portet ★★★★☆

870–872 Maroondah Highway, Coldstream, Vic 3770 **REGION** Yarra Valley
T (03) 5962 5760 **F** (03) 5962 4938 **WEB** www.dominiqueportet.com **OPEN** 7 days 10–5
WINEMAKER Dominique Portet, Scott Bakea **EST.** 2000 **CASES** 7500
SUMMARY Dominique Portet was bred in the purple. He spent his early years at Chateau Lafite (where his father was regisseur) and was one of the very first Flying Winemakers, commuting to Clos du Val in the Napa Valley where his brother is winemaker. Since 1976 he has lived in Australia, spending more than 20 years as managing director of Taltarni, and also developing the Clover Hill Vineyard in Tasmania. After retiring from Taltarni, he set himself up in the Yarra Valley, a region he had been closely observing since the mid-1980s. In 2001 he found the site he had long looked for, and in a twinkling of an eye built his winery and cellar door, and planted a quixotic mix of viognier and merlot next to the winery; he also undertakes contract winemaking for others. Exports to the UK, the US and other major markets.

ŸŸŸŸŸ **Heathcote Shiraz 2003** Dark but bright colour; medium to full-bodied; opens with abundant black fruits, then spicy, ripe, fine persistent tannins. Quality cork. **RATING** 94 **DRINK** 2018 $ 42.50

ŸŸŸŸŸ **Yarra Valley Cabernet Sauvignon Merlot 2003** Medium-bodied; savoury, earthy, cedary black olive and blackcurrant fruit; has considerable length; Bordeaux style. Quality cork. **RATING** 90 **DRINK** 2013 $ 40

ŸŸŸŸ **Fontaine Yarra Valley Sauvignon Blanc 2004** Firm mineral/slate aromas; the palate is similarly minerally, with a touch of herb; quite complex, but not particularly intense. **RATING** 88 **DRINK** 2007 $ 18.50

Fontaine Rose 2004 Faint salmon touch to the colour; twists of herb, grass and mineral with a delicate red fruit gloss; appealingly dry finish. **RATING** 87 **DRINK** 2007 $ 18.50

Donnelly River Wines NR

Lot 159 Vasse Highway, Pemberton, WA 6260 **REGION** Pemberton
T (08) 9776 2052 **F** (08) 9776 2053 **OPEN** 7 days 9.30–4.30
WINEMAKER Blair Meiklejohn **EST.** 1986 **CASES** 15 000
SUMMARY Donnelly River Wines draws upon 16 ha of estate vineyards; they were planted in 1986 and produced the first wines in 1990. It has performed consistently well with its Chardonnay. Exports to the UK, Denmark, Germany, Singapore, Malaysia and Japan.

Donnybrook Estate NR

Hacket Road, Donnybrook, WA 6239 **REGION** Geographe
T (08) 9731 0707 **F** (08) 9731 0707 **OPEN** 7 days 10–5.30
WINEMAKER Gary Greirson **EST.** 1997 **CASES** 5000
SUMMARY Gary Greirson and wife Sally have completed the long-planned move to Donnybrook Estate from Cape Bouvard. The new winery was completed during the 2003 vintage, and Gary Greirson contract-makes a small amount of wine for others in the Donnybrook area. The wines are estate-grown from 11 acres of vineyards.

Donovan Wines NR

RMB 2017, Pomonal Road, Stawell, Vic 3380 **REGION** Grampians
T (03) 5358 2727 **F** (03) 5358 2727 **OPEN** Mon–Sat 10–5, Sun 12–5
WINEMAKER Chris Peters **EST.** 1977 **CASES** 250
SUMMARY Donovan quietly makes some concentrated, powerful Shiraz, with several vintages of the latter typically on offer. Limited distribution in Melbourne; most of the wine is sold by mail order with some bottle age. Has 5 ha of estate plantings.

Doonkuna Estate ★★★★

Barton Highway, Murrumbateman, NSW 2582 **REGION** Canberra District
T (02) 6227 5811 **F** (02) 6227 5085 **WEB** www.doonkuna.com.au **OPEN** 7 days 11–4
WINEMAKER Malcolm Burdett **EST.** 1973 **CASES** 4000

SUMMARY Following the acquisition of Doonkuna by Barry and Maureen Moran in late 1996, the plantings have been increased from a little under 4 ha to 20 ha. The cellar door prices remain modest, and increased production has followed in the wake of the new plantings.

🍷🍷🍷🍷🍷 **Shiraz 2003** Blackberry, plum and a touch of spice; good balance and, in particular, length; controlled oak and extract. **RATING** 90 **DRINK** 2013 $ 23.40

🍷🍷🍷🍷 **Sauvignon Blanc Semillon 2004** Good texture and mouthfeel; quite complex and ripe fruit flavours; 70% Sauvignon Blanc, 30% Semillon, 5% barrel-fermented. Screwcap. **RATING** 89 **DRINK** 2008 $ 14.40
Cabernet Merlot 2002 Savoury/earthy but ripe edges to blackcurrant fruit; good texture and length; good tannins. **RATING** 89 **DRINK** 2012 $ 21.60
Rising Ground Sauvignon Blanc Semillon 2004 Clean, sweet, gooseberry and herb aromas and flavours; relatively soft acidity; 55% Sauvignon Blanc, 45% Semillon. Screwcap. **RATING** 88 **DRINK** 2007 $ 10.80
Rose 2004 Right on the Rose money; bright red fruits and lemony acidity; fresh and not sweet. Juice run-off. Screwcap. **RATING** 88 **DRINK** Now $ 14

🍷🍷🍷🍷 **Riesling 2004** **RATING** 86 **DRINK** 2008 $ 18
Rising Ground Chardonnay 2004 **RATING** 86 **DRINK** 2008 $ 14
Rising Ground Shiraz 2001 **RATING** 86 **DRINK** 2008 $ 14
Rising Ground Cabernet Sauvignon 2001 **RATING** 85 **DRINK** 2007 $ 14

🍇 Dos Rios ★★★☆

PO Box 343, Nyah, Vic 3594 **REGION** Swan Hill
T (03) 5030 3005 **F** (03) 5030 3006 **WEB** www.dosrios.com.au **OPEN** Not
WINEMAKER Alan Cooper **EST.** 2003 **CASES** NA
SUMMARY Bruce Hall entered the wine business as a small vineyard contract grower for McGuigan Simeon Wines. From this point on, the story goes in reverse: instead of McGuigan Simeon saying it no longer required the grapes, it purchased the vineyard outright in 2003. In the meantime, Hall had hand-picked the grapes left at the end of the rows after the mechanical harvester had passed through, and had the wines made by Alan Cooper of Cobaw Ridge. In 2004 he purchased a small property northwest of Swan Hill with plantings of 20-year-old shiraz, to be extended by small areas of viognier, tempranillo, durif and merlot. The wines are available by mail order and at local clubs and restaurants.

🍷🍷🍷🍷 **Chardonnay 2003** A mix of tropical, stone fruit and melon aromas and flavours; good mouthfeel; clever oak handling and winemaking. **RATING** 89 **DRINK** 2008 $ 12.10
Shiraz 2003 Light to medium-bodied; elegant and polished; blackberry and spice; minimal oak. **RATING** 87 **DRINK** 2008 $ 13.20

🍷🍷🍷🍷 **Pinot Grigio 2003** Complex and mouthfilling texture and apricot/spice flavour. Sophisticated winemaking. **RATING** 86 **DRINK** Now $ 12.10
Verdelho 2003 **RATING** 86 **DRINK** Now $ 12.10
Cabernet Sauvignon Merlot 2003 **RATING** 85 **DRINK** 2007 $ 12.10

Dowie Doole ★★★☆

Tatachilla Road, McLaren Vale, SA 5171 (postal) **REGION** McLaren Vale
T (08) 8323 7428 **F** (08) 8323 7305 **WEB** www.dowiedoole.com.au **OPEN** At Penny's Hill
WINEMAKER Brian Light (Contract) **EST.** 1996 **CASES** 9000
SUMMARY The imaginatively packaged and interestingly named Dowie Doole was a joint venture between two McLaren Vale grapegrowers: architect Drew Dowie and one-time international banker Norm Doole. Between them they have over 40 ha of vineyards, and only a small proportion of their grapes are used to produce the Dowie Doole wines. In 1999 the partnership was expanded to include industry marketing veteran Leigh Gilligan, who returned to his native McLaren Vale after 5 years in Coonawarra (Gilligan is also involved with Boar's Rock). Exports to Canada, Alaska, Germany, Denmark, Fiji, Singapore and Hong Kong.

🍷🍷🍷🍷🍷 **Shiraz 2002** Strongly regional dark chocolate/savoury cast to the fruit; medium-bodied; good tannin structure and support. **RATING** 90 **DRINK** 2014 $ 23

🍷🍷🍷🍷 **Cabernet Sauvignon 2002** Savoury, earthy black fruits and bitter chocolate; strong and powerful; has good length. **RATING** 89 **DRINK** 2012 $ 21

ŦŦŦ♀ **McLaren Vale Merlot 2003** Has the texture and weight of Merlot, but struggles to express varietal character; overall, an easy-drinking red. **RATING** 86 **DRINK** 2008 $ 21

ŦŦŦ **Chenin Blanc 2004** **RATING** 83 **DRINK** Now $ 15.50

Downing Estate Vineyard   NR

19 Drummonds Lane, Heathcote, Vic 3523 **REGION** Heathcote
T (03) 5433 3387 **F** (03) 5433 3389 **OPEN** By appointment
WINEMAKER Bob Downing, Joy Downing **EST.** 1994 **CASES** NA
SUMMARY Bob and Joy Downing purchased 24 ha of undulating land in 1994, and have since established the estate vineyard from which all the wines are made; 75% of the plantings are shiraz, 20% cabernet sauvignon and 5% merlot.

Drakesbrook Wines   NR

PO Box 284, Waroona, WA 6215 **REGION** Peel
T (08) 9446 1383 **F** (08) 9446 1383 **WEB** www.drakesbrookwines.com.au **OPEN** Not
WINEMAKER Bernard Worthington **EST.** 1998 **CASES** NA
SUMMARY Bernard (Bernie) Worthington, a Perth-based property specialist, developed a serious interest in wine, and spent 4 years looking for a site which met all his criteria: ample water, easy access to a major population, and supporting tourist attractions. During that time he also completed a winegrowing course at Charles Sturt University. All his interests coalesced when he found Drakesbrook, a 216-ha property taking its name from the Drakesbrook River which flows through it. One hour's drive from Perth, it has views out to the ocean and is adjacent to the Lake Navarino tourist resort. He has subdivided the property, retaining 121 ha. The 11.9-ha vineyard is planted to semillon, chardonnay, shiraz, merlot, petit verdot, cabernet franc and cabernet sauvignon.

Drayton's Family Wines   ★★★

Oakey Creek Road, Cessnock, NSW 2321 **REGION** Lower Hunter Valley
T (02) 4998 7513 **F** (02) 4998 7743 **WEB** www.draytonswines.com.au **OPEN** Mon–Fri 8–5, weekends & public hols 10–5
WINEMAKER Trevor Drayton **EST.** 1853 **CASES** 90 000
SUMMARY A family-owned and run stalwart of the Hunter Valley, producing honest, full-flavoured wines which sometimes excel themselves and are invariably modestly priced. The size of the production will come as a surprise to many, but it is a clear indication of the good standing of the brand, notwithstanding the low profile of recent years. It is not to be confused with Reg Drayton Wines. National retail distribution, with exports to New Zealand, the US, Japan, Singapore, Taiwan, Samoa and Switzerland.

Drews Creek Wines   NR

558 Wollombi Road, Broke, NSW 2330 **REGION** Lower Hunter Valley
T (02) 6579 1062 **F** (02) 6579 1062 **OPEN** By appointment
WINEMAKER David Lowe (Contract) **EST.** 1993 **CASES** 300
SUMMARY Graeme Gibson and his partners are developing Drews Creek step by step. The initial planting of 2 ha of chardonnay and 3 ha of merlot was made in 1991, and the first grapes were produced in 1993. A further 2.5 ha of sangiovese were planted in September 1999. Most of the grapes are sold to contract winemaker David Lowe, but a small quantity of wine is made for sale to friends and through the mailing list. A cellar door has opened, and holiday cabins overlooking the vineyard and Wollombi Brook are planned.

Driftwood Estate   ★★★☆

Lot 13 Caves Road, Yallingup, WA 6282 **REGION** Margaret River
T (08) 9755 6323 **F** (08) 9755 6343 **OPEN** 7 days 11–4.30
WINEMAKER Barney Mitchell, Mark Pizzuto **EST.** 1989 **CASES** 15 000
SUMMARY Driftwood Estate is now a well-established landmark on the Margaret River scene. Quite apart from offering a brasserie restaurant capable of seating 200 people (open 7 days for lunch and

dinner) and a mock Greek open-air theatre, its wines feature striking and stylish packaging (even if strongly reminiscent of that of Devil's Lair) and opulent flavours. The winery architecture is, it must be said, opulent rather than stylish. The wines are exported to Singapore.

ŸŸŸŸ **Chardonnay 2003** Ripe stone fruit; rich and round mouthfeel; controlled oak. **RATING** 89 **DRINK** 2008

ŸŸŸŸ **Merlot 2002 RATING** 85 **DRINK** 2008

drinkmoor wines ★★★☆

All Saints Road, Wahgunyah, Vic 3687 **REGION** Rutherglen
T (02) 6033 5544 **F** (02) 6033 5645 **WEB** www.drinkmoorwines.com **OPEN** 7 days 10–5
WINEMAKER Damien Cofield **EST.** 2002 **CASES** 2500
SUMMARY This is a separate venture of Max and Karen Cofield (who also own Cofield Wines) and son Damien, with a very clear vision and marketing plan. It is to encourage people to make wine their beverage of choice; in other words, don't drink beer or spirits, drink wine instead, or drink more wines. Thus the wines are made in an everyday, easy-drinking style, with the cost kept as low as possible. The labelling, too, is designed to take the pretentiousness out of wine drinking, and to provide a bit of fun. Although the Cofields don't say so, this is the heartland of Generation X.

ŸŸŸŸ **Shiraz NV** Abundant plum and blackberry; good weight, texture and length; fruit-driven; admirable value. Screwcap. **RATING** 89 **DRINK** 2010 **$** 13.80
Traveller NV Relatively young Tokay-dominant fortified wine; good balance, and although young, does have some complexity, and a pleasingly dry finish. Good value. **RATING** 89 **DRINK** Now **$** 13.80
Cabernet Merlot NV Fresh and light to medium-bodied; good expression of the varietal blend; fresh finish, minimal oak. Screwcap. **RATING** 87 **DRINK** 2008 **$** 13.80

ŸŸŸŸ **Chenin Blanc NV** Full-on cellar door style; crammed with tropical fruit; distinctly sweet but has good acid balance. Screwcap. **RATING** 86 **DRINK** Now **$** 11.80
Petit Verdot NV Light to medium-bodied; unusual but eminently drinkable version of the variety; juicy sweet berry. Screwcap. **RATING** 86 **DRINK** 2007 **$** 13.80
Sticky 375 ml NV RATING 86 **DRINK** 2008 **$** 11.80
Cabernets NV RATING 85 **DRINK** Now **$** 13.80
Chardonnay NV RATING 84 **DRINK** Now **$** 11.80

ŸŸŸ **Al Dente White NV RATING** 83 **$** 11.80
Al Dente Red NV RATING 83 **$** 13.80

Dromana Estate ★★★★★

555 Old Moorooduc Road, Tuerong, Vic 3933 **REGION** Mornington Peninsula
T (03) 5974 4400 **F** (03) 9600 3245 **WEB** www.dromanaestate.com.au **OPEN** Wed–Sun 11–5
WINEMAKER Rollo Crittenden **EST.** 1982 **CASES** 30 000
SUMMARY Since it was established, Dromana Estate has always been near or at the cutting edge, both in marketing terms and in terms of development of new varietals, most obviously the Italian range under the 'i' label. Rollo Crittenden has taken over winemaking responsibilities after the departure of father Garry, and the business is now majority-owned by outside investors. The capital provided has resulted in the Yarra Valley Hills and Mornington Estate wines coming under the Dromana Estate umbrella. It is distributed domestically by Domaine Wine Shippers in all states, and exports to the UK.

ŸŸŸŸŸ **Dromana Estate Reserve Chardonnay 2002** Despite massive winemaking inputs, retains the core of the Dromana Estate style, with creamy/nutty/figgy flavours; finesse and elegance. Wild yeast, malolactic fermentation, 18 months barrel age. **RATING** 95 **DRINK** 2010 **$** 45
Dromana Estate Reserve Pinot Noir 2002 Excellent purple-red colour; rich, velvety, dark plum fruit; lovely texture, line and length; high-class Pinot. **RATING** 95 **DRINK** 2008 **$** 45
Chardonnay 2002 Typically fine and elegant; harmonious and gentle barrel ferment and malolactic inputs on delicate melon and stone fruit; bright finish. **RATING** 94 **DRINK** 2008 **$** 29
Pinot Noir 2002 Complex black cherry, plum and spice aromas; excellent structure and flavour; fine tannins and a long finish. **RATING** 94 **DRINK** 2007 **$** 29

ŸŸŸŸŸ **Sauvignon Blanc Semillon 2004** Clean, fresh and bright; gooseberry and grass; bright finish; squeaky acidity. Small percentage Semillon. Screwcap. **RATING** 91 **DRINK** 2007 $ 20
Mornington Estate Shiraz Viognier 2003 Excellent colour; a very successful marriage, with vibrant plum, spice and the touch of apricot ex Viognier; supple and smooth; fine tannins. Screwcap. **RATING** 91 **DRINK** 2010 $ 20
Yarra Valley Hills Chardonnay 2003 Powerful melon, grapefruit and stone fruit; well-integrated French oak. Screwcap. **RATING** 90 **DRINK** 2009 $ 19

ŸŸŸŸ **Garry Crittenden i Rosato 2004** Light but attractive allspice and fruit aromas and flavours; long, clean, dry finish; excellent style. Screwcap. **RATING** 89 **DRINK** Now $ 18
Pinot Noir 2003 Light but complex savoury/sappy style; plum, forest floor and spices; good length. **RATING** 89 **DRINK** 2007 $ 20
Yarra Valley Hills Yarra Valley Cabernet Sauvignon 2003 Clean, attractive cassis/blackcurrant on entry and mid-palate; slightly furry tannins. Screwcap. **RATING** 89 **DRINK** 2012 $ 21
Garry Crittenden i Sangiovese 2002 Fragrant cherry, rose petal and spice aromas; light to medium-bodied; supple fine tannins. Pyrenees and King Valley. **RATING** 89 **DRINK** 2007 $ 25
Gary Crittenden i Arneis 2003 Tight, but quite complex, minerally, flinty structure; subtle pear and apple fruit. **RATING** 88 **DRINK** 2007 $ 20
Yarra Valley Hills Yarra Valley Pinot Noir 2003 Light to medium-bodied; clean plummy fruit, touches of spice; not particularly concentrated. Screwcap. **RATING** 88 **DRINK** 2007 $ 21
Cabernet Merlot 2003 Light to medium-bodied; elegant leaf, spice and berry; just on the cusp of ripeness. Cork. **RATING** 87 **DRINK** 2009 $ 29
Garry Crittenden i Sangiovese 2003 Savoury, spicy, lingering; gently earthy tannins; some cherry and vanilla. Cork. **RATING** 87 **DRINK** 2007 $ 20

ŸŸŸŸ **Mornington Estate Rose 2004** **RATING** 85 **DRINK** Now $ 20
Garry Crittenden i Nebbiolo 2000 **RATING** 85 **DRINK** Now $ 20

Dromana Valley Wines   NR

Cnr Nepean Highway/Pickings Lane, Dromana, Vic 3936 **REGION** Mornington Peninsula
T (03) 5987 2093 **F** (03) 5987 2093 **WEB** www.dvwines.com.au **OPEN** Weekends & public hols 11–5
WINEMAKER Greg Ray **EST.** 1974 **CASES** NA
SUMMARY The Stavropoulos family established Dromana Valley Wines in 1974, planting a small block of shiraz. When the Hickinbotham family purchased the property across the road in 1988 it led to the first Dromana Valley wines being made by Andrew Hickinbotham, and to the extension of the vineyard in 1989, with further plantings in 1997. There is now a little under 2 ha of chardonnay, over 1 ha of pinot noir, the remaining 2 ha divided between shiraz and cabernet sauvignon. In 1997 a new winery was built, and in Easter 1998 the cellar door was opened and wine sales commenced, with a number of vintages on offer. Since 1999 winemaking has been carried out onsite by Greg Ray.

Drummonds Corrina Vineyard   ★★★☆

85 Wintles Road, Leongatha South, Vic 3953 **REGION** Gippsland
T (03) 5664 3317 **OPEN** Weekends 12.30–4.30
WINEMAKER Phillip Jones (Contract) **EST.** 1983 **CASES** NA
SUMMARY The Drummond family has 3 ha of vines (1 ha each of pinot noir and sauvignon blanc, and 0.5 ha each of cabernet sauvignon and merlot) which was slowly established without the aid of irrigation. The viticultural methods are those practised by Phillip Jones, who makes the wines for Drummonds: north–south row orientation, leaf plucking on the east side of the rows, low yields, and all fruit picked by hand. Similarly restrained winemaking methods (no pumping, no filters and low SO$_2$) follow in the winery. The wines are sold through the cellar door and by mail order only.

ŸŸŸŸ **Dinah's Block Pinot Noir 2001** Savoury/spicy/foresty/stemmy/briary aromas and flavours; has length; once better; stained cork has done it no favours. **RATING** 86 **DRINK** Now $ 28

Dudley Partners   NR

Porky Flat Vineyard, Penneshaw, Kangaroo Island, SA 5222 (postal) **REGION** Kangaroo Island
T (08) 8553 1509 **F** (08) 8553 1509 **OPEN** Not
WINEMAKER Wine Network (James Irvine) **EST.** 1994 **CASES** NA

SUMMARY Colin Hopkins, Jeff Howard, Alan Willson and Paul Mansfield have formed a partnership to bring together 3 vineyards on Kangaroo Island's Dudley Peninsula: the Porky Flat vineyard (5 ha), Hog Bay River (2 ha) and Sawyers (4 ha). It is the quirky vineyard names which give the products their distinctive identities. The partners not only look after viticulture, but also join in the winemaking process. To date, most of the wines are sold through licensed outlets on Kangaroo Island, supplemented by retail sales in Adelaide.

Due South   NR

PO Box 72, Denmark, WA 6333 **REGION** Denmark
T (08) 9848 3399 **F** (08) 9848 1690 **OPEN** Not
WINEMAKER Harewood Estate (Contract) **EST.** 1999 **CASES** NA
SUMMARY Another substantial new development in the Great Southern, with 100 ha of sauvignon blanc, semillon, chardonnay, pinot noir, shiraz, merlot, cabernet franc and cabernet sauvignon. Part of the grapes produced each year go to make wine under the Due South brand, which is stocked exclusively by Vintage Cellars. The remainder is sold as grapes or processed wine to others. Due South wines are also exported to the UK and available by mail order.

Duke's Vineyard   ★★★★

Porongurup Road, Porongurup, WA 6324 **REGION** Porongurup
T (08) 9853 1107 **F** (08) 9853 1107 **WEB** www.dukesvineyard.com **OPEN** 7 days 10–4.30
WINEMAKER Mike Garland (Contract) **EST.** 1998 **CASES** 2500
SUMMARY When Hilde and Ian (Duke) Ranson sold their clothing manufacturing business in 1998 they were able to fulfil a long-held dream of establishing a vineyard in the Porongurup subregion of Great Southern. It took two abortive efforts before they became third-time-lucky with the acquisition of a 65-ha farm at the foot of the Porongurup Range. They planted 3 ha each of shiraz and cabernet sauvignon and 4 ha of riesling. Hilde Ranson is a successful artist, and it was she who designed the beautiful scalloped, glass-walled cellar door sale area with its mountain blue cladding. The wines have limited New South Wales distribution through Lewis Fine Wines.

▼▼▼▼▽ **Great Southern Shiraz 2003** Medium-bodied; complex spice, licorice, blackberry and game Rhône-style aromas and flavours; fine, ripe tannins; subtle oak. Screwcap. **RATING** 92 **DRINK** 2013 $ 24
Great Southern Riesling 2004 Spotlessly clean; apple, pear and citrus aromas; sweet citrus and ripe apple palate; gentle acidity on a long finish. Screwcap. **RATING** 91 **DRINK** 2012 $ 18

▼▼▼▼ **Great Southern Autumn Riesling 2004** Delicate, gently sweet lime aromas; lower alcohol (than 12.8°) might be better still. Screwcap. **RATING** 87 **DRINK** 208 $ 16

▼▼▼▽ **Great Southern Cabernet Sauvignon 2003** **RATING** 85 **DRINK** 2007 $ 22
Cabernet Sauvignon Rose 2004 **RATING** 84 **DRINK** Now $ 18

Dulcinea   NR

Jubilee Road, Sulky, Ballarat, Vic 3352 **REGION** Ballarat
T (03) 5334 6440 **F** (03) 5334 6828 **WEB** www.dulcinea.com.au **OPEN** 7 days 10–6
WINEMAKER Rod Stott **EST.** 1983 **CASES** 3000
SUMMARY Rod Stott is passionate grapegrower and winemaker (with 6 ha of vineyard) who chose the name Dulcinea from *The Man of La Mancha,* where only a fool fights windmills. With winemaking help from various sources, he has produced a series of interesting and often complex wines. Exports to Japan, Fiji and China.

Dumaresq Valley Vineyard   NR

Bruxner Highway, Tenterfield, NSW 2372 **REGION** Northern Slopes Zone
T (02) 6737 5281 **F** (02) 6737 5293 **WEB** www.dumaresqvalleyvineyard.com.au **OPEN** 7 days 9–5
WINEMAKER Contract **EST.** 1997 **CASES** NA
SUMMARY Three generations of the Zappa family have been involved in the establishment of what is now a very large mixed farming property on 1600 ha, all beginning when the first generation arrived from Italy in the late 1940s to work as cane-cutters in Queensland. Today, Martin and Amelia, with

three of their sons and wives, have a property sustaining 120 cattle, 5000 super-fine wool Merino sheep, 140 ha of fresh produce, 250 ha of cereal crops and a 25-ha vineyard. The vineyard was progressively established between 1997 and 2000, with plantings of chardonnay, semillon, sauvignon blanc, shiraz, merlot, cabernet sauvignon, barbera and tempranillo.

Dusty Hill Estate ★★★☆

Barambah Road, Moffatdale via Murgon, Qld 4605 **REGION** South Burnett
T (07) 4168 4700 **F** (07) 4168 4888 **WEB** www.dustyhill.com.au **OPEN** 7 days 9.30–5
WINEMAKER Stuart Pierce (Contract) **EST.** 1996 **CASES** 3000
SUMMARY Joe Prendergast and family have established 2 ha each of shiraz and cabernet sauvignon, 1 ha each of verdelho and semillon and 0.5 ha each of merlot and black muscat. The vines are crop-thinned to obtain maximum ripeness in the fruit and to maximise tannin extract, although the winery's specialty is the Dusty Rose, continuing a long tradition of Rose/Beaujolais-style wines from Queensland. They also have a luxury B&B cottage (with 3 queen-sized bedrooms), which takes advantage of the 20 km of waterfront to Lake Barambah.

▼▼▼▼ **Forbidden Shiraz 2001** Riper and sweeter than the varietal, with greater tannin structure; impressive power. **RATING** 89 **DRINK** 2010 $ 30

Dutschke Wines ★★★★☆

PO Box 107, Lyndoch, SA 5351 **REGION** Barossa Valley
T (08) 8524 5485 **F** (08) 8524 5489 **WEB** www.dutschkewines.com **OPEN** Not
WINEMAKER Wayne Dutschke **EST.** 1998 **CASES** 4000
SUMMARY Wayne Dutschke had over 20 years working in Australia and overseas for companies large and small before joining his uncle (and estate grapegrower), Ken Semmler to form Dutschke Wines in 1990. In addition to outstanding table wines, he has a once-yearly release of fortified wines (doubtless drawing on his time at Baileys of Glenrowan); these sell out overnight, and have received the usual stratospheric points from Robert Parker. Exports to the UK, the US and other major markets.

▼▼▼▼▽ **The Tawny NV** Rich, biscuity brandy snap, butterscotch flavours; good rancio; at the sweet end of the spectrum. Average 22 years old. **RATING** 92 **DRINK** Now $ 25
The Tokay NV Fresh, lively tea leaf characters; crystal clear varietal character; elegant, balanced palate; lovely, fresh style. **RATING** 91 **DRINK** Now $ 20
The Muscat NV Rich, luscious raisin plum pudding flavours; long finish, cleansing acidity. **RATING** 91 **DRINK** Now $ 20

Dyson Wines ★★★★

Sherriff Road, Maslin Beach, SA 5170 **REGION** McLaren Vale
T (08) 8386 1092 **F** (08) 8327 0066 **OPEN** 7 days 10–5
WINEMAKER Allan Dyson **EST.** 1976 **CASES** 2000
SUMMARY Allan Dyson, who describes himself as 'a young man of 50-odd years' has recently added to his 1.5 ha of viognier with 2.5 ha each of chardonnay and cabernet sauvignon, and has absolutely no thoughts of slowing down or retiring. All wines are estate-grown, made and bottled. Some retail distribution in South Australia, the ACT and New South Wales supplements cellar door sales.

▼▼▼▼▽ **Viognier 2004** Powerful, but not the least phenolic; ripe fruits; long palate, excellent acidity. High-quality cork. **RATING** 90 **DRINK** 2008 $ 20

▼▼▼▼ **Chardonnay 2003** Medium-bodied; moderately ripe yellow peach balanced by subtle oak and good acidity on the finish. Quality cork. **RATING** 88 **DRINK** 2007 $ 25

Eagle Vale ★★★★

51 Caves Road, Margaret River, WA 6285 **REGION** Margaret River
T (08) 9757 6477 **F** (08) 9757 6199 **WEB** www.eaglevalewine.com **OPEN** 7 days 10–5
WINEMAKER Guy Gallienne **EST.** 1997 **CASES** 7500
SUMMARY Eagle Vale is a joint venture between the property owners, Steve and Wendy Jacobs, and the operator/winemaking team of Guy, Chantal and Karl Gallienne. It is a united nations team: Steve Jacobs was born in Colorado, and has business interests in Bali. The Galliennes come from the Loire Valley, although Guy secured his winemaking degree at Roseworthy College/Adelaide University.

The vineyard, now 11.5 ha, is managed on a low-impact basis, without pesticides (guinea fowls do the work) and with minimal irrigation. All the wines are made from estate-grown grapes. Exports to the UK, Germany, The Netherlands, Indonesia, Singapore and the US.

🍷🍷🍷🍷🍷 **Shiraz 2003** Earthy, spicy, stemmy background to tangy red and black fruits; fine tannins; good length and finish. **RATING** 91 **DRINK** 2010 $ 28

🍷🍷🍷🍷 **Sur Lie Semillon 2003** Quite intense fruit has absorbed the 6 months in new oak; long, intense herb and lemon fruits; good acidity. **RATING** 89 **DRINK** 2007 $ 26
Semillon Sauvignon Blanc 2004 Lively, fresh and tangy; herb, grass and citrus; lingering lemony/minerally acidity. **RATING** 89 **DRINK** 2008 $ 18
Merlot 2003 Savoury olive and bramble backdrop to red fruits; fine-grained tannins, integrated oak. **RATING** 89 **DRINK** 2010 $ 26
Sauvignon Blanc Fume 2004 Gently oaked; faintly nutty/smoky flavours; crisp, flinty acidity. **RATING** 88 **DRINK** 2007 $ 32
Cabernet Sauvignon Merlot Cabernet Franc Petit Verdot 2002 Attractive, medium-bodied, complex wine; cedar, spice and black fruit mix; ripe tannins, subtle oak. **RATING** 88 **DRINK** 2012 $ 28

East Arm Vineyard   ★★★☆

111 Archers Road, Hillwood, Tas 7250 **REGION** Northern Tasmania
T (03) 6334 0266 **F** (03) 6334 1405 **OPEN** Weekends & public hols, or by appointment
WINEMAKER Bert Sundstrup, Nicholas Butler (Contract) **EST.** 1993 **CASES** 1200
SUMMARY East Arm Vineyard was established by Launceston gastroenterologist Dr John Wettenhall and partner Anita James, who happens to have completed the Charles Sturt University Diploma in Applied Science (winegrowing). The 2 ha of vineyard, which came into full production in 1998, are more or less equally divided among riesling, chardonnay and pinot noir. It is established on a historic block, part of a grant made to retired British soldiers of the Georgetown garrison in 1821, and slopes down to the Tamar River. The property is 25 ha, and there are plans for further planting and, somewhere down the track, a winery. The Riesling is usually excellent. Exports to Hong Kong.

Eastern Peake   NR

Clunes Road, Coghills Creek, Vic 3364 **REGION** Ballarat
T (03) 5343 4245 **F** (03) 5343 4365 **OPEN** 7 days 10–5
WINEMAKER Norman Latta **EST.** 1983 **CASES** 3000
SUMMARY Norm Latta and Di Pym commenced the establishment of Eastern Peake, 25 km northeast of Ballarat on a high plateau overlooking the Creswick Valley, almost 15 years ago. In the early years the grapes were sold to Trevor Mast of Mount Chalambar and Mount Langi Ghiran, but the 5 ha of vines are now dedicated to the production of Eastern Peake wines. The Pinot Noir is on the minerally/stemmy side; earlier bottling might preserve more of the sweet fruit. Exports to the UK.

🐌 Eden Hall   ★★★★★

8 Martin Avenue, Fitzroy, SA 5082 (postal) **REGION** Eden Valley
T (08) 8562 4590 **F** (08) 8342 3950 **WEB** www.edenhall.com.au **OPEN** Not
WINEMAKER James Irvine, Joanne Irvine **EST.** 2002 **CASES** 1200
SUMMARY David and Mardi Hall purchased the historic Avon Brae property in 1996. The 120-ha property has now been planted to 32 ha of cabernet sauvignon (the lion's share), shiraz, merlot, cabernet franc, riesling (over 9 ha), and viognier. The majority of the production is contracted to Yalumba, St Hallett and McGuigan Simeon, with 10% of the best grapes held back for winemaking by James and Joanne Irvine. The Riesling, Shiraz Viognier and Cabernet Sauvignon are all excellent, the red wines outstanding. They are available through the website, and are distributed nationally by Prime Wines.

🍷🍷🍷🍷🍷 **Shiraz Viognier 2002** Impressive wine; spicy shiraz fruit with an excellent tweak ex the Viognier; long, supple palate; fine tannins. **RATING** 94 **DRINK** 2015 $ 32
Cabernet Sauvignon 2002 Deep colour; full, ripe but not over the top, fleshy blackcurrant and cassis; soft, velvety tannins; lots of integrated oak. Typical James Irvine style. **RATING** 94 **DRINK** 2012 $ 32

🍷🍷🍷🍷 **Riesling 2004** Full aromas; a mix of lime and a hint of mineral; a rich, full palate, very generous; early developing. **RATING** 89 **DRINK** 2007 $ 20

Eden Springs

NR

Boehm Springs Road, Springton, SA 5235 **REGION** Eden Valley
T (08) 8564 1166 **F** (08) 8564 1265 **WEB** www.edensprings.com.au **OPEN** Not
WINEMAKER Andrew Ewart (Contract) **EST.** 2000 **CASES** 1500
SUMMARY Richard Wiencke and Meredith Hodgson opened the Eden Springs wine doors on 1 July 2000. It is a remote vineyard (6 km by dirt road from Springton) and sells its wine through a high-quality newsletter to mailing list customers and the website. Exports to the UK, the US, Canada, Denmark, Hong Kong, Malaysia and Singapore.

Edwards & Chaffey

 ★★★☆

Tanunda Road, Nuriootpa, SA 5355 **REGION** South Australia
T (08) 8568 9389 **F** (08) 8568 9489 **WEB** www.edwardsandchaffey.com.au **OPEN** Not
WINEMAKER Various **EST.** 1850 **CASES** NFP
SUMMARY After a near-death experience, the Edwards & Chaffey range of sparkling wines has been revived with the Seaview and Minchinbury labels.

ỹỹỹỹỹ **Seaview Chardonnay Brut 1999** Quite complex biscuity, bready lees contact characters; plenty of mid-palate flavour and length. **RATING** 90 **DRINK** Now $19.95

ỹỹỹỹ **Seaview Pinot Chardonnay Brut 1999 RATING** 86 **DRINK** Now $17.70
Seaview Blanc de Blancs 2001 RATING 85 **DRINK** Now $17.65
Seaview Sparkling Shiraz NV RATING 85 **DRINK** Now $8.27
Seaview Grande Cuvee NV RATING 84 **DRINK** Now $12.95

ỹỹỹ **Minchinbury Brut de Brut Private Brut NV RATING** 83 $6.95
Minchinbury White Seal Private Cuvee NV RATING 83 $6.95

Edwards Vineyard

 ★★★★☆

Cnr Caves Road/Ellensbrook Road, Cowaramup, WA 6284 **REGION** Margaret River
T (08) 9755 5999 **F** (08) 9755 5988 **WEB** www.edwardsvineyard.com.au **OPEN** 7 days 10.30–5
WINEMAKER Michael Edwards **EST.** 1994 **CASES** 6000
SUMMARY This is very much a family affair, headed by parents Brian and Jenny Edwards. Michael Edwards is the assistant winemaker at Voyager Estate, and also oversees the winemaking of the Edwards Vineyard wines; Chris Edwards is vineyard manager; and Fiona and Bianca Edwards are involved in sales and marketing. They have a 20-ha vineyard, planted to chardonnay, semillon, sauvignon blanc, shiraz and cabernet sauvignon. One of the local attractions is the Tiger Moth 'Matilda', flown from England to Australia in 1990 as a fundraiser: it is now kept at the Edwards Vineyard and can be seen flying locally. Exports to the US, Denmark, Singapore and Spain.

ỹỹỹỹỹ **Margaret River Shiraz 2003** Deep colour; powerful, rich and complex; abundant blackberry fruit; attractive spicy components; long finish. Screwcap. **RATING** 94 **DRINK** 2015 $26

ỹỹỹỹ **Margaret River Sauvignon Blanc 2004** Spotlessly clean; tightly focused, clean and crisp; excellent lemony acidity; lingering finish. Screwcap. **RATING** 91 **DRINK** 2007 $19
Margaret River Semillon Sauvignon Blanc 2004 A skilled touch of partial barrel ferment adds both aroma and texture; lemon, spice and mineral; has real substance. Screwcap. **RATING** 91 **DRINK** 2007 $19
Margaret River Chardonnay 2003 Brilliant colour; medium-bodied; subtle complexity throughout; melon, fig, cream and cashew; very well made. Screwcap. **RATING** 91 **DRINK** 2008 $24
Margaret River Cabernet Sauvignon 2003 In typical vineyard style, powerful and concentrated; blackcurrant, earth and chocolate; good, ripe tannins; positive oak. Cork. **RATING** 91 **DRINK** 2013 $29

Elan Vineyard

 ★★★☆

17 Turners Road, Bittern, Vic 3918 **REGION** Mornington Peninsula
T (03) 5983 1858 **F** (03) 5983 2821 **WEB** www.elanvineyard.com.au **OPEN** First weekend of month, public hols 11–5, or by appointment

WINEMAKER Selma Lowther **EST.** 1980 **CASES** 400
SUMMARY Selma Lowther, then fresh from Charles Sturt University (as a mature-age student) made an impressive debut with her spicy, fresh, crisp Chardonnay, and has continued to make tiny quantities of appealing and sensibly priced wines. Most of the grapes from the 2.5 ha of estate vineyards are sold; production remains minuscule.

Elderton ★★★★☆

3 Tanunda Road, Nuriootpa, SA 5355 **REGION** Barossa Valley
T (08) 8568 7878 **F** (08) 8568 7879 **WEB** www.eldertonwines.com.au **OPEN** Mon–Fri 8.30–5, weekends & hols 11–4
WINEMAKER Richard Langford, James Irvine (Consultant) **EST.** 1984 **CASES** 32 000
SUMMARY The wines are based on some old, high-quality Barossa floor estate vineyards, and all are driven to a lesser or greater degree by American oak; the Command Shiraz is at the baroque end of the spectrum and has to be given considerable respect within the parameters of its style. National retail distribution, with exports to all major markets.

▼▼▼▼▼ **Barossa Cabernet Sauvignon 2002** Excellent blackcurrant and a touch of chocolate; medium-bodied; superb fruit flow; ripe tannins, good oak. Quality cork. **RATING** 94 **DRINK** 2015 $ 24

▼▼▼▼▽ **Command Shiraz 2001** Medium-bodied; a mix of black fruits, vanilla, spice, sweet earth and chocolate; good overall mouthfeel and balance; fine, silky tannins; 3 years in oak polishes the wine. Screwcap. **RATING** 92 **DRINK** 2014 $ 85

Eldredge ★★★★☆

Spring Gully Road, Clare, SA 5453 **REGION** Clare Valley
T (08) 8842 3086 **F** (08) 8842 3086 **OPEN** 7 days 11–5
WINEMAKER Leigh Eldredge **EST.** 1993 **CASES** 6000
SUMMARY Leigh and Karen Eldredge have established their winery and cellar door sales area in the Sevenhill Ranges at an altitude of 500m, above the town of Watervale. Both the Rieslings and red wines have had considerable success in recent years. The wines are distributed in Victoria and Queensland and exported to the UK, the US and Canada.

▼▼▼▼▼ **Blue Chip Shiraz 2002** Rich, dark fruits and black chocolate, with nice spicy splashes; excellent mouthfeel and fruit profile. **RATING** 95 **DRINK** 2017 $ 26

▼▼▼▼▽ **Blue Chip Shiraz 2003** Rich, powerful, concentrated blackberry fruit; firm but ripe and balanced tannins; oak in support role. Screwcap. **RATING** 92 **DRINK** 2018 $ 25
Clare Valley Cabernet Sauvignon 2002 Blackberry, dark chocolate and spicy/savoury notes; rich, but not over the top; sweet vanilla oak; 13% Shiraz. Screwcap. **RATING** 91 **DRINK** 2017 $ 25

▼▼▼▼ **Watervale Riesling 2004** Big, solid, ripe and mouthfilling fruit; lime juice and fruit salad. Screwcap. **RATING** 88 **DRINK** 2007 $ 17

Eldridge Estate ★★★★★

120 Arthurs Seat Road, Red Hill, Vic 3937 **REGION** Mornington Peninsula
T (03) 5989 2644 **F** (03) 5989 2644 **WEB** www.eldridge-estate.com.au **OPEN** Weekends, public hols & 1–26 January 11–5
WINEMAKER David Lloyd **EST.** 1985 **CASES** 800
SUMMARY The Eldridge Estate vineyard, with 7 varieties included in its 3.5 ha, was purchased by Wendy and David Lloyd in 1995. Major retrellising work has been undertaken, changing to Scott-Henry, and all the wines will now be estate-grown and made. David Lloyd has also planted several Dijon-selected pinot noir clones (114, 115 and 777) which have made their contribution since 2004. The wines are available at the Victorian Wine Centre and Tastings, Armadale, in Melbourne, and in a few leading restaurants in Melbourne and Sydney.

▼▼▼▼▼ **Chardonnay 2003** Excellent length and intensity; melon and touches of citrus supported by subtle French oak and perfectly balanced acidity. **RATING** 95 **DRINK** 2013 $ 35
Clonal Selection Pinot Noir 2002 Very good colour, still red; abundant and concentrated rich plum fruit; long and impressive finish; still in its infancy. **RATING** 95 **DRINK** 2012 $ 48

ŸŸŸŸŸ **Pinot Noir 2003** Deep colour; rich, ripe, luscious black cherry, damson plum and spice; integrated oak, soft tannins. Screwcap. **RATING** 92 **DRINK** 2010 $ 42

Gamay 2003 Heady plum, almond and spice aromas and flavours; smooth and supple, fresh acidity to close. The leader of a small Gamay band in Australia. Screwcap. **RATING** 90 **DRINK** 2007 $ 28

Elgee Park ★★★

RMB 5560, Wallaces Road, Merricks North, Vic 3926 **REGION** Mornington Peninsula
T (03) 5989 7338 **F** (03) 5989 7338 **WEB** www.elgeeparkwines.com.au **OPEN** One day a year – Sunday of Queen's Birthday weekend
WINEMAKER Contract **EST.** 1972 **CASES** 1800
SUMMARY The pioneer of the Mornington Peninsula in its 20th century rebirth, owned by Baillieu Myer and family. The wines are now made at Stonier and T'Gallant, Elgee Park's own winery having been closed, and the overall level of activity decreased. Melbourne retail distribution through Flinders Wholesale.

ŸŸŸ **Pinot Gris 2003** **RATING** 83

Elgo Estate ★★★★

Upton Road, Upton Hill via Longwood, Vic 3665 **REGION** Strathbogie Ranges
T (03) 5798 5563 **F** (03) 5798 5524 **WEB** www.elgoestate.com.au **OPEN** By appointment
WINEMAKER Cameron Atkins **EST.** 1999 **CASES** 15 000
SUMMARY The Taresch family began the development of their vineyard, at an altitude of 500m, in the Upton area, adjacent to Mount Helen, Alexander Park and Plunkett's Blackwood Ridge vineyards. Grant Taresch manages the vineyard, while Cameron Atkins, who has overseen the vintages made between 2001 and 2003 at other venues, runs the new 800 tonne winery (erected in time for the 2004 vintage). Striking packaging is a feature.

ŸŸŸŸŸ **Strathbogie Ranges Riesling 2004** Quite intense mineral and lime flavours run through the length of a flavoursome palate. Screwcap. **RATING** 90 **DRINK** 2010 $ 16

ŸŸŸŸ **Strathbogie Ranges Sauvignon Blanc Semillon 2004** Good mouthfeel; touches of passionfruit, ripe apple and tropical fruit; has good length. Screwcap. **RATING** 89 **DRINK** 2007 $ 16

Cabernet Sauvignon 2003 Very good colour; elegant, light to medium-bodied cassis/berry fruit; minimal tannins and oak, but has nice flavours. **RATING** 88 **DRINK** 2010 $ 28

Allira Riesling 2004 Clean, relatively soft lime and passionfruit; balanced acidity; early drinking; value. Screwcap. **RATING** 87 **DRINK** 2007 $ 12

Allira Sauvignon Blanc Semillon 2004 Delicate, fresh, gently tropical fruit; fleeting sweetness adds to the finish. Screwcap. **RATING** 87 **DRINK** Now $ 12

ŸŸŸŸ **Allira Chardonnay 2004** **RATING** 85 **DRINK** 2007 $ 12

Strathbogie Ranges Pinot Noir Rose 2004 **RATING** 84 **DRINK** Now $ 16

Eling Forest Winery ★★★

Hume Highway, Sutton Forest, NSW 2577 **REGION** Southern New South Wales Zone
T (02) 4878 9499 **F** (02) 4878 9499 **WEB** www.elingforest.com.au **OPEN** 7 days 10–5
WINEMAKER Michelle Crockett **EST.** 1987 **CASES** 11 500
SUMMARY Eling Forest's mentally agile and innovative founder Leslie Fritz celebrated his 80th birthday not long after he planted the first vines here, in 1987. He proceeded to celebrate his 88th birthday by expanding the vineyards from 3 ha to 4 ha, primarily with additional plantings of the Hungarian varieties. He has also developed a Cherry Port and is using the spinning cone technology to produce various peach-based liqueurs, utilising second-class peach waste. Details of the award-winning restaurant and B&B accommodation from the website.

Ellender Estate ★★★☆

260 Green Gully Road, Glenlyon, Vic 3461 **REGION** Macedon Ranges
T (03) 5348 7785 **F** (03) 5348 7784 **WEB** www.ellenderwines.com **OPEN** Weekends & public hols
11–5, or by appointment
WINEMAKER Graham Ellender **EST.** 1996 **CASES** 1200
SUMMARY The Ellenders have established 4 ha of pinot noir, chardonnay, sauvignon blanc and pinot
gris, and also source shiraz and sauvignon blanc from Cowra, cabernet sauvignon from Harcourt,
cabernet franc from Macedon and pinot noir from Narre Warren. Formerly called Leura Glen Estate,
marketplace confusion with similar names, and other considerations, led to the change to Ellender
Estate.

ΨΨΨΨΨ Rosetta Macedon Ranges Rose 2004 Pale pink; aromatic, spicy, strawberry bouquet;
lively, fresh, dry palate; crisp finish. Serious Rose style. Screwcap. **RATING** 90 **DRINK** 2007
$ 18

ΨΨΨΨ Macedon Ranges Chardonnay 2004 Complex citrussy fruit on bouquet and palate; a
touch of oak in the background; brisk acidity. Screwcap. **RATING** 87 **DRINK** 2007 $ 24
Pinot Chardonnay 2002 Pinot dominant; a big wine, slightly brawny and muscular.
RATING 87 **DRINK** 2008 $ 38
Pinot Chardonnay NV Bright salmon-pink; very bright, crisp strawberry and citrus; high
acidity; needs more time on lees or higher dosage. **RATING** 87 **DRINK** 2010 $ 38

ΨΨΨΨ Moonstruck Vineyard Chardonnay 2004 RATING 86 **DRINK** 2007 $ 24
Macedon Pinot Noir 2002 RATING 86 **DRINK** 2008 $ 33
Fortified Chardonnay 2001 RATING 86 **DRINK** 2007 $ 22
Sauvignon Blanc 2004 RATING 84 **DRINK** Now $ 20

ΨΨΨ Metcalfe Shiraz 2002 RATING 79 $ 18

Elliot Rocke Estate ★★★★

Craigmoor Road, Mudgee, NSW 2850 **REGION** Mudgee
T (02) 6372 7722 **F** (02) 6372 0680 **WEB** www.elliotrockeestate.com.au **OPEN** 7 days 9–4
WINEMAKER Jim Chatto, Greg Silkman (Monarch Winemaking Services) **EST.** 1999 **CASES** 6000
SUMMARY Elliot Rocke Estate has 24.2 ha of vineyards dating back to 1987, when the property was
known as Seldom Seen. Plantings are made up of around 9 ha of semillon, 4.3 ha shiraz and
chardonnay, 2.2 ha merlot and 2 ha each of cabernet sauvignon and traminer, with 0.5 ha of
doradillo. Contract winemaking by Jim Chatto and Greg Silkman have resulted in medals at the
Mudgee and Rutherglen wine shows. The wines are available through the cellar door, by mailing list,
and through a number of Sydney retailers. Exports to South Korea.

ΨΨΨΨΨ Mudgee Merlot 2003 Light to medium-bodied; a clean mix of small red fruits and gentle
savoury tannins; attractive varietal flavour and texture. High-quality cork. **RATING** 90
DRINK 2010 $ 19.95

ΨΨΨΨ Mudgee Semillon 2004 Gentle grass and lanolin mix; softer style than usual; citrussy
fruit, lemony finish. Screwcap. **RATING** 89 **DRINK** 2008 $ 16.95
Premium Mudgee Chardonnay 2003 Some colour development; medium-bodied;
plenty of yellow peach and stone fruit; good oak handling, has length. Cork. **RATING** 89
DRINK 2008 $ 17.95
Mudgee Shiraz 2003 Full-bodied; extremely robust and powerful; black fruits, big
tannins; needs time. Cork. **RATING** 88 **DRINK** 2015 $ 19.95
Mudgee Cabernet Sauvignon 2003 Powerful, rustic and earthy; blackcurrant, mocha
and chocolate; like the Shiraz, needs time. Cork. **RATING** 88 **DRINK** 2010 $ 19.95
Ice Wine 2004 Clean; very sweet fruit; not complex, though fair acid balance. **RATING** 87
DRINK 2008 $ 24.95

ΨΨΨΨ Mudgee Unwooded Chardonnay 2004 RATING 86 **DRINK** 2007 $ 15.95
Mudgee Traminer 2004 RATING 85 **DRINK** Now $ 15.95

Elmslie ★★☆

Upper McEwans Road, Legana, Tas 7277 **REGION** Northern Tasmania
T (03) 6330 1225 **F** (03) 6330 2161 **OPEN** By appointment
WINEMAKER Ralph Power **EST.** 1972 **CASES** 600
SUMMARY A small, specialist red winemaker, from time to time blending Pinot Noir with Cabernet.
The fruit from the now fully mature vineyard (0.5 ha of pinot noir and 1.5 ha of cabernet sauvignon)
has depth and character, but operational constraints mean that the style of the wine is often
somewhat rustic.

Elmswood Estate ★★★★

75 Monbulk–Seville Road, Wandin East, Vic 3139 **REGION** Yarra Valley
T (03) 5964 3015 **F** (03) 5964 3405 **WEB** www.elmswoodestate.com.au **OPEN** 7 days 10–5
WINEMAKER Paul Evans **EST.** 1981 **CASES** 2000
SUMMARY Rod and Dianne Keller purchased their 9.5-ha vineyard in June 1999; it had been planted
in 1981 on the red volcanic soils of the far southern side of the valley. Prior to their acquisition of the
vineyard, the grapes had been sold to other Yarra Valley winemakers, but the Kellers immediately set
about having their own wine made from the estate. The cellar door offers spectacular views across the
Upper Yarra Valley to Mt Donna Buang and Warburton. The wines are sold chiefly through the cellar
door and by mailing list; there are limited restaurant listings.

ΥΥΥΥΥ **Yarra Valley Chardonnay 2003** Complex and rich, ripe stone fruit and barrel ferment
oak; powerful structure, good length. **RATING** 91 **DRINK** 2010 $ 23
Cabernet Sauvignon 2003 Powerful, ripe, sweet blackcurrant fruit; nice touches of spicy
oak; good structure and length. Diam. **RATING** 90 **DRINK** 2013 $ 30

ΥΥΥΥ **Cabernet Merlot 2003** Good concentration and focus; blackcurrant fruit is still relatively
austere and needing to loosen up; will do so. Diam. **RATING** 89 **DRINK** 2013 $ 26

ΥΥΥΥ **Yarra Valley Cabernet Rose 2004** **RATING** 85 **DRINK** Now $ 20
Yarra Valley Unoaked Chardonnay 2004 **RATING** 84 **DRINK** Now $ 20

Elsewhere Vineyard ★★★☆

42 Dillons Hill Road, Glaziers Bay, Tas 7109 **REGION** Southern Tasmania
T (03) 6295 1228 **F** (03) 6295 1591 **WEB** www.elsewherevineyard.com **OPEN** Not
WINEMAKER Andrew Hood (Contract), Steve Lubiana (Contract) **EST.** 1984 **CASES** 4000
SUMMARY Kylie and Andrew Cameron's evocatively named Elsewhere Vineyard used to jostle for
space with a commercial flower farm. The estate-produced range comes from the 6 ha of pinot noir,
3 ha of chardonnay and 1 ha of riesling which constitute the immaculately tended vineyard.

ΥΥΥΥ **Somewhere Else Gewurztraminer 2004** Nicely balanced and clean; varietal character a
little subdued, but will become more obvious with some bottle age. **RATING** 88 **DRINK** 2009
$ 18

ΥΥΥΥ **Somewhere Else Pinot Noir 2004** **RATING** 86 **DRINK** 2007 $ 20

Elsmore's Caprera Grove ★★★

657 Milbrodale Road, Broke, NSW 2330 **REGION** Lower Hunter Valley
T (02) 6579 1344 **F** (02) 6579 1355 **WEB** www.elsmorewines.com.au **OPEN** Weekends & public hols
10–5, or by appointment
WINEMAKER Jim Chatto, Gary Reid (Contract) **EST.** 1995 **CASES** 800
SUMMARY Bindy and Chris Elsmore purchased their 16-ha property at Broke in 1995, subsequently
establishing a little over 4 ha of chardonnay, verdelho and shiraz, with chardonnay taking the lion's
share of the plantings. Their interest in wine came not from their professional lives – Chris is a
retired commodore of the RAN and Bindy had a career in advertising, marketing and personnel – but
from numerous trips to the wine regions of France, Italy and Spain.

Eltham Vineyards

NR

225 Shaws Road, Arthurs Creek, Vic 3099 **REGION** Yarra Valley
T (03) 9439 4144 **F** (03) 9439 5121 **OPEN** By appointment
WINEMAKER George Apted, John Graves **EST.** 1990 **CASES** 600
SUMMARY Drawing upon vineyards at Arthurs Creek and Eltham, John Graves (brother of David Graves, of the illustrious Californian Pinot producer Saintsbury) produces tiny quantities of quite stylish Chardonnay and Pinot Noir, the former showing nice barrel-ferment characters. The wines have been consistent medal winners in regional Victorian wine shows.

Elysium Vineyard

★★★☆

393 Milbrodale Road, Broke, NSW 2330 **REGION** Lower Hunter Valley
T (02) 9664 2368 **F** (02) 9664 2368 **WEB** www.winecountry.com.au/accommodation/elysium **OPEN** Weekends 10–5, or by appointment
WINEMAKER Nick Paterson (Tyrrell's) **EST.** 1990 **CASES** 450
SUMMARY Elysium was once part of a much larger vineyard established by John Tulloch. Tulloch (not part of the Tulloch operation previously owned by Southcorp) continues to look after the viticulture, with the 1 ha of verdelho being vinified at Tyrrell's. The Elysium Cottage, large enough to accommodate 6 people, has won a number of tourism awards; proprietor Victoria Foster, in partnership with Ben Moechtar (Vice-President of the Australian Sommeliers Association), conduct wine education weekends on request, with meals prepared by a chef brought in for the occasion. The cost per person for a gourmet weekend is $300–400, depending on numbers. Exports to the US and Canada.

▼▼▼▼ **Limited Release Fordwich Verdelho 2002** Unusually lively, brisk and fresh lemony acidity, more to Semillon in style; developing slowly and surely. Quality cork. **RATING** 88 **DRINK** 2007 **$** 25

Emerald Hill Winery

NR

218 Donges Road, Severnlea, Qld 4352 **REGION** Granite Belt
T 0411 487 226 **OPEN** Weekends & public hols 10–5
WINEMAKER Tom Jimenez **EST.** 1998 **CASES** 900
SUMMARY Tom Jimenez planted his 2-ha vineyard as a lifestyle change. The varieties chosen were chardonnay, merlot (0.25 ha each), tempranillo, shiraz and cabernet sauvignon (0.5 ha each). The wines, which have received recognition in both wine shows and *Winestate* magazine, are sold through the cellar door (appointment necessary), by mail order and at Pizzani's Restaurant, Brisbane.

Emma's Cottage Vineyard

NR

Wilderness Road, Lovedale, NSW 2320 **REGION** Lower Hunter Valley
T (02) 4998 7734 **F** (02) 4998 7209 **WEB** www.emmascottage.com.au **OPEN** Fri–Mon, public & school hols 10–5, or by appointment
WINEMAKER David Hook (Contract) **EST.** 1987 **CASES** NA
SUMMARY Rob and Toni Powys run a combined boutique winery and accommodation business on their 12-ha property at Lovedale; 4 ha of semillon, chardonnay, verdelho, merlot, pinot noir and shiraz have been planted, and a range of varietals and vintages are on offer.

Empress Vineyard

★★★★

Drapers Road, Irrewarra, Vic 3250 (postal Amberley House, 391 Sandy Bay Road, Hobart, Tas 7005)
REGION Western Victoria Zone
T (03) 6225 1005 **F** (03) 6225 0639 **WEB** www.empress.com.au **OPEN** By appointment
WINEMAKER Robin Brockett, Cate Looney, Lisa Togni **EST.** 1998 **CASES** 1000
SUMMARY If the address of Empress and its Geographic Zone seem schizophrenic, don't be alarmed. Allistair Lindsay is in the course of moving to Tasmania: he is selling the restaurant at Irrewarra (although not, so far, the vineyard) seeking to re-establish both restaurant and vineyard/winemaking near Hobart. It is uncertain whether both vineyard operations will be kept going; the quality of the wines from the existing Empress Vineyard must tempt Lindsay to maintain the operation.

England's Creek

NR

PO Box 6, Murrumbateman, NSW 2582 **REGION** Canberra District
T (02) 6227 5550 **F** (02) 6227 5605 **WEB** www.barrique.com.au **OPEN** At Barrique Café, Murrumbateman
WINEMAKER Ken Helm (Contract) **EST.** 1995 **CASES** 250
SUMMARY The diminutive England's Creek was established in 1995 by Stephen Carney and Virginia Rawling with the planting of 1 ha each of riesling and shiraz; both areas have subsequently been doubled. The wines are available at selected Canberra restaurants and Vintage Cellars, Manuka or from the winery.

Ensay Winery

NR

Great Alpine Road, Ensay, Vic 3895 **REGION** Gippsland
T (03) 5157 3203 **F** (03) 5157 3372 **OPEN** Weekends, public & school hols 11–5, or by appointment
WINEMAKER David Coy **EST.** 1992 **CASES** 1500
SUMMARY A weekend and holiday business for the Coy family, headed by David Coy, with 2.5 ha of chardonnay, pinot noir, merlot, shiraz and cabernet sauvignon.

Eppalock Ridge

633 North Redesdale Road, Redesdale, Vic 3444 **REGION** Heathcote
T (03) 5443 7841 **WEB** www.eppalockridge.com **OPEN** By appointment
WINEMAKER Rod Hourigan **EST.** 1979 **CASES** 1500
SUMMARY While continuing to maintain a low profile as a winemaking operation, the estate plantings have increased to 17 ha, dominated by shiraz with 10 ha, and as well as limited domestic retail distribution, exports have been established to the US, New Zealand and Fiji.

ΥΥΥΥΥ **Heathcote Shiraz 2002** Powerful and concentrated; a rich array of black fruits, licorice and spice; balanced French and American oak. **RATING** 94 **DRINK** 2017 $ 33

ΥΥΥΥΥ **Kylix Shiraz 2002** Arguably more elegant than the varietal release, with more length and finesse, but not as generous on the mid-palate. **RATING** 91 **DRINK** 2012

ΥΥΥΥ **Heathcote Cabernet Merlot 2002** Lashings of sweet cassis and blackcurrant fruit; medium-bodied; fine tannins. **RATING** 89 **DRINK** 2011 $ 33

Ermes Estate

NR

2 Godings Road, Moorooduc, Vic 3933 **REGION** Mornington Peninsula
T (03) 5978 8376 **F** (03) 5978 8396 **OPEN** Weekends & public hols 11–5
WINEMAKER Ermes Zucchet, Denise Zucchet **EST.** 1989 **CASES** 700
SUMMARY Ermes and Denise Zucchet commenced planting of the 2.5-ha estate in 1989 with chardonnay, riesling, cabernet sauvignon and merlot, adding pinot gris in 1991. In 1994 an existing piggery on the property was converted to a winery and cellar door area (in the Zucchets' words, 'the pigs having been evicted'); the modestly priced wines are on sale there.

🍇 Ernest Hill Wines

NR

307 Wine Country Drive, Nulkaba, NSW 2325 **REGION** Lower Hunter Valley
T (02) 4991 4418 **F** (02) 4991 7724 **WEB** www.ernesthillwines.com.au **OPEN** 7 days 10–5
WINEMAKER Mark Woods **EST.** 1999 **CASES** 1400
SUMMARY The Wilson family has owned the Ernest Hill property since 1999; the vineyard has 3 ha of semillon, and 1 ha each of chardonnay, traminer and verdelho; an additional hectare of shiraz is leased. The business has had great success with the wines so far released, none more so than the 2002 Alexander Chardonnay (made by previous winemaker Adrian Lockhart), with a string of medals (including a gold medal and trophy for the Cyril Semillon).

ese Vineyards ★★★★

1013 Tea Tree Road, Tea Tree, Tas 7017 **REGION** Southern Tasmania
T 0417 319 875 **OPEN** 7 days 10–5
WINEMAKER Julian Alcorso (Contract) **EST.** 1994 **CASES** 2700
SUMMARY Elvio and Natalie Brianese are an architect and graphic designer couple whose extended
family have centuries-old viticultural roots in the Veneto region of northern Italy. They have 2.5 ha of
bearing vineyard. The Pinot Noir can be outstanding.

ΨΨΨΨ **Pinot Noir 2003** Strong colour; extremely ripe, almost essency, plum aromas; similar
flavours, but avoids going over the top. High-quality cork. **RATING** 92 **DRINK** 2011 $ 24.50

ΨΨΨΨ **Chardonnay 2003** The bouquet shows some stressed yeast characters, but the palate is
bright and vibrant, with citrus fruit and crisp Tasmanian acidity. Quality cork. **RATING** 87
DRINK 2008 $ 24.50

Etain NR

c/- Prime Wines, PO Box 392, Melbourne, Vic 3057 **REGION** Margaret River
T 1300 720 006 **WEB** www.primewines.au.com **OPEN** Not
WINEMAKER Conor Lagan, Jurg Muggli **EST.** 2001 **CASES** 5000
SUMMARY Etain is a private label of Conor Lagan, available only to trade through distributor Prime
Wines. In Gaelic mythology Etain is the horse goddess, representing birth and rebirth. It is in turn
linked to the fascinating story of Conor Lagan's life, which can be found on www.primewines.au.com.
The wines are sourced from vineyards in the Margaret and Frankland River regions.

Eumundi Winery NR

2 Bruce Highway, Eumundi, Qld 4562 **REGION** Queensland Coastal
T (07) 5442 7444 **F** (07) 5442 7455 **OPEN** 7 days 10–6
WINEMAKER Andrew Hickinbotham (Contract) **EST.** 1996 **CASES** 2500
SUMMARY Eumundi Vineyard is set on 21 ha of river-front land in the beautiful Eumundi Valley,
12 km inland from Noosa Heads. The climate is hot, wet, humid and maritime, the only saving grace
being the regular afternoon northeast sea breeze. It is a challenging environment for growing grapes:
the owners, Robyn and Gerry Humphrey, have trialled 14 different grape varieties and three different
trellis systems. Currently they have tempranillo, shiraz, chambourcin, petit verdot, durif, mourvedre
and verdelho. Plantings in 2001 included tannat and others, which gives some idea of their eclectic
approach. The establishment of the vineyard was financed by the sale of a 19m charter yacht which
used to sail the oceans around northern Australia. Quite a change in lifestyle!

🐚 Eurabbie Estate ★★★

251 Dawson Road, Avoca, Vic 3467 **REGION** Pyrenees
T (03) 5465 3799 **OPEN** 7 days 10–5
WINEMAKER John Higgins **EST.** 2000 **CASES** 1000
SUMMARY John and Kerry Higgins have established Eurabbie Estate 2.5 km west of Avoca township
in an 80-ha forest property overlooking a 4-ha natural lake. Two separate blocks of cabernet
sauvignon, shiraz and merlot, with a dash of pinot noir, give rise to the Eurabbie Estate range. From
2004, grapes have been purchased from three small Pyrenees growers to produce the Pyrenees
Villages range: Percydale Chardonnay, Percydale Cabernet Franc, Amherst Shiraz, Stuart Mill Shiraz
and Avoca Cabernet Sauvignon. The wines are made onsite in a mud-brick winery powered by solar
energy. The wines are currently sold by mail order or through the cellar door, but a distributor will
likely be appointed, as production tripled between 2002 and 2005.

ΨΨΨΨ **Avoca Stephen James Shiraz 2003** Light to medium-bodied; ripe red and black fruits;
soft tannins; not particularly concentrated. **RATING** 86 **DRINK** 2007 $ 19.75
Avoca Matthew John Merlot 2003 RATING 86 **DRINK** 2008 $ 19.75
Pyrenees Village Dalys Cottage Percydale Chardonnay 2004 RATING 84 **DRINK** Now
$ 19.75

Evans & Tate ★★★★☆

Metricup Road, Wilyabrup, WA 6280 **REGION** Margaret River
T (08) 9755 6244 **F** (08) 9755 6346 **WEB** www.evansandtate.com.au **OPEN** 7 days 10.30–5
WINEMAKER Richard Rowe **EST.** 1970 **CASES** NFP
SUMMARY From its Swan Valley base 30 years ago, Evans & Tate is now the largest Margaret River winery and producer. Having increased its estate vineyard holdings with the establishment of a large planting in the Jindong area, it raised substantial capital by successfully listing on the Stock Exchange. It then turned its attention eastwards, with the acquisition of Oakridge Estate in the Yarra Valley, followed by Cranswick Wines (renamed Barramundi and now an export-only label) in March 2003. Wine quality is always polished, and, within the Margaret River context, at the lighter end of the spectrum. National distribution and exports to all major markets.

ΨΨΨΨΨ **Redbrook Chardonnay 2002** Still pale green-straw; elegant and fine; lovely melon, stone fruit and subtle cashew/cream barrel and malolactic fermentation inputs; excellent balance. Screwcap. **RATING** 95 **DRINK** 2012 $ 63

ΨΨΨΨ♀ **Margaret River Sauvignon Blanc Semillon 2004** Fresh, crisp, bright and lively; light-bodied but intense in the mineral/herbaceous spectrum; good finish and aftertaste. Screwcap. **RATING** 92 **DRINK** 2007 $ 20
Margaret River Semillon 2003 Sophisticated winemaking (partial barrel ferment and lees contact) adds as much to texture as flavour; ripe, lemongrass-accented fruit; crisp finish. Screwcap. **RATING** 91 **DRINK** 2010 $ 20
Margaret River Chardonnay 2004 Clean, fresh; light to medium-bodied; nectarine, melon and cashew; subtle, spicy oak. Screwcap. **RATING** 91 **DRINK** 2009 $ 20.99
Redbrook Shiraz 2002 Complex licorice, spice and game on the bouquet; medium-bodied palate; spicy licorice and black cherry fruit; still knitting. Cork. **RATING** 90 **DRINK** 2012
Margaret River Classic Red 2003 Medium-bodied; red berry fruit; good control of extract and oak use. **RATING** 90 **DRINK** 2010 $ 17.99

ΨΨΨΨ **Redbrook Cabernet Sauvignon 2001** Cedary, spicy aromas; tight, earthy and savoury fruit takes no prisoners; excellent austere varietal expression reminiscent of '79 Leeuwin Estate as a young wine. Leave for 10 years. Quality cork. **RATING** 89 **DRINK** 2016 $ 63
Margaret River Classic White 2004 Water white; light-bodied, but no reduction; nice lemony fruit and minerality. **RATING** 87 **DRINK** Now $ 19.50
Margaret River Cabernet Merlot 2002 Medium-bodied; distinctly savoury varietal edges to the fruit; fine, persistent tannins. **RATING** 87 **DRINK** 2008 $ 20.95

ΨΨΨ♀ **Gnangara Sauvignon Blanc 2004** **RATING** 86 **DRINK** Now $ 13.50
Margaret River Verdelho 2004 **RATING** 85 **DRINK** 2007 $ 18
Gnangara Unwooded Chardonnay 2004 **RATING** 84 **DRINK** Now $ 14

Evans & Tate Salisbury ★★★

Campbell Avenue, Irymple, Vic 3498 **REGION** Murray Darling
T (03) 5024 6800 **F** (03) 5024 6605 **OPEN** Mon–Sat 10–4.30, Sun 12–4
WINEMAKER Krister Jonsson, Donna Stephens, Tony Pla Bou **EST.** 1977 **CASES** NFP
SUMMARY This is the former Milburn Park winery; the positions of the Salisbury and Milburn brands have been reversed, with Salisbury now the senior and the relaunched Milburn Park label sold at cellar door and as export only. Mosaic is a new, alternative variety, label.

ΨΨΨΨ **Milburn Park Shiraz 2002** Firm, quite savoury and tight; clean black cherry; minimal oak. Good cork. **RATING** 89 **DRINK** 2009 $ 15
Mosaic Viognier 2003 Medium-bodied, smooth and soft; varietal apricot notes, good balance; clean finish. Screwcap. **RATING** 87 **DRINK** Now $ 13.50

ΨΨΨ♀ **Milburn Park Chardonnay 2003** **RATING** 85 **DRINK** Now $ 15
Mosaic Sangiovese Shiraz 2002 **RATING** 85 **DRINK** Now $ 13.50

ΨΨΨ **Chardonnay 2004** **RATING** 83 $ 9
Chardonnay Semillon 2004 **RATING** 83 $ 9

ΨΨ♀ **Mosaic Petit Verdot 2003** **RATING** 79 $ 13.50

Evans Family Wines ★★★★

151 Palmers Lane, Pokolbin, NSW 2321 **REGION** Lower Hunter Valley
T (02) 4998 7237 **F** (02) 4998 7201 **OPEN** 7 days 10–5
WINEMAKER Toby Evans **EST.** 1979 **CASES** 2600
SUMMARY In the wake of the acquisition of Rothbury by Mildara Blass, Len Evans' wine interests now focus on Evans Family (estate-grown and produced from vineyards around the family home), the Evans Wine Company (a quite different, part-maker, part-negociant business) and, most recently, Tower Estate. Len Evans continues to persist with the notion that the Hunter Valley can produce Gamay and Pinot Noir of quality and, irritatingly, occasionally produces evidence to suggest he may be half-right. There is, of course, no such reservation with the Semillon, the Chardonnay or the Shiraz. Exports to the US.

Evelyn County Estate ★★★★

55 Eltham–Yarra Glen Road, Kangaroo Ground, Vic 3097 **REGION** Yarra Valley
T (03) 9437 2155 **F** (03) 9437 2188 **WEB** www.evelyncountyestate.com.au **OPEN** Mon–Wed 11–5, Thurs–Fri 11–10, Sat 9–midnight, Sun 9am–10pm
WINEMAKER Robyn Male, James Lance, David Lance (Contract) **EST.** 1994 **CASES** 3000
SUMMARY The 8-ha Evelyn County Estate has been established by former Coopers & Lybrand managing partner Roger Male and his wife Robyn, who has completed a degree in Applied Science (wine science) at Charles Sturt University. David and James Lance (of Diamond Valley) are currently making the wines, and an architect-designed cellar door sales, gallery and restaurant opened in April 2001. As one would expect, the quality of the wines is very good. A small planting of tempranillo bore its first crop in 2004 and the wine made onsite by Robyn Male.

▼▼▼▼♀ **Black Paddock Chardonnay 2003** Intense and long stone fruit, grapefruit and melon; excellent balance and drive; subtle oak; clean, lively finish. **RATING** 93 **DRINK** 2010 $ 35

▼▼▼▼ **Black Paddock Sauvignon Blanc 2004** Clean, gently tropical gooseberry aromas and flavours; falters slightly on the finish. **RATING** 87 **DRINK** Now $ 23

▼▼▼♀ **Black Paddock Pinot Noir 2003 RATING** 86 **DRINK** 2013 $ 35
Black Paddock Cabernet Sauvignon 2003 Very savoury, lean style; herb and briar overtones; slightly green tannins; does have length. **RATING** 86 **DRINK** 2009 $ 30
Black Paddock Merlot 2003 RATING 85 **DRINK** 2008 $ 30

Excelsior Peak NR

PO Box 269, Tumbarumba, NSW 2653 **REGION** Tumbarumba
T (02) 6948 5102 **F** (02) 6948 5102 **OPEN** Not
WINEMAKER Contract **EST.** 1980 **CASES** 700
SUMMARY Excelsior Peak proprietor Juliet Cullen established the first vineyard in Tumbarumba in 1980. That vineyard was thereafter sold to Southcorp, and Juliet Cullen subsequently established another vineyard, now releasing wines under the Excelsior Peak label. Plantings total over 10 ha, with most of the grapes sold. Sales by mail order only.

Ey Estate ★★★☆

Main Road, Coonawarra, SA 5263 **REGION** Coonawarra
T (08) 8739 3063 **F** (08) 8739 3069 **WEB** www.eyestatewines.com **OPEN** Not
WINEMAKER Pat Tocaciu (Contract) **EST.** 1989 **CASES** 900
SUMMARY The Ey family arrived in Coonawarra in 1908, establishing a mixed farming business on terra rossa soil just to the north of the Coonawarra township. Between 1988 and 1998, third generation Robin Ey, and fourth generation son Peter Ey have established 20 ha of cabernet sauvignon, 4 ha of chardonnay and 2 ha of shiraz, planted in five separate blocks. Most of the grapes are sold to Southcorp under contract, with a small amount made by Pat Tocaciu.

Eyre Creek NR

PO Box 162, Auburn, SA 5451 **REGION** Clare Valley
T 0418 818 400 **F** (08) 8849 2266 **OPEN** Not
WINEMAKER Stephen John (Contract) **EST.** 1999 **CASES** NA

SUMMARY John Osborne established Auburn Vintners, the maker of Eyre Creek, in 1999, with 2 ha of riesling, grenache, cabernet sauvignon and shiraz. The tiny output is sold by mail order and through limited wholesale distribution.

Faber Vineyard ★★★★★

233 Hadrill Road, Baskerville, WA 6056 (postal) **REGION** Swan Valley
T (08) 9296 0619 **F** (08) 9296 0681 **OPEN** Not
WINEMAKER John Griffiths **EST.** 1997 **CASES** 800
SUMMARY Former Houghton winemaker and now university lecturer and consultant John Griffiths has teamed with his wife, Jane Micallef, to found Faber Vineyard. Since 1997 they have established 1 ha of shiraz, and 0.5 ha each of chardonnay, verdelho, cabernet sauvignon, petit verdot and brown muscat. Says John Griffiths, 'It may be somewhat quixotic, but I'm a great fan of traditional warm area Australia wine styles – those found in areas such as Rutherglen and the Barossa. Wines made in a relatively simple manner that reflect the concentrated ripe flavours one expects in these regions. And when one searches, some of these gems can be found from the Swan Valley.' Possessed of an excellent palate, and with an impeccable winemaking background, the quality of John Griffiths' wines is guaranteed.

ŸŸŸŸŸ **Reserve Shiraz 2003** Opaque purple-red; full-bodied; extremely complex, rich and concentrated; blackberry, prune and spice; Swan Valley's answer to the Barossa. Quality cork. **RATING** 94 **DRINK** 2015 $40
Frankland River Cabernet Sauvignon 2003 Strong purple-red; spicy black fruit aromas; medium-bodied; satin-smooth flow to spicy blackcurrant fruit; quality oak; fine, ripe tannins. Quality cork. **RATING** 94 **DRINK** 2017 $35

ŸŸŸŸŸ **Riche Shiraz 2003** Striking purple-red; potent blackberry and plum fruit plus vanilla oak on both bouquet and palate; simply needs 10 years. **RATING** 91 **DRINK** 2018 $16.50
Riche Shiraz 2004 Rich indeed; excellent blackberry, vanilla and soft tannins; medium to full-bodied, but retains grace. Quality cork. **RATING** 90 **DRINK** 2011 $16.50

ŸŸŸŸ **Reserve Shiraz 2002** Attractive savoury style with good length and intensity. Sweet, cedary oak, fine tannins. **RATING** 89 **DRINK** 2009 $40
Margaret River Cabernet Sauvignon 2002 Tight, savoury, earthy aromas; sweetens up somewhat on the palate, and has good length. **RATING** 88 **DRINK** 2010 $35
Swan Valley Chardonnay 2003 Very similar in style to the 2004, but has built a little on the back palate. **RATING** 87 **DRINK** 2007 $12
Swan Valley Verdelho 2004 Fresh, elegant fruit salad aromas and flavours; nice length; not obviously sweet. **RATING** 87 **DRINK** Now $12
Petit Verdot 2004 Powerful black fruits and hints of earth on the bouquet; structure not as strong as expected, nor tannins in particular. Young vines and/or warm-grown? Cork. **RATING** 87 **DRINK** 2008 $19.50

ŸŸŸŸ **Swan Valley Chardonnay 2004** Very pale; some oak inputs to the bouquet, the palate tight, light and fresh; slightly one-dimensional. **RATING** 86 **DRINK** 2008 $12

ŸŸŸ **Swan Valley Shiraz Cabernet 2003** **RATING** 83 $12

Fairview Wines

422 Elderslie Road, Branxton, NSW 2335 **REGION** Lower Hunter Valley
T (02) 4938 1116 **F** (02) 4938 1116 **WEB** www.fairviewwines.com.au **OPEN** Fri–Mon 10–5, or by appointment
WINEMAKER Rhys Eather (Contract) **EST.** 1997 **CASES** 2000
SUMMARY Greg and Elaine Searles purchased the property on which they have established Fairview Wines in 1997. For the previous 90 years it had sustained an orchard, but since that time 2 ha of shiraz, 1 ha each of barbera and semillon and 0.5 ha of chambourcin and verdelho have been established, using organic procedures wherever possible. The Searles operate the cellar door in person; retail distribution in Sydney and exports to the UK. Accommodation (in a relocated church) is now available.

Faisan Estate NR

Amaroo Road, Borenore, NSW 2800 **REGION** Orange
T (02) 6365 2380 **OPEN** Not
WINEMAKER Col Walker **EST.** 1992 **CASES** 500

SUMMARY Faisan Estate, within sight of Mt Canobolas and 20 km west of the city of Orange, has been established by Trish and Col Walker. They now have almost 10 ha of vineyards and have also purchased grapes from other growers in the region.

Falls Wines ★★★

Belubula Way, Canowindra, NSW 2804 REGION Cowra
T (02) 6344 1293 F (02) 6344 1290 WEB www.fallswines.com OPEN 7 days 10–4
WINEMAKER Jon Reynolds (Contract) EST. 1997 CASES 3200
SUMMARY Peter and Zoe Kennedy have established Falls Vineyard and Retreat (to give it its full name) on the outskirts of Canowindra. They have planted chardonnay, semillon, merlot, cabernet sauvignon and shiraz, with luxury B&B accommodation offering large spa baths, exercise facilities, fishing and a tennis court.

Faranda Wines NR

768 Wanneroo Road, Wanneroo, WA 6065 REGION Swan District
T (08) 9306 1174 OPEN Mon–Fri 9–5
WINEMAKER Basil Faranda EST. NA CASES NA
SUMMARY Basil Faranda has 3 ha of mixed wine and table grapes, planted to grenache, shiraz, muscat, chasselas, cardinal and italia. He makes the wine onsite, selling through local outlets and the cellar door.

Farmer's Daughter Wines ★★★☆

791 Cassilis Road, Mudgee, NSW 2850 REGION Mudgee
T (02) 6373 3177 F (02) 6373 3759 WEB www.farmersdaughterwines.com.au OPEN 7 days 9–5
WINEMAKER Joe Lesnik (Contract) EST. 1995 CASES 6000
SUMMARY The intriguingly named Farmer's Daughter Wines is a family-owned vineyard, run by the daughters of a feed-lot farmer, with winemaking by Joe Lesnik. Much of the production from the substantial vineyard of 20 ha, planted to shiraz (7 ha), merlot (6 ha), chardonnay and cabernet sauvignon (3 ha each) and semillon (1 ha), is sold to other makers, but 6000 cases are made for the Farmer's Daughter label. As well as local retail distribution (and 7-day cellar door sales), the wines are available through selected outlets in Sydney and New South Wales regional areas.

ŶŶŶŶŶ **Cabernet Sauvignon 2003** Strong colour; medium-bodied, ripe blackcurrant fruit and supporting tannins; supple mouthfeel, good finish. Quality cork. RATING 90 DRINK 2012 $19

ŶŶŶŶ **Shiraz 2003** RATING 86 DRINK 2010 $22

Farosa Estate NR

1157 Port Wakefield Road, Waterloo Corner, SA 5110 (postal) REGION Adelaide Plains
T 0412 674 655 F (08) 8280 6450 OPEN Not
WINEMAKER Frank Perre (Contract) EST. 2000 CASES NA
SUMMARY The family-owned Farosa Estate has 11 ha of shiraz and 3.6 ha of mourvedre (mataro) in production. The aim is to produce a full-bodied wine with as little preservative as possible, with open fermentation and oak maturation varying between 10 and 18 months. The first release of Farosa Estate Shiraz was in 2003, and the price has not yet been finally determined. To date, winemaking has taken place in the Barossa Valley, but the family is contemplating building its own winery.

Farrawell Wines ★★☆

60 Whalans Track, Lancefield, Vic 3435 REGION Macedon Ranges
T (03) 9817 5668 F (03) 9817 7215 WEB www.farrawellwines.com.au OPEN By appointment
WINEMAKER Trefor Morgan, David Cowburn (Contract) EST. 2000 CASES 250
SUMMARY Farrawell had a dream start to its commercial life when its 2001 Chardonnay was awarded the Trophy for Best Chardonnay at the 2003 Macedon Ranges Wine Exhibition. Given that slightly less than 1 ha each of chardonnay and pinot noir are the sole source of wines, production will always

be limited. Trefor Morgan is the owner/winemaker of Mount Charlie Winery, but perhaps better known as a Professor of Physiology at Melbourne University

ΨΨΨ **Pinot Noir 2003** RATING 83 $ 25

Farrell's Limestone Creek

NR

Mount View Road, Mount View, NSW 2325 **REGION** Lower Hunter Valley
T (02) 4991 2808 **F** (02) 4991 3414 **OPEN** 7 days 10–5
WINEMAKER Neil McGuigan (Contract) **EST.** 1980 **CASES** 3500
SUMMARY The Farrell family purchased 20 ha on Mount View in 1980 and gradually established 7.3 ha of vineyards planted to semillon, verdelho, chardonnay, shiraz, cabernet sauvignon and merlot. Most of the grapes are sold to McWilliam's, with a lesser amount made for cellar door and mailing list orders.

Farr Rising

 ★★★★☆

27 Maddens Road, Bannockburn, Vic 3331 (postal) **REGION** Geelong
T (03) 5281 1979 **F** (03) 5281 1979 **OPEN** Not
WINEMAKER Nicholas Farr **EST.** 2001 **CASES** 2000
SUMMARY Nicholas Farr is the son of Gary Farr, and with encouragement from his father has launched his own brand. He has learnt his winemaking in France and Australia, and has access to some excellent base material, hence the quality of the wines. Exports to Denmark, Hong Kong and Japan.

ΨΨΨΨΨ **Mornington Peninsula Pinot Noir 2003** Clean and expressive; black plums and spice; immaculate structure, balance and length. RATING 94 DRINK 2010 $ 35

ΨΨΨΨΨ **Geelong Pinot Noir 2003** Bright but light red; highly fragrant cherry and small red fruits; light but elegant. RATING 91 DRINK 2007 $ 35

ΨΨΨΨ **Truckin Clare Valley Riesling 2004** Apple, pear and spice aromas; minerally flavour, just a fraction grippy. Cork. RATING 89 DRINK 2008 $ 13.43
Geelong Saignee 2004 Plenty of depth and length; spicy strawberry and cherry flavours; has texture. Cork. RATING 88 DRINK Now $ 16.13
Geelong Merlot 2003 Ultra-herbal, spicy style; some green olive rather than black olive; just gets over the line. Cork. RATING 87 DRINK 2009 $ 34.50

🍇 Feet First Wines

 ★★★

32 Parkinson Lane, Kardinya, WA 6163 (postal) **REGION** Southeast Australia
T (08) 9314 7133 **F** (08) 9314 7134 **OPEN** Not
WINEMAKER Contract **EST.** 2004 **CASES** 4500
SUMMARY This is the business of Ross and Ronnie (Veronica) Lawrence, who have been fine wine wholesalers in Perth since 1987, handling top-shelf Australian and imported wines. It is a virtual winery, with both grapegrowing and winemaking provided by contract, the aim being to produce easy-drinking, good-value wines under $20; the deliberately limited portfolio includes Semillon Sauvignon Blanc, Cabernets Merlot and Cabernet Merlot.

ΨΨΨΨ **Cabernet Merlot 2003** Clean, fresh, lively juicy berry flavours; fruit-driven, low tannins. From Geographe. RATING 86 DRINK Now $ 14
Cabernet Merlot 2001 RATING 85 $ 16

Felsberg Winery

 ★★★

116 Townsends Road, Glen Aplin, Qld 4381 **REGION** Granite Belt
T (07) 4683 4332 **F** (07) 4683 4377 **OPEN** 7 days 9–5
WINEMAKER Otto Haag **EST.** 1983 **CASES** 2500
SUMMARY Felsberg has a spectacular site, high on a rocky slope, with the winery itself built on a single huge boulder. It has been offering wine for sale via the cellar door (and mailing list) made by former master brewer Otto Haag for many years; the red wines are the strength.

ΥΥΥΥ **Merlot 2003** Long and savoury, but with slightly green tannins on the finish. **RATING** 88 **DRINK** 2009 $20

ΥΥΥΫ **Cabernet Sauvignon 2002** Light to medium-bodied; fresh red and blackcurrant fruit; a hint of sweetness on the finish. Cork. **RATING** 86 **DRINK** 2008 $18

Fenton Views Winery   NR

182 Fenton Hill Road, Clarkefield, Vic 3430 **REGION** Sunbury
T (03) 5428 5429 **F** (03) 5428 5304 **OPEN** Weekends 11–5, or by appointment
WINEMAKER David Spiteri **EST.** 1994 **CASES** 800
SUMMARY Situated on the north-facing slopes of Fenton Hill at Clarkefield, just northeast of Sunbury, the Hume and Macedon Ranges provide a spectacular and tranquil setting. It is a small family operation, with plantings of shiraz, chardonnay, pinot noir and cabernet sauvignon. Co-owner David Spiteri studied winemaking at Charles Sturt University, and has had vintage experience in Australia and California.

Ferguson Falls Estate   NR

Pile Road, Dardanup, WA 6236 **REGION** Geographe
T (08) 9728 1083 **F** (08) 9728 1616 **OPEN** 11–5 weekends & public hols, or by appointment
WINEMAKER David Crawford (Contract) **EST.** 1983 **CASES** 1000
SUMMARY Peter Giumelli and family are dairy farmers in the lush Ferguson Valley, 180 km south of Perth. In 1983 they planted 3 ha of cabernet sauvignon, chardonnay and merlot, making their first wines for commercial release from the 1995 and 1996 vintages, which confirmed the suitability of the region for the production of premium wine. This led to a doubling of the plantings, including 1 ha of tempranillo and 0.6 ha of nebbiolo.

🐌 Ferguson Hart Estate

Cnr Pile Road/Garden Court Drive, Ferguson Valley, WA 6236 **REGION** Geographe
T (08) 9728 0144 **F** (08) 9728 0144 **OPEN** Weekends 11–5
WINEMAKER Contract **EST.** 1994 **CASES** 400
SUMMARY Merv Hart and family have established 2.7 ha of shiraz, sauvignon blanc and semillon on gravelly soils on northern slopes. Start-of-the-art viticultural techniques are used to keep vigour and yield under control. An art gallery and coffee shop operate on weekends.

ΥΥΥΫ **Sauvignon Blanc Semillon 2004** Lots of CO_2 spritz; sweet fruit at the tropical end of the spectrum. Screwcap. **RATING** 86 **DRINK** 2008 $16

Fergusson

Wills Road, Yarra Glen, Vic 3775 **REGION** Yarra Valley
T (03) 5965 2237 **F** (03) 5965 2405 **WEB** www.fergussonwinery.com.au **OPEN** 7 days 11–5
WINEMAKER Christopher Keyes, Peter Fergusson **EST.** 1968 **CASES** 10 000
SUMMARY One of the very first Yarra wineries to announce the rebirth of the Valley, now best known as a favoured destination for tourist coaches, offering hearty fare in comfortable surroundings and wines of both Yarra and non-Yarra Valley origin. For this reason the limited quantities of its estate wines are often ignored, but they should not be. Exports to the UK.

ΥΥΥΥΫ **LJK Pinot Noir 2002** Has the intensity typical of the vintage; smoky, spicy, savoury edges to intense plum, spice and mocha fruit; good length. Screwcap. **RATING** 93 **DRINK** 2009 $25
Victoria Chardonnay 2004 Elegant melon, nectarine and citrus; clean, harmonious palate; soft, accessible style. Screwcap. **RATING** 90 **DRINK** 2008 $25

ΥΥΥΥ **Benjamyn Cabernet Sauvignon 2003** Blackcurrant, mocha, vanilla and chocolate come together on a light to medium-bodied palate; fine tannins. Dodgy cork. **RATING** 87 **DRINK** 2009 $25

ΥΥΥΫ **Yarra Valley Brut Pinot Noir Chardonnay 2003** **RATING** 86 **DRINK** 2009 $25

Fermoy Estate ★★★★

Metricup Road, Wilyabrup, WA 6280 **REGION** Margaret River
T (08) 9755 6285 **F** (08) 9755 6251 **WEB** www.fermoy.com.au **OPEN** 7 days 11–4.30
WINEMAKER Michael Kelly **EST.** 1985 **CASES** 25 000
SUMMARY A long-established estate-based winery with 14 ha of semillon, sauvignon blanc, chardonnay, cabernet sauvignon and merlot. Notwithstanding its substantial production, it is happy to keep a relatively low profile. Exports to the UK, Holland, Switzerland and the US.

Fernbrook Estate Wines NR

Bolganup Dam Road, Porongurup, WA 6324 **REGION** Porongurup
T (08) 9853 1030 **F** (08) 9853 1030 **OPEN** By appointment
WINEMAKER David McNamara **EST.** 1978 **CASES** NA
SUMMARY Run by Danuta Faulkner and Michelle Faulkner-Pearce, the Estate (formerly Bolganup Heritage Wines) has 4 ha of cabernet sauvignon and gamay, and makes table, sparkling and organic wines under the Fernbrook Estate label. Exports to the UK, Germany and Sweden are the primary outlet; domestic sales by mail order and through the cellar door by appointment.

Ferngrove Vineyards ★★★★★

Ferngrove Road, Frankland, WA 6396 **REGION** Frankland River
T (08) 9855 2378 **F** (08) 9855 2368 **WEB** www.ferngrove.com.au **OPEN** 7 days 10–4
WINEMAKER Kim Horton **EST.** 1997 **CASES** 20 000
SUMMARY After 90 years of family beef and dairy farming heritage, Murray Burton decided in 1997 to venture into premium grapegrowing and winemaking. Since that time he has moved with exceptional speed, establishing 414 ha of grapes on 3 vineyards in the Frankland River subregion, and a fourth at Mount Barker. The operation centres around the Ferngrove Vineyard, where a large rammed-earth winery and tourist complex was built in time for the 2000 vintage. Part of the vineyard production is sold as grapes; part is sold as juice or must; part is sold as finished wine; and part is made under the Ferngrove Vineyards label. Exports to the UK and the US.

ŸŸŸŸŸ **Majestic Cabernet Sauvignon 2003** Strong colour; clear blackcurrant and cassis varietal aromas; firm, well-structured medium-bodied palate; very good cabernet expression throughout; subtle oak. **RATING** 94 **DRINK** 2015 $ 24.99
King Malbec 2003 Powerful mouthfilling style with much more structure than normally encountered with malbec, but juicy/jammy varietal fruit there nonetheless. **RATING** 94 **DRINK** 2012 $ 24.99

ŸŸŸŸŸ **Cossack Riesling 2004** Powerful and intense, with a faint touch of reduction; tightly focused mineral and herb flavours; long finish. **RATING** 93 **DRINK** 2014 $ 20
Semillon Sauvignon Blanc 2004 Clean and aromatic tropical passionfruit bouquet leads into a fresh, crisp palate with herb and grass joining the band of flavours. **RATING** 93 **DRINK** 2007 $ 14.99
King Malbec 2002 Arguably the best definition of malbec in Australia; particularly juicy, jammy fruit with fine, long tannins. **RATING** 92 **DRINK** 2010 $ 25
Riesling 2004 Lively, crisp, minerally; touches of spice and herb; good balance; needs time. **RATING** 90 **DRINK** 2014 $ 17.99
Diamond Chardonnay 2003 Fine, restrained style; melon, fig and citrus components; good overall balance. **RATING** 90 **DRINK** 2008 $ 22.99
Majestic Cabernet Sauvignon 2002 Entirely fruit-driven; medium-bodied, blackcurrant, blackberry and cassis; fine tannins to close; elegant style. **RATING** 90 **DRINK** 2012 $ 25

ŸŸŸŸ **Sauvignon Blanc 2004** Clean and crisp, with no reduction; a light, fresh and delicate mix of tropical, gooseberry and capsicum flavours. **RATING** 88 **DRINK** 2007 $ 17
Dragon Shiraz 2003 Abundant satsuma plum and prune; touches of spice; slight break in the palate line. **RATING** 88 **DRINK** 2013 $ 24.99

Fern Gully Winery   NR

63 Princes Highway, Termeil, NSW 2539 **REGION** Shoalhaven Coast
T (02) 4457 1124 **WEB** www.shoalhavencoast.com.au/wineries **OPEN** Weekends & hols 11–5.30
(except winter)
WINEMAKER Max Staniford **EST.** 1996 **CASES** 350
SUMMARY Glenda and Max Staniford planted a 0.25 ha each of chardonnay, shiraz, cabernet sauvignon
and chambourcin in the 1996 and 1997 planting seasons, producing the first grapes in 1998. The wines
are all estate-grown (hence the limited production) and all the winemaking takes place onsite. The
vineyard is enclosed in permanent netting, and hand-picking the grapes ensures the exclusion of
diseased fruit. The wines have won a number of silver and bronze medals at (unspecified) shows.

Fern Hill Estate

Ingoldby Road, McLaren Flat, SA 5171 **REGION** McLaren Vale
T (08) 8383 0167 **F** (08) 8383 0107 **OPEN** At Marienberg Limeburners Centre
WINEMAKER Peter Orr **EST.** 1975 **CASES** 5000
SUMMARY Fernhill Estate, along with Marienberg and Basedow, became part of the James Estate
empire in 2003. The wines are made under the direction of Peter Orr and sold through the
Marienberg cellar door. Exports to the UK and the US.

Fighting Gully Road

RMB 1315, Whorouly South, Vic 3735 **REGION** Beechworth
T (03) 5727 1434 **F** (03) 5727 1434 **OPEN** By appointment
WINEMAKER Mark Walpole **EST.** 1997 **CASES** 300
SUMMARY Mark Walpole (chief viticulturist for Brown Brothers) and partner Carolyn De Poi have begun
the development of their Aquila Audax vineyard, planting the first vines in 1997. It is situated between
530 and 580m above sea level: the upper eastern slopes are planted to pinot noir and the warmer western
slopes to cabernet sauvignon; there are also small quantities of tempranillo, sangiovese and merlot.

🍷🍷🍷🍷 **Tempranillo 2002** Spice, red and black fruits; good structure and complexity; ripe
tannins, good balance; impressive; from one of Australia's oldest plantings of the variety.
RATING 91 **DRINK** 2010

🍷🍷🍷🍷 **Beechworth Pinot Noir 2002** Some spicy aspects to both bouquet and palate, plus hints
of mocha and caramel; long finish; slightly diminished varietal character. **RATING** 89
DRINK 2007
Beechworth Cabernet Sauvignon 2000 Cedary, earthy, briary style with fine tannins and
good length; bottle-developed; extensive cork staining. **RATING** 87 **DRINK** 2008

Fireblock

St Vincent Street, Watervale, SA 5452 **REGION** Clare Valley
T 0414 441 925 **F** (02) 9144 1925 **OPEN** Not
WINEMAKER David O'Leary, Nick Walker (Contract) **EST.** 1926 **CASES** 3000
SUMMARY Fireblock (formerly Old Station Vineyard) is owned by Alastair Gillespie and Bill and Noel
Ireland, who purchased the 6 ha, 70-year-old vineyard in 1995. Watervale Riesling, Old Vine Shiraz
and Old Vine Grenache are skilfully contract-made, winning trophies and gold medals at capital city
wine shows. Exports to the US.

🍷🍷🍷🍷🍷 **Old Station Vineyard Old Vine Shiraz 2002** Excellent balance, structure and overall
mouthfeel; delicious satsuma plum and blackberry fruit; seriously underpriced wine.
Single 1926 vineyard. Screwcap. **RATING** 94 **DRINK** 2017 $ 20

🍷🍷🍷🍷 **Old Station Vineyard Old Vine Grenache 2002** Finely balanced and structured;
medium-bodied; gentle array of black fruits and chocolate; fine tannins. **RATING** 90
DRINK 2010 $ 20

🍷🍷🍷🍷 **Old Station Vineyard Watervale Riesling 2004** Rich and full ripe fruit; tropical and
lime; no need to wait. Screwcap. **RATING** 89 **DRINK** 2008 $ 20

🍷🍷🍷 **Old Station Vineyard Dry Rose 2004** **RATING** 86 **DRINK** Now $ 16

Fire Gully ★★★★

Metricup Road, Wilyabrup, WA 6280 **REGION** Margaret River
T (08) 9755 6220 **F** (08) 9755 6308 **OPEN** By appointment
WINEMAKER Dr Michael Peterkin **EST.** 1998 **CASES** 5000
SUMMARY The Fire Gully vineyard has been established on what was first a dairy and then a beef farm. A 6-ha lake created in the gully ravaged by bushfires gave the property its name, and is stocked with marron. The vineyard was planted in 1988. In 1998 Mike Peterkin, of Pierro, purchased the property; he now manages the vineyard in conjunction with former owners Ellis and Margaret Butcher. He regards the Fire Gully wines as entirely separate from those of Pierro, being estate-grown: just under 9 ha is planted to cabernet sauvignon, merlot, shiraz, semillon, sauvignon blanc, chardonnay and viognier. Exports to the US, Europe, Asia and Russia.

ΤΤΤΤΥ **Chardonnay 2004** No reduction; subtle melon and cashew fruit; medium-bodied and well balanced; gentle oak handling. **RATING** 90 **DRINK** 2012 $ 25
Shiraz 2002 Elegant, spicy; medium-bodied; red and black fruits; gentle tannins. **RATING** 90 **DRINK** 2008 $ 22

ΤΤΤΤ **Sauvignon Blanc Semillon 2004** Light straw-green; delicate, well balanced, but with modest varietal fruit. **RATING** 87 **DRINK** Now $ 22

ΤΤΤΥ **Cabernet Sauvignon Merlot 2002 RATING** 86 **DRINK** 2007 $ 22

First Creek Wines

Cnr McDonalds Road/Gillards Road, Pokolbin, NSW 2321 **REGION** Lower Hunter Valley
T (02) 4998 7293 **F** (02) 4998 7294 **WEB** www.firstcreekwines.com.au **OPEN** 7 days 9.30–5
WINEMAKER Greg Silkman, Jim Chatto **EST.** 1984 **CASES** 25 000
SUMMARY First Creek is the shop-front of Monarch Winemaking Services, which has acquired the former Allanmere wine business and offers a complex range of wines under both the First Creek and the Allanmere labels. The quality is very reliable.

ΤΤΤΤΥ **Orange Cabernet Sauvignon 2003** Good colour; spotlessly clean and very elegant expression of cabernet; medium-bodied; fine, silky, but persistent tannins; very good oak. Cork. **RATING** 93 **DRINK** 2015 $ 20
Durham Hunter Valley Chardonnay 2004 Light green-yellow; light to medium-bodied; well-handled barrel ferment inputs evident but not too heavy; melon, white peach and a touch of cashew. Screwcap. **RATING** 90 **DRINK** 2008 $ 16
Hunter Valley Shiraz 2003 Ultra-regional smoky, savoury, leathery aromas; medium-bodied; sweet plum fruit; fine tannins; excellent balance. Quality cork. **RATING** 90 **DRINK** 2013 $ 20

ΤΤΤΤ **Three Degrees Semillon Sauvignon Blanc 2004** Fresh, lively and crisp; an extra extension to the fruit flavour on the finish courtesy of the Tumbarumba Sauvignon Blanc component; touches of sweet citrus; very good value. Screwcap. **RATING** 88 **DRINK** 2007 $ 11.99
Three Degrees Chardonnay 2003 Fresh; light to medium-bodied; light and crisp; stone fruit, a touch of minerality, and a flick of oak. Screwcap. **RATING** 87 **DRINK** Now $ 11.99
Hunter Valley Verdelho 2004 Very well made; light to medium-bodied; smooth line and flow; gentle fruit salad; fruit, not sweet. Screwcap. **RATING** 87 **DRINK** 2007 $ 14.50

5 Corners Wines ★★★

785 Henry Lawson Drive, Mudgee, NSW 2850 **REGION** Mudgee
T (02) 6373 3745 **F** (02) 6373 3749 **WEB** www.5corners.biz **OPEN** Fri–Mon 10–5
WINEMAKER Contract **EST.** 2001 **CASES** NA
SUMMARY 5 Corners Wines has come together in a hurry. Grant and Suzie Leonard came to Mudgee in 2001 for an overnight visit, and promptly fell in love with the region. They purchased a 40-ha property with 5 ha of established vineyard and a small cottage. The property now includes the family's house (5 children and 6 dogs come and go), the original cottage (occupied by the vineyard manager), and plantings which have been increased by a further 3 ha.

Five Geese/Hillgrove Wines ★★★★

RSD 587, Chapel Hill Road, Blewitt Springs, SA 5171 (postal) **REGION** McLaren Vale
T (08) 8383 0576 **F** (08) 8383 0629 **WEB** www.fivegeese.com **OPEN** Not
WINEMAKER Mike Farmilo (Contract) **EST.** 1999 **CASES** 1500
SUMMARY Five Geese is produced by Hillgrove Wines, a partnership established between Sue Trott, Joanne Watt and Rob Sumner in July 1999. The wines come from 32 ha of vines separately owned by Sue Trott, 1 vineyard planted in 1927, and the other in 1963. The grapes have been sold for many years to companies such as Southcorp and Orlando, but in 1999 Sue Trott decided to establish a partnership and make a strictly limited amount of wine from the pick of the vineyards. Exports to the US, Canada and Singapore.

ТТТТ **Five Geese McLaren Vale Shiraz 2003** Light to medium-bodied; round, soft blackberry, plum and chocolate fruit; smooth; a light touch of vanilla oak. Screwcap. **RATING** 89 **DRINK** 2009 $24.50
Five Geese McLaren Vale Grenache Shiraz 2003 Bright colour; fresh and vibrant red fruits; touches of spice; ready to roll. Screwcap. **RATING** 87 **DRINK** 2008 $19.99

Five Oaks Vineyard ★★★★

60 Aitken Road, Seville, Vic 3139 **REGION** Yarra Valley
T (03) 5964 3704 **F** (03) 5964 3064 **WEB** www.fiveoaks.com.au **OPEN** Weekends & public hols 10–5, and by appointment
WINEMAKER Wally Zuk **EST.** 1997 **CASES** 2000
SUMMARY Wally Zuk and wife Judy run all aspects of Five Oaks; this is far removed from Wally's background in nuclear physics. He has, however, completed his wine science degree at Charles Sturt University, and is thus more than qualified to make the Five Oaks wines. Exports to Canada.

ТТТТ **Yarra Valley Chardonnay 2003** Light to medium-bodied; melon fruit and spicy French oak; harmonious mouthfeel, good length. Cork. **RATING** 89 **DRINK** 2008 $19
Yarra Valley Cabernet Sauvignon Merlot 2002 Savoury, earthy, spicy cool region/cool vintage characters; light to medium-bodied; finish not bitter, just needed a touch more flesh. Cork. **RATING** 88 **DRINK** 2009 $25
Yarra Valley Riesling 2004 Soft, gently tropical aromas and flavours; a touch of sweetness. Screwcap. **RATING** 87 **DRINK** 2008 $20
Yarra Valley Cabernet Rose 2004 Bright colour; herbaceous redcurrant aromas and flavours; good length, crisp, dry finish. Screwcap. **RATING** 87 **DRINK** Now $18

ТТТҮ **Yarra Valley Cabernet Sauvignon 2003** **RATING** 85 **DRINK** 2010 $29

572 Richmond Road NR

590 Richmond Road, Cambridge, Tas 7170 **REGION** Southern Tasmania
T 0408 484 040 **F** (03) 6223 6487 **OPEN** Not
WINEMAKER Wellington Wines (Contract) **EST.** 1994 **CASES** 450
SUMMARY Dean and Wendy Cooper purchased the property from founders John and Sue Carney (who lived at 572 Richmond Road) in July 2005. Just to confuse matters a little, Dean and Wendy Cooper live at 590 Richmond Road Cambridge.

Five Sons Estate ★★★★

85 Harrison's Road, Dromana, Vic 3936 **REGION** Mornington Peninsula
T (03) 5987 3137 **F** (03) 5981 0572 **WEB** www.fivesonsestate.com.au **OPEN** Mon–Fri & public hols, 11–5, 7 days in Jan
WINEMAKER Contract **EST.** 1998 **CASES** 2500
SUMMARY Bob and Sue Peime purchased the most historically significant viticultural holding in the Mornington Peninsula in 1998. Development of the 68-ha property began in the early 1930s. In the 1940s it was sold to a member of the Seppelt family, who planted riesling in 1948. Two years later the property was sold to the Broadhurst family, close relatives of Doug Seabrook, who persisted with growing and making riesling until a 1967 bushfire destroyed the vines. Since 1998, 10 ha of pinot noir, 5 ha of chardonnay, 2.5 ha of shiraz and 1.2 ha each of pinot gris and cabernet sauvignon have been planted.

ŶŶŶŶŶ **The Boyz Mornington Peninsula Cabernet Shiraz 2003** Light to medium-bodied; the blend works quite well; gently sweet black and red fruits and spices; lingering, ripe tannins. Elegant. Good cork. **RATING** 90 **DRINK** 2010 $18

ŶŶŶŶ **The Boyz Mornington Peninsula Pinot Noir 2003** More robust character; plum, spice and earth; stands up to its more pricey brother very well. Cork. **RATING** 88 **DRINK** 2007 $18
Mornington Peninsula Pinot Noir 2003 Light-bodied; tangy and spicy red cherry fruit; hints of forest, stem and mint. Cork. **RATING** 87 **DRINK** Now $28

ŶŶŶŶŶ **The Boyz Mornington Peninsula Rose 2004** **RATING** 85 **DRINK** Now $18

Flinders Bay ★★★★

Wilson Road, Karridale, WA 6288 **REGION** Margaret River
T (08) 9757 6281 **F** (08) 9757 6353 **OPEN** Not
WINEMAKER O'Leary & Waker (Contract) **EST.** 1995 **CASES** 30 000
SUMMARY A joint venture between Alastair Gillespie and Bill and Noel Ireland, the former a grapegrower and viticultural contractor in the Margaret River region for over 25 years, the latter two Sydney wine retailers for an even longer period. The wines are made from grapes grown on the 50-ha Karridale Vineyard (planted between 1995 and 1998), with the exception of a Verdelho, which is purchased from the northern Margaret River. Part of the grape production is sold, and part made under the Flinders Bay and Dunsborough Hills brands. Exports to the UK and the US.

ŶŶŶŶŶ **Shiraz 2002** Elegant but complex; spice, blackberry and bitter chocolate; fine tannins. **RATING** 92 **DRINK** 2011 $17
Margaret River Chardonnay 2004 Clean; elegant nectarine, white peach and citrus fruit; a light touch of smoky oak; has length. Screwcap. **RATING** 90 **DRINK** 2008 $18

ŶŶŶŶ **Margaret River Sauvignon Blanc Semillon 2004** Powerful, mouthfilling style; good length; minerally acidity. **RATING** 87 **DRINK** Now $17

ŶŶŶŶŶ **Margaret River Verdelho 2004** **RATING** 86 **DRINK** 2007 $18
Pericles Sauvignon Blanc Semillon 2004 **RATING** 84 $18

Flint's of Coonawarra ★★★★

PO Box 8, Coonawarra, SA 5263 **REGION** Coonawarra
T (08) 8736 5046 **F** (08) 8736 5146 **WEB** www.flintsofcoonawarra.com.au **OPEN** Not
WINEMAKER Bruce Gregory (Contract) **EST.** 2000 **CASES** 700
SUMMARY Six generations of the Flint family have lived and worked in Coonawarra since 1840. Damian Flint and his family began the development of 21 ha of cabernet sauvignon, shiraz and merlot in 1989, but it was not until 2000 that they decided to keep a small portion of cabernet sauvignon back and have it made by Bruce Gregory at Majella, which is owned by their lifelong friends the Lynn brothers. Ten tonnes (around 700 cases) were vinified, and the wine had immediate show success in Melbourne; another 10 tonnes were diverted from the 2001 vintage, and the first wines were released in 2003.

ŶŶŶŶŶ **Gammon's Crossing Cabernet Sauvignon 2002** medium-bodied; blackberry, earth and cedar; good balance and length; savoury tannins. **RATING** 90 **DRINK** 2012 $23

Fluted Cape Vineyard ★★★☆

28 Groombridge Road, Kettering, Tas 7155 **REGION** Southern Tasmania
T (03) 6267 4262 **OPEN** 7 days 10–5
WINEMAKER Andrew Hood (Contract) **EST.** 1993 **CASES** 170
SUMMARY For many years Val Dell was the senior wildlife ranger on the central plateau of Tasmania, his wife Jan running the information centre at Liawenee. I met them there on trout fishing expeditions, staying in one of the park huts. They have now retired to the Huon Valley region, having established 0.25 ha each of pinot noir and chardonnay overlooking Kettering and Bruny Island, said to be a spectacularly beautiful site. The high-quality wines are made for them by Andrew Hood and are sold through the cellar door and Hartzview Cellars in Gardners Bay.

ŶŶŶŶ **Chardonnay 2004** Fresh, citrussy, tangy fruit; crunchy acidity; good length. **RATING** 87 **DRINK** 2008 $15

Flying Fish Cove ★★★★

Lot 125 Caves Road, Wilyabrup, WA 6284 REGION Margaret River
T (08) 9755 6688 F (08) 9755 6788 WEB www.flyingfishcove.com OPEN 7 days 11–5
WINEMAKER Matthew Tydeman EST. 2000 CASES 15 000
SUMMARY A group of 20 shareholders got together to acquire the 130-ha property on which the
Flying Fish Cove winery was subsequently built. It has two strings to its bow: contract winemaking
for others, and the development of three product ranges, partly based on 20 ha of estate plantings,
with another 10 ha underway. Exports to Indonesia.

ŸŸŸŸŸ **Margaret River Semillon Sauvignon Blanc 2004** Plenty of juicy fruit; a mix of tropical,
gooseberry and grassy flavours; good balance and length. RATING 90 DRINK 2007 $ 18
Margaret River Cabernet Sauvignon Merlot 2003 Bright blackcurrant fruit; gentle, ripe
tannins; good texture and structure. RATING 90 DRINK 2010 $ 20

ŸŸŸŸ **Margaret River Shiraz 2004** Sophisticated winemaking; medium-bodied; blackberry
and spice aromas and flavours; soft, feathery tannins; ready now. Screwcap. RATING 89
DRINK 2008 $ 19.99
Margaret River Shiraz 2003 Medium-bodied; dark plum/black fruits; fine savoury
tannins; subtle oak. RATING 89 DRINK 2011 $ 20
Margaret River Cabernet Sauvignon 2003 Powerful and concentrated; blackberry, black
olive and herb; has length. Screwcap. RATING 89 DRINK 2010 $ 19.99
Margaret River Cabernet Sauvignon Merlot 2004 Spotlessly clean; light to medium-
bodied; bright red fruits, slightly chalky tannins. Screwcap. RATING 87 DRINK 2009
$ 19.99

ŸŸŸŸ **Margaret River Rose 2004** RATING 86 DRINK Now $ 19.99

Foate's Ridge ★★★

241 Fordwich Road, Broke, NSW 2330 REGION Lower Hunter Valley
T (02) 6579 1284 F (02) 9922 4397 WEB www.foate.com.au OPEN By appointment
WINEMAKER Steve Dodd (Contract) EST. 1992 CASES 1000
SUMMARY The Foate family, headed by Tony Foate, planted a total of 10 ha, chardonnay (4 ha) and
verdelho, merlot and cabernet sauvignon (2 ha each), between 1992 and 2001 on the 36-ha property
purchased in 1991. The soils are the typical light alluvial loam of the region, which promote vigorous
vine growth and generous yields, yields which need to be controlled if quality is to be maximised.
Using a Scott Henry trellis, bunch thinning and fewer spur positions have been utilised to reduce the
15 tonne per hectare yields to 10 tonnes per hectare.

🐌 Foggo Wines ★★★★★

Lot 21 Foggos Road, McLaren Vale, SA 5171 REGION McLaren Vale
T (08) 8323 0131 F (08) 8323 7626 WEB www.foggowines.com.au OPEN Mon–Fri 10.30–4.30,
weekends & public hols 11–5
WINEMAKER Herb Van De Wiel EST. 1999 CASES 3000
SUMMARY Herb and Sandie Van De Wiel have been grapegrowers in McLaren Vale for 16 years,
but their viticultural roots go back further, to Renmark in the Riverland, where Herb grew up on
his father's vineyard. In 1999 they were able to purchase the former Curtis winery, which, after
refurbishment, gave them the opportunity to establish Foggo Wines. They have 3 vineyards: the
oldest (on Foggo Road) is 9 ha of shiraz dating back to 1915; their 80-year-old grenache, 45-year-
old cinsaut and 20-year-old chardonnay and sauvignon blanc come from their other vineyards,
totalling 25 ha in all. With help from their recently graduated winemaker son Ben, they have
wasted no time in establishing a formidable reputation for a range of Shiraz, Grenache,
Grenache Shiraz Cinsaut and Cabernet Sauvignon equal to the best. Exports to the US, Canada
and Taiwan.

ŸŸŸŸŸ **Hubertus Reserve Shiraz 2002** Medium to full-bodied; tightly focused and structured;
very intense and very long black fruits; fine tannins. RATING 95 DRINK 2017 $ 45
Cabernet Sauvignon 2002 Very powerful, focused and concentrated; lashings of
blackcurrant fruit, a whisper of dark chocolate; persistent tannins. RATING 94 DRINK 2017
$ 28

ŸŸŸŸŸ **Grenache Shiraz Cinsaut 2002** Fragrant, elegant and expressive; light to medium-bodied, utterly belying its 14.7° alcohol; fine-grained tannins; long finish. **RATING** 91 **DRINK** 2008 **$** 22

Chardonnay 2003 Extremely well made; nectarine fruit with perfectly balanced and integrated oak; good length and mouthfeel. **RATING** 90 **DRINK** 2007 **$** 25

Old Vine Shiraz 2003 Medium-bodied; elegant, well-balanced wine; black fruits; fine, spicy tannins a feature, adding to length. **RATING** 90 **DRINK** 2013 **$** 28

Old Bush Vine Grenache 2002 Light to medium-bodied, but slightly firmer and slightly more focused than the '03; the tannins are slightly riper and more evident; 15.3° alcohol. **RATING** 90 **DRINK** 2009 **$** 28

Cabernet Sauvignon 2003 Elegant; medium-bodied; blackcurrant fruit and fine persistent tannins. **RATING** 90 **DRINK** 2012 **$** 28

ŸŸŸŸ **Old Bush Vine Grenache 2003** Light to medium-bodied; spicy, strongly varietal, but in soft, southern Rhône style; 15.7° alcohol barely noticeable. **RATING** 89 **DRINK** 2008 **$** 28

Cinsaut Rose 2003 Quite complex; spiced plum and prune aromas; medium to full-bodied for a Rose; subliminal sweetness. **RATING** 88 **DRINK** 2007 **$** 15

Sauvignon Blanc 2004 Light to medium-bodied and quite elegant; tropical fruits, the residual sugar just a little overdone. **RATING** 87 **DRINK** Now **$** 18

ŸŸŸŸ **Unwooded Chardonnay 2004** **RATING** 85 **DRINK** Now **$** 18

Fonty's Pool Vineyards ★★★★☆

Seven Day Road, Manjimup, WA 6258 **REGION** Manjimup
T (08) 9777 0777 **F** (08) 9777 0788 **WEB** www.fontyspoolwines.com.au **OPEN** 7 days 10–4.30
WINEMAKER Eloise Jarvis, Mark Morton **EST.** 1998 **CASES** 30 000
SUMMARY This is a joint venture between Cape Mentelle (which makes the wine) and Fonty's Pool Farm. The Fonty's Pool vineyards are part of the original farm owned by pioneer settler Archie Fontanini, who was granted land by the government in 1907. In the early 1920s a large dam was created to provide water for the intensive vegetable farming which was part of the farming activities. The dam became known as Fonty's Pool, and to this day remains a famous local landmark and recreational facility. The first grapes were planted in 1989, and at 110 ha, the vineyard is now one of the region's largest, supplying grapes to a number of leading WA wineries. An increasing amount of the production is used for Fonty's Pool, which has now established an onsite cellar door. Exports to the UK and Europe supplement domestic distribution by Möet Hennessy.

ŸŸŸŸŸ **Chardonnay 2003** Very attractive barrel ferment/malolactic ferment aromas; elegant melon, nectarine and a touch of grapefruit on the palate; very good mouthfeel. Screwcap. **RATING** 93 **DRINK** 2008 **$** 20.75

Shiraz 2002 Potent licorice, black fruits and a dash of black pepper; plenty of weight and good tannin structure. **RATING** 93 **DRINK** 2012 **$** 20.75

Pinot Noir 2002 Intense savoury/foresty aromas; lingering finish and aftertaste; lots of class. **RATING** 92 **DRINK** 2007 **$** 20.75

Merlot 2003 Has the concentration missing from some of the other Fonty's Pool wines of the vintage; attractive, positive dark fruits and touches of spice; controlled oak. Screwcap. **RATING** 92 **DRINK** 2013 **$** 20.75

Viognier 2003 A subtle but complex interwoven mix of honey, apricot, lemon and cream flavours; very good mouthfeel. Screwcap. **RATING** 90 **DRINK** 2007 **$** 20.75

Cabernet Merlot 2003 Attractive, well balanced, medium-bodied wine; supple, gently sweet blackcurrant fruit; fine tannins, subtle oak. Screwcap. **RATING** 90 **DRINK** 2012 **$** 15.99

ŸŸŸŸ **Sauvignon Blanc Semillon 2004** Water white; not particularly expressive in fruit, but has excellent mouthfeel, line and length; subtle oak; should develop well. Screwcap. **RATING** 89 **DRINK** 2008 **$** 15.99

Shiraz 2003 Light-bodied; spicy red fruits; pleasant, but lacks concentration. Screwcap. **RATING** 87 **DRINK** 2008 **$** 20.75

ŸŸŸŸ **Pinot Noir 2003** **RATING** 86 **DRINK** 2007 **$** 20.75

Forester Estate ★★★★

Lot 11 Wildwood Road, Yallingup, WA 6282 **REGION** Margaret River
T (08) 9755 2788 **F** (08) 9755 2766 **WEB** www.foresterestate.com.au **OPEN** By appointment
WINEMAKER Kevin McKay, Michael Langridge **EST.** 2001 **CASES** 20 000
SUMMARY The Forester Estate business partners are Kevin McKay and Redmond Sweeny. Winemaker Michael Langridge has a Bachelor of Arts (Hons) in Psychology and a Bachelor of Applied Science (wine science, Charles Sturt). As Bill McKay says, 'he is the most over-qualified forklift driver in Australia'. Langridge also has 6 vintages in the Margaret River region under his belt. Together they have built and designed a 500-tonne winery, half devoted to contract winemaking, the other half for the Forester label. Part of the intake comes from the 4.5-ha estate plantings of sauvignon blanc, cabernet and shiraz, the remainder from nearby growers, one of whom is the operating viticulturist at Forester Estate.

▼▼▼▼▽ **Sauvignon Blanc 2004** Spotlessly clean and fragrant; intense and potent passionfruit, herb and gooseberry mix. **RATING** 92 **DRINK** 2007 $ 20

▼▼▼▼ **Semillon Sauvignon Blanc 2004** Clean, fresh, floral; a similarly concentrated palate; lemon, thyme and gooseberry flavours. **RATING** 89 **DRINK** 2008 $ 17
Cabernet Merlot 2003 Closed bouquet; quite rich black and red fruit on the mid-palate; balanced tannins. **RATING** 87 **DRINK** 2009 $ 17

Forest Hill Vineyard ★★★★

South Coast Highway, Denmark, WA 6333 **REGION** Mount Barker
T (08) 9381 2911 **F** (08) 9381 2955 **WEB** www.foresthillwines.com.au **OPEN** 7 days 10–5
WINEMAKER Shand McKerran, Liz Richardson **EST.** 1965 **CASES** 10 000
SUMMARY This is one of the oldest 'new' winemaking operations in Western Australia, and was the site for the first grape plantings for the Great Southern region: in 1966, on a farming property owned by the Pearce family. The Forest Hill brand became well known, aided by the fact that a 1975 Riesling made by Sandalford from Forest Hill grapes won nine trophies in national wine shows. In 1997 the property was acquired by interests associated with Perth stockbroker Tim Lyons, and a program of renovation and expansion of the vineyards commenced. A new winery near Denmark was completed in time for the 2003 vintage, and a new cellar door opened in September 2004.

▼▼▼▼▽ **Chardonnay 2003** Complex barrel ferment aromas with ripe nectarine and stone fruit; a touch of malolactic/lees input; well balanced and proportioned. **RATING** 92 **DRINK** 2010 $ 19.99
Sauvignon Blanc 2004 Water white; spotlessly clean gooseberry aromas, moving into a mix of mineral, slate, asparagus and gooseberry on the palate. **RATING** 90 **DRINK** 2007 $ 16.99

▼▼▼▼ **Cabernet Sauvignon 2001** Potent, concentrated, still very youthful; black fruits with tight structure and tannins; leave it alone for 3 years plus. **RATING** 89 **DRINK** 2014 $ 21.99

▼▼▼▽ **Sauvignon Blanc Semillon 2004** **RATING** 86 **DRINK** Now $ 16.99
Unwooded Chardonnay 2004 **RATING** 86 **DRINK** 2007 $ 16.99

🍇 Four Winds Vineyard NR

PO Box 131, Murrumbateman, NSW 2582 **REGION** Canberra District
T (02) 6226 8182 **F** (02) 6226 8257 **WEB** www.fourwindsvineyard.com.au **OPEN** Not
WINEMAKER Graeme Lunney **EST.** 1998 **CASES** NA
SUMMARY Graeme and Suzanne Lunney conceived the idea for Four Winds in 1997, planting the first vines in 1998, moving to the property full-time in 1999, and making the first vintage in 2000. Son Tom manages the day-to-day operations of the vineyard; daughter Sarah looks after events and promotions; and youngest daughter Jaime, complete with a degree in Forensic Biology, joins the party at the most busy times of the year. Graeme Lunney makes the wine, and Suzanne tends the gardens and the 100 rose bushes at the end of the vine rows.

Fox Creek Wines ★★★★

Malpas Road, Willunga, SA 5172 **REGION** McLaren Vale
T (08) 8556 2403 **F** (08) 8556 2104 **WEB** www.foxcreekwines.com **OPEN** 7 days 10–5
WINEMAKER Chris Dix, Scott Zrna **EST.** 1995 **CASES** 36 000
SUMMARY Fox Creek has made a major impact since coming on-stream late in 1995. It is the venture of the Watts and Roberts families, headed respectively by a surgeon and an anaesthetist; it was the Watts family which established the vineyard back in 1985. The Reserve red wines, especially the Reserve Shiraz, are outstanding and have enjoyed considerable show success. Comprehensive distribution throughout Australia; exports to the UK, the US and other major markets.

ŸŸŸŸŸ **Reserve Cabernet Sauvignon 2002** Medium to full-bodied; black fruits interwoven with savoury tannins and a touch of regional chocolate. **RATING** 92 **DRINK** 2012 $ 36
Fox & Hounds McLaren Vale Shiraz Cabernet 2003 Medium to full-bodied; good structure; blackcurrant and blackberry fruit plus ripe, persistent tannins; good length. Cork. **RATING** 91 **DRINK** 2013 $ 25
Short Row Shiraz 2003 Deep colour; strong plum, prune and dark chocolate supported by abundant tannins; needs time. **RATING** 90 **DRINK** 2013 $ 26

ŸŸŸŸ **McLaren Vale Chardonnay 2004** Light to medium-bodied; a mix of melon, cashew and mineral; good length, clean finish. Screwcap. **RATING** 89 **DRINK** 2008 $ 16
JSM 2003 Attractive, soft, fresh savoury blackberry fruit; hints of spice and vanilla; soft tannins. Shiraz/Cabernet Franc. Screwcap. **RATING** 89 **DRINK** 2009 $ 22
Duet McLaren Vale Cabernet Merlot 2003 Medium-bodied; spicy blackcurrant, with hints of olive, leaf and earth; quite ripe tannins; comes together well. Screwcap. **RATING** 89 **DRINK** 2013 $ 19
McLaren Vale Shiraz Grenache 2003 Sweet juicy berry and touches of chocolate; light to medium-bodied; easy-access style. Screwcap. **RATING** 88 **DRINK** 2007 $ 17
Semillon Sauvignon Blanc 2003 Full-bodied, rich; sweet citrus and some honey; slightly old-fashioned. Screwcap. **RATING** 87 **DRINK** Now $ 16
Shadow's Run Shiraz Cabernet Sauvignon 2003 Medium-bodied; firm, tangy fruit flavours; a slight nip on the heels to finish. Screwcap. **RATING** 87 **DRINK** 2008 $ 12

ŸŸŸŸ **South Australia Chardonnay 2002 RATING** 86 **DRINK** Now $ 16
McLaren Vale Shiraz Grenache 2002 RATING 86 **DRINK** 2007 $ 17
Sauvignon Blanc 2004 RATING 85 **DRINK** Now $ 16
Shadow's Run The White 2004 RATING 85 **DRINK** Now $ 12
Verdelho 2004 RATING 84 **DRINK** Now $ 16

Foxeys Hangout ★★★★☆

795 White Hill Road, Red Hill, Vic 3937 **REGION** Mornington Peninsula
T 0402 117 104 **F** (03) 9809 0495 **WEB** www.foxeys-hangout.com.au **OPEN** Not
WINEMAKER Tony Lee **EST.** 1998 **CASES** 3000
SUMMARY Brothers Michael and Tony Lee spent 20 years in the hospitality business, acquiring a considerable knowledge of wine through the selection of wine lists for two decades, opting for a change of lifestyle and occupation when they planted 2.2 ha of pinot noir, 2 ha of chardonnay and 0.5 ha of pinot gris on the northeast-facing slopes of an old farm. The name (and the catchy label) stems from the true tale of two Mornington Peninsula fox-hunters who began a competition with each other in 1936, hanging their kills on the branches of an ancient eucalypt tree to keep count. The corpses have gone, but not the nickname for the area in which the vineyard is planted.

ŸŸŸŸŸ **Mornington Peninsula Chardonnay 2003** Complex and rich wine; barrel ferment characters evident but not overdone; ripe stone fruit; good balance and finish. **RATING** 92 **DRINK** 2008 $ 21
Mornington Peninsula Late Harvest Pinot Gris 2004 Attractive, sweet lemon essence and spiced apple flavours; good balance; cordon-cut. Diam. **RATING** 90 **DRINK** 2008 $ 20

ŸŸŸŸ **Mornington Peninsula Pinot Gris 2004** Very fresh and crisp; bone-dry apple and mineral; more to Grigio in style; attractive squeaky acidity. Screwcap. **RATING** 89 **DRINK** 2007 $ 20
Mornington Peninsula Shiraz 2003 While the colour is not deep, has surprising weight and power; ripe plum fruit and substantial tannins. **RATING** 89 **DRINK** 2010 $ 23

Mornington Peninsula Pinot Noir 2003 Solid black plum aromas; quite powerful, robust style; firm tannins on the plummy palate need to settle and soften. Cork. **RATING** 88 **DRINK** 2010 $ 30

Mornington Peninsula Rose 2004 Very clever cellar door style; bright, light colour, strawberry fruit; sugar part of the palate, off-set by acidity. **RATING** 87 **DRINK** Now $ 15

Francois Jacquard

NR

14 Neil Street, Osborne Park, WA 6017 **REGION** Perth Hills
T (08) 9380 9199 **F** (08) 9380 9199 **OPEN** Not
WINEMAKER Francois Jacquard **EST.** 1997 **CASES** 2000
SUMMARY Francois (Franky) Jacquard graduated from Dijon University in 1983. He worked that vintage as a cellar hand at Domaine Dujac, then came to Australia for Bannockburn in 1985. Between then and 1992 he worked in both the northern and southern hemispheres, before moving back to become chief winemaker at Chittering Estate in the Perth Hills in 1992, a position he held until 1997 when he established his own brand. He has since kept a consistently low profile.

Frankland Estate

Frankland Road, Frankland, WA 6396 **REGION** Frankland River
T (08) 9855 1544 **F** (08) 9855 1549 **OPEN** Mon–Fri 10–4, public hols & weekends by appointment
WINEMAKER Barrie Smith, Judi Cullam **EST.** 1988 **CASES** 15 000
SUMMARY A significant Frankland River operation, situated on a large sheep property owned by Barrie Smith and Judi Cullam. The 29-ha vineyard has been established progressively since 1988, and a winery was built on the site for the 1993 vintage. The recent introduction of an array of single-vineyard Rieslings has been a highlight. All the wines are energetically promoted and marketed by Judi Cullam, especially the Riesling. Frankland Estate has held several important International Riesling tastings and seminars over recent years. Exports to the UK, the US and other major markets.

Isolation Ridge Vineyard Riesling 2004 Very tight, spotless and clean; immaculately balanced; great mouthfeel, line and flow. **RATING** 94 **DRINK** 2015 $ 23

Isolation Ridge Vineyard Chardonnay 2003 Elegant, fine and tightly focused bouquet; subtle oak; very good mouthfeel to the grapefruit, nectarine and melon flavours. **RATING** 93 **DRINK** 2012 $ 23

Cooladerra Vineyard Riesling 2004 Tight, clean, focused mineral and lime; quite powerful, particularly on the back palate and finish. **RATING** 92 **DRINK** 2012 $ 23

Poison Hill Vineyard Riesling 2004 More open, with some tropical fruit aromas; the palate follows suit with soft, tropical fruit. Late-picked style with some alcohol sweetness. **RATING** 90 **DRINK** 2009 $ 23

Rocky Gully Shiraz Viognier 2003 High-toned, very expressive wine; lifted Viognier (though only 3%) with vibrant red fruits. **RATING** 90 **DRINK** 2008 $ 18

Isolation Ridge Vineyard Shiraz 2001 Herb, leather, spice and blackberry; plenty of weight and depth; savoury finish. Best for years. **RATING** 90 **DRINK** 2011 $ 27

Rocky Gully Riesling 2004 Clean, fine and crisp; lots of lime juice running through the length of the palate; great value. **RATING** 89 **DRINK** 2010 $ 16

Isolation Ridge Vineyard Cabernet Sauvignon 2002 Medium-bodied; red and blackcurrant fruit off-set by slightly savoury notes on the finish; no problems with oak. **RATING** 89 **DRINK** 2012 $ 25

Isolation Ridge Vineyard Cabernet Sauvignon 2001 Powerful, chunky black fruits and touches of bitter chocolate; abundant tannins. Be patient. **RATING** 89 **DRINK** 2014 $ 24

Olmo's Reward 2001 Savoury and lean; decidedly tannic; food style, but does have presence and length. **RATING** 87 **DRINK** 2011 $ 35

Isolation Ridge Vineyard Shiraz 2002 **RATING** 85 **DRINK** 2009 $ 28
Rocky Gully Cabernets 2003 **RATING** 84 **DRINK** 2008 $ 18

Fratin Brothers Vineyard

Byron Road, Ararat, Vic 3377 **REGION** Grampians
T (03) 5352 3322 **F** (03) 5352 3322 **OPEN** 7 days 10–5
WINEMAKER Michael Fratin **EST.** 1996 **CASES** 500

SUMMARY The Fratin Brothers Vineyard was planted by Dino and Michael Fratin in 1996, 30 years after their father Serge and uncles Dom and Lino established Mount Langi Ghiran Vineyards. Shiraz cuttings were supplied by Mount Langi Ghiran, and 2 ha of shiraz, 1 ha of chardonnay and 0.5 ha of merlot have been planted. The wines are made in open fermentation tanks and basket pressed.

ΥΥΥΥ **Shiraz 2002** Estery, essency aromas suggesting some shrivel/dead fruit characters; fairly sharp acid profile. Twin Top. **RATING** 87 **DRINK** 2009 $ 22

ΥΥΥ? **Cabernet Sauvignon Merlot 2002** **RATING** 84 **DRINK** 2007 $ 20

Frazer Woods Wines   ★★☆

c/- Post Office, Yallingup, WA 6282 **REGION** Margaret River
T (08) 9755 6274 **F** (08) 9755 6295 **OPEN** Not
WINEMAKER Various (Contract) **EST.** 1996 **CASES** 1000
SUMMARY John Frazer has set up a contract sparkling wine business, called the Champagne Shed, although the winemaking is done offsite. He makes the Frazer Woods wines from 2 ha of estate-grown shiraz; the white grapes for the pinot chardonnay sparkling are bought in. The wines are sold through the Margaret River Wine Cellars and the Witchcliffe Liquor Store.

Freeman Vineyards   ★★★★

RMB 101, Prunevale, NSW 2587 (postal) **REGION** Hilltops
T (02) 6384 4299 **F** (02) 6384 4299 **WEB** www.brianfreeman.com.au **OPEN** Not
WINEMAKER Dr Brian Freeman **EST.** 2000 **CASES** 250
SUMMARY Dr Brian Freeman has spent much of his long life in research and education, in the latter role as head of Charles Sturt University's viticulture and oenology campus. In 2004 he purchased the 30-year-old vineyard and winery previously known as Demondrille. He has also established a new vineyard, and in all has 14 varieties totalling 40.5 ha; these range from staples such as shiraz, cabernet sauvignon, semillon and riesling through to the more exotic, trendy varieties such as tempranillo, and on to corvina and rondinella. It is the latter two grapes which have been used to make the first release. He has had a long academic interest in the effect of partial drying of grapes on the tannins, and (living at Prunevale) was easily able to obtain a prune dehydrator to partially raisin the two varieties, which were then made at the Centennial Winery in Bowral. However, in future vintages, the wine will be made onsite.

ΥΥΥΥ **Rondinella Corvina 2002** Interesting texture and structure; ripe red fruits, firm but ripe tannins, and relatively high acidity. The rating is given for the wine as it is, without any additional points reflecting (in diving terms) the degree of difficulty. **RATING** 89 **DRINK** 2008 $ 35

Freycinet   ★★★★★

15919 Tasman Highway via Bicheno, Tas 7215 **REGION** East Coast Tasmania
T (03) 6257 8574 **F** (03) 6257 8454 **WEB** www.freycinetvineyard.com.au **OPEN** 7 days 9.30–4.30
WINEMAKER Claudio Radenti, Lindy Bull, Paula Kloosterman (Assistant) **EST.** 1980 **CASES** 5000
SUMMARY The original 9-ha Freycinet vineyards are beautifully situated on the sloping hillsides of a small valley. The soils are brown dermosol on top of jurasic dolerite, and the combination of aspect, slope, soil and heat summation produce red grapes with unusual depth of colour and ripe flavours. One of Australia's foremost producers of Pinot Noir, with a wholly enviable track record of consistency – rare with such a temperamental variety. The Radenti (sparkling), Riesling and Chardonnay are also wines of the highest quality. Exports to the UK.

ΥΥΥΥΥ **Radenti 1998** Wonderfully fragrant orange blossom aromas; lively, lemony, fresh and exuberant in the mouth; incredibly youthful. **RATING** 95 **DRINK** 2010 $ 45
Riesling 2004 Very tight and focused; a steely core of acidity, but with plenty of lime sherbet fruit; long finish. **RATING** 94 **DRINK** 2019 $ 22
Pinot Noir 2003 Excellent wine; rich plum, black cherry and spice; long, finely balanced palate; good tannin finish and aftertaste. **RATING** 94 **DRINK** 2009 $ 62

ΥΥΥΥ? **Chardonnay 2003** Medium straw-green; very fragrant stone fruit and grapefruit aromas, then a bright, fresh palate, with the acidity cleverly balanced. **RATING** 91 **DRINK** 2010 $ 30

ΥΥΥΥ **Louis Unwooded Chardonnay 2004** As intended, uncomplicated, but has good intensity and length to the nectarine and citrus fruit; nice acidity. **RATING** 89 **DRINK** 2007 $ 22
Louis Riesling Schonburger 2004 Fresh, spotlessly clean aromas; excellent cellar door style; a mix of sweet, spicy, grapey/lychee fruit flavours; faintest touch of residual sugar. **RATING** 88 **DRINK** 2007 $ 18
Cabernet Sauvignon Merlot 2001 Ultra savoury/briary style; slippery tannins and brisk acidity. **RATING** 88 **DRINK** 2009 $ 34

Frog Choir Wines

PO Box 515, Margaret River, WA 6285 **REGION** Margaret River
T (08) 9757 6510 **F** (08) 9757 6501 **WEB** www.frogchoir.com **OPEN** Not
WINEMAKER Mark Lane (Contract) **EST.** 1997 **CASES** 550
SUMMARY Eddie Sawiris and partner Sharon Martin have a micro vineyard of 1.2 ha, equally split between shiraz and cabernet sauvignon. It has immaculate address credentials: adjacent to Leeuwin Estate and Voyager Estate. The wines are available through the website, a handful of chosen restaurants, and the Margaret River Regional Wine Centre.

ΥΥΥΥ **Cabernet Shiraz 2002** Herb, spice, earth, blackberry and blackcurrant aromas and flavours; has length; finishes with savoury tannins. **RATING** 87 **DRINK** 2012 $ 12
Cabernet Shiraz 2001 Powerful dark fruits/blackcurrant, the tannins still softening and needing to continue to do so; lots of stuffing. **RATING** 87 **DRINK** 2011 $ 12

Frog Island ★★★☆

PO Box 423, Kingston SE, SA 5275 **REGION** Limestone Coast Zone
T (08) 8768 5000 **F** (08) 8768 5008 **WEB** www.frogisland.com.au **OPEN** At Ralph Fowler
WINEMAKER Sarah Squire **EST.** 2003 **CASES** 10 000
SUMMARY Sarah Squire (née Fowler) has decided to do her own thing, with full support from father Ralph. The quixotic name is taken from a small locality inland from the seaside town of Robe, and the wine is deliberately made in a fresh, fruit-forward style. Exports to Europe and Asia.

ΥΥΥΥ **Cabernet Merlot 2003** medium-bodied; clean, vibrant red and blackcurrant fruit; fine tannins. **RATING** 90 **DRINK** 2008 $ 18

ΥΥΥ **Rose 2004** **RATING** 84 **DRINK** Now $ 18
Sparkling Red NV **RATING** 84 **DRINK** Now $ 18

ΥΥΥ **Chardonnay 2004** **RATING** 83 $ 15

Frogmore Creek ★★★★☆

Brinktop Road, Penna, Tas 7171 **REGION** Southern Tasmania
T (03) 6224 6788 **F** (03) 6224 6788 **OPEN** At Wellington/Hood Wines
WINEMAKER Andrew Hood (Contract) **EST.** 1997 **CASES** 3500
SUMMARY Frogmore Creek is a Pacific Rim joint venture, the two owners being Tony Scherer of Tasmania, and Jack Kidwiler of California. They have commenced the establishment of the only organically certified commercial vineyard in Tasmania, and plan to take the area under vine to 80 ha over the next 4 years. An onsite winery will be constructed; when completed, the development will offer a visitor centre and cellar door sales area; an environmental centre with walking trails and lakeside picnic areas; an organic garden; and a restaurant, accommodation and event facilities. The name is taken from the creek which runs through the property. In late 2003 the Frogmore Creek owners acquired the Wellington wine business of Andrew Hood, and for the foreseeable future will run the two operations in tandem, handling all organically grown fruit at the Frogmore Creek winery, and the remainder at the Wellington winery.

ΥΥΥΥΥ **Chardonnay 2003** Light to medium-bodied; complex barrel ferment and malolactic ferment inputs; nectarine/peach/citrus fruit; good balance and length. **RATING** 94 **DRINK** 2008 $ 26

ΥΥΥΥ **Pinot Noir 2003** Spotlessly clean and fragrant; elegant red fruits of strawberry and cherry; also plum; fine tannins, good length. **RATING** 90 **DRINK** 2008 $ 50

ŢŢŢŢ **Riesling 2003** Very minerally and grainy, with pronounced acidity; needs more time. **RATING** 87 **DRINK** 2013 $ 24

ŢŢŢŢ **Riesling 2004 RATING** 85 **DRINK** 2007 $ 24

Frog Rock Wines ★★★☆

Edgell Lane, Mudgee, NSW 2850 **REGION** Mudgee
T (02) 6372 2408 **F** (02) 6372 6924 **WEB** www.frogrockwines.com **OPEN** 7 days 10–5
WINEMAKER Simon Gilbert, David Lowe, Jane Wilson (Contract) **EST.** 1973 **CASES** 20 000
SUMMARY Frog Rock is the former Tallara Vineyard, established over 30 years ago by leading Sydney chartered accountant Rick Turner. There are now 60 ha of vineyard, with 22 ha each of shiraz and cabernet sauvignon, and much smaller plantings of chardonnay, semillon, merlot, petit verdot and chambourcin. Exports to Ireland, the US, Canada, Singapore and Hong Kong.

ŢŢŢŢ **Premium Shiraz 2002** Light to medium-bodied; good colour; red and black cherry fruit; slightly elevated acidity; fine tannins. **RATING** 88 **DRINK** 2009 $ 35
Sticky Frog 2004 Golden orange; not really very sticky, but has length and fresh acidity to balance the cumquat and vanilla flavours. **RATING** 87 **DRINK** 2008 $ 30

ŢŢŢŢ **Premium Cabernet Sauvignon 2002 RATING** 86 **DRINK** 2008 $ 35

Frogspond ★★★☆

400 Arthurs Seat Road, Red Hill, Vic 3937 **REGION** Mornington Peninsula
T (03) 5989 2941 **F** (03) 9824 7659 **WEB** www.frogspond.com.au **OPEN** By appointment
WINEMAKER David Lloyd **EST.** 1994 **CASES** 160
SUMMARY The Nelson family has established 2 ha of chardonnay and pinot noir on an ideal north-facing slope. The low yields produce grapes with intense fruit flavours, but only a tiny amount of wine is made. It is sold primarily by mail order.

ŢŢŢŢ **Mornington Peninsula Chardonnay 2003** Very elegant; strong winemaker inputs via malolactic, barrel ferment and lees contact take the wine into secondary characters; a touch more fruit strength needed. Diam. **RATING** 89 **DRINK** 2008 $ 32

ŢŢŢŢ **Mornington Peninsula Pinot Noir 2003 RATING** 85 **DRINK** 2007 $ 32

FUSE ★★★★☆

PO Box 441, South Melbourne, Vic 3205 **REGION** Clare Valley & Adelaide Hills
T (03) 9696 7018 **F** (03) 9686 4015 **OPEN** Not
WINEMAKER Neil Pike **EST.** 2004 **CASES** 5000
SUMMARY FUSE is a joint venture of the Pikes Vintners (Clare Valley), Pike & Joyce (Adelaide Hills) and well-known Melbourne wine distributors Trembath & Taylor. It takes low-cropped grape varieties from terroir that best suits them: riesling, cabernet, merlot, shiraz, grenache and mourvedre from the Clare Valley, and semillon, sauvignon blanc, chardonnay and pinot noir from the Adelaide Hills. Distinctive packaging, and a simple price range, makes the proposition easy to understand.

ŢŢŢŢŢ **Clare Valley Cabernet Merlot 2003** Medium-bodied; skilfully melded red and black fruits, chocolate, sweet oak and silky tannins. **RATING** 91 **DRINK** 2003 $ 18.95
Clare Valley Riesling 2004 Clean, no reduction; plenty of weight and presence; mineral, spice and lime; good length and finish. **RATING** 90 **DRINK** 2012 $ 16.25
Adelaide Hills Pinot Noir 2003 Very fragrant, almost into citrus blossom; medium-bodied cherry and plum fruit; good tannins and acidity on a long finish. **RATING** 90 **DRINK** 2007 $ 18.95

ŢŢŢŢ **Adelaide Hills Semillon Sauvignon Blanc 2004** Clean, well made; a powerful grassy/gooseberry mix on the powerful palate; balanced finish. **RATING** 88 **DRINK** 2007 $ 18.95
Adelaide Hills Chardonnay 2004 Very delicate, light-bodied style; melon-accented; redeemed by the length of the palate rather than the depth of fruit flavour. **RATING** 87 **DRINK** 2008 $ 18.95
Clare Valley Shiraz Grenache Mourvedre 2004 Savoury/earthy/forest characters run throughout; spicy, slightly dry tannins to close. **RATING** 87 **DRINK** 2009 $ 18.95

Fyffe Field   NR

1417 Murray Valley Highway, Yarrawonga, Vic 3730 **REGION** Goulburn Valley
T (03) 5748 4282 **F** (03) 5748 4284 **WEB** www.fyffefieldwines.com.au **OPEN** 7 days 10–5
WINEMAKER Contract **EST.** 1993 **CASES** 1300
SUMMARY Fyffe Field has been established by Graeme and Liz Diamond near the Murray River
between Cobram and Yarrawonga in a mudbrick and leadlight tasting room opposite a historic
homestead. They have 2 ha of shiraz, 1 ha each of semillon, verdelho, merlot and cabernet sauvignon,
and 0.5 ha each of touriga and petit verdot. A highlight is the collection of ornamental pigs, a display
set up long before Babe was born.

Gabriel's Paddocks Vineyard   NR

Deasys Road, Pokolbin, NSW 2320 **REGION** Lower Hunter Valley
T (02) 4998 7650 **F** (02) 4998 7603 **WEB** www.gabrielspaddocks.com.au **OPEN** Thurs–Mon 9–5
WINEMAKER Contract **EST.** 1979 **CASES** NA
SUMMARY Formerly Sutherlands Wines, Gabriel's Paddocks is as much about general tourism and
small conference accommodation as it is about wine production, and has two separate buildings able
to accommodate more than 20 people altogether. The 13.6-ha vineyards are planted to chardonnay,
chenin blanc, pinot noir, merlot, shiraz and cabernet sauvignon; the wines are all contract-made.

Galafrey   ★★★

Quangellup Road, Mount Barker, WA 6324 **REGION** Mount Barker
T (08) 9851 2022 **F** (08) 9851 2324 **OPEN** 7 days 10–5
WINEMAKER Ian Tyrer **EST.** 1977 **CASES** 10 000
SUMMARY Relocated to a new purpose-built but utilitarian winery after previously inhabiting the
exotic surrounds of the old Albany wool store, Galafrey makes wines with plenty of robust, if not
rustic, character, drawing grapes in the main from nearly 13 ha of estate plantings at Mount Barker.
Exports to Belgium, Holland, Japan and Singapore.

Galah   ★★★★

Tregarthen Road, Ashton, SA 5137 **REGION** Adelaide Hills
T (08) 8390 1243 **F** (08) 8390 1243 **OPEN** At Ashton Hills
WINEMAKER Stephen George **EST.** 1986 **CASES** 1500
SUMMARY Over the years, Stephen George has built up a network of contacts across South Australia
from which he gains some very high-quality small parcels of grapes or wine for the Galah label. These
are all sold direct at extremely low prices for the quality. Exports to the UK and the US.

ΨΨΨΨ **Adelaide Hills Riesling 2004** Intense spice, mineral and green apple aromas, apple
dominant on the palate; slightly unusual, but certainly appealing. Screwcap. **RATING** 93
DRINK 2014 **$** 14.50

Gallagher Wines   ★★★★

2779 Dog Trap Road, Murrumbateman, NSW 2582 **REGION** Canberra District
T (02) 6227 0555 **F** (02) 6227 0666 **WEB** www.gallagherwines.com.au **OPEN** Not
WINEMAKER Greg Gallagher **EST.** 1995 **CASES** 2500
SUMMARY Greg Gallagher was senior winemaker at Taltarni for 20 years; he worked with Dominique
Portet. He began planning a change of career at much the same time as did Dominique, and started
establishing a small vineyard at Murrumbateman in 1995, planting a little over 1 ha each of
chardonnay and shiraz. He and his family have now moved to the region. Retail distribution in
Victoria, New South Wales and the ACT.

ΨΨΨΨ **Canberra District Riesling 2004** Spotlessly clean; crisp, slippery, minerally style; lemony
acid gives length. Screwcap. **RATING** 90 **DRINK** 2012 **$** 17
Canberra District Shiraz 2003 Unusual, potent herb, spice and licorice aromas; bitter
chocolate, black fruits and licorice on the palate. Screwcap. **RATING** 90 **DRINK** 2015 **$** 20

▼▼▼▼ **Canberra District Chardonnay 2002** Light to medium-bodied, linear style; tight melon fruit; a touch of citrus; invisible oak. Screwcap. **RATING** 87 **DRINK** 2008 **$** 17
Canberra District Shiraz 2002 A ripe mix of spice and faintly jammy fruit; light to medium-bodied; soft tannins. Cork. **RATING** 87 **DRINK** 2009 **$** 20

Galli Estate   ★★★★☆

1507 Melton Highway, Rockbank, Vic 3335 **REGION** Sunbury
T (03) 9747 1444 **F** (03) 9747 1481 **WEB** www.galliestate.com.au **OPEN** 7 days 11–5
WINEMAKER Stephen Phillips **EST.** 1997 **CASES** 12 000
SUMMARY Galli Estate may be a relative newcomer to the scene, but it is a substantial one. Lorenzo and Pam Galli planted 38 ha of vineyard, the lion's share to cabernet sauvignon and shiraz, but with 1.5–2.5 ha of semillon, sauvignon blanc, pinot grigio, chardonnay, sangiovese and pinot noir. A large underground cellar has been constructed; already 50m long, it is to be extended in the future. A cellar door sales, bistro and administration centre were completed in March 2002, with former Coldstream Hills winemaker Stephen Phillips now in charge. Exports to Japan.

▼▼▼▼▽ **Sunbury Semillon Sauvignon Blanc 2004** Spotlessly clean; potent, powerful wine; lemon and honey fruit; good balance and length. **RATING** 92 **DRINK** 2010 **$** 18
Sunbury Pinot Grigio 2004 Super-elegant, finely tuned; lemon and musk fruit; excellent balance and line. **RATING** 91 **DRINK** 2007 **$** 18

▼▼▼▼ **Heathcote Sangiovese 2003** Fragrant, elevated herb, cherry and mint aromas and flavours; just a touch brisk on the finish. **RATING** 88 **DRINK** 2007 **$** 18

Gapsted Wines   ★★★★☆

Great Alpine Road, Gapsted, Vic 3737 **REGION** Alpine Valleys
T (03) 5751 1383 **F** (03) 5751 1368 **WEB** www.gapstedwines.com.au **OPEN** 7 days 10–5
WINEMAKER Michael Cope-Williams, Shayne Cunningham **EST.** 1997 **CASES** 20 000
SUMMARY Gapsted is the premier brand of the Victorian Alps Wine Co., which is primarily a contract-crush facility which processes grapes for 48 growers in the King and Alpine Valleys. The estate plantings total 10 ha of shiraz, cabernet sauvignon, petit verdot and merlot, but the Gapsted wines come both from these estate plantings and from contract-grown fruit. The 'Ballerina Canopy' is a reference to the open nature of a particular training method which is ideally suited to these regions. Exports to New Zealand, Japan and Germany.

▼▼▼▼▽ **Victorian Alps Semillon Sauvignon Blanc 2004** Excellent balance, texture and structure; tropical gooseberry on the one hand, lemony grassy notes on the other. Screwcap. **RATING** 92 **DRINK** 2007 **$** 14
Ballerina Canopy Chardonnay 2002 Light to medium-bodied; excellent balance and integration of fruit and French oak; creamy, nutty notes, then cleansing acidity on the finish. **RATING** 91 **DRINK** 2010 **$** 20
Ballerina Canopy Cabernet Sauvignon 2001 Powerful dark berry fruit and equally powerful tannins; elements of bitter chocolate; ageing well. Cork. **RATING** 91 **DRINK** 2010 **$** 23
Limited Release Tempranillo 2003 Fragrant and spicy; a smooth cascade of red fruits, cherries and spices; silky tannins, fresh finish. Cork. **RATING** 91 **DRINK** 2008 **$** 25
Ballerina Canopy Sauvignon Blanc 2004 Potent, complex and ripe, with a touch of funk; powerful, textured palate; good length and finish. **RATING** 90 **DRINK** 2007 **$** 19
Limited Release Saperavi 2002 Intense, dark purple-red; luscious but powerful, with a mix of bitter chocolate, blackberry, plum and licorice; excellent structure, bright acidity. Cork. **RATING** 90 **DRINK** 2010 **$** 25

▼▼▼▼ **Ballerina Canopy Shiraz 2001** Clever integration of sweet fruit and sweet oak to off-set the savoury underlay. **RATING** 89 **DRINK** 2011 **$** 23
Ballerina Canopy Rose 2004 Well above average; has vinosity and length; strawberry-accented fruit; very good balance. Screwcap. **RATING** 88 **DRINK** Now **$** 18
Ballerina Canopy Durif 2002 Potent cigar box, black fruits and prune; tannins to spare, but not too dry. **RATING** 88 **DRINK** 2012 **$** 30
Moscato 2004 Flavoursome but distinctly sweet, the residual slightly off-set by lots of spritz. **RATING** 87 **DRINK** Now **$** 14

ΥΥΥΨ   **Victorian Alps Chardonnay 2004** RATING 86 DRINK 2007 $14
        Ballerina Canopy Merlot 2001 RATING 86 DRINK 2007 $23
        Victorian Alps Cabernet Merlot 2001 RATING 85 DRINK 2007 $14
        Ballerina Canopy Riesling 2003 RATING 84 DRINK 2007 $18

Garbin Estate

209 Toodyay Road, Middle Swan, WA 6056 **REGION** Swan Valley
T (08) 9274 1747 **F** (08) 9274 1747 **OPEN** Tues–Sun & public hols 10.30–5.30
WINEMAKER Peter Garbin, Peter Grimwood **EST.** 1956 **CASES** 4500
SUMMARY Peter Garbin, winemaker by weekend and design draftsman by week, decided in 1990 that
he would significantly upgrade the bulk fortified winemaking business commenced by his father in
1956. The 11-ha vineyards were replanted, 2 ha of chardonnay was planted at Gin Gin, the winery was
re-equipped, and the first of the new-generation wines was produced in 1994. Exports to Hong
Kong; otherwise sold direct from the winery.

ΥΥΥΥ   **Cabernet Merlot 2003** Good colour; medium-bodied; an impressive varietal blend given
        the region; gently ripe blackcurrant fruit, fine tannins; very well made. Quality cork.
        RATING 90 **DRINK** 2010 $19

ΥΥΥΥ   **Basket Pressed Reserve Shiraz 2003** Medium-bodied; blackberry, earth and dark
        chocolate; good length, moderate tannins. High-quality cork. **RATING** 89 **DRINK** 2010 $25

ΥΥΥΨ   **Semillon 2004** Plenty of flavour; a touch of French oak; residual sugar is evident but
        balanced. Screwcap. **RATING** 86 **DRINK** 2007 $14

Garden Gully Vineyards   NR

1477 Western Highway, Great Western, Vic 3377 **REGION** Grampians
T (03) 5356 2400 **F** (03) 5356 2405 **WEB** www.gardengully.com.au **OPEN** 7 days 10–5
WINEMAKER Warren Randall **EST.** 1987 **CASES** 1000
SUMMARY In mid-2005 a 5-family team purchased Garden Gully. The team is Tom and Sarah Guthrie
(owners of Grampians Estate), Robyn and Bruce Dalkin (owners of Westgate Vineyard), Paul Dakis
(vineyard manager at Seppelt), Bill and Helen Francis (owners of a small olive grove near Great
Western) and Mike and Kate Connellan (local doctor and lawyer). They have reopened the cellar
door, selling Garden Gully, Grampians Estate and Westgate Wines, various olive oils and other local
produce. The old 5.5-ha vineyard is to be rejuvenated.

Garlands

Marmion Street off Mount Barker Hill Road, Mount Barker, WA 6324 **REGION** Mount Barker
T (08) 9851 2737 **F** (08) 9851 1062 **WEB** www.garlandswines.com.au **OPEN** 7 days 10.30–4.30; winter
Thurs–Sun 10.30–4.30, or by appointment
WINEMAKER Michael Garland **EST.** 1996 **CASES** 5000
SUMMARY Garlands is a partnership between Michael and Julie Garland and their vigneron
neighbours, Craig and Caroline Drummond and Patrick and Christine Gresswell. Michael Garland
has come to grapegrowing and winemaking with a varied background, in biological research,
computer sales and retail clothing; he is now enrolled at Charles Sturt University for his degree in
oenology, but already has significant practical experience behind him. A small but highly functional
winery was erected prior to the 2000 vintage; the earlier wines were made elsewhere. The winery has
a capacity of 150 tonnes, and will continue contract-making for other small producers in the region
as well as making the wine from the 9.25 ha of estate vineyards (planted to shiraz, riesling, cabernet
sauvignon, cabernet franc, chardonnay, sauvignon blanc and semillon). Cabernet Franc is the winery
specialty, but the quality of all the wines has risen. Exports to the UK, Switzerland, Trinidad, Hong
Kong and Singapore.

ΥΥΥΥΨ   **Shiraz 2002** Nice mix of spicy oak and spicy black fruits; good texture and balance.
        RATING 90 **DRINK** 2010 $20

ΥΥΥΨ   **Saros 2002** RATING 85 DRINK 2007 $25

Gartelmann Hunter Estate ★★★★☆

Lovedale Road, Lovedale, NSW 2321 **REGION** Lower Hunter Valley
T (02) 4930 7113 **F** (02) 4930 7114 **WEB** www.gartelmann.com.au **OPEN** 7 days 10–5
WINEMAKER Monarch Winemaking Services (Contract) **EST.** 1970 **CASES** 10 000
SUMMARY In 1996 Jan and Jorg Gartelmann purchased what was previously the George Hunter Estate – 16 ha of mature vineyards – established by Sydney restaurateur Oliver Shaul in 1970. They produced a limited amount of wine under the Gartelmann label in 1997, and moved to full production in 1998. Diedrich Shiraz is the flagship, and is consistently good. Exports to UK, Germany and Canada.

🍷🍷🍷🍷 **Diedrich Shiraz 2003** Medium-bodied; fragrant red berries and spice; elegant, well balanced; fine, silky tannins; controlled oak. Screwcap. **RATING** 92 **DRINK** 2015 $ 32
Benjamin Semillon 2003 Fine but intense lemon and lanolin mid-palate fruit; minerally acidity on the finish gives length and persistence. **RATING** 91 **DRINK** 2013 $ 18
Benjamin Semillon 2004 Substantial; unusual weight and concentration; fine lemon and citrus palate; good length. Screwcap. **RATING** 90 **DRINK** 2014 $ 18
Chardonnay 2003 Melon, fig and stone fruit; squeaky acidity tightens up the palate and provides length. Screwcap. **RATING** 90 **DRINK** 2008 $ 20

🍷🍷🍷🍷 **Merlot 2003** Potent, bright, redcurrant/blackcurrant mix; supple and smooth; structure weakens slightly on the finish. Screwcap. **RATING** 89 **DRINK** 2008 $ 20

🍷🍷🍷🍷 **Vintage Brut 2001 RATING** 86 **DRINK** 2007 $ 22
Rose 2004 RATING 84 **DRINK** Now $ 16

Gawler River Grove NR

PO Box 280, Virginia, SA 5120 **REGION** Adelaide Plains
T 0438 506 097 **F** (08) 8380 9787 **OPEN** Not
WINEMAKER Steve Black (Contract) **EST.** 2001 **CASES** 200
SUMMARY The vineyards at Gawler River Grove go back to the late 1940s, with 7.7 ha of grenache bush vines. Since then, 5.8 ha of chardonnay and 1.5 ha of shiraz have been added. It was not until 2003 that a small amount of Chardonnay was vinified for the Gawler River Grove label; Grenache followed in 2004.

Gecko Valley ★★☆

Bailiff Road via 700 Glenlyon Road, Gladstone, Qld 4680 **REGION** Queensland Coastal
T (07) 4979 0400 **F** (07) 4979 0500 **OPEN** 7 days 10–5
WINEMAKER Bruce Humphery-Smith (Contract) **EST.** 1997 **CASES** 1000
SUMMARY Gecko Valley extends the viticultural map of Queensland yet further: it is little more than 50 km off the Tropic of Capricorn in an area better known for beef farming and mineral activities. The 3-ha vineyard (chardonnay, verdelho and shiraz) was established by Tony (an engineer) and Coleen McCray (an accountant). The coastal belt between Gladstone and Rockhampton has a unique climate, with lower rainfall than the more northern and the more southern coastal strips. The climate is hot, but the vineyard is only 1 km from the tempering influence of the sea. It has been planted on free-draining, shallow soil, so excessive vigour is not a problem.

🍷🍷🍷🍷 **Special Reserve Verdelho 2004 RATING** 85 **DRINK** Now

Geebin Wines NR

3729 Channel Highway, Birchs Bay, Tas 7162 **REGION** Southern Tasmania
T (03) 6267 4750 **F** (03) 6267 5090 **OPEN** 7 days 10–5
WINEMAKER Andrew Hood (Contract) **EST.** 1983 **CASES** 100
SUMMARY Although production is minuscule, quality has been consistently high. The Riesling is well made, but the interesting wine from this far southern vineyard is Cabernet Sauvignon – clearly, the vineyard enjoys favourable ripening conditions. With 0.9 ha of vineyards, Geebin claims to be the smallest commercial producer in Australia, but isn't: Scarp Valley and Jollymont are (or were) smaller. The vineyard, incidentally, was once called Milnathort.

Gehrig Estate

NR

Cnr Murray Valley Highway/Howlong Road, Barnawartha, Vic 3688 REGION Rutherglen
T (02) 6026 7296 F (02) 6026 7424 OPEN Mon–Sat 9–5, Sun 10–5
WINEMAKER Ross Gehrig EST. 1858 CASES 5000
SUMMARY A historic winery and adjacent house are superb legacies of the 19th century. Progressive
modernisation of the winemaking facilities and operations has seen the quality of the white wines
improve significantly; the red wines now receive a percentage of new oak. Another recent innovation
has been the introduction of the Gourmet Courtyard, which serves lunch on weekends, public
holidays and Victorian school holidays.

Gembrook Hill

★★★★★

Launching Place Road, Gembrook, Vic 3783 REGION Yarra Valley
T (03) 5968 1622 F (03) 5968 1699 WEB www.gembrookhill.com.au OPEN By appointment
WINEMAKER Timo Mayer EST. 1983 CASES 2000
SUMMARY The 6-ha Gembrook Hill Vineyard is situated on rich, red volcanic soils 2 km north of
Gembrook in the coolest part of the Yarra Valley. The vines are not irrigated, with consequent natural
vigour control, and naturally low yields. Harvest usually spans mid-April, 3 weeks later than the
traditional northern parts of the valley, and the style is consistently elegant.

ΨΨΨΨΨ **Yarra Valley Sauvignon Blanc 2003** Herb and gooseberry aromas; excellent length, focus
and intensity; bright, lemony acidity to close. RATING 94 DRINK 2007 $ 30
Yarra Valley Chardonnay 2003 Light straw-green; poised, precise and intense; grapefruit
and melon; very good oak balance and integration; long and lingering. RATING 94
DRINK 2008 $ 30

ΨΨΨΨΨ **Yarra Valley Pinot Noir 2003** Complex; a touch of farmyard to the bouquet; a mix of black
and red cherry fruit with notes of stem and spice. RATING 91 DRINK 2011 $ 35
Mayer Vineyard Yarra Valley Pinot Noir 2003 Scented, spicy, stemmy aromas; intense,
almost biting palate; long finish; needs time. RATING 90 DRINK 2010 $ 23

Gemtree Vineyards

★★★★★

PO Box 164, McLaren Vale, SA 5171 REGION McLaren Vale
T (08) 8323 8199 F (08) 8323 7889 OPEN Not
WINEMAKER Mike Brown EST. 1998 CASES 10 000
SUMMARY The Buttery family, headed by Paul and Jill, and with the active involvement of Melissa as
viticulturist for Gemtree Vineyards, have been grapegrowers in McLaren Vale since 1980, when they
purchased their first vineyard. Today the family owns a little over 130 ha of vines. The oldest block, of
25 ha on Tatachilla Road at McLaren Vale, was planted in 1970. Recent releases have been especially
good. Exports to the US, Canada, the UK, The Netherlands, Switzerland and Singapore.

ΨΨΨΨΨ **Uncut Shiraz 2003** A very complex array of flavours supported by great texture;
blackberry, plum, raspberry and mulberry; fine, ripe, lingering tannins. High-quality cork.
RATING 94 DRINK 2018 $ 25
Obsidian Shiraz 2002 Rich and supple, with abundant blackberry and dark chocolate
fruit flavours; very good balance. RATING 94 DRINK 2017 $ 40

ΨΨΨΨ **Citrine Chardonnay 2004** Light-bodied; subtle cashew and cream interwoven with fresh
melon and peach fruit; sophisticated but unforced winemaking; good length. Screwcap.
RATING 89 DRINK 2008 $ 15
Tatty Road 2003 Fresh, supple and smooth; light to medium-bodied; bright red and black
fruits; soft tannins. Cabernet Sauvignon/Petit Verdot/Merlot. Screwcap. RATING 89
DRINK 2008 $ 18
Bloodstone Tempranillo 2003 Spicy medium-bodied wine; some smoky notes; sweet
berry fruit and quite varietal; 350 cases made. Screwcap. RATING 88 DRINK 2010 $ 25

ΨΨΨΨ **Cinnibar Grenache Tempranillo Shiraz 2003** A very curious blend of convenience
though nominally the Cadenzia theme based around Grenache; driven by sweet, soft fruit
and a hint of sweetness. Zork. RATING 86 DRINK Now $ 25

Gentle Annie ★★★

455 Nalinga Road, Dookie, Vic 3646 **REGION** Central Victoria Zone
T (03) 5828 6333 **F** (03) 9602 1349 **WEB** www.gentle-annie.com **OPEN** By appointment
WINEMAKER David Hodgson, Tony Lacy **EST.** 1997 **CASES** 8000
SUMMARY Gentle Annie was established by Melbourne businessman Tony Cotter; wife Anne and five daughters assist with sales and marketing. The name Gentle Annie refers to an early settler renowned for her beauty and gentle temperament. The vineyard is a substantial one, with 4 ha of verdelho, 37 ha of shiraz and 22 ha of cabernet sauvignon planted on old volcanic ferrosol soils, similar to the red Cambrian loam at Heathcote. The winemaking team is headed by David Hodgson, who also heads up the Oenology faculty at Dookie College. Gentle Annie has hitherto sold the major part of its grape production, winning the Brown Brothers Grower of the Year title for the last two vintages. Other sales are to Southcorp. The increasing production of Gentle Annie wines has a substantial export component, likely to grow in the future.

ΤΤΤΤ **Shiraz 2001** **RATING** 84 **DRINK** 2007 $25

Geoff Hardy Wines

c/- Pertaringa Wines, Cnr Hunt Road/Rifle Range Road, McLaren Vale, SA 5171 **REGION** Adelaide Hills
T (08) 8323 8125 **F** (08) 8323 7766 **WEB** www.k1.com.au **OPEN** At Pertaringa
WINEMAKER Geoff Hardy, Ben Riggs **EST.** 1993 **CASES** 3000
SUMMARY Geoff Hardy wines come from 20 ha of vines, with a large percentage of the grape production being sold to other makers. The new premium K1 range is impressive in both quality and value. Retail distribution through South Australia, New South Wales, Victoria and Queensland; exports to Germany, Denmark, Canada and Hong Kong.

ΤΤΤΤΤ **K1 Adelaide Hills Chardonnay 2003** Restrained elegance; sweet apple, pear, melon and cashew flavours; restrained oak, moderate alcohol and dry finish. **RATING** 93 **DRINK** 2010 $28
K1 Adelaide Hills Shiraz 2002 Intense, ripe, bordering essency, aromas; blackberry and licorice flavours more in keeping with 14.5° alcohol; velvety and long. Quality cork. **RATING** 92 **DRINK** 2012 $28
K1 Adelaide Hills Cabernet Sauvignon 2002 Black fruits and attractive oak aromas; very powerful and concentrated; forceful tannins need to settle down; 420 cases made. High-quality cork. **RATING** 90 **DRINK** 2015 $28
The Full Fronti NV Complex and intense; excellent grapey fruit; clean fortifying spirit; biscuity Christmas cake flavours; good balance. **RATING** 90 **DRINK** 2007 $18

ΤΤΤΤ **K1 Adelaide Hills Merlot 2002** Powerful, long, brooding black fruits and savoury tannins; not easy to cuddle up to; may mellow with age. **RATING** 88 **DRINK** 2010 $28

ΤΤΤΤ **K1 Adelaide Hills Pinot Noir 2003** **RATING** 86 **DRINK** 2007 $28

Geoff Merrill Wines

291 Pimpala Road, Woodcroft, SA 5162 **REGION** McLaren Vale
T (08) 8381 6877 **F** (08) 8322 2244 **WEB** www.geoffmerrillwines.com **OPEN** Mon–Fri 10–5, weekends 12–5
WINEMAKER Geoff Merrill, Scott Heidrich **EST.** 1980 **CASES** 75 000
SUMMARY If Geoff Merrill ever loses his impish sense of humour or his zest for life, high and not-so-high, we shall all be the poorer. The product range consists of three tiers: premium (varietal); reserve, being the older (and best) wines, reflecting the desire for elegance and subtlety of this otherwise exuberant winemaker; and at the top, Henley Shiraz. Mount Hurtle wines are sold exclusively through Vintage Cellars/Liquorland. National retail distribution; exports to all major markets.

ΤΤΤΤΤ **Henley Shiraz 1998** Medium-bodied; elegant bottle-developed style; supple and smooth, the fruit holding beautifully, offering plum, chocolate, mocha and spice; good oak integration and balance. Cork. **RATING** 94 **DRINK** 2018 $150
Pimpala Vineyard Cabernet Merlot 2000 A complex mix of savoury, blackcurrant and dark chocolate fruits; fine lingering tannins, good French/American oak; 430 cases made. **RATING** 94 **DRINK** 2010 $30

TTTTY **McLaren Vale Grenache Rose 2004** Vivid fuchsia; vividly flowery, aromatic rose petal aromas; fresh, well-balanced palate; very good example of Australian Rose style. Screwcap. RATING 90 DRINK Now $ 18
Liquid Asset McLaren Vale Shiraz Grenache Viognier 2003 Fragrant bouquet; light to medium-bodied; well balanced, bright and fresh red fruits; finest tannins; great summer red. RATING 90 DRINK 2007 $ 20
Coonawarra/McLaren Vale Cabernet Sauvignon 2001 Clean, elegant and well balanced; nice interplay of fruit, oak and tannins; medium-bodied, but flavoursome. RATING 90 DRINK 2011 $ 19.50

TTTT **Merlot 2001** Well-made, stylish wine; not muscly, but has length and intensity; mix of olive and red fruits. RATING 89 DRINK 2007 $ 19.50

TTTY **McLaren Vale Sauvignon Blanc 2004** RATING 86 DRINK Now $ 18
Mount Hurtle Victoria Sauvignon Blanc 2004 RATING 86 DRINK Now $ 8
Mount Hurtle Coonawarra Cabernet Sauvignon 2002 RATING 86 DRINK 2008 $ 22.50
Mount Hurtle McLaren Vale Shiraz 2001 RATING 85 DRINK 2007 $ 22.50

TTT **Mount Hurtle McLaren Vale Chardonnay 2001** RATING 83 $ 8

Geoff Weaver ★★★★☆

2 Gilpin Lane, Mitcham, SA 5062 (postal) **REGION** Adelaide Hills
T (08) 8272 2105 **F** (08) 8271 0177 **WEB** www.geoffweaver.com.au **OPEN** Not
WINEMAKER Geoff Weaver **EST.** 1982 **CASES** 5000
SUMMARY This is now the full-time business of former Hardys chief winemaker Geoff Weaver. He draws upon a little over 11 ha of vineyard established between 1982 and 1988, and invariably produces immaculate Riesling and Sauvignon Blanc, and one of the longest-lived Chardonnays to be found in Australia, with intense grapefruit and melon flavour. The beauty of the labels ranks supreme, equal to Pipers Brook. Exports to the UK and the US.

TTTTY **Lenswood Riesling 2004** Spotlessly clean passionfruit and lime aromas; delicate, fresh, minerally palate; long finish. Screwcap. RATING 93 DRINK 2012 $ 19.50
Pinot Noir 2002 Intense, fragrant, spicy/foresty aromas; a long, intense and very savoury palate. RATING 93 DRINK 2010 $ 35
Lenswood Sauvignon Blanc 2004 Palest straw-green; clean, fresh and crisp; delicate fruit yet to express itself. RATING 92 DRINK Now $ 23
Pinot Noir 2003 Light to medium-bodied; savoury/foresty/stemmy complexity; red berries on the mid-palate; long finish, not over-extracted. RATING 90 DRINK 2008 $ 31

Ghost Rock Vineyard ★★★★

PO Box 311, Devonport, Tas 7310 **REGION** Northern Tasmania
T (03) 6423 1246 **OPEN** Due to open November 2006
WINEMAKER Tamar Ridge (Contract) **EST.** 2001 **CASES** 450
SUMMARY Cate and Colin Arnold purchased the former Patrick Creek Vineyard (itself planted in 1989) in August 2001. They run a printing and design business in Devonport, and were looking for a suitable site to establish a vineyard, when the opportunity to buy Patrick Creek came up. The 1-ha vineyard is half chardonnay and a quarter each of pinot noir and sauvignon blanc, planted on a northeasterly aspect on a sheltered slope. In November 2004 the vineyard was increased, with an additional 3 ha of vines.

TTTTY **Chardonnay 2002** Elegant, long and fine; citrussy, with good acidity and balance; some cork problems. RATING 93 DRINK 2010 $ 18
Pinot Noir 2003 An attractive mix of ripe, red and black fruits; good tannins. RATING 90 DRINK 2010 $ 20

TTTT **Sauvignon Blanc 2004** Elegant, light to medium-bodied; pleasing gooseberry fruit; finesse and balance. RATING 89 DRINK 2007 $ 22

TTT **Chardonnay 2004** RATING 83 $ 18

Giaconda ★★★★★

McClay Road, Beechworth, Vic 3747 **REGION** Beechworth
T (03) 5727 0246 **F** (03) 5727 0246 **WEB** www.giaconda.com.au **OPEN** By appointment
WINEMAKER Rick Kinzbrunner **EST.** 1985 **CASES** 2000
SUMMARY These wines have a super-cult status and, given the tiny production, are extremely difficult to find; they are sold chiefly through restaurants and by mail order. All have a cosmopolitan edge befitting Rick Kinzbrunner's international winemaking experience. The Chardonnay and Pinot Noir are made in contrasting styles: the Chardonnay tight and reserved, the Pinot Noir more variable, but usually opulent and ripe. The rating is based on tastings over the years. Exports to the UK and the US.

Giant Steps ★★★★

10–12 Briarty Road, Gruyere, Vic 3770 **REGION** Yarra Valley
T (03) 5962 6111 **F** (03) 5962 6199 **WEB** www.giant-steps.com.au **OPEN** By appointment
WINEMAKER Phil Sexton, Allison Sexton **EST.** 1998 **CASES** 15 000
SUMMARY Phil Sexton made his first fortune as a pioneer micro-brewer, and invested a substantial part of that fortune in establishing Devil's Lair. Late in 1996 he sold Devil's Lair to Southcorp, which had purchased Coldstream Hills earlier that year. Two years later he and Allison Sexton purchased a hillside property less than 1 km from Coldstream Hills, and sharing the same geological structure and aspect. The name Giant Steps comes in part from their love of jazz and John Coltrane's album of that name, and in part from the rise and fall of the property across a series of ridges ranging from 120m to 360m. The 34-ha vineyard is predominantly planted to pinot noir and chardonnay, but with significant quantities of cabernet sauvignon and merlot, plus small plantings of cabernet franc and petit verdot. The wines are distributed nationally through Tucker Seabrook; exports to the US.

🍷🍷🍷🍷🍷(half) **Pinot Noir 2003** Focused, concentrated and rich; smooth, supple fruit-forward red and black fruit; good balance; a faint twist of stem on the finish. **RATING** 92 **DRINK** 2010 **$** 24.95
Sexton Dijon Clones Pinot Noir 2003 Powerful, concentrated black fruits and plum on both bouquet and palate; extraction just a little over the top, but very impressive. **RATING** 92 **DRINK** 2013 **$** 44.95
Sexton Harry's Monster 2003 Attractive, almost glossy fruit; medium-bodied; fine tannins to balance the fruit and give moderate length. **RATING** 90 **DRINK** 2013 **$** 45

🍷🍷🍷🍷 **Sexton Bernard Clones Chardonnay 2003** A delicate wine, with nice balance and length; melon fruit with a touch of creaminess, and nice acidity. **RATING** 89 **DRINK** 2008 **$** 39.95

🍷🍷🍷(half) **Chardonnay 2003** **RATING** 86 **DRINK** 2008 **$** 24.95

Gibraltar Rock ★★★★★

Woodlands Road, Porongurup, WA 6324 **REGION** Porongurup
T (08) 9481 2856 **F** (08) 9481 2857 **OPEN** Wed–Sun 10–5
WINEMAKER Larry Cherubino **EST.** 1979 **CASES** 400
SUMMARY A once-tiny Riesling specialist in the wilds of the Porongurups, forced to change its name from Narang because Lindemans felt it could be confused with its (now defunct) Nyrang Shiraz brand; truly a strange world. This beautifully sited vineyard and its long-lived Riesling were acquired by Perth orthopaedic surgeon Dr Peter Honey prior to the 2001 vintage. The vineyard now has 26 ha of riesling, sauvignon blanc, chardonnay, pinot noir, merlot, shiraz and cabernet franc. Most of the grapes are sold to Houghton under a 10-year contract, but Dr Honey intends to slowly increase production from the older vines under the Gibraltar Rock label.

🍷🍷🍷🍷🍷 **Porongurup Riesling 2004** Fine, fragrant and flowery; spotlessly clean; lovely light-bodied apple, passionfruit and lime; clean finish. Screwcap. **RATING** 94 **DRINK** 2016 **$** 20
Porongurup Chardonnay 2002 Very elegant and subtle malolactic and barrel ferment influences interwoven with fine melon and stone fruit; light-bodied, but perfectly poised and balanced. Quality cork. **RATING** 94 **DRINK** 2012 **$** 22

🍷🍷🍷🍷(half) **Porongurup Chardonnay 2004** Light green-straw; elegant; subtle barrel ferment complexity on medium-bodied nectarine and white peach palate; good length and balance. Screwcap. **RATING** 90 **DRINK** 2008 **$** 22

🍷🍷🍷🍷 **Porongurup Pinot Noir 2004** Light red-purple; falls in the savoury, spicy, earthy, foresty, stemmy spectrum; has length, but not fruit sweetness. **RATING** 87 **DRINK** 2008 **$** 18

Gibson ★★★★☆

Willows Road, Light Pass, SA 5355 **REGION** Barossa Valley
T (08) 8562 3193 **F** (08) 8562 4490 **WEB** www.barossavale.com **OPEN** Fri–Mon & public hols 11–5
WINEMAKER Rob Gibson **EST.** 1996 **CASES** 3500
SUMMARY Rob Gibson spent much of his working life as a senior viticulturist for Penfolds. While at
Penfolds he was involved in research tracing the characters that particular parcels of grapes give to a
wine, which left him with a passion for identifying and protecting what is left of the original vineyard
plantings in wine regions around Australia. He plans to release tiny quantities of wines from other
regions, drawing upon old vineyards; this led to the acquisition of an additional 8 ha of old shiraz,
mourvedre and grenache, plus some of the oldest chardonnay vines in the Barossa (recent arrivals in
comparison with shiraz, but planted in 1982). A carefully designed and built cellar door has also
opened. Exports to the UK and Hong Kong.

🍷🍷🍷🍷🍷 **BarossaVale Old Vine Collection Shiraz 2002** Medium-bodied; excellent texture and
structure; finely balanced black and red fruits; lingering, silky tannins. **RATING** 94
DRINK 2015 **$** 85

🍷🍷🍷🍷🍷 **BarossaVale Wilfreda Blend 2003** Much more depth than many such blends; an
attractive mix of black fruits, chocolate and red fruits; supple, ripe tannins.
Mourvedre/Grenache. **RATING** 92 **DRINK** 2013 **$** 27.50
BarossaVale Reserve Merlot 2002 Focused and intense; beautifully ripe
redcurrant/blackcurrant fruit; good French oak; ripe tannins. Dodgy cork. **RATING** 91
DRINK 2012 **$** 36.90
Loose End Adelaide Hills SBS 2004 Clean, fresh, vigorous lime, lemon and gooseberry
aromas and flavours; good drive and finish. **RATING** 90 **DRINK** 2007 **$** 14.90
Loose End Barossa GSM 2004 Fresh but not callow; a spray of red fruits and small
berries; nice mouthfeel; clever winemaking. **RATING** 90 **DRINK** 2007 **$** 16.90

🍷🍷🍷🍷 **BarossaVale Merlot 2002** Soft and very ripe blackcurrant and raspberry fruit; complex
flavours, though diminished varietal character. **RATING** 89 **DRINK** 2008 **$** 26.50

Gidgee Estate Wines NR

441 Weeroona Drive, Wamboin, NSW 2620 **REGION** Canberra District
T (02) 6236 9506 **F** (02) 6236 9070 **OPEN** Weekends 12–4
WINEMAKER Andrew McEwin (Contract) **EST.** 1996 **CASES** 500
SUMMARY Brett and Cheryl Lane purchased the 1-ha vineyard in 1996; it had been planted to riesling,
chardonnay, cabernet sauvignon, cabernet franc and merlot over a 10-year period prior to its
acquisition, but had been allowed to run down and needed to be rehabilitated.

Gilberts ★★★★☆

RMB 438, Albany Highway, Kendenup via Mount Barker, WA 6323 **REGION** Mount Barker
T (08) 9851 4028 **F** (08) 9851 4021 **OPEN** 7 days 10–5
WINEMAKER Plantagenet (Contract) **EST.** 1980 **CASES** 4000
SUMMARY A part-time occupation for sheep and beef farmers Jim and Beverly Gilbert, but a very
successful one. The now mature vineyard, coupled with contract winemaking at Plantagenet, has
produced small quantities of high-quality Riesling and Chardonnay. The Riesling won the trophy for
Best Wine of Show at the Qantas West Australian Wines Show in both 2000 and 2001. The wines sell
out quickly each year, with retail distribution through New South Wales, Victoria, the ACT and
Western Australia, and exports to the US, the UK, Singapore and The Netherlands. A restaurant and
function area opened in April 2003, and further plantings are planned.

🍷🍷🍷🍷🍷 **Mount Barker Riesling 2004** Spotlessly clean; intense, flowery lime, apple and spice
aromas; powerful, intense and focused palate. All class. Screwcap. **RATING** 94 **DRINK** 2014
$ 17

🍷🍷🍷🍷🍷 **Reserve Mount Barker Shiraz 2002** Clean, smooth and elegant; spicy black fruits; fine
tannins and quality French oak. High-quality cork. **RATING** 93 **DRINK** 2012 **$** 25
Mount Barker Chardonnay 2003 Restrained style; some minerally characters; stone fruit
and a touch of citrus; subtle oak. Cork. **RATING** 90 **DRINK** 2008 **$** 18
Three Devils Shiraz 2003 Medium-bodied; an attractive mix of red and black fruits; fine,
silky mouthfeel; fine tannins. Screwcap. **RATING** 90 **DRINK** 2010 **$** 16

ŸŸŸŸ **Alira Riesling 2004** Rich, late-picked style; no botrytis, simply tropical/pineapple fruit. Made for a particular market sector. Screwcap. **RATING** 88 **DRINK** 2007 $ 14

Gilead Estate   ★★★★

1868 Wanneroo Road, Neerabup, WA 6031 (postal) **REGION** Swan District
T (08) 9407 5076 **F** (08) 9407 5187 **OPEN** Not
WINEMAKER Gerry Gauntlett **EST.** 1995 **CASES** 400
SUMMARY A retirement – but nonetheless serious – venture for Judy and Gerry Gauntlett, who planted 1.2 ha on the Tuart sands of Wanneroo in 1990. The name comes from the Balm of Gilead. This was produced from trees on the hills northeast of Galilee in Biblical times, and was said to have had healing and purifying qualities. The tiny production is mainly sold by mail order, with occasional tasting days.

ŸŸŸŸŸ **Shiraz 2003** Medium-bodied; spicy blackberry, black cherry and sweet spice; nice oak, fine tannins. Stained Diam. **RATING** 90 **DRINK** 2013 $ 15
Cabernet Sauvignon 2003 Medium-bodied; clean, fresh; nicely balanced and framed black fruits; gentle spicy, ripe tannins; integrated oak. Stained Diam. **RATING** 90 **DRINK** 2014 $ 15

Gilgai Winery   NR

Tingha Road, Gilgai, NSW 2360 **REGION** Northern Slopes Zone
T (02) 6723 1204 **OPEN** 7 days 10–5
WINEMAKER Keith Whish **EST.** 1968 **CASES** 550
SUMMARY Inverell medical practitioner Dr Keith Whish has been quietly producing wines from his 6-ha vineyard for almost 30 years. All the production is sold through the cellar door.

🍃 Gilligan   ★★★★☆

PO Box 235, McLaren Vale, SA 5172 **REGION** McLaren Vale
T (08) 8323 8379 **F** (08) 8323 8379 **OPEN** Not
WINEMAKER Mark Day, Leigh Gilligan **EST.** 2001 **CASES** 750
SUMMARY Leigh Gilligan is a 20-year marketing veteran, most of the time with McLaren Vale wineries (including Wirra Wirra). The Gilligan family (including Jen, brother Ross and son Sami) have 6 ha of shiraz and 2 ha of grenache on their Old Rifle Range Vineyard, selling the lion's share to Southcorp. In 2001 they persuaded next-door neighbour Drew Noon to make a barrel of Shiraz, which they drank and gave away. Realising they needed more than one barrel, and with no space at Noon's, they moved to Maxwell Wines for 2002 and 2003, with help from Maxwell Wines winemaker Mark Day. They have now migrated to Mark's new Koltz Winery at Blewitt Springs. The longer-term plan is to take all the fruit when the Southcorp contract terminates; they have also planted more grenache, and small parcels of mourvedre, marsanne and roussanne on another property they have acquired in the heart of McLaren Vale. The wines sell out rapidly, and are currently available only by mail order. Exports to the US, Canada, Germany and Denmark.

ŸŸŸŸŸ **McLaren Vale Shiraz Grenache 2003** Fragrant, savoury, spicy verging on pepper aromas; a fresh array of red and black fruits; brushes off 15° alcohol with ease; overall, light to medium-bodied. Quality cork. **RATING** 90 **DRINK** 2008 $ 20
McLaren Vale Shiraz Grenache Mourvedre 2002 Mourvedre adds stiffening and structure; a touch more black fruits coming from the cool '02 vintage; considerable length. Quality cork. **RATING** 90 **DRINK** 2010 $ 20

Gin Gin Wines   NR

Gin Gin Historical Village, Mulgrave Street, Gin Gin, Qld 4671 **REGION** Queensland Coastal
T (07) 4157 3099 **F** (07) 4157 3088 **OPEN** 7 days 10–5
WINEMAKER Lyla McLaren **EST.** 2002 **CASES** NA
SUMMARY The 2.5-ha vineyard of Lyla and John McLaren may not be large, but it is planted to a Joseph's Coat of varieties: sauvignon blanc, gewurztraminer, semillon, chardonnay, colombard, verdelho, pinot noir, merlot, grenache, cabernet sauvignon, malbec, shiraz, petit verdot, sangiovese and tempranillo. Similarly, the cellar door offers wine tourists everything they could wish for.

Gisborne Peak ★★★★

69 Short Road, Gisborne South, Vic 3437 REGION Macedon Ranges
T (03) 5428 2228 F (03) 5428 4816 WEB www.gisbornepeakwines.com.au OPEN 7 days 11–5
WINEMAKER John Ellis (Contract) EST. 1978 CASES 1500
SUMMARY Bob Nixon began the development of Gisborne Peak way back in 1978, planting his dream vineyard row-by-row, then acre-by-acre (chardonnay, semillon and pinot noir). Bob is married to Barbara Nixon, founder of Victoria Winery Tours; she has been in and out of cellar doors around Australia with greater frequency than any other living person. So it is that the tasting room has wide shaded verandahs, plenty of windows and sweeping views of the Chardonnay Bowl and the Semillon Flats. Wood-fired pizza is served on weekends and public holidays, and cheese platters are available daily. Exports to the US.

TTTTT **Mawarra Estate Macedon Pinot Noir 2003** Very deep colour; aromatic; concentrated smoky, briary plum fruit; fine tannins; great future. Screwcap. RATING 93 DRINK 2013 $35

TTTT **Mawarra Estate Macedon Chardonnay 2003** Citrussy lemony fruit and good length; good acidity, and still building complexity, which will come with time. RATING 89 DRINK 2010 $25
Mawarra Macedon Unwooded Chardonnay 2004 Light-bodied; fresh and lively, with strong citrus component; good balance, though the fruit dips towards the finish. Screwcap. RATING 87 DRINK 2008 $16.50

TTTT **Mawarra Estate Macedon Chardonnay 2004** RATING 86 DRINK 2007 $22

Glaetzer Wines ★★★★☆

34 Barossa Valley Way, Tanunda, SA 5352 REGION Barossa Valley
T (08) 8563 0288 F (08) 8563 0218 WEB www.glaetzer.com OPEN Mon–Sat 10.30–4.30, public hols 1–4.30
WINEMAKER Colin Glaetzer, Ben Glaetzer EST. 1996 CASES 5000
SUMMARY Colin (recently installed as a Baron of the Barossa) and Ben Glaetzer are almost as well known in South Australian wine circles as Wolf Blass winemaker John Glaetzer, and, needless to say, they are all closely related. Glaetzer Wines purchases its grapes from third and fourth-generation Barossa Valley growers and makes an array of traditional Barossa styles. The Shiraz comes predominantly from vines that are 80 years or more old. National retail distribution; exports to the UK, the US and other major markets.

TTTTT **Amon-Ra Unfiltered Shiraz 2003** Dense, deep colour; rich, concentrated and powerful black fruits; ripe but powerful tannins; some heat from 15.5° alcohol. High-quality cork. RATING 93 DRINK 2023 $80
Bishop Shiraz 2002 Medium to full-bodied; smooth, supple and luscious blackberry and black cherry fruit; fine, ripe tannins; despite its size, has elegance; good oak. Quality cork. RATING 91 DRINK 2015 $49
Barossa Valley Shiraz 2002 Ripe, rich, round black and red fruits; chocolate, mocha and vanilla overtones; soft tannins. From 80-year-old vines. Stained cork. RATING 91 DRINK 2015 $49

TTTT **Wallace Shiraz Grenache 2003** Medium-bodied; distinctive, slightly jammy, confection fruit from the Grenache, very typical; spicy black cherry and plum from Shiraz. Screwcap. RATING 88 DRINK 2007 $19

Glastonbury Estate Wines ★★★

Shop 4, 104 Memorial Drive, Eumundi, Qld 4562 REGION Queensland Coastal
T (07) 5442 8557 F (07) 5442 8745 WEB www.glastonburyvineyard.com.au OPEN Tues 12–5, Wed 9–8, Thurs 12–8, Fri 12–5, Sat 9–8, Sun 12–5
WINEMAKER Peter Scudamore-Smith MW (Consultant) EST. 2001 CASES 4000
SUMMARY Glastonbury Estate is situated in the hills of Glastonbury, high up in the Sunshine Coast hinterland, 50 minutes from Noosa. It is the vision of managing director Steve Davoren, who (in typical Queensland tradition) has established a combined wine and tourism venture. Chardonnay, merlot and cabernet sauvignon have been established on terraces cut into the hillsides, with further plantings underway. A large lodge comfortably sleeping three couples has been built. Glastonbury

Estate intends to become one of the first developments in Queensland to offer building sites amongst the vines (further details are available from the website).

ŸŸŸ **Shiraz Cabernet 2002** RATING 83 $16

Gledswood Homestead & Winery NR

900 Camden Valley Way, Catherine Fields, NSW 2171 REGION Sydney Basin
T (02) 9606 5111 WEB www.gledswood.com.au OPEN 7 days 10–5
WINEMAKER Contract EST. 2000 CASES NA
SUMMARY The Gledswood Homestead & Winery complex is one of the most historically important properties in Australia, with the collection of buildings dating back to 1810, and the homestead to around 1820. The owners live in the homestead, but the homestead and all its ancillary buildings are devoted to a wide range of tourist activities, supported by the restaurant, which is open 7 days.

Glenalbyn

84 Halls Road, Kingower, Vic 3517 REGION Bendigo
T (03) 5438 8255 F (03) 5438 8255 OPEN 10.30–4.30 most days
WINEMAKER Lee (Leila) Gillespie EST. 1997 CASES 500
SUMMARY When Leila Gillespie's great-grandfather applied for his land title in 1856, he had already established a vineyard on the property (in 1853). A survey plan of 1857 shows the cultivation paddocks, one marked the Grape Paddock, and a few of the original grape vines have survived in the garden which abuts the National Trust and Heritage homestead. In 1986 Leila and John Gillespie decided on a modest diversification of their sheep, wool and cereal crop farm, and began the establishment of 4 ha of vineyards. Since 1997 Leila Gillespie has made the wine (she is self-taught), starting with Cabernet Sauvignon, then adding Pinot Noir and Sauvignon Blanc. In 2003 she commemorated 150 years of family ownership of the property; ironically, the 2003 drought meant that no grapes were picked.

ŸŸŸŸŸ **Sauvignon Blanc 2004** Fresh and clean; no reduction whatsoever; gentle tropical fruits; crunchy acidity, long finish. Screwcap. RATING 90 DRINK 2007

GlenAyr

Back Tea Tree Road, Richmond, Tas 7025 REGION Southern Tasmania
T (03) 6260 2388 F (03) 6260 2691 OPEN Mon–Fri 8–5
WINEMAKER Andrew Hood (Contract) EST. 1975 CASES 500
SUMMARY The substantial and now fully mature Tolpuddle Vineyard, managed by Warren Schasser, who is completing a Bachelor of Applied Science (viticulture) at Charles Sturt University, provides the grapes which go to make the GlenAyr wines. The major part of the grape production continues to be sold to Domaine Chandon and Hardys, with most going to make premium still table wine, and a lesser amount to premium sparkling.

Glenburnie Vineyard NR

Black Range Road, Tumbarumba, NSW 2653 REGION Tumbarumba
T (02) 6948 2570 F (02) 6948 2570 OPEN 7 days 10–5
WINEMAKER Cofield Wines (Contract) EST. 1992 CASES 800
SUMMARY Robert Parkes has established 12 ha of vineyard planted to riesling, sauvignon blanc, chardonnay and pinot noir. The production is marketed under the Black Range Wines. The cellar door offers barbecue facilities, and accommodation is also available.

Glen Creek Wines NR

Glen Creek Road, Barjarg, Vic 3722 REGION Upper Goulburn
T (03) 5776 4271 F (03) 9873 5088 WEB www.glencreekwines.com.au OPEN By appointment
WINEMAKER MasterWineMakers (Contract) EST. 2001 CASES NA
SUMMARY Geoff Alford commenced the establishment of the vineyard in Mt Strathbogie at Barjarg, around 30 km northwest of Mansfield, with the planting of 500 chardonnay vines in 1995. The estate has since grown to 6 ha, with the addition of pinot gris, merlot, cabernet sauvignon and nebbiolo;

other local vineyards contribute shiraz, pinot noir and additional cabernet sauvignon. There is a complementary planting of olives. Part of the wine is made onsite, part offsite by MasterWineMakers. The wines are available by mail order, with limited retail distribution.

Glendonbrook ★★★

Lot 2 Park Street, East Gresford, NSW 2311 **REGION** Upper Hunter Valley
T (02) 4938 9666 **F** (02) 4938 9766 **WEB** www.glendonbrook.com **OPEN** Mon–Fri 9–5, weekends & public hols 10.30–4.30
WINEMAKER Geoff Broadfield **EST.** 2000 **CASES** 15 000
SUMMARY Highly successful Sydney businessman Tom Smith and wife Terese purchased the Bingleburra homestead at East Gresford in the mid-1990s. The 600-ha property raises beef cattle, but in 1997 the decision was taken to plant 12.5 ha of vines (8.3 ha shiraz, 4.2 ha verdelho). This in turn led to the construction (in 2001) of a $2 million, 300-tonne capacity winery, lifting their total investment in the wine industry to $3 million. The estate production is supplemented by contract-grown grapes, and the winery has sufficient capacity to offer contract winemaking facilities for others. It marks a major return to the Gresford area, where Dr Henry Lindeman established his Cawarra vineyards in the mid-1800s.

TTTT **Verdelho 2002 RATING** 84 **DRINK** Now $ 17.99

Glen Eldon Wines ★★★★

Cnr Koch's Road/Nitschke Road, Krondorf, SA 5235 **REGION** Eden and Barossa Valleys
T (08) 8568 2996 **F** (08) 8568 1833 **WEB** www.gleneldonwines.com.au **OPEN** Mon–Fri 8.30–5, weekends 11–5
WINEMAKER Richard Sheedy **EST.** 1997 **CASES** 4000
SUMMARY The Sheedy family – brothers Richard and Andrew, and wives Mary and Sue – have established their base at the Glen Eldon property (which was given its name over 100 years ago); it is today the home of Richard and Mary. The riesling is planted here; the shiraz and cabernet sauvignon come from their vineyards in the Barossa Valley. National distribution; exports to the UK, the US and Canada. A new winery and cellar door opened in July 2005.

TTTTT **Dry Bore Barossa Shiraz 2002** Powerful blackberry fruit; perfect ripeness typical of 2002; very good structure; fine, ripe tannins; carries 14.5° alcohol with ease. Screwcap. **RATING** 94 **DRINK** 2018

TTTT **Eden Valley Riesling 2004** Light, spice, mineral and lime aromas and flavours; correct, but shows the vintage dilution. Screwcap. **RATING** 88 **DRINK** 2009
Barossa Merlot 2002 Powerful and concentrated mix of lush, dark berry and more savoury/spicy varietal character; dries off nicely on the finish. Screwcap. **RATING** 88 **DRINK** 2017
Dry Bore Barossa Cabernet Sauvignon 2002 Huge wine; lashings of sweet black fruits, but the tannins needed more work before bottling. Try again in 10 years. Screwcap. **RATING** 88 **DRINK** 2017

Glen Erin Vineyard Retreat ★★★★

Rochford Road, Lancefield, Vic 3435 **REGION** Macedon Ranges
T (03) 5429 1041 **F** (03) 5429 2053 **WEB** www.glenerinretreat.com.au **OPEN** Weekends & public hols 10–6
WINEMAKER Brian Scales, John Ellis **EST.** 1993 **CASES** 400
SUMMARY Brian Scales acquired the former Lancefield Winery and renamed it Glen Erin. Wines are contract-made from Macedon and other grapes and sold only through the cellar door and restaurant; conferences and events are the major business activity, supported by 24 accommodation rooms.

TTTTY **Mystic Park Chardonnay Pinot NV** Complex; well-balanced bready notes; nice, lingering tannins. **RATING** 93 **DRINK** 2007 $ 35

Glenfinlass NR

Elysian Farm, Parkes Road, Wellington, NSW 2820 **REGION** Western Plains Zone
T (02) 6845 2011 **F** (02) 6845 3329 **OPEN** Sat 9–5, or by appointment

WINEMAKER Brian G Holmes **EST.** 1971 **CASES** 500
SUMMARY The weekend and holiday hobby of Wellington solicitor Brian Holmes, who has wisely decided to leave it at that. I have not tasted the wines for many years, but the last wines I did taste were competently made. Wines are in short supply owing to drought (1998), frost (1999) and flooding (2000), promptly followed by three more years of drought.

Glengariff Estate Winery   NR

3234 Mount Mee Road, Dayboro Valley, Qld 4521 **REGION** Queensland Coastal
T (07) 3425 1299 **F** (07) 3425 2255 **WEB** www.glengariff.com.au **OPEN** By appointment
WINEMAKER Contract **EST.** 1999 **CASES** 350
SUMMARY The word 'historic' is as much overused as the word 'passionate', but this is a historic property with a quite remarkable story. The twice-married Honorah Mullins, first to a Mr Doyle and later to a Mr Mullins, moved with her husband from County Cork, Ireland to Australia in 1875. In 1876 they established the family dairy farm, now Glengariff Estate. At the age of 90, Honorah Mullins was still milking a herd of 40 cows, and when 111 she continued to take her morning walk with one of her sons, Dennis Doyle. When she died on 1 May 1926, one day before her 115th birthday, she had lived through the reign of six English monarchs, from George III to George V. Tracey Wrightson, the great-great-granddaughter of Honorah Mullins, together with husband Andrew and children, now own and run the 100-ha Glengariff Estate. It operates as a tourist attraction, with a restaurant and wedding function venue and (since 1999) as a grapegrower and wine producer.

Glenguin   ★★★★

Milbrodale Road, Broke, NSW 2330 **REGION** Lower Hunter Valley
T (02) 6579 1009 **F** (02) 6579 1009 **OPEN** At Boutique Wine Centre, Broke Road, Pokolbin
WINEMAKER Robin Tedder MW **EST.** 1993 **CASES** 9000
SUMMARY Glenguin's vineyard has been established along the banks of the Wollombi Brook by Robin (MW) and Rita Tedder; Robin is a grandson of Air Chief Marshal Tedder, made Baron of Glenguin by King George VI in recognition of his wartime deeds. There are now two distinct ranges: the Glenguin wines come solely from the 19 ha of estate plantings at Wollombi, and the Maestro label matching grape varieties and site climates in regions as diverse as Orange and the Adelaide Hills. Exports to the UK, Germany and New Zealand.

ΨΨΨΨ**Y** **The Old Broke Block Semillon 2004** Crisp and clean; very good mouthfeel, balance and length; appealing lemony acidity on the finish and aftertaste. Screwcap. **RATING** 91 **DRINK** 2014 **$** 19

ΨΨΨΨ **Maestro Merlot 2002** A powerful, foresty/savoury style; black fruits and olives; fine tannins; has length. **RATING** 89 **DRINK** 2012 **$** 25
Maestro Pinot Grigio 2004 Nicely balanced and weighted; ripe pear, spice and apple fruit. Orange. Screwcap. **RATING** 88 **DRINK** 2007 **$** 23
Schoolhouse Block Shiraz 2002 Savoury, earthy, spicy regional characters to the black fruits; fine-grained tannins. Cork. **RATING** 88 **DRINK** 2012 **$** 30
River Terrace Chardonnay 2003 Light to medium-bodied; well balanced and structured; melon and a hint of citrus; good length; no visible oak. Screwcap. **RATING** 87 **DRINK** 2008 **$** 19

ΨΨΨ**Y** **Stonybroke Shiraz 2002** **RATING** 86 **DRINK** 2009 **$** 21

Glen Isla Estate   NR

107 Glen Isla Road, Bickley, WA 6076 **REGION** Perth Hills
T (08) 9293 5293 **F** (08) 9293 5293 **WEB** www.glenislaestate.com.au **OPEN** By appointment
WINEMAKER John Griffiths (Contract) **EST.** 1998 **CASES** 350
SUMMARY Jim Winterhalder has established 0.84 ha each of merlot and pinot noir, and 2.38 ha of shiraz, on slopes which straddle Piesse Brook, facing variously west, east and north. The wine is made by the highly skilled John Griffiths; apart from a couple of retail outlets, sold only by mail order.

Gloucester Ridge Vineyard   NR

Lot 7489 Burma Road, Pemberton, WA 6260 **REGION** Pemberton
T (08) 9776 1035 **F** (08) 9776 1390 **WEB** www.gloucester-ridge.com.au **OPEN** 7 days 10–5 (until late Saturday)
WINEMAKER Brenden Smith **EST.** 1985 **CASES** 6000
SUMMARY Gloucester Ridge is the only vineyard located within the Pemberton town boundary. It is owned and operated by Don and Sue Hancock. Retail distribution in Queensland, New South Wales, Victoria and WA.

Gnadenfrei Estate   ★★★★☆

Seppeltsfield Road, Marananga via Nuriootpa, SA 5355 **REGION** Barossa Valley
T (08) 8562 2522 **F** (08) 8562 3470 **OPEN** Tues–Sun 11–5.30
WINEMAKER Malcolm Seppelt **EST.** 1979 **CASES** 750
SUMMARY A strictly cellar door operation, which relies on a variety of sources for its wines but has a core of 2 ha of estate shiraz and 1 ha of grenache. The red wines are from old estate, dry-grown vines and are not filtered.

▼▼▼▼▼ **St Michael's Shiraz 2003** Opaque, dense purple; massive wine in every respect; black fruits, tannins and oak. In its style, very good; Parker special. **RATING** 94 **DRINK** 2023 **$** 40

▼▼▼▼♀ **Grenache 2003** Spicy, sweet, blackberry jam fruit; powerful structure and savoury tannins. **RATING** 90 **DRINK** 2016 **$** 20

▼▼▼▼ **Shiraz Grenache 2003** Inky purple; another massively constructed and slightly extractive wine, the tannins forceful and needing to settle. **RATING** 89 **DRINK** 2023 **$** 30

Gold Dust Wines   NR

Southpark, Tallwood Road, Millthorpe, NSW 2798 **REGION** Orange
T (02) 6366 5168 **F** 902) 6361 9165 **OPEN** By appointment
WINEMAKER Contract **EST.** 1993 **CASES** 700
SUMMARY John and Jacqui Corrie have established 3 ha each of riesling and chardonnay, electing to sell two-thirds of the production, and have the remainder contract-made. Most of the wine is sold by mail order.

Golden Ball   ★★★★

1175 Beechworth–Wangaratta Road, Beechworth, Vic 3747 **REGION** Beechworth
T (03) 5727 0284 **OPEN** By appointment
WINEMAKER James McLaurin **EST.** 1996 **CASES** 625
SUMMARY The Golden Ball vineyard is established on one of the original land grants in the Beechworth region. The 2.4-ha vineyard was planted by James and Janine McLaurin in 1996, the major parts being cabernet sauvignon, shiraz and merlot, with lesser plantings of grenache and malbec. All the wines are vinified separately and aged in one-third new French oak, the remainder 2–3 years old. The low yields result in intensely flavoured wines which are to be found in a Who's Who of Melbourne's best restaurants and a handful of local and Melbourne retailers, including Randall's at Albert Park.

▼▼▼▼♀ **Gallice Beechworth Cabernet Merlot Malbec 2002** Medium to full-bodied; round, velvety, sweet black fruits; gentle oak, ripe tannins; delicious overall flavour. Cork. **RATING** 91 **DRINK** 2012 **$** 32

▼▼▼▼ **Beechworth Shiraz 2002** Light to medium-bodied; elegant, spicy, savoury, peppery notes to the black fruits; subtle oak; fine, powdery tannins. Quality cork. **RATING** 89 **DRINK** 2010 **$** 32

Golden Grape Estate   NR

Oakey Creek Road, Pokolbin, NSW 2321 **REGION** Lower Hunter Valley
T (02) 4998 7588 **F** (02) 4998 7730 **OPEN** 7 days 10–5

WINEMAKER Neil McGuigan (Consultant) **EST.** 1985 **CASES** NFP
SUMMARY German-owned and unashamedly directed at the tourist, with a restaurant, barbecue and picnic areas, a wine museum and a separate tasting room for bus tours. The substantial range of wines are of diverse origins and style. The operation now has over 42 ha of Hunter Valley plantings.

Golden Grove Estate ★★★

Sundown Road, Ballandean, Qld 4382 **REGION** Granite Belt
T (07) 4684 1291 **F** (07) 4684 1247 **OPEN** 7 days 9–5
WINEMAKER Sam Costanzo **EST.** 1993 **CASES** 10 000
SUMMARY Golden Grove Estate was established by Mario and Sebastiana Costanzo in 1946, producing stone fruits and table grapes for the fresh fruit market. The first wine grapes (shiraz) were planted in 1972, but it was not until 1985, when ownership passed to son Sam Costanzo and wife Grace, that the use of the property started to change. In 1993 chardonnay and merlot joined the shiraz, followed by cabernet sauvignon, sauvignon blanc and semillon. Wine quality has steadily improved; national (though limited) retail distribution.

ΥΥΥ **Chardonnay 2003** **RATING** 82 **$** 16

Golden Gully Wines NR

5900 Mid Western Highway, Mandurama, NSW 2792 **REGION** Orange
T (02) 6367 5148 **F** (02) 6367 4148 **OPEN** Weekends 10–4, or by appointment
WINEMAKER Contract **EST.** 1994 **CASES** 1300
SUMMARY Kevin and Julie Bate have progressively established over 5 ha of vineyard (2 ha cabernet sauvignon, 1.6 shiraz, 0.5 merlot and 0.5 each of semillon and sauvignon blanc). The first commercial crop came in 2001, but tiny makes in 1999 (Cabernet Shiraz) and 2000 (Cabernet Sauvignon) both won bronze medals at the Bathurst Cool Climate Wine Show.

Golden Mile Wines NR

47 Whitewood Drive, Upper Stuart, SA 5156 (postal) **REGION** Riverland
T (08) 8370 8041 **F** (08) 8370 8984 **OPEN** Not
WINEMAKER Tim Mader, Jane Mader **EST.** 2000 **CASES** NA
SUMMARY Tim and Jane Mader have set up what, by Riverland standard, is a micro-boutique, based on 8 ha of merlot and shiraz at Barmera. Part of the production is sold, part vinified for the Big River and Aged Vine Shiraz labels. The wine is chiefly sold by mail order.

Golders Vineyard ★★★★

Bridport Road, Pipers Brook, Tas 7254 **REGION** Northern Tasmania
T (03) 6395 4142 **F** (03) 6395 4142 **WEB** www.geocities.com/goldersvineyard **OPEN** By appointment
WINEMAKER Richard Crabtree **EST.** 1991 **CASES** 400
SUMMARY The initial plantings of 1.5 ha of pinot noir have been supplemented by a hectare of chardonnay. The quality of the Pinot Noir has been good from the initial vintage in 1995.

ΥΥΥΥ **Pinot Noir 2003** Considerable intensity and length; spicy, savoury fruit accents; lingering tannins. **RATING** 90 **DRINK** 2007 **$** 28

ΥΥΥΥ **Chardonnay 2004** Tangy, citrussy fruit typical of the vintage; crunchy acidity; good length. **RATING** 88 **DRINK** 2008 **$** 24

Gomersal Wines ★★★☆

Lyndoch Road, Gomersal, SA 5352 **REGION** Barossa Valley
T (08) 8563 3611 **F** (08) 8563 3776 **OPEN** 7 days 10–5
WINEMAKER Contract **EST.** 2000 **CASES** 2000
SUMMARY In 1887 Friedrich W Fromm planted the Wonganella Vineyards; he followed that with a winery on the edge of the Gomersal Creek in 1891. During the following 90 years the winery remained in operation. It was finally closed in 1983. In 2000 a group of friends 'with strong credentials in both the making and consumption end of the wine industry' bought the winery and re-

established the vineyard, planting 17 ha of shiraz, 2.25 ha of mourvedre and 1 ha of grenache via terraced bush vines. The Riesling comes from purchased grapes, the Grenache Rose, Grenache Shiraz Mataro and Shiraz from the replanted vineyard.

ŸŸŸŸ **Grenache Rose 2004** Vivid purple-red; fresh red cherry and raspberry; plenty of flavour, dry finish. Excellent value. **RATING** 89 **DRINK** Now $12
Shiraz 2003 Good fruit weight and richness; blackberry and plum; no tricks, traditional Barossa style; little oak influence. **RATING** 89 **DRINK** 2010 $18

ŸŸŸŸ **Riesling 2004** Pale straw; light thyme/herb nuances; slightly thin, but crisp. **RATING** 86 **DRINK** 2007 $12
Grenache Shiraz Mataro 2002 RATING 86 **DRINK** 2007 $16

Goona Warra Vineyard ★★★★☆

Sunbury Road, Sunbury, Vic 3429 **REGION** Sunbury
T (03) 9740 7766 **F** (03) 9744 7648 **WEB** www.goonawarra.com.au **OPEN** 7 days 10–5
WINEMAKER John Barnier, Mark Matthews **EST.** 1863 **CASES** 3000
SUMMARY A historic stone winery, established under this name by a 19th-century Victorian premier. A brief interlude as part of The Wine Investment Fund in 2001 is over, the Barniers having bought back the farm. Excellent tasting facilities; an outstanding venue for weddings and receptions; Sunday lunch is also served. Exports to the UK.

ŸŸŸŸŸ **Sunbury Shiraz 2002** Strong colour; black cherry, spice, licorice and blackberry; archetypal cool-grown Shiraz; tannins fine but ripe, giving great mouthfeel. High-quality cork. **RATING** 94 **DRINK** 2015 $29.50

ŸŸŸŸ **Sunbury Cygnet 2001** Medium-bodied; complex, spicy, earthy, savoury interplay with blackcurrant fruits; tannins still resolving. High-quality cork. Merlot/Cabernet Franc/Cabernet Sauvignon. **RATING** 90 **DRINK** 2014 $45

ŸŸŸŸ **Sunbury Semillon Sauvignon Blanc 2004** Crisp, clean, grass, herb and mineral; fresh palate, crisp acid; will grow. Screwcap. **RATING** 88 **DRINK** 2009 $18.50
Sunbury Roussanne Chardonnay 2003 Glowing green-yellow; smooth mouthfeel, though not high-toned or aromatic; questionable synergy in the blend. Screwcap. **RATING** 88 **DRINK** 2007 $29.50

ŸŸŸŸ **Sunbury Baldini Rose 2004 RATING** 86 **DRINK** Now $16

Goorambath ★★★★

103 Hooper Road, Goorambat, Vic 3725 **REGION** Glenrowan
T (03) 5764 1380 **F** (03) 5764 1320 **WEB** www.goorambath.com.au **OPEN** By appointment
WINEMAKER David Hodgson **EST.** 1997 **CASES** 650
SUMMARY Lyn and Geoff Bath have had a long association with the Victorian wine industry. Since 1982 Geoff Bath has been senior lecturer in viticulture with the University of Melbourne at Dookie campus; he and wife Lyn also owned (in conjunction with two other couples) a vineyard at Whitlands for 18 years. In July 2000 they sold their interest in that vineyard to focus on their small vineyard at Goorambat, hence the clever name. Planting had begun in 1998 with 1 ha of shiraz, subsequently joined by 1 ha of verdelho, 0.5 ha of orange muscat and 0.2 ha of tannat.

ŸŸŸŸ **Shiraz 2003** Ultra-powerful, slightly rustic; blackberry and spice fruit; powerful tannins yet to fully integrate. Quality cork. **RATING** 89 **DRINK** 2010 $18

Gordon Sunter Wines NR

PO Box 12, Tanunda, SA 5352 **REGION** Barossa Valley
T (08) 8563 2349 **OPEN** Not
WINEMAKER Stuart Blackwell **EST.** 1982 **CASES** NA
SUMMARY Gordon Sunter Wines has lived a shadowy existence for over 20 years, as the part-time private label of St Hallett winemaker Stuart Blackwell. The deliberately low profile is not hard to understand.

Goulburn Terrace ★★★

340 High Street, Nagambie, Vic 3608 **REGION** Goulburn Valley
T (03) 5794 2828 **F** (03) 5794 1854 **WEB** www.goulburnterrace.com.au **OPEN** Weekends 10–5
WINEMAKER Dr Mike Boudry, Greta Moon **EST.** 1993 **CASES** 1000
SUMMARY Dr Mike Boudry and Greta Moon have established their 7-ha vineyard on the west bank of the Goulburn River, around 8 km south of Lake Nagambie. Planting began in 1993; chardonnay on the alluvial soils (10 000 years old, adjacent to the river), and cabernet sauvignon on a gravelly rise based on 400 million-year-old Devonian rocks. The wines are made in small volumes, with open fermentation and hand plunging of the reds; all are basket pressed. The wines are sold by mail order, and at the cellar door in High Street, Nagambie.

▼▼▼▼ **Chardonnay 2003** Light to medium-bodied; pleasant stone fruit and subtle oak inputs; good acidity provides length. **RATING** 87 **DRINK** Now $ 22

▼▼▼▽ **Cabernet Sauvignon 2001 RATING** 85 **DRINK** 2010 $ 25
Midnight Shiraz 2001 RATING 84 **DRINK** 2007 $ 22

▼▼▼ **Cabernet Pressings 2001 RATING** 83 $ 18

Goulburn Valley Estate Wines ★★☆

340 Trotter Road, Mooroopna North, Vic 3629 **REGION** Goulburn Valley
T (03) 5829 0278 **F** (03) 5829 0014 **OPEN** By appointment
WINEMAKER Rocky Scarpari **EST.** 2001 **CASES** NA
SUMMARY Rocky Scarpari heads Goulburn Valley Estate Wines, the wine being under the direction of the vastly experienced Lee Clarnette. Goulburn Valley Estate has a nominal 1.2 ha of vines; the major part of its substantial production comes from growers in the Mooroopna area. The wines are sold under the Goulburn Shed brand, with exports to Hong Kong and Malaysia, and limited cellar door and mail order sales.

Goundrey ★★★★

Muirs Highway, Mount Barker, WA 6324 **REGION** Mount Barker
T (08) 9892 1777 **F** (08) 9851 1997 **WEB** www.goundreywines.com.au **OPEN** 7 days 10–4.30
WINEMAKER David Martin, Michael Perkins, Stephen Craig **EST.** 1976 **CASES** 375 000
SUMMARY Jack Bendat acquired Goundrey when it was on its knees; through significant expenditure on land, vineyards and winery capacity, it became the House that Jack Built. In late 2002 it was acquired by Vincor, Canada's largest wine producer, for a price widely said to be more than $30 million, a sum which would have provided Bendat with a very satisfactory return on his investment. National distribution; exports to all major markets.

▼▼▼▼▽ **Reserve Cabernet Sauvignon 2002** Medium-bodied; nicely proportioned blackcurrant/cassis fruit; subtle oak; good length and tannins. **RATING** 90 **DRINK** 2012 $ 34

▼▼▼▼ **Homestead Riesling 2004** Big, full, robust, strongly flavoured wine; slightly old-fashioned. Screwcap. **RATING** 89 **DRINK** 2008 $ 14.99
Offspring Shiraz 2003 Medium-bodied; attractive red and black fruits; fine tannins, minimal oak. Great Southern/Margaret River. Screwcap. **RATING** 88 **DRINK** 2010 $ 19.99
Homestead Sauvignon Blanc Semillon 2004 Solid, quite ripe mid-palate fruit; lemony acidity. **RATING** 87 **DRINK** 2009 $ 14.99

▼▼▼▽ **Homestead Unwooded Chardonnay 2004 RATING** 86 **DRINK** Now $ 14.99
Fox River Shiraz 2002 RATING 86 **DRINK** 2009 $ 13
Homestead Shiraz Cabernet 2002 RATING 86 **DRINK** 2009 $ 14.99
Fox River Cabernet Shiraz 2002 RATING 86 **DRINK** 2007 $ 15
Langton Margaret River Sauvignon Blanc Semillon 2003 RATING 85 **DRINK** Now $ 14.99
WA Cabernet Merlot 2002 RATING 85 **DRINK** 2007 $ 14.99
Homestead Chenin Blanc 2004 RATING 84 $ 14.99

▼▼▼ **Fox River Classic White 2004 RATING** 83 $ 15

Governor Robe Selection ★★★

Waterhouse Range Vineyards, Lot 11 Old Naracoorte Road, Robe, SA 5276
REGION Limestone Coast Zone
T (08) 8768 2083 **F** (08) 8768 2190 **WEB** www.waterhouserange.com.au **OPEN** At The Attic House,
Victoria Street, Robe
WINEMAKER Cape Jaffa Wines (Contract) **EST.** 1998 **CASES** 2500
SUMMARY Brothers Bill and Mick Quinlan-Watson, supported by a group of investors, began the
development of Waterhouse Range Vineyards Pty Ltd in 1995, planting 15 ha of vines that year, with
further plantings over the following few years lifting the total area under vine to just under 60 ha.
The majority of the grapes are sold; what is retained is contract-made at Cape Jaffa winery. The
unusual name comes from the third Governor of South Australia, Frederick Holt Robe, who in 1845
selected the site for a port and personally put in the first survey peg at Robe.

TTTT **Shiraz 2002** Plenty of plum and blackberry fruit; ripe tannins; a little too much oak.
RATING 87 **DRINK** 2010 $ 22

TTT **Unwooded Chardonnay 2003** **RATING** 80 $ 15

Governor's Choice Winery NR

Berghofer Road, Westbrook via Toowoomba, Qld 4350 **REGION** Queensland Zone
T (07) 4630 6101 **F** (07) 4630 6701 **WEB** www.governorschoice.com.au **OPEN** 7 days 9–5
WINEMAKER James Yates **EST.** 1999 **CASES** 1500
SUMMARY This is a part winery, part premium guesthouse accommodation venture situated 18 km
from the town of Toowoomba. The estate plantings (3 ha) produce chardonnay, shiraz, verdelho,
cabernet sauvignon and malbec, made onsite and sold through the cellar door or to those using the
accommodation.

Gowrie Mountain Estate ★★★

2 Warrego Highway, Kingsthorpe, Qld 4400 **REGION** Darling Downs
T (07) 4630 0566 **F** (07) 4630 0366 **OPEN** 7 days 10–5
WINEMAKER Peter Howland, Rod McPherson (Contract) **EST.** 1998 **CASES** 6000
SUMMARY Situated northeast of Toowoomba, in the heart of the Darling Downs, this is a substantial
new entrant, having already established 32 ha to mainstream varieties, and to the new breed in the
form of tempranillo (4 ha) and gamay (2 ha). Part of the production goes to Peter Howland in the
Hunter Valley, who makes the red wines, and part to Preston Peak, where the white wines and
Tempranillo are made. An underground barrel and bottled wine storage area has been completed,
with a sales, restaurant and general tourist facility planned. All the Newberry family members,
headed by father Ron, are involved in the venture.

TTTT **Verdelho 2003** **RATING** 85 **DRINK** Now $ 16

TTT **Chardonnay 2002** **RATING** 83 $ 18

Gracedale Hills Estate ★★★★☆

770 Healesville–Kooweerup Road, Healesville, Vic 3777 **REGION** Yarra Valley
T (03) 5967 3403 **F** (03) 5967 3581 **OPEN** Not
WINEMAKER Gary Mills (Contract) **EST.** 1996 **CASES** 250
SUMMARY Dr Richard Gutch has established 1.2 ha of chardonnay and 2 ha of shiraz at a time when
most would be retiring from active business, but it represents the culmination of a life-long love of
fine wine, and Richard has no hard feelings towards me – it was I who encouraged him, in the mid-
1990s to plant vines on the north-facing slopes of his property. Here, too, the grapes have been sold to
others, but he is now retaining sufficient to make around 250 cases a year.

TTTTT **Hill Paddock Yarra Valley Chardonnay 2003** Shows the best side of wild yeast
fermentation, giving a complex but fine, minerally cast to the fruit and mouthfeel; long,
clean, classy finish; excellent French oak use. Cork. **RATING** 94 **DRINK** 2008 $ 25

ƳƳƳƳ **Hill Paddock Yarra Valley Shiraz 2003** Light to medium-bodied; elegant cool-grown Shiraz style; red fruits, spice and pepper; fine tannins, subtle French oak. **RATING** 89 **DRINK** 2008 $ 25

Grace Devlin Wines ★★★

53 Siddles Road, Redesdale, Vic 3444 **REGION** Heathcote
T (03) 5425 3101 **OPEN** By appointment
WINEMAKER Brian Paterson, Lee Paterson **EST.** 1998 **CASES** 200
SUMMARY Brian and Lee Paterson have 2 ha of cabernet sauvignon and 0.5 ha of merlot at Redesdale. It is one of the most southerly vineyards in the Heathcote region, and most of the vines are over 12 years old. The name comes from the middle names of Brian Paterson's grandmother, mother and daughters. Although production is small, it is available in a number of local outlets.

ƳƳƳƳ **Cabernet Sauvignon 2003** **RATING** 85 **DRINK** 2008 $ 20

Gralaine Vineyard ★★★★

65 Feehan's Road, Mount Duneed, Vic 3216 (postal) **REGION** Geelong
T 0429 009 973 **F** (03) 9886 7377 **OPEN** At Hanging Rock Winery
WINEMAKER John Ellis (Hanging Rock Winery) **EST.** 1983 **CASES** NA
SUMMARY Graeme and Elaine Carroll have gradually established 4 ha of low-yielding merlot (with a few cabernet sauvignon vines). There are no cellar door sales, but the wine can be tasted at Hanging Rock Winery.

ƳƳƳƳƳ **Cabernet Sauvignon 2001** Clean, fragrant and elegant; cassis and redcurrant fruit off-set by well-balanced and integrated oak. **RATING** 94 **DRINK** 2009

ƳƳƳƳ **Merlot 2001** **RATING** 85 **DRINK** Now

Gralyn Estate ★★★★☆

Caves Road, Wilyabrup, WA 6280 **REGION** Margaret River
T (08) 9755 6245 **F** (08) 9755 6136 **WEB** www.gralyn.com.au **OPEN** 7 days 10.30–4.30
WINEMAKER Graham Hutton, Merilyn Hutton, Bradley Hutton **EST.** 1975 **CASES** 2500
SUMMARY The move from primarily fortified wine to table wine production has been completed, and has brought considerable success. The red wines are made in a distinctively different style from most of those from the Margaret River region, with an opulence (in part from American oak) which is reminiscent of some of the bigger wines from McLaren Vale. The age of the vines (30 years) and the site are also significant factors. Exports to the US.

ƳƳƳƳƳ **Cabernet Sauvignon 2003** Very good colour; classic cassis and blackcurrant varietal character; medium to full-bodied; balanced, persistent but fine tannins. Good oak. High-quality cork. **RATING** 94 **DRINK** 2010 $ 90

ƳƳƳƳƳ **Reserve Shiraz 2003** Slightly finer and more spicy/savoury than the Old Vine; medium to full-bodied; long and balanced palate, though far from ready. Cork. **RATING** 93 **DRINK** 2015 $ 60
Old Vine Shiraz 2003 Medium to full-bodied; powerful blackberry fruit; full-on extract and tannins; oak in the background. Quality cork. **RATING** 92 **DRINK** 2015 $ 60
Single Barrel Reserve 2003 While elegant, quite dry tannins need to soften before the fruit, and it is not entirely certain that they will. Shiraz/Cabernet Sauvignon. High-quality cork. **RATING** 90 **DRINK** 2018 $ 90

Grampians Estate ★★★★★

Mafeking Road, Willaura, Vic 3379 **REGION** Grampians
T (03) 5354 6245 **F** (03) 5354 6257 **WEB** www.grampiansestate.com.au **OPEN** By appointment
WINEMAKER Simon Clayfield (Contract) **EST.** 1989 **CASES** 1000
SUMMARY Over a decade ago local farmers and graziers Sarah and Tom Guthrie decided to diversify their activities, while continuing to run their fat lamb and wool production. So they planted 2 ha of shiraz and 1.2 ha of chardonnay, and opened the Thermopylae Host Farm business. This offers two farm-stay buildings, a 5 bedroom shearer's cottage which sleeps 12, and a 5 room miner's cottage

which sleeps 10. They also secured the services of immensely experienced local winemaker Simon Clayfield to produce the Grampians Estate wines. These are sold to those who stay on the farm, which is able to offer an unusually wide range of activities; the wines are also available by direct mail order and at one or two local hotels, including the Kookaburra Rest at Halls Gap.

ㅗㅗㅗㅗㅗ **Streeton Reserve Shiraz 2001** Holding hue well; medium to full-bodied; excellent focus and intensity, with a mix of predominantly black fruits and some spices; notably long finish. **RATING** 94 **DRINK** 2016 $ 45

Grancari Estate Wines ★★★☆

50 Northumberland Road, Onkaparinga Hills, SA 5163 **REGION** McLaren Vale
T (08) 8382 4465 **F** (08) 8382 4465 **OPEN** By appointment
WINEMAKER Rino Ozzella, Greta Ozzella, James Hastwell (Consultant) **EST.** 1999 **CASES** 3000
SUMMARY In 1983 Rino and Greta Ozzella purchased a small vineyard in McLaren Vale which had been planted in the early 1940s to a little under 3 ha of grenache; the grapes were sold to other winemakers. In 1993 the Ozzellas purchased two properties at Loxton in the Riverland. After 3 years developing the vineyards there, the Ozzellas sold the blocks and returned to McLaren Vale. They planted a further 2.5 ha of shiraz on a westerly slope facing the sea, and decided to establish their own brand. At the same time they began the conversion to organic production, which has now been certified (in conversion). Production has increased significantly, from 850 to 3000 cases.

Grandview Vineyard ★★★

59 Devlyns Road, Birchs Bay, Tas 7162 **REGION** Southern Tasmania
T (03) 6267 4099 **F** (03) 6267 4779 **WEB** www.grandview.au.com **OPEN** 7 days 10–5
WINEMAKER Andrew Hood (Contract) **EST.** 1996 **CASES** 350
SUMMARY Ryan Hartshorn has acquired the vineyard formerly burdened by the impossible name 2 Bud Spur. It is a pocket-handkerchief mix of varieties: 0.35 ha gewurztraminer, 0.7 ha chardonnay, 0.6 ha pinot noir, 0.3 ha sauvignon blanc and 0.05 ha gamay which are now organic.

ㅗㅗㅗ **Chardonnay 2003 RATING** 83 $ 25

Granite Hills ★★★★☆

1481 Burke & Wills Track, Baynton, Kyneton, Vic 3444 **REGION** Macedon Ranges
T (03) 5423 7264 **F** (03) 5423 7288 **WEB** www.granitehills.com.au **OPEN** Mon–Sat 10–6, Sun 12–6
WINEMAKER Llew Knight, Ian Gunter **EST.** 1970 **CASES** 7000
SUMMARY Granite Hills is one of the enduring classics, pioneering the successful growing of riesling and shiraz in an uncompromisingly cool climate. It is based on 11 ha of riesling, chardonnay, shiraz, cabernet sauvignon, merlot and pinot noir (the last used in its sparkling wine). After a quiet period in the 1990s, it has been reinvigorated, with its original two icons once again to the fore. The Rieslings age superbly, and the shiraz is at the forefront of the cool-climate school in Australia. Exports to the US and the UK.

ㅗㅗㅗㅗㅗ **Knight Macedon Ranges Riesling 2004** Delicate, fine, fresh, super-elegant; flowing lime juice and passionfruit; will grow in bottle over a decade. Screwcap. **RATING** 94 **DRINK** 2014 $ 20

ㅗㅗㅗㅗㅗ **Knight Macedon Ranges Chardonnay 2004** Bright green-yellow; lively, quite intense grapefruit and melon; delicate finish; excellent unwooded style. Screwcap. **RATING** 90 **DRINK** 2008 $ 18

ㅗㅗㅗㅗ **Knight Macedon Ranges Merlot 2003** Light to medium-bodied; fine, savoury black olive and blackcurrant fruit; fine tannins; harmonious mouthfeel. Screwcap. **RATING** 89 **DRINK** 2008 $ 24

ㅗㅗㅗㅗ **Knight Macedon Ranges Cabernet Sauvignon 2002 RATING** 86 **DRINK** 2008 $ 26

Granite Ridge Wines ★★★★

Sundown Road, Ballandean, Qld 4382 **REGION** Granite Belt
T (07) 4684 1263 **F** (07) 4684 1250 **WEB** www.graniteridgewines.com.au **OPEN** 7 days 9–5
WINEMAKER Dennis Ferguson, Juliane Ferguson **EST.** 1995 **CASES** 1500

SUMMARY Formerly known as Denlana Ferguson Estate Wines, Granite Ridge had considerable success in the mid-1990s. Its Goldies Unwooded Chardonnay was the first Queensland wine to be chosen as the official Parliamentary Wine of the Queensland Government. Most of the production comes from its 5-ha vineyard, which is planted to pinot gris, chardonnay, verdelho, merlot, shiraz, petit verdot, tempranillo and cabernet sauvignon.

ŢŢŢŢŸ **Crystals Sauvignon Blanc Semillon 2004** Fine, elegant and crisp; entirely fruit-driven, with bright and frisky lemon/mineral fruit. **RATING** 93 **DRINK** 2007 $ 20
Traminer 2004 Surprising lychee and spice varietal fruit; very well made; clean and fresh.
RATING 92 **DRINK** 2007 $ 18

ŢŢŢŢ **The Ridge Cabernet Sauvignon Merlot 2002** Big, powerful, rich and chunky black fruits; slightly rustic. **RATING** 87 **DRINK** 2008 $ 18
Bilby Red 2002 Lots of chocolate; a mix of ripe and less ripe fruit; moderate length.
RATING 87 **DRINK** 2010 $ 16

ŢŢŢŸ **Goldies Unwooded Chardonnay 2004 RATING** 86 **DRINK** Now $ 14
Verdelho 2004 RATING 84 **DRINK** Now $ 14

ŢŢŢ **Granite Rock Shiraz 2002 RATING** 83 $ 20
First Oak Chardonnay 2003 RATING 82 $ 18

Grant Burge   ★★★★☆

Jacobs Creek, Barossa Valley, SA 5352 **REGION** Barossa Valley
T (08) 8563 3700 **F** (08) 8563 2807 **WEB** www.grantburgewines.com.au **OPEN** 7 days 10–5
WINEMAKER Grant Burge **EST.** 1988 **CASES** 200 000
SUMMARY As one might expect, this very experienced industry veteran makes consistently good, full-flavoured and smooth wines chosen from the pick of the crop of his extensive vineyard holdings, which total an impressive 200 ha; the immaculately restored/rebuilt stone cellar door sales buildings are another attraction. The provocatively named the Holy Trinity (Grenache/Shiraz/Mourvedre) joins Shadrach and Meshach at the top of the range. In 1999 Grant Burge repurchased the farm from Mildara Blass by acquiring the Krondorf winery (not the brand) in which he made his first fortune. He has renamed it Barossa Vines (it is in Krondorf Road, Tanunda) and, taking advantage of the great views it offers, has opened a cellar door offering casual food, featuring local produce wherever possible. A third cellar door (Illaparra) is open at Murray Street, Tanunda. Exports to the UK, Europe, the US, Canada and Asia.

ŢŢŢŢŢ **Meshach Shiraz 2001** Skilful winemaking; a fusion of sweet black fruits and oak; fine tannins, balance and length; great finesse. **RATING** 95 **DRINK** 2016 $ 99

ŢŢŢŢŸ **Thorn Vineyard Riesling 2004** Lime, spice and herb; fine and elegant; long palate and finish. **RATING** 92 **DRINK** 2010 $ 16.50
Summers Eden Valley Chardonnay 2003 Delicious wine; supple melon and fig; good line and length; balanced oak. **RATING** 92 **DRINK** 2007 $ 19
Cameron Vale Cabernet Sauvignon 2002 Clean, sweet cassis and black fruits with neatly juxtaposed fruit, oak and tannins; medium-bodied, good length. **RATING** 91 **DRINK** 2010 $ 19.80
Lily Farm Frontignac 2004 Lots of vivacious tropical fruits with a twist of lemon on an appealing sweet finish; as good as they come; great bargain; Chinese food special. **RATING** 90 **DRINK** Now $ 12

ŢŢŢŢ **Barossa Vines Riesling 2004** Generous citrus/lime aromas and flavours carry through to the finish; lots of weight; good value. **RATING** 89 **DRINK** 2009 $ 9.95
Hillcott Merlot 2003 Spicy, savoury varietal character plus 10% Cabernet input; medium-bodied; fine tannins, subtle oak. **RATING** 89 **DRINK** 2008 $ 18.95
Shadrach Cabernet Sauvignon 2000 Uncertain colour; spice, herb, berry and leaf; overall, reflects the vintage. **RATING** 88 **DRINK** 2007 $ 45
Pinot Noir Chardonnay NV Generously flavoured; quite ripe fruit flavours and creamy cashew notes; ready to roll. **RATING** 88 **DRINK** Now $ 19.50
Zerk Semillon 2004 Full flavoured and rich; skin contact and oak; in particular style.
RATING 87 **DRINK** Now $ 16.50
Adelaide Hills Viognier 2003 Well balanced and quite rich; solid pastille/spice/musk/apricot varietal characters. **RATING** 87 **DRINK** Now $ 19.90

Barossa Vines Shiraz 2003 Direct, straightforward plum and blackberry fruit; doesn't show 14.5° alcohol; fine tannins. Twin Top. **RATING** 87 **DRINK** 2008 $14.90

TTTT **Barossa Vines Semillon 2004** **RATING** 86 **DRINK** Now $9.95
Barossa Vines Semillon Sauvignon Blanc 2004 **RATING** 86 **DRINK** Now $12
Adelaide Hills Pinot Grigio 2003 **RATING** 86 **DRINK** Now $19.90
Tawny Tawny Port NV **RATING** 86 **DRINK** Now $14
Barossa Vines Chardonnay 2004 **RATING** 85 **DRINK** Now $12

Grassy Point/Coatsworth Wines ★★★★

145 Coatsworth Road, Portarlington, Vic 3223 **REGION** Geelong
T 0409 429 608 **WEB** www.grassypointwines.com.au **OPEN** Weekends & public hols 11–5
WINEMAKER Dr Paul Champion (Mermerus) **EST.** 1997 **CASES** 500
SUMMARY Partners David Smith and Robert Bennett and Kerry Jones purchased this 32-ha undeveloped grazing property in 1997. Coatsworth Farm, as the property is known, now has 7.4 ha of vines (chardonnay, sauvignon blanc, pinot noir, shiraz, merlot, malbec and cabernet franc), South Devon beef cattle and Perendale/White Suffolk-cross lambs. The first crops were sold to Mermerus, but have since been made by Dr Paul Champion for Grassy Point.

TTTTT **Grassy Point Bellarine Peninsula Sauvignon Blanc 2004** Clean, fresh, clear kiwifruit/passionfruit aromas and flavours; bright and lively palate; crisp, clean finish. **RATING** 92 **DRINK** Now $16
Grassy Point Bellarine Peninsula Chardonnay 2003 Complex rich fruit supported by gentle oak handling; abundant ripe, sweet stone fruit on the mid-palate; cleansing finish. **RATING** 90 **DRINK** 2008 $18

TTTT **Grassy Point Bellarine Peninsula Rose 2004** Spotlessly clean, bright pink; drier style, with punchy acidity on the finish after red fruits on the mid-palate. **RATING** 87 **DRINK** Now $14

TTTY **Grassy Point Bellarine Peninusla Shiraz 2003** **RATING** 85 **DRINK** 2008 $18
Grassy Point Bellarine Peninsula Pinot Noir 2003 **RATING** 84 **DRINK** Now $18

TTY **Grassy Point Bellarine Peninsula Cabernets 2002** **RATING** 79 $17

Great Lakes Wines NR

115 Herivals Road, Wootton, NSW 2423 **REGION** Northern Rivers Zone
T (02) 4997 7255 **F** (02) 4997 7450 **OPEN** 7 days 10–5
WINEMAKER David Hook (Contract), Steve Attkins **EST.** 1990 **CASES** NA
SUMMARY Great Lakes Wines is situated south of the Hastings River region but well north of Newcastle. Robyn Piper and Steve Attkins have 4 ha of semillon, chardonnay, verdelho, cabernet sauvignon, shiraz and chambourcin planted, and make the wine onsite with David Hook overseeing proceedings. The wines are sold by mail order and through the cellar door, which offers light meals, and barbecue and picnic facilities.

Green Ant Wines ★★★☆

Dookie–Malinga Road, Dookie, Vic 3646 **REGION** Central Victoria Zone
T (03) 5833 9295 **F** (03) 5833 9296 **WEB** www.greenantwines.com **OPEN** By appointment
WINEMAKER Anthony Lacy **EST.** 2005 **CASES** 5000
SUMMARY This is a separate, stand-alone venture of Anthony Lacy (winemaker at Yengari Wine Company), using contract-grown grapes from Rutherglen, Glenrowan, King Valley, Alpine Valley, Goulburn Valley and Nagambie.

TTTT **Barrel-Fermented Chardonnay 2002** Light to medium-bodied; sophisticated but gentle cashew, cream malolactic/barrel ferment inputs on melon and stone fruit. Twin Top. **RATING** 89 **DRINK** 2007 $14
Shiraz Cabernet 2003 Spicy, savoury black fruits, mocha, cedar and spice; underlying sweetness. Cork. **RATING** 87 **DRINK** 2009 $9.50

TTTY **Unoaked Chardonnay 2003** **RATING** 86 **DRINK** 2007 $9.50
Cabernet Merlot 2003 **RATING** 86 **DRINK** 2008 $14

Greenock Creek Wines

NR

Radford Road, Seppeltsfield, SA 5360 **REGION** Barossa Valley
T (08) 8562 8103 **F** (08) 8562 8259 **OPEN** Wed–Mon 11–5 when wine available
WINEMAKER Michael Waugh **EST.** 1978 **CASES** 2500
SUMMARY Michael and Annabelle Waugh are disciples of Rocky O'Callaghan of Rockford Wines, and have deliberately accumulated a series of old dryland, low-yielding Barossa vineyards, aiming to produce wines of unusual depth of flavour and character. They have succeeded handsomely in this aim, achieving icon status and stratospheric prices in the US, making the opinions of Australian scribes irrelevant. They also offer superior accommodation in 'Miriam's' the ancient but beautifully restored 2-bedroom cottage; Michael Waugh is a skilled stonemason.

Green Valley Vineyard

★★★★

3137 Sebbes Road, Forest Grove, WA 6286 **REGION** Margaret River
T (08) 9757 7510 **F** (08) 9757 7510 **WEB** www.greenvalleyvineyard.com.au **OPEN** 7 days 10–6
WINEMAKER Moss Wood (Contract) **EST.** 1980 **CASES** 3500
SUMMARY Owners Ed and Eleanore Green began developing Green Valley Vineyard in 1980. It is still a part-time operation, production has grown steadily from the 7.7 ha of vines, and the Cabernet Sauvignon has been a consistent medal winner. Exports to Singapore and the US.

Gregory's Wines

★★★☆

1 Lizard Park Drive, Kilkerran, SA 5573 **REGION** The Peninsulas Zone
T (08) 8834 1258 **F** (08) 8834 1287 **OPEN** 7 days 10–4.30
WINEMAKER Stephen John (Contract) **EST.** 1997 **CASES** 500
SUMMARY Rod and Toni Gregory have established 11 ha of vineyard near Maitland, on the western side of the York Peninsula. The plantings are of chardonnay, viognier, shiraz and cabernet sauvignon, and are chiefly sold through the cellar door and by mail order. The site has facilities to cater for concerts or festivals, and tours by arrangement.

▼▼▼▼ **Barley Stacks The Peninsulas Shiraz 2003** Deep colour; ripe, black fruits off-set by a hint of olive and sweet oak; slight dip in the palate, then lengthens on the finish. **RATING** 89 **DRINK** 2010 $ 25
Barley Stacks The Peninsulas Shiraz 2002 Light to medium-bodied; tangy, spicy, savoury, with hints of olive and leaf; has length, and brisk acidity. **RATING** 89 **DRINK** 2009 $ 25

▼▼▼ **Barley Stacks The Peninsulas Liqueur Chardonnay NV RATING** 83 $ 20

Grevillea Estate

★★★☆

Buckajo Road, Bega, NSW 2550 **REGION** South Coast Zone
T (02) 6492 3006 **F** (02) 6492 5330 **WEB** www.grevilleawines.com **OPEN** Sept–May Mon–Fri 9–5, weekends 10–5; June–Aug 7 days 10–4
WINEMAKER Nicola Collins **EST.** 1980 **CASES** 2000
SUMMARY A tourist-oriented winery which successfully sells all its production through the cellar door and local restaurants. The consistency and quality of the wines has improved out of sight; a further label redesign has also lifted the appeal.

Grey Sands

★★★★

Cnr Kerrisons Road/Frankford Highway, Glengarry, Tas 7275 **REGION** Northern Tasmania
T (03) 6396 1167 **F** (03) 6396 1153 **WEB** www.tassie.net.au/greysands **OPEN** Last Sunday of each month 10–5, or by appointment
WINEMAKER Bob Richter **EST.** 1989 **CASES** 800
SUMMARY Bob and Rita Richter began the establishment of Grey Sands in 1988, slowly increasing the plantings over the ensuing 10 years to the present total of 2.5 ha. The ultra-high density of 8900 vines per ha reflects the experience gained by the Richters during a 3-year stay in England, during which time they visited many vineyards across Europe, and Bob Richter's graduate diploma in wine from Roseworthy College.

ŸŸŸŸ♀ **Pinot Gris 2004** Classic Pinot Gris; faint pear and musk aromas and flavours; it is the excellent mouthfeel and squeaky acidity which do the work. Screwcap. **RATING** 93 **DRINK** 2009 $ 26

ŸŸŸ♀ **Merlot 2002** Tangy, earthy, spicy, lemony; green olive rather than black olive; nice structure. Cork. **RATING** 86 **DRINK** 2008 $ 30

🐚 Griffin Wines   NR

PO Box 221, Clarendon, SA 5157 **REGION** Adelaide Hills
T (08) 8377 1300 **F** (08) 8377 3015 **WEB** www.griffinwines.com **OPEN** Not
WINEMAKER Phil Christiansen, Shaw & Smith, Kangarilla Road (Contract) **EST.** 1997 **CASES** 1000
SUMMARY The Griffin family (Trevor, Tim, Mark and Val) planted 26.5 ha of pinot noir, chardonnay, sauvignon blanc, merlot and shiraz in 1997, having owned the property for over 30 years. It is situated 3 km from Kuitpo Hall; its 350-m elevation gives sweeping views south down the valley below. Part of the grape production is sold; a small amount is made offsite, and sold through the website.

Grosset   ★★★★★

King Street, Auburn, SA 5451 **REGION** Clare Valley
T (08) 8849 2175 **F** (08) 8849 2292 **WEB** www.grosset.com.au **OPEN** Wed–Sun 10–5 from 1st week of September for approx 6 weeks
WINEMAKER Jeffrey Grosset **EST.** 1981 **CASES** 9000
SUMMARY Jeffrey Grosset served part of his apprenticeship at the vast Lindeman Karadoc winery, moving from the largest to one of the smallest when he established Grosset Wines in its old stone winery. He now crafts the wines with the utmost care from grapes grown to the most exacting standards; all need a certain amount of time in bottle to achieve their ultimate potential, not the least the Rieslings and Gaia, which are among Australia's best examples of their kind. He is also a passionate advocate of the use of screwcaps on all wines. Exports to all major markets mean a continuous shortage of the wines in all markets.

ŸŸŸŸŸ **Polish Hill Riesling 2004** Potent lime and apple blossom aromas flow through into the palate, where flecks of herb and slate add to the complexity of the long finish. **RATING** 96 **DRINK** 2014 $ 39
Piccadilly Chardonnay 2003 Stylish and fragrant; incisive melon and stone fruit with seamless oak; clean, lingering finish. **RATING** 95 **DRINK** 2010 $ 54
Watervale Riesling 2004 Light green-yellow; spotlessly clean; classic Clare with great finesse and length; lime/tropical fruit; balanced acidity. **RATING** 94 **DRINK** 2014 $ 33
Semillon Sauvignon Blanc 2004 Glowing yellow-green; as ever, beautifully crafted and balanced, building flavour through the length of the palate. Clare semillon/Adelaide Hills sauvignon blanc. **RATING** 94 **DRINK** 2009 $ 30
Pinot Noir 2003 Bright red-purple; classic texture, weight, line and mouthfeel; a mix of small fruits and spice; long finish. **RATING** 94 **DRINK** 2008 $ 59.50
Gaia 2002 A vibrant array of red and blackcurrant/cassis fruit; substantial but fine and balanced tannins; good oak. **RATING** 94 **DRINK** 2022 $ 54.60

Grove Estate   ★★★★☆

Murringo Road, Young, NSW 2594 **REGION** Hilltops
T (02) 6382 6999 **F** (02) 6382 4527 **WEB** www.groveestate.com.au **OPEN** Weekends 10–5, or by appointment
WINEMAKER Tim Kirk, Chris Derrez (Clonakilla) **EST.** 1989 **CASES** 3000
SUMMARY A partnership of Brian Mullany, John Kirkwood and Mark Flanders has established a 30-ha vineyard planted to semillon, chardonnay, merlot, shiraz, cabernet sauvignon and zinfandel. Some of the grapes are sold (principally to Southcorp), but an increasing amount of very good and interesting wine is contract-made by Clonakilla for the Grove Estate label. Exports to the UK.

ŸŸŸŸŸ **The Cellar Block Shiraz 2003** Densely coloured; extremely concentrated, but not extractive or alcoholic (only 13.5°); a cascade of dark berry and chocolate fruits; a dash of Viognier all to the good. Low yield. **RATING** 94 **DRINK** 2018 $ 30

ŸŸŸŸŸ **Hilltops Semillon 2000** Straw-yellow; light to medium-bodied; toasty, honeyed development on the bouquet; fresh and lively in the mouth; excellent length courtesy of acidity. **RATING** 90 **DRINK** 2007 $ 20
The Partners Cabernet Sauvignon 2002 Fresh, fragrant, vibrant cassis, red/blackcurrant fruit; firm but balanced tannins. **RATING** 90 **DRINK** 2017 $ 19
Hilltops Zinfandel 2003 Dense colour; powerful, deep, concentrated and complex black fruits and a touch of licorice; ripe tannins; impressive. Points for patience. **RATING** 90 **DRINK** 2016 $ 17

ŸŸŸŸ **Murringo Way Chardonnay 2003** **RATING** 86 **DRINK** 2007 $ 15
Hilltops The Partners Cabernet Sauvignon Petit Verdot 2003 Huge potential, but unbalanced by overpowering tannins on the finish. **RATING** 86 **DRINK** 2007 $ 19

Grove Hill ★★★★

120 Old Norton Summit Road, Norton Summit, SA 5136 **REGION** Adelaide Hills
T (08) 8390 1437 **F** (08) 8390 1437 **OPEN** Sunday 11–5, or by appointment
WINEMAKER Neville Falkenberg (Contract) **EST.** 1978 **CASES** 500
SUMMARY Grove Hill is a heritage property established in 1846; the original homestead and outbuildings have been held by the same family since that time. Very tight, slow-developing wines.

ŸŸŸŸŸ **Adelaide Hills Riesling 2004** Light-bodied; clean apple, mineral, spice and slate; has length and focus. Screwcap. **RATING** 90 **DRINK** 2012 $ 22
Adelaide Hills Chardonnay 2002 Light green-straw; still restrained and elegant, but has more intensity than the '03; crisp, minerally acidity; still evolving. Stained cork. **RATING** 90 **DRINK** 2010 $ 40
Adelaide Hills Pinot Noir 2002 A complex mix of spicy, savoury, foresty, stemmy plum fruit; good length and balance; starting to open up. Quality cork. **RATING** 90 **DRINK** 2008 $ 40

ŸŸŸŸ **Adelaide Hills Marguerite Blanc de Noir 1997** Pale salmon; still very crisp and youthful; low dosage; has length, not depth (11.5° alcohol). **RATING** 87 **DRINK** 2010 $ 45

ŸŸŸŸ **Adelaide Hills Chardonnay 2003** Extremely tight minerally and restrained style; has length, but the flavour is yet to evolve. Dodgy cork. **RATING** 86 **DRINK** 2009 $ 40
Adelaide Hills Pinot Noir 2001 **RATING** 85 **DRINK** Now $ 40

Growlers Gully ★★★☆

354 Shaws Road, Merton, Vic 3715 **REGION** Upper Goulburn
T (03) 5778 9615 **F** (03) 5778 9615 **OPEN** Weekends & public hols 10–5, or by appointment
WINEMAKER MasterWineMakers (Contract) **EST.** 1997 **CASES** 380
SUMMARY Les and Wendy Oates began the establishment of the Growlers Gully vineyard in 1997, extending it in 1998 to a total of 4 ha of shiraz and 1 ha of cabernet sauvignon. It sits at an elevation of 375m on fertile brown clay loam soil. A rammed-earth cellar door sales outlet opened in early 2002, the aim is to offer light meals and barbecue facilities.

ŸŸŸŸ **Upper Goulburn Cabernet Sauvignon 2002** Slightly rustic/earthy/minty edges to blackberry/blackcurrant fruit; does have length and intensity. **RATING** 87 **DRINK** 2012 $ 18

ŸŸŸŸ **Cabernet Sauvignon Shiraz 2003** **RATING** 86 **DRINK** 2010 $ 18

Guichen Bay Vineyards ★★★☆

PO Box 582, Newport, NSW 2106 **REGION** Mount Benson
T (02) 9997 6677 **F** (02) 9997 6177 **WEB** www.guichenbay.com.au **OPEN** Not
WINEMAKER Contract **EST.** 2003 **CASES** 600
SUMMARY Guichen Bay Vineyards is one of the three adjacent vineyards known collectively as the Mount Benson Community Vineyards. Between 1997 and 2001, 120 ha of vines were planted to chardonnay, sauvignon blanc, shiraz, merlot and cabernet sauvignon. While the major part of the production is sold under long-term contracts, the three owners have obtained a producer's licence, so a small quantity of grapes is held back and made by local contract winemakers under the Guichen Bay Vineyards label.

ƟƟƟƟ **Mount Benson Shiraz 2003** Good purple-red colour; light to medium-bodied; black cherry and spice; fine tannins, but needs more flesh. **RATING** 89 **DRINK** 2010 $ 20

Haan Wines ★★★★★

Siegersdorf Road, Tanunda, SA 5352 **REGION** Barossa Valley
T (08) 8562 4590 **F** (08) 8562 4590 **WEB** www.haanwines.com.au **OPEN** Not
WINEMAKER Mark Jamieson (Contract) **EST.** 1993 **CASES** 5000
SUMMARY Hans and Fransien Haan established their business in 1993 when they acquired a 19-ha vineyard near Tanunda (since extended to 36.7 ha). The primary focus was on Merlot, in particular the luxury Merlot Prestige, supported by Semillon, Viognier and Shiraz. Exports to all major markets.

ƟƟƟƟƟ **Wilhelmus 2002** A 5-variety Bordeaux blend matured in a mix of new and 1-year-old French oak. All these components are perfectly synthesised and balanced, supported by fully ripe, velvety tannins giving the palate great length. **RATING** 95 **DRINK** 2015 $ 42
Merlot Prestige 2002 In Haan style, a fusion between fruit and oak; medium-bodied, long and fluid; clear-cut olive and berry varietal fruit, fine tannins. **RATING** 94 **DRINK** 2014 $ 38

ƟƟƟƟƟ **Viognier Prestige 2004** The bouquet is still to develop, but distinctive varietal fruit on the palate; pastille and some musk; sweetness ex alcohol. **RATING** 90 **DRINK** 2008 $ 35
Shiraz Prestige 2002 Unconvincing colour; medium-bodied; red and black fruits; controlled oak inputs. Slightly disappointing for the vintage. **RATING** 90 **DRINK** 2010 $ 40

Hackersley ★★★★☆

Ferguson Road, Dardanup, WA 6236 **REGION** Geographe
T (08) 9384 6247 **F** (08) 9383 3364 **WEB** www.hackersley.com.au **OPEN** Fri–Sun 10–4
WINEMAKER Tony Davis (Contract) **EST.** 1997 **CASES** 1000
SUMMARY Hackersley is a partnership between the Ovens, Stacey and Hewitt families, friends since their university days, and with (so they say) the misguided belief that growing and making their own wine would be cheaper than buying it. They found what they describe as a 'little piece of paradise in the Ferguson Valley just south of Dardanup', and in September 1998 they planted a little under 8 ha, extended in August 2000 to 9.5 ha of the mainstream varieties; interestingly, they turned their back on chardonnay. Most of the crop is sold to Houghton, but a small quantity of immaculately packaged wines have been made for release under the Hackersley label.

ƟƟƟƟƟ **Ferguson Valley Sauvignon Blanc 2004** Intense tropical gooseberry and lemon flavours hold through the length of the palate and aftertaste. Exceptional wine; great value. Screwcap. **RATING** 94 **DRINK** 2007 $ 16

ƟƟƟƟƟ **Ferguson Valley Shiraz 2002** Medium to full-bodied; blackberry, plum, licorice, spice and dark chocolate; ripe tannins, good oak. Slightly suspect cork. **RATING** 92 **DRINK** 2012 $ 20
Ferguson Valley Cabernet Sauvignon 2002 Medium-bodied; elegant, earthy, black olive cabernet fruit; good balance, line and length; judicious oak. Cork. **RATING** 91 **DRINK** 2015 $ 20
Semillon 2004 Fragrant herb and grass aromas plus a twist of lemon; fresh, well balanced. **RATING** 90 **DRINK** 2007 $ 19

ƟƟƟƟ **Merlot 2003** Elegant, light to medium-bodied, foresty savoury wine; easy, accessible style. **RATING** 88 **DRINK** 2008 $ 24.50

ƟƟƟƟ **Ferguson Valley Verdelho 2004** **RATING** 84 **DRINK** Now $ 19

Hahndorf Hill Winery ★★★★

Lot 10 Pains Road, Hahndorf, SA 5245 **REGION** Adelaide Hills
T (08) 8388 7512 **F** (08) 8388 7618 **WEB** www.hahndorfhillwinery.com.au **OPEN** 7 days 10–5
WINEMAKER Geoff Weaver (Consultant) **EST.** 2002 **CASES** 3000
SUMMARY Larry Jacobs and Marc Dobson, both originally from South Africa, purchased Hahndorf Hill Winery in January 2002. Jacobs gave up a career in intensive care medicine in 1988 when he purchased an abandoned property in Stellenbosch. He proceeded to establish one of Capetown's

best-known sauvignon blanc producers, Mulderbosch. When Mulderbosch was purchased at the end of 1996, the pair migrated to Australia and eventually found their way to Hahndorf Hill. A new winery was upgraded to deal with the ultra-strict effluent disposal requirements of the Adelaide Hills. Trollinger and lemberger were planted by the prior owners; both are rare German varieties.

▼▼▼▽ **Sauvignon Blanc 2004** Pale straw-green; a ghost of reduction dissipates on the tightly focused and balanced palate; apple, herb, spice and grass; excellent acidity and length. **RATING** 93 **DRINK** 2007 $18.50

▼▼▼▼ **Shiraz 2002** An undeveloped yet curiously light colour; supple red fruits, fine tannins and subtle oak; elegant style. **RATING** 89 **DRINK** 2010 $24
Lemberger 2002 Fresh, clean cherry, raspberry and a touch of mint; smooth, medium-bodied and well balanced; altogether promising. **RATING** 89 **DRINK** 2010 $24
Trollinger & Lemberger Rose 2004 Bright, light fuchsia; spice, wild berries and lemon; minerally, dry finish. **RATING** 88 **DRINK** 2007 $17.50

Haig   NR

Square Mile Road, Mount Gambier, SA 5290 **REGION** Mount Gambier
T (08) 8725 5414 **F** (08) 8725 5414 **OPEN** 7 days 11–5
WINEMAKER Martin Slocombe (Contract) **EST.** 1982 **CASES** 1000
SUMMARY The 4 ha of estate vineyards are planted on the rich volcanic soils near the slopes of the famous Blue Lake of Mt Gambier. I have neither seen nor tasted the wines.

Hainault   NR

255 Walnut Road, Bickley, WA 6076 **REGION** Perth Hills
T (08) 9293 8339 **WEB** www.hainault.com.au **OPEN** Weekends & public hols 11–5, or by appointment
WINEMAKER Tony Davis (Contract) **EST.** 1980 **CASES** 2200
SUMMARY Lyn and Michael Sykes became the owners of Hainault in 2002, after Bill Mackey and wife Vicki headed off elsewhere. The 11 ha of close-planted vines are hand-pruned and hand-picked, and the pinot noir is very sensibly used to make a sparkling wine, rather than a table wine. A restaurant is planned.

🐌 Halifax Wines   NR

Lot 501 Binney Road, McLaren Vale, Willunga, SA 5172 **REGION** McLaren Vale
T (08) 8557 1000 **F** (08) 8367 0333 **WEB** www.halifaxwines.com.au **OPEN** By appointment
WINEMAKER Peter Butcher **EST.** 2000 **CASES** 800
SUMMARY Halifax is owned and operated by Elizabeth Tasker (background in advertising and marketing) and Peter Butcher (20 years in the wine industry, in marketing, sales, distribution, education and winemaking). A passionate proponent of wine's 'sense of place', Peter has worked with some of Australia's most well-known winemakers – Jeffrey Grosset, Peter Leske, Mike Farmilo and Peter Gago – and has also been influenced by visits to France and Italy. Currently produces a single-vineyard Shiraz from 4 ha of estate plantings, with plans for a Shiraz/Cabernet Franc/Merlot blend and Vermentino (planted spring 2005).

🐌 Halina Brook Estate   NR

Bindoon Moora Road, Bindoon WA 6502 **REGION** Perth Hills
T (08) 9576 2030 **OPEN** By appointment
WINEMAKER Rayko Boehlke, Rob Marshall (Contract) **EST.** 2001 **CASES** NA
SUMMARY The Halina Brook Estate cellar door is in an old shearing shed with panoramic views of the Bindoon area. A little over 16 ha of verdelho, shiraz, chenin blanc and grenache is planted. The wines sell for $12.50.

Hamelin Bay   ★★★★★

McDonald Road, Karridale, WA 6288 **REGION** Margaret River
T (08) 9758 6779 **F** (08) 9758 6779 **WEB** www.hbwines.com.au **OPEN** 7 days 10–5
WINEMAKER Julian Scott **EST.** 1992 **CASES** 10 000

SUMMARY The 25-ha Hamelin Bay vineyard was established by the Drake-Brockman family. The initial releases were contract-made, but a winery with cellar door sales facility was opened in 2000; this has enabled an increase in production. Exports to all major markets.

ŸŸŸŸŸ **Five Ashes Reserve Chardonnay 2003** Clean and pure; excellent fruit and oak balance on the bouquet; the palate is more intense, long and penetrating than the varietal version; fruit forward. **RATING** 95 **DRINK** 2010 $ 42.23

Five Ashes Vineyard Chardonnay 2003 Elegant and harmonious; a subtle and balanced infusion of oak and malolactic fermentation influences; creamy, nutty, figgy; good length and balance. **RATING** 94 **DRINK** 2010 $ 42.25

ŸŸŸŸŸ **Five Ashes Reserve Shiraz 2001** Medium-bodied; a complex mix of spicy and riper red fruits; sure oak handling and tannin extract. **RATING** 91 **DRINK** 2011 $ 43

Five Ashes Reserve Sauvignon Blanc 2004 Extremely lively; CO_2 spritz needs to settle down, but there is ample minerally acidity and fruit flavour. **RATING** 90 **DRINK** 2007 $ 19

Five Ashes Reserve Cabernet Merlot 2002 A distinctive edge of olive aroma ex the Merlot; medium-bodied; quite savoury tannins; good length and persistence. **RATING** 90 **DRINK** 2012 $ 42.25

Rampant Red 2002 Attractive medium-bodied wine; sweet red and blackcurrant fruit; ripe tannins. **RATING** 90 **DRINK** 2008 $ 19.43

ŸŸŸŸ **Semillon Sauvignon Blanc 2004** Builds progressively through the palate to the finish after a slightly smoky/sweaty start; quite lemony, which is typical of the vintage. **RATING** 89 **DRINK** 2007 $ 19.43

Five Ashes Reserve Cabernet Sauvignon 2002 Strongly savoury/earthy overtones to both the bouquet and palate give a certain austerity; does have length. **RATING** 89 **DRINK** 2012 $ 43

ŸŸŸŸ **Rampant White 2004** **RATING** 85 **DRINK** 2007 $ 17

Hamiltons Bluff ★★★

Longs Corner Road, Canowindra, NSW 2804 **REGION** Cowra
T (02) 6344 2079 **F** (02) 6344 2165 **WEB** www.hamiltonsbluff.com.au **OPEN** By appointment
WINEMAKER Alasdair Sutherland (Contract) **EST.** 1995 **CASES** 2000
SUMMARY Hamiltons Bluff is owned and operated by the Andrews family, which planted 45 ha of vines in 1995, with the first crop in 1998. Cellar door sales opened in early 1999, heralding a new stage of development for the Cowra region. Chardonnay, Shiraz, Sangiovese and sparkling wines are made. Exports to the US.

Hamilton's Ewell Vineyards ★★★★★

Siegersdorf Vineyard, Barossa Valley Way, Nuriootpa, SA 5355 **REGION** Barossa Valley
T (08) 8231 0088 **F** (08) 8231 0355 **WEB** www.hamiltonewell.com.au **OPEN** 7 days 10–5
WINEMAKER Robert Hamilton **EST.** 1837 **CASES** 11 000
SUMMARY Mark Hamilton, an Adelaide lawyer by profession, is a sixth-generation direct descendant of Richard Hamilton, who arrived in South Australia in 1838 (a year after the State was proclaimed) and made his first wine in 1841. Hamilton's Ewell Vineyards remained in the family until 1979, when it was acquired by Mildara Blass, much to Mark Hamilton's dismay. Since 1991 he has set about building another Hamilton wine business by a series of astute vineyard acquisitions, and by buying back the name Hamilton's Ewell from Mildara. Most of the grapes are sold, but there is scope to increase production. Exports to the UK, the US and other major markets.

ŸŸŸŸŸ **Railway Shiraz 2002** Very ripe luscious plum, blackberry and blueberry; nice balancing tannins; good length; not over the top. **RATING** 94 **DRINK** 2015 $ 28

Fuller's Barn Shiraz 2002 Medium-bodied; supple, smooth; the beautiful balance and ripeness typical of 2002; blackberry and plum fruit; fine, silky tannins; subservient oak. Slightly stained cork. **RATING** 94 **DRINK** 2015 $ 39

ŸŸŸŸŸ **Fuller's Barn Shiraz 2001** Impressive depth of flavour; succulent black cherry and blackberry; subtle oak, long finish. **RATING** 93 **DRINK** 2016 $ 39

Stonegarden Eden Valley Riesling 2004 Strong regional lime aromas; intense, mouthfilling fruit; good length. **RATING** 90 **DRINK** 2011 $ 18

Stonegarden Shiraz Cabernet 2001 Medium to full-bodied; black fruits, spice and chocolate; persistent but ripe tannins; balanced oak. **RATING** 90 **DRINK** 2014 $18

Stonegarden Grenache Shiraz Mourvedre 2002 Clean and fresh; medium-bodied; fruit-driven throughout by raspberry and black cherry flavours. **RATING** 90 **DRINK** 2007 $18

▼▼▼▽ **Stonegarden Grenache Shiraz Mourvedre 2003** **RATING** 86 **DRINK** Now $18

Sturt River Cabernet Sauvignon 2002 **RATING** 85 **DRINK** 2007 $14

Stonegarden Chardonnay 2003 **RATING** 84 **DRINK** Now $18

Stonegarden Rose 2004 **RATING** 84 **DRINK** Now $18

▼▼▼ **Sturt River Chardonnay 2004** **RATING** 83 $14

Hanging Rock Winery ★★★★☆

88 Jim Road, Newham, Vic 3442 **REGION** Macedon Ranges
T (03) 5427 0542 **F** (03) 5427 0310 **WEB** www.hangingrock.com.au **OPEN** 7 days 10–5
WINEMAKER John Ellis **EST.** 1982 **CASES** 40 000
SUMMARY The Macedon area has proved very marginal in spots, and the Hanging Rock vineyards, with their lovely vista towards the Rock, are no exception. John Ellis has thus elected to source additional grapes from various parts of Victoria to produce an interesting and diverse range of varietals at different price points. The low-priced Rock series, with its bold packaging, has replaced the Picnic wines. Exports to the UK, Denmark, Sweden, Canada, New Zealand, Hong Kong, Singapore, The Philippines, Malaysia and Japan.

▼▼▼▼▼ **The Jim Jim Sauvignon Blanc 2004** Spotlessly clean aromas, with no hint of sweatiness; tropical passionfruit flavour, with good length and balance. **RATING** 94 **DRINK** 2007 $27

▼▼▼▼▽ **The Jim Jim Pinot Gris 2004** Outstanding example of the variety; fragrant aromas, with vibrant touch of acacia; great length. **RATING** 93 **DRINK** 2007 $25

The Jim Jim Gewurztraminer 2004 Intense; abundant fruit and spicy varietal character; fractionally short. **RATING** 92 **DRINK** 2007 $25

The Jim Jim Gewurztraminer 1998 Excellent green-yellow; not overmuch varietal character, but really good length and balance. Extraordinarily youthful. **RATING** 92 **DRINK** 2009 $25

Cambrian Rise Heathcote Shiraz 2002 Clean and supple; medium-bodied; attractive array of soft black fruits; good tannin and oak extract. **RATING** 90 **DRINK** 2012 $27

Hanging Tree Wines ★★★

Lot 2 O'Connors Road, Pokolbin, NSW 2321 **REGION** Lower Hunter Valley
T (02) 4998 6601 **F** (02) 4998 6602 **WEB** www.hangingtreewines.com.au **OPEN** By appointment
WINEMAKER Andrew Thomas (Contract) **EST.** 2003 **CASES** 1250
SUMMARY Hanging Tree Wines is the former Van De Scheur Estate. A little under 3 ha of semillon, chardonnay, shiraz and cabernet sauvignon provide the grapes for the wines.

▼▼▼▼ **Unwooded Chardonnay 2004** Plenty of peachy stone fruit flavour, and balanced oak inputs. **RATING** 87 **DRINK** Now $24

Hankin Estate ★★★☆

2 Johnsons Lane, Northwood via Seymour, Vic 3660 **REGION** Goulburn Valley
T (03) 5792 2396 **F** (03) 9353 2927 **OPEN** Weekends & public hols 10–5
WINEMAKER Dr Max Hankin **EST.** 1975 **CASES** 1700
SUMMARY Hankin Estate is now the principal occupation of Dr Max Hankin, who has retired from full-time medical practice. He has to contend with phylloxera, which decimated the original plantings, but has successfully replanted most of the vineyard.

Hanson-Tarrahill Vineyard ★★★★

49 Cleveland Avenue, Lower Plenty, Vic 3093 (postal) **REGION** Yarra Valley
T (03) 9439 7425 **F** (03) 9439 4217 **OPEN** Not
WINEMAKER Dr Ian Hanson **EST.** 1983 **CASES** 1300

SUMMARY Dental surgeon Ian Hanson planted his first vines in the late 1960s, close to the junction of the Yarra and Plenty Rivers; in 1983 those plantings were extended (with 3000 vines), and in 1988 the Tarrahill property at Yarra Glen was established with a further 4 ha. Hanson is the name which appears most prominently on the newly designed labels; Tarrahill Vineyard is in much smaller type. Exports to the UK.

♼♼♼♼♼ Tarra's Block Cabernets 2003 Clean, fresh, ripe redcurrant fruit; very good balance and structure; silky tannins. A style revolution for the vineyard; 95% Cabernet Franc, 5% Cabernet Sauvignon. **RATING** 92 **DRINK** 2015 $ 26

Happs ★★★★★

571 Commonage Road, Dunsborough, WA 6281 **REGION** Margaret River
T (08) 9755 3300 **F** (08) 9755 3846 **WEB** www.happs.com.au **OPEN** 7 days 10–5
WINEMAKER Erl Happ, Mark Warren **EST.** 1978 **CASES** 16 000
SUMMARY Former schoolteacher turned potter and winemaker Erl Happ is an iconoclast and compulsive experimenter. Many of the styles he makes are unusual, and the future is likely to be even more so: the Karridale vineyard planted in 1994 has no less than 28 different varieties established. Merlot has been a winery specialty for a decade. Limited retail distributed through New South Wales, Victoria and Queensland; exports to the US.

♼♼♼♼♼ Three Hills Shiraz 2002 Brilliant, full purple-red; excellent structure, texture and focus; supple black fruits, subtle oak and a long finish. **RATING** 95 **DRINK** 2017 $ 55
Three Hills Shiraz 2003 Deep colour; potent licorice, leather, spice and blackberry aromas and flavours; very good balance and length. Cork. **RATING** 94 **DRINK** 2018 $ 55

♼♼♼♼♼ Three Hills Charles Andreas Cabernet Sauvignon 2002 Very fine, elegant and savoury; long in the mouth; not the typical show style at all. **RATING** 93 **DRINK** 2012 $ 36
Margaret River Cabernets 2001 Quite rich; an amalgam of black fruits, chocolate and sweet earth; medium to full-bodied; good tannins. **RATING** 92 **DRINK** 2014 $ 20
Margaret River Semillon Sauvignon Blanc 2004 Light to medium-bodied; clean and fresh; gooseberry/grassy flavours; partial barrel fermentation giving more to texture than to flavour; good length. **RATING** 90 **DRINK** Now $ 16
Pinot Noir 2002 Light-bodied style, but very well balanced and long; gently savoury fruit. Skilled winemaking. **RATING** 90 **DRINK** 2007 $ 18
Three Hills Merlot 2003 Super-powerful and concentrated, somewhat over the top for the variety; exudes red and black fruits; needs taming in bottle. **RATING** 90 **DRINK** 2015 $ 36

♼♼♼♼ Three Hills Charles Andreas Cabernet Sauvignon 2003 **RATING** 86 **DRINK** 2012 $ 36

Harbord Wines ★★★★

PO Box 41, Stockwell, SA 5355 **REGION** Barossa Valley
T (08) 8562 2598 **F** (08) 8562 2598 **WEB** www.harbordwines.com.au **OPEN** Not
WINEMAKER Roger Harbord **EST.** 2003 **CASES** 3000
SUMMARY Roger Harbord is a well-known and no less respected Barossa winemaker, with over 20 years' experience, the last 10 as chief winemaker for Cellarmaster Wines, Normans and Ewinexchange. He has set up his own virtual winery as a complementary activity; the grapes are contract-grown, and he leases winery space and equipment to make and mature the wines. Exports to the UK, the US and other major markets.

♼♼♼♼♼ Barossa Shiraz 2002 Medium-bodied; clean, elegant and restrained style; blackberry and spice mix; fine tannins, restrained oak. High-quality cork. **RATING** 91 **DRINK** 2015 $ 22

♼♼♼♼ Barossa Chardonnay 2004 **RATING** 85 **DRINK** Now $ 18

Harcourt Valley Vineyards ★★★☆

3339 Calder Highway, Harcourt, Vic 3453 **REGION** Bendigo
T (03) 5474 2223 **F** (03) 5474 2293 **WEB** www.bendigowine.org.au/harcourtvalley **OPEN** 7 days 11–5 (11–6 during daylight saving)
WINEMAKER Contract **EST.** 1976 **CASES** 1000

SUMMARY Established by Ray and Barbara Broughton, the vineyard was handed over to John and Barbara Livingstone in 1998. Barbara's Shiraz was created by Barbara Broughton, but with the arrival of the new 'Barbara' it lives on as the flagship of the vineyard. The Livingstones planted a further 2 ha of shiraz on north-facing slopes with the aid of two sons, who, says Barbara, 'have since bolted, vowing never to have anything to do with vineyards, but having developed fine palates'. John Livingstone died in mid-2004, but Barbara continues her role of viticulturist; winemaking is being overseen by local vignerons for the time being.

▼▼▼▼ **Cabernet Sauvignon 2002** Juicy, intense blackcurrant and cassis; medium-bodied; spicy notes and earthy, savoury tannins. Stained cork. **RATING** 89 **DRINK** 2012 $ 25

▼▼▼▽ **Riesling 2004** Ripe apple and sweet citrus fruit, bordering Spaetlese sweetness; can improve; cellar door special. Screwcap. **RATING** 86 **DRINK** 2008 $ 16
Chardonnay 2004 RATING 85 **DRINK** 2007 $ 20

Hardys ★★★★☆

Reynell Road, Reynella, SA 5161 **REGION** McLaren Vale
T (08) 8392 2222 **F** (08) 8392 2202 **WEB** www.hardys.com.au **OPEN** Mon–Fri 10–4.30, Sat 10–4, Sun 11–4, closed public hols
WINEMAKER Peter Dawson, Paul Lapsley, Ed Carr, Tom Newton **EST.** 1853 **CASES** 16 000
SUMMARY The 1992 merger of Thomas Hardy and the Berri Renmano group may well have had some of the elements of a forced marriage when it took place, but the merged group prospered mightily over the next 10 years. So successful was it that a further marriage followed in early 2003, with Constellation Wines of the US the groom, and BRL Hardy the bride. It has created the largest wine group in the world. The Hardys wine brands are many and various, from the lowest price point to the highest, and covering all the major varietals. They also happen to make outstanding Vintage Port and fine, wood-aged Brandy.

▼▼▼▼▼ **Reynell Basket Pressed Cabernet Sauvignon 1998** Very rich; layer upon layer of flavour and texture; dark chocolate, blackcurrant and blackberry; very good oak and tannins; will live forever. High-quality cork. Tucker Seabrook Trophy 2004. **RATING** 96 **DRINK** 2023 $ 50
Hardys Reynella Eileen Hardy Chardonnay 2002 A marvellous combination of hyper-intense nectarine and citrus-tinged fruit with barrel ferment and malolactic inputs, still retaining elegance, fruit the last word. **RATING** 96 **DRINK** 2012 $ 40
Hardys Reynella Eileen Hardy Shiraz 2001 One of the most elegant to date under this label; medium-bodied, silky texture and very long in the mouth; perfect aftertaste. **RATING** 96 **DRINK** 2016 $ 105
Hardys Reynella Arras 1999 Crisp, fine and elegantly poised; subtle bready autolysis characters alongside lingering lemon, citrus, apple and stone fruit; faultless balance. **RATING** 95 **DRINK** 2008 $ 50
Hardys Reynella Thomas Hardy Cabernet Sauvignon 2000 Elegant, fragrant cassis and berry aromas; the fruit is ripe, and the finish long; controlled oak; skilled winemaking response to the vintage. **RATING** 94 **DRINK** 2010 $ 105

▼▼▼▼▽ **Reynell Basket Pressed Shiraz 2002** Elegant, but tightly focused and structured; fine dark fruits and bitter chocolate; equally fine, savoury tannins. Quality cork. **RATING** 93 **DRINK** 2015 $ 45
Reynell McLaren Vale Grenache 2002 Soft, supple, rounded raspberry, cherry and plum; shows McLaren Vale Grenache to full advantage; gentle tannins. Cork. **RATING** 93 **DRINK** 2007 $ 30
Hardys Reynella Sir James Vintage 2001 Super-fine and elegant, bringing together pear, apple and brioche aromas and flavours; impeccably balanced, it has the long, clean finish and aftertaste which is the hallmark of all fine sparkling wines. **RATING** 93 **DRINK** Now $ 25
Hardys Reynella Oomoo Shiraz 2003 Laden with plum and blackberry fruit and a wrapping of regional chocolate, it has excellent balance, depth and structure. Almost embarrassingly good value. **RATING** 92 **DRINK** 2008 $ 13
Hardys Reynella Chateau Reynella Shiraz 2002 Full-bodied, masculine style with powerful, dense black fruits and bitter chocolate. Should loosen up with age. **RATING** 92 **DRINK** 2017 $ 52
Hardys Reynella Padthaway Shiraz 2002 Medium-bodied; well-balanced red and black fruits and fine, ripe tannins; integrated oak. **RATING** 90 **DRINK** 2009 $ 21

Hardys Reynella Padthaway Unwooded Chardonnay 2003 Bright colour; light, crisp fruit-driven style, with a good finish. **RATING** 89 **DRINK** 2006 $14.95

ŶŶŶŶ **Nottage Hill Cabernet Sauvignon Shiraz 2003** Medium-bodied; blackcurrant fruit; nice balance and texture. **RATING** 88 **DRINK** 2009 $8.95

Hardys Sir James Cuvee Brut NV Scented acacia and citrus aromas; appealing citrus flavours on a delicate palate; neat dosage, neither sweet nor dry. Amazingly, given the price, it is bottle-fermented and spends 18 months on yeast lees. **RATING** 87 **DRINK** Now $15

Hardys Reynella Voyage Colombard Semillon Sauvignon Blanc 2004 A well-balanced mix of tropical and citrus fruit; simple, but fresh and clean. Spectacular value. **RATING** 87 **DRINK** Now $6

Hardys Reynella Voyage Cabernet Sauvignon Petit Verdot Merlot 2003 A smooth and soft mix of raspberry and plum fruits and soft tannins, the seeming absence of oak irrelevant. **RATING** 87 **DRINK** Now $6

ŶŶŶŶ **Hardys Reynella Nottage Hill Shiraz 2002** **RATING** 85 **DRINK** 2010 $8.99

Sir James Sparkling Pinot Noir Shiraz NV Not phenolic, sweet or oaky (all traps for red sparkling wine) but, ironically, shortens on the finish; does have strawberry and beetroot flavours; good value. **RATING** 86 **DRINK** Now $15

Savy Rouge Cabernet Sauvignon NV **RATING** 84 **DRINK** Now $11

ŶŶŶ **Hardys Reynella Woodcroft Shiraz 2002** **RATING** 83 $18.20

Savy Blonde NV **RATING** 83 $11

Savy Sparkle NV **RATING** 83 $11

Hardys Tintara ★★★★★

202 Main Road, McLaren Vale, SA 5171 **REGION** McLaren Vale
T (08) 8329 4110 **F** (08) 8329 4100 **WEB** www.hardys.com.au **OPEN** 7 days 10–4.30
WINEMAKER Robert Mann **EST.** 1876 **CASES** 45 000
SUMMARY Hardys Tintara is run as a separate winemaking entity, although all the Hardys wines are offered at the cellar door. The Limited Release wines are first class; the Tintara Cellars appeal on the grounds of price.

ŶŶŶŶŶ **Tintara Cellars Chardonnay 2002** Smoky barrel ferment characters woven through nectarine fruit; good acidity and intensity; exceptional length. **RATING** 95 **DRINK** 2012 $15.99

Limited Release Shiraz 2001 Rich but not jammy; spicy blackberry, plum and chocolate fruit; very good oak and tannin management. Quality cork. **RATING** 94 **DRINK** 2015 $48.95

ŶŶŶŶŶ **Grenache 2002** Complex licorice, spice, anise and game aromas; touches of regional dark chocolate; very good structure. **RATING** 93 **DRINK** 2012 $35

Tintara Cellars Shiraz 2001 Powerful and luscious blackberry and licorice fruit; ripe tannins, skilled oak handling. Great value. **RATING** 91 **DRINK** 2016 $16

ŶŶŶŶ **Tintara Cellars Shiraz 2000** Light to medium-bodied; black fruits, leather and spice. **RATING** 87 **DRINK** 2010 $15.99

Hare's Chase ★★★★☆

PO Box 46, Melrose Park, SA 5039 **REGION** Barossa Valley
T (08) 8277 3506 **F** (08) 8277 3543 **WEB** www.hareschase.com.au **OPEN** Not
WINEMAKER Peter Taylor **EST.** 1998 **CASES** 2500
SUMMARY Hare's Chase is the creation of two families who own this 100-year-old vineyard in the Marananga Valley subregion of the Barossa Valley. The simple, functional winery sits at the top of a rocky hill in the centre of the vineyard, which has some of the best red soil available for dry-grown viticulture. The winemaking arm of the partnership is provided by Peter Taylor, a senior red winemaker with Penfolds for over 20 years, and now Southcorp chief winemaker. Exports to the UK, the US and Switzerland.

ŶŶŶŶŶ **Barossa Blend 2003** Elegantly complex spice, chocolate and black fruits; medium-bodied, with good texture and structure; ripe tannins, silky mouthfeel. Five varieties, Shiraz dominant; 1% Cabernet Sauvignon, 1% Tempranillo. Quality cork. **RATING** 93 **DRINK** 2013 $20

Barossa Shiraz 2003 Dense colour; medium to full-bodied; supple, rich blackberry fruit and chocolate; well-handled oak. Quality cork. **RATING** 92 **DRINK** 2015 $ 45

Harewood Estate ★★★★★

Scotsdale Road, Denmark, WA 6333 **REGION** Denmark
T (08) 9840 9078 **F** (08) 9840 9053 **WEB** www.harewoodestate.com.au **OPEN** 7 days 10–4
WINEMAKER James Kellie **EST.** 1988 **CASES** 4000
SUMMARY In July 2003 James Kellie, who for many years was a winemaker with Howard Park, and was responsible for the contract making of Harewood Wines since 1998, purchased the estate with his father and sister as partners. Events moved quickly thereafter: a 300-tonne winery was constructed, offering both contract winemaking services for the Great Southern region, and the ability to expand the Harewood range to include subregional wines that showcase the region, hence the already much-expanded production.

▼▼▼▼▼ **Mount Barker Riesling 2004** Pale straw-green; fragrant, floral apple blossom bouquet; fine, elegant, intense and lingering. Screwcap. **RATING** 94 **DRINK** 2014 $ 19.50
Denmark Sauvignon Blanc Semillon 2004 Fragrant and flowery aromas; intense passionfruit and gooseberry flavours; great line and flow. Screwcap. **RATING** 94 **DRINK** 2009 $ 19.50

▼▼▼▼▽ **Denmark Chardonnay 2003** Fragrant, fresh, delicate nectarine and citrus fruit; subtly interwoven French oak; lovely finish. Screwcap. **RATING** 93 **DRINK** 2010 $ 25

▼▼▼▼ **Great Southern Classic White 2004** Bright, light green-straw; fresh melon and citrus, nice acidity. Chardonnay-based blend. Screwcap. **RATING** 88 **DRINK** Now $ 16
Great Southern Late Harvest Riesling 2004 Very delicate now and seemingly slightly simple, but will flower given 5–10 years. Points for now, not what it will become. Screwcap. **RATING** 87 **DRINK** 2014 $ 15

▼▼▼▽ **Denmark Pinot Noir 2003** **RATING** 86 **DRINK** 2007 $ 25

Harmans Ridge Estate NR

Cnr Bussell Highway/Harmans Mill Road, Wilyabrup, WA 6284 **REGION** Margaret River
T (08) 9755 7444 **F** (08) 9755 7400 **WEB** www.harmansridge.com.au **OPEN** Wed–Mon 10–4
WINEMAKER Paul Green **EST.** 1999 **CASES** 20 000
SUMMARY Harmans Ridge Estate, with a crush capacity of 1600 tonnes, is primarily a contract winery for larger producers in the Margaret River region which do not have their own winery/winemaker. It does, however, have 2 ha of shiraz, and does make wines under the Harmans Ridge Estate label from grapes grown in Margaret River. A cellar door opened in mid-2003. The wines are sold in Western Australia, and exported to Asia and the US.

🌿 Harrington Glen Estate ★★★☆

88 Townsend Road, Glen Aplin, Qld 4381 **REGION** Granite Belt
T (07) 4683 4388 **F** (07) 4683 4388 **OPEN** 7 days 10–4, Sat 10–5
WINEMAKER Various regional contract makers **EST.** 2003 **CASES** 1200
SUMMARY The Ireland family has established 2.8 ha of cabernet sauvignon, shiraz, merlot and verdelho. Until the vineyard comes into full production (planting began in 1997), grapes are being purchased from local growers. The leading wines are both varietal and reserve versions of Shiraz and Cabernet Sauvignon, with Simply Red and Simply White at the bottom end of the price scale.

▼▼▼▼▽ **Queensland Chardonnay 2004** Excellent unwooded Chardonnay; major surprise; vibrant, fresh nectarine and citrus fruit; good balance and length. Screwcap. **RATING** 90 **DRINK** 2007 $ 16

▼▼▼▽ **Queensland Verdelho 2004** Light to medium-bodied; good balance and length with a touch of the sweetness the market expects. **RATING** 86 **DRINK** Now $ 18
Vineyard 88 Reserve Cabernet Sauvignon 2002 More concentration than most of the wines in tone range; fully ripe, dusty, earthy notes; some tannins; adjusted acidity shows. **RATING** 86 **DRINK** 2008 $ 20
Vineyard 88 Reserve Shiraz 2002 **RATING** 85 **DRINK** 2007 $ 18

Vineyard 88 Cabernet Sauvignon 2002 RATING 85 DRINK Now $15
Vineyard 88 Shiraz 2002 RATING 84 DRINK Now $15

ΥΥΥ **Vineyard 88 Verdelho 2004** RATING 83 $20

Harris Estate

NR

Paracombe Road, Paracombe, SA 5132 REGION Adelaide Hills
T (08) 8380 5353 F (08) 8380 5353 OPEN By appointment
WINEMAKER Trevor Harris EST. 1994 CASES 1000
SUMMARY Trevor and Sue Harris have established 2.5 ha of chardonnay, shiraz and cabernet sauvignon at Paracombe. The wines are distributed by The Wine Group, Victoria, and Jonathan Tolley, South Australia, and sold by mail order.

Hartley Estate

260 Chittering Valley Road, Lower Chittering, WA 6084 REGION Perth Hills
T (08) 9481 4288 F (08) 9481 4291 OPEN By appointment
WINEMAKER Steve Hagan (Contract) EST. 1999 CASES 1700
SUMMARY Bernie and Erin Stephens purchased the property now named Hartley Estate without any forethought. While driving the Chittering Valley one Sunday with his daughter Angela, and reminiscing about the times he had spent there with his father Hartley, Stephen saw a For Sale sign on the property, and later that day the contract for sale was signed. Planting of 17 ha of vines began, with Cabernet Sauvignon and Shiraz released in 2003. They form part of the Generations Series, recognising the involvement of three generations of the family: the founders, their children and the grandchildren born to three of the daughters in 2003. The major part of the crop goes to Western Range Wines; the remainder are under the Hartley Estate label.

ΥΥΥΥ **Classic White 2004** RATING 84 DRINK Now $14

Hartz Barn Wines

1 Truro Road, Moculta, SA 5353 REGION Eden Valley
T (08) 8563 9002 F (08) 8563 9002 WEB www.hartzbarnwines.com.au OPEN By appointment
WINEMAKER David Barnett EST. 1997 CASES 2000
SUMMARY Hartz Barn Wines was formed in 1997 by Penny Hart (operations director), David Barnett (winemaker/director), Katrina Barnett (marketing director) and Matthew Barnett (viticulture/cellar director), which may suggest that the operation is rather larger than it in fact is. The business name and label have an unexpectedly complex background, too, involving elements from all the partners. The grapes come from the estate vineyards, which are planted to riesling, lagrein, merlot, shiraz and cabernet sauvignon. Exports to Canada, Japan and New Zealand.

ΥΥΥΥ **General Store Eden Valley Riesling 2004** Clean, soft and round lime/tropical fruit; quite fleshy; early-developing. Screwcap. RATING 88 DRINK 2009 $19
Mail Box Barossa Merlot 2003 Medium-bodied; dark fruits, with a hint of jam in the mix; robust tannins, rustic style. High-quality cork. RATING 87 DRINK 2009 $25

Hartzview Wine Centre

NR

70 Dillons Road, Gardners Bay, Tas 7112 REGION Southern Tasmania
T (03) 6295 1623 F (03) 6295 1723 WEB www.hartzview.com.au OPEN 7 days 9–5
WINEMAKER Andrew Hood (Contract), Robert Patterson EST. 1988 CASES 2000
SUMMARY A combined wine centre, offering wines from a number of local Huon Valley wineries; also, newly erected and very comfortable accommodation for 6 people in a separate, self-contained house. Hartzview table wines (produced from 3 ha of estate plantings) are much to be preferred to the self-produced Pig & Whistle Hill fruit wines.

Harvey River Bridge Estate

Third Street, Harvey, WA 6220 REGION Geographe
T (08) 9729 2199 F (08) 9729 2298 WEB www.harveyfresh.com.au OPEN 7 days 10–4

WINEMAKER Greg Jones **EST.** 2000 **CASES** 35 000
SUMMARY This is a highly focused business which is a division of parent company Harvey Fresh (1994) Ltd, a producer of fruit juice and dairy products exported to more than 12 countries. It has 10 contract growers throughout the Geographe region, with the wines being made in a company-owned winery and juice factory. Exports to the US, Japan, Malaysia, Singapore, Germany and Ireland; a wide range of marketing activities (including a wine club and website) are utilised for the domestic market.

Haselgrove ★★★★

150 Main Road, McLaren Vale, SA 5171 **REGION** McLaren Vale
T (08) 8323 8706 **F** (08) 8323 8049 **WEB** www.haselgrove.com.au **OPEN** 7 days 11–4
WINEMAKER Simon Parker **EST.** 1981 **CASES** 45 000
SUMMARY Haselgrove has been through a tumultuous period following its acquisition by Barrington Estates and the subsequent collapse of Barrington. The underlying winemaking operations of Haselgrove have continued. Domestic retail distribution is exclusive to the Vintage Cellars, Liquorland and Theo's wine chains of Coles Myer; also limited on-premise distribution. Exports to the UK, Denmark, Hong Kong and Taiwan.

ŸŸŸŸŸ **'H' Reserve Shiraz 2003** Deep colour; excellent texture; fine, ripe tannins run through blackberry, licorice and spice flavours. Screwcap. **RATING** 93 **DRINK** 2015 $ 24.95
'H' Reserve Adelaide Hills Chardonnay 2004 Fine, elegant and focused; nectarine, citrus and apple; good balance, excellent length. Screwcap. **RATING** 92 **DRINK** 2010 $ 24.95

ŸŸŸŸ **MVS McLaren Vale Cabernet Sauvignon 2003** Attractive, sweet blackcurrant and dark chocolate mix; not jammy; nice ripe tannins. **RATING** 89 **DRINK** 2010 $ 14.95
Sovereign Series Semillon Sauvignon Blanc 2004 Good length and balance; grass and citrus flavours; quite long, minerally acidity; surprise packet. **RATING** 88 **DRINK** Now $ 9.95
MVS McLaren Vale Chardonnay 2004 Peach, nectarine and fig fruit; good structure, and, in particular, length. Screwcap. **RATING** 88 **DRINK** 2007 $ 14.95
Sovereign Series Chardonnay 2004 Pleasant wine; good balance and mouthfeel; gentle creamy/figgy flavours. Screwcap. **RATING** 87 **DRINK** 2007 $ 9.95
'H' Reserve Adelaide Hills Viognier 2004 Very subtle; has texture and structure, but not much varietal character. **RATING** 87 **DRINK** 2007 $ 24.95
Grenache Shiraz Viognier 2004 Fresh, juicy red and black fruit mix; a nice touch of soft tannins. Screwcap. **RATING** 87 **DRINK** 2007 $ 14.95

ŸŸŸŸ **Sovereign Shiraz 2004** **RATING** 86 **DRINK** 2009 $ 9.95
Sovereign Series Cabernet Merlot 2004 **RATING** 85 **DRINK** 2008 $ 9.95
MVS Dam Block Shiraz 2003 **RATING** 84 **DRINK** 2008 $ 14.95
Sovereign Series Cabernet Merlot 2003 **RATING** 84 **DRINK** 2008 $ 9.95

ŸŸŸ **McLaren Dam Block Chardonnay 2004** **RATING** 81 $ 14.95

Hastwell & Lightfoot ★★★★☆

Foggos Road, McLaren Vale, SA 5171 **REGION** McLaren Vale
T (08) 8323 8692 **F** (08) 8323 8098 **WEB** www.hastwellandlightfoot.com.au **OPEN** By appointment
WINEMAKER Goe DiFabio (Contract) **EST.** 1990 **CASES** 2000
SUMMARY Hastwell & Lightfoot is an offshoot of a rather larger grapegrowing business, with the majority of the grapes from the 16 ha of vineyard being sold to others; the vineyard was planted in 1988 and the first grapes produced in 1990. Incidentally, the labels are once seen, never forgotten. Exports to the US, Singapore and New Zealand.

ŸŸŸŸ **McLaren Vale Shiraz 2002** An abundance of rich, ripe, sweet red and black fruits; ripe tannins and nice vanilla oak ex 24 months in barrel. Cork. **RATING** 91 **DRINK** 2012 $ 20.95
McLaren Vale Cabernet Franc 2002 Generously endowed, unusually so for the variety; sweet cassis and raspberry fruit; fine tannins, good length. Cork. **RATING** 91 **DRINK** 2012 $ 20.95
McLaren Vale Cabernet 2002 Some minty edges to the aromas; swells to rich blackcurrant and chocolate on the palate; excellent length and persistence. Stained cork. **RATING** 90 **DRINK** 2011 $ 20.95

ΨΨΨΨ **McLaren Vale Viognier 2004** Medium-bodied; ripe, mouthfilling apricot and pear fruit; a very subtle touch of oak. Screwcap. **RATING** 88 **DRINK** 2007 $ 20.95

Hawkers Gate ★★★★☆

Lot 31 Foggo Road, McLaren Flat, SA 5171 **REGION** McLaren Vale
T 0403 809 990 **F** (08) 8323 9981 **WEB** www.hawkersgate.com.au **OPEN** By appointment
WINEMAKER James Hastwell **EST.** 2000 **CASES** 380
SUMMARY James Hastwell (son of Mark and Wendy Hastwell of Hastwell & Lightfoot) decided he would become a winemaker when he was 9 years old, and duly obtained his wine science degree from the University of Adelaide, working each vintage during his degree course at Haselgrove Wines and later Kay Bros. It is a long way from Hawkers Gate, which takes its name from the gate at the border of Australia's dog fence between South Australia and New South Wales, 250 km north of Broken Hill. A small onsite winery in Foggo Road was completed in time for the 2003 vintage; as well as giving greater control over the making of the Hawkers Gate wines, it acts as a barrel storage facility for Hastwell & Lightfoot wines. A few rows of saperavi have been planted. Exports to the US.

ΨΨΨΨΨ **McLaren Vale Shiraz 2002** Deep, clear red-purple; sweet, not jammy, black fruits, supple tannins and good mouthfeel; harmonious oak. Quality cork. **RATING** 92 **DRINK** 2014
McLaren Vale Cadenzia NV Attractive fruit-driven style, bursting with flavours ranging through red, blue and black fruit spectrum; firm finish. A blend of '04 Grenache and '02 Shiraz. Zork. **RATING** 90 **DRINK** 2007 $ 18

Hawley Vineyard NR

Hawley Beach, Hawley, Tas 7307 **REGION** Northern Tasmania
T (03) 6428 6221 **F** (03) 6428 6844 **WEB** www.view.com.au/hawley **OPEN** 7 days
WINEMAKER Julian Alcorso (Contract) **EST.** 1988 **CASES** 1000
SUMMARY Hawley Vineyard overlooks Hawley Beach and thence northeast to Bass Strait. It is established on a historic 200-ha farming property, with Hawley House offering dining and accommodation in a grand style. There are no other vineyards in this unique winegrowing region, and few hoteliers-cum-viticulturists as flamboyant as owner Simon Houghton. Limited distribution in Sydney.

Hay River Wines NR

'The Springs', RMB 570, Mount Barker, WA 6324 (postal) **REGION** Mount Barker
T (08) 9857 6012 **F** (08) 9857 6112 **OPEN** Not
WINEMAKER Michael Kerrigan **EST.** 1974 **CASES** 200
SUMMARY Hay River first appeared in my *Wines and Wineries of Western Australia*, published in 1982. The then very remote vineyard had been planted in 1974, and I visited the tractor shed-cum-winery with diesel engine-generated power, watching Jane Paul make the 1981 vintage, which turned out very well. These days the grapes from the 6 ha of cabernet sauvignon and 5 ha of chardonnay are sold to Howard Park, but a small amount of wine is made for release under the Hay River label.

Hay Shed Hill Wines

Harmans Mill Road, Wilyabrup, WA 6280 **REGION** Margaret River
T (08) 9755 6046 **F** (08) 9755 6305 **WEB** www.hayshedhill.com.au **OPEN** 7 days 10.30–5
WINEMAKER Nigel Kinsman, Virginia Willcock **EST.** 1987 **CASES** 30 000
SUMMARY When erected in 1987, the winery was a landmark in the Margaret River region, and over the ensuing years the 'sold out' sign was often displayed. Quality wobbled in the lead-up to its ill-fated acquisition by Barrington Estate in 2000, but in November 2002 it joined Alexandra Bridge and Chestnut Grove as part of Mike Calneggia's Australian Wine Holdings Limited group.

ΨΨΨΨΨ **Margaret River Sauvignon Blanc Semillon 2004** Spotlessly clean; very attractive mix of grass, herb and sweet tropical/passionfruit flavours; fresh acidity to close. Screwcap.
RATING 94 **DRINK** 2008 $ 19.75

ΨΨΨΨΨ **Pitchfork Semillon Sauvignon Blanc 2004** Clean and fresh; plenty of flavour and structure, albeit driven by Semillon; grass, herb and lemon zest; nicely balanced, hint of sweetness. Screwcap. **RATING** 90 **DRINK** 2007 $ 16.30

Margaret River Chardonnay 2003 Stone fruit and melon; subtle French oak; notwithstanding 14.5° alcohol, does not heat up on the finish. Quality cork. **RATING** 90 **DRINK** 2008 $ 30.86

Margaret River Shiraz 2002 Light to medium-bodied; elegant, gentle spice and sweet red fruits; fine tannins. Screwcap. **RATING** 90 **DRINK** 2009 $ 32.92

ΨΨΨΨ **Margaret River Cabernet Merlot 2003** Strong colour; powerful black fruits; still all arms and legs; leave for 3 years to settle down. Screwcap. **RATING** 88 **DRINK** 2013 $ 22.29

ΨΨΨΨ **Pitchfork Pink 2004** Heady, spicy aromas; phenolics counterbalanced by closing sweetness. Screwcap. **RATING** 86 **DRINK** Now $ 16.30

Hayward's Whitehead Creek   NR

80 Hall Lane, Seymour, Vic 3660 **REGION** Goulburn Valley
T (03) 5792 3050 **F** (03) 5792 3030 **OPEN** Mon–Sat 9–6, Sun 10–6
WINEMAKER Sid Hayward, David Hayward **EST.** 1975 **CASES** Nil
SUMMARY The 4.5 ha of low-yielding 25-year-old vines make powerful wines in a somewhat rustic mode, perhaps, but at low prices. Hayward's has a number of back vintages across all varieties in stock, and has taken the decision to sell all the grape production in the future.

Hazyblur Wines   NR

Lot 5, Angle Vale Road, Virginia, SA 5120 **REGION** Adelaide Plains
T (08) 8380 9307 **F** (08) 8380 8743 **OPEN** By appointment
WINEMAKER Ross Trimboli **EST.** 1998 **CASES** 2000
SUMMARY Robyne and Ross Trimboli hit the jackpot with their 2000 vintage red wines, sourced from various regions in South Australia, including one described by Robert Parker as 'Barotta, the most northerly region in South Australia' (it is in fact Baroota, and is not the most northerly), with Parker points ranging between 91 and 95. One of the wines included a Late Harvest Shiraz, tipping the scales at 17° alcohol, and contract-grown at Kangaroo Island. It is here that the Trimbolis have established their own 4.7-ha vineyard, planted principally to cabernet sauvignon and shiraz (first vintage 2004). Needless to say, almost all the wine is exported to the US (lesser amounts to Canada), the importer being the one and only Dan Phillips, aka The Grateful Palate.

Healesville Wine Co.   NR

189–191a Maroondah Highway, Healesville, Vic 3777 **REGION** Yarra Valley
T (03) 5962 1800 **F** (03) 5962 1833 **OPEN** 7 days 11–6
WINEMAKER Paul Evans (Contract) **EST.** 2002 **CASES** 1000
SUMMARY This is the venture of John Reith and Roger Hocking, who have a small vineyard, planted with chardonnay in 1997, off Don Road, Healesville, plus pinot noir and chardonnay from the Kiah Yallambee Vineyard in Old Don Road. Small amounts of shiraz, cabernet sauvignon, cabernet franc and merlot are obtained from Yarra Valley vineyards managed or controlled by the Healesville Wine Co. The cellar door also has a café, art gallery and local produce for sale.

Heartland Vineyard   ★★★★

PO Box 78, Greta, NSW 2334 **REGION** Lower Hunter Valley
T (02) 4938 6272 **F** (02) 4938 6004 **WEB** www.heartlandvineyard.com.au **OPEN** Not
WINEMAKER David Hook **EST.** 1998 **CASES** 1500
SUMMARY Duncan and Libby Thomson, cardiac surgeon and cardiac scrub nurse respectively, say Heartland Vineyard is the result of a sea-change that got a little out of hand: 'After looking one weekend at some property in the Hunter Valley to escape the Sydney rat-race, we stumbled upon the beautiful 90 acres that has become our vineyard.' They have built a rammed-earth house on the property, and the vineyard is now a little over 5 ha, with an exotic mix of shiraz, semillon, merlot, barbera, verdelho and viognier.

ΨΨΨΨ **Semillon 2004** Spotlessly clean; pure herb, grass, spice and lanolin aromas; lingering finish; classy wine. Screwcap. **RATING** 93 **DRINK** 2014 $ 11.60

Semillon 2003 Spotless; similar style to the '04; slightly less fruit; chalky minerality on a long finish. Screwcap. **RATING** 91 **DRINK** 2013 $ 11.60

ŸŸŸŸ **Merlot 2003** Clean; hints of olive; firm mouthfeel, but nonetheless only light to medium-bodied; fine-grained tannins. Screwcap. **RATING** 88 **DRINK** 2011 $13.30
Shiraz Viognier 2003 Light to medium-bodied; fresh and lively, but 16% Viognier diminishes the structure too radically; raspberry, plum and apricot nuances don't compensate. Screwcap. **RATING** 87 **DRINK** 2008 $13.30
Sticky Monster 2004 Nowhere near 'monster'; simply a nicely balanced sweet wine with good acidity. Screwcap. **RATING** 87 **DRINK** 2008 $10

ŸŸŸŸ **Verdelho 2004** **RATING** 84 **DRINK** 2007 $12.50

Heartland Wines ★★★★

Level 1, 205 Greenhill Road, Eastwood, SA 5063 **REGION** Limestone Coast Zone
T (08) 8357 9344 **F** (08) 8357 9388 **WEB** www.heartlandwines.com.au **OPEN** Not
WINEMAKER Ben Glaetzer **EST.** 2001 **CASES** 20 000
SUMMARY This is a joint venture of four industry veterans: winemakers Ben Glaetzer and Scott Collett, viticulturist Geoff Hardy and wine industry management specialist Grant Tilbrook. It draws upon grapes grown in the Limestone Coast, Barossa Valley and McLaren Vale, predominantly from vineyards owned by the partners. Its sights are firmly set on exports and it has already had impressive results. The wines are principally contract-made at Barossa Vintners, but there are no local or cellar door sales facilities. Value for money is excellent. Exports to the UK, the US and other major markets.

ŸŸŸŸŸ **Director's Cut Shiraz 2003** Bright, fresh blackberry, plum and spice fruit; medium-bodied and accessible; soft tannins. Stained cork. **RATING** 90 **DRINK** 2012 $30

ŸŸŸŸ **Limestone Coast Shiraz 2003** Delicious fruit-driven style; red and black berries, plus a hint of mint; soft finish. Cork. **RATING** 88 **DRINK** 2007 $17
Limestone Coast Cabernet Sauvignon 2003 Light to medium-bodied; smooth and supple texture; blackcurrant and hints of leaf, olive and mint. Cork. **RATING** 87 **DRINK** 2008 $17

ŸŸŸŸ **Stickleback Red 2003** Plenty of dark fruits; soft and round; overall flavour rather more than expected. Cabernet/Shiraz/Grenache blend. Screwcap. **RATING** 86 **DRINK** Now $12
Limestone Coast Viognier Pinot Gris 2004 **RATING** 85 **DRINK** Now $20

ŸŸŸ **Stickleback White 2004** **RATING** 83 $12

Heathcote Estate ★★★★★

206 Bourke Street, Melbourne, Vic 3000 (postal) **REGION** Heathcote
T (03) 9251 5375 **F** (03) 9639 1540 **WEB** www.heathcoteestate.com **OPEN** Not
WINEMAKER Tod Dexter, Larry McKenna (Consultant) **EST.** 1999 **CASES** 3000
SUMMARY Heathcote Estate is a thoroughly professional venture, a partnership between Louis Bialkower, founder of Yarra Ridge Winery, and Robert G Kirby, owner of Yabby Lake Vineyards, Director of Escarpment Vineyards (New Zealand) and Chairman of Village Roadshow Ltd. They purchased a prime piece of Heathcote red Cambrian soil on Drummonds Lane in 1999, and have an experienced and skilled winemaking team in the form of Tod Dexter (ex Stonier) and Larry McKenna (of New Zealand) as consultant; these two are also responsible for the Yabby Lake wines. They have planted 40 ha of vines, 85% shiraz and 15% grenache, the latter an interesting variant on viognier. A single wine is to be produced, and one suspects that the percentage of grenache will vary from year to year: it was 8% in 2002. The wines are matured exclusively in French oak, 50% new and 50% old.

ŸŸŸŸŸ **Shiraz 2002** Excellent wine; shows the Heathcote regional style to best advantage; a cascade of black fruits; long, savoury tannins; balanced oak. **RATING** 94 **DRINK** 2017 $45

Heathcote Winery ★★★★

183–185 High Street, Heathcote, Vic 3523 **REGION** Heathcote
T (03) 5433 2595 **F** (03) 5433 3081 **OPEN** 7 days 11–5
WINEMAKER Jonathan Mepham **EST.** 1978 **CASES** 7000
SUMMARY The Heathcote Winery is back in business with a vengeance. The wines are being produced predominantly from the 26 ha of estate vineyard, and some from local and other growers under long-term contracts, and the tasting room facilities have been restored and upgraded. Exports to the UK.

Craven's Place Shiraz 2002 Lush, plush blackberry, plum and spice fruit; touches of dark chocolate; fine, savoury tannins. **RATING** 91 **DRINK** 2012 $ 17

Mail Coach Shiraz 2003 Scented, spicy blackberry aromas; medium-bodied; good balance of blackberry and plum fruit, oak and tannins. A splash of Viognier. Screwcap. **RATING** 90 **DRINK** 2015 $ 24

Mail Coach Viognier 2004 Medium-bodied; gently ripe, creamy fruit; barrel ferment and 6 months in French oak have contributed much to the texture and structure. Screwcap. **RATING** 89 **DRINK** 2008 $ 20

Curagee Shiraz 2003 Excellent dark plum aroma, the subliminal influence of 3% Viognier; enters the mouth well, with plush fruit, but then excessive, dry tannins take over. Drought effect, perhaps. Screwcap. **RATING** 88 **DRINK** 2015 $ 40.50

Thomas Craven Shiraz 2002 Light to medium-bodied; spicy, earthy blackberry fruit; tannins provide most of the structure. Screwcap. **RATING** 87 **DRINK** 2009 $ 16

Heathfield Ridge Wines ★★★

PO Box 94, Kensington Park, SA 5068 **REGION** Limestone Coast Zone
T (08) 8363 5800 **F** (08) 8363 1980 **WEB** www.heathfieldridgewines.com.au **OPEN** Not
WINEMAKER Irvine Consultancy (Contract) **EST.** 1997 **CASES** 20 000
SUMMARY The former Heathfield Ridge Winery is now operated by Orlando Wyndham, which is now called Russet Ridge. However, the Tidswell family have retained ownership of the 2 large vineyards, totalling 114 ha, the lion's share planted to shiraz and cabernet sauvignon, with smaller plantings of merlot, chardonnay and sauvignon blanc. Part of the grape production is retained by the owners and vinified under the Heathfield Ridge label; the remainder is sold to Russet Ridge.

Caves Road Shiraz 2002 RATING 85 **DRINK** 2008 $ 12

Heathvale ★★★☆

Saw Pit Gully Road, via Keyneton, SA 5353 **REGION** Eden Valley
T (08) 8564 8248 **F** (08) 8564 8248 **WEB** www.heathvalewines.com.au **OPEN** By appointment
WINEMAKER Ben Radford **EST.** 1987 **CASES** 1250
SUMMARY The origins of Heathvale go back to 1865, when William Heath purchased the property, building the Heathvale home and establishing the fruit orchard and 8 ha of vineyard. The property is now 65 ha and has 10 ha of vineyard in production, with future plantings planned. The wine was made in the cellar of the house which still stands on the property; the house is now occupied by owners Trevor and Faye March. The vineyards were re-established in 1987, and consist of shiraz, cabernet sauvignon, chardonnay and riesling, with a 1000-vine sagrantino trial planted in 2004. Exports to the UK and the US.

Heath Wines ★★★

21–23 Fourth Street, Bowden, SA 5007 (postal) **REGION** Warehouse
T (08) 8346 8488 **F** (08) 8346 4088 **WEB** www.heathwines.com.au **OPEN** Not
WINEMAKER Contract **EST.** 2002 **CASES** NA
SUMMARY Since Alan Heath founded the eponymously named winery in 2002, it has built up exports to eight countries, with a major presence in North America and the Asia Pacific. There are three labels: Lizard Flat Cabernet Sauvignon Merlot Sangiovese blend (under $10); Southern Roo Cabernet Sauvignon Shiraz and Chardonnay Viognier blends (under $15); and four Southern Sisters wines – Cabernet Sauvignon, Sauvignon Blanc, Riesling and Chardonnay (under $25).

Southern Roo Cabernet Shiraz 2002 Good colour; robust style with plenty of structure; red and black fruits; savoury tannins. **RATING** 87 **DRINK** 2009 $ 15

Southern Roo Chardonnay Viognier 2004 RATING 84 **DRINK** 2008 $ 15

Heggies Vineyard ★★★★☆

Heggies Range Road, Eden Valley, SA 5235 **REGION** Eden Valley
T (08) 8565 3203 **F** (08) 8565 3380 **WEB** www.heggiesvineyard.com **OPEN** At Yalumba
WINEMAKER Peter Gambetta **EST.** 1971 **CASES** 13 000

SUMMARY Heggies was the second of the high-altitude (570m) vineyards established by S Smith & Sons (Yalumba). Plantings on the 120-ha former grazing property began in 1973, and 62 ha is now under vine. The view of Heggies as a better white than red wine producer has changed, with the pendulum swinging backwards and forwards according to vintage. Plantings of both chardonnay and viognier were increased in 2002. Exports to all major markets.

ᵀᵀᵀᵀᵀ **Viognier 2003** Bright, light green-yellow; very aromatic; clear-cut varietal character; abundant pastille fruit, neither phenolic nor heavy. Outstanding example. **RATING** 94 **DRINK** Now $26.95

ᵀᵀᵀᵀ♀ **Eden Valley Riesling 2004** Flavoursome but focused flinty/toasty edges to the lime juice core; excellent length, persistence and aftertaste. **RATING** 93 **DRINK** 2014 $18.95
Eden Valley Merlot 2001 Distinguished, elegant style; fine savoury tannins run through the black fruits palate; subtle oak. **RATING** 93 **DRINK** 2011 $24.95
Museum Reserve Eden Valley Riesling 1999 Very complex traditional style; toasty, kerosene, lime mix; long finish; still some CO_2; will go on. **RATING** 92 **DRINK** 2009
Chardonnay 2003 Elegant; light to medium-bodied; melon and a touch of cashew; very subtle, well-integrated oak. **RATING** 90 **DRINK** 2007 $24.95

Helen's Hill Estate
NR

16 Ingram Road, Lilydale, Vic 3140 **REGION** Yarra Valley
T (03) 9739 1573 **F** (03) 9739 0350 **WEB** www.helenshillestate.com.au **OPEN** Wed 11–6, Thurs 11–9, Fri & Sat 11–11, Sun & public hols 11–9
WINEMAKER Scott McCarthy (MasterWineMakers) **EST.** 1984 **CASES** 4000
SUMMARY Helen's Hill Estate is named after the previous owner of the property, Helen Fraser. Allan Nalder, Roma and Lewis Nalder and Andrew and Robyn McIntosh, with backgrounds in banking and finance, grazing and medicine respectively, are the partners in the venture. A small planting of pinot noir and chardonnay dating from the mid-1980s is retained for the Helen's Hill Estate wines; the grapes from the newer plantings are sold to Domaine Chandon and Coldstream Hills. The plantings now cover chardonnay, pinot noir, shiraz, merlot and cabernet sauvignon. A very elegant and relatively large restaurant, with a private function room, looks out over the Yarra Valley.

Helm
★★★★

Butt's Road, Murrumbateman, NSW 2582 **REGION** Canberra District
T (02) 6227 5953 **F** (02) 6227 0207 **WEB** www.helmwines.com.au **OPEN** Thurs–Mon 10–5
WINEMAKER Ken Helm **EST.** 1973 **CASES** 3000
SUMMARY Ken Helm is well known as one of the more stormy petrels of the wine industry and is an energetic promoter of his wines and of the Canberra district generally. His wines have been consistent bronze medal winners, with silvers and the occasional gold dotted here and there. The wines have limited retail distribution in New South Wales, the ACT and Victoria.

ᵀᵀᵀᵀ♀ **Classic Dry Riesling 2003** Elegant and aromatic; clean; plenty of expression; lime and mineral; good finish. Screwcap. **RATING** 91 **DRINK** 2010 $25
Riesling 2004 Slightly more concentrated and longer palate than the Classic; lingering finish. Screwcap. **RATING** 90 **DRINK** 2012 $33

ᵀᵀᵀᵀ **Classic Dry Riesling 2004** Clean, minerally aromas; light to medium-bodied lime and passionfruit; good length and aftertaste. Screwcap. **RATING** 89 **DRINK** 2011 $25
Cabernet Sauvignon 2002 Light to medium-bodied; herb, spice, earth and blackcurrant; no-frills style; minimal oak. Cork. **RATING** 87 **DRINK** 2010 $20

ᵀᵀᵀ **Unwooded Chardonnay 2004** **RATING** 83 $20

Henderson Hardie
NR

PO Box 554, Wangaratta, Vic 3676 **REGION** King Valley
T (03) 5722 1850 **F** (03) 5721 5577 **OPEN** Not
WINEMAKER Howard Anderson (Contract) **EST.** 2000 **CASES** NA
SUMMARY Gayle and Jim Hardie have established 12 ha of gewurztraminer, chardonnay, pinot gris, pinot noir and pinot meunier in their Whitlands vineyard. Jim Hardie has had a long and high-

profile career in viticulture and in viticultural research, and the choice of the varieties planted in this high altitude vineyard reflects that knowledge. Howard Anderson, too, has many years under his belt as a winemaker in various parts of Victoria.

Henke

NR

175 Henke Lane, Yarck, Vic 3719 **REGION** Upper Goulburn
T (03) 5797 6277 **F** (03) 5797 6277 **OPEN** By appointment
WINEMAKER Tim Miller, Caroline Miller **EST.** 1974 **CASES** 250
SUMMARY Produces tiny quantities of estate-grown deep-coloured, full-flavoured, minty red wines known only to a chosen few. The 1.5 ha of shiraz and 0.5 ha of cabernet sauvignon are low-yielding, hence the power and longevity of the wines. A range of back vintages up to 5 years of age are usually available at the cellar door.

Henkell Wines

NR

Melba Highway, Dixons Creek, Vic 3775 **REGION** Yarra Valley
T (03) 9417 4144 **WEB** www.henkellvineyards.com.au **OPEN** Thurs & Sun 11–5, Fri–Sat 11–9
WINEMAKER Contract **EST.** 1988 **CASES** 500
SUMMARY Hans Henkell started with a 57-variety Heinz mix in the vineyard, but has now rationalised it to a total of 25 ha of sauvignon blanc, chardonnay, pinot noir, shiraz and cabernet sauvignon. Most of the grapes are sold, with small amounts contract-made each year. And yes, Hans Henkell is part of the family. Dinner concerts are held regularly throughout the summer months; bookings essential.

Henley Park Wines

NR

6 Swan Street, Henley Brook, WA 6055 **REGION** Swan Valley
T (08) 9296 4328 **F** (08) 9296 1313 **WEB** www.henleywine.com **OPEN** Tues–Sun 10–5
WINEMAKER Claus Petersen, Lisbet Petersen **EST.** 1935 **CASES** 5000
SUMMARY Henley Park, like so many Swan Valley wineries, was founded by a Yugoslav family, but it is now jointly owned by Danish and Malaysian interests, a multicultural mix if ever there was one. Majority owner and winemaker Claus Petersen arrived in 1986 and had his moment of glory in 1990, when Henley Park was the Most Successful Exhibitor at the Mount Barker Wine Show. Much of the production is sold through the cellar door (and exported to Denmark and Japan).

Henry's Drive

★★★★

Hodgsons Road, Padthaway, SA 5271 **REGION** Padthaway
T (08) 8765 5251 **F** (08) 8765 5180 **WEB** www.henrysdrive.com **OPEN** 7 days 10–4
WINEMAKER Kim Johnston, Chris Ringland (Consultant) **EST.** 1998 **CASES** 100 000
SUMMARY The Longbottom families have been farming in Padthaway since the 1940s, with a diverse operation, ranging from sheep and cattle to growing onions. In 1992 they decided to plant a few vines. Now there is almost 300 ha of vineyard consisting mainly of shiraz and cabernet sauvignon, plus some chardonnay, merlot, verdelho and sauvignon blanc. Henry's Drive is owned and operated by Brian and Kay Longbottom. Exports to the US, Canada, South-East Asia, the UK, Japan, Germany and Switzerland.

ΨΨΨΨ **Reserve Shiraz 2003** Powerful blackberry, licorice and dark chocolate fruit; fractionally sharp tannins; will evolve. **RATING** 90 **DRINK** 2013 $ 48

ΨΨΨΨ **Shiraz 2003** Very concentrated, powerful black fruits; massive wine; a trifle aldehydic. **RATING** 87 **DRINK** 2010 $ 32
Parson's Flat Padthaway Shiraz Cabernet 2003 Very ripe blackberry, prune and blackcurrant; soft tannins; overall sweetness from 15.5° alcohol. **RATING** 87 **DRINK** 2009 $ 35

Henschke

★★★★★

Henschke Road, Keyneton, SA 5353 **REGION** Eden Valley
T (08) 8564 8223 **F** (08) 8564 8294 **WEB** www.henschke.com.au **OPEN** Mon–Fri 9–4.30, Sat 9–12, public hols 10–3

WINEMAKER Stephen Henschke **EST.** 1868 **CASES** 40 000

SUMMARY Regarded as the best medium-sized red wine producer in Australia, and has gone from strength to strength over the past two decades under the guidance of Stephen and Prue Henschke. The red wines fully capitalise on the very old, low-yielding, high-quality vines and are superbly made with sensitive but positive use of new small oak: Hill of Grace is second only to Penfolds Grange as Australia's red wine icon. Exports to all major markets.

ŸŸŸŸŸ **Joseph Hill Gewurztraminer 2004** Delicate but bell-clear rose petal and spice varietal fruit; a dry but very long and fine palate; one of the very best examples of the variety. **RATING** 94 **DRINK** 2010 $ 27.80

Lenswood Croft Chardonnay 2003 Fragrant stone fruit and a touch of citrus; gentle barrel ferment inputs to the bouquet and palate; fine and elegant mouthfeel. **RATING** 94 **DRINK** 2010 $ 37.60

ŸŸŸŸŸ **Crane's Eden Valley Chardonnay 2002** Complex barrel ferment and bottle-developed aromas emerging; powerful creamy/nutty overlay to stone fruit; long carry. **RATING** 93 **DRINK** 2007 $ 22.60

Mount Edelstone 2001 Licorice, spice, red cherry/berry fruit and plum; good intensity, depth and length; ripe tannins. **RATING** 93 **DRINK** 2016 $ 62

Keyneton Estate Euphonium 2001 Deep red-purple; fragrant, spicy red and black fruit aromas; medium-bodied, with ripe, fine tannins and well-integrated oak. **RATING** 93 **DRINK** 2015 $ 32

Cyril Henschke Cabernet 2001 Medium-bodied; elegant, finely structured style; a subtle interplay of blackcurrant, earth, olive and fine French oak; long, balanced finish. Cabernet Sauvignon/Cabernet Franc/Merlot. Cork. **RATING** 92 **DRINK** 2017 $ 88

Coralinga Sauvignon Blanc 2004 Very pale straw-green; spotlessly clean; the fine, reserved palate is likewise on the shy side as yet. **RATING** 91 **DRINK** Now $ 21.90

Julius Eden Valley Riesling 2004 Clean and fresh; light to medium-bodied; regional lime blossom and flavour; soft finish. Screwcap. **RATING** 90 **DRINK** 2009 $ 23.50

Henry's Seven 2003 Highly aromatic juicy red berry fruits; fine, ripe tannins; minimal oak influence. Screwcap. **RATING** 90 **DRINK** 2009 $ 27.30

ŸŸŸŸ **Louis Eden Valley Semillon 2003** Flavoursome, soft and rounded; quite creamy; early-developing style. **RATING** 89 **DRINK** 2007 $ 19.50

Sauvignon Blanc Semillon 2004 Nicely balanced; medium-bodied; some gooseberry and a faint touch of more tropical fruit; good balance and length. **RATING** 89 **DRINK** Now $ 20.90

Littlehampton Innes Vineyard Pinot Gris 2003 Spice and musk aromas; round and mouthfilling weight and texture. **RATING** 89 **DRINK** Now $ 22.50

Tilly's Vineyard 2004 Fragrant stone fruit and fruit salad; fresh and lively; seems to have (wisely) abandoned oak. Very good value. Screwcap. **RATING** 89 **DRINK** 2007 $ 12.80

Johann's Garden Grenache Shiraz Mourvedre 2003 Lovely juicy, grapey aromas leap from the glass; fruit leads into the mouth, then unexpected tannins take over. A wine in two parts. **RATING** 89 **DRINK** 2008 $ 34

Crane's Eden Valley Chardonnay 2003 Strong, biscuity/toasty malolactic and oak inputs; complex, but the fruit struggles. **RATING** 88 **DRINK** 2007 $ 22.60

ŸŸŸŸ **Tilly's Vineyard 2003** **RATING** 84 **DRINK** Now $ 12.80

Henty Brook Estate NR

Box 49, Dardanup, WA 6236 **REGION** Geographe
T (08) 9728 1459 **F** (08) 9728 1459 **OPEN** Weekends 10–4, Mon–Fri by appointment
WINEMAKER James Pennington (Contract) **EST.** 1994 **CASES** 400

SUMMARY Shiraz and sauvignon blanc (1 ha each) and semillon (0.5 ha) were planted in the spring of 1994. It has a very low profile.

Heritage Estate ★★★

Granite Belt Drive, Cottonvale, Qld 4375 **REGION** Granite Belt
T (07) 4685 2197 **F** (07) 4685 2112 **WEB** www.heritagewines.com.au **OPEN** 7 days 9–5
WINEMAKER Paola Andrea Cabezas Rhymer **EST.** 1992 **CASES** 5000

SUMMARY Bryce and Paddy Kassulke operate a very successful winery, with many awards in recent years. It also showcases its wines through its cellar door at Mt Tamborine (cnr Bartle Road/The Shelf Road, telephone (07) 5545 3144): it is an old church converted into a tasting and sales area, with views over the Gold Coast hinterland, and includes a restaurant, barbecue area and art gallery. The estate plantings, established in 1993, are chardonnay (2.5 ha), merlot (1 ha), shiraz (0.4 ha) and cabernet sauvignon (0.1 ha). The quality of the wines has been consistently good, in the top ten of the now innumerable Queensland wineries.

ΥΥΥΥ **Cabernet Merlot Reserve 2003 RATING** 86 **DRINK** 2008 $ 25

ΥΥΥ **Verdelho 2004 RATING** 83 $ 18.50
Unwooded Chardonnay 2004 RATING 80 $ 15.50

Heritage Farm Wines

NR

RMB 1005, Murray Valley Highway, Cobram, Vic 3655 **REGION** Goulburn Valley
T (03) 5872 2376 **F** (03) 5872 2376 **OPEN** 7 days 9–5
WINEMAKER Roy Armfield **EST.** 1987 **CASES** 2000
SUMMARY Heritage Farm claims to be the only vineyard and orchard in Australia still using horsepower, with Clydesdales used for most of the general farm work. The winery and cellar door area also boasts a large range of restored horse-drawn farm machinery and a bottle collection. All the wines are sold by mailing list and through the cellar door.

Heritage Wines

★★★★☆

106a Seppeltsfield Road, Marananga, SA 5355 **REGION** Barossa Valley
T (08) 8562 2880 **F** (08) 8562 2692 **OPEN** 7 days 11–5
WINEMAKER Stephen Hoff **EST.** 1984 **CASES** 6000
SUMMARY This little-known winery deserves a far wider audience, for Stephen Hoff is apt to produce some startlingly good wines. At various times the Chardonnay, Riesling (from old Clare Valley vines) and Rossco's Shiraz (now the flagbearer) have all excelled. Exports to the UK, the US, Malaysia and The Netherlands.

ΥΥΥΥΥ **Rossco's Shiraz 2002** Deeply saturated colour; concentrated but supple dark fruits with touches of dark chocolate and licorice; ripe tannins. **RATING** 95 **DRINK** 2017 $ 35

ΥΥΥΥΥ **Barossa Cabernet Malbec 2002** Dense red-purple; rich blackberry and dark chocolate fruit; ripe tannins; delicious now or in 10 years. **RATING** 92 **DRINK** 2012 $ 18

ΥΥΥΥ **Steve Hoff Barossa Cabernet Sauvignon 2003** Powerful blackberry, earth and bitter chocolate; ripe tannins, integrated oak. Cork. **RATING** 89 **DRINK** 2013 $ 25
Steve Hoff Barossa Semillon 2004 Unoaked, but powerful, rich and mouthfilling; perhaps some skin contact; early maturing. Screwcap. **RATING** 87 **DRINK** 2008 $ 15

Hermes Morrison Wines

NR

253 Swan Ponds Road, Woodstock, NSW 2793 **REGION** Central Ranges Zone
T (02) 6345 0153 **F** (02) 6345 0153 **OPEN** 7 days 10–5 summer, winter weekends & public hols
WINEMAKER Jill Lindsay (Contract) **EST.** 1990 **CASES** 180
SUMMARY The Morrison family established Hermes Poll Dorset Stud in 1972; it continues but has now been joined by Hermes Morrison Wines. The cellar door has been built by the side of a large lake fed by cold, clear water welling up from subterranean caves, and a 10-minute walk takes you to the summit of Mt Palatine, one of the highest peaks in the shire, and with a spectacular view of the Canobolas Mountains 80 km away.

🐚 Heron Lake Estate

★★★★☆

Lot 27, Rendezvous Road, Vasse, WA 6280 **REGION** Margaret River
T (08) 9336 5711 **F** (08) 9433 1297 **WEB** www.heronlake.com.au **OPEN** 7 days 10–4
WINEMAKER Frank Kittler **EST.** 1984 **CASES** 1200
SUMMARY Di and Rob Goodwin (plus children Hannah and Callum) purchased the Heron Lake Vineyard from its founders, Mike and Faith Sparrow, in 2001, by which time the vineyard was 20 years old. There is a little over 6 ha of vines, chardonnay accounting for 2.6 ha, the remainder

verdelho, semillon, sauvignon blanc, cabernet and merlot. Both Rob and Di Goodwin are involved in postgraduate viticulture studies at various West Australian campuses. Di is actively involved in the management of the vineyard while Rob continues his involvement in a US sales training consultancy. The wines are available through the cellar door, by mail order and via the website, and are stocked by the Margaret River Regional Wine Centre. The quality is consistently good.

ΨΨΨΨΨ **Margaret River Chardonnay 2004** Strong, funky, charry, Burgundian barrel ferment aromas; complex palate; inputs work well, the wine tightening up rather than blowing out on the palate. High-quality cork. **RATING** 94 **DRINK** 2010 $19

ΨΨΨΨ **Margaret River Semillon Sauvignon Blanc 2004** Very fresh, delicate and appealing mix of passionfruit, ripe apple and citrus. Spotlessly clean opening and finish. **RATING** 90 **DRINK** 2007 $18

ΨΨΨΨ **Margaret River Sauvignon Blanc 2004** Spotlessly clean; fresh, fragrant and ripe aromas; plenty of flavour and depth, with a mix of tropical and gooseberry fruit; slightly cloying finish. Screwcap. **RATING** 89 **DRINK** Now $17

Margaret River Merlot 2002 Powerful and concentrated, but keeps varietal character; a core of red and black fruits, then long, fine, savoury tannins. **RATING** 89 **DRINK** 2012 $27

Margaret River Shiraz 2002 Light to medium-bodied; red cherry fruit, gently savoury tannins and a hint of vanilla oak; nicely balanced. **RATING** 88 **DRINK** 2010 $19

Margaret River Verdelho 2004 Gentle tropical fruit; nicely made; light-bodied and with some elegance; not sweet. **RATING** 87 **DRINK** Now $16

ΨΨΨ **Margaret River Cabernet Sauvignon 2003** Light-bodied; fresh, clean and well made; not enough depth; young vines? Twin Top. **RATING** 86 **DRINK** 2009 $19

ΨΨΨ **Rendezvous Rose 2004** **RATING** 83 $14

Herons Rise Vineyard   NR

Saddle Road, Kettering, Tas 7155 **REGION** Southern Tasmania
T (03) 6267 4339 **F** (03) 6267 4245 **WEB** www.heronsrise.com.au **OPEN** By appointment
WINEMAKER Andrew Hood (Contract) **EST.** 1984 **CASES** 250
SUMMARY Sue and Gerry White run a small stone country guesthouse in the D'Entrecasteaux Channel area and basically sell the wines produced from the surrounding hectare of vineyard to those staying at the two self-contained cottages.

Hesperos Wines   NR

PO Box 882, Margaret River, WA 6285 **REGION** Margaret River
T (08) 9757 6565 **F** (08) 9757 6565 **WEB** www.hesperoswines.com.au **OPEN** Not
WINEMAKER Jurg Muggli **EST.** 1993 **CASES** 2000
SUMMARY Hesperos is the venture of Jurg Muggli and Sandra Hancock. It supplies Jurg Muggli's winemaking skills to Xanadu, where Muggli has been resident winemaker for many years. It also has a 30-ha property near Witchcliffe, between Cape Mentelle and Devil's Lair, with the potential of 15 ha of vineyard. Planting commenced in the winter of 1999. Exports to Japan, Switzerland and Germany.

Hewitson   ★★★★★

The Old Dairy Cold Stores, 66 London Road, Mile End, SA 5031 **REGION** Southeast Australia
T (08) 8443 6466 **F** (08) 8443 6866 **WEB** www.hewitson.com.au **OPEN** By appointment
WINEMAKER Dean Hewitson **EST.** 1996 **CASES** 18 000
SUMMARY Dean Hewitson was a Petaluma winemaker for 10 years, and during that time managed to do three vintages in France and one in Oregon as well as undertaking his Masters at UC Davis, California. It is hardly surprising that the Hewitson wines are immaculately made from a technical viewpoint. However, he has also managed to source 30-year-old riesling from the Eden Valley and 70-year-old shiraz from McLaren Vale, and makes a Barossa Valley Mourvedre from 145-year-old vines at Rowland Flat and a Barossa Valley Shiraz and Grenache from 60-year-old vines at Tanunda. The vineyards are now under long-term contracts to Dean Hewitson. Exports to the UK, the US and other major markets.

YYYYY **Private Cellar McLaren Vale Shiraz Mourvedre 2002** Glorious bouquet of dark berry fruit; classic regional mix of blackberry, plum and bitter chocolate; Shiraz does most of the talking; no Grenache confection; 250 cases. Screwcap. **RATING** 94 **DRINK** 2015 $ 49
Old Garden Mourvedre 2003 Scented, highly fruity varietal aromas and flavours; relies more on elegance than power or extract; delicious now. From 1853 vineyard plantings. **RATING** 94 **DRINK** 2010 $ 51

YYYY **Miss Harry Dry Grown and Ancient 2003** A supple, fleshy array of red fruit flavours; soft, ripe, gentle tannins; overall attractive sweetness. **RATING** 93 **DRINK** 2008 $ 22
The Mad Hatter McLaren Vale Shiraz 2002 Very regional; pervasive dark chocolate, blackberry, plum and alcohol; savoury tannins prolong the finish; 2 years in French oak. Screwcap. **RATING** 92 **DRINK** 2017 $ 49

YYYY **Mermaids Muscadelle Dry 2004** Pushes the envelope convincingly; 10° alcohol; feathery, tangy, lemony mouthfeel; good balance. Perfect aperitif style. **RATING** 87 **DRINK** Now $ 16

Heytesbury Ridge ★★★★☆

1170 Cooriemungle Road, Timboon, Vic 3268 **REGION** Geelong
T (03) 5598 7394 **F** (03) 5598 7396 **WEB** www.heytesburyridge.com.au **OPEN** 7 days 11–5 Nov–Apr, or by appointment
WINEMAKER David Newton **EST.** 1998 **CASES** 1000
SUMMARY David and Dot Newton say that after milking cows for 18 years, they decided to investigate the possibility of planting a northeast-facing block of land which they also owned. Their self-diagnosed mid-life crisis also stemmed from a lifelong interest in wine as consumers. They planted 2 ha of chardonnay and pinot noir in December 1998, and another 2 ha of pinot gris, pinot noir and sauvignon blanc the following year. Having done a short winemaking course at Melbourne University (Dookie campus), the Newtons completed a small winery and in 2003. There is 4.5-star B&B accommodation on the property.

YYYYY **Limited Release Chardonnay 2004** Elegant and fine; subtle complexity with great structure; very sensitive oak; lingering, Chablis-like finish. Screwcap. **RATING** 94 **DRINK** 2010 $ 28

YYYY **Shiraz 2004** Light to medium red-purple; bright, fresh red and black cherry, and touches of spice; silky, fine tannins. Screwcap. **RATING** 89 **DRINK** 2010 $ 20
Chardonnay 2004 Very delicate, fine citrus, grapefruit and melon; has balance and length. Screwcap. **RATING** 87 **DRINK** 2008 $ 18
Pinot Grigio 2004 Cleverly made; a balance of pear, acidity and residual sugar neatly achieved. Screwcap. **RATING** 87 **DRINK** 2007 $ 15

Hickinbotham of Dromana ★★★

Nepean Highway (near Wallaces Road), Dromana, Vic 3936 **REGION** Mornington Peninsula
T (03) 5981 0355 **F** (03) 5987 0692 **WEB** www.hickinbotham.biz **OPEN** 7 days 11–5
WINEMAKER Andrew Hickinbotham **EST.** 1981 **CASES** 5000
SUMMARY After a peripatetic period and a hiatus in winemaking, Hickinbotham established a permanent vineyard and winery base at Dromana. It now makes only Mornington Peninsula wines, drawing in part on 5 ha of estate vineyards, and in part on contract-grown fruit. The wines are principally sold through the cellar door and by mail order.

YYYY **Cabernet Merlot 2000** Light red; light-bodied and distinctly developed; some spicy notes and fine, ripe tannins. **RATING** 87 **DRINK** Now $ 28

Hidden Creek NR

Eukey Road, Ballandean, Qld 4382 **REGION** Granite Belt
T (07) 4684 1383 **F** (07) 4684 1355 **WEB** www.hiddencreek.com.au **OPEN** Mon–Fri 11–3, weekends 10–4
WINEMAKER Jim Barnes **EST.** 1997 **CASES** 1000
SUMMARY A beautifully located vineyard and winery on a 1000-m high ridge overlooking the Ballandean township and the Severn River Valley, separated from Girraween National Park by Doctors Creek. The granite boulder-strewn hills mean that the 70-ha property will only provide a little over 6 ha of vineyard, in turn divided into six different blocks.

Hidden River Estate ★★★☆

Mullineaux Road, Pemberton, WA 6260 **REGION** Pemberton
T (08) 9776 1437 **F** (08) 9776 0189 **WEB** www.hiddenriver.com.au **OPEN** 7 days 9–4
WINEMAKER Brenden Smith, Phil Goldring **EST.** 1994 **CASES** 2000
SUMMARY Phil and Sandy Goldring spent 10 years operating farm chalets in the Pemberton area
before selling the business and retiring to become grapegrowers, with the intention of selling the
grapes to others. However, they found old habits hard to kick, so opened a cellar door and
café/restaurant. It is a successful business with a very strong marketing push; a 1901 Kalgoorlie tram
(the streetcar named Desire) has been purchased, renovated and installed onsite to provide more
seating for the award-winning restaurant. I hope the Goldrings did not pay much for the tram.

Highbank NR

Riddoch Highway, Coonawarra, SA 5263 **REGION** Coonawarra
T (08) 8736 3311 **F** (08) 8736 3122 **WEB** www.highbank.com.au **OPEN** By appointment
WINEMAKER Dennis Vice, Trevor Mast (Contract) **EST.** 1986 **CASES** 1000
SUMMARY Mt Gambier lecturer in viticulture Dennis Vice makes a tiny quantity of smooth, melon-
accented Chardonnay and stylish, good-quality Coonawarra Cabernet Blend; they are sold through
local restaurants and the cellar door, with limited Melbourne distribution. Intermittent exports to
various countries.

Higher Plane Wines ★★★★☆

Location 1077, Wintarru Rise via Warner Glen Road, Forrest Grove, WA 6286 (postal) **REGION**
Margaret River
T (08) 9336 7855 **F** (08) 9336 7866 **WEB** www.higherplanewines.com.au **OPEN** Not
WINEMAKER Keith Mugford (Contract) **EST.** 1997 **CASES** 6000
SUMMARY Plastic and hand surgeon Dr Craig Smith, and wife Cathie, left nothing to chance in
planning and establishing Higher Plane. As a prelude, Cathie obtained a Master of Business in wine
marketing from Edith Cowan University, and Craig began the wine marketing course at the
University of Adelaide. An exhaustive search for the right property ended in 1997, and 7.13 ha of vines
were planted, followed by a further 6.58 ha in late 2004, covering all the classic varieties. Its eastern
and northern boundaries adjoin Devil's Lair, and the two have similar gravelly, loamy, sandy soil. The
wines are sold through an active mailing list with copious information; limited retail distribution in
Western Australia, New South Wales, Victoria and Tasmania.

ΥΥΥΥΥ **Margaret River Chardonnay 2004** Very elegant; light to medium-bodied; gentle citrus
and melon; subtle barrel ferment oak; excellent length and balance. Screwcap. **RATING** 94
DRINK 2010 $ 31

ΥΥΥΥ♀ **Margaret River Chardonnay 2003** Quite complex, tangy, citrus-tinged aromas; lively
nectarine palate; good acidity. Screwcap. **RATING** 92 **DRINK** 2009 $ 31

ΥΥΥΥ **Margaret River Merlot 2003** High-toned, high-flavoured mix of wild herbs, spices, olives
and red fruits. Screwcap. **RATING** 89 **DRINK** 2010 $ 33
Margaret River Pinot Noir 2004 Strong colour; powerful smoky, briary edges to plummy
fruit; slightly stemmy finish; goes closer to Pinot than many from the region. Screwcap.
RATING 87 **DRINK** 2009 $ 26
Margaret River Cabernet Sauvignon 2003 Light to medium-bodied; savoury green olive
behind blackcurrant fruit; needs more ripe flesh. Screwcap. **RATING** 87 **DRINK** 2008 $ 33

ΥΥΥ **Margaret River Cabernet Merlot 2002** **RATING** 83 $ 32

Highland Heritage Estate NR

Mitchell Highway, Orange, NSW 2800 **REGION** Orange
T (02) 6361 3612 **F** (02) 6361 3613 **OPEN** Mon–Fri 9–3, weekends 9–5
WINEMAKER John Hordern, Rex D'Aquino **EST.** 1984 **CASES** 3500
SUMMARY The estate plantings have increased from 4 ha to over 15 ha, with 1995 and 1997 plantings
now in full production. The tasting facility is unusual: a converted railway carriage overlooking the
vineyard.

High Valley Wines
★★★☆

137 Cassilis Road, Mudgee, NSW 2850 **REGION** Mudgee
T (02) 6372 1011 **F** (02) 6372 1033 **WEB** www.highvalley.com.au **OPEN** 7 days 10–5
WINEMAKER Ian MacRae, David Lowe (Contract) **EST.** 1995 **CASES** 2000
SUMMARY The Francis family, headed by Ro and Grosvenor Francis, have operated a sheep, wheat
and cattle property at Dunedoo for several generations. When they handed over the property to their
sons in 1995, Ro and Grosvenor subdivided and retained a 40-ha block on which they have since
established 11 ha of shiraz, 6 ha of cabernet sauvignon and 5 ha of chardonnay. A grape supply
agreement was entered into with Rothbury Estate, but in 1998 they decided to also retain a portion of
the grapes and develop the High Valley Wines label. Also features a gas and wood-fired working
pottery, and vineyard and farm tours.

ỸỸỸỸ **Mudgee Chardonnay 2002** Pale straw-green; very delicate, crisp and fresh; strong
minerally substrate has absorbed the oak; utterly belies its 14° alcohol; interesting wine,
and could improve substantially. Screwcap. **RATING** 89 **DRINK** 2012 $ 23

Highway Wines
NR

612 Great Northern Highway, Herne Hill, WA 6056 **REGION** Swan Valley
T (08) 9296 4354 **OPEN** Mon–Sat 8.30–6
WINEMAKER Tony Bakranich **EST.** 1954 **CASES** 4000
SUMMARY A survivor of another era, when literally dozens of such wineries plied their business in the
Swan Valley. It still enjoys a strong local trade, selling much of its wine in fill-your-own-containers,
and 2-litre flagons, with lesser quantities sold by the bottle.

Hillbillé
★★★★☆

Blackwood Valley Estate, Balingup Road, Nannup, WA 6275 **REGION** Blackwood Valley
T (08) 9481 0888 **F** (08) 9486 1899 **WEB** www.hillbille.com **OPEN** Weekends & hols 10–4
WINEMAKER David Watson, Stuart Watson (Woodlands Wines) **EST.** 1998 **CASES** 2500
SUMMARY Gary Bettridge began the establishment of 19 ha of shiraz, cabernet sauvignon, merlot,
chardonnay and semillon in 1998. The vineyard is situated in the Blackwood Valley between
Balingup and Nannup, which the RAC describes as 'the most scenic drive in the southwest of
Western Australia'. A significant part of the grape production is sold to Goundrey, Vasse Felix,
Plantagenet and Evans & Tate, but since the 2003 vintage, part has been vinified by the Watsons.

ỸỸỸỸỸ **Reserve Shiraz 2003** Complex spice, pepper and licorice aromas; fine, elegant cool-
grown style (13.5° alcohol); silky black fruits; fine tannins. High-quality cork. **RATING** 94
DRINK 2013 $ 25

ỸỸỸỸ **Rose 2004** Strong purple-red for Rose; powerful, into light bodied dry red, but has
balance, and attractive cherry, raspberry, cassis fruit. Screwcap. **RATING** 88 **DRINK** 2007
$ 15

Hillbrook
★★★

639 Doust Road, Gearys Gap via Bungendore, NSW 2621 **REGION** Canberra District
T (02) 6236 9455 **F** (02) 6236 9455 **OPEN** Weekends & public hols 10–5
WINEMAKER Contract **EST.** 1994 **CASES** 2000
SUMMARY Adolf and Levina Zanzert began the establishment of 8.5 ha of vines at Gearys Gap in 1994.
The wines have retail distribution in the ACT, Bungendore and Cooma, and are also available
through the cellar door and via a mailing list.

ỸỸỸỸ **Merlot 2003 RATING** 84 **DRINK** 2007

Hillbrook Wines
NR

Cnr Hillbrook Road/Wheatley Coast Road, Quinninup, WA 6258 **REGION** Pemberton
T (08) 9776 7202 **F** (08) 9776 7202 **OPEN** By appointment
WINEMAKER Castle Rock Estate (Contract) **EST.** 1996 **CASES** 350

SUMMARY Brian Ede and partner Anne Walsh have established 1 ha of sauvignon blanc and 3 ha of merlot, and have the wines made for them by Robert Diletti at Castle Rock Estate. They are sold through the cellar door and via a mailing list, and – increasingly – by word of mouth.

Hillcrest Vineyard ★★★★★

31 Phillip Road, Woori Yallock, Vic 3139 REGION Yarra Valley
T (03) 5964 6689 F (03) 5961 5547 WEB www.hillcrestvineyard.com.au OPEN By appointment
WINEMAKER Phillip Jones (Contract) EST. 1971 CASES 400
SUMMARY David and Tanya Bryant may or may not realise it, but my association with Hillcrest goes back to 1985, when Coldstream Hills first started purchasing grapes from the then owners, Graeme and Joy Sweet. Although there was never a written contract, that arrangement continued until Hillcrest was sold, by which time the tiny amount of grapes coming from it was of no particular significance to Coldstream Hills. But the Sweets had stood by Coldstream Hills in the years of acute grape shortages, and we reciprocated further down the track.

TTTTT **Yarra Valley Chardonnay 2003** Bright green-yellow; poised and focused stone fruit and a hint of citrus; oak swallowed up; long finish; ultra-stylish. RATING 94 DRINK 2010 $ 36
Yarra Valley Pinot Noir 2003 Complex spice, black plums and forest; intense, long, lingering aftertaste. Beautifully made. RATING 94 DRINK 2009 $ 40

TTTT **Yarra Valley Cabernet Sauvignon 2003** Unconvincing colour; savoury, earthy, with obvious development; elegant but light on, though does have length. Oxidation somewhere or other. RATING 88 DRINK 20102010 $ 36

Hillside Estate Wines NR

Marrowbone Road, Pokolbin, NSW 2320 REGION Lower Hunter Valley
T (02) 4991 4370 F (02) 4991 4371 OPEN By appointment
WINEMAKER Trevor Drayton (Contract) EST. 1995 CASES NA
SUMMARY Rena and former noted journalist Ed Barnum have a substantial vineyard of 46 ha, planted to chardonnay, verdelho, traminer, shiraz and cabernet sauvignon; this is substantially more than a quiet retirement hobby. The wines are contract-made by district veteran Trevor Drayton.

Hill Smith Estate ★★★★☆

Flaxmans Valley Road, Eden Valley, SA 5235 REGION Eden Valley
T (08) 8561 3200 F (08) 8561 3393 WEB www.hillsmithestate.com OPEN At Yalumba
WINEMAKER Louisa Rose EST. 1979 CASES 5000
SUMMARY Part of the Yalumba stable, drawing upon estate plantings, including 15 ha of sauvignon blanc. Over the years has produced some excellent wines, but the style (and perhaps quality) does seem to vary significantly with vintage, and the winery rating is a compromise between the best and the least. Exports to all major markets.

TTTTY **Sauvignon Blanc 2004** Voluminous aromatic, gooseberry and grapefruit aromas flow through to a well-balanced and long palate. Clean finish. RATING 93 DRINK Now $ 18.95

Hills of Plenty NR

370 Yan Yean Road, Yarrambat, Vic 3091 REGION Yarra Valley
T (03) 9436 2264 F (03) 9436 2264 WEB www.hillsofplenty.com.au OPEN Last Sun of each month 11–6, or by appointment
WINEMAKER Karen Coulston EST. 1998 CASES 400
SUMMARY Hills of Plenty is just outside the Melbourne metropolitan area, a few minutes' drive north of Greensborough. There is a tiny 0.2-ha vineyard of riesling, chardonnay and cabernet sauvignon around the winery, but most of the fruit is purchased from other regions, notably Geelong, Gippsland and Swan Hill. The limited production means that the cellar door only opens once a month, but these are festive occasions, with live music, and picnics or barbecues welcome.

Hills View Vineyards ★★★☆

42 Crittenden Road, Findon, SA 5023 **REGION** McLaren Vale
T (08) 8445 7337 **F** (08) 8445 7367 **WEB** www.hillsview.com.au **OPEN** Not
WINEMAKER Brett Howard **EST.** 1998 **CASES** 30 000
SUMMARY District veteran Brett Howard, with 20 years' winemaking experience, is now the winemaker for Hills View Vineyards, producing its range of wines: the Blewitt Springs range and Howard label, a Fleurieu Semillon and a Coonawarra Shiraz are released only in the best vintages. Exports to the UK, the US and Germany.

Hillwood Vineyard NR

55 Innocent Street, Kings Meadows, Tas 7249 (postal) **REGION** Northern Tasmania
T 0418 500 672 **OPEN** Not
WINEMAKER Geoff Carr **EST.** NA **CASES** NA
SUMMARY Geoff Carr, the owner, viticulturist and winemaker, has established his vineyard on the east bank of the Tamar River, looking out over the river. He supplements his estate-grown grapes by purchasing some chardonnay and pinot gris from local growers.

Hochkirch Wines NR

Hamilton Highway, Tarrington, Vic 3301 **REGION** Henty
T (03) 5573 5200 **F** (03) 5573 5200 **OPEN** 11–5 by appointment
WINEMAKER John Nagorcka **EST.** 1997 **CASES** 3000
SUMMARY Jennifer and John Nagorcka have developed Hochkirk in response to the very cool climate: growing season temperatures are similar to those in Burgundy. A high-density planting pattern was implemented, with a low fruiting wine taking advantage of soil warmth in the growing season, and the focus was placed on pinot noir (4.5 ha), with lesser quantities of riesling, cabernet sauvignon, semillon and shiraz. The vines are not irrigated, and no synthetic fungicides, pesticides or fertilisers are used; the Nagorckas are trialling biodynamic practice. Wines with considerable complexity and interest are the result, the Pinot Noir having received critical acclaim in a number of quarters.

Hoddles Creek Estate ★★★★☆

505 Gembrook Road, Hoddles Creek, Vic 3139 **REGION** Yarra Valley
T (03) 5967 4692 **F** (03) 5967 4692 **WEB** www.hoddlescreekestate.com.au **OPEN** By appointment
WINEMAKER Franco D'Anna **EST.** 1997 **CASES** 10 000
SUMMARY In 1997, the D'Anna family decided to establish a vineyard on the property which had been in the family since 1960. There are now two vineyard blocks totalling 18.5 ha, split by Gembrook Road and Hoddles Creek; the vineyards are hand-pruned and hand-harvested. A 300-tonne, split-level winery was completed in time for the 2003 vintage. Son Franco D'Anna is the viticulturist and winemaker, having started to work in the family liquor store at 13, graduating to chief wine buyer by the time he was 21, then completing a Bachelor of Commerce degree at Melbourne University before studying viticulture at Charles Sturt University. A vintage at Coldstream Hills, then consulting help from Peter Dredge of Red Edge and Mario Marson (ex Mount Mary) has put an old head on young shoulders. Together with his uncle Bruno and one other worker, he is solely responsible for the vineyard and winery.

ŸŸŸŸŸ **Yarra Valley Chardonnay 2003** Elegant and fresh citrus and stone fruit; excellent length and finesse. Trophy Victorian Wines Show 2004. **RATING** 96 **DRINK** 2010 $16.99

ŸŸŸŸŸ **Yarra Valley Pinot Noir 2003** Light to medium-bodied; quite complex spice, plum and earth aromas and flavours; good length; spicy finish, almost minerally. **RATING** 91 **DRINK** 2008 $16.99

ŸŸŸŸ **Yarra Valley Sauvignon Blanc 2004** Clear varietal character; kiwifruit, gooseberry and a touch of smoke; shortens fractionally. **RATING** 89 **DRINK** 2007 $16.99
Yarra Valley Pinot Gris 2004 Again a touch of smoke/reduction; impressively powerful and long apple/pear palate; lingering aftertaste. Screwcap. **RATING** 89 **DRINK** 2008 $16.99

Hoffmann's ★★★☆

Ingoldby Road, McLaren Flat, SA 5171 **REGION** McLaren Vale
T (08) 8383 0232 **F** (08) 8383 0232 **OPEN** 7 days 11–5
WINEMAKER Nick Holmes, Hamish McGuire (Consultant) **EST.** 1996 **CASES** 2500
SUMMARY Peter and Anthea Hoffmann have been growing grapes at their property in Ingoldby Road since 1978, and Peter Hoffmann has worked at various wineries in McLaren Vale since 1979. Both he and Anthea have undertaken courses at the Regency TAFE Institute in Adelaide, and (in Peter's words), 'in 1996 we decided that we knew a little about winemaking and opened a small cellar door'. Exports to the UK, the US and other major markets.

ŶŶŶŶ **McLaren Vale Merlot 2003** Medium-bodied; sweet fruits and round, ripe tannins; good balance, controlled oak. Cork. **RATING** 87 **DRINK** 2009 $ 18
McLaren Vale Cabernet Sauvignon 2003 Soft, fleshy blackcurrant fruit; medium-bodied; ripe tannins; minimal oak. Cork. **RATING** 87 **DRINK** 2010 $ 21

ŶŶŶŶ **McLaren Vale Chardonnay 2004** **RATING** 86 **DRINK** 2007 $ 16
McLaren Vale Shiraz 2003 **RATING** 86 **DRINK** 2008 $ 21

Holley Hill ★★★★

136 Ronalds Road, Willung, Vic 3847 **REGION** Gippsland
T (03) 5198 2205 **F** (03) 5198 2205 **OPEN** Thurs–Sun & public hols 10–6
WINEMAKER David Packham **EST.** 1998 **CASES** 500
SUMMARY David Packham has used his background as a Master of Applied Science, formerly a research scientist with the CSIRO, and more recently with the Bureau of Meteorology, to plan the establishment of Holley Hill. He served his apprenticeship at another winery for 2 years before acquiring the then 2-year-old Holley Hill vineyard, planted to 0.5 ha each of chardonnay, sauvignon blanc and pinot noir. A large hay shed on the property was converted to a winery, and the cellar door opened in November 2002.

ŶŶŶŶŶ **Shiraz 2003** Dense colour; a super-abundance of blackberry, licorice and spice; still to fully form shape, but will do so. Stained Diam cork. **RATING** 91 **DRINK** 2078 $ 18

ŶŶŶŶ **Pinot Noir 2003** Opaque purple; very concentrated; almost mono-dimensional dark plum and blackberry; presumably microscopic crop levels. Dry reddish. Diam. **RATING** 87 **DRINK** 2013 $ 15

ŶŶŶŶ **Sauvignon Blanc 2004** **RATING** 86 **DRINK** 2007 $ 15
Pinot Rose 2004 Fuchsia; sweet strawberry and cherry fruit; charming cellar door style. Diam. **RATING** 86 **DRINK** Now $ 15

Hollick ★★★★☆

Riddoch Highway, Coonawarra, SA 5263 **REGION** Coonawarra
T (08) 8737 2318 **F** (08) 8737 2952 **WEB** www.hollick.com **OPEN** 7 days 9–5
WINEMAKER Ian Hollick, David Norman **EST.** 1983 **CASES** 40 000
SUMMARY Winner of many trophies (including the most famous of all, the Jimmy Watson), its wines are well crafted and competitively priced. A $1 million cellar door and restaurant complex opened in June 2002. National distribution in all states; exports to Europe and Asia.

ŶŶŶŶŶ **Cabernet Sauvignon 2002** Good colour; dense, powerful style with blackcurrant fruit and a touch of chocolate; big tannins; very long palate. Multiple trophies 2004 Limestone Coast Wine Show. **RATING** 95 **DRINK** 2017 $ 29

ŶŶŶŶŶ **Reserve Chardonnay 2003** Considerable intensity; fruit-driven, with good acidity and a clean, lingering finish. **RATING** 93 **DRINK** 2010 $ 22
Shiraz Cabernet 2002 Medium red-purple; slightly lean earth and olive overtones to the blackberry and blackcurrant fruit; very fine texture and structure. **RATING** 93 **DRINK** 2017 $ 19
Coonawarra Cabernet Sauvignon Merlot 2002 Abundant, round blackberry fruit on the mid-palate; ripe tannins to close; good oak. **RATING** 92 **DRINK** 2012 $ 24

ŶŶŶŶ **Wilgha Shiraz 2002** Long, savoury and spicy; slightly lean, needing a touch more sweet fruit on the mid-palate. **RATING** 89 **DRINK** 2012 $ 45

Sauvignon Blanc Semillon 2004 Fragrant and clean; citrus and lemon fruit with minerally acid which is likely to cause some to flinch. **RATING** 87 **DRINK** 2007 $ 17

ŸŸŸŸ **The Nectar 2004 RATING** 86 **DRINK** 2007 $ 22

ŸŸŸ **Hollaia Varietal Trial Sangiovese Cabernet Sauvignon 2003 RATING** 79 $ 17.50

Hollyclare

NR

940 Milbrodale Road, Broke, NSW 2330 **REGION** Lower Hunter Valley
T (02) 6579 1193 **F** (02) 6579 1269 **OPEN** Weekends 10–5 by appointment
WINEMAKER Tamburlaine (Contract) **EST.** 1987 **CASES** 2000
SUMMARY John Holdsworth established the Hollyclare Vineyard (now totalling 3 ha each of chardonnay, semillon, shiraz and 1 ha of aleatico) 10 years ago, but the Hollyclare label is a relatively new one on the market. While the wines are made under contract at Tamburlaine, Hollyclare has its own dedicated wine tanks and all the wines are estate-grown.

Holm Oak

★★★★

RSD 256, Rowella, West Tamar, Tas 7270 **REGION** Northern Tasmania
T (03) 6394 7577 **F** (03) 6394 7350 **OPEN** 7 days 10–5
WINEMAKER Nick Butler, Julian Alcorso (Contract) **EST.** 1983 **CASES** 3000
SUMMARY The Butler family produces tremendously rich and strongly flavoured red wines from their vineyard on the banks of the Tamar River; it takes its name from its grove of oak trees, planted around the turn of the 20th century, and originally intended for the making of tennis racquets.

Home Hill

★★★★

38 Nairn Street, Ranelagh, Tas 7109 **REGION** Southern Tasmania
T (03) 6264 1200 **F** (03) 6264 1069 **WEB** www.homehillwines.com.au **OPEN** 7 days 10–5
WINEMAKER Peter Dunbaven **EST.** 1994 **CASES** 3000
SUMMARY Terry and Rosemary Bennett planted their first 0.5 ha of vines in 1994 on gentle slopes in the beautiful Huon Valley. The plantings were quickly extended to 3 ha, with another hectare planted in 1999. A 70-seat restaurant is open for lunch Wednesday to Sunday and dinner on Saturday.

ŸŸŸŸŸ **Kelly's Reserve Chardonnay 2004** Light-bodied; subtle malolactic and barrel ferment inputs give a touch of elegance; good length. **RATING** 93 **DRINK** 2008 $ 23
Kelly's Reserve Pinot Noir 2003 Vivid red-purple; fragrant, vibrant black and red cherry fruit; spotlessly clean, but very firm, low pH style; needs time to soften. Screwcap. **RATING** 90 **DRINK** 2013 $ 35

ŸŸŸŸ **Pinot Noir 2003** A powerful entry, with strong plum and cherry fruit; complex oak with hints of spice and leather; huge-impact style. Beware cork taint. **RATING** 88 **DRINK** 2009 $ 25

ŸŸŸŸ **Chardonnay 2004 RATING** 86 **DRINK** 2007 $ 19
Sylvaner 2004 RATING 86 **DRINK** 2007 $ 19
Reserve Sticky 2003 RATING 85 **DRINK** 2007 $ 19

ŸŸŸ **Rose 2004 RATING** 83 $ 19

Honeytree Estate

16 Gillards Road, Pokolbin, NSW 2321 **REGION** Lower Hunter Valley
T (02) 4998 7693 **F** (02) 4998 7693 **WEB** www.honeytreewines.com **OPEN** Wed–Fri 11–4, weekends 10–5
WINEMAKER Jim Chatto (Contract) **EST.** 1970 **CASES** 3600
SUMMARY The Honeytree Estate vineyard was first planted in 1970, and for a period of time wines were produced under the Honeytree Estate label. It then disappeared, but the vineyard has since been revived by Dutch-born Henk Strengers and family. Its 10 ha of vines are of shiraz, cabernet sauvignon, semillon and a little clairette, known in the Hunter Valley as blanquette, and a variety

which has been in existence there for well over a century. Jancis Robinson comments that the wine 'tends to be very high in alcohol, a little low in acid and to oxidise dangerously fast', but in a sign of the times, the first Honeytree Clairette sold out so quickly (in 4 weeks) that 2.2 ha of vineyard has been grafted over to additional clairette. Exports to The Netherlands.

ŦŦŦŦ **Paul Alexander Shiraz 2003** Savoury regional undertones to attractive ripe plum and black fruits; sweet, ripe tannins; subtle oak. Cork. **RATING** 89 **DRINK** 2010 $ 20

Hood Wines/Wellington ★★★★★

Cnr Richmond Road/Denholms Road, Cambridge, Tas 7170 **REGION** Southern Tasmania
T (03) 6248 5844 **F** (03) 6248 5855 **OPEN** First Sunday of every month 12–4, or by appointment
WINEMAKER Andrew Hood, Jeremy Dineen **EST.** 1990 **CASES** 5000
SUMMARY In late 2003 Wellington was acquired by Tony Scherer and Jack Kidwiler of Frogmore Creek; it has since been renamed Hood Wines. The Wellington winery will continue to operate as previously, making both its own label wines and wines for its other contract customers while a new winery is constructed on the Frogmore Creek property. The latter will be exclusively devoted to organically grown wines; Andrew Hood will remain in charge of winemaking both at Wellington and at the new Frogmore Creek operation.

ŦŦŦŦŦ **Wellington Riesling 2004** Fragrant lime, herb, spice and blossom aromas; delicate but intense; lingering, perfectly balanced finish. **RATING** 95 **DRINK** 2015 $ 19
Wellington Chardonnay 2003 Unusually rich and ripe, even luscious, for Tasmania; white peach and nectarine fruit does all the talking; long, balanced finish. Multiple trophies 2005 Tasmanian Wines Show. **RATING** 95 **DRINK** 2010 $ 24
Wellington Sauvignon Blanc 2004 Faintly smoky, but impressively complex and strongly varietal, with a nice mix of tropical and more herbal flavours. Trophy 2005 Tasmanian Wines Show. **RATING** 94 **DRINK** 2007 $ 19

ŦŦŦŦⵖ **Wellington Riesling 2004** Lovely lime juicey/tangy fruit; beautiful balance and length; spot-on Mosel style. **RATING** 92 **DRINK** 2015 $ 19
Wellington Chardonnay 2003 Very funky barrel ferment bouquet; exceptionally complex palate, just that fraction over the top, but will appeal greatly to Burgundy lovers. **RATING** 92 **DRINK** 2012 $ 24
Wellington Chardonnay 2004 Quite ripe; touches of tropical fruit and nectarine; crisp acidity. **RATING** 90 **DRINK** 2008 $ 24
Wellington Pinot Noir 2003 Light to medium-bodied; sweet red fruits; good line and length. **RATING** 90 **DRINK** 2009 $ 32
Wellington Sparkling 2000 Quite spicy, the pinot noir component of this; still youthful and still developing. **RATING** 90 **DRINK** 2008
Wellington Riesling 375 ml 2004 Intense, piercing acidity and considerable underlying sweetness, all adding up to balance. Needs time. **RATING** 90 **DRINK** 2009 $ 19

ŦŦŦŦ **Wellington Pinot Gris 2004** Clean and fresh; neutral fruit as ever, but well balanced, with fresh acidity. **RATING** 89 **DRINK** 2007 $ 19

ŦŦŦ **Wellington Pinot Noir 2004** **RATING** 83 $ 32

Hope Estate NR

Cobcroft Road, Broke, NSW 2330 **REGION** Lower Hunter Valley
T (02) 6579 1161 **F** (02) 6579 1373 **WEB** www.hopeestate.com **OPEN** 7 days 10–4
WINEMAKER Josh Steele **EST.** 1996 **CASES** 30 000
SUMMARY Pharmacist Michael Hope has come a long way since acquiring his first vineyard in the Hunter Valley in 1994. His Hunter Valley empire now encompasses three substantial vineyards and the former Saxonvale Winery, acquired in 1996, renamed Hope Estate, and refurbished at a cost of over $1 million. That, however, proved to be only the first step, for Hope has acquired most of the assets of the former public-listed Vincor, including its Donnybrook Vineyard in Western Australia, and the Virgin Hills brand, which includes its original 14-ha vineyard, another nearby 32-ha vineyard at Glenhope, a lease of the historic winery, and all Virgin Hills stocks. Exports to the UK, the US and other major markets.

Hoppers Hill Vineyards

NR

Googodery Road, Cumnock, NSW 2867 **REGION** Western Plains Zone
T (02) 6367 7270 **OPEN** By appointment
WINEMAKER Robert Gilmore **EST.** 1990 **CASES** NFP
SUMMARY The Gilmores planted their vineyard in 1980, using organic growing methods; they use no preservatives or filtration in the winery, which was established in 1990. Not surprisingly, the wines cannot be judged or assessed against normal standards, but may have appeal in a niche market.

Horndale

NR

Fraser Avenue, Happy Valley, SA 5159 **REGION** McLaren Vale
T (08) 8387 0033 **F** (08) 8387 0033 **OPEN** Mon–Sat 9–5, Sun & public hols 10–5.30
WINEMAKER Phil Albrecht **EST.** 1896 **CASES** NFP
SUMMARY Established in 1896 and has remained continuously in production in one way or another since that time, though with a number of changes of ownership and direction. The wines are only available from the cellar door and by mail order. A personal connection is the Horndale Brandy my father used to buy 60 years ago, but it no longer appears on the extensive price list.

Horseshoe Vineyard

NR

Horseshoe Road, Horseshoe Valley via Denman, NSW 2328 **REGION** Upper Hunter Valley
T (02) 6547 3528 **OPEN** Weekends 9–5
WINEMAKER John Hordern **EST.** 1986 **CASES** NFP
SUMMARY Fell by the wayside after its wonderful start in 1986, with rich, full-flavoured, barrel-fermented Semillons and Chardonnays. These days John Hordern's main occupation seems to be as a highly successful contract winemaker, particularly for Penmara.

Horvat Estate

★★★

2444 Burke Street, Landsborough, Vic 3384 **REGION** Pyrenees
T (03) 5356 9296 **F** (03) 5356 9264 **OPEN** 7 days 10–5
WINEMAKER Andrew Horvat, Gabriel Horvat **EST.** 1995 **CASES** 1500
SUMMARY The Horvat family (including Janet, Andrew and Gabriel) began developing their 5-ha vineyard of shiraz in 1995, supplementing production with contract-grown grapes. The wine is made onsite using traditional methods and ideas, deriving in part from the family's Croatian background.

 Premium Family Reserve Shiraz 2003 Moderately complex leather, spice and herb aromas and flavours; drying, grippy tannins detract. **RATING** 87 **DRINK** 2009 $ 30

Traditional Cabernet 2002 RATING 85 **DRINK** 2007 $ 20

Houghton

★★★★★

Dale Road, Middle Swan, WA 6056 **REGION** Swan Valley
T (08) 9274 9450 **F** (08) 9274 5372 **WEB** www.houghton-wines.com.au **OPEN** 7 days 10–5
WINEMAKER Robert Bowen, Ross Pamment, Simon Osicka **EST.** 1836 **CASES** 280 000
SUMMARY The 5-star rating was once partially justified by Houghton White Burgundy, one of Australia's largest-selling white wines: it was almost entirely consumed within days of purchase, but was superlative with seven or so years' bottle age. The Jack Mann red, Gladstones Shiraz, Houghton Reserve Shiraz, the Margaret River reds and Frankland Riesling are all of the highest quality, and simply serve to reinforce the rating. To borrow a saying of the late Jack Mann, 'There are no bad wines here.'

 Gladstones Cabernet Sauvignon 2001 In normal super-heroic style; densely packed with fruit, oak and tannins, all integrated and well balanced. **RATING** 96 **DRINK** 2021 $ 62
Jack Mann 2001 Immensely powerful and concentrated, yet not the least jammy or alcoholic. Glorious blackcurrant, spice, earth and bitter chocolate; fine, long tannins; very good oak management. High-quality cork. **RATING** 96 **DRINK** 2021 $ 105
Gladstones Shiraz 2001 Massively powerful upscale version of the Frankland River Shiraz; dense, spicy, savoury black fruits and long finish. Do not approach before 2010. **RATING** 95 **DRINK** 2021 $ 62

Frankland River Justin Vineyard Shiraz 2001 Bursting with luscious black fruits and spices complemented by French oak; fine, supple tannins; long finish. **RATING** 95 **DRINK** 2016 $ 32

Pemberton Chardonnay 2003 Bright green-straw; super-elegant grapefruit, melon and stone fruit; delicate malolactic and barrel ferment influences; long and supple. Quality cork. **RATING** 94 **DRINK** 2010

Margaret River Cabernet Sauvignon 2001 Clarion-clear cassis, red and blackcurrant varietal fruit; fine tannins, good oak. **RATING** 94 **DRINK** 2011 $ 32

♥♥♥♥♀ **Crofters Cabernet Merlot 2001** A substantial wine; powerful structure; cassis and blackcurrant fruit, lingering tannins. **RATING** 93 **DRINK** 2016 $ 25

Pemberton Chardonnay Pinot Noir 2000 Elegant creamy/nutty overtones to supple stone fruit; harmonious and stylish. **RATING** 92 **DRINK** Now $ 28

Crofters Sauvignon Blanc Semillon 2004 Abundant tropical fruit off-set by crisp, herbal/mineral acidity; good length. **RATING** 91 **DRINK** Now $ 18

Pemberton Merlot 2001 Medium-bodied; ripe redcurrant and blackcurrant varietal fruit; fine, ripe tannins; controlled French oak. Cork. **RATING** 90 **DRINK** 2010

Cabernet Shiraz Merlot 2003 Abundant and expansive red and black fruits provide delicious mouthfeel and flavour; fantastic value for a lovely drink-now wine. **RATING** 90 **DRINK** 2007 $ 11

♥♥♥♥ **Pemberton Sauvignon Blanc 2004** Very pale colour; tight, reserved, clean and balanced, but needs more fruit. **RATING** 89 **DRINK** Now $ 24

White Burgundy 2004 A medium-bodied and balanced mix of tropical fruit salad and a twist of lemon; nice acidity. Value and development potential. **RATING** 88 **DRINK** 2009 $ 10

Margaret River Cabernet Sauvignon 2003 Good colour; medium-bodied; blackcurrant, chocolate and vanilla; ripe tannins; honest style. Twin Top. **RATING** 88 **DRINK** 2010

♥♥♥♀ **Chardonnay 2004** **RATING** 85 **DRINK** Now $ 10

Chardonnay Verdelho 2004 **RATING** 85 **DRINK** Now

House of Certain Views ★★★★☆

1238 Milbrodale Road, Broke, NSW 2330 **REGION** Lower Hunter Valley
T (02) 6579 1317 **F** (02) 6579 1317 **WEB** www.margan.com.au **OPEN** Not
WINEMAKER Andrew Margan **EST.** 2001 **CASES** 1500
SUMMARY A stand-alone business owned by Andrew and Lisa Margan, with a fascinating portfolio of wines based on exclusive or fairly new winegrowing regions on the western side of the Great Dividing Range. The selection of the vineyard sites (via contract growers) involves a careful correlation of latitude, altitude, soil type and variety – the French catch it all in the single word: terroir. The packaging of the wines, incidentally, is brilliant.

♥♥♥♥♥ **Coonabarabran Cabernet Sauvignon 2002** Deep colour; clean, luscious and powerful blackcurrant/cassis/blackberry; fine, ripe tannins; lovely wine. **RATING** 94 **DRINK** 2015 $ 30

♥♥♥♥ **Orange Viognier 2004** Not assertive in varietal aromas, but some apricot/pastille fruit; nice mouthfeel. **RATING** 88 **DRINK** Now $ 25

Mt Kaputar Merlot 2002 Strongly savoury/olivaceous aromas and flavours; classic austere varietal style; doesn't shows its 14° alcohol. **RATING** 87 **DRINK** 2009 $ 30

Howard Park (Denmark) ★★★★★

Scotsdale Road, Denmark, WA 6333 **REGION** Denmark
T (08) 9848 2345 **F** (08) 9848 2064 **WEB** www.howardparkwines.com.au **OPEN** 7 days 10–4
WINEMAKER Michael Kerrigan, Andy Browning, Matt Burton **EST.** 1986 **CASES** 100 000
SUMMARY All the Howard Park wines are made here at the new, large winery. However, there are three groups of wines: those sourced from either Great Southern or Margaret River; the icon Howard Park Riesling and Cabernet Sauvignon Merlot; and the multi-regional MadFish range. Thus the Leston wines come from Margaret River, the Scotsdale from Great Southern. All are very impressive. Exports to all major markets.

♥♥♥♥♥ **Riesling 2004** Pale straw-green; spotlessly clean apple and lime blossom; lovely palate, with sweet lime fruit and a dry finish. **RATING** 95 **DRINK** 2014 $ 25

Scotsdale Great Southern Shiraz 2002 Elegant, but intense; medium-bodied; long palate; firm but not aggressive tannins. Pure class. Screwcap. **RATING** 94 **DRINK** 2017 $ 35

Howard Park (Margaret River)   ★★★★★

Miamup Road, Cowaramup, WA 6284 **REGION** Margaret River
T (08) 9756 5200 **F** (08) 9756 5222 **WEB** www.howardparkwines.com.au **OPEN** 7 days 10–5
WINEMAKER Michael Kerrigan, Andy Browning, Matt Burton **EST.** 1986 **CASES** 100 000
SUMMARY In the wake of its acquisition by the Burch family, and the construction of a large state-of-the-art winery at Denmark, a capacious cellar door (incorporating Feng Shui principles) has been opened in the Margaret River, where there are also significant estate plantings. The Margaret River flagships are the Leston Shiraz and Leston Cabernet Sauvignon, but the Margaret River vineyards routinely contribute to all the wines in the range, from MadFish at the bottom, to the icon Cabernet Sauvignon Merlot at the top. Exports to all major markets.

ŸŸŸŸŸ **Chardonnay 2003** A seamless and super-fine palate reflects precision engineering of nectarine fruit and barrel-fermented French oak; the epitome of elegance, and at the start of its life. **RATING** 96 **DRINK** 2010 $ 35
Cabernet Sauvignon 2001 Classy wine; abundant structure but not the least extractive; blackcurrant and sweet fruit; long and silky. Great Southern 71%, Margaret River 29%. **RATING** 96 **DRINK** 2021 $ 75
MadFish Riesling 2004 Intense lime, herb and apple aromas; delicate yet intense; spotlessly clean; long and impeccably balanced citrussy fruit. Three trophies Western Australian Wine Show 2004, including Best White of Show. **RATING** 95 **DRINK** 2015 $ 16
Best Barrels Merlot 2003 Very serious wine; concentrated and intense; crystal-clear varietal character; dark currant with faint hints of spice and olive; great structure. **RATING** 95 **DRINK** 2018 $ 75
Cabernet Sauvignon 2002 Perfectly ripened cabernet fruit; luscious blackcurrant tempered by just a touch of olive and earth; tannins and oak (20 months French) perfectly integrated. **RATING** 95 **DRINK** 2022 $ 75

ŸŸŸŸ⅃ **MadFish Chardonnay 2003** Smooth, seamless fusion of melon, citrus and oak; excellent balance and finish. **RATING** 92 **DRINK** 2008 $ 22
MadFish Shiraz 2003 Very aromatic; bright, cool-grown varietal red fruits, spice and fine tannins; good structure, weight and depth. **RATING** 92 **DRINK** 2009 $ 24
Leston Margaret River Shiraz 2002 Spicy red and black fruits well integrated with French oak; fine, lingering, soft tannins. **RATING** 92 **DRINK** 2012 $ 35
MadFish Sauvignon Blanc Semillon 2004 Clean; delicate hints of passionfruit, apple and gooseberry; lively finish with lemony acidity. **RATING** 90 **DRINK** 2008 $ 18
MadFish Premium White 2004 Elegant; quite intense nectarine/citrus fruit; outstanding example of unwooded chardonnay. **RATING** 90 **DRINK** Now $ 17

ŸŸŸŸ **MadFish Rose 2004** Light, bright red-purple; a fresh mix of red fruits and leaf on the bouquet and palate. **RATING** 87 **DRINK** Now $ 18

ŸŸŸ⅃ **MadFish Carnelian 2003** Substantial red wine; tannins too powerful for the fruit, but may settle down; atypical for the MadFish style. Cabernet/grenache/carignan cross. **RATING** 86 **DRINK** 2010 $ 24

Howards Lane Vineyard   NR

Howards Lane, Welby, Mittagong, NSW 2575 **REGION** Southern Highlands
T (02) 4872 1971 **F** (02) 4872 1971 **WEB** www.howardslane.com.au **OPEN** 7 days 10–5
WINEMAKER Michelle Crockett (Contract) **EST.** 1994 **CASES** 650
SUMMARY Tony and Mary Betteridge have developed the plantings over a 10-year period, establishing the Corrie Vineyard first, and recently the McCourt Vineyard. The cellar door, open daily, has light meals and picnic facilities. Back vintages of Chardonnay are available.

HPR Wines   NR

260 Old Moorooduc Road, Tuerong, Vic 3933 (postal) **REGION** Mornington Peninsula
T (03) 5974 2097 **F** (03) 5974 3099 **OPEN** Not
WINEMAKER Hugh Robinson **EST.** 1988 **CASES** 250

SUMMARY Hugh Robinson is a Mornington Peninsula veteran, and has no less than 22 ha of sauvignon blanc, semillon, chardonnay, pinot gris, pinot noir, merlot and shiraz. The major part of the production is sold as grapes to other makers, with the remainder made by Hugh Robinson onsite. Retail distribution through Rutherglen Wine and Spirit, or by mail order.

Hudson's Peak Wines
NR

92 Hillsborough Road, Hillsborough, NSW 2320 **REGION** Lower Hunter Valley
T 0409 660 883 **F** (02) 4930 0759 **OPEN** 7 days 10–5
WINEMAKER John Cassegrain (Contract) **EST.** 1998 **CASES** NFP
SUMMARY Hudson's Peak Wines come from a historic property, first gazetted in 1829, and taken up by Beresford Hudson, who gave his name both to a nearby mountain top and (now) this substantial wine venture. The 53-ha property includes 18 ha of vines, almost half to shiraz, the remainder to semillon, chardonnay, verdelho and merlot. Part of the production is sold as grapes, and part is contract-made.

Hugh Hamilton
 ★★★★

McMurtrie Road, McLaren Vale, SA 5171 **REGION** McLaren Vale
T (08) 8323 8689 **F** (08) 8323 9488 **WEB** www.hughhamiltonwines.com.au **OPEN** Mon–Fri 10–5.30, weekends & public hols 11–5.30
WINEMAKER Hugh Hamilton **EST.** 1991 **CASES** 8000
SUMMARY Hugh Hamilton is the most recent member of the famous Hamilton winemaking family to enter the business with a label of his own. Production comes from 18.2 ha of estate plantings, supplemented by contract-grown material. Recent plantings go beyond the mainstream to sangiovese, tempranillo, petit verdot and saperavi. Retail distribution in most states; exports to the US, Canada, the UK, Denmark and Malaysia.

TTTTY The Rascal Shiraz 2003 Dense but better hue than the Jekyll and Hyde. Despite its alcohol (15.5°), has some bitterness and reduction; certainly needs time to resolve. Screwcap. **RATING** 92 **DRINK** 2013 $ 24.50
Jekyll & Hyde Shiraz Viognier 2003 Strong colour; powerful wine; blackberry and dark chocolate; 7% Viognier influence subtle; ripe tannins; 16° alcohol heats up the finish. Stained cork. **RATING** 92 **DRINK** 2013 $ 28.50

TTTT Menage a Trois 2004 Spicy, fresh sour and red cherries; vibrant and racy; brasserie special; 85% Sangiovese, 10% Cabernet Sauvignon, 5% Merlot. Screwcap. **RATING** 87 **DRINK** Now $ 19.50

TTTY The Villain Cabernet Sauvignon 2003 RATING 86 **DRINK** 2010 $ 24.50
The Loose Cannon Viognier 2004 RATING 85 **DRINK** Now $ 19.50
The Trickster Verdelho 2004 RATING 84 **DRINK** Now $ 18.50

TTT The Scallywag Unwooded Chardonnay 2004 RATING 83 $ 17.50

Hugo
★★★☆

Elliott Road, McLaren Flat, SA 5171 **REGION** McLaren Vale
T (08) 8383 0098 **F** (08) 8383 0446 **WEB** www.hugowines.com.au **OPEN** Mon–Fri 9–5, Sat 12–5, Sun 10.30–5
WINEMAKER John Hugo **EST.** 1982 **CASES** 12 000
SUMMARY A winery which came from relative obscurity to prominence in the late 1980s with some lovely ripe, sweet reds which, while strongly American oak-influenced, were quite outstanding. Has picked up the pace again after a dull period in the mid-1990s. There are 32 ha of estate plantings, with part of the grape production sold to others. Exports to all major markets.

TTTT McLaren Vale Sauvignon Blanc 2004 Authentic varietal character from the first moment; good length and finish, likewise balance. **RATING** 89 **DRINK** 2007 $ 18
McLaren Vale Cabernet Sauvignon 2002 Clean, medium-bodied blend of blackcurrant and dark chocolate fruit; persistent but ripe tannins. **RATING** 89 **DRINK** 2012 $ 21.50
McLaren Vale Cabernet Rose 2004 Fresh, light to medium-bodied; zesty, leafy, almost minerally palate; good length and acidity; dry finish. **RATING** 87 **DRINK** Now $ 19

TTTY McLaren Vale Unwooded Chardonnay 2004 RATING 86 **DRINK** 2007 $ 16
McLaren Vale Shiraz 2002 RATING 84 **DRINK** 2011 $ 21.50

🐛 Humbug Reach Vineyard ★★★★☆

72 Nobelias Drive, Legana, Tas 7277 **REGION** Northern Tasmania
T (03) 6330 2875 **F** (03) 6330 2739 **OPEN** Not
WINEMAKER Julian Alcorso (Contract) **EST.** 1988 **CASES** NA
SUMMARY The Humbug Reach Vineyard was established in the late 1980s on the banks of the Tamar River, with plantings of pinot noir. Riesling and chardonnay followed thereafter. Owned by Paul and Sally McShane since 1999, who proudly tend the 5000 or so vines on the property. The wines are stocked at various Tasmanian outlets and at Randall's Wine Merchant in Victoria.

🍷🍷🍷🍷🍷 **Riesling 2004** Lemon peel/zest and mineral; well balanced; intense drive and length. **RATING** 94 **DRINK** 2014 $ 22

🍷🍷🍷🍷🍷 **Chardonnay 2004** Long, citrus and melon fruit; smooth and quite supple; squeaky acidity on the finish; fresh as a daisy. Screwcap. **RATING** 91 **DRINK** 2010 $ 20
Pinot Noir 2002 Good colour; very attractive plum and spice fruit; medium-bodied; gaining complexity and mouthfeel as it ages. Cork. **RATING** 91 **DRINK** 2009 $ 40
Chardonnay 2003 Developing slowly; attractive fresh-cut sweet nectarine fruit; good length; still evolving. Screwcap. **RATING** 90 **DRINK** 2008 $ 20

🍷🍷🍷🍷 **Pinot Noir 2003** Light to medium-bodied; smooth, fine, silky texture; gentle plum and touches of black cherry and spice; balanced and harmonious. Screwcap. **RATING** 89 **DRINK** 2010 $ 40

🍷🍷🍷🍷 **Chardonnay 2002** Opens well, but the acid is simply too strong on the finish; will it ever soften? Cork. **RATING** 86 **DRINK** 2010 $ 27

Hundred Tree Hill ★★★

c/- Redbank Winery, 1 Sallys Lane, Redbank, Vic 3478 **REGION** Pyrenees
T (03) 5467 7255 **F** (03) 5467 7248 **WEB** www.sallyspaddock.com.au **OPEN** Mon–Sat 9–5, Sun 10–5
WINEMAKER Huw Robb, Scott Hutton, Sasha Robb **EST.** 1973 **CASES** 6000
SUMMARY The next generation of the Robb family (Emily, Huw and Sasha) have established their own vineyard, with 6 ha each of shiraz, cabernet sauvignon and cabernet franc, plus 2 ha of pinot noir. Hundred Tree Hill was so named to commemorate the 100 trees which went into the building of the Hundred Tree Homestead. For the time being, the focus is on export sales, but the Robbs intend to diversify into the domestic market in the near future. Exports to the US, Germany and The Philippines.

Hungerford Hill ★★★★☆

1 Broke Road, Pokolbin, NSW 2321 **REGION** Lower Hunter Valley
T 1800 187 666 **F** (02) 4998 7375 **WEB** www.hungerfordhill.com.au **OPEN** 7 days 10–5
WINEMAKER Phillip John **EST.** 1967 **CASES** 20 000
SUMMARY Hungerford Hill, sold by Southcorp to the Kirby family in 2002, has emerged with its home base at the impressive winery on the corner of Allandale and Broke Roads, previously known as One Broke Road. The development of the One Broke Road complex proved wildly uneconomic, and the rationalisation process has resulted in Hungerford Hill being the sole owner. Terroir Restaurant and Wine Bar are run by award-winning chef Darren Ho. Exports to all major markets.

🍷🍷🍷🍷🍷 **Tumbarumba Chardonnay 2004** Elegant and very fine; creamy malolactic with melon and citrus/grapefruit, interwoven with subtle oak; beautifully crafted. **RATING** 94 **DRINK** 2012 $ 25

🍷🍷🍷🍷🍷 **Tumbarumba Pinot Noir 2004** Deep purple-red; powerful, deep, ripe black cherry and satsuma plum have absorbed the new French oak. Patience required. **RATING** 92 **DRINK** 2014 $ 25
Hunter Valley Semillon 2004 Spotlessly clean; gentle lemon with faint tropical overtones; well balanced; deceptive length. **RATING** 91 **DRINK** 2014 $ 23
Clare Valley Riesling 2004 Lime and nettle aromas; full, rich and generous tropical fruit palate; early-drinking style. **RATING** 90 **DRINK** 2008 $ 23
Hilltops Cabernet Sauvignon 2002 Potent, earthy, savoury aromas and flavours; long, quite intense. Will outlive another very dodgy cork. **RATING** 90 **DRINK** 2012 $ 23

ﾔﾔﾔﾔ **Fish Cage Sauvignon Blanc Chardonnay 2003** Tangy, lively; citrus and passionfruit; excellent length; major surprise. No regional claim of origin. **RATING** 89 **DRINK** Now $ 12.99

Orange Merlot 2003 An interesting mix of savoury olive and sweet berry fruit; light to medium-bodied; fine, gently savoury tannins. Dodgy cork. **RATING** 89 **DRINK** 2008 $ 28

ﾔﾔﾔﾖ **Fish Cage Cabernet Merlot 2002** **RATING** 86 **DRINK** Now $ 12.99

Hunter Park   NR

PO Box 815, Muswellbrook, NSW 2333 **REGION** Upper Hunter Valley
T (02) 6541 4000 **F** (02) 6543 2456 **OPEN** Not
WINEMAKER Contract **EST.** 1977 **CASES** NA
SUMMARY The origins of Hunter Park go back more than 25 years; the business is based on 80 ha of sauvignon blanc, chardonnay, merlot, cabernet sauvignon and cabernet franc managed by Andrew Dibley. The wines are not widely distributed in Australia (although they are available by mail order) but exports have been established to England, Germany and the US.

Hunting Lodge Estate

703 Mt Kilcoy Road, Mount Kilcoy, Qld 4515 **REGION** South Burnett
T (07) 5498 1243 **F** (07) 5498 1025 **WEB** www.huntinglodgeestate.com.au **OPEN** 7 days 10–5
WINEMAKER Daryl Higgins **EST.** 1999 **CASES** 9000
SUMMARY Daryl and Vicki Higgins opened Hunting Lodge Estate on their 140-ha cattle property in 1999, originally with a cellar door and B&B. A winery was opened in early 2002, and there is now a kaleidoscopic array of table and fortified wines available, mostly with African game park associations. For good measure, there is a personal museum of hunting trophies.

Huntington Estate

Cassilis Road, Mudgee, NSW 2850 **REGION** Mudgee
T (02) 6373 3825 **F** (02) 6373 3730 **WEB** www.huntingtonestate.com.au **OPEN** Mon–Fri 9–5, Sat 10–5, Sun 10–3
WINEMAKER Susie Roberts **EST.** 1969 **CASES** 20 000
SUMMARY The remarkable Roberts family members have a passion for wine which is equalled only by their passion for music, with the Huntington Music Festival a major annual event. The red wines of Huntington Estate are outstanding and sell for relatively low prices. The wines are seldom exported; almost all are sold via cellar door and mailing list.

ﾔﾔﾔﾔﾔ **Special Reserve Shiraz 2002** Bin FB15. Even richer and denser than FB13; ripe blackberry, chocolate and currant fruit; ripe, soft tannins, controlled oak. **RATING** 94 **DRINK** 2022 $ 30.50

Special Reserve Cabernet Sauvignon 2002 Bin FB20. Excellent blackcurrant fruit; supple, smooth and long; ripe but balanced tannins; subtle oak; stylish wine. Cork. **RATING** 94 **DRINK** 2015 $ 30.50

ﾔﾔﾔﾔﾖ **Special Reserve Shiraz 2002** Bin FB13. Powerful blackberry fruit and tannins; concentrated, full-bodied; long palate. **RATING** 93 **DRINK** 2017 $ 30.50

Special Reserve Cabernet Sauvignon 2002 Bin FB19. Powerful, fully ripe blackcurrant fruit; chunky tannins; good oak; big wine, needs much time. Cork. **RATING** 92 **DRINK** 2017 $ 30.50

Shiraz 2002 Bin FB14. Very good colour; attractive medium-bodied to medium-full-bodied wine; blackberry, mint fruit; a touch of vanilla; ripe, spicy tannins. Value. **RATING** 90 **DRINK** 2012 $ 18.50

Shiraz 2002 Bin FB16. Much more savoury, earthy and oaky than FB14; perhaps more regional, with touches of dark chocolate; good balance. **RATING** 90 **DRINK** 2011 $ 18.50

ﾔﾔﾔﾔ **Cabernet Sauvignon 2002** Bin FB22. Savoury/earthy notes to black fruits and ripe tannins; more medium-bodied than full-bodied. Cork. **RATING** 88 **DRINK** 2012 $ 18.50

ﾔﾔﾔﾖ **Cabernet Sauvignon 2002** Bin FB21. **RATING** 86 **DRINK** 2012 $ 18.50

Huntleigh Vineyards

NR

38 Tunnecliffes Lane, Heathcote, Vic 3523 **REGION** Heathcote
T (03) 5433 2795 **F** (03) 5433 2795 **WEB** www.heathcotewinegrowers.com.au **OPEN** 7 days 10–5.30
WINEMAKER Leigh Hunt **EST.** 1975 **CASES** 500
SUMMARY The wines are all made at the winery by former stockbroker Leigh Hunt from 5 ha of
estate-grown grapes; the last-tasted Cabernet Sauvignon (1998) was of exemplary quality.

Hunt's Foxhaven Estate

NR

Canal Rocks Road, Yallingup, WA 6282 **REGION** Margaret River
T (08) 9755 2232 **F** (08) 9755 2249 **WEB** www.netserv.net.au/foxhaven **OPEN** Weekends & hols 11–5,
or by appointment
WINEMAKER David Hunt **EST.** 1978 **CASES** 1000
SUMMARY A low-profile operation, based on 4.5 ha of vines progressively established, the oldest being
25-year-old riesling. It seems that some of the grapes are sold, some swapped for semillon and
sauvignon blanc. All the wine is sold through the cellar door and by mail order.

Hurley Vineyard

101 Balnarring Road, Balnarring, Vic 3926 **REGION** Mornington Peninsula
T (03) 5931 3000 **F** (03) 5931 3200 **OPEN** First weekend of each month, or by appointment
WINEMAKER Kevin Bell **EST.** 1998 **CASES** 500
SUMMARY It's never as easy as it seems. Though Kevin Bell is now a Victorian Supreme Court judge,
and his wife Tricia Byrnes has a busy legal life as a family law specialist in a small Melbourne law
firm, they have done most of the hard work in establishing Hurley Vineyard themselves, with family
and friends. Most conspicuously, Kevin Bell has completed the Applied Science (Wine Science)
degree at Charles Sturt University, and has drawn on Matt White for consultancy advice, and
occasionally from Phillip Jones of Bass Phillip, and Domaine Fourrier and Gevrey Chambertin. The
2001 release was a dream start for the business.

Hutton Vale Vineyard

NR

Stone Jar Road, Angaston, SA 5353 **REGION** Eden Valley
T (08) 8564 8270 **F** (08) 8564 8385 **WEB** www.huttonvale.com **OPEN** By appointment
WINEMAKER David Powell, Chris Ringland (both Contract) **EST.** 1960 **CASES** 500
SUMMARY John Howard Angas (who arrived in South Australia in 1843, aged 19, charged with the
responsibility of looking after the affairs of his father, George Fife Angas) named part of the family
estate Hutton Vale. It is here that John Angas, John Howard's great-great-grandson, and wife Jan
tend a little over 26 ha of vines and produce (or, at least, Jan does) a range of jams, chutneys and
preserves. Almost all the grapes are sold, but a tiny quantity has been made by the Who's Who of the
Barossa Valley, notably David Powell of Torbreck and Chris Ringland of Rockford. Most of the wine is
sold by mail order, and what is left is exported. I haven't tasted the wines, but I'm prepared to wager
they are of outstanding quality.

Ibis Wines

239 Kearneys Drive, Orange, NSW 2800 **REGION** Orange
T (02) 6362 3257 **F** (02) 6362 5779 **WEB** www.ibiswines.com.au **OPEN** Weekends & public hols 11–5,
or by appointment
WINEMAKER Phil Stevenson **EST.** 1988 **CASES** 1600
SUMMARY Ibis Wines is located just north of Orange (near the botanic gardens) on what was once a
family orchard. Planting of the vineyard commenced in 1988, and a new winery was completed on the
property in 1998. The grapes are sourced from the home vineyards (at an altitude of 800m), the Habitat
Vineyard (at 1100m on Mt Canobolas) (pinot noir and merlot) and the Kanjara Vineyard (shiraz).

TTTT **Habitat Orange Riesling 2004** Very pale; light-bodied, fresh, clean and crisp; mineral,
flint, herb and spice; lively finish. Screwcap. **RATING** 89 **DRINK** 2010 **$** 16
Habitat Orange Sauvignon Blanc 2004 Pronounced fresh herb and fresh-cut grass over
gooseberry; minerally acidity; powerful, punchy wine. Screwcap. **RATING** 89 **DRINK** 2007 **$** 16

Unwooded Chardonnay 2004 Stone fruit, passionfruit and citrus; abundant fruit flavour and depth; slightly sweet, slightly grippy finish. **RATING** 87 **DRINK** 2008 $16

ŸŸŸŸ **Habitat Sir Jasper Late Picked Sauvignon Blanc 2004** **RATING** 86 **DRINK** 2008 $16
Habitat Orange Pinot Gris 2004 **RATING** 85 **DRINK** Now $20

ŸŸŸ **Habitat Pagan 2001** **RATING** 83 $18
Habitat Orange Merlot 2001 **RATING** 80 $14

Idlewild ★★★☆

70 Milbrodale Road, Broke, NSW 2330 **REGION** Lower Hunter Valley
T (02) 6574 5188 **F** (03) 6574 5199 **WEB** www.wildbrokewines.com.au **OPEN** At Broke Estate
WINEMAKER Matthew Ryan **EST.** 1999 **CASES** 400
SUMMARY Idlewild is a spin-off from Broke Estate/Ryan Family Wines; it is a partnership between Matthew Ryan (who continues as viticulturist for Ryan Family Wines on Broke Estate and Minimbah Vineyards) and wife Tina Ryan (who continues to run Wild Rhino PR Marketing & Events in Sydney). It shares the 25 ha of vineyards with Broke Estate/Ryan Family Wines, although the product range is different. Since 2003, Matthew Ryan has been the hands-on winemaker.

ŸŸŸŸ **Cabernet Shiraz 1999** Mature, soft; light to medium-bodied; fruit still at the top end of sweetness, verging on jammy; ripe tannins. Cork. **RATING** 88 **DRINK** 2009 $40

ŸŸŸŸ **Barbera 2001** **RATING** 86 **DRINK** 2007 $40

Ilnam Estate ★★★

750 Carool Road, Carool, NSW 2486 **REGION** Northern Rivers Zone
T (07) 5590 7703 **F** (07) 5590 7922 **WEB** www.ilnam.com.au **OPEN** Wed–Mon 10–5
WINEMAKER Mark Quinn **EST.** 1998 **CASES** 3000
SUMMARY This is the first vineyard and winery to be established in the Tweed Valley, 30 minutes from the Gold Coast. There are 2 ha each of chardonnay, cabernet sauvignon and shiraz, plus a small planting of chambourcin. In addition, Ilnam Estate has a number of growers in the Stanthorpe area who supply grapes to complete the two series of wine. Ione, Lachlan, Nathan, Andrew and Mark Quinn are all involved in the family business.

Immerse ★★★★

1548 Melba Highway, Yarra Glen, Vic 3775 **REGION** Yarra Valley
T (03) 5965 2444 **F** (03) 5965 2460 **WEB** www.immerseyourself.com.au **OPEN** Thurs–Mon 11–5
WINEMAKER Contract **EST.** 1989 **CASES** 700
SUMMARY Steve and Helen Miles have purchased the restaurant, accommodation and function complex previous known as Lovey's. A spa-based health farm has 8 rooms, with a full range of services. I have to say that the name chosen both for the facility and for the wines is as far left of centre as it is possible to go. As previously, a substantial portion of the grapes produced is sold to other makers in the Yarra Valley, the 6.9-ha vineyards having been rehabilitated.

ŸŸŸŸŸ **Yarra Valley Chardonnay 2003** Good balance of melon, citrus and cashew; bright, fresh and long finish. Cork. **RATING** 90 **DRINK** 2008 $24

ŸŸŸŸ **Yarra Valley Pinot Noir 2002** Much lighter-bodied than most from the vintage; spicy, savoury, stemmy, but not green, flavours; good length. **RATING** 88 **DRINK** 2009 $24
Yarra Valley Sauvignon Blanc 2004 Light-bodied; crisp, clean herbaceous/mineral stye. Screwcap. **RATING** 87 **DRINK** 2007 $22

ŸŸŸŸ **Yarra Valley Shiraz 2003** **RATING** 86 **DRINK** 2007 $26

Inchiquin Wines NR

PO Box 865, Clare, SA 5453 **REGION** Clare Valley
T (08) 8843 4210 **OPEN** Not
WINEMAKER Stephen McInerney **EST.** 1998 **CASES** 1000
SUMMARY Stephen McInerney learnt his trade on the winery floor in various parts of the world: he started in 1985 at Jim Barry Wines, and spent a number of years there before moving to Pikes. He

also worked as a Flying Winemaker in France, Oregon, Spain and Argentina. He is now assistant winemaker at the large new Kirribilly Winery in the Clare Valley. He established Inchiquin Wines with his partner Kate Strachan; she too has great industry credentials, primarily as the viticulturist for Taylor's (previously Southcorp), which has the largest vineyards in the Clare Valley. The wines are made by Stephen McInerney at Pikes. Exports to Ireland.

Indigo Ridge ★★★☆

Icely Road, Orange, NSW 2800 **REGION** Orange
T (02) 6362 1851 **F** (02) 6362 1851 **WEB** www.indigowines.com.au **OPEN** First & second weekend of the month 12–5, or by appointment
WINEMAKER Contract **EST.** 1995 **CASES** 800
SUMMARY Indigo Ridge has 4.5 ha of vineyard planted to cabernet sauvignon, sauvignon blanc and merlot. Production is still very small. The wines are sold through the cellar door and by mail order; also, limited on and off-premise distribution in Orange and Sydney.

Inghams Skilly Ridge Wines NR

Gillentown Road, Sevenhill via Clare, SA 5453 **REGION** Clare Valley
T (08) 8843 4330 **F** (08) 8843 4330 **OPEN** Weekends 10–5
WINEMAKER Clark Ingham, David O'Leary (Contract) **EST.** 1994 **CASES** 2000
SUMMARY Clark Ingham has established a substantial vineyard of shiraz, cabernet sauvignon, chardonnay, riesling, merlot, tempranillo and semillon. Part of the production is made by contract winemaker David O'Leary (with input from Clark Ingham); the remaining grape production is sold.

Ingoldby ★★★★☆

Ingoldby Road, McLaren Flat, SA 5171 **REGION** McLaren Vale
T (08) 8383 0005 **F** (08) 8383 0790 **WEB** www.ingoldby.com.au **OPEN** 7 days 10–4
WINEMAKER Matt O'Leary **EST.** 1983 **CASES** 170 000
SUMMARY A sister operation to Andrew Garrett, also within the Beringer Blass wine group, with many of the wines now not having a sole McLaren Vale source but instead being drawn from regions across southeastern Australia. Over the past few years, Ingoldby has produced some excellent wines which provide great value for money.

ŸŸŸŸŸ **Shiraz 2003** Dense blackberry and chocolate; lush mouthfeel; ripe tannins, controlled oak. Unanimous top gold medal 2004 National Wine Show. **RATING** 94 **DRINK** 2013

ŸŸŸŸŸ **Shiraz 2002** Powerful, complex and concentrated; savoury, earthy black fruits; slightly dusty oak. **RATING** 90 **DRINK** 2012 $16

ŸŸŸŸ **Semillon Sauvignon Blanc 2004** A solid wine, with herb/grass semillon dominant; well balanced but not particularly long. **RATING** 88 **DRINK** Now $18
Rose 2004 Clean, fresh cherry and raspberry fruit; fuller style; dry finish. **RATING** 88 **DRINK** Now $18

ŸŸŸŸ **Cabernet Sauvignon 2002** **RATING** 86 **DRINK** 2011 $16

Injidup Point NR

Caves Road, Wilyabrup, WA 6280 **REGION** Margaret River
T 0408 955 770 **F** (08) 9386 8352 **OPEN** By appointment
WINEMAKER Belinda Gould, Michael Standish **EST.** 1993 **CASES** 1000
SUMMARY The development of the substantial Injidup Point vineyard began in 1993; there are now 16 ha planted of cabernet sauvignon, shiraz, cabernet franc, merlot, sauvignon blanc, pinot noir and semillon. Most of the grapes are sold to other makers, with a small amount of wine reserved for mail order sale and other local distribution. An extensive native garden surrounds the property, which has views to the adjacent Leeuwin Naturaliste National Park.

Inneslake Vineyards

The Ruins Way, Inneslake, Port Macquarie, NSW 2444 **REGION** Hastings River
T (02) 6581 1332 **F** (02) 6581 0391 **OPEN** Mon–Fri 10–4, weekends 10–5
WINEMAKER Nick Charley, John Cassegrain (Contract) **EST.** 1988 **CASES** 1200
SUMMARY The property upon which the Inneslake vineyard is established has been in the Charley family's ownership since the turn of the 20th century, but had been planted to vines by a Major Innes in the 1840s. After carrying on logging and fruit growing at various times, the Charley family planted vines in 1988 with the encouragement of John Cassegrain. Around 4.5 ha of vines have been established.

TTTT **Charley Brothers Shiraz 2002** Light to medium-bodied; gently earthy, spicy background; fine but balanced tannins; well made. Stained Twin Top. **RATING** 86 **DRINK** 2008 $18

Innisfail Vineyards

Cross Street, Batesford, Vic 3221 **REGION** Geelong
T (03) 5276 1258 **F** (03) 5276 1258 **OPEN** By appointment
WINEMAKER Nick Farr **EST.** 1980 **CASES** 2000
SUMMARY This 6-ha estate-based producer released its first wines way back in 1988, but has had a very low profile, notwithstanding the quality of its early wines. Nick Farr, son of Gary Farr, is now the winemaker and the profile has increased, as has the quality of the wines.

International Vintners Australia NR

11 Biralee Road, Regency Park, SA 5010 (postal) **REGION** Yarra Valley
T (08) 8440 6300 **F** (08) 8244 5553 **OPEN** Not
WINEMAKER Mark Jamieson **EST.** 1995 **CASES** 100 000
SUMMARY International Vintners arose from the ashes in 2001 when it provided the capital necessary to sustain the former Andrew Garrett business. The brands have extensive distribution in Australia and overseas.

Ironbark Ridge Vineyard NR

Middle Road Mail Service 825, Purga, Qld 4306 **REGION** Queensland Coastal
T (07) 5464 6787 **F** (07) 5464 6858 **WEB** www.ironbarkridge.com **OPEN** Tues–Sun & public hols 10–5
WINEMAKER Contract **EST.** 1984 **CASES** 250
SUMMARY Ipswich is situated on the coastal side of the Great Dividing Range, and the high summer humidity and rainfall will inevitably provide challenges for viticulture here. Chardonnay has impressed most.

Iron Gate Estate NR

Oakey Creek Road, Pokolbin, NSW 2320 **REGION** Lower Hunter Valley
T (02) 4998 6570 **F** (02) 4998 6571 **WEB** www.iron-gate-estate.com.au **OPEN** 7 days 10–4
WINEMAKER Carig Perry, Roger Lilliott **EST.** 2001 **CASES** 5000
SUMMARY Iron Gate Estate would not be out of place in the Napa Valley, which favours bold architectural statements made without regard to cost. No expense has been spared in equipping the winery, or on the lavish cellar door facilities. The business, headed by Roger Lilliott, plans to sell all its wine through an active members club (with three levels, each carrying a larger discount) and through local and Newcastle region restaurants, bypassing normal retail trade altogether. The wines are made from 8 ha of estate plantings of semillon, verdelho, chardonnay, cabernet sauvignon and shiraz, and include such exotic offerings as a sweet shiraz and a chardonnay made in the style of a fino sherry.

Iron Pot Bay Wines

766 Deviot Road, Deviot, Tas 7275 **REGION** Northern Tasmania
T (03) 6394 7320 **F** (03) 6394 7346 **WEB** www.ironpotbay.com.au **OPEN** Thurs–Sun 11–5 Sept–May, June–Aug by appointment

WINEMAKER Andrew Pirie **EST.** 1988 **CASES** 2100
SUMMARY Iron Pot Bay is now part of the syndicate which has established Rosevears Estate, with its large, state-of-the-art winery on the banks of the Tamar. The vineyard takes its name from a bay on the Tamar River (now called West Bay) and is strongly maritime-influenced, producing delicate but intensely flavoured unwooded white wines. It has 4.58 ha of vines, over half being chardonnay, the remainder semillon, sauvignon blanc, pinot gris, gewurztraminer and riesling.

ŸŸŸŸ **Riesling 2004** RATING 85 DRINK 2009 $ 21
Chardonnay 2004 RATING 84 DRINK 2007 $ 21
Pinot Grigio 2004 RATING 84 DRINK 2007 $ 22
Sweet Semillon 2002 RATING 84 DRINK Now $ 15

Ironwood Estate ★★★☆

RMB 1288, Porongurup, WA 6234 **REGION** Porongurup
T (08) 9853 1126 **F** (08) 9853 1172 **OPEN** By appointment
WINEMAKER Dianne Miller, Bill Crappsley (Consultant) **EST.** 1996 **CASES** 2000
SUMMARY Ironwood Estate was established in 1996; the first wines were made from purchased grapes. In the same year, chardonnay, shiraz and cabernet sauvignon were planted on a northern slope of the Porongurup Range. The twin peaks of the Porongurups, seen on the label, rise above the vineyard. The first estate-grown grapes were vinified at the new Porongurup Winery, erected for the 1999 vintage and co-owned with Jingalla, Chatsfield and Montgomery's Hill.

ŸŸŸŸ **Reserve Chardonnay 2003** Light-bodied; fresh and lively citrus and stone fruit; barrel ferment oak inputs nicely controlled. RATING 87 DRINK 2008 $ 19.50
Rocky Road Great Southern Rose 2004 Deep purple-red for a Rose style; full-on cross between light-bodied dry red and Rose; plum and cherry fruit; cellar door sweetness. Screwcap. RATING 87 DRINK Now
Great Southern Shiraz 2003 Light to medium-bodied; supple black and red fruits, spice, leaf and pepper; fine tannins, subtle oak. Dodgy cork. RATING 87 DRINK 2009

ŸŸŸŸ **Porongurup Merlot 2003** RATING 86 DRINK 2008

Irvine ★★★★☆

PO Box 308, Angaston, SA 5353 **REGION** Eden Valley
T (08) 8564 1046 **F** (08) 8564 1314 **OPEN** At Eden Valley Hotel
WINEMAKER James Irvine, Joanne Irvine **EST.** 1983 **CASES** 7000
SUMMARY Industry veteran Jim Irvine, who has successfully guided the destiny of so many South Australian wineries, quietly introduced his own label in 1991. The vineyard from which the wines are sourced was begun in 1983 and now comprises a patchwork quilt of a little over 12 ha of vines. The flagship is the rich Grand Merlot. Exports to all major markets. The top wines were not submitted for this edition.

ŸŸŸŸŸ **Eden Crest Pinot Gris 2004** Pungent herb, spice, blossom and musk aromas and flavours; real presence; long finish; excellent example of the variety. RATING 94 DRINK 2007 $ 22

ŸŸŸŸ **Springhill Merlot 2002** Distinctive varietal olive, savoury fruit aromas and flavours; good balance and length. RATING 89 DRINK 2007 $ 18
Eden Crest Merlot 2001 Light to medium-bodied; savoury varietal fruit off-set by some sweeter oak notes. RATING 89 DRINK 2007 $ 24
Eden Crest Merlot Cabernet 2001 Cedary, spicy overtones to a mix of sweet red and black fruits; integrated oak; clever making. RATING 89 DRINK 2008 $ 24
The Baroness NV A blend of 41% Merlot from the '99 vintage, 28% Cabernet Franc, 22% Cabernet Sauvignon and 9% Merlot from '01; 50% Eden Valley/50% Barossa Valley. The sum is presumably greater than the parts. RATING 87 DRINK Now $ 35

Irymple Estate Winery NR

2086 Karadoc Avenue, Irymple, Vic 3498 **REGION** Murray Darling
T (03) 5024 5759 **F** (03) 5024 5759 **OPEN** Not
WINEMAKER Contract **EST.** 1999 **CASES** 1500

SUMMARY Irymple is a paradox. On the one hand, it is estate-based, with 2 ha each of chardonnay and shiraz, and less than 1 ha of merlot and cabernet sauvignon. On the other hand, the contract-made wines are sold in the old-fashioned way, at distinctly old-fashioned prices: on last advice, in the case of the Chardonnay, either cleanskin at under $5 a bottle; labelled at a little over $5 a bottle; or in a 10-litre cask costing $21.30. The Shiraz is offered only cleanskin or labelled, but at the same price as the Chardonnay. Wine quality is appropriate to the price.

Island Brook Estate ★★★

Bussell Highway, Metricup, WA 6280 **REGION** Margaret River
T (08) 9755 7501 **F** (08) 9755 7008 **WEB** www.islandbrook.com.au **OPEN** 7 days 10–5
WINEMAKER Flying Fish Cove (Contract) **EST.** 1985 **CASES** 2000
SUMMARY Linda and Peter Jenkins purchased Island Brook from Ken and Judy Brook in early 2001, and undertook major renovations, including extensive vineyard retrellising, before opening their cellar door in November 2001. Luxurious accommodation set among 45 acres of forest has since been completed.

▼▼▼▽ **Merlot 2002 RATING** 85 **DRINK** 2008 **$** 26

Ivanhoe Wines

Marrowbone Road, Pokolbin, NSW 2320 **REGION** Lower Hunter Valley
T (02) 4998 7325 **F** (02) 4998 7848 **WEB** www.ivanhoewines.com.au **OPEN** 7 days 10–5
WINEMAKER Stephen Drayton, Tracy Drayton **EST.** 1995 **CASES** 7000
SUMMARY Stephen Drayton is the son of the late Reg Drayton and, with wife Tracy, is the third branch of the family to be actively involved in winemaking in the Hunter Valley. The property on which the vineyard is situated has been called Ivanhoe for over 140 years, and 25 ha of 30-year-old vines provide high-quality fruit for the label. The plans are to build a replica of the old homestead (burnt down, along with much of the winery, in the 1968 bushfires) to operate as a sales area.

Jackson's Hill Vineyard ★★★☆

Mount View Road, Mount View, NSW 2321 **REGION** Lower Hunter Valley
T 1300 720 098 **F** 1300 130 220 **WEB** www.jacksonshill.com.au **OPEN** By appointment
WINEMAKER Christian Gaffey **EST.** 1983 **CASES** 1500
SUMMARY One of the low-profile operations on the spectacularly scenic Mount View Road, making small quantities of estate-grown (3 ha) wine sold exclusively through the cellar door and Australian Wine Selectors.

Jadran NR

445 Reservoir Road, Orange Grove, WA 6109 **REGION** Perth Hills
T (08) 9459 1110 **OPEN** Mon–Sat 10–8, Sun 11–5
WINEMAKER Steve Radojkovich **EST.** 1967 **CASES** NFP
SUMMARY A quite substantial operation which basically services local clientele, occasionally producing wines of quite surprising quality from a variety of fruit sources.

JAG Wine

72 William Street, Norwood, SA 5067 (postal) **REGION** Warehouse
T (08) 8364 4497 **F** (08) 8364 4497 **OPEN** Not
WINEMAKER Grant Anthony White **EST.** 2001 **CASES** 350
SUMMARY The name is doubtless derived from that of owners Julie and Grant White, but might cause raised eyebrows in clothing circles. The project developed from their lifelong love of wine; it started with a hobby vineyard (along with friends) in the Adelaide Hills, then more formal wine studies, then highly successful amateur winemaking. The Whites obtained their producers' licence (and trademark) in 2001, purchasing grapes from the major South Australian regions, bringing them to their suburban house to be fermented and pressed, and then storing the wine offsite in French and American oak until ready for sale. Most of the wine is sold via the internet, direct mail orders and phone orders, with a small amount sold through cafés in the suburb of Norwood.

▼▼▼▼ **Cabernet Sauvignon 2002** Blackcurrant, blackberry and spice; medium-bodied; a nice touch of sweet oak, and ripe tannins. Adelaide Plains/Langhorne Creek. Cork. **RATING** 88 **DRINK** 2010 $ 25

▼▼▼♀ **Shiraz 2002 RATING** 86 **DRINK** 2007 $ 22

James Estate ★★★☆

951 Bylong Valley Way, Baerami via Denman, NSW 2333 **REGION** Upper Hunter Valley
T (02) 6547 5168 **F** (02) 6547 5164 **WEB** www.jamesestatewines.com.au **OPEN** 7 days 10–4.30
WINEMAKER Peter Orr **EST.** 1971 **CASES** 50 000
SUMMARY David James (chief executive and principal shareholder of James Estate) laid the base for what is now a very substantial wine business with the acquisition of the former Serenella Estate in 1997. Having secured the funds to significantly expand the James Estate production, and recruited former McWilliam's Mount Pleasant and Allandale winemaker Peter Orr, the business was already on the road to success. However, the demise of Hill International Wines (owner of Basedow, Fern Hill and Marienberg Wines in South Australia) presented James Estate with an opportunity to take over four well-established brands along with a major distribution company. Now Australian Beverage Distributors distributes the four major brands in all states; exports to the UK and the US.

▼▼▼▼ **Semillon 2003** Light to medium-bodied; some lemon, citrus, herb and lanolin; nice flavours; slightly short. **RATING** 89 **DRINK** 2007 $ 14
Cabernet Sauvignon Petit Verdot 2003 Tending slightly butch and angular, but there is some nice blackberry, plum and blackcurrant fruit there. Cork. **RATING** 87 **DRINK** 2009 $ 15

▼▼▼♀ **Hunter Valley Verdelho 2004 RATING** 84 **DRINK** Now $ 14

Jamiesons Run ★★★★

Penola–Naracoorte Road, Coonawarra, SA 5263 **REGION** Coonawarra
T (08) 8736 3380 **F** (08) 8736 3307 **WEB** www.jamiesonsrun.com.au **OPEN** Mon–Fri 9–4.30, weekends 10–4
WINEMAKER Andrew Hales **EST.** 1955 **CASES** 160 000
SUMMARY Once the prized possession of a stand-alone Mildara, which spawned a child called Jamiesons Run to fill the need for a cost-effective second label. Now the name Mildara is very nearly part of ancient wine history, and the child has usurped the parent. Worldwide distribution via Beringer Blass.

▼▼▼▼♀ **McShane's Block Coonawarra Shiraz 2002** Firm, tight, focused red and blackcurrant fruits; slightly brittle tannins. **RATING** 92 **DRINK** 2012
O'Dea's Block Coonawarra Cabernet Sauvignon 2002 Dense colour; massively powerful and deep blackcurrant; tannins to burn. Needs decades. **RATING** 91 **DRINK** 2022
Limestone Coast Chardonnay 2004 Strong green-yellow; complex barrel ferment with a nice touch of funk; ripe stone fruit flavours. **RATING** 90 **DRINK** 2007
Robertson's Well Shiraz 2001 Savoury, earthy black fruits and a touch of bitter chocolate; good tannins and length. **RATING** 90 **DRINK** 2011 $ 24

▼▼▼▼ **Coonawarra Shiraz 2002** Elegant, light-bodied wine with fine, soft tannins and sophisticated oak. **RATING** 87 **DRINK** 2008
Mildara Coonawarra Cabernet Sauvignon 2002 Savoury, leafy, minty; very callow; worked enough before going under screwcap? **RATING** 87 **DRINK** 2010 $ 29
Coonawarra Cabernet Shiraz Merlot 2002 Light to medium-bodied; appealing mix of sundry savoury fruit characters; long finish, though slightly tweaky. **RATING** 87 **DRINK** 2009 $ 15

▼▼▼♀ **Coonawarra Merlot 2003 RATING** 86 **DRINK** 2007
Coonawarra Merlot 2002 RATING 86 **DRINK** 2009 $ 15
Coonawarra Cabernet Sauvignon 2002 RATING 86 **DRINK** 2009 $ 15

Jane Brook Estate ★★★☆

229 Toodyay Road, Middle Swan, WA 6056 **REGION** Swan Valley
T (08) 9274 1432 **F** (08) 9274 1211 **WEB** www.janebrook.com.au **OPEN** Mon–Fri 10–5, weekends & public hols 12–5

WINEMAKER Julie Smith, David Atkinson **EST.** 1972 **CASES** 20 000
SUMMARY Beverley and David Atkinson have worked tirelessly to build up the Jane Brook Estate wine business over the past 30 years. The most important changes during that time have been the establishment of a Margaret River vineyard, and sourcing grapes from other southern wine regions in Western Australia; winemaker Julie Smith (née White) has also played a major role in lifting wine quality since her appointment as chief winemaker in 2000. Retail distribution in Perth, Sydney, Canberra and Melbourne; exports to the UK, the US and Asia.

ㅇㅇㅇㅇ **Back Block Shiraz 2003** Light to medium-bodied; smooth, supple blackberry fruit; unforced; light oak and tannins; 60-year-old estate vines. Twin Top. **RATING** 88 **DRINK** 2009 $ 20.50
Plain Jane Shiraz 2004 Light-bodied; bright, fresh, clean and lively; entirely fruit-driven; early access. Screwcap. **RATING** 87 **DRINK** Now $ 11

ㅇㅇㅇㅇ **Plain Jane Chenin Blanc Chardonnay 2004** **RATING** 86 **DRINK** Now $ 11
Verdelho 2004 **RATING** 85 **DRINK** Now $ 18
Merlot 2003 **RATING** 85 **DRINK** 2007 $ 24

Jansz ★★★★★

1216b Pipers Brook Road, Pipers Brook, Tas 7254 **REGION** Northern Tasmania
T (03) 6382 7066 **F** (03) 6382 7088 **WEB** www.jansz.com.au **OPEN** 7 days 10–5
WINEMAKER Natalie Fryar **EST.** 1985 **CASES** 15 000
SUMMARY Jansz is part of the S Smith & Son/Yalumba group, and was one of the early sparkling wine labels in Tasmania, stemming from a short-lived relationship between Heemskerk and Louis Roederer. Its 15 ha of chardonnay, 12 ha of pinot noir and 3 ha of pinot meunier correspond almost exactly to the blend composition of the Jansz wines. It is the only Tasmanian winery entirely devoted to the production of sparkling wine, which is of high quality.

ㅇㅇㅇㅇㅇ **Premium 2000** Fragrant, citrussy aromas; bright and fresh; very good length and, in particular, balance; still very youthful. **RATING** 94 **DRINK** 2007 $ 36.95

ㅇㅇㅇㅇ **Cuvee NV** Some colour development; complex, bready autolysis overtones to the nectarine fruit; good length. **RATING** 89 **DRINK** Now $ 21.95

Jarrah Ridge Winery ★★★☆

651 Great Northern Highway, Herne Hill, WA 6056 **REGION** Perth Hills
T 1800 800 047 **F** (08) 9409 8010 **WEB** www.jarrahridge.com.au **OPEN** By appointment
WINEMAKER Rob Marshall (Contract) **EST.** 1998 **CASES** 8000
SUMMARY Syd and Julie Pond have established a 13.5-ha vineyard with shiraz the most important, the remainder chenin blanc, chardonnay, cabernet sauvignon, verdelho, viognier and merlot. Children Michael and Lisa are also involved in the business, and the experienced Rob Marshall is contract winemaker. Most of the wines have a degree of sweetness which will doubtless appeal to cellar door and restaurant customers.

ㅇㅇㅇㅇ **Shiraz 2003** Very powerful and concentrated black fruits and lingering tannins; obvious cellaring potential. **RATING** 90 **DRINK** 2013 $ 16

ㅇㅇㅇㅇ **Milly Milly Shiraz 2003** Spicy, savoury overtones to black fruits; medium-bodied; nice, persistent tannins. Cork. **RATING** 89 **DRINK** 2010 $ 16

ㅇㅇㅇㅇ **Balladonia Chenin Blanc 2003** **RATING** 85 **DRINK** Now $ 13
Merlot 2003 **RATING** 84 **DRINK** 2007 $ 14

Jarretts of Orange ★★★★☆

Annangrove Park, Cargo Road, Orange, NSW 2800 **REGION** Orange
T (02) 6364 3118 **F** (02) 6364 3048 **OPEN** By appointment
WINEMAKER Chris Derrez **EST.** 1995 **CASES** 2000
SUMMARY Justin and Pip Jarrett have established a very substantial vineyard (140 ha), planted to chardonnay, cabernet sauvignon, shiraz, sauvignon blanc, merlot, pinot noir, riesling, marsanne, cabernet franc and verdelho. As well as managing this vineyard, they provide management and development services to growers of another 120 ha in the region. Most of the grapes are sold, with a limited amount produced for local distribution and by mail order. The wines are modestly priced.

ΥΥΥΥΥ **Finger & Thumb Shiraz 2002** A fragrant and appealing array of spicy/savoury aromas; the palate delivers on the promise; medium-bodied; satiny texture; dark berry flavours and spice. **RATING** 94 **DRINK** 2012

ΥΥΥΥ **Sauvignon Blanc 2004** A mix of stoney, herbaceous, mineral and gooseberry/kiwifruit; a fraction angular, but will soften. Screwcap. **RATING** 89 **DRINK** Now $ 15
Finger & Thumb Cabernet Sauvignon 2002 Not 100% ripe; light to medium-bodied; leafy/sappy/berry fruits, slightly sweet and sour; does have length. **RATING** 87 **DRINK** 2010

ΥΥΥΥ **Chardonnay 2003 RATING** 85 **DRINK** 2007 $ 16

Jarvis Estate ★★★

Lot 13, Wirring Road, Margaret River, WA 6285 **REGION** Margaret River
T (08) 9758 7526 **F** (08) 9758 8017 **WEB** www.jarvisestate.com.au **OPEN** By appointment
WINEMAKER Mike Lemos (Contract) **EST.** 1995 **CASES** 3000
SUMMARY Matt and Jackie Jarvis carefully researched the Margaret River region, and in particular the Bramley locality, before purchasing their property, where they now live. It is planted to cabernet sauvignon, shiraz, merlot, chardonnay and cabernet franc (8.4 ha). The first vintage was 2002, with the wines made under contract by well-known local winemakers. Not surprisingly, some show young vine character, but they have been well made. Exports to Taiwan, Greece and Ireland; retail distribution in Victoria (DC Fine Wines).

Jasper Hill ★★★★★

Drummonds Lane, Heathcote, Vic 3523 **REGION** Heathcote
T (03) 5433 2528 **F** (03) 5433 3143 **OPEN** By appointment
WINEMAKER Ron Laughton **EST.** 1975 **CASES** 3500
SUMMARY The red wines of Jasper Hill are highly regarded and much sought after, invariably selling out at the cellar door and through the mailing list within a short time of release. These are wonderful wines in admittedly Leviathan mould, reflecting the very low yields and the care and attention given to them by Ron Laughton. The oak is not overdone, and the fruit flavours show Heathcote at its best. There has been comment (and some criticism) in recent years about the alcohol level of the wines. Laughton responds by saying he picks the grapes when he judges them to be at optimum ripeness, and is in no way chasing high alcohol, whether to suit the US market or otherwise. I believe he is correct, and that the power of the fruit carries the alcohol.

ΥΥΥΥΥ **Georgia's Paddock Shiraz 2003** Very powerful, dense and concentrated; some tannin elevation and mid-palate diminution; drought stress? May come around with time. High-quality cork. **RATING** 92 **DRINK** 2015 $ 65.50
Emily's Paddock Shiraz Cabernet Franc 2003 Complex, savoury, spicy aromas; medium-bodied; slightly less vibrant entry than Georgia's, but tannins slightly less obtrusive, though still dry and lingering; same issues. High-quality cork. **RATING** 91 **DRINK** 2015 $ 43.75
Georgia's Paddock Nebbiolo 2003 Intense aromas; cigar box, cedar, spice and cherry; Italianate tannins; will likely please Nebbiolo lovers. Good example of a terribly difficult variety. High-quality cork. **RATING** 90 **DRINK** 2012 $ 27.25

ΥΥΥΥ **Georgia's Paddock Riesling 2004** Powerful, minerally aromas; ripe but subdued fruit; round and relatively soft. High-quality cork. **RATING** 89 **DRINK** 2007 $ 29

Jasper Valley NR

RMB 880, Croziers Road, Berry, NSW 2535 **REGION** Shoalhaven Coast
T (02) 4464 1596 **F** (02) 4464 1595 **WEB** www.jaspervalleywines.com.au **OPEN** 7 days 9.30–5.30
WINEMAKER Contract **EST.** 1976 **CASES** 1500
SUMMARY A strongly tourist-oriented winery, with most of its wine purchased as cleanskins from other makers, but with 2 ha of estate shiraz planted in 1976 by former owner Sidney Mitchell; these are the oldest vines in the region. Features around 1 ha of lawns, barbecue facilities, and sweeping views.

Jeanneret Wines ★★★★☆

Jeanneret Road, Sevenhill, SA 5453 **REGION** Clare Valley
T (08) 8843 4308 **F** (08) 8843 4251 **OPEN** Mon–Fri 11–5, weekends & public hols 10–5
WINEMAKER Ben Jeanneret **EST.** 1992 **CASES** 10 000
SUMMARY Jeanneret's fully self-contained winery has a most attractive outdoor tasting area and equally attractive picnic facilities, on the edge of a small lake surrounded by bushland. While it did not open the business until October 1994, its first wine was in fact made in 1992 (Shiraz) and it had already established a loyal following. National wholesale distribution; exports to the UK, Canada, Malaysia and Japan.

ΥΥΥΥΥ **Denis Reserve Shiraz 2002** Velvety, supple, harmonious blood plum and blackberry fruit; quality oak and fine, ripe tannins; seamless and long. From 138-year-old vines. Quality cork. **RATING** 94 **DRINK** 2022 **$** 55

ΥΥΥΥΥ **Clare Valley Grenache Shiraz 2003** Excellent texture and structure; blackberry, prune, plum and spice; ripe tannins; less confronting than the '02. **RATING** 93 **DRINK** 2012 **$** 18
Clare Valley Cabernets 2002 A rich, powerful array of black fruits, dark chocolate and vanilla; a long, fruit-driven finish; very attractive wine. **RATING** 93 **DRINK** 2017 **$** 20

ΥΥΥΥ **Clare Valley Riesling 2004** Big, rich, powerful, ripe and mouthfilling; soft finish; fast-developing. Screwcap. **RATING** 88 **DRINK** 2007 **$** 18
Clare Valley Shiraz 2003 Powerful wine; blackberry and chocolate fruit; persistent, slightly rough tannins need time to settle. Will undoubtedly improve. Screwcap. **RATING** 88 **DRINK** 2010 **$** 22

Jeir Creek NR

Gooda Creek Road, Murrumbateman, NSW 2582 **REGION** Canberra District
T (02) 6227 5999 **F** (02) 6227 5900 **WEB** www.jeircreekwines.com.au **OPEN** Thurs–Mon & hols 10–5
WINEMAKER Rob Howell **EST.** 1984 **CASES** 4500
SUMMARY Rob Howell came to part-time winemaking through a love of drinking fine wine, and is intent on improving both the quality and the consistency of his wines. It is now a substantial (and still growing) business, with the vineyard plantings increased to 11 ha by the establishment of more cabernet sauvignon, shiraz, merlot and viognier.

Jenke Vineyards ★★★★

Barossa Valley Way, Rowland Flat, SA 5352 **REGION** Barossa Valley
T (08) 8524 4154 **F** (08) 8524 5044 **OPEN** 7 days 11–5
WINEMAKER Kym Jenke **EST.** 1989 **CASES** 8000
SUMMARY The Jenkes have been vignerons in the Barossa since 1854 and have over 45 ha of vineyards; a small part of the production is now made and marketed through a charming restored stone cottage cellar door. Wholesale distribution in Victoria and New South Wales; exports to Singapore, Switzerland and New Zealand.

ΥΥΥΥΥ **Barossa Shiraz 2002** Good colour; supple, smooth and round; medium-bodied; blackberry and blood plum; fine, ripe, sweet tannins; good oak. Screwcap. **RATING** 91 **DRINK** 2015 **$** 28
Barossa Reserve Shiraz 1999 Medium-bodied; elegant, restrained style developing well; fine, savoury tannins; fresh finish. Quality cork. **RATING** 90 **DRINK** 2011 **$** 35

ΥΥΥΥ **Barossa Semillon 2004** Delicate, fresh, crisp, grassy, new Barossa Valley style; crisp acidity; will develop well. Screwcap. **RATING** 89 **DRINK** 2010 **$** 15
Barossa Merlot 2002 Elegant light to medium-bodied mix of spicy, savoury and sweet red fruits; attractive early-drinking style. Screwcap. **RATING** 89 **DRINK** 2008 **$** 20
Barossa Cabernet Sauvignon 2002 Ripe, supple blackberry and blackcurrant; polished tannins, nice oak. Synthetic cork inappropriate. **RATING** 89 **DRINK** 2008 **$** 20
Barossa Cabernet Franc 2003 Spicy edges; touches of varietal tobacco leaf and herb; eclectic. Screwcap. **RATING** 87 **DRINK** 2008 **$** 18

ΥΥΥΥ **Barossa Grenache Shiraz 2003** **RATING** 85 **DRINK** 2007

ΥΥΥ **Barossa Cabernet Franc Rose 2004** **RATING** 83

Jester Hill Wines ★★★☆

292 Mount Stirling Road, Glen Aplin, Qld 4381 **REGION** Granite Belt
T (07) 4683 4380 **F** (02) 6622 3190 **WEB** www.jesterhillwines.com.au **OPEN** Fri–Mon 9–5
WINEMAKER Mark Ravenscroft (Contract) **EST.** 1993 **CASES** 8500
SUMMARY A family-run vineyard situated in the pretty valley of Glen Aplin in the Granite Belt. The owners, John and Genevieve Ashwell, aim to concentrate on small quantities of premium-quality wines reflecting the full-bodied style of the region. Believing that good wine is made in the vineyard, John and Genevieve spent the first 7 years establishing healthy, strong vines on well-drained soil.

TTTT **Touchstone Cabernet Sauvignon 2002** Strongly accented and powerful black fruits; slightly extractive, dry tannins. **RATING** 88 **DRINK** 2012 $ 28

Jim Barry Wines ★★★★

Craig's Hill Road, Clare, SA 5453 **REGION** Clare Valley
T (08) 8842 2261 **F** (08) 8842 3752 **OPEN** Mon–Fri 9–5, weekends & hols 9–4
WINEMAKER Mark Barry **EST.** 1959 **CASES** 80 000
SUMMARY The patriarch of this highly successful wine business, Jim Barry, died in October 2004, but the business continues under the very active management of various of his many children. There is a full range of wine styles across most varietals, but with special emphasis on Riesling, Shiraz and Cabernet Sauvignon. The ultra-premium release is The Armagh Shiraz, with the McCrae Wood red wines not far behind. Jim Barry Wines is able to draw upon 247 ha of mature Clare Valley vineyards, plus a small holding in Coonawarra. Worldwide distribution.

TTTTT **Lodge Hill Riesling 2004** Lively herb, mineral, slate and spice aromas; fine palate, crisp and long; still developing. **RATING** 91 **DRINK** 2012 $ 19.95
First Eleven Coonawarra Cabernet Sauvignon 2000 Medium-bodied; an attractive mix of raspberry, cassis and blackcurrant; fine, ripe tannins; integrated oak. Quality cork. **RATING** 90 **DRINK** 2010 $ 45

TTTT **The Cover Drive Cabernet Sauvignon 2003** Medium-bodied; an ultra-Coonawarra mix of earth and blackcurrant; the fruit grows on the back palate. **RATING** 89 **DRINK** 2013 $ 18
Lodge Hill Shiraz 2003 Lots of upfront, smooth, black fruits, then tails off somewhat. **RATING** 88 **DRINK** 2009 $ 18
Watervale Riesling Florita Vineyard 2004 Solid wine; apple, citrus and lime, but needs more focus. **RATING** 87 **DRINK** 2009 $ 14.95

TTTT **Lavender Hill 2004** **RATING** 85 **DRINK** Now $ 12.95

TTT **The Family Vineyards Shiraz Cabernet 2003** **RATING** 83 $ 13

Jimbour Wines ★★★☆

Jimbour Station, Jimbour, Qld 4406 **REGION** Queensland Zone
T (07) 3878 8909 **F** (07) 3878 8920 **WEB** www.jimbour.com **OPEN** 7 days 10–4.30
WINEMAKER Peter Scudamore-Smith MW **EST.** 2000 **CASES** 15 000
SUMMARY Jimbour Station was one of the first properties opened in the Darling Downs: the heritage-listed homestead was built in 1876. The property, which has been owned by the Russell family since 1923, has diversified by establishing a 22-ha vineyard and opening a cellar door. Increasing production is an indication of its intention to become one of Queensland's major wine producers. Exports to Canada, Germany, Japan, the US and South Korea.

TTTT **Jimbour Station Ludwig Leichhardt Reserve Merlot 2003** Extremely ripe, complex fruit aromas and flavours, bordering on raisined; abundant richness, but unusual for Merlot. Screwcap. **RATING** 88 **DRINK** 2009 $ 27.99
Jimbour Station Merlot 2004 Good, rich berry fruit; tannins just over the top; a pity. **RATING** 87 **DRINK** 2008 $ 15.99

TTTT **Jimbour Station Verdelho 2004** **RATING** 86 **DRINK** Now $ 15.99
Jimbour Station Darling Downs Viognier 2004 **RATING** 86 **DRINK** 2008 $ 15.99
Rose Cabernet Shiraz Merlot 2004 **RATING** 86 **DRINK** Now $ 15.99
Jimbour Station Shiraz 2002 **RATING** 85 **DRINK** 2012 $ 16.99

TTT **Jimbour Station Queensland Rose 2004** **RATING** 83 $ 15.99
Jimbour Station Cabernet Sauvignon 2002 **RATING** 83 $ 15.99

Jindalee Estate ★★★★

265 Ballan Road, Moorabool, North Geelong, Vic 3221 **REGION** Geelong
T (03) 5276 1280 **F** (03) 5276 1537 **WEB** www.jindaleewines.com.au **OPEN** 7 days 10–5
WINEMAKER Andrew Byers, Chris Sargeant **EST.** 1997 **CASES** 500 000
SUMMARY Jindalee made its debut with the 1997 vintage. It is part of the Littore Group, which currently has 550 ha of premium wine grapes in wine production and under development in the Riverland. Corporate offices are now at the former Idyll Vineyard, acquired by Jindalee in late 1997. Here 14 ha of estate vineyards have been retrellised and upgraded, and produce the Fettlers Rest range. The Jindalee Estate Chardonnay can offer spectacular value. Exports to the UK, Sweden, the US and Canada.

▼▼▼▼▼ **Fettlers Rest Chardonnay 2003** Ultra-complex barrel ferment characters on the bouquet, then long, rippling and complex fruit on the palate. **RATING** 94 **DRINK** 2012 $ 19.95

▼▼▼▼▽ **Fettlers Rest Shiraz 2002** Very complex and intense spice, herb and licorice; very long finish. Possible touch of brett ignored. **RATING** 93 **DRINK** 2012 $ 19.95

▼▼▼▽ **Shiraz 2003** **RATING** 86 **DRINK** 2007 $ 9
Sauvignon Blanc 2004 **RATING** 84 **DRINK** Now $ 9

Jingalla ★★★☆

RMB 1316, Bolganup Dam Road, Porongurup, WA 6324 **REGION** Porongurup
T (08) 9853 1023 **F** (08) 9853 1023 **WEB** www.jingallawines.com.au **OPEN** 7 days 10.30–5
WINEMAKER Diane Miller, Bill Crappsley (Consultant) **EST.** 1979 **CASES** 5000
SUMMARY Jingalla is a family business, owned and run by Geoff and Nita Clarke and Barry and Shelley Coad, the latter the ever-energetic wine marketer of the business. The 8 ha of hillside vineyards are low-yielding, with the white wines succeeding best, but they also produce some lovely red wines. A partner in the new Porongurup Winery, which means it no longer has to rely on contract winemaking. Exports to the UK, Taiwan and Singapore.

▼▼▼▼ **Sauvignon Blanc Verdelho 2004** Fresh, clean and aromatic; tropical fruits with a twist of lemon; works very well. Screwcap. **RATING** 88 **DRINK** Now $ 15

▼▼▼▽ **CabRouge 2004** **RATING** 84 **DRINK** Now $ 13
Shiraz Reserve 2003 **RATING** 84 **DRINK** 2009 $ 25

Jinglers Creek Vineyard ★★★★

288 Relbia Road, Relbia, Tas 7258 **REGION** Northern Tasmania
T (03) 6344 3966 **F** (03) 6344 3966 **OPEN** Thurs–Sun 11–5
WINEMAKER Graham Wiltshire, Michael Fogarty (Contract) **EST.** 1998 **CASES** 1300
SUMMARY One of the newer arrivals on the Tasmanian scene, with 2 ha of pinot noir, pinot gris and chardonnay. Winemaking is done by industry veteran Graham Wiltshire, who knows more about growing grapes and making wine in Tasmania than any other active winemaker.

▼▼▼▼▽ **Pinot Grigio 2003** Still bright and fresh; crisp, balanced palate of green apple and pear; a flick of residual sugar. **RATING** 90 **DRINK** 2008 $ 15

▼▼▼▼ **Chardonnay 2003** Citrus and stone fruit mix; light to medium-bodied; nice balance, subtle oak. **RATING** 88 **DRINK** 2007 $ 15
Chardonnay 2004 Light-bodied; citrus, grapefruit and nectarine supported by the usual acidity. **RATING** 87 **DRINK** 2007 $ 17
Pinot Grigio 2004 Interesting pear skin flavours cross-cut by piercing acidity. **RATING** 87 **DRINK** 2008 $ 17

Jinks Creek Winery ★★★★☆

Tonimbuk Road, Tonimbuk, Vic 3815 **REGION** Gippsland
T (03) 5629 8502 **F** (03) 5629 8551 **WEB** www.jinkscreekwinery.com.au **OPEN** By appointment
WINEMAKER Andrew Clarke **EST.** 1981 **CASES** 1000
SUMMARY Jinks Creek Winery is situated between Gembrook and Bunyip, bordering the evocatively named Bunyip State Park. While the winery was not built until 1992, planting of the 3.64-ha

vineyard started back in 1981 and all the wines are estate-grown. The 'sold out' sign goes up each year – small wonder in vintages such as 2000, '02 and '03. Exports to the US and Singapore.

ҬҬҬҬҬ **Gippsland Shiraz 2003** Flooded with licorice, black cherry, blackberry and spicy fruit; medium to full-bodied; sweet, fine tannins provide structure; restrained French oak; 14° alcohol. High-quality cork. **RATING** 94 **DRINK** 2015

ҬҬҬҬҬ **Gippsland Pinot Noir 2003** Light but bright; fragrant strawberry and cherry aromas; fresh, lively and expressive fruit-forward style. **RATING** 93 **DRINK** 2008 $ 28
Yarra Valley Shiraz 2003 Fresh, bright red fruits and French oak; medium-bodied; well balanced and structured; fine tannins. **RATING** 93 **DRINK** 2013 $ 28
Heathcote Shiraz 2003 Dense colour; full-bodied, powerful and concentrated blackberry, dark plum and bitter chocolate; savoury, powerful tannins; drought year wine. High-quality cork. **RATING** 93 **DRINK** 2020

Jinnunger Vineyard ★★★☆

588 Nanarup Road, Lower Kalgan, Albany, WA 6330 **REGION** Albany
T (08) 9846 4374 **F** (08) 9846 4474 **WEB** www.jinnunger.com.au **OPEN** By appointment
WINEMAKER Robert Diletti (Contract) **EST.** 1996 **CASES** 800
SUMMARY Jinnunger Vineyard is owned by research scientist Colin Sanderson. There is 1 ha each of chardonnay and pinot noir, and while he expects to increase the plantings, it will always be a small, hand-tended vineyard. It is ideally situated, on a north-facing slope of Mt Mason close to the Southern Ocean, 18 km east of Albany. The name comes from the local Aboriginal (Nyungah) language, and means 'good views': the property looks out over the Porongorup and Stirling Ranges.

ҬҬҬҬ **Albany Chardonnay 2003** Bright colour; medium-bodied; ripe, generous peach and melon fruit; subtle barrel ferment inputs; slightly hot (14.1° alcohol) finish. **RATING** 89 **DRINK** 2007 $ 20

ҬҬҬҬ **Albany Pinot Noir 2003** Light-bodied; stemmy, spicy overtones to light, sweet fruit; just there. **RATING** 86 **DRINK** Now $ 24

Joadja Vineyards NR

Joadja Road, Berrima, NSW 2577 **REGION** Southern Highlands
T (02) 4878 5236 **F** (02) 4878 5236 **WEB** www.joadja.com **OPEN** 7 days 10–5
WINEMAKER Kim Moginie **EST.** 1983 **CASES** 2000
SUMMARY The strikingly labelled Joadja Vineyards wines, first made in 1990, are principally drawn from 7 ha of estate vineyards situated in the cool hills adjacent to Berrima. Mature vines and greater experience of this emerging region has solved early difficulties in securing full ripeness.

John Duval Wines ★★★★☆

9 Park Street, Tanunda, SA 5352 (postal) **REGION** Barossa Valley
T (08) 8563 2591 **OPEN** Not
WINEMAKER John Duval **EST.** 2003 **CASES** 1000
SUMMARY John Duval is an internationally recognised winemaker, having been the custodian of Penfolds Grange for almost 30 years as part of his role as chief red winemaker at Penfolds. He remains involved with Penfolds as a consultant, but these days is concentrating on establishing his own brand, and providing consultancy services to other clients in various parts of the world. On the principle of if not broken, don't fix, he is basing his business on Shiraz and Shiraz blends from old-vine vineyards in the Barossa Valley. Plexus, incidentally, denotes a network in an animal body that combines elements into a coherent structure.

ҬҬҬҬ **Plexus Barossa Valley Shiraz Grenache Mourvedre 2003** Medium-bodied; subtle and refined combination of spicy, savoury red and black berry fruit; fine, ripe tannins; skilled French oak use. Quality cork. **RATING** 93 **DRINK** 2013 $ 33.10

John Gehrig Wines ★★★★

Oxley–Milawa Road, Oxley, Vic 3678 **REGION** King Valley
T (03) 5727 3395 **F** (03) 5727 3699 **WEB** www.johngehrigwines.com.au **OPEN** 7 days 9–5

WINEMAKER John Gehrig **EST.** 1976 **CASES** 5600
SUMMARY Honest wines are the norm, but with occasional offerings such as the 2004 Riesling (a cool vintage) of thoroughly impressive quality, all the more given that it comes from the vineyard adjacent to the winery, rather than high in the King Valley.

ΨΨΨΨΨ **Riesling 2004** Fine, fragrant lime juice aromas and flavours, and a hint of spicy minerality; delicate but fine and long palate. Exceptional achievement. **RATING** 93 **DRINK** 2014 $20

John Kosovich Wines ★★★

Cnr Memorial Avenue/Great Northern Highway, Baskerville, WA 6056 **REGION** Swan Valley
T (08) 9296 4356 **F** (08) 9296 4356 **WEB** www.johnkosovichwines.com.au **OPEN** 7 days 10–5.30
WINEMAKER John Kosovich **EST.** 1922 **CASES** 4000
SUMMARY The name change from Westfield to John Kosovich Wines does not signify any change in either philosophy or direction for this much-admired producer of a surprisingly elegant and complex Chardonnay; the other wines are more variable, but from time to time there have been attractive Verdelho and excellent Cabernet Sauvignon. In 1998, wines partly or wholly from the family's new planting at Pemberton were released: Swan/Pemberton blends released under the Bronze Wing label. Limited retail distribution in Perth, Melbourne and Brisbane; exports to Singapore.

ΨΨΨΨ **Westfield Chardonnay 2003** **RATING** 84 **DRINK** Now $15

Johnston Oakbank ★★★★☆

18 Oakwood Road, Oakbank, SA 5243 **REGION** Adelaide Hills
T (08) 8388 4263 **F** (08) 8388 4278 **WEB** www.johnston-oakbank.com.au **OPEN** Mon–Fri 8–5
WINEMAKER David O'Leary (Contract), Geoff Johnston **EST.** 1843 **CASES** 4000
SUMMARY The origins of this business, owned by the Johnston Group, date back to 1839, making it the oldest known family-owned business in South Australia. The vineyard at Oakbank is substantial, with 7 ha each of sauvignon blanc and pinot noir, 6 ha of shiraz, 5 ha of chardonnay and 4 ha of merlot. Retail distribution in South Australia (Porter & Co) and Victoria (Yarra Valley Wine Consultants).

ΨΨΨΨΨ **Adelaide Hills Sauvignon Blanc 2004** Spotlessly clean; tropical passionfruit aromas; lively palate, finishing with minerally, squeaky acidity. Screwcap. **RATING** 93 **DRINK** 2007 $17.95
Adelaide Hills Shiraz 2002 Very attractive spicy, cool-grown style; tangy, intense black fruits; long palate, fine tannins. Screwcap. **RATING** 93 **DRINK** 2015 $20
Adelaide Hills Chardonnay 2004 Very pale; delicate, elegant, light-bodied stone fruit, melon and citrus; crisp finish, unforced. Screwcap. **RATING** 90 **DRINK** 2009 $17.95

John Wade Wines NR

PO Box 23, Denmark, WA 6633 **REGION** Denmark
T (08) 9848 2462 **F** (08) 9848 2087 **OPEN** By appointment
WINEMAKER John Wade, Stephanie Wade, Alex Wade **EST.** 2000 **CASES** 1500
SUMMARY John Wade is arguably the most experienced winemaker in Western Australia, with over 20 years' experience following his role as chief winemaker at Wynns Coonawarra Estate. He is best known for his involvement with Plantagenet and then Howard Park. Having sold his interest in Howard Park, he has become a consultant winemaker to a substantial number of producers; his own label is a relatively small part of his total wine business. The wines are chiefly sold through premium retail outlets and restaurants.

Jollymont NR

145 Pullens Road, Woodbridge, Tas 7162 (postal) **REGION** Southern Tasmania
T (03) 6267 4594 **F** (03) 6267 4594 **OPEN** Not
WINEMAKER Andrew Hood (Contract) **EST.** 1988 **CASES** 100
SUMMARY However briefly, Jollymont displaced Scarp Valley as the smallest producer in Australia, its 1998 vintage (the first) producing 10 cases, the next 20, now 100. The vines are not irrigated, nor will they be, and Peter and Heather Kreet do not intend to sell any wine younger than 3–4 years old. Their aim is to produce wines of maximum intensity and complexity.

Jones Winery & Vineyard

Jones Road, Rutherglen, Vic 3685 **REGION** Rutherglen
T (02) 6032 8496 **F** (02) 6032 8495 **WEB** www.joneswinery.com **OPEN** Fri–Sun & public hols 10–5
WINEMAKER Mandy Jones **EST.** 1864 **CASES** 1500
SUMMARY Late in 1998 the winery was purchased from Les Jones by Leanne Schoen and Mandy and
Arthur Jones (nieces and nephew of Les). The cellar door sales area is in a building from the 1860s,
still with the original bark ceiling and walls made of handmade bricks fired onsite; it was completely
renovated in 2002/03.

ΨΨΨΨ **LJ Shiraz 2002** Complex, powerful and intense array of black fruits; very good tannin and
extract control, to the point of unexpected elegance. Quality cork. **RATING** 92 **DRINK** 2017
$ 40

ΨΨΨΨ **The Winemaker Shiraz 2003** Rich satsuma/blood plum fruit; smooth and supple;
surprisingly fine tannins. Cork. **RATING** 89 **DRINK** 2010 $ 21
The Winemaker Marsanne 2002 Floral honeysuckle varietal characters on the bouquet
and palate, filled out by bottle development; quite rich. Cork. **RATING** 88 **DRINK** 2007 $ 20

ΨΨΨΨ **The Winemaker Merlot 2003** **RATING** 86 **DRINK** 2012 $ 20
Apero NV **RATING** 85 **DRINK** Now $ 20

Journeys End Vineyards

248 Flinders Street, Adelaide, SA 5000 (postal) **REGION** Southeast Australia
T 0431 709 305 **WEB** www.journeysendvineyards.com.au **OPEN** Not
WINEMAKER Ben Riggs (Contract) **EST.** 2001 **CASES** 5000
SUMMARY A particularly interesting business in the virtual winery category which, while focused on
McLaren Vale shiraz, also has contracts for other varieties in the Adelaide Hills and Langhorne
Creek. The shiraz comes in four levels, and, for good measure, uses five different clones of shiraz to
amplify the complexity which comes from having grapegrowers in many different parts of McLaren
Vale. The wines are distributed through a limited number of fine wine retailers, particularly in
Melbourne, and through the website. Exports to the US, the UK, Canada and Singapore.

ΨΨΨΨΨ **Arrival Shiraz 2002** Super-powerful, but not extractive; like the Ascent, flooded with
superb regional fruit; excellent lingering and surprisingly fine tannins. **RATING** 96
DRINK 2017 $ 45
Ascent Shiraz 2002 Absolutely crammed to the gills with luscious blackberry,
blackcurrant, plum and dark chocolate fruit; soft, ripe tannins. **RATING** 94 **DRINK** 2017
$ 27.50

ΨΨΨΨ **Fleurieu Shiraz 2003** Generous, ripe, complex bouquet; unmistakable bitter chocolate,
blackberry and spice regional mix; good balance; handles its 15° alcohol well. High-quality
cork. **RATING** 90 **DRINK** 2013 $ 22.50

ΨΨΨΨ **Footprints on Maslin Chardonnay 2004** Light-bodied; delicate melon and citrus;
moderate length; nice unforced, unwooded, style. Cork. **RATING** 87 **DRINK** 2007 $ 17.50

ΨΨΨΨ **Three Brothers Reunion Shiraz 2003** **RATING** 86 **DRINK** 2008 $ 15

ΨΨΨ **Made in the Vineyard Verdelho 2004** **RATING** 83 $ 15

Judds Warby Range Estate

Jones Road, Taminick via Glenrowan, Vic 3675 **REGION** Glenrowan
T (03) 5765 2314 **WEB** www.warbyrange-estate.com.au **OPEN** Thurs–Mon 10–5, or by appointment
WINEMAKER Ralph Judd **EST.** 1989 **CASES** 500
SUMMARY Ralph and Margaret Judd began the development of their vineyard in 1989 as contract
growers for Southcorp. They have gradually expanded the plantings to 4 ha of shiraz and 0.5 ha of
durif; they also have 100 vines each of zinfandel, ruby cabernet, cabernet sauvignon, petit verdot,
nebbiolo, tempranillo and sangiovese for evaluation. Until 1995, all the grapes were fermented and
then sent by tanker to Southcorp, but in 1996 the Judds made their first barrel of wine. They have
now opened a small cellar door sales area. The wines are monumental in flavour and depth, in best
Glenrowan tradition, and will richly repay extended cellaring.

▼▼▼▼▽ **Shiraz 2003** Voluminous blackberry, plum and spice fruit is supported by soft, ripe tannins and well-integrated vanilla oak. **RATING** 91 **DRINK** 2008 $ 15
Durif 2003 Intensely aromatic and lively; spiced prunes and plums; low tannins, but quite long. **RATING** 90 **DRINK** 2007 $ 15

Juniper Estate ★★★★☆

Harmans Road South, Cowaramup, WA 6284 **REGION** Margaret River
T (08) 9755 9000 **F** (08) 9755 9100 **WEB** www.juniperestate.com.au **OPEN** 7 days 10–5
WINEMAKER Mark Messenger **EST.** 1973 **CASES** 15 000
SUMMARY This is the reincarnation of Wrights, which was sold by founders Henry and Maureen Wright in 1998. The 10-ha vineyard has been retrellised, and the last 1.5 ha of plantable land has seen the key plantings of shiraz and cabernet sauvignon increase a little. A major building program was completed in February 2000, giving Juniper Estate a new 250-tonne capacity winery, barrel hall and cellar door facility. Juniper Crossing wines use a mix of estate-grown and purchased grapes from other Margaret River vineyards. The Juniper Estate releases are made only from the 28-year-old estate plantings. Immaculate packaging and background material. Exports to the US, the UK, Denmark, Germany, Hong Kong and Japan.

▼▼▼▼▼ **Cabernet Sauvignon 2001** Fragrant cassis and blackcurrant aromas; perfectly modulated and balanced; generous fruit, oak and tannins. **RATING** 95 **DRINK** 2016 $ 32

▼▼▼▼▽ **Semillon 2004** Subtle barrel ferment inputs to both bouquet and palate; long and intense; excellent acidity; barrel-fermented and matured. Screwcap. **RATING** 92
DRINK 2010 $ 23
Semillon 2003 Excellent supple mouthfeel, line and length; delicate barrel ferment inputs; long, balanced finish. **RATING** 92 **DRINK** 2010 $ 22
Juniper Crossing Semillon Sauvignon Blanc 2004 Very lively, fresh and crisp; delicate aromas and flavours of grass, passionfruit and pear; lingering finish. Screwcap. **RATING** 91
DRINK 2008 $ 16
Juniper Crossing Chardonnay 2003 Neatly balanced complex fruit and oak integration; classic Margaret River chardonnay with ripe stone fruit richness and length. **RATING** 91
DRINK 2009 $ 19
Juniper Crossing Cabernet Merlot 2003 Good colour; medium-bodied; supple, ripe blackcurrant and cassis; fine, ripe tannins; subtle oak. Screwcap. **RATING** 90 **DRINK** 2010
$ 16

▼▼▼▼ **Shiraz 2001** Fragrant, lifted red fruit aromas; more structure on the medium-bodied palate; slightly dusty tannins. **RATING** 89 **DRINK** 2008 $ 29
Juniper Crossing Cabernet Merlot 2002 Deep colour; powerful structure in classic regional mould; black fruits, touches of olive and herb, savoury tannins. Top value.
RATING 89 **DRINK** 2012 $ 16
Cabernet Sauvignon 2002 Clean and fresh; distinctly savoury and less ripe than the '01; earthy fruit, savoury tannins. High-quality cork. **RATING** 89 **DRINK** 2011 $ 33

▼▼▼▽ **Juniper Crossing Shiraz 2002 RATING** 86 **DRINK** 2007 $ 19
Cane Cut Riesling 2003 RATING 85 **DRINK** Now $ 24

Jupiter Creek Winery NR

10 Queen Street, Thebarton, SA 5031 (postal) **REGION** Adelaide Hills
T (08) 8354 3744 **F** (08) 8354 3822 **OPEN** Not
WINEMAKER Paul Lindner (Contract) **EST.** 1999 **CASES** NA
SUMMARY Jupiter Creek has 8.9 ha of vineyard at Echunga, under the control of viticulturist Michael Clarken. The varieties planted are sauvignon blanc, grenache, cabernet sauvignon, merlot and shiraz.

🐌 Jylland Vineyard NR

77 Ashby Road, Gingin, WA 6503 **REGION** Perth Hills
T (08) 9575 1442 **OPEN** Tues–Sun 10–5
WINEMAKER Alon Arbel **EST.** 1999 **CASES** 2000

314 | James Halliday

SUMMARY Edel and Terry Grocke have planted 6 ha of chardonnay, verdelho, chenin blanc, cabernet sauvignon, shiraz, carnelian and sangiovese. Shady picnic spots are available, as are vignerons' platters, tea, coffee and cakes.

Kabminye Wines ★★★★★

Krondorf Road, Tanunda, SA 5352 **REGION** Barossa Valley
T (08) 8563 0889 **F** (08) 8563 3828 **WEB** www.kabminye.com **OPEN** 7 days 11–5
WINEMAKER Contract **EST.** 2001 **CASES** 3000
SUMMARY Rick and Ingrid Glastonbury have established a combined café (serving traditional Barossa Valley lunches all day), art gallery and cellar door, with a surrounding 1.5 ha of vineyard. Architect Rick Glastonbury has been a home winemaker for 30 years, but almost all the wines under the Kabminye label are contract-made from purchased grapes.

ΨΨΨΨΨ **Hubert Shiraz 2002** Elegant, intense and focused; long and powerful red fruits plus spice and super-fine tannins; integrated French oak. Cork. **RATING** 95 **DRINK** 2017 $ 37.50
HWG Cabernet Sauvignon 2002 Dense colour; black fruits and dark chocolate; rich and round; not overly extracted or worked; subtle oak. **RATING** 94 **DRINK** 2017 $ 37.50

ΨΨΨΨΨ **Barossa Shiraz 2002** Medium-bodied; lusciously ripe and sweet plum and blackberry fruit; substrate of American oak; ripe tannins. Cork. **RATING** 92 **DRINK** 2012 $ 24

ΨΨΨΨ **Three Posts Eden Valley Riesling 2004** Lime and green apple aromas and flavours; full-bodied, generous style. Screwcap. **RATING** 89 **DRINK** 2008 $ 19.50
Irma Adeline 2002 Scented, spicy, sweet raspberry, cherry and plum fruit; fine tannins. Screwcap. **RATING** 88 **DRINK** 2007 $ 22.50
Schliebs Block 2003 Light to medium-bodied; fresh, juicy red berry fruit; minimal tannins; good summer lunch wine. Screwcap. **RATING** 87 **DRINK** 2007

ΨΨΨΨ **Barossa Valley Semillon 2004** **RATING** 85 **DRINK** 2007 $ 19.50

Kaesler Wines ★★★★★

Barossa Valley Way, Nuriootpa, SA 5355 **REGION** Barossa Valley
T (08) 8562 4488 **F** (08) 8562 4499 **WEB** www.kaesler.com.au **OPEN** Mon–Sat 10–5, Sunday & public hols 11.30–4
WINEMAKER Reid Bosward **EST.** 1990 **CASES** 12 000
SUMMARY The Kaesler name dates back to 1845, when the first members of the family settled in the Barossa Valley. The Kaesler vineyards date back to 1893, but the Kaesler ownership ended in 1968. After several changes, the present (much-expanded) Kaesler Wines was acquired by a Swiss banking family in conjunction with former Flying Winemaker Reid Bosward and wife Bindy. Bosward's experience shows through in the wines, which now come from 24 ha of estate vineyards which, as well as the 1893 shiraz, grenache and mourvedre, have grenache and mourvedre planted in the 1930s. A new winery was completed in time for the 2002 vintage. Exports to the US, Canada, Switzerland, Denmark, Sweden, Japan, Hong Kong and New Zealand.

ΨΨΨΨΨ **Old Bastard Shiraz 2002** Gloriously concentrated and intense essence of Shiraz; seamless black fruits and tannins; immaculate oak handling. From 1893 plantings. Indifferent-quality cork. **RATING** 96 **DRINK** 2022 $ 180
Old Vine Shiraz 2002 Medium to full-bodied; gains momentum and strength as it travels along the palate towards the finish; fine, silky tannins. From 1961 and 1893 plantings. **RATING** 95 **DRINK** 2017 $ 60
The Bogan Shiraz 2002 Deep, intense colour; extremely powerful and concentrated; huge black fruits, huge tannins and masses of extract; will live forever if the cork holds. Mega 15.5° alcohol. **RATING** 94 **DRINK** 2022 $ 50
W.O.M.S. Shiraz Cabernet 2002 Deep purple-red; lusciously ripe and powerful black fruits/blackberry/blackcurrant fruit; powerful lingering tannins; oak absorbed. Indeed, a Weapon of Mass Seduction. **RATING** 94 **DRINK** 2020 $ 70

ΨΨΨΨ **Avignon Shiraz Grenache Mataro 2003** Medium-bodied; attractive red fruits; fine, long and silky tannins. Shiraz 70%, Grenache and Mourvedre 30% (from 70-year-old vines). **RATING** 92 **DRINK** 2010 $ 30
The Fave Grenache 2003 More structure than most Barossa Grenaches; medium-bodied, with some varietal jammy fruit and plenty of ripe tannins; subtle oak. **RATING** 92 **DRINK** 2010 $ 40

Cabernet Sauvignon 2002 Solid wine; blackcurrant, earth and chocolate; powerful, persistent tannins, subtle oak; needs a decade. **RATING** 92 **DRINK** 2017 $ 25
Stonehorse Shiraz 2003 Medium-bodied, supple and smooth; attractive red and black fruits; has line. **RATING** 91 **DRINK** 2012 $ 30
Old Vine Semillon 2004 Intense lemon citrus aromas and flavours; long, lingering, modern style; neither phenolics nor oak. Vines planted in 1961. **RATING** 90 **DRINK** 2014 $ 16.50
Stonehorse Grenache Shiraz Mataro 2003 Bright colour; plenty of ripe red fruits; overall, quite soft; fine tannins. **RATING** 90 **DRINK** 2010 $ 17.50

TTTT **Chardonnay 2002** Full-flavoured, powerful wine; ripe fruit; does show bottle development; drink soon. **RATING** 87 **DRINK** Now $ 25

Kalari Wines   NR

120 Carro Park Road, Cowra, NSW 2794 **REGION** Cowra
T (02) 6342 1465 **F** (02) 6342 1465 **OPEN** Fri–Mon & public hols 9–5
WINEMAKER Jill Lindsay (Contract) **EST.** 1995 **CASES** 500
SUMMARY Kalari Vineyards is yet another of the new brands to appear in the Cowra region. It has 14.5 ha of vines, with a Verdelho, Chardonnay and Shiraz in the initial release.

Kalleske   ★★★★☆

Vinegrove Road, Greenock, SA 5360 **REGION** Barossa Valley
T 0409 339 599 **F** (08) 8562 8118 **WEB** www.kalleske.com **OPEN** Not
WINEMAKER Troy Kalleske **EST.** 1999 **CASES** 4000
SUMMARY The Kalleske family has been growing and selling grapes on a mixed farming property at Greenock for over 100 years. Fifth-generation John and Lorraine Kalleske embarked on a trial vintage for a fraction of the grapes in 1999. It was an immediate success, and led to the construction of a small winery with son Troy Kalleske as winemaker. The vineyards, with an average age of 50 years, see no chemical fertilisers or pesticides; some blocks are certified fully organic. The density of the flavour of the Shiraz and Grenache is awesome.

TTTTY **Greenock Shiraz 2003** Dense colour; very powerful, ripe and concentrated black fruits, prune and dark chocolate; tannins entirely appropriate. Long future. **RATING** 93 **DRINK** 2018 $ 40
Shiraz Viognier 2002 Intense fruit; luscious, not jammy, black cherry; oak balanced and integrated; fine, savoury tannins. **RATING** 93 **DRINK** 2015 $ 32.99

TTTY **Clarry's Barossa White 2004** **RATING** 86 **DRINK** Now $ 17.99

Kamberra   ★★★★

Cnr Northbourne Avenue/Flemington Road, Lyneham, ACT 2602 **REGION** Canberra District
T (02) 6262 2333 **F** (02) 6262 2300 **WEB** www.kamberra.com.au **OPEN** 7 days 10–5
WINEMAKER Alex McKay, Ed Carr **EST.** 2000 **CASES** 18 000
SUMMARY Kamberra is part of the Hardys group, established in 2000 with the planting of 40 ha of vines and a new winery in the Australian Capital Territory, only a few hundred metres from the showground facilities where the national wine show is held every year. Riesling and Shiraz are fully estate-grown, and most of the wines have a Kamberra component.

Kancoona Valley Wines   NR

123 Morgan's Creek Road, Kancoona South, Vic 3691 **REGION** Alpine Valleys
T (02) 6028 9419 **F** (02) 6028 9051 **WEB** www.kancoonavalleywines.com.au **OPEN** By appointment
WINEMAKER Joseph Birti **EST.** 1989 **CASES** NFP
SUMMARY Joseph and Lena Birti began planting their vineyard, situated in a natural amphitheatre 12 km from the Kiewa River, halfway between Myrtleford and Mt Beauty, in 1989. Thermal breezes rising from the Kiewa River valley help protect the vines from fungal disease, and the Birtis do not use any pesticides. They made their first wines in 1999, and from the word go have offered preservative-free alternatives.

Kangarilla Road Vineyard

★★★★☆

Kangarilla Road, McLaren Vale, SA 5171 **REGION** McLaren Vale
T(08) 8383 0533 **F**(08) 8383 0044 **OPEN** Mon–Fri 9–5, weekends 11–5
WINEMAKER Kevin O'Brien **EST.** 1975 **CASES** 40 000
SUMMARY Kangarilla Road Vineyard and Winery was formerly known as Stevens Cambrai. Long-time industry identity Kevin O'Brien and wife Helen purchased the property in July 1997, and have now fully established the strikingly labelled Kangarilla Road brand in place of Cambrai, steadily increasing production as well. Exports to all major markets.

▼▼▼▼▼ **McLaren Vale Shiraz Viognier 2003** Greater aromatic complexity than the varietal Shiraz, but also better structure and expression even though, once again, full-bodied; lingering, savoury tannins (15° alcohol). **RATING** 94 **DRINK** 2017

▼▼▼▼▽ **McLaren Vale Shiraz 2003** Powerful, dense and complex full-bodied wine; ripe, almost sweet blackberry fruit (only 14.5° alcohol); good tannins and oak. **RATING** 93 **DRINK** 2013 $ 19

▼▼▼▼ **Chardonnay 2004** Lively, tangy citrussy aromas and flavours; ultra-subtle oak; good length and style. **RATING** 89 **DRINK** Now $ 15
Cabernet Sauvignon 2002 Comes alive on a rich palate with chocolate, cassis, blackcurrant and soft tannins; subtle oak. **RATING** 89 **DRINK** 2012 $ 20
Cadenzia Grenache Zinfandel Shiraz 2003 Fresh, juicy berry lunch red; minimal oak and tannins. **RATING** 87 **DRINK** Now $ 19
Fleurieu Zinfandel 2003 Light to medium-bodied in terms of fruit weight; strongly varietal juicy/lemony/spicy fruit. Does not have the extreme alcohol heat of the McLaren Vale Zinfandel. **RATING** 87 **DRINK** 2008 $ 17

▼▼▼▽ **McLaren Vale Viognier 2004** **RATING** 86 **DRINK** 2007 $ 20
McLaren Vale Zinfandel 2003 **RATING** 85 **DRINK** 2008 $ 30

Kangaroo Island Vines

★★★☆

c/- 413 Payneham Road, Felixstow, SA 5070 **REGION** Kangaroo Island
T(08) 8365 3411 **F**(08) 8336 2462 **OPEN** Not
WINEMAKER Caj Amadio **EST.** 1990 **CASES** 600
SUMMARY Kangaroo Island is another venture of Caj and Genny Amadio, with the wines being sold through the Chain of Ponds cellar door. The Amadios have been the focal point of the development of vineyards on Kangaroo Island, producing the wines from their own tiny planting of 450 vines on quarter of an acre, and from grapes from other vignerons on the island. The tiny quantities of wine so far produced, particularly the excellent Florance Cabernet Merlot, strongly support the notion that Kangaroo Island has an excellent climate for Bordeaux-style reds.

Kangderaar Vineyard

NR

Wehla–Kingower Road, Rheola, Vic 3517 **REGION** Bendigo
T(03) 5438 8292 **F**(03) 5438 8292 **OPEN** Mon–Sat 9–5, Sun 10–5
WINEMAKER James Nealy **EST.** 1980 **CASES** 800
SUMMARY The 4.5-ha vineyard is near the Melville Caves, said to have been the hideout of the bushranger Captain Melville in the 1850s, and surrounded by the Kooyoora State Park. It is owned by James and Christine Nealy.

Kara Kara Vineyard

★★★★

Sunraysia Highway, St Arnaud, Vic 3478 (10 km sth St Arnaud) **REGION** Pyrenees
T(03) 5496 3294 **F**(03) 5496 3294 **WEB** www.pyrenees.org.au/karakara.htm **OPEN** Mon–Fri 10.30–6, weekends 9–6
WINEMAKER John Ellis (Contract), Steve Zsigmond **EST.** 1977 **CASES** 1200
SUMMARY Hungarian-born Steve Zsigmond comes from a long line of vignerons and sees Kara Kara as the eventual retirement occupation for himself and wife Marlene. He is a graduate of the Adelaide University Roseworthy campus wine marketing course, and worked for Yalumba and Negociants as a sales manager in Adelaide and Perth. He looks after sales and marketing from the Melbourne

premises of Kara Kara, and the wine is made at Hanging Rock, with consistent results. Draws upon 9 ha of estate plantings.

ΨΨΨΨ **Cabernet Sauvignon 2002** Cool vintage characters show in savoury/olive elements to stylish, medium-bodied palate; blackcurrant fruit, lingering, fine tannins. Cork. **RATING** 91 **DRINK** 2014 $ 26
Shiraz 2003 Powerful blackberry and plum fruit; controlled tannins and oak. Clean. Screwcap. **RATING** 90 **DRINK** 2013 $ 26
Shiraz 2002 Very ripe, very dense, very powerful flow of dark fruits and dark chocolate; ripe, chewy tannins; needs more time. Cork. **RATING** 90 **DRINK** 2015 $ 26
Cabernet Sauvignon 2003 Fresh, positive black and redcurrant fruit; firm and lively, fine but ripe tannins. Screwcap. **RATING** 90 **DRINK** 2014 $ 26

ΨΨΨΨ **Classic White 2003** Nicely balanced, gently ripe array of fruit flavours; nice touch of bottle development; balanced acidity. Cork. **RATING** 87 **DRINK** 2007 $ 18

ΨΨΨΨ **Sauvignon Blanc 2004** **RATING** 85 **DRINK** Now $ 18

🐚 Karatta Wine ★★★★☆

43/22 Liberman Close, Adelaide, SA 5000 (postal) **REGION** Mount Benson
T (08) 8215 0250 **F** (08) 8215 0450 **OPEN** Not
WINEMAKER Contract **EST.** 1994 **CASES** 1400
SUMMARY This is the former Anthony Dale vineyard, planted to 12 ha of shiraz, cabernet sauvignon, pinot noir, malbec, and more recently sauvignon blanc and chardonnay. It is owned by Karatta Wine Company in association with the Tenison Vineyard. The wines are sold through regional outlets, and by mail order, but with further developments planned.

ΨΨΨΨΨ **Lake Butler Reserve Tenison Vineyard Shiraz 2003** Spotless black plum and blackberry aromas; perfectly integrated French oak and gently sweet fruit; great mouthfeel and balance, supple, fine tannins. **RATING** 94 **DRINK** 2013 $ 18

ΨΨΨΨ **The 12 Mile Vineyard Shiraz Cabernet Sauvignon 2002** Medium-bodied; an appealing mix of black fruits, chocolate and more savoury notes; lingering tannins. **RATING** 90 **DRINK** 2012 $ 15

ΨΨΨΨ **The 12 Mile Vineyard Shiraz Cabernet Sauvignon 2003** Good structure and tannins to red and black fruit flavours; oak a little too obvious. **RATING** 88 **DRINK** 2007 $ 15

🐚 Karee Estate ★★★★

PO Box 38, Goornong, Vic 3557 **REGION** Bendigo
T (03) 5432 2268 **F** (03) 5432 2274 **OPEN** By appointment
WINEMAKER Greg Dedman (Contract) **EST.** 2002 **CASES** NA
SUMMARY The earlier wines were made by Mal Stewart, but since 2004 they have been made in collaboration with the Bendigo Institute of TAFE winery, now run by Greg Dedman.

ΨΨΨΨ **Merlot 2003** Very attractive and consistent varietal fruit expression on both bouquet and palate; a mix of black olive, blackcurrant, cedar and spice; fine, lingering tannins; very good balance. High-quality cork. **RATING** 91 **DRINK** 2014
Shiraz 2003 Firm blackberry and spice aromas and flavours; medium-bodied; fine, persistent tannins; good balance; no drought stress obvious. Quality cork. **RATING** 90 **DRINK** 2013

ΨΨΨΨ **Cabernet Sauvignon 2002** Elegant; light to medium-bodied; blackcurrant and black olive, some spice; balanced, fine tannins; (12.8° alcohol). Quality cork. **RATING** 88 **DRINK** 2012
Cabernet Sauvignon 2003 Spicy, cedary, leafy, olive edges to medium-bodied blackcurrant fruit; does show its slightly low (12.5°) alcohol. High-quality cork. **RATING** 87 **DRINK** 2010

Karina Vineyard ★★★★

35 Harrisons Road, Dromana, Vic 3936 **REGION** Mornington Peninsula
T (03) 5981 0137 **F** (03) 5981 0137 **OPEN** Weekends 11–5, 7 days in January

WINEMAKER Gerard Terpstra **EST.** 1984 **CASES** 2000

SUMMARY A typical Mornington Peninsula vineyard, situated in the Dromana/Red Hill area on rising, north-facing slopes, just 3 km from the shores of Port Phillip Bay, immaculately tended and with picturesque garden surrounds. Fragrant Riesling and cashew-accented Chardonnay are usually its best wines. Retail distribution in Victoria; exports to Japan.

🍷🍷🍷🍷🍷 **Sauvignon Blanc 2004** Very lively, fresh, lemony gooseberry fruit; bright and long finish. **RATING** 90 **DRINK** Now **$** 19

🍷🍷🍷🍷 **Cabernet Merlot 2003** Good colour; medium-bodied; well balanced, attractive dark fruits and fine but ripe tannins. Excellent for the region. **RATING** 89 **DRINK** 2008 **$** 20

Karl Seppelt

NR

Ross Dewells Road, Springton, SA 5235 **REGION** Eden Valley
T (08) 8568 2378 **F** (08) 8568 2799 **OPEN** 7 days 10–5
WINEMAKER Karl Seppelt **EST.** 1981 **CASES** 5000
SUMMARY After experimenting with various label designs and names, Karl Seppelt (former marketing director of Seppelt) has decided to discontinue the brand name Grand Cru (although retaining it as a business name) and henceforth market the wines from his estate vineyards, now made at a small winery constructed on the property, under his own name. The quality is consistent across the range. Exports to Canada and Germany.

Karri Grove Estate

PO Box 432, Margaret River, WA 6285 **REGION** Margaret River
T (08) 9757 6281 **F** (08) 9757 6353 **OPEN** Not
WINEMAKER Flying Fish Cove (white), David O'Leary (red) (Contract) **EST.** 1991 **CASES** 3000
SUMMARY Karri Grove Estate is loosely associated with Flinders Bay, from which it purchases most of its grapes. The white wines are made at Flying Fish Cove in the Margaret River region; the grapes for the red wines are transported to South Australia, where they are contract-made by David O'Leary. Distribution is via wholesale distributors in New South Wales (Young & Rashleigh), Victoria (Sullivan Wine Agencies) and Queensland (Premier Small Vineyards); limited availability by mail order.

Karriview

★★★★

Cnr Scotsdale Road/Roberts Road, Denmark, WA 6333 **REGION** Denmark
T (08) 9840 9381 **F** (08) 9855 1549 **WEB** www.karriviewwines.com.au **OPEN** Fri–Sun 11–4, school & public hols 7 days 11–4
WINEMAKER Elizabeth Smith **EST.** 1986 **CASES** 550
SUMMARY A small (1.5 ha each) of immaculately tended pinot noir and chardonnay on ultra-close spacing produce tiny quantities of two wines of at times remarkable intensity, quality and style. Available only from the winery, but worth the effort. There is some vintage variation; the winery rating is based upon the successes, not the disappointments. Typically, back vintages are available; with age, the Pinot Noir acquires strong foresty characters which are quite Burgundian.

🍷🍷🍷🍷🍷 **Chardonnay 2003** Light green-straw, quite brilliant; complex aromas with some barrel ferment smoke; intense grapefruit, pear and melon fruit. **RATING** 92 **DRINK** 2010

🍷🍷🍷🍷 **Pinot Noir 2003 RATING** 84 **DRINK** Now

🍂 Kassebaum Wines

Nitschke Road, Marananga, SA 5355 **REGION** Barossa Valley
T (08) 8562 2731 **F** (08) 8562 4751 **OPEN** By appointment
WINEMAKER Rod Chapman (Contract) **EST.** 2003 **CASES** 160
SUMMARY David and Dianne Kassebaum are third-generation grapegrowers. David has been involved in the wine industry for 20 years, working first with Penfolds in bottling, microbiology and maturation laboratories, and most recently in the Vinpac International laboratory. They have 5.4 ha of shiraz and 1.5 ha of semillon, most of which is sold to Southcorp with a top-quality grade. Yields vary from 1 to 1.5 tonnes per acre. The small amount of shiraz retained for the Kassebaum Magdalena brand is matured in new French and American oak for 12 months.

ΥΥΥΥΥ Magdalena Shiraz 2003 Inky purple-red; luscious blackberry, plum and prune fruit; good oak handling and soft tannins; archetypal Barossa. **RATING** 92 **DRINK** 2013

Katnook Estate ★★★★☆

Riddoch Highway, Coonawarra, SA 5263 **REGION** Coonawarra
T (08) 8737 2394 **F** (08) 8737 2397 **WEB** www.katnookestate.com.au **OPEN** Mon–Fri 9–4.30, Sat 10–4.30, Sun 12–4.30
WINEMAKER Wayne Stehbens **EST.** 1979 **CASES** 100 000
SUMMARY Still one of the largest contract grapegrowers and suppliers in Coonawarra, selling more than half its grape production to others. The historic stone woolshed in which the second vintage in Coonawarra (1896) was made, and which has served Katnook since 1980, is being restored. The 1997 launch of the flagship Odyssey and the 2000 follow-up of Prodigy Shiraz point the way to a higher profile for the winemaking side of the venture. Several years ago, Freixenet, the Spanish Cava producer, acquired 60% of the business. Exports to the UK, the US and other major markets.

ΥΥΥΥΥ Odyssey Cabernet Sauvignon 2000 Fragrant red berry fruits; masses of cedar, cigar box and sandalwood; fine, ripe tannins. **RATING** 94 **DRINK** 2010 $ 80

ΥΥΥΥΥ Sauvignon Blanc 2004 Very light straw-green; clean and flowery aromas; delicate gooseberry fruit; crisp finish, excellent length. Major success. **RATING** 93 **DRINK** Now $ 28
Riddoch Coonawarra Shiraz 2002 Spicy, savoury aromas; medium-bodied and elegant; good tension between sweet black fruit, oak and tannins. **RATING** 92 **DRINK** 2012
Riddoch Sauvignon Blanc 2004 Punchy herb and grass aromas; plenty of attack on the palate; minerally acidity. **RATING** 90 **DRINK** Now $ 20
Chardonnay Brut 2002 Fragrant citrus blossom aromatics; elegant, fresh and lively aperitif style. **RATING** 90 **DRINK** Now $ 32

ΥΥΥΥ Riesling 2004 Tight, fine, crisp and delicate, and will always be on the elegant side. **RATING** 89 **DRINK** 2012 $ 20
Shiraz 2002 Some colour development; medium-bodied, with spicy/savoury edges to the fruit; balanced tannins and cedary oak. **RATING** 89 **DRINK** 2012 $ 40
Riddoch Sparkling Shiraz 2002 Complex boot leather, spice and earth aromas and flavours; moderately sweet dosage. **RATING** 87 **DRINK** 2008 $ 22

ΥΥΥΥ Riddoch Coonawarra Chardonnay 2002 RATING 86 **DRINK** Now $ 17

Kay Bros Amery ★★★★☆

Kay Road, McLaren Vale, SA 5171 **REGION** McLaren Vale
T (08) 8323 8211 **F** (08) 8323 9199 **WEB** www.kaybrothersamerywines.com **OPEN** Mon–Fri 9–5, weekends & public hols 12–5
WINEMAKER Colin Kay **EST.** 1890 **CASES** 14 000
SUMMARY A traditional winery with a rich history and nearly 20 ha of priceless old vines; while the white wines have been variable, the red wines and fortified wines can be very good. Of particular interest is Block 6 Shiraz, made from 100-year-old vines; both vines and wine are going from strength to strength. Exports to the UK, the US and other major markets.

ΥΥΥΥΥ McLaren Vale Shiraz 2002 Dense colour; powerful, concentrated blackberry/dark chocolate; good overall balance and extract; subtle oak. Screwcap. **RATING** 94 **DRINK** 2022 $ 50

ΥΥΥΥΥ Founders Very Old Tawny Solera (375 ml) 2003 High-flavoured, good rancio; attractive spicy, biscuity flavours; clean finish. **RATING** 90 **DRINK** Now $ 22

ΥΥΥΥ Hillside Shiraz 2002 Elegant, medium-bodied style; does not show its 15° alcohol, partly due to balancing acidity; savoury, dark fruits. Screwcap. **RATING** 89 **DRINK** 2010 $ 22
McLaren Vale Shiraz 2002 Medium-bodied, savoury, elegant style similar to Hillside; slightly more ripe fruit, but an even bigger surprise with 15.5° alcohol not heating the finish. Screwcap. **RATING** 89 **DRINK** 2010 $ 22
McLaren Vale Cabernet Sauvignon 2002 Medium-bodied; attractive blackberry and blueberry fruit; faint twist of regional chocolate; fine tannins. Screwcap. **RATING** 89 **DRINK** 2008 $ 22
Founders Very Old Muscat (375 ml) 2003 Age evident in the concentration of sweet, raisined fruit; notes of coffee and caramel. **RATING** 88 **DRINK** Now $ 22

🍷🍷🍷🍷 **Merlot 2002** RATING 85 DRINK 2008 $ 22
McLaren Vale Semillon 2003 RATING 84 DRINK 2007 $ 17
MGM Merlot Grenache Mataro 2002 RATING 84 DRINK 2008 $ 17

Keith Tulloch Wine ★★★★★

Hunter Ridge Winery, Hermitage Road, Pokolbin, NSW 2320 **REGION** Lower Hunter Valley
T (02) 4998 7500 **F** (02) 4998 7211 **WEB** www.keithtullochwine.com.au **OPEN** Thurs–Fri 10–4, Sat 10–5, or by appointment
WINEMAKER Keith Tulloch **EST.** 1997 **CASES** 6500
SUMMARY Keith Tulloch is, of course, a member of the Tulloch family which has played such a lead role in the Hunter Valley for over a century. Formerly a winemaker at Lindemans and then Rothbury Estate, he is responsible for the production of Evans Family Wines as well as developing his own label since 1997. I cannot remember being more impressed with an initial release of wines than those under the Keith Tulloch label. The only problem is the small scale of their production. There is the same almost obsessive attention to detail, the same almost ascetic intellectual approach, the same refusal to accept anything but the best. Exports to all major markets.

🍷🍷🍷🍷🍷 **Semillon 2004** The Hunter Valley Wine Show is the ultimate testing ground for semillon. Repeated success here for production minnow Keith Tulloch is especially significant. Sophisticated crafting results in a silken web of complexity and an alluring future. **RATING** 95 **DRINK** 2019 **$** 26

Kellermeister/Trevor Jones ★★★☆

Barossa Valley Highway, Lyndoch, SA 5351 **REGION** Barossa Valley
T (08) 8524 4303 **F** (08) 8524 4880 **WEB** www.kellermeister.com.au **OPEN** 7 days 9–6
WINEMAKER Trevor Jones **EST.** 1979 **CASES** 20 000
SUMMARY Trevor Jones is an industry veteran, with vast experience in handling fruit from the Barossa Valley, the Eden Valley and the Adelaide Hills. He finally introduced his own label, using grapes purchased from various contract growers, with the first wines going on sale in 1996. Exports to the US (very successful), Japan, Switzerland and France.

🍷🍷🍷🍷 **Trevor Jones Size 04 Boots Gris Blanc 2004** Clean, spicy; lots of fruit; good length, augmented by a touch of sweetness. Delphic label. **RATING** 87 **DRINK** Now **$** 14

Kells Creek Vineyards NR

Kells Creek Road, Mittagong, NSW 2575 **REGION** Southern Highlands
T (02) 4878 5096 **F** (02) 4878 5097 **WEB** www.kellscreekvineyards.com.au **OPEN** By appointment
WINEMAKER Eric Priebee **EST.** 2001 **CASES** 800
SUMMARY Kells Creek is one of the newer businesses in the rapidly expanding Southern Highlands region. It has been established by Eric Priebee and wife Gaby Barfield, drawing principally on other vineyards around Mittagong, Moss Vale and Aylmerton. The one wine not to come from the Southern Highlands is a 2000 Pinot Noir, made before the establishment of Kells Creek, but which is of excellent quality. Kells Creek itself has 1 ha of riesling planted, and operates an energetic marketing program under the direction of industry veteran Douglas Hamilton. Full details are available on the website and/or via email. In 2003 a joint venture was set up with Littledale Estates of the Hunter Valley: Kells Creek will make the wines for both partners, and the wines will be marketed under the Littledale Estates Brand. Exports to Canada.

Kellybrook ★★★★

Fulford Road, Wonga Park, Vic 3115 **REGION** Yarra Valley
T (03) 9722 1304 **F** (03) 9722 2092 **WEB** www.kellybrookwinery.com.au **OPEN** Mon 11–5, Tues–Sat 9–6, Sun 11–6
WINEMAKER Darren Kelly, Philip Kelly **EST.** 1960 **CASES** 3000
SUMMARY The 8-ha vineyard is at Wonga Park, at the entrance to the principal winegrowing areas of the Yarra Valley, and has a picnic area and a full-scale restaurant. As well as table wine, a very competent producer of both cider and apple brandy (in Calvados style). When it received its winery licence in 1960, it became the first winery in the Yarra Valley to open its doors in the 20th century, a

distinction often ignored or forgotten (by this author as well as others). Retail distribution through Victoria, New South Wales and Queensland; exports to the UK and Denmark.

𝖸𝖸𝖸𝖸𝖸 **Yarra Valley Shiraz 2003** Spicy, tangy, peppery; lively red fruits underneath the pepper; light to medium-bodied and lively; 60 cases made. Cork. RATING 90 DRINK 2009 $ 35

𝖸𝖸𝖸𝖸 **Yarra Valley Riesling 2004** Clean, fresh, light-bodied; gentle passionfruit and apple; well made; basically wrong region. Quality cork. RATING 88 DRINK 2007 $ 24
Yarra Valley Chardonnay 2003 Elegant, light-bodied; creamy cashew inputs; fruit slightly suppressed, and into secondary characters. Cork. RATING 88 DRINK 2009 $ 24
Yarra Valley Pinot Noir 2001 Bottle-developed, and into a gently savoury, spicy spectrum; light-bodied, and close to its best-by date. Cork. RATING 87 DRINK Now $ 27
Late Harvest Gewurztraminer 2004 Fresh, bright, crisp green apple and lemon zest; a curious manifestation of late-harvest gewurztraminer, but nice, slightly off-dry wine. Twin Top. RATING 87 DRINK 2008 $ 30

𝖸𝖸𝖸𝖸 **Yarra Valley Cabernet Merlot 2003** RATING 86 DRINK 2008 $ 27

Kelly's Creek ★★★★

RSD 226a, Lower Whitehills Road, Relbia, Tas 7258 REGION Northern Tasmania
T (03) 6234 9696 F (03) 6231 6222 OPEN Not
WINEMAKER Andrew Hood (Contract) EST. 1992 CASES 650
SUMMARY Kelly's Creek draws on 1 ha of riesling and 0.2 ha each of chardonnay, pinot noir and cabernet sauvignon. Its majority owner is Darryl Johnson, who runs the vineyard with help from Guy Wagner, who describes himself as 'merely a marketing minion'. Small quantities of Riesling are made for Kelly's Creek; all vintages have had success at the Tasmanian Wines Show.

𝖸𝖸𝖸𝖸𝖸 **Unwooded Chardonnay 2004** Nectarine and grapefruit; well above average fruit weight and intensity; good balance. RATING 90 DRINK 2009

𝖸𝖸𝖸 **Riesling 2004** RATING 83
Chardonnay 2003 RATING 83

Kelman Vineyards ★★★★

Cnr Oakey Creek Road/Mount View Road, Pokolbin, NSW 2320 REGION Lower Hunter Valley
T (02) 4991 5456 F (02) 4991 7555 WEB www.kelmanvineyards.com.au OPEN 7 days 10–5
WINEMAKER Cameron Webster (Contract) EST. 1999 CASES 3000
SUMMARY Kelman Vineyards is a California-type development on the outskirts of Cessnock. A 40-ha property has been subdivided into 80 residential development lots, but with 8 ha of vines wending between the lots, which are under common ownership. Part of the chardonnay has already been grafted across to shiraz before coming into full production, and the vineyard has the potential to produce 8000 cases a year. In the meantime, each owner will receive 12 cases a year of the wines produced by the vineyard; the balance is available for sale via mail order (telephone (02) 4991 5456 for details) and through a single Sydney retail outlet.

𝖸𝖸𝖸𝖸𝖸 **Chairman's Reserve Shiraz 2003** Spotlessly clean; full-bodied; very concentrated blackberry and earth; good handling of oak and extract, but needs many years. Stained cork. RATING 93 DRINK 2018 $ 48
Lakeview Lane Shiraz 2003 Strong colour; medium to full-bodied, with early signs of regional earth and leather under potent blackberry fruit. Stained cork. RATING 91 DRINK 2016 $ 23.50

𝖸𝖸𝖸𝖸 **Old Block Pokolbin Semillon 2003** Consistent ripe, soft style (12° alcohol), gentle citrus; late picking. Screwcap. RATING 89 DRINK 2007 $ 19.50
Chairman's Reserve Semillon 2002 Developed yellow-green; earlier-picked (11° alcohol) but still in softer, fuller style; lemon and honey; ready now. Cork. RATING 89 DRINK Now $ 25
Catherine's Blush Rose 2004 Delicious raspberry and strawberry red fruits; good balance and length; not sweet. From 5 red varieties. RATING 89 DRINK Now $ 19
Orchard Block Semillon 2004 Clean and fresh; soft, lemon/citrus fruit and squeaky acidity; at 11.7° alcohol, on the ripe side; early-maturing. Screwcap. RATING 88 DRINK 2007 $ 19.50

Kelso

NR

Princes Highway, Narrawong, Vic 3285 **REGION** Henty
T (03) 5529 2334 **OPEN** By appointment
WINEMAKER Contract **EST.** NA **CASES** NA
SUMMARY Howard and Glenda Simmonds have established their vineyard 11 km east of Portland, and produce Riesling and Cabernet Sauvignon.

Kelvedon

★★★★★

PO Box 126, Swansea, Tas 7190 **REGION** Southern Tasmania
T (03) 6257 8283 **F** (03) 6257 8179 **OPEN** Not
WINEMAKER Julian Alcorso (Contract) **EST.** 1998 **CASES** 280
SUMMARY Jack and Gill Cotton began the development of Kelvedon by planting 1 ha of pinot noir in 1998. The plantings were extended in 2000/01 by an additional 5 ha, half to pinot noir and half to chardonnay; all the production from this is under contract to the Hardy Wine Company. The Pinot Noirs from 2002 and 2003 have been of outstanding quality.

 Pinot Noir 2003 Deep colour; plush, opulent black plum fruit; ripe tannins, good oak and a touch of spice. **RATING** 95 **DRINK** 2011 $ 25

Kenilworth Bluff Wines

★★☆

Lot 13 Bluff Road, Kenilworth, Qld 4574 **REGION** Queensland Coastal
T (07) 5472 3723 **F** (07) 5522 8620 **OPEN** Weekends & public hols 10–4
WINEMAKER Stuart Pierce **EST.** 1993 **CASES** 800
SUMMARY Brian and Colleen Marsh modestly describe themselves as 'little more than hobbyists', but also admit that 'our wines show tremendous promise'. They began planting the vineyards in 1993 in a hidden valley at the foot of Kenilworth Bluff, and now have 4 ha of shiraz, cabernet sauvignon, merlot, semillon and chardonnay. Presently the wines are made offsite, but one day the Marshes hope it will be feasible to establish an onsite winery.

 Chardonnay 2004 **RATING** 84 **DRINK** 2007 $ 15
 Shiraz 2003 **RATING** 79 $ 18

Kennedys Keilor Valley

NR

Lot 3 Overnewton Road, Keilor, Vic 3036 **REGION** Sunbury
T (03) 9311 6246 **F** (03) 9331 6246 **OPEN** By appointment
WINEMAKER Peter Dredge (Contract) **EST.** 1994 **CASES** 300
SUMMARY A small Chardonnay specialist, producing its only wine from 1.8 ha of estate vineyards; half is sold as grapes, half contract-made and sold by mailing list and word of mouth.

Kevin Sobels Wines

NR

Cnr Broke Road/Halls Road, Pokolbin, NSW 2321 **REGION** Lower Hunter Valley
T (02) 4998 7766 **F** (02) 4998 7475 **WEB** www.sobelswines.com.au **OPEN** 7 days (no fixed hours)
WINEMAKER Kevin Sobels **EST.** 1992 **CASES** 9000
SUMMARY Veteran winemaker Kevin Sobels draws upon 8 ha of vineyards (originally planted by the Ross Jones family) to produce wines sold almost entirely through the cellar door and by mail order, with limited retail representation. The cellar door offers light meals and picnic and barbecue facilities.

Kies Family Wines

★★★★☆

Barossa Valley Way, Lyndoch, SA 5381 **REGION** Barossa Valley
T (08) 8524 4110 **F** (08) 8524 4544 **WEB** www.kieswines.com.au **OPEN** 7 days 9.30–4.30
WINEMAKER Jim Irvine, Jo Irvine (Contract) **EST.** 1969 **CASES** 4000
SUMMARY The Kies family has been resident in the Barossa Valley since 1857, with the present generation of winemakers being the fifth, their children the sixth. Until 1969 the family sold almost

all the grapes to others, but in that year they launched their own brand, Karrawirra. The co-existence of Killawarra forced a name change in 1983 to Redgum Vineyard; this business was subsequently sold. Later still, Kies Family Wines opened for business, drawing upon vineyards (up to 100 years old) which had remained in the family throughout the changes, offering a wide range of wines through the 1880 cellar door. Exports to the UK, Canada, Singapore, Hong Kong, China and Japan.

ΨΨΨΨΨ **Dedication Ken Kies 1929–1996 Shiraz 2000** Complex, long and lingering; gently spicy, savoury fruits swathed in sweet vanilla oak; typical Jim Irvine style (maker). Dodgy cork. RATING 92 DRINK 2010 $ 39
Monkey Nut Tree Merlot 2002 Powerful, quite luscious blackcurrant/blackberry with a varietal twist of olive and herb; good structure and balanced oak. RATING 92 DRINK 2012 $ 28
Hill Block Riesling 2002 Distinct herb and grass notes; tightly focused minerally palate; still very youthful. Value-plus. Screwcap. RATING 91 DRINK 2012 $ 15
Klauber Block Shiraz 2002 Bright red-purple; medium-bodied, with smooth black fruits off-set by mocha oak and spicy tannins; sophisticated winemaking. RATING 90 DRINK 2012 $ 25
Chaff Mill Cabernet Sauvignon 2002 Medium to full-bodied; has the focus and concentration of the vintage; blackberry fruit, integrated oak; good, persistent tannins. Cork. RATING 90 DRINK 2015 $ 25

ΨΨΨΨ **Spring Cabernet 2004** Vivid pink colour; highly aromatic blossom aromas; a lively palate, but excessive sweetness a disappointment. RATING 86 DRINK Now $ 15
Monkey Nut Tree Sparkling Merlot 2002 RATING 86 DRINK 2007 $ 25
Deer Stalker Merlot 2004 RATING 85 DRINK 2007 $ 15
Monkey Nut Tree Sparkling Merlot 2004 RATING 85 DRINK 2007 $ 25

Kilgour Estate ★★★

85 McAdams Lane, Bellarine, Vic 3223 REGION Geelong
T (03) 5251 2223 F (03) 5251 2223 OPEN Wed–Sun 10.30–6, 7 days in Jan
WINEMAKER Karen Coulstone (Contract) EST. 1989 CASES 4000
SUMMARY Kilgour Estate has 7 ha of vines, and the wines are contract-made. Fruit-driven Pinot Noir and Chardonnay are winery specialties, the Pinot Noir having won at least one gold medal. The beautifully situated cellar door has a restaurant and barbecue facilities.

ΨΨΨΨ **Kilgour Views Pinot Gris 2004** RATING 84 DRINK Now

Kilikanoon ★★★★★

Penna Lane, Penwortham, SA 5453 REGION Clare Valley
T (08) 8843 4377 F (08) 8843 4246 WEB www.kilikanoon.com.au OPEN Thurs–Sun & public hols 11–5
WINEMAKER Kevin Mitchell EST. 1997 CASES 25 000
SUMMARY Kilikanoon has over 300 ha of vineyards, predominantly in the Clare Valley, but spreading to all regions around Adelaide and the Barossa Valley. It had the once-in-a-lifetime experience of winning five of the six trophies awarded at the 2002 Clare Valley Wine Show, spanning Riesling, Shiraz and Cabernet, and including Best Wine of Show. Hardly surprising, then, that production has risen sharply. Wholesale distribution in South Australia, Victoria and Western Australia; exports to the UK, the US and other major markets.

ΨΨΨΨΨ **Oracle Shiraz 2002** Dense colour; rich blackberry and blackcurrant run through an intense and long palate, with excellent balance and structure; exemplary tannins and oak. RATING 96 DRINK 2017 $ 49
Mort's Block Reserve Riesling 2004 Intense, rich, potent fruit, even more opulent than Mort's Block. Echoes of Rheingau in a ripe year. RATING 94 DRINK 2017 $ 30
Covenant Shiraz 2002 Medium-bodied; well structured and balanced; gently earthy touches to the fruit; quite sweet; quality oak. RATING 94 DRINK 2017 $ 40
Secret Places Barossa Valley Shiraz 2002 Lush, plush sweet fruit; satsuma plums and dark berries; ripe tannins, good oak. RATING 94 DRINK 2017 $ 40

ΨΨΨΨ **Morts Block Riesling 2004** Powerful and intense; ripe lime and tropical fruit; touches of slate and spice. RATING 93 DRINK 2014 $ 22

McLaren Vale Parable Shiraz 2002 Medium-bodied; utterly authentic regional characters; dark chocolate with gently spicy aspects to the fruit; soft, ripe tannins. RATING 93 DRINK 2017 $ 36

Medley Grenache Shiraz Mourvedre 2002 Rich but not jammy mix of black fruits and sundry spices; excellent texture and structure; good finish. RATING 93 DRINK 2010 $ 25

Blacket's Vineyard Eden Valley Riesling 2004 Aromas of mineral, spice, slate, herb and lime; firmly delineated varietal fruit; long finish. Screwcap. RATING 92 DRINK 2013 $ 20

Barrel-Fermented Clare Valley Semillon 2004 Barrel ferment influence more evident on the bouquet than the palate; while light to medium-bodied, has particular focus and great length; lingering finish. Screwcap. RATING 92 DRINK 2012 $ 20

Block's Road Cabernet Sauvignon 2002 Deep red-purple; profound, layered blackcurrant, tannins and oak; overall Bordeaux-like austerity. RATING 92 DRINK 2015 $ 29

Killerman's Run Adelaide Hills Sauvignon Blanc 2004 Clean, fresh, crisp, minerally aromas; moves up a gear on a long and intense lemon and herb palate. Screwcap. RATING 91 DRINK 2009 $ 20

Second Fiddle Grenache Rose 2004 Raspberry and a touch of plum; more structure than many; good acidity, dry finish. RATING 90 DRINK Now $ 18

ΥΥΥΥ **Killerman's Run Shiraz Grenache 2002** Well balanced and constructed; nice red berry fruits and tannins to match. RATING 89 DRINK 2008 $ 20

Prodigal Grenache 2002 Juicy, slightly jammy raspberry/cherry fruit, with some varietal spice. RATING 88 DRINK Now $ 25

Killerman's Run Shiraz 2002 Medium-bodied and well balanced; smooth red fruits, gentle oak. From premium South Australian regions. RATING 87 DRINK 2008 $ 20

ΥΥΥΥ **Secret Places 0404 Red 2004** RATING 85 DRINK Now $ 19

Killara Park Estate ★★★☆

Kylie Lane, Seville East, Vic 3139 REGION Yarra Valley
T (03) 9790 1255 F (03) 9790 1633 WEB www.killarapark.com.au OPEN Weekends & public hols 11–5
WINEMAKER Michael Kyberd EST. 1997 CASES 5500
SUMMARY The striking label design hints at the involvement of the Palazzo family, the owners, in winemaking in Lombardia (Italy) since the 16th century. It also tells you that this is a highly-focused, modern, wine-producing company. With just over 60 ha of vineyards established since 1997, Killara Park is one of the larger grape suppliers in the Yarra Valley, capable of producing fruit of high quality from its steeply sloping vineyards. Around 90% of the grapes are sold to companies such as Coldstream Hills and McWilliam's, but 10% is now being vinified for the label. Sales through the cellar door, mailing list and website; exports to the UK.

ΥΥΥΥ **Yarra Valley Pinot Noir 2004** Light-bodied; savoury, spicy, stemmy; some dilution, though varietal character is there, and not over-extracted. Screwcap. RATING 87 DRINK 2008 $ 20

Yarra Valley Shiraz 2004 Fresh, clean, bright red and black fruits; linear, light to medium-bodied and fresh, simply lacking intensity. Screwcap. RATING 87 DRINK 2009 $ 20

Yarra Valley Merlot 2004 Nice olive, blueberry and redcurrant mix; light-bodied; super-fine tannins; lacks concentration, but not forced. Screwcap. RATING 87 DRINK 2008 $ 20

ΥΥΥΥ **Yarra Valley Chardonnay 2004** RATING 86 DRINK 2007 $ 20
Yarra Valley Cabernet Sauvignon 2004 RATING 85 DRINK 2007 $ 20

ΥΥΥ **Yarra Valley Pinot Noir 2003** RATING 83 $ 20

Killerby ★★★☆

Caves Road, Wilyabrup, WA 6280 REGION Margaret River
T 1800 655 722 F 1800 679 578 WEB www.killerby.com.au OPEN Not
WINEMAKER Simon Keall EST. 1973 CASES 15 000
SUMMARY Has moved from Geographe to Margaret River following the acquisition of a vineyard with 25-year-old chardonnay vines on Caves Road. It has kept its substantial mature vineyards in Geographe, where the wines are still made. Exports to the US and Denmark.

ΥΥΥΥ **Chardonnay 2003** Pleasant, medium-bodied; peachy fruit, balanced oak. **RATING** 87 **DRINK** Now $ 34

🥝 Kiltynane Estate ★★★☆

Cnr School Lane/Yarra Glen–Healesville Road, Tarrawarra, Vic 3775 **REGION** Yarra Valley
T(03) 5962 1897 **F**(03) 5962 1897 **WEB** www.kiltynane.com.au **OPEN** By appointment
WINEMAKER Kate Kirkhope, Frederic Blanck **EST.** 2000 **CASES** 400
SUMMARY Kate Kirkhope has owned and run Kiltynane Estate since 1994. Having completed a local viticulture course in 1997, she began the development of the 3.8-ha vineyard, planted to seven clones of pinot noir, in 2000. Her son's education at the Rudolf Steiner School had given her an interest in biodynamics, and biodynamic practices are followed wherever possible, though she will use sprays, including systemics, if absolutely necessary. The vines are not irrigated, and no pesticides are used. The winemaking has been carried out with help from Frederic Blanck, of the highly regarded Alsace winery Paul Blanck et Fils. He has been a regular visitor to Australia and the Yarra Valley over the years, and guided the making of the Preliminaire. Winemaker Matt Aldridge also provides consulting advice on technical issues. The wines are sold by mail order or by appointment onsite.

ΥΥΥΥ **Pinot Noir 2004** Light-bodied, reflecting the big berry, big bunch vintage; fresh cherry and strawberry fruit; controlled French oak; good length. Quality cork. **RATING** 89 **DRINK** 2009 $ 35
Preliminaire 2004 Delicate pink; good structure; strawberry, spice and mineral; ripe fruit (13.5° alcohol) and a strong finish. A Blanc de Noir made from pinot noir; barrel-fermented and wild yeast. **RATING** 88 **DRINK** 2009 $ 32

Kimbarra Wines ★★★★

422 Barkly Street, Ararat, Vic 3377 **REGION** Grampians
T(03) 5352 2238 **F**(03) 5342 1950 **WEB** www.kimbarrawines.com.au **OPEN** Mon–Fri 9–5
WINEMAKER Peter Leeke, Ian MacKenzie **EST.** 1990 **CASES** 1000
SUMMARY Peter and David Leeke have established 12 ha of riesling, shiraz and cabernet sauvignon, the three varieties which have proved best suited to the Grampians region. The particularly well-made wines deserve a wider audience.

ΥΥΥΥΥ **Great Western Shiraz 2002** Medium-bodied; elegant but intense blackberry and spice fruits; fine, persistent tannins; good oak handling. High-quality cork. **RATING** 93 **DRINK** 2015 $ 25
Great Western Riesling 2003 Potent apple, talc and herb aromas; focused, intense palate; not obviously heavy, but the flavours penetrate all corners of the mouth (13.3° alcohol). Screwcap. **RATING** 92 **DRINK** 2010 $ 15

ΥΥΥΥ **Great Western Late Picked Riesling 2003** Lime juice, mineral and squeaky acidity; nice flavour and feel. Screwcap. **RATING** 88 **DRINK** 2007 $ 12

ΥΥΥΥ **Great Western Cabernet Sauvignon 2001** **RATING** 86 **DRINK** 2008 $ 22

Kimber Wines ★★☆

Chalk Hill Road, McLaren Vale, SA 5171 **REGION** McLaren Vale
T(08) 8323 9773 **F**(08) 8323 9773 **WEB** www.kimberwines.com **OPEN** 7 days Dec–Apr 9–6, or by appointment
WINEMAKER Reg Wilkinson **EST.** 1996 **CASES** 400
SUMMARY Kimber Wines is primarily a grapegrower, selling its production from 2.5 ha each of chardonnay and cabernet sauvignon, and 1.2 ha of petit verdot to larger producers. A very small amount of its grapes are vinified under the Kimber Wines label; they tend to sell out within a few months of release through the cellar door (hence the restricted opening hours). An added attraction is pick-your-own fruit (peaches, apricots and plums) during the summer months.

ΥΥΥΥ **McLaren Vale Petit Verdot 2003** **RATING** 84 **DRINK** Now $ 18

ΥΥΥ **McLaren Vale Unwooded Chardonnay 2004** **RATING** 83 $ 14

King River Estate ★★★★

3556 Wangaratta–Whitfield Road, Wangaratta, Vic 3678 **REGION** King Valley
T (03) 5729 3689 **F** (03) 5729 3688 **WEB** www.kingriverestate.com.au **OPEN** Weekends, or by appointment
WINEMAKER Trevor Knaggs **EST.** 1996 **CASES** 6000
SUMMARY Trevor Knaggs, with the assistance of his father Collin (sic), began the establishment of King River Estate in 1990, making the first wines in 1996. The initial plantings were of 3.3 ha each of chardonnay and cabernet sauvignon, followed by 8 ha of merlot and 3 ha of shiraz. More recent plantings have extended the varietal range with verdelho, viognier, barbera and sangiovese, lifting the total plantings to a substantial 24 ha. Home-stay accommodation is available in the farm-style guesthouse. Needless to say, bookings are essential.

ŸŸŸŸŸ **King Valley Reserve Merlot 2003** A complex wine; strong olive and blackcurrant fruit; integrated French oak; excellent texture and weight. Stained cork. **RATING** 93 **DRINK** 2012 $45

ŸŸŸŸ **King Valley Cabernet Sauvignon 2002** Rich blackcurrant and cassis aromas and flavours; medium-bodied; good mouthfeel; fine, ripe tannins. Cork. **RATING** 89 **DRINK** 2010 $20
King Valley Merlot 2003 Light to medium-bodied; clear-cut savoury, black olive, herb and blackcurrant varietal character; fine tannins, subtle oak. Cork. **RATING** 88 **DRINK** 2009 $22
King Valley Sangiovese 2003 Good colour; abundant black cherry and sour cherry mix with a dash of spice; at the big end of the town for the variety. May be interesting with bottle age. Cork. **RATING** 88 **DRINK** 2009 $25
King Valley Chardonnay 2004 Light-bodied, understated style; melon and fig; a touch of cashew. Screwcap. **RATING** 87 **DRINK** 2008 $18
King Valley Shiraz Viognier 2002 Light to medium-bodied; distinctive apricot fruit lift from Viognier to black cherry core; minimal tannins and oak. Quality cork. **RATING** 87 **DRINK** 2009 $25
King Valley Barbera 2003 Ripe, round medium-bodied, soft black fruits on entry, which is all you can expect. Cork. **RATING** 87 **DRINK** 2008 $25

ŸŸŸŸ **King Valley Reserve Viognier 2002 RATING** 86 **DRINK** 2007 $35
King Valley Sparkling Shiraz 2001 RATING 86 **DRINK** 2007 $22

ŸŸŸ **King Valley Verdelho 2003 RATING** 83 $22

Kingsley Grove ★★★

49 Stuart Valley Drive, Kingaroy, Qld 4610 (postal) **REGION** South Burnett
T (07) 4163 6433 **F** (07) 4162 2201 **WEB** www.kingsleygrove.com **OPEN** Not
WINEMAKER Michael Berry, Patricia Berry **EST.** 1998 **CASES** NA
SUMMARY Michael and Patricia Berry have established a substantial vineyard of 8.7 ha near Kingaroy. It is planted to verdelho, chardonnay, semillon, shiraz, merlot, sangiovese, chambourcin and cabernet sauvignon, and the wines are made onsite in a winery built in 2001 and extended in 2003, Michael Berry having undertaken viticulture studies at Melbourne University. The wines are sold by mail order and via the internet.

ŸŸŸŸ **Cabernet Sauvignon 2003** Light to medium-bodied; very respectable Cabernet, with a nice mix of blackcurrant and cassis fruit; good line and mouthfeel. Twin Top. **RATING** 87 **DRINK** 2009 $14.50

ŸŸŸŸ **Hilltop Shiraz 2003 RATING** 85 **DRINK** 2008 $15

ŸŸŸ **Sweet Berry Red 2004 RATING** 83 $13.50

Kings of Kangaroo Ground NR

15 Graham Road, Kangaroo Ground, Vic 3097 **REGION** Yarra Valley
T (03) 9712 0666 **F** (03) 9712 0566 **WEB** www.kkg.com.au **OPEN** Mon–Sat 10–6, Sun 12–6
WINEMAKER Ken King, Geoff Anson, Neil Johannesen **EST.** 1990 **CASES** 600

SUMMARY Ken King's involvement in wine began back in 1984 as an amateur member of the Eltham and District Winemakers Guild. Around that time, the Guild was asked to manage a tiny (.13 ha) experimental vineyard planted on the rich volcanic soil of Kangaroo Ground. In 1988 Ken King purchased a little under 3 ha of similar land, which he describes as 'chocolate cake'; he established 1 ha of chardonnay and 0.6 ha of pinot noir in 1990. Up until 2000, the grapes were sold to Diamond Valley, but each year King retained sufficient grapes to produce a barrel or two of Pinot Noir, and began experimenting with multi-vintage blends of pinot with up to 5 years of continuous ageing in French barriques. The wines have been well received at amateur wine shows, and the planned cellar door has now opened.

Kingston Estate ★★★★

Sturt Highway, Kingston-on-Murray, SA 5331 **REGION** Southeast Australia
T (08) 8130 4500 **F** (08) 8130 4511 **WEB** www.kingstonestatewines.com **OPEN** By appointment
WINEMAKER Bill Moularadellis **EST.** 1979 **CASES** 100 000
SUMMARY Kingston Estate, under the direction of Bill Moularadellis, still has its production roots in the Riverland region, but it has also set up long-term purchase contracts with growers in the Clare Valley, the Adelaide Hills, Coonawarra, Langhorne Creek and Mount Benson. It has also spread its net to take in a wide range of varietals, mainstream and exotic, under a number of different brands at various price points. Overall wine quality has increased significantly. Exports to Europe.

ŸŸŸŸŸ **Ambleside Adelaide Hills Chardonnay 2003** Light to medium-bodied; attractive nectarine and peach; gently spicy oak; well balanced. Screwcap. **RATING** 90 **DRINK** 2008
Ashwood Grove Shiraz 2003 Firm red and black fruits; quite elegant; fine tannins. Surprise performer. **RATING** 90 **DRINK** 2010
Empiric Selection Durif 2002 Rich, ripe blackberry, plum and prune aromas; well-balanced and elegant palate; fine tannins, long finish. **RATING** 90 **DRINK** 2007 $ 18.95

ŸŸŸŸ **Shiraz 2003** Unexpected weight and structure to the palate, with plenty of ripe black fruit flavours, even if it does shorten fractionally. **RATING** 88 **DRINK** 2008 $ 10.95
Baritone Limestone Coast Cabernet Shiraz 2000 Plenty of richness and depth; spicy aromas and an array of sweet fruit and caramel flavours; very clever winemaking and packaging in a 1000 ml bottle. **RATING** 88 **DRINK** 2007 $ 10.99
Petit Verdot 2002 Quite savoury, lean and long, with a mix of chocolate and slightly earthy tannins. **RATING** 88 **DRINK** 2009 $ 12
Sarantos Soft Press Sauvignon Blanc 2004 Good varietal aroma and flavour; soft, ripe, tropical/gooseberry fruit. **RATING** 87 **DRINK** Now $ 13.94
Empiric Selection Pinot Gris 2004 Pale salmon-blush; ripe pear, apple and spice; clear varietal character throughout. Screwcap. **RATING** 87 **DRINK** Now $ 18
Empiric Selection Viognier 2003 Interesting contrast to the barrel-fermented version; less complex, but the finish is brighter and cleaner; honeysuckle and peach fruit. **RATING** 87 **DRINK** 2007 $ 19
Barrel-Fermented Viognier 2003 Honeyed and rich; the barrel ferment inputs quite subtle; well balanced, though a slightly thick finish. **RATING** 87 **DRINK** Now $ 19
Sarantos Soft Press Shiraz 2004 Generous and, indeed, soft blackberry fruit; fine, soft tannins; honest and flavoursome. **RATING** 87 **DRINK** 2008 $ 15
Sarantos Soft Press Shiraz 2003 Ripe plums and spices give some complexity; good balance. **RATING** 87 **DRINK** 2008 $ 13.95
Baritone Limestone Coast Cabernet Shiraz 2001 Light to medium-bodied; savoury, lemony twist around a core of red fruits; fine tannins. **RATING** 87 **DRINK** Now $ 10.95
Empiric Tempranillo 2003 Good colour; light to medium-bodied; some spicy, savoury notes to fresh red berry fruit; nonetheless, doesn't make the world stop. **RATING** 87 **DRINK** 2008 $ 19

ŸŸŸ **Sarantos Soft Press Chardonnay 2004** **RATING** 86 **DRINK** Now $ 13.95
Ashwood Grove Chardonnay 2003 **RATING** 86 **DRINK** Now
Ambleside Adelaide Hills Pinot Gris 2004 **RATING** 86 **DRINK** 2007
Sarantos Soft Press Verdelho 2004 **RATING** 86 **DRINK** Now $ 13.95
Sarantos Soft Press Australian Sparkling NV **RATING** 86 **DRINK** Now $ 12.95
Chardonnay 2003 **RATING** 85 **DRINK** Now $ 10.95
Verdelho 2004 **RATING** 85 **DRINK** Now $ 13.99
Sarantos Soft Press Scarlet Rose 2004 **RATING** 85 **DRINK** Now $ 13.95
Outback Chase Coonawarra Shiraz 2003 **RATING** 84 **DRINK** Now $ 9.95

ŸŸŸ   **Sauvignon Blanc 2004** RATING 83 $13.99
    Ashwood Grove Chardonnay 2002 RATING 83 $12.95
    Outback Chase White Shiraz 2004 RATING 83 $9.50

Kingtree Wines
NR

Kingtree Road, Wellington Mills via Dardanup, WA 6326 REGION Geographe
T (08) 9728 3050 F (08) 9728 3113 OPEN 7 days 12–5.30
WINEMAKER Contract EST. 1991 CASES 1000
SUMMARY Kingtree Wines, with 2.5 ha of estate plantings, is part of the Kingtree Lodge development,
a four and a half-star luxury retreat in dense Jarrah forest.

Kinloch Wines

Kainui, Wairere Road, Booroolite, Vic 3723 REGION Upper Goulburn
T (03) 5777 3447 F (03) 5777 3449 WEB www.kinlochwines.com.au OPEN Weekends & public hols
10–5, or by appointment
WINEMAKER Al Fencaros (Contract) EST. 1996 CASES 2500
SUMMARY In 1996 Susan and Malcolm Kinloch began the development of their vineyard, at an
altitude of 400m on the northern slopes of the Great Dividing Range, 15 minutes' drive from
Mansfield. One of the unusual varieties in the portfolio is Pinot Meunier. The grapes are hand-picked
and taken to the Yarra Valley for contract making. Light meals are available.

ŸŸŸŸ   **Pinot Noir 2003** Cherry, plum, spice and leaf; good texture and structure; fine tannins
    undoubtedly contribute; unexpected. RATING 89 DRINK 2008 $23
    Chardonnay 2003 Restrained; creamy cashew notes; also touches of minerality. Gentle
    oak. RATING 88 DRINK 2007 $22
    Wild Ferment Chardonnay 2003 Spotlessly clean; quite soft flavour and mouthfeel; stone
    fruit and fig; no obvious evidence of oak. RATING 88 DRINK 2008 $34
    Merlot 2003 Earthy, savoury, olive aromas, but not minty; light to medium-bodied; good
    varietal definition; minimal tannins and oak. RATING 88 DRINK 2009 $25
    Unwooded Chardonnay 2003 Quite aromatic stone fruit; light-bodied, fresh and crisp;
    balanced acidity; good example, developing slowly. RATING 87 DRINK 2007 $17
    Pinot Meunier 2003 Very sappy, spicy, savoury style, but has length and presence, and is
    strongly varietal. RATING 87 DRINK 2007 $23

ŸŸŸŸ   **Sauvignon Blanc 2004** RATING 86 DRINK Now $22

Kinvarra Estate
★★★☆

RMB 5141, New Norfolk, Tas 7140 REGION Southern Tasmania
T (03) 6286 1333 F (03) 6286 2026 OPEN Not
WINEMAKER Andrew Hood (Contract) EST. 1990 CASES 90
SUMMARY Kinvarra is the part-time occupation of David and Sue Bevan; their wonderful 1827
homestead is depicted on the label. There is only 1 ha of vines, half riesling and half pinot noir, and
most of the crop is sold to Wellington Wines.

ŸŸŸŸ   **Riesling 2004** Solid; plenty of rich lime/citrus fruit; depth more than length. RATING 88
    DRINK 2009
    Pinot Noir 2003 Light to medium-bodied; a mix of plum and more sappy/savoury fruits;
    has length. RATING 87 DRINK 2008

ŸŸŸ   **Pinot Noir 2002** RATING 82

Kirkham Estate
NR

3 Argyle Street, Camden, NSW 2570 REGION Sydney Basin
T (02) 4655 7722 F (02) 4655 7722 OPEN 7 days 11–5
WINEMAKER Stan Aliprandi EST. 1993 CASES 3000
SUMMARY Kirkham Estate is one of six or so wine producers near Camden. This is a far cry from the
18 producers of the mid-19th century, but still indicative of the growth of vineyards and winemakers
everywhere. It is the venture of Leif Karlsson and Stan Aliprandi, the latter a former Riverina

winemaker. It draws upon 9 ha of vineyards, planted to chardonnay, semillon, verdelho, petit verdot, shiraz, merlot, pinot noir and cabernet sauvignon, supplemented, it would seem, by grapes (and wines) purchased elsewhere.

Kirrihill Estates ★★★★☆

Wendouree Road, Clare, SA 5453 **REGION** Clare Valley
T (08) 8842 4087 **F** (08) 8842 4089 **WEB** www.kirrihillwines.com.au **OPEN** 7 days 10–4
WINEMAKER Richard Rowe, David Mavor **EST.** 1998 **CASES** 25 000
SUMMARY One of the larger vineyard and winery developments over the past 5 years, with a 7000-tonne, $10 million, winery designed for modular expansion to 20 000 tonnes, and currently storing 3 million litres of wine. It is associated with the Kirribilly Wine Group, which has developed and now manages 1300 ha of vineyards in the Clare Valley, the Adelaide Hills and Langhorne Creek. Small parcels of its managed vineyards' grapes are taken for the Kirrihill Estates wine range, with a Cabernet Sauvignon from each of the Clare and Langhorne Creek, plus a Sauvignon Blanc from the Adelaide Hills completing the range. Richard Rowe, the chief winemaker, was responsible for many years for the Leasingham Classic Clare range; assistant David Mavor has worked both in France and for Tyrrell's in the Hunter Valley. The quality of the wines is thus no surprise.

ŸŸŸŸŸ **Adelaide Hills Sauvignon Blanc 2003** Intense and fragrant; powerful, ripe tropical/gooseberry fruit; long finish. **RATING** 93 **DRINK** Now $ 17.95
Adelaide Hills Sauvignon Blanc 2004 Very clean; herb, asparagus, gooseberry and grass; a remarkably intense and tight palate; mineral, spice and grass flavours; punchy acidity, good length. Screwcap. **RATING** 91 **DRINK** Now $ 17.95
Clare Valley Riesling 2004 Clean herb, mineral and spice; plenty of weight and mouthfeel; some lemon rind. **RATING** 90 **DRINK** 2008 $ 18.95
Clare Valley Shiraz 2002 Abundant blackberry fruit; a big, powerful wine, slightly alcohol-pushed; well-handled oak. **RATING** 90 **DRINK** 2017 $ 22

ŸŸŸŸ **Shiraz Mourvedre Grenache 2002** **RATING** 86 **DRINK** 2008 $ 20

Kirwan's Bridge Wines NR

Lobb's Lane/Kirwan's Bridge Road, Nagambie, Vic 3608 **REGION** Nagambie Lakes
T (03) 5794 1777 **F** (03) 5794 1993 **OPEN** 7 days 10–5
WINEMAKER Anna Hubbard **EST.** 1997 **CASES** 1500
SUMMARY A major development, with over 35 ha planted: a major emphasis on the Rhône varietals (7.9 ha marsanne, 2.7 ha viognier, 1.3 ha of roussanne; and 11.2 ha shiraz, 2.7 ha mourvedre and 2.5 ha grenache). A side bet on 4.8 ha cabernet sauvignon, 2.4 ha merlot and 1.3 ha riesling rounds off the planting. The cellar door complex includes a restaurant (open for lunch and dinner Thursday to Sunday – dinner bookings essential), conference facility and art gallery. A protracted family inheritance dispute has severely impacted on the business.

🍇 Kithbrook Estate NR

RMB 4480, Strathbogie, Vic 3666 (postal) **REGION** Strathbogie Ranges
T (03) 5790 8627 **F** (03) 5790 8630 **OPEN** Not
WINEMAKER Contract **EST.** 1994 **CASES** NA
SUMMARY Kithbrook Estate (formerly Gemleigh Meadows) has 2 vineyards on Broughtons Road, Strathbogie: the first and larger is at an altitude of 480–500m, the second is higher up the hillside at the 560–580m contour lines. By far the most important part of the business is grapegrowing for others, coming from 30 ha of sauvignon blanc, 27 ha of merlot, 15 ha of pinot noir and 14 ha of chardonnay, plus a dash of shiraz. The wines are available in local stores at low prices, and have scored consistently well at the Strathbogie Ranges Wine Show.

🍇 Kladis Estate NR

Princes Highway, Wandanian, NSW 2650 **REGION** Shoalhaven Coast
T (02) 4443 5606 **F** (02) 4443 6485 **OPEN** Weekends & public hols 10–5
WINEMAKER Steve Dodd (Briar Ridge) **EST.** 1996 **CASES** 5000

SUMMARY Jim and Nikki Kladis have developed 11 ha of shiraz, cabernet sauvignon, grenache, verdelho, merlot and muscadelle at their Shoalhaven property, and 4 ha of traminer and cabernet sauvignon in the Hunter Valley. The inspiration has been the medium-bodied red wines Jim Kladis grew up with on the Greek island of Zante. With Steve Dodd as winemaker, all the wines on release have received some show recognition.

Knappstein Wines   ★★★★★

2 Pioneer Avenue, Clare, SA 5453 **REGION** Clare Valley
T (08) 8842 2600 **F** (08) 8842 3831 **WEB** www.knappsteinwines.com.au **OPEN** Mon–Fri 9–5, Sat 11–5, Sun & public hols 11–4
WINEMAKER Paul Smith **EST.** 1976 **CASES** 30 000
SUMMARY Very much part of the Petaluma empire, with Paul Smith having taken over from Andrew Hardy, who has returned to Petaluma headquarters. The 90 ha of mature estate vineyards in prime locations supply grapes both for the Knappstein brand and for wider Petaluma use. Exports to the UK, Canada, Japan and New Zealand.

🍷🍷🍷🍷🍷 **Single Vineyard Watervale Riesling 2004** Spicily fragrant; very delicate, almost feather-light, but with a lovely, long finish. **RATING** 94 **DRINK** 2014 **$** 25
Hand Picked Riesling 2004 A blend of Clare and Watervale fruit, the wine has a fragrant and floral bouquet of apple, lime and passionfruit, and a delicate but intense palate of pure riesling fruit. **RATING** 94 **DRINK** 2012 **$** 20
Single Vineyard Clare Valley Cabernet Sauvignon 2002 Dense red-purple; abundant, rich blackcurrant/blackberry fruit; excellent texture and structure; ripe tannins, good oak. **RATING** 94 **DRINK** 2017 **$** 32

🍷🍷🍷🍷♡ **Fortified Shiraz 1998** Complex; developing nicely as the fruit starts to dry out; chocolate, earth and spice; good extract. **RATING** 91 **DRINK** 2010 **$** 21
Semillon Sauvignon Blanc 2004 Solidly built; ripe passionfruit flavours and a whisper of honey; good length. **RATING** 90 **DRINK** 2008 **$** 19.99
Clare Valley Chardonnay 2004 Remarkably good for the region; clean, tangy citrus melon fruit; well-controlled touch of gently smoky oak. Screwcap. **RATING** 90 **DRINK** 2008 **$** 16.99

🍷🍷🍷🍷 **Shiraz 2002** Clever winemaking; nice oak sweetening of sturdy fruit; soft tannins. **RATING** 89 **DRINK** 2012 **$** 20
Cabernet Merlot 2001 Medium-bodied; black and red fruits, sweet oak and soft tannins. Mouthfilling. **RATING** 89 **DRINK** 2008 **$** 19.99
Viognier 2003 Yellow-gold; colossal oak and rich fruit flavours; 100% barrel-fermented in new oak; love or hate it. Screwcap. **RATING** 88 **DRINK** Now **$** 18
Thr3e 2004 A quixotic blend of Gewurztraminer, Riesling and Pinot Gris; Gewurztraminer leads the way, the others merely making up the numbers. **RATING** 88 **DRINK** Now **$** 20
Cabernet Merlot 2002 Powerful, savoury style; leathery/briary overtones to blackcurrant fruit. Cork. **RATING** 87 **DRINK** 2010 **$** 19.99

Knights Vines   ★★☆

655 Henry Lawson Drive, Mudgee, NSW 2850 **REGION** Mudgee
T (02) 6373 3954 **F** (02) 6373 3750 **WEB** www.eurundereewines.com.au **OPEN** Wed–Fri & Sun 10–4, Sat 10–5
WINEMAKER Peter Knights **EST.** 1985 **CASES** 1500
SUMMARY Sometimes called Knights Vines, although the wines are marketed under the Eurunderee Flats label. There are 5 ha of vineyards producing white wines of variable quality, and rather better dry red table wines. Exports to Hong Kong.

Knots Wines   ★★★★☆

A8 Shurans Lane, Heathcote, Vic 3552 **REGION** Heathcote
T (03) 5441 5429 **F** (03) 5441 5429 **WEB** www.bendigowine.org.au/knots **OPEN** Select weekends, or by appointment
WINEMAKER Lindsay Ross **EST.** 1997 **CASES** 1000

SUMMARY This is the venture of erstwhile Balgownie winemaker Lindsay Ross and wife Noeline, and is part of a broader business known as Winedrops, which acts as a wine production and distribution network for the Bendigo wine industry. The Knots wines are sourced from long-established Heathcote and Bendigo vineyards, providing 0.5 ha each of semillon and chardonnay, and 4 ha each of shiraz and cabernets. The viticultural accent is on low-cropping vineyards with concentrated flavours, the winemaking emphasis on flavour, finesse and varietal expression.

ŸŸŸŸŸ **The Bridge Shiraz 2002** Very supple, smooth and elegant red and black fruits; fine, silky tannins. RATING 94 DRINK 2015 $ 45

ŸŸŸŸ **Sheepshank Shiraz 2002** Good focus and tight structure; cherry-accented fruit, not overripe; lingering, savoury tannins. RATING 89 DRINK 2015 $ 25
Rose Lashing 2002 Faintly nutty almond aromas; quite intense and long; well balanced, but better even when younger. RATING 87 DRINK Now $ 20
Lark's Head Cabernet Merlot 2002 Light to medium-bodied, particularly given the vintage; sweet fruits at the core, and does have length. RATING 87 DRINK 2008 $ 25

Knowland Estate   NR

Mount Vincent Road, Running Stream, NSW 2850 REGION Mudgee
T (02) 6358 8420 F (02) 6358 8423 OPEN By appointment
WINEMAKER Peter Knowland EST. 1990 CASES 250
SUMMARY The former Mount Vincent Winery, at an altitude of 1080m, which sells much of its grape production from the 4 ha of vineyards to other makers.

Koltz   NR

5 Adams Road, Blewitt Springs, SA 5171 (postal) REGION McLaren Vale
T (08) 8383 0023 F (08) 8383 0023 OPEN Not
WINEMAKER Mark Day EST. 1994 CASES 2000
SUMMARY Mark Day and Anna Koltunow released their first wine in 1995, using grapes from the Bottin Vineyard in McLaren Vale. Mark Day had worked as winemaker at Maxwell Wines and Wirra Wirra in McLaren Vale, and has been a Flying Winemaker for six consecutive vintages in Europe. Day and Koltunow have decided to specialise in shiraz and shiraz blends from the McLaren Vale region, but have added sangiovese and mourvedre to the mix since the 2002 vintage. The wines are exported to England and the US, and can be ordered by mail.

Kominos Wines   ★★★★

27, 145 New England Highway, Severnlea, Qld 4352 REGION Granite Belt
T (07) 4683 4311 F (07) 4683 4291 WEB www.kominoswines.com OPEN 7 days 9–5
WINEMAKER Tony Comino EST. 1976 CASES 4000
SUMMARY Tony Comino is a dedicated viticulturist and winemaker and, together with his father, has battled hard to prevent ACI obtaining a monopoly on glass production in Australia, foreseeing many of the things which have in fact occurred. Kominos Wines keeps a very low profile, selling all its wine through the cellar door and by mailing list. Exports to the US and Taiwan.

ŸŸŸŸŸ **Merlot 2002** Elegant, medium-bodied wine; attractive savoury variety character and style. RATING 90 DRINK 2009
Reserve Merlot 2002 Brilliant clarity; gently savoury olive, redcurrant and blackcurrant fruit; fine tannins, very good length. Twin Top. RATING 90 DRINK 2010

ŸŸŸŸ **Reserve Cabernet Merlot 2002** Powerful wine; concentrated blackcurrant, blackberry, chocolate and earth; ripe tannins; oak merely a vehicle. Stained Twin Top. RATING 89 DRINK 2010
Unwooded Chardonnay 2002 Good colour; light to medium-bodied; some delicate stone fruit flavours, but needs more back palate intensity for higher points. RATING 87 DRINK Now
Reserve Shiraz 2002 Light to medium-bodied; quite firm, direct plum and blackberry fruit; minimal oak influence. Twin Top. RATING 87 DRINK 2009

ŸŸŸŸ **Vin Doux NV** RATING 86 DRINK Now
Cabernet Merlot 2003 RATING 85 DRINK 2007

ŸŸŸ **Nouvelle 2003** RATING 82

Kongwak Hills Winery

NR

1030 Korumburra–Wonthaggi Road, Kongwak, Vic 3951 **REGION** Gippsland
T (03) 5657 3267 **F** (03) 5657 3267 **OPEN** Weekends & public hols 10–5
WINEMAKER Peter Kimmer **EST.** 1989 **CASES** 600
SUMMARY Peter and Jenny Kimmer started the development of their vineyard in 1989 and now have
0.5 ha each of cabernet sauvignon, shiraz and pinot noir, together with lesser quantities of malbec,
merlot and riesling. Most of the wines are sold at the cellar door; limited distribution in Melbourne
through Woods Wines Pty Ltd of Fitzroy.

Koonara

★★★

Skinner Road, Coonawarra, SA 5263 **REGION** Coonawarra
T (08) 8736 3267 **F** (08) 8736 3020 **WEB** www.koonara.com **OPEN** By appointment
WINEMAKER Dru Resckke, Peter Douglas (Consultant) **EST.** 1988 **CASES** NA
SUMMARY Koonara is a sister, or, more appropriately, brother company to Reschke Wines. The latter
is run by Burke Reschke, Koonara by his brother Dru. Both are sons of Trevor Reschke, who planted
the first vines on the Koonara property in 1988. The initial planting was of cabernet sauvignon,
followed by shiraz in 1993 and additional cabernet sauvignon in 1998. Peter Douglas, formerly
Wynn's chief winemaker before moving overseas for some years, has returned to the district and is
consultant winemaker.

♥♥♥♀ **Ezra's Gift Shiraz 2002** **RATING** 86 **DRINK** 2007

Kooroomba Vineyards

★★☆

168 FM Bells Road, Mount Alford via Boonah, Qld 4310 **REGION** Queensland Zone
T (07) 5463 0022 **F** (07) 5463 0441 **OPEN** Wed–Sun & public hols 10–5
WINEMAKER Ballandean Estate (Contract) **EST.** 1998 **CASES** 3000
SUMMARY Kooroomba Vineyards is little more than 1 hour's drive from the Brisbane CBD, and offers
cellar door wine tasting and sales, a vineyard restaurant and a lavender farm. The 7.5-ha vineyard is
planted to verdelho, marsanne, merlot, shiraz and cabernet sauvignon and chardonnay.

♥♥♥♀ **Merlot 2002** **RATING** 85 **DRINK** 2007
     Verdelho Marsanne 2003 **RATING** 84 **DRINK** Now $ 18.50

Kooyong

★★★★☆

PO Box 153, Red Hill South, Vic 3937 **REGION** Mornington Peninsula
T (03) 5989 7355 **F** (03) 5989 7677 **WEB** www.kooyong.com **OPEN** At Port Phillip Estate
WINEMAKER Sandro Mosele **EST.** 1996 **CASES** 5000
SUMMARY Kooyong, owned by Giorgio and Dianne Gjergja, is one of the larger new entrants on the
Mornington Peninsula scene, releasing its first wines in June 2001. The 34-ha vineyard is planted to
pinot noir and chardonnay. Winemaker Sandro Mosele is a graduate of Charles Sturt University,
having previously gained a science degree. He has worked at Rochford and learnt from Sergio Carlei,
of Green Vineyards, and makes the wine at an onsite winery which also provides contract
winemaking services for others. The wines are distributed through Negociants Australia, and the
quality is impressive. Exports to the UK, the US and Singapore.

♥♥♥♥♥ **Pinot Noir 2003** Very good colour; powerful, rich and concentrated; lashings of plum and
     black cherry fruit; very good structure and oak. Diam. **RATING** 95 **DRINK** 2010 $ 42
     Chardonnay 2003 Bright yellow-green; perfectly modulated and balanced melon, stone
     fruit, fig and malolactic/barrel ferment inputs. Diam. **RATING** 94 **DRINK** 2009 $ 39

♥♥♥♥♀ **Massale Pinot Noir 2003** A complex and rich mix of new French oak and potent damson
     plum fruit; good length. Diam. **RATING** 90 **DRINK** 2008 $ 26

Kopparossa Wines

★★★☆

PO Box 922, Naracoorte, SA 5271 **REGION** Wrattonbully
T 1800 620 936 **F** (08) 8762 0937 **OPEN** Not
WINEMAKER Gavin Hogg, Mike Press **EST.** 1996 **CASES** 5000

SUMMARY Kopparossa has undergone several transformations since its establishment in 1996, but the partnership of Gavin Hogg and Mike Press, with more than 60 years' winemaking and grapegrowing experience between them, has continued throughout. The business is now based on two estate vineyards, one in the Adelaide Hills, the other in Coonawarra, plus contract-grown grapes from Wrattonbully. The Adelaide Hills property, developed by the Press family and known as Kenton Valley, has 24 ha of pinot noir, merlot, shiraz, cabernet sauvignon and chardonnay planted in 1998 and 1999. The Coonawarra vineyard is (at first sight, controversially, but the vineyard is in fact on Stentiford Road) called Stentiford, and is, quite literally, Gavin and Julie Hogg's back yard. It was planted in 1992 and 1993 with cabernet sauvignon, merlot and chardonnay.

ȚȚȚȚ **Coonawarra Cabernet Merlot 2002** Light to medium-bodied; quite elegant, with good length and fine tannins, RATING 89 DRINK 2010

ȚȚȚ **Coonawarra Unwooded Chardonnay 2004** RATING 79

Kotai Estate

South Western Highway, Harvey, WA 6220 REGION Geographe
T (08) 9729 1755 F (08) 9729 1755 OPEN Wed–Sun 10–5
WINEMAKER Peter Stanlake (Contract) EST. 2001 CASES 2000
SUMMARY Carol and Peter Jackson have planted 4.2 ha of chenin blanc, semillon, chardonnay, cabernet sauvignon and merlot, using contract-winemaking services for the wines. Sales are by mail order and through the cellar door.

Kouark Vineyard

300 Thompson Road, Drouin South, Vic 3818 REGION Gippsland
T (03) 5627 6337 F (03) 5627 6337 WEB www.gourmetgippsland.com OPEN Weekends 12–5
WINEMAKER Phil Gray EST. 1997 CASES 1000
SUMMARY Dairy farmers Phil and Jane Gray decided to diversify with the establishment of a 4-ha vineyard on part of their farm. They have planted 1.3 ha each of chardonnay and pinot noir, and 0.7 ha each of shiraz and cabernet sauvignon (and a few vines of pinot gris and viognier) on a northeasterly slope, bordered on the east by a 2.4-ha lake. As well as their general farming background, they have undertaken various Charles Sturt University grape and wine production courses, and similar short courses from other education facilities. A simple but appropriately equipped winery has been established onsite, and the wines are sold through local stores and cafés. The name is believed to be the word for kookaburra in the language of the local Kurnai tribe.

ȚȚȚȚ **Gippsland Pinot Noir 2003** Stemmy, gamey aromas moving to sweet red cherry and plum fruit on the mid-palate; slightly brisk finish. RATING 88 DRINK Now $ 20

ȚȚȚȚ **Gippsland Cabernet Sauvignon 2001** RATING 85 DRINK 2008 $ 23

ȚȚȚ **Gippsland Chardonnay 2002** RATING 83 $ 20

Kraanwood

8 Woodies Place, Richmond, Tas 7025 REGION Southern Tasmania
T (03) 6260 2540 OPEN Not
WINEMAKER Frank van der Kraan EST. 1994 CASES 150
SUMMARY Frank van der Kraan and wife Barbara established their 0.5-ha vineyard Kraanwood in 1994 and 1995, with approximately equal plantings of pinot noir, chardonnay and cabernet sauvignon. Frank van der Kraan also manages the 1-ha Pembroke Vineyard, and procures from it small quantities of schonburger, chardonnay, riesling and sauvignon blanc.

ȚȚȚȚ **Pinot Noir 2003** RATING 84 DRINK 2007

ȚȚȚ **Schonburger 2004** RATING 81

ȚȚȚ **Chardonnay 2004** RATING 79

Krinklewood ★★★★

712 Wollombi Road, Broke, NSW 2330 **REGION** Lower Hunter Valley
T (02) 6579 1322 **F** (02) 9968 3435 **WEB** www.krinklewood.com **OPEN** Weekends, long weekends &
by appointment
WINEMAKER Contract **EST.** 1981 **CASES** 5000
SUMMARY Rod and Suzanne Windrim first ventured to the Hunter Valley in 1981, establishing
Krinklewood Cottage at Pokolbin and a 1-ha vineyard. In 1996 they sold that property and moved to
the Broke/Fordwich region, where they planted 17.5 ha with Dr Richard Smart as their viticultural
consultant. They struck gold with their first vintage in 2000. Leading restaurant listings of the
imaginatively packaged wines have followed, as have favourable reviews in various magazines.
Exports to Canada.

ŸŸŸŸŸ **Hunter Valley Chardonnay 2003** Opposite to the Semillon; has greater tightness and
structure than usual in the region; stone fruit and mineral more in Chablis style despite 9
months in oak. Screwcap. **RATING** 90 **DRINK** 2010 $ 22

ŸŸŸŸ **Hunter Valley Semillon 2004** Developed though bright colour; a quite soft, generous
palate; ripe citrus and even stone fruit; early-developing. Screwcap. **RATING** 88
DRINK 2007 $ 18
Hunter Valley Verdelho 2004 Considerable aromatic fruit salad aromas and flavours;
nice tangy finish; good varietal example. Screwcap. **RATING** 88 **DRINK** 2009 $ 18
Hunter Valley Rose 2004 Crisp, lively and fresh; good extension to red fruit flavours;
lingering acidity. Screwcap. **RATING** 87 **DRINK** Now $ 18

ŸŸŸŸ **Hunter Valley Shiraz 2003** **RATING** 86 **DRINK** 2009 $ 28

Kulkunbulla ★★★★☆

Brokenback Estate, 1595 Broke Road, Pokolbin, NSW 2320 **REGION** Lower Hunter Valley
T (02) 4998 7140 **F** (02) 4998 7142 **WEB** www.kulkunbulla.com.au **OPEN** 7 days 9–5
WINEMAKER Gavin Lennard, Duane Roy **EST.** 1996 **CASES** 5000
SUMMARY Kulkunbulla is owned by a relatively small Sydney-based company headed by Gavin
Lennard, which has purchased part of the Brokenback Estate in the Hunter Valley formerly owned
by Rothbury. A cellar door with scenic views opened in 2004, supplementing mail order and retail
distribution through all Vintage Cellars outlets. A small amount of wine is exported to the US.

ŸŸŸŸŸ **The Glandore Semillon 2004** Flowing line and mouthfeel; caresses the tongue; long,
lemony/minerally finish; 10° alcohol. Screwcap. **RATING** 94 **DRINK** 2016 $ 40

ŸŸŸŸŸ **Hunter Valley Semillon 2004** Elegant, finely drawn and crisp; citrus and lemon; fresh
finish; 10.5° alcohol. Screwcap. **RATING** 92 **DRINK** 2014 $ 20
Hunter Valley Shiraz 2002 Medium-bodied; firm, fresh blackberry/earthy fruit; precise
and focused; subtle oak. Screwcap. **RATING** 90 **DRINK** 2012 $ 35
Hilltops Cabernet Merlot 2002 As powerful and concentrated as the Hilltops Shiraz;
savoury blackcurrant and bitter chocolate; long, persistent tannins still to soften; 24
months in French oak. Screwcap. **RATING** 90 **DRINK** 2017 $ 35

ŸŸŸŸ **Hilltops Shiraz 2002** Full-bodied; extremely powerful, dense wine, the spicy licorice and
black fruits dominated by persistent tannins; needs much patience. Screwcap. **RATING** 89
DRINK 2017 $ 35
Hunter Valley Verdelho 2004 Well made; tangy fruit salad flavour with lemony acidity
providing both length and character. Screwcap. **RATING** 87 **DRINK** 2008 $ 20

Kurabana ★★★★

74 Burrows Road, Lethbridge, Vic 3331 (postal) **REGION** Geelong
T (03) 5266 1273 **F** (03) 5266 1116 **WEB** www.kurabana.com **OPEN** Not
WINEMAKER Ray Nadeson **EST.** 1987 **CASES** 2000
SUMMARY The development of the quite extensive Kurabana Vineyard, west of Geelong in the
foothills of Mt Moriac, began in 1987. Pinot noir (7.5 ha) is the largest portion, followed by (in
descending order) shiraz, chardonnay, sauvignon blanc and pinot gris. While some of the grapes are
sold, there are also limited purchases from the Geelong area. There are no cellar door sales, but
orders can be placed through the website or by mail; retailers and restaurants can be supplied direct.

ᵂᵂᵂᵂᵂ **Reserve Pinot Noir 2002** Intense, sappy, spicy aromas; very long and stylish palate, with strong foresty notes and black cherry; fine tannins. **RATING** 93 **DRINK** 2007 $ 39.95
Shiraz 2003 Excellent colour; elegant, gently spicy, cool-climate style; controlled tannin and oak extract and use. **RATING** 90 **DRINK** 2013 $ 23.95

ᵂᵂᵂᵂ **Pinot Gris 2004** Pale salmon colour; sweet fruit aromas; plenty of mid-palate fruit and balancing acidity. **RATING** 89 **DRINK** Now $ 19.95
Estate Pinot Noir 2003 Complex herb and spice aromas; light to medium-bodied dark berry fruit; good length and aftertaste. **RATING** 89 **DRINK** 2007 $ 22.95
Red Shed Pinot Noir 2003 Good colour; plenty of fruit, and although not complex, shows varietal character. May well have bypassed oak on the way to bottle. Excellent value. **RATING** 87 **DRINK** Now $ 13.95

ᵂᵂᵂᵂ **Chardonnay 2004** Elegant; distinct fruit sweetness, but a relatively dry finish. **RATING** 86 **DRINK** Now $ 24.95
Mt Moriac Sauvignon Blanc Chardonnay 2004 RATING 85 **DRINK** Now $ 14.95
Pinot Gris 2003 RATING 84 **DRINK** Now $ 19.95

ᵂᵂᵂ **Rose 2003 RATING** 82 $ 17.95

Kurrajong Downs ★★★★

Casino Road, via Tenterfield, NSW 2372 **REGION** Northern Slopes Zone
T (02) 6736 4590 **F** (02) 6736 1983 **WEB** www.kurrajongdownswines.com **OPEN** Thurs–Mon 10–4
WINEMAKER Mark Ravenscroft, Blair Duncan **EST.** 2000 **CASES** 2600
SUMMARY Jonus Rhodes arrived at Tenterfield in 1858, lured by the gold he mined for the next 40 years, until his death in 1898. He was evidently successful, for the family now runs a 2800-ha cattle grazing property on which Lynton and Sue Rhodes have planted a 5.2-ha vineyard at an altitude of 850m. Development of the the vineyard started in the spring of 1996, and continued the following year. The substantial cellar door, restaurant and function centre overlooking the vineyard are open 10 am–4 pm Monday to Thursday, and for dinner on Friday and Saturday evening (capacity 100 people).

ᵂᵂᵂᵂᵂ **Louisa Mary Semillon 2002** Classic young semillon aromas of herb, lanolin and lemon blossom; good length and balance; clean minerally finish. **RATING** 90 **DRINK** 2012 $ 14

ᵂᵂᵂᵂ **The Forge Cabernet Sauvignon 2003** Light to medium-bodied; well balanced and structured; sweet blackcurrant fruit; fine, ripe tannins; minimal oak. **RATING** 89 **DRINK** 2010 $ 16
Timbarra Gold Chardonnay 2004 Light-bodied but well made; melon and gently tangy fruit; a neat touch of oak. **RATING** 87 **DRINK** 2008 $ 15

ᵂᵂᵂᵂ **All Nations Pinot Noir 2003** Distinctive somewhat stemmy varietal character; foresty, bramble flavours; stained/pitted cork a worry. **RATING** 86 **DRINK** Nqw $ 22
Reserve Pinot Noir 2002 RATING 85 **DRINK** 2008 $ 22
Pinot Noir 2002 RATING 84 **DRINK** 2007 $ 22

ᵂᵂᵂ **Reserve Merlot 2002 RATING** 82 $ 22

Kurtz Family Vineyards NR

PO Box 460, Nuriootpa, SA 5355 **REGION** Barossa Valley
T 0418 810 982 **F** (08) 8564 8278 **OPEN** Not
WINEMAKER John Zilm (Contract) **EST.** 1996 **CASES** NA
SUMMARY The Kurtz family has 20 ha of vineyard at Light Pass, planted to semillon, chardonnay, grenache, cabernet sauvignon, merlot, shiraz, cabernet franc, mourvedre and petit verdot. The wines are distributed in Victoria through Woods Wines, with exports to the US and Hong Kong. They are also available by mail order.

Kyeema Estate ★★★☆

43 Shumack Street, Weetangera, ACT 2614 (postal) **REGION** Canberra District
T (02) 6254 7557 (AH) **F** (02) 6254 7536 **OPEN** Not
WINEMAKER Andrew McEwin **EST.** 1986 **CASES** 1200

SUMMARY Part-time winemaker, part-time wine critic (with *Winewise* magazine) Andrew McEwin produces wines full of flavour and character; every wine released under the Kyeema Estate label has won a show award of some description. Limited retail distribution.

Kyneton Ridge Estate ★★★★☆

90 Blackhill School Road, Kyneton, Vic 3444 **REGION** Macedon Ranges
T (03) 5422 7377 **F** (03) 5422 3747 **WEB** www.kynetonridge.com.au **OPEN** Weekends & public hols 10–5, or by appointment
WINEMAKER John Boucher **EST.** 1997 **CASES** 500
SUMMARY Kyneton Ridge Estate has been established by a family team of winemakers with winemaking roots going back four generations in the case of John and Ann Boucher. Together with Pauline Russell they found what they believe is a perfect pinot noir site near Kyneton, and planted 2.5 ha of pinot noir in 1997; 1.5 ha of chardonnay and 0.5 ha of shiraz were added in 2002.

▼▼▼▼▽ **Pinot Noir 2003** Very powerful, compact, dense dark fruits and plum; will be long-lived. **RATING** 93 **DRINK** 2010 $ 25

🐦 Kyotmunga Estate NR

287 Chittering Valley Road, Lower Chittering, WA 6084 **REGION** Perth Hills
T (08) 9571 8001 **OPEN** Weekends 11–5 April–Dec
WINEMAKER Trevor Wallis **EST.** 2000 **CASES** 500
SUMMARY Lynette Chester and Trevor Wallis have 2.4 ha of shiraz, chenin blanc, taminga, grenache and barbera. Prices are low ($13–14); olive oil, Mediterranean platters and Devonshire teas are also available at the cellar door.

Laanecoorie ★★★★★

4834 Bendigo/Maryborough Road, Betley, Vic 3472 **REGION** Bendigo
T (03) 5468 7260 **F** (03) 5468 7388 **OPEN** Weekends & by appointment
WINEMAKER Graeme Jukes (Contract) **EST.** 1982 **CASES** 150
SUMMARY John McQuilten's 7.5-ha vineyard produces grapes of high quality, and competent contract-winemaking has done the rest.

▼▼▼▼▼ **McQuilterns Reserve Shiraz 2003** Full-bodied; rich, ripe and luscious; drought concentration, but keeps mid-palate black fruits; ripe tannins; has eaten up the oak. Quality cork. **RATING** 94 **DRINK** 2013 $ 39.50

Labyrinth NR

PO Box 7372, Shepparton, Vic 3632 **REGION** Yarra Valley
T (03) 5831 2793 **F** (03) 5831 2982 **WEB** www.labyrinthwine.com **OPEN** Not
WINEMAKER Rick Hill **EST.** 2000 **CASES** 1100
SUMMARY Rick Hill is running a unique wine business, the name Labyrinth being well chosen. While it is a pinot noir-only specialist, one is produced in the southern hemisphere (from the Yarra Valley) and one from the northern hemisphere (Santa Barbara, California) each year. Moreover, the wines come from individual vineyards: the Bien Nacido Vineyard has a deserved reputation as one of the best sources of pinot noir in California. Rick Hill uses leased space in California and at Goulburn Valley Estate to make the wines, and also has active consultancy work in California. The wines are distributed in Australia through Steve Naughton at Pinot Now.

La Cantina King Valley NR

5 Honey's Lane, King Valley, Vic 3678 **REGION** King Valley
T (03) 5729 3615 **F** (03) 5729 3613 **WEB** www.lacantinakingvalley.com.au **OPEN** 7 days 10–5 (10–6 during daylight saving)
WINEMAKER Gino Corsini **EST.** 1996 **CASES** 1500
SUMMARY Gino and Peter Corsini have 22 ha of riesling, chardonnay, shiraz, merlot and cabernet sauvignon, selling most but making a small amount onsite in a winery 'made of Glenrowan granite stone in traditional Tuscan style'. The wines are made without the use of sulphur dioxide; in other words, they are organic.

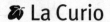 La Curio ★★★★

11 Sextant Avenue, Seaford, SA 5169 (postal) **REGION** McLaren Vale
T (08) 8327 1442 **F** (08) 8327 1442 **WEB** www.lacuriowines.com **OPEN** Not
WINEMAKER Adam Hooper, Elena Golakova **EST.** 2003 **CASES** 500
SUMMARY La Curio has been established by Adam Hooper and partner Elena Golakova, who purchased small parcels of grapes from 5 vineyards in McLaren Vale with an average age of 40 years, the oldest 80 years. They make the wines at Redheads Studio, a boutique winery in McLaren Vale which has been established to cater for a number of small producers. The manacles depicted on the striking label are those of Harry Houdini, and the brand proposition is very cleverly worked through. Winemaking techniques, too, are avant garde, and highly successful. Exports to the US.

ŸŸŸŸŸ Reserve McLaren Vale Shiraz 2003 Scented, spicy oak aromatics; medium-bodied; very good mouthfeel and length; blackberry, plum and some spice. Cork. **RATING** 91 **DRINK** 2013 $28
Reserve McLaren Vale Bush Vine Grenache 2003 Good colour; luscious red berry fruit shot through with fine, ripe tannins; does show its 15° alcohol. Cork. **RATING** 90 **DRINK** 2010 $24

ŸŸŸŸ The Nubile McLaren Vale Grenache Shiraz 2003 Rich black fruits; quite pronounced tannins in relation to the fruit, but within bounds. Cork. **RATING** 89 **DRINK** 2009 $19

Ladbroke Grove ★★★★☆

Riddoch Highway, Coonawarra, SA 5263 **REGION** Coonawarra
T (08) 8737 3777 **F** (08) 8737 3777 **WEB** www.ladbrokegrove.com.au **OPEN** Wed–Sun 10–5, or by appointment
WINEMAKER Contract **EST.** 1982 **CASES** 5000
SUMMARY Having been established in 1982, Ladbroke Grove is a relatively old Coonawarra brand. However, while the vineyards remained, winemaking and marketing lapsed until the business was purchased by John Cox and Marie Valenzuela, who have quietly gone about the re-establishment and rejuvenation of the label, and have been rewarded by a string of wine show results in 2002 and 2003. It has extensive grape sources, including the Killian vineyard (10 ha), planted in 1990 to cabernet sauvignon, merlot and chardonnay. It also leases a little over 1 ha of dry-grown shiraz planted in 1965 in the centre of the Coonawarra township. In the spring of 2002 it planted another 11 ha at the northern end of Coonawarra to cabernet sauvignon, shiraz, viognier, riesling and merlot.

ŸŸŸŸŸ Township Block Shiraz 2002 Powerful, complex spice, licorice and boot leather aromas; a highly focused and particularly long palate. **RATING** 94 **DRINK** 2017 $28

ŸŸŸŸŸ Compadres Blend Cabernet Merlot 2002 Supple and ripe cassis and blackcurrant fruit; fine tannins; well-balanced and integrated oak. **RATING** 93 **DRINK** 2012 $26
Reserve Shiraz 2002 Very good colour; medium-bodied, with good balance and structure; needed a touch more mid-palate sweet fruit. **RATING** 90 **DRINK** 2010 $28

ŸŸŸŸ Shiraz Viognier 2002 RATING 86 **DRINK** 2008 $26
Reserve Cabernet Sauvignon 2002 RATING 84 **DRINK** 2009 $28

ŸŸŸ Flat Broke Lad Unwooded Chardonnay 2004 RATING 83

Lake Barrington Estate ★★★★

1133–1136 West Kentish Road, West Kentish, Tas 7306 **REGION** Northern Tasmania
T (03) 6491 1249 **F** (03) 6334 2892 **OPEN** Wed–Sun 10–5 (Nov–Apr)
WINEMAKER Steve Lubiana (Sparkling), Andrew Hood (Table) (both Contract) **EST.** 1986 **CASES** 500
SUMMARY Lake Barrington Estate is owned by the vivacious and energetic Maree Taylor; it is adjacent to Lake Barrington, 30 km south of Devonport, on the northern coast of Tasmania. There are picnic facilities at the 3-ha vineyard, and, needless to say, the scenery is very beautiful.

ŸŸŸŸŸ Alexandra Methode Champenoise 1998 Deep colour; rich, generous, round and mouthfilling style, yet retains elegance. Trophy Tasmanian Wines Show 2005. **RATING** 95 **DRINK** 2007

ŸŸŸ Pinot Noir 2002 RATING 83

Lake Breeze Wines ★★★★☆

Step Road, Langhorne Creek, SA 5255 **REGION** Langhorne Creek
T (08) 8537 3017 **F** (08) 8537 3267 **WEB** www.lakebreeze.com.au **OPEN** 7 days 10–5
WINEMAKER Greg Follett **EST.** 1987 **CASES** 12 000
SUMMARY The Folletts have been farmers at Langhorne Creek since 1880, grapegrowers since the 1930s. Since 1987, increasing amounts of their grapes have been made into wine; a cellar door sales facility was opened in early 1991. The quality of the releases has been exemplary, with the red wines particularly appealing. Retail distribution in Victoria, NSW, Queensland and Western Australia; exports to the UK, the US and other major markets.

▼▼▼▼▼ **Arthur's Reserve Cabernet Petit Verdot 2002** Bell-clear line and length; not heavy, but tighter than the other wines (doubtless Petit Verdot and French oak at work); has length and balance. Cork. **RATING** 93 **DRINK** 2012 $ 29
Bernoota 2002 Sweet, spicy blackberry and black cherry; medium-bodied; fine but round tannins; whisk of American oak. Cork. **RATING** 93 **DRINK** 2015 $ 20
Winemaker's Selection Shiraz 2002 Smooth, supple, round, plum and blackberry fruit; soft tannins, balanced oak; long finish and a touch of bitter chocolate. Quality cork.
RATING 92 **DRINK** 2015 $ 38
Langhorne Creek Cabernet Sauvignon 2002 Rich, supple, smooth blackcurrant; soft, rounded tannins; cedary oak. Cork. **RATING** 92 **DRINK** 2015 $ 23

▼▼▼▼ **Langhorne Creek Grenache 2003** Strong red-purple; spicy, juicy berry; touches of earth and chocolate; good mouthfeel; smart Grenache. Cork. **RATING** 89 **DRINK** 2010 $ 17
Arthur's Reserve Cabernet Petit Verdot 2001 Light to medium-bodied; a mix of black fruits, earth and mint; fine tannins. **RATING** 88 **DRINK** 2007 $ 30

Lake Charlotte Wines NR

4750 Ballup Road, Wooroloo, WA 6558 **REGION** Perth Hills
T (08) 9573 1219 **F** (08) 9573 1616 **OPEN** Weekends & public hols 10–5
WINEMAKER Jim Elson (Contract) **EST.** 2001 **CASES** NA
SUMMARY There is no doubt the Perth Hills is a very pretty wine region, its twisting roads and multiple sub-valleys reminding me in some ways of the Clare Valley. It also has the great advantage of being an easy drive from Perth. Peter and Edwina Carter have set up their cellar door in an idyllic setting on the edge of Lake Charlotte, with a typical wide and open verandah under a low-sloping roof. They have 2.5 ha of verdelho, cabernet sauvignon, shiraz and merlot, and their wines are contract-made by long-term Perth Hills winemaker Jim Elson.

Lake Cooper Estate ★★★★☆

1608 Midland Highway, Corop, Vic 316 **REGION** Heathcote
T (03) 9397 7781 **F** (03) 9397 8502 **OPEN** 7 days 11–5
WINEMAKER Peter Kelliher, Donald Risstrom **EST.** 1998 **CASES** 600
SUMMARY Lake Cooper Estate is another new and substantial venture in the burgeoning Heathcote region. Planting began in 1998 with 12 ha of shiraz, and has since been extended to 18 ha of shiraz, 10 ha of cabernet sauvignon and small plantings of merlot and chardonnay; additional small blocks of more exotic varieties will follow. Owners Gerry and Geraldine McHarg completed an onsite winery in 2003 (the wine was made elsewhere by Peter Kelliher till then) and a new cellar door in 2005. Both vineyard and winery are set on the side Mt Camel Range, with panoramic views of Lake Cooper, Greens Lake and the Corop township.

▼▼▼▼▼ **Heathcote Reserve Shiraz 2003** A relatively quiet bouquet; swells massively on the fruit-saturated palate; black cherry, dark mocha suffused with gentle oak. **RATING** 94
DRINK 2015 $ 25

▼▼▼▼▼ **Heathcote Shiraz Cabernet Sauvignon 2003** Rich, dense and powerful; swollen with black fruit flavours; an earlier picking or less extractive winemaking might be even better.
RATING 92 **DRINK** 2014 $ 20
Cabernet Sauvignon 2003 Medium-bodied; very good structure with blackcurrant woven through with ripe, savoury tannins. Good length. **RATING** 91 **DRINK** 2013 $ 20

Dry Lake Heathcote Shiraz 2001 Softer, smoother and more supple than the '02 Dry Lake Shiraz; appealing mix of red and black fruits; medium-bodied; soft tannins and subtle oak. **RATING** 90 **DRINK** 2010 $ 30

▼▼▼▼ **Dry Lake Heathcote Cabernet Sauvignon 2002** Attractive medium-bodied blackcurrant fruit; fine, savoury tannins; subtle oak. Poor-quality cork. **RATING** 89 **DRINK** 2008 $ 28
Shiraz 2003 On the savoury end of the spectrum, with bitter chocolate, briar and moderately ripe tannins. **RATING** 88 **DRINK** 2010 $ 25
Dry Lake Heathcote Shiraz 2002 Full-bodied blackberry fruit; slightly dry tannins and mouthfeel, but plenty there. Inferior cork (staining and imperfections) a worry. **RATING** 88 **DRINK** 2007 $ 28
Heathcote Sparkling Shiraz 2003 Juicy black fruits and licorice; needs 10 years on lees; would be outstanding; time in bottle may give half the result. **RATING** 87 **DRINK** 2010 $ 18

Lake George Winery ★★☆

Federal Highway, Collector, NSW 2581 **REGION** Canberra District
T (02) 4848 0039 **F** (02) 4848 0039 **WEB** www.lakegeorgewinery.com.au **OPEN** By appointment
WINEMAKER Sam Karelas **EST.** 1971 **CASES** 1000
SUMMARY Dr Edgar Riek was an inquisitive, iconoclastic winemaker who was not content with his role as Godfather and founder of the Canberra District, and so was forever experimenting and innovating. His fortified wines, vintaged in northeastern Victoria but matured at Lake George, were very good. Major cork/oxidation problems evident in the 2002 vintage wines.

▼▼▼▼▽ **Botrytis Semillon 375 ml 2000** Glowing gold; complex, rich cumquat, apricot and peach fruit; good balancing acidity and length. Cork. **RATING** 90 **DRINK** 2007 $ 39

▼▼▼▽ **Unfiltered Pinot Noir 2002** **RATING** 85 **DRINK** 2007 $ 49
Unfiltered Merlot Cabernet Sauvignon 2002 **RATING** 84 **DRINK** Now $ 35

▼▼▽ **Unfiltered Semillon 2002** **RATING** 79 $ 25
Unfiltered Chardonnay 2002 **RATING** 79 $ 29

Lake Moodemere Vineyard ★★★☆

McDonalds Road, Rutherglen, Vic 3685 **REGION** Rutherglen
T (02) 6032 9449 **F** (02) 6032 9449 **WEB** www.moodemerewines.com.au **OPEN** Weekends & public hols 10–5, Mon, Thurs, Fri 10–3.30
WINEMAKER Michael Chambers **EST.** 1995 **CASES** 2500
SUMMARY Michael, Belinda, Peter and Helen Chambers are all members of the famous Chambers family of Rutherglen. They have 30 ha of vineyards (tended by Peter), with the Italian grape variety biancone a vineyard specialty, made as a light-bodied late-harvest-style wine. The cellar door sits high above Lake Moodemere, and gourmet hampers can be arranged with 24 hours' notice.

▼▼▼▼▽ **Rutherglen Shiraz 2002** Medium-bodied; red and black fruit focused; fine, supple tannins. Very well made. **RATING** 90 **DRINK** 2012 $ 18

▼▼▼▽ **Rutherglen Chardonnay 2003** **RATING** 86 **DRINK** Now $ 16.50
Late Harvest Biancone 2003 **RATING** 84 **DRINK** Now $ 15.50

Lake's Folly

Broke Road, Pokolbin, NSW 2320 **REGION** Lower Hunter Valley
T (02) 4998 7507 **F** (02) 4998 7322 **WEB** www.lakesfolly.com.au **OPEN** 7 days 10–4 while wine available
WINEMAKER Rodney Kempe **EST.** 1963 **CASES** 4500
SUMMARY The first of the weekend wineries to produce wines for commercial sale, long revered for its Cabernet Sauvignon and thereafter its Chardonnay. Very properly, terroir and climate produce a distinct regional influence and thereby a distinctive wine style. Some find this attractive, others are less tolerant. The winery continues to enjoy an incredibly loyal clientele, with much of each year's wine selling out quickly by mail order. Lake's Folly no longer has any connection with the Lake family, having been acquired some years ago by Perth businessman Peter Fogarty. Mr Fogarty's family company has previously established the Millbrook Winery in the Perth Hills, so is no stranger to the joys and agonies of running a small winery.

ΨΨΨΨΨ **Chardonnay 2003** Very stylish; controlled complexity; beautifully balanced and structured melon, stone fruit and cashew; fresh, bright finish. **RATING** 96 **DRINK** 2010
Chardonnay 2002 Bright green-yellow, this proclaims its class from start to finish, with immaculately handled barrel ferment oak supporting white peach fruit and fine acidity. **RATING** 96 **DRINK** 2009 $45
Cabernets 2003 Clean; elegant, medium-bodied style; red and black fruits with silky tannins; subtle oak; fine and long. **RATING** 94 **DRINK** 2013 $45

ΨΨΨΨΨ **Cabernets 2002** Slightly lighter than the 2003; long and fine; all the elements surrounding red and black fruits, in mainstream Folly style. **RATING** 93 **DRINK** 2010 $45

Lambert Vineyards   NR

810 Norton Road, Wamboin, NSW 2620 **REGION** Canberra District
T (02) 6238 3866 **F** (02) 6238 3855 **OPEN** Thurs–Sun 10–5, or by appointment
WINEMAKER Ruth Lambert, Steve Lambert **EST.** 1998 **CASES** 6000
SUMMARY Ruth and Steve Lambert have established 8 ha of riesling, chardonnay, pinot gris, pinot noir, cabernet sauvignon, merlot and shiraz. Steve Lambert makes the wines onsite; they are sold by mail order and through the cellar door. The café is open Thurs–Sat evening, Fri–Sun for lunch.

Lamont's   ★★★★☆

85 Bisdee Road, Millendon, WA 6056 **REGION** Swan Valley
T (08) 9296 4485 **F** (08) 9296 1663 **WEB** www.lamonts.com.au **OPEN** Wed–Sun 10–5
WINEMAKER Keith Mugford (Consultant) **EST.** 1978 **CASES** 10 000
SUMMARY Corin Lamont is the daughter of the late Jack Mann, and, with the recent involvement of Keith Mugford as consultant, oversees the making of wines in a style which would have pleased her father. Lamont's also boasts a superb restaurant run by granddaughter Kate Lamont, plus a gallery for the sale and promotion of local arts. The wines are going from strength to strength, utilising both estate grown and contract-grown (from southern regions) grapes. There are two cellar doors, the second (open 7 days) in the Margaret River at Gunyulgup Valley Drive, Yallingup, telephone (08) 9755 2434.

ΨΨΨΨΨ **Chardonnay 2003** Excellent balance, texture and mouthfeel; creamy stone fruit, melon and fig; subtle oak, long finish. **RATING** 94 **DRINK** 2010 $22

ΨΨΨΨΨ **Frankland River Riesling 2004** Spotlessly clean; vibrantly fresh and focused; pure lime and citrus; considerable length. **RATING** 93 **DRINK** 2012 $18

ΨΨΨΨ **Shiraz 2002** Sweet raspberry and blackberry fruit; integrated and balanced vanilla oak; ripe tannins. **RATING** 89 **DRINK** 2015 $25
Margaret River Semillon Sauvignon Blanc 2004 Fresh, no reduction; powerful mineral and herb; good length and aftertaste. **RATING** 87 **DRINK** 2008 $20

Lancefield Winery   ★★☆

Scrubby Camp Road, Emu Flat, Lancefield, Vic 3435 **REGION** Macedon Ranges
T (03) 5433 5292 **F** (03) 5433 5114 **WEB** www.wineandmusic.net **OPEN** By appointment
WINEMAKER Rod Schmidt **EST.** 1985 **CASES** 1000
SUMMARY Lancefield Winery was established by Andrew Pattison, with plantings of 1 ha each of chardonnay and shiraz, and 0.5 ha each of gewurztraminer, pinot noir and cabernets/merlot. With Rod Schmidt in charge from June 2004, it is in the course of developing its own labels, the other brands having moved across to Pattison's newly established Burke and Wills winery.

ΨΨΨ **Reserve Chardonnay 2001** **RATING** 82 $25

Landsborough Valley Estate   ★★★★

850 Landsborough–Elmhurst Road, Landsborough, Vic 3385 **REGION** Pyrenees
T (03) 5356 9390 **F** (03) 5356 9130 **OPEN** Mon–Fri 10–4, weekends by appointment
WINEMAKER Wal Henning **EST.** 1996 **CASES** 6000
SUMMARY LVE (for short) originated in 1963, when civil engineering contractor Wal Henning was engaged to undertake work at Chateau Remy (now Blue Pyrenees). He was so impressed with the potential of the region for viticulture that he began an aerial search for sites with his close friend

Geoff Oliver. Their first choice was not available; they chose a site which is now Taltarni, developing 40 ha. Taltarni was then sold, and the pair (with Geoff's brother Max) moved on to establish Warrenmang Vineyard. When it, too, was sold the pair was left without a vineyard, but in 1996 they were finally able to purchase the property they had identified 33 years previously, which is now partly given over to LVE and part to the giant Glen Kara vineyard. They have established 20 ha on LVE, the lion's share to shiraz, with lesser amounts of cabernet sauvignon, pinot noir, chardonnay and riesling.

ƳƳƳƳƳ Geoff Oliver Classic Shiraz 2004 Strong purple-red; masses of dark fruits, blackberry, spice and licorice; tannins yet to integrate. Cork. **RATING** 92 **DRINK** 2014 $40

ƳƳƳƳ Cabernet Sauvignon 2003 Powerful blackcurrant fruit on bouquet and fore-palate; dry, dusty tannins out of balance and unlikely to fully soften. A pity. Cork. **RATING** 88 **DRINK** 2015 $30

ƳƳƳƳ Geoff Oliver Classic Shiraz 2003 **RATING** 85 **DRINK** 2018 $40

Lane's End Vineyard ★★★★

PO Box 87, Lancefield, Vic 3435 **REGION** Macedon Ranges
T (03) 5429 1760 **F** (03) 5429 1760 **OPEN** Not
WINEMAKER Howard Matthews, Ken Murchison, David Cowburn (Kilchurn Wines) **EST.** 1985 **CASES** 450
SUMMARY In September 2000 pharmacist Howard Matthews (and family) purchased the former Woodend Winery, with 1.8 ha of chardonnay and pinot noir (and a small amount of cabernet franc) dating back to the mid-1980s. For the first 2–3 years, the grapes were sold, but by 2003 Howard Matthews was ready to make the first wines. For the two preceding vintages he had worked with next-door neighbour Ken Murchison of Portree Wines, gaining winemaking experience; with the exception of the Unoaked Chardonnay, made by David Cowburn, the wines are made there.

ƳƳƳƳƳ Macedon Ranges Pinot Noir 2003 Light but good hue; good varietal expression in a light to medium-bodied frame; fresh, plum fruit; slightly brisk acidity. Quality cork. **RATING** 91 **DRINK** 2009 $34

ƳƳƳƳ Macedon Ranges Unoaked Chardonnay 2004 Intensely aromatic; sweet peach and melon fruit off-set by squeaky acidity; lots of character. **RATING** 89 **DRINK** 2007 $17
Macedon Ranges Cabernet Franc 2003 Spicy, leafy, herbal characters emphasising the difficulty the variety poses, but with some sweet fruit notes popping out. High-quality cork. **RATING** 87 **DRINK** 2008 $20

Langanook Wines ★★★★

91 McKittericks Road, Sutton Grange, Vic 3448 **REGION** Bendigo
T (03) 5474 8250 **F** (03) 5474 8250 **WEB** www.bendigowine.org.au/langanook **OPEN** Weekends & public hols 11–5, or by appointment
WINEMAKER Matt Hunter **EST.** 1985 **CASES** 1250
SUMMARY The Langanook vineyard was established back in 1985 (the first wines came much later), at an altitude of 450m on the granite slopes of Mt Alexander. The climate is much cooler than in other parts of Bendigo, with a heat summation on a par with the Yarra Valley. The 20-tonne winery allows minimal handling of the wines. Exports to Belgium and Canada.

ƳƳƳƳƳ Cabernet Sauvignon Merlot Cabernet Franc 2002 Aromatic, scented, mint and leaf on black fruit aromas; lots of juicy berry fruits on the palate. **RATING** 90 **DRINK** 2012 $24

ƳƳƳƳ Reserve Cabernet Sauvignon Merlot Cabernet Franc 2000 Cedary, earthy bottle-developed overtones; leaf, berry, mint and blackcurrant flavours; subtle oak. **RATING** 89 **DRINK** 2008 $35

Langbrook Estate Vineyard NR

65 Summerhill Road, Yarra Junction, Vic 3797 **REGION** Yarra Valley
T (03) 5967 1320 **F** (03) 5967 1182 **WEB** www.langbrook.com **OPEN** By appointment
WINEMAKER MasterWineMakers (Contract) **EST.** 1996 **CASES** 360
SUMMARY Langbrook Estate has 9 ha of pinot noir, 5 ha of sauvignon blanc, 4 ha each of chardonnay and merlot and 1 ha of cabernet sauvignon planted; this will provide the base for a substantial output in future years. There is also a B&B cottage and studio.

Langleyvale Vineyard NR

43 Blackhill School Road, Kyneton, Vic 3444 **REGION** Macedon Ranges
T 0417 359 106 **F** (03) 9576 2966 **OPEN** By appointment
WINEMAKER Richard Beniac **EST.** 2000 **CASES** 250
SUMMARY Richard Beniac purchased his property at Macedon after completing a part-time university viticulture course; he also conducted soil tests and collected weather data before deciding to take on the challenge of cool-climate viticulture. The first plantings were 2.6 ha of merlot, followed by 0.6 ha each of shiraz and cabernet franc. Merlot was the first wine produced, in 2004; it will be followed in 2006/07 by Shiraz and Cabernet Franc.

Langmeil Winery

Cnr Para Road/Langmeil Road, Tanunda, SA 5352 **REGION** Barossa Valley
T (08) 8563 2595 **F** (08) 8563 3622 **WEB** www.langmeilwinery.com.au **OPEN** 7 days 11–4.30
WINEMAKER Paul Lindner **EST.** 1996 **CASES** 15 000
SUMMARY Vines were first planted at Langmeil in the 1840s, and the first winery on the site, known as Paradale Wines, opened in 1932. In 1996, cousins Carl and Richard Lindner plus brother-in-law Chris Bitter formed a partnership to acquire and refurbish the winery and its 5-ha vineyard (planted to shiraz, and including 2 ha planted in 1846). This vineyard was supplemented by another vineyard acquired in 1998, taking total plantings to 14.5 ha and including cabernet sauvignon and grenache. Distribution in New South Wales and Victoria; exports to the UK, the US and other major markets.

ΨΨΨΨΨ **The Freedom Shiraz 2002** Dense, velvety plum fruit; restrained French oak; ripe tannins and a luscious finish. High-quality cork. **RATING** 94 **DRINK** 2017 **$** 65
Jackaman's Cabernet Sauvignon 2002 Dense colour; powerful but not overripe blackcurrant, cassis and mulberry; fine, gently savoury tannins and excellent French oak handling. Very high-quality Barossa Cabernet. High-quality cork. **RATING** 94 **DRINK** 2017 **$** 45

ΨΨΨΨY **Valley Floor Shiraz 2002** Excellent structure; savoury, fine-grained tannins run through the medium-bodied, black-fruited palate; well-balanced finish. **RATING** 92 **DRINK** 2012 **$** 22.50
The Fifth Wave Grenache 2002 Luscious, rich varietal fruit on both bouquet and palate carries both the alcohol and the oak well; soft, ripe tannins to close. **RATING** 90 **DRINK** 2010 **$** 30

ΨΨΨΨ **Valley Floor Shiraz 2003** Quite luscious; ripe blackberry and plum mix; medium-bodied; soft vanilla oak. Quality cork. **RATING** 89 **DRINK** 2011 **$** 27.50
Shiraz 2000 Fully traditional Port style; rich, luscious blackberry and bitter chocolate; neutral spirit, needs years. Creased, stained cork is ominous. **RATING** 89 **DRINK** 2015 **$** 25
Three Gardens Shiraz Grenache Mourvedre 2003 Good colour; generous, ripe, complex fruit runs right through the palate to the finish. **RATING** 89 **DRINK** 2010 **$** 27.50
Single Vineyard Chardonnay 2004 Light to medium-bodied; nicely balanced nectarine fruit and a touch of French oak; pleasing length and mouthfeel. Screwcap. **RATING** 88 **DRINK** 2007 **$** 14.50
The Blacksmith Cabernet Sauvignon 2002 Ultra-ripe cassis and blackcurrant; touches of prune and chocolate. **RATING** 88 **DRINK** 2009 **$** 24
Eden Valley Riesling 2004 Pleasant; soft, easy access; early-drinking. Screwcap. **RATING** 87 **DRINK** Now **$** 19.50

ΨΨΨY **Barossa Valley Semillon 2003** **RATING** 86 **DRINK** 2007 **$** 16

Lark Hill

521 Bungendore Road, Bungendore, NSW 2621 **REGION** Canberra District
T (02) 6238 1393 **F** (02) 6238 1393 **WEB** www.larkhillwine.com.au **OPEN** Wed–Mon 10–5
WINEMAKER Dr David Carpenter, Sue Carpenter **EST.** 1978 **CASES** 4000
SUMMARY The Lark Hill vineyard is situated at an altitude of 860m, level with the observation deck on Black Mountain Tower, and offers splendid views of the Lake George escarpment. The Carpenters have made wines of real quality, style and elegance from the start, but have defied all the odds (and conventional thinking) with the quality of their Pinot Noirs. Exports to the UK and the US.

ΨΨΨΨΨ **Chardonnay 2002** Elegant, fresh, citrus and stone fruit aromas and flavours; excellent mouthfeel and balance; clever use of barrel ferment and partial malolactic ferment. **RATING** 94 **DRINK** 2007 $ 28

ΨΨΨΨΨ **Pinot Noir 2003** Sappy, spicy, stemmy whole-bunch characters; complex smoky oak; fractionally dry tannins on the finish. **RATING** 91 **DRINK** 2008 $ 28
Shiraz 2001 Smoky, leathery, spicy aromas and flavours; supple, medium-bodied palate; fine tannins. **RATING** 90 **DRINK** 2009 $ 28
Cabernet Merlot 2001 Good colour; ripe blackcurrant fruit; supple and sweet tannin and oak inputs. **RATING** 90 **DRINK** 2010 $ 28

ΨΨΨΨ **Riesling 2004** Clean, no reduction; tropical fruit notes give plenty of flavour throughout, but the line is slightly broken. Screwcap. **RATING** 89 **DRINK** 2009 $ 22
Chardonnay 2003 Light to medium-bodied; clean citrus and stone fruit; good balance and length. **RATING** 89 **DRINK** 2009 $ 28
Rose 2004 Attractive style; plenty of fresh, juicy red fruit flavours; gently dry finish. **RATING** 88 **DRINK** Now $ 20
Exaltation Shiraz 2001 Good colour; very powerful wine; black fruits and licorice; dry tannins on the finish detract. **RATING** 87 **DRINK** 2010

ΨΨΨ **Exaltation Pinot Noir 2002** **RATING** 82 $ 40

Lashmar ★★★☆

c/- 24 Lindsay Terrace, Belair, SA 5052 **REGION** Kangaroo Island
T (08) 8278 3669 **F** (08) 8278 3998 **WEB** www.lashmarwines.com **OPEN** Not
WINEMAKER Colin Cooter **EST.** 1996 **CASES** 1000
SUMMARY Colin and Bronwyn Cooter (who are also part of the Lengs & Cooter business) are the driving force behind Antechamber Bay Wines. The wines are in fact labelled and branded Lashmar; the Kangaroo Island Cabernet Sauvignon comes from vines planted in 1991 on the Lashmar family property, which is on the extreme eastern end of Kangaroo Island overlooking Antechamber Bay. The first commercial wines were made in 1999 and released in October 2000. The Three Valleys and Sisters wines (from other regions) give the business added volume. Exports to the US, Canada, Singapore and Japan.

ΨΨΨΨ **McLaren Vale Viognier 2003** Bright green-yellow; light to medium-bodied, but quite complex; hints of smoke, pastille, apricot and pear. Screwcap. **RATING** 89 **DRINK** 2007 $ 26
Kangaroo Island Cabernet 2002 Spice, cedar, tobacco and blackcurrant; slightly pushed fruit flavours, the tannins slightly wobbly. Stained cork. **RATING** 87 **DRINK** 2008 $ 30

ΨΨΨΨ **Sister's Blend 2002** **RATING** 85 **DRINK** 2008 $ 20

Latara NR

Cnr McDonalds Road/Deaseys Road, Pokolbin, NSW 2320 **REGION** Lower Hunter Valley
T (02) 4998 7320 **OPEN** Sat 9–5, Sun 9–4
WINEMAKER Iain Riggs (Contract) **EST.** 1979 **CASES** 250
SUMMARY The bulk of the grapes produced on the 6-ha Latara vineyard, which was planted in 1979, are sold to Brokenwood. As one would expect, the wines are very competently made, and are of show medal standard.

Laurance of Margaret River ★★☆

Lot 549 Caves Road, Wilyabrup, WA 6280 **REGION** Margaret River
T (08) 9755 6199 **F** (08) 9755 6276 **WEB** www.laurancewines.com **OPEN** Wed–Sun 11–4
WINEMAKER Bruce Dukes (Consultant) **EST.** 2001 **CASES** 5000
SUMMARY Dianne Laurance is the driving force of this business, but her husband Bruce Carr and son Brendon Carr (plus wife Kerrianne) are also involved. Brendon is vineyard manager, living on the property with his wife and child. The 40-ha property had 21 ha planted when it was purchased, and since its acquisition it has been turned into a showplace, with a rose garden to put that of Voyager Estate to shame. While the wine is made offsite by Bruce Dukes, a substantial wine storage facility has been built onsite, and a new cellar door opened in 2005. But it is the tenpin bowling, ceramic-baked labels which will gain the most attention – and doubtless secondary uses for the bottles as lamp stands. Exports to Singapore and Japan.

ŦŦŦ⑨ **Rose 2003** RATING 86 DRINK Now $ 30
White 2003 RATING 84 DRINK 2007 $ 32
Red 2002 RATING 84 DRINK 2007 $ 34

ŦŦŦ **Just a Sweetie NV** RATING 83 $ 22
Aussie Jean Red Rock 2003 RATING 81 $ 17

Laurel Bank ★★★

130 Black Snake Lane, Granton, Tas 7030 REGION Southern Tasmania
T (03) 6263 5977 F (03) 6263 3117 OPEN By appointment
WINEMAKER Julian Alcorso (Contract) EST. 1987 CASES 850
SUMMARY Laurel (hence Laurel Bank) and Kerry Carland began planting their 3-ha vineyard in 1986.
They delayed the first release of their wines for some years and (by virtue of the number of entries
they were able to make) won the trophy for Most Successful Exhibitor at the 1995 Royal Hobart Wine
Show. Things have settled down since; wine quality is solid and reliable.

ŦŦŦŦ **Pinot Noir 2003** Light to medium-bodied; long, linear palate and silky tannins; fruit
slightly diminished. RATING 89 DRINK 2007 $ 24

ŦŦŦ⑨ **Sauvignon Blanc 2004** RATING 86 DRINK 2007 $ 20
Cabernet Sauvignon Merlot 2002 RATING 85 DRINK 2012 $ 24
Cabernet Sauvignon Merlot 2003 RATING 84 DRINK 2007 $ 24

Lauren Brook NR

Eedle Terrace, Bridgetown, WA 6255 REGION Blackwood Valley
T (08) 9761 2676 F (08) 9761 1879 WEB www.laurenbrook.com.au OPEN Fri–Wed 11–4.30
WINEMAKER Stephen Bullied EST. 1993 CASES 500
SUMMARY Lauren Brook is on the banks of the beautiful Blackwood River; an 80-year-old barn on the
property has been renovated to contain a micro-winery and a small gallery. There is 1 ha of estate
chardonnay, supplemented by grapes purchased locally.

Lawrence Victor Estate NR

Arthur Street, Penola, SA 5277 REGION Coonawarra
T (08) 8737 3572 F (08) 8739 7344 WEB www.lawrencevictorestate.com.au OPEN Not
WINEMAKER Contract EST. 1994 CASES 1500
SUMMARY Lawrence Victor Estate is part of a large South Australian company principally engaged
in harvesting and transport of plantation softwood. The company was established by Lawrence
Victor Dohnt in 1932, and the estate has been named in his honour by the third generation of the
family. Though a small part of the group's activities, the plantings (principally contracted to
Southcorp) are substantial, with 11 ha of shiraz and 20 ha of cabernet sauvignon established
between 1994 and 1999. An additional 12 ha of cabernet sauvignon and 6 ha of pinot noir were
planted in 2000.

Lawson Hill Estate NR

Henry Lawson Drive, Eurunderee, Mudgee, NSW 2850 REGION Mudgee
T (02) 6373 3953 F (02) 6373 3948 OPEN Sat 10–5, Sun 10–1, public hols 10–3, or by appointment
WINEMAKER Rhys Eather (Meerea Park) EST. 1985 CASES 2500
SUMMARY The 5.6-ha Lawson Hill Estate vineyard was purchased from its founders by a group of
business associates and friends in 2001. The new cellar door takes advantage of the sweeping views
out over the vineyards and to the west. A full varietal range is now made by noted Hunter winemaker
Rhys Eather.

Lazy River Estate NR

29R Old Dubbo Road, Dubbo, NSW 2830 REGION Western Plains Zone
T (02) 6882 2111 F (02) 6882 2111 WEB www.lazyriverestate.com.au OPEN By appointment
WINEMAKER Briar Ridge (Contract) EST. 1997 CASES 1400

SUMMARY The Scott family have planted 3 ha each of chardonnay and semillon, 1 ha of merlot, and 1.5 ha each of petit verdot and cabernet sauvignon. The property is a little under 3 km from the end of the main street of Dubbo. The wines are made at Briar Ridge.

Leabrook Estate ★★★★☆

24 Tusmore Avenue, Leabrook, SA 5068 **REGION** Adelaide Hills
T (08) 8331 7150 **F** (08) 8364 1520 **WEB** www.leabrookestate.com **OPEN** By appointment
WINEMAKER Colin Best **EST.** 1998 **CASES** 4500
SUMMARY With a background as an engineer, and having dabbled in home winemaking for 30 years, Colin Best took the plunge and moved into commercial scale winemaking in 1998. His wines are now to be found in a Who's Who of restaurants, and in some of the best independent wine retailers on the east coast. Best says 'I consider that my success is primarily due to the quality of my grapes, since they have been planted on a 1.2 x 1.2m spacing and very low yields.' I won't argue with that; he has also done a fine job in converting the grapes into wine. A cellar door is planned for the near future. Exports to the UK, Singapore and Japan.

ΥΥΥΥΥ **Adelaide Hills Chardonnay 2003** Elegant, deft malolactic and barrel ferment inputs; quite powerful drive through the palate to a long finish; a certain austerity. Cork. **RATING** 92 **DRINK** 2010 $ 25
Adelaide Hills Cabernet Franc 2003 Light to medium-bodied; scented red cherry, tobacco leaf and spice varietal fruit; very fine tannins; has more length than anticipated; creeps up on you. Quality cork. **RATING** 92 **DRINK** 2010 $ 24
Adelaide Hills Pinot Gris 2004 Spotlessly clean; vibrant and pure apple, pear and mineral; good length and acidity. Quality cork. **RATING** 90 **DRINK** 2008 $ 24
Three Region Shiraz 2003 Light to medium-bodied; fresh and supple; red and black fruits; gentle, savoury tannins run throughout; good balance, nice oak. Adelaide Hills/Langhorne Creek/Adelaide Plains. Cork. **RATING** 90 **DRINK** 2012 $ 30

ΥΥΥΥ **Adelaide Hills Sauvignon Blanc 2004** Powerful, though slightly reduced bouquet; full flavoured, sweet, tropical passionfruit. Cork. **RATING** 89 **DRINK** 2007 $ 24
Charleston Rose 2004 Salmon pink; complex Rose, strongly proclaiming its varietal Pinot Noir origin; savoury and spicy, off the mainstream. Cork. **RATING** 88 **DRINK** Now $ 17

Leasingham ★★★★☆

7 Dominic Street, Clare, SA 5453 **REGION** Clare Valley
T (08) 8842 2555 **F** (08) 8842 3293 **WEB** www.leasingham-wines.com.au **OPEN** Mon–Fri 8.30–5.30, weekends 10–4
WINEMAKER Kerri Thompson **EST.** 1893 **CASES** 70 000
SUMMARY Successive big-company ownerships and various peregrinations in labelling and branding have not resulted in any permanent loss of identity or quality. With a core of high-quality, aged vineyards to draw on, Leasingham is in fact going from strength to strength under Hardys' direction. The stentorian red wines take no prisoners, compacting densely rich fruit and layer upon layer of oak into every long-lived bottle; the Bin 7 Riesling also often excels.

ΥΥΥΥΥ **Bin 7 Riesling 2004** More potent and powerful fruit than most from 2004, with intense mineral and citrus aromas and flavours, the palate deep and long. **RATING** 95 **DRINK** 2014 $ 20

ΥΥΥΥΥ **Classic Clare Cabernet Sauvignon 2001** Powerful blackcurrant fruit with touches of dark chocolate; smooth, supple tannins. **RATING** 92 **DRINK** 2016 $ 45
Classic Clare Shiraz 2002 Dense blackberry and dark chocolate; maximum extract and oak; the tannins remain just in the field of play. **RATING** 90 **DRINK** 2017
Classic Clare Shiraz 2001 Deep colour; big, brawny, ripe black fruits; ripe tannins and balanced oak. **RATING** 90 **DRINK** 2016 $ 45

ΥΥΥΥ **Bastion Riesling 2003** **RATING** 86 **DRINK** 2008

ΥΥΥ **Bastion Cabernet Sauvignon 2003** **RATING** 82

346 | James Halliday

Leconfield ★★★★☆

Riddoch Highway, Coonawarra, SA 5263 **REGION** Coonawarra
T (08) 8737 2326 **F** (08) 8737 2385 **WEB** www.leconfieldwines.com **OPEN** Mon–Fri 9–5, weekends &
public hols 10–4.30
WINEMAKER Paul Gordon, Tim Bailey (Assistant) **EST.** 1974 **CASES** 15 000
SUMMARY A distinguished estate with a proud history. Long renowned for its Cabernet Sauvignon, its
repertoire has steadily grown with the emphasis on single-variety wines. The style overall is fruit-
rather than oak-driven. Exports to the UK, the US and other major markets.

ＹＹＹＹＹ **Old Vines Coonawarra Riesling 2004** Delicate, floral apple blossom and hints of slate
and spice; considerable length. **RATING** 93 **DRINK** 2012 $ 19.95
McLaren Vale Shiraz 2003 Dense, deep colour; rich, dense, fruit-flooded; blackberry and
dark chocolate; fine, ripe tannins provide structure. **RATING** 93 **DRINK** 2015
Synergy Shiraz 2003 Powerful wine; a blend of McLaren Vale and Coonawarra; aromatic
spicy notes of Coonawarra plus an edge to the McLaren Vale black fruits. **RATING** 91
DRINK 2012
Coonawarra Sparkling Shiraz 2003 Clean and fresh; nicely balanced, not too oaky or
sweet; spicy licorice fruit, and good finish. Major surprise. **RATING** 91 **DRINK** 2010 $ 25.95
Coonawarra Cabernet Sauvignon 2002 Elegant, distinctly savoury wine; long, lingering
black fruits and fine tannins; a certain austerity. **RATING** 90 **DRINK** 2010

ＹＹＹＹ **Synergy Chardonnay 2004** Quite elegant, but has plenty of melon fruit flavour and subtle
oak. Coonawarra/McLaren Vale blend. **RATING** 89 **DRINK** 2009
Coonawarra Merlot 2003 Good colour; extremely ripe red and black fruits carry through
the length of the palate; somewhat in-your-face style. **RATING** 89 **DRINK** 2011
Synergy Cabernet Merlot 2003 Good colour; abundant juicy, plummy berry fruit; soft
tannins, frugal oak. **RATING** 89 **DRINK** 2010

LedaSwan ★★★☆

179 Memorial Avenue, Baskerville, WA 6065 **REGION** Swan Valley
T (08) 9296 0216 **WEB** www.ledaswan.com.au **OPEN** 7 days 11–4.30
WINEMAKER Duncan Harris **EST.** 1998 **CASES** 250
SUMMARY LedaSwan claims to be the smallest winery in the Swan Valley. It uses organically grown
grapes, partly coming from its own vineyard, and partly from contract-grown grapes; the intention is
to move to 100% estate-grown in the future, from the 2 ha of estate vineyards. Duncan Harris moved
from the coast to Baskerville in 1998, and retired from engineering in 2001 to become a full-time
vintner; he has already won several awards. Tours of the underground cellar are offered, and there is
an extensive range of back vintages on offer.

ＹＹＹＹ **Organic Shiraz 2002** Medium-bodied; complex, savoury, gamey, earthy nuances to gentle
black fruits; overall, sweet oak and sweet fruit. Cork. **RATING** 88 **DRINK** 2009 $ 25

ＹＹＹＹ **Cabernet Sauvignon 2001 RATING** 84 **DRINK** Now $ 23

Leeuwin Estate ★★★★★

Stevens Road, Margaret River, WA 6285 **REGION** Margaret River
T (08) 9759 0000 **F** (08) 9759 0001 **WEB** www.leeuwinestate.com.au **OPEN** 7 days 10–4.30, Saturday
evening dinner
WINEMAKER Bob Cartwright, Paul Atwood **EST.** 1974 **CASES** 60 000
SUMMARY Leeuwin Estate's Chardonnay is, in my opinion, Australia's finest example, based on the
wines of the last 20 vintages, and it is this wine alone which demands a 5-star rating for the winery.
The Cabernet Sauvignon can be an excellent wine with great style and character in warmer vintages,
and Shiraz has made an auspicious debut. Almost inevitably, the other wines in the portfolio are not
in the same Olympian class, although the Prelude Chardonnay and Sauvignon Blanc are impressive
at their lower price level. This edition fell between release dates for the Chardonnay. Exports to all
major markets.

ＹＹＹＹＹ **Art Series Chardonnay 2002** Fragrant nectarine, citrus and melon with subtly
interwoven oak through both bouquet and palate; immaculate balance, great length. Cork.
RATING 96 **DRINK** 2012 $ 79.96

Prelude Vineyards Chardonnay 2003 Elegant, long, tightly focused nectarine and grapefruit; subtle barrel ferment oak inputs; excellent length; great value if you can't afford the Art Series. Cork. **RATING** 94 **DRINK** 2011 $ 30

ΨΨΨΨΨ **Siblings Sauvignon Blanc Semillon 2004** Fragrant, flowery lemon blossom; delicate but long palate; finely balanced acidity. **RATING** 92 **DRINK** Now $ 19.99

ΨΨΨΨ **Art Series Riesling 2004** Very pale straw-green; well balanced and made; typically restrained varietal character; won't frighten the horses. Screwcap. **RATING** 87 **DRINK** 2008 $ 23.50

Leland Estate ★★★★

PO Lenswood, SA 5240 **REGION** Adelaide Hills
T (08) 8389 6928 **WEB** www.lelandestate.com.au **OPEN** Not
WINEMAKER Robb Cootes **EST.** 1986 **CASES** 1250
SUMMARY Former Yalumba senior winemaker Robb Cootes, with a Master of Science degree, deliberately opted out of mainstream life when he established Leland Estate, living in a split-level, one-roomed house built from timber salvaged from trees killed in the Ash Wednesday bushfires. The Sauvignon Blanc is usually good. Retail distribution in Victoria, New South Wales and Queensland via Prime Wines; exports to the US, Canada and Japan.

Le 'Mins Winery NR

40 Lemins Road, Waurn Ponds, Vic 3216 (postal) **REGION** Geelong
T (03) 5241 8168 **OPEN** Not
WINEMAKER Steve Jones **EST.** 1994 **CASES** 80
SUMMARY Steve Jones presides over 0.5 ha of pinot noir planted in 1998 to the MV6 clone, and 0.25 ha of the same variety planted 4 years earlier to Burgundy clone 114. The tiny production is made for Le 'Mins at Prince Albert Vineyard, and the wine is basically sold by word of mouth.

Lengs & Cooter ★★★★☆

24 Lindsay Terrace, Belair, SA 5042 **REGION** Southeast Australia
T (08) 8278 3998 **F** (08) 8278 3998 **WEB** www.lengscooter.com.au **OPEN** Not
WINEMAKER Contract **EST.** 1993 **CASES** 8000
SUMMARY Carel Lengs and Colin Cooter began making wine as a hobby in the early 1980s. Each had (and has) a full-time occupation outside the wine industry, and it was all strictly for fun. One thing has led to another, and although they still possess neither vineyards nor what might truly be described as a winery, the wines graduated to big-boy status, winning gold medals at national wine shows and receiving critical acclaim from writers across Australia. Exports to the UK, Canada, Singapore and Malaysia.

ΨΨΨΨΨ **Reserve McLaren Vale Shiraz 2002** Medium-bodied; complex flavours; earth, bitter chocolate, spice, blackberry and plum all there; good tannins and oak. Stained cork. **RATING** 94 **DRINK** 2013 $ 45

ΨΨΨΨΨ **Watervale Riesling 2004** Spotless, aromatic lime bouquet; good structure and focus; intense lime and lemon; long, clean, fruit-driven finish. Screwcap. **RATING** 93 **DRINK** 2014 $ 16
Old Vines Clare Valley Shiraz 2002 Dense colour; powerful, concentrated, focused blackberry, prune and plum; tannins unexpectedly fine and silky. The oldest vines from 1892. Stained cork. **RATING** 93 **DRINK** 2014 $ 25
Swinton McLaren Vale Cabernet Sauvignon 2002 Powerful blackberry and bitter chocolate; has the great texture and mouthfeel of this remarkable vintage. Cork. **RATING** 92 **DRINK** 2015 $ 22

ΨΨΨΨ **Clare Valley Rose 2004** Raspberry, strawberry and cherry; good length and balance; nice dry finish. Made from old vine Grenache. Screwcap. **RATING** 87 **DRINK** Now $ 16

ΨΨΨΨ **The Victor 2003 RATING** 86 **DRINK** 2010 $ 18

Lenton Brae Wines ★★★★

Wilyabrup Valley, Margaret River, WA 6285 **REGION** Margaret River
T (08) 9755 6255 **F** (08) 9755 6268 **WEB** www.lentonbrae.com **OPEN** 7 days 10–6
WINEMAKER Edward Tomlinson **EST.** 1983 **CASES** NFP
SUMMARY Former architect and town planner Bruce Tomlinson built a strikingly beautiful winery which is now in the hands of winemaker son Edward, making elegant wines in classic Margaret River style. Retail distribution through all states, and exports to the UK, Singapore, the US and Canada.

ŶŶŶŶŶ Semillon Sauvignon Blanc 2004 Spotless, clean and crisp; minerally herb and lemon cast; lively, fresh finish; 55% Semillon, 45% Sauvignon Blanc. Screwcap. **RATING** 91 **DRINK** 2009 $18

ŶŶŶŶ Margaret River Chardonnay 2003 Medium to full-bodied; an abundance of ripe, peachy fruit and oak to match. **RATING** 89 **DRINK** 2008 $38

Leo Buring ★★★★☆

Tanunda Road, Nuriootpa, SA 5355 **REGION** Barossa Valley
T (08) 8560 9408 **F** (08) 8563 2804 **WEB** www.leoburing.com.au **OPEN** Not
WINEMAKER Matthew Pick **EST.** 1931 **CASES** NFP
SUMMARY Earns its high rating by being Australia's foremost producer of Rieslings over a 35-year period, with a rich legacy left by former winemaker John Vickery. After veering away from its core business with other varietal wines, has now been refocused as a specialist Riesling producer.

ŶŶŶŶŶ Leonay Riesling 2004 Discreet and tightly focused; mineral and lime; very good balance and length; built to stay. **RATING** 94 **DRINK** 2019 $32.95

ŶŶŶŶŶ Eden Valley Riesling 2004 Fragrant apple, spice and lime aromas; fresh and elegant; good line and length. **RATING** 93 **DRINK** 2012 $17.95
Clare Valley Riesling 2004 Solid citrus and apple aromas; powerful palate; good length and balance. **RATING** 92 **DRINK** 2010 $17.95

Lerida Estate ★★★

The Vineyards, Old Federal Highway, Lake George, NSW 2581 **REGION** Canberra District
T (02) 4848 0231 **F** (02) 4848 0232 **WEB** www.leridaestate.com **OPEN** 7 days 11–4.30, or by appointment
WINEMAKER Charles Vivet, Greg Gallagher **EST.** 1999 **CASES** 1500
SUMMARY Lerida Estate continues the planting of vineyards along the escarpment sloping down to Lake George. It is immediately to the south of the Lake George vineyard established by Edgar Riek 30 years ago. Inspired by Edgar Riek's success with pinot noir, Lerida founder Jim Lumbers has planted 6 ha of pinot noir, together with 1 ha each of chardonnay and merlot, and 0.5 ha of pinot gris (plus shiraz and cabernet franc). The Glenn Murcutt-designed winery, barrel room and cellar door complex (available for weddings and other functions) has spectacular views over Lake George.

ŶŶŶŶ Lake George Pinot Gris 2004 Water-white colour; mineral and distinct citrussy/lemony acidity off-set by fruit sweetness. Screwcap. **RATING** 88 **DRINK** 2007 $35

ŶŶŶ Lake George Chardonnay 2003 RATING 81 $22

ŶŶŶ Lake George Merlot 2002 RATING 79 $24

Lethbridge Wines ★★★★

74 Burrows Road, Lethbridge, Vic 3222 **REGION** Geelong
T (03) 5281 7221 **F** (03) 5281 7221 **WEB** www.lethbridgewines.com **OPEN** Fri–Sun & public hols 10.30–5, or by appointment
WINEMAKER Ray Nadeson, Maree Collis **EST.** 1996 **CASES** 1500
SUMMARY Lethbridge was founded by three scientists: Ray Nadeson, Maree Collis and Adrian Thomas. In Ray Nadeson's words, 'Our belief is that the best wines express the unique character of special places. With this in mind our philosophy is to practise organic principles in the vineyard complemented by traditional winemaking techniques to allow the unique character of the site to be expressed in our fruit and captured in our wine.' As well as understanding the importance of terroir,

the partners have built a unique load-bearing straw-bale winery, designed for its ability to recreate the controlled environment of cellars and caves in Europe. Winemaking is no less ecological: hand-picking, indigenous yeast fermentations, small open fermenters, pigeage (treading the grapes) and minimal handling of the wine throughout the maturation process are all part and parcel of the highly successful Lethbridge approach.

ŸŸŸŸŸ **Merlot 2003** Strong savoury herb and olive varietal aromas and flavours, with an appropriate core of small red berry fruits. **RATING** 92 **DRINK** 2010 $35
Chardonnay 2003 Strongly citrussy, lemony, fruit-driven wine, almost into sauvignon blanc flavours, but long in the mouth. **RATING** 90 **DRINK** 2009 $30
Indra Shiraz 2002 Intense, spicy black fruit/Christmas cake aromas; good finish and aftertaste. **RATING** 90 **DRINK** 2010 $38

ŸŸŸŸ **Pinot Noir 2003** Deep colour; a massive wine, slightly over-extracted. **RATING** 87 **DRINK** 2010 $28

ŸŸŸŸ **Pinot Gris 2004** **RATING** 86 **DRINK** Now $22
Shiraz 2003 **RATING** 85 **DRINK** 2008

ŸŸŸ **Rose 2004** **RATING** 83 $18

Leura Park Estate ★★★☆

1400 Portarlington Road, Curlewis, Vic 3222 **REGION** Geelong
T (03) 5253 3180 **F** (03) 5251 1262 **OPEN** Weekends 11–5
WINEMAKER Steve Webber (De Bortoli) **EST.** 1995 **CASES** 600
SUMMARY Stephen and Lisa Cross gained fame as restaurateurs in the 1990s, first at Touché and then at the outstanding Saltwater at Noosa Heads. They have established a very substantial vineyard, with 8 ha of chardonnay and 3+ ha each of pinot gris, pinot noir and sauvignon blanc, with 1 ha of shiraz yet to come into bearing. Most of the production is sold to De Bortoli, where the wines for the Leura Park label are made.

ŸŸŸŸ **25 d'Gris Pinot Gris 2004** Very powerful wine, with overtones of Alsace, and some phenolics. **RATING** 87 **DRINK** 2007 $30

ŸŸŸŸ **Sauvignon Blanc 2004** Tangy and citrussy, but very light-bodied; high acidity and suppressed varietal fruit. **RATING** 86 **DRINK** Now $18.50

Leven Valley Vineyard ★★☆

321 Raymond Road, Gunns Plains, Tas 7315 **REGION** Northern Tasmania
T (03) 6429 1186 **F** (03) 6429 1369 **WEB** www.levenvalleyvineyard.com.au **OPEN** Wed–Mon 10–5, Tues by appointment
WINEMAKER Richard Richardson (Contract) **EST.** 1997 **CASES** 700
SUMMARY John and Wendy Weatherly have acquired the former Moonrakers Vineyard from Stephen and Diana Usher, and have changed the name, but otherwise left well alone. The vineyard consists of 0.5 ha each of chardonnay and pinot noir on a north-facing slope above the picturesque valley of Gunns Plains. The deep loam over limestone soil holds much promise.

ŸŸŸ **Pinot Noir 2004** **RATING** 82
Unwooded Chardonnay 2004 **RATING** 80

Liebich Wein

Steingarten Road, Rowland Flat, SA 5352 **REGION** Barossa Valley
T (08) 8524 4543 **F** (08) 8524 4543 **WEB** www.liebichwein.com.au **OPEN** Wed–Mon 11–5
WINEMAKER Ron Liebich **EST.** 1992 **CASES** 2500
SUMMARY Liebich Wein is Barossa Deutsch for 'Love I wine'. The Liebich family have been grapegrowers and winemakers at Rowland Flat since 1919, with CW 'Darkie' Liebich one of the great local characters. His nephew Ron began making wine in 1969, but it was not until 1992 that he and his wife Janet began selling wine under the Liebich Wein label. Exports to the US, the UK and Germany.

ŸŸŸŸŸ **The Darkie Barossa Valley Shiraz 2003** Impenetrable purple-red; massive wine, way beyond normal full-bodied boundaries; prune, blackberry and plum; formidable tannins; 1.1. tonnes per acre; pray for the cork to last. **RATING** 92 **DRINK** 2018 $40

Leveret Barossa Valley Shiraz 2003 Dense, dark colour; very powerful black fruits, bitter chocolate and leather; vanilla oak in the background; carries 15.3° alcohol. Screwcap. **RATING** 90 **DRINK** 2013 $ 23

ΥΥΥΥ **Crackerjack Barossa Valley Cabernet Merlot 2003** Very ripe, robust wine; black fruits, and abundant tannins needing to soften; 85% Cabernet Sauvignon, 15% Merlot. Screwcap. **RATING** 89 **DRINK** 2013 $ 23

ΥΥΥ♀ **The Potter's Barossa Valley Merlot 2003** **RATING** 86 **DRINK** 2010
Barossa TeMPt 2004 **RATING** 85 **DRINK** 2017 $ 23
Barossa Valley Unwooded Chardonnay 2004 **RATING** 84 **DRINK** Now $ 14

ΥΥΥ **Late Picked Riesling Traminer 2004** **RATING** 83 $ 13.50

Lighthouse Peak   NR

Tumbarumba–Khancoban Road, Bringenbrong, NSW 3707 **REGION** Tumbarumba
T 0500 524 444 **F** 0500 524 445 **OPEN** Not
WINEMAKER Kerry Potocky-Pacay **EST.** 1996 **CASES** NA
SUMMARY Ian Tayles has established a 2-ha vineyard on this historic road. It is planted to sauvignon blanc, chardonnay, verdelho, pinot noir, cabernet sauvignon and merlot, and the wines are sold by mail order.

Lilac Hill Estate

55 Benara Road, Caversham, WA 6055 **REGION** Swan Valley
T (08) 9378 9945 **F** (08) 9378 9946 **WEB** www.lilachillestate.com.au **OPEN** Tues–Sun 10.30–5.00
WINEMAKER Stephen Murfit **EST.** 1998 **CASES** 15 000
SUMMARY Lilac Hill Estate is part of the renaissance which is sweeping the Swan Valley. Just when it seemed it would die a lingering death, supported only by Houghton, Sandalford and the remnants of the once Yugoslav-dominated cellar door trade, wine tourism has changed the entire scene. Thus Lilac Hill Estate, drawing in part upon 4 ha of estate vineyards, has already built a substantial business, relying on cellar door trade and limited retail distribution. Considerable contract winemaking onsite fleshes out the business even further.

ΥΥΥΥ **Reserve Noble Semillon 2000** Bright yellow-gold; only Spaetlese sweetness, but has developed well, and has time to go. Cork. **RATING** 88 **DRINK** 2010 $ 18

ΥΥΥ♀ **Swan Valley Chenin Blanc 2004** Very well made; nice gentle tropical fruit; good balance, not sweet. Screwcap. **RATING** 86 **DRINK** Now $ 15
Swan Valley White Zinfandel 2004 Better than expected, and much better than its Californian counterparts; gentle strawberry fruit, not too sweet. Curious use of zinfandel, nonetheless. Screwcap. **RATING** 86 **DRINK** Now $ 15
Cape White 2004 **RATING** 86 **DRINK** Now $ 15
Swan Valley Verdelho 2004 **RATING** 84 **DRINK** Now $ 15

Lillian

Box 174, Pemberton, WA 6260 **REGION** Pemberton
T (08) 9776 0193 **F** (08) 9776 0193 **OPEN** Not
WINEMAKER John Brocksopp **EST.** 1993 **CASES** 400
SUMMARY Long-serving (and continuing consultant) viticulturist to Leeuwin Estate John Brocksopp established 3-ha of the Rhône trio of marsanne, roussanne and viognier and the south of France trio of shiraz, mourvedre and graciano (first vintage in 1998). The varietal mix may seem à la mode, but it in fact comes from John's early experience working for Seppelt at Barooga in New South Wales, and his formative years in the Barossa Valley. The wines are sold via the (email) mailing list and word of mouth; exports to the UK through Domaine Direct.

ΥΥΥΥ♀ **Pemberton Marsanne 2003** Pale green-yellow; clean, fresh honeysuckle; finely chiselled and balanced; long finish, very impressive. Cork. **RATING** 92 **DRINK** 2010
Shiraz Mataro 2001 Good colour; medium-bodied; supple texture and mouthfeel; spicy black cherry fruit; fine, ripe tannins. Quality cork. **RATING** 91 **DRINK** 2011 $ 21
Pemberton Marsanne Roussanne 2004 Lively, fresh lemony aspects; honeysuckle, a touch of mineral and chalk; good balance and finish. Cork. **RATING** 90 **DRINK** 2009

Lilliput Wines NR

Withers Road, Springhurst, Vic 3602 **REGION** Rutherglen
T (03) 5726 5055 **F** (03) 5726 5056 **OPEN** By appointment
WINEMAKER P Hellema **EST.** 2002 **CASES** NA
SUMMARY The Hellema family has established 6 ha of cabernet sauvignon, merlot, shiraz and petit verdot. The as-yet tiny production is sold by mail order and through the cellar door.

Lillydale Estate ★★★★

45 Davross Court, Seville, Vic 3139 **REGION** Yarra Valley
T (03) 5964 2016 **F** (03) 5964 3009 **WEB** www.mcwilliams.com.au **OPEN** 7 days 11–5
WINEMAKER Jim Brayne, Max McWilliam **EST.** 1975 **CASES** NFP
SUMMARY Acquired by McWilliam's Wines in 1994; Max McWilliam is in charge of the business. With a number of other major developments, notably Coonawarra and Barwang, on its plate, McWilliam's has adopted a softly, softly approach to Lillydale Estate; a winery restaurant opened in February 1997.

🍷🍷🍷🍷🍷 **Sauvignon Blanc 2004** Fragrant and delicately crisp herb, citrus and passionfruit aromas and flavours. **RATING** 93 **DRINK** Now **$** 20

🍷🍷🍷🍷 **Cabernet Merlot 2002** Cool-grown savoury/earthy/leafy aromas and flavours; medium-bodied; savoury tannins. **RATING** 88 **DRINK** 2009

Rose 2004 Clean, fresh, bright and crisp red berries and pleasing minerally finish. **RATING** 87 **DRINK** Now **$** 18

Lillypilly Estate ★★★★

Lillypilly Road, Leeton, NSW 2705 **REGION** Riverina
T (02) 6953 4069 **F** (02) 6953 4980 **WEB** www.lillypilly.com **OPEN** Mon–Sat 10–5.30, Sun by appointment
WINEMAKER Robert Fiumara **EST.** 1982 **CASES** 15 000
SUMMARY Botrytised white wines are by far the best from Lillypilly, with the Noble Muscat of Alexandria unique to the winery; these wines have both style and intensity of flavour and can age well. However, table wine quality is always steady. Exports to the UK, the US and Canada.

🍷🍷🍷🍷🍷 **Noble Blend 2003** Rich cumquat, mandarin and peach; not excessively luscious but quite intense; good balancing acidity. Screwcap. **RATING** 91 **DRINK** 2007 **$** 27.30

Noble Muscat of Alexandria 2003 Glowing yellow-green; very rich and complex; candied fruit off-set by good acidity. **RATING** 90 **DRINK** 2008 **$** 16.50

Noble Riesling 2003 Orange, lime, mandarin and citrus mix; vibrant palate, good acidity. Screwcap. **RATING** 90 **DRINK** 2007 **$** 18.75

Noble Blend 2002 Botrytis influence evident; very complex; some bottle development adding; long, lingering finish. **RATING** 90 **DRINK** 2008 **$** 22.50

🍷🍷🍷🍷 **Petit Verdot 2002** Strong licorice and anise aromas, somewhat atypical; plenty of colour and black fruit flavour; sweet, ripe tannins. **RATING** 88 **DRINK** 2012 **$** 16.50

Sauvignon Blanc 2003 Light but positive varietal fruit expression on both bouquet and palate; tropical flavours balanced by acidity; well made. **RATING** 87 **DRINK** Now **$** 14.50

Petit Verdot 2003 Fresh, juicy black fruits and a touch of chocolate; light to medium-bodied, but good tannin structure. **RATING** 87 **DRINK** 2008 **$** 16.50

🍷🍷🍷🍷 **Chardonnay 2002** Still remarkably fresh; melon, fig and stone fruit; sweetness for the cellar door. **RATING** 86 **DRINK** 2007 **$** 14.50

Chardonnay 2003 **RATING** 85 **DRINK** Now **$** 14.50

Red Velvet 2002 **RATING** 85 **DRINK** Now **$** 13.50

Lilyvale Wines ★★★☆

Riverton Road, via Texas, Qld 4385 **REGION** Darling Downs
T (07) 3391 1848 **F** (07) 3391 3903 **WEB** www.lilyvalewines.com **OPEN** By appointment 10–4
WINEMAKER John Hordern, Peter Scudamore-Smith MW (Contract) **EST.** 1997 **CASES** 4000

SUMMARY Yet another new but substantial winery in Queensland. It has established 5 ha each of shiraz and chardonnay, 3 ha of cabernet sauvignon, around 2.5 ha each of semillon and verdelho, and 1.5 ha of merlot. The vineyard is near the Dumaresq River on the border between Queensland and New South Wales. Exports to the US, Canada, Singapore and Japan.

TTTT **Silver Downs Semillon 2003** Clear varietal character on the bouquet and palate; solid grass, herb and lemon; just a tad phenolic, but impressive nonetheless. Screwcap. **RATING** 88 **DRINK** 2009 $15

Watson's Crossing Chardonnay 2003 Stone fruit flavours; subtle oak influence; fractionally hard acidity. **RATING** 87 **DRINK** Now $15

Inca's Lily Verdelho 2003 Fresh and clean; light to medium-bodied; gentle tropical fruit salad flavours. **RATING** 87 **DRINK** Now $15

Limbic ★★★★☆

295 Morrison Road, Pakenham Upper, Vic 3810 **REGION** Port Phillip Zone
T (03) 5942 7723 **F** (03) 5942 7723 **OPEN** By appointment
WINEMAKER Michael Pullar **EST.** 1997 **CASES** 600
SUMMARY Jennifer and Michael Pullar have established a vineyard on the hills between Yarra Valley and Gippsland, overlooking the Mornington Peninsula and Westernport Bay (thus entitled only to the Port Phillip Zone appellation). They have planted 3.1 ha of pinot noir, 1.8 ha of chardonnay and 1.3 ha of sauvignon blanc, increasingly using organic and thereafter biodynamic practices. The first 5 years of grape production was sold, with trial vintages under the Limbic label commencing in 2001, followed by the first commercial releases in 2003. A winery and cellar door have been constructed, and the 2005 vintage was made onsite; production will now increase from 600 to 1200 cases. 'Limbic' is the word for a network of neural pathways in the brain that link smell, taste and emotion.

TTTTT **Sauvignon Blanc 2004** Clean, fresh, crisp and lively; lovely gooseberry, kiwifruit and lemon juice mix; long finish; something special. Quality cork. **RATING** 95 **DRINK** 2008 $20

TTTTY **Chardonnay 2003** Bright green-yellow; light to medium-bodied; gentle melon and nectarine fruit; subtle French oak; very good length and balance. High-quality cork. **RATING** 93 **DRINK** 2010 $30

Pinot Noir 2003 Clear-cut black cherry and plum varietal expression to both bouquet and palate; perfectly handled oak and extract. High-quality cork. **RATING** 93 **DRINK** 2009 $30

Limb Vineyards NR

PO Box 145, Greenock, SA 5360 **REGION** Barossa Valley
T 0419 846 549 **F** (08) 8347 7484 **OPEN** Not
WINEMAKER Contract **EST.** 1997 **CASES** NA
SUMMARY Julie Limb manages the business, based on 15 ha of cabernet sauvignon, shiraz and mourvedre. The wines are contract-made, the principal market being the US; they are available by mail order within Australia.

Lindemans (Coonawarra) ★★★★

Memorial Drive, Coonawarra, SA 5263 **REGION** Coonawarra
T (08) 8737 2613 **F** (08) 8737 2959 **WEB** www.lindemans.com.au **OPEN** Not
WINEMAKER Greg Clayfield **EST.** 1908 **CASES** NFP
SUMMARY Lindemans is clearly the strongest brand other than Penfolds (and perhaps Rosemount) in the Southcorp Group, with some great vineyards and a great history. The Coonawarra vineyards are of ever-increasing significance because of the move towards regional identity in the all-important export markets, which has led to the emergence of a new range of regional/varietal labels. Whether the fullest potential of the vineyards (from a viticultural viewpoint) is being realised has been a matter of debate, but there are distinct signs of change for the better. Exports to all major markets.

TTTTY **Rouge Homme Cabernet Sauvignon 2003** A supple and rich range of red fruits through to blackcurrant; medium-bodied; subtle oak, savoury tannins, good length. **RATING** 90 **DRINK** 2008 $14.99

TTTT **Rouge Homme Shiraz Cabernet 2003** Soft blackberry and plum fruit on entry, followed by a somewhat tannic finish. **RATING** 87 **DRINK** 2008 $14.99

Rouge Homme Cabernet Merlot 2003 Quite juicy, ripe red and black fruits; minimal oak and tannin inputs; easy style. **RATING** 87 **DRINK** 2007 $14.99

Rouge Homme Cabernet Merlot 2002 Ample blackcurrant and mulberry fruit, with touches of chocolate and earth; soft tannins. **RATING** 87 **DRINK** 2008 $14.99

Lindemans (Hunter Valley) ★★★☆

McDonalds Road, Pokolbin, NSW 2320 **REGION** Lower Hunter Valley

T (02) 4998 7684 **F** (02) 4998 7324 **WEB** www.lindemans.com.au **OPEN** 7 days 10–5

WINEMAKER Wayne Falkenberg, Greg Clayfield **EST.** 1843 **CASES** NFP

SUMMARY One way or another, I have intersected with the Hunter Valley in general and Lindemans in particular for almost 50 years. The wines are no longer made in the Lower Hunter, and the once mighty Semillon is a mere shadow of its former self. However, the refurbished historic Ben Ean winery (while no longer making wine) is a must-see for the wine tourist.

Lindemans (Karadoc) ★★★

Edey Road, Karadoc via Red Cliffs, Vic 3496 **REGION** Murray Darling

T (03) 5051 3333 **F** (03) 5051 3390 **WEB** www.lindemans.com **OPEN** 7 days 10–4.30

WINEMAKER Greg Clayfield, Wayne Falkenberg **EST.** 1974 **CASES** 8 million

SUMMARY Now the production centre for all the Lindemans and Leo Buring wines, with the exception of special lines made in Coonawarra. The very large winery allows all-important economies of scale, and is the major processing centre for Southcorp's beverage wine sector (casks, flagons and low-priced bottles). Its achievement in making several million cases of Bin 65 Chardonnay a year is extraordinary given the quality and consistency of the wines. Exports to all major markets.

TTTT **Bin 50 Shiraz 2003** Deep purple-red colour; surprising depth and fruit concentration; blackberry and plum fruit; minimal oak. Excellent value; do not cellar (synthetic cork). **RATING** 88 **DRINK** Now $8.99

Bin 95 Sauvignon Blanc 2004 Obvious tropical varietal fruit on both bouquet and palate; a slightly thick finish does not unduly detract from the overall impact. **RATING** 87 **DRINK** Now $8.99

TTTY **Bin 65 Chardonnay 2004** **RATING** 86 **DRINK** Now $8.99

Bin 35 Rose 2004 **RATING** 86 **DRINK** Now $8.99

Bin 50 Shiraz 2004 **RATING** 85 **DRINK** Now $8.99

TTT **Bin 55 Shiraz Cabernet 2003** **RATING** 83 $8.99

Lindemans (Padthaway) ★★★☆

Naracoorte Road, Padthaway, SA 5271 **REGION** Padthaway

T (02) 4998 7684 **F** (02) 4998 7682 **WEB** www.lindemans.com.au **OPEN** Not

WINEMAKER Greg Clayfield **EST.** 1908 **CASES** NFP

SUMMARY Lindemans Padthaway Chardonnay is one of the better premium Chardonnays on the market in Australia, with a proven capacity to age. However, all the wines under the Padthaway label offer consistent quality and value for money.

TTTT **Padthaway Reserve Shiraz 2003** Quite elegant and well balanced; medium-bodied; fine black fruits and tannins; good value. **RATING** 87 **DRINK** 2008 $12.99

Limestone Coast Reserve Cabernet Merlot 2002 Slightly savoury and lean, but redeemed by its balance and good length. **RATING** 87 **DRINK** 2009 $12.50

TTTY **Reserve Limestone Coast Chardonnay 2003** **RATING** 86 **DRINK** Now $12.50

Lindenderry at Red Hill NR

142 Arthurs Seat Road, Red Hill, Vic 3937 **REGION** Mornington Peninsula

T (03) 5989 2933 **F** (03) 5989 2936 **WEB** www.lindenderry.com.au **OPEN** 7 days 11–5

WINEMAKER Lindsay McCall (Paringa Estate) **EST.** 1999 **CASES** 1500

SUMMARY Lindenderry at Red Hill is a sister operation to Lancemore Hill in the Macedon Ranges and Lindenwarrah at Milawa. It has a 5-star country house hotel, conference facilities, a function area, day spa and à la carte restaurant on 16 ha of park-like gardens, but also has a little over 3 ha of vineyards, planted equally to pinot noir and chardonnay 10 years ago. The wines are made by the famed Lindsay McCall, using similar techniques to those he uses for his estate wines.

Lindrum ★★★

c/- Level 29, Chifley Tower, 2 Chifley Square, Sydney, NSW 2000 (postal) **REGION** Langhorne Creek
T (02) 9375 2185 **F** (02) 9375 2121 **WEB** www.lindrum.com **OPEN** Not
WINEMAKER Michael Potts (Bleasdale Winery) **EST.** 2001 **CASES** 12 000
SUMMARY The Lindrum story is a fascinating one; few Australians will not have heard of Walter Lindrum, who reigned as World Professional Billiards and Snooker Champion for over 30 years. What few would know is that his great-grandfather, Frederick Wilhelm von Lindrum, was a renowned vigneron in Norwood, South Australia, and also became Australia's first professional billiards champion, beating the English champion, John Roberts, in 1869. The wines are made from purchased grapes by Michael Potts at his Bleasdale Winery; distribution through an active website and retail sources.

🐌 Linfield Road Wines ★★★★☆

PO Box 6, Williamstown, SA 5351 **REGION** Barossa Valley
T (08) 8524 6140 **F** (08) 8524 6427 **WEB** www.annandalevineyards.com.au **OPEN** Not
WINEMAKER Steve Wilson, Deb Wilson **EST.** 2002 **CASES** 1500
SUMMARY The Wilson family has been growing grapes at their estate vineyard for over 100 years; Steve and Deb Wilson are the fourth generation of Wilson vignerons. The vineyard is in one of the coolest parts of the Barossa Valley, in an elevated position near the Adelaide Hills boundary. The estate's 19 ha are planted to riesling, cabernet sauvignon, semillon, shiraz, merlot, grenache and chardonnay. In 2002 the Wilsons decided to vinify part of the production. Within 12 months of the release of the first wines under the Linfield Road label, the wines had accumulated three trophies and five gold medals. While there is B&B accommodation on the property, there is as yet no cellar door; the wines are sold through the website, and by a few restaurants and retailers in South Australia.

🍷🍷🍷🍷 **Limited Release Merlot 2002** Solid blackcurrant and blackberry fruit; considerable depth and length; power and presence. **RATING** 94 **DRINK** 2012 $ 25

🍷🍷🍷🍷 **Limited Release Shiraz 2002** Medium-bodied; silky, supple red and black fruits; very good line and length; fruit-driven. Stained cork. **RATING** 92 **DRINK** 2012 $ 28
Limited Release Cabernet Sauvignon 2002 Full-bodied; powerful, ripe blackcurrant/blackberry fruit supported by solid, sweet, ripe tannins and vanilla oak. Stained cork. **RATING** 90 **DRINK** 2012 $ 19

🍷🍷🍷🍷 **Limited Release Chardonnay 2003** Well above average for the region; still has fresh melon and stone fruit flavour; crisp finish. Screwcap. **RATING** 87 **DRINK** Now $ 16

Lirralirra Estate ★★★★

15 Paynes Road, Chirnside Park, Vic 3116 **REGION** Yarra Valley
T (03) 9735 0224 **F** (03) 9735 0224 **OPEN** Weekends & hols 10–6, Jan 7 days
WINEMAKER Alan Smith **EST.** 1981 **CASES** 400
SUMMARY Alan Smith started Lirralirra with the intention of specialising in a Sauternes-style blend of botrytised semillon and sauvignon blanc. It seemed a good idea – in a sense it still does on paper – but it simply didn't work. He has had to change direction to a more conventional mix, but has done so with dignity and humour.

🍷🍷🍷🍷 **Sauvignon Blanc 2004** Clean, fresh; good varietal expression on the bouquet; excellent drive to gooseberry, kiwifruit and snow pea palate. **RATING** 93 **DRINK** 2008 $ 19
Reserve Pinot Noir 2003 Deep colour; very intense, complex and powerful, but has good balance; rich plum and black cherry, then a suggestion of slightly dank oak. Controversial. **RATING** 90 **DRINK** 2014 $ 30

🍷🍷🍷🍷 **Semillon 2004** Clean, tight, reserved style; citrus rind, some stone/mineral notes; good length. **RATING** 89 **DRINK** 2010 $ 19
Semillon Sauvignon Blanc 2003 Pale straw-green; clean and highly aromatic herb and mineral aromas; plenty of flavour, but toughens off slightly on the finish. **RATING** 87 **DRINK** Now $ 19

Little Brampton Wines ★★★★

PO Box 61, Clare, SA 5453 **REGION** Clare Valley
T (08) 8843 4201 **F** (08) 8843 4244 **WEB** www.littlebramptonwines.com.au **OPEN** Not
WINEMAKER Contract **EST.** 2001 **CASES** 800
SUMMARY Little Brampton Wines is a boutique, family-owned business operated by Alan and Pamela Schwarz. They purchased their 24-ha property in the heart of the Clare Valley in the early 1990s; Alan graduated from Roseworthy in 1981. The property has produced grapes since the 1860s, but the vineyard had been removed during the Vine Pull Scheme of the 1980s. The Schwarzes have replanted 10 ha to riesling, shiraz and cabernet sauvignon on northwest slopes at 520m; a small proportion of the production is vinified for the Little Brampton label. Available at selected restaurants, mail order or from the website.

♥♥♥♥♀ **Shiraz 2003** Good colour; flooded with sweet plum and blackberry fruit; vanilla oak in support; good acidity. Screwcap. **RATING** 91 **DRINK** 2013 $ 24

♥♥♥♥ **Riesling 2004** A quiet beginning; springs to life on the palate; lime, slate mix; good length and intensity. Screwcap. **RATING** 89 **DRINK** 2010 $ 19
Cabernet Sauvignon 2003 Light to medium-bodied; savoury berry fruit with some earthy tones sweetened by oak; fine, ripe tannins. **RATING** 87 **DRINK** 2012 $ 22

Little Bridge ★★★★

PO Box 499, Bungendore, NSW 2621 **REGION** Canberra District
T (02) 6251 5242 **F** (02) 6251 4379 **WEB** www.littlebridgewines.com.au **OPEN** Not
WINEMAKER Greg Gallagher (Jeir Creek Winery), Sue Carpenter, David Carpenter (Lark Hill Winery), John Leyshon **EST.** 1996 **CASES** 1000
SUMMARY Little Bridge Vineyard is a partnership between long-term friends John and Val Leyshon, and Rowland and Madeleine Clark. The establishment date of 1996 marks the formation of the business partnership; 2 ha of Chardonnay, Pinot Noir, Riesling and Merlot were planted in 1997 on Rowland Clark's property at Butmaroo near Bungendore, at a height of 860m. A further 2.5 ha were planted in the spring of 2004. Greg Gallagher makes the white wines; the Pinot Noir is made by Sue and David Carpenter, in each case with John Leyshon in close attendance.

Little River Estate NR

c/- 147 Rankins Road, Kensington, Vic 3031 (postal) **REGION** Upper Goulburn
T 0418 381 722 **OPEN** Not
WINEMAKER Philip Challen, Oscar Rosa, Nick Arena **EST.** 1986 **CASES** 250
SUMMARY Philip (a chef and hotelier) and Christine Challen began the establishment of their vineyard in 1986 with the planting of 0.5 ha of cabernet sauvignon. Several years later, 2 ha of chardonnay (and a few vines of pinot noir) followed. Vineyard practice and soil management are based on organic principles; there are low yields, notwithstanding the age of the vines. While made in small quantities, they are available in virtually every hotel, restaurant and liquor store in the region, and in a considerable number of outlets in Melbourne.

Little River Wines NR

Cnr West Swan Road/Forest Road, Henley Brook, WA 6055 **REGION** Swan Valley
T (08) 9296 4462 **F** (08) 9296 1022 **WEB** www.littleriverwinery.com **OPEN** 7 days 10–5
WINEMAKER Bruno de Tastes **EST.** 1934 **CASES** 3000
SUMMARY The former Glenalwyn now has as its winemaker the eponymously named Count Bruno de Tastes; the wines come from 4 ha of estate vineyards. Exports to Hong Kong and Malaysia.

Littles ★★★☆

Cnr Palmers Lane/McDonalds Road, Pokolbin, NSW 2321 **REGION** Lower Hunter Valley
T (02) 4998 7626 **F** (02) 4998 7867 **WEB** www.littleswinery.com.au **OPEN** Fri–Mon 10–4.30
WINEMAKER Contract **EST.** 1984 **CASES** 6000

SUMMARY Littles winery is owned and operated by Peter Kindred, who acquired it in or about 2000. The Kindred family has 41 ha of vines, and part of the production is vinified under the Littles brand, the trademark of a company owned by Peter Kindred.

ΨΨΨΨ **Semillon Sauvignon Blanc 2004** Light-bodied and fresh; more at the herbaceous than tropical end of the spectrum; bright, brisk finish. Hunter Valley Semillon/Tumbarumba Sauvignon Blanc. Screwcap. **RATING** 89 **DRINK** 2009 $ 16
Hunter Valley Gewurztraminer 2002 Crisp, clean, fresh and lively; a touch of citrus, but little or no varietal character. Screwcap. **RATING** 87 **DRINK** 2008 $ 16
Hunter Valley Reserve Shiraz 2003 Light to medium-bodied; blackberry, plum and raspberry; nicely balanced though not intense; subtle oak. Quality cork. **RATING** 87 **DRINK** 2009 $ 24
Hunter Valley Dessert Semillon 2002 Bright green-gold; moderately luscious wine; nice lemony acidity; good balance. **RATING** 87 **DRINK** 2008 $ 18

ΨΨΨΨ **Hunter Valley Reserve Shiraz 2002** **RATING** 86 **DRINK** 2010 $ 24
Hunter Valley Reserve Shiraz 2001 **RATING** 85 **DRINK** 2008 $ 24
Hunter Valley Cabernet Shiraz Merlot 2002 **RATING** 85 **DRINK** 208 $ 16

Little Valley ★★★★

RMB 6047, One Chain Road, Merricks North, Vic 3926 **REGION** Mornington Peninsula
T (03) 5989 7564 **F** (03) 5989 7564 **OPEN** By appointment
WINEMAKER Richard McIntyre (Moorooduc) **EST.** 1998 **CASES** 600
SUMMARY Wesley College teacher Sue Taylor and part-time Anglican minister husband Brian have planted 0.8 ha each of chardonnay and pinot noir on their Little Valley property, simultaneously building their house there. They have Ian MacRae as consultant viticulturist, and Rick McIntyre makes the wines. The Mornington Peninsula is a beautiful place, and the Little Valley property itself a prime example of that beauty, providing a return which cannot be measured in dollars and cents.

ΨΨΨΨ **Mornington Peninsula Chardonnay 2003** Complex wine, with obvious barrel fermentation; plenty of flavour and richness; the Achilles heel is a touch of sweetness. **RATING** 91 **DRINK** 2009 $ 20

ΨΨΨΨ **Mornington Peninsula Chardonnay 2004** Light to medium-bodied; clean, fresh, gentle stone fruit; subtle touches of spice, cashew and cream; will build. Diam. **RATING** 89 **DRINK** 2008 $ 25
Mornington Peninsula Pinot Noir 2004 Very good colour; medium-bodied; plenty of plum and rich black cherry fruit; fraction extractive, suggesting some juice run-off. Diam. **RATING** 89 **DRINK** 2009 $ 25

Llangibby Estate ★★★☆

Old Mount Barker Road, Echunga, SA 5153 **REGION** Adelaide Hills
T (08) 8338 5529 **F** (08) 8338 7118 **WEB** www.llangibbyestate.com **OPEN** By appointment
WINEMAKER Ben Riggs (Contract) **EST.** 1998 **CASES** 13000
SUMMARY Chris Addams Williams and John Williamson have established a substantial vineyard cresting a ridge close to Echunga, at a height of 360m. The varietal choice is eclectic, the lion's share to a little over 5 ha each of shiraz and cabernet sauvignon, then 1.95 ha of tempranillo, 1.4 ha of sauvignon blanc, and a tiny planting of pinot noir. Until 2002 this was used to provide a Pinot Hermitage blend, but from that year both a varietal Tempranillo and Pinot Noir have joined the product range alongside Sauvignon Blanc and Shiraz Cabernet. Exports to the UK.

ΨΨΨΨ **Adelaide Hills Sauvignon Blanc 2004** Spotlessly clean aromas; a citrus and gooseberry fruit mix off-set by crisp acidity; good length. Screwcap. **RATING** 88 **DRINK** 2007 $ 19
Adelaide Hills Red Talbot 2003 Light to medium-bodied; fresh, juicy redcurrant, raspberry and cherry fruit, allied with some spicy notes. Predominantly Tempranillo. Interesting wine. **RATING** 87 **DRINK** Now $ 13

ΨΨΨΨ **Adelaide Hills Pinot Noir 03/02** **RATING** 85 **DRINK** Now $ 8

Loch Luna   NR

Morgan Road, Overland Corner, SA 5345 **REGION** Riverland
T (08) 8588 7210 **F** (08) 8588 7210 **WEB** www.riverland.net.au/~lochluna **OPEN** By appointment
most days 1–5
WINEMAKER Grant Semmens (Contract) **EST.** 1999 **CASES** NA
SUMMARY Raymond Neindorf and Louise Spangler run a small eco-business taking full advantage of the
national heritage-listed wetlands reserves; Loch Luna Eco-Stay is part of the world network of
biosphere reserves. A cottage for 2–3 people is 300m from the homestead/cellar door. The wines come
from 10 ha of vineyards, and are made in limited quantities. The website gives full details of the venture.

Lochmoore   ★★★☆

PO Box 430, Trafalgar, Vic 3824 **REGION** Gippsland
T 0402 216 622 **OPEN** Not
WINEMAKER Owen Schmidt (Contract) **EST.** 1997 **CASES** NA
SUMMARY The 2 ha of chardonnay and pinot noir at Lochmoore are tended by one of the most highly
qualified viticulturists one is ever likely to meet. Sue Hasthorpe grew up in Trafalgar, but went on to
obtain a Bachelor of Science (Hons) and Doctor of Philosophy in Physiology at the University of
Melbourne; then she worked and travelled as a medical research scientist in Australia, the UK, the
US and Europe, including a year at the Pasteur Institute in Paris, and after returning to Australia
studied viticulture via the University of Melbourne Dookie College campus (by distance education).
If this were not enough, she is now doing a Masters of Agribusiness at the University of Melbourne.
The wines are sold through a number of local restaurants and shops, and by mail order.

▼▼▼▼   **Pinot Noir 2003** Light colour, good hue; light-bodied but clear varietal definition; spicy
        wild strawberries; not forced. **RATING** 87 **DRINK** 2008 $ 18

▼▼▼▽   **Chardonnay 2003 RATING** 85 **DRINK** Now $ 16

Logan Wines   ★★★☆

1320 Castlereagh Highway, Mudgee, NSW 2850 **REGION** Orange
T (02) 9958 1817 **F** (02) 9958 1258 **WEB** www.loganwines.com.au **OPEN** Weekends 10–4
WINEMAKER Peter Logan **EST.** 1997 **CASES** 20 000
SUMMARY Logan Wines is a family operation, founded by businessman Mal Logan and assisted by
three of his children: Peter, who just happens to be an oenology graduate from the University of
Adelaide, Greg (advertising) and Kylie (office administrator). Retail distribution in all states; exports
to the UK, the US, Canada, Germany, Sweden, New Zealand, Singapore and Hong Kong.

▼▼▼▼   **Orange Shiraz 2001** Medium-bodied; distinctly savoury, spicy notes to both fruit and
        tannins; a mix of mulberry, raspberry and blackberry fruit. Quality cork. **RATING** 89 **DRINK**
        2009 $ 20.95
        Orange Chardonnay 2001 Light-bodied; still youthful and fresh; a mix of apple, melon
        and citrus, with the barest flick of vanilla oak. Screwcap. **RATING** 88 **DRINK** 2007 $ 19.95
        M Cuvee 1999 Fragrant spicy strawberry aromas; bright, fresh and crisp; lemony acidity.
        Chardonnay/Pinot Noir/Pinot Meunier. **RATING** 88 **DRINK** Now $ 25
        Apple Tree Flat Semillon Sauvignon Blanc 2004 Spotlessly clean aromas; very light-
        bodied, but has varietal character, and considerable length. Mudgee/Orange blend. Good
        value. **RATING** 87 **DRINK** Now $ 9.95
        Hannah Rose 2004 Good colour; light-bodied; fresh, clean red fruits; relatively crisp and
        dry. Cork. **RATING** 87 **DRINK** Now $ 17.95
        Orange Cabernet Merlot 1999 Light-bodied; some elegance and bottle development;
        savoury, lemony berry fruit and fine tannins. **RATING** 87 **DRINK** Now $ 19.95

▼▼▼▽   **Orange Sauvignon Blanc 2004 RATING** 86 **DRINK** Now $ 17.95

London Lodge Estate   NR

Muswellbrook Road, Gungal, NSW 2333 **REGION** Upper Hunter Valley
T (02) 6547 6122 **F** (02) 6547 6122 **OPEN** 7 days 10–9
WINEMAKER Gary Reed (Contract) **EST.** 1988 **CASES** NA

SUMMARY The 16-ha vineyard of Stephen and Joanne Horner is planted to Chardonnay, Pinot Noir, Shiraz and Cabernet Sauvignon, and sold through a cellar door (and restaurant) with a full array of tourist attractions, including arts and crafts.

🐦 Lone Crow Wines ★★★☆

RSM 343, Busselton, WA 6280 (postal) **REGION** Geographe
T (08) 9753 3023 **F** (08) 9753 3032 **OPEN** Not
WINEMAKER Mark Messenger (Contract) **EST.** 1996 **CASES** 600
SUMMARY The Kennedy (David and Michelle) and Espinos (Kim and Jodie) families progressively established 14 ha of sauvignon blanc, semillon, shiraz, merlot and cabernet sauvignon between 1996 and 1999 in the foothills of the Whicher Ranges, 15 km inland from Busselton. Most of the grapes are sold, principally to Evans & Tate; limited quantities are made under the Lone Crow label.

ꔼꔼꔼꔼ **Shiraz 2003** Light to medium-bodied; spice, pepper and black fruits; fine, savoury tannins. **RATING** 87 **DRINK** 2008 $18

ꔼꔼꔼꔼ **Cabernet Sauvignon 2003** **RATING** 86 **DRINK** 2007 $18
Semillon Sauvignon Blanc 2004 **RATING** 85 **DRINK** Now $12.50

🐦 Longboard Wines NR

520 Great Ocean Road, Bellbrae, Vic 3228 **REGION** Geelong
T (03) 5264 8480 **F** (03) 5222 6182 **WEB** www.bellbraeestate.com.au **OPEN** Weekends 11–5 (winter), Thurs–Mon 11–5 (summer)
WINEMAKER Matthew di Sciascio, Peter Flewellyn **EST.** 1999 **CASES** 1800
SUMMARY Longboard Wines (also known as Bellbrae Estate) is the venture of two friends, Richard Macdougall and Matthew di Sciascio, both with strong family connections to the nearby beach and surfing. Sharing a common love of wine, surf and coastal life, they decided to establish a vineyard and produce their own wine. In 1998 Richard Macdougall purchased a small sheep grazing property with 8 ha of fertile, sheltered north-facing slopes on the Great Ocean Road near Bellbrae, and with Matthew's help as business associate, Bellbrae Estate was born. The early vintages, from 1999, were made from purchased grapes in shared winery space, but from 2003 all the wines have been Geelong-sourced, and include estate Shiraz and Pinot Noir. A cellar door and micro-winery were opened in 2004.

Long Gully Estate ★★★★

Long Gully Road, Healesville, Vic 3777 **REGION** Yarra Valley
T (03) 9510 5798 **F** (03) 9510 9859 **WEB** www.longgullyestate.com **OPEN** 7 days 11–5
WINEMAKER Luke Houlihan **EST.** 1982 **CASES** 16 000
SUMMARY One of the larger Yarra Valley producers to have successfully established a number of export markets, doubtless due to a core of mature vineyards; it is able to offer a range of wines with 2–3 years' bottle age. Recent vineyard extensions underline Long Gully's commercial success. Exports to the UK, Switzerland and Singapore.

ꔼꔼꔼꔼꔼ **Yarra Valley Pinot Noir 2003** Relatively forward style; strong whole-bunch/stem characters and a touch of tomato vine; in a particular, but complex, style. **RATING** 90 **DRINK** 2010 $20
Yarra Valley Shiraz 2001 Gently spicy, ripe, soft plum and black fruits; some mocha and vanilla; elegant, light to medium-bodied wine. Cork. **RATING** 90 **DRINK** 2009 $20
Reserve Ice Riesling 2003 Clean, fresh, intense luscious tropical riesling fruit; good length and balance. Cork. **RATING** 90 **DRINK** 2007 $17.90

ꔼꔼꔼꔼ **Yarra Valley Sauvignon Blanc Semillon 2003** Clean and fresh cut grass, mineral and kiwifruit; light-bodied, but well balanced. Indifferent cork. **RATING** 89 **DRINK** Now $16.50
Yarra Valley Chardonnay 2003 Quite intense and powerful; melon grapefruit, minimal oak; 14.5° alcohol heats the finish somewhat. Indifferent cork. **RATING** 89 **DRINK** 2008 $20

Long Point Vineyard NR

6 Cooinda Place, Lake Cathie, NSW 2445 **REGION** Hastings River
T (02) 6585 4598 **F** (02) 6584 8915 **OPEN** Thurs–Sun & public hols 10–6, or by appointment
WINEMAKER Graeme Davies **EST.** 1995 **CASES** 600

SUMMARY In turning their dream into reality, Graeme (an educational psychologist) and Helen (a chartered accountant) Davies took no chances. After becoming interested in wine as consumers through wine appreciation courses, the Davies moved from Brisbane so that 36-year-old Graeme could begin his study for a postgraduate diploma in wine from Roseworthy. Late in 1993 they purchased a 5-ha property near Lake Cathie, progressively establishing 2 ha of chardonnay, shiraz, chambourcin, cabernet sauvignon and frontignac. As well as having a full-time job at Cassegrain and establishing the vineyard, Graeme Davies built the house, which was designed by Helen and has a pyramid-shaped roof and an underground cellar. All the wines are made onsite.

Longview Vineyard ★★★★

Pound Road, Macclesfield, SA 5153 **REGION** Adelaide Hills
T (08) 8388 9694 **F** (08) 8388 9693 **WEB** www.longviewvineyard.com.au **OPEN** Sunday 11–5, or by appointment
WINEMAKER Shaw & Smith, Kangarilla Road (Contract) **EST.** 1995 **CASES** 8500
SUMMARY In a strange twist of fate, Longview Vineyard came to be through the success of Two Dogs, the lemon-flavoured alcohol drink created by Duncan MacGillivray and sold in 1995 to the Pernod Ricard Group (also the owners of Orlando). Over 60 ha have been planted: shiraz and cabernet sauvignon account for a little over half, and there are significant plantings of chardonnay and merlot, and smaller plantings of viognier, semillon, riesling, sauvignon blanc, zinfandel and nebbiolo. The majority of the production is sold to Southcorp, but $1.2 million has been invested in a cellar door and function area, barrel rooms and an administration centre for the Group's activities. All the buildings have a spectacular view over the Coorong and Lake Alexandrina. Exports to the UK, the US and Canada.

ΤΤΤΤ **Single Vineyard Blue Cow Chardonnay 2004** Delicate yet intense nectarine and citrus fruit travels right across the palate; very stylish. Screwcap. **RATING** 89 **DRINK** 2008 $ 19.90
Single Vineyard Yakka Shiraz Viognier 2003 Medium-bodied; fragrant and lifted; the small percentage of Viognier works very well; spice and apricot nuances all soften the wine; user-friendly, has length. **RATING** 89 **DRINK** 2009 $ 27.50
Single Vineyard Iron Knob Riesling 2004 Clean, crisp, minerally aromas and flavours; good acidity the main feature, providing length. May develop. Screwcap. **RATING** 88 **DRINK** 2010 $ 22.10
Red Bucket Semillon Sauvignon Blanc 2004 Above-average intensity for the vintage; sweet citrus fruit; lemony/minerally finish. Screwcap. **RATING** 88 **DRINK** 2007 $ 16.25
Yakka Single Vineyard Shiraz 2003 Light to medium-bodied; spicy, savoury style belies the 14.5° alcohol; elegant palate, good length, but lacking richness. Stained cork. **RATING** 88 **DRINK** 2010 $ 27
Devil's Elbow Cabernet Sauvignon 2003 Fragrant cassis/berry aromas; light to medium-bodied; slightly hollow mid-palate accentuating fractionally gritty tannins on the finish. Should come together well with time. Cork. **RATING** 88 **DRINK** 2012 $ 27.50
Single Vineyard Whippet Sauvignon Blanc 2004 Light-bodied; clean, fresh and correct; gooseberry, herbaceous and mineral flavours. Screwcap. **RATING** 87 **DRINK** Now $ 19.90
Single Vineyard My Fat Goose Semillon Sauvignon Blanc 2004 Clean, fresh, herbal and citrus mix; minerally finish; not intense. Screwcap. **RATING** 87 **DRINK** 2008 $ 19.90
Red Bucket Cabernet Shiraz 2003 Appealing spicy, berry nuances; light to medium-bodied; early-drinking; minimal tannins, but has flavour. Screwcap. **RATING** 87 **DRINK** 2008 $ 16.25

ΤΤΤΥ **Single Vineyard Beau Sea Viognier 2004 RATING** 86 **DRINK** 2009 $ 26
Single Vineyard The Mob Zinfandel 2003 RATING 85 **DRINK** 2007 $ 29.25

Lost Lake ★★★

Lot 3 Vasse Highway, Pemberton, WA 6260 **REGION** Pemberton
T (08) 9776 1251 **F** (08) 9776 1919 **WEB** www.lostlake.com.au **OPEN** Wed–Sun 10–4
WINEMAKER Justin Hearn, Melanie Bowater **EST.** 1990 **CASES** 5000
SUMMARY Previously known as Eastbrook Estate, its origins go back to 1990, to the acquisition of a 80-ha farming property which was subdivided into three portions: 16 ha, now known as Picardy, were acquired by Dr Bill Pannell, 18 ha became the base for Lost Lake, and the remainder was sold. The initial plantings in 1990 were of pinot noir and chardonnay, followed by shiraz, sauvignon blanc,

merlot and cabernet sauvignon between 1996 and 1998 – 9 ha are now planted. A jarrah and cedar winery with a crush capacity of 300 tonnes was built in 1995, together with a large restaurant. In 1999 the business was acquired by four Perth investors. Exports to the UK.

Lost Valley Winery   ★★★☆

Strath Creek, Vic 3658 (postal) **REGION** Upper Goulburn
T (03) 9592 3531 **F** (03) 9592 6396 **WEB** www.lostvalleywinery.com **OPEN** Not
WINEMAKER Alex White (Contract) **EST.** 1995 **CASES** 4500
SUMMARY Dr Robert Ippaso planted the Lost Valley vineyard at an elevation of 450m on the slopes of Mt Tallarook, with 12 ha of merlot, shiraz, cortese and sauvignon blanc. This cortese is the only planting in Australia. It pays homage to Dr Ippaso's birthplace: Savoie, in the Franco-Italian Alps, where cortese flourishes. Exports to the UK and Canada.

ŸŸŸŸ **Hazy Mountain Merlot 2003** A mix of savoury olive and earth with red fruits; medium-bodied; good tannin balance. Cork. **RATING** 89 **DRINK** 2010 $ 32
Sauvignon Blanc 2004 Clean, fresh, grass, herb and gooseberry aromas and flavours; a light, neatly balanced palate. Screwcap. **RATING** 87 **DRINK** Now $ 25

ŸŸŸŸ **Shiraz 2002** **RATING** 86 **DRINK** 2009 $ 32
Cortese 2004 **RATING** 85 **DRINK** Now $ 30

Louee   ★★★★

Cox's Creek Road, Rylstone, NSW 2849 **REGION** Mudgee
T (02) 8923 5373 **F** (02) 8923 5362 **WEB** www.louee.com.au **OPEN** Mon–Sat 10–4, Sun & public hols 11–2
WINEMAKER David Lowe, Jane Wilson (Contract) **EST.** 1998 **CASES** 2500
SUMMARY Jointly owned by Rod James and Tony Maxwell; while a relative newcomer on the scene, Louee is a substantial operation. Its home vineyard at Rylstone has over 32 ha of plantings, led by cabernet sauvignon, shiraz, petit verdot and merlot, with chardonnay, cabernet franc and verdelho making up the balance. The second vineyard is on Nullo Mountain, bordered by the Wollemi National Park, at an altitude of 1100m, high by any standards. Here 4 ha (in all) of the cool-climate varieties of riesling, sauvignon blanc, pinot noir, pinot gris and nebbiolo have been planted.

ŸŸŸŸŸ **Nullo Mountain Rylstone Pinot Gris 2004** Floral aromas; apple, citrus, spice, pear and mineral; good balance and length. Screwcap. **RATING** 90 **DRINK** 2008 $ 18

ŸŸŸŸ **Rylstone Petit Verdot 2003** Full-bodied; powerful, concentrated black fruits hovering between lusciousness and astringency; tannins just under control. Stained cork. **RATING** 89 **DRINK** 2010 $ 19
Rumkers Peak Rylstone Shiraz 2003 Good colour; blackberry and black cherry fruit; touches of spice; firm tannins. Questionable cork. **RATING** 88 **DRINK** 2010 $ 18
Nullo Mountain Rylstone Riesling 2004 Clean; strongly herbal aromas; appreciable residual sugar for cellar door clients, it would seem. Screwcap. **RATING** 87 **DRINK** 2008 $ 18
Cox's Crown Rystone Verdelho 2004 A pretty wine; fruit salad flavours; nice balance; acidity gives length. Screwcap. **RATING** 87 **DRINK** Now $ 15

ŸŸŸŸ **Nullo Mountain Late Picked Riesling 2003** **RATING** 85 **DRINK** Now $ 18
Tongbong Chardonnay 2003 **RATING** 84 **DRINK** 2007 $ 18

Louis-Laval Wines   NR

160 Cobcroft Road, Broke, NSW 2330 **REGION** Lower Hunter Valley
T (02) 6579 1105 **F** (02) 6579 1105 **WEB** www.louislaval.com **OPEN** By appointment
WINEMAKER Roy Meyer **EST.** 1987 **CASES** 1200
SUMMARY It is ironic that the winery name should have associations with Alfa Laval, the giant Swiss food and wine machinery firm. Roy Meyer runs an organic vineyard (using only sulphur and copper sprays) and is proud of the fact that the winery has no refrigeration and no stainless steel. The wines produced from the 2.5-ha vineyard are fermented in open barrels or cement tanks, and maturation is handled entirely in oak.

Lovegrove Vineyard and Winery

NR

1420 Heidelberg–Kinglake Road, Cottles Bridge, Vic 3099 **REGION** Yarra Valley
T (03) 9718 1569 **F** (03) 9718 1028 **OPEN** Weekends & public hols 11–6, Mon–Fri by appointment
WINEMAKER Stephen Bennett **EST.** 1983 **CASES** 1500
SUMMARY Lovegrove is a long-established winery in the Diamond Valley subregion, and while production is limited, it offers the visitor much to enjoy, with picturesque gardens overlooking the Kinglake Ranges; antipasto, soup and cheese lunch; barbecue and picnic tables; and live music on the second Sunday of the month. Intermittent art exhibitions are staged, and the winery caters for private functions. The wines are produced from 4 ha of estate plantings which are now fully mature, and a range of vintages is available.

Lowe Family Wines

Tinja Lane, Mudgee, NSW 2850 **REGION** Mudgee
T (02) 6372 0800 **F** (02) 6372 0811 **WEB** www.lowewine.com.au **OPEN** Fri–Mon 10–5, or by appointment
WINEMAKER David Lowe, Jane Wilson **EST.** 1987 **CASES** 6000
SUMMARY Former Rothbury winemaker David Lowe and Jane Wilson have consolidated their operations in Mudgee, moving back from the cellar door in the Hunter Valley. As if to make sure that life is not too simple, they have started a new Mudgee business, Mudgee Growers, at the historic Fairview winery (see separate entry). Exports to the UK, Germany and Canada.

TTTTT **Hunter Valley Semillon 2004** Crystal-bright and clear; herb, grass, mineral and spice; excellent length, structure and aftertaste. Screwcap. **RATING** 94 **DRINK** 2017 $ 21

TTTTY **Mudgee Reserve Shiraz 2003** Very good colour; light to medium-bodied; good texture and tannin management; spicy blackberry fruit, long finish; 160 cases made. Cork. **RATING** 92 **DRINK** 2013
Hunter Valley Mudgee Orange Chardonnay 2003 Very tightly structured and focused; oak simply a medium, as whole-bunch pressing, wild yeast and lees have more impact; good length, needs time. Cork. **RATING** 91 **DRINK** 2008 $ 23
Tinja Orange Sauvignon Blanc 2004 Elegant and delicate, but with appealing passionfruit, ripe apple and gooseberry flavours. Screwcap. **RATING** 90 **DRINK** 2007 $ 18
Mudgee Shiraz 2003 Medium purple-red; good mouthfeel, medium-bodied; blackberry fruit; fine, ripe tannins; subtle oak. Cork. **RATING** 90 **DRINK** 2011 $ 28

TTTT **Mudgee Sangiovese Blend 2003** Tangy, savoury, fine tannins run through the palate; appropriately Italianate; sour morello cherry to a T. Very dodgy cork. **RATING** 87 **DRINK** 2008 $ 28

TTTY **Mudgee Merlot 2003** **RATING** 86 **DRINK** 2009 $ 25
Mudgee Zinfandel 2003 Solid, dark berry fruit; some spice, solid tannins; dry red more than Zinfandel. Stained, dodgy cork. **RATING** 86 **DRINK** 2009 $ 28
Tinja Mudgee Botrytis Semillon 2004 Very high botrytis, but has been fermented a long way; orange-gold colour a worry, but the balance is good. Diam. **RATING** 86 **DRINK** 2007 $ 18

Loxley Vineyard

NR

362 Pastoria East Road, Pipers Creek near Kyneton, Vic 3444 **REGION** Macedon Ranges
T (03) 9616 6598 **F** (03) 9614 2249 **OPEN** Not
WINEMAKER Alison Cash, John Ellis, Llew Knight (Contract) **EST.** 1999 **CASES** 1200
SUMMARY A partnership is developing a vineyard/resort/entertainment complex at Loxley; 17 ha of vineyard have been planted. Wines will be produced under two labels, as part of the crop is being sold to Hanging Rock. The first commercial release (Pinot Noir) was in 2004.

Lucas Estate

Donges Road, Severnlea, Qld 4352 **REGION** Granite Belt
T (07) 4683 6365 **F** (07) 4683 6356 **WEB** www.lucasestate.com.au **OPEN** 7 days 10–5
WINEMAKER Colin Sellars, Jim Barnes **EST.** 1999 **CASES** 1000

SUMMARY Louise Samuel and husband Colin Sellars purchased Lucas Estate in 2003. A cellar door has been completed, with light food available; production has risen, with all the grapes from the 2.5 ha of estate plantings being used in addition to contract-grown grapes.

ŢŢŢŸ **The Joyce Mary Verdelho 2004** Light green-straw; very well made; ripe fruit salad flavours; obvious residual sugar, but targeted at the market. Screwcap. **RATING** 86 **DRINK** 2007 $18

Lucy's Run ★★★☆

1274 Wine Country Drive, Rothbury, NSW 2335 **REGION** Lower Hunter Valley
T (02) 4938 3594 **F** (02) 4938 3592 **WEB** www.lucysrun.com **OPEN** 7 days 10–5
WINEMAKER David Hook (Contract) **EST.** 1998 **CASES** 1000
SUMMARY The Lucy's Run business has a variety of offerings of wine, cold-pressed extra virgin olive oil and self-catered farm accommodation. The wines are made from 4.5 ha of verdelho, merlot and shiraz. The feisty label design is the work of local artist Paula Rengger, who doubles up as the chef at Shakey Tables Restaurant, itself the deserving winner of numerous awards.

ŢŢŢŢ **Shiraz 2003** Medium-bodied; clean, fresh blackberry and plum; fine tannins, moderate length; 13.3° alcohol. Screwcap. **RATING** 89 **DRINK** 2009 $20
Merlot 2004 Lusty style; robust red and black fruits; rather less finesse. Screwcap. **RATING** 87 **DRINK** 2008 $25

Lyre Bird Hill ★★★★

370 Inverloch Road, Koonwarra, Vic 3954 **REGION** Gippsland
T (03) 5664 3204 **F** (03) 5664 3206 **WEB** www.lyrebirdhill.com.au **OPEN** Wed–Mon 10–5
WINEMAKER Owen Schmidt **EST.** 1986 **CASES** 2500
SUMMARY Former Melbourne professionals Owen and Robyn Schmidt make small quantities of estate-grown wine (the vineyard is 2.4 ha in size), and offers accommodation for three couples (RACV 4-star rating) in their spacious guesthouse and self-contained cottage. Various weather-related viticulture problems have seen the Schmidts supplement their estate-grown intake with grapes from contract growers in Gippsland and the Yarra Valley, and also provide contract winemaking services.

ŢŢŢŢŸ **Traminer 2003** Intense, spicy lychee varietal character and flavour; full-on Alsace depth; faint phenolics on finish are nigh-on inevitable. Remarkable wine. Good cork. **RATING** 92 **DRINK** 2008 $15

ŢŢŢŢ **Riesling 2004** Powerful minerally style; fractionally grippy; may soften with age. Screwcap. **RATING** 88 **DRINK** 2010 $15
Sauvignon Blanc 2004 Powerful style; shares some of the slightly grippy characters evident in the Riesling, probably ex solids; certainly has presence. Screwcap. **RATING** 87 **DRINK** 2007 $18

ŢŢŢŸ **Salut! Cabernet Shiraz Merlot 2003** **RATING** 86 **DRINK** Now $15
Shiraz 2000 **RATING** 85 **DRINK** Now $20
Unwooded Chardonnay 2004 **RATING** 84 **DRINK** 2007 $12
Pinot Noir 2001 **RATING** 84 **DRINK** Now $20
Pinot Noir Cellar Reserve 2001 **RATING** 84 **DRINK** Now $30
Cabernet Sauvignon 2000 **RATING** 84 **DRINK** Now $18

ŢŢŸ **Unwooded Chardonnay 2001** **RATING** 79 $20

Lyrebird Ridge Organic Winery NR

270 Budgong Road, Budgong via Nowra and Kangaroo Valley, NSW 2541 **REGION** South Coast Zone
T (02) 4446 0648 **F** (02) 4446 0649 **OPEN** Weekends & public hols 10–5
WINEMAKER Larry Moreau **EST.** 1993 **CASES** 600
SUMMARY This is the ultimate organic winery, with no sprays whatsoever being used in the vineyard, and no chemicals – and in particular, no sulphur dioxide – added to the wines. No oak is used, nor are the wines filtered. Chambourcin is, and always will be, the most important grape, its hybrid heritage making it resistant to most of the moulds requiring spraying. The absence of SO_2 in the wine means early consumption is essential.

ŢŢŢŢ **Chambourcin 2004** **RATING** 84 **DRINK** Now $25

Mabrook Estate

NR

258 Inlet Road, Bulga, NSW 2330 **REGION** Lower Hunter Valley
T (02) 9971 9994 **F** (02) 9971 9924 **WEB** www.mabrookestate.com **OPEN** Weekends 10–4
WINEMAKER Larissa Kalt, Tony Kalt **EST.** 1996 **CASES** 800
SUMMARY The Swiss-born Kalt family began the establishment of Mabrook Estate in 1996, planting
3 ha of semillon, 2 ha of shiraz and 1 ha of verdelho. Parents Mona and Tony Kalt decided to use
organic growing methods from the word go, and the vineyard is now certified organic by NASAA
(National Association for Sustainable Agriculture Australia). Daughter Larissa, having obtained an
Honours degree in Medical Science at the University of Sydney, decided to pursue winemaking by
working as a 'lab rat' and cellar hand at a local winery, and visited Switzerland and Italy to observe
small-scale family winemaking in those countries. The red wines are all very light in structure and
extract, which may be intentional.

Macaw Creek Wines

Macaw Creek Road, Riverton, SA 5412 **REGION** Mount Lofty Ranges Zone
T (08) 8847 2237 **F** (08) 8847 2237 **WEB** www.macawcreekwines.com.au **OPEN** Sun & public hols 11–4
WINEMAKER Rodney Hooper **EST.** 1992 **CASES** 4000
SUMMARY The property on which Macaw Creek Wines is established has been owned by the Hooper
family since the 1850s, but development of the estate vineyards did not begin until 1995; 10 ha have
been planted since that time, with a further 20 ha planted in the winter/spring of 1999. Rodney and
Miriam Hooper established the Macaw Creek brand previously (in 1992) with wines made from
grapes from other regions, including the Preservative-Free Yoolang Cabernet Shiraz. Rodney Hooper
is a highly qualified and skilled winemaker with experience in many parts of Australia and in
Germany, France and the US. Exports to the US, Canada and Malaysia.

🐛 McCrae Mist Wines

21 Bass Street, McCrae, Vic 3938 (postal) **REGION** Mornington Peninsula
T 0416 008 630 **F** (03) 5986 6973 **OPEN** Not
WINEMAKER Brien Cole **EST.** 2003 **CASES** 2000
SUMMARY Dr Stephen Smith acquired the Kings Creek Vineyard & Winery after it went into
liquidation, inheriting 15.5 ha of pinot grigio, pinot noir, shiraz and sangiovese, and adding another
4 ha of chardonnay in 2005. The wines are sold by mail order, with limited retail distribution in the
eastern states.

🍷🍷🍷🍷🍷 **Mornington Peninsula Chardonnay 2004** Light to medium-bodied; attractive nectarine
and stone fruit aromas and flavours; a nice touch of cashew; good texture and structure.
Quality cork. **RATING** 92 **DRINK** 2009 $ 15
Mornington Peninsula Shiraz 2003 Quite luscious black cherry and spice fruit; fine,
balanced, ripe tannins; subtle oak. Cork. **RATING** 91 **DRINK** 2010 $ 15

🍷🍷🍷🍷 **Mornington Peninsula Pinot Grigio 2003** Light-bodied; a nicely balanced mix of ripe
apple, pear and spice; possible contribution to texture ex used barriques. Twin Top.
RATING 88 **DRINK** Now $ 15
Mornington Peninsula Pinot Noir 2003 Light to medium red; fragrant, sappy, spicy,
slightly minty overtones to cherry fruit; clean, fresh, bright finish. Quality cork. **RATING** 88
DRINK 2007 $ 15

McGee Wines

NR

1710 Wattlevale Road, Nagambie, Vic 3608 **REGION** Nagambie Lakes
T (03) 5794 1530 **F** (03) 5794 1530 **OPEN** By appointment
WINEMAKER Contract **EST.** 1995 **CASES** 750
SUMMARY Andrew McGee and partner Kerry Smith (the latter the viticulturist) have established
12 ha of vines on the banks of the Goulburn River, the majority planted to shiraz, with lesser
quantities of grenache, viognier and mourvedre. Currently, 95% of the production is sold to
Mitchelton, where the McGee wines are presently made, but the plan is for the partners to make the
wine themselves, and to increase production. The wines are distributed through Woods Wines, 35
Greeves Street, Fitzroy.

McGlashan's Wallington Estate

225 Swan Bay Road, Wallington, Vic 3221 **REGION** Geelong
T (03) 5250 5760 **F** (03) 5250 5760 **OPEN** By appointment
WINEMAKER Robin Brockett (Scotchmans Hill) **EST.** 1996 **CASES** 1000
SUMMARY Russell and Jan McGlashan began the establishment of their 10-ha vineyard in 1996. Chardonnay and pinot noir make up the bulk of the plantings, with the remainder shiraz, and the wines are made by Robin Brockett. Local restaurants around Geelong and the Bellarine Peninsula take much of the wine, but cellar door sales are available by appointment.

YYYY **Pinot Noir 2003** Light to medium-bodied; elegant, savoury, spicy style with considerable length and persistence. **RATING** 93 **DRINK** 2010
Chardonnay 2003 Melon, cashew and stone fruit; well balanced, elegant style; well-handled oak. **RATING** 91 **DRINK** 2009

McGlashan Wines

Nyrang Creek Vineyard, Canowindra, NSW 2904 **REGION** Cowra
T (02) 6344 7153 **F** (02) 6344 7105 **OPEN** By appointment
WINEMAKER Murray Smith (Canobolas-Smith Wines) **EST.** 1992 **CASES** 1500
SUMMARY Anthony and Margaret Wallington began their Nyrang Creek Vineyard with 2 ha of cabernet sauvignon in 1992, followed by 7 ha of chardonnay in 1994, then shiraz (2 ha) and semillon (0.75 ha) in 1995, 0.75 ha each of cabernet franc and pinot noir in 1998, thereafter adding a mix of grenache, mourvedre, tempranillo and viognier. Most of the production is sold, but Arrowfield makes the Chardonnay and Murray Smith, at Orange, makes the Cabernet Sauvignon and Shiraz. The quality of the wines is such that exports to the US have already commenced.

YYYY **Chardonnay 2003** Fresh, lively and long; nectarine/grapefruit has soaked up 12 months of French oak; lingering finish. **RATING** 92 **DRINK** 2008
Pinot Noir 2003 A particularly long and intense palate, though only light to medium-bodied in weight; red fruits dominant, plus a touch of spice. **RATING** 90 **DRINK** 2009

McGuigan Wines ★★★☆

Cnr Broke Road/McDonald Road, Pokolbin, NSW 2321 **REGION** Lower Hunter Valley
T (02) 4998 7700 **F** (02) 4998 7401 **WEB** www.mcguiganwines.com.au **OPEN** 7 days 9.30–5
WINEMAKER Peter Hall **EST.** 1992 **CASES** 1.2 million
SUMMARY A public-listed company which is the ultimate logical expression of Brian McGuigan's marketing drive and vision, on a par with that of Wolf Blass in his heyday. Highly successful in its chosen niche market notwithstanding some labels which are garish. Has been particularly active in export markets, notably the US and more recently China. The overall size of the company has been measurably increased by the acquisition of Simeon Wines; Yaldara and Miranda are now also part of the empire. Exports to all major markets.

YYYY **Bin 2000 Shiraz 2003** Medium-bodied, clean and smooth; pleasant plum and blackberry fruit. **RATING** 87 **DRINK** 2008 $ 13.50

YYYY **Bin 7000 Chardonnay 2003** **RATING** 84 **DRINK** Now $ 13.50

McIvor Creek NR

Costerfield Road, Heathcote, Vic 3523 **REGION** Heathcote
T (03) 5433 4000 **F** (03) 5433 3456 **OPEN** 7 days 10–5.30
WINEMAKER Peter Turley **EST.** 1973 **CASES** 1000
SUMMARY The beautifully situated McIvor Creek winery is well worth a visit and does offer wines in diverse styles; the red wines are the most regional. Peter Turley has 5 ha of cabernet sauvignon and 2.5 ha of cabernet franc and merlot, and supplements this with grapes from other growers.

McIvor Estate

80 Tooborac–Baynton Road, Tooborac, Vic 3522 **REGION** Heathcote
T (03) 5433 5266 **F** (03) 5433 5358 **WEB** www.mcivorestate.com.au **OPEN** Weekends & public hols 10–5, or by appointment

WINEMAKER Adrian Munari (Contract) **EST.** 1997 **CASES** 2000
SUMMARY McIvor Estate is situated at the base of the Tooborac Hills, at the southern end of the Heathcote wine region, 5 km southwest of the Tooborac township towards Lancefield. Gary and Cynthia Harbor have planted 5.5 ha of marsanne, roussanne, shiraz, cabernet sauvignon, merlot, nebbiolo and sangiovese. Competent contract winemaking.

ŸŸŸŸŸ **Shiraz 2002** Intense and very savoury/spicy style, seemingly using some Burgundian techniques. **RATING** 93 **DRINK** 2013 $ 28
Shiraz 2003 A strong overlay of mint to the aroma and black cherry and blackberry flavour; supple tannins; distinctly regional. Cork. **RATING** 90 **DRINK** 2012 $ 28

ŸŸŸŸ **Merlot 2003** Extremely ripe, dense, drought-stressed fruit; full-bodied dry red, not Merlot. **RATING** 88 **DRINK** 2013

ŸŸŸŸ **Marsanne Roussanne 2003** **RATING** 86 **DRINK** 2007 $ 22
Nebbiolo 2003 **RATING** 85 **DRINK** 2007
Sangiovese 2003 **RATING** 84 **DRINK** 2007 $ 32

McKellar Ridge Wines ★★★

40 Rohan Rivett Crescent, McKellar, ACT 2617 (postal) **REGION** Canberra District
T (02) 6258 1556 **F** (02) 6258 9770 **WEB** www.mckellarridgewines.com.au **OPEN** Not
WINEMAKER Contract **EST.** 2000 **CASES** 300
SUMMARY Dr Brian Johnston and his wife Janet are the partners in McKellar Ridge Wines. He is studying wine science at Charles Sturt University, and in the interim is making the wines at Jeir Creek under the guidance of Rob Howell, Bryan Martin and Greg Gallagher.

ŸŸŸŸ **Semillon Chardonnay 2003** **RATING** 86 **DRINK** 2009 $ 14

McLaren Vale III Associates ★★★★

130 Main Road, McLaren Vale, SA 5171 **REGION** McLaren Vale
T 1800 501 513 **F** (08) 8323 7422 **WEB** www.associates.com.au **OPEN** Mon–Fri 9–5, tasting by appointment
WINEMAKER Brian Light **EST.** 1999 **CASES** 12 000
SUMMARY The three associates in question all have a decade or more of wine industry experience; Mary Greer is managing partner, Reginald Wymond chairing partner, and Christopher Fox partner. The partnership owns 34 ha of vines spanning 2 vineyards, one owned by Mary and John Greer, the other by Reg and Sue Wymond. The label was first introduced in 1999, the aim being to produce affordable quality wine. A thoroughly impressive portfolio. Exports to the US, Canada, Germany and China.

ŸŸŸŸŸ **Sabbatical Sauvignon Blanc 2004** Spotless herb, grass, nettle and spice aromas and flavours; bright and firm; very good wine. Screwcap. **RATING** 93 **DRINK** Now $ 17.90
Squid Ink Elite Shiraz 2003 Archetypal mocha, dark chocolate and blackberry fruit; soft tannins; well-handled American oak. High-quality cork. **RATING** 93 **DRINK** 2016 $ 40
The Elder Merlot 2003 Medium-bodied; ripe and chocolatey; more strongly regional than varietal, but has good texture and structure. **RATING** 90 **DRINK** 2010 $ 22.90
Memento Cabernet Sauvignon 2003 Elegant, medium-bodied style; gently ripe blackcurrant fruit; fine savoury tannins, subtle oak. **RATING** 90 **DRINK** 2013 $ 24.90

ŸŸŸŸ **Renaissance Merlot Cabernet Petiti verdot 2003** **RATING** 86 **DRINK** 2009 $ 22.90

ŸŸŸ **Pink Diamond Rose 2004** **RATING** 83 $ 18.90

McLean's Farm Wines ★★★★★

PO Box 403, Tanunda, SA 5352 **REGION** Barossa Valley
T (08) 8564 3340 **F** (08) 8564 3340 **OPEN** Not
WINEMAKER Bob McLean **EST.** 2001 **CASES** 5000
SUMMARY At various times known as the Jolly Green Giant and Sir Lunchalot, Bob McLean has gone perilously close to being a marketing legend in his own lifetime, moving from Orlando to Petaluma and then (for longer and more importantly) St Hallett. He is now free to do his own thing, starting with what he terms as 'The Virtual Winery' in partnership with long-term friends Dean and Rod

Schubert (the latter a notable Australian artist). Around the corner lies barr-eden, a very real vineyard and winery in the course of establishment on top of Mengler's Hill at an altitude of 520m. Important exports to the UK; wholesale distribution through The Wine Group in Victoria and Chase Agency in South Australia.

ŸŸŸŸŸ **Trinity Corner Barossa Shiraz 2002** Spicy, earthy blackberry fruit; potent and intense, but not heavy (14° alcohol); fine tannins, subtle oak; long finish. Poor cork a real pity. **RATING** 94 **DRINK** 2012 $ 28.99
Reserve Shiraz Cabernet 2003 Medium to full-bodied; an array of luscious blackberry and blackcurrant fruit; good tannins; has soaked up the oak. Screwcap. Hooray. **RATING** 94 **DRINK** 2018 $ 28.99
Reserve Barossa 2002 Fragrant blackberry, blackcurrant and spice aromas and flavours; medium-bodied; silky tannins and mouthfeel; innate elegance (13.5° alcohol). Cork. **RATING** 94 **DRINK** 2012 $ 28.99

ŸŸŸŸŸ **Schubert McLean Shiraz Cabernet 2003** Powerful structure, savoury dark fruits and spicy tannins; remarkable value. Terrible cork. **RATING** 90 **DRINK** 2010 $ 15.99

McLeish Estate

Lot 3 De Beyers Road, Pokolbin, NSW 2320 **REGION** Lower Hunter Valley
T (02) 4998 7754 **F** (02) 4998 7754 **WEB** www.mcleishhunterwines.com.au **OPEN** 7 days 10–5, or by appointment
WINEMAKER Andrew Thomas **EST.** 1985 **CASES** 4000
SUMMARY Bob and Maryanne McLeish started planting their vineyard in 1985, and have now planted over 10 ha. They have also opened up their cellar door to the public, having accumulated a number of gold medals for their wines. However, claiming a gold medal and trophy at the 2003 Hunter Valley Boutique Wine Show for all six wines submitted for tasting, spanning 2002 to 2004, is not on.

ŸŸŸŸŸ **Hunter Valley Semillon 2004** Powerful, concentrated, zesty lime and lemon flavours run right through the length of the palate. Now or later. Cork. **RATING** 93 **DRINK** 2012 $ 15
Reserve Hunter Valley Shiraz 2003 Medium-bodied; attractive plum and blackberry fruit; good mouthfeel; fine, ripe tannins and good oak management. High-quality cork. **RATING** 92 **DRINK** 2013 $ 35
Reserve Hunter Valley Chardonnay 2004 Light-bodied; nicely handled barrel ferment inputs don't dominate the delicate melon, stone fruit and pear flavours; balanced acidity. Cork. **RATING** 90 **DRINK** 2008 $ 25
Jessica's Botrytis Semillon 2002 Vibrant, fresh, tangy cumquat, lemon and mandarin; lemony acidity gives balance; trophy winner as a young wine, and ageing nicely. **RATING** 90 **DRINK** 2008 $ 25

ŸŸŸŸ **Hunter Valley Semillon Sauvignon Blanc 2004** Strong lemon juice flavours; pointed acidity adds to the length. Cork. **RATING** 89 **DRINK** 2007 $ 15
Hunter Valley Shiraz 2003 Light to medium-bodied; fresh, juicy berry fruit; clean finish, fine tannins. Twin Top. **RATING** 88 **DRINK** 2009 $ 20

ŸŸŸŸ **Hunter Valley Verdelho 2004** **RATING** 86 **DRINK** 2007 $ 16
Hunter Valley Cabernet Sauvignon 2002 **RATING** 86 **DRINK** 2009 $ 20
Hunter Valley Merlot 2002 **RATING** 85 **DRINK** 2009 $ 20

McPherson Wines

PO Box 529, Artarmon, NSW 1570 **REGION** Nagambie Lakes
T (02) 9436 1644 **F** (02) 9436 3144 **WEB** www.mcphersonwines.com **OPEN** Not
WINEMAKER Andrew McPherson, Geoff Thompson **EST.** 1993 **CASES** 300 000
SUMMARY McPherson Wines is not well known in Australia but is, by any standards, a substantial business. Its wines are almost entirely produced for the export market, with sales in Australia through the Woolworths group (Safeway and First Estate). The wines are made at various locations from contract-grown grapes and represent very good value. For the record, McPherson Wines is a joint venture between Andrew McPherson and Alister Purbrick of Tahbilk. Both have had a lifetime of experience in the industry. Exports to all major markets.

ŸŸŸŸ **Basilisk Shiraz Mourvedre 2002** Deep red-purple; powerful and remarkably fresh red fruits and plums; persistent tannins provide structure; good acidity. **RATING** 89 **DRINK** 2010 $ 13

ŶŶŶŶ **Murray Darling Verdelho 2004** Nice wine; clear-cut fruit salad off-set by lemony acidity. Twin Top. **RATING** 86 **DRINK** Now $8.99
Murray Darling Semillon Sauvignon Blanc 2004 **RATING** 84 **DRINK** Now $8.99
Murray Darling Shiraz 2003 **RATING** 84 **DRINK** 2007 $8.99

ŶŶŶ **Murray Darling Chardonnay 2004** **RATING** 83 $8.99
Murray Darling Rose 2004 **RATING** 83 **DRINK** Now $8.99
Basilisk Marsanne Viognier 2003 **RATING** 82 $13

Macquariedale Estate ★★★★

170 Sweetwater Road, Rothbury, NSW 2335 **REGION** Lower Hunter Valley
T (02) 6574 7012 **F** (02) 6574 7013 **WEB** www.macquariedale.com.au **OPEN** By appointment
WINEMAKER Ross McDonald **EST.** 1993 **CASES** 5000
SUMMARY Macquariedale is an acorn to oak story, beginning with a small hobby vineyard in Branxton many years ago, and now extending to three certified organic (in conversion) vineyards around the Lower Hunter with a total 13 ha of semillon, chardonnay, shiraz, merlot and cabernet sauvignon. This has led to Ross McDonald (and his family) leaving a busy Sydney life to be full-time grapegrower and winemaker. The wines are sold by mailing list, through the Boutique Wine Centre in Pokolbin and via the 30 or so restaurants that list the wines. Exports to the US, Canada and Japan.

ŶŶŶŶŶ **Old Vine Semillon 2002** Very good colour; elegant, light to medium-bodied; lively, fresh and tangy palate; minerally acidity; good length. From 34-year-old vines. **RATING** 90 **DRINK** 2012 $16
Four Winds Chardonnay 2002 Excellent light green-yellow colour; elegant, light-bodied style; excellent oak handling (30% barrel ferment); creamy overtones to the fig and melon fruit. **RATING** 90 **DRINK** 2007 $20

ŶŶŶŶ **Cabernet Sauvignon 2002** Well balanced, medium-bodied wine; a nice mix of blackcurrant, earth and chocolate; fine, lingering tannins. **RATING** 89 **DRINK** 2011 $22
Thomas Shiraz 2001 Light to medium-bodied; graceful and balanced; an almost lemony cast to the fruit; fine tannins. **RATING** 88 **DRINK** 2010 $20
Shiraz 2002 Very earthy, very regional savoury characters; has length to compensate for the diminished fruit; fine tannins. **RATING** 87 **DRINK** 2009 $22

McVitty Grove ★★★★

Wombeyan Caves Road, Mittagong, NSW 2575 **REGION** Southern Highlands
T (02) 4878 5044 **F** (02) 4878 5524 **WEB** www.mcvittygrove.com.au **OPEN** Mon–Fri 8–5, weekends 8–5
WINEMAKER Madew Wines (Contract) **EST.** 1998 **CASES** 1500
SUMMARY Notwithstanding his 20-year career in finance, Mark Phillips also had 6 years of tertiary qualifications in horticulture when he and wife Jane began the search for a Southern Highlands site suited to premium grapegrowing and olive cultivation. In 1998 they bought 42 ha of farm land on the Wombeyan Caves Road, just out of Mittagong. They have now established 5.5 ha of pinot noir and pinot gris on deep, fertile soils at the front of the property. In addition, a 1.5-ha olive grove has been planted; it provides the backdrop for the cellar door and café, which opened in April 2004.

ŶŶŶŶŶ **Pinot Noir 2003** Sultry, spicy, smoky bouquet; complex, powerful palate; satsuma plum and spice; firm finish. Perhaps a hint of brett. **RATING** 90 **DRINK** 2010 $26

ŶŶŶŶ **Rose 2004** Pale salmon; a firm style, with a hint of citrus overlay to the red fruits; dry finish. **RATING** 87 **DRINK** Now $15

ŶŶŶŶ **Pinot Gris 2004** **RATING** 85 **DRINK** Now $23
Endymion Cuvee NV **RATING** 85 **DRINK** Now $25
Cut Arm Pinot Gris 2004 **RATING** 84 **DRINK** Now $25

McWilliam's ★★★★★

Jack McWilliam Road, Hanwood, NSW 2680 **REGION** Riverina
T (02) 6963 0001 **F** (02) 6963 0002 **WEB** www.mcwilliams.com.au **OPEN** Mon–Sat 9–5
WINEMAKER Jim Brayne, Martin Cooper, Russell Cody, Stephen Cook **EST.** 1916 **CASES** NFP

SUMMARY The best wines to emanate from the Hanwood winery are from other regions, notably the Barwang Vineyard at Hilltops in New South Wales, Coonawarra and Eden Valley. As McWilliam's viticultural resources have expanded, they have been able to produce regional blends from across southeastern Australia under the Hanwood label; in the last few years, these have been startlingly good. Exports to many countries via a major distribution joint venture with Gallo.

🍷🍷🍷🍷🍷 **Clare Valley Riesling 2004** Crystal-clear varietal character, offering lingering lime juice and grapefruit flavours with a minerally acid cross-cut, giving structure and length. **RATING** 95 **DRINK** 2015 $18.50
1877 Cabernet Sauvignon Shiraz 2001 An unusual scented, spicy array of sweet red and black fruits; excellent tannins and oak management; long life ahead. **RATING** 95 **DRINK** 2021 $83

🍷🍷🍷🍷🍷 **Margaret River Chardonnay 2003** Fine, elegant but quite intense; typical regional stone fruit and a touch of citrus; subtle oak. **RATING** 90 **DRINK** 2007 $18.50

🍷🍷🍷🍷 **Eden Valley Riesling 2004** Light but fragrant; curiously, lacks the intensity of the Clare Valley version; needs time. **RATING** 88 **DRINK** 2015 $18.50
Margaret River Cabernet Merlot 2002 A fragrant bouquet; light to medium-bodied palate ranging through savoury earth and chocolate notes to blackcurrant; good tannins. **RATING** 88 **DRINK** 2009 $18
Margaret River Semillon Sauvignon Blanc 2004 Clean, crisp and fresh; light-bodied, minerally acidity; not concentrated. **RATING** 87 **DRINK** Now $18.50
Hanwood Shiraz 2003 Medium-bodied; good balance, structure and mouthfeel to small black fruits; good acidity. **RATING** 87 **DRINK** 2009 $12

🍷🍷🍷🍷 **Hanwood Sauvignon Blanc 2004** **RATING** 86 **DRINK** Now $12
Hanwood Chardonnay 2003 **RATING** 86 **DRINK** Now $12
Inheritance Semillon Sauvignon Blanc 2004 **RATING** 85 **DRINK** 2007
Hanwood Verdelho 2004 **RATING** 85 **DRINK** Now $12
Inheritance Shiraz Merlot 2003 **RATING** 85 **DRINK** 2008

🍷🍷🍷 **Redvale Cabernet Sauvignon 2002** **RATING** 83

McWilliam's Mount Pleasant ★★★★★

Marrowbone Road, Pokolbin, NSW 2320 **REGION** Lower Hunter Valley
T (02) 4998 7505 **F** (02) 4998 7761 **WEB** www.mcwilliams.com.au **OPEN** 7 days 10–5
WINEMAKER Phillip Ryan, Andrew Leembruggen **EST.** 1921 **CASES** NFP
SUMMARY McWilliam's Elizabeth and the glorious Lovedale Semillon are generally commercially available with 4–5 years of bottle age and are undervalued treasures with a consistently superb show record. The three individual vineyard wines, together with the Maurice O'Shea memorial wines, add to the lustre of this proud name. Exports to many countries, the most important being the UK, the US, Germany and New Zealand.

🍷🍷🍷🍷🍷 **Lovedale Semillon 1999** Glowing green-gold; gentle honey, toast and citrus; outstanding length and balance; great acidity. **RATING** 96 **DRINK** 2009 $46.50
Rosehill Shiraz 2000 Super-refined and elegant; red fruits wrapped in a more savoury/earthy regional coat; only light to medium-bodied, but has great depth and will develop for decades. **RATING** 94 **DRINK** 2020 $32

🍷🍷🍷🍷🍷 **Maurice O'Shea Chardonnay 2003** Complex aromas from barrel fermentation; the palate is finer than the bouquet suggests; stone fruit and white peach; good acidity. **RATING** 93 **DRINK** 2008 $32
Early Release Elizabeth Semillon 2002 Punchy herb, mineral, lemon and spice aromas; great line; very precise acidity and length. Screwcap guarantees the long life. **RATING** 92 **DRINK** 2017 $18

🍷🍷🍷🍷 **Hunter Valley Chardonnay 2003** Soft, peachy fruit; touches of cashew and fig; gentle oak. **RATING** 87 **DRINK** Now $16.50
Merlot 2002 A mix of regional and varietal influences; very savoury/briary. **RATING** 87 **DRINK** Now $18

Madew Wines

NR

Westering, Federal Highway, Lake George, NSW 2581 **REGION** Canberra District
T (02) 4848 0026 **F** (02) 4848 0026 **OPEN** Weekends, public hols 11–5
WINEMAKER David Madew **EST.** 1984 **CASES** 2500
SUMMARY Madew Wines bowed to the urban pressure of Queanbeyan and purchased the Westering
Vineyard from Captain GP Hood some years ago. Plantings there have now increased to 9.5 ha, with
1 ha each of shiraz and pinot gris coming into bearing. Madew's restaurant, grapefoodwine, which is
open Friday to Saturday for lunch and dinner and Sunday for breakfast and lunch, won the Best
Restaurant in a Winery award in 2001, and also hosts monthly music concerts.

Madigan Vineyard

NR

Lot 1 Wilderness Road, Rothbury, NSW 2320 **REGION** Lower Hunter Valley
T (02) 4998 7815 **F** (02) 4998 7116 **OPEN** Weekends 10–5
WINEMAKER Contract **EST.** 1996 **CASES** 1000
SUMMARY Bob and Ann Rich have 3 ha of shiraz, chardonnay and verdelho at Rothbury, with the
infinitely experienced Keith Holder as viticulturist. Virtually all the wine is sold by mailing list and
through the cellar door.

Maglieri of McLaren Vale

Douglas Gully Road, McLaren Flat, SA 5171 **REGION** McLaren Vale
T (08) 8383 0177 **F** (08) 8383 0735 **WEB** www.maglieri.com.au **OPEN** Mon–Sat 9–4, Sun 12–4
WINEMAKER Charles Hargrave **EST.** 1972 **CASES** 14 000
SUMMARY Was one of the better-kept secrets among the wine cognoscenti, but not among the many
customers who drink thousands of cases of white and red Lambrusco every year, an example of niche
marketing at its profitable best. It was a formula which proved irresistible to Beringer Blass, which
acquired Maglieri in 1999. Its dry red wines are invariably generously proportioned and full of
character, the Shiraz particularly so.

▼▼▼▼♡ **Shiraz 2002** Big chocolate and blackberry style; soft tannins and abundant oak.
RATING 90 **DRINK** 2012

🐦 Magpie Estate

PO Box 126, Tanunda, SA 5352 **REGION** Barossa Valley
T (08) 8562 3300 **F** (08) 8562 1177 **OPEN** Not
WINEMAKER Rolf Binder, Noel Young **EST.** 1993 **CASES** 6000
SUMMARY This is a partnership between Rolf Binder of Veritas and Cambridge (England) wine
merchant Noel Young. It came about in 1993 when there was limited demand for or understanding
of Southern Rhône-style blends based on shiraz, grenache and mourvedre. Initially a small, export-
only brand, the quality of the wines was such that it has grown substantially over the years, although
the intention is to limit production to 7500 cases. The majority of the wines are very reasonably
priced (The Schnell! Shiraz Grenache, The Black Sock Mourvedre, The Fakir Grenache, the Callbag
Grenache Mourvedre, The Sack Shiraz and The Wit and the Shanker Cabernet); the two super-
premiums (The Gomersal Grenache and The Election Shiraz) are more expensive. The labelling is
strongly reminiscent of Torbreck and other subsequent ventures, but the quality of the wine needs no
assistance. Exports to the UK, the US and other major markets.

▼▼▼▼♡ **The Election Shiraz 2002** Powerful and focused; abundant black fruits and a touch of
chocolate; lingering tannins and integrated oak. Needs time. **RATING** 91 **DRINK** 2015 **$** 55

Main Ridge Estate

80 William Road, Red Hill, Vic 3937 **REGION** Mornington Peninsula
T (03) 5989 2686 **F** (03) 5931 0000 **WEB** www.mre.com.au **OPEN** Mon–Fri 12–4, weekends 12–5
WINEMAKER Nat White **EST.** 1975 **CASES** 1100
SUMMARY Nat White gives meticulous attention to every aspect of his viticulture and winemaking,
doing annual battle with one of the coolest sites on the Peninsula. The same attention to detail
extends to the winery and the winemaking. Despite such minuscule production, domestic sales
through the cellar door and by mail order, and exports to the UK and Singapore.

ŸŸŸŸŸ Chardonnay 2003 Developed green-gold; complex, ripe melon and fig fruit has all the weight needed to carry the oak and malolactic fermentation; superbly rich. **RATING** 95 **DRINK** 2010 $47

Half Acre Pinot Noir 2003 Deep colour; rich and powerful dark plum and some spice; long palate; will age well. Screwcap. **RATING** 94 **DRINK** 2010 $48

Half Acre Pinot Noir 2002 Appealing mix of cherry, raspberry and strawberry fruits and sweet spices; elegant and seductive. **RATING** 94 **DRINK** 2009 $50

Maiolo Wines   ★★★★

Bussell Highway, Carbunup River, WA 6282 **REGION** Margaret River
T (08) 9755 1060 **F** (08) 9755 1060 **WEB** www.maiolowines.com.au **OPEN** 7 days 10–5
WINEMAKER Charles Maiolo **EST.** 1999 **CASES** 4000
SUMMARY Charles Maiolo has established a 28-ha vineyard planted to semillon, sauvignon blanc, chardonnay, pinot noir, shiraz, merlot and cabernet sauvignon. He has a wine science degree from Charles Sturt University, and presides over a winery with a capacity of 250–300 tonnes. The red wines, in particular, show great promise, with Shiraz and Cabernet Sauvignon to the fore. Exports to Canada and Singapore.

ŸŸŸŸŸ Margaret River Cabernet Merlot 2002 Medium-bodied mix of red and black fruits, spice and a touch of French oak; ripe tannins. Stained cork. **RATING** 90 **DRINK** 2012 $30

ŸŸŸŸ Margaret River Semillon Sauvignon Blanc 2004 Crisp, clean, light-bodied; gentle tropical/mineral mix. Screwcap. **RATING** 87 **DRINK** Now $16

Margaret River Chardonnay 2003 Delicate grapefruit and melon; integrated, gentle French oak. **RATING** 87 **DRINK** 2008 $18

Majella   ★★★★★

Lynn Road, Coonawarra, SA 5263 **REGION** Coonawarra
T (08) 8736 3055 **F** (08) 8736 3057 **WEB** www.majellawines.com.au **OPEN** 7 days 10–4.30
WINEMAKER Bruce Gregory **EST.** 1969 **CASES** 14 000
SUMMARY Majella is one of the more important contract grapegrowers in Coonawarra, with 61 ha of vineyard, principally shiraz and cabernet sauvignon, and with a little riesling and merlot. Common gossip has it that part finds its way into the Wynns John Riddoch Cabernet Sauvignon and Michael Shiraz, or their equivalent within the Southcorp Group. The Malleea is one of Coonawarra's best wines. Production under the Majella label has increased substantially over the past few years, from 2000 to 14 000 cases; exports to the UK, the US and other major markets.

ŸŸŸŸŸ Cabernet Sauvignon 2002 Bright cassis, redcurrant and blackcurrant mix; firm acidity and balanced spicy vanilla oak. **RATING** 94 **DRINK** 2015 $32

The Malleea 2002 Good colour; classic restraint; blackcurrant, blackberry, earth and spice; very good texture and structure; cedary French oak. Quality cork. **RATING** 94 **DRINK** 2022 $66

ŸŸŸŸ Shiraz 2002 Very fragrant, high-toned black cherry and blackberry aromas; lively and fresh; good texture and length. **RATING** 92 **DRINK** 2012 $31

Malcolm Creek Vineyard   ★★★★☆

Bonython Road, Kersbrook, SA 5231 **REGION** Adelaide Hills
T (08) 8389 3235 **F** (08) 8389 3235 **OPEN** Weekends & public hols 11–5, or by appointment
WINEMAKER Reg Tolley **EST.** 1982 **CASES** 700
SUMMARY Malcolm Creek is the retirement venture of Reg Tolley, and he keeps a low profile. However, the wines are invariably well made and develop gracefully; they are worth seeking out, and are usually available with some extra bottle age at a very modest price. Exports to the UK.

ŸŸŸŸ Adelaide Hills Chardonnay 2003 Smooth melon and stone fruit; good oak integration; balanced acidity; has style. Poor cork. **RATING** 90 **DRINK** 2007 $19

Adelaide Hills Cabernet Sauvignon 2002 Nicely modulated, medium-bodied; blackcurrant, blackberry and dark chocolate; fine, ripe tannins; subtle oak. Quality cork. **RATING** 90 **DRINK** 2011 $22

Mandalay Estate   NR

Mandalay Road, Mumballup, WA 6010 **REGION** Geographe
T (08) 9372 2006 **F** (08) 9384 5962 **OPEN** Weekends & public hols 10–5
WINEMAKER Contract **EST.** 1997 **CASES** NA
SUMMARY Terry and Bernice O'Connell have established 4 ha of chardonnay, shiraz, cabernet
sauvignon and zinfandel on their 40-ha property, previously owned by Bunnings Tree Farms and
hence abounding with tree stumps. The tasting room has been established in an old plant shed on the
property, and the wines are sold through the cellar door and by mail order.

Mandurang Valley Wines   NR

77 Fadersons Lane, Mandurang, Vic 3551 **REGION** Bendigo
T (03) 5439 5367 **F** (03) 5439 3850 **OPEN** Weekends & hols 11–5
WINEMAKER Wes Vine **EST.** 1994 **CASES** 2000
SUMMARY Wes and Pamela Vine have slowly built Mandurang Valley Wines, using 2.5 ha of estate
vines and a further 6 ha of estate-grown grapes. Café lunches complement the outdoor seating and
barbecue facilities. The wines are chiefly sold through the cellar door and by mailing list, with limited
distribution through Bacchus Wines, Armadale (Vic).

Mann   NR

105 Memorial Avenue, Baskerville, WA 6056 **REGION** Swan Valley
T (08) 9296 4348 **F** (08) 9296 4348 **OPEN** Weekends 10–5 and by appointment
from 1 Aug until sold out
WINEMAKER Dorham Mann **EST.** 1988 **CASES** 600
SUMMARY Industry veteran Dorham Mann has established a one-wine label for what must be
Australia's most unusual wine: a dry, only faintly pink, sparkling wine made exclusively from
cabernet sauvignon and cygne blanc grown on the 2.5-ha estate surrounding the cellar door. Dorham
Mann explains, 'Our family has made and enjoyed the style for more than 30 years, although just in a
private capacity until recently.'

Mansfield Wines   ★★★

204 Eurunderee Lane, Mudgee, NSW 2850 **REGION** Mudgee
T (02) 6373 3871 **F** (02) 6373 3708 **OPEN** Thurs–Tues & public hols 10–5, or by appointment
WINEMAKER Bob Heslop **EST.** 1975 **CASES** 2000
SUMMARY Mansfield Wines has moved with the times, moving the emphasis from fortified wines to
table wines (though still offering some fortifieds) and expanding the product range to take in cutting-
edge varietal reds such as Touriga and Zinfandel.

♥♥♥♥ **Touriga 2003** Powerful; bramble, spice, black fruits and bitter chocolate; good ripeness
and intensity; stained low-quality cork does not do justice to the wine. **RATING** 88
DRINK 2010 $ 18

♥♥♥♡ **Acacia Spectabilis Mudgee Wattle Cabernet Merlot 2001 RATING** 84 **DRINK** 2007 $ 20

♥♥♥ **Acacia Spectabilis Mudgee Wattle Zinfandel 2003 RATING** 83 $ 20

Mantons Creek Vineyard

240 Tucks Road, Main Ridge, Vic 3928 **REGION** Mornington Peninsula
T (03) 5989 6264 **F** (03) 5989 6348 **WEB** www.mantonscreekvineyard.com.au **OPEN** 7 days 11–5
WINEMAKER Alex White (Contract) **EST.** 1990 **CASES** 3500
SUMMARY The 19-ha property was originally an orchard, herb farm and horse stud. After the vineyard
was established, the grapes were sold to other wineries in the region until 1998, when the first
Mantons Creek wines were made from the 10-ha vineyard planted in 1994. A purpose-built cellar
door, restaurant and 4-bedroom accommodation unit was opened in December 1998; the property
was purchased by Dr Michael Ablett, a retired cardiologist, and his wife Judy in March 2001. Exports
to Hong Kong and Japan.

ŶŶŶŶŶ **Gewurztraminer 2004** Delicate but clear-cut rose petal and lychee aromas and flavours; excellent balance and length; the price is justified. Screwcap. **RATING** 93 **DRINK** 2009 $ 35
Pinot Gris 2003 Fragrant apple blossom aromas; a hint of citrus and lively acidity on the expressive palate. **RATING** 92 **DRINK** 2007
Sauvignon Blanc 2004 Potent, challenging mown grass/smoky bouquet; the palate settles down with gently tropical fruit and lemony acid counterbalance. Screwcap.
RATING 90 **DRINK** 2007 $ 22.50

ŶŶŶŶ **Jessica Chardonnay 2002** Glowing yellow-green; extremely concentrated, very complex and rich, though all up front. Possible botrytis. Good food style. Screwcap. **RATING** 89
DRINK Now $ 20
Jessica Pinot Gris 2002 Expressive, rich wine with almost tropical fruit flavour; plenty of character, although varietal flavour subdued. **RATING** 88 **DRINK** Now $ 22
Tempranillo 2003 Light-bodied, but has the usual spicy raspberry red fruit varietal character plus good acidity. Very pricey. Screwcap. **RATING** 87 **DRINK** 2009 $ 45

ŶŶŶŶ **Pinots Rose 2004** **RATING** 86 **DRINK** Now $ 18
Pinot Noir 2003 **RATING** 86 **DRINK** 2008 $ 30
Muscat 2004 **RATING** 84 $ 15

Marandoo Estate   NR

Ground Floor, 62 Greenhill Road, Wayville, SA 5034 (postal) **REGION** Langhorne Creek
T (08) 8373 9977 **F** (08) 8373 9988 **WEB** www.fabal.com.au **OPEN** Not
WINEMAKER Michael Potts (Contract) **EST.** 1990 **CASES** NFP
SUMMARY Marandoo Estate (and Marandoo Run) are the visible but very small part of a very large and complex vineyard owning, vineyard management and grapegrowing group with 1100 ha of vineyards under management around Australia, extending from Langhorne Creek to Padthaway, Margaret River, Barossa Valley, Canberra District and Young.

Margan Family   ★★★★

1238 Milbrodale Road, Broke, NSW 2330 **REGION** Lower Hunter Valley
T (02) 6579 1317 **F** (02) 6579 1317 **WEB** www.margan.com.au **OPEN** 7 days 10–5
WINEMAKER Andrew Margan **EST.** 1997 **CASES** 30 000
SUMMARY Andrew Margan followed in his father's footsteps by entering the wine industry 20 years ago and has covered a great deal of territory since, working as a Flying Winemaker in Europe, then for Tyrrell's, first as a winemaker then as marketing manager. His wife Lisa, too, has had many years of experience in restaurants and marketing. They now have over 80 ha of fully yielding vines at their Ceres Hill homestead property at Broke, and lease the nearby Vere Vineyard. The first stage of a 700-tonne onsite winery was completed in 1998. Wine quality (and packaging) is consistently good. Café Beltree is open for light meals and coffee. Exports to the UK, the US and other major markets.

ŶŶŶŶŶ **Botrytis Semillon 2004** Glowing green-gold; complex and luscious, the oak balanced and integrated with cumquat, peach, mandarin and almond. **RATING** 93 **DRINK** 2009 $ 25
Semillon 2004 Clean, fresh and lively; lemon, grass, lanolin and mineral flavours; very good length and potential for ageing. **RATING** 92 **DRINK** 2019 $ 16
Chardonnay 2003 Bright yellow-green; complex barrel ferment inputs to stone fruit/peach flavours; nice balancing acidity. **RATING** 90 **DRINK** 2010 $ 19

ŶŶŶŶ **Shiraz 2003** Strongly regional style; a mix of black fruits and earth; persistent tannins; needs patience. **RATING** 89 **DRINK** 2013 $ 19

ŶŶŶŶ **Shiraz Saignee 2004** **RATING** 86 **DRINK** Now $ 16
Merlot 2003 **RATING** 86 **DRINK** 2007 $ 19
Verdelho 2004 **RATING** 85 **DRINK** 2008 $ 16

Marienberg   ★★★

2 Chalk Hill Road, McLaren Vale, SA 5171 **REGION** McLaren Vale
T (08) 8323 9666 **F** (08) 8323 9600 **OPEN** 7 days 10–5
WINEMAKER Peter Orr **EST.** 1966 **CASES** 30 000

SUMMARY Another long-established business (founded by Australia's first female owner/vigneron, Ursula Pridham) acquired by James Estate in 2003. Exports to the UK and the US.

YYYY   **Reserve Shiraz 2002** Ripe and sweet red fruits; medium-bodied; gentle tannins and subtle oak; pretty wine. Cork. **RATING** 89 **DRINK** 2010 $ 30

Marinda Park Vineyard ★★★★

238 Myers Road, Balnarring, Vic 3926 **REGION** Mornington Peninsula
T (03) 5989 7613 **F** (03) 5989 7613 **WEB** www.marindapark.com **OPEN** Thurs–Mon 11–5, 7 days in January
WINEMAKER Sandro Mosele (Contract) **EST.** 1999 **CASES** 2500
SUMMARY Mark and Belinda Rodman have established 10 ha of chardonnay, sauvignon blanc, pinot noir and merlot on their vineyard on the outskirts of Balnarring. They operate the business in conjunction with American partners Norm and Fanny Winton, who are involved in the sale and distribution of the wines in the US and Singapore. The wines are principally sold overseas, but are available locally by mail order, and have been sold at the cellar door at the small French Provincial-style café since October 2003. Exports to the US and Singapore.

YYYYY   **Sauvignon Blanc 2004** Spotlessly clean; initially subdued aromas and flavours but gathers momentum on the back palate and finish. **RATING** 90 **DRINK** 2007 $ 21

YYYY   **Pinot Noir 2003** Ripe, plummy cake spice aromas; full mid-palate; slightly firm, acid finish. Diam. **RATING** 89 **DRINK** 2008 $ 28

YYYY   **Rose 2004** **RATING** 86 **DRINK** Now $ 19.50

Mariners Rest ★★★

Jamakarri Farm, Roberts Road, Denmark, WA 6333 **REGION** Denmark
T (08) 9840 9324 **F** (08) 9840 9321 **OPEN** 7 days 11–5
WINEMAKER Brenden Smith **EST.** 1996 **CASES** 750
SUMMARY Mariners Rest is the reincarnation of the now defunct Golden Rise winery. A new 2.5-ha vineyard was planted in the spring of 1997, and a slightly odd selection of replacement wines are being marketed.

Maritime Estate ★★★★

Tucks Road, Red Hill, Vic 3937 **REGION** Mornington Peninsula
T (03) 9848 2926 **F** (03) 9848 2926 **OPEN** Weekends & public hols 11–5, 7 days Dec 27–Jan 26
WINEMAKER Clare Halloran (Contract) **EST.** 1988 **CASES** 2000
SUMMARY John and Linda Ruljancich and Kevin Ruljancich have enjoyed great success since their first vintage in 1994, no doubt due in part to skilled winemaking but also to the situation of their vineyard, looking across the hills and valleys of the Red Hill subregion.

Marius Wines ★★★★

PO Box 545, Willunga, SA 5172 **REGION** McLaren Vale
T 0402 344 340 **F** (08) 8407 5717 **WEB** www.mariuswines.com.au **OPEN** Not
WINEMAKER Mark Day **EST.** 1994 **CASES** 500
SUMMARY Roger Pike says he has loved wine for over 30 years; that for 15 years he has had the desire to add a little bit to the world of wine; and that 9 years ago he decided to do something about it, ripping the front paddock and planting 1.6 ha of shiraz in 1994. He sold the grapes from the 1997–99 vintages, but when the 1998 vintage became a single-vineyard wine (made by the purchaser of the grapes) selling in the US at $40, the temptation to have his own wine became irresistible. The wines are available by mail order and via the website. Exports to the US.

YYYYY   **Single Vineyard McLaren Vale Shiraz 2003** Complex, rich, typical of 2003; blackberry, chocolate and plum; heats up slightly on the finish courtesy of 15° alcohol; good oak. Screwcap. **RATING** 90 **DRINK** 2013 $ 25

Markwood Estate   NR

Morris Lane, Markwood, Vic 3678 **REGION** King Valley
T (03) 5727 0361 **F** (03) 5727 0361 **OPEN** 7 days 9–5
WINEMAKER Rick Morris **EST.** 1971 **CASES** 200
SUMMARY A member of the famous Morris family, Rick Morris shuns publicity and relies virtually
exclusively on cellar door sales for what is a small output. Of a range of table and fortified wines tasted
some years ago, the Old Tawny Port (a cross between Port and Muscat, showing more of the character
of the latter than the former) and a White Port (seemingly made from Muscadelle) were the best.

Maroochy Springs   NR

Musavale Road, Erwah Vale near Eumundi, Qld 4562 **REGION** Queensland Coastal
T (07) 5442 8777 **F** (07) 5442 8745 **WEB** www.sunshinecoastwine.com.au **OPEN** 7 days 12–6
WINEMAKER Kevin Watson (Contract) **EST.** 2001 **CASES** NA
SUMMARY Jack and Margaret Connolly have established their winery in the beautiful Erwah Valley at
the foothills of the Blackall Range, 30 minutes' drive from Noosa and only 6 km west of Eumundi.
They have the usual range of general tourist facilities and attractions, including an air-conditioned
cellar door and barbecue/picnic area.

Marquis Phillips   NR

2 Riviera Court, Pasadena, SA 5042 (postal) **REGION** Fleurieu/Limestone Coast Zone
T (08) 8357 4560 **F** (08) 8357 4234 **OPEN** Not
WINEMAKER Sparky Marquis, Sarah Marquis, Kim Johnston **EST.** 1998 **CASES** NA
SUMMARY Marquis Phillips is the export-oriented brand created by the high-profile Sparky and Sarah
Marquis winemaking duo. The very large production is directed to the Canadian, German, Singapore
and the US markets, but is nominally available by mail order.

Marribrook   ★★★★

Albany Highway, Kendenup, WA 6323 **REGION** Mount Barker
T (08) 9851 4651 **F** (08) 9851 4652 **OPEN** Wed–Sun & public hols 10.30–4.30
WINEMAKER Richard Robson **EST.** 1990 **CASES** 2000
SUMMARY The Brooks family purchased the former Marron View 5.6-ha vineyard from Kim Hart in
1994 and renamed the venture Marribrook Wines. Those wines are now made at Plantagenet, having
been made at Alkoomi up to 1994. The Brooks have purchased an additional property on the Albany
Highway north of Mount Barker and immediately south of Gilberts. Retail distribution in WA and
Victoria; exports to the UK and Singapore.

ΨΨΨΨ♡ **Frankland River Semillon Sauvignon Blanc 2004** Clean; very intense and tightly
focused; mineral, lemon and spice; considerable length. **RATING** 93 **DRINK** 2009 $ 15

ΨΨΨΨ **Cabernet Malbec Merlot 2002** Light to medium-bodied; earth and olive tinges to the
black fruits; lingering finish with fine, savoury, olive-accented tannins. **RATING** 89
DRINK 2010 $ 20

ΨΨΨ♡ **Botanica Chardonnay 2004** **RATING** 85 **DRINK** 2008 $ 15

Marri Wood Park   ★★★★

Cnr Caves Road/Whittle Road, Yallingup, WA 6282 **REGION** Margaret River
T 0438 525 580 **F** (08) 9315 2855 **OPEN** Weekends & public hols 10.30–5.30
WINEMAKER Mark Messenger (Juniper Estate) **EST.** 1993 **CASES** 1800
SUMMARY With plantings commencing back in 1993, Marri Wood Park has 6.5 ha of vineyards: 2 ha
of chenin blanc and 1.5 ha each of semillon, sauvignon blanc and cabernet sauvignon. Part of the
grapes are sold to other makers, the wine for Marri Wood Park being made by Mark Messenger. The
budget-priced Guinea Run range takes its name from the guinea fowl which are permanent vineyard
residents, busily eating the grasshoppers, weevils and bugs which cluster around the base of the
vines, thus reducing the need for pesticides. The premium Marri Wood Park range takes its name
from the giant Marri gum tree depicted on the label.

▼▼▼▼▽ Margaret River Semillon Sauvignon Blanc 2004 Not reduced, as is the Sauvignon Blanc; light-bodied; fresh juicy lemon and gooseberry fruit; attractive finish. Screwcap. **RATING** 90 **DRINK** 2008 $13.50

▼▼▼▼ Guinea Run Margaret River Cabernet Merlot 2004 Bright purple-red; abundant sweet berry fruit aromas; the palate is slightly raw and disjointed; needed more work one way or the other. Screwcap. **RATING** 87 **DRINK** 2008 $12.50

▼▼▼▽ Guinea Run Margaret River Chenin Blanc 2004 RATING 86 **DRINK** Now $12
Guinea Run Classic White 2004 Tangy, fresh, crisp, light-bodied; fruity, but nicely dry finish; no claims to complexity. Screwcap. **RATING** 86 **DRINK** 2007 $12
Margaret River Cabernet Sauvignon 2004 RATING 86 **DRINK** 2008 $13.50
Margaret River Sauvignon Blanc 2004 RATING 85 **DRINK** 2007 $13.50

Marschall Groom Cellars ★★★★

28 Langmeil Road, Tanunda, SA 5352 (postal) **REGION** Barossa Valley
T (08) 8563 1101 **F** (08) 8563 1102 **OPEN** Not
WINEMAKER Daryl Groom **EST.** 1997 **CASES** 2500
SUMMARY This is a family venture involving Daryl Groom, former Penfolds but now long-term Geyser Peak winemaker in California, Jeannette Marschall and David Marschall. It is an export-focused business, the principal market being the US.

▼▼▼▼▽ Barossa Valley Shiraz 2003 Powerful, dense black fruits and savoury chocolate; typical bombastic style of the '03 vintage; balanced tannins and oak. Quality cork. **RATING** 91 **DRINK** 2013 $58

▼▼▼▼ Adelaide Hills Sauvignon Blanc 2004 Very complex barrel ferment toasty oak aromas and flavours tend to dominant the ripe fruit. **RATING** 87 **DRINK** Now $24

Marsh Estate NR

Deasy's Road, Pokolbin, NSW 2321 **REGION** Lower Hunter Valley
T (02) 4998 7587 **F** (02) 4998 7884 **OPEN** Mon–Fri 10–4.30, weekends 10–5
WINEMAKER Andrew Marsh **EST.** 1971 **CASES** 7000
SUMMARY Through sheer consistency, value for money and unrelenting hard work, the Marsh family (who purchased the former Quentin Estate in 1978) has built up a sufficiently loyal cellar door and mailing list clientele to allow all the considerable production to be sold direct. Wine style is always direct, with oak playing a minimal role, and prolonged cellaring paying handsome dividends. No recent tastings.

Martins Hill Wines ★★☆

Sydney Road, Mudgee, NSW 2850 **REGION** Mudgee
T (02) 6373 1248 **F** (02) 6373 1248 **OPEN** Not
WINEMAKER Pieter Van Gent (Contract) **EST.** 1985 **CASES** 600
SUMMARY Janette Kenworthy and Michael Sweeny are committed organic grapegrowers and are members of the Organic Vignerons Association. It is a tiny operation at the moment, with 0.5 ha each of sauvignon blanc and pinot noir, 1 ha of cabernet sauvignon and 1.5 ha of shiraz in production. While there is no cellar door (only a mailing list), organic vineyard tours and talks can be arranged by appointment.

Marybrook Vineyards NR

Vasse–Yallingup Road, Marybrook, WA 6280 **REGION** Margaret River
T (08) 9755 1143 **F** (08) 9755 1112 **OPEN** Fri–Mon 10–5, 7 days 10–5 school hols
WINEMAKER Aub House **EST.** 1986 **CASES** 2000
SUMMARY Marybrook Vineyards is owned by Aub and Jan House. They have 8 ha of vineyards in production, with back vintages often available.

Mary Byrnes Wine NR

Rees Road, Ballandean, Qld 4382 **REGION** Granite Belt
T (07) 4684 1111 **F** (07) 4684 1312 **OPEN** 7 days 10–5 Easter–Oct

WINEMAKER Mary Byrnes **EST.** 1991 **CASES** 3500

SUMMARY Mary Byrnes, who has a wine science degree, acquired her property in 1991, and has since planted 4 ha of shiraz, and 1 ha each of marsanne, viognier, roussanne and mourvedre, and 0.5 ha each of grenache and black hamburg muscat. She has deliberately grown the vines without irrigation, thereby limiting yield and (in her words) ensuring a distinctive regional quality and flavour. Exports to the UK and New Zealand.

Maslin Old Dunsborough Wines   NR

90 Naturaliste Terrace, Dunsborough, WA 6281 **REGION** Margaret River
T (08) 9755 3578 **F** (08) 9755 3578 **OPEN** Weekends, or by appointment
WINEMAKER Robert Maslin **EST.** 1999 **CASES** NA

SUMMARY Yet another new entrant in the Margaret River region, established by Robert and Leonie Maslin. They have planted semillon, sauvignon blanc, chenin blanc, pinot noir, merlot and cabernet sauvignon and make the wines onsite. Accommodation is available, and the cellar door offers barbecue facilities.

Massena Vineyards   NR

PO Box 54, Tanunda, SA 5352 **REGION** Barossa Valley
T (08) 8564 3037 **F** (08) 8564 3037 **OPEN** Not
WINEMAKER Dan Standish, Jaysen Collins **EST.** 2000 **CASES** NA

SUMMARY Massena Vineyards draws upon 2 ha of grenache, shiraz, mourvedre, durif and tinta amarella at Nuriootpa. It is an export-oriented business, selling to the US, Denmark and England. The wines can, however, be purchased by mail order.

Massoni   ★★★★

PO Box 13261, Law Courts Post Office, Melbourne, Vic 8010 **REGION** Pyrenees/Mornington Peninsula
T 1300 131 175 **F** 1300 131 185 **WEB** www.massoniwines.com **OPEN** Not
WINEMAKER Michael Unwin (Punt Road) **EST.** 1984 **CASES** 20 000

SUMMARY Massoni, under the direction of the Ursini family, has regained control of its destiny after the proposed public issue was terminated. The main grape source for Massoni is the very large GlenKara vineyard in the Pyrenees, with a yield well in excess of 1000 tonnes in 2005. Notwithstanding the 2004 drought, GlenKara was awarded Brown Brothers Grower of the Year, as well as Producer of Best Cabernet and Best Merlot. Massoni has also appointed Punt Road winemakers Rob Dolan and Kate Goodman, in conjunction with Michael Unwin, as contract winemakers.

ŸŸŸŸŸ **Barbera 2003** Deep, dense colour; concentrated, powerful but not extractive; bitter chocolate, blackberry and spice flavours. GlenKara vineyard. Screwcap. **RATING** 90 **DRINK** 2013 $ 25

ŸŸŸŸ **Cabernet Sauvignon 2002** Medium-bodied; earth, mint and blackcurrant; fine tannins, savoury finish. GlenKara vineyard. Cork. **RATING** 88 **DRINK** 2012 $ 25

Matilda's Estate   ★★★★

RMB 654, Hamilton Road, Denmark, WA 6333 **REGION** Denmark
T (08) 9848 1951 **F** (08) 9848 1957 **WEB** www.matildasestate.com **OPEN** Tues–Sun 10–5, 7 days during school hols
WINEMAKER Gavin Berry, Dave Cleary **EST.** 1990 **CASES** 4000

SUMMARY In September 2002 the founders of Matilda's Meadow (as it was then known), Don Turnbull and Pamela Meldrum, sold the business to former citizen of the world Steve Hall. It is a thriving business based on 6 ha of estate plantings; a restaurant offers morning and afternoon tea, lunch Tuesday to Sunday and dinner Thursday to Saturday.

ŸŸŸŸŸ **Fossil Series Semillon Sauvignon Blanc 2004** Spotlessly clean; fresh, delicate but clearly articulated herb, grass and passionfruit flavours. Screwcap. **RATING** 90 **DRINK** 2007 $ 16.50

ΨΨΨΨ **Fossil Series Cabernet Sauvignon Cabernet Franc 2003** Light to medium-bodied; bright, fresh red fruits; attractive summer red, neither green nor mean. **RATING** 88 **DRINK** Now $20
Fossil Series Unwooded Chardonnay 2004 Citrus, stone fruit and melon; simple, easy style; drink now. **RATING** 87 **DRINK** Now $18

ΨΨΨΨ **Fossil Series Pinot Noir 2003** **RATING** 85 **DRINK** Now $24.50

Mawson Ridge NR

24–28 Main Road, Hahndorf, SA 5066 **REGION** Adelaide Hills
T (08) 8338 0828 **F** (08) 8338 0828 **WEB** www.mawsonridge.com **OPEN** Summer Tues–Sat 11–5, Winter Wed–Sat 11–5, Sun 12–5
WINEMAKER Michael Scarpantoni (Contract) **EST.** 1998 **CASES** 400
SUMMARY You might be forgiven for thinking the winery name carries the cool-climate association a little bit too far. In fact, Sir Douglas Mawson, also a conservationist and forester, arrived in the Lenswood region in the early 1930s, harvesting the native stringybarks and replanting the cleared land with pine trees. A hut that Mawson built on the property still stands today on Mawson Road, which the vineyard fronts. Here Raymond and Madeline Marin have established 5.5 ha of vines, having added 2 ha of pinot gris in 2002.

Maximilian's Vineyard NR

Main Road, Verdun, SA 5245 **REGION** Adelaide Hills
T (08) 8388 7777 **F** (08) 8388 1371 **WEB** www.maximilians.com.au **OPEN** Wed–Mon 11–5
WINEMAKER Contract **EST.** 1994 **CASES** 2000
SUMMARY Maximilian and Louise Hruska opened Maximilian's Restaurant in 1976, in a homestead built in 1851. They planted 2 ha of chardonnay and 6 ha of cabernet sauvignon in 1994, surrounding the restaurant. The Cabernet Sauvignon is made by Grant Burge, the Chardonnay at Scarpantoni Estate under the direction of the Hruska's eldest son, Paul. Since graduating from Roseworthy, Paul Hruska has completed vintages in Burgundy, Bordeaux, Spain, Margaret River and the Clare Valley; he is winemaker/vineyard manager at The Islander on Kangaroo Island.

Maxwell Wines ★★★★

Olivers Road, McLaren Vale, SA 5171 **REGION** McLaren Vale
T (08) 8323 8200 **F** (08) 8323 8900 **WEB** www.maxwellwines.com.au **OPEN** 7 days 10–5
WINEMAKER Mark Maxwell, Adam Hooper **EST.** 1979 **CASES** 12 000
SUMMARY Maxwell Wines has come a long way since opening for business in 1979 using an amazing array of Heath Robinson equipment in cramped surroundings. A state-of-the-art and much larger winery was built on a new site in time for the 1997 vintage. The brand has produced some excellent white and red wines in recent years. Exports to the UK, Switzerland, Austria, Germany, Belgium, Hong Kong, Singapore, Thailand, Malaysia, New Zealand, Canada and the US.

ΨΨΨΨΨ **Ellen Street Shiraz 2002** Dense, powerful structure; black fruits, earth and chocolate; solid tannins, good length. **RATING** 93 **DRINK** 2015 $29

ΨΨΨΨ **Where's Molly Rose 2004** Plenty of flavour in the red cherry spectrum; good balance as a summer red. Molly is the winery dog. **RATING** 87 **DRINK** Now $12
Four Roads 2002 Complex spice and red fruit flavours, but a slightly hollow texture. Shiraz/Grenache/Viognier. **RATING** 87 **DRINK** 2007 $19
Cabernet Merlot 2002 Juicy berry fruits and regional dark chocolate; slightly disjointed tannins need to marry. **RATING** 87 **DRINK** 2009 $16

ΨΨΨ **Box 111 Chardonnay 2004** **RATING** 83 $14
The Mistress Verdelho 2004 **RATING** 83 $16

Maygars Hill Winery ★★★★☆

53 Longwood–Mansfield Road, Longwood, Vic 3665 **REGION** Strathbogie Ranges
T (03) 5798 5417 **F** (03) 5798 5457 **WEB** www.strathbogieboutiquewines.com **OPEN** By appointment
WINEMAKER Sam Plunkett (Contract) **EST.** 1997 **CASES** 1200

SUMMARY The 8-ha property known as Maygars Hill was purchased by Jenny Houghton in 1994. The plan, now a reality, was to establish onsite B&B accommodation, and to plant a small vineyard, which now comprises 1.6 ha of shiraz and 0.8 ha of cabernet sauvignon. The name comes from Lieutenant Colonel Maygar, who fought with outstanding bravery in the Boer War in South Africa in 1901, where he won the Victoria Cross. In World War I he rose to command of the 8th Light Horse Regiment, winning yet further medals for bravery. He died on 1 November 1917.

ΨΨΨΨΨ **Reserve Shiraz 2003** Supple, smooth, deliciously sweet blackberry and plum fruit; mid-palate vinosity retained despite the '100-year drought'; long, balanced finish. Quality cork. **RATING** 94 **DRINK** 2018 $ 32

ΨΨΨΨΨ **Reserve Cabernet Sauvignon 2003** Very ripe cassis, blackcurrant, almost into jam; some drought stress evident, though big flavour. Stained cork. **RATING** 90 **DRINK** 2015 $ 32

M. Chapoutier Australia ★★★☆

PO Box 437, Robe, SA 5276 **REGION** Mount Benson
T(08) 8768 5076 **F**(08) 8768 5073 **WEB** www.chapoutier.com **OPEN** Not
WINEMAKER Benjamin Darnault **EST.** 1998 **CASES** 10 0000
SUMMARY M. Chapoutier Australia is the offshoot of the famous Rhône Valley producer. It has established 3 vineyards in Australia: Domaine Tournon at Mount Benson (17 ha shiraz, 10 ha cabernet sauvignon, 4 ha marsanne, 3 ha viognier), Domaine Terlato Chapoutier in the Pyrenees (30 ha shiraz, 2 ha viognier) and a third at Heathcote (10 ha shiraz). It seems likely that in future increasing emphasis will be placed on the two Victorian vineyards. The business is in the course of re-establishing all of its operations in Heathcote, with a winery and office to be built in the not-too-distant future. Exports to Europe, Asia, the US, New Zealand, Hong Kong, Japan, Singapore and Indonesia.

Meadowbank Estate ★★★★

699 Richmond Road, Cambridge, Tas 7170 **REGION** Southern Tasmania
T(03) 6248 4484 **F**(03) 6248 4485 **WEB** www.meadowbankwines.com.au **OPEN** 7 days 10–5
WINEMAKER Andrew Hood (Contract) **EST.** 1974 **CASES** 10 000
SUMMARY Now an important part of the Ellis family business on what was once (but is no more) a large grazing property on the banks of the Derwent. Increased plantings are under contract to Hardys, and a splendid winery has been built to handle the increased production. The winery has expansive entertainment and function facilities, capable of handling up to 1000 people, and offering an arts and music program throughout the year, plus a large restaurant (open 7 days). Exports to the UK, Hong Kong and Denmark.

ΨΨΨΨΨ **Riesling 2004** Attractive wine, almost fleshy; tropical overtones to citrus and lime fruit. **RATING** 90 **DRINK** 2014 $ 25

ΨΨΨΨ **Chardonnay 2004** Clean; no reduction; fresh, elegant and long; gentle melon and citrus, the citrus and brisk acidity substituting for oak and giving length. **RATING** 89 **DRINK** 2008 $ 25.50
Cabernet 2003 Fragrant; light to medium-bodied, almost delicate cassis/redcurrant/blackcurrant fruit; fractionally green tannins. **RATING** 89 **DRINK** 2009 $ 31

ΨΨΨΨ **Sauvignon Blanc 2004 RATING** 85 **DRINK** 2007 $ 27.50
Pinot Gris 2004 RATING 84 **DRINK** 2007 $ 28.50
Henry James Pinot Noir 2003 RATING 84 **DRINK** 2007 $ 41

ΨΨΨ **Cabernet Sauvignon 2003 RATING** 83 $ 31

Meerea Park ★★★★☆

Lot 3 Palmers Lane, Pokolbin, NSW 2320 **REGION** Lower Hunter Valley
T(02) 4998 7474 **F**(02) 4930 7100 **WEB** www.meereapark.com.au **OPEN** At The Boutique Wine Centre, Broke Road, Pokolbin
WINEMAKER Rhys Eather **EST.** 1991 **CASES** 10 000
SUMMARY All the wines are produced from grapes purchased from growers, primarily in the Pokolbin, Broke-Fordwich and Upper Hunter regions, but also from as far afield as Orange and

Young. It is the brainchild of Rhys Eather, a great-grandson of Alexander Munro, a leading vigneron in the mid-19th century; he makes the wine at the former Little's Winery on Palmer's Lane in Pokolbin. Retail distribution in most states; exports to the UK, The Netherlands, Germany, Canada and Singapore.

ŸŸŸŸŸ **Terracotta Shiraz 2002** Lifted aromas and flavours so typical of Shiraz with a touch of Viognier (8%); stylish and long palate; well balanced, fine tannins. **RATING** 94 **DRINK** 2017 $55

ŸŸŸŸŸ **Epoch Semillon 2004** Intense lemongrass and spice fruit aromas; generous flavour but not heavy; good focus and length; now or later. Screwcap. **RATING** 93 **DRINK** 2012 $19
The Aunts Shiraz 2003 Medium to full-bodied; rich and ripe blackberry and plum fruit; round, ripe tannins. Exceptionally good for the Hunter Valley. **RATING** 93 **DRINK** 2018 $26
Alexander Munro Shiraz 2002 Strong colour; complex regional leather, earth and spice; firm blackberry fruit entry; attractive soft tannins and oak on the finish. Screwcap. **RATING** 92 **DRINK** 2017 $40
Terracotta Shiraz 2003 Clean, aromatic, full-bodied; very powerful and firm palate; austere tannins. Demands 5 years, perhaps 20. Screwcap. **RATING** 91 **DRINK** 2023 $55
The Aunts Shiraz 2002 Strongly regional earthy, spicy aromas; excellent length and structure, more to red fruits; clever use of American oak. **RATING** 90 **DRINK** 2012 $25

ŸŸŸŸ **Epoch Semillon 2003** Powerful, quite deep lemon and herb fruit; shows its 12° alcohol. **RATING** 88 **DRINK** 2009 $18

ŸŸŸŸ **Alexander Munro Chardonnay 2003** **RATING** 86 **DRINK** 2008 $25
Shiraz Viognier 2003 **RATING** 86 **DRINK** 2010 $19

Melaleuca Grove   ★★★★

8 Melaleuca Court, Rowville, Vic 3178 (postal) **REGION** Upper Goulburn
T (03) 9752 7928 **F** (03) 9752 7928 **WEB** www.melaleucawines.com.au **OPEN** Not
WINEMAKER Jeff Wright **EST.** 1999 **CASES** 1000
SUMMARY Jeff and Anne Wright are both Honours graduates in biochemistry who have succumbed to the lure of winemaking after lengthy careers elsewhere; in the case of Jeff, 20 years in research and hospital science. He commenced his winemaking apprenticeship in 1997 at Green Vineyards, backed up by vintage work in 1999 and 2000 at Bianchet and Yarra Valley Hills, both in the Yarra Valley. At the same time he began the external Bachelor of Applied Science (Wine Science) course at Charles Sturt University, while still working in biochemistry in the public hospital system. They purchase grapes from various cool-climate regions, including Yea and the Yarra Valley. The wines are available through selected Melbourne retailers and restaurants, and by mailing list. Exports to Canada.

ŸŸŸŸŸ **Limited Release Chardonnay 2002** Light-bodied, but intense and stylish; minerally, citrussy edges to stone fruit and melon; subtle oak; good length. Yarra Valley/Upper Goulburn. Cork. **RATING** 90 **DRINK** 2010 $16.50

ŸŸŸŸ **Central Victoria Sauvignon Blanc 2004** A slatey, minerally bouquet with not overmuch varietal fruit; picks up the pace on the palate, with lingering acidity. Good value. Screwcap. **RATING** 86 **DRINK** Now $11.30

Melange Wines   NR

Farm 1291, Harward Road, Griffith, NSW 2680 **REGION** Riverina
T (02) 6962 7783 **F** (02) 6962 7783 **OPEN** 7 days 10–5
WINEMAKER Angelo D'Aquino **EST.** 2000 **CASES** NA
SUMMARY Melange Wines is a relative newcomer in the Riverina region, although Angelo D'Aquino comes from a family with considerable viticultural experience. There are 25 ha of sauvignon blanc, semillon, chardonnay, verdelho, trebbiano, muscat gordo blanco, shiraz and durif planted. The cellar door offers light meals and winery tours plus tutored tastings.

Mengler View Wines   NR

Magnolia Road, Tanunda, SA 5352 **REGION** Barossa Valley
T (08) 8563 2217 **F** (08) 8563 2408 **OPEN** By appointment
WINEMAKER Bob Mitchell, Stuart Blackwell **EST.** 1995 **CASES** 1300

SUMMARY This is the project of the Faith Lutheran School, which began making small batches of wine in 1992 as part of the Year 10 agricultural studies program. Stuart Blackwell of St Hallett has mentored the program since its inception, during which time the crush has grown from 0.5 tonne (in 1995) to 15 tonnes (2004). The wines have been exhibited with success in the Barossa Valley Wine Show, and Faith became the first school in Australia to construct a purpose-built winery: the Faith Wine Education Centre opened in October 2002. The executive manager in charge is Bob Mitchell, agricultural co-ordinator and winery manager.

Merli   NR

19 One Chain Road, Merricks North, Vic 3926 **REGION** Mornington Peninsula
T (03) 5989 7435 **F** (03) 9380 2555 **OPEN** By appointment
WINEMAKER Ennio Merli, David Merli **EST.** 2000 **CASES** NA
SUMMARY Ennio, David and Jonathan Merli have established 4 ha of chardonnay, pinot noir, shiraz, cabernet sauvignon and merlot at Merricks North. The relatively small production is made onsite, and sold by mail order and throught the cellar door when open.

Mermerus Vineyard   ★★★★☆

60 Soho Road, Drysdale, Vic 3222 **REGION** Geelong
T (03) 5253 2718 **F** (03) 5226 1683 **OPEN** First Sunday of each month & every Sunday in January 11–4
WINEMAKER Paul Champion **EST.** 2000 **CASES** 600
SUMMARY Commencing in 1996, Paul Champion has established 1.5 ha of pinot noir, 1 ha of chardonnay and 0.2 ha of riesling at Mermerus, making the wine onsite (the winery was built in 2000), also acting as contract winemaker for small growers in the region. The first commercial wines were made in the following year, and are sold through the cellar door/mailing list and selected restaurants.

♟♟♟♟♟ **Chardonnay 2003** Potent, complex barrel ferment and oak inputs along with potent, deep fruit; mega-style which works well. **RATING** 94 **DRINK** 2010 $ 18

♟♟♟♟♐ **Pope's Eye Rose 2004** Bright pink; delicate, clean and fresh; an elegant, light but well-balanced wine with a lingering finish. **RATING** 90 **DRINK** Now $ 14

♟♟♟♟ **Pinot Noir 2003** Ultra-ripe, highly polished red and black cherry fruit; just avoids jamminess. **RATING** 89 **DRINK** 2009 $ 18

🐦 Merops Wines   ★★★

243 Caves Road, Margaret River, WA 6825 **REGION** Margaret River
T (08) 9757 2691 **F** (08) 9757 3193 **WEB** www.meropswines.com.au **OPEN** By appointment
WINEMAKER Mark Lane (Contract) **EST.** 2000 **CASES** 1320
SUMMARY Jim and Yvonne Ross have been involved in horticulture for over 25 years, in production, retail nurseries and viticulture. They established a nursery and irrigation business in the Margaret River township in 1985 on a 3-ha property in town before establishing a rootstock nursery. In 2000 they removed the nursery and planted 6.3 ha of cabernet sauvignon, cabernet franc, merlot and shiraz on the laterite gravel over clay soils. They use the practices developed by Professor William Albrecht in the US 50 years ago, providing mineral balance and thus eliminating the need for insecticides and toxic sprays. The wines are sold by mail order and through the website.

♟♟♟♐ **Shiraz 2003** Avant garde labelling works quite well. Medium-bodied, spicy, savoury; needs a little more sweet fruit. **RATING** 86 **DRINK** 2008 $ 17
Ornatus 2003 **RATING** 85 **DRINK** 2007 $ 20

♟♟♟ **Cabernet Merlot 2003** **RATING** 83 $ 17

Merrebee Estate   NR

Lot 3339 St Werburghs Road, Mount Barker, WA 6234 **REGION** Mount Barker
T (08) 9851 2424 **F** (08) 9851 2425 **WEB** www.merrebee.ozware.com **OPEN** By appointment
WINEMAKER Contract **EST.** 1986 **CASES** 500
SUMMARY Planting of the Merrebee Estate vineyards commenced in 1986 and have now reached a little under 9 ha. The wines are available from selected retailers in Western Australia and from Rathdowne Cellars, Melbourne, and Ultimo Wine Centre, Sydney; exports to the UK, the US and Canada.

Merricks Creek Wines

44 Merricks Road, Merricks, Vic 3916 **REGION** Mornington Peninsula
T (03) 5989 8868 **F** (03) 5989 9070 **WEB** www.pinot.com.au **OPEN** By appointment
WINEMAKER Nick Farr, Peter Parker **EST.** 1998 **CASES** 330
SUMMARY Peter and Georgina Parker retained Gary Farr (of Bannockburn) as viticultural consultant before they began establishing of their 2-ha pinot noir vineyard. They say, 'He has been an extraordinarily helpful and stern taskmaster from day one. He advised on clonal selection, trellis design and planting density, and visits the vineyard regularly to monitor canopy management.' (Son Nick Farr completes the circle as contract winemaker.) The vineyard is planted to a sophisticated and rare collection of new pinot noir clones, and is being planted at the ultra-high density of 500 mm spacing on 1-m high trellising.

ỸỸỸỸỸ **Nick Farr Pinot Noir 2003** Very deep colour; rich, mouthfilling plum, cherry and blackberry fruits; very different style with great depth. **RATING** 94 **DRINK** 2013 $ 45

ỸỸỸỸỸ **Close Planted Pinot Noir 2003** Good hue, albeit light colour; a restrained, elegant bouquet; fine, silky, supple red and black cherry fruits. **RATING** 92 **DRINK** 2010 $ 43
Pinot Noir 2003 Similar to the Close Planted Pinot Noir; slightly more intensity and some plummy characters; more length, but the same restraint. **RATING** 92 **DRINK** 2010 $ 34

ỸỸỸỸ **Young Vines Pinot Noir 2003** Pale but bright hue; distinct stemmy/stalky/minty edges to the red fruits, but not significantly lower alcohol. **RATING** 88 **DRINK** 2007 $ 18

Merricks Estate

Thompsons Lane, Merricks, Vic 3916 **REGION** Mornington Peninsula
T (03) 5989 8416 **F** (03) 9613 4242 **OPEN** First weekend of each month, each weekend in Jan & public holiday weekends 12–5
WINEMAKER Paul Evans **EST.** 1977 **CASES** 2000
SUMMARY Melbourne solicitor George Kefford, with wife Jacquie, runs Merricks Estate as a weekend and holiday enterprise. Right from the outset it has produced distinctive, spicy, cool-climate Shiraz which has accumulated an impressive array of show trophies and gold medals.

ỸỸỸỸỸ **Shiraz 2000** All the precursors for development are here; black fruits, licorice and plum aromas, then mouthfilling, round, supple and sweet black fruits, licorice and spice; excellent length. '94 and '97 tasted by comparison, both very good. **RATING** 94 **DRINK** 2010 $ 25

ỸỸỸỸ **Pinot Noir 2002** Good colour; fragrant, spicy, foresty edges to strong varietal fruit; low-crop intensity, but not at all over the top; satiny tannins. Cork. **RATING** 93 **DRINK** 2011

ỸỸỸỸ **Chardonnay 2001** Very rich, ripe, mouthfilling yellow peach, fig and melon fruit; soft finish. Cork. **RATING** 88 **DRINK** Now

Merum ★★★★★

Hillbrook Road, Quinninup, WA 6258 **REGION** Pemberton
T (08) 9776 6011 **F** (08) 9776 6022 **WEB** www.merum.com.au **OPEN** By appointment
WINEMAKER Jan Davies (Contract) **EST.** 1996 **CASES** 1500
SUMMARY Merum is owned and managed by viticulturist Mike Melsom and partner Julie Roberts. The 6.3-ha vineyard, planted in 1996, consists of semillon, shiraz and chardonnay. The first wine was made in 1999 by the late Maria Melsom. Exports to the UK and Hong Kong.

ỸỸỸỸỸ **Pemberton Semillon 2004** Complex, rich, rounded but not heavy; ripe lemon almost into stone fruit; very good mouthfeel. Consistent vineyard style and quality. Screwcap. **RATING** 94 **DRINK** 2010 $ 27

ỸỸỸỸ **Pemberton Shiraz 2003** Light-bodied; fresh, spicy red fruits; not forced, but not as much depth as usual. Screwcap. **RATING** 87 **DRINK** 2008

Metcalfe Valley ★★★★★

283 Metcalfe–Malmsbury Road, Metcalfe, Vic 3448 **REGION** Macedon Ranges
T (03) 5423 2035 **OPEN** By appointment
WINEMAKER Ian Pattison **EST.** 1994 **CASES** 600

SUMMARY Ian Pattison, who has a PhD in metallurgy, and a Diploma in horticultural science and viticulture from Melbourne University/Dookie College, purchased Metcalfe Valley from the Frederiksens in 2003. He has a little under 5 ha of shiraz and sauvignon blanc, and production is increasing.

🍷🍷🍷🍷🍷 **Shiraz 2003** Beautiful young wine; a mix of red and black fruit; perfect balance and texture. Trophy winner 2004 Macedon Ranges Wine Exhibition. **RATING** 94 **DRINK** 2013 $ 20

Metier Wines ★★★★★

Tarraford Vineyard, 440 Healesville Road, Yarra Glen, Vic 3775 (postal) **REGION** Yarra Valley
T 0419 678 918 **F** (03) 5962 2194 **WEB** www.metierwines.com.au **OPEN** Not
WINEMAKER Martin Williams MW **EST.** 1995 **CASES** 2000
SUMMARY Metier is the French word for craft, trade or profession; the business is that of Yarra Valley-based Martin Williams MW, who has notched up an array of degrees and had winemaking stints in France, California and Australia which are, not to put too fine a word on it, extraordinary. The focus of Metier is individual vineyard wines, initially based on grapes from the Tarraford and Schoolhouse Vineyards, both in the Yarra Valley. Exports to the UK, the US and Hong Kong.

🍷🍷🍷🍷🍷 **Tarraford Vineyard Yarra Valley Chardonnay 2002** Great finesse and elegance; sublimely subtle barrel ferment and malolactic inputs to melon and stone fruit; very long life. Screwcap. **RATING** 95 **DRINK** 2012
Schoolhouse Vineyard Yarra Valley Chardonnay 2002 In typical super-elegant, refined style; a subtle interplay of malolactic and barrel ferment inputs seamlessly woven through a long, lingering finish. Cork. **RATING** 94 **DRINK** 2012 $ 32

🍷🍷🍷🍷🍷 **Milkwood Adelaide Hills Sauvignon Blanc 2004** Spotlessly clean; fresh, delicate grass, citrus and a hint of passionfruit. Screwcap. **RATING** 90 **DRINK** 2007

🍷🍷🍷🍷 **Milkwood Central Victoria/Yarra Valley Chardonnay 2003** Gently sweet stone fruit and melon; fresh, has length, though not particularly complex. Screwcap. **RATING** 87 **DRINK** 2007

Meure's Wines ★★★★

16 Fleurtys Lane, Birchs Bay, Tas 7162 **REGION** Southern Tasmania
T (03) 6267 4483 **F** (03) 6267 4483 **OPEN** By appointment
WINEMAKER Louise Brightman, Dirk Meure, Michael Vishacki (Consultant) **EST.** 1991 **CASES** 300
SUMMARY Dirk Meure has established 1 ha of vineyard on the shores of D'Entrecasteaux Channel, overlooking Bruny Island. The Huon Valley is the southernmost wine region in Australia, and it was here that Dirk Meure's parents settled on their arrival from The Netherlands in 1950. He says he has been heavily influenced by his mentors, Steve and Monique Lubiana. The philosophy is to produce low yields from balanced vines and to interfere as little as possible in the winemaking and maturation process.

Miceli ★★★★☆

60 Main Creek Road, Arthurs Seat, Vic 3936 **REGION** Mornington Peninsula
T (03) 5989 2755 **F** (03) 5989 2755 **OPEN** First weekend each month 12–5, public hols, every weekend, and by appointment in Jan
WINEMAKER Anthony Miceli **EST.** 1991 **CASES** 3000
SUMMARY This may be a part-time labour of love for general practitioner Dr Anthony Miceli, but that hasn't prevented him taking the whole venture very seriously. He acquired the property in 1989 specifically to establish a vineyard. He planted 1.8 ha in November 1991, followed by a further hectare of Pinot Gris in 1997. Between 1991 and 1997 Dr Miceli did the Wine Science course at Charles Sturt University; he now manages both vineyard and winery. Retail distribution through Haviland Wine Merchants in Sydney and Australian Wine Agencies in Melbourne.

🍷🍷🍷🍷🍷 **Olivia's Chardonnay 2001** Great green-gold colour; intense grapefruit and melon; perfectly balanced and integrated oak; great length. Perfect development under screwcap. **RATING** 94 **DRINK** 2011 $ 26

YYYY **Iolanda Pinot Grigio 2003** Quite deep and powerful; lemony, minerally acidity gives balance and length. **RATING** 91 **DRINK** Now $ 20

YYYY **Lucy's Choice Pinot Noir 2001** Developed colour; bottle-developed, complex, spicy, gamey flavours; light-bodied; good balance. Screwcap. **RATING** 88 **DRINK** 2007 $ 26

Michael Unwin Wines ★★★☆

2 Racecourse Road, Beaufort, Vic 3373 **REGION** Grampians
T (03) 5349 2021 **F** (03) 5349 2032 **WEB** www.michaelunwinwines.com **OPEN** 7 days 10–6
WINEMAKER Michael Unwin **EST.** 2000 **CASES** 1000
SUMMARY Established at Ararat, Victoria by winemaker Michael Unwin and wife and business partner Catherine Clark. His track record as a winemaker spans 17 years, and includes extended winemaking experience in France, New Zealand and Australia; he has found time to obtain a postgraduate degree in oenology and viticulture at Lincoln University, Canterbury, New Zealand. He also does contract winemaking and consulting; the winemaking takes place in a converted textile factory.

YYYY **Acrobat Botrytised Riesling 2003** More into Kabinett/Spatlese style than full-on botrytis; considerable acidity; needs time. **RATING** 87 **DRINK** 2012 $ 25

YYY **Black Hen Chardonnay NV** **RATING** 83 $ 28
Black Hen Cabernet Sauvignon NV **RATING** 83 $ 28

Michelini Wines ★★★

Great Alpine Road, Myrtleford, Vic 3737 **REGION** Alpine Valleys
T (03) 5751 1990 **F** (03) 5751 1410 **WEB** www.micheliniwines.com.au **OPEN** 7 days 10–5
WINEMAKER Greg O'Keefe **EST.** 1982 **CASES** 5000
SUMMARY The Michelini family are among the best-known grapegrowers in the Buckland Valley of northeast Victoria. Having migrated from Italy in 1949, the Michelinis originally grew tobacco, diversifying into vineyards in 1982. They now have a little over 42 ha of vineyard on terra rossa soil at an altitude of 300m, mostly with frontage to the Buckland River. The major part of the production is sold (to Orlando and others), but since 1996 an onsite winery has permitted the Michelinis to vinify part of their production. The winery has the capacity to handle 1000 tonnes of fruit, which eliminates the problem of moving grapes out of a declared phylloxera area.

Middlebrook Estate NR

RSD 43, Sand Road, McLaren Vale, SA 5171 **REGION** McLaren Vale
T (08) 8383 0600 **F** (08) 8383 0557 **WEB** www.middlebrookestate.com.au **OPEN** Mon–Fri 10.30–4, weekends 11.30–4.30
WINEMAKER Joseph Cogno, Michael Petrucci **EST.** 1947 **CASES** 65 000
SUMMARY After a brief period of ownership by industry veteran Bill Clappis (who renovated and reopened the winery), ownership has now passed to the Cogno brothers family, which has been winemaking at Cobbity, near Camden, NSW, since 1964. Through Middlebrook the family has become one of the largest producers of Lambrusco in Australia; it is available Australia-wide through Liquorland stores. Many other wines (18 in all) are produced under the Cogno Brothers label; the Middlebrook cask hall has been given over to production of the Medlow chocolate range. The top wines are still sold under the Middlebrook label.

Middlesex 31 NR

PO Box 367, Manjimup, WA 6258 **REGION** Manjimup
T (08) 9771 2499 **F** (08) 9771 2499 **OPEN** Not
WINEMAKER Brenden Smith, Dave Cleary, Mark Aitken **EST.** 1990 **CASES** 1000
SUMMARY Dr John Rosser (a local GP who runs the Manjimup Medical Centre) and Rosemary Davies have planted 6.5 ha of vines, predominantly to shiraz, chardonnay and verdelho, but with a little patch of pinot noir.

Middleton Wines ★★★

Flagstaff Hill Road, Middleton, SA 5213 **REGION** Currency Creek
T (08) 8555 4136 **F** (08) 8555 4108 **OPEN** Fri–Sun 11–5
WINEMAKER Robert Alexandre **EST.** 1979 **CASES** 6000
SUMMARY The Bland family has acquired Middleton Wines and has changed the entire focus of the business. Previously, all the production from the 12 ha of estate plantings was sold either as grapes or as bulk wine; now much is made into wine at the onsite winery.

TTTT **Alexandre's Special Reserve Cabernet Sauvignon 2001** Blackcurrant, mocha, cedar and spice aromas; light to medium-bodied; some bottle development; fine tannins. **RATING** 88 **DRINK** 2008 $18

TTTY **Currency Creek Shiraz 2003** **RATING** 86 **DRINK** 2008 $15

Midhill Vineyard ★★★

PO Box 30, Romsey, Vic 3434 **REGION** Macedon Ranges
T (03) 5429 5565 **OPEN** Not
WINEMAKER Contract **EST.** 1993 **CASES** 200
SUMMARY The Richards family has been breeding Angus cattle for the past 35 years, and diversified into grapegrowing in 1993. The vineyard has been planted on a northeast-facing slope on red volcanic clay loam which is free-draining and moderately fertile. There are 2 ha of chardonnay and 0.5 ha each of pinot noir and gewurztraminer in production. Sparkling Vintage Blancs de Blanc and lightly wooded Chardonnay are made from this planting; the other wine is Gewurztraminer. The wines have quite extensive distribution in local restaurants, and are available by mail order.

TTTT **Chardonnay 2003** Scored strongly at the 2004 Macedon Ranges Wine Exhibition, but did show some bottling SO_2 which will settle down. **RATING** 89 **DRINK** 2008 $20

Milford Vineyard NR

Tasman Highway, Cambridge, Tas 7170 **REGION** Southern Tasmania
T (03) 6248 5029 **F** (03) 6248 5076 **OPEN** Not
WINEMAKER Andrew Hood (Contract) **EST.** 1984 **CASES** 200
SUMMARY Given the tiny production, Milford is understandably not open to the public; the excellent Pinot Noir is quickly sold by word of mouth. The 150-ha grazing property (the oldest Southdown sheep stud in Australia) has been in Charlie Lewis's family since 1830. Only 15 minutes from Hobart, and with an absolute water frontage to the tidal estuary of the Coal River, it is a striking site. The vineyard is on a patch of 1.5m-deep sand over a clay base with lots of lime impregnation.

Milimani Estate NR

92 The Forest Road, Bungendore, NSW 2621 **REGION** Canberra District
T (02) 6238 1421 **F** (02) 6238 1424 **OPEN** Weekends & public hols 10–5
WINEMAKER Lark Hill, Kyeema Estate (Contract) **EST.** 1989 **CASES** 1400
SUMMARY The Preston family (Mary, David and Rosemary) have established a 3-ha vineyard at Bungendore planted to sauvignon blanc, chardonnay, pinot noir, merlot and cabernet franc.

Millbrook Estate NR

Lot 18/19 Mount View Road, Millfield, NSW 2325 **REGION** Lower Hunter Valley
T (02) 4998 1155 **F** (02) 4998 1155 **WEB** www.millbrookestate.com.au **OPEN** 7 days 10–5
WINEMAKER John Lyons **EST.** 1996 **CASES** 800
SUMMARY The 2.6 ha of Millbrook Estate vineyards produces between 400 cases (in a dry year) and 800 cases (in a good year). Interestingly, the vineyard is on a geological fault line, and is in fact an uplifted ancient creek bed. The wines are sold only through the cellar door and the vineyard cottage operated by the Lyons family.

Millbrook Winery ★★★★

Old Chestnut Lane, Jarrahdale, WA 6124 **REGION** Perth Hills
T (08) 9525 5796 **F** (08) 9525 5672 **WEB** www.millbrookwinery.com.au **OPEN** 7 days 10–5
WINEMAKER Tony Davis **EST.** 1996 **CASES** 16 000
SUMMARY The strikingly situated Millbrook Winery, opened in December 2001, is owned by the highly successful Perth-based entrepreneur Peter Fogarty and wife Lee. They also own Lake's Folly in the Hunter Valley, and Deep Woods Estate in Margaret River, and have made a major commitment to the quality end of Australian wine. Millbrook draws on 7.5 ha of vineyards in the Perth Hills, planted to sauvignon blanc, semillon, chardonnay, viognier, cabernet sauvignon, merlot, shiraz and petit verdot. It also purchases grapes from the Perth Hills and Geographe regions. The wines under both labels (Millbrook and Barking Owl) are of consistently high quality. Lunch is available from the restaurant 7 days. Exports to the UK, the US, Singapore and Germany.

ŦŦŦŦ¶ **Sauvignon Blanc 2004** Clean, fresh, complex gooseberry and passionfruit; excellent intensity, drive and length; minerally acidity. **RATING** 92 **DRINK** 2007 **$** 19.90
Shiraz 2002 Medium to full-bodied; a mix of dark and red berry fruit; solid but balanced tannins. **RATING** 92 **DRINK** 2015 **$** 32
Margaret River Semillon Sauvignon Blanc 2004 Spotlessly clean; mineral, herb and passionfruit; good length and fruit expression. Screwcap. **RATING** 91 **DRINK** 2007 **$** 21.50
Barking Owl Semillon Sauvignon Blanc 2004 Not particularly aromatic or expressive, but has excellent length and mouthfeel; herb and citrus; typical Semillon. Screwcap.
RATING 90 **DRINK** 2007 **$** 16.95

ŦŦŦŦ **Chardonnay 2003** Light-bodied; unforced style; melon and touches of cashew and cream ex barrel ferment and malolactic; harmonious finish. Cork. **RATING** 89 **DRINK** 2010 **$** 24
Viognier 2003 Luscious, rich varietal fruit with an inevitable touch of heat; apricots and peaches. Cork. **RATING** 89 **DRINK** Now **$** 21.50
Barking Owl Shiraz 2002 Retains youthful hue; spicy, tangy overtones to mint and red berry fruit; fresh, low pH style. Twin Top. **RATING** 87 **DRINK** 2008 **$** 16.95

ŦŦŦ¶ **Barking Owl Chardonnay 2003** **RATING** 86 **DRINK** 2007 **$** 16.95
Viognier 2004 **RATING** 86 **DRINK** 2007 **$** 22
Cabernet Merlot 2002 **RATING** 86 **DRINK** 2008 **$** 30.65
Barking Owl Cabernet Sauvignon Merlot 2003 **RATING** 85 **DRINK** 2007 **$** 16.95

Millers Samphire   NR

Watts Gully Road, Robertson Road, Kersbrook, SA 5231 **REGION** Adelaide Hills
T (08) 8389 3183 **F** (03) 8389 3183 **OPEN** 7 days 9–5 by appointment
WINEMAKER Tom Miller **EST.** 1982 **CASES** 80
SUMMARY Next after Scarp Valley, one of the smallest wineries in Australia offering wine for sale; pottery also helps. Tom Miller has one of the more interesting and diverse CVs, with an early interest in matters alcoholic leading to the premature but happy death of a laboratory rat at Adelaide University and his enforced switch from biochemistry to mechanical engineering. The Riesling is a high-flavoured wine with crushed herb and lime aromas and flavours.

Millfield ★★☆

Lot 341, Mount View Road, Millfield, NSW 2325 **REGION** Lower Hunter Valley
T (02) 4998 1571 **F** (02) 4998 0172 **WEB** www.millfieldwines.com **OPEN** Weekends 10–4
WINEMAKER David Lowe **EST.** 1997 **CASES** 500
SUMMARY Situated on the picturesque Mount View Road, Millfield made its market debut in June 2000. The neatly labelled and packaged wines have won gold medals and trophies right from the first vintage in 1998, and praise from wine writers and critics in Australia and the UK. The wines are sold through the cellar door and by mailing list, and through a limited number of fine wine retail and top-quality restaurants. Exports to the UK through Corney & Barrow.

Millinup Estate ★★★★

RMB 1280, Porongurup Road, Porongurup, WA 6324 **REGION** Porongurup
T (08) 9853 1105 **F** (08) 9853 1105 **OPEN** Weekends 10–5, or by appointment

WINEMAKER Mike Garland (Red), Diane Miller (White) **EST.** 1989 **CASES** 250

SUMMARY The Millinup Estate vineyard was planted in 1978, when it was called Point Creek. Owners Peter and Lesley Thorn purchased it in 1989, renaming it and having the limited production (from 0.5 ha of riesling, supplemented by purchased red grapes) vinified at Garlands and the Porongurup Winery.

Milvine Estate Wines ★★★

108 Warren Road, Heathcote, Vic 3523 **REGION** Heathcote
T 0407 332 772 **OPEN** Weekends 2–5, or by appointment
WINEMAKER Jonathan Mephan (Contract) **EST.** 2002 **CASES** 275

SUMMARY Jo and Graeme Millard planted 2.3 ha of clonally selected shiraz in 1995, picking their first grapes in 1998; in that and the ensuing four vintages the grapes were sold to Heathcote Winery, but in 2003 part of the production was vinified by Heathcote Winery for the Millards under the Milvine label. Production will increase in the years ahead, and the Millards have a carefully thought-out business plan to market the wine.

YYYY **Heathcote Shiraz 2003** Deep colour; lots of black fruit flavours, but even more tannins; needed additional barrel work or fining. Will benefit from age. **RATING** 87 **DRINK** 2013 $ 29.50

Minko Wines ★★★

13 High Street, Willunga, SA 5172 **REGION** Southern Fleurieu
T (08) 8556 4987 **F** (08) 8556 2688 **OPEN** 7 days 10–5
WINEMAKER James Hastwell (Hawkers Gate) **EST.** 1997 **CASES** NA

SUMMARY Mike Boerema, Inger Kellett, and children Nick and Margo (the winery name uses letters from each of the family names) established their vineyard on slopes of Mt Compass at an altitude of 300m. Minko practises sustainable eco-agriculture, and is a member of the the Compass Creek Care group; the Nangkita and Tookayerta creeks flow through the property, providing wetlands and associated native vegetation.

YYYY **Mount Compass Merlot Rose 2004** Bright crimson; raspberry, strawberry and cherry fruit; plenty of intensity and length; balance the strong point. Screwcap. **RATING** 87 **DRINK** Now $ 14.50

YYYY **Mount Compass Merlot 2003** Light to medium-bodied; clear black olive, herb and spice overtones to the blackcurrant fruit; good varietal character; light touch of oak. **RATING** 86 **DRINK** 2008 $ 18.50
Sparkling Merlot 2003 **RATING** 85 **DRINK** 2007 $ 16.50
Mount Compass Unwooded Chardonnay 2004 **RATING** 84 **DRINK** 2007 $ 13.50

Minot Vineyard ★★★☆

Lot 4 Harrington Road, Margaret River, WA 6285 **REGION** Margaret River
T (08) 9757 3579 **F** (08) 9757 2361 **OPEN** By appointment 10–5
WINEMAKER Harmans Estate (Contract) **EST.** 1986 **CASES** 2000

SUMMARY Minot, which takes its name from a small chateau in the Loire Valley in France, is the husband and wife venture of the Miles family, and produces just two wines from the 4.5-ha plantings of semillon, sauvignon blanc and cabernet sauvignon.

YYYY **Margaret River Semillon Sauvignon Blanc 2004** Crisp, dry, grass, lemon and mineral; driven by Semillon; firm finish. Screwcap. **RATING** 89 **DRINK** 2009 $ 18
Margaret River Cabernet Sauvignon Reserve 2001 Medium-bodied; savoury, spicy blackcurrant fruit; quite soft and supple fruit and tannin profile; nice oak. Cork. **RATING** 89 **DRINK** 2011 $ 35
Margaret River Cabernet Sauvignon 2002 Light to medium-bodied; savoury, spicy, leafy berry; fine tannins, some elegance. Cork. **RATING** 87 **DRINK** 2009 $ 28

Mintaro Wines ★★★☆

Leasingham Road, Mintaro, SA 5415 **REGION** Clare Valley
T (08) 8843 9150 **F** (08) 8843 9050 **WEB** www.mintarowines.com.au **OPEN** 7 days 10–4.30
WINEMAKER Peter Houldsworth **EST.** 1984 **CASES** 4000

SUMMARY Has produced some very good Riesling over the years, developing well in bottle. The red wines are formidable, massive in body and extract, built for the long haul. Exports to Singapore.

▼▼▼▼ **Belles Femmes et Grand Vin Shiraz 2001** Light to medium-bodied; savoury, spicy, lifted fruit; long palate; nice wine, seductive label. **RATING** 89 **DRINK** 2010 $ 30
Clare Valley Riesling 2002 Mineral, kerosene, flint and smoke aromas; powerful, robust style; slightly grippy. **RATING** 88 **DRINK** 2009 $ 18
Clare Valley Cabernet Sauvignon 2002 Powerful, earthy blackberry fruit; rustic tannins; needs time. **RATING** 88 **DRINK** 2012 $ 30

Minto Wines   NR

'Minto', Faraday via Castlemaine, Vic 3450 **REGION** Bendigo
T (03) 5473 3278 **OPEN** By appointment
WINEMAKER Alan Elliot **EST.** 1998 **CASES** 130
SUMMARY Alan and Heather Elliot have established a substantial business, anchored around 8 ha of chardonnay, pinot noir, shiraz and cabernet sauvignon, supplemented by contract-grown grapes. Sales are by mail order and through the cellar door (when open), which is housed in the former Faraday school.

Miramar   ★★★☆

Henry Lawson Drive, Mudgee, NSW 2850 **REGION** Mudgee
T (02) 6373 3874 **F** (02) 6373 3854 **WEB** www.miramarwines.com.au **OPEN** 7 days 9–5
WINEMAKER Ian MacRae **EST.** 1977 **CASES** 6000
SUMMARY Industry veteran Ian MacRae has demonstrated his skill with every type of wine over the decades, ranging from Rose to Chardonnay to full-bodied reds. All have shone under the Miramar label at one time or another, although the Ides of March are pointing more to the red than the white wines these days. The majority of the production from the 35 ha of estate vineyard is sold to others, the best being retained for Miramar's own use. From 2002 all wines have been sealed with screwcap.

▼▼▼▼▼ **Chardonnay 2000** Clean, still quite fresh; entirely fruit-driven by melon, stone fruit and citrus flavours; good balance. **RATING** 90 **DRINK** 2007 $ 15

▼▼▼▼ **Eurunderee Rose 2003 RATING** 86 **DRINK** Now $ 12
Riesling 2004 RATING 85 **DRINK** 2009 $ 12

Miranda Wines   ★★★☆

57 Jondaryan Avenue, Griffith, NSW 2680 **REGION** Riverina
T (02) 6960 3000 **F** (02) 6962 6944 **WEB** www.mirandawines.com.au **OPEN** 7 days 9–5
WINEMAKER Sam F Miranda, Garry Wall, Hope Golding, Luis E Simian **EST.** 1939 **CASES** 2.5 million
SUMMARY In 2003 Miranda Wines was purchased by the McGuigan/Simeon group; it has kept the brand portfolio largely intact, perhaps investing more in the most successful brands and markets.

Mistletoe Wines   ★★★★

771 Hermitage Road, Pokolbin, NSW 2320 **REGION** Lower Hunter Valley
T (02) 4998 7770 **F** (02) 4998 7792 **WEB** www.mistletoe.com.au **OPEN** 7 days 10–6
WINEMAKER Ken Sloan **EST.** 1989 **CASES** 4000
SUMMARY Mistletoe Wines, owned by Ken and Gwen Sloan, can trace its history back to 1909, when a substantial vineyard was planted on what was then called Mistletoe Farm. The Mistletoe Farm brand made a brief appearance in the late 1970s but disappeared until being revived under the Mistletoe Wines label by the Sloans. All wine is now made at the onsite winery. No retail distribution, but worldwide delivery available ex winery. The art gallery features works by local artists.

▼▼▼▼▼ **Reserve Hunter Valley Semillon 2004** Classic lanolin, wet wool, mineral and lemon aromas; crisp, long and lively; very good balance. Screwcap. **RATING** 93 **DRINK** 2014 $ 23
Reserve Hunter Valley Chardonnay 2004 Despite 100% barrel ferment in French oak, peach and spice fruit flavours drive the wine; balanced acidity. Screwcap. **RATING** 90 **DRINK** 2009 $ 23

ŦŦŦŦ **Reserve Hunter Valley Shiraz 2003** Powerful wine with lots of black fruits; tannins a little pokey, possibly slightly reduced ex screwcap. All it needs is time. **RATING** 89 **DRINK** 2013 $ 23

ŦŦŦŦ **New England Merlot 2003 RATING** 86 **DRINK** 2008 $ 25

Mitchell ★★★★

Hughes Park Road, Sevenhill via Clare, SA 5453 **REGION** Clare Valley
T (08) 8843 4258 **F** (08) 8843 4340 **WEB** www.mitchellwines.com **OPEN** 7 days 10–4
WINEMAKER Andrew Mitchell **EST.** 1975 **CASES** 30 000
SUMMARY One of the stalwarts of the Clare Valley, producing long-lived Rieslings and Cabernet Sauvignons in classic regional style. The range now includes very creditable Semillon, Grenache and Shiraz. A lovely old stone apple shed provides the cellar door and upper section of the compact winery. National retail distribution; exports to the US.

ŦŦŦŦŦ **Watervale Riesling 2004** Firm structure; mineral, herb, spice and citrus; good length.
RATING 92 **DRINK** 2014 $ 20
Peppertree Vineyard Shiraz 2003 Medium-bodied; gently ripe, spicy damson plum/blackberry fruit; fine, lingering tannins; well-made, subtle oak. Screwcap.
RATING 90 **DRINK** 2013

ŦŦŦŦ **Peppertree Vineyard Sparkling Shiraz NV** Light to medium-bodied style; spice and vanilla flavours; nice balance and length, neither phenolic nor sweet. A blend of vintages, 2 years on lees. **RATING** 88 **DRINK** 2010

Mitchelton ★★★★

Mitchellstown via Nagambie, Vic 3608 **REGION** Nagambie Lakes
T (03) 5736 2222 **F** (03) 5736 2266 **WEB** www.mitchelton.com.au **OPEN** 7 days 10–5
WINEMAKER Toby Barlow, Neville Rowe **EST.** 1969 **CASES** 200 000
SUMMARY Acquired by Petaluma in 1994, having already put the runs on the board in no uncertain fashion with gifted winemaker Don Lewis (who retired in 2004). Boasts an impressive array of wines across a broad spectrum of style and price, each carefully aimed at a market niche. Exports to all major markets.

ŦŦŦŦŦ **Print Shiraz 2000** Excellent clearly profiled red and black fruits; silky tannins and quality oak perfectly integrated and balanced. **RATING** 94 **DRINK** 2015 $ 49

ŦŦŦŦ **Blackwood Park Estate Riesling 2004** Quite intense aromas; solid, moderately powerful stone/mineral/citrus flavours; some length. Screwcap. **RATING** 88 **DRINK** 2008 $ 17
Preece Shiraz 2002 Good colour; firm black and red fruits; subtle oak; still developing, but poor-quality cork. **RATING** 88 **DRINK** 2009 $ 14.99

ŦŦŦŦ **Preece Sauvignon Blanc 2004 RATING** 86 **DRINK** Now $ 14.99
Blackwood Park Chardonnay 2003 RATING 86 **DRINK** Now $ 17

Mitolo Wines ★★★★★

PO Box 520, Virginia, SA 5120 **REGION** McLaren Vale
T (08) 8282 9012 **F** (08) 8282 9062 **WEB** www.mitolowines.com.au **OPEN** Not
WINEMAKER Ben Glaetzer **EST.** 1999 **CASES** 8000
SUMMARY Frank Mitolo began making wine in 1995 as a hobby, and soon progressed to undertaking formal studies in winemaking. His interest grew year by year, but it was not until 2000 that he took the plunge into the commercial end of the business, retaining Ben Glaetzer to make the wines for him. Since that time, a remarkably good series of wines have been released. Imitation being the sincerest form of flattery, part of the complicated story behind each label name is pure Torbreck, but Mitolo then adds a Latin proverb or saying to the name. A natty little loosely tied explanation/translation booklet tied to the neck of each bottle would be useful. Exports to the UK, the US and other major markets.

ŦŦŦŦŦ **Savitar McLaren Vale Shiraz 2003** Full-bodied but supple and long in the mouth; spice, dark chocolate and blackberry; fine tannins. **RATING** 95 **DRINK** 2015 $ 72.65
G.A.M. McLaren Vale Shiraz 2003 Herb and spice edges to the aroma; full-bodied, powerful and dense blackberry and bitter chocolate palate fruit; controlled but ample tannins; 14.5° alcohol. **RATING** 94 **DRINK** 2018 $ 55.75

TTTTT **Reiver Barossa Shiraz 2003** Medium to full-bodied; black fruits and plums, with savoury tannins in contrast; good oak. **RATING** 93 **DRINK** 2015 $ 55.75

TTTT **Serpico McLaren Vale Cabernet Sauvignon 2003** Powerful red berry fruits and even more powerful tannins; still coming together. **RATING** 89 **DRINK** 2013 $ 72.65

Molly Morgan Vineyard ★★★★

Talga Road, Lovedale, NSW 2321 **REGION** Lower Hunter Valley
T (02) 9816 4088 **F** (02) 9816 2680 **WEB** www.mollymorgan.com **OPEN** By appointment
WINEMAKER John Baruzzi (Consultant) **EST.** 1963 **CASES** 5500
SUMMARY Molly Morgan has been acquired by Andrew and Hady Simon, who established the Camperdown Cellars Group in 1971, becoming the largest retailer in Australia before moving on to other pursuits. They have been recently joined by Grant Breen, their former general manager at Camperdown Cellars. The property has 5.5 ha of 42-year-old unirrigated semillon, which goes to make the Old Vines Semillon, 0.8 ha for Joe's Block Semillon, 2.5 ha of chardonnay and 1.35 ha of shiraz. The wines are contract-made, but to a high standard. Exports to the US, Canada, Ireland, China and Japan.

TTTTT **Rosellas Rest Semillon Sauvignon Blanc 2004** Light to medium-bodied; slightly fuller than the varietal Semillons; underlying touches of tropical fruit; good line and length. **RATING** 93 **DRINK** 2012 $ 22
Woodpecker Wooded Semillon 2004 Very delicate oak influence; long and harmonious; more even flow and line than the Lizards Lair. **RATING** 92 **DRINK** 2014 $ 24
Lizards Lair Old Vines Semillon 2004 Spotless lemon zest aromas; abundant fore-palate flavour; slight dip in the mid-palate will fill with age. **RATING** 90 **DRINK** 2014 $ 22

TTTT **Back Patch Chardonnay 2003** Peachy, nutty, creamy, mouthfilling; attractive early-drinking style. **RATING** 87 **DRINK** Now $ 24
Verde Verdelho 2004 Tangy; quite lemony and fresh aromas; lemon tingle and tropical mix in the mouth. **RATING** 87 **DRINK** Now $ 22

TTTT **Unwooded Chardonnay 2004** **RATING** 86 **DRINK** 2007 $ 22
Shiraz 2003 **RATING** 86 **DRINK** 2008 $ 25
Red Mistress Sparkling Shiraz NV **RATING** 86 **DRINK** 2007 $ 23

TTT **Fair Lady Sparkling NV** **RATING** 83 $ 20

Monahan Estate ★★★

319 Wilderness Road, Rothbury, NSW 2320 **REGION** Lower Hunter Valley
T (02) 4930 9070 **F** (02) 4930 7679 **WEB** www.monahanestate.com.au **OPEN** Wed–Sun 10–5
WINEMAKER Monarch Winemaking Services (Contract) **EST.** 1997 **CASES** 2000
SUMMARY Having become partners with founder Matthew Monahan in 1999, John and Patricia Graham now own the estate outright. It is bordered by Black Creek in the Lovedale district, an area noted for its high-quality semillon; the old bridge adjoining the property is displayed on the wine label; the wines themselves have been consistent silver and bronze medal winners at the Hunter Valley Wine Show.

TTTT **Old Bridge Hunter Valley Chardonnay 2004** Early picked to successfully retain fresh fruit; melon and citrus; no oak influence; 12.2° alcohol. Screwcap. **RATING** 86 **DRINK** 2007 $ 14

Monbulk Winery NR

Macclesfield Road, Monbulk, Vic 3793 **REGION** Yarra Valley
T (03) 9756 6965 **F** (03) 9756 6965 **OPEN** Weekends & public hols 12–5, or by appointment
WINEMAKER Paul Jabornik **EST.** 1984 **CASES** 500
SUMMARY Originally concentrated on kiwifruit wines but now extending to table wines; the very cool Monbulk subregion should be capable of producing wines of distinctive style, but the table wines are not of the same standard as the kiwifruit wines, which are quite delicious.

🍇 Mongrel Creek Vineyard ★★★★

Lot 72, Hayes Road, Yallingup Siding, WA 6281 **REGION** Margaret River
T 0417 991 065 **F** (08) 9755 5708 **OPEN** Weekends, school & public hols 10–5
WINEMAKER Michael Kerrigan, Matt Burton **EST.** 1996 **CASES** 700
SUMMARY Larry and Shirley Schoppe both have full-time occupations, the former as vineyard supervisor at Howard Park's Leston Vineyard, the latter as a full-time nurse. Thus the 2.8-ha vineyard, planted to shiraz, semillon, sauvignon blanc in 1996, is still a weekend and holiday business. Given the viticultural and winemaking expertise of those involved, it is hardly surprising that the wines have been consistent show medal winners.

🍷🍷🍷🍷 **Margaret River Semillon Sauvignon Blanc 2003** Quite fragrant, driven by the 70% grassy Semillon component; crisp, clean, fresh finish. Screwcap. **RATING** 89 **DRINK** 2008 $ 12

Margaret River Shiraz 2003 Light to medium-bodied; fresh, spicy black and red fruits; lively palate and finish. Screwcap. **RATING** 89 **DRINK** 2010 $ 18

Margaret River Semillon Sauvignon Blanc 2004 Good depth of flavour, a mixture of herbal and slightly sweet fruit. Screwcap. **RATING** 87 **DRINK** Now $ 12

Margaret River Shiraz 2002 Fresh red cherry and blood plum; light-bodied; brisk finish. Poor-quality cork. **RATING** 87 **DRINK** 2009 $ 18

Monichino Wines ★★★☆

1820 Berrys Road, Katunga, Vic 3640 **REGION** Goulburn Valley
T (03) 5864 6452 **F** (03) 5864 6538 **WEB** www.monichino.com.au **OPEN** Mon–Sat 9–5, Sun 10–5
WINEMAKER Carlo Monichino, Terry Monichino **EST.** 1962 **CASES** 22 000
SUMMARY This winery was an early pacemaker for the region, with clean, fresh wines in which the fruit character was (and is) carefully preserved; also showed a deft touch with its Botrytis Semillon. It has moved with the times, introducing an interesting range of varietal wines while preserving its traditional base.

🍷🍷🍷🍷 **Chardonnay 2003** Very complex, funky/smoky barrel aromas; plenty of flavour; fractionally sweet. **RATING** 88 **DRINK** 2007 $ 15

Shiraz 2002 Light to medium-bodied; nice traditional savoury style; blackberry, earth and vanilla oak all come together well. Cork. **RATING** 87 **DRINK** 2011 $ 15

Cabernet Sauvignon 2002 Elegant, savoury, light to medium-bodied; blackberry fruit; fine, savoury tannins; subtle oak. **RATING** 87 **DRINK** 2012 $ 15

🍷🍷🍷🍷 **Riesling 2004** Pale straw-green; soft, ripe, floral apple blossom aromas; shortens on the finish, but good value. Screwcap. **RATING** 86 **DRINK** 2007 $ 13

Pinot Grigio 2004 RATING 86 **DRINK** 2007 $ 18

Sauvignon Blanc 2004 RATING 85 **DRINK** Now $ 13

Montalto Vineyards ★★★★★

33 Shoreham Road, Red Hill South, Vic 3937 **REGION** Mornington Peninsula
T (03) 5989 8412 **F** (03) 5989 8417 **WEB** www.montalto.com.au **OPEN** 7 days 11–5
WINEMAKER Robin Brockett **EST.** 1998 **CASES** 4000
SUMMARY John Mitchell and family established Montalto Vineyards in 1998, but the core of the vineyard goes back to 1986. There are 3 ha of chardonnay and 5.6 ha of pinot noir, with 0.5 ha each of semillon, riesling and pinot meunier. Intensive vineyard work opens up the canopy, with yields ranging between 1.5 and 2.5 tonnes per acre, with the majority of the fruit hand-harvested. Wines are released under two labels, the flagship Montalto and Pennon, the latter effectively a lower-priced, second label. The high-quality restaurant, open daily for lunch and on Friday and Saturday evenings, also features guest chefs and cooking classes. A new star in the Peninsula sky.

🍷🍷🍷🍷🍷 **Chardonnay 2003** This wine has a fragrant, delicate yet intense array of white peach and grapefruit aromas and flavours which marry with perfect, almost sweet, acidity. Quite delicious. **RATING** 95 **DRINK** 2008 $ 27

Pinot Noir 2003 Clean; powerful dark plum aromas and flavours; good length and structure. **RATING** 94 **DRINK** 2010 $ 35

ＹＹＹＹＹ **Riesling 2004** Spotlessly clean apple, pear and spice aromas; intense and balanced palate; lingering finish. Screwcap. **RATING** 91 **DRINK** 2012 $ 23

Pennon Hill Chardonnay 2004 Light-bodied but beautifully sculpted wine; citrus and melon fruit underpinned by a touch of French oak. Screwcap. **RATING** 90 **DRINK** 2008 $ 18.50

ＹＹＹＹ **Pennon Hill Pinot Noir 2003** Rich, ripe plum fruit aromas and flavours; slightly one-dimensional. **RATING** 89 **DRINK** 2008 $ 23

Pennon Hill Pinot Grigio 2004 Fresh, lively and moderately crisp; saved from anonymity by a twist of lemony acidity giving length. Screwcap. **RATING** 87 **DRINK** 2007 $ 18.50

Pennon Hill Rose 2004 Delicious strawberry fruit in a dry, delicate frame; lingering finish. Pinot Noir/Pinot Meunier. Screwcap. **RATING** 87 **DRINK** 2007 $ 18.50

ＹＹＹＹ **Pennon Hill Semillon Sauvignon Blanc 2004** **RATING** 86 **DRINK** Now $ 18.50

Montara ★★★

Chalambar Road, Ararat, Vic 3377 **REGION** Grampians
T (03) 5352 3868 **F** (03) 5352 4968 **WEB** www.montara.com.au **OPEN** Mon–Sat 10–5, Sun 12–4
WINEMAKER Mike McRae **EST.** 1970 **CASES** NFP
SUMMARY Achieved considerable attention for its Pinot Noirs during the 1980s, but other regions (and other makers) have come along since. It continues to produce wines of distinctive style, and smart label designs help. Limited national distribution; exports to the UK, Switzerland, Canada and Hong Kong.

ＹＹＹＹ **Riesling 2004** Light to medium-bodied; clean, relying in part on a flick of residual sugar to the primary mix of minerally citrus and slate. **RATING** 87 **DRINK** 2008 $ 17

ＹＹＹＹ **Sauvignon Blanc 2004** Fractionally smoky/sweaty bouquet; light to medium-bodied palate; a tweak of sweetness off-set by acidity. **RATING** 86 **DRINK** 2007 $ 15

ＹＹＹ **Shiraz 2001** **RATING** 82 $ 25

Montgomery's Hill ★★★★★

Hassell Highway, Upper Kalgan, Albany, WA 6330 **REGION** Albany
T (08) 9844 3715 **F** (08) 9844 1104 **OPEN** 7 days 11–5
WINEMAKER Robert Lee (Porongurup Winery), John Wade (Consultant) **EST.** 1996 **CASES** 2000
SUMMARY Montgomery's Hill is 16 km northeast of Albany on a north-facing slope on the banks of the Kalgan River. The vineyard is on a site which was previously an apple orchard; it is a diversification for the third generation of the Montgomery family, which owns the property. Chardonnay, cabernet sauvignon and cabernet franc were planted in 1996, followed by sauvignon blanc, shiraz and merlot in 1997.

ＹＹＹＹＹ **Albany Chardonnay 2003** Fresh, clean, bright, fresh-cut nectarine fruit plus nuances of grapefruit; oak in pure support role; still youthful; delicious mouthfeel. Screwcap. **RATING** 94 **DRINK** 2010

ＹＹＹＹ **Albany Shiraz 2003** Medium-bodied; black cherry, blackberry, licorice and spice; fine structure and tannins. Diam. **RATING** 92 **DRINK** 2013

🍇 Montvalley NR

150 Mitchells Road, Mount View, NSW 2325 (postal) **REGION** Lower Hunter Valley
T (02) 4991 1936 **F** (02) 4991 7994 **WEB** www.montvalley.com.au **OPEN** Not
WINEMAKER James Chatto (Monarch Winemaking Services) **EST.** 2002 **CASES** 3000
SUMMARY Having looked at dozens of properties over the previous decade, and having detailed soil analyses done before finalising the deal, John and Deirdre Colvin purchased their 80-ha property in January 1998. They chose the name Montvalley in part because it reflects the beautiful valley in the Brokenback Ranges of which the property forms part, and in part because the name Colvin originates from France, 'col' meaning valley and 'vin' meaning vines. Between 1998 and 2001 they have planted a total of 5.7 ha of vines, the lion's share to shiraz, with lesser amounts of chardonnay and semillon. The wines are contract-made under the watchful eye of James Chatto, and are primarily sold by mail order.

Monument Vineyard ★★★★

Cnr Escort Way/Manildra Road, Cudal, NSW 2864 **REGION** Central Ranges Zone
T (02) 9686 4605 **F** (02) 9686 4605 **WEB** www.monumentvineyard.com.au **OPEN** By appointment
WINEMAKER Alison Eisermann **EST.** 1998 **CASES** 1500
SUMMARY In the early 1990s five mature-age students at Charles Sturt University, successful in their own professions, decided to form a partnership to develop a substantial vineyard and winery on a scale that they could not individually afford, but could do so collectively. After a lengthy search, a large property at Cudal was identified, with ideal terra rossa basalt-derived soil over a limestone base. The property now has 110 ha under vine, as a result of planting in the spring of 1998 and 1999.

ҮҮҮҮ**Ÿ** **Shiraz 2003** Deep, bright red-purple; clean and powerful blackberry and plum on a sweet mid-palate; more savoury on the finish. **RATING** 92 **DRINK** 2013 $ 18
Shiraz Viognier 2003 Slightly less intense colour; similar to the Shiraz, but shows the life and lift injected by the Viognier; medium-bodied and supple, but the 12% Viognier is that little bit too much. **RATING** 91 **DRINK** 2012 $ 16
Sangiovese 2003 Good colour; a thoroughly interesting wine; strong rose petal and cherry aromas; bright red cherry fruit and nice ripe and soft tannins. **RATING** 90 **DRINK** 2008 $ 16

ҮҮҮҮ **Pinot Grigio 2003** Medium weight; ripe, but not fat, fruit runs through the length of the palate; just a little low on acidity on the finish. **RATING** 89 **DRINK** Now $ 15
Cabernet Sauvignon 2003 Elevated aromatics; very powerful blackcurrant and earth flavours; persistent tannins. **RATING** 88 **DRINK** 2010 $ 16
Cabernets 2003 Plenty of sweet juicy berry/cassis fruit; fine, ripe tannins, and just a hint of vanilla oak; fruit-driven; very good value. **RATING** 88 **DRINK** 2010 $ 12

ҮҮҮ**Ÿ** **Cabernets 2002 RATING** 86 **DRINK** 2008 $ 16

🐌 Moombaki Wines ★★★★☆

RMB 1277, Parker Road, Kentdale via Denmark, WA 6333 **REGION** Denmark
T (08) 9840 8006 **F** (08) 9840 8006 **WEB** www.moombaki.com **OPEN** By appointment
WINEMAKER Robert Diletti, James Kellie **EST.** 1997 **CASES** 650
SUMMARY David Britten and Melissa Boughey (with three young sons in tow) have established 2 ha of vines on a north-facing gravel hillside with a picturesque Kent River frontage. Not content with establishing the vineyard, they have put in significant mixed tree plantings to increase wildlife habitats and fenced off wetlands and river from stock grazing and degradation. It is against this background that they chose Moombaki as their vineyard name: it is a local Aboriginal word meaning 'where the river meets the sky'. They have had a number of mentors along the way, not the least a Swiss wine merchant who encouraged them to find and plant the property in the first place. After a few disappointments with early contract winemaking, the quality of the grapes is now coming through in the wines, with Robert Diletti making the 2003 vintage, and James Kellie the 2004 and subsequent vintages (his winery is much closer).

ҮҮҮҮ**Ÿ** **Shiraz 2003** Strong purple-red colour; intense spice, black cherry, blackberry fruit; spicy. Good oak handling. **RATING** 91 **DRINK** 2012 $ 22
Cabernet Sauvignon 2003 Medium-bodied; excellent balance and structure; blackcurrant and blackberry fruit; fine, ripe tannins. **RATING** 90 **DRINK** 2010 $ 22

ҮҮҮҮ **Chardonnay 2003** Medium-bodied; neatly balanced and integrated French oak with melon fruit; falters ever so slightly on the finish. **RATING** 89 **DRINK** 2007 $ 25

Moonbark Estate Vineyard NR

Lot 11, Moonambel–Natte Yallock Road, Moonambel, Vic 3478 (postal) **REGION** Pyrenees
T 0439 952 263 **F** (03) 9870 6116 **OPEN** Not
WINEMAKER Warrenmang Estate (Contract) **EST.** 1998 **CASES** 300
SUMMARY Rod Chivers and his family have been slowly establishing their vineyard over the past 7 years, with 0.5 ha of shiraz in bearing. A further 1+ ha of cabernet sauvignon and merlot are due to be planted over the next few years. The wines are sold through local restaurants and retailers.

Moondah Brook ★★★★

c/- Houghton, Dale Road, Middle Swan, WA 6056 **REGION** Swan Valley
T (08) 9274 5172 **F** (08) 9274 5372 **WEB** www.moondahbrook.com.au **OPEN** Not
WINEMAKER Robert Bowen, Ross Pamment, Simon Osicka **EST.** 1968 **CASES** 80 000
SUMMARY Part of the BRL Hardy wine group which has its own special character, as it draws part of its fruit from the large Gingin vineyard, 70 km north of the Swan Valley, and part from the Margaret River and Great Southern. In recent times it has excelled even its own reputation for reliability with some quite lovely wines, in particular honeyed, aged Chenin Blanc, generous Shiraz and finely structured Cabernet Sauvignon.

🍷🍷🍷🍷 **Cabernet Rose 2004** Bright red-purple; fragrant red fruits; bright flavours, balanced acidity. **RATING** 91 **DRINK** Now $ 13
Cabernet Sauvignon 2001 Blackcurrant and cassis fruit are matched by fine tannins and subtle oak; medium-bodied, with very good texture and structure. Outstanding value. **RATING** 91 **DRINK** 2008 $ 13

🍷🍷🍷🍷 **Verdelho 2004** **RATING** 85 **DRINK** Now $ 13

Moondarra ★★★☆

Browns Road, Moondarra, Vic 3825 (postal) **REGION** Gippsland
T (03) 9598 3049 **F** (03) 9598 0677 **OPEN** Not
WINEMAKER Neil Prentice **EST.** 1991 **CASES** NA
SUMMARY In 1991 Neil Prentice and family established their Moondarra Vineyard in Gippsland, planted to 1.5 ha of 11 low-yielding clones of pinot noir, to which they have recently added a 0.25 ha each of nebbiolo and piccolit. The vines are not irrigated, and vineyard management is predicated on the minimum use of any sprays; the aim is to eventually move to Biodynamic/Pagan farming methods. The winemaking techniques are strongly influenced by the practices of controversial Burgundy consultant Guy Accad, with 10 days pre-fermentation maceration and whole bunches added prior to fermentation. Distribution in Melbourne and Sydney by Select Vineyards; exports to the US, Japan and Singapore.

Moorebank Vineyard NR

Palmers Lane, Pokolbin, NSW 2320 **REGION** Lower Hunter Valley
T (02) 4998 7610 **F** (02) 4998 7367 **WEB** www.moorebankvineyard.com.au **OPEN** Fri–Mon 10–5, or by appointment
WINEMAKER Iain Riggs (Contract) **EST.** 1977 **CASES** 2000
SUMMARY Ian Burgess and Debra Moore own a mature 6-ha vineyard planted to chardonnay, semillon, gewurztraminer and merlot, with a small cellar door operation offering immaculately packaged wines in avant-garde style. The peachy Chardonnay has been a medal winner at Hunter Valley Wine Shows.

Moores Hill Estate ★★★★★

3343 West Tamar Highway, Sidmouth, Tas 7270 **REGION** Northern Tasmania
T (03) 6394 7649 **F** (03) 6394 7649 **WEB** www.mooreshill.com.au **OPEN** Oct–June Wed–Sun 10–5, Mon–Tues by appointment for group bookings
WINEMAKER Julian Alcorso (Contract) **EST.** 1997 **CASES** 3000
SUMMARY Karen and Rod Thorpe, the latter with a background in catering, together with Bob Harness, have established their vineyard on the gentle slopes of the west Tamar Valley. They have planted 4.9 ha of riesling, chardonnay, pinot noir, merlot and cabernet sauvignon, with additional newly planted riesling. It represents a full circle for the Thorpes, because when they purchased the property a little over 20 years ago there was an old vineyard which they pulled out. A wine tasting and sales area made from Tasmanian timber opened at the end of 2002.

🍷🍷🍷🍷🍷 **Riesling 2004** Elegant, clean and fresh; delicate mineral and citrus; fine balance. **RATING** 94 **DRINK** 2014 $ 18
Pinot Noir 2003 Supple red and black cherry fruit; fine, ripe tannins; long finish. **RATING** 94 **DRINK** 2010 $ 20

🍷🍷🍷🍷 **Chardonnay 2003** Attractive, gently ripe melon and stone fruit; good mouthfeel and line; fractionally sweet finish. **RATING** 91 **DRINK** 2009 $ 18

ΥΥΥΥ   **Cabernet Sauvignon Merlot 2003** Powerful and rich, with initially luscious fruit and lots of oak; acidity very strong on the finish. **RATING** 88 **DRINK** 2012 $20

ΥΥΥ   **Unwooded Chardonnay 2004 RATING** 83 $16

Moorilla Estate   ★★★★★

655 Main Road, Berriedale, Tas 7011 **REGION** Southern Tasmania
T (03) 6277 9900 **F** (03) 6249 4093 **WEB** www.moorilla.com.au **OPEN** 7 days 10–5
WINEMAKER Michael Glover **EST.** 1958 **CASES** 16 000
SUMMARY Moorilla Estate is an icon in the Tasmanian wine industry and is thriving. Wine quality continues to be unimpeachable, and the opening of the museum in the marvellous Alcorso house designed by Sir Roy Grounds adds even more attraction for visitors to the estate, which is a mere 15–20 minutes from Hobart. Five-star self-contained chalets are available, with a restaurant open for lunch 7 days. Exports to the US, Hong Kong and Denmark.

ΥΥΥΥΥ   **Riesling 1998** Totally delicious; fresh as a daisy; abundant lime juice flavour, and great length. Trophy winner Tasmanian Wines Show 2005. **RATING** 96 **DRINK** 2008
White Label Chardonnay 2002 Still very fine and delicate; classy focus and definition; long citrus and stone fruit; subtle oak. Cork. **RATING** 94 **DRINK** 2009 $26

ΥΥΥΥ   **Black Label Riesling 2004** Fragrant, crisp aromas; lovely Mosel Kabinett sweetness off-set by slippery, squeaky acidity. Twin Top. **RATING** 93 **DRINK** 2010 $25
Sauvignon Blanc 2004 Spotlessly clean, fresh and intense; stylish gooseberry and passionfruit flavours; long and balanced. Cork. **RATING** 93 **DRINK** 2008
Black Label Pinot Noir 2000 Light to medium-bodied; very attractive and harmonious; holding very well indeed. **RATING** 93 **DRINK** 2007 $24.50
Claudio's Reserve Pinot Noir 2003 Very deep colour; extremely powerful and concentrated; dark, savoury fruits; curiously, acid, rather than tannin, drives the finish. Cork. **RATING** 91 **DRINK** 2010 $38
Winter Collection Reserve Merlot 2002 Light to medium-bodied; fine structure, not the least extractive; silky, smooth and sweet red berry fruit; gossamer tannins. High-quality cork. **RATING** 91 **DRINK** 2015 $39.50
Black Label Sauvignon Blanc 2004 Aromatic tropical, passionfruit and kiwifruit aromas and flavours; good line and length. **RATING** 90 **DRINK** 2007 $23.50
Black Label Chardonnay 2003 Gently complex; ripe stone fruit and tangy citrus mix; good length and balance. Twin Top. **RATING** 90 **DRINK** 2008 $22.50
Reserve Chardonnay 2003 Superb green-tinged colour; light to medium-bodied; sauvignon blanc/chardonnay crossover with fine oak. Destined for development down the track. **RATING** 90 **DRINK** 2013 $38.50
White Label Pinot Noir 2003 Plenty of depth and character; strongly structured plum and damson fruit; fine tannins, good length. **RATING** 90 **DRINK** 2010 $38

ΥΥΥΥ   **Reserve Chardonnay 2001** Gently nutty/creamy flavours, with nice mouthfeel, though length slightly compromised by the malolactic fermentation inputs. **RATING** 89 **DRINK** 2008 $38.50
Brut 2001 Scented, spicy strawberry aromas; crystal-bright acidity; long and lingering; needs time on cork. **RATING** 89 **DRINK** 2010 $29.50
Riesling 2004 Interesting wine, apparently made in a German Kabinett style, with very appreciable residual sugar balanced by acidity. **RATING** 88 **DRINK** 2009 $25
White Label Cabernet Sauvignon 2003 Medium-bodied; blackberry fruits; long, penetrating savoury tannins; for Bordeaux lovers. **RATING** 87 **DRINK** 2009 $31.50
White Label Cabernet Sauvignon 2002 Great colour; potentially excellent wine, but with overwhelming tannin extract which will take years to soften, if it ever does. **RATING** 87 **DRINK** 2010 $31

ΥΥΥΥ   **Reserve Merlot 2003 RATING** 86 **DRINK** 2008 $39

Moorooduc Estate   ★★★★★

501 Derril Road, Moorooduc, Vic 3936 **REGION** Mornington Peninsula
T (03) 5971 8506 **F** (03) 5971 8550 **WEB** www.moorooduc-estate.com.au **OPEN** Weekends 11–5, 7 days in January
WINEMAKER Dr Richard McIntyre **EST.** 1983 **CASES** 2500

SUMMARY Richard McIntyre has taken Moorooduc Estate to new heights as he has completely mastered the difficult art of gaining maximum results from wild yeast fermentations. While the Chardonnays remain the jewels in the crown, the Pinot Noirs and other wines are also impressive. From the 2004 vintage, all the wines have been sealed with screwcap, notwithstanding the high-quality corks used up to that time.

ΨΨΨΨΨ **The Moorooduc Chardonnay 2003** Super-stylish wine with complex making inputs, but intense, yet delicate, stone fruit and melon cutting through; wonderfully elegant wine. High-quality cork. **RATING** 96 **DRINK** 2011 $58
The Moorooduc Pinot Noir 2003 Very complex aromas of spice and small black fruits plus quality French oak; an extra degree of concentration in both fruit and structure. Screwcap. **RATING** 95 **DRINK** 2013 $58
Pinot Noir 2002 Pristine varietal character and fragrance; an elegant mix of red fruits (dominant) plus touches of spice and forest; impeccable balance and length. **RATING** 95 **DRINK** 2009 $34.95
Chardonnay 2003 Very good colour; the full bag of complex techniques – wild yeast, malolactic and barrel ferment, extended lees contact. Great mouthfeel and balance. High-quality cork. **RATING** 94 **DRINK** 2010 $30
Wild Yeast Pinot Noir 2003 Smooth, supple and silky but substantial mouthfeel; sultry black cherry and plum; fine tannins make their appearance. Screwcap. **RATING** 94 **DRINK** 2011 $35

ΨΨΨΨΨ **Pinot Gris 2004** Flawless texture and balance; seamless aromas and flavours; musk and pear. Screwcap. **RATING** 90 **DRINK** 2007 $30
Devil Bend Creek Pinot Noir 2003 Very spicy, savoury, foresty aromas; plum and spice fruit drives the light to medium-bodied, linear palate. Screwcap. **RATING** 90 **DRINK** 2009 $23

ΨΨΨΨ **Devil Bend Creek Chardonnay 2001** Elegant and fragrant; juicy, sweet peach and nectarine fruit; not particularly complex, but ageing nicely. **RATING** 88 **DRINK** Now $25

Morambro Creek Wines ★★★☆

Riddoch Highway, Padthaway, SA 5271 (postal) **REGION** Padthaway
T (08) 8765 6043 **F** (08) 8765 6011 **OPEN** Not
WINEMAKER Nicola Honeysett **EST.** 1994 **CASES** 6000
SUMMARY The Bryson family has been involved in agriculture for more than a century, moving to Padthaway in 1955 as farmers and graziers. In the early 1990s they began the establishment of 125 ha of vines, planted principally to chardonnay, shiraz and cabernet sauvignon; further plantings are planned. The wines have been consistent winners of bronze and silver medals at Australian wine shows since their release.

ΨΨΨΨΨ **Chardonnay 2004** Aromatic, almost floral; entirely driven by nectarine and citrus fruit; very long. **RATING** 92 **DRINK** 2008

ΨΨΨΨ **Shiraz 2003 RATING** 84 **DRINK** 2008

ΨΨΨ **Chardonnay 2003 RATING** 82

🐚 Moranghurk Vineyard ★★★★

1516 Sturt Street, Ballarat, Vic 3350 (postal) **REGION** Geelong
T (03) 5331 2105 **F** (03) 5332 9244 **OPEN** Not
WINEMAKER Dan Buckle (Contract) **EST.** 1996 **CASES** 340
SUMMARY Ross and Liz Wilkie have established a tiny vineyard on the historic Moranghurk property, which was first settled in 1840. They have planted 0.6 ha of clonally selected pinot noir and 0.5 ha of chardonnay on volcanic soil overlying shale and clay. The vineyard is mulched, and is in the course of being converted to organic, with yields of less than 5 tonnes per hectare.

ΨΨΨΨΨ **Pinot Noir 2003** Aromatic, fruit-forward plum, black cherry and spice; more depth and complexity on the palate; good mouthfeel, depth and length. **RATING** 92 **DRINK** 2009 $20

ΨΨΨΨ **Chardonnay 2003 RATING** 85 **DRINK** 2007 $20

🐦 MorganField ★★★☆

104 Ashworths Road, Lancefield, Vic 3435 **REGION** Macedon Ranges
T (03) 5429 1157 **OPEN** Weekends & public hols 10–5
WINEMAKER John Ellis (Hanging Rock Winery) **EST.** 2003 **CASES** 400
SUMMARY The vineyard was first planted in 1980 to pinot noir, shiraz, pinot meunier and cabernet sauvignon. It was then known as Ashworths Hill. When purchased by Mark and Gina Morgan, additional pinot noir and chardonnay plantings increased the area under vine to 4 ha. Pinot gris may well follow soon. The wines are deliberately made in a light-bodied, easy-access fashion.

🍷🍷🍷🍷   **Macedon Ranges Pinot Noir 2004** Clean, bright, fresh red cherry; light-bodied, but nice feel and flow. Screwcap. **RATING** 89 **DRINK** 2009 $22
          Macedon Ranges Unwooded Chardonnay 2004 Some colour development; more character than the majority of Unwooded Chardonnays; quite ripe, peachy fruit; good balancing acidity. Screwcap. **RATING** 87 **DRINK** 2007 $18

Morgan Simpson ★★★★

PO Box 39, Kensington Park, SA 5068 **REGION** McLaren Vale
T 0417 843 118 **F** (08) 8364 3645 **WEB** www.morgansimpson.com.au **OPEN** Not
WINEMAKER Richard Simpson **EST.** 1998 **CASES** 2000
SUMMARY Morgan Simpson was founded by South Australian businessman George Morgan (since retired) and winemaker Richard Simpson, who is a wine science graduate of Charles Sturt University. The grapes are sourced from the Clos Robert Vineyard (where the wine is made) established by Robert Allen Simpson in 1972. The aim was – and is – to provide drinkable wines at a reasonable price. It succeeds admirably. Exports to the US and New Zealand.

🍷🍷🍷🍷🍷   **McLaren Vale Shiraz 2003** Deep purple-red; rich plum and strong, regional dark chocolate flavours; ripe tannins and a flick of vanilla. oak. Stained cork. **RATING** 91 **DRINK** 2013 $18

🍷🍷🍷🍷   **Row 42 McLaren Vale Cabernet Sauvignon 2003** Elegant, cedary, earthy spicy overtones to cabernet black fruits; medium-bodied; fine tannins. Cork. **RATING** 89 **DRINK** 2011 $16.50
          McLaren Vale Chardonnay 2003 Melon, citrus and subtle oak; squeaky acidity provides length and vibrancy. Cork. **RATING** 88 **DRINK** Now $13.50

🍷🍷🍷   **McLaren Vale Semillon 2003** **RATING** 82

Morgan Vineyards ★★★☆

30 Davross Court, Seville, Vic 3139 **REGION** Yarra Valley
T (03) 5964 4807 **WEB** www.morganvineyards.com.au **OPEN** Mon–Fri 11–4, weekends & public hols 11–5
WINEMAKER Roger Morgan **EST.** 1987 **CASES** 1500
SUMMARY Roger and wife Ally Morgan have brought Morgan Vineyards along slowly. In 1987 they purchased a 1.6-ha vineyard of cabernet sauvignon and pinot noir which had been planted in 1971. They extended the plantings in 1989 (more pinot), in 1991 (more cabernet sauvignon plus merlot) and in 1995 (chardonnay), bringing the total area under vine to 5.66 ha. In 1997 Roger Morgan completed the wine science degree course at Charles Sturt University, and finally embarked on making the wines under the Morgan Vineyards label. An onsite winery and elegant tasting room have been established. Roger Morgan's aim is to build a reputation for making elegant wines at reasonable prices.

🍷🍷🍷🍷🍷   **Heathcote Shiraz 2003** Elegant spicy black cherry and plum; disguises 14.8° alcohol very well; fine, ripe tannins; subtle oak. Stained cork. **RATING** 92 **DRINK** 2015 $30

🍷🍷🍷🍷   **Yarra Valley Chardonnay 2004** Pale straw-green; light-bodied; crisp, citrussy/minerally fruit-driven style; needs a few years to fill out. Cork. **RATING** 87 **DRINK** 2009 $24

🍷🍷🍷   **Yarra Valley Pinot Noir 2003** Light-bodied; savoury spicy cherry aromas; crisp acidity; seems over-adjusted to excessively low pH. Cork. **RATING** 86 **DRINK** 2009 $28
          Yarra Valley Cabernet Sauvignon 2002 **RATING** 84 **DRINK** 2008 $25

Morialta Vineyard

195 Norton Summit Road, Norton Summit, SA 5136 **REGION** Adelaide Hills
T (08) 8390 1061 **F** (08) 8390 1585 **WEB** www.visitadelaidehills.com.au/morialta **OPEN** By appointment
WINEMAKER Jeffrey Grosset (Contract) **EST.** 1989 **CASES** 500
SUMMARY Morialta Vineyard was planted in 1989 on a site first planted to vines in the 1860s by John Baker, who named his property Morialta Farm. The Bunya pine depicted on the label is one of the few surviving trees from that era, and indeed one of the few surviving trees of that genus. The 20-ha property has 11 ha under vine, planted to chardonnay, pinot noir, cabernet sauvignon, sauvignon blanc, shiraz and merlot. Most of the grapes are sold to Southcorp. Given the age of the vineyard and winemaking by Jeffrey Grosset, it is not surprising that the wines have done well in the Adelaide Hills Wine Show. They are sold through selected restaurants in Adelaide and by mail order.

TTTTY **Adelaide Hills Pinot Noir 2002** Vibrant colour; strong primary plum fruit; powerful; with time will become even more complex. **RATING** 91 **DRINK** 2010

Morningside Wines

711 Middle Tea Tree Road, Tea Tree, Tas 7017 **REGION** Southern Tasmania
T (03) 6268 1748 **F** (03) 6268 1748 **OPEN** By appointment
WINEMAKER Peter Bosworth **EST.** 1980 **CASES** 600
SUMMARY The name Morningside was given to the old property on which the vineyard stands because it gets the morning sun first; the property on the other side of the valley was known as Eveningside. Consistent with the observation of the early settlers, the Morningside grapes achieve full maturity with good colour and varietal flavour. Production will increase as the 2.9-ha vineyard matures, and as recent additions of clonally selected pinot noir (including 8104, 115 and 777) come into bearing. Available through the Tasmanian Wine Centre; retail distribution in Melbourne.

TTTTY **Riesling 2004** Very well constructed; tightly focused mineral, spice and slate; very good mouthfeel. **RATING** 92 **DRINK** 2014 $ 20
Pinot Noir 2003 Elegant, perfumed; light to medium-bodied; appealing balance of savoury and sweeter fruits. **RATING** 90 **DRINK** 2008 $ 34

TTTY **Rose 2003 RATING** 85 **DRINK** Now $ 20

TTY **Chardonnay 2003 RATING** 79 $ 23

Morning Star Estate

1 Sunnyside Road, Mount Eliza, Vic 3930 **REGION** Mornington Peninsula
T (03) 9787 7760 **F** (03) 9787 7160 **WEB** www.morningstarestate.com.au **OPEN** 7 days 10–4
WINEMAKER Sandro Mosele (Kooyong Estate) **EST.** 1992 **CASES** 4000
SUMMARY In 1992 Judy Barrett purchased this historic property, the house built in 1867; she and her family spent the next 10 years repairing it. Over the same timeframe, 10 ha each of pinot gris, chardonnay and pinot noir were planted. Most of the grapes are sold, with a lesser amount going to make the Morning Star wines. The wines – all sold through the Estate's accommodation, conference and function centre and cellar door – are made by Sandro Mosele.

TTTTY **Merlot Cabernet 2001** Powerful, focused blackcurrant/berry aromas; similarly powerful palate, which does catch on the finish with a hint of brett. **RATING** 92 **DRINK** 2010 $ 30

Morning Sun Vineyard

NR

337 Main Creek Road, Main Ridge, Vic 3928 **REGION** Mornington Peninsula
T (03) 5989 6571 **OPEN** By appointment
WINEMAKER Rod Bourchier (Contract) **EST.** 1995 **CASES** NA
SUMMARY Mario Toniolo has managed the development of 6 ha of vineyard at the Main Ridge area of Red Hill. The varieties planted are semillon, chardonnay, pinot gris, pinot noir and barbera, and the wines are made onsite under the direction of Rod Bourchier. Sales are by mail order and through the cellar door by appointment; meals are available by arrangement.

Morris ★★★★★

Mia Mia Road, Rutherglen, Vic 3685 **REGION** Rutherglen
T (02) 6026 7303 **F** (02) 6026 7445 **WEB** www.morriswines.com **OPEN** Mon–Sat 9–5, Sun 10–5
WINEMAKER David Morris **EST.** 1859 **CASES** 100 000
SUMMARY One of the greatest of the fortified winemakers, ranking with Chambers Rosewood. If you wish to test that view, try the Old Premium Rare Muscat and Old Premium Rare Tokay, which are absolute bargains given their age and quality; these give rise to the winery rating. The Durif table wine is a winery specialty; the others are dependable. The white wines are made by owner Orlando.

🍷🍷🍷🍷🍷 **Old Premium Rare Rutherglen Tokay NV** Deep, aged olive-brown; super-intense, with a resplendent array of spices, cake and tea leaf surrounded by smoky rancio which cuts the richness and provides a lingering, intense but pleasingly dry aftertaste. **RATING** 97 **DRINK** Now
Old Premium Liqueur Rare Muscat NV Deep mahogany brown with an olive rim; the ultra-rich bouquet has a complex mix of plum pudding, spice, toffee and coffee; the almost explosive flavour of the palate is intensely raisiny/dried raisin, then a cleansing finish invests the wine with enormous length. **RATING** 97 **DRINK** 2010
Old Premium Rare Rutherglen Muscat NV Deep olive brown; dense spice, plum pudding and raisin aromas; utterly exceptional intensity and length; altogether in another dimension; while based upon some very old wine, is as fresh as a daisy. **RATING** 97 **DRINK** Now
Grand Rutherglen Tokay NV Very rich, very complex tea leaf, spice and Christmas cake aromas, some honey and butterscotch lurking; floods the mouth, intense and long, with a pronounced rancio cut, yet not sharp nor volatile. **RATING** 95 **DRINK** Now
Grand Rutherglen Muscat NV Full olive brown, green rim. A powerful and intense bouquet, rancio, spice and raisin; while less unctuous than some of its peers, the palate has outstanding texture, intensity and length. **RATING** 94 **DRINK** Now

🍷🍷🍷🍷🍸 **Classic Rutherglen Liqueur Tokay NV** Olive-brown; a very complex, classic mix of tea leaf, honey, butterscotch and some fish oil flavours is supported by excellent texture and balance. **RATING** 93 **DRINK** Now
Rutherglen Shiraz 2002 Big, rich, ripe voluptuous blackberry and plum; abundant, round tannins. In heroic style. **RATING** 92 **DRINK** 2015
Classic Rutherglen Liqueur Muscat NV A multiplicity of flavours, centred around raisin muscat fruit, but with a spicy jab of rancio to liven up the finish. **RATING** 92 **DRINK** Now
Rutherglen Durif 2001 Powerful and concentrated black fruits; potent tannins which are nonetheless in balance. Touches of spice; almost elegant. **RATING** 91 **DRINK** 2021 **$** 20
Old Premium Tawny Port NV Obvious age, true tawny colour; richly robed and textured into a Liqueur Tawny style; biscuity aftertaste. **RATING** 90 **DRINK** Now **$** 44.95

🍷🍷🍷🍷 **Blue Imperial Cinsaut 2001** Fragrant raspberry and red cherry aromas and flavours; light to medium-bodied and soft tannins; drink now. **RATING** 88 **DRINK** Now **$** 17.99
Cabernet Sauvignon 2000 Light to medium-bodied; pleasant red and blackberry varietal fruit; balanced tannins. **RATING** 87 **DRINK** 2008 **$** 14.99

🍷🍷🍷🍸 **Chardonnay 2003** **RATING** 84 **DRINK** Now **$** 13.99

Morrisons Riverview Winery NR

Lot 2, Merool Lane, Moama, NSW 2731 **REGION** Perricoota
T (03) 5480 0126 **F** (03) 5480 7144 **WEB** www.riverviewestate.com.au **OPEN** 7 days 10–5
WINEMAKER John Ellis (Hanging Rock Winery) **EST.** 1996 **CASES** 2500
SUMMARY Alistair and Leslie Morrison purchased this historic piece of land in 1995. Plantings began in 1996 with shiraz and cabernet sauvignon, followed in 1997 by sauvignon blanc, frontignac and grenache in 1998, totalling 6 ha. The cellar door and restaurant opened in spring 2000, serving light lunches, platters, picnic baskets, coffee and gourmet cakes; wines are sold by the glass, bottle or box and tastings are free of charge.

Mortimers of Orange NR

'Chestnut Garth', 786 Burrendong Way, Orange, NSW 2800 **REGION** Orange
T (02) 6365 8689 **F** (02) 6365 8689 **OPEN** 7 days 10–4
WINEMAKER Jim Chatto (Contract) **EST.** 1996 **CASES** 2250

SUMMARY Peter and Julie Mortimer began the establishment of their vineyard (named after a quiet street in the Humberside village of Burton Pidsea in the UK) in 1996. They now have just over 4 ha of chardonnay, shiraz, cabernet sauvignon, merlot and pinot noir.

Moss Brothers ★★★★

Caves Road, Wilyabrup, WA 6280 **REGION** Margaret River
T (08) 9755 6270 **F** (08) 9755 6298 **WEB** www.mossbrothers.com.au **OPEN** 7 days 10–5
WINEMAKER David Moss, Paul Dixon **EST.** 1984 **CASES** 30 000
SUMMARY Established by long-term viticulturist Jeff Moss and his family, notably sons Peter and David and Roseworthy graduate daughter Jane. A 100-tonne rammed-earth winery was constructed in 1992 and draws upon both estate-grown and purchased grapes. Wine quality has improved dramatically, first the white wines, and more recently the reds. National wholesale distribution; exports to the UK, the US and other major markets.

🍷🍷🍷🍷½ **Semillon 2004** Herb, grass and spice; complex fruit flavours with hints of honey and acacia; long and even flow through the palate; soft acidity. **RATING** 92 **DRINK** 2010 **$** 20

Jane Moss Semillon Sauvignon Blanc 2004 Aromatic; an attractive array of tropical and more herbal fruits; good balance and length. **RATING** 92 **DRINK** 2007 **$** 20

Sauvignon Blanc 2004 Fresh mineral, herb and grass aromas; lively palate, good length and persistence. **RATING** 91 **DRINK** Now **$** 20

Shiraz 2002 Quite fragrant and fresh red fruits; medium-bodied, but well balanced, fine, ripe tannins. **RATING** 90 **DRINK** 2012 **$** 30

🍷🍷🍷🍷 **Shiraz 2003** A ripe mix of spice, bramble, black fruits and prune; medium-bodied; savoury tannins, good balance; gentle oak. Quality cork. **RATING** 89 **DRINK** 2013 **$** 29

Jane Moss Rose 2004 Clean, fresh strawberry/red fruits; bone-dry finish. **RATING** 87 **DRINK** Now **$** 17

Moss Wood ★★★★★

Metricup Road, Wilyabrup, WA 6284 **REGION** Margaret River
T (08) 9755 6266 **F** (08) 9755 6303 **WEB** www.mosswood.com.au **OPEN** By appointment
WINEMAKER Keith Mugford **EST.** 1969 **CASES** 18 000
SUMMARY Widely regarded as one of the best wineries in the region, capable of producing glorious Semillon in both oaked and unoaked forms, unctuous Chardonnay and elegant, gently herbaceous, superfine Cabernet Sauvignon which lives for many years. In 2000 Moss Wood acquired the Ribbon Vale Estate, which is now merged within its own business; the Ribbon Vale wines are now treated as vineyard-designated within the Moss Wood umbrella. Exports to all major markets.

🍷🍷🍷🍷🍷 **Margaret River Cabernet Sauvignon 2001** Spotlessly clean, this is a gorgeous, silky wine flooded with redcurrant, cassis and blackcurrant fruit in a web of fine tannins. Elegance personified, the screwcap guaranteeing a very long life. **RATING** 96 **DRINK** 2026 **$** 85

Lefroy Brook Vineyard Pemberton Chardonnay 2003 Intense, lively and tangy citrus and stone fruit aromas and flavours; fruit-driven; very long finish. Polar opposite to the Margaret River Chardonnay. **RATING** 94 **DRINK** 2015

🍷🍷🍷🍷½ **Margaret River Chardonnay 2003** Ultra-complex bouquet, quite Burgundian; a powerful and complex palate which does, however, shorten fractionally. **RATING** 93 **DRINK** 2013 **$** 49

The Amy's Blend Cabernet Sauvignon 2003 Medium-bodied; deliciously sweet cassis and blackcurrant; fruit-driven, but has fine tannins in support. **RATING** 93 **DRINK** 2013 **$** 26

Ribbon Vale Estate Semillon Sauvignon Blanc 2004 Spotlessly clean; very rich, ripe passionfruit and honeycomb flavours; long finish. **RATING** 91 **DRINK** 2007 **$** 20

Margaret River Cabernet Sauvignon 2002 Powerful, austere, and at the savoury end of the Moss Wood spectrum; tight black fruits and tannins; clean finish, but questionable whether the screwcap is helping right now. Screwcap. **RATING** 91 **DRINK** 2015

Semillon 2004 Very powerful and rich, even by Margaret River standards; honey, lemon and mineral mix; does show its 14° alcohol. **RATING** 90 **DRINK** 2008 **$** 28.50

Ribbon Vale Vineyard Merlot 2002 Bright colour; clean and fragrant, with no reduction; fresh, lively redcurrant fruit and a background filigree of tannins. Screwcap. **RATING** 90 **DRINK** 2012

ŦŦŦŦ **Ribbon Vale Vineyard Cabernet Sauvignon Merlot 2002** Fragrant and savoury aromas; dark fruit flavours; slightly aggressive tannins yet to soften. **RATING** 87 **DRINK** 2012 $ 34

ŦŦŦ♈ **Pinot Noir 2002 RATING** 85 **DRINK** 2007 $ 45

🐚 Motton Terraces ★★★

119 Purtons Road, North Motton, Tas 7315 **REGION** Northern Tasmania
T (03) 6425 2317 **WEB** www.cradlecoastwines.info/ **OPEN** Weekends 10–5, or by appointment
WINEMAKER Flemming Aaberg **EST.** 1990 **CASES** 120
SUMMARY Another of the micro-vineyards which seem to be a Tasmanian specialty; Flemming and Jenny Aaberg planted slightly less than 0.5 ha of chardonnay and riesling in 1990, and are only now increasing that to 1 ha with more riesling and some sauvignon blanc. The exercise in miniature is emphasised by the permanent canopy netting to ward off possums and birds. Winemaking has been brought onsite in the Aabergs' carport.

ŦŦŦ♈ **Riesling 2004 RATING** 86 **DRINK** 2007 $ 13.50

Mountadam ★★★☆

High Eden Road, Eden Valley, SA 5235 **REGION** Eden Valley
T (08) 8564 1900 **F** (08) 8564 1999 **OPEN** 7 days 11–4
WINEMAKER Tim Heath **EST.** 1972 **CASES** 25 000
SUMMARY One of the leading small wineries, founded by David Wynn and run by winemaker son Adam Wynn, initially offering only the Mountadam range at relatively high prices. The subsequent development of the three ranges of wines has been very successful, judged from both a winemaking and a wine-marketing viewpoint. Mountadam has built up an extensive export network over many years, with Canada, Hong Kong, Japan and the UK being the major markets, but extending across the breadth of Europe and most Asian markets. This was strengthened following the acquisition of Mountadam by Cape Mentelle in 2000.

ŦŦŦŦ **Eden Valley Chardonnay 2002** Very developed colour; soft, nutty, thoroughly old-fashioned, but does have flavour. **RATING** 87 **DRINK** Now $ 37

Mount Anakie Wines NR

130 Staughton Vale Road, Anakie, Vic 3221 **REGION** Geelong
T (03) 5284 1256 **F** (03) 5284 1405 **OPEN** 7 days 11–5
WINEMAKER Otto Zambelli **EST.** 1968 **CASES** 6000
SUMMARY Also known as Zambelli Estate; once produced some excellent wines (under its various ownerships and winemakers), all distinguished by their depth and intensity of flavour. No recent tastings; prior to that, the wines tasted were but a shadow of their former quality. The level of activity seems relatively low.

🐚 Mount Appallan Vineyards ★★★

239 Mitchell Road, Biggenden, Qld 4621 **REGION** Queensland Coastal
T (07) 4127 1390 **F** (07) 4127 1090 **WEB** www.mtappallan.com.au **OPEN** By appointment
WINEMAKER Andrew Hickinbotham (Contract) **EST.** 1998 **CASES** 400
SUMMARY The Goodchild family settled on the Draycot property in 1912, successive generations carrying on first wool growing and thereafter dairying. The 160-ha farm is 75 km west of Maryborough, in what is known locally as the Wide Bay–Burnett area, where the rich volcanic soils and semi-maritime mild climate is not very different from that of South Burnett. The family has established 7.6 ha of vineyards planted to verdelho, shiraz, merlot, cabernet sauvignon, petit verdot and viognier, with a small amount each of grenache and mourvedre. Third-generation Syd Goodchild returned as a mature-age student to study viticulture at Adelaide University (adding a fourth academic degree), and fourth-generation Bernie Wixon manages the property, including the dairy side. Pending the granting of a full liquor licence, the wines are available through the website.

ŦŦŦŦ **Middle Burnett Shiraz 2003** Good colour; abundant ripe blackcurrant and plum fruit; medium-bodied; soft tannins; fruit-driven and impressive. Screwcap. **RATING** 88 **DRINK** 2011 $ 18

ŶŶŶŶ **Biggenden Shire Verdelho 2002** Gentle fruit salad; fair length; well made; said to be the first commercial wine from the shire; 50 cases made. Screwcap. **RATING** 86 **DRINK** Now $ 14

ŶŶŶ **Unwooded Chardonnay 2003** **RATING** 79 $ 14

Mount Avoca Winery ★★★★

Moates Lane, Avoca, Vic 3467 **REGION** Pyrenees
T (03) 5465 3282 **F** (03) 5465 3544 **WEB** www.mountavoca.com **OPEN** Mon–Fri 9–5, weekends 10–5
WINEMAKER Matthew Barry **EST.** 1970 **CASES** 15 000
SUMMARY A substantial winery which has long been one of the stalwarts of the Pyrenees region, and is steadily growing, with 23.7 ha of vineyards. There has been a significant refinement in the style and flavour of the red wines over the past few years. I suspect a lot of worthwhile work has gone into barrel selection and maintenance. Reverted to family ownership in July 2003 after a short period as part of the ill-fated Barrington Estates group. Exports to Asia.

ŶŶŶŶŶ **Sauvignon Blanc 2004** Delicate, fresh tropical gooseberry and passionfruit mix; balanced acidity and finish. Pro Cork. **RATING** 90 **DRINK** 2007 $ 17

ŶŶŶŶ **Shiraz 2002** Medium-bodied; nicely balanced fruit and fine, ripe tannins; not sweet; good texture. **RATING** 89 **DRINK** 2010 $ 20
Merlot 2001 Quite complex olive, leather, earth and tannin aromas and flavours; Bordeaux aspects; fraction bitter. **RATING** 87 **DRINK** 2008 $ 20
Cabernet Sauvignon 2001 Light to medium-bodied; earthy, cedary, blackberry/blackcurrant fruit; savoury tannins. Stained and fractured Pro Cork. **RATING** 87 **DRINK** 2008 $ 20

ŶŶŶŶ **Semillon Sauvignon Blanc 2004** **RATING** 86 **DRINK** 2007 $ 15
Chardonnay 2002 **RATING** 85 $ 20

Mount Beckworth ★★★☆

RMB 915, Learmonth Road, Tourello via Ballarat, Vic 3363 **REGION** Ballarat
T (03) 5343 4207 **F** (03) 5343 4207 **WEB** www.ballarat.com/clunes/beckworth.htm **OPEN** Weekends 10–6, and by appointment
WINEMAKER Paul Lesock **EST.** 1984 **CASES** 1000
SUMMARY The 4-ha Mount Beckworth vineyard was planted between 1984 and 1985, but it was not until 1995 that the full range of wines under the Mount Beckworth label appeared. Until that time much of the production was sold to Seppelt Great Western for sparkling wine use. It is owned and managed by Paul Lesock, who studied viticulture at Charles Sturt University, and his wife Jane. The wines reflect the very cool climate except in warm years. Limited Victorian retail distribution.

ŶŶŶŶ **Unwooded Chardonnay 2004** Light-bodied; fresh and clean; nice citrus and stone fruit mix; appropriate unoaked style. Twin Top. **RATING** 88 **DRINK** 2007 $ 16
Clunes Vineyard Chardonnay 2004 Elegant, light-bodied; good texture and mouthfeel; slightly subdued fruit. Twin Top. **RATING** 87 **DRINK** 2007 $ 18
Pinot Noir 2003 Light-bodied; strongly savoury, earthy, spicy style; has length; just a touch more red fruits needed. Cork. **RATING** 87 **DRINK** 2008 $ 18

ŶŶŶŶ **Cabernet Merlot 2003** **RATING** 85 **DRINK** 2008 $ 16

Mt Billy ★★★★☆

18 Victoria Street, Victor Harbor, SA 5211 (postal) **REGION** Southern Fleurieu
T (08) 8552 7200 **F** (08) 8552 8333 **WEB** www.mtbillywines.com.au **OPEN** Not
WINEMAKER Contract **EST.** 2000 **CASES** 1700
SUMMARY John Edwards became a resident dentist at Victor Harbor in 1983, having been an avid wine collector (and consumer) since 1973. John and wife Pauline purchased a 3.75-ha property on the hills behind Victor Harbor, and the sheep and goats ultimately gave way to plantings of 1.2 ha each of chardonnay and pinot meunier. The original intention was to sell the grapes, but low yields quickly persuaded Edwards that making and selling a bottle-fermented sparkling wine was the way to go. Additionally, in 1999 1 tonne each of grenache and shiraz were purchased in the Barossa Valley,

and David Powell of Torbreck agreed to make the wine. Mt Billy was born. Since 1999, quality red grapes from the Barossa Valley have been purchased. Exports to the UK and the US.

ŸŸŸŸŸ **Antiquity Barossa Valley Shiraz 2002** A lovely wine, with perfect black fruits and spice ripeness; great texture, structure and mouthfeel. Cork. **RATING** 96 **DRINK** 2015 $45

ŸŸŸŸŸ **Harmony Barossa Valley Shiraz Mataro Grenache 2002** Strongly varietal, sweet juicy berry aromas and flavours; fine, slippery tannins; minimal oak. Screwcap. **RATING** 90 **DRINK** 2008 $23

ŸŸŸŸ **Southern Fleurieu Chardonnay 2004** Clean, rich, ripe yellow peach fruit; full-bodied style; 14.5° alcohol evident. Screwcap. **RATING** 88 **DRINK** 2009 $22

Mount Broke Wines ★★★★

130 Adams Peak Road, Broke, NSW 2330 **REGION** Lower Hunter Valley
T (02) 6579 1314 **F** (02) 6579 1314 **WEB** www.mtbrokewines.com.au **OPEN** Weekends 11–4
WINEMAKER Contract **EST.** 1997 **CASES** 1000
SUMMARY Phil and Jo McNamara began planting 9.6-ha vineyard to shiraz, merlot, verdelho, barbera, semillon, chardonnay and cabernet sauvignon in 1997 on the west side of Wollombi Brook. They have already established a wine club and have opened The Cow Café, with wine tasting and wine functions capacity.

ŸŸŸŸŸ **Quince Tree Paddock Semillon 2004** Powerful, robust; medium-bodied, though only 10.5° alcohol; very good minerally acidity tightens the finish and gives length. Screwcap. **RATING** 91 **DRINK** 2010 $16

ŸŸŸŸ **Adam's Peak Chardonnay 2004** Light to medium-bodied; gentle melon and fig; subtle oak, good balance and mouthfeel. Screwcap. **RATING** 88 **DRINK** 2008 $25
River Bank Shiraz 2003 Light to medium-bodied; fresh, direct red fruits; minimal tannins; well balanced, early-drinking style. Screwcap. **RATING** 87 **DRINK** 2008 $25

ŸŸŸŸ **River Bank Verdelho 2004** **RATING** 86 **DRINK** 2007 $16
Harrowby Cabernet Merlot 2003 **RATING** 85 **DRINK** 2007 $20

Mount Buninyong Winery NR

Platts Road, Scotsburn, Vic 3352 **REGION** Ballarat
T (03) 5341 8360 **F** (03) 5341 2442 **WEB** www.mountbuninyong.com **OPEN** 7 days
WINEMAKER Peter Armstrong **EST.** 1993 **CASES** NA
SUMMARY Mount Buninyong Winery is the venture of Peter and Jan Armstrong, assisted by son and daughter-in-law Malcolm and Sandra Armstrong. It is situated just south of Ballarat, with 4 ha of riesling, chardonnay, pinot noir and cabernet sauvignon established near Scotsburn. A range of table, fortified, sparkling and organic wines are made under the Mount Buninyong, Ballarat Wines and Ballarat Regional Wines labels. The cellar door has barbecue and picnic facilities.

Mount Burrumboot Estate ★★★★☆

3332 Heathcote–Rochester Road, Colbinabbin, Vic 3559 **REGION** Heathcote
T (03) 5432 9238 **F** (03) 5432 9238 **WEB** www.burrumboot.com **OPEN** Weekends & public hols 11–5, or by appointment
WINEMAKER Cathy Branson **EST.** 1999 **CASES** 900
SUMMARY To quote, 'Mount Burrumboot Estate was born in 1999, when Andrew and Cathy Branson planted vines on the Home Block of the Branson family farm, Donore, on the slopes of Mt Burrumboot, on the Mt Camel Range, above Colbinabbin. Originally the vineyard was just another diversification of an already diverse farming enterprise. However, the wine bug soon bit Andrew and Cathy, and so a winery was established. The first wine was made in 2001 by contract – however, 2002 vintage saw the first wine made by Cathy in the machinery shed, surrounded by headers and tractors. Very primitive, and the appearance of the new 50-tonne winery in August 2002 was greeted with great enthusiasm!' And then you taste the wines. Amazing.

ŸŸŸŸŸ **Winemaker's Reserve Shiraz 2002** A rich and velvety mix of black fruits, licorice and a touch of spice; fine, ripe tannins; long, supple and silky palate and finish. Good cork. **RATING** 94 **DRINK** 2015 $35

▼▼▼▼⟁ **Heathcote Shiraz 2003** Very ripe juicy, jammy blackberry, plum and spice; controlled extract. Quality cork. **RATING** 90 **DRINK** 2013 $25

Mad Uncle Jack's Petit Verdot 2003 Dark red-purple; abundant blackcurrant and blackberry fruit, touches of dark chocolate; controlled tannins. **RATING** 90 **DRINK** 2015 $20

▼▼▼▼ **Old Soolum Red 2003** Medium to full-bodied; nicely balanced and rounded texture and structure; black fruits, touches of chocolate and oak; substantial tannins on the finish need time. High-quality cork. **RATING** 89 **DRINK** 2013 $20

▼▼▼⟁ **Elle Rougit Rose 2004** **RATING** 84 **DRINK** Now $17

Mount Cathedral Vineyards
NR

125 Knafl Road, Taggerty, Vic 3714 **REGION** Upper Goulburn
T 0409 354 069 **F** (03) 9354 0994 **OPEN** By appointment
WINEMAKER Oscar Rosa, Nick Arena **EST.** 1995 **CASES** 400
SUMMARY The Rosa and Arena families established Mount Cathedral Vineyards 1995, the vines being planted at an elevation of 300m on the north face of Mt Cathedral. The first plantings were of 1.2 ha of merlot and 0.8 ha of chardonnay, followed by 2.5 ha of cabernet sauvignon and 0.5 ha of cabernet franc in 1996. Oscar Rosa, chief winemaker, has completed two TAFE courses in viticulture and winemaking, and completed a Bachelor of Wine Science course at Charles Sturt University in 2002. He gained practical experience working at Yering Station during 1998 and 1999.

Mount Charlie Winery
★★★★

228 Mount Charlie Road, Riddells Creek, Vic 3431 **REGION** Macedon Ranges
T (03) 5428 6946 **F** (03) 5428 6946 **WEB** www.mountcharlie.com.au **OPEN** Most Sundays, and by appointment
WINEMAKER Trefor Morgan **EST.** 1991 **CASES** 900
SUMMARY Mount Charlie's wines are sold principally by mail order and through selected restaurants. A futures program encourages mailing list sales with a discount of over 25% on the release price. Owner/winemaker Trefor Morgan is perhaps better known as a Professor of Physiology at Melbourne University. He also acts as a contract maker for others in the region.

▼▼▼▼⟁ **Chardonnay 2003** Medium-bodied; citrus and stone fruit flavours; smooth and supple. **RATING** 90 **DRINK** 2009 $19.99

▼▼▼▼ **Red 2003** Developed colour; light-bodied, but elegant and attractive; gently ripe fruit; no green notes. Shiraz/Merlot/Cabernet Sauvignon. **RATING** 88 **DRINK** 2008 $22

▼▼▼⟁ **Sauvignon Blanc 2004** **RATING** 86 **DRINK** 2007 $14.99

Mount Coghill Vineyard
★★★☆

Clunes–Learmonth Road, Coghills Creek, Vic 3364 **REGION** Ballarat
T (03) 5343 4329 **F** (03) 5343 4329 **WEB** www.mtcoghillwinery.com **OPEN** Weekends 10–5
WINEMAKER Norman Latta **EST.** 1993 **CASES** 350
SUMMARY Ian and Margaret Pym began planting their tiny vineyard in 1995 with 1280 pinot noir rootlings, and added 450 chardonnay rootlings the next year. Since 2001 the wine has been made and released under the Mount Coghill Vineyard label.

▼▼▼▼ **Ballarat Chardonnay 2003** Bright, crisp citrus, grapefruit and mineral flavours have absorbed the French oak; crunchy acidity to close. Screwcap. **RATING** 87 **DRINK** 2008 $20

▼▼▼⟁ **Ballarat Rose 2004** **RATING** 85 **DRINK** Now $18
Ballarat Pinot Noir 2003 **RATING** 85 **DRINK** 2007 $22

▼▼▼ **Ballarat Unwooded Chardonnay 2004** **RATING** 82 $18

Mount Delancey Winery
NR

60 De Lancey Road, Wandin North, Vic 3139 **REGION** Yarra Valley
T (03) 5964 4964 **OPEN** Weekends 10–5.30, or by appointment
WINEMAKER Jordan Metlikovec **EST.** 1985 **CASES** 200

SUMMARY Jordan Metlikovec makes a tiny quantity of wine and fruit wine from a mixed planting of 1 ha which includes chardonnay, pinot noir and cabernet sauvignon. He also purchases approximately 2 tonnes of grapes from other small Yarra Valley vineyards and berry growers.

Mount Duneed NR

Feehan's Road, Mount Duneed, Vic 3216 **REGION** Geelong
T (03) 5264 1281 **F** (03) 5264 1281 **OPEN** Public hols & weekends 11–5, or by appointment
WINEMAKER Ken Campbell, John Darling **EST.** 1970 **CASES** 1000
SUMMARY Rather idiosyncratic wines are the order of the day. Some can develop surprisingly well in bottle; the Botrytis Noble Rot Semillon has, from time to time, been of very high quality. A significant part of the production from the 7.5 ha of vineyards is sold to others.

Mount Eliza Estate

Cnr Sunnyside Road/Nepean Highway, Mount Eliza, Vic 3930 **REGION** Mornington Peninsula
T (03) 9787 0663 **F** (03) 9708 8355 **OPEN** 7 days 11–5
WINEMAKER Scott Ireland (Provenance) **EST.** 1997 **CASES** 8500
SUMMARY Robert and Jenny Thurley planted the 7.84-ha vineyard at Mount Eliza Estate in 1997; the varieties are riesling, chardonnay, sauvignon blanc, shiraz, pinot noir and cabernet sauvignon. Son James, presently studying viticulture, has worked at the vineyard since day one under the direction of viticulturist Graeme Harrip, making the business a family affair. The cellar door, which has great views across Port Phillip Bay to the Melbourne city skyline, was opened in November 2000. The contract winemaker, Scott Ireland, has had many years' experience in making wines from the Port Phillip Zone.

Mount Eyre Vineyards ★★★

1325 Broke Road, Broke, NSW 2330 **REGION** Lower Hunter Valley
T 0438 683 973 **F** (02) 6842 4513 **WEB** www.mounteyre.com **OPEN** By appointment
WINEMAKER CP Lin (Contract) **EST.** 1970 **CASES** 9000
SUMMARY Mount Eyre draws on 2 vineyards, the first a 24-ha estate at Broke, planted to semillon, chardonnay, shiraz, chambourcin, cabernet franc and cabernet sauvignon, and the second, Holman Estate, in Gillards Road, Pokolbin, with 4 ha of shiraz and 1.8 ha of merlot. CP Lin, the winemaker, must surely be the only blind Chinese maker in the world. For good measure, having completed the Hunter vintage he crosses to Mountford Winery, near Christchurch, New Zealand to work with pinot noir each year. Most amazingly of all, he has translated the *Oxford Companion to Wine* into braille. Exports to Canada, Thailand, Cambodia, Singapore and Finland.

ȲȲȲȲ **Three Ponds Semillon 2004** Light green-straw, with some traces of reduction on the bouquet; tight slate/mineral palate, fresh and crisp; needs to build character. **RATING** 87 **DRINK** 2010 $ 24.95

ȲȲȲȲ **Shiraz 2003** **RATING** 86 **DRINK** 2007 $ 14.95
Merlot 2003 **RATING** 85 **DRINK** Now $ 14.95
Rose 2004 **RATING** 84 **DRINK** Now $ 14.95
Double Cabernet 2004 **RATING** 84 **DRINK** Now $ 14.95

Mountford ★★★☆

Bamess Road, West Pemberton, WA 6260 **REGION** Pemberton
T (08) 9776 1345 **F** (08) 9776 1345 **WEB** www.mountfordwines.com.au **OPEN** Mon–Fri 10–4, weekends 10–5
WINEMAKER Andrew Mountford, Saxon Mountford **EST.** 1987 **CASES** 3000
SUMMARY English-born and trained Andrew Mountford and wife Sue migrated to Australia in 1983, and were one of the early movers to select Pemberton for their vineyard. The cool climate and spectacular forested countryside were important considerations in the move. Their strikingly packaged wines are produced from 6 ha of permanently netted, dry-grown vineyards.

ȲȲȲȲ **Sauvignon Blanc 2004** Clean, fresh and crisp; light-bodied; delicate herb and gooseberry; a subliminal hint of sweetness. Screwcap. **RATING** 87 **DRINK** Now $ 19.50

Blanc de Noir 2004 Pale salmon; free-run pinot noir juice; nice balance of sweetness and acidity provides length. Still, Rose style. Screwcap. **RATING** 87 **DRINK** Now $ 16

ҮҮҮҮ **Reserve Pinot Noir 2001** **RATING** 86 **DRINK** Now $ 35
Reserve Merlot 2001 Elegant savoury style; light to medium-bodied; berry, olive and forest flavours, but slightly aggressive tannins. Stained cork. **RATING** 86 **DRINK** 2009 $ 35
Cabernet Sauvignon Cabernet Franc Merlot 2002 Light-bodied; very savoury and earthy; despite the lack of red fruit, has balance and length. Good-quality cork, but stained. **RATING** 86 **DRINK** 2009 $ 25
Pinot Noir 2004 **RATING** 84 **DRINK** 2007 $ 16.50

Mount Gisborne Wines ★★★★

83 Waterson Road, Gisborne, Vic 3437 **REGION** Macedon Ranges
T (03) 5428 2834 **F** (03) 5428 2834 **OPEN** Weekends 10–5
WINEMAKER Stuart Anderson **EST.** 1986 **CASES** 1500
SUMMARY Mount Gisborne Wines is very much a weekend and holiday occupation for proprietor David Ell, who makes the wines from the 7-ha vineyard under the watchful and skilled eye of industry veteran Stuart Anderson, now living in semi-retirement high in the Macedon Hills. All the wines are 100% estate-grown from plantings between 1986 and 1990, and are estate-bottled.

ҮҮҮҮҮ **Chardonnay 2003** Complex barrel ferment aromas, with some French funk; equally complex and rich palate; considerable mouthfeel. Cork. **RATING** 92 **DRINK** 2010 $ 20.80

ҮҮҮҮ **Pinot Noir Rose 2004** Strawberry and red cherry fruit; crisp-cut, dry finish; good acidity. Excellent style. Cork. **RATING** 89 **DRINK** Now $ 10
Pinot Noir 2003 Very light-bodied though unforced style; some complex, spicy notes; very fine tannins. High-quality cork. **RATING** 87 **DRINK** 2008 $ 26.25

Mount Horrocks ★★★★★

The Old Railway Station, Curling Street, Auburn, SA 5451 **REGION** Clare Valley
T (08) 8849 2243 **F** (08) 8849 2265 **WEB** www.mounthorrocks.com **OPEN** Weekends & public hols 10–5
WINEMAKER Stephanie Toole **EST.** 1982 **CASES** 4500
SUMMARY Mount Horrocks has well and truly established its own identity in recent years, aided by positive marketing and, equally importantly, wine quality which has resulted in both show success and critical acclaim. Exports to the UK, the US, Belgium, Switzerland, Holland, Italy and Japan. Lunches available on weekends.

ҮҮҮҮҮ **Clare Valley Shiraz 2002** Spotlessly clean; intense, concentrated, focused blackberry and dark plum fruit; perfect structure and balance. **RATING** 94 **DRINK** 2022 $ 35
Clare Valley Cabernet Merlot 2002 Very good colour; rich black fruits and dark chocolate; fine, ripe tannins; exemplary oak handling. **RATING** 94 **DRINK** 2019 $ 35

ҮҮҮҮҮ **Cordon Cut Riesling 2004** Intense, glowing green-yellow; very youthful; sweet lime juice flavours and soft acidity; fascinating to watch development. Screwcap in beautiful half-bottle. **RATING** 93 **DRINK** 2014 $ 32.75
Watervale Riesling 2004 Quite full in the mouth; ripe lemon/citrus fruit, followed by crunchy acidity on the aftertaste. **RATING** 91 **DRINK** 2014 $ 28
Semillon 2003 Typical full-bodied style; the oak obvious but integrated with ripe fruit flavours. **RATING** 90 **DRINK** 2008 $ 27
Chardonnay 2003 Generous stone fruit, fig and cashew, held together with good acidity on the finish; a particularly good outcome for the Clare Valley. **RATING** 90 **DRINK** 2007 $ 24.95

Mount Ida ★★★★☆

Northern Highway, Heathcote, Vic 3253 **REGION** Heathcote
T (03) 8626 3340 **OPEN** Not
WINEMAKER Matt Steel **EST.** 1978 **CASES** 2000
SUMMARY Established by the famous artist Leonard French and Dr James Munro but purchased by Tisdall after the 1987 bushfires and by Beringer Blass when it acquired Tisdall. Up to the time of the

fires, wonderfully smooth, rich red wines with almost voluptuous sweet, minty fruit were the hallmark. After a brief period during which the name was used as a simple brand (with various wines released), has returned to a single estate-grown wine.

ŶŶŶŶŶ **Heathcote Shiraz 2002** Medium to full-bodied; abundant, layered, rich plum, blackberry and spice fruit supported by vanillin oak and soft, ripe tannins. **RATING** 93 **DRINK** 2017 $ 45

Mountilford   NR

Mount Vincent Road, Ilford, NSW 2850 **REGION** Mudgee
T (02) 6358 8544 **F** (02) 6358 8544 **OPEN** 7 days 10–4
WINEMAKER Contract **EST.** 1985 **CASES** 1800
SUMMARY Surprisingly large cellar door operation which has grown significantly over the past few years, utilising 7 ha of estate vineyards. Roughly half the production is sold to other winemakers. I have not, however, had the opportunity to taste the wines.

Mt Jagged Wines   ★★★★

Main Victor Harbor Road, Mt Jagged, SA 5211 **REGION** Southern Fleurieu
T (08) 8554 9532 **F** (08) 8224 0727 **WEB** www.mtjaggedwines.com.au **OPEN** 7 days 10–5
WINEMAKER Mike Farmilo (Contract) **EST.** 1989 **CASES** 5000
SUMMARY Jerry White immigrated to Australia in 1970, and after a successful business career, purchased 100 ha at Mt Jagged in 1988. The land is on the main road to Victor Harbor, which he believed would generate ample cellar door sales demand. Being the first to plant in the region, he decided to plant 28 ha, thus producing sufficient grapes to supply large companies, and duly entered into a contract with Penfolds, with semillon, chardonnay, merlot, cabernet sauvignon and shiraz all being sold. It was not until 1996 that the first Mt Jagged wine appeared; more and more fruit has since been diverted to the Mt Jagged label. The cool, maritime environment was described by John Gladstones as 'what appears to be the best climate in mainland South Australia for making table wines'. The white wines are exemplary; the red wines, however, seem to struggle for ripeness. Exports to the US.

ŶŶŶŶŶ **Southern Fleurieu Chardonnay 2003** Bright green-yellow; quality wine; intense grapefruit and stone fruit length and power; not phenolic. Screwcap. **RATING** 91 **DRINK** 2009 $ 12
Southern Fleurieu Adelaide Hills Semillon Sauvignon Blanc 2003 Considerable depth and intensity to the palate; lime juice and gooseberry; Sauvignon Blanc the driver. Screwcap. **RATING** 90 **DRINK** 2007 $ 12

ŶŶŶŶ **Southern Fleurieu Single Vineyard Shiraz 2003** Light to medium-bodied; savoury, spicy fruit; leafy red berries; struggles for ripeness. **RATING** 87 **DRINK** 2008 $ 20

ŶŶŶŶ **Southern Fleurieu Single Vineyard Cabernet Merlot 2003 RATING** 85 **DRINK** 2007 $ 18
Sparkling Red NV RATING 85 **DRINK** 2010 $ 12

Mount Langi Ghiran Vineyards   ★★★★★

Warrak Road, Buangor, Vic 3375 **REGION** Grampians
T (03) 5354 3207 **F** (03) 5354 3277 **WEB** www.langi.com.au **OPEN** Mon–Fri 9–5, weekends 12–5
WINEMAKER Trevor Mast, Dan Buckle **EST.** 1969 **CASES** 45 000
SUMMARY A maker of outstanding cool-climate peppery Shiraz, crammed with flavour and vinosity, and very good Cabernet Sauvignon. The Shiraz points the way for cool-climate examples of the variety. The business was acquired by the Rathbone family group in November 2002, and hence has been integrated with the Yering Station product range, a synergistic mix with no overlap. Trevor Mast continues to run the Langi Ghiran operation. Exports to all major markets.

ŶŶŶŶŶ **Langi Shiraz 2002** Elegant, stylish, spicy blackberry aromas; medium-bodied; silky tannins and mouthfeel; beautifully poised wine. Quality cork. **RATING** 94 **DRINK** 2015 $ 55

ŶŶŶŶ **Riesling 2004** Herb, spice and mineral aromas; lively and fresh; quite intense apple and lime fruit; impressive style. Best for years. **RATING** 93 **DRINK** 2014 $ 20
Pinot Gris 2004 Very pale pink; strawberry, pear and musk aromas and flavours show ultra-clear varietal character; retains delicacy without sacrificing length. **RATING** 90 **DRINK** 2007 $ 22

ΤΤΤΤ   **Cliff Edge Shiraz 2002** Similar flavours to the Billi Billi Creek Shiraz; just a little more concentration to the satsuma plum and spice fruit. Stained cork. **RATING** 89 **DRINK** 2010 $25

      Billi Billi Creek Shiraz 2002 Gently sweet, slightly essency red fruit aromas; light to medium-bodied; fine tannins; nice early-consumption red. Screwcap. **RATING** 87 **DRINK** 2007 $16

Mt Lofty Ranges Vineyard   ★★★★☆

Harris Road, Lenswood, SA 5240 **REGION** Adelaide Hills
T (08) 8389 8339 **F** (08) 8389 8349 **OPEN** Weekends 11–5, or by appointment
WINEMAKER Peter Leske (Nepenthe) **EST.** 1992 **CASES** 800
SUMMARY Mt Lofty Ranges Vineyard is owned by Alan Herath and Jan Reed, who have been involved from the outset in planting, training and nurturing the 5.8-ha vineyard. Both had professional careers but are now full-time vignerons. Skilled winemaking by Peter Leske has already brought rewards and recognition to the vineyard. Retail distribution through Domaine Wine Shippers in South Australia; elsewhere direct from the winery. The 2002 Old Pump Shed Pinot Noir was the top wine among the 265 entries at the 2004 Adelaide Hills Regional Wine Show.

ΤΤΤΤΫ   **Old Pump Shed Pinot Noir 2003** Lively, spicy, tangy violet aromas; forest, wild strawberry and a touch of plum on the palate; long finish. Screwcap. **RATING** 92 **DRINK** 2009 $20

      Sauvignon Blanc 2004 Pleasing gently tropical aromas; light-bodied; passionfruit, gooseberry and mineral; good balance. Screwcap. **RATING** 90 **DRINK** 2007 $18

      Chardonnay 2003 Fine, elegant citrus and melon; finely suffused oak; good length and aftertaste. Screwcap. **RATING** 90 **DRINK** 2008 $16

ΤΤΤΤ   **Five Vines Riesling 2004** Light, fine, minerally; well-made; slightly diminished fruit intensity of the vintage; touches of apple and passionfruit. Screwcap. **RATING** 88 **DRINK** 2008 $16

Mount Macedon Winery   ★★★

433 Bawden Road, Mount Macedon, Vic 3441 **REGION** Macedon Ranges
T (03) 5427 2735 **F** (03) 5427 1071 **OPEN** 7 days 10–6 (10–5 in winter)
WINEMAKER Alan Cooper (Cobaw Ridge) **EST.** 1989 **CASES** 800
SUMMARY The property on which Mount Macedon Winery is situated was purchased by David and Ronda Collins in August 2003. The 32-ha property, at an altitude of 68m, has 8 ha of gewurztraminer, chardonnay, pinot noir and pinot meunier.

ΤΤΤΤ   **Estate Grown Gewurztraminer 2004** Very potent, spicy gewurz varietal character, lifted and intense; a rich, spicy, lychee, almost essency, palate. Twin Top. **RATING** 88 **DRINK** Now $20

ΤΤΤΫ   **Unoaked Chardonnay 2004** Citrus blossom aromas; nectarine and citrus fruit; nicely balanced palate. Screwcap. **RATING** 86 **DRINK** 2008 $20

ΤΤΤ   **Estate Grown Rose 2004** **RATING** 83 $20

Mount Majura Vineyard   ★★★★

RMB 314, Majura Road, Majura, ACT 2609 **REGION** Canberra District
T (02) 6262 3070 **F** (02) 6262 4288 **WEB** www.mountmajura.com.au **OPEN** Sun & long weekends 10–5
WINEMAKER Dr Frank van de Loo **EST.** 1988 **CASES** 2000
SUMMARY The first vines were planted in 1988 by Dinny Killen on a site on her family property which had been especially recommended by Dr Edgar Riek; its attractions were red soil of volcanic origin over limestone, with reasonably steep east and northeast slopes providing an element of frost protection. The 1-ha vineyard was planted to pinot noir, chardonnay and merlot in equal quantities; the pinot noir grapes were sold to Lark Hill and used in their award-winning Pinot Noir, while the Chardonnay and Merlot were made for Mount Majura by Lark Hill, both wines enjoying show success. The syndicate which purchased the property in 1999 has extended the plantings, and Dr Frank van de Loo makes the wines in leased space at Brindabella Hills.

ΥΥΥΥΥ **Riesling 2004** Attractive lime and passionfruit aromas and flavours; dry talc/mineral on the back palate and finish. **RATING** 90 **DRINK** 2012 $ 16

ΥΥΥΥ **Canberra District Chardonnay 2003** Crisp, tight citrus, stone fruit and melon; good structure; subtle oak. Screwcap. **RATING** 89 **DRINK** 2010 $ 20

Tempranillo 2003 Interesting wine; light to medium-bodied; predominantly red fruits interwoven with spicy, fine tannins; good length. Obvious potential. **RATING** 89 **DRINK** 2008 $ 25

Pinot Gris 2004 Very pale, clean, spicy/musky aromas; similar musk and spice flavours bolstered by alcohol on the palate. **RATING** 87 **DRINK** 2009 $ 16

Mount Markey

NR

1346 Cassilis Road, Cassilis, Vic 3896 **REGION** Gippsland
T (03) 5159 4264 **F** (03) 5159 4599 **WEB** www.omeoregion.com.au/winery **OPEN** Wed–Mon 10–5
WINEMAKER Howard Reddish **EST.** 1991 **CASES** 650
SUMMARY Howard and Christine Reddish have established 2 vineyards, one of 2 ha surrounding the winery, the other of 3 ha on the slopes of Mt Markey, at an altitude of nearly 500m. The winery is built on the site of the Cassilis Wine Palace, which served the local goldmining families for almost 70 years until the gold ran out in the 1940s. A sheltered barbecue spot is among the many attractions.

Mount Mary

 ★★★★★

Coldstream West Road, Lilydale, Vic 3140 **REGION** Yarra Valley
T (03) 9739 1761 **F** (03) 9739 0137 **OPEN** Not
WINEMAKER Dr John Middleton **EST.** 1971 **CASES** 3000
SUMMARY Superbly refined, elegant and intense Cabernets and usually outstanding and long-lived Pinot Noirs fully justify Mount Mary's exalted reputation. The Triolet blend is very good; more recent vintages of Chardonnay are even better. Limited quantities of the wines are sold through the wholesale/retail distribution system in Victoria, NSW, Queensland and South Australia.

Mount Moliagul

 ★★★★☆

Clay Gully Lane, Moliagul, Vic 3472 **REGION** Bendigo
T (03) 9809 2113 **WEB** www.mountmoliagulwines.com.au **OPEN** By appointment, call 0427 221 641
WINEMAKER Terry Flora **EST.** 1991 **CASES** 400
SUMMARY Terry and Bozenka Flora began their tiny vineyard in 1991, gradually planting 0.5 ha each of shiraz and cabernet sauvignon, and 0.2 ha of chardonnay. Terry Flora has completed two winemaking courses, one with Winery Supplies and the other at Dookie College, and has learnt his craft very well.

ΥΥΥΥΥ **Cabernet Sauvignon 2003** Strong colour; ripe blackcurrant fruit; medium to full-bodied; well-ripened tannins, integrated oak. Pitted, stained cork. **RATING** 92 **DRINK** 2015 $ 25

Shiraz 2003 Deep colour; medium to full-bodied; abundant, ripe blackberry fruit; ripe, chunky tannins; vanilla oak. Cork. **RATING** 90 **DRINK** 2013 $ 30

Mount Panorama Winery

 ★★★★

117 Mountain Straight, Mount Panorama, Bathurst, NSW 2795 **REGION** Central Ranges Zone
T (02) 6331 5368 **OPEN** 7 days 10.30–5
WINEMAKER Desmond McMahon **EST.** 1991 **CASES** 600
SUMMARY For all the obvious reasons, Mount Panorama Winery makes full use of its setting: on Mountain Straight after 'Hell Corner' on the famous motor racing circuit. All the winemaking is done onsite, from picking and using the hand-operated basket press through to bottling, labelling, etc. The owners are gradually extending both the size and scope of the cellar door facilities to take advantage of the tourist opportunities of the site.

ΥΥΥΥΥ **Unwooded Chardonnay 2003** A complex but harmonious and balanced bouquet; abundant stone fruit, nice length, and a clean finish and aftertaste. **RATING** 91 **DRINK** 2007

Mount Prior Vineyard ★★★★

Gooramadda Road, Rutherglen, Vic 3685 **REGION** Rutherglen
T (02) 6026 5591 **F** (02) 6026 5590 **WEB** www.rutherglenvic.com **OPEN** 7 days 9–5
WINEMAKER Brian Devitt **EST.** 1860 **CASES** 5 000
SUMMARY A full-scale tourist facility, with yet more in the pipeline. Full accommodation packages at the historic Mount Prior House; a restaurant operating weekends under the direction of Trish Hennessy (for groups of six or more), with four consecutive *Age Good Food Guide* awards to its credit; picnic and barbecue facilities; and a California-style gift shop. The wines are basically sold through the cellar door and an active mailing list. The 112 ha of vineyards were expanded in 1998 by a further 5 ha of durif, a mark both of the success of Mount Prior and of interest in Durif.

ŶŶŶŶ♀ **Black Label Durif 2002** Deep colour; masses of soft, black fruits, licorice, prune and spice; ripe, fine tannins. Quality cork. **RATING** 90 **DRINK** 2012 $29

ŶŶŶŶ **Director's Selection Muscat NV** Raisined and rich; strong varietal expression; simply a little young. **RATING** 89 **DRINK** Now $17
Reserve Port Museum Release NV Christmas cake and spice aromas and flavours show the obvious wood age; chocolate, spice and biscuit. **RATING** 88 **DRINK** Now $50
Directors Selection Tokay NV Pale golden brown; attractive, relatively young, but sweet Tokay tea leaf varietal character. **RATING** 88 **DRINK** Now $18.50
Merlot 2002 Powerful and concentrated; a core of savoury olive fruit; the tannins firm, but not dry. Cork. **RATING** 87 **DRINK** 2012 $23
Shiraz 2002 A solid, substantial wine with black fruits and slightly rustic tannins; a Rutherglen/Southeast Australia blend. **RATING** 87 **DRINK** 2009 $23
Directors Selection Port NV Rich liqueur style, but does pull up unexpectedly short. **RATING** 87 **DRINK** Now $16

ŶŶŶ♀ **Domain Chardonnay Durif Rose NV** **RATING** 86 **DRINK** Now
Domain Chardonnay Durif Rose 2001 Now there's a blend to end all blends; strong colour; sweet aspects to a powerful cellar door style. **RATING** 86 **DRINK** Now
Sparkling Shiraz Durif NV Powerful, potent, dry style; will improve in bottle. **RATING** 86 **DRINK** 2010 $27
Cabernet Merlot 2002 **RATING** 85 **DRINK** 2009 $19.50
Chenin Blanc 2000 **RATING** 84 **DRINK** Now $19.50

ŶŶŶ **Chardonnay 2000** **RATING** 83 $17.50

Mt Samaria Vineyard ★★★☆

RMB 1626, Midland Highway, Lima South, Vic 3673 **REGION** Upper Goulburn
T (03) 5768 2550 **WEB** www.m-s-v.com.au **OPEN** By appointment
WINEMAKER Michael Reid (Auldstone), Roger Cowan **EST.** 1992 **CASES** 400
SUMMARY The 3-ha Mt Samaria Vineyard, with shiraz (1.7 ha) and tempranillo (0.8 ha) having the lion's share, accompanied by a little cabernet and pinot gris, is owned and operated by Judy and Roger Cowan. Plantings took place over an 8-year period, and in the early days the grapes were sold to Delatite; the Cowans ventured into wine production in 1999. Michael Reid makes part of the shiraz, and Roger Cowan (who has completed a short winemaking course at Dookie College) makes another portion, together with cabernet shiraz. The production sells out each year, most of the sales at the annual tastings at the winery and in Melbourne in May. Apart from a few local restaurants and the Tatong Farmers Market, the remainder is sold by mail order.

ŶŶŶŶ **Shiraz 2003** Riper and more robust dark fruits and depth, notwithstanding lower alcohol (13°) and price; strange role reversal. **RATING** 88 **DRINK** 2009 $15
Black Label Shiraz 2003 Mint, spice, leaf and berry aromas and flavours; light to medium-bodied (13.5° alcohol); bright finish; early-drinking. **RATING** 87 **DRINK** 2007 $16

ŶŶŶ♀ **Pinot Gris 2004** Spice, herb, apple and musk on a well balanced, light to medium-bodied palate, showing the limitation of the variety. **RATING** 86 **DRINK** Now $18

ŶŶŶ **White Shiraz Rose 2004** **RATING** 82 $12

Mt Surmon Wines ★★★☆

Scarlattis Cellar Door Gallery, Basham Road, Stanley Flat, SA 5453 **REGION** Clare Valley
T (08) 8842 1250 **F** (08) 8842 4064 **WEB** www.mtsurmon.com.au **OPEN** Fri–Sun 10–5
WINEMAKER Contract **EST.** 1995 **CASES** 800
SUMMARY The Surmon family has established just under 20 ha of vineyard, half to shiraz, the remainder to cabernet sauvignon, nebbiolo, chardonnay, pinot gris and viognier. Most of the grapes are sold to other wineries (some on a swap basis for riesling and merlot), but small quantities are contract-made and sold through Scarlattis Cellar Door Gallery and a few local hotels. The first wines were made in 1999 (Cabernet Merlot and Shiraz); white wines were added later.

▼▼▼▼ **Pinot Gris 2004** Pink, halfway to rose in colour; flowery aromas and flavours; good use of acidity on a clean, fresh finish. **RATING** 89 **DRINK** 2007 $ 16
Chardonnay 2004 Clean, fresh, tangy and lively; light-bodied, and no evidence of oak. **RATING** 87 **DRINK** Now $ 17
Nebbiolo 2003 Less tannic than the Reserve version; savoury, cedary, lemony edges to the mid-palate sweet fruit; then lingering tannins. **RATING** 87 **DRINK** 2009 $ 20
Clare Valley Sparkling Pinot Gris 2004 Pale pink; amazingly, works quite well; fresh and lively, with a sweet fruit core; good balance. **RATING** 87 **DRINK** 2008 $ 20

▼▼▼▽ **Viognier 2004** **RATING** 86 **DRINK** 2007 $ 17
Cabernet Sauvignon 2003 **RATING** 86 **DRINK** 2007 $ 20
Reserve Nebbiolo 2003 **RATING** 86 **DRINK** Now
Shiraz Viognier 2003 **RATING** 85 **DRINK** 2008 $ 20
Sparkling Nebbiolo 2003 **RATING** 85 **DRINK** Now $ 20

Mount Torrens Vineyards NR

PO Box 1679, Mount Torrens, SA 5244 **REGION** Adelaide Hills
T (08) 8389 4229 **F** (08) 8389 4229 **OPEN** Not
WINEMAKER David Powell (Contract) **EST.** 1996 **CASES** NA
SUMMARY Mount Torrens Vineyards has 3 ha of shiraz and viognier, and the distinguished team of Mark Whisson as viticulturist and David Powell as contract winemaker. The wines are available by mail order, but are chiefly exported to England and the US.

Mount Trio Vineyard ★★★★

Cnr Castle Rock Road/Porongurup Road, Porongurup WA 6324 **REGION** Porongurup
T (08) 9853 1136 **F** (08) 9853 1120 **OPEN** By appointment
WINEMAKER Gavin Berry **EST.** 1989 **CASES** 6500
SUMMARY Mount Trio was established by Gavin Berry and Gill Graham shortly after they moved to the Mt Barker district in late 1988. They have slowly built up the Mount Trio business, based in part on estate plantings of 2 ha of pinot noir and 0.5 ha of chardonnay and in part on purchased grapes. An additional 6 ha was planted in the spring of 1999. Exports to the UK.

▼▼▼▼▽ **Great Southern Sauvignon Blanc 2004** Pale green-straw; spotlessly clean, no reduction; intense but elegant gooseberry fruit on the palate; lemony acidity; very good value. **RATING** 93 **DRINK** 2007 $ 14.90
Great Southern Cabernet Merlot 2003 Bright colour; medium-bodied, but intense and precise; a long, pure line of blackcurrant with a twist of olive. **RATING** 92 **DRINK** 2015 $ 17.50
Great Southern Shiraz 2002 Medium-bodied; an attractive mix of red and black fruits and spices; elegant style, fine tannins. **RATING** 90 **DRINK** 2012 $ 22

▼▼▼▽ **Great Southern Pinot Noir 2003** **RATING** 86 **DRINK** 2007 $ 19

Mount View Estate ★★★★☆

Mount View Road, Mount View, NSW 2325 **REGION** Lower Hunter Valley
T (02) 4990 3307 **F** (02) 4991 1289 **OPEN** 7 days 10–5
WINEMAKER Andrew Thomas (Consultant) **EST.** 1971 **CASES** 4000

SUMMARY The Tulloch family has neither owned nor had any interest in Mount View Estate since 2000. Winemaking has passed to the capable hands of former Tyrrell's winemaker Andrew Thomas. The 30-year-old vines are paying big dividends.

ΨΨΨΨΨ **Flagship Merlot 2003** Deep red-purple; deliciously ripe, but not over-ripe, mix of redcurrant, olive and blackcurrant; balanced tannins, good oak; remarkable for the region; only 500 bottles made. High-quality cork. **RATING** 94 **DRINK** 2015 $48

ΨΨΨΨ♀ **Pinot Noir 2003** Round, rich, ripe, medium-bodied dry red; nicely made; varietal character gone missing in action as ever, but could please with more bottle age. Cork. **RATING** 93 **DRINK** 2018 $25

Flagship Shiraz 2003 Exotic plum, spice, prune and blackberry aromas; rich and opulent; excellent structure; fine, silky tannins. Trophy winner; 280 cases made. Stained cork. **RATING** 93 **DRINK** 2018 $48

Reserve Semillon 2004 Spotlessly bright, crisp and clear; mineral and herb; crunchy acidity; good length and finish. Screwcap. **RATING** 92 **DRINK** 2014 $19

Reserve Shiraz 2003 Medium-bodied; seems lower in alcohol than the Flagship, but has the same level (14.5°); more regional, savoury, earthy characters; good length and balance. Cork. **RATING** 90 **DRINK** 2013 $30

Cabernet Sauvignon 2003 Bright, clear colour; very good, fresh, medium-bodied balance and structure; fine, sweet, savoury tannins; again, out-performs regional expectations. Cork. **RATING** 90 **DRINK** 2013 $22

ΨΨΨΨ **Reserve Chardonnay 2004** A subtle interplay of gentle melon fruit with malolactic barrel ferment cashew notes; light to medium-bodied; good acidity. Screwcap. **RATING** 89 **DRINK** 2008 $19

Reserve Hunter Valley Cabernet Sauvignon 2003 Clean, attractive dark fruit aromas; medium-bodied; doesn't quite deliver on the mid-palate as yet, but should fill out. Quality cork. **RATING** 89 **DRINK** 2010 $18

Tawny Port NV Rich, toffee, Christmas cake and molasses style; clean spirit; well balanced. Estate-grown and made from a Shiraz Solera commenced in 1983. **RATING** 88 **DRINK** 2007 $20

Reserve Verdelho 2004 Gentle, well-balanced fruit salad and melon; light to medium-bodied; won't frighten the horses. Screwcap. **RATING** 87 **DRINK** 2007 $17

Shiraz Rose 2004 Aromatic cherry blossom fruit; long palate; good balance, dry finish. Serious style. Screwcap. **RATING** 87 **DRINK** Now $16

ΨΨΨ♀ **Basalt Hill 2002** **RATING** 86 **DRINK** 2007 $16

Mountview Wines

★★★★☆

Mount Stirling Road, Glen Aplin, Qld 4381 **REGION** Granite Belt
T (07) 4683 4316 **F** (07) 4683 4111 **WEB** www.mountviewwines.com.au **OPEN** Fri–Sun 9.30–4.30, 7 days during school & public hols
WINEMAKER Jim Barnes **EST.** 1990 **CASES** 1250
SUMMARY Mountview Wines has changed hands and is now owned by Pauline Stewart. The quality of the wines is exemplary; one of the top producers in the region.

ΨΨΨΨΨ **Reserve Semillon 2004** Powerful evocation of varietal characters; herb, lanolin, grass and mineral; excellent length and intensity. Screwcap. **RATING** 94 **DRINK** 2019 $18

ΨΨΨΨ♀ **Flagship Shiraz 2003** Deep, dense colour; powerful and concentrated blackberry fruit; slight back-palate break should fill in with time in bottle. Stained cork. **RATING** 92 **DRINK** 2015 $48

Reserve Shiraz 2003 Clean, medium-bodied; nicely ripened blackberry fruit; balanced tannins and extract; good length. Stained cork. **RATING** 90 **DRINK** 2013 $25

ΨΨΨΨ **Flagship Merlot 2003** Strong colour; very deep, concentrated and powerful; Merlot on steroids, but impressively muscled. Needs much time. Cork. **RATING** 89 **DRINK** 2020 $48

ΨΨΨ♀ **Reserve Chardonnay 2003** **RATING** 86 **DRINK** 2007 $16
Reserve Verdelho 2004 **RATING** 85 **DRINK** 2007 $16

Mt Vincent Estate

NR

8 Main Road, Mount Vincent, NSW 2323 **REGION** Lower Hunter Valley
T (02) 4938 0078 **F** (02) 4938 0048 **WEB** www.mvewines.com.au **OPEN** By appointment
WINEMAKER Contract **EST.** NA **CASES** NA
SUMMARY If you drive from Sydney to the Hunter Valley by the most conventional and quickest route, Mt Vincent Estate is the first vineyard you will come to. It is on the right-hand side of the road, at the foot of Mt Vincent in the Mulbring Valley. The 50-ha property includes a 2-ha lake stocked with fish and yabbies, a 5-bedroom accommodation retreat, and a cellar door. There is also a club membership order system which offers various incentives. Semillon, Verdelho, Chardonnay, Shiraz and Merlot are the principal wines on offer. Has produced a number of wines that have won gold medals in recent years.

Mount William Winery

★★★★

Mount William Road, Tantaraboo, Vic 3764 **REGION** Macedon Ranges
T (03) 5429 1595 **F** (03) 5429 1998 **WEB** www.mtwilliamwinery.com.au **OPEN** 7 days 11–5
WINEMAKER Murray Cousins, Esther Cousins, David Cowburn (Contract) **EST.** 1987 **CASES** 3500
SUMMARY Adrienne and Murray Cousins established 7.5 ha of vineyards, planted to pinot noir, cabernet franc, merlot and chardonnay, between 1987 and 1999. The wines are made under contract and are sold through a stone cellar door, and through a number of fine wine retailers around Melbourne.

ΥΥΥΥΥ **Pinot Noir 2003** Light to medium-bodied; fragrant, spicy, savoury red berries; good length and balance. Screwcap. **RATING** 92 **DRINK** 2009 $ 25
2000 Crisp and attractive spicy notes to citrus and pear fruit; long finish; crisp and clean. **RATING** 90 **DRINK** 2010 $ 28

ΥΥΥΥ **Louise Clare NV** **RATING** 86 **DRINK** 2008 $ 28

Mr Riggs Wine Company

★★★★☆

PO Box 584, McLaren Vale, SA 5171 **REGION** McLaren Vale
T (08) 8556 4460 **F** (08) 8556 4462 **WEB** www.pennyshill.com.au **OPEN** Not
WINEMAKER Ben Riggs **EST.** 2001 **CASES** 10 600
SUMMARY After 14 years as winemaker at Wirra Wirra, and another six at various Australian wineries as well as numerous northern hemisphere vintages, Ben Riggs has decided to establish his own business. His major activity is as consultant winemaker to Penny's Hill, Pertaringa, Coriole and Geoff Hardy, plus keeping his hand in consulting for Cazal Viel in the south of France and for UK-based distributor, Western Wines. His domestic winemaking includes making commercial batches of wine for wholesale and retail entities in Australia, adopting a 'grape to plate' approach. He also makes wine for his Mr Riggs label, initially buying select parcels of grapes from old vines in McLaren Vale, and in due course also using grapes from his own vineyard at Piebald Gully, where he has planted shiraz, viognier and petit verdot. Exports to the US, Canada, Denmark, Malaysia, New Zealand and Hong Kong.

ΥΥΥΥΥ **McLaren Vale Shiraz 2003** Black fruits and lots of new oak which is well integrated; fine structure, particularly tannins; stylish. **RATING** 94 **DRINK** 2015 $ 38

ΥΥΥΥΥ **Adelaide Hills Riesling 2004** Full of flavour in full-on spatlese style; sweet apple and lime juice. **RATING** 93 **DRINK** 2015 $ 22

ΥΥΥΥ **Adelaide Hills Tempranillo 2004** Bright, fresh red fruits; low tannins; subliminal touch of citrus. **RATING** 89 **DRINK** 2007 $ 26
Adelaide Viognier 2004 Fresh, lively and neatly balanced; scores for mouthfeel more than any overt varietal character. **RATING** 88 **DRINK** 2007 $ 26

Mudgee Growers

★★★☆

Henry Lawson Drive, Mudgee, NSW 2580 **REGION** Mudgee
T (02) 6372 2855 **F** (02) 6372 2811 **WEB** www.mudgeegrowers.com.au **OPEN** 7 days 10–5
WINEMAKER David Lowe, Jane Wilson **EST.** 2004 **CASES** 1200

SUMMARY After closing their operation in the Hunter Valley, David Lowe and Jane Wilson have set up a new business in Mudgee, using grapes from various vineyards in the region. The cellar door is in the heritage winery at Fairview (formerly known as Platt's), which has been returned to working order, once more housing tanks, oak casks and barrels.

TTTT **Mudgee Growers Semillon 2004** Spicy lemon blossom aromas; a relatively soft palate with a touch of residual sugar; for immediate drinking. **RATING** 89 **DRINK** 2007 $ 15
Mudgee Growers Petit Verdot 2003 Strong varietal expression; powerful black fruits with built-in tannins. Should evolve well. **RATING** 89 **DRINK** 2013 $ 22
Mudgee Growers Verdelho 2004 Lemon peel/rind aromas; a pleasant mix of guava, peach and tropical fruit salad; not too sweet. **RATING** 87 **DRINK** 2007 $ 18
Mudgee Growers Rose 2004 Ample rose style; good colour; cherry/berry fruit; again, not too sweet. **RATING** 87 **DRINK** Now $ 15

TTTY **Mudgee Growers Chardonnay 2004** Very rich, ripe, mouthfilling, tropical style; sweetness designed for the cellar door; a pity. **RATING** 86 **DRINK** 2007 $ 18
Mudgee Growers Shiraz 2003 **RATING** 86 **DRINK** 2007 $ 22
Mudgee Growers West Court Vintage Port 2004 **RATING** 86 **DRINK** 2014 $ 20

Mudgee Wines   NR

Henry Lawson Drive, Mudgee, NSW 2850 **REGION** Mudgee
T (02) 6372 2258 **OPEN** Thurs–Mon 10–5, hols 7 days
WINEMAKER David Conway **EST.** 1963 **CASES** 600
SUMMARY Following the acquisition of Mudgee Wines by the Conway family, the organic winemaking practices of the former owner Jennifer Meek have been discontinued; conventional viticultural and winemaking practices have now been adopted.

Mulcra Estate Wines   ★★★☆

PO Box 182, Irymple, Vic 3498 **REGION** Murray Darling
T (03) 5022 8991 **F** (03) 5022 8991 **WEB** www.mulcraestate.com.au **OPEN** At The Enjoy Wine Cafe, 8th St, Mildura
WINEMAKER Glen Olsen **EST.** 2002 **CASES** 1000
SUMMARY Samuel and Anna Andriske were part of a wave of Germans who left their homeland in the 1840s to escape poverty, wars and religious differences. The majority settled in the Barossa Valley, but one group was brought to Geelong by its then Mayor. Grapegrowing was part of a mixed farming business for Andriskes, but in the wake of phylloxera the third generation (Charles Andriske) moved to Mildura. His sons established Mulcra Estate in 1933, selling grapes to the Mildara winery and also producing table grapes. Finally, the fifth generation, Marlene Andriske and son Mark, have made the move from grapegrowing to winemaking, with 3 ha of chardonnay, supplemented by grapes purchased from a local grower.

TTTT **Henry Andriske Reserve Shiraz 2003** Dense colour; massively ripe, rich and concentrated prune, jam and blackberry. **RATING** 89 **DRINK** 2010 $ 45
Petit Verdot 2003 Above-average weight and depth of flavour so typical of the variety; dark berry fruits; fine tannins, good acidity. **RATING** 87 **DRINK** 2010 $ 28

TTTY **Merlot 2003** **RATING** 85 **DRINK** 2008 $ 24.50
Reserve Cabernet Sauvignon 2003 **RATING** 84 **DRINK** 2008 $ 25

TTY **Windmill Reserve Chardonnay 2003** **RATING** 79 $ 24.50

Mulligan Wongara Vineyard   ★★★

603 Grenfell Road, Cowra, NSW 2794 **REGION** Cowra
T (02) 6342 9334 **F** (02) 6342 9334 **OPEN** Sat, public hols (Sundays if a public holiday weekend) 10–4
WINEMAKER Nick Millichip (Consultant) **EST.** 1993 **CASES** 2000
SUMMARY Andrew and Emma Mulligan began the establishment of their 16-ha vineyard in 1993; chardonnay (14 ha), shiraz (2.5 ha), cabernet (3.5 ha) and sangiovese (1 ha) have been planted. A significant proportion of the grapes is sold to others. A striking tower cellar door and cellar is now open, and the wines are sold direct to Sydney restaurants and retailers.

Mulyan ★★★

North Logan Road, Cowra, NSW 2794 **REGION** Cowra
T (02) 6342 1336 **F** (02) 6341 1015 **OPEN** Weekends & public hols 10–5, or by appointment
WINEMAKER Drew Tuckwell (Contract) **EST.** 1994 **CASES** 2000
SUMMARY Mulyan is a 1350-ha grazing property purchased by the Fagan family in 1886 from Dr
William Redfern, a leading 19th century figure in Australian history. The current-generation owners,
Peter and Jenni Fagan, began planting in 1994, and intend the vineyard area to be 100 ha in all.
Presently there are 29 ha of shiraz and 15 ha of chardonnay, plus an experimental plot of sangiovese.
The label features a statue of the Roman God Mercury which has stood in the Mulyan homestead
garden since being brought back from Italy in 1912 by Peter Fagan's grandmother.

ΨΨΨΨ **Cowra Shiraz 2002** Solid blackberry and plum fruit; savoury, earthy notes add to the
structure. Stained cork. **RATING** 87 **DRINK** 2009 **$** 25

ΨΨΨΨ **Bush Rangers Bounty Shiraz 2002** **RATING** 85 **DRINK** Now **$** 15
Bush Rangers Bounty Chardonnay 2001 **RATING** 84 **DRINK** Now **$** 11

ΨΨΨ **Cowra Chardonnay 2003** **RATING** 82 **$** 18

Munari Wines ★★★★

1129 Northern Highway, Heathcote, Vic 3523 **REGION** Heathcote
T (03) 5433 3366 **F** (03) 5433 3095 **WEB** www.munariwines.com **OPEN** 7 days 10–5
WINEMAKER Adrian Munari, Deborah Munari **EST.** 1993 **CASES** 2000
SUMMARY Adrian and Deborah Munari made a singularly impressive entry into the winemaking
scene, with both their initial vintages winning an impressive array of show medals, and have carried
on in similar vein since then. With a little under 8 ha of estate vines, production will be limited, but
the wines are well worth seeking out. Exports to Singapore, Malaysia Indonesia and South Korea.

ΨΨΨΨΨ **The Ridge Shiraz 2003** Dense colour; rich, round black cherry, plum and blackberry;
utterly different structure from Lady's Pass; soft and mouthfilling. Stained-quality cork.
RATING 93 **DRINK** 2017
Lady's Pass Heathcote Shiraz 2003 Medium-bodied; smooth, supple spicy, gently
savoury black cherries; elegant; good length and fine tannins. Very nice wine. Slightly
stained-quality cork. **RATING** 93 **DRINK** 2013

ΨΨΨΨ **The Bendigo Shiraz Mourvedre 2003** Elegant, medium-bodied, softened to a degree by
Mourvedre; spicy berry fruit; fine tannins. Cork. **RATING** 89 **DRINK** 2011
Heathcote Cabernet Sauvignon 2003 Sweet, juicy berry notes of jam and mint; some
drought stress evident. Cork. **RATING** 89 **DRINK** 2011
Schoolhouse Red 2003 Light to medium-bodied; juicy red fruits and spice; supple and
fine; attractive blend of Merlot, Cabernet Sauvignon, Malbec and Shiraz. Stained cork.
RATING 88 **DRINK** 2007

Mundoonen ★★★★

1457 Yass River Road, Yass, NSW 2582 **REGION** Canberra District
T (02) 6227 1353 **F** (02) 6227 1453 **WEB** www.mundoonen.com.au **OPEN** Sun & public hols, or by
appointment
WINEMAKER Terry O'Donnell **EST.** 2003 **CASES** 700
SUMMARY Jenny and Terry O'Donnell released their first wines in August 2003. The estate winery is
situated beside the Yass River, behind one of the oldest settler's cottages in the Yass River Valley,
dating back to 1858. Estate plantings of shiraz and viognier are supplemented by contract-grown
riesling, sauvignon blanc and cabernet sauvignon. The barrel shed has been created by refurbishing
and insulating a 140-year-old building on the property.

ΨΨΨΨΨ **Canberra District Riesling 2002** Developed colour; immensely powerful, broad Alsace
style; some body building has gone on in the making; seems much riper than 11.5° alcohol.
Certainly very different. Screwcap. **RATING** 90 **DRINK** 2008 **$** 18

ΨΨΨΨ **Canberra District Late Harvest Riesling 2003** Glowing yellow-green; plenty of lime
juice fruit; will grow further in bottle; only marginal sweetness. Screwcap. **RATING** 88
DRINK 2010 **$** 22

Mundrakoona Estate

Sir Charles Moses Lane, Old Hume Highway, Mittagong, NSW 2575 **REGION** Southern Highlands
T (02) 4872 1311 **F** (02) 4872 1322 **WEB** www.mundrakoona.com.au **OPEN** Mon–Fri 10–5, weekends
& public hols 9–6
WINEMAKER Anton Balog **EST.** 1997 **CASES** 8500
SUMMARY During 1998 and 1999 Anton Balog progressively planted 3.2 ha of pinot noir, sauvignon
blanc and tempranillo at an altitude of 680m. He is using wild yeast ferments, hand-plunging and
other 'natural' winemaking techniques, with the aim of producing Burgundian-style Pinot and
Chardonnay and Bordeaux-style Sauvignon Blanc and Cabernet Sauvignon. For the foreseeable
future, estate production will be supplemented by grapes grown in local vineyards.

ŸŸŸŸŸ **Artemis Pinot Noir 2003** Complex aromas, flavours and structure; black fruits with
touches of spice and briar; lingering, silky tannins. As surprising as it is impressive. Cork.
RATING 93 **DRINK** 2010 $ 35

ŸŸŸŸ **Artemis Grand Crux Shiraz 2003** Clean spice, berry and mint aromas; savoury, minty
palate with fractionally green notes. Quality cork. **RATING** 88 **DRINK** 2010 $ 45

ŸŸŸŸ **Artemis Tempranillo 2003 RATING** 86 **DRINK** 2007 $ 28

Murchison Wines

105 Old Weir Road, Murchison, Vic 3610 **REGION** Goulburn Valley
T (03) 5826 2294 **F** (03) 5826 2510 **WEB** www.murchisonwines.com.au **OPEN** Fri–Mon & public hols
10–5, or by appointment
WINEMAKER Guido Vazzoler **EST.** 1975 **CASES** 4000
SUMMARY Sandra (ex kindergarten teacher turned cheesemaker) and Guido Vazzoler (ex Brown
Brothers) acquired the long-established Longleat Estate vineyard in 2003, renaming it Murchison
Wines; they had lived on the property (as tenants) for some years. The wines are estate-grown;
limited distribution through Tasman Liquor Traders, plus cellar door, mail order and website sales.

ŸŸŸŸŸ **Longleat Estate Semillon 2004** Abundant sweet, ripe semillon fruit flavours, but
avoids heaviness/over-extraction; a quite silky mouthfeel. Clean. Screwcap. **RATING** 90
DRINK 2010 $ 15

ŸŸŸŸ **Longleat Estate Riesling 2004** Plenty of depth and flavour; ripe apple and spice; good
persistence. Screwcap. **RATING** 89 **DRINK** 2008 $ 15
Longleat Estate Cabernet Sauvignon 2002 Medium-bodied; sweet cassis/berry fruit;
fine tannins, fractionally pointy acidity. **RATING** 89 **DRINK** 2010 $ 18.50
Longleat Estate Shiraz 2002 Savoury, earthy style; medium-bodied; red fruits, bramble
and olive. Cork. **RATING** 88 **DRINK** 2009 $ 19.90

ŸŸŸ **Longleat Estate Late Harvest Riesling 2004 RATING** 83 $ 13

Murdoch Hill

Mappinga Road, Woodside, SA 5244 **REGION** Adelaide Hills
T (08) 8389 7081 **F** (08) 8389 7991 **WEB** www.murdochhill.com.au **OPEN** By appointment
WINEMAKER Brian Light (Contract) **EST.** 1998 **CASES** 2500
SUMMARY A little over 21 ha of vines have been established on the undulating, gum-studded
countryside of the Downer family's Erinka property, 4 km east of Oakbank. In descending order of
importance, the varieties established are sauvignon blanc, shiraz, cabernet sauvignon and
chardonnay. The wines are distributed by Australian Prestige Wines in Melbourne and Sydney.

ŸŸŸŸ **Sauvignon Blanc 2004** Clean and fresh; quite powerful and intense; herb, lemon peel
and gooseberry flavours. **RATING** 87 **DRINK** Now $ 17

ŸŸŸ **Cabernet Sauvignon 2001 RATING** 78 $ 18

Murdock

Riddoch Highway, Coonawarra, SA 5263 **REGION** Coonawarra
T (08) 8737 3700 **F** (08) 8737 2107 **WEB** www.murdockwines.com **OPEN** Not
WINEMAKER Peter Bissell (Balnaves) **EST.** 1998 **CASES** 3000

SUMMARY The Murdock family has established 10.4 ha of cabernet sauvignon, 2 ha of shiraz, 1 ha of merlot, and 0.5 ha each of chardonnay and riesling, and produces small quantities of an outstanding Cabernet Sauvignon, contract-made by Peter Bissell. A second vineyard has been added in the Barossa Valley, with 5.8 ha of shiraz and 2.1 ha each of semillon and cabernet sauvignon. Retail distribution in the eastern states; exports to the US and Asia. The labels, incidentally, are ultra-minimalist; no flood of propaganda here.

ŸŸŸŸŸ Riesling 2004 Fragrant, flowery apple blossom; delicate but has some intensity; lingering aftertaste; good acidity. **RATING** 92 **DRINK** 2012 $ 20

ŸŸŸŸ The Merger Cabernet Shiraz 2003 Very youthful, indeed slightly aggressive; not the typical polished style of Murdock; leaf and pine needle; low-pH style. Should sort itself out with bottle age. **RATING** 87 **DRINK** 2009 $ 20

Murdup Wines ★★★☆

Southern Ports Highway, Mount Benson, SA 5275 **REGION** Mount Benson
T (08) 8768 6190 **F** (08) 8768 6190 **WEB** www.murdupwines.com.au **OPEN** 7 days 10–4
WINEMAKER Ralph Fowler (Contract) **EST.** 1996 **CASES** 1400
SUMMARY Andy and Melinda Murdock purchased their property in 1996; when first settled as a grazing property in the 1860s, it was called Murdup. Beginning in 1997, they have established 10.5 ha of vineyard, the lion's share going to cabernet sauvignon and shiraz, with smaller plantings of chardonnay and sauvignon blanc.

ŸŸŸŸŸ Sauvignon Blanc 2004 Bright green-yellow; zesty, lively, intense lemon rind, gooseberry and passionfruit; clean, bright finish. Screwcap. **RATING** 92 **DRINK** 2007 $ 17

ŸŸŸŸ Shiraz 2003 RATING 86 **DRINK** 2008 $ 22

🐦 Murray Darling Collection ★★★☆

PO Box 84, Euston, NSW 2737 **REGION** Murray Darling
T (03) 5026 1932 **F** (03) 5026 3228 **WEB** www.murraydarlingcollection.com **OPEN** Not
WINEMAKER Sandro Mosele (Contract) **EST.** 1989 **CASES** 3000
SUMMARY This is the project of Bruce and Jenny Chalmers, who run the largest vine nursery propagation business in Australia, and Stefano di Pieri. As well as supplying rootlings to vignerons all over Australia, the Chalmers have established substantial plantings of a range of varietals, running from mainstream to rare. By using fine, misty, water sprays in the vineyard, Chalmers is able to radically reduce the canopy temperatures in summer, thus achieving unexpected results with varieties which theoretically require a far cooler climate. The grapes are taken to the Mornington Peninsula, where the wines are made by Sandro Mosele. Strikingly labelled and branded, they are distributed by Cellarhand in NSW and Victoria.

ŸŸŸŸ A Murray Cod Called Bruce Vermentino 2004 Quite bright, crisp and fresh floral aromas; light to medium-bodied; lemony acidity; interesting. A native of Sardinia and the north coast of Tuscany. Diam. **RATING** 87 **DRINK** 2007 $ 21.50
Piano Del Bacino Lagrein 2004 Dark red-purple; plenty of plum, black cherry, bordering luscious; very soft tannins. Diam. **RATING** 87 **DRINK** 2009 $ 22

ŸŸŸŸ Mungo Lunette Viognier 2003 Clean, fresh, soft fruit salad and pastille fruit; well balanced, though the 14° alcohol shows. Diam. **RATING** 86 **DRINK** 2007 $ 21.50
Salt Pan Shiraz 2003 Deep purple-red; medium-bodied; opens with damson plum and blackberry; the tannins a tad aggressive, the acidity seemingly tweaked a little bit too far. Diam. **RATING** 86 **DRINK** 2012 $ 21.50
1902 Corowa Sangiovese 2003 Light-bodied; fresh, fine, savoury notes; varietal sour cherry, lemony tannins; well made. Diam. **RATING** 86 **DRINK** 2009 $ 21.50
El Fuente Tempranillo 2004 Bright, fresh, light-bodied juicy fruit; as fresh and clean as a daisy. Diam. **RATING** 86 **DRINK** 2007 $ 21.50

Murray Estate NR

Tocumwal–Barooga Road, Yarrawonga, Vic 3730 **REGION** Murray Darling
T (03) 5745 8345 **F** (03) 5745 8346 **WEB** www.murrayestatewines.com.au **OPEN** Weekends 11–5
WINEMAKER John Weinert **EST.** 1997 **CASES** NA

SUMMARY John and Sue Weinert were involved from the ground up in planting their 2.6-ha vineyard to riesling, chenin blanc, merlot, shiraz and cabernet sauvignon. They make the wines onsite, selling them through the cellar door and by mail order.

🍇 Murray Street Vineyard ★★★★

Lot 723, Murray Street, Greenock, SA 5360 **REGION** Barossa Valley
T (08) 8562 8373 **F** (08) 8562 8414 **OPEN** 7 days 10–4.30
WINEMAKER Andrew Seppelt **EST.** 2003 **CASES** 2000
SUMMARY Andrew and Vanessa Seppelt have moved with a degree of caution in setting up Murray Street Vineyard, possibly because of inherited wisdom. Andrew Seppelt is a direct descendant of Benno and Sophia Seppelt, who built Seppeltsfield and set the family company bearing their name on its path to fame. They have 46 ha of vineyards, one block at Gomersal, the other at Greenock, with the lion's share going to shiraz, followed by grenache, mourvedre, viognier, marsanne, semillon and zinfandel. Most of the grapes are sold, with a small (but hopefully increasing) amount retained for the Murray Street Vineyard brand. The Benno Shiraz Mataro is one icon tribute on the masculine side; an intended Sophia Shiraz Grenache will be the feminine icon. Domestic distribution is handled direct from the winery; exports to the UK, the US, Canada and Denmark.

ΨΨΨΨΨ **Benno Barossa Valley Shiraz Mataro 2002** Elegant, supple, medium-bodied; a fine, seamless blend of blackberry fruits and oak; fine-grained tannins. High-quality cork. **RATING** 94 **DRINK** 2015

ΨΨΨΨ **Barossa Valley Grenache Mataro 2002** Light to medium-bodied; gently spicy, softly sweet fruit; 14.2° alcohol; has elegance. **RATING** 89 **DRINK** 2008
Barossa Valley Shiraz 2002 Medium-bodied; sweet, juicy red and black berry fruits; subtle oak, minimal tannins; lighter than many '02 wines. Cork. **RATING** 88 **DRINK** 2009
Barossa Valley Shiraz 2001 Medium-bodied, showing the first signs of development, with gently earthy/savoury notes to the sweet, plummy fruit; soft tannins and controlled American oak. **RATING** 87 **DRINK** 2008

Murrin Bridge Wines NR

PO Box 16, Lake Cargelligo, NSW 2672 **REGION** Riverina
T (02) 6898 2264 **F** (02) 6898 2263 **WEB** www.murrinbridgewines.com.au **OPEN** Not
WINEMAKER Dom Piromalli (Contract) **EST.** 1999 **CASES** 3500
SUMMARY The Murrin Bridge Vineyard arose out of a program between the Aboriginal and Torres Strait Islander Commission (ATSIC) undertaken in 1999 by five members of the Murrin Bridge Aboriginal community, who had received training for a diploma in viticulture from the TAFE college at Griffith. Plantings began with 2 ha of shiraz in 1999, followed by a further 8 ha in 2000, and another extension in 2002 with shiraz, semillon and chardonnay. Very attractive wine bottle stands are handmade from local hardwoods gathered from the paddocks and banks of the Lachlan River.

Murrindindi ★★★★☆

Cummins Lane, Murrindindi, Vic 3717 **REGION** Upper Goulburn
T (03) 5797 8448 **F** (03) 5797 8448 **OPEN** At Marmalades Café, Yea
WINEMAKER Alan Cuthbertson **EST.** 1979 **CASES** 1500
SUMMARY Situated in an unequivocally cool climate, which means that special care has to be taken with the viticulture to produce ripe fruit flavours. In more recent vintages, Murrindindi has succeeded handsomely in so doing. Limited Sydney and Melbourne distribution through Wine Source.

Murrumbateman Winery NR

Barton Highway, Murrumbateman, NSW 2582 **REGION** Canberra District
T (02) 6227 5584 **OPEN** Thurs–Sun 10–5
WINEMAKER Duncan Leslie **EST.** 1972 **CASES** 1500
SUMMARY Revived after a change of ownership, the Murrumbateman Winery draws upon 4.5 ha of vineyards, and also incorporates an à la carte restaurant and function room, together with picnic and barbecue areas.

Myrtaceae

53 Main Creek Road, Main Ridge, Vic 3928 **REGION** Mornington Peninsula
T (03) 5989 2045 **F** (03) 5989 2845 **OPEN** First weekend of each month & public hols
WINEMAKER Julie Trueman **EST.** 1985 **CASES** 200
SUMMARY The development of the Myrtaceae vineyard began in 1985 with the planting of 0.7 ha of
cabernet sauvignon, cabernet franc and merlot intended for a Bordeaux-style red blend. Between
1988 and 1996 the grapes were sold, but it became evident that these late-ripening varieties were not
well suited to the site, so between then and 2000 the vineyard was converted to 0.5 ha each of pinot
noir and chardonnay. John Trueman (viticulturist) and Julie Trueman (winemaker) are the
proprietors. Part of the property is devoted to the Land for Wildlife Scheme, and there is an extensive
garden.

ΨΨΨΨΫ **Mornington Peninsula Chardonnay 2003** Complex barrel ferment inputs on light to
medium-bodied nectarine fruit, but which is not overwhelmed; elegant wine; clean, long
finish. Cork. **RATING** 91 **DRINK** 2009 **$** 25

Naked Range Wines

★★★☆

125 Rifle Range Road, Smiths Gully, Vic 3760 **REGION** Yarra Valley
T (03) 9710 1575 **F** (03) 9710 1655 **WEB** www.nakedrangewines.com **OPEN** By appointment
WINEMAKER Rob Dolan, Kate Goodman (Punt Road) **EST.** 1996 **CASES** 2500
SUMMARY Mike Jansz began the establishment of the Jansz Estate vineyard at Smiths Gully, in the
Diamond Valley area of the Yarra Valley, in 1996. He has established 7 ha of vineyard, one-third
sauvignon blanc, a small patch of pinot noir and the remainder cabernet sauvignon (predominant),
merlot and chardonnay. The wines are made at the Punt Road winery, and marketed under the
striking Naked Range label, with a second label for overseas markets using grapes from other
Victorian regions. Limited retail distribution in Victoria; exports to Indonesia.

ΨΨΨΨΫ **Yarra Valley Cabernet Sauvignon 2003** Good colour; clear-cut blackcurrant, olive and
earth varietal aromas; medium-bodied; nicely structured and balanced; good tannins.
Quality cork. **RATING** 90 **DRINK** 2013

ΨΨΨΨ **Yarra Valley Sauvignon Blanc 2004** Clean, fresh, brisk, minerally; well made, but needs
more varietal fruit for higher points. Cork. **RATING** 87 **DRINK** 2007

ΨΨΨΫ **Yarra Valley Chardonnay 2004** **RATING** 86 **DRINK** 207
Yarra Valley Merlot 2003 **RATING** 84 **DRINK** 2007

Nandroya Estate

NR

262 Sandfly Road, Margate, Tas 7054 **REGION** Southern Tasmania
T (03) 6267 2377 **OPEN** By appointment
WINEMAKER Andrew Hood (Contract) **EST.** 1995 **CASES** 400
SUMMARY John Rees and family have established 0.75 ha each of sauvignon blanc and pinot noir; the
wines are sold through the cellar door and to one or two local restaurants. The Reeses regard it as a
holiday and retirement project and modestly wonder whether they deserve inclusion in this work.
They certainly do, for wineries of this size are an indispensable part of the Tasmanian fabric.

Narkoojee

170 Francis Road, Glengarry, Vic 3854 **REGION** Gippsland
T (03) 5192 4257 **F** (03) 5192 4257 **WEB** www.narkoojee.com **OPEN** 7 days 10.30–4.30
WINEMAKER Harry Friend, Axel Friend **EST.** 1981 **CASES** 3500
SUMMARY Narkoojee Vineyard is within easy reach of the old goldmining town of Walhalla and looks
out over the Strzelecki Ranges. The wines are produced from a little over 10 ha of estate vineyards,
with chardonnay accounting for half the total. Harry Friend was an amateur winemaker of note
before turning to commercial winemaking with Narkoojee; his skills show through with all the
wines, none more so than the Chardonnay. Small amounts are exported; much is sold through the
cellar door and by mailing list.

ΨΨΨΨΨ **Reserve Chardonnay 2003** Very complex and rich, ripe stone fruit; creamy texture,
balanced oak. Ready now. Stylish new packaging also a plus. **RATING** 94 **DRINK** 2008 **$** 32

ŢŢŢŢŢ **Lily Grace Chardonnay 2003** Light to medium-bodied; elegant style; creamy cashew characters foremost on melon and stone fruit; cleverly made. Cork. **RATING** 92 **DRINK** 2009 $23

Trafalgar Chardonnay 2003 Trademark unforced elegance of the Narkoojee style; quite fragrant; gentle stone fruit; belies its 14° alcohol. Cork. **RATING** 90 **DRINK** 2008 $18

ŢŢŢŢ **Myrtle Point Shiraz 2003** Light to medium-bodied; elegant, dark cherry-accented fruit; fine tannins, subtle oak. Cork. **RATING** 88 **DRINK** 2009 $18

Yorkies Gully Rose 2003 Exotic spice and dried fruits bouquet and entry to the mouth; unexpectedly dry, crisp finish. Cork. **RATING** 87 **DRINK** Now $15

Nashdale Wines   NR

Borenore Lane, Nashdale, NSW 2800 **REGION** Orange
T (02) 6365 2463 **F** (02) 6361 4495 **OPEN** Weekends 2–6
WINEMAKER Mark Davidson (Contract) **EST.** 1990 **CASES** 1000
SUMMARY Orange solicitor Edward Fardell began establishing the 10-ha Nashdale Vineyard in 1990. At an elevation of 1000m, it offers panoramic views of Mt Canobolas and the Lidster Valley; a restaurant/café is open on weekends.

Nassau Estate   NR

Fish Fossil Drive, Canowindra, NSW 2804 **REGION** Cowra
T (02) 9267 4785 **F** (02) 9267 3844 **OPEN** Not
WINEMAKER Andrew Margan (Contract) **EST.** 1996 **CASES** 1500
SUMMARY The Curran family established its 110-ha vineyard adjacent to the Belubula River at Canowindra in 1996. The vineyard was named in honour of forebear Joseph Barbeler, who had been involved in a similar endeavour 140 years early in the Duchy of Nassau on the river Rhine near Frankfurt. A significant proportion of the grapes is contracted for sale to one of Australia's largest wineries; selected amounts are retained and contract-made for the Nassau Estate label.

Nazaaray   ★★★☆

266 Meakins Road, Flinders, Vic 3929 **REGION** Mornington Peninsula
T (03) 9585 1138 **F** (03) 9585 1140 **WEB** www.nazaaray.com.au **OPEN** By appointment 1st weekend of each month
WINEMAKER Paramdeep Ghumman **EST.** 1996 **CASES** 600
SUMMARY Paramdeep Ghumman is, as far as I am aware, the only Indian-born winery proprietor and winemaker in Australia. He and his wife migrated from India 22 years ago, and purchased the Nazaaray vineyard property in 1991. An initial trial planting of 400 vines in 1996 was gradually expanded to the present level of 1.6 ha of pinot noir, 0.4 ha of pinot gris and 0.15 ha of chardonnay. Notwithstanding the micro size of the estate, all the wines are made and bottled onsite.

ŢŢŢŢ **Mornington Peninsula Pinot Gris 2003** Good mouthfeel and weight; plenty of varietal character on the mid-palate; good length. **RATING** 88 **DRINK** Now $18

Mornington Peninsula Pinot Noir 2003 Spicy aromas; spicy, stemmy, light to medium-bodied; quite intense, long and penetrating; slightly hard finish. **RATING** 88 **DRINK** 2008 $30

Mornington Peninsula Pinot Gris 2004 Plenty of depth and mouthfeel; musk, pear and spice; 13.5° alcohol spot on. Cork. **RATING** 87 **DRINK** Now $18

ŢŢŢŢ **Mornington Peninsula Pinot Noir 2003** **RATING** 86 **DRINK** Now $30

ŢŢŢ **Mornington Peninsula Merlot 2003** **RATING** 82 $18

ŢŢŢ **Mornington Peninsula Chardonnay 2003** **RATING** 79 $18

Neagles Rock Vineyards

Lot 1 & 2 Main North Road, Clare, SA 5453 **REGION** Clare Valley
T (08) 8843 4020 **F** (08) 8843 4021 **WEB** www.neaglesrock.com **OPEN** 7 days 10–5
WINEMAKER Neil Pike (Consultant), Steve Wiblin **EST.** 1997 **CASES** 7500

SUMMARY Owner-partners Jane Willson and Steve Wiblin have taken the plunge in a major way, simultaneously raising a young family, resuscitating two old vineyards, and – for good measure – stripping a dilapidated house to the barest of bones and turning it into a first-rate, airy restaurant-cum-cellar door. They bring decades of industry experience, gained at all levels of the wine industry, to Neagles Rock, and built upon this by the September 2003 acquisition of the outstanding and mature vineyards of Duncan Estate, adding another level of quality to their wines; these now draw on a total of 25 ha. Exports to the UK, The Netherlands and Malaysia.

ŸŸŸŸŸ **Frisky Filly Reserve Clare Valley Riesling 2004** Mineral, slate and apple aromas; tightly focused, crisp, crunchy apple and lime flavours; will build further. Screwcap. **RATING** 94 **DRINK** 2014 $ 30

One Black Dog Reserve Clare Valley Cabernet Shiraz 2002 Excellent mouthfeel, texture and weight; seamless marriage of varieties, tannins and oak; long and finely balanced finish. **RATING** 94 **DRINK** 2017 $ 35

ŸŸŸŸ **Clare Valley Semillon Sauvignon Blanc 2004** Complex, mouthfilling style; generous texture and ripe fruit flavours. Screwcap. **RATING** 89 **DRINK** 2007 $ 18

Misery Clare Valley Grenache Shiraz 2004 Medium-bodied; typical juicy berry Grenache bolstered by the structure from the Shiraz; good length. Screwcap. **RATING** 89 **DRINK** 2009 $ 18

Clare Valley Riesling 2004 Not particularly aromatic, but clean, and slowly but steadily builds through to the finish. Screwcap. **RATING** 87 **DRINK** 2008 $ 18

Clare Valley Semillon Sauvignon Blanc 2003 Big, generous, early-drinking style; almost tropical ripe fruit. **RATING** 87 **DRINK** Now $ 18

Needham Estate Wines   NR

Ingoldby Road, McLaren Flat, SA 5171 **REGION** McLaren Vale
T (08) 8383 0301 **F** (08) 8383 0301 **OPEN** Not
WINEMAKER Contract **EST.** 1997 **CASES** 2800
SUMMARY Clive Needham has 2 vineyards; the first, of 4 ha, is newly planted and came into full production in 2001. The second has less than 0.5 ha of 100-year-old shiraz vines, which go to produce the White House Shiraz, with an annual production of only 120 cases.

Neighbours Vineyards   NR

75 Fullarton Road, Kent Town, SA 5067 (postal) **REGION** McLaren Vale
T (08) 8331 8656 **F** (08) 8331 8443 **OPEN** Not
WINEMAKER Chester Osborn **EST.** 1995 **CASES** 500
SUMMARY Esteemed (and dare I say now senior) journalist Bob Mayne planted 1.6 ha of shiraz in McLaren Vale in 1995, without any clear objective in mind; he was certainly not venturing into winemaking. However, one thing leads to another, and in 1998 he formed Neighbours Vineyards Pty Ltd, its 14 shareholders all being McLaren Vale grapegrowers.

Nelson Touch   NR

Hamilton Road, Denmark, WA 6333 **REGION** Denmark
T (08) 9385 3552 **F** (08) 9286 2060 **OPEN** Not
WINEMAKER Michael Staniforth (Contract) **EST.** 1990 **CASES** 2000
SUMMARY Barbara and Brett Nelson began the development of their vineyard back in 1990, and until 1999 sold all the grapes to other wineries, including Howard Park. While Howard Park continues to receive some grapes, the lion's share of the plantings of the 1.5 ha each of sauvignon blanc, pinot noir and cabernet sauvignon, plus 0.5 ha of merlot, is now used for the Nelson Touch label. The name comes from the saying that Admiral Nelson had the 'Nelson touch' when he defeated the French, because everything he did turned to naval gold.

Nepenthe Vineyards   ★★★★

Jones Road, Balhannah, SA 5242 **REGION** Adelaide Hills
T (08) 8398 8888 **F** (08) 8388 1100 **WEB** www.nepenthe.com.au **OPEN** 7 days 10–4
WINEMAKER Peter Leske, Michael Paxton **EST.** 1994 **CASES** 70 000

SUMMARY The Tweddell family has established a little over 160 ha of close-planted vineyards at Lenswood since 1994, with an exotic array of varieties. In late 1996 it obtained the second licence to build a winery in the Adelaide Hills (Petaluma was the only prior successful applicant, back in 1978). Nepenthe has quickly established itself as one of the most exciting newer wineries in Australia. Distribution through most states; exports to the UK, the US, Canada, Denmark, Holland, Sweden, Japan and Hong Kong.

ΥΥΥΥ️ **Adelaide Hills Riesling 2004** Delicate aromas of slate, apple and herb; dry and fresh finish and aftertaste. **RATING** 92 **DRINK** 2012 $ 19.99

Tryst Semillon Sauvignon Blanc 2004 A rich array of tropical fruits and abundant flavour; the long finish is neither coarse nor phenolic. **RATING** 92 **DRINK** 2007 $ 12.99

The Rogue 2003 A complex array of spicy, cedary, savoury fruits with a skein of sweetness running through the middle. Cabernet Sauvignon/Merlot/Shiraz. Screwcap. **RATING** 90 **DRINK** 2013 $ 20

ΥΥΥΥ **Adelaide Hills Sauvignon Blanc 2004** Clean and crisp, with squeaky acidity; balance and length, but where is the fruit? **RATING** 89 **DRINK** Now $ 20.99

Adelaide Hills Pinot Gris 2004 Faint blush of pink; delicate, fresh and lively; touches of pear and spice; clean aftertaste; partial barrel ferment in older French oak. Screwcap. **RATING** 89 **DRINK** 2008 $ 20

Charleston Pinot Noir 2003 Colour showing some development; spicy, stemmy red fruits; good length and balance; rather dodgy cork. **RATING** 89 **DRINK** Now $ 20.99

Charleston Pinot Noir 2002 Powerful wine; black fruits/plums/spice; does dip slightly on the back palate, but very good value. **RATING** 89 $ 20

Adelaide Hills Unoaked Chardonnay 2004 Slight reduction; relatively complex, from nectarine through to spice and mineral on the finish. Screwcap. **RATING** 87 **DRINK** 2008 $ 17

Tryst Cabernet Tempranillo Zinfandel 2003 Light to medium-bodied; bracing fresh fruits with a slightly green finish. A psychedelic blend of Cabernet, Zinfandel and Tempranillo. **RATING** 87 **DRINK** Now $ 14.99

ΥΥΥ️ **Adelaide Hills Tempranillo 2003** **RATING** 86 **DRINK** 2007 $ 22

New England Estate   NR

Delungra, NSW 2403 **REGION** Northern Slopes Zone
T (02) 6724 8508 **F** (02) 6724 8507 **OPEN** 7 days 10–5
WINEMAKER John Cassegrain (Contract) **EST.** 1997 **CASES** NA
SUMMARY New England Estate is 33 km west of Inverell; Ross Thomas has established a very substantial vineyard of 36 ha planted to chardonnay, cabernet sauvignon, merlot and shiraz. The wines are sold by mail order and through the cellar door, which has barbecue and picnic facilities. There is also a museum, and accommodation available.

New Era Vineyard   NR

PO Box 239, Woodside, SA 5244 **REGION** Adelaide Hills
T (08) 8389 7562 **F** (08) 8389 7562 **OPEN** Not
WINEMAKER Paracombe (Contract) **EST.** 1988 **CASES** NA
SUMMARY Patricia Wark's 12.5-ha vineyard, planted to chardonnay, cabernet sauvignon, merlot and shiraz, is under long-term contract to Wolf Blass, providing grapes for the Wolf Blass Adelaide Hills Cabernet Merlot. A tiny proportion of cabernet sauvignon is retained and contract-made.

New Glory   NR

931 Murray Valley Highway, Echuca, Vic 3564 **REGION** Goulburn Valley
T (03) 5480 7090 **F** (03) 5480 7096 **OPEN** 7 days 10–5
WINEMAKER Don Buchanan, Paul Smart **EST.** 2000 **CASES** 30 000
SUMMARY New Glory is the reincarnation of Echuca Estate Wines, which had New Glory Vineyard as its largest supplier amongst a matrix of contributing growers. The operation now has a total of 39 ha of shiraz, cabernet sauvignon, durif, petit verdot, sangiovese and mourvedre, the only white variety being verdelho. Radical changes will continue to flow following the arrival of industry veteran Don Buchanan as winemaker.

New Mediterranean Winery ★★★

Lot 2 McMillans Road, Boort, Vic 3537 REGION Central Victoria Zone
T (03) 5455 2274 F (03) 5455 2615 WEB www.akrasiwine.com.au OPEN By appointment
WINEMAKER George Tallis EST. 1997 CASES 500
SUMMARY It is unlikely that you will come across Boort by accident. It falls roughly between the Calder and Loddon Highways as they wend their way north towards the Murray River and the NSW border; Kerang, 51 km to the north, is the nearest landmark of any significance. George Tallis commenced home winemaking in the early 1990s, initially simply for the benefit of himself and his immediate family. Success led to relatively small commercial winemaking under the Akrasi brand, strongly influenced by Tallis' Greek ancestry. Indeed, the word 'Akrasi' comes from the Greek name of George Tallis' home town. Taking away the letter A you are left with 'krasi' which in Greek means wine.

ΤΤΤ♀ **Gordo 2003** Well made; retains grapey flavour without an unduly sweet finish; faintly phenolic. RATING 86 DRINK Now $12

Next Generation Wines ★★★

Grants Gully Road, Clarendon, SA 5157 REGION Adelaide Hills
T (08) 8383 5555 F (08) 8383 5551 WEB www.nxg.com.au OPEN Mon–Fri 9–5
WINEMAKER Natasha Mooney EST. 2001 CASES 300 000
SUMMARY After 3 years of ownership by Xanadu, Normans and Next Generation Wines were sold in early 2005, taking Xanadu back to its base, and leaving the future of the Normans and Next Generation brands in temporary limbo.

Nicholson River ★★★☆

Liddells Road, Nicholson, Vic 3882 REGION Gippsland
T (03) 5156 8241 F (03) 5156 8433 WEB www.nicholsonriverwinery.com.au OPEN 7 days 10–4
WINEMAKER Ken Eckersley EST. 1978 CASES 3000
SUMMARY The fierce commitment to quality in the face of the temperamental Gippsland climate and the frustratingly small production has been handsomely repaid by some massive Chardonnays and quixotic red wines (from 9 ha of estate plantings), mostly sold through the cellar door; a little is exported to the UK, Thailand and the US. Ken Eckersley refers to his Chardonnays not as white wines but as gold wines, and lists them accordingly in his newsletter.

Nick Haselgrove/Blackbilly ★★★☆

Range Road, Willunga Hill, SA 5172 REGION McLaren Vale
T (08) 8556 7340 F (08) 8556 7340 OPEN By appointment
WINEMAKER Nick Haselgrove EST. 1993 CASES NA
SUMMARY This is the personal winemaking venture of Nick Haselgrove, using contract-grown grapes from McLaren Vale and Fleurieu. Exports to the US.

ΤΤΤΤ♀ **Blackbilly McLaren Vale Shiraz 2002** Medium-bodied; a supple palate with fine, sweet tannins running throughout mocha, chocolate and black cherry fruit. Cork. RATING 90 DRINK 2010 $22

ΤΤΤΤ **Blackbilly Sparkling Shiraz NV** Some age evident; quite complex spicy, mocha notes to the base wine; not over-liqueured; dry finish. RATING 88 DRINK 2009 $28

ΤΤΤ♀ **Blackbilly Pinot Gris 2004** RATING 86 DRINK 2007 $22

Nightingale Wines ★★★

1239 Milbrodale Road, Broke, NSW 2330 REGION Lower Hunter Valley
T (02) 6579 1499 F (02) 6579 1477 WEB www.nightingalewines.com.au OPEN 7 days 10–4
WINEMAKER Nigel Robinson (Contract), Paul Nightingale EST. 1997 CASES 18 000
SUMMARY Paul and Gail Nightingale have wasted no time since establishing their business in 1997. They have planted 3 ha each of verdelho and merlot, 2 ha of shiraz, 1.5 ha each of chardonnay and cabernet sauvignon and 1 ha of chambourcin. The wines are contract-made, and are sold through the cellar door and an actively promoted wine club, and to selected local restaurants. Exports to New Zealand.

▼▼▼▼ **Shiraz 2003** Solid, powerful, nuggety wine; an array of black fruits; well-managed tannins. Twin Top. **RATING** 89 **DRINK** 2012 $ 21
Chambourcin 2003 Deep colour, of course; unusually rich and quite long black fruits; normal soft tannin profile. Twin Top. **RATING** 88 **DRINK** 2008 $ 25

▼▼▼▽ **Unwooded Chardonnay 2003 RATING** 86 **DRINK** 2007 $ 19
Cabernet Sauvignon 2003 Red fruits/cassis/blackcurrant; lacks the structure for higher points. Twin Top. **RATING** 86 **DRINK** 2009 $ 21

▼▼▼ **Verdelho 2004 RATING** 83 $ 19
Sparkling Chambourcin NV RATING 83 $ 25

Nillahcootie Estate ★★★

RMB 1637, Lima South, Vic 3673 **REGION** Upper Goulburn
T (03) 5768 2685 **F** (03) 5768 2678 **WEB** www.nillahcootieestate.com.au **OPEN** By appointment
WINEMAKER Sam Plunkett, David Coburn (Contract) **EST.** 1988 **CASES** 700
SUMMARY Karen Davy and Michael White decided to diversify their primary business of beef cattle production on their 280-ha property in 1988. Between then and 2001 they planted a little over 8 ha of grapes, initially content to sell the production to other local wineries, but in 2001 they retained a small proportion of the grapes for winemaking, increasing it the following year to its current level. In 2001 they also purchased a 20-ha property overlooking Lake Nillahcootie. They have since renovated a homestead (available for rent) and commenced construction of the cellar door. The wines have limited local and Melbourne retail distribution.

▼▼▼▼ **Shiraz Cabernet Merlot 2003** Light to medium-bodied; bright red fruits; cassis and spice; very fine tannins. Quality cork. **RATING** 87 **DRINK** 2008 $ 18

▼▼▼▽ **Maggies Paddock Cabernet Merlot 2003 RATING** 85 **DRINK** 2007 $ 18
Unwooded Chardonnay 2004 RATING 84 **DRINK** Now $ 16

Nirvana Estate NR

339 Sandy Creek Road, Kilcoy, Qld 4515 **REGION** Queensland Coastal
T (07) 5498 1055 **F** (07) 5498 1099 **OPEN** Tues–Sun & public hols 10–5
WINEMAKER Contract **EST.** 1996 **CASES** NA
SUMMARY Julie Doolan has 5.3 ha planted to sauvignon blanc, semillon, chardonnay, cabernet sauvignon, merlot and shiraz, contract-made offsite. The cellar door offers light meals, and can cater for concerts.

Noon Winery NR

Rifle Range Road, McLaren Vale, SA 5171 **REGION** McLaren Vale
T (08) 8323 8290 **F** (08) 8323 8290 **OPEN** Weekends 10–5 in November (while stock is available)
WINEMAKER Drew Noon MW **EST.** 1976 **CASES** 3000
SUMMARY Drew Noon returned to McLaren Vale and purchased Noon's from his parents (though father David still keeps an eye on things), having spent many years as a consultant oenologist and viticulturist in Victoria, and thereafter as winemaker at Cassegrain. Some spectacular and unusual wines have followed, such as the 17.9° alcohol Solaire Grenache, styled like an Italian Amarone. Low prices mean each year's release sells out in 4–5 weeks, during which time the cellar door is open; all wines are subject to quantity limits. Small amounts are exported to the UK, the US and other markets.

Noosa Valley Winery NR

855 Noosa–Eumundi Road, Doonan, Qld 4562 **REGION** Queensland Coastal
T (07) 5449 1675 **F** (07) 5449 1679 **OPEN** Wed–Sat 11–5
WINEMAKER Robinsons Family Vineyards (Contract) **EST.** 1999 **CASES** NA
SUMMARY Irish-born George and Sue Mullins came to Australia over 30 years ago, but it was not until 1999 that they purchased the property and opened a B&B business. The potential for wine became obvious, and 550 chambourcin vines were planted in 2000 at the front of the 5-ha property, giving rise to the first vintage in 2003. The cellar door also acts as a satellite door for Robinsons Family Vineyards.

No Regrets Vineyard

40 Dillons Hill Road, Glaziers Bay, Tas 7109 **REGION** Southern Tasmania
T(03) 6295 1509 **F**(03) 6295 1509 **OPEN** By appointment, also at Salamanca Market, Hobart, most Saturdays
WINEMAKER Andrew Hood, Jeremy Dineen (Contract) **EST.** 2000 **CASES** 400
SUMMARY Having sold Elsewhere Vineyard, Eric and Jette Phillips have turned around and planted another vineyard almost next door, called No Regrets. This is their 'retirement' vineyard: they will be producing only one wine from the 1 ha of pinot noir.

ŸŸŸŸŸ Chardonnay 2000 Supple nectarine and citrus fruit; excellent length and aftertaste. Deserved Top Gold Tasmanian Wines Show 2005. **RATING** 95 **DRINK** 2008 $ 22

ŸŸŸŸ Pinot Noir 2003 RATING 85 **DRINK** 2007 $ 20

Norfolk Rise Vineyard

Limestone Coast Road, Mount Benson, SA 5265 **REGION** Mount Benson
T(08) 8768 5080 **F**(08) 8768 5083 **WEB** www.norfolkrise.com.au **OPEN** Mon–Fri 9–5
WINEMAKER Steve Grimley **EST.** 2000 **CASES** 85 000
SUMMARY This is by far the largest and most important development in the Mount Benson region. It is ultimately owned by a privately held Belgian company, G & C Kreglinger, established in 1797. Kreglinger Australia was established in 1893 as an agribusiness export company specialising in sheep skins. In early 2002 it acquired Pipers Brook Vineyard; it will maintain the separate brands of the two ventures. The Mount Benson development commenced in 2000, with an 160-ha vineyard and a 2000-tonne winery, primarily aimed at the export market.

ŸŸŸŸŸ Vintage Brut 1998 Crammed with all the right flavours; creamy/yeasty brioche around a stone fruit and mineral core, then powers through to a long finish. **RATING** 95 **DRINK** Now $ 40
Mount Benson Shiraz 2002 Blackberry, plum, chocolate and licorice; good structure and texture; plenty of oak. **RATING** 94 **DRINK** 2012 $ 30

Normanby Wines

Rose-Lea Vineyard, Dunns Avenue, Harrisville, Qld 4307 **REGION** Queensland Zone
T(07) 5467 1214 **F**(07) 5467 1023 **WEB** www.normanbywines.com.au **OPEN** 7 days Winter 10–5, Summer 10–7
WINEMAKER Blair Duncan **EST.** 1999 **CASES** 600
SUMMARY Normanby Wines, about 50 km due south of Ipswich, fills in more of the Queensland viticultural jigsaw puzzle. The vineyard has 1 ha each of verdelho and shiraz, and 0.2 ha each of chambourcin, durif and grenache. In a commendable display of courage, Normanby describes its 2002 Shiraz as 'a territorial Shiraz showing the unique quality and flavours of this region, which will soon be recognised as one of Australia's best'.

ŸŸŸŸ Verdelho 2004 Nice wine; light to medium-bodied; good balance, line and length; cunning touch of residual sugar. **RATING** 89 **DRINK** 2007 $ 19

Normans

Grant's Gully Road, Clarendon, SA 5157 **REGION** Adelaide Hills
T(08) 8383 5555 **F**(08) 8383 5551 **WEB** www.xanadunormans.com.au **OPEN** Mon–Sat 9–4
WINEMAKER Natasha Mooney, Hugh Thomson **EST.** 1853 **CASES** 50 000
SUMMARY After 3 years of ownership by Xanadu, Normans and Next Generation Wines were sold in early 2005, taking Xanadu back to its base, and leaving the future of the Normans and Next Generation brands in temporary limbo.

ŸŸŸŸŸ Old Vine Shiraz 2003 A complex amalgam of dark spicy fruit and vanillin oak; ample depth, good length. **RATING** 91 **DRINK** 2013 $ 24.99
Chais Clarendon Cabernet Sauvignon 2002 Fresh red-purple; medium-bodied; clean cassis blackcurrant fruit and touches of chocolate; soft tannins. Mclaren Vale/Langhorne Creek/Adelaide Plains. **RATING** 90 **DRINK** 2010 $ 40

ᵀᵀᵀᵀ **Old Vine Cabernet Sauvignon 2002** Pleasant; light to medium-bodied; nicely balanced red and black fruits; gentle oak and tannins. **RATING** 88 **DRINK** 2007 $ 24.99
Encounter Bay Chardonnay 2004 Elegant to the point of outright delicacy; seemingly unoaked, fresh, fruit-driven style. **RATING** 87 **DRINK** Now $ 14

ᵀᵀᵀᵀ **Encounter Bay Chardonnay 2004** **RATING** 86 **DRINK** Now $ 13.99

Norse Wines   NR

24 Damascus Road, Gin Gin, Qld 4671 **REGION** Queensland Coastal
T (07) 4157 3636 **F** (07) 4157 3637 **OPEN** 7 days 10–5
WINEMAKER Thomas Janstrom, Peter Janstrom **EST.** 1998 **CASES** NA
SUMMARY Peter and Dianna Janstrom have established their 2-ha vineyard 37 km due west of Bundaberg. Here they have chardonnay, verdelho, shiraz, cabernet sauvignon and touriga nationale, producing both table and fortified wines. The cellar door offers all the usual facilities.

Norton Estate   ★★★★☆

758 Plush Hannan Road, Lower Norton, Vic 3400 **REGION** Western Victoria Zone
T (03) 5384 8235 **F** (03) 5384 8235 **OPEN** 7 days 10–4
WINEMAKER Hamish Seabrook (Contract) **EST.** 1997 **CASES** 800
SUMMARY Donald Spence worked for the Victorian Department of Forests for 36 years before retiring. In 1996 he and his family purchased a farm at Lower Norton, and instead of farming wool, meat and wheat, trusted their instincts and planted vines on the lateritic buckshot soil. The vineyard is 6 km northwest of the Grampians GI, and will have to be content with the Western Victoria Zone until a sufficient number of others follow suit and plant on the around 1000 ha of suitable soil in the area. The quality of the wines is encouragement enough. A purpose-built cellar door facility opened mid-2005.

ᵀᵀᵀᵀᵀ **Limited Release Shiraz 2002** Deep colour; dense, deep black fruits; built-in, but balanced, tannins; 20 months' French oak merely in support. Needs patience. Cork a worry. **RATING** 93 **DRINK** 2022 $ 25
Shiraz 2002 Fully ripe but not jammy or dead fruit; aromatic red berry aromas, moving more to plum and spice on the palate. Quality cork. **RATING** 90 **DRINK** 2012 $ 25

ᵀᵀᵀᵀ **Sauvignon Blanc 2004** Fresh, lively and crisp; squeaky, tingling acidity gives length and interest; delicate herbaceous fruit. Screwcap. **RATING** 88 **DRINK** 2007 $ 17.95
Limited Release Cabernet Sauvignon 2002 Ripe black fruits, dark chocolate, plum and prune; classical dip/doughnut palate profile. Grungy cork. **RATING** 88 **DRINK** 2012 $ 25
Cabernet Sauvignon 2002 Herb, mint and earth overlays to blackberry fruit. Good cork. **RATING** 87 **DRINK** 2010 $ 25

🐚 Nowra Hill Vineyard   NR

222 BTU Road, Nowra Hill, NSW 2540 **REGION** Shoalhaven Coast
T (02) 4447 8362 **F** (02) 4447 8362 **OPEN** Weekends & public hols 10–4
WINEMAKER Bevan Wilson, Bruce McLeod **EST.** 1998 **CASES** 450
SUMMARY Bruce and Judy McLeod progressively established a micro-vineyard of chambourcin, verdelho, malbec, chardonnay and cabernet sauvignon between 1998 and 2004. It is situated on a northfacing slope, with sweeping views of the Cambewarra Mountains, and all the wine is sold through the adjacent cellar door, by mail order and through a handful of local outlets. The quaintly named BTU Road, incidentally, runs off the Princes Highway south of Nowra, and leads to the HMAS *Albatross* Base.

Nugan Estate   ★★★★

60 Banna Avenue, Griffith, NSW 2680 **REGION** Riverina
T (02) 6962 1822 **F** (02) 6962 6392 **OPEN** Mon–Fri 9–5
WINEMAKER Daren Owers **EST.** 1999 **CASES** 400 000
SUMMARY Nugan Estate has arrived on the scene like a whirlwind. It is an offshoot of the Nugan group, a family company established over 60 years ago in Griffith as a broad-based agricultural business. It is headed by Michelle Nugan, inter alia the recipient of an Export Hero Award 2000. Nine years ago the company began developing vineyards, and is now a veritable giant, with 310 ha at

426 | James Halliday

Darlington Point, 52 ha at Hanwood and 120 ha at Hillston (all in New South Wales), 100 ha in the King Valley, and 10 ha in McLaren Vale. In addition, it has contracts in place to buy 1000 tonnes of grapes per year from Coonawarra. It sells part of the production as grapes, part as bulk wine and part under the Cookoothama and Nugan Estate labels. Exports to the US, Canada, Ireland, Norway, Denmark, Sweden and New Zealand.

YYYYY **Cookoothama King Valley Sauvignon Blanc Semillon 2004** Highly aromatic grass, gooseberry and kiwifruit aromas; good length and intensity; impressive wine at the price. **RATING** 90 **DRINK** Now $14.95

YYYY **Frasca's Lane Vineyard Sauvignon Blanc 2003** Plenty of ripe gooseberry and tropical fruit; full-bodied style; just carries the sweetness. **RATING** 88 **DRINK** Now $19.95
Cookoothama Darling Point Botrytis Semillon 2003 Orange-gold; soft apricot, cumquat and almond mix; rapid development. **RATING** 88 **DRINK** Now $22.95
Cookoothama King Valley Riesling 2004 Pleasant medium-bodied, lime-accented fruit; good balance and length. **RATING** 87 **DRINK** Now $14.95
Frasca's Lane Vineyard Pinot Grigio 2004 Quite floral aromatics; lively, lemony acidity; just achieves ripeness. **RATING** 87 **DRINK** Now $19.95

YYYY **Cookoothama Chardonnay 2003 RATING** 86 **DRINK** 2007
Cookoothama King Valley Sauvignon Blanc Semillon 2003 RATING 85 **DRINK** Now $14.95
Cookoothama Cabernet Merlot 2002 RATING 84 **DRINK** 2007

Nuggetty Vineyard ★★★★☆

280 Maldon–Shelbourne Road, Nuggetty, Vic 3463 **REGION** Bendigo
T (03) 5475 1347 **F** (03) 5475 1647 **WEB** www.nuggettyvineyard.com.au **OPEN** Weekends & public hols 10–4, or by appointment
WINEMAKER Greg Dedman, Jackie Dedman **EST.** 1993 **CASES** 2000
SUMMARY The family-owned vineyard was established in 1993 by Greg and Jackie Dedman. Greg is a Charles Sturt University graduate, while Jackie (having spent 18 months at Bowen Estate in 1997/8) has simultaneously undertaken the wine marketing degree at Charles Sturt University and the winemaking degree at the University of Adelaide. They share the vineyard and winery tasks (including contract winemaking for others); these include 6.5 ha of estate plantings (semillon, shiraz and cabernet sauvignon). Mailing list and cellar door sales are available while stocks last.

YYYYY **Shiraz 2002** Good colour; rich, ripe plum and blackberry fruit; fine tannins, good oak. Cork. **RATING** 94 **DRINK** 2017 $25

YYYYY **Cabernet Sauvignon 2002** Strong colour; powerful, tightly focused wine still to open up; blackcurrant fruit on a long palate. Good cork. **RATING** 93 **DRINK** 2015 $25
Barrel-Fermented Semillon 2004 Attractive wine; ripe pear and some grass and herb in the background; subtle oak; excellent acidity and mouthfeel. Screwcap. **RATING** 91 **DRINK** 2010 $18

Nursery Ridge Estate ★★★

Calder Highway, Red Cliffs, Vic 3496 **REGION** Murray Darling
T (03) 5024 3311 **F** (03) 5024 3114 **OPEN** By appointment
WINEMAKER Bob Shields **EST.** 1999 **CASES** 5000
SUMMARY The estate takes its name from the fact that it is situated on the site of the original vine nursery at Red Cliffs. It is a family-owned and operated affair, with shiraz, cabernet sauvignon, chardonnay, petit verdot and viognier. A cellar door and winery site on the Calder Highway opened in 2001. The well-priced wines are usually well made, with greater richness and depth of fruit flavour than most other wines from the region. Production has risen substantially, and, if all goes well, will continue to do so.

Oak Dale Wines NR

40 Titford Road, Tresco, Vic 3583 **REGION** Swan Hill
T (03) 5037 2911 **F** (03) 5037 2911 **OPEN** By appointment
WINEMAKER Robert Zagar (Contract) **EST.** 2000 **CASES** NA

SUMMARY Glen and Anne Cook have established 6.3 ha of mourvedre, muscat and sultana, the latter two especially suited to fortified wines, and the mourvedre dual purpose. The relatively small amount of wine made is sold locally, by mail order and through the cellar door when open.

Oakover Estate ★★★☆

14 Yukich Close, Middle Swan, WA 6056 REGION Swan Valley
T (08) 9274 0777 F (08) 9274 0788 WEB www.oakoverwines.com.au OPEN 7 days 11–4
WINEMAKER Rob Marshall EST. 1990 CASES 10 000
SUMMARY Owned by the Yukich family, and part of the Dalmatian Coast/Croatian cultural group in the Swan Valley, whose roots go back to the early 1900s. However, Oakover Estate is very much part of the new wave in the area, with a very large vineyard holding of 64 ha, planted predominantly to chardonnay, shiraz, chenin blanc and verdelho. Part of the production is sold to others, with increasing amounts made under the Oakover label, selling (among the other usual ways) at the large café/restaurant and function centre in the heart of the vineyard.

Oakridge ★★★★☆

864 Maroondah Highway, Coldstream, Vic 3770 REGION Yarra Valley
T (03) 9739 1920 F (03) 9739 1923 WEB www.oakridgeestate.com.au OPEN 7 days 10–5
WINEMAKER David Bicknell EST. 1978 CASES NFP
SUMMARY The 1997 capital raising by Oakridge Vineyards Limited led to the opening of a new winery in 1998 on a prominent Maroondah Highway site. In 2001 the then struggling company was acquired by Evans & Tate. The appointment of David Bicknell (formerly for many years at De Bortoli) has revitalised the winemaking. Exports to the US, Canada, Switzerland and The Philippines.

TTTTT **Chardonnay 2003** Well-balanced barrel ferment inputs provide very good texture and mouthfeel to the melon and stone fruit flavours. RATING 95 DRINK 2012 $ 24.99

TTTTT **Sauvignon Blanc 2004** Herb and nettle aromas; very intense, precise and long; lemony acidity. Screwcap. RATING 92 DRINK 2007 $ 19.99
Merlot 2003 Excellent medium-bodied style; abundant small red and black berry fruits; fine tannins, fruit-driven. Screwcap. RATING 91 DRINK 2013 $ 29.99
Cabernet Sauvignon 2003 Smooth, supple blackberry and cassis mix; fine tannins; integrated oak. Screwcap. RATING 90 DRINK 2015 $ 29.99

TTTT **Pinot Noir 2003** Light-bodied; cherry and strawberry fruit; good balance and length. Screwcap. RATING 89 DRINK 2009 $ 24.99
Shiraz 2003 Medium to full-bodied; dark plum fruit on entry to the mouth; slight break in the line through to the finish, but plenty of flavour. RATING 89 DRINK 2010 $ 24.99
Pinot Gris 2004 Stone/mineral aromas; crisp, well-focused and with above-average intensity. RATING 88 DRINK Now $ 20

TTTT **Cabernet Merlot 2003** RATING 86 DRINK 2009 $ 19.99

Oakvale ★★★☆

Broke Road, Pokolbin, NSW 2320 REGION Lower Hunter Valley
T (02) 4998 7088 F (02) 4998 7077 WEB www.oakvalewines.com.au OPEN 7 days 10–5
WINEMAKER Cameron Webster EST. 1893 CASES 17 000
SUMMARY All the literature and promotional material emphasises the fact that Oakvale has been family-owned since 1893. What it does not mention is that three quite unrelated families have been the owners: first, and for much of the time, the Elliott family; then former Sydney solicitor Barry Shields; and, since 1999, Richard and Mary Owens, who also own the separately run Milbrovale winery at Broke. Be that as it may, the original slab hut homestead of the Elliott family which is now a museum, and the atmospheric Oakvale winery, are in the 'must visit' category. The winery complex offers a delicatessen, espresso coffee shop, a bookshop and has picnic and playground facilities. Live entertainment each weekend between 11 am and 3 pm. Exports to the UK, the US, Japan and Singapore.

TTTT **Peach Tree Chardonnay 2002** Colour holding well; nice bottle-developed characters; gentle barrel ferment/toasty oak on ripe stone fruit and melon. Soggy cork. RATING 88 DRINK 2007 $ 24.50

2004 Clean, nice varietal fruit salad with a twist of lemon; modest overall intensity. Surprising Blue Gold Sydney International Wine Competition 2005. Twin Top. **RATING** 87 **DRINK** Now $ 19.50

Observatory Hill Vineyard

107 Centauri Drive, Mount Rumney, Tas 7170 (postal) **REGION** Southern Tasmania
T (03) 6238 5380 **OPEN** Not
WINEMAKER Andrew Hood (Contract) **EST.** 1991 **CASES** 50
SUMMARY Chris and Glenn Richardson have developed their vineyard slowly since acquiring the property in 1990. In 1991 50 vines were planted, another 300 were planted in 1992, with further plantings over the intervening years lifting the total to 1.2 ha in 2002. Whatever wine is not sold by mail order is sometimes available at the nearby Mornington Inn.

ΤΤΤΫ **Chardonnay 2004 RATING** 86 **DRINK** 2008
Cabernet Sauvignon 2003 RATING 86 **DRINK** 2007

Occam's Razor

c/- Jasper Hill, Drummonds Lane, Heathcote, Vic 3523 (postal) **REGION** Heathcote
T (03) 5433 2528 **F** (03) 5433 3143 **OPEN** By appointment
WINEMAKER Emily Laughton **EST.** 2001 **CASES** 300
SUMMARY Emily Laughton has decided to follow in her parents' footsteps after first seeing the world and having a range of casual jobs. Having grown up at Jasper Hill, winemaking was far from strange, but she decided to find her own way, buying the grapes from a small vineyard owned by Jasper Hill employee Andrew Conforti and his wife Melissa. She then made the wine 'with guidance and inspiration from my father, and with assistance from winemaker Mario Marson'. The name comes from William of Ockham (also spelt Occam) (1285–1349), a theologian and philosopher responsible for many sayings, including that appearing on the back label of the wine: 'what can be done with fewer is done in vain with more'. Only 300 cases are made, and the wine is being exclusively distributed in fine restaurants across Australia. Exports to the US, Canada and Singapore.

ΤΤΤΤ **Shiraz 2003** Spicy, peppery nuances on the bouquet; medium-bodied; slightly astringent tannins shadow the fruit on the palate. Cork. **RATING** 88 **DRINK** 2012 $ 37

Oddfellows Wines ★★★★

Bremer Place, Langhorne Creek, SA 5255 **REGION** Langhorne Creek
T (08) 8537 3326 **F** (08) 8537 3319 **OPEN** 7 days 11–5
WINEMAKER Greg Follett **EST.** 1997 **CASES** 2000
SUMMARY Oddfellows is the name taken by a group of five individuals who decided to put their expertise, energy and investments into making premium wine. Greg Follett leads the winemaking side, David Knight the viticultural side, the others the financial and marketing side. Exports to the US and Asia.

ΤΤΤΤΫ **Langhorne Creek Shiraz 2002** Above-average intensity and extract for Langhorne Creek; abundant blackberry fruit; good tannin support and oak integration; good length. Quality cork. **RATING** 93 **DRINK** 2015

ΤΤΤΤ **Langhorne Creek Shiraz Cabernet 2003** Ripe, rich, sweet dark fruits and chocolate; some spice and vanilla; soft tannins. Terrible cork. **RATING** 89 **DRINK** 2010 $ 18

O'Donohoe's Find

PO Box 460, Berri, SA 5343 **REGION** Riverland
T 0414 765 813 **F** (08) 8583 2228 **WEB** www.tomsdrop.com.au **OPEN** Not
WINEMAKER Michael O'Donohoe **EST.** 2002 **CASES** 600
SUMMARY Michael O'Donohoe pays tribute to his Irish grandfather, Thomas O'Donohoe, and 6 great-uncles, who arrived from Ireland in 1881 to join their father in the search for gold, ending up distilling salty bore water into fresh water. A century later Michael O'Donohoe runs a small vineyard in the Riverland which was certified organic in 1990, receives very little water, and crops at around 2 tonnes per acre. The wines (released under the Tom's Drop label) are made using a tiny crusher, a small hand-operated basket press, and open fermenters. They deserve to be taken seriously.

ȲȲȲȲȲ **Tom's Drop Shiraz 2003** Attractive, medium-bodied, ripe black cherry, plum and blackberry; fine, persistent tannins in support. Twin Top. **RATING** 90 **DRINK** 2010

ȲȲȲȲ **Tom's Drop Mourvedre Shiraz 2003** Good varietal Mourvedre (contributing 80% of the blend) giving savoury aspects; Shiraz contributing the structure; fine, lingering tannins. **RATING** 89 **DRINK** 2009 $ 16.50

Old Caves Winery

NR

New England Highway, Stanthorpe, Qld 4380 **REGION** Granite Belt
T (07) 4681 1494 **F** (07) 4681 2722 **WEB** www.oldcaveswinery.com.au **OPEN** Mon–Sat 9–5, Sun 10–4
WINEMAKER David Zanatta **EST.** 1980 **CASES** 2400
SUMMARY Old Caves is a family business run by David, his wife Shirley and their three sons, Tony, Jeremy and Nathan, drawing on 5 ha of estate vineyards. The wines are sold locally, through the cellar door and by mail order.

Old Kent River

Turpin Road, Rocky Gully, WA 6397 **REGION** Frankland River
T (08) 9855 1589 **F** (08) 9855 1660 **WEB** www.valleyofthegiants.com.au/oldkentriver **OPEN** At Kent River, South Coast Highway
WINEMAKER Alkoomi (Contract), Michael Staniford **EST.** 1985 **CASES** 3000
SUMMARY Mark and Debbie Noack have done it tough all their lives but have earned respect from their neighbours and from the other producers to whom they sell more than half the production from the 16.5-ha vineyard on their sheep property. The quality of their wines has gone from strength to strength. Exports to Canada, the UK, The Netherlands, Hong Kong and Japan.

ȲȲȲȲȲ **Frankland River Sauvignon Blanc 2004** Considerable tropical fruit, passionfruit and kiwifruit on both bouquet and palate, without losing freshness and crispness. Screwcap. **RATING** 94 **DRINK** 2007 $ 18
Diamontina 2000 Ultra-fragrant blossom aromas, quite striking; intense yet feathery delicacy to strawberry, nectarine and citrus fruit; 70% Pinot Noir, 30% Chardonnay. **RATING** 94 **DRINK** 2010 $ 30

ȲȲȲȲ **Frankland River Pinot Noir 2003** Fragrant spice and plum; elegant, intense and complex; savoury plum fruit; fine, lingering tannins. Quality cork. **RATING** 92 **DRINK** 2009 $ 25
Backtrack Frankland River Chardonnay 2004 Supple, fresh-cut nectarine and melon; delicious flavour and mouthfeel; top example of unwooded Chardonnay. Screwcap. **RATING** 91 **DRINK** 2008 $ 14.95
Burls Reserve Pinot Noir 2002 Intense, sappy, foresty/spicy aromas; long, tight and lingering; courageous, austere style; 11.5° alcohol. Quality cork. **RATING** 91 **DRINK** 2012 $ 68
Frankland River Chardonnay 2002 Some bottle development; ripe, melon, fig and nectarine; rounded mouthfeel; subtle oak. Cork. **RATING** 90 **DRINK** 2009 $ 20

ȲȲȲȲ **Frankland River Shiraz 2003** Savoury, spicy, earthy style; light to medium-bodied; good length. **RATING** 87 **DRINK** 2008 $ 22

ȲȲȲȲ **Frankland River Pinot Noir 2002** Early-picked style (11° baume); long and savoury; a mix of this and the normal late-picked wine would be the way to go. **RATING** 86 **DRINK** Now $ 25

Old Loddon Wines

5 Serpentine Road, Bridgewater, Vic 3516 **REGION** Bendigo
T (03) 5437 3197 **F** (03) 5438 3502 **OPEN** Weekends 12–5, Mon–Fri by appointment
WINEMAKER Graeme Leith **EST.** 1995 **CASES** 5000
SUMMARY A boutique winery overlooking the scenic Loddon River in Bridgewater, owned and managed by Jill Burdett. The 6-ha vineyard is planted to cabernet franc, merlot, cabernet sauvignon and shiraz. The first vintage was in 1995, and the winery produces full-bodied wines.

ȲȲȲȲ **Cabernet Franc 2003** Bright, clear red-purple; fine, supple raspberry and redcurrant fruit; ripe, tobacco leaf, tannins. Diam. **RATING** 88 **DRINK** 2009

ȲȲȲȲ **Merlot 2003** Medium to full-bodied; robust, rustic; abundant black fruits and also tannins; needs patience. Cork. **RATING** 86 **DRINK** 2010
Cabernet 2003 **RATING** 86 **DRINK** 2009

O'Leary Walker Wines ★★★★★

Main Road, Leasingham, SA 5452 (PO Box 49, Watervale, SA 5452) **REGION** Clare Valley
T (08) 8843 0022 **F** (08) 8843 0156 **WEB** www.olearywalkerwines.com **OPEN** Not
WINEMAKER David O'Leary, Nick Walker **EST.** 2001 **CASES** 14 000
SUMMARY David O'Leary and Nick Walker together have more than 30 years' experience as winemakers working for some of the biggest Australian wine groups. They then took the plunge, and backed themselves to establish their own winery and brand. Their main vineyard is at Watervale in the Clare Valley, with over 36 ha of riesling, shiraz, cabernet sauvignon, merlot and semillon. In the Adelaide Hills they have established 14 ha of chardonnay, cabernet sauvignon, pinot noir, shiraz, sauvignon blanc and merlot. Exports to the US, Canada, the UK, Indonesia and Singapore.

TTTTT **Watervale Riesling 2004** Pale straw-green, with a lively, fragrant, spice and citrus bouquet and a fresh palate with tingling fruit and crunchy acidity; overall delicacy and finesse. **RATING** 94 **DRINK** 2010 $ 20
Claire Reserve Shiraz 2002 Strongly savoury, earthy, spicy aromas along with profound licorice, chocolate and blackberry fruit; ripe, persistent tannins; extremely long finish. From 100-year-old vines. Screwcap. **RATING** 94 **DRINK** 2022 $ 90

TTTTY **Clare Valley McLaren Vale Shiraz 2003** Rich, opulent blackberry and plum and a whisk of dark chocolate; ripe, smooth tannins; positive oak. Screwcap. **RATING** 92 **DRINK** 2015 $ 22
Polish Hill River Riesling 2004 Powerful lime and apple aromas; ripe fruit flavours with weight and length. **RATING** 91 **DRINK** 2010 $ 20
Adelaide Hills Chardonnay 2003 Elegant stone fruit, apple and citrus; well-handled oak; good length. Will develop. **RATING** 90 **DRINK** 2008 $ 22
Adelaide Hills Pinot Noir 2003 Fragrant spice, cherry and strawberry; light-bodied but long; elegant. **RATING** 90 **DRINK** 2007 $ 22

TTTT **Watervale Semillon 2004** Glowing yellow-green; gentle oak adds complexity but not varietal character; overall, soft. **RATING** 88 **DRINK** 2007 $ 18
Hurtle Adelaide Hills Chardonnay Pinot 2002 Fine, tight and elegant, but not particularly complex; lemon, citrus and mineral; fresh finish. **RATING** 88 **DRINK** 2009 $ 31

Olive Farm NR

77 Great Eastern Highway, South Guildford, WA 6055 **REGION** Swan Valley
T (08) 9277 2989 **F** (08) 9277 6828 **WEB** www.olivefarm.com.au **OPEN** Wed–Sun 10–5.30 Cellar Sales, 11.30–2.30 Café
WINEMAKER Ian Yurisich **EST.** 1829 **CASES** 3500
SUMMARY The oldest winery in Australia in use today, and arguably the least communicative. The ultra-low profile in no way inhibits flourishing cellar door sales. The wines come from 14 ha of estate plantings of 11 different varieties.

Oliverhill NR

Seaview Road, McLaren Vale, SA 5171 **REGION** McLaren Vale
T (08) 8323 8922 **F** (08) 8323 8916 **OPEN** By appointment
WINEMAKER Stuart Miller **EST.** 1973 **CASES** 3000
SUMMARY Stuart and Linda Miller purchased the property in a thoroughly run-down state in 1993, and gradually restored the vineyard and winery. The wines are sold through the cellar door, the online retailer auswine.com.au; small exports to the US and Canada.

Olivers Taranga Vineyards ★★★★

Olivers Road, McLaren Vale, SA 5171 **REGION** McLaren Vale
T (08) 8323 8498 **F** (08) 8323 7498 **OPEN** By appointment
WINEMAKER Corrina Rayment **EST.** 1839 **CASES** 3000
SUMMARY 1839 was the year in which William and Elizabeth Oliver arrived from Scotland to settle at McLaren Vale. Six generations later, members of the family are still living on the Whitehill and Taranga farms, 2 km north of McLaren Vale. The Taranga property has 12 varieties planted on 92 ha; historically, grapes from the property have been sold to up to five different wineries, but since 1994

some of the old vine shiraz has been made under the Oliver's Taranga label. From the 2000 vintage, the wine has been made by Corrina Rayment (the Oliver family's first winemaker and a sixth-generation family member). Exports to the UK, the US and other major markets.

TTTTY **McLaren Vale Corrina's Cabernet Shiraz 2002** Rich, full black fruits, bitter chocolate and licorice neatly balanced by tannins and integrated oak. Quality cork. **RATING** 90 **DRINK** 2013 $29.95

Olsen ★★★

RMB 252, Osmington Road, Osmington, WA 6285 **REGION** Margaret River
T (08) 9757 4536 **F** (08) 9757 4114 **WEB** www.olsen.com.au **OPEN** By appointment
WINEMAKER Bernard Abbott **EST.** 1986 **CASES** 2500
SUMMARY Steve and AnnMarie Olsen have planted 3.25 ha of cabernet sauvignon, and 2 ha each of semillon and chardonnay, which they tend with the help of their 4 children. It was the desire to raise their children in a healthy, country environment that prompted the move to establish the vineyard, coupled with a longstanding dream to make their own wine. The wines are sold through a wide range of restaurants and specialist retailers in most states, distributed direct ex the vineyard.

TTTT **Shiraz 2003** Very rich, very ripe fruit and substantial tannins. Some dead fruit characters, but certainly flavoursome. **RATING** 87 **DRINK** 2010 $18

TTTY **Sauvignon Blanc Semillon 2003** **RATING** 85 **DRINK** Now $14
Margaret River Merlot 2002 **RATING** 85 **DRINK** 2010 $18

Olssens of Watervale ★★★★

Sollys Hill Road, Watervale, SA 5452 **REGION** Clare Valley
T (08) 8843 0065 **F** (08) 8843 0065 **OPEN** Thurs–Sun & public hols 11–5, or by appointment
WINEMAKER Contract **EST.** 1994 **CASES** 1500
SUMMARY Kevin and Helen Olssen first visited the Clare Valley in December 1986. Within 2 weeks they and their family decided to sell their Adelaide home and purchased a property in a small, isolated valley 3 km north of the township of Watervale. As a result of the acquisition of the Bass Hill Vineyard, estate plantings have risen to more than 32 ha, including unusual varieties such as carmenere and primitivo di Gioia. The Bass Hill project is a joint venture between parents Kevin and Helen and children David and Jane Olssen.

TTTTY **Bass Hill Vineyard Clare Valley Mataro 2003** Sweet, rich licorice, spice and black fruits; ripe tannins, subtle oak; nice wine. From a new vineyard planting. **RATING** 90 **DRINK** 2013 $35

TTTT **Clare Valley Riesling 2004** Subdued aromas, possibly entering a shut-down phase; mineral and slate characters are lifted by appealing lemony acidity on the finish; should develop. **RATING** 89 **DRINK** 2010 $19
Clare Valley Cabernet Sauvignon 2002 Powerful; some earthy, gamey aromas and flavours give a slightly angular mouthfeel. **RATING** 87 **DRINK** 2012 $20

Orange Country Wines NR

Underwood Road, Borenore, NSW 2800 **REGION** Orange
T (02) 6365 2221 **F** (02) 6365 2227 **OPEN** 7 days 10–5
WINEMAKER Don MacLennan, David MacLennan **EST.** 1999 **CASES** NA
SUMMARY Don and David MacLennan have planted sauvignon blanc, semillon, chardonnay, pinot noir, cabernet sauvignon and shiraz, and are making the wines onsite in a winery constructed with sawdust blocks and ironbark posts. They are sold by mail order and through the cellar door (9 km from Orange), which also offers local crafts and paintings.

Orange Mountain Wines ★★★

Cnr Forbes Road/Radnedge Lane, Orange, NSW 2800 **REGION** Orange
T (02) 6365 2626 **WEB** www.orangemountain.com.au **OPEN** Weekends & public hols 9–5
WINEMAKER Terry Dolle **EST.** 1997 **CASES** 500

SUMMARY Terry Dolle has a total of 6 ha of vineyards, part at Manildra (established 1997) and the remainder at Orange (in 2001). The Manildra climate is distinctly warmer than that of Orange, and the plantings reflect the climatic difference, with pinot noir and sauvignon blanc at Orange, shiraz, cabernet sauvignon, merlot and viognier at Manildra.

Orani Vineyard   NR

Arthur Highway, Sorrel, Tas 7172 **REGION** Southern Tasmania
T(03) 6225 0330 **F**(03) 6225 0330 **OPEN** Weekends & public hols 9.30–6.30
WINEMAKER Julian Alcorso (Contract) **EST.** 1986 **CASES** NA
SUMMARY The first commercial release from Orani was of a 1992 Pinot Noir, with Chardonnay and Riesling following in the years thereafter; since that time Orani has continued to do well with its Pinot Noir. Owned by Tony and Angela McDermott, the latter the President of the Royal Hobart Wine Show. The wines are released with some years' bottle age.

Oranje Tractor Wine/Lincoln & Gomm   ★★★★

198 Link Road, Albany, WA 6330 **REGION** Albany
T(08) 9842 5175 **F**(08) 9842 5175 **WEB** www.oranjetractor.com **OPEN** Sunday, or by appointment
WINEMAKER Rob Diletti (Contract) **EST.** 1998 **CASES** 1000
SUMMARY The name tells part of the story of the vineyard owned by Murray Gomm and Pamela Lincoln. Murray Gomm was born next door, but moved to Perth to work in physical education and health promotion. Here he met nutritionist Pamela Lincoln, who completed the wine science degree at Charles Sturt University in 2000, before being awarded a Churchill Fellowship to study organic grape and wine production in the US and Europe. When the partners established their 3-ha vineyard, they went down the organic path, with the aid of a 1964 vintage Fiat tractor, which is orange.

▼▼▼▼▽ **Oranje Tractor Sauvignon Blanc 2004** Spotlessly clean; squeaky, slippery acidity; gentle passionfruit, then a long, lingering finish. Screwcap. **RATING** 90 **DRINK** 2007 $ 18

▼▼▼▼ **Oranje Tractor Riesling 2004** Bright green-straw; powerful bouquet with a ghost of reduction; equally powerful and crisp citrus/lime palate; long finish, worth cellaring. Screwcap. **RATING** 88 **DRINK** 2012 $ 18.50
Oranje Tractor Cabernet Merlot 2003 Clean, fresh, light to medium-bodied; bright red fruits and fine tannins still softening and coming together. Screwcap. **RATING** 87 **DRINK** 2010 $ 20.50

Orchard Road   ★★★

PO Box 769, Cessnock, NSW 2325 **REGION** Orange
T 0417 693 310 **F**(02) 4930 7100 **OPEN** At Boutique Wine Centre, Broke Road, Pokolbin
WINEMAKER Rhys Eather **EST.** 2001 **CASES** 1100
SUMMARY This is a stand-alone venture of Rhys Eather (of Meerea Park). The grapes are sourced from the Angullong Vineyard, established at a height of 600m on the slopes of Mt Conabolas, and the wines are made by Rhys Eather at Meerea Park. They are available by mail order, and via the Boutique Wine Centre in Pokolbin; World Wine Estates distribute the wines in Sydney. Angullong Vineyard has its own separate winemaking operation and brand.

▼▼▼▼ **Angullong Vineyard Pinot Gris 2003** Fragrant blossom and spice; nicely weighted; good acidity and length. **RATING** 87 **DRINK** Now $ 20

▼▼▼▽ **Barbera 2002** Interesting aromas; confronting flavours with a mix of lemon rind and raspberry, then a spine of acidity. **RATING** 86 **DRINK** 2007 $ 24

O'Regan Creek Vineyard and Winery   NR

969 Pialba–Burrum Heads Road, Hervey Bay, Qld 4655 (postal) **REGION** Queensland Coastal
T(07) 4128 7636 **OPEN** Not
WINEMAKER John Fuerst, Cathy Fuerst **EST.** 1998 **CASES** NA
SUMMARY John and Kathy Fuerst have established their vineyard right on the Queensland Coast, planting cabernet sauvignon, shiraz, chambourcin (doubtless suited to the climate) and zinfandel.

🍇 Organic Vignerons Australia ★★★☆

Section 395 Derrick Road, Loxton North, SA 5333 **REGION** Riverland
T (08) 8541 3616 **F** (08) 8541 3616 **WEB** www.ova.com.au **OPEN** Mon–Fri 9.30–4.30
WINEMAKER David Bruer **EST.** 2002 **CASES** 3700
SUMMARY Organic Vignerons Australia is a very interesting winemaking business. It consists of the owners of five certified organic South Australian properties: Claire and Kevin Hansen at Padthaway, Bruce and Sue Armstrong at Waikerie, Brett and Melissa Munchenberg at Loxton, Terry Markou at Adelaide Plains and David and Barbara Bruer at Langhorne Creek. The wines are made by David Bruer at Temple Bruer, which is itself a certified organic producer. The wines are distributed by Bay Wines in South Australia and Rutherglen Wine & Spirit Company Limited in New South Wales, Victoria and Queensland; exports to Japan.

ᵀᵀᵀᵀ **Shiraz Cabernet Sauvignon 2002** Shows the extra power and depth from this exceptional Riverland vintage; savoury, spicy, blackberry fruit; good tannin structure. **RATING** 89 **DRINK** 2012 **$** 18
Merlot 2003 Juicy red berry, plum and mulberry fruits; light to medium-bodied; nice varietal expression. Padthaway/Adelaide Plains. **RATING** 87 **DRINK** 2008 **$** 18

ᵀᵀᵀ♀ **Rose Grenache Viognier 2004** Strawberry, apricot and spice aromas and flavours; unashamedly sweet, but the balance is good. Chinese food. **RATING** 86 **DRINK** Now **$** 16.50
Viognier 2004 **RATING** 85 **DRINK** Now **$** 16.50

Orlando ★★★★★

Jacob's Creek Visitor Centre, Barossa Valley Way, Rowland Flat, SA 5352 **REGION** Barossa Valley
T (08) 8521 3000 **F** (08) 8521 3003 **WEB** www.orlandowines.com **OPEN** 7 days 10–5
WINEMAKER Philip Laffer, Bernard Hicken, Sam Kurtz **EST.** 1847 **CASES** NFP
SUMMARY Jacob's Creek is one of the largest-selling brands in the world and is almost exclusively responsible for driving the fortunes of this French-owned (Pernod Ricard) company. A colossus in the export game, chiefly to the UK and Europe, but also to the US and Asia. Wine quality across the full spectrum from Jacob's Creek upwards has been exemplary, driven by the production skills of Philip Laffer. The global success of the basic Jacob's Creek range has had the perverse effect of prejudicing many critics and wine writers who fail (so it seems) to objectively look behind the label and taste what is in fact in the glass. Prejudice, real or imagined, does not enter into the question with the outstanding Lawson's Padthaway Shiraz, Jacaranda Ridge Cabernet Sauvignon, Steingarten Riesling and the Jacob's Creek Limited Release range.

ᵀᵀᵀᵀᵀ **Lawson's Padthaway Shiraz 1999** Medium purple-red; powerful, complex dark fruit aromas lead into a palate with massive extract and depth of dark fruit/plum/dark chocolate flavours; needs many years for the tannins to fully soften. **RATING** 95 **DRINK** 2016 **$** 59.99
Jacaranda Ridge Cabernet Sauvignon 1999 Potent, powerful, black fruits; long and intense, persistent but ripe tannins provide structure; good oak. **RATING** 95 **DRINK** 2014 **$** 54.99
Centenary Hill Shiraz 1998 Medium-bodied; smooth, supple and rounded; gently ripe fruit, quality oak and tannins all coalesce; entering maturity. Quality cork. **RATING** 94 **DRINK** 2013

ᵀᵀᵀᵀ♀ **St Helga Eden Valley Riesling 2004** Fragrant and elegant; apple, passionfruit and lime juice; long, fresh finish. **RATING** 93 **DRINK** 2012 **$** 15.99
Steingarten Riesling 2002 Generous wine; lots of tropical lime and citrus fruit; will come into full flower circa 2007. **RATING** 93 **DRINK** 2012 **$** 24.99
Jacob's Creek Reserve Shiraz 2002 Elegant but intense; spicy, tangy black fruits; lingering tannins, quality oak. Good cork. **RATING** 92 **DRINK** 2017 **$** 15.99
Jacob's Creek Limited Release Shiraz Cabernet 1999 Rich and opulent; lots of oak and extract; dark fruits; carefully pitched to wine shows, succeeding in Melbourne, Rutherglen, Cowra and Perth, but not in the best shows. **RATING** 91 **DRINK** 2009 **$** 74.99
Steingarten Riesling 2003 Zippy, lively and intense; high acidity balanced by the faintest hint of sweetness, but does dip slightly on the back palate. **RATING** 90 **DRINK** 2013 **$** 24.99
Gramp's Cabernet Merlot 2002 Rich, ripe, generous mix of red and black fruits; supple mouthfeel and tannins. **RATING** 90 **DRINK** 2008 **$** 15.99

ŸŸŸŸ **Jacob's Creek Reserve Chardonnay 2003** Fresh stone fruit/grapefruit aromas and flavours; subtle barrel ferment French oak; moderate length. RATING 89 DRINK 2007 $ 15.99

Trilogy White 2004 Tangy, slippery wine; lemony fruit salad; brisk acidity. Semillon/Sauvignon Blanc/Viognier. RATING 89 DRINK Now $ 14.99

Gramp's Shiraz 2002 Generous, round blackberry and plum fruit; good tannin and oak management; plenty of stuffing. RATING 88 DRINK 2009 $ 15.99

Trilogy Brut NV Crisp and elegant, with a mix of apple and nectarine; good length and aftertaste. No frills, but honest and to the point. RATING 88 DRINK Now $ 14.99

Jacob's Creek Chardonnay 2004 Citrus, stone fruit and melon; good varietal character and overall flavour; faintest touch of oak. RATING 87 DRINK Now $ 9.99

Trilogy 2002 Fresh, vibrant red fruits; bright and crisp; low tannins. RATING 87 DRINK Now $ 15

ŸŸŸŸ **Gramp's Barossa Chardonnay 2003** RATING 86 DRINK Now $ 15.99

Jacob's Creek Semillon Chardonnay 2004 RATING 86 DRINK Now $ 9.99

Jacob's Creek Limited Release Shiraz Cabernet 2002 RATING 86 DRINK 2008 $ 69.99

Jacob's Creek Cabernet Merlot 2003 RATING 86 DRINK 2007

Jacob's Creek Cabernet Sauvignon 2002 RATING 86 DRINK 2007 $ 9.99

Jacob's Creek Chardonnay Pinot Brut Cuvee NV RATING 86 DRINK Now $ 10.99

Gramp's Noble Late Harvest 2002 Moderately luscious and nicely balanced; as yet simple, but should develop complexity. RATING 86 DRINK 2007 $ 15.99

Jacob's Creek Semillon Sauvignon Blanc 2004 RATING 85 DRINK Now $ 9.99

Jacob's Creek Shiraz Rose 2004 RATING 85 DRINK Now

Jacob's Creek Merlot 2003 RATING 85 DRINK Now $ 9.99

Osborns ★★★★

166 Foxeys Road, Merricks North, Vic 3926 REGION Mornington Peninsula
T (03) 5989 7417 F (03) 5989 7510 WEB www.osborns.com.au OPEN Weekends Oct–June, and by appointment
WINEMAKER Frank Osborn, Richard McIntyre (Moorooduc) EST. 1988 CASES 1500
SUMMARY Frank and Pamela Osborn are now Mornington Peninsula veterans, having purchased the vineyard land in Ellerina Road in 1988 and (with help from son Guy) planted the vineyard over the following 4 years. The first release of wines in 1997 offered six vintages each of Chardonnay and Pinot Noir and five vintages of Cabernet Sauvignon, quite a debut (since drastically trimmed). Part of the production from the 5.5 ha of vineyards is sold to others. The wine is fermented at Moorooduc Estate by Richard McIntyre, then matured in barrel at the Osborns barrel store, monitored by Frank Osborn and daughter Lucinda.

ŸŸŸŸŸ **Reserve Pinot Noir 2002** Stylish, very complex and long sustained spicy notes; considerable textural complexity; dark fruit spectrum. Screwcap. RATING 93 DRINK 2009 $ 35

Sienna Reserve Pinot Noir 2003 Silkier texture and slightly more red fruit expression than the varietal version; similar light to medium-bodied weight; long finish. Screwcap. RATING 92 DRINK 2011 $ 35

ŸŸŸŸ **Pinot Noir 2002** Complex touches of spice as well as forest to the plum fruit; supple and smooth; fine tannins. Screwcap. RATING 89 DRINK 2007 $ 25

Pinot Noir 2003 Light to medium-bodied; firm, briary, foresty, savoury style through bouquet and palate; good length. Screwcap. RATING 88 DRINK 2009 $ 25

Rose 2004 Delicate strawberry, rose petal and a touch of spice; faint sweetness; good package. Screwcap. RATING 87 DRINK Now $ 18

O'Shea & Murphy Rosebery Hill Vineyard ★★★☆

Rosebery Hill, Pastoria Road, Pipers Creek, Vic 3444 REGION Macedon Ranges
T (03) 5423 5253 F (03) 5424 5253 WEB www.osheamurphy.com OPEN By appointment
WINEMAKER Barry Murphy, John O'Shea EST. 1984 CASES 3000
SUMMARY Planting of the 8-ha vineyard began in 1984 on a north-facing slope of red basalt soil which runs at the 550-m elevation line; it is believed the hill was the site of a volcanic eruption 7 million years ago. The vines were established without the aid of irrigation (and remain unirrigated), and produced the first small crop in 1990. No grapes were produced between 1993 and 1995 owing to

mildew: Murphy and O'Shea say, 'We tried to produce fruit with no sprays at all, and learned the hard way'. Part of the current production is sold to others, all of whom attest to the quality of the fruit.

ΥΥΥΥ **Pipers Creek Macedon Shiraz 2002** Relatively light-bodied with smooth and supple spicy black fruits; fine-grained tannins; minimal French oak. Cork. **RATING** 89 **DRINK** 2010
Chardonnay 2003 Light, crisp, clean green apple, citrus and melon fruit; good acidity; will develop. **RATING** 87 **DRINK** 2008

ΥΥΥΥ **Chardonnay 2004** **RATING** 85 **DRINK** 2007

Otway Estate ★★★★

20 Hoveys Road, Barongarook, Vic 3249 **REGION** Geelong
T (03) 5233 8400 **F** (03) 5233 8343 **WEB** www.otwayestate.com.au **OPEN** Mon–Fri 11–4.30, weekends 10–5
WINEMAKER Ian Deacon **EST.** 1983 **CASES** 3200
SUMMARY The history of Otway Estate dates back to 1983, when the first vines were planted by Stuart and Eileen Walker. The current group of nine family and friends, including winemaker Ian Deacon, have substantially expanded the scope of the business: there are now 6 ha of vineyard, planted primarily to chardonnay (3 ha) and pinot noir (2 ha) with small patches of riesling, semillon, sauvignon blanc and cabernet making up the remainder. The wines made from these plantings are sold under the Otway Estate label; wines made from contract-grown grapes in the region are marketed under the Yahoo Creek label. These are aimed at cafés and brasseries, with significant distribution around the region. In late 2000 three luxury self-contained cottages were built in the bush surrounding the vineyard, adding a further dimension to the business. Exports to Canada.

ΥΥΥΥΥ **Semillon Sauvignon Blanc 2004** Strong herb and grass varietal aromas; crisp and clean, with minerally acidity. **RATING** 90 **DRINK** Now $ 15
Chardonnay 2002 Good barrel ferment and oak handling; nicely balanced melon fruit. **RATING** 90 **DRINK** 2008 $ 20

ΥΥΥΥ **Chardonnay 2003** Solid stone fruit, the oak strong and still to integrate; has length. **RATING** 87 **DRINK** 2007 $ 20

ΥΥΥΥ **Pinot Noir 2003** **RATING** 84 **DRINK** Now $ 20

🐌 Outlook Hill ★★★★

97 School Lane, Tarrawarra, Vic 3777 **REGION** Yarra Valley
T (03) 5962 2890 **F** (03) 5962 2890 **WEB** www.outlookhill.com.au **OPEN** Thurs–Mon 11–4.30
WINEMAKER Al Fencaros (Dixons Creek Winery) **EST.** 2000 **CASES** 2100
SUMMARY After several years overseas, former Melbourne professionals Peter and Lydia Snow returned in 1997 planning to open a wine tourism business in the Hunter Valley. However, they had second thoughts, and in 2000 returned to the Yarra Valley, where they have now established two tourist B&B cottages, 5.5 ha of vineyard, a terrace restaurant and adjacent cellar door outlet, backed by a constant temperature wine storage cool room. The wines are made by Al Fencaros at Dixons Creek Winery. Victorian distribution through Victorian Fine Wine Merchants.

ΥΥΥΥΥ **Chardonnay 2003** A complex wine; some colour development; bigger, richer style, fractionally old-fashioned. **RATING** 92 **DRINK** 2010 $ 25

ΥΥΥΥ **Pinot Noir 2003** Vibrant colour; fresh, very firm plum fruit, rather like an austere Burgundy. Needs more time. **RATING** 88 **DRINK** 2009 $ 20

ΥΥΥΥ **Pinot Gris 2004** Clean, fresh and crisp; simply lacks varietal conviction. **RATING** 86 **DRINK** 2007 $ 16
Cabernet Merlot 2003 **RATING** 85 **DRINK** 2007 $ 22

Outram Estate ★★★☆

PO Box 621, Broadway, NSW 2007 **REGION** Lower Hunter Valley
T (02) 9481 7576 **F** (02) 9481 7879 **WEB** www.outramestate.com **OPEN** Not
WINEMAKER Peter Howland (Contract) **EST.** 1995 **CASES** 1150
SUMMARY Dr Geoff Cutter says his inspiration to start Outram Estate came from Max Lake, a visit to St Emilion/Pomerol in Bordeaux, and my account of the establishment of Coldstream Hills, which he

read in one of my books. His aim is to produce quality, not quantity, and with Peter Howland in charge of winemaking, there is no reason why he should not do so. He has 5 ha of merlot on rich red volcanic basalt, and 13 ha of verdelho and chardonnay on the sandy grey alluvial soils of Wollombi Creek. Distribution by Pacific Wine Connections; exports to the UK, Fiji, Taiwan and the US. The wines are also available by mail order.

Oyster Cove Vineyard NR

134 Manuka Road, Oyster Cove, Tas 7054 **REGION** Southern Tasmania
T (03) 6267 4512 **F** (03) 6267 4635 **OPEN** By appointment
WINEMAKER Andrew Hood (Contract) **EST.** 1994 **CASES** 100
SUMMARY The striking label of Oyster Cove, with a yacht reflected in mirror-calm water, is wholly appropriate, for Jean and Rod Ledingham have been quietly growing tiny quantities of grapes from the 1 ha of chardonnay and pinot noir since 1994.

Padthaway Estate

Riddoch Highway, Padthaway, SA 5271 **REGION** Padthaway
T (08) 8734 3148 **F** (08) 8734 3188 **WEB** www.padthawayestate.com **OPEN** 7 days 10–4
WINEMAKER Ulrich Grey-Smith **EST.** 1980 **CASES** 6000
SUMMARY For many years, until the opening of Stonehaven, this was the only functioning winery in Padthaway, set in the superb grounds of the Estate in a large and gracious old stone woolshed; the homestead is in the Relais et Chateaux mould, offering luxurious accommodation and fine food. Sparkling wines are the specialty. Padthaway Estate also acts as a tasting centre for other Padthaway-region wines.

ΨΨΨΨ **Unwooded Chardonnay 2004** Light to medium-bodied; nice, even flow of melon and stone fruit; good balance, if a little light on. **RATING** 89 **DRINK** 2007 $ 15
Limited Release Shiraz 2002 Supple black fruits; fine, ripe tannins; technically flawed by brett. **RATING** 88 **DRINK** 2009 $ 23

ΨΨΨΨ **Limited Release Rose 2004** Crisp, fresh and bone-dry; unusually, would have been better with a little more sweetness. **RATING** 86 **DRINK** Now $ 15
Cabernet Sauvignon 2002 **RATING** 84 **DRINK** 2008 $ 19

Palandri Wines

Bussell Highway, Cowaramup, WA 6284 **REGION** Margaret River
T (08) 9755 5711 **F** (08) 9755 5722 **WEB** www.palandri.com.au **OPEN** 7 days 10–5
WINEMAKER Sarah Siddons **EST.** 1999 **CASES** 250 000
SUMMARY A state-of-the-art winery completed just prior to the 2000 vintage now has a capacity of 2500 tonnes. The vineyards, which are scheduled to supply Palandri Wines with 50% of its intake, are situated in the Frankland River subregion of the Great Southern. In 1999, 150 ha of vines were planted at Frankland River; the major varieties are shiraz, merlot, cabernet sauvignon, riesling, chardonnay and sauvignon blanc. A further 60 ha were planted in early September 2000; a second block has been purchased south of the Frankland River vineyard, and a further 140 ha are being developed there. Exports to all major markets.

ΨΨΨΨΨ **Baldivis Estate Semillon 2003** Excellent balance, flavour and mouthfeel; distinctive WA style with good mid-palate weight. Clean, crisp finish. **RATING** 94 **DRINK** 2010

ΨΨΨΨ **Semillon Sauvignon Blanc 2004** Highly aromatic and fragrant; lively, bracing lemony and more tropical/passionfruit flavours; long, clean finish. **RATING** 92 **DRINK** Now $ 16.95
Frankland River Riesling 2004 Crisp, spotless blossom, mineral and apple aromas; well balanced, long palate; lingering aftertaste. **RATING** 91 **DRINK** 2012 $ 16.95
Chardonnay 2003 An elegant wine; very good balance and integration of oak with the stone fruit flavours; good length. **RATING** 91 **DRINK** 2009 $ 24.95

ΨΨΨΨ **Shiraz 2002** Abundant black fruits, blackberry and chocolate; nice, ripe tannins; subtle oak. **RATING** 89 **DRINK** 2008 $ 24.95
Baldivis Estate Cabernet Merlot 2003 Fresh fruit flavours with plenty of depth and texture. **RATING** 88 **DRINK** 2009 $ 11.95

ΥΥΥΥ **Merlot 2003** RATING 86 DRINK 2007 $16.95

ΥΥΥ **Baldivis Estate Chardonnay 2004** RATING 83 $11.95
Baldivis Estate Cabernet Shiraz 2002 RATING 81 $11.95

Palmara NR

1314 Richmond Road, Richmond, Tas 7025 REGION Southern Tasmania
T (03) 6260 2462 F (03) 6260 2462 WEB www.palmara.com.au OPEN Sept–May 7 days 12–6
WINEMAKER Allan Bird EST. 1985 CASES 300
SUMMARY Allan Bird makes the Palmara wines in tiny quantities. (The vineyard is slightly less than
1 ha.) The Pinot Noir has performed consistently well since 1990. The Exotica Siegerrebe blend is
unchallenged as Australia's most exotic and unusual wine, with pungent jujube/lanolin aromas and
flavours.

Palmers Wines NR

Lot 152 Palmers Lane, Pokolbin, NSW 2321 REGION Lower Hunter Valley
T (02) 4998 7452 F (02) 9949 9884 OPEN Weekends 10–5, or by appointment
WINEMAKER Contract EST. 1986 CASES 1100
SUMMARY The name of the vineyard and that of the lane on which it is established came from Henry
Palmer, who arrived in 1862. Three generations of the family continued to work the 40-ha property
as a mixed farming enterprise, but when the last (William) died in the 1970s, the property was to all
intents and purposes abandoned. Purchased in 1986, the new owners set about rebuilding the
original Palmer homestead, which now serves as the cellar door, and establishing 2.6 ha of vineyard
(chardonnay, verdelho, semillon and shiraz). Part of the grapes are sold to other winemakers.

Palmer Wines

Caves Road, Wilyabrup, WA 6280 REGION Margaret River
T (08) 9756 7388 F (08) 9756 7399 OPEN 7 days 10–5
WINEMAKER Bruce Dukes EST. 1977 CASES 7000
SUMMARY Stephen and Helen Palmer planted their first hectare of vines way back in 1977, but a series
of events (including a cyclone and grasshopper plagues) caused them to lose interest and instead turn
to thoroughbred horses. But with encouragement from Dr Michael Peterkin of Pierro, and after a gap
of almost 10 years, they again turned to viticulture and now have 15 ha planted to the classic varieties.

ΥΥΥΥΥ **Shiraz 2003** Powerful, medium to full-bodied; blackberry, spice and dark chocolate; fully
ripe fruit and tannins. Screwcap. RATING 93 DRINK 2018 $18.99

ΥΥΥΥ **Chardonnay 2003** Funky, slightly reduced barrel ferment characters and flavours; good
length and persistence. Soggy cork. RATING 89 DRINK 2008 $14.99

Pankhurst

Old Woodgrove, Woodgrove Road, Hall, NSW 2618 REGION Canberra District
T (02) 6230 2592 F (02) 6230 2592 WEB www.pankhurstwines.com.au OPEN Weekends, public hols,
or by appointment
WINEMAKER Dr David Carpenter, Sue Carpenter, Dr Roger Harris (Lark Hill) EST. 1986 CASES 4000
SUMMARY Agricultural scientist and consultant Allan Pankhurst and wife Christine (with a degree in
pharmaceutical science) have established a 5.7-ha split-canopy vineyard. The first wines produced
showed considerable promise. In recent years Pankhurst has shared success with Lark Hill in the
production of good Pinot Noir. Says Christine Pankhurst, 'the result of good viticulture here and
great winemaking at Lark Hill', and she may well be right.

ΥΥΥΥΥ **Pinot Noir 2003** Ultra-concentrated and powerful, almost painfully so, but nonetheless
very correct. Spicy, stemmy, briary undergrowth to potent plum and varietal fruit;
demands food. Cork. RATING 94 DRINK 2010

ΥΥΥΥΥ **Chardonnay 2003** Light to medium-bodied; cashew, melon, fig and stone fruit;
malolactic and barrel ferment inputs well balanced and integrated; good length. Good
cork. RATING 90 DRINK 2008

Panorama ★★★☆

1848 Cygnet Coast Road, Cradoc, Tas 7109 **REGION** Southern Tasmania
T (03) 6266 3409 **F** (03) 6266 3482 **WEB** www.panoramavineyard.com.au **OPEN** Wed–Mon 10–5
WINEMAKER Michael Vishacki **EST.** 1974 **CASES** 210
SUMMARY Michael and Sharon Vishacki purchased Panorama from Steve Ferencz in 1997, and have since spent considerable sums in building a brand new winery and an attractive cellar door sales outlet, and in trebling the vineyard size.

🍷🍷🍷🍷 **Chardonnay 2001** Glowing yellow-green; has length and freshness, though dips slightly on the mid-palate. **RATING** 90 **DRINK** 2008 $28

🍷🍷🍷🍷 **Estate Pinot Noir 2003** **RATING** 84 **DRINK** 2007 $39

🍷🍷🍷 **Botrytis Sauvignon Blanc 2003** **RATING** 82 $20

🍷🍷🍷 **Sauvignon Blanc 2004** **RATING** 79 $22

Panton Hill Winery NR

145 Manuka Road, Panton Hill, Vic 3759 **REGION** Yarra Valley
T (03) 9719 7342 **F** (03) 9719 7362 **WEB** www.pantonhillwinery.com.au **OPEN** Weekends & public hols 11–5, or by appointment
WINEMAKER Dr Teunis AP Kwak **EST.** 1988 **CASES** 700
SUMMARY Melbourne academic Dr Teunis Kwak has a 4-ha fully mature vineyard, part planted in 1976, the remainder in 1988. Part of the production is sold to others. The vineyard, established on a fairly steep hillside, is picturesque, and there is a large stone hall available for functions.

Paperbark Vines NR

PO Box 2553, Kent Town, SA 5071 **REGION** Southeast Australia
T (08) 8431 3675 **F** (08) 8431 3674 **OPEN** Not
WINEMAKER Contract **EST.** 2000 **CASES** NA
SUMMARY Paperbark Vines is a virtual winery owned by Mark Cohen of Malesco Imports and Export Pty Ltd. Chardonnay, cabernet sauvignon and shiraz are made under the Paperbark Vines label, and sold only into Malaysia, Singapore, Thailand and the US.

Paracombe Wines ★★★★☆

Main Road, Paracombe, SA 5132 (postal) **REGION** Adelaide Hills
T (08) 8380 5058 **F** (08) 8380 5488 **WEB** www.paracombewines.com **OPEN** Not
WINEMAKER Paul Drogemuller **EST.** 1983 **CASES** 5000
SUMMARY The Drogemuller family have established 12 ha of vineyards at Paracombe, reviving a famous name in South Australian wine history. The wines are stylish and consistent; they are sold by mail order and through retailers in South Australia. Exports to the the UK, Sweden, Switzerland, the US, Canada, Singapore and Japan.

🍷🍷🍷🍷 **Adelaide Hills Sauvignon Blanc 2004** Fragrant, gentle passionfruit/tropical blossom aromas; delicate but positive fruit. Another good outcome. Screwcap. **RATING** 92 **DRINK** 2007 $21

Somerville Shiraz 2002 Light to medium-bodied; fragrant and beguiling wine; ululating sweet fruit flavours; delicate tannin and oak; clean, dry, long finish Radically different from the '01. Cork. **RATING** 92 **DRINK** 2015 $69

Holland Creek Riesling 2004 Floral apple and lime blossom; delicate but intensely focused palate; lime and green apple; good outcome for the vintage. Screwcap. **RATING** 90 **DRINK** 2013 $21

The Reuben 2002 Sweet, juicy blackberry, plum, blackcurrant and cassis fruit do all the talking; oak and tannins incidental music. **RATING** 90 **DRINK** 2012 $25

🍷🍷🍷🍷 **Adelaide Hills Chardonnay 2003** Bright, medium-yellow-green; less developed than the bouquet suggests; elegant, light-bodied citrus, apple and stone fruit. Screwcap. **RATING** 89 **DRINK** 2010 $25

Adelaide Hills Cabernet Sauvignon 2002 High-toned cassis and blackcurrant; quite strong oak; milky tannins. Cork. **RATING** 88 **DRINK** 2011 $ 27

ΥΥΥΥ **Adelaide Hills Cabernet Franc 2003** **RATING** 86 **DRINK** 2007 $ 27

Paradigm Hill ★★★★

26 Merricks Road, Merricks, Vic 3916 **REGION** Mornington Peninsula
T 0438 114 480 **F** (03) 5989 2191 **WEB** www.paradigmhill.com.au **OPEN** By appointment
WINEMAKER Dr George Mihaly **EST.** 1999 **CASES** 1000
SUMMARY Dr George Mihaly (with a background in medical research, then thereafter the biotechnology and pharmaceutical industries) and wife Ruth (a former chef and caterer) have realised a 30-year dream of establishing their own vineyard and winery, abandoning their previous careers to do so. George Mihaly had all the necessary scientific qualifications, and built on those by making the 2001 Merricks Creek wines, moving to home base at Paradigm Hill for the 2002 vintage, all along receiving guidance and advice from Nat White from Main Ridge Estate. The vineyard, under Ruth's control with advice from Shane Strange, is planted to 2.1 ha of pinot noir, 1 ha of shiraz, 0.9 ha of riesling and 0.4 ha of pinot gris. The back labels are a mine of technical information. Exports to the UK.

ΥΥΥΥΥ **VH-DOC Shiraz 2003** Highly aromatic, fresh and flavour-packed black cherry fruit and spice, yet not the least heavy; long, fine palate; low pH will prolong the life, cork permitting. **RATING** 93 **DRINK** 2015 $ 35
Mornington Peninsula Pinot Gris 2004 Abundant pear and spice fruit; a minerally spine for the clever use of French oak and malolactic fermentation; pricey but stylish. Screwcap. **RATING** 90 **DRINK** 2007 $ 35

ΥΥΥΥ **Mornington Peninsula Riesling 2004** Delicate apple, pear and lime aromas and flavours; soft acid, ready now. Screwcap. **RATING** 87 **DRINK** 2008 $ 24
Transition Pinot Noir Rose 2004 Unusual style; spicy aromatics, some strawberry; long, bone-dry, firm acid finish. Food style-plus. Pricey. Screwcap. **RATING** 87 **DRINK** Now $ 27

Paradise Enough NR

Stewarts Road, Kongwak, Vic 3951 **REGION** Gippsland
T (03) 5657 4241 **F** (03) 5657 4229 **OPEN** Sun, public hols 12–5
WINEMAKER John Bell, Sue Armstrong **EST.** 1987 **CASES** 600
SUMMARY Phillip Jones of Bass Phillip persuaded John Bell and Sue Armstrong to establish a small vineyard on a substantial dairy and beef cattle property.

Paringa Estate ★★★★★

44 Paringa Road, Red Hill South, Vic 3937 **REGION** Mornington Peninsula
T (03) 5989 2669 **F** (03) 5931 0135 **WEB** www.paringaestate.com.au **OPEN** 7 days 11–5
WINEMAKER Lindsay McCall **EST.** 1985 **CASES** 5000
SUMMARY Schoolteacher-turned-winemaker Lindsay McCall has shown an absolutely exceptional gift for winemaking across a range of styles, but with immensely complex Pinot Noir and Shiraz leading the way. The wines have an unmatched level of success in the wine shows and competitions Paringa Estate is able to enter, the limitation being the relatively small size of the production. His skills are no less evident in contract winemaking for others. The restaurant is open 7 days 10–3.

ΥΥΥΥΥ **Reserve Special Barrel Selection Pinot Noir 2003** Beautifully fragrant, with long and silky red fruits; ultra-classic style, elegant and perfumed. Sheer class. **RATING** 97 **DRINK** 2010 $ 80
Pinot Noir 2003 Very powerful and intense, but not over-extracted; dark plum, spice and a touch of forest floor; great depth and length. **RATING** 96 **DRINK** 2012 $ 55
Pinot Noir 2002 Spotless, pristine varietal character; a long, lingering and intense palate; a perfect match of red fruits, spices, oak and finest tannins. **RATING** 96 **DRINK** 2009 $ 55
Reserve Shiraz 2003 Deep colour, good hue; a complex and layered array of black cherry, licorice and spice; fine tannins. **RATING** 95 **DRINK** 2015 $ 70
Peninsula Pinot Noir 2003 Very good colour; a highly fragrant and spicy mix of red and black fruits; lively, intense and long palate; delicious. **RATING** 94 **DRINK** 2008 $ 25

ŤŤŤŤ♀ Shiraz 2003 Vivid red-purple; very elegant and precise cool-climate style; earthy spicy edges; lingering tannins. **RATING** 93 **DRINK** 2013 $42

Peninsula Chardonnay 2003 100% barrel-fermented in French oak, 20% new. The elegant, moderately intense grapefruit and melon palate is perfectly balanced, the fruit having eaten the oak. **RATING** 92 **DRINK** 2012 $15

Peninsula Pinot Noir 2004 Purple hue; abundant dark cherry and plum fruit; a nice touch of smoky barrel ferment oak; good length and finish. Screwcap. **RATING** 92 **DRINK** 2009 $25

Riesling 2004 Clean, fresh, crisp; gentle herb/spice/citrus/lime/apple; fresh, slatey finish. Screwcap. **RATING** 90 **DRINK** 2012 $19

Pinot Gris 2004 Powerful and mouthfilling; 15° alcohol plays a big part in texture, but doesn't heat the finish; correct pear, apple and spice flavours. Screwcap. **RATING** 90 **DRINK** 2009 $20

ŤŤŤŤ Riesling 2003 Generous, ripe, full-blown wine; hint of botrytis; high flavour. **RATING** 89 **DRINK** 2008 $19

Peninsula Shiraz 2003 Fragrant berry, mint, leaf and spice aromas and flavours; minimal tannins. **RATING** 89 **DRINK** 2010 $28

White Pinot 2004 Bright, fresh strawberry and cherry; vibrant and long; subliminal sweetness, then acidity. Saignee style; 5 months on lees. Screwcap. **RATING** 88 **DRINK** Now $15

Parish Hill Wines ★★★

Parish Hill Road, Uraidla, SA 5142 **REGION** Adelaide Hills
T (08) 8390 3927 **F** (08) 8390 0394 **WEB** www.parishhillwines.com.au **OPEN** By appointment
WINEMAKER Andrew Cottell **EST.** 1998 **CASES** 1000
SUMMARY Andrew Cottell and Joy Carlisle have a tiny 1.6-ha vineyard on a steep, sunny, exposed slope adjacent to their house, and a micro-onsite winery (which has approval for a total crush of 15 tonnes), but have taken the venture very seriously. Andrew Cottell studied wine science and viticulture at Charles Sturt University, where he was introduced to the Italian varieties; this led to the planting of 0.2 ha of arneis and 0.5 ha of nebbiolo. The other two varieties are new French clones selected by Professor Bernard at Dijon University. An attempt to use an organic spray program in 2002 failed, and while they adopt integrated pest management, soft environmental practices and beneficial insects, they have moved to conventional vineyard management for the time being at least.

ŤŤŤŤ Piccadilly Valley Nebbiolo Rose 2004 Very pale; lemony acidity runs through gentle strawberry flavours; crisp, fresh and balanced. **RATING** 87 **DRINK** Now $25

Nebbiolo 2003 Light-bodied; a mix of cherry, strawberry and more savoury fruit; minimal tannins; does show varietal character. **RATING** 87 **DRINK** Now $25

ŤŤŤ♀ Pinot Noir 2003 RATING 86 **DRINK** 2007 $25

Arneis 2004 RATING 84 **DRINK** Now $25

Parker Coonawarra Estate ★★★★☆

Riddoch Highway, Coonawarra, SA 5263 **REGION** Coonawarra
T (08) 8737 3525 **F** (08) 8737 3527 **WEB** www.parkercoonawarraestate.com.au **OPEN** 7 days 10–4
WINEMAKER Peter Bissell (Contract) **EST.** 1985 **CASES** 5000
SUMMARY Parker Coonawarra Estate is at the southern end of Coonawarra, on rich terra rossa soil over limestone. Cabernet Sauvignon is the predominant variety, with minor plantings of merlot and petit verdot. Acquired by the Rathbone family in May 2004. Exports to the UK, the US and other major markets.

ŤŤŤŤ♀ Terra Rossa Cabernet Sauvignon 2002 Medium-bodied; nicely balanced blackcurrant fruit with touches of earth and cedar; particularly long palate and finish. **RATING** 91 **DRINK** 2017

ŤŤŤŤ♀ Terra Rossa Merlot 2002 RATING 86 **DRINK** 2009

Park Wines NR

RMB 6291, Sanatorium Road, Allan's Flat, Yackandandah, Vic 3691 **REGION** Alpine Valleys
T (02) 6027 1564 **F** (02) 6027 1561 **OPEN** Weekends & public hols 10–5
WINEMAKER Rod Park, Julia Park **EST.** 1995 **CASES** NA

SUMMARY Rod and Julia Park have a 6-ha vineyard of riesling, chardonnay, merlot, cabernet franc and cabernet sauvignon, set in the beautiful hill country of the Ovens Valley. Part of the vineyard is still coming into bearing, and the business is still in its infancy.

Parri Estate ★★★★

Sneyd Road, Mount Compass, SA 5210 **REGION** Southern Fleurieu
T (08) 8383 0462 **F** (08) 8554 9505 **WEB** www.parriestate.com.au **OPEN** 7 days 11–5
WINEMAKER Linda Domas **EST.** 1998 **CASES** 10 000
SUMMARY Alice, Peter and John Phillips have established a substantial business with a clear marketing plan and an obvious commitment to quality. The 33-ha vineyard is planted to chardonnay, viognier, sauvignon blanc, semillon, pinot noir, cabernet sauvignon and shiraz, using modern trellis and irrigation systems. The protected valley in which the vines are planted has a creek which flows throughout the year, and which has been rejuvenated by the planting of 3000 trees. A second vineyard in McLaren Vale with 5.6 ha of shiraz, grenache and cabernet sauvignon has also been acquired. Exports to the UK, Canada, Germany, Japan, Hong Kong and China.

▼▼▼▼▽ **Semillon 2004** Lively, fresh lemon zest; excellent balance and length; has real finesse; 11° alcohol spot on. Screwcap. **RATING** 93 **DRINK** 2012 $14

▼▼▼▼ **Sauvignon Blanc 2004** Light-bodied; quite elegant, gentle passionfruit and gooseberry; crisp, clean finish. Screwcap. **RATING** 89 **DRINK** 2007 $18
Viognier Chardonnay 2004 Lively, fresh, light to medium-bodied; melon, fruit salad, guava and apricot; nice acidity. High-quality cork. **RATING** 88 **DRINK** 2007 $18

▼▼▼▽ **Pinot Noir 2003** **RATING** 86 **DRINK** 2007 $25
Shiraz 2003 **RATING** 86 **DRINK** 2008 $20
Cabernet Sauvignon 2003 **RATING** 86 **DRINK** 2008 $20
Shiraz Cabernet 2003 **RATING** 84 **DRINK** 2007 $15

Passing Clouds ★★★★

RMB 440, Kurting Road, Kingower, Vic 3517 **REGION** Bendigo
T (03) 5438 8257 **F** (03) 5438 8246 **WEB** www.passingclouds.com.au **OPEN** Weekends 12–5, Mon–Fri by appointment
WINEMAKER Graeme Leith **EST.** 1974 **CASES** 4000
SUMMARY In 1974 Graeme Leith and Sue Mackinnon planted the first vines at Passing Clouds, 60 km northwest of Bendigo. Graeme Leith is one of the great personalities of the wine industry, with a superb sense of humour, and makes lovely regional reds with cassis, berry and mint fruit. Sheltered by hills of ironbark forest, the valley offers an ideal growing climate for premium red wine. The main varieties planted on the 6-ha vineyard are shiraz, cabernet sauvignon, and pinot noir. Additional varieties are sourced from local grapegrowers. Exports to the US.

▼▼▼▼▽ **Reserve Shiraz 2003** Medium-bodied; a combination of spice, satsuma plum and blackberry; fine, ripe tannins; good oak. Quality cork. **RATING** 92 **DRINK** 2013 $35
Angel Blend 2003 Medium-bodied combination of mint, chocolate, earth, spice and black fruits; fine tannins; good length. Quality cork. **RATING** 90 **DRINK** 2012 $30
Cabernet Franc 2002 Medium to full-bodied, at the ripe end of the spectrum; hints of dark chocolate; ripe tannins. **RATING** 90 **DRINK** 2010 $20

▼▼▼▼ **Graeme's Blend Shiraz Cabernet 2003** Powerful, medium to full-bodied mix of dark berry fruit and some minty notes; does shorten slightly on the finish. Quality cork. **RATING** 89 **DRINK** 2012 $25
Yarra Valley Pinot Noir 2003 Powerful wine; complex black fruits in a plummy spectrum; lots of oak. **RATING** 87 **DRINK** 2008 $23
Merlot 2002 Light to medium-bodied; savoury olive and briar aromas and flavours; varietal, but needs a touch more sweetness. **RATING** 87 **DRINK** 2008 $23

Pasut Family Wines NR

Block 445 Calder Highway, Sunnycliffs, Vic 3496 **REGION** Murray Darling
T (03) 5024 2361 **OPEN** By appointment
WINEMAKER Stuart Kilmister (Contract) **EST.** 2000 **CASES** NA

SUMMARY Denis and Pauline Pasut have 10 ha of vineyards, with a very interesting range of varietals planted: pinot gris, sangiovese, barbera, fragola, nebbiolo and vermentino, all of which (with the qualified exception of pinot gris) are grapes grown chiefly in Italy. If the varieties planted are exotic, the brands are more so: Pasut, Pinkbits, Fatbelly and Alpino Misto.

Paternoster NR

17 Paternoster Road, Emerald, Vic 3782 **REGION** Yarra Valley
T (03) 5968 3197 **F** (03) 5968 3197 **WEB** www.paternosterwines.com.au **OPEN** Weekends 11–6
WINEMAKER Philip Hession **EST.** 1985 **CASES** 700
SUMMARY The densely planted, non-irrigated vines (at a density of 5000 vines to the hectare) cascade down a steep hillside in one of the coolest parts of the Yarra Valley. Pinot Noir is the specialty of the winery: it produces intensely flavoured wines with a strong eucalypt mint overlay.

Paterson's Gundagai Vineyard ★★★☆

474 Old Hume Highway Road,Tumblong, NSW 2729 **REGION** Gundagai
T (02) 6944 9227 **OPEN** 7 days 9.30–5
WINEMAKER Celine Rousseau (Contract) **EST.** 19971466 **CASES** 700
SUMMARY The Paterson family began developing the 12-ha vineyard in 1996. It is a powerful team: Robert Paterson (M.Ec. – Sydney, PMD – Harvard) was a Senior Vice-President of Coca Cola and his wife Rhondda was a teacher, before both turned to cattle farming in the early '80s and grapegrowing in the mid-1990s. Son Stuart Paterson has a PhD in Chemical Engineering from the University of New South Wales, and is studying viticulture and wine science at Charles Sturt University in Wagga; wife Rainny is an architect. Most of the grapes grown elsewhere in Gundagai are sold to major wine companies for blended wines; Paterson's is one of the few estate-based operations.

Patrick's Vineyard ★★★★☆

Croziers Road, Cobaw via Mount Macedon, Vic 3441 (postal) **REGION** Macedon Ranges
T 0419 598 401 **F** (03) 9521 6266 **OPEN** Not
WINEMAKER Alan Cooper (Contract) **EST.** 1996 **CASES** 400
SUMMARY Noell and John McNamara and Judy Doyle planted 2 ha of pinot noir over the 1996 and 1997 planting seasons. The vineyard stands high on the southern slopes of the Cobaw Ranges with an 1862 settler's cottage still standing and marking the first land use in the region. At an altitude of 600m, even pinot ripens very late in the season, typically at the end of April or early May, but in the right years, when the canopy has turned entirely from green to yellow-gold, the results can be impressive. After the marvellous 2002 vintage (still available at the cellar door as at December 2004) heartbreak struck one week before the 2003 vintage when a Department of Environment Controlled Fire destroyed the grapes by smoke contamination.

TTTTT **Pinot Noir 2002** An intense, stylish and complex mix of dark berries, plums and multi-spices; excellent oak; long, lingering finish. **RATING** 94 **DRINK** 2009 $16.50

Patrick T Wines ★★★★

Cnr Ravenswood Lane/Riddoch Highway, Coonawarra, SA 5263 **REGION** Coonawarra
T (08) 8737 3687 **F** (08) 8737 3689 **OPEN** 7 days 10–4.30
WINEMAKER Pat Tocaciu **EST.** 1996 **CASES** 1500
SUMMARY Patrick Tocaciu is a district veteran, setting up Patrick T Winemaking Services after prior careers at Heathfield Ridge Winery and Hollick Wines. He and his partners have almost 44 ha of vines at Wrattonbully, and another 2 ha of cabernet sauvignon in Coonawarra. The Wrattonbully plantings cover all the major varieties, while the Coonawarra plantings give rise to the Home Block Cabernet Sauvignon. Patrick also carries out contract winemaking for others.

TTTTT **The Caves Vineyard Riesling 2003** Extremely aromatic lime and toast; vibrant, flavoursome palate with more lime and toast; good lemony acidity; a bargain. Screwcap. **RATING** 94 **DRINK** 2009 $15

TTTT **The Caves Vineyard Shiraz 2001** Medium to full-bodied; solid dark fruits and balanced extract; will repay cellaring. **RATING** 89 **DRINK** 2014 $25

Home Block Cabernet Sauvignon 2001 Elegant, medium-bodied, tangy, savoury style, with nigh-on lemony aspects, but not green or bitter; 750 cases made. Screwcap. **RATING** 88 **DRINK** 2010 $18

Home Block Cabernet Sauvignon 1998 Elegant, medium-bodied wine with notes of herb and earth; balanced finish. **RATING** 88 **DRINK** 2009 $35

Patritti Wines ★★★★

13–23 Clacton Road, Dover Gardens, SA 5048 **REGION** Adelaide Zone
T(08) 8296 8261 **F**(08) 8296 5088 **OPEN** Mon–Sat 9–6
WINEMAKER G Patritti, J Mungall **EST.** 1926 **CASES** 100 000
SUMMARY A traditional, family-owned business offering wines at modest prices, but with impressive vineyard holdings of 10 ha of shiraz in Blewitt Springs and 6 ha of grenache at Aldinga North.

ŸŸŸŸŸ **Dover McLaren Vale Shiraz 2002** Powerful, ripe, blackberry and dark chocolate aromas and flavours; medium to medium-full bodied; excellent balance and structure. Cork. **RATING** 93 **DRINK** 2015 $25

Marion Liqueur Verdelho 1977 Powerful but not abrasive; lovely old fortified white with a gently biscuity finish. A piece of history from the last vintage before the vineyard gave way to houses. **RATING** 92 **DRINK** Now $30

ŸŸŸŸ **Blewitt Springs Estate Chardonnay 2004** Light-bodied, but quite complex; 50% malolactic fermentation works well; delicate creamy cashew and gentle melon flavours coalesce. Screwcap. **RATING** 87 **DRINK** 2008 $12.50

Patterson Lakes Estate NR

Riverend Road, Bangholme, Vic 3175 (postal) **REGION** Port Phillip Zone
T(03) 9773 1034 **F**(03) 9772 5634 **OPEN** Not
WINEMAKER Bill Christophersen **EST.** 1998 **CASES** 1500
SUMMARY Former property developer James Bate has followed in the footsteps of the late Sid Hamilton (who established Leconfield in Coonawarra when he was 80) by starting Patterson Lakes Estate not long before he turned 80. The original planting was of 3 ha of shiraz, with a further 3 ha of shiraz, 0.8 ha each of viognier and tempranillo, a patch of cabernet franc, petit verdot, and merlot for a Bordeaux blend, and small amounts of mourvedre, cinsaut and grenache to go with the shiraz. A small winery was completed in time for the 2004 vintage. Sullivan Wine Agencies handles the domestic distribution; exports to the US.

Pattersons ★★★★

St Werburghs Road, Mount Barker, WA 6234 **REGION** Mount Barker
T(08) 9851 2063 **F**(08) 9851 2063 **OPEN** Sat–Wed 10–5, or by appointment
WINEMAKER Plantagenet (Contract) **EST.** 1982 **CASES** 500
SUMMARY Schoolteachers Sue and Arthur Patterson have grown chardonnay, shiraz and pinot noir and grazed cattle as a weekend relaxation for a decade. The cellar door is in a recently completed and very beautiful rammed-earth house, and a number of vintages are on sale at any one time. Good Chardonnay and Shiraz have been complemented by the occasional spectacular Pinot Noir.

Paul Conti Wines ★★★★

529 Wanneroo Road, Woodvale, WA 6026 **REGION** Greater Perth Zone
T(08) 9409 9160 **F**(08) 9309 1634 **WEB** www.paulcontiwines.com.au **OPEN** Mon–Sat 9.30–5.30, Sun by appointment
WINEMAKER Paul Conti, Jason Conti **EST.** 1948 **CASES** 7000
SUMMARY Third-generation winemaker Jason Conti has now assumed day-to-day control of winemaking, although father Paul (who succeeded his father in 1968) remains interested and involved in the business. Over the years Paul Conti challenged and redefined industry perceptions and standards; the challenge for Jason Conti was to achieve the same degree of success in a relentlessly and increasingly competitive market environment, and he is doing just that. Exports to the UK, Indonesia, Singapore, Malaysia and Japan.

ΥΥΥΥ♀ **Mariginiup Shiraz 2002** Bright, clear red-purple; clean, fresh cherry and plum fruit on the bouquet and palate; structure through ripe, balanced tannins; subtle oak. Minor classic. Cork. **RATING** 92 **DRINK** 2012 $ 28

ΥΥΥΥ **The Tuarts Cabernet Sauvignon 2003** Spotlessly clean aromas; restrained, relatively austere cabernet varietal character; blackcurrant and black olive; fine tannins, good French oak. Cork. **RATING** 89 **DRINK** 2013 $ 18
Medici Ridge Pinot Noir 2003 Attractive spicy plum aromas; light to medium-bodied; correct and clear varietal character; nice wine. Quality cork. **RATING** 88 **DRINK** 2007 $ 18
Late Harvest Muscat Fronti 2004 Delicate spicy/grapey flavours; beautifully judged flick of residual sugar on the palate. Cork. **RATING** 87 **DRINK** 2007 $ 12

ΥΥΥ♀ **The Tuarts Chenin Blanc 2004** **RATING** 84 **DRINK** Now $ 12

Paulett

★★★★☆

Polish Hill Road, Polish Hill River, SA 5453 **REGION** Clare Valley
T (08) 8843 4328 **F** (08) 8843 4202 **WEB** www.paulettwines.com.au **OPEN** 7 days 10–5
WINEMAKER Neil Paulett **EST.** 1983 **CASES** 12 500
SUMMARY The Paulett story is a saga of Australian perseverance, commencing with the 1982 purchase of a property with 1 ha of vines and a house, promptly destroyed by the terrible Ash Wednesday bushfires of the following year. Son Matthew has joined Neil and Alison Paulett as a partner in the business, responsible for viticulture, and the plantings now total 25 ha on a much-expanded property holding of 147 ha. The winery and cellar door have wonderful views over the Polish Hill River region, the memories of the bushfires long gone. Exports to the UK and New Zealand.

ΥΥΥΥΥ **Polish Hill River Aged Release Riesling 1997** Glowing light yellow-green; clean lime and toast; drinking superbly; flavour with freshness; lime, mineral and toast; long, crisp finish. Rebottled with a Screwcap! **RATING** 96 **DRINK** 2010 $ 25

ΥΥΥΥ♀ **Polish Hill River Riesling 2004** Spotlessly clean; lime and blossom aromas; attractive, rounded lime/tropical fruit, yet retains delicacy. Screwcap. **RATING** 93 **DRINK** 2014 $ 18

ΥΥΥΥ **Polish Hill River Shiraz 2002** Spicy, savoury, leafy berry aromas and flavours; light to medium-bodied; not as concentrated as most from the vintage. Screwcap. **RATING** 88 **DRINK** 2009 $ 22
Polish Hill River Cabernet Merlot 2002 Powerful, fairly austere earthy notes to blackcurrant and spice fruit. Screwcap. **RATING** 87 **DRINK** 2008 $ 22

Paul Osicka

NR

Majors Creek Vineyard at Graytown, Vic 3608 **REGION** Heathcote
T (03) 5794 9235 **F** (03) 5794 9288 **OPEN** Mon–Sat 10–5, Sun 12–5
WINEMAKER Paul Osicka **EST.** 1955 **CASES** NFP
SUMMARY A low-profile producer but reliable, particularly when it comes to its smooth but rich Shiraz. The wines are distributed in Melbourne and Sydney by Australian Prestige Wines; exports to the UK, Hong Kong and Japan.

Paulmara Estate

★★★☆

47 Park Avenue, Rosslyn Park, SA 5072 (postal) **REGION** Barossa Valley
T (08) 8364 3019 **F** (08) 8364 3019 **WEB** www.paulmara.com.au **OPEN** Not
WINEMAKER Paul Georgiadis, Neil Pike **EST.** 1999 **CASES** 600
SUMMARY Paul Georgiadis is one of many personal success stories. Born to an immigrant Greek family, he grew up in Waikerie, where his family owned vineyards and orchards. His parents worked sufficiently hard to send him first to St Peters College in Adelaide and then to do a marketing degree at Adelaide University. He became the whirlwind grower relations manager for Southcorp, and one of the best-known faces in the Barossa Valley. His wife Mara comes from California; she has a degree in agribusiness and experience in California tasting rooms and marketing departments. They established a 13-ha vineyard in 1995, planted to semillon, shiraz, sangiovese, merlot and cabernet sauvignon. Yields are limited to 5–7 tonnes per hectare; part of the production is sold, and the best shiraz goes to make the Syna Shiraz ('syna' being Greek for together). A small amount is exported to the US, the remainder sold through the website.

▼▼▼▼ **Syna Shiraz 2000** Unexpectedly, slightly more depth than the '01; black fruits with a touch of sweet vanilla. **RATING** 88 **DRINK** 2009 $ 15

Syna Shiraz 2001 Medium-bodied, traditional, honest, regional no-frills style with nice black fruits; soft oak and tannins. **RATING** 87 **DRINK** 2008 $ 15

Paxton Wines ★★★★

Wheaton Road, McLaren Vale, SA 5171 **REGION** McLaren Vale
T (08) 8323 8645 **F** (08) 8323 8903 **WEB** www.paxtonvineyards.com **OPEN** Weekends & public hols 10–5
WINEMAKER Michael Paxton **EST.** 1997 **CASES** 1500
SUMMARY David Paxton is one of Australia's best-known viticulturists and consultants. He founded Paxton Vineyards in McLaren Vale with his family in 1979, and has since been involved in various capacities in the establishment and management of vineyards in the Adelaide Hills, Coonawarra, the Clare Valley, Yarra Valley, Margaret River and Great Southern. Sons Ben (now general manager) and Michael (with 14 years' experience in Spain, South America, France and Australia) are responsible for making the wines. There are 4 vineyards in the family holdings: the Thomas Block, the Jones Block, Quandong Farm and Landcross Farm Settlement. The first 2 vineyards provide the shiraz (some dating back to 1880), and the last is home to a 100-year-old stone barn cellar door.

▼▼▼▼▽ **McLaren Vale Chardonnay 2004** Elegant, light to medium-bodied; melon, stone fruit and subtle malolactic and barrel ferment creamy cashew inputs. Screwcap. **RATING** 90 **DRINK** 2007 $ 27

Peacetree Estate ★★★

Harmans South Road, Wilyabrup, WA 6280 **REGION** Margaret River
T (08) 9755 5170 **F** (08) 9755 9275 **WEB** www.peacetreeestate.com **OPEN** 7 days 10–6
WINEMAKER Paul Green (Contract) **EST.** 1995 **CASES** 1300
SUMMARY Three generations of the Tucker family were involved in the first plantings at Peacetree Estate in 1995; however, it was of olive trees, not vines. The latter soon followed, with sauvignon blanc and cabernet sauvignon. For the first two vintages the grapes were sold to Hay Shed Hill; in the third year they went to Palandri. In 2001 the Tuckers decided to have the wine bottled under the Peacetree Estate label, and in 20002 they opened the cellar door – they haven't regretted the decision. A little semillon and merlot is also grown and made.

▼▼▼▼ **Semillon Sauvignon Blanc 2003** A gentle mix of blossom and more minerally aromas; a delicate palate; clever use of a touch of residual sugar. **RATING** 87 **DRINK** 2008 $ 19

Peacock Hill Vineyard ★★☆

29 Palmers Lane, Pokolbin, NSW 2320 **REGION** Lower Hunter Valley
T (02) 4998 7661 **F** (02) 4998 7661 **WEB** www.peacockhill.com.au **OPEN** Thurs–Mon, public & school hols 10–5, or by appointment
WINEMAKER George Tsiros, Bill Sneddon, Rod Russell (Contract) **EST.** 1969 **CASES** 1500
SUMMARY The Peacock Hill Vineyard was first planted in 1969 as part of the Rothbury Estate, originally being owned by a separate syndicate but then moving under the direct control and ownership of Rothbury. After several further changes of ownership as Rothbury sold many of its vineyards, George Tsiros and Silvi Laumets acquired the 8-ha property in October 1995. Since that time they have rejuvenated the vineyard and built a small but attractive accommodation lodge for two people. They have a tennis court and petanque rink for their exclusive enjoyment.

▼▼▼▽ **Good Company NV RATING** 85 **DRINK** Now $ 40

Pearson Vineyards NR

Main North Road, Penwortham, SA 5453 **REGION** Clare Valley
T (08) 8843 4234 **F** (08) 8843 4141 **OPEN** Mon–Fri 11–5, weekends 10–5
WINEMAKER Jim Pearson **EST.** 1993 **CASES** 800
SUMMARY Jim Pearson makes the Pearson Vineyard wines at Mintaro Cellars. The 1.5-ha estate vineyards surround the beautiful little stone house which acts as a cellar door – and which appears on the cover of my book, *The Wines, The History, The Vignerons of the Clare Valley.*

Peel Estate ★★★★

Fletcher Road, Baldivis, WA 6171 **REGION** Peel
T (08) 9524 1221 **F** (08) 9524 1625 **WEB** www.peelwine.com.au **OPEN** 7 days 10–5
WINEMAKER Will Nairn **EST.** 1974 **CASES** 6000
SUMMARY The icon wine is the Shiraz, a wine of considerable finesse and with a remarkably consistent track record. Every year Will Nairn holds a Great Shiraz Tasting for 6-year-old Australian Shirazs, and pits Peel Estate (in a blind tasting attended by 60 or so people) against Australia's best. It is never disgraced. The white wines are workmanlike, the wood-matured Chenin Blanc another winery specialty, although not achieving the excellence of the Shiraz. Exports to the UK, the US, Malaysia, Hong Kong and Japan.

ŶŶŶŶŶ **Shiraz 2000** Good colour; smooth, supple and silky medium-bodied wine; red and black fruits; well-balanced and integrated French and American oak. High-quality cork.
RATING 92 **DRINK** 2010 $ 36
Chardonnay 2003 Light to medium-bodied; melon and fig fruit; a gentle touch of barrel ferment; good length, structure and balance. Cork. **RATING** 90 **DRINK** 2008 $ 20
Chardonnay 2001 Complex nutty, oaky aromas; powerful deep and long palate; cashew, fig and stone fruit. Wet cork disregarded. **RATING** 90 **DRINK** 2007 $ 20
Wood Matured Chenin Blanc 2001 Ageing slowly and impressively; oak a subtle framework for honeydew and melon fruit, still relatively tight; good balance. Quality cork.
RATING 90 **DRINK** 2009 $ 21
Shiraz 1999 Elegant, fresh, medium-bodied; appealing cherry and plum red fruits; unexpected tweak of acidity on the finish. **RATING** 90 **DRINK** 2009 $ 36
Cabernet Sauvignon 2000 Rich, warm-grown, earthy, chocolatey overtones to a well of blackberry fruit; soft tannins, plenty of substance. **RATING** 90 $ 30

ŶŶŶŶ **Wood Matured Chenin Blanc 2000** Flavoursome wine with oak and bottle age adding to the character; complex, big hitter. **RATING** 89 **DRINK** Now $ 21
Baroque Shiraz Cremant 1994 Elegant, long and relatively dry; spicy red fruits; good length and balance; not phenolic. Surprise (sparkling) package. **RATING** 88 **DRINK** 2010 $ 55

ŶŶŶŶ **Sauvignon Blanc Chenin Blanc 2004** **RATING** 86 **DRINK** 2007 $ 14
Premium Red 2002 **RATING** 86 **DRINK** 2008 $ 16
Zinfandel 2000 Extraordinarily powerful, ripe and sweet; super-hot finish; an unfortified 18° alcohol monster; lots of tannins too. Guinness Book of Records. **RATING** 86
DRINK 2010 $ 35

ŶŶŶ **Verdelho 2004** **RATING** 83 **DRINK** 2007 $ 17
Verdelho 2003 **RATING** 83 $ 17

Peerick Vineyard ★★★★

Wild Dog Track, Moonambel, Vic 3478 **REGION** Pyrenees
T (03) 5467 2207 **F** (03) 5467 2207 **WEB** www.peerick.com.au **OPEN** Weekends & public hols 11–4
WINEMAKER Contract **EST.** 1990 **CASES** 3000
SUMMARY Peerick is the venture of Chris Jessup and wife Meryl. They have mildly trimmed their Joseph's coat vineyard by increasing the plantings to 5.6 ha and eliminating the malbec and semillon, but still grow cabernet sauvignon, shiraz, cabernet franc, merlot, sauvignon blanc and viognier. Quality has improved as the vines have approached maturity. Exports to New Zealand.

ŶŶŶŶŶ **Viognier 2004** Complex, multi-flavoured; strong barrel ferment influence; creamy apricot flavours, twist of lemon to close. Cork. **RATING** 90 **DRINK** 2007 $ 22.50
Shiraz 2002 Very good colour; attractive juicy berry red and black fruits; lively, good length. **RATING** 90 **DRINK** 2012 $ 20

ŶŶŶŶ **Shiraz Viognier 2003** Disappointing colour for the blend; nice spicy, savoury texture and mouthfeel. Stained cork. **RATING** 89 **DRINK** 2009 $ 28
Cabernet Sauvignon 2002 Similar developed colour; fine, savoury texture and structure; elegant, light to medium-bodied; some red and black fruits. Cork. **RATING** 89 **DRINK** 2012 $ 22.50
Sauvignon Blanc 2004 Delicate, precise and fresh; partial barrel ferment all but invisible; nice line and flow. Clean. Screwcap. **RATING** 88 **DRINK** Now $ 17
Merlot 2002 Developed colour; light to medium-bodied; quite good varietal character; slippery/savoury/lemony cast to the fruit. Cork. **RATING** 87 **DRINK** 2010 $ 18.50

Pegeric Vineyard   NR

PO Box 227, Woodend, Vic 3442 **REGION** Macedon Ranges
T (03) 9354 4961 **F** (03) 9354 4961 **OPEN** Not
WINEMAKER Chris Cormack, Ian Gunter, Llew Knight (Contract) **EST.** 1987 **CASES** 100
SUMMARY Owner and viticulturist Chris Cormack accumulated an oenological degree and experience
in every facet of the wine industry here and overseas before beginning the establishment of the close-
planted, non-irrigated, low-yielding Pegeric Vineyard at an altitude of 640m on red volcanic basalt
soil. As a separate exercise, he has also made several vintages of a cross-regional blend of Cabernet
Shiraz named Tumbetin. He has recently planted a small block of riesling.

Pembroke   NR

Richmond Road, Cambridge, Tas 7170 **REGION** Southern Tasmania
T (03) 6248 5139 **F** (03) 6234 5481 **WEB** www.pembrokewines.com **OPEN** By appointment
WINEMAKER Andrew Hood (Contract) **EST.** 1980 **CASES** 300
SUMMARY The 2.2-ha Pembroke vineyard was established in 1980 by the McKay and Hawker families
and is still owned by them. It is predominantly planted to pinot noir and chardonnay, with tiny
quantities of riesling and sauvignon blanc.

Penbro Estate

Cnr Melba Highway/Murrindindi Road, Glenburn, Vic 3717 **REGION** Upper Goulburn
T 0408 548 717 **F** (03) 9215 2346 **WEB** www.penbroestate.com.au **OPEN** At Glenburn Pub
WINEMAKER Scott McCarthy (Contract) **EST.** 1997 **CASES** 3200
SUMMARY Since 1997 the Bertalli family has established 40 ha of premium cool-climate vineyards on
their highly regarded Black Angus cattle farm. The vineyards are high up in the rolling hills of the
Great Dividing Range, flanked by the Toolangi Forest and the alluvial plains of the Yea River, halfway
between Yarra Glen and Yea. Part of the grape production is sold. Distribution in Victoria by The
Wine Group.

ŢŢŢŢ   **Chardonnay 2003** Restrained but quite complex malolactic and barrel ferment inputs;
creamy cashew, fig and melon; older oak used. Cork. **RATING** 89 **DRINK** 2008 $ 19.95
Shiraz 2003 Attractive, light to medium-bodied; supple black fruits, spice and well-
integrated oak; fine tannins; good length. Grossly misleading silver medal on the label
awarded to the '02 vintage at the '03 Victorian Wines Show. Quality cork. **RATING** 89
DRINK 2009 $ 21.50
Pinot Noir 2003 Medium-bodied; strongly savoury, foresty, spicy background to plum
fruit and fine tannins. Stained, creased cork. **RATING** 88 **DRINK** 2007 $ 21.60
Unwooded Chardonnay 2004 Light, fresh grapefruit and melon; has length rather than
depth, but nonetheless a good example of the style. Screwcap. **RATING** 87 **DRINK** Now
$ 18.45
Merlot 2003 Medium-bodied; olive, spice, leaf and berry; fruit varietal character good;
tannins assertive. Cork. **RATING** 87 **DRINK** 2008 $ 21.50
Cabernet Sauvignon 2003 Light to medium-bodied; sweet cassis berry fruit; light
tannins, minimal oak; role reversion with Merlot. Cork. **RATING** 87 **DRINK** 2009 $ 21.50

Pendarves Estate

110 Old North Road, Belford, NSW 2335 **REGION** Lower Hunter Valley
T (02) 6574 7222 **F** (02) 9970 6152 **OPEN** Weekends 11–5, Mon–Fri by appointment
WINEMAKER Greg Silkman (Contract) **EST.** 1986 **CASES** 12 000
SUMMARY The perpetual-motion general practitioner and founder of the Australian Medical Friends
of Wine, Dr Philip Norrie, is a born communicator and marketer as well as a wine historian of note.
He also happens to be a passionate advocate of the virtues of Verdelho, inspired in part by the high
regard held for that variety by vignerons around the turn of the century. His ambassadorship for the
cause of wine and health, in Australia and overseas, has led to a joint venture to produce and export a
large-volume brand, 'The Wine Doctor'; exports to Singapore, the UK, Germany, China, India,
Russia and Malaysia (and national distribution).

Penfolds ★★★★★

Tanunda Road, Nuriootpa, SA 5355 **REGION** Barossa Valley
T (08) 8568 9290 **F** (08) 8568 9493 **WEB** www.penfolds.com.au **OPEN** Mon–Fri 10–5, weekends & public hols 11–5
WINEMAKER Peter Gago **EST.** 1844 **CASES** 1.4 million
SUMMARY Senior among the numerous wine companies or stand-alone brands in Southcorp Wines and undoubtedly one of the top wine companies in the world in terms of quality, product range and exports. The consistency of the quality of the red wines and their value for money is recognised worldwide; the white wines, headed by the ultra-premium Yattarna Chardonnay, are steadily improving in quality.

🍷🍷🍷🍷🍷 **Yattarna Chardonnay 2002** Bright, light green-straw; complex, toasty barrel ferment aromas; very elegant, tight and refined; white peach, nectarine and citrus; long, clean finish. Cork. **RATING** 96 **DRINK** 2012 $ 119.95

Grange 2000 Good depth to the colour; seamless blackberry fruit and vanilla/cedar oak; abundant power and concentration; sultry blackberry, dark chocolate and spice; persistent but balanced tannins. Exceptional outcome for an ordinary vintage; obviously strict selection criteria used. Stained cork broke on extraction. **RATING** 96 **DRINK** 2025 $ 400

Reserve Bin Adelaide Hills Semillon 2000 Bright yellow-green; top-class example of barrel-fermented Semillon in quality French oak; both fruit and oak have full expression, yet both are seamlessly balanced and integrated. Quality cork. **RATING** 95 **DRINK** 2010 $ 19.50

Reserve Bin Chardonnay 2003 Bin 03A. Very complex, toasty, charry barrel ferment aromas; intense, fine melon, citrus and white peach fruit more than holds its own with the oak; long, elegant finish. Needs time. Screwcap. **RATING** 95 **DRINK** 2011 $ 79.95

Yattarna Chardonnay 2001 Super-refined and elegant cashew and stone fruit; a very pure wine; long future. **RATING** 95 **DRINK** 2011 $ 95

Cellar Reserve Grenache 2002 Intense raspberry/blackberry aromas, then a rich, beautifully textured and structured palate; fine tannins and superb mouthfeel. **RATING** 95 **DRINK** 2012 $ 45

Bin 707 Cabernet Sauvignon 2002 Powerful blackberry, earth fruit punctuates both bouquet and palate; intense, no-compromise tannins; has chewed up the oak; long finish. High-quality cork showing overflow stain. **RATING** 95 **DRINK** 2027 $ 143.95

RWT Shiraz 2002 Deep colour; lots of new French oak on both bouquet and palate, but also plenty of dark fruits; very good mouthfeel and texture, ripe tannins; given the benefit of the oak doubt. Quality cork, but, surprisingly, stained. **RATING** 94 **DRINK** 2017 $ 143.95

RWT Shiraz 2001 Powerful blackberry fruit aromas; similarly powerful and concentrated dark fruit palate; oak and tannin extract in balance. **RATING** 94 **DRINK** 2021 $ 120

Old Vine Barossa Valley Bin 138 Grenache Shiraz Mourvedre 2003 A luscious array of red and black fruit aromas; powerful wine in the mouth, much more in the direction of black fruits; good tannin and oak; no cosmetics. Cork. **RATING** 94 **DRINK** 2013 $ 25

Bin 389 Cabernet Shiraz 2002 Powerful but silky smooth; elegance and fruit freshness beyond the normal; black fruits running through the length of the palate; ripe tannins, restrained oak. Another testament to 2002. Cork. **RATING** 94 **DRINK** 2022 $ 42.90

🍷🍷🍷🍷🍸 **Kalimna Bin 28 Shiraz 2002** Fragrant black fruits, earth, spice and vanilla; medium-bodied; very good structure, flow and mouthfeel; at the elegant end of the '02 spectrum (14.5° alcohol). Cork. **RATING** 93 **DRINK** 2013 $ 25

Eden Valley Riesling 2004 Spotlessly clean; lime, mineral, slate and herb; distinct spritz ex CO_2 will diminish, but demands longer-term cellaring. Screwcap. **RATING** 91 **DRINK** 2016 $ 25.95

Thomas Hyland Shiraz 2002 Opulent black fruits so typical of the vintage; medium-bodied; excellent balance and mouthfeel. Cork. **RATING** 91 **DRINK** 2012 $ 19.95

Bin 128 Coonawarra Shiraz 2002 Solid blackberry and damson plum fruit, with a nice twist of spice; powerful, long finish. **RATING** 91 **DRINK** 2012 $ 24.90

Bin 407 Cabernet Sauvignon 2002 Medium-bodied; savoury black fruits, earth and spice; well-balanced oak; very good, but not great in the context of the vintage. Cork. **RATING** 91 **DRINK** 2012 $ 30.50

Cellar Reserve Sangiovese 2003 Smoky bacon spice and red cherry aromas and flavours; fine tannins; left field, perhaps. **RATING** 91 **DRINK** 2007 $ 45

Eden Valley Reserve Riesling 2004 Gentle citrus and lime juice; moderately intense; good balance. **RATING** 90 **DRINK** 2010 $ 24.95

Cellar Reserve Adelaide Hills Pinot Noir 2002 Powerful, dense, complex and concentrated, bordering on dry red; will be long-lived, and may develop more varietal character; certainly has abundant fruit. Quality cork. **RATING** 90 **DRINK** 2013 $ 41.90
St Henri Shiraz 2000 Black cherry and blackcurrant aromas; moves up a gear on the back palate and finish; mix of spicy, savoury notes. **RATING** 90 **DRINK** 2010 $ 60
Koonunga Hill Shiraz Cabernet 2002 Excellent blackberry and blackcurrant fruit aromas and flavours; velvety tannins and subtle oak. **RATING** 90 **DRINK** 2012 $ 14

ΥΥΥΥ **Koonunga Hill Semillon Sauvignon Blanc 2004** Fresh, tangy, mineral herb, citrus and gooseberry fruit; lively finish; nice wine. Screwcap. **RATING** 89 **DRINK** 2008 $ 14.95
Thomas Hyland Chardonnay 2003 Gentle nectarine and melon fruit; medium-bodied; well-integrated and balanced oak. **RATING** 89 **DRINK** Now $ 19
Koonunga Hill Shiraz 2002 Medium-bodied but quite complex; soft blackberry and vanilla flavours; soft, ripe tannins. Screwcap. **RATING** 89 **DRINK** 2012 $ 14.95
Thomas Hyland Cabernet Sauvignon 2002 Savoury, earthy blackcurrant fruit; relatively austere, but long. Cork. **RATING** 89 **DRINK** 2010 $ 19.95
Thomas Hyland Shiraz 2003 Medium-bodied; a typical mix of black fruits and vanilla oak; soft tannins. Cork. **RATING** 88 **DRINK** 2010 $ 18.50
Rawson's Retreat Chardonnay 2004 Well-balanced stone fruit, melon and fig; squeaky acidity; fresh finish. Synthetic. **RATING** 87 **DRINK** 2008 $ 9.99
Club Reserve Aged Tawny NV A more than useful style at the price; lots of biscuit, caramel and Christmas cake showing aged components. **RATING** 87 **DRINK** Now $ 12.95

ΥΥΥϘ **Koonunga Hill Cabernet Merlot 2002** **RATING** 86 **DRINK** 2007 $ 14
Rawson's Retreat Riesling 2004 **RATING** 85 **DRINK** Now $ 9.99
Rawson's Retreat Chardonnay 2003 **RATING** 85 **DRINK** Now $ 9.99
Koonunga Hill Semillon Chardonnay 2003 **RATING** 85 **DRINK** Now $ 14
Killawarra Non Vintage Brut NV **RATING** 85 **DRINK** Now $ 10.65
Koonunga Hill Chardonnay 2003 **RATING** 84 **DRINK** Now $ 14

Penfolds Magill Estate ★★★★☆

78 Penfold Road, Magill, SA 5072 **REGION** Adelaide Zone
T (08) 8301 5569 **F** (08) 8301 5588 **WEB** www.penfolds.com.au **OPEN** 7 days 10.30–4.30
WINEMAKER Peter Gago **EST.** 1844 **CASES** NFP
SUMMARY The birthplace of Penfolds, established by Dr Christopher Rawson Penfold in 1844; his house is still part of the immaculately maintained property. It includes: 6 ha of precious shiraz used to make Magill Estate; the original and subsequent winery buildings, most still in operation or in museum condition; Penfolds' corporate headquarters; and the much-acclaimed Magill Restaurant, with panoramic views back to the city, a great wine list and fine dining. All this a 20-minute drive from Adelaide's CBD.

ΥΥΥΥϘ **Shiraz 2002** Medium-bodied; fine, elegant, spicy, cedary, savoury aspects to restrained but balanced black fruits; fine, ripe tannins. Cork. **RATING** 92 **DRINK** 2017 $ 79.95

Penley Estate ★★★★☆

McLeans Road, Coonawarra, SA 5263 **REGION** Coonawarra
T (08) 8736 3211 **F** (08) 8736 3124 **WEB** www.penley.com.au **OPEN** 7 days 10–4
WINEMAKER Kym Tolley **EST.** 1988 **CASES** 50 000
SUMMARY Owner winemaker Kym Tolley describes himself as a fifth-generation winemaker, the family tree involving both the Penfolds and the Tolleys. He worked 17 years in the industry before establishing Penley Estate and has made every post a winner since, producing a succession of rich, complex, full-bodied red wines and stylish Chardonnays. These are made from 91 ha of estate plantings. Exports to all major markets.

ΥΥΥΥΥ **Reserve Coonawarra Cabernet Sauvignon 2002** Classic restraint; blackcurrant, cassis and blackberry, subliminal earth; perfect tannin structure and oak handling. Cork. **RATING** 95 **DRINK** 2022 $ 62

ΥΥΥΥϘ **Ausvetia Shiraz 2002** Complex array of red and black fruit aromas and flavours plus spice components; 24 months in oak largely integrated. Brittle cork. **RATING** 92 **DRINK** 2017 $ 75.30

Phoenix Cabernet Sauvignon 2003 Medium-bodied; very attractive sweet blackcurrant and cassis mix; fine tannins; subtle oak works well. Cork. **RATING** 90 **DRINK** 2013 $ 24

ŢŢŢŢ **Special Select Coonawarra Shiraz 2002** Vibrant, fresh and lively; some spice, mint and leaf overtones to berry fruit; belies its 14.5° alcohol. Stained cork. **RATING** 89 **DRINK** 2012 $ 62

Shiraz Cabernet Sauvignon 2002 Medium-bodied; balanced and elegant; cedar, blackcurrant and blackberry; integrated oak, fine tannins. Cork. **RATING** 89 **DRINK** 2010 $ 29.70

Pinot Noir Chardonnay 1997 Strong mousse; very fine and tight; crisp acidity; just a fraction lean. **RATING** 89 **DRINK** 2007 $ 33.20

Hyland Shiraz 2003 Medium-bodied; well balanced, the fruit tending savoury; has particularly good length. **RATING** 87 **DRINK** 2010 $ 20.50

Chardonnay 2003 Ripe, soft peach and stone fruit, with some oak-push; alcohol shows. **RATING** 87 **DRINK** Now $ 19.50

ŢŢŢ **Pinot 2003 RATING** 83 $ 15
Over The Moon 2004 RATING 83 $ 17.99

Penmara ★★☆

Bridge Street, Muswellbrook, NSW 2333 **REGION** Upper Hunter Valley
T (02) 9362 5157 **F** (02) 9362 5157 **WEB** www.penmarawines.com.au **OPEN** Not
WINEMAKER John Horden **EST.** 2000 **CASES** 30 000
SUMMARY Penmara was formed with the banner '5 Vineyards: 1 Vision'. In fact a sixth vineyard has already joined the group, the vineyards pooling most of their grapes, with a central processing facility, and marketing focused exclusively on exports. The members are Lilyvale Vineyards, in the Northern Slopes region near Tenterfield; Tangaratta Vineyards at Tamworth; Birnam Wood, Rothbury Ridge and Martindale Vineyards in the Hunter Valley; and Highland Heritage at Orange. In all these vineyards give Penmara access to 128 ha of shiraz, chardonnay, cabernet sauvignon, semillon, verdelho and merlot. Exports to the US, Canada, Singapore and Japan.

ŢŢŢŢ **Reserve Shiraz 2002 RATING** 86 **DRINK** 2007 $ 17.95

ŢŢŢ **Five Families Chardonnay 2003 RATING** 83 $ 11.95
The Five Families Orange Pinot Noir 2002 RATING 80 $ 14.95

Penna Lane Wines ★★★★

Lot 51, Penna Lane, Penwortham via Clare, SA 5453 **REGION** Clare Valley
T (08) 8843 4364 **F** (08) 8843 4349 **WEB** www.pennalanewines.com.au **OPEN** Thurs–Sun & public hols 11–5, or by appointment
WINEMAKER Contract **EST.** 1998 **CASES** 3500
SUMMARY Ray and Lynette Klavin, then living and working near Waikerie in the Riverland, purchased their 14-ha property in the Skilly Hills in 1993. It was covered with rubbish, Salvation Jane, a derelict dairy and a tumbledown piggery, and every weekend they travelled from Waikerie to clean up the property, initially living in a tent and thereafter moving into the dairy, which had more recently been used as a shearing shed. Planting began in 1996, and in 1997 the family moved to the region, Lynette to take up a teaching position and Ray to work at Knappstein Wines. Ray had enrolled at Roseworthy in 1991, and met Stephen Stafford-Brookes, another mature-age student. Both graduated from Roseworthy in 1993, having already formed a winemaking joint venture for Penna Lane. Picnic and barbecue facilities are available at the cellar door, and light lunches are served. Exports to the US.

ŢŢŢŢŢ **Riesling 2004** Glowing yellow-green; herb and spice aromas moving to touches of lime and more tropical fruit on the generous mid-palate. Screwcap. **RATING** 90 **DRINK** 2010 $ 19

ŢŢŢŢ **Semillon 2004** Complex flavours and aromas; spicy oak contribution; mid-palate sweet citrus fruit delivers more than the finish. Partial barrel ferment. Screwcap. **RATING** 89 **DRINK** 2009 $ 17

Rambling Rose 2004 More light-bodied dry red than conventional Rose; cherry and raspberry; unconventional but works well; good balance. Screwcap. **RATING** 89 **DRINK** 2007 $ 18

Pennyfield Wines

Pennyfield Road, Berri, SA 5343 **REGION** Riverland
T (08) 8582 3595 **F** (08) 8582 3205 **WEB** www.pennyfieldwines.com.au **OPEN** Not
WINEMAKER David Smallacombe **EST.** 2000 **CASES** 3500
SUMMARY Pennyfield Wines is named in memory of the pioneering family which originally developed the property, part of which is now owned by the Efrosinis family. Pennyfield draws on 17.7 ha of estate vineyards (principally planted to cabernet sauvignon and shiraz) but is also supplied with chardonnay, merlot, petit verdot, touriga and viognier by four local growers. It is also part of Riverland Boutique Wines Incorporated, which has over 20 members with, or soon to be with, producer's licences. Exports to the US, Canada, Denmark, Hong Kong, China and Japan.

▼▼▼▼ **Viognier 2004** Rich, ripe texture and mouthfeel; 14.5° alcohol elevates tropical flavour, but balanced by good acidity on the finish. Part barrel ferment. Poor cork. **RATING** 88 **DRINK** 2007 $ 20
Basket Pressed Shiraz Viognier 2003 Light to medium-bodied; a supple and smooth array of red and black fruits; a touch of apricot ex Viognier; fine tannins. Dodgy cork. **RATING** 88 **DRINK** 2008 $ 20
Late Picked Viognier 2004 Plenty of flavour with abundant tropical pastille and vanilla; sweetness is not very obvious, but it is there. **RATING** 88 **DRINK** 2009 $ 20
Basket Pressed Cabernet Sauvignon 2003 Powerful, very ripe black fruits; prune, dark chocolate and licorice; slightly over the top. **RATING** 87 **DRINK** 2010 $ 22

▼▼▼▽ **Cragg's Creek Cabernet Merlot 2003** **RATING** 85 **DRINK** 2007 $ 13
Liqueur Chardonnay Viognier 2004 **RATING** 85 **DRINK** Now $ 20
Cragg's Creek Shiraz Cabernet 2003 **RATING** 84 **DRINK** Now $ 13

Penny's Hill ★★★★☆

Main Road, McLaren Vale, SA 5171 **REGION** McLaren Vale
T (08) 8556 4460 **F** (08) 8556 4462 **WEB** www.pennyshill.com.au **OPEN** 7 days 10–5
WINEMAKER Ben Riggs (Contract) **EST.** 1988 **CASES** 11 500
SUMMARY Penny's Hill is owned by Adelaide advertising agency businessman Tony Parkinson and wife Susie. The Penny's Hill vineyard is 43.5 ha and, unusually for McLaren Vale, is close-planted with a thin vertical trellis/thin vertical canopy, the work of consultant viticulturist David Paxton. The innovative red dot packaging was the inspiration of Tony Parkinson, recalling the red dot sold sign on pictures in an art gallery and now giving rise to the Red Dot Art Gallery opening at Penny's Hill. Exports to the UK, the US and other major markets.

▼▼▼▼▼ **Footprint McLaren Vale Shiraz 2002** Significantly richer and riper than the standard wine; luscious blackcurrant, plum, prune and chocolate fruit; controlled oak and tannins. **RATING** 95 **DRINK** 2017 $ 40

▼▼▼▼▽ **Shiraz 2002** Redolent with regional chocolate and earth overtones to the blackberry fruit; fine tannins. **RATING** 92 **DRINK** 2012 $ 29

▼▼▼▼ **Red Dot Chardonnay Viognier 2004** An intriguing varietal fruit mix with lemon pastille from the Viognier; entirely fruit-driven; nice feel. **RATING** 88 **DRINK** 2007 $ 16.13
Specialized Shiraz Cabernet Merlot 2003 Very powerful and dense; masses of flavour but slightly dead fruit characters, and hence too much extract. **RATING** 88 **DRINK** 2009 $ 24.99
Goss Corner Semillon 2003 Still-water white; light to medium-bodied; lemony-accented fruit; soft acidity and a hint of sweetness. **RATING** 87 **DRINK** 2007 $ 18.50
Red Dot Fleurieu Shiraz 2003 Archetypal regional mix of blackberry and dark chocolate in a sweet fruit base; controversial Zork closure. **RATING** 87 **DRINK** Now $ 17.75
McLaren Vale Cadenzia Grenache 2003 Jammy, juicy varietal fruit; pleasantly fruity, early-drinking style. Zork. **RATING** 87 **DRINK** Now $ 22.60

Pennyweight Winery ★★★

Pennyweight Lane, Beechworth, Vic 3747 **REGION** Beechworth
T (03) 5728 1747 **F** (03) 5728 1704 **WEB** www.pennyweight.com.au **OPEN** 7 days 10–5
WINEMAKER Stephen Newton Morris **EST.** 1982 **CASES** 1000

SUMMARY Pennyweight was established by Stephen Morris, great-grandson of GF Morris, founder of Morris Wines. The 4 ha of vines are not irrigated and are organically grown. The business is run by Stephen, together with his wife Elizabeth and assisted by their three sons; Elizabeth Morris says, 'It's a perfect world', suggesting that Pennyweight is more than happy with its lot in life.

ＹＹＹＹ **Beechworth Cabernet Sauvignon Cabernet Franc Merlot 2002** **RATING** 85 **DRINK** 2008 $ 26

Peos Estate ★★★

Graphite Road, Manjimup, WA 6258 **REGION** Manjimup
T (08) 9772 1378 **F** (08) 9772 1372 **WEB** www.peosestate.com.au **OPEN** 7 days 10–4
WINEMAKER Shane McKerrow (Contract) **EST.** 1996 **CASES** 3000
SUMMARY The Peos family has farmed the West Manjimup district for 50 years, the third generation of four brothers commencing the development of a substantial vineyard in 1996; there is a little over 33 ha of vines, with shiraz (10 ha), merlot (7 ha), chardonnay (6.5 ha), cabernet sauvignon (4 ha) and pinot noir, sauvignon blanc and verdelho (2 ha each). Exports to Denmark.

Pepperton Estate ★★★☆

c/- Australian Wine Supply, 74 Chandos Street, St Leonards, NSW 2065 (postal) **REGION** Southeast Australia
T (02) 9906 3061 **F** (02) 9906 3081 **OPEN** Not
WINEMAKER Contract **EST.** 2002 **CASES** NA
SUMMARY Pepperton Estate is another virtual winery, with three ranges: at the bottom Goodwyn, exclusively for on-premise; in the middle, Two Thumbs; and at the top, Pepperton Estate.

ＹＹＹＹ **Two Thumbs Sauvignon Blanc 2004** Clean, crisp and correct; subtle but clear-cut varietal flavours, passionfruit and lemon; good length and line. Alpine and King Valleys. Screwcap. **RATING** 89 **DRINK** 2007
Two Thumbs Chardonnay 2004 Quite fragrant citrus and nectarine; clean and fresh, good acidity; light-bodied, no sign of oak. Frankland and Margaret Rivers. Screwcap. **RATING** 87 **DRINK** 2007
Two Thumbs Frankland River Shiraz 2003 Deep colour; powerful black fruits and savoury tannins; needs time. **RATING** 87 **DRINK** 2010 $ 14.99

ＹＹＹＹ **The Regional Classics Adelaide Hills Chardonnay 2003** **RATING** 86 **DRINK** Now $ 18.99
The Regional Classics Clare Shiraz 2002 **RATING** 86 **DRINK** 2007 $ 18.99
The Regional Classics Coonawarra Cabernet Sauvignon 2002 **RATING** 85 **DRINK** 2007 $ 18.99

ＹＹＹ **The Regional Classics King Valley Sauvignon Blanc 2002** **RATING** 83 $ 18.99
Two Thumbs Chardonnay 2003 **RATING** 82 $ 14.99

Pepper Tree Wines ★★★★☆

Halls Road, Pokolbin, NSW 2321 **REGION** Lower Hunter Valley
T (02) 4998 7539 **F** (02) 4998 7746 **WEB** www.peppertreewines.com.au **OPEN** Mon–Fri 9–5, weekends 9.30–5
WINEMAKER Chris Cameron **EST.** 1993 **CASES** 50 000
SUMMARY The Pepper Tree winery is part of the complex which also contains The Convent guesthouse and Roberts Restaurant. In October 2002 it was acquired by a company controlled by Dr John Davis, who owns 50% of Briar Ridge and has substantial vineyard interests throughout NSW and SA. Pepper Tree has made a determined, and quite successful, effort to establish its reputation as one of Australia's leading producers of Merlot. Exports to the UK, the US and other major markets.

ＹＹＹＹＹ **Grand Reserve Hunter Valley Shiraz 2003** Strong colour; lush, ripe red and black cherry fruit reflecting the vintage; good balance and length with controlled oak extract. Cork. **RATING** 94 **DRINK** 2018 $ 50

ＹＹＹＹＹ **Grand Reserve Wrattonbully Shiraz 2003** Generous, medium to full-bodied; plum and blackberry fruit; good texture and length; nice oak. **RATING** 93 **DRINK** 2013 $ 50

Grand Reserve Coonawarra Cabernet Sauvignon 2002 Deep, dense red-purple; rich, layered blackcurrant fruit; oak and tannins fully ripe but not over the top. RATING 93 DRINK 2017 $50

Reserve Hunter Valley Museum Release Semillon 1995 Bright green-yellow; lime, honey and some toast, still with a spine of acidity. The saturated, wet cork limits the future of a very good wine. RATING 91 DRINK 2007 $35

Sauvignon Blanc Semillon 2004 Clean, fresh, crisp and lively, the blend working well with lively varietal Sauvignon Blanc leading the way; 41% Marlborough (NZ) Sauvignon Blanc/Orange Sauvignon Blanc/Hunter Semillon. Screwcap. RATING 90 DRINK Now $18

▼▼▼▼ **Reserve Orange Chardonnay 2004** Quite delicate; sweet apple and melon fruit with a touch of creamy cashew. Cork. RATING 89 DRINK 2007 $23

Reserve Wrattonbully Chardonnay 2004 Light to medium-bodied, elegant and restrained; grapefruit and passionfruit; subliminal oak. Screwcap. RATING 89 DRINK 2008 $23

Reserve Orange Shiraz 2003 Good colour; bright, lively, spicy berry fruit; quite long, a brisk finish. Cork. RATING 89 DRINK 2008 $30

▼▼▼▽ **Grand Reserve Wrattonbully Chardonnay 2003** RATING 86 DRINK Now $41

Reserve Orange Verduzzo 2004 RATING 85 DRINK 2007 $27

Peppin Ridge ★★★★

Peppin Drive, Bonnie Doon, Vic 3720 REGION Upper Goulburn
T (03) 5778 7430 F (03) 5778 7430 OPEN 7 days 11–5
WINEMAKER Don Adams EST. 1997 CASES 400
SUMMARY Peppin Ridge is planted on the shores of Lake Eildon; the land forms part of a vast station property established in 1850, and now partly under Lake Eildon. The property in question was then acquired by the Peppin family, who developed the Peppin Merino sheep, said to be the cornerstone of the Australian wool industry. The plantings of marsanne, verdelho, shiraz and merlot cover 4 ha, and the wine is made onsite.

▼▼▼▼▽ **Shiraz 2002** Licorice, spice, blackberry and blackcurrant; perfect ripeness; supple and long. Good cork. RATING 92 DRINK 2015 $20

▼▼▼▼ **Merlot 2003** Aromatic cherry/red fruits with hints of mint and leaf; juicy style; fine tannins, minimal oak. RATING 89 DRINK 2011 $18

Perrini Estate NR

Bower Road, Meadows, SA 5201 REGION Adelaide Hills
T (08) 8388 3210 F (08) 8388 3210 OPEN Wed–Sun & public hols 10–5
WINEMAKER Antonio Perrini EST. 1997 CASES 3500
SUMMARY Perrini Estate is very much a family affair; Tony and Connie Perrini had spent their working life in the retail food business, and Tony purchased the land in 1988 as a hobby farm and retirement home (or so he told Connie). In 1990 Tony planted his first few grapevines, began to read everything he could about making wine, and thereafter obtained vintage experience at a local winery. Next came highly successful entries into amateur winemaker competitions, and that was that. Together the family established the 6 ha of vineyard and built the winery and cellar door. The first commercial releases came with the 1997 vintage; production has steadily increased since. Exports to Singapore.

Pertaringa

Cnr Hunt Road/Rifle Range Road, McLaren Vale, SA 5171 REGION McLaren Vale
T (08) 8323 8125 F (08) 8323 7766 WEB www.pertaringa.com.au OPEN Mon–Fri 10–5, weekends & public hols 11–5
WINEMAKER Geoff Hardy, Ben Riggs EST. 1980 CASES 15 000
SUMMARY The Pertaringa wines are made from part of the grapes grown by by leading viticulturists Geoff Hardy and Ian Leask. The Pertaringa vineyard of 31 ha was acquired in 1980 and rejuvenated. The ultra-cool Kuitpo vineyard in the Adelaide Hills was begun in 1987 and now supplies leading makers such as Southcorp and Petaluma. Retail distribution through South Australia, New South Wales, Victoria and Queensland; exports to Germany, Switzerland, Denmark, Hong Kong, Malaysia, Canada and the US.

▼▼▼▼▼ **Over The Top Shiraz 2002** Deeply coloured, with a wonderful array of luscious black fruits, dark chocolate and ripe tannins. The handling of the French and American oak is faultless. **RATING** 95 **DRINK** 2017 $ 30

▼▼▼▼♀ **Undercover McLaren Vale Shiraz 2003** Fully ripe prune, blackberry, spice and bitter chocolate; medium to full-bodied; good length. Screwcap. **RATING** 91 **DRINK** 2015 $ 20

▼▼▼▼ **Two Gentlemen's Grenache 2002** Much more structure and texture than is often the case with grenache; spicy red and black fruits; savoury underlay. **RATING** 89 **DRINK** 2007 $ 18
Rifle & Hunt Cabernet Sauvignon 2002 Distinctly savoury/earthy/leafy overtones to black fruits; medium-bodied, with tannins to match. **RATING** 87 **DRINK** 2010 $ 30

▼▼▼♀ **Scarecrow Sauvignon Blanc 2004** Fresh herbs and spices to a background of citrus/lemon fruit; light-bodied. **RATING** 86 **DRINK** Now $ 15
The Final Fronti 2004 RATING 86 **DRINK** Now $ 15

Peschar's   NR

179 Wambo Road, Bulga, NSW 2330 **REGION** Lower Hunter Valley
T (02) 4927 1588 **F** (02) 4927 1589 **WEB** www.peschar.com.au **OPEN** Not
WINEMAKER Tyrrell's (Contract) **EST.** 1995 **CASES** 8000
SUMMARY In 1995 John and Mary Peschar purchased the historic Meerea Park property; it had been in the ownership of the Eather family, and the name continues to be used by the Eathers for a quite separate winemaking operation. The property acquired by the Peschars is at the foot of the Wollemi National Park, which rises steeply behind the vineyard, which is planted on sandy alluvial soils. There are 16 ha of chardonnay. While the focus is on Chardonnay, the Peschars have sourced 6 ha of vines in the Limestone Coast Zone (South Australia) for the production of Shiraz and Cabernet Merlot.

Petaluma   ★★★★★

Spring Gully Road, Piccadilly, SA 5151 **REGION** Adelaide Hills
T (08) 8339 9300 **F** (08) 8339 9301 **WEB** www.petaluma.com.au **OPEN** At Bridgewater Mill, Mount Barker Road, Bridgewater
WINEMAKER Brian Croser **EST.** 1976 **CASES** 30 000
SUMMARY The Petaluma empire comprises Knappstein Wines, Mitchelton, Stonier and Smithbrook. In late 2001 the Petaluma group was acquired by New Zealand brewer Lion Nathan, but left Brian Croser in place. Croser has never compromised his fierce commitment to quality, and doubtless never will. The Riesling is almost monotonously good; the Chardonnay is a category leader, the Merlot another marvellously succulent wine to buy without hesitation. Bridgewater Mill is the second label, which consistently provides wines most makers would love to have as their top label. Exports to the UK, the US and Japan.

▼▼▼▼▼ **Adelaide Hills Shiraz 2002** Very complex lifted aromas and flavours ex 5% Viognier; black cherry, blackberry and spice; perfect oak; excellent mouthfeel and structure. High-class wine. **RATING** 96 **DRINK** 2017 $ 42
Tiers Chardonnay 2002 Spice and cashew inputs to the bouquet, then a super-fine palate hastening slowly; apple and stone fruit have swallowed up the oak; great length and persistence. High-quality cork. **RATING** 95 **DRINK** 2012
Hanlin Hill Riesling 2004 Intensely floral aromas of apple blossom, a touch of passionfruit and a twist of lime lead into a very well balanced and long palate, with a core of minerally acidity. **RATING** 94 **DRINK** 2014 $ 23
Piccadilly Vineyard Chardonnay 2003 An exercise in delicate, refined elegance; a mix of apple, stone fruit and grapefruit flavours with super-fine oak; lovely squeaky acidity. High-quality cork. **RATING** 94 **DRINK** 2011
Piccadilly Vineyard Chardonnay 2002 Elegant and refined; pear, apple and stone fruit in a fine skein of oak; impeccable balance and length. **RATING** 94 **DRINK** 2010 $ 42
Summertown Chardonnay 2001 Unmistakable Petaluma style; ripe apple, pear and stone fruit; textural complexity from barrel ferment and malolactic ferment, yet flavour inputs subtle. High-quality cork. **RATING** 94 **DRINK** 2011
Adelaide Hills Viogner 2003 B+V Vineyard. Excellent balance and profile; none of the often cloying characters; unusually crisp finish thanks to acidity. Clever barrel fermentation inputs. **RATING** 94 **DRINK** 2007 $ 38

Coonawarra 2002 Strong purple-red colour; an attractive medium-bodied mix of blackcurrant, cedar, mocha and earth; ripe tannins; excellent mouthfeel and texture. High-quality cork. **RATING** 94 **DRINK** 2015

Croser 2002 As ever, very fine and discreet; immaculately balanced pear and stone fruit with a touch of creamy brioche. **RATING** 94 **DRINK** 2007 $ 36

♥♥♥♥ **Bridgewater Mill Three Districts Sauvignon Blanc 2004** Clean, crisp and minerally aromas; light tropical fruit; good length and balance. **RATING** 89 **DRINK** Now $ 20

Bridgewater Mill Chardonnay 2001 Nice wine; plenty of weight and richness to the pear and stone fruit flavours; subtle oak. **RATING** 89 **DRINK** 2007 $ 21

Peter Howland Wines ★★★★

2/14 Portside Crescent, Wickham, NSW 2293 **REGION** Southeast Australia
T (02) 4920 2622 **F** (02) 4920 2699 **WEB** www.peterhowlandwines.com **OPEN** By appointment
WINEMAKER Peter Howland **EST.** 2001 **CASES** 4000
SUMMARY Peter Howland graduated from Adelaide University in 1997 with a first-class Honours degree in oenology. He has worked in the Hunter Valley, Margaret River, the Hastings Valley, the Macedon Ranges and Puglia in Italy. Newcastle may seem a strange place for a winery cellar door, but this is where his insulated and refrigerated barrel shed is located. As from 2004 he has fermented his wines at Serenella Estate, where he also acts as contract winemaker. If he maintains the quality of his initial releases – and there seems no reason why he should not – this will become a very well-known label.

♥♥♥♥♀ **Mouthpiece Hunter Valley Shiraz 2003** Medium-bodied; elegant red and black fruits; lacks the richness on the mid-palate of the best wines of the vintage, but finishes well. The label design does it no favours. **RATING** 90 **DRINK** 2013 $ 29

Peter Lehmann ★★★★★

Para Road, Tanunda, SA 5352 **REGION** Barossa Valley
T (08) 8563 2100 **F** (08) 8563 3402 **WEB** www.peterlehmannwines.com **OPEN** Mon–Fri 9.30–5, weekends & public hols 10.30–4.30
WINEMAKER Andrew Wigan, Leonie Lange, Ian Hongell, Kerry Morrison **EST.** 1979 **CASES** 200 000
SUMMARY After one of the more emotional and intense takeover battles in the latter part of 2003, Peter Lehmann fought off the unwanted suit of Allied Domeq, and is now effectively controlled by the Swiss/Californian Hess Group. The takeover has reinforced the core business, and protect the interests of employees, and of Peter Lehmann's beloved Barossa Valley grapegrowers. Exports to the UK, the US and other major markets.

♥♥♥♥♥ **The 1885 Shiraz 2001** Lovely intense, fine savoury/spicy/cedary edges to blackberry and plum fruit; balanced oak, silky tannins. Simply beautiful. Single 1885 vineyard. Cork. **RATING** 96 **DRINK** 2021 $ 35

Stonewell Shiraz 1999 Lovely wine in all respects; medium-bodied, with great regional character and fruit; filled with flavour, yet retains great elegance. Only 14° alcohol. **RATING** 96 **DRINK** 2019 $ 75

Reserve Semillon 1999 Bright green-yellow; very complex, toasty aromas; distinctive honeycomb, beeswax and lemon fruit; soft but balanced acidity. **RATING** 95 **DRINK** 2009 $ 24

Eden Valley Reserve Riesling 2000 Lime and toast aromas on the entry to the mouth, then crisp acidity to balance the finish. **RATING** 94 **DRINK** 2010 $ 24

The Futures Shiraz 2002 Great bouquet; lashings of dark fruit aromas and French oak; a quite restrained palate; fine tannins run throughout; counter-cultural 14.5° alcohol. **RATING** 94 **DRINK** 2015 $ 30

♥♥♥♥♀ **Eden Valley Riesling 2004** Flowery and fragrant lime blossom; clean, long and moderately intense; will build. **RATING** 93 **DRINK** 2012 $ 16

Shiraz Muscadelle 2002 Strong colour; utterly seductive but powerful mix of black fruits and spicy, lifted components; sure oak and tannin handling. An echo of the Shiraz Tokay of 20 years ago. Quality cork. **RATING** 93 **DRINK** 2015 $ 25

The Mentor 2000 Medium-bodied; sweet, spicy cedary oak inputs on supple black fruits and a touch of warm chocolate; 79% cabernet sauvignon, 16% malbec, 5% merlot. Top result. **RATING** 93 **DRINK** 2008 $ 40

The King 1996 Intensely spicy and savoury; quite dry; closing in on Portuguese style Vintage Port. Touriga/Shiraz/Cabernet Sauvignon. **RATING** 92 **DRINK** 2016 $25

Black Queen Sparkling Shiraz 1997 Complex wine; multi-spice aromas and flavours plus plum and blackberry; dry finish a real plus; good length. Disgorged July 2004. **RATING** 92 **DRINK** 2010 $35

Eden Valley Shiraz 2001 Curious spicy scent to bouquet far from unpleasant; medium-bodied red and black fruits; ripe tannins still softening. Cork. **RATING** 91 **DRINK** 2015 $28

Cabernet Sauvignon 2002 Cedary, briary black fruit aromas and flavours; savoury palate; good length and persistent tannins. **RATING** 91 **DRINK** 2012 $18

Barossa Shiraz 2002 Elegant, medium-bodied plum, spice and blackberry; gentle extract and oak; good length. **RATING** 90 **DRINK** 2008 $18

Shiraz Muscadelle 2001 Fine, nice bottle-developed earthy, savoury red and black fruits; fine tannins. Recreation of a bygone era. **RATING** 90 **DRINK** 2011 $25

Barossa Merlot 2002 Good length, weight and intensity; distinctive varietal character; twang of olive on blackcurrant fruit; balanced tannins and oak. Surprise packet. **RATING** 90 **DRINK** 2008 $18

ŸŸŸŸ **Cellar Reserve Cabernet Franc 1999** Cedary, leafy, spicy, showing both bottle development and varietal character at the savoury end of the spectrum. Certainly is different. High-quality cork. **RATING** 89 **DRINK** 2009 $24

Barossa Semillon 2003 Rich, full and rounded; lemon tart, and nice balancing acidity. **RATING** 88 **DRINK** 2009 $12

Clancy's 2003 Medium-bodied; soft, supple and smooth; spicy, gently savoury black fruits mix; gentle tannins and oak. Poor cork. **RATING** 88 **DRINK** 2008 $13

Botrytis Semillon 2002 Glowing yellow-green; light to medium-bodied; well balanced, sweetness neatly off-set by lemony acidity; will improve. **RATING** 88 **DRINK** 2009 $16

Chenin Blanc 2004 Lively, fresh, crisp; juicy lemony fruit and excellent balancing acidity; clever winemaking. **RATING** 87 **DRINK** 2007 $13

Barossa Merlot 2003 Medium-bodied; dark berries, spice and olive components; good texture and weight; the profile of Merlot. Cork. **RATING** 87 **DRINK** 2008 $18

ŸŸŸ︎ **Semillon Chardonnay 2004** **RATING** 86 **DRINK** Now $12

Rose 2004 Fragrant, fresh, crisp red fruits; light but dry finish. **RATING** 86 **DRINK** Now $15

Barossa Riesling 2004 **RATING** 85 **DRINK** 2008 $12

Cellar Reserve Pinot Noir 2001 **RATING** 85 **DRINK** 2007 $22

Chardonnay 2004 **RATING** 84 **DRINK** Now $15

Peterson Champagne House

NR

Cnr Broke Road/Branxton Road, Pokolbin, NSW 2320 **REGION** Lower Hunter Valley
T (02) 4998 7881 **F** (02) 4998 7882 **OPEN** 7 days 9–5
WINEMAKER Contract **EST.** 1994 **CASES** 7000
SUMMARY Prominently and provocatively situated on the corner of Broke and Branxton Roads as one enters the main vineyard and winery district in the Lower Hunter Valley. It is an extension of the Peterson family empire and, no doubt, very deliberately aimed at the tourist. While the dreaded word 'Champagne' has been retained in the business name, the wine labels now simply say Peterson House, which is a big step in the right direction. Almost all the wine is sold through the cellar door and the wine club mailing list.

Petersons

★★★★☆

Mount View Road, Mount View, NSW 2325 **REGION** Lower Hunter Valley
T (02) 4990 1704 **F** (02) 4991 1344 **WEB** www.petersonswines.com.au **OPEN** Mon–Sat 9–5, Sun 10–5
WINEMAKER Colin Peterson, Gary Reed **EST.** 1971 **CASES** 15 000
SUMMARY Ian and Shirley Peterson were among the early followers in the footsteps of Max Lake, contributing to the Hunter Valley renaissance which has continued to this day. Grapegrowers since 1971 and winemakers since 1981, the second generation of the family, headed by Colin Peterson, now manages the business. It has been significantly expanded to include 16 ha at Mount View, a 42-ha vineyard in Mudgee (Glenesk), and an 8-ha vineyard near Armidale (Palmerston).

▼▼▼▼▼ Glenesk Mudgee Cabernet Sauvignon 2002 Good colour; medium-bodied; smooth and supple; blackcurrant/black fruits; silky, ripe tannins; good oak, excellent mouthfeel. **RATING** 94 **DRINK** 2012

Pettavel ★★★★

65 Pettavel Road, Waurn Ponds, Vic 3216 **REGION** Geelong
T (03) 5266 1120 **F** (03) 5266 1140 **WEB** www.pettavel.com **OPEN** 7 days 10–5.30
WINEMAKER Peter Flewellyn **EST.** 2000 **CASES** 20 000
SUMMARY This is a major new landmark in the Geelong region. Mike and wife Sandi Fitzpatrick sold their large Riverland winery and vineyards, and moved to Geelong, where, in 1990, they began developing vineyards at Sutherlands Creek. Here they have been joined by daughter Robyn (who has overseas management of the business) and son Reece (who coordinates the viticultural resources). A striking and substantial winery was opened in time for the 2002 vintage, prior to which time the wines were contract-made at Mount Langi Ghiran. The development also includes a modern tasting area adjacent to a restaurant (open 7 days for lunch). The development can accommodate private functions and corporate events for up to 180 seated guests. Exports to the UK, the US, Sweden and Germany.

▼▼▼▼▼ Southern Emigre Shiraz 2002 Savoury, spicy complexity; medium-bodied, with good tannins and length. **RATING** 91 **DRINK** 2013 **$** 40
Evening Star Riesling 2004 Lots of lime juice aroma and flavour; good vinosity and length. **RATING** 90 **DRINK** 2007 **$** 18

▼▼▼▼ Platina Chardonnay 2002 Developed colour; full-bodied yellow peach, tropical and fig fruit; malolactic and barrel ferment inputs obvious; big middle palate. Cork. **RATING** 89 **DRINK** 2007 **$** 27
Evening Star Chardonnay 2004 Very developed colour; rich, complex, forward yellow peach, spice and cashew oak and malolactic inputs. Screwcap. **RATING** 88 **DRINK** 2007 **$** 18

▼▼▼▼ Evening Star Sauvignon Blanc Semillon 2004 RATING 86 **DRINK** Now **$** 18
Evening Star Chardonnay 2003 RATING 86 **DRINK** 2007 **$** 18
Evening Star Shiraz 2003 RATING 86 **DRINK** 2009 **$** 18

Pewsey Vale ★★★★★

PO Box 10, Angaston, SA 5353 **REGION** Eden Valley
T (08) 8561 3200 **F** (08) 8561 3393 **WEB** www.pewseyvale.com **OPEN** At Yalumba
WINEMAKER Louisa Rose **EST.** 1961 **CASES** 18 000
SUMMARY Pewsey Vale was a famous vineyard established in 1847 by Joseph Gilbert, and it was appropriate that when S Smith & Son (Yalumba) began the renaissance of the high Adelaide Hills plantings in 1961, they should do so by purchasing Pewsey Vale and establishing 40 ha of riesling and 2 ha each of gewurztraminer and pinot gris. After a dip in form, Pewsey Vale has emphatically bounced back to its very best. The Riesling has also finally benefited from being the first wine to be bottled with a Stelvin screwcap in 1977. While public reaction forced the abandonment of the initiative for almost 20 years, Yalumba/Pewsey Vale never lost faith in the technical advantages of the closure. Exports to all major markets.

▼▼▼▼▼ Museum Release The Contours Riesling 2000 Pure class; youthful and vibrant; clearly focused; great line and length. Fully deserving of its trophy for Best White Wine at the National Wine Show 2004. Screwcap. **RATING** 96 **DRINK** 2015 **$** 25.95
The Contours Eden Valley Riesling 2002 Considerable complexity and intensity; superb developing riesling characters; on its way to greatness. Screwcap. **RATING** 94 **DRINK** 2017 **$** 25.95

▼▼▼▼ Individual Vineyard Selection Eden Valley Riesling 2004 Clean, crisp, mineral aromas with a hint of fruit spice; power and palate drive right through to a long finish. **RATING** 93 **DRINK** 2014 **$** 16.95
Eden Valley Pinot Gris 2004 Notable concentration, focus and length; ripe pear and apple; spicy finish and aftertaste. **RATING** 90 **DRINK** 2007 **$** 22.95

▼▼▼▼ Eden Valley Riesling 2004 Solid and weighty; ripe tropical/lime fruit. **RATING** 88 **DRINK** 2009 **$** 16.95

Pfeiffer ★★★★

167 Distillery Road, Wahgunyah, Vic 3687 **REGION** Rutherglen
T (02) 6033 2805 **F** (02) 6033 3158 **WEB** www.pfeifferwines.com.au **OPEN** Mon–Sat 9–5, Sun 10–5
WINEMAKER Christopher Pfeiffer, Jen Pfeiffer **EST.** 1984 **CASES** 20 000
SUMMARY Ex-Lindeman fortified winemaker Chris Pfeiffer occupies one of the historic wineries (built 1880) which abound in northeast Victoria and which is worth a visit on this score alone. The fortified wines are good, and the table wines have improved considerably over recent vintages, drawing upon 32 ha of estate plantings. The winery offers barbecue facilities, a children's playground, gourmet picnic hampers, and dinners (by arrangement). Exports to the UK, Canada, Malaysia and China (under the Carlyle and Three Chimneys labels).

ΨΨΨΨ♀ **Carlyle Marsanne 2003** Floral honeysuckle and citrus; excellent mouthfeel and balance; long, clean finish. Screwcap. **RATING** 92 **DRINK** 2009
Christopher's Rutherglen Vintage Port 2003 Spicy black fruits; excellent spirit on both bouquet and palate; very good balance; impressive. Cork. **RATING** 92 **DRINK** 2013 $ 22.50
Chardonnay 2003 Subtle but complex; some appealing minerality behind melon fruit and more creamy, cashew notes; gentle hint of oak; good style. Screwcap. **RATING** 90 **DRINK** 2010 $ 16.50

ΨΨΨΨ **Carlyle Riesling 2004** Clean but subdued bouquet; attractive, soft, tropical citrus and ripe apple fruit; balanced finish; should develop. Screwcap. **RATING** 89 **DRINK** 2012 $ 15.90
Shiraz 2001 Clean, fresh, with a nice touch of bottle development; light to medium-bodied black cherry and blackberry fruit; good tannin and oak management; smooth, supple finish. Quality cork. **RATING** 89 **DRINK** 2009 $ 18.50
Cabernet Sauvignon 2001 Medium-bodied; smooth, supple blackcurrant, earth and chocolate; ripe tannins, minimal oak, good balance. Cork. **RATING** 89 **DRINK** 2011 $ 18.50
Gamay 2004 Vivid colour; light to medium-bodied; clean spiced cherry and plum; distinctive varietal character; well made. Screwcap. **RATING** 88 **DRINK** 2007 $ 15.50
Riesling 2004 Similarly subdued bouquet; light to medium-bodied; well made, but doesn't have the focus of the best; gentle tropical fruits. Screwcap. **RATING** 87 **DRINK** 2010 $ 16.50
Carlyle Shiraz 2002 Light to medium-bodied; gently ripe black fruits and a lick of vanilla oak; balanced tannins. Screwcap. **RATING** 87 **DRINK** 2008
Carlyle Cabernet Merlot 2002 Light to medium-bodied; fresh redcurrant and blackcurrant; minimal tannin and oak input. Screwcap. **RATING** 87 **DRINK** 2009

ΨΨΨ♀ **Carlyle Merlot 2002** **RATING** 86 **DRINK** 2012
Auslese Tokay 2004 **RATING** 86 **DRINK** 2008 $ 15.90
Ensemble Rose 2004 **RATING** 85 **DRINK** Now $ 13.50
Sparkling Pinot Noir 2002 **RATING** 85 **DRINK** 2007 $ 29.90
Chardonnay 2000 **RATING** 84 **DRINK** Now $ 15
Pinot Noir 2001 **RATING** 84 **DRINK** Now $ 17.90

Pfitzner ★★★★☆

PO Box 1098, North Adelaide, SA 5006 **REGION** Adelaide Hills
T (08) 8390 0188 **F** (08) 8390 0188 **OPEN** Not
WINEMAKER Petaluma (Contract) **EST.** 1996 **CASES** 1500
SUMMARY The subtitle to the Pfitzner name is Eric's Vineyard. The late Eric Pfitzner purchased and aggregated a number of small, subdivided farmlets to protect the beauty of the Piccadilly Valley from ugly rural development. His three sons inherited the vision, with a little under 6 ha of vineyard planted principally to chardonnay and pinot noir, plus small amounts of sauvignon blanc and merlot. Half the total property has been planted, the remainder preserving the natural eucalypt forest. Roughly half the production is sold in the UK. The remainder is sold through retail outlets in Adelaide and Melbourne.

ΨΨΨΨΨ **Eric's Vineyard Piccadilly Valley Chardonnay 2001** Opens quietly, building to a long, fruit-driven, lingering finish; subtle barrel ferment and malolactic overtones to stone fruit, apple and creamy cashew flavours; great length. **RATING** 94 **DRINK** 2010 $ 19.95

ΨΨΨΨ **Piccadilly Valley Merlot 2001** Spice, herbs, olive and snow peas aromas; small red berry fruits; still very youthful; low pH style. **RATING** 89 **DRINK** 2008 $ 14.95

Phaedrus Estate

220 Mornington–Tyabb Road, Moorooduc, Vic 3933 **REGION** Mornington Peninsula
T 903) 5978 8134 **F** (03) 5978 8134 **WEB** www.phaedrus.com.au **OPEN** Weekends & public hols 11–5
WINEMAKER Ewan Campbell, Maitena Zantvoort **EST.** 1997 **CASES** 1500
SUMMARY Ewan Campbell and Maitena Zantvoort established Phaedrus Estate in 1997. At that time both had already had winemaking experience with large wine companies, and were at the point of finishing their wine science degrees at Adelaide University. They decided they wished to (in their words) 'produce ultra-premium wine with distinctive and unique varietal flavours, which offer serious (and light-hearted) wine drinkers an alternative to mainstream commercial styles'. Campbell and Zantvoort believe that quality wines involve both art and science, and I don't have any argument with that.

TTTTY **Reserve Pinot Noir 2003** Not 100% bright (unfiltered), but good hue; complex, powerful, ripe plummy fruit and fractionally dry tannins; 400 bottles made. **RATING** 92 **DRINK** 2009 $ 65
Chardonnay 2003 Light straw-green; nicely made wine showing wild yeast and malolactic inputs; supple cashew and cream notes; good length, line and balance. Screwcap. **RATING** 90 **DRINK** 2008 $ 18
Pinot Gris 2004 Pale green-straw; very tangy, grassy/lemony elements unusual, but provide interest and length. **RATING** 90 **DRINK** 2007 $ 18

TTTT **Shiraz 2003** Flavoursome red cherry and spice plus hints of game and licorice; arresting style. Screwcap. **RATING** 89 **DRINK** 2009 $ 20

TTTY **Pinot Noir 2003** **RATING** 84 **DRINK** 2007 $ 20

Phillip Island Vineyard

Berrys Beach Road, Phillip Island, Vic 3922 **REGION** Gippsland
T (03) 5956 8465 **F** (03) 5956 8465 **WEB** www.phillipislandwines.com.au **OPEN** 7 days 11–6
(Nov–March), 11–5 (April–Oct)
WINEMAKER David Lance, James Lance **EST.** 1993 **CASES** 3000
SUMMARY 1997 marked the first harvest from the 2.5 ha of the Phillip Island vineyard, which is totally enclosed in the permanent silon net which acts both as a windbreak and protection against birds. The quality of the wines across the board make it clear that this is definitely not a tourist-trap cellar door; it is a serious producer of quality wine. Exports to South-East Asia.

TTTTT **Chardonnay 2002** Vivid green-yellow; totally delicious melon and nectarine fruit; outstanding length and balance; malolactic and barrel ferment notes in the background. Quality cork. **RATING** 96 **DRINK** 2009 $ 28
Sauvignon Blanc 2004 Powerful and intense, yet not heavy; classic gooseberry and passionfruit mix; lingering acidity to close. Screwcap. **RATING** 94 **DRINK** 2008 $ 28
Pinot Noir 2003 Rich, ripe, very powerful and complex array of spicy, smoky plum aromas and flavours; long palate, balanced tannins. Quality cork. **RATING** 94 **DRINK** 2012 $ 30
Merlot 2002 Intensely aromatic spice and black olive aromas; vibrant redcurrant and raspberry fruit; fine tannins, great length. Quality cork. **RATING** 94 **DRINK** 2012 $ 30

TTTT **Cabernet Sauvignon 2002** Aromatic, lifted, leafy berry; slightly lemony notes; struggled for ripeness. Quality cork. **RATING** 89 **DRINK** 2008 $ 28

TTTY **The Nobbies Pinot Noir 2003** **RATING** 86 **DRINK** 2009 $ 24

Phillips Brook Estate
NR

118 Redmond–Hay River Road, Redmond, WA 6332 **REGION** Albany
T (08) 9845 3124 **F** (08) 9845 3126 **OPEN** By appointment
WINEMAKER James Kellie (Contract) **EST.** 1975 **CASES** 1200
SUMMARY Bronwen and David Newbury first became viticulturists near the thoroughly unlikely town of Bourke, in western New South Wales. They were involved with Dr Richard Smart in setting up the First Light vineyard, with the aim of making the first wine in the world each calendar year. Whatever marketing appeal the idea may have had, the wine was never going to be great, so in May 2001 they moved back to the Great Southern region. The name comes from the adjoining Phillips Brook Nature Reserve, and the permanent creek on their property. Riesling and cabernet sauvignon (4.5 ha in all)

had been planted in 1975, but thoroughly neglected. The Newburys have rehabilitated the old plantings, and have added 7.5 ha of chardonnay, merlot, cabernet franc and sauvignon blanc.

ŢŢŢŢ **Great Southern Riesling 2004** RATING 84 DRINK Now $15

Phillips Estate ★★★

Lot 964a Channybearup Road, Pemberton, WA 6230 REGION Pemberton
T (08) 9776 0381 F (08) 9776 0381 OPEN 7 days 10.30–4
WINEMAKER Phillip Wilkinson EST. 1996 CASES 5000
SUMMARY Phillip Wilkinson has developed 4.5 ha of vines framed by an old-growth Karri forest on one side and a large lake on the other. As well as the expected varieties, he has planted 1 ha of zinfandel; as far as I know, it is the only zinfandel in the Pemberton region. Sophisticated winemaking techniques are used at the fermentation stage, but fining and filtration are either not used at all, or employed to a minimum degree. Exports to the UK.

Pialligo Estate NR

18 Kallaroo Road, Pialligo, ACT 2609 REGION Canberra District
T (02) 6247 6060 F (02) 6262 6074 WEB www.pialligoestate.com.au OPEN Thurs–Sun & public hols 10–5
WINEMAKER Andrew McEwin, Greg Gallagher (Contract) EST. 1999 CASES 1200
SUMMARY In 1999 Sally Milner and John Nutt began establishing their 4-ha vineyard (1.5 ha of merlot, 1 ha of riesling and 0.5 ha each of shiraz, cabernet sauvignon and sangiovese). The cellar door sales area and café opened July 2002, with views of Mt Ainslie, Mt Pleasant, Duntroon, the Telstra Tower, Parliament House and the Brindabella Ranges beyond. The property, which has a 1-km frontage to the Molonglo River, also includes an olive grove, yet is only 5 minutes' drive from the centre of Canberra. Experienced contract-winemaking should underwrite the quality of the wines.

Piano Gully NR

Piano Gully Road, Manjimup, WA 6258 REGION Manjimup
T (08) 9772 3140 F (08) 9316 0336 WEB www.pianogully.com.au OPEN By appointment
WINEMAKER Ashley Lewkowski EST. 1987 CASES 4000
SUMMARY The 5-ha vineyard was established in 1987 on rich Karri loam, 10 km south of Manjimup, with the first wine made from the 1991 vintage. The name of the road (and the winery) commemorates the shipping of a piano from England by one of the first settlers in the region. The horse and cart carrying the piano on the last leg of the long journey were within sight of their destination when the piano fell from the cart and was destroyed.

Picardy ★★★★★

Cnr Vasse Highway/Eastbrook Road, Pemberton, WA 6260 REGION Pemberton
T (08) 9776 0036 F (08) 9776 0245 WEB www.picardy.com.au OPEN By appointment
WINEMAKER Dr Bill Pannell, Dan Pannell EST. 1993 CASES 5000
SUMMARY Picardy is owned by Dr Bill Pannell, his wife Sandra and son Daniel; Bill and Sandra were the founders of Moss Wood winery in the Margaret River region (in 1969). Picardy reflects Bill Pannell's view that the Pemberton area has proved to be one of the best regions in Australia for Pinot Noir and Chardonnay, but it is perhaps significant that the wines include a Shiraz, and a Bordeaux-blend of 50% Merlot, 25% Cabernet Franc and 25% Cabernet Sauvignon. Time will tell whether Pemberton has more Burgundy, Rhône or Bordeaux in its veins. National distribution, and exports to the UK, the US and other major markets.

ŢŢŢŢŢ **Chardonnay 2003** A complex, stylish wine; seamless balance and integration of melon, stone fruit, cashew and oak. RATING 94 DRINK 2010 $35

Piccadilly Fields NR

185 Piccadilly Road, Piccadilly, SA 5151 REGION Adelaide Hills
T (08) 8370 8800 OPEN Not
WINEMAKER Sam Virgara EST. 1989 CASES 2000

SUMMARY Piccadilly Fields has only a passing resemblance to its original state. The Virgara family has joined with a syndicate of investors which jointly own 176 ha of vineyards in various parts of the Adelaide Hills, producing up to 1000 tonnes per year. The lion's share is sold as grapes to other winemakers; 30 tonnes or so are held for the Piccadilly Fields label.

Pierro ★★★★☆

Caves Road, Wilyabrup via Cowaramup, WA 6284 **REGION** Margaret River
T (08) 9755 6220 **F** (08) 9755 6308 **OPEN** 7 days 10–5
WINEMAKER Dr Michael Peterkin **EST.** 1979 **CASES** 7500
SUMMARY Dr Michael Peterkin is another of the legion of Margaret River medical practitioners; for good measure, he married into the Cullen family. Pierro is renowned for its stylish white wines, which often exhibit tremendous complexity. The Chardonnay can be monumental in its weight and complexity. Exports to the UK, the US, Japan and Indonesia.

ᵀᵀᵀᵀᵀ **Chardonnay 2003** Slightly more restrained than usual; beautiful balance and mouthfeel, with nectarine fruit to the fore. **RATING** 95 **DRINK** 2013 $ 65

ᵀᵀᵀᵀ **Semillon Sauvignon Blanc LTC 2004** Pale straw-green; the flavour is bolstered by a touch of sweetness; smooth and supple. **RATING** 89 **DRINK** 2007 $ 25

Pier 10 NR

10 Shoreham Road, Shoreham, Vic 3916 **REGION** Mornington Peninsula
T (03) 5989 8848 **F** (03) 5989 8848 **WEB** www.pier10.com.au **OPEN** Wed–Sun 11–5, 7 days Dec–Mar
WINEMAKER Kevin McCarthy (Contract) **EST.** 1996 **CASES** NA
SUMMARY Eric Baker and Sue McKenzie began the development of Pier 10 with the aim of creating first a lifestyle, then perhaps a retirement business. Both helped set up the vineyard while continuing to work in Melbourne before handing over viticultural management of the 3.2 ha to Mark Danaher. The varieties planted are chardonnay, pinot gris and pinot noir, and with ultra-competent winemaking, the sold-out sign goes up regularly. The cellar door offers light meals and barbecue and picnic facilities.

Piesse Brook NR

226 Aldersyde Road, Bickley, WA 6076 **REGION** Perth Hills
T (08) 9293 3309 **F** (08) 9293 3309 **OPEN** Sat 1–5, Sun, public hols 10–5, and by appointment
WINEMAKER Di Bray, Ray Boyanich **EST.** 1974 **CASES** 1200
SUMMARY Surprisingly good red wines made in tiny quantities; they have received consistent accolades over the years. The first Chardonnay was made in 1993; a trophy-winning Shiraz was produced in 1995. Now has 4 ha of chardonnay, shiraz, merlot and cabernet sauvignon under vine. Exports to the UK.

Pieter van Gent NR

Black Springs Road, Mudgee, NSW 2850 **REGION** Mudgee
T (02) 6373 3807 **F** (02) 6373 3910 **WEB** www.pvgwinery.com.au **OPEN** Mon–Sat 9–5, Sun 11–4
WINEMAKER Pieter van Gent, Philip van Gent **EST.** 1978 **CASES** 10 000
SUMMARY Many years ago Pieter van Gent worked for Lindemans, then Craigmoor; he moved to his own winery in 1979. He and his family have forged a strong following here, initially for fortified wines, but now also for the table wines. Accommodation is available at the Bushman's Cottage.

Piggs Peake ★★★★

697 Hermitage Road, Pokolbin, NSW 2321 **REGION** Lower Hunter Valley
T (02) 6574 7000 **F** (02) 6574 7070 **WEB** www.piggspeake.com **OPEN** 7 days 10–5 (10–6 during daylight saving)
WINEMAKER Steve Langham **EST.** 1998 **CASES** 2000
SUMMARY The derivation of the name remains a mystery to me; if it is a local landmark, I have not heard of it. This is one of the newer wineries in the Hunter Valley, sourcing its grapes from a wide variety of places, to make a range of wines which are well outside the straight and narrow. Piggs

Peake has secured listings at a number of leading Sydney metropolitan and NSW country restaurants. The arrival of Steve Langham (having previously worked four vintages at Allandale) has seen a very marked increase in quality.

▼▼▼▼▼ **Wiggly Tail Marsanne 2004** Altogether surprising wine; chalk, mineral, honeysuckle, lemon and herb aromas and flavours; a hint of oak adds to the mix; has attitude. Screwcap. **RATING** 90 **DRINK** 2009 $ 24
House of Sticks Shiraz 2003 Powerful structure and concentration; blackberry plus hints of spice and plum; ripe tannins. High-quality cork. **RATING** 90 **DRINK** 2012 $ 26

▼▼▼▼ **Suckling Pig Zinfandel 2004** A trap for the unwary, 'super-ripe' zinfandel from Cargo Road, Orange; luscious, very sweet dessert wine; 15° alcohol, not fortified. Delphic label. **RATING** 87 **DRINK** 2008 $ 35

Pike & Joyce ★★★★

Mawson Road, Lenswood, SA 5240 (postal) **REGION** Adelaide Hills
T (08) 8843 4370 **F** (08) 8843 4353 **WEB** www.pikeswines.com.au **OPEN** Not
WINEMAKER Neil Pike, John Trotter **EST.** 1998 **CASES** 4000
SUMMARY As the name suggests, this is a partnership between the Pike family (of Clare Valley fame) and the Joyce family, related to Andrew Pike's wife Cathy. The Joyce family have been orchardists at Lenswood for over 100 years, but also have extensive operations in the Riverland. Together with Andrew Pike (formerly chief viticulturist for the Southcorp group) they have established 18.5 ha of vines; the lion's share go to pinot noir, sauvignon blanc and chardonnay, followed by merlot, pinot gris and semillon. The wines are made at Pikes Clare Valley winery. National distribution by Tucker Seabrook; exports to the UK, the US and other major markets.

▼▼▼▼▼ **Adelaide Hills Chardonnay 2003** Complex, rich, ripe stone fruit; strong oak inputs to both bouquet and palate; plenty of total flavour; food style. Cork. **RATING** 90 **DRINK** 2007 $ 28

▼▼▼▼ **Adelaide Hills Pinot Gris 2004** Spotlessly clean and correct; nice bracing citrussy acidity; good length. **RATING** 88 **DRINK** 2007 $ 20
Adelaide Hills Sauvignon Blanc 2004 Very pale; crisp and correct, but very light-bodied lemon and gooseberry flavours. **RATING** 87 **DRINK** Now $ 20
Adelaide Hills Pinot Noir 2003 Clean, firm plum and cherry; relatively high acid and low pH sharpen the palate a little too much. Cork. **RATING** 87 **DRINK** 2008 $ 28

Pikes ★★★★★

Polish Hill River Road, Sevenhill, SA 5453 **REGION** Clare Valley
T (08) 8843 4370 **F** (08) 8843 4353 **WEB** www.pikeswines.com.au **OPEN** 7 days 10–4
WINEMAKER Neil Pike, John Trotter **EST.** 1984 **CASES** 35 000
SUMMARY Owned by the Pike brothers: Andrew was for many years the senior viticulturist with Southcorp, Neil was a winemaker at Mitchell. Pikes now has its own winery, with Neil Pike presiding. Generously constructed and flavoured wines are the order of the day. Exports to the UK, the US and other major markets.

▼▼▼▼▼ **The EWP Reserve Shiraz 2002** Rich, complex, blackberry, satsuma plum and chocolate; round, long and supple mouthfeel. Quality cork. **RATING** 95 **DRINK** 2015
The Merle Reserve Riesling 2004 Voluminous lime and tropical aromas and flavours; rich, mouthfilling style; now or later. Screwcap. **RATING** 94 **DRINK** 2014 $ 34
Clare Valley Cabernet Sauvignon 2002 Rich, medium to full-bodied; lush blackcurrant, chocolate and cedar; ripe tannins, long finish; very good balance. Quality cork. **RATING** 94 **DRINK** 2015 $ 22

▼▼▼▼▼ **Clare Valley Riesling 2004** Floral lime blossom and spice aromas; a delicate and elegant palate, but has good length and balance. **RATING** 92 **DRINK** 2014 $ 22
Clare Valley Shiraz 2002 Concentrated, powerful black fruits; touches of earth and spice; long finish, lingering tannins. **RATING** 92 **DRINK** 2017 $ 22
Clare Valley Sauvignon Blanc Semillon 2004 Altogether substantial, yet not phenolic; much more flavour and structure than most from the vintage; semillon component important. **RATING** 91 **DRINK** 2012 $ 18

Clare Valley Chardonnay 2003 Pale straw-green; sophisticated winemaking, with a hint of French funk; tangy citrus and melon; malolactic and barrel ferment creamy notes; very good outcome for the region. Cork. **RATING** 90 **DRINK** 2009 $ 20

ΨΨΨΨ **Clare Valley Shiraz Grenache Mourvedre 2002** Light to medium-bodied mix of savoury, earthy and more jammy fruit; just struggles over the line. Quality cork. **RATING** 87 **DRINK** 2009 $ 20

Pinelli   NR

30 Bennett Street, Caversham, WA 6055 **REGION** Swan Valley
T (08) 9279 6818 **F** (08) 9377 4259 **OPEN** Mon–Fri 9–5.30, weekends 10–5
WINEMAKER Robert Pinelli, Daniel Pinelli **EST.** 1979 **CASES** 10 000
SUMMARY Dominic Pinelli and son Robert – the latter a Roseworthy Agricultural College graduate – sell 75% of their production in flagons but are seeking to place more emphasis on bottled wine sales in the wake of recent show successes with Chenin Blanc.

Pinnacle Wines   NR

50 Pinnacle Road, Orange, NSW 2800 **REGION** Orange
T (02) 6365 3316 **OPEN** By appointment
WINEMAKER David Lowe, Jane Wilson (Contract) **EST.** 1999 **CASES** 400
SUMMARY Peter Gibson began Pinnacle Wines in 1999, with the planting of 2 ha of pinot gris on the slopes of Mt Canobolas, at an elevation of around 1000m. The vineyard is close to Brangayne of Orange, and Peter Gibson says that Brangayne's success played a considerable part in his decision to plant the vineyard. Just over 1 ha of viognier and 1.6 ha of pinot noir (using the new Burgundy clones 777 115 and 114 in conjunction with MV6), plus a little riesling, have been added.

Pipers Brook Vineyard

1216 Pipers Brook Road, Pipers Brook, Tas 7254 **REGION** Northern Tasmania
T (03) 6382 7527 **F** (03) 6382 7226 **WEB** www.pipersbrook.com **OPEN** 7 days 10–5
WINEMAKER Rene Bezemer **EST.** 1974 **CASES** 90 000
SUMMARY The Pipers Brook Tasmanian empire has over 220 ha of vineyard supporting the Pipers Brook and Ninth Island labels, with the major focus, of course, being on Pipers Brook. As ever, fastidious viticulture and winemaking, immaculate packaging and enterprising marketing create a potent and effective blend. Pipers Brook operates two cellar door outlets, one at headquarters, the other at Strathlyn (ph: (03) 6330 2388). In 2001 it became yet another company to fall prey to a takeover, in this instance by Belgian-owned sheepskin business Kreglinger, which has also established a large winery and vineyard at Mount Benson in South Australia. Exports to all major markets.

ΨΨΨΨΨ **Estate Riesling 2004** Pale straw-green; very tight and discreet, bordering on austere, but the balance good, the acidity controlled. **RATING** 92 **DRINK** 2014 $ 27.50
Estate Chardonnay 2001 Attractive hint of grapefruit/citrus over stone fruit; slightly leaner style, with minerally acidity; some malolactic influences evident. **RATING** 92 **DRINK** 2008 $ 44.95
Ninth Island Pinot Noir 2004 Strong colour; considerable power and density to plum and black cherry fruit; good tannin, structure and length; will flower further as it softens. Screwcap. **RATING** 91 **DRINK** 2008 $ 23.50
Estate Chardonnay 2002 Extremely reserved and tight, with good length, and still building character; Tasmanian Wines Show result an abberration. **RATING** 90 **DRINK** 2010 $ 33.95
Estate Pinot Noir 2003 Fine, elegant red and black cherry fruit; subtle oak; very fine tannins. **RATING** 90 **DRINK** 2009 $ 36.50

ΨΨΨΨ **Ninth Island Riesling 2003** Rich tropical lime aromas; full mid-palate flavour; slightly short finish. **RATING** 89 **DRINK** 2007 $ 18.25
Ninth Island Sauvignon Blanc 2004 Clean, nicely balanced, with the faintest touch of sweetness, albeit diminished varietal character. **RATING** 89 **DRINK** Now $ 21.50
Ninth Island Pinot Grigio 2004 Minerally, with touches of citrus blossom; light to medium-bodied; balance quite good. **RATING** 89 **DRINK** Now $ 21.50

Ninth Island Chardonnay 2004 Bracing, fresh and crisp citrussy fruit; spotlessly clean; bright, minerally acidity. Screwcap. **RATING** 88 **DRINK** 2007 $ 22.50
Estate Gewurztraminer 2004 Clean, nicely balanced; some rose petal and spice, but the varietal character struggles to express itself. **RATING** 87 **DRINK** 2009 $ 27.50
Estate Pinot Gris 2004 Pale pink tinges; light-bodied; pleasant apple, pear, musk and spice fruit; fair finish. **RATING** 87 **DRINK** 2007 $ 27.50

ỲỲỲỲ **Ninth Island Brut NV RATING** 86 **DRINK** 2007 $ 25.95

Piromit Wines

NR

113 Hanwood Avenue, Hanwood, NSW 2680 **REGION** Riverina
T (02) 6963 0200 **F** (02) 6963 0277 **WEB** www.piromitwines.com.au **OPEN** Mon–Fri 9–5
WINEMAKER Dom Piromalli, Pat Mittiga **EST.** 1998 **CASES** 60 000
SUMMARY I simply cannot resist quoting directly from the background information kindly supplied to me. 'Piromit Wines is a relatively new boutique winery situated in Hanwood, New South Wales. The winery complex, which crushed 1000 tonnes this season (2000), was built for the 1999 vintage on a 14-acre site which was until recently used as a drive-in. Previous to this, wines were made on our 100-acre vineyard. The winery site is being developed into an innovative tourist attraction complete with an Italian restaurant and landscaped formal gardens.' It is safe to say this extends the concept of a boutique winery into new territory, but then it is a big country. It is a family business run by Pat Mittiga, Dom Piromalli and Paul Hudson.

Pirramimma

★★★★★

Johnston Road, McLaren Vale, SA 5171 **REGION** McLaren Vale
T (08) 8323 8205 **F** (08) 8323 9224 **WEB** www.pirramimma.com.au **OPEN** Mon–Fri 9–5, Sat 11–5, Sun, public hols 11.30–4
WINEMAKER Geoff Johnston **EST.** 1892 **CASES** 50 000
SUMMARY A long-established, conservative, family-owned company with outstanding vineyard resources. It is now turning those resources to full effect, with a series of intense old-vine varietals including Shiraz, Grenache, Cabernet Sauvignon and Petit Verdot, all fashioned without over-embellishment.

ỲỲỲỲỲ **McLaren Vale Shiraz 2002** Complex and scented, yet elegant, bouquet; has intensity and power without clumsiness; fine, ripe tannins. Great vintage. **RATING** 95 **DRINK** 2017 $ 26.50
McLaren Vale Cabernet Sauvignon 2002 On the mark from the first whiff; nigh-on perfect balance of cabernet fruit, tannins and oak; long and harmonious. **RATING** 94 **DRINK** 2017 $ 26.50
McLaren Vale Petit Verdot 2002 Cedar, cigar box, black fruits and earth; hyper-concentrated and powerful, reflecting both the 20-year-old vines and the vintage. **RATING** 94 **DRINK** 2022 $ 26.50

ỲỲỲỲỲ **Stock's Hill Semillon Sauvignon Blanc 2004** Good flavour, intensity and length; lilting mix of tropical and herbaceous aromas and flavours. Trophy McLaren Vale Wine Show 2004. **RATING** 92 **DRINK** 2008 $ 14
Stock's Hill Shiraz 2002 Powerfully structured; abundant blackberry fruit, and strong but ripe tannins. Very good value. **RATING** 90 **DRINK** 2012 $ 16
Stock's Hill Cabernet Sauvignon 2002 Aromatic bouquet; light to medium-bodied spicy, savoury fruit strengthened by attractive ripe tannins; good length; value. **RATING** 90 **DRINK** 2012 $ 16

ỲỲỲỲ **McLaren Vale Stock's Hill Rose 2004** Crisp spice and herb aromas; flowing cassis/strawberry fruit; good balance and mouthfeel; carries slight sweetness. Free-run cabernet. **RATING** 87 **DRINK** Now $ 14

ỲỲỲỲ **Hillsview Cabernet Merlot 2002 RATING** 86 **DRINK** 2008 $ 16

Pizzini

★★★☆

Lano–Trento Vineyard, 175 King Valley Road, Whitfield, Vic 3768 **REGION** King Valley
T (03) 5729 8278 **F** (03) 5729 8495 **WEB** www.pizzini.com.au **OPEN** 7 days 12–5
WINEMAKER Alfred Pizzini, Joel Pizzini, Mark Walpole **EST.** 1980 **CASES** 10 000

SUMMARY Fred and Katrina Pizzini have been grapegrowers in the King Valley for over 20 years, with over 100 ha of vineyard. Grapegrowing (rather than winemaking) still continues to be the major focus, but their move into winemaking has been particularly successful, and I can personally vouch for their Italian cooking skills. It is not surprising, then, that their wines should span both Italian and traditional varieties. Exports to Hong Kong and China.

King Valley Sauvignon Blanc 2004 Clean, very correct, long palate; minerally limey tropical mix; lively acidity. Screwcap. **RATING** 88 **DRINK** 2007 $ 15

King Valley Arneis 2003 Apple, spice and pear aromas and flavours; delicate, but has intensity and character. Cork. **RATING** 88 **DRINK** 2007 $ 20

Rosetta 2004 Bright, light, fuchsia; light cherry and strawberry aromas and flavours; pleasantly dry; good Rose style. Screwcap. **RATING** 87 **DRINK** Now

King Valley Cabernet Sauvignon 2001 Light to medium-bodied; savoury, earthy, spicy aromas; fine blackberry fruit; supple, savoury tannins. Stained cork. **RATING** 87 **DRINK** 2011 $ 20

King Valley Sangiovese 2003 Fine, dusty, almost lemony tannins run through the sour cherry palate; light to medium-bodied; food style. Cork. **RATING** 87 **DRINK** 2008 $ 24

King Valley Verduzzo Dolce 2004 Auslese sweetness; could develop the complexity it lacks now. Screwcap. **RATING** 86 **DRINK** 2009 $ 14

King Valley Shiraz 2001 **RATING** 85 **DRINK** 2007 $ 25

King Valley Nebbiolo 1998 **RATING** 85 **DRINK** 2010 $ 45

Plantagenet ★★★★☆

Albany Highway, Mount Barker, WA 6324 **REGION** Mount Barker
T (08) 9851 2150 **F** (08) 9851 1839 **WEB** www.plantagenetwines.com **OPEN** 7days 9–5
WINEMAKER Richard Robson **EST.** 1974 **CASES** 130 000
SUMMARY The senior winery in the Mount Barker region, making superb wines across the full spectrum of variety and style: highly aromatic Riesling, tangy citrus-tinged Chardonnay, glorious Rhône-style Shiraz and ultra-stylish Cabernet Sauvignon. Exports to all major markets.

Mount Barker Chardonnay 2003 Light straw-green; complex barrel ferment characters; citrus and stone fruit with excellent focus and length; crisp, elegant finish. **RATING** 94 **DRINK** 2010 $ 23

Margaret River Semillon Sauvignon Blanc 2004 Spotlessly clean; light-bodied, lively and fresh; gently ripe gooseberry and passionfruit flavours. **RATING** 90 **DRINK** 2007 $ 23

Omrah Shiraz 2002 A medium-bodied mix of blackberry and raspberry fruits; good length and fine tannins; good value. **RATING** 89 **DRINK** 2008 $ 17

Mount Barker Cabernet Sauvignon 2002 Medium-bodied; nice structure and attractive savoury components. **RATING** 89 **DRINK** 2010 $ 35

Mount Barker Shiraz 2002 Medium-bodied; clean, well-balanced black fruits; subtle oak. **RATING** 88 **DRINK** 2012 $ 38

Great Southern/Pemberton Pinot Noir 2003 Light to medium-bodied; savoury, spicy, stemmy aromas and flavours; some length, but rather dry. **RATING** 87 **DRINK** Now $ 25

Omrah Cabernet Merlot 2002 **RATING** 86 **DRINK** 2008 $ 17

Hazard Hill Shiraz 2003 **RATING** 85 **DRINK** 2008

Platypus Lane Wines ★★★

PO Box 1140, Midland, WA 6936 **REGION** Swan District
T (08) 9250 1655 **F** (08) 9274 3045 **OPEN** Not
WINEMAKER Brenden Smith (Contract) **EST.** 1996 **CASES** NA
SUMMARY Platypus Lane, with a small core of 2.5 ha of chardonnay, shiraz and muscat, gained considerable publicity for owner Ian Gibson when its Shiraz won the inaugural John Gladstones Trophy at the Qantas Western Australian Wines Show for the wine showing greatest regional and varietal typicity. Much of the credit can no doubt go to winemaker Brenden Smith, who handles significant quantities of grapes brought in from other producers as well as from the core vineyards. National distribution through National Liquor; exports to the UK and the US.

Plunkett Wines ★★★☆

Cnr Hume Highway/Lambing Gully Road, Avenel, Vic 3664 **REGION** Strathbogie Ranges
T (03) 5796 2150 **F** (03) 5796 2147 **WEB** www.plunkett.com.au **OPEN** 7 days 10–5 (cellar door),
Thurs–Mon 10–5 (restaurant)
WINEMAKER Sam Plunkett, Victor Nash **EST.** 1980 **CASES** 13 000
SUMMARY The Plunkett family first planted grapes way back in 1968, establishing 1.2 ha with 25
experimental varieties. Commercial plantings commenced in 1980, with 100 ha now under vine, and
more coming. Though holding a vigneron's licence since 1985, the Plunketts did not commence
serious marketing of the wines until 1992. They now produce an array of wines which are pleasant
and well priced; the Reserves are in another quality and price league. Wholesale distribution to all
states; exports to the US, Canada, the UK, Germany, Malaysia, Indonesia, Vietnam and Hong Kong.

🍷🍷🍷🍷♀ **Strathbogie Ranges Riesling 2004** Talc, slate, herb and mineral aromas lead into an
intense, lively and long palate with lemony acidity. Cork-finished – a pity. **RATING** 91
DRINK 2009 $ 18

🍷🍷🍷♀ **Strathbogie Ranges Gewurztraminer 2004 RATING** 86 **DRINK** 2007 $ 18
Blackwood Ridge Sauvignon Blanc 2004 RATING 85 **DRINK** Now $ 18

Poacher's Ridge Vineyard ★★★★☆

163 Jersey Street, Wembley, WA 6014 (postal) **REGION** Mount Barker
WEB www.prv.com.au **OPEN** Not
WINEMAKER Robert Diletti (Contract) **EST.** 2000 **CASES** 2000
SUMMARY Alex and Janet Taylor purchased the Poacher's Ridge property in 1999; before then it had
been used for cattle grazing. In 2000, 7 ha of vineyard (in descending order, shiraz, cabernet
sauvignon, merlot, riesling, marsanne and viognier) were planted. The first small crop came in 2003,
a larger one in 2004, together making an auspicious debut. A cellar door and café was under
construction in 2005.

🍷🍷🍷🍷🍷 **Late Harvest Riesling 2004** Aromatic and flowery; totally delicious and vibrant lime and
passionfruit flavours; perfectly balanced residual sugar and acidity; classic Kabinett style.
Screwcap. **RATING** 94 **DRINK** 2010 $ 16.50

🍷🍷🍷🍷♀ **Riesling 2003** Potent herb, nettle and mineral aromas; lime juice comes through on the
palate; long finish. Screwcap. **RATING** 92 **DRINK** 2013 $ 15
Louis' Block Cabernet Sauvignon 2003 Medium-bodied; elegant and focused;
blackcurrant fruits; silky, supple and long. High-quality cork. **RATING** 92 **DRINK** 2013 $ 17

🍷🍷🍷🍷 **Riesling 2004** Spotlessly clean; delicate passionfruit and lime; crisp, clean, lingering
finish. Screwcap. **RATING** 89 **DRINK** 2009
Marsanne 2003 Very intense honeysuckle, spicy and musk aromas; good length and
acidity. Screwcap. **RATING** 89 **DRINK** 2008 $ 14
Marsanne 2004 Opens quietly enough, but runs through to a clean, lingering and
persuasive finish. Screwcap. **RATING** 87 **DRINK** 2007

Poet's Corner ★★★★

Craigmoor Road, Mudgee, NSW 2850 **REGION** Mudgee
T (02) 6372 2208 **F** (02) 6372 4464 **WEB** www.poetscornerwines.com **OPEN** Mon–Sat 10–4.30, Sun
& public hols 10–4
WINEMAKER Trent Nankivell **EST.** 1858 **CASES** 150 000
SUMMARY Poet's Corner is located in one of the oldest wineries in Australia to remain in more or less
continuous production. Craigmoor (as it was previously known) was built by Adam Roth in
1858/1860; his grandson Jack Roth ran the winery until the early 1960s. It is the public face for Poet's
Corner, Montrose and Craigmoor wines.

🍷🍷🍷🍷♀ **Henry Lawson Shiraz 2002** Strong purple-red colour; medium-bodied; excellent texture
and structure; a mix of black plums and blackberry; lingering but balanced tannins. Great
value. **RATING** 93 **DRINK** 2012 $ 15.99

🍷🍷🍷🍷 **Unwooded Chardonnay 2004** Bright and fresh citrus and melon; crisp acidity helps.
RATING 87 **DRINK** Now $ 9.99

Henry Lawson Chardonnay 2002 Pleasantly mature; ripe stone fruit and cashew; good length. RATING 87 DRINK Now $12.99
Henry Lawson Cabernet Sauvignon 2002 A supple, medium-bodied mix of red and black fruits; gentle tannins; minimal oak. RATING 87 DRINK Now $15.99

TTTT Shiraz Cabernet Sauvignon 2003 RATING 86 DRINK 2009 $9.99
Semillon Sauvignon Blanc Chardonnay 2004 RATING 85 DRINK Now $9.99
Montrose Black Shiraz 2002 RATING 85 DRINK 2009
Montrose Barbera 2000 RATING 85 DRINK Now $20.99

Pokolbin Estate ★★★★

McDonalds Road, Pokolbin, NSW 2321 REGION Lower Hunter Valley
T (02) 4998 7524 F (02) 4998 7765 WEB www.pokolbinestate.com.au OPEN 7 days 10–6
WINEMAKER Andrew Thomas (Contract) EST. 1980 CASES 2500
SUMMARY If you go to the lengths that Pokolbin Estate has done to hide its light under a bushel, you end up with something like 7 vintages of Semillon, 6 of Riesling, 7 of Shiraz, 3 of Tempranillo, 2 each of Nebbiolo and Sangiovese and sundry other wines adding up to more than 30 in total. Between 1998 and 2000 Neil McGuigan and Gary Reid shared the winemaking tasks; since 2001 Andrew Thomas has skilfully made the wines from vineyards up to 25 years old. I have included a selection of tasting notes, to give some idea of the treasures waiting to be discovered.

TTTTT Hunter Valley Riesling 1999 Starting to show fully mature expression; honey and toast; good length and balance. Cork. RATING 92 DRINK 2009 $26
Hunter Valley Semillon 2004 Quite intense lemon rind characters running through a long palate; good acidity, much potential. Screwcap. RATING 92 DRINK 2014 $26
Belebula Hunter Valley Nebbiolo 2003 Considerable power, depth and extract; remarkable varietal character with those earth, olive and black stemmy fruit flavours; fine tannins, real length. RATING 92 DRINK 2010 $28
Hunter Valley Shiraz 2003 Good colour; concentrated, rich dark plum and blackberry fruit; plenty of substance but tannins controlled. Cork. RATING 91 DRINK 2013 $30
Hunter Valley Shiraz 2000 Medium-bodied; savoury, earthy, regional characters starting to emerge; fine, persistent tannins; nicely ripened fruit. Cork. RATING 91 DRINK 2011 $25
Hunter Valley Riesling 2001 Firm, lively, lime; crisp, clean finish; good acidity. Cork. RATING 90 DRINK 2010 $20
Hunter Valley Semillon 2003 Crisp and intense; a spine of lemony/minerally acidity; long finish. Cork. RATING 90 DRINK 2009 $30
Hunter Valley Semillon 2002 Fresh; light to medium-bodied; good balance; citrussy, lemony acidity. RATING 90 DRINK 2012 $20
Reserve Hunter Valley Shiraz 2002 Attractive black cherry, black plum and blackberry mix; smooth, supple tannins; hint of oak. Cork. RATING 90 DRINK 2012 $44
George's Tawny Port (500 ml) NV Powerful and complex, with obvious rancio; a clever mix of old and younger material. RATING 90 DRINK 2007 $50

TTTT Hunter Valley Riesling 2002 Light-bodied; some honeyed characters developing; good acidity and length. Cork. RATING 89 DRINK 2010 $20
Hunter Valley Semillon 1998 Starting to show some development; hints of honey; still lemony; no toast showing yet. Slightly wet cork. RATING 89 DRINK 2009 $32
Hunter Valley Shiraz 2002 Light to medium-bodied; balanced black fruits; soft tannins; very consistent unforced style. Cork. RATING 89 DRINK 2008 $30
Belebula Hunter Valley Tempranillo 2004 Considerable intensity and authenticity; spicy red fruits and a touch of mint; fine, gently ripe tannins; minimal oak intrusion. RATING 89 DRINK 2008 $32
Belebula Hunter Valley Sangiovese 2004 Light, fragrant spice and red cherry aromas; fine texture; gentle tannins. RATING 88 DRINK 2009 $25
Belebula Hunter Valley Tempranillo 2002 Dense colour; powerful, earthy black fruits; plenty of substance; perhaps less varietal character. RATING 88 DRINK 2012 $48
Belebula Hunter Valley Nebbiolo 2004 As is often the case, not much depth to the colour; light to medium-bodied; harmonious, supple mouthfeel. RATING 87 DRINK 2010 $28
Belebula Hunter Valley Tempranillo 2003 Medium-bodied; smooth and supple; sweeter red and black fruits than the '02; a touch of spice. RATING 87 DRINK 2010 $32

ŦŦŦŸ **Belebula Hunter Valley Sangiovese 2003** RATING 86 DRINK 2009 $ 25
Neil's Autumn Riesling 2003 RATING 86 DRINK Now $ 22
Hunter Valley Chardonnay 2002 RATING 85 DRINK 2007 $ 22
Reserve Hunter Valley Shiraz 2003 RATING 85 DRINK 2008 $ 48
Neil's Autumn Riesling 2004 RATING 85 DRINK Now $ 22
6 Year Old Verdelho Solera NV RATING 84 DRINK Now $ 24

Polin & Polin Wines

Wyameta, Bell's Lane, Denman, NSW 2328 REGION Upper Hunter Valley
T (02) 6547 2955 F (02) 9969 9665 WEB www.polinwines.com.au OPEN Not
WINEMAKER Peter Orr (Contract) EST. 1997 CASES 1200
SUMMARY The 6-ha vineyard was established by Lexie and Michael Polin (and family) in 1997. It is
not named for them, as one might expect, but to honour Peter and Thomas Polin, who migrated from
Ireland in 1860, operating a general store in Coonamble. Limb of Addy has a distinctly Irish twist to
it, but is in fact a hill immediately to the east of the vineyard.

Politini Wines ★★★

65 Upper King River Road, Cheshunt, Vic 3678 REGION King Valley
T (03) 5729 8277 F (03) 5729 8373 WEB www.politiniwines.com.au OPEN 7 days 11–5
WINEMAKER Contract EST. 1989 CASES 2200
SUMMARY The Politini family have been grapegrowers in the King Valley supplying major local
wineries since 1989, selling to Brown Brothers, Miranda and the Victorian Alps Winery. In 2000
they decided to withold 20 tonnes per year for the Politini Wines label; they have established sales
outlets at a number of high-class Melbourne restaurants and clubs. The wines are also available
through mail order and the cellar door.

ŦŦŦŦ **King Valley Sangiovese 2003** Bright, clear, red-purple; as the colour promises, fresh and
clear red fruits/raspberry; balanced acidity; subliminal oak. Quality cork. RATING 89
DRINK 2008
King Valley Chardonnay 2002 Light to medium-bodied; clean melon and peach; subtle
oak; good balance and length. Poor cork. RATING 88 DRINK 2007 $ 17

ŦŦŦŸ **Amoroso 2004** RATING 85 DRINK Now $ 14

Polleters ★★★★

Polleters Road, Moonambel, Vic 3478 REGION Pyrenees
T (03) 9569 5030 OPEN Weekends 10–5
WINEMAKER Mark Summerfield EST. 1994 CASES 450
SUMMARY Pauline and Peter Bicknell purchased the 60-ha property on which their vineyard now
stands in 1993, at which time it was part of a larger grazing property. The first vines were planted in
spring 1994, and there are now 2 ha each of shiraz and cabernet sauvignon, 1.25 ha of cabernet
franc and 0.75 ha of merlot. In the first few years the grapes were sold, but as from 2001 part of the
production has been taken to produce the impressively rich and powerful wines. The grapes are
hand-picked, fermented in open vats with hand-plunging, and matured for 18 months in American
oak.

Pondalowie Vineyards ★★★★★

6 Main Street, Bridgewater-on-Loddon, Vic 3516 REGION Bendigo
T (03) 5437 3332 F (03) 5437 3332 WEB www.pondalowie.com.au OPEN Weekends & public hols
12–5, or by appointment
WINEMAKER Dominic Morris, Krystina Morris EST. 1997 CASES 1500
SUMMARY Dominic and Krystina Morris both have strong winemaking backgrounds, gained from
working in Australia, Portugal and France. Dominic has worked alternate vintages in Australia and
Portugal since 1995, and Krystina has worked there, at St Hallett, Boar's Rock and currently for
Portavin wine bottlers. They have established 5.5 ha of shiraz, 2 ha each of tempranillo and cabernet
sauvignon, and a little viognier, malbec and touriga. The wines have been eagerly sought in the UK
market, leaving only a small amount to be sold through trendy Melbourne bars and bistros and a few
country outlets.

ŦŦŦŦŦ **Special Release Shiraz 2003** Deep colour; luscious and opulent, yet not over-extracted; a velvety array of plum, blackberry and spice has soaked up the oak. Half a tonne to the acre; 130 dozen made. Screwcap. **RATING** 96 **DRINK** 2020

Shiraz Viognier 2003 The fusion with Viognier works as it should, with lifted, faintly floral aromas, and supple, silky mouthfeel; perfect control of extract and tannins; 5% Viognier. Screwcap. **RATING** 94 **DRINK** 2015 $ 21.50

ŦŦŦŦŶ **Shiraz 2003** Dense purple-red; medium to full-bodied; a rich, round and supple array of predominantly black fruits; fine, ripe tannins; subtle oak. Screwcap. **RATING** 93 **DRINK** 2013 $ 17.80

Special Release Tempranillo 2003 Deep purple-red; extremely concentrated, powerful and rich; drought-exaggerated, perhaps, brooding black fruits and cherry. Like Tempranillo (Cencibel) from La Mancha. Screwcap. **RATING** 92 **DRINK** 2023 $ 29.50

ŦŦŦŦ **MT Unoaked Tempranillo 2004** Strong purple-red; intense spice and freshly rolled tobacco leaf aromas; touches of cola, then persistent tannins. **RATING** 88 **DRINK** 2009 $ 25

Vineyard Blend 2003 Intense aromas, but a touch of bitterness from reduction; light to medium-bodied; fruit-driven, not complex. Shiraz/Cabernet/Tempranillo blend, co-fermented. Screwcap. **RATING** 87 **DRINK** 2009 $ 14.50

Pontville Station ★★★

948 Midland Highway, Pontville, Tas 7030 **REGION** Southern Tasmania
T (03) 6268 1635 **OPEN** Not
WINEMAKER Peter Rundle **EST.** 1990 **CASES** 90
SUMMARY Peter and Jane Rundle have a tiny vineyard of 0.5 ha, mainly planted to pinot noir. Because the vineyard has been established in a frost-prone site, they have from time to time purchased small quantities of grapes from other growers, but in February 2002 were able to make the first commercial vineyard release, hot on the heels of winning a silver medal with each wine at the 2002 Tasmanian Wines Show, the Pinot Noir in one of the strongest Pinot classes ever seen in Australia, and the Dessert Riesling coming second in its class. No further news, however.

ŦŦŦ **Pinot Noir 2003 RATING** 83

Poole's Rock ★★★

De Beyers Road, Pokolbin, NSW 2321 **REGION** Lower Hunter Valley
T (02) 9563 2500 **F** (02) 9563 2555 **WEB** www.poolesrock.com.au **OPEN** 7 days 10–5
WINEMAKER Patrick Auld **EST.** 1988 **CASES** 42 000
SUMMARY Sydney merchant banker David Clarke has had a long involvement with the wine industry. The 18-ha Poole's Rock vineyard, planted purely to chardonnay, is his personal venture; it was initially bolstered by the acquisition of the larger, adjoining Simon Whitlam Vineyard. However, the purchase of the 74-ha Glen Elgin Estate, upon which the 2500-tonne former Tulloch winery is situated, takes Poole's Rock (and its associated brands, Cockfighter's Ghost and Firestick) into another dimension. Retail distribution throughout Australia; exports to the UK, the US and other major markets.

ŦŦŦŦ **Firestick Shiraz Cabernet 2002** Neatly balanced and constructed; ripe black fruits; above-average mouthfeel. South Australian. **RATING** 87 **DRINK** 2010 $ 14.50

ŦŦŦŶ **Firestick Langhorne Creek Chardonnay 2003 RATING** 86 **DRINK** Now $ 9.89

Firestick Langhorne Creek Chardonnay 2002 RATING 85 **DRINK** Now $ 14.50

Pooley Wines ★★★★☆

Cooinda Vale Vineyard, Barton Vale Road, Campania, Tas 7026 **REGION** Southern Tasmania
T (03) 6224 3591 **F** (03) 6224 3591 **WEB** www.pooleywines.com.au **OPEN** 7 days 10–5
WINEMAKER Matt Pooley, Andrew Hood (Contract) **EST.** 1985 **CASES** 2500
SUMMARY Three generations of the Pooley family have been involved in the development of the Cooinda Vale Estate; the winery was previously known as Cooinda Vale. Plantings have now reached 8 ha on a property which covers both sides of the Coal River in a region which is substantially warmer and drier than most people realise. Retail distribution in Victoria, the ACT and Tasmania.

🍷🍷🍷🍷🍷 **Coal River Riesling 2002** Glowing, bright green-gold; a lovely wine, with bright acidity woven through powerful lime juice flavours. Cork. **RATING** 94 **DRINK** 2012 $ 20

🍷🍷🍷🍷🍸 **Family Reserve Pinot Noir 2003** Strong colour; complex savoury, spicy aromas; slightly unusual but appealing flavours; super-fine tannins. **RATING** 93 **DRINK** 2010 $ 40
Coal Valley Reserve Pinot Noir 2003 Substantial and powerful; plum and black cherry; lingering tannins. **RATING** 90 **DRINK** 2010 $ 40

🍷🍷🍷🍷 **Coal River Pinot Noir 2003** Light to medium-bodied; some bramble starting to develop underlying red cherry fruit; crisp finish. **RATING** 88 **DRINK** 2007 $ 26
Margaret Pooley Tribute Riesling 2004 A big, powerful style; plenty of depth of ripe fruit. **RATING** 87 **DRINK** 2010 $ 28
Nellie's Nest Pinot Noir 2004 Red cherry fruit with some briary/savoury edges; light to medium-bodied; pronounced acidity and needs time. **RATING** 87 **DRINK** 2008 $ 18

🍷🍷🍷🍸 **Cabernet Sauvignon Merlot 2003** **RATING** 86 **DRINK** 2008 $ 35
Family Reserve Cabernet Merlot 2003 **RATING** 86 **DRINK** 2009 $ 35
Coal River Riesling 2004 **RATING** 84 **DRINK** Now $ 20
Coal River Pinot Grigio 2004 **RATING** 84 **DRINK** Now $ 24

🍷🍷🍷 **Cabernet 2002** **RATING** 82

Poplar Bend   NR

RMB 8655, Main Creek Road, Main Ridge, Vic 3928 **REGION** Mornington Peninsula
T (03) 5989 6046 **F** (03) 5989 6460 **OPEN** Weekends & public hols 10–5, and by appointment
WINEMAKER David Briggs **EST.** 1988 **CASES** 350
SUMMARY Poplar Bend was the child of Melbourne journalist, author and raconteur Keith Dunstan and wife Marie, who moved into full-scale retirement in 1997, selling Poplar Bend to David Briggs. The changes are few; the label still depicts Chloe in all her glory, which could be calculated to send the worthy inhabitants of the Bureau of Alcohol, Tobacco and Firearms (of the US) into a state of cataleptic shock.

Port Phillip Estate   ★★★★★

261 Red Hill Road, Red Hill, Vic 3937 **REGION** Mornington Peninsula
T (03) 5989 2708 **F** (03) 5989 3017 **WEB** www.portphillip.net **OPEN** Weekends & public hols 11–5
WINEMAKER Sandro Mosele **EST.** 1987 **CASES** 4000
SUMMARY Established by leading Melbourne QC Jeffrey Sher, who, after some prevarication, sold the estate to Giorgio and Dianne Gjergja in February 2000. The Gjergjas are rightly more than content with the quality and style of the wines; the main changes are enhanced cellar door facilities and redesigned labels. Exports to the UK and the US.

🍷🍷🍷🍷🍷 **Sauvignon Blanc 2004** Aromatic, floral and spotlessly clean; very intense, focused and long; herb, gooseberry and mineral. Diam. **RATING** 94 **DRINK** 2007 $ 22
Chardonnay 2003 Bright green-yellow; elegant and stylish; medium-bodied, with super-smooth nectarine fruit which has absorbed the oak; long, balanced finish. Diam. **RATING** 94 **DRINK** 2009 $ 30

🍷🍷🍷🍷🍸 **Shiraz 2003** Complex spice, licorice, game and black fruit aromas and flavours; lively and elegant; fresh mouthfeel. Diam. **RATING** 93 **DRINK** 2013 $ 35
Pinot Noir 2003 Elegant, light to medium-bodied; cherry, plum and spice flavours; long finish. Diam. **RATING** 91 **DRINK** 2008 $ 35

Portree   ★★★★☆

72 Powells Track via Mt William Road, Lancefield, Vic 3455 **REGION** Macedon Ranges
T (03) 5429 1422 **F** (03) 5429 2205 **WEB** www.portreevineyard.com.au **OPEN** Weekends & public hols 11–5
WINEMAKER Ken Murchison **EST.** 1983 **CASES** 1500
SUMMARY Owner Ken Murchison selected his 5-ha Macedon vineyard after studying viticulture at Charles Sturt University and being strongly influenced by Dr Andrew Pirie's doctoral thesis. All the wines show distinct cool-climate characteristics, the Quarry Red having clear similarities to the

wines of Chinon in the Loire Valley. However, Portree has done best with Chardonnay; this is its principal wine (in terms of volume). Exports to Hong Kong.

ΨΨΨΨΨ **Macedon Ranges Chardonnay 2001** Fine, tangy/citrussy and melon; good length and lingering minerally acidity. Has developed magically well. **RATING** 94 **DRINK** 2008 $ 28

ΨΨΨΨ♀ **Pinot Noir 2003** Intense berry/stem/tomato vine aromas and flavours; considerable length and aftertaste. **RATING** 92 **DRINK** 2009 $ 33

ΨΨΨΨ **Macedon Ranges Chardonnay 2003** A citrus and stone fruit mix, with good length and balanced acidity. Will develop. **RATING** 89 **DRINK** 2010 $ 28
Damask 2004 Lively, fresh spice, leaf and red berry aroma; crisp, minerally acidity; dry finish. Screwcap. **RATING** 87 **DRINK** Now $ 18

ΨΨΨ♀ **Cabernet Franc 2001** **RATING** 86 **DRINK** 2007 $ 25
Amveeta Dessert Wine NV **RATING** 86 **DRINK** 2008 $ 20

ΨΨΨ **Greenstone Chardonnay 2004** **RATING** 83 $ 20

Port Stephens Winery   NR

69 Nelson Bay Road, Bobs Farm, NSW 2316 **REGION** Northern Rivers Zone
T (02) 4982 6411 **F** (02) 4982 6766 **WEB** www.portstephenswinery.com **OPEN** 7 days 10–5
WINEMAKER Contract **EST.** 1984 **CASES** 3500
SUMMARY Planting of the quite substantial Port Stephens Winery vineyard began in 1984, and there are now 4 ha of vines in production. The wines are made under contract in the Hunter Valley but sold through the attractive Boutique Wine Centre onsite, which has recently been extended: it now offers over 100 wines from 30 wineries (as far afield as Manjimup in Western Australia).

Possums Vineyard   ★★★★

31 Thornber Street, Unley Park, SA 5061 (postal) **REGION** McLaren Vale
T (08) 8272 3406 **F** (08) 8272 3406 **OPEN** Not
WINEMAKER Brian Light (Consultant) **EST.** 2000 **CASES** 8000
SUMMARY Possums Vineyard is owned by the very distinguished wine scientist and researcher Dr John Possingham, and Carol Summers. They have 22 ha of shiraz, 16.9 ha of cabernet sauvignon, 13.6 ha of chardonnay and 0.5 ha of grenache established in 2 vineyards, one at Blewitt Springs, the other at Willunga. They regard themselves as grapegrowers, rather than winemakers, with the bulk of the grapes sold to Beringer Blass and d'Arenberg. However, with the advent of Boar's Rock Winery, and the contract-making facilities it offered, they have embarked on making wines under the Possums Vineyard label. Exports to the US, the UK and elsewhere; in Australia the wines are available only by mail order.

ΨΨΨΨ♀ **McLaren Vale Shiraz 2003** Fragrant red and black fruit aromas and flavours; fine tannins; underlay of vanillin oak. Cork. **RATING** 90 **DRINK** 2012 $ 15

Pothana   ★★★★☆

Pothana Lane, Belford, NSW 2335 **REGION** Lower Hunter Valley
T (02) 6574 7164 **F** (02) 6574 7209 **WEB** www.davidhookwines.com.au **OPEN** 7 days 10–5
WINEMAKER David Hook **EST.** 1984 **CASES** 5000
SUMMARY David Hook has over 20 years' experience, as a winemaker for Tyrrell's and Lake's Folly, also doing the full Flying Winemaker bit, with jobs in Bordeaux, the Rhône Valley, Spain, the US and Georgia. He and his family began establishing the vineyard in 1984, the winery in 1990. In 2004 they moved the winery home to the former Peppers Creek Winery (a cellar door is open at Peppers Creek 7 days 10–5). The wines are available by mailing list; distribution by Grapelink in NSW and Victoria, Prime Wines in Queensland and Tasmania.

ΨΨΨΨΨ **Belford Hunter Valley Semillon 2004** Elegant, clean and fresh; delicate yet intense lemon zest flavour; very good acidity and aftertaste. Screwcap. **RATING** 94 **DRINK** 2015 $ 22

ΨΨΨΨ♀ **Belford Hunter Valley Chardonnay 2004** Gently sweet stone fruit, melon and fig; supple and smooth; good length, subtle oak. Screwcap. **RATING** 92 **DRINK** 2010 $ 30

Belford Hunter Valley Shiraz 2003 Very good colour; sweet blackberry, earth and leather fruit; good oak, ripe tannins; shortens fractionally. Screwcap. **RATING** 91 **DRINK** 2016 $ 30

ТТТТ **The Gorge Hunter Valley Viognier 2004** Mouthfilling, rich, textured honey and pastille fruit; a fraction phenolic. Screwcap. **RATING** 87 **DRINK** 2008 $ 16

ТТТ♀ **The Gorge Hunter Valley Chardonnay 2004 RATING** 86 **DRINK** 2007 $ 16
The Gorge Hunter Valley Pinot Gris 2004 RATING 85 **DRINK** Now $ 16
The Gorge Hunter Valley Verdelho 2004 RATING 84 **DRINK** Now $ 16

Potters Clay Vineyards ★★★

Main Road, Willunga, SA 5172 **REGION** McLaren Vale
T (08) 8556 2799 **F** (08) 8556 2922 **OPEN** Not
WINEMAKER John Bruschi **EST.** 1994 **CASES** 900
SUMMARY John and Donna Bruschi are second-generation grapegrowers who assumed full ownership of the 16-ha Potters Clay Vineyard in 1994 with the aim of establishing their own winery and label. In 1999 they completed stage one of a two-stage boutique winery. Stage one is a winery production facility; stage two (at some future date) is to be cellar door, restaurant and garden/picnic area. At least this is in the correct order; all too often the cellar door and restaurant come first. The clever packaging and high-quality promotional literature should do much to enhance sales.

ТТТ♀ **Chardonnay 2001 RATING** 85 **DRINK** Now $ 13.95
Cabernet Franc Shiraz 2001 RATING 84 **DRINK** Now $ 14.95

ТТТ **Semillon Chardonnay 2002 RATING** 83 $ 12.95
Shiraz 2000 RATING 83 $ 15.95
Merlot Cabernet Sauvignon 2000 RATING 81 $ 13.95

Preston Peak ★★★

31 Preston Peak Lane, Toowoomba, Qld 4352 **REGION** Granite Belt
T (07) 4630 9499 **F** (07) 4630 9499 **WEB** www.prestonpeak.com **OPEN** Wed–Sun 10–5
WINEMAKER Rod MacPherson **EST.** 1994 **CASES** 4000
SUMMARY Dentist owners Ashley Smith and Kym Thumpkin have a substantial tourism business. The large, modern cellar door can accommodate functions of up to 150 people, and is often used for weddings and other events. It is situated less than 10 minutes' drive from the Toowoomba city centre, with views of Table Top Mountain, the Lockyer Valley and the Darling Downs.

ТТТТ **Reserve Shiraz 2002** Well-crafted wine; neatly balanced American oak and blackberry/red berry fruits; ripe tannins. Sophisticated making including 90% barrel ferment in new oak. **RATING** 89 **DRINK** 2012 $ 24
Reserve Cabernet Sauvignon 2002 Powerful black fruits; substantial oak, some slightly green tannins to close. **RATING** 89 **DRINK** 2010

ТТТ **Leaf Series Chardonnay 2002 RATING** 83 $ 17
Reserve Chardonnay 2003 RATING 81
Verdelho 2004 RATING 80

Pretty Sally Estate ★★★☆

PO Box 549, Kilmore East, Vic 3764 **REGION** Central Victoria Zone
T (03) 5783 3082 **F** (03) 5783 2027 **WEB** www.prettysally.com **OPEN** Not
WINEMAKER John Ellis (Hanging Rock) **EST.** 1996 **CASES** 900
SUMMARY The McKay, Davies and Cornew families have joined to create the Pretty Sally business. It is based on estate plantings of 11.7 ha of shiraz, 23.8 ha of cabernet sauvignon and a splash of sauvignon blanc. The vineyard is still coming into production, the first commercial vintage being made in 2001. The wines are chiefly exported to the US, where Pretty Sally has a permanent office.

ТТТТ **Sauvignon Blanc 2004** Well balanced, gentle tropical kiwifruit aromas; harmonious, supple and smooth; different profile from the '03, but well made. Screwcap. **RATING** 89 **DRINK** 2007
Shiraz 2003 Very powerful wine; abundant black fruits; some drought effects; dry tannins need to soften. Diam. **RATING** 88 **DRINK** 2013

ТТТ♀ **Cabernet Sauvignon 2002 RATING** 86 **DRINK** 2009

Preveli Wines

Bessell Road, Rosa Brook, Margaret River, WA 6285 **REGION** Margaret River
T (08) 9757 2374 **F** (08) 9757 2790 **WEB** www.preveliwines.com.au **OPEN** At Prevelly General Store
WINEMAKER Andrew Gaman Jnr, Frank Kittler, Mike Lemmes (all Contract) **EST.** 1995 **CASES** 8000
SUMMARY Andrew and Greg Home have turned a small business into a substantial one, with 15 ha of
vineyards at Rosabrook (supplemented by contracts with local growers), and winemaking spread
among a number of contract makers. The wines are of impressive quality. Retail distribution in NSW
(Irvines Fine Wines) and in Perth; the Prevelly General Store (owned by the Homes) is the main local
outlet.

ＹＹＹＹ **Shiraz 2003** Layered texture; oak and tannins surrounding sweet fruit; clever
winemaking. **RATING** 90 **DRINK** 2012 $ 32.95

Primo Estate ★★★★★

Old Port Wakefield Road, Virginia, SA 5120 **REGION** Adelaide Plains
T (08) 8380 9442 **F** (08) 8380 9696 **WEB** www.primoestate.com.au **OPEN** June–Aug Mon–Sat 10–4,
Sep–May Mon–Fri 10–4
WINEMAKER Joseph Grilli **EST.** 1979 **CASES** 20 000
SUMMARY Roseworthy dux Joe Grilli has risen way above the constraints of the hot Adelaide Plains to
produce innovative and always excellent wines. The biennial release of the Joseph Sparkling Red (in
its tall Italian glass bottle) is eagerly awaited, the wine immediately selling out. Also unusual and
highly regarded are the vintage-dated extra virgin olive oils. However, the core lies with the La
Biondina (Colombard), the Il Briccone Shiraz Sangiovese and the Joseph Cabernet Merlot. National
distribution through Negociants; exports to all major markets.

ＹＹＹＹＹ **Joseph Moda Cabernet Merlot 2002** Complex aromas and flavours of tobacco,
blackcurrant, cedar and spice are flanked by ripe, spicy tannins and very good oak. An
overall impression of delectably ripe fruit. **RATING** 95 **DRINK** 2017 $ 55
Joseph Sparkling Red NV Elegant; the driest sparkling red on the market; spicy
complexity; good acidity and length. **RATING** 94 **DRINK** 2010

ＹＹＹＹＹ **Joseph Pinot Grigio d'Elena 2004** Excellent mouthfeel and positive, supple fruit
flavours; honeysuckle and citrus. **RATING** 92 **DRINK** 2007 $ 28

ＹＹＹＹ **La Biondina Colombard 2004** While predominantly colombard, now incorporates lesser
amounts of riesling and sauvignon blanc. As ever, fresh, crisp and lively, with
slippery/squeaky mouthfeel, and a clean, dry finish and aftertaste. **RATING** 89 **DRINK** Now
$ 14.50
Il Briccone Shiraz Sangiovese 2003 High flavour profile, yet elegant, light to medium-
bodied, with fine tannins. **RATING** 89 **DRINK** 2008 $ 19.50
Joseph La Magia 2004 Good balance and length; fully sweet, but nice balancing acidity;
preserved lemon/lime flavours. **RATING** 88 **DRINK** 2009 $ 26

ＹＹＹＹ **Joseph Nebbiolo 2002 RATING** 85 **DRINK** 2010 $ 55

Prince Albert ★★★☆

100 Lemins Road, Waurn Ponds, Vic 3216 **REGION** Geelong
T (03) 5241 8091 **F** (03) 5241 8091 **OPEN** By appointment
WINEMAKER Bruce Hyett **EST.** 1975 **CASES** 100
SUMMARY Australia's true Pinot Noir specialist (it has only ever made the one wine), which also made
much of the early running with the variety: the wines always show good varietal character and have
rebounded after a dull patch in the second half of the 1980s. In 1998 the vineyard and winery was
certified organic by OVAA Inc. Apart from the mailing list, the wine is sold through fine wine
retailers in Sydney and Melbourne, with a little finding its way to the UK. The impact of the drought
resulted in a radically decreased production of the 2002 and 2003 vintages.

ＹＹＹＹ **Pinot Noir 2003 RATING** 86 **DRINK** 2009 $ 25.80

Prince of Orange ★★★★

'Cimbria', The Escort Way, Borenore, NSW 2800 **REGION** Orange
T (02) 6365 2396 **F** (02) 6365 2396 **OPEN** Sat 11–5, or by appointment
WINEMAKER Greg Silkman, Jim Chatto (Contract) **EST.** 1996 **CASES** 2400
SUMMARY Harald and Coral Brodersen purchased the 40-ha Cimbria property in 1990, and planted 3 ha of Sauvignon Blanc and 2 ha of Cabernet Sauvignon in 1996, followed by more recent and smaller plantings of merlot, viognier, shiraz and semillon. The name and label design were inspired by the link between Thomas Livingstone Mitchell, Surveyor-General of New South Wales, who served in the British Army during the Peninsular Wars against Napoleon alongside Willem, Prince of Orange, who was aide-de-camp to the Duke of Wellington. It was Mitchell who named the town Orange in honour of his friend, who had by then been crowned King Willem II of The Netherlands.

ΨΨΨΨΨ **Sauvignon Blanc 2004** Excellent varietal expression; firm and spotlessly clean herb, redcurrant and red capsicum fruit; great length and focus. Screwcap. **RATING** 94 **DRINK** 2007 $18

ΨΨΨΨ **Cabernet Sauvignon 2003** Light to medium-bodied; redcurrant and mint aromas and flavours; nice mouthfeel, fine tannins; unforced. **RATING** 87 **DRINK** 2009 $23

ΨΨΨ♀ **Cabernet Rose 2004** Raspberry and redcurrant fruit; fresh, crisp and dry; lively acidity. Quixotic cork (not screwcap) closure. **RATING** 86 **DRINK** Now $18

ΨΨΨ **Mistelle Blanc 2004** **RATING** 83 $19

Principia ★★★★

139 Main Creek Road, Red Hill, Vic 3937 (postal) **REGION** Mornington Peninsula
T (03) 5931 0010 **WEB** www.principiawines.com.au **OPEN** Not
WINEMAKER Rebecca Gaffy **EST.** 1995 **CASES** 400
SUMMARY Darren and Rebecca Gaffy spent their honeymoon in South Australia, and awakened their love of wines. In due course they gravitated to Burgundy, and in 1994 began the search in Australia for a suitable cool-climate site to grow pinot noir and chardonnay. In 1995 they began to develop the vineyard, with 2.6 ha of pinot noir, and 0.8 ha of chardonnay. Darren continues to work full-time as a toolmaker (and in the vineyard on weekends and holidays); while Rebecca's career as a nurse took second place to the Bachelor of Applied Science (Wine Science) course at Charles Sturt University – she graduated in 2002. Along the way she worked at Red Hill Estate, Bass Phillip, Virgin Hills and Tuck's Ridge, and as winemaker at Massoni Homes. They built a rammed-earth house onsite, where they live with their two boys. Construction of a cellar door is to commence soon.

ΨΨΨΨ♀ **Pinot Noir 2003** Clean; light to medium-bodied; attractive plum, cherry and raspberry fruit mix; fine tannins, subtle oak. Well-made. Diam. **RATING** 90 **DRINK** 2008 $32.50

Printhie Wines ★★★☆

Yuranigh Road, Molong, NSW 2866 **REGION** Orange
T (02) 6366 8422 **F** (02) 6366 9328 **WEB** www.printhiewines.com.au **OPEN** Mon–Sat 10–4
WINEMAKER Robert Black **EST.** 1996 **CASES** 18 000
SUMMARY Jim and Ruth Swift have planted 32 ha of viognier, cabernet sauvignon, merlot and shiraz, and built the largest winery in the region. As well as making the Printhie wines, full-time winemaker Robert Black oversees contract winemaking for others. Adding further weight, Printhie supplements the estate-grown grapes with grapes purchased from growers in the region. The wines are modestly priced, and will gain weight as the vines mature.

ΨΨΨΨ **Orange Riesling 2004** Clean, fine, minerally blossom aromas; the palate ebbs and flows between sweeter fruit and drier, savoury characters. Screwcap. **RATING** 89 **DRINK** 2010 $14

Orange Cabernet Merlot 2004 Light to medium-bodied; an attractive mix of red fruits and spice; fine-grained tannins; good mouthfeel. Screwcap. **RATING** 88 **DRINK** 2009 $14

Orange Chardonnay 2004 Light-bodied; unforced, light nectarine and melon; a subtle hint of French oak. Screwcap. **RATING** 87 **DRINK** 2008 $14

ΨΨΨ♀ **Orange Sauvignon Blanc 2004** **RATING** 86 **DRINK** 2007 $14

Provenance Wines ★★★★

870 Steiglitz Road, Sutherlands Creek, Vic 3331 **REGION** Geelong
T (03) 5281 2230 **F** (03) 5281 2205 **WEB** www.provenancewines.com.au **OPEN** By appointment
WINEMAKER Scott Ireland **EST.** 1995 **CASES** 2000
SUMMARY A joint venture between Pam and Richard Austin of Austin's Barrabool wines and Scott Ireland has resulted in a new winery being built on land owned by the Austins at Sutherlands Creek, and leased to winemaker Scott Ireland. Here he will make the Provenance wines, the Austin's Barrabool wines, and provide contract winemaking services for small companies in the region.

ΨΨΨΨΨ **Geelong Pinot Noir 2003** Attractive, warm and soft varietal fruit; nice touch of spice. **RATING** 93 **DRINK** 2012 $ 30
Geelong Pinot Gris 2004 Full-bodied, supple and smooth; good weight and varietal fruit. **RATING** 90 **DRINK** 2007 $ 27.90

ΨΨΨΨ **Geelong Chardonnay 2003 RATING** 86 **DRINK** 2009 $ 23.50

Providence Vineyards ★★★★☆

236 Lalla Road, Lalla, Tas 7267 **REGION** Northern Tasmania
T (03) 6395 1290 **F** (03) 6395 2088 **WEB** www.providence-vineyards.com.au **OPEN** 7 days 10–5
WINEMAKER Andrew Hood (Contract) **EST.** 1956 **CASES** 1000
SUMMARY Providence incorporates the pioneer vineyard of Frenchman Jean Miguet, now owned by the Bryce family, which purchased it in 1980. The original 1.3-ha vineyard has been expanded to a little over 3 ha, and unsuitable grenache and cabernet (left from the original plantings) have been grafted over to chardonnay, pinot noir and semillon. Miguet called the vineyard 'La Provence', reminding him of the part of France he came from, but after 40 years the French authorities forced a name change to Providence. The cellar door offers 70 different wines from all over Tasmania.

ΨΨΨΨΨ **Chardonnay 2003** Very complex wine with positive barrel ferment and malolactic inputs; strong melon and nectarine fruit to sustain those inputs. **RATING** 94 **DRINK** 2009 $ 23.50

ΨΨΨΨ **Pinot Noir 2003 RATING** 86 **DRINK** 2008 $ 25
Riesling 2004 RATING 85 **DRINK** 2007 $ 19

Puddleduck Vineyard ★★★☆

992 Richmond Road, Richmond, Tas 7024 **REGION** Southern Tasmania
T (03) 6260 2301 **F** (03) 6260 2301 **WEB** www.puddleduckvineyard.com.au **OPEN** 7 days 10–5
WINEMAKER Andrew Hood (Contract) **EST.** 1997 **CASES** 500
SUMMARY The cutely named Puddleduck Vineyard is owned and run by Darren and Jackie Brown. Darren's career began at Moorilla Estate, mowing lawns (aged 16); he ended up as assistant winemaker to Julian Alcorso, and also as vineyard manager. With the changing of the guard at Moorilla Darren left to become vineyard manager of both Craigow and 572 Richmond Road in the Coal Valley. Jackie moved to Craigow when its cellar door opened, then worked in the restaurant and cellar door at Coal Valley Vineyard (formerly Treehouse). In the meantime, they had purchased a house with a block of land suitable for viticulture. So far, they have planted 0.6 ha of pinot noir and 0.4 ha of sauvignon blanc; they are sourcing grapes from other vineyards in the region (particularly those managed by Darren) until they have sufficient vineyards of their own.

ΨΨΨΨ **Chardonnay 2004** Quite complex, with a lot of activity on the bouquet; tangy grapefruit and nectarine palate; long finish. **RATING** 89 **DRINK** 2008 $ 24

ΨΨΨΨ **Sauvignon Blanc 2004 RATING** 86 **DRINK** Now $ 22
Riesling 2004 RATING 85 **DRINK** 2008 $ 27

Punters Corner ★★★★★

Cnr Riddoch Highway/Racecourse Road, Coonawarra, SA 5263 **REGION** Coonawarra
T (08) 8737 2007 **F** (08) 8737 3138 **WEB** www.punterscorner.com.au **OPEN** 7 days 10–5
WINEMAKER Peter Bissell (Contract) **EST.** 1988 **CASES** 10 000
SUMMARY Punters Corner started off life in 1975 as James Haselgrove, but in 1992 was acquired by a group of investors who evidently had few delusions about the uncertainties of viticulture and

winemaking, even in a district as distinguished as Coonawarra. The arrival of Peter Bissell as winemaker at Balnaves paid immediate (and continuing) dividends. Sophisticated packaging and label design add to the appeal of the wines. National retail distribution; exports to the UK, the US, Hong Kong, China, Malaysia, Singapore and Japan.

ŶŶŶŶŶ **Spartacus Reserve Shiraz 2002** Deeply coloured; the potent, penetrating bouquet leads into lusciously abundant mid-palate blackberry and spice, balanced by fine tannins and faintly smoky oak on the finish. **RATING** 96 **DRINK** 2015 $ 65
Cabernet Sauvignon 2002 Attractive bright cassis and blackcurrant fruit leads the way; fine ripe tannins and good oak; elegant style. **RATING** 94 **DRINK** 2012 $ 30

ŶŶŶŶŶ **Triple Crown 2002** Medium-bodied; very typical 2002 vintage character; nice touch of vanilla oak, and the tannins ripe. **RATING** 90 **DRINK** 2012 $ 24

ŶŶŶŶ **Single Vineyard Coonawarra Chardonnay 2003** A mix of peach, stone fruit and spicy oak; overall, medium-bodied, soft and accessible. **RATING** 89 **DRINK** 2007 $ 26
Coonawarra Shiraz 2002 Very firm savoury, earthy fruit; at the austere end of the spectrum; the '02 vintage in Coonawarra at work. Cork. **RATING** 89 **DRINK** 2010 $ 20

Punt Road   ★★★★☆

10 St Huberts Road, Coldstream, Vic 3770 **REGION** Yarra Valley
T (03) 9739 0666 **F** (03) 9739 0633 **WEB** www.puntroadwines.com.au **OPEN** 7 days 10–5
WINEMAKER Kate Goodman **EST.** 2000 **CASES** 6000
SUMMARY Punt Road was originally known as The Yarra Hill, a name abandoned because of the proliferation of wineries with the word 'Yarra' as part of their name. The winery (still opposite St Huberts) produces the Punt Road wines, as well as undertaking substantial contract winemaking for others. The Punt Road wines are made from the best parcels of fruit grown on 100 ha of vineyards owned by members of the Punt Road syndicate, and represent the tip of the iceberg.

ŶŶŶŶŶ **MVN Shiraz 2001** Very good, deep red-purple; intense spice, sweet leather and abundant dark fruit flavours. Super-premium release to honour one of Punt Road's founders, Michael Vivian Napoleone. **RATING** 96 **DRINK** 2021 $ 48

ŶŶŶŶŶ **Yarra Valley Sauvignon Blanc 2004** Crisp, clean and mineral, with a hint of passionfruit to the bouquet; tight, crisp and long in the mouth; lemony minerality to the finish.
RATING 90 **DRINK** 2007 $ 20
Yarra Valley Pinot Gris 2004 Apple, pear and musk aromas; considerable varietal expression, yet the palate avoids heaviness; whiff of oak a further plus. **RATING** 90
DRINK 2007 $ 21.99
Yarra Valley Cabernet Sauvignon 2002 Fine, elegant, medium-bodied; blackcurrant, with touches of earth and olive; fine, ripe tannins and subtle oak. **RATING** 90 **DRINK** 2012
$ 25.99
Botrytis Semillon 2003 Yellow-gold; nicely balanced peachy/apricot fruit; good acidity, good length. **RATING** 90 **DRINK** 2008 $ 31.99

ŶŶŶŶ **Yarra Valley Merlot 2003** Bright red-purple; fresh, clean and firm bright fruit aromas and flavours; not complex, but has length, and may build with time. **RATING** 87
DRINK 2010 $ 25

Purple Patch Wines   NR

101 Main Avenue, Merbein, Vic 3505 **REGION** Murray Darling
T (03) 5025 3558 **F** (03) 5025 2253 **OPEN** By appointment
WINEMAKER Brian Davey **EST.** 2001 **CASES** NA
SUMMARY The neatly named Purple Patch Wines has been established by Brian Davey with a 2.5 ha planting of cabernet sauvignon, merlot and shiraz. The wines are made onsite by Brian with assistance from a contract winemaker. The small production is principally sold by mail order.

Pycnantha Hill Estate

Benbournie Road, Clare, SA 5453 (postal) **REGION** Clare Valley
T (08) 8842 2137 **F** (08) 8842 2137 **WEB** www.pycnanthahill.com.au **OPEN** Not
WINEMAKER Jim Howarth **EST.** 1997 **CASES** 1000

SUMMARY The Howarth family progressively established 2.4 ha of vineyard from 1987, and made its first commercial vintage in 1997. *Acacia pycnantha* is the botanic name for the golden wattle which grows wild over the hills of the Howarth farm, and they say it was 'a natural choice to name our vineyards Pycnantha Hill'. I am not too sure that marketing gurus would agree, but there we go.

♟♟♟♟♡ **Clare Valley Riesling 2004** Spotlessly clean; herb, mineral, apple and citrus blossom aromas; very lively, fresh and elegant in the mouth; good length and balance; bargain price. Screwcap. **RATING** 93 **DRINK** 2010 $15

♟♟♟♟ **Clare Valley Cabernet Merlot 2003** Savoury, spicy earthy overtones to dark berry fruit; medium-bodied; subtle oak. **RATING** 87 **DRINK** 2012 $16

♟♟♟♡ **Clare Valley Chardonnay 2003** **RATING** 86 **DRINK** 2007 $18
Clare Valley Shiraz 2003 **RATING** 86 **DRINK** 2008 $16

Pyramid Hill Wines ★★★★

194 Martindale Road, Denman, NSW 2328 **REGION** Upper Hunter Valley
T (02) 6547 2755 **F** (02) 6547 2735 **WEB** www.pyramidhillwines.com **OPEN** 7 days 10–5
WINEMAKER Jim Chatto (Monarch Winemaking Services) **EST.** 2002 **CASES** 6000
SUMMARY Pyramid Hill is a partnership between the Adler and Hilder families. Richard Hilder is a veteran viticulturist who oversaw the establishment of many of the Rosemount vineyards. Nicholas Adler and Caroline Sherwood made their mark in the international film industry before moving to Pyramid Hill in 1997 with their four young children. There are now 72 ha of chardonnay, semillon, verdelho, shiraz, merlot, cabernet sauvignon and ruby cabernet, with a computer-controlled irrigation system backed up by a network of radio-linked weather and soil moisture sensors which constantly relay data detailing the amount of available moisture at different soil depths to a central computer, thus avoiding excess irrigation and preventing stress. Most of the grapes are sold to leading makers (guess who), but a small amount has been vinified under the Pyramid Hill label, with cautious expansion in the years ahead. The wines are very competently contract-made by Jim Chatto. Exports to the UK.

♟♟♟♟♡ **Semillon 2004** Lively, fresh, lemony tang to both bouquet and palate; crisp finish; best now? Screwcap. **RATING** 91 **DRINK** 2010 $17

♟♟♟♟ **Verdelho 2004** Good varietal character; fruit salad balanced and extended by citrussy/lemony acidity. Screwcap. **RATING** 88 **DRINK** 2007 $17
Chardonnay 2004 Light-bodied but quite stylish; good French oak handling; nectarine and melon, spicy finish. Screwcap. **RATING** 87 **DRINK** 2008 $20
Chardonnay 2003 Very much in the Pyramid Hill style; gentle fruit and well-controlled French oak; melon and cashew. Cork. **RATING** 87 **DRINK** 2007 $20
Merlot 2003 Very good colour; fragrant, fresh and clean red berry fruit aromas and flavours; light to medium-bodied. Cork. **RATING** 87 **DRINK** 2009 $22

♟♟♟♡ **Shiraz 2003** **RATING** 86 **DRINK** 2009 $22
Rose Saignee 2004 **RATING** 84 **DRINK** Now $17

Pyramids Road Wines ★★★★

Pyramids Road, Wyberba, Qld 4382 **REGION** Granite Belt
T (07) 4684 5151 **F** (07) 4684 5151 **OPEN** Weekends & public hols 10–4.30
WINEMAKER Warren Smith **EST.** 1999 **CASES** 500
SUMMARY Warren Smith and partner Sue moved to the Granite Belt region in 1999. With encouragement and assistance from the team at Ballandean Estate, the first vines were planted in November 1999; the first vintage was 2002. Current vineyard area is just 2 ha; further plantings are planned but will not exceed 4 ha. The 2002 Shiraz won Best Queensland Shiraz at the 2003 Australian Small Winemakers Show. All wines are made onsite and the production area can be viewed from the cellar door.

♟♟♟♟♡ **Granite Belt Shiraz 2002** Medium-bodied; smoky, briary vanilla aromas; blackberry and plum fruit; good mouthfeel and ripe tannins, though trophy at the Small Winemakers Show a surprise. **RATING** 90 **DRINK** 2010 $32

♟♟♟♟ **Granite Belt Bernie's Blend 2002** Quite powerful mix of Cabernet, Shiraz and Merlot; black fruits, bitter chocolate, leaf and spice; substantial but ripe tannins; has the structure to develop. Twin Top. **RATING** 88 **DRINK** 2010 $24

Granite Belt Cabernet Sauvignon 2002 Dried gum leaf and spice aromas; more conventional palate; light-bodied, but creditable, particularly the fine tannin finish. Cork. **RATING** 87 **DRINK** 2009 $ 20

ҮҮҮҮ **Granite Belt Verdelho 2004** **RATING** 84 **DRINK** 2007 $ 18

Pyrenees Ridge Vineyard ★★★★☆

532 Caralulup Road, Lamplough via Avoca, Vic 3467 **REGION** Pyrenees
T (03) 5465 3710 **F** (03) 5465 3320 **WEB** www.pyreneesridge.com.au **OPEN** Thurs–Mon & public hols 10–5
WINEMAKER Graeme Jukes **EST.** 1998 **CASES** 1800
SUMMARY Notwithstanding the quite extensive winemaking experience (and formal training) of Graeme Jukes, this started life as a small-scale, winemaking in the raw version of the French garagiste approach. Graeme and his wife, Sally-Ann, have planted 2 ha each of cabernet sauvignon and shiraz; the grape intake is supplemented by purchases from other growers in the region. The success of the wines has been such that the winery size will be doubled, another 1.5 ha of estate plantings will be completed, and contract purchases increased. Contract winemaking for others will also be expanded. Limited retail distribution; most is sold by through the website and the cellar door. Exports (tiny) to the US.

ҮҮҮҮҮ **Reserve Shiraz 2003** Powerful, focused and complex; intense spice, black fruits and blackberry; integrated American oak and lingering tannins. **RATING** 94 **DRINK** 2015 $ 45

ҮҮҮҮҮ **Shiraz 2003** Abundant, rich plum and blackberry fruits; plush, medium to full-bodied style; soft, ripe tannins; balanced oak. **RATING** 92 **DRINK** 2010 $ 25
Cabernet Shiraz 2003 Good colour; clean, rich and powerful, the tannins poking through a little more; good oak handling. **RATING** 90 **DRINK** 2013 $ 23

Queen Adelaide ★★☆

Eddy Road, Karadoc, Vic 3496 **REGION** Southeast Australia
T (03) 5051 3333 **F** (03) 5051 3390 **OPEN** Not
WINEMAKER Various **EST.** 1858 **CASES** NFP
SUMMARY The famous brand established by Woodley Wines and some years ago, subsumed into the Seppelt and now Southcorp Group. It is a pure brand, without any particular home either in terms of winemaking or fruit sources, but is hugely successful; Queen Adelaide Chardonnay is and has for some time been the largest-selling bottled white wine in Australia. The move away from agglomerate to screwcap closures has ended the glue-taint problems of prior years. The 2002 releases had synthetic corks, inappropriate for anything other than immediate consumption.

ҮҮҮҮ **Brut NV** Excellent mousse, plenty of grapey flavour, and controlled sweetness. Adding a dash of orange juice would not be a capital offence. **RATING** 85 **DRINK** Now $ 6.82
Regency Red 2004 **RATING** 85 **DRINK** Now $ 7.45

ҮҮҮ **Chardonnay 2004** **RATING** 83 $ 7.45

Racecourse Lane Wines ★★★

PO Box 215, Balgowlah, NSW 2093 **REGION** Lower Hunter Valley
T 0418 242 490 **F** (02) 9949 7185 **WEB** www.racecourselane.com.au **OPEN** Not
WINEMAKER David Fatches (Contract) **EST.** 1998 **CASES** 800
SUMMARY Mike and Helen McGorman purchased the 15-ha property now known as Racecourse Lane Wines in 1998. They have established 1.6 ha of shiraz and 0.8 ha each of semillon, verdelho and sangiovese. Consultancy viticultural advice from Brian Hubbard, and winemaking by David Fatches, a long-term Hunter Valley winemaker (who also makes wine in France each year) has paid dividends. The wines are sold only by mail order and to a handful of top restaurants, including Rockpool in Sydney. Exports to the UK.

ҮҮҮҮ **Hunter Valley Semillon 2004** Clean, correct aromas; light-bodied; balanced, but lacks intensity. Screwcap. **RATING** 87 **DRINK** 2008 $ 19
Hunter Valley Sangiovese 2004 A mix of spice, earth and sour cherries; light to medium-bodied; good balance, positive varietal character. **RATING** 87 **DRINK** 2009 $ 19

ҮҮҮҮ **Hunter Valley Verdelho 2004** **RATING** 85 **DRINK** Now $ 19

🐦 Rahona Valley Vineyard ★★★☆

PO Box 256, Red Hill South, Vic 3939 **REGION** Mornington Peninsula
T (03) 5989 2924 **F** (03) 5989 2924 **WEB** www.rahonavalley.com.au **OPEN** Not
WINEMAKER John Salmons, Rebecca Gaffy (Consultant) **EST.** 1991 **CASES** 200
SUMMARY John and Leonie Salmons have one of the older and more interesting small vineyards in the Mornington Peninsula, on a steep north-facing slope of a small valley in the Red Hill area. The area takes its name from the ancient red basalt soils. In all there are 1.3 ha of pinot noir planted to 5 different clones and a few hundred vines of pinot meunier.

ΨΨΨΨ **Reserve Red Hill Pinot Noir 2003** Far more complex and intense than the varietal; good oak input and greater texture; interestingly, same alcohol (13.9°). **RATING** 91 **DRINK** 2009 $ 27

ΨΨΨΨ **Red Hill Pinot Meunier 2003** Very good colour hue; lively, vibrant, sappy, citrussy tang to crisp, red fruits; good example of the variety in the table wine mode. **RATING** 88 **DRINK** 2008 $ 20
Red Hill Pinot Noir 2003 Ripe plum, cherry and spice; light to medium-bodied; a fraction linear; slightly hard finish. Cork. **RATING** 87 **DRINK** 2007 $ 20

Raleigh Winery NR

Queen Street, Raleigh, NSW 2454 **REGION** Northern Rivers Zone
T (02) 6655 4388 **F** (02) 6655 4265 **WEB** www.raleighwines.com **OPEN** Wed–Sun 10–5, 7 days during school hols
WINEMAKER Lavinia Dingle **EST.** 1982 **CASES** 500
SUMMARY Raleigh Winery lays claim to being Australia's most easterly vineyard. The vineyard was begun in 1982 and purchased by Lavinia and Neil Dingle in 1989. The wine is produced in part from 1 ha of vines planted to no less than six varieties, and have won bronze medals at the Griffith Wine Show.

Ralph Fowler Wines ★★★★

Limestone Coast Road, Mount Benson, SA 5275 **REGION** Mount Benson
T (08) 8768 5000 **F** (08) 8768 5008 **OPEN** 7 days 10–5
WINEMAKER Sarah Squires **EST.** 1999 **CASES** 4000
SUMMARY Established in February 1999 by the Fowler family, headed by well-known winemaker Ralph Fowler, with wife Deborah and children Sarah (Squires) and James all involved in the 40-ha vineyard property. Ralph Fowler began his winemaking career at Tyrrell's, moving to the position of chief winemaker before moving to Hungerford Hill, then the Hamilton/Leconfield group. In 2005 he passed on the operation of the business to Sarah. Exports to Europe and Asia.

ΨΨΨΨ **Limestone Coast Shiraz 2001** Ripe blackberry, plum, licorice and chocolate aromas and flavours; medium-bodied; good structure and balance; fine tannins, long finish. High-quality cork. **RATING** 92 **DRINK** 2016 $ 25
Limestone Coast Botrytis Semillon 2003 Extremely luscious and complex; apricot, cumquat, lime and vanilla flavours; long finish. **RATING** 92 **DRINK** 2009 $ 25

ΨΨΨΨ **Mount Benson Sauvignon Blanc 2004** Clean, crisp and minerally; good mouthfeel largely driven by lively acidity; hints of herb and gooseberry along the way. Screwcap. **RATING** 89 **DRINK** 2007 $ 18
Mount Benson Viognier 2004 Dried apricot/apple/spice varietal fruit; good weight. **RATING** 87 **DRINK** Now $ 25
Limestone Coast Cabernet Sauvignon 2002 Uncompromisingly light-bodied, but has some elegance and ripe fruit. **RATING** 87 **DRINK** 2009 $ 25

ΨΨΨ **Shiraz Viognier 2003 RATING** 83 $ 25

Ramsay's Vin Rose ★★★☆

30 St Helier Road, The Gurdies, Vic 3984 **REGION** Gippsland
T (03) 5997 6531 **F** (03) 5997 6158 **OPEN** 7 days 1—5
WINEMAKER Dianne Ramsay **EST.** 1995 **CASES** 500

SUMMARY The slightly curious name (which looks decidedly strange in conjunction with Riesling and Cabernet Sauvignon) stems from the original intention of Alan and Dianne Ramsay to grow roses on a commercial scale on their property. Frank Cutler, at Western Port Winery, persuaded them to plant wine grapes instead; they established the first 2 ha of vines in 1995. They opened their micro-winery in 1999, and have four 2-bedroom self-contained units set around their 800-bush rose garden.

ᵀᵀᵀᵀ **Riesling 2003** Bright straw-green colour; extremely powerful Alsatian style; rich and some phenolics; demands food. Good cork. **RATING** 89 **DRINK** 2007 $ 15

Random Valley Organic Wines   NR

PO Box 11, Karridale, WA 6288 **REGION** Margaret River
T (08) 9758 6707 **F** (08) 9758 6707 **WEB** www.randomvalley.com **OPEN** Not
WINEMAKER Saxon Mountford **EST.** 1995 **CASES** 3000
SUMMARY The Little family has established 7 ha of sauvignon blanc, semillon, shiraz and cabernet sauvignon, with a no-holds-barred organic grapegrowing program. No chemical-based fertilisers, pesticides or herbicides are used in the vineyard, building humus and biological activity in the soil. Given that the 7 ha produce 50 tonnes per year, it is evident that the approach has worked well. The wines are sold by mail order and the website.

Rangemore Estate   NR

366 Malling–Boundary Road, Maclagan, Qld 4352 **REGION** Darling Downs
T (07) 4692 1338 **F** (07) 4692 1338 **OPEN** Fri–Sun 10–5
WINEMAKER Mark Ravenscroft (Contract) **EST.** 1999 **CASES** 600
SUMMARY The 4.5-ha vineyard of Rangemore Estate, planted to verdelho, shiraz, cabernet and merlot, is high in the southern foothills of the Bunya Mountains. The soil is a sandy loam over sandstone, and the low-yielding vines are grown with little or no irrigation. The founding Allen family operate a cellar door and café, with B&B accommodation, offering spectacular views of the Bunya Mountains. Winemaking is carried out by the experienced and skilled Mark Ravenscroft.

Ravens Croft Wines   ★★★★

274 Spring Creek Road, Stanthorpe, Qld 4380 **REGION** Granite Belt
T (07) 4683 3252 **F** (07) 4683 3252 **OPEN** Fri–Sun, or by appointment
WINEMAKER Mark Ravenscroft **EST.** 2002 **CASES** 600
SUMMARY Mark Ravenscroft is the South African-born and trained winemaker at Robert Channon Wines, where he has had outstanding success. He makes small quantities of wine from 0.3 ha of verdelho and 0.2 ha of cabernet sauvignon, all sold through his cellar door, mailing list and independent bottle shops and restaurants.

ᵀᵀᵀᵀᵞ **Chardonnay 2004** Slightly old-fashioned but ripe; full-flavoured wine; controlled oak. **RATING** 90 **DRINK** 2008

Ravensworth   ★★★★

Rosehill Vineyard, PO Box 116, Mawson, ACT 2607 **REGION** Canberra District
T (02) 6226 8368 **F** (02) 6226 8378 **WEB** www.ravensworthwines.com.au **OPEN** Not
WINEMAKER Bryan Martin **EST.** 2000 **CASES** 1000
SUMMARY Winemaker, vineyard manager and partner Bryan Martin (with dual wine science and winegrowing degrees from Charles Sturt University) had a background of wine retail, and food and beverages in the hospitality industry; he teaches part-time in that field. He is also assistant winemaker to Tim Kirk at Clonakilla, after 7 years at Jeir Creek. Judging at wine shows is another arrow to his bow. Ravensworth has 7 ha of vineyards spread over two sites: Rosehill, planted in 1998 to cabernet sauvignon, merlot and sauvignon blanc, and Martin Block, (planted 2000/01) to shiraz, viognier, marsanne and sangiovese.

ᵀᵀᵀᵀᵀ **Canberra District Shiraz 2003** Rich, concentrated blackberry, mulberry, licorice and spice fruit; neatly balanced touch of French oak; ripe tannins. **RATING** 94 **DRINK** 2018 $ 25

ᵀᵀᵀᵀ **Canberra District Cabernet Merlot 2003** A medium-bodied mix of black and red fruits; ripe, slightly spicy tannins; balanced oak. **RATING** 89 **DRINK** 2013 $ 18

Canberra District Marsanne 2003 A complex wine; strong winemaker inputs but varietal character is still evident courtesy of honeysuckle and citrus. **RATING** 87 **DRINK** 2008 $16
Canberra District Sangiovese Merlot 2003 Light, spicy, savoury/earthy cherry fruit; a seamless blend of two similar varieties. **RATING** 87 **DRINK** 2007 $18

Raydon Estate ★★★★

Lake Plains Road, Langhorne Creek, SA 5255 **REGION** Langhorne Creek
T (08) 8537 3158 **F** (08) 8537 3158 **OPEN** At Bremer Place, Langhorne Creek
WINEMAKER Wayne Dutschke (Contract) **EST.** 1999 **CASES** 1200
SUMMARY The establishment date of any winery business can have a wide number of meanings. In this instance it is the date of the first vintage, but Colleen and Joe Borrett planted 8 ha each of shiraz and cabernet sauvignon many years ago, selling the majority of the grapes to Bleasdale and Southcorp. A small parcel of shiraz not under contract allowed them to move into the winemaking business; they have now added a little cabernet sauvignon. Exports to the US and Malaysia.

Ray-Monde ★★★☆

250 Dalrymple Road, Sunbury, Vic 3429 **REGION** Sunbury
T (03) 5428 2657 **F** (03) 5428 3390 **OPEN** Sundays, or by appointment
WINEMAKER John Lakey **EST.** 1988 **CASES** 700
SUMMARY The Lakey family has established 5 ha of pinot noir on their 230-ha grazing property at an altitude of 400m. Initially the grapes were sold to Domaine Chandon, but in 1994 son John Lakey (who had gained experience at Tarrawarra, Rochford, Virgin Hills and Coonawarra, plus a vintage in Burgundy) began making the wine – and very competently.

Reads NR

Evans Lane, Oxley, Vic 3678 **REGION** King Valley
T (03) 5727 3386 **F** (03) 5727 3386 **OPEN** Mon–Sat 9–5, Sun 10–6
WINEMAKER Kenneth Read **EST.** 1972 **CASES** 1900
SUMMARY Limited tastings have not impressed, but there may be a jewel lurking somewhere, such as the medal-winning though long-gone 1990 Sauvignon Blanc. No tastings for some time.

Redbank Winery ★★★★☆

1 Sally's Lane, Redbank, Vic 3467 **REGION** Pyrenees
T (03) 5467 7255 **F** (03) 5467 3478 **WEB** www.sallyspaddock.com.au **OPEN** Mon–Sat 9–5, Sun 10–5
WINEMAKER Neill Robb **EST.** 1973 **CASES** 8000
SUMMARY Neill Robb makes very concentrated wines, full of character; the levels of volatile acidity can be intrusive, but are probably of more concern to technical tasters than to the general public. Sally's Paddock is the star, a single-vineyard block with an esoteric mix of cabernet, shiraz and malbec; over the years, it has produced many great wines. Exports to the US, Canada and The Philippines.

♥♥♥♥♥ **Sally's Paddock 2002** Very powerful and tightly structured; full-bodied black fruits, spice, cedar and earth; long, lingering finish; ripe tannins. Quality cork. **RATING** 94
DRINK 2022 $47.30

♥♥♥♥ **The Anvil Heathcote Shiraz 2001** Colour less dense than many from Heathcote; light to medium-bodied; clean, red berry fruits, gentle tannins; very subtle French oak. **RATING** 89
DRINK 2008 $50

Red Clay Estate ★★☆

269 Henry Lawson Drive, Mudgee, NSW 2850 **REGION** Mudgee
T (02) 6372 4569 **F** (02) 6372 4596 **OPEN** Jan–Sept 7 days 10–5, Oct–Dec Mon–Fri 10–5, or by appointment
WINEMAKER Ken Heslop **EST.** 1997 **CASES** NA

SUMMARY Ken Heslop and Annette Bailey are among the recent arrivals in Mudgee, with a 2.5-ha vineyard planted to a diverse range of varieties. The wines are sold only through the cellar door and by mail order.

Red Earth Estate Vineyard ★★★

18L Camp Road, Dubbo, NSW 2830 REGION Western Plains Zone
T (02) 6885 6676 F (02) 6882 8297 WEB www.redearthestate.com.au OPEN Thurs–Tues 10–5
WINEMAKER Ken Borchardt EST. 2000 CASES 3000
SUMMARY Ken and Christine Borchardt look set to be the focal point of winegrowing and making in the future Macquarie Valley region of the Western Plains Zone. They have planted 1.3 ha each of riesling, verdelho, frontignac, grenache, shiraz and cabernet sauvignon at the winery, and gamay, tempranillo, barbera and carmenere at the Macquarie Grove Vineyard at Narromine. The winery has a capacity of 14 000 cases, and the Borchardts are offering contract winemaking facilities in addition to making and marketing their own brand.

ΥΥΥΫ **Macquarie Grove Tempranillo 2003** Has some varietal flavour, but the structure is rather awkward. RATING 86 DRINK 2008 $ 38
Macquarie Grove Gamay 2003 RATING 84 DRINK Now $ 25

ΥΥΥ **Winemakers Blend 2002** RATING 80

Red Edge

Golden Gully Road, Heathcote, Vic 3523 REGION Heathcote
T (03) 9337 5695 F (03) 9337 7550 OPEN By appointment
WINEMAKER Peter Dredge, Judy Dredge EST. 1971 CASES 1000
SUMMARY Red Edge is a relatively new name on the scene, but the vineyard dates back to 1971, at the renaissance of the Victorian wine industry, and in the early 1980s it produced the wonderful wines of Flynn & Williams. It has now been rehabilitated by Peter and Judy Dredge. They produced two quite lovely wines in their inaugural vintage and have continued that form in succeeding vintages. They now have a little over 15 ha under vine, and Red Edge has become a full-time occupation for Peter Dredge. Exports to the US and the UK.

ΥΥΥΥΫ **Heathcote Shiraz 2003** Very powerful and intense; voluminous blackberry and bitter chocolate fruit; protracted tannins; much patience required. High-quality cork. RATING 93 DRINK 2018 $ 48
Jackson's Vineyard Heathcote Shiraz 2003 Fragrant, lifted, spicy, tangy red cherry, raspberry and plum; fine, dusty tannins. Younger Shiraz, some Mourvedre and a touch of Riesling. High-quality cork. RATING 91 DRINK 2013 $ 25

Redesdale Estate Wines

North Redesdale Road, Redesdale, Vic 3444 REGION Heathcote
T (03) 5425 3236 F (03) 5425 3122 WEB www.redesdale.com OPEN Nov–April weekends 11–4, or by appointment
WINEMAKER Tobias Ansted (Contract) EST. 1982 CASES 1000
SUMMARY Planting of the Redesdale Estate vines began in 1982 on the northeast slopes of a 25-ha grazing property, fronting the Campaspe River on one side. The rocky quartz and granite soil meant the vines had to struggle for existence, and when Peter Williams and wife Suzanne Arnall-Williams purchased the property in 1988 the vineyard was in a state of disrepair. They have rejuvenated the vineyard, planted an olive grove, and, more recently, erected a self-contained 2-storey cottage surrounded by a garden which is part of the Victorian open garden scheme (and cross-linked to a villa in Tuscany).

ΥΥΥΥΥ **Heathcote Shiraz 2003** Dense purple-red; medium to full-bodied; rich, supple, velvety, round and fleshy plum and blackberry fruit; ripe tannins. High-quality cork. RATING 94 DRINK 2013 $ 42

ΥΥΥΥΫ **Heathcote Cabernet Sauvignon Cabernet Franc 2003** Medium to full red-purple; medium-bodied; complex black fruits, cedar, spice, blackcurrant and cassis; flows along the tongue. Quality cork. RATING 92 DRINK 2013 $ 42

Redgate ★★★★

Boodjidup Road, Margaret River, WA 6285 **REGION** Margaret River
T (08) 9757 6488 **F** (08) 9757 6308 **WEB** www.redgatewines.com.au **OPEN** 7 days 10–5
WINEMAKER Andrew Forsell **EST.** 1977 **CASES** 12 000
SUMMARY A little over 21 ha of mature estate plantings (the majority to sauvignon blanc, semillon, cabernet sauvignon, cabernet franc, shiraz and chardonnay) provides the base for this well-established quality producer. The wines are distributed in Perth, Melbourne, Sydney and Brisbane; exports to all major markets.

ΨΨΨΨ **Sauvignon Blanc Semillon 2004** Pleasantly ripe gooseberry and tropical fruit; the palate progressively builds power through to a long finish. **RATING** 91 **DRINK** 2008 **$** 18.50
Sauvignon Blanc Reserve 2004 Clean, fresh and lively; very gentle and well-integrated barrel ferment oak; fluid mouthfeel; slippery acidity and length. **RATING** 90 **DRINK** 2007 **$** 22.50

ΨΨΨΨ **Bin 588 2002** Lively, fresh, savoury, tangy style; fine-grained tannins. Cabernet Sauvignon/Shiraz/Cabernet Franc. **RATING** 87 **DRINK** 2009 **$** 22.50

ΨΨΨΨ **Anastasia's Delight Margaret River (375 ml) 2003 RATING** 86 **DRINK** Now **$** 22.50
Ezabella White Port 2003 RATING 85 **DRINK** Now **$** 22.50

Red Hill Estate ★★★★☆

53 Shoreham Road, Red Hill South, Vic 3937 **REGION** Mornington Peninsula
T (03) 5989 2838 **F** (03) 5989 2855 **WEB** www.redhillestate.com.au **OPEN** 7 days 11–5
WINEMAKER Michael Kyberd, Luke Curry **EST.** 1989 **CASES** 25 000
SUMMARY Red Hill Estate was established by Sir Peter Derham and family, and has three vineyard sites: Range Road, with a little over 31 ha, Red Hill Estate (the home vineyard) with 10 ha, and The Briars with 2 ha. Taken together, the vineyards make Red Hill Estate one of the larger producers of Mornington Peninsula wines. The tasting room and ever-busy restaurant have a superb view across the vineyard to Westernport Bay and Phillip Island. Production continues to surge, and the winery goes from strength to strength. Exports to the US, Canada, the UK and Sweden.

ΨΨΨΨΨ **Classic Release Pinot Noir 2001** Exudes spice, bramble and plum aromas; very complex and powerful, with great finish and length. High-quality cork. **RATING** 94 **DRINK** 2009 **$** 35

ΨΨΨΨΨ **Classic Release Chardonnay 2002** Complex barrel ferment and bottle-developed aromas; ripe stone fruit; super-powerful and long. **RATING** 93 **DRINK** 2008 **$** 30
Bimaris Pinot Noir 2003 A mix of spice, plum and stem; medium-bodied; good structure and long, fine, ripe tannins. **RATING** 90 **DRINK** 2009 **$** 14

ΨΨΨΨ **Chardonnay 2003** Rich, ripe peach and apricot; soft mouthfeel; good oak handling.
RATING 89 **DRINK** 2007 **$** 20
Bimaris Rose 2004 Salmon colour; spicy aromas to an interesting wine with texture and length; very good balance; top Rose style. **RATING** 89 **DRINK** Now **$** 14
Pinot Grigio 2004 Some apple blossom, spice and musk fragrance; light to medium-bodied; good flow and mouthfeel. **RATING** 88 **DRINK** 2007 **$** 22

Redman ★★★

Riddoch Highway, Coonawarra, SA 5263 **REGION** Coonawarra
T (08) 8736 3331 **F** (08) 8736 3013 **WEB** www.redman.com.au **OPEN** Mon–Fri 9–5, weekends 10–4
WINEMAKER Bruce Redman, Malcolm Redman **EST.** 1966 **CASES** 11 000
SUMMARY After a prolonged period of mediocrity, the Redman wines are showing sporadic signs of improvement, partly through the introduction of modest amounts of new oak, even if principally American. It would be nice to say the wines now reflect the full potential of the vineyard, but there is still some way to go.

ΨΨΨΨ **Cabernet Sauvignon Merlot 2000** Medium-bodied; elegant, nicely ripened fresh blackcurrant/cassis/redcurrant fruits; subtle oak; fine tannins. Best for some time.
RATING 90 **DRINK** 2008 **$** 30

ΨΨΨΨ **Shiraz 2002 RATING** 84 **DRINK** 2007
Cabernet Sauvignon 2002 RATING 84 **DRINK** 2008

Red Mud

NR

PO Box 237, Paringa, SA 5340 **REGION** Riverland
T (08) 8595 8042 **F** (08) 8595 8042 **WEB** www.nelwood.com **OPEN** Not
WINEMAKER Mike Farmilo **EST.** 2002 **CASES** NA
SUMMARY The Red Mud wines come from large plantings of shiraz, chardonnay, petit verdot and
cabernet sauvignon near Nelwood, 32 km east of Renmark near the SA border. The grapegrowers
who are shareholders in the company have been growing grapes for up to three generations in the
Riverland.

Red Rock Winery

NR

Red Rock Reserve Road, Alvie, Vic 3249 **REGION** Western Victoria Zone
T (03) 5234 8382 **F** (03) 5234 8382 **WEB** www.redrockwinery.com.au **OPEN** 7 days 10–5
WINEMAKER Rohan Little **EST.** 1981 **CASES** 5000
SUMMARY Red Rock Winery has progressively established 10 ha of sauvignon blanc, semillon, pinot
noir and shiraz, and is a part-time occupation for Rohan Little. It takes its name from the now
dormant Red Rock Volcano which created the lakes and craters of the Western District when it last
erupted, 8000 years ago. The winery café opened in early 2002.

Red Tail Wines

NR

15 Pinnacle Place, Marlee, NSW 2429 **REGION** Northern Rivers Zone
T (02) 6550 5084 **F** (02) 6550 5084 **OPEN** By appointment
WINEMAKER Serenella Estate (Contract) **EST.** 1992 **CASES** 900
SUMMARY Warren and Sue Stiff have planted 0.5 ha each of colombard, semillon and verdelho, and
0.25 ha of merlot, at their property northwest of Taree. The vineyard takes its name from the red-
tailed black cockatoo which inhabits the area; the very reasonably priced wines are available by
phone, fax or mail order.

Reedy Creek Vineyard

NR

Reedy Creek, via Tenterfield, NSW 2372 **REGION** Northern Slopes Zone
T (02) 6737 5221 **F** (02) 6737 5200 **WEB** www.reedycreekwines.com.au **OPEN** 7 days 9–5
WINEMAKER Contract **EST.** 1971 **CASES** 2800
SUMMARY Like so many Italian settlers in the Australian countryside, the De Stefani family has been
growing grapes and making wine for its own consumption for over 30 years at its Reedy Creek
property in the far north of NSW. What is more, like their compatriots in the King Valley, the family's
principal activity until 1993 was growing tobacco, but the continued rationalisation of the tobacco
industry prompted the De Stefanis to turn a hobby into a commercial exercise. The vineyard has now
been expanded to 6.1 ha; the first commercial vintage of Shiraz was made in 1995, with Chardonnay
following in 1998. The wines are sold through the cellar door; the maturation cellar opened in 1997.

Rees Miller Estate

 ★★★☆

5355 Goulburn Highway, Yea, Vic 3717 **REGION** Upper Goulburn
T (03) 5797 2101 **F** (03) 5797 3276 **WEB** www.reesmiller.com **OPEN** Weekends & public hols 10–5
WINEMAKER David Miller **EST.** 1996 **CASES** 3000
SUMMARY Partners Sylke Rees and David Miller purchased the 64-ha property in 1998. It then had
1 ha of pinot noir (planted in 1996). They have added another block of pinot noir, 3 ha of cabernet
sauvignon, 1 ha each of merlot and shiraz, and 0.5 ha of cabernet franc, all of which came into
production in 2002. They use integrated pest management (no insecticides) and deliberately irrigate
sparingly, the upshot being yields of 2.5 tonnes per hectare (a ton to the acre in the old money). All
the wines are made onsite, some named after the original owners of the property, Daniel Joseph and
Wilhemina Therese Sier. Exports to Canada.

Reg Drayton Wines   NR

Cnr Pokolbin Mountain Road/McDonalds Road, Pokolbin, NSW 2321 **REGION** Lower Hunter Valley
T (02) 4998 7523 **F** (02) 4998 7523 **WEB** www.regdraytonwines.com.au **OPEN** 7 days 10–5
WINEMAKER Tish Cecchini, Robyn Drayton **EST.** 1989 **CASES** 5500
SUMMARY Reg and Pam Drayton were among the victims of the Seaview/Lord Howe Island air crash
in October 1984, having established Reg Drayton Wines after selling their interest in the long-
established Drayton Family Winery. Their daughter Robyn (a fifth-generation Drayton and billed as
the Hunter's first female vigneron) and husband Craig continue the business, which draws chiefly
upon the Pokolbin Hills Estate but also takes fruit from the historic Lambkin Estate vineyard.

Reilly's Wines   NR

Cnr Hill Street/Burra Street, Mintaro, SA 5415 **REGION** Clare Valley
T (08) 8843 9013 **F** (08) 8843 9013 **WEB** www.reillyswines.com **OPEN** 7 days 10–5
WINEMAKER Justin Ardill **EST.** 1994 **CASES** 10 000
SUMMARY Cardiologist Justin and Julie Ardill are no longer newcomers in the Clare Valley, with 10 or
so vintages under their belt. An unusual sideline of Reilly's Cottage is the production of Extra Virgin
Olive Oil; it is unusual in that it is made from wild olives found in the Mintaro district of the Clare
Valley. Justin Ardill also does some contract making for others. The restaurant is open 7 days for
lunch and Monday, Wednesday, Friday and Saturday for dinner. Exports to the US, Ireland, Malaysia
and Singapore.

Remo & Son's Vineyard   NR

58 Blaxland Ridge Road, Kurrajong, NSW 2758 **REGION** South Coast Zone
T (02) 4576 1539 **F** (02) 4576 0072 **OPEN** Weekends by appointment
WINEMAKER Remo Crisante **EST.** 1998 **CASES** NA
SUMMARY Remo and Mark Crisante have pushed the viticultural envelope that little bit further by
planting 2 ha of chardonnay, verdelho, merlot, cabernet sauvignon and traminer at Kurrajong, for
long a holiday destination for Sydneysiders. The fact that Kurrajong is in the South Coast Zone may
come as a surprise, since it is 100 km northwest of Sydney, but the zone boundaries have always been
a matter of convenience, and had to be so drawn as to cover all of the State. A restaurant and
accommodation are available onsite, pointing to the conference and function market.

Renewan Murray Gold Wines   ★★★

Murray Valley Highway, Piangil, Vic 3597 **REGION** Swan Hill
T (03) 5030 5525 **F** (03) 5030 5695 **OPEN** 7 days 9–5
WINEMAKER John Ellis (Contract) **EST.** 1989 **CASES** 220
SUMMARY In 1990 former senior executive at Nylex Corporation in Melbourne, Jim Lewis, and artist
wife Marg, retired to what is now Renewan Vineyard, set on the banks of the Murray River. It is a
small business, based on 2.5 ha of estate plantings, and the production is sold through the cellar door
and by mail order, with limited distribution to local hotels, bottle shops and restaurants.

Reschke Wines   ★★★★

Level 183 Melbourne Street, North Adelaide, SA 5006 (postal) **REGION** Coonawarra
T (08) 8239 0500 **F** (08) 8239 0522 **WEB** www.reschke.com.au **OPEN** Not
WINEMAKER Peter Douglas (Contract) **EST.** 1998 **CASES** 6000
SUMMARY It's not often that the first release from a new winery is priced at $100 per bottle (since
increased to $115), but that is precisely what Reschke Wines achieved with its 1998 Cabernet
Sauvignon. The family has been a landholder in the Coonawarra region for almost 100 years, with a
large landholding which is partly terra rossa, part woodland. There are 15.5 ha of merlot, 105 ha of
cabernet sauvignon, 0.5 ha of cabernet franc and 2.5 ha of shiraz in production, with a further 26 ha
planted before the end of 2001, mostly to shiraz, and with a little petit verdot. Exports to the US,
Canada and Singapore.

ҮҮҮҮ **Empyrean Cabernet Sauvignon 2002** Deep colour; earthy notes typical of the variety in Coonawarra; blackcurrant fruit, touch of bitter chocolate; controlled oak and tannins. Good cork. **RATING** 93 **DRINK** 2017

ҮҮҮ **Coonawarra Sauvignon Blanc 2004 RATING** 86 **DRINK** Now $ 18

Rex Vineyard

NR

Beaufort, WA 6315 **REGION** Central Western Australia Zone
T (08) 9384 3210 **F** (08) 9384 3210 **OPEN** Not
WINEMAKER Julie White (Contract) **EST.** 1991 **CASES** 500
SUMMARY Peter and Gillian Rex have established 2 ha of chardonnay, cabernet sauvignon, merlot and shiraz. Approximately half of each year's production is sold as grapes; the remainder is made by the highly competent Julie White in the Swan Valley.

Ribarits Estate Wines

NR

Sturt Highway, Trentham Cliffs, NSW 2738 (postal) **REGION** Murray Darling
T 0409 330 997 **F** (03) 5024 0332 **OPEN** Not
WINEMAKER Contract **EST.** 1998 **CASES** 4000
SUMMARY Adrian Ribarits has developed over 82 ha of chardonnay, merlot, shiraz and cabernet sauvignon, primarily as a contract grapegrower for Simeon Wines. A small part of the grape production is vinified for Ribarits Estate and sold by mail order at yesterday's prices; the wines have various bronze medals to their credit.

Richard Hamilton

Main Road, Willunga, SA 5172 **REGION** McLaren Vale
T (08) 8556 2288 **F** (08) 8556 2868 **WEB** www.richardhamiltonwines.com **OPEN** Mon–Fri 10–5, weekends & public hols 11–5
WINEMAKER Paul Gordon, Tim Bailey (Assistant) **EST.** 1972 **CASES** 20 000
SUMMARY Richard Hamilton has outstanding estate vineyards, some of great age, all fully mature. The arrival (in 2002) of former Rouge Homme winemaker Paul Gordon has allowed the full potential of those vineyards to be expressed. Exports to all major markets.

ҮҮҮҮҮ **Hamilton Almond Grove Chardonnay 2004** Complex wine; excellent melon and stone fruit with classy barrel ferment inputs; medium-bodied; impeccable balance and length; squeaky acidity. Screwcap. **RATING** 94 **DRINK** 2010
Hamilton Centurion 110 Year Old Vine Shiraz 2002 An elegant mix of spicy, savoury blackberry fruit; fine texture and structure; has real finesse and length. **RATING** 94 **DRINK** 2017
Hut Block Cabernet Sauvignon 2002 Sweet cassis and blackcurrant flavours in an elegant frame; fine but quite intense tannins and oak provide perfectly balanced support. **RATING** 94 **DRINK** 2015 $ 19.95

ҮҮҮҮ **Cadenzia Burton's Vineyard Old Bush Vine Grenache Shiraz 2002** Spicy red and black fruit aromas; an intense, round, mouthfilling style as only McLaren Vale can deliver with the variety. Zork. **RATING** 93 **DRINK** 2009
Marion Vineyard Old Vine Grenache Shiraz 2002 Very ripe juicy jammy Grenache aromas and flavours but with a stylish, silky texture. From the last urban vineyard in the Marion suburb. **RATING** 92 **DRINK** 2012
Slate Quarry Riesling 2004 Rich and powerful; more style than most McLaren Vale rieslings; tropical and citrus fruit. **RATING** 90 **DRINK** 2009 $ 15.95
Hamilton Lot 148 Merlot 2002 Another tribute to 2002; aromatic red fruits with some savoury elements; fine tannins, good length. **RATING** 90 **DRINK** 2007 $ 19.95

ҮҮҮҮ **Hamilton Colton Ruins GSM 2002** Light to medium-bodied; juicy berry fruit; gentle tannins. **RATING** 87 **DRINK** 2007 $ 19.95

ҮҮҮ **Hamilton Gumprs' Block Shiraz 2002 RATING** 86 **DRINK** 2007 $ 19.95

Richfield Estate ★★★☆

Bonshaw Road, Tenterfield, NSW 2372 **REGION** Northern Slopes Zone
T (07) 5545 1711 **F** (07) 5545 3522 **WEB** www.richfieldvineyard.com.au **OPEN** 7 days 10–4
WINEMAKER John Cassegrain **EST.** 1997 **CASES** 15 000
SUMMARY Singapore resident Bernard Forey is the Chairman and majority shareholder of Richfield
Estate. The 500-ha property, at an altitude of 720m, was selected after an intensive survey by soil
specialists. Just under 30 ha of shiraz, cabernet sauvignon, merlot, ruby cabernet, semillon,
chardonnay and verdelho have been planted, the first vintage being made in 2000. Winemaker John
Cassegrain is a shareholder in the venture, and it is expected that the bulk of the sales will come from
the export markets of southeast Asia and Japan.

ΨΨΨΨΨ **Tenterfield Semillon 2002** Interesting floral, herb and crushed lemon leaf aromas; light-bodied; clean, fresh and bright; developing slowly; good acidity. Twin Top. **RATING** 90 **DRINK** 2008 $ 14.75

ΨΨΨΨ **Tenterfield Shiraz 2002** Quite fragrant; light to medium-bodied mix of red fruits and gently earthy savoury notes; fine tannins. Twin Top. **RATING** 87 **DRINK** 2008 $ 15.80

ΨΨΨΨ **Tenterfield Chardonnay 2002 RATING** 86 **DRINK** 2007 $ 14.75
Tenterfield Merlot 2002 RATING 86 **DRINK** 2008 $ 15.50
Tenterfield Cabernet Merlot 2002 RATING 86 **DRINK** 2007 $ 14.75
Tenterfield Verdelho Semillon 2002 RATING 85 **DRINK** Now $ 14.75

Richmond Estate NR

99 Gadds Lane, North Richmond, NSW 2754 **REGION** Sydney Basin
T (02) 4573 1048 **OPEN** Weekends 11–6
WINEMAKER Tony Radanovic **EST.** 1967 **CASES** 600
SUMMARY While this is the second time Richmond Estate has been listed in the *Wine Companion*, it
was also featured in a number of books I wrote between 1979 and 1984, as then-proprietor Barry
Bracken (a Sydney orthopaedic surgeon) was making excellent Shiraz and Cabernet Sauvignon.
However, late in 1984 he sold the property, and it went through several owners before being
purchased by Monica and Tony Radanovic in 1987. The Radanovics have restored the vineyard,
which had been run down in the years prior to their purchase, and while only 3 ha are under vine, the
vineyard is used by the University of Western Sydney as its field laboratory for undergraduate and
wine production courses.

Richmond Grove ★★★★

Para Road, Tanunda, SA 5352 **REGION** Barossa Valley
T (08) 8563 7300 **F** (08) 8563 2804 **WEB** www.richmondgrovewines.com **OPEN** 7 days 10.30–4.30
WINEMAKER Steve Clarkson **EST.** 1983 **CASES** 150 000
SUMMARY Richmond Grove now has two homes, including one in the Barossa Valley. It is owned by
Orlando Wyndham and draws its grapes from diverse sources. The Richmond Grove Barossa Valley
and Watervale Rieslings made by the team directed by former winemaker John Vickery represent
excellent value for money (for Riesling) year in, year out. If these were the only wines produced by
Richmond Grove, it would have 5-star rating. Exports to the UK.

ΨΨΨΨΨ **Watervale Riesling 2004** Lime, herb and spice; good mouthfeel, balance and length; fresh acidity. **RATING** 92 **DRINK** 2014 $ 15.99
Coonawarra Cabernet Sauvignon 2002 Very good colour; excellent bouquet; nice blackcurrant and dark chocolate on entry; tannins do need to soften. **RATING** 92 **DRINK** 2017

ΨΨΨΨ **French Cask Chardonnay 2003** Tangy citrus and stone fruit; good balance and length and a nice touch of oak; surprise packet. **RATING** 89 **DRINK** Now $ 13.99
Padthaway Chardonnay 2003 Elegant, light-bodied; classic regional grapefruit; fresh, fruit-driven. Cork. **RATING** 89 **DRINK** 2008
Chardonnay Pinot Noir NV Citrus and apple aromas and flavours; lively and fresh; good balance. **RATING** 87 **DRINK** Now $ 13.99

ΨΨΨΨ **Riesling 2004 RATING** 86 **DRINK** 2009 $ 13.99

ΨΨΨ **Cabernet Merlot 2002 RATING** 79

Richmond Park Vineyard ★★★★

Logie Road, Richmond, Tas 7025 (postal) **REGION** Southern Tasmania
T (03) 6265 2949 **F** (03) 6265 3166 **OPEN** Not
WINEMAKER Andrew Hood (Contract) **EST.** 1989 **CASES** 250
SUMMARY A small vineyard owned by Tony Park, which gives the clue to the clever name. It is 20 minutes' drive from Hobart; a particular (and uncommon) attraction for mailing list clients is the availability of 375 ml bottles.

ŸŸŸŸŸ **Pinot Noir 2002** Light style, but has elegance, balance and length. **RATING** 90 **DRINK** 2007

ŸŸŸ **Pinot Noir 2003** **RATING** 82

Rickety Gate ★★★★

RMB 825, Scotsdale Road, Denmark, WA 6333 **REGION** Denmark
T (08) 9840 9503 **F** (08) 9840 9502 **WEB** www.ricketygate.com.au **OPEN** By appointment
WINEMAKER John Wade (Contract) **EST.** 2000 **CASES** 2000
SUMMARY The 3-ha vineyard of Rickety Gate is situated on north-facing slopes of the Bennet Ranges, in an area specifically identified by Dr John Gladstones as highly suited to cool-climate viticulture. The property was purchased by Russell and Linda Hubbard at the end of 1999, and after vineyard preparation work directed by veteran consultant viticulturist Ted Holland, 1.8 ha of merlot, 0.8 ha of riesling and 0.5 ha of chardonnay and pinot noir were planted by September 2000. John Wade makes the wines at the small onsite winery.

ŸŸŸŸŸ **Riesling 2004** Very tight, focused and crisp; herb and mineral; crunchy acidity, clean finish. **RATING** 90 **DRINK** 2010 $ 22.50
Merlot 2003 Elegant and very well-balanced and constructed wine; savoury varietal fruit and balanced oak. **RATING** 90 **DRINK** 2009 $ 24.50

Riddells Creek Winery ★★★★☆

296 Gap Road, Riddells Creek, Vic 3431 **REGION** Macedon Ranges
T (03) 5428 6295 **F** (03) 5428 7221 **OPEN** Wed–Sun 11–5, or by appointment
WINEMAKER John Ellis, Trefor Morgan (both Contract), Peter Evans **EST.** 1998 **CASES** 2300
SUMMARY Partners Peter Evans, Sonia Mailer, Craig Wellington and Susan Wellington commenced planting the 18.5-ha vineyard in 1998; the varieties chosen were riesling, chardonnay, cabernet sauvignon, shiraz and merlot. While it is situated at the extreme southern end of the Macedon Ranges, only 8 km from Sunbury, the partners correctly anticipated that achieving full ripeness with the red varieties might be difficult in cooler vintages. However, winemakers John Ellis and Trefor Morgan, with input from Peter Evans, have done an excellent job with the white wines since the inaugural vintage of 2001. All the wines are sold direct from the winery.

ŸŸŸŸŸ **Amee Alyce Riesling 2004** Fragrant and youthful; very bright minerally mouthfeel and flavours; exceptional length; needs time. **RATING** 94 **DRINK** 2014 $ 17

ŸŸŸŸŸ **The Sarah Ivy Chardonnay 2003** Light to medium yellow-green; smooth, supple grapefruit and stone fruit off-set by subtle malolactic and subtle barrel ferment cashew and spicy oak; good balance. **RATING** 93 **DRINK** 2010 $ 19
Unwooded Chardonnay 2004 Lively, tangy, grapefruit, melon and paw paw flavours; nice balance; clear finish. Excellent example of the style. **RATING** 90 **DRINK** 2008 $ 12

ŸŸŸŸ **The Leigh Craig Cabernet Sauvignon 2003** **RATING** 84 **DRINK** Now $ 17

Ridgeback Wines ★★★★

New Chum Gully Estate, Howards Road, Panton Hill, Vic 3759 **REGION** Yarra Valley
T (03) 9719 7687 **F** (03) 9719 7667 **WEB** www.ridgebackwines.com.au **OPEN** By appointment
WINEMAKER MasterWineMakers (Contract) **EST.** 2000 **CASES** 1200
SUMMARY Ron and Lynne Collings purchased their Panton Hill property in March 1990, clearing the land and making it ready for the first vine planting in 1992; there are now a little over 4 ha on the hillside slopes beneath their house. Ron Collings completed the degree in winegrowing at Charles Sturt University in 1997, with the Dean's Award for Academic Excellence. Most of the grapes were

sold to Coldstream Hills, but Ron Collings made small batches of wine himself each year, which ultimately led to the decision to establish the Ridgeback label, with contract winemaking, although Collings is never far from the scene at vintage. The name, incidentally, is intended to reflect in part the rolling hillside of Panton Hill, and to salute the Collings' Rhodesian Ridgeback dogs, Jana being the most recent arrival. Exports to the UK.

♥♥♥♥ Yarra Valley Chardonnay 2003 Light to medium-bodied; elegant melon fruit; restrained oak, good length. Cork. **RATING** 89 **DRINK** 2008 **$** 22
Yarra Valley Cabernet Merlot 2003 Medium-bodied; a mix of blackcurrant, redcurrant and savoury, spicy notes; fractionally dry tannins should soften. Quality cork. **RATING** 89 **DRINK** 2012 **$** 23
Yarra Valley Pinot Noir 2003 Strong, deep colour; very powerful and slightly extractive style; black fruits/plums/savoury tannins. Perhaps some fruit shrivel. Cork. **RATING** 88 **DRINK** 2009 **$** 22
Yarra Valley Merlot 2003 Savoury but light bouquet; more small, red and black fruits on the palate; gentle tannins. Stained cork. **RATING** 87 **DRINK** 2010 **$** 29

♥♥♥♥ Yarra Valley Rose 2004 RATING 84 **DRINK** Now **$** 15

Ridgeline   NR

PO Box 695, Healesville, Vic 3777 **REGION** Yarra Valley
T 0421 422 154 **F** (03) 5962 2670 **OPEN** By appointment
WINEMAKER Mark Haisma **EST.** 2001 **CASES** 800
SUMMARY Mark Haisma has established 2 ha of pinot noir, shiraz, cabernet sauvignon and merlot on a small hillside vineyard on Briarty Road; his neighbours include such well-known producers as Yarra Yering and Giant Steps, and two substantial vineyards, one owned by Coldstream Hills, the other by Malcolm Fell.

Rigel Wines

PO Box 18062, Collins Street East, Melbourne, Vic 8004 **REGION** Mornington Peninsula
T 1300 131 081 **F** 1300 131 281 **WEB** www.rigelwines.com.au **OPEN** At the General Store, Merricks
WINEMAKER MasterWineMakers (Contract) **EST.** 1989 **CASES** 5000
SUMMARY Rigel Wine Company is owned by Dr Damian and Sue Ireland and Michael and Mary Calman; the Irelands own the Mornington Peninsula vineyard at Shoreham, which provides the grapes for the super-premium Rigel label. The second property is at Tocumwal and has 80 ha of vines with 6 km of Murray River frontage. Most of the grapes are sold to other winemakers, but part of the production is vinified for both the local and export markets.

♥♥♥♥♥ Mornington Peninsula Pinot Noir 2002 Very good colour; powerful, complex and concentrated dark plum and spice; good tannins; impressive, long-lived style. Cork. **RATING** 93 **DRINK** 2012 **$** 24
Mornington Peninsula Chardonnay 2002 Green-gold; concentrated, powerful, stone fruit, melon and fig; the low yield evident, but doesn't coarsen the wine. Quality cork. **RATING** 90 **DRINK** 2009 **$** 24

♥♥♥♥ Barooga Road Shiraz 2002 Shows the 2002 class, even in the Riverland; light to medium-bodied, but good texture, structure and flavour; not forced; fine tannins give length. **RATING** 87 **DRINK** 2009 **$** 16

♥♥♥♥ Barooga Road Merlot 2002 RATING 86 **DRINK** 2007 **$** 16
XLV Sangiovese 2002 RATING 85 **DRINK** 2007 **$** 18
Barooga Road Chardonnay 2002 RATING 84 **DRINK** Now **$** 16

♥♥♥ XLV Nebbiolo 2002 RATING 83 **$** 18

Rimfire Vineyards

Bismarck Street, Maclagan, Qld 4352 **REGION** Darling Downs
T (07) 4692 1129 **F** (07) 4692 1260 **WEB** www.rimfirewinery.com.au **OPEN** 7 days 10–5
WINEMAKER Tony Connellan **EST.** 1991 **CASES** 6500
SUMMARY The Connellan family (parents Margaret and Tony and children Michelle, Peter and Louise) began planting the 12-ha, 14-variety Rimfire Vineyards in 1991 as a means of diversification

of their very large (1500-ha) cattle stud in the foothills of the Bunya Mountains, 45 minutes' drive northeast of Toowoomba. They produce a kaleidoscopic array of wines, the majority without any regional claim of origin. The wine (and variety) simply called 1893 is said to be made from a vine brought to the property by a German settler in about 1893; the vineyard ceased production in the early 1900s, but a single vine remained, and DNA testing has established that the vine does not correspond to any vine cultivar currently known in Australia. Rimfire propagated cuttings, and a small quantity is made each year. The Black Bull Café is open daily 10–5 (blackboard menu and wine by the glass). Annual Jazz on the Lawn concert each spring. An impressive display of estate-grown varietal wines.

ΥΥΥΥ **Graciano 2003** Deep colour; unexpectedly powerful and rich; spicy black fruits and good structure; major surprise. **RATING** 89 **DRINK** 2010 $18
Cabernet Sauvignon 2002 Light to medium-bodied; surprisingly good varietal character; berry, leaf and mint spectrum; fine, ripe tannins underpin the wine. Estate-grown. Screwcap. **RATING** 88 **DRINK** 2009 $18
Verdelho 2004 Rather gritty/grainy acidity, but does have impact and length. **RATING** 87 **DRINK** Now $17
Vin Gris Aleatico 2004 Pale pink; distinct spicy, grapey, strawberry fruit; good length, not sweet; well made. Estate-grown. Screwcap. **RATING** 87 **DRINK** Now $18
Musque 2004 Intensely grapey aroma and flavour; sweetness well controlled and balanced. Estate-grown. Screwcap. **RATING** 87 **DRINK** Now $17

ΥΥΥΥ **Dolce 2004** **RATING** 86 **DRINK** Now $17
Tinta 2004 **RATING** 86 **DRINK** Now $18
Sangiovese 2003 **RATING** 86 **DRINK** 2007 $18
Cabernets 2003 **RATING** 85 **DRINK** 2007 $18
Chardonnay 2003 **RATING** 84 **DRINK** 2008 $17
1893 2004 **RATING** 84 **DRINK** Now $17
Rose 2004 **RATING** 84 **DRINK** Now $13.50

ΥΥΥ **Touriga Nacional 2003** **RATING** 82 $20

Riseborough Estate ★★★☆

Lot 21, Petersen Rise, off Mooliabeenee Road, Gingin, WA 6503 **REGION** Swan District
T (08) 9575 1211 **F** (08) 9575 1211 **OPEN** Wed–Sun 10–4
WINEMAKER Flying Fish Cove (Contract), Rob Marshall (Oakover Wines) **EST.** 1998 **CASES** 5000
SUMMARY Don Riseborough and Susan Lamp began developing their 8.7-ha vineyard, a stone's throw from Moondah Brook, in 1998. They have planted shiraz, cabernet sauvignon, merlot, cabernet franc and grenache; the grapes take the slightly unusual trip south to Margaret River where the red wines are made by Flying Fish Cove. A small selection of non-estate white wines (Chenin Blanc, Chardonnay and Verdelho, all with a small amount of residual sweetness) are made by Rob Marshall in the Swan Valley. The spacious, purpose-built cellar door has expansive views across the Gingin Valley.

ΥΥΥΥ **Grenache Rose 2004** Clean, fresh and crisp; small, red berry fruits; dry finish; well made. Screwcap. **RATING** 87 **DRINK** 2007 $12
Cabernet Sauvignon 2003 Light to medium-bodied; clean, fresh raspberry and blackcurrant; good length and mouthfeel. Cork. **RATING** 87 **DRINK** 2008 $12
Cabernet Sauvignon Merlot Cabernet Franc 2003 Bright colour; light to medium-bodied; fresh, tight red fruits; minimal tannins and oak; brisk acid finish. Quality cork. **RATING** 87 **DRINK** 2009 $16

ΥΥΥΥ **Shiraz 2003** **RATING** 86 **DRINK** 2008 $12
Shiraz 2002 **RATING** 86 **DRINK** 2007 $12

ΥΥΥ **Cabernet Sauvignon 2002** **RATING** 83 $12

Rivendell ★★★★

Lot 328, Wildwood Road, Yallingup, WA 6282 **REGION** Margaret River
T (08) 9755 2090 **F** (08) 9755 2301 **WEB** www.rivendellwines.com.au **OPEN** 7 days 10.30–5
WINEMAKER James Pennington **EST.** 1987 **CASES** 3000

SUMMARY Rivendell was established in 1987 by a local family and became recognised for its gardens, restaurant, jams, preserves and wines. The property has recently been purchased by private investors who intend to upgrade the property. The new owners wish to lift wine quality and have employed James Pennington to oversee the improvements to the winery and its production.

ҰҰҰҰҰ **Chardonnay 2002** Aromatic, fragrant nectarine white peach aromas and flavours; elegant, fine silky mouthfeel; balanced and integrated oak. Cork. **RATING** 93 **DRINK** 2010 **$** 20

Shiraz 2002 Clean and fresh black cherry, spice and pepper; tannins still coming back into the wine; subtle oak. Quality cork. **RATING** 90 **DRINK** 2012 **$** 17

The Cabernets 2002 Cedary, spicy aromas and flavours around a core of blackberry; earthy but sweet, fine tannins; elegant style which grows on you. Doubtful cork. **RATING** 90 **DRINK** 2012 **$** 20

ҰҰҰҰ **Semillon Sauvignon Blanc 2004** Harmonious blend, the Semillon providing structure, Sauvignon Blanc dominating the flavour with gentle tropical fruit. Chalky finish. Screwcap. **RATING** 89 **DRINK** 2008 **$** 15

Semillon 2004 Oak maturation adds weight; the trade-off is obscuration of varietal character; less overt oak might have been a better option. Twin Top. **RATING** 87 **DRINK** 2008 **$** 17

RiverBank Estate ★★★☆

126 Hamersley Road, Caversham, WA 6055 **REGION** Swan Valley
T (08) 9377 1805 **F** (08) 9377 2168 **WEB** www.riverbankestate.com.au **OPEN** 7 days 10–5
WINEMAKER Robert James Bond, Phoebe Thomas **EST.** 1993 **CASES** 6000
SUMMARY Robert Bond, a graduate of Charles Sturt University and a Swan Valley viticulturist for 20 years, established RiverBank Estate in 1993. He draws upon 11 ha of estate plantings and, in his words, 'The wines are unashamedly full bodied, produced from ripe grapes in what is recognised as a hot grapegrowing region.' Wines extending back over several vintages are available at the cellar door. Bond conducts 8-week wine courses affiliated with the Wine Industry Association of WA. A large restaurant is also open 7 days 11–5. Exports to Poland.

ҰҰҰҰҰ **Riesling 2004** Spotless citrus blossom aromas; medium-bodied; smooth, flowing lime and tropical fruit; very good now (or later). From Mount Barker. Screwcap. **RATING** 90 **DRINK** 2012 **$** 18

ҰҰҰҰ **Padlock Paddock Cabernet 2002** Slightly funky, spicy bouquet; sweet, warm-grown chocolate and blackcurrant fruit flavours; older vintages show the wines age very well. Cork. **RATING** 87 **DRINK** 2012 **$** 20

ҰҰҰҰ **Sauvignon Blanc 2004** **RATING** 85 **DRINK** Now **$** 18
Verdelho 2004 **RATING** 85 **DRINK** 2007 **$** 18

ҰҰҰ **Unwooded Chardonnay 2004** **RATING** 83 **$** 15

Riverina Estate ★★★☆

700 Kidman Way, Griffith, NSW 2680 **REGION** Riverina
T (02) 6963 8300 **F** (02) 6962 4628 **WEB** www.riverinaestate.com **OPEN** Mon–Fri 9–5, Sat 10–4
WINEMAKER Sam Trimboli, Moreno Chiappin, Roberto Delgado, Sally Whittaker **EST.** 1969
CASES 650 000
SUMMARY One of the large producers of the region, drawing upon 1100 ha of estate plantings. While much of the wine is sold in bulk to other producers, selected parcels of the best of the grapes are made into table wines, with at one time spectacular success. Current tastings are more as one would expect. Exports to the US.

ҰҰҰҰҰ **1164 Family Reserve Shiraz 2001** Sweet plum and blackberry fruit; soft and round in the mouth; clever winemaking although on the oaky side. **RATING** 92 **DRINK** 2011 **$** 35

ҰҰҰҰ **Warburn Estate Show Reserve Shiraz 2003** Attractive red and black fruit flavours on entry and mid-palate; the tannic kick on the aftertaste is a pity. **RATING** 89 **DRINK** 2008 **$** 17.99

ҰҰҰ **Bushman's Gully Chardonnay 2003** **RATING** 79

River Park ★★★☆

River Park Road, Cowra, NSW 2794 **REGION** Cowra
T (02) 6342 3596 **F** (02) 6341 3711 **OPEN** Mon–Fri 9–5, weekends 10–5
WINEMAKER John Hordern (Contract) **EST.** 1994 **CASES** 600
SUMMARY Bill and Chris Murphy established River Park with 10 ha each of chardonnay and cabernet sauvignon on the banks of the Lachlan River, on the outskirts of Cowra, in 1994. Most of the grapes are sold to major wine companies; some is made under contract and has been stocked by Liquorland, Woolworths and Dan Murphy.

ΨΨΨΨ **Cowra Chardonnay 2003** Stylish wine; melon and stone fruit; creamy mouthfeel; good length and weight. Major surprise. **RATING** 90 **DRINK** Now $ 13

ΨΨΨ **Cowra Cabernet Sauvignon 2002** **RATING** 85 **DRINK** 2007 $ 13

Riversands Vineyards ★★★

Whytes Road, St George, Qld 4487 **REGION** Queensland Zone
T (07) 4625 3643 **F** (07) 4625 5043 **WEB** www.riversandswines.com **OPEN** Mon–Sat 8–6, Sunday 9–4
WINEMAKER Ballandean Estate (Contract) **EST.** 1990 **CASES** 4000
SUMMARY Riversands is on the banks of the Balonne River in the southwest corner of Queensland. It is a mixed wine grape and table grape business, acquired by present owners Alison and David Blacket in 1996. The wines have already won a number of silver and bronze medals.

ΨΨΨΨ **Explorer's Chardonnay 2003** Medium-bodied; stone fruit and melon; subtle oak; a little short. **RATING** 88 **DRINK** Now $ 16

ΨΨΨ **Dr Seidel's Soft Red Aleatico Red Muscat 2003** **RATING** 85 **DRINK** Now $ 12.50

ΨΨΨ **Shiraz Ruby Cabernet 2002** **RATING** 82

RiverStone Wines NR

105 Skye Road, Coldstream, Vic 3770 **REGION** Yarra Valley
T (03) 5962 3947 **F** (03) 5962 6616 **WEB** www.riverstonewine.com.au **OPEN** Thurs–Mon 10–6
WINEMAKER Punt Road (Contract) **EST.** 1995 **CASES** NA
SUMMARY Peter and Jenny Inglese began the establishment of 10 ha of sauvignon blanc, chardonnay, pinot noir, shiraz and cabernet sauvignon in 1995. They also built a bluestone homestead and cellar door, incorporating 100-year-old reclaimed timber. The site has 360-degree views of the Yarra Valley and surrounding mountains, and antipasto platters are available for those who wish to stay a little longer and absorb the beauty of the valley. The wines are available only through the cellar door and by mail order.

Robert Channon Wines ★★★★

Bradley Lane, Stanthorpe, Qld 4380 **REGION** Granite Belt
T (07) 4683 3260 **F** (07) 4683 3109 **WEB** www.robertchannonwines.com **OPEN** 7 days 10–5
WINEMAKER Mark Ravenscroft **EST.** 1998 **CASES** 3500
SUMMARY Peggy and Robert Channon have established 8 ha of chardonnay, verdelho, shiraz, merlot and cabernet sauvignon under permanent bird protection netting. The initial cost of installing permanent netting is high, but in the long term it is well worth it: it excludes birds and protects the grapes against hail damage. Also, there is no pressure to pick the grapes before they are fully ripe.

ΨΨΨΨ **Reserve Chardonnay 2002** Light yellow-green; a light to medium-bodied palate, quite elegant and fresh; gentle fruit and integrated oak; developing reassuringly and slowly; no oak issues. **RATING** 90 **DRINK** 2007 $ 24.50
Verdelho 2004 Clean; medium-bodied; fruit salad, with a touch of sweetness on the finish; does have length. Screwcap. **RATING** 90 **DRINK** Now $ 24.50

ΨΨΨΨ **Merlot 2002** Medium-bodied; blackcurrant, black olive and spice; fine, ripe tannins; subtle oak; good varietal character. Cork. **RATING** 88 **DRINK** 2010 $ 18.50

ΨΨΨ **Chardonnay 2003** Toasty oak; fruit intensity is simply not there to support the oak. **RATING** 86 **DRINK** 2007 $ 21.50

Singing Lake Rose 2004 Bright fuchsia; distinctly ripe underlying fruit; good length, crisp acidity. Screwcap. **RATING** 86 **DRINK** Now $ 14.50

Cabernet Sauvignon 2002 Savoury, leafy and a touch of green; light to medium-bodied; the Merlot much better. Cork. **RATING** 86 **DRINK** 2008 $ 18.50

Cabernet Merlot 2003 **RATING** 85 **DRINK** 2008

Merlot Shiraz 2002 **RATING** 85 **DRINK** Now

Merlot 2003 **RATING** 84 **DRINK** 2007 $ 18.50

🐦 Robert Johnson Vineyards ★★★★☆

PO Box 6708 Halifax Street, Adelaide, SA 5000 **REGION** Eden Valley
T (08) 8227 2800 **F** (08) 8227 2833 **OPEN** Not
WINEMAKER Robert Johnson **EST.** 1997 **CASES** 2500
SUMMARY The home base for Robert Johnson is a 12-ha vineyard and olive grove purchased in January 1996, with 0.4 ha of merlot (previously sold to Irvine Wines for Grand Merlot) and 5 ha of dilapidated olive trees. The olive grove has been rehabilitated, and 2.1 ha of shiraz, 1.2 ha of merlot and a small patch of viognier have been established. Wines made from the estate-grown grapes are released under the Robert Johnson label; these are supplemented by the Alan & Veitch wines purchased from the Sam Virgara vineyard in the Adelaide Hills, and named after Robert Johnson's parents. Retail distribution in NSW is through Vinous Solutions.

🍷🍷🍷🍷🍷 **Alan & Veitch Adelaide Hills Merlot 2003** Stylish wine; perfect balance and structure; clearly expressed varietal character through olive and spice-tinged fruit; fine silky tannins. **RATING** 94 **DRINK** 2012

🍷🍷🍷🍷🍷 **Alan & Veitch Adelaide Hills Viognier 2004** Honeysuckle, fruit pastille and poached pear flavours not overly alcoholic and thick. **RATING** 90 **DRINK** 2007

🍷🍷🍷🍷 **Alan & Veitch Adelaide Hills Sauvignon Blanc 2004** Potent bouquet; grass, gooseberry and asparagus flavours; long, firm palate; big-framed style. **RATING** 89 **DRINK** Now

Eden Valley Merlot 2001 Light to medium-bodied; quite fragrant; delicate savoury fruit, with touches of mint and leaf. **RATING** 89 **DRINK** 2008

Eden Valley Shiraz Viognier 2003 Strong Viognier influence on both bouquet and palate a little too obvious; light to medium-bodied spicy fruits. **RATING** 87 **DRINK** 2008

Alan & Veitch Adelaide Hills Merlot 2002 Aromatic spice and herb bouquet; light-bodied, with slightly jammy fruit, but finishes with nice tannins. **RATING** 87 **DRINK** 2008

🍷🍷🍷🍷 **Eden Valley Merlot 2002** **RATING** 84 **DRINK** Now

Roberts Estate ★★★

Game Street, Merbein, Vic 3505 **REGION** Murray Darling
T (03) 5024 2944 **F** (03) 5024 2877 **WEB** www.robertsestatewines.com **OPEN** Not
WINEMAKER John Pezzaniti **EST.** 1998 **CASES** 20 000
SUMMARY A very large winery acting as a processing point for grapes grown up and down the Murray River. Over 10 000 tonnes are crushed each vintage; much of the wine is sold in bulk to others, but a small amount is vinified under the Roberts Estate label.

🍷🍷🍷🍷 **Shiraz 2003** Light to medium-bodied; nice spicy/savoury edges to red fruits; gentle tannins. **RATING** 90 **DRINK** 2008 $ 11

🍷🍷🍷 **Merlot 2003** **RATING** 83 $ 10

Cabernet Sauvignon 2002 **RATING** 80 $ 10

Robert Stein Vineyard ★★★☆

Pipeclay Lane, Mudgee, NSW 2850 **REGION** Mudgee
T (02) 6373 3991 **F** (02) 6373 3709 **WEB** www.robertstein.com.au **OPEN** 7 days 10–4.30
WINEMAKER Robert Stein, Moore Haszard **EST.** 1976 **CASES** 8500
SUMMARY The sweeping panorama from the winery is its own reward for cellar door visitors. Right from the outset this has been a substantial operation but has managed to sell the greater part of its production direct from the winery by mail order and cellar door, with retail distribution in Sydney, Victoria and South Australia. Wine quality, once variable, albeit with top wines from time to time, has become much more consistent. Exports to the UK and Germany.

ŸŸŸŸ   **Cabernet Rose 2004** Light, bright purple-red; good mid-palate fruit and intensity; raspberry and blackcurrant; balanced, dry finish. Deserves its show medals. **RATING** 89 **DRINK** Now $ 13.50

Robinsons Family Vineyards   ★★★

Curtin Road, Ballandean, Qld 4382 **REGION** Granite Belt
T (07) 4684 1216 **F** (07) 4684 1216 **OPEN** 7 days 10–5
WINEMAKER Craig Robinson **EST.** 1969 **CASES** 3000
SUMMARY One of the pioneers of the Granite Belt, with the second generation of the family Robinson now in control. One thing has not changed: the strongly held belief of the Robinsons that the Granite Belt should be regarded as a cool, rather than warm, climate. It is a tricky debate, because some climatic measurements point one way, others the opposite. Embedded in all this are semantic arguments about the meaning of 'cool' and 'warm'. Suffice it to say that shiraz and (conspicuously) cabernet sauvignon are the most suitable red varieties for the region; semillon, verdelho and chardonnay are the best white varieties.

ŸŸŸŸŸ   **Chardonnay 2000** Still youthful and elegant; excellent colour; good length and style. Gold Museum class Queensland Wine Awards 2004. **RATING** 93 **DRINK** Now

ŸŸŸ   **Merlot 2003** **RATING** 81

ŸŸŸ   **Chardonnay 2002** **RATING** 79

Robinvale   ★★★

Sea Lake Road, Robinvale, Vic 3549 **REGION** Murray Darling
T (03) 5026 3955 **F** (03) 5026 1123 **WEB** www.organicwines.com.au **OPEN** Mon–Fri 9–6, Sun 1–6
WINEMAKER Bill Caracatsanoudis **EST.** 1976 **CASES** 10 000
SUMMARY Robinvale was one of the first Australian wineries to be fully accredited with the Biodynamic Agricultural Association of Australia. Most, but not all, of the wines are produced from organically grown grapes, with some made preservative-free. Production has grown dramatically, no doubt reflecting the interest in organic and biodynamic viticulture and winemaking. Exports to the UK, Japan, Belgium, Canada and the US.

Roche Wines   ★★★★☆

Broke Road, Pokolbin, NSW 2320 **REGION** Lower Hunter Valley
T (02) 4998 7600 **F** (02) 4998 7706 **WEB** www.hvg.com.au **OPEN** 7 days 10–5
WINEMAKER Sarah-Kate Dineen (Contract) **EST.** 1999 **CASES** 10 000
SUMMARY Roche Wines, with its 45.77 ha of semillon, shiraz and chardonnay (plus a few bits and pieces), is but the tip of the iceberg of the massive investment made by Bill Roche in the Pokolbin subregion. He has transformed the old Hungerford Hill development on the corner of Broke and McDonalds Roads, and built a luxurious resort hotel with extensive gardens and an Irish pub on the old Tallawanta Vineyard, as well as resuscitating the vines on Tallawanta. The wines are all sold onsite through the various outlets in the overall development; excess grapes are sold to other makers.

ŸŸŸŸŸ   **Tallawanta Reserve IJR Shiraz 2003** Classic earthy, regional overtones to intense plum, blackberry and mulberry fruit; excellent oak and tannin balance; a long life and evolution. From 100-year-old vines. Cork. **RATING** 94 **DRINK** 2018 $ 55

ŸŸŸŸ   **Tallawanta Chardonnay 2003** Attractive wine; nectarine and melon woven through with smoky barrel ferment aromas; light to medium-bodied; good flow, line and mouthfeel. Quality cork. **RATING** 90 **DRINK** 2008 $ 19
Tallawanta Botrytis Semillon 2004 Deep gold; cumquat, mandarin, honey, vanilla and lemon zest; particularly bright acidity. Quality cork. **RATING** 90 **DRINK** 2008 $ 25

ŸŸŸŸ   **Tallawanta Premium Reserve Steven Vineyard Shiraz 2003** Attractive spicy/savoury edges to the dark berry fruit and tannins. **RATING** 89 **DRINK** 2012 $ 55

Rochford Wines

Cnr Maroondah Highway/Hill Road, Coldstream, Vic 3770 **REGION** Yarra Valley
T (03) 5962 2119 **F** (03) 5962 5319 **WEB** www.rochfordwines.com.au **OPEN** 7 days 10–5 (10–6 during daylight saving)
WINEMAKER David Creed **EST.** 1988 **CASES** 25 000
SUMMARY Following the acquisition of Eyton-on-Yarra by Helmut and Yvonne Konecsny, major changes have occurred. Most obvious is the renaming of the winery and brand, slightly less so the move of the winemaking operations of Rochford to the Yarra Valley.

TTTTT **Macedon Ranges Reserve Pinot Noir 2003** Very complex sous bois aromas; intense but relatively fine spice and forest flavours; excellent length. Good cork. **RATING** 94 **DRINK** 2010 $54

TTTTT **Macedon Ranges Chardonnay 2003** Tight, fragrant grapefruit, citrus and melon; nice touches of barrel ferment and malolactic; good length. Cork. **RATING** 92 **DRINK** 2010 $27
Yarra Valley Reserve Pinot Noir 2003 Radically different from the varietal; deeper colour; medium to full-bodied; ripe plum, spice and bramble; oak push, too. High-quality cork. **RATING** 91 **DRINK** 2008 $44
Yarra Valley Shiraz 2002 Neatly balanced redcurrant, raspberry and blackcurrant, with notes of spice; medium-bodied; fine tannins and length. **RATING** 91 **DRINK** 2010 $26
Macedon Ranges Pinot Noir 2003 Fresh bright cherry fruit then spicy, savoury, fine-grained tannins; good length. Cork. **RATING** 90 **DRINK** 2008 $41

TTTT **Yarra Valley Sauvignon Blanc 2004** Nicely balanced and weighted wine; ripe gooseberry fruit; crisp finish. Screwcap. **RATING** 89 **DRINK** Now $21
Yarra Valley Pinot Noir 2003 Spicy, foresty aromas; light-bodied, elegant palate, again spice-dominant; doesn't show its alcohol of 14.5°. Screwcap. **RATING** 89 **DRINK** 2007 $27
Yarra Valley Cabernet Merlot 2001 Firm, earthy savoury edges built around blackcurrant, olive and cedar fruit; distinctly regional. Good cork. **RATING** 89 **DRINK** 2011 $23
Yarra Valley Chardonnay 2003 Ripe yellow peach and tropical fruit; unusual for the region; barrel ferment oak and malolactic inputs. Cork. **RATING** 88 **DRINK** 2008 $21
Yarra Valley Arneis 2004 Faint lemon blossom and slate; mineral, lemon zest and spice, bright finish. Screwcap. **RATING** 88 **DRINK** 2007 $23
Victoria Chardonnay 2003 Melon and citrus; light-bodied but balanced; hints of oak. Screwcap. **RATING** 87 **DRINK** 2009 $18

TTTT **Macedon Ranges Pinot Gris 2004** **RATING** 86 **DRINK** 2007 $27

RockBare Wines

PO Box 63, Mt Torrens, SA 5244 **REGION** McLaren Vale
T (08) 8389 9584 **F** (08) 8389 9587 **WEB** www.rockbare.com.au **OPEN** Not
WINEMAKER Tim Burvill **EST.** 2000 **CASES** 10 000
SUMMARY A native of Western Australia, Tim Burvill moved to South Australia in 1993 to do the winemaking course at the University of Adelaide Roseworthy Campus. Having completed an Honours degree in oenology, he was recruited by Southcorp, and quickly found himself in a senior winemaking position, with responsibility for super-premium whites including Penfolds Yattarna. He makes the RockBare wines under lend-lease arrangements with other wineries. National distribution by Red+White. Exports to the US, Canada and New Zealand.

TTTTT **Barossa Valley Shiraz 2002** Very good colour; potent, focused black fruits; immaculate fruit and oak balance and integration; fine, persistent tannins, long finish. **RATING** 95 **DRINK** 2017 $21

TTTTT **Adelaide Hills Chardonnay 2003** Subtle barrel ferment complexities; elegant, tangy grapefruit and stone fruit flavours; lingering finish. **RATING** 93 **DRINK** 2008 $19
McLaren Vale Chardonnay 2004 Excellent line, balance and structure; driven by tangy grapefruit and melon; oak invisible. **RATING** 90 **DRINK** 2009 $18

TTTT **McLaren Vale Shiraz 2003** **RATING** 86 **DRINK** 2008 $18.99

Rockfield Estate ★★★★☆

Rosa Glen Road, Margaret River, WA 6285 **REGION** Margaret River
T(08) 9757 5006 **F**(08) 9757 5006 **WEB** www.rockfield.com.au **OPEN** 7 days 11–5
WINEMAKER Andrew Gaman Jr **EST.** 1997 **CASES** 8000
SUMMARY Rockfield Estate Vineyard is very much a family affair. Dr Andrew Gaman wears the hats of chief executive officer, assistant winemaker and co-marketing manager; wife Anne Gaman is a Director; Alex Gaman and Nick McPherson are viticulturists; Andrew Gaman Jr is winemaker; and Anna Walter (née Gaman) helps Dr Andrew Gaman with the marketing. Chapman Brook meanders through the property, the vines running from its banks up to the wooded slopes above the valley floor. The winery café offers light refreshments and food throughout the day. Exports to the US.

▼▼▼▼▼ **Semillon 2004** Fragrant and flowery, unusually so for Semillon; intensely focused, building flavour progressively through the palate; good now, even better in the future. Good value. Screwcap. **RATING** 95 **DRINK** 2014 $ 17

▼▼▼▼▽ **Semillon Sauvignon Blanc 2004** Partial barrel ferment adds texture and structure, though takes a little edge off the varietal fruit expression; lifted by squeaky acidity on the finish. Screwcap. **RATING** 90 **DRINK** 2008 $ 17
Cabernet Merlot 2002 Medium-bodied; elegant blackcurrant and savoury mix; some Bordeaux qualities; balanced tannins and oak. Quality cork. **RATING** 90 **DRINK** 2012 $ 24

Rockford ★★★★★

Krondorf Road, Tanunda, SA 5352 **REGION** Barossa Valley
T(08) 8563 2720 **F**(08) 8563 3787 **OPEN** Mon–Sat 11–5
WINEMAKER Robert O'Callaghan, Chris Ringland **EST.** 1984 **CASES** NFP
SUMMARY The wines are sold only through Adelaide retailers (and the cellar door) and are unknown to most eastern Australian wine-drinkers, which is a great pity because these are some of the most individual, spectacularly flavoured wines made in the Barossa today, with an emphasis on old, low-yielding dryland vineyards. This South Australian slur on the palates of Victoria and NSW is exacerbated by the fact that the wines are exported to Switzerland, the UK, the US, Canada and New Zealand; it all goes to show we need proper authority to protect our living treasures.

▼▼▼▼▼ **Handpicked Eden Valley Riesling 2001** Powerful, potent, touch of old-fashioned kerosene; excellent structure and balance; crammed with mineral and spice; long aftertaste. **RATING** 94 **DRINK** 2011 $ 17.50
Basket Press Shiraz 2002 Medium-bodied; classic exercise in restraint; an array of black fruits on a long palate; fine, savoury tannins; minimal oak. **RATING** 94 **DRINK** 2017 $ 44.50
Black Shiraz NV Complex spicy wine; black fruits and truffles; excellent balance – long, but neither sweet nor phenolic; persistent mousse. **RATING** 94 **DRINK** 2015 $ 53

▼▼▼▼▽ **Rod & Spur 2002** Good colour; abundant, gently sweet blackberry and blackcurrant fruit; ripe tannins, subtle oak, long finish; carries its 15° alcohol with ease. Cabernet Sauvignon/Shiraz. **RATING** 93 **DRINK** 2015 $ 28
Rifle Range Cabernet Sauvignon 2002 Lively, juicy cassis berry fruit; medium-bodied; not extractive, and gentle oak. **RATING** 92 **DRINK** 2015 $ 33
Rod & Spur 2001 Elegant, understated style; a gently ripe array of red and black berry fruits; fine, ripe tannins. **RATING** 92 **DRINK** 2010 $ 28
Shiraz Vintage Port 1998 Good style; chocolate and black fruits on a stick; good spirit; not too sweet. **RATING** 91 **DRINK** 2015
Moppa Springs 2000 Medium-bodied; a savoury, spicy mix; ripe tannins add to the flavour and structure; very good for vintage and age. **RATING** 90 **DRINK** 2008 $ 22.50

▼▼▼▼ **Handpicked Eden Valley Riesling 2002** Still bright, pale yellow-green; powerful, generous style; depth and flavour rather than finesse. **RATING** 89 **DRINK** 2008 $ 17.50
PS Marion Tawny NV Good rancio style; nice dry biscuit aftertaste; good length. **RATING** 89 **DRINK** Now
Alicante Bouchet 2004 Vivid purple-red; fresh, spicy/minty edge to red fruits; seems a little too sweet. **RATING** 87 **DRINK** Now $ 16

▼▼▼▽ **White Frontignac 2004 RATING** 86 **DRINK** Now $ 13
Local Growers Barossa Valley Semillon 2001 RATING 85 **DRINK** Now $ 17

Rock House   NR

St Agnes Hill, Calder Highway, Kyneton, Vic 3444 (postal) **REGION** Macedon Ranges
T (03) 5422 2205 **F** (03) 9388 9355 **OPEN** Not
WINEMAKER Malcolm Stewart **EST.** 1990 **CASES** 350
SUMMARY Ray Lacey and partners have established 6 ha of riesling, cabernet sauvignon and merlot.
By far the greatest percentage of the production is sold as grapes, with 5 tonnes being used for the
Rock House wines. All the wine is sold through local retail outlets and by mail order.

Rocklea Vineyard   NR

Londons Road, Lovedale, NSW 2325 (postal) **REGION** Lower Hunter Valley
T (02) 9980 7000 **F** (02) 9980 2833 **OPEN** Not
WINEMAKER Bill Sneddon (Contract) **EST.** 1989 **CASES** NA
SUMMARY Allan Brown has 10 ha planted to semillon, chardonnay and shiraz. The wine is available
by mail order, and limited amounts are exported.

Rocland Wines   NR

PO Box 679, Nuriootpa, SA 5355 **REGION** Barossa Valley
T (08) 8562 202 **F** (08) 8562 2182 **OPEN** Not
WINEMAKER Tim Smith (Contract) **EST.** 2000 **CASES** NA
SUMMARY Rocland Wines is primarily a bulk winemaking facility for contract work, but Frank Rocca
does have 6 ha of shiraz which is used to make Rocland Wines; they are largely destined for the
Canadian market.

Rodericks   NR

90 Goshnicks Road, Murgon, Qld 4605 **REGION** South Burnett
T (07) 4168 4768 **F** (07) 4168 4768 **OPEN** 7 days 10–5
WINEMAKER Colin Roderick, Robert Roderick **EST.** 1996 **CASES** NA
SUMMARY The Roderick family (Wendy, Colin and Robert) have a 22-ha vineyard planted to semillon,
chardonnay, colombard, verdelho, cabernet sauvignon, merlot, malbec, shiraz, white muscat, muscat
hamburg and tarrango, and make the wine onsite. The production is largely sold by mail order and
through the cellar door, which offers the full gamut of facilities, including light meals.

Roehr   ★★★★

Roehr Road, Ebenezer near Nuriootpa, SA 5355 **REGION** Barossa Valley
T (08) 8565 6242 **F** (08) 8565 6242 **OPEN** Not
WINEMAKER Contract **EST.** 1995 **CASES** NFP
SUMMARY Karl Wilhelm Roehr arrived in Australia in 1841, and was amongst the earliest settlers at
Ebenezer, in the northern end of the Barossa Valley. His great-great grandson Elmor Roehr is the
custodian of 20 ha of shiraz, grenache, mataro on a vineyard passed down through the generations. In
1995 he decided to venture into winemaking and produced a Shiraz from 80-year-old vines which
typically crop at less than 1.5 tonnes to the acre; he has subsequently expanded the range significantly.

TTTTT **Elmor's Ebenezer Old Vine Shiraz 1998** Powerful black fruits, blood plum jam and warm
spice; supple and smooth; nice bottle-developed characters developing; 80-year-old vines.
Cork. **RATING** 90 **DRINK** 2012

TTTT **Ebenezer Ridge Cabernet Sauvignon 2002** Solid blackcurrant and blackberry fruit;
vanilla oak; ripe tannins. **RATING** 89 **DRINK** 2012

TTTT **GMS Ebenezer Ridge Grenache Shiraz 2000** **RATING** 86 **DRINK** 2007

Rogues Gallery   NR

PO Box 10295, Adelaide BC, SA 5000 **REGION** McLaren Vale
T 0413 263 713 **F** (08) 8410 0918 **WEB** www.roguesgallery.com.au **OPEN** Not
WINEMAKER Contract **EST.** 1996 **CASES** NA

SUMMARY Stephen Inglis sources the material for the Rogues Gallery wines in various ways: from 4 ha of vineyards in the heart of McLaren Vale, 2.4 ha at Blewitt Springs and 1.7 ha on the Willunga Scarp. Less than 20 tonnes are crushed for the Rogues Gallery label; the remainder goes elsewhere. Exports to Canada, England and the US, and the limited distribution in Victoria by Yarra Valley Wine Consultants; wines are also available via mail order.

Rojo Wines   NR

34 Breese Street, Brunswick, Vic 3056 **REGION** Port Phillip Zone
T (03) 9386 5688 **F** (03) 9386 5699 **OPEN** Weekends 10–6
WINEMAKER Graeme Rojo **EST.** 1999 **CASES** NA
SUMMARY Rojo Wines is part of Melbourne's urban winery at Brunswick. Core production is cool-climate wines from the Strathbogie Ranges (Sauvignon Blanc, Chardonnay, Shiraz and Merlot). Fruit is also sourced from various regions in Victoria. Production is low, allowing maximum time to be spent with each wine through its development.

Romavilla   ★★☆

Northern Road, Roma, Qld 4455 **REGION** Queensland Zone
T (07) 4622 1822 **F** (07) 4622 1822 **WEB** www.romavilla.com **OPEN** Mon–Fri 8–5, Sat 9–12, 2–4
WINEMAKER David Wall, Richard Wall **EST.** 1863 **CASES** 2000
SUMMARY An amazing historic relic, seemingly untouched since its 19th-century heyday, producing conventional table wines but still providing some extraordinary fortifieds, including a truly stylish Madeira made from Riesling and Syrian (the latter variety originating in Persia). David Wall has now been joined by son Richard in the business, which will hopefully ensure continuity for this important part of Australian wine history. The vineyard has been increased with the planting of 0.4 ha of the Italian grape garganega. Exports to Hong Kong and Canada.

ŦŦŦŦ **Rose Black Muscat 2004** **RATING** 86 **DRINK** Now $ 11
        Gold Reserve Riesling Crouchen 2002 **RATING** 84 **DRINK** Now $ 15

Rosabrook Estate   ★★★★☆

Rosabrook Road, Margaret River, WA 6285 **REGION** Margaret River
T (08) 9757 2286 **F** (08) 9757 3634 **OPEN** 7 days 10–4
WINEMAKER Bill Crappsley **EST.** 1980 **CASES** 4000
SUMMARY The first Rosabrook vineyard plantings took place in 1980; these were further plantings in 1985, '89, '94, '95 and '96. A second vineyard, a few kilometres further down Rosabrook Road, is known as the Rosabrook Mowen Vineyard. The vineyards are planted to sauvignon blanc, semillon, chardonnay, shiraz, merlot, cabernet sauvignon and petit verdot. The cellar door was formerly the first commercial abattoir in the region, hence the slightly challenging name of the icon red (Slaughterhouse Block). Rosabrook is now owned by a group of Australian and international investors.

ŦŦŦŦŦ **Chardonnay 2003** Elegant, intense and focused; bright nectarine and grapefruit underpinned by subtle oak; great length; carries 14.5° alcohol. Screwcap. **RATING** 94 **DRINK** 2011 $ 22

ŦŦŦŦ **Semillon Sauvignon Blanc 2004** Fragrant herb, gooseberry and citrus aromas; 10% barrel ferment works very well, adding to texture; long, clean line and fruit expression. Screwcap. **RATING** 93 **DRINK** 2008 $ 17.50
        Estate Reserve Slaughterhouse Block 2002 Vibrant colour; clean, bright, fresh and harmonious array of cassis, blackcurrant and raspberry; fine, ripe tannins; subtle oak. Bordeaux blend. Screwcap. **RATING** 93 **DRINK** 2017 $ 33

ŦŦŦŦ **Pioneers Chardonnay 2002** Scented and aromatic; extremely tight minerally/citrussy palate; crunchy acidity. Peter Pan? Screwcap. **RATING** 89 **DRINK** 2012 $ 22
        Shiraz 2002 Spicy black and red cherry aromas and flavours; light to medium-bodied; tannins still a little obtrusive. Needs a few years. Screwcap. **RATING** 89 **DRINK** 2013 $ 25
        Petalon Hocus Pocus Cabernet Sauvignon 2002 Medium-bodied; lively, juicy black and redcurrant fruit; light tannins, fruit-forward style. **RATING** 89 **DRINK** 2008 $ 13.50
        Petalon Love Potion Rose of Cabernet 2004 Aromatic, classic Cabernet Rose style; hints of herb and leaf alongside red fruits; not too sweet. **RATING** 88 **DRINK** Now $ 13.50

Cabernet Merlot 2003 Light to medium-bodied; smooth, supple, fresh red and black fruits; fine tannins; no patience required. Screwcap. **RATING** 88 **DRINK** 2007 $ 22
Petalon Hocus Pocus Cabernet Sauvignon 2003 Bell-clear cabernet varietal character; obviously not much barrel work; lingering tannins. Style and brand image inconsistent. Screwcap. **RATING** 87 **DRINK** 2010 $ 13.50

▼▼▼ **Petalon Seduction Classic Dry White 2004** **RATING** 83 $ 13.50

Rosebrook Estate ★★★

1092 Maitlandvale Road, Rosebrook, NSW 2320 **REGION** Lower Hunter Valley
T (02) 4930 6961 **F** (02) 4930 6963 **WEB** www.rosebrookestatewines.com.au **OPEN** By appointment
WINEMAKER Graeme Levick **EST.** 2000 **CASES** 2000
SUMMARY Graeme and Tania Levick run Rosebrook Estate and Hunter River Retreat as parallel operations. They include self-contained cottages, horse-riding, tennis, canoeing, swimming, bushwalking, fishing, riverside picnic area, recreation room and minibus for winery tours and transport to functions or events in the area. Somewhere in the middle of all this they have established 2.5 ha each of chardonnay and verdelho, purchasing shiraz and muscat to complete the product range.

▼▼▼▼ **Shiraz 2003** Medium red-purple; clean, fresh and focused; light to medium-bodied; nice red and black fruits; fine tannins, subtle oak. Cork. **RATING** 89 **DRINK** 2012 $ 17

Rosemount Estate (Hunter Valley) ★★★★

Rosemount Road, Denman, NSW 2328 **REGION** Upper Hunter Valley
T (02) 6549 6450 **F** (02) 6549 6499 **WEB** www.rosemountestate.com.au **OPEN** 7 days 10–4
WINEMAKER Charles Whish, Matt Koch, Briony Hoare **EST.** 1969 **CASES** NFP
SUMMARY Rosemount Estate achieved a miraculous balancing act, maintaining wine quality while presiding over an ever-expanding empire and dramatically increasing production. The wines were consistently of excellent value; all had real character and individuality, and more than a few were startlingly good. The outcome was the merger with Southcorp in March 2001; what seemed to be a powerful and synergistic merger turned out to be little short of a disaster. Southcorp lost more than its market capitalisation and more than half of its most effective and talented employees, inviting takeover offers.

▼▼▼▼▽ **Roxburgh Chardonnay 2002** At once complex yet more restrained and less idiosyncratic than many of its predecessors; oak just a fraction overt. **RATING** 93 **DRINK** 2008 $ 40.95
Orange Vineyard Chardonnay 2002 Elegant, tight, focused, almost minerally, aromas; palate more to melon, with creamy cashew notes; long finish, good acidity. **RATING** 92 **DRINK** 2008 $ 25.95
Orange Vineyard Shiraz 2002 Much greater depth of blackberry fruit than is typical; sweeter, riper, too; a dash of chocolate and ripe tannins. Cork. **RATING** 92 **DRINK** 2015 $ 29.50
Mountain Blue Shiraz Cabernet 2001 Full-bodied, concentrated and rich; strong structure; black and red fruits; ripe tannins, balanced oak. Cork. **RATING** 92 **DRINK** 2016 $ 53
Hill of Gold Mudgee Cabernet Sauvignon 2003 Medium-bodied; supple, smooth blackcurrant; very good fine, ripe tannins and mouthfeel; skilled oak handling. Cork. **RATING** 91 **DRINK** 2013 $ 17.90
Diamond Label Cabernet Sauvignon 2002 Medium to full-bodied; powerful blackcurrant fruit, unusually ripe for the region; plenty of depth to the structure and tannins; will develop. Cork. **RATING** 91 **DRINK** 2013 $ 20.90
Hill of Gold Mudgee Chardonnay 2004 Good structure and texture; nice spare frame around stone fruit, apple and mineral; elegant and controlled. Cork. **RATING** 90 **DRINK** 2008 $ 17.90
Orange Vineyard Chardonnay 2003 Super-refined and elegant; long, lingering grapefruit/stone fruit has absorbed the oak; all its life in front of it. Cork. **RATING** 90 **DRINK** 2012 $ 20.90
Mountain Blue Shiraz Cabernet 2002 Spicy, earthy, savoury, leathery aromas and flavours; considerable length is its strong suit. **RATING** 90 **DRINK** 2009 $ 53

ŸŸŸŸ **Show Reserve Chardonnay 2003** Generous but not flabby; yellow peach and stone fruit; soft and ready. Cork. **RATING** 89 **DRINK** 2007 $ 20.90

Diamond Label Limited Edition Shiraz Grenache Viognier 2002 Medium-bodied; full of flavour with sweet spicy/berry fruit, and some Viognier lift; the three varieties mesh well; soft tannins. Well priced. **RATING** 89 **DRINK** Now $ 14.95

Hill of Gold Mudgee Shiraz 2003 Savoury, earthy, spicy style; medium-bodied; black fruits and lingering, earthy tannins. Cork. **RATING** 88 **DRINK** 2010 $ 17.90

Diamond Label Sangiovese 2004 More substance than many; abundant cherry fruit, more sweet than sour; fine, ripe tannins. Synthetic cork. **RATING** 88 **DRINK** 2009 $ 13.50

Diamond Label Chardonnay 2004 Honest wine; plenty of peach and melon fruit, not too much oak. Dry finish. **RATING** 87 **DRINK** Now $ 14.95

Diamond Label Pinot Noir 2004 Medium-bodied; plenty of depth; trembles on the brink of dry red, but does have plummy, varietal fruit. Honest. Cork. **RATING** 87 **DRINK** 2008 $ 13.50

Diamond Label Shiraz 2003 Medium-bodied; pleasant black cherry, plum and blackberry fruits; subtle oak. **RATING** 87 **DRINK** 2008 $ 14.95

ŸŸŸŸ **Roxburgh Chardonnay 2003** **RATING** 86 **DRINK** 2007 $ 36.90

Giants Creek Chardonnay Viognier 2002 **RATING** 86 **DRINK** Now $ 19.45

Diamond Label Pinot Noir 2003 **RATING** 86 **DRINK** 2008 $ 14.95

Diamond Label Cabernet Merlot 2003 **RATING** 86 **DRINK** Now $ 11

Diamond Label Riesling 2003 **RATING** 85 **DRINK** 2007 $ 13.50

Grenache Shiraz 2003 **RATING** 85 **DRINK** Now $ 10.95

Chardonnay Pinot NV **RATING** 84 **DRINK** Now $ 13.50

ŸŸŸ **Diamond Label Shiraz Cabernet 2003** **RATING** 83 $ 11

Jigsaw Riesling Frontignac Verdelho 2003 **RATING** 81 $ 7.99

Jigsaw Chardonnay Verdelho Sauvignon Blanc 2003 **RATING** 81 $ 7.99

Rosemount Estate (McLaren Vale) ★★★★

Chaffeys Road, McLaren Vale, SA 5171 **REGION** McLaren Vale
T (08) 8323 8250 **F** (08) 8323 9308 **WEB** www.rosemountestate.com.au **OPEN** Mon–Sat 10–5, Sun & public hols 11–4
WINEMAKER Charles Whish **EST.** 1888 **CASES** NFP
SUMMARY The specialist red wine arm of Rosemount Estate, responsible for its prestigious Balmoral Syrah, Show Reserve Shiraz and GSM, as well as most of the other McLaren Vale-based Rosemount brands. These wines come in large measure from 325 ha of estate plantings.

ŸŸŸŸŸ **GSM 2002** Fragrant and aromatic; a rippling array of black and red fruits, spice and a touch of chocolate; fine, ripe tannins. Very nice wine. Cork. **RATING** 93 **DRINK** 2010 $ 22

GSM 2001 Very good balance, flavour and texture; a marriage of red and black fruits with some juicy notes and ripe tannins. **RATING** 93 **DRINK** 2008 $ 27.95

Traditional 2002 Dense colour; powerful, concentrated and compact; ripe but potent overtones; overall savoury and with Bordeaux overtones. **RATING** 93 **DRINK** 2015 $ 27.95

ŸŸŸŸ **Traditional 2003** Powerful, earthy black fruits; surprisingly edgy tannins. Still to soften and integrate. Cork. **RATING** 87 **DRINK** 2010 $ 27.95

Rosenvale Wines ★★★★

Lot 385 Railway Terrace, Nuriootpa, SA 5355 **REGION** Barossa Valley
T 0407 390 788 **F** (08) 8565 7206 **WEB** www.rosenvale.com.au **OPEN** By appointment
WINEMAKER James Rosenzweig, Mark Jamieson **EST.** 2000 **CASES** 1600
SUMMARY The Rosenzweig family has 80 ha of vineyards, some old and some new, planted to riesling, semillon, pinot noir, grenache, shiraz and cabernet sauvignon. Most of the grapes are sold to other producers, but since 1999 select parcels have been retained and vinified for release under the Rosenvale label. Exports to the UK, the US, Singapore, China and Taiwan.

Rosevears Estate ★★★☆

1a Waldhorn Drive, Rosevears, Tas 7277 **REGION** Northern Tasmania
T (03) 6330 1800 **F** (03) 6330 1810 **WEB** www.rosevearsestate.com.au **OPEN** 7 days 10–4
WINEMAKER Andrew Pirie **EST.** 1999 **CASES** 8000

summary The multi-million dollar Rosevears Estate winery and restaurant complex was opened by the Tasmanian premier in November 1999. Built on a steep hillside overlooking the Tamar River, it is certain to make a lasting and important contribution to the Tasmanian wine industry. It is owned by a syndicate of investors headed by Dr Mike Beamish, and incorporates both Notley Gorge and Ironpot Bay. Spacious, high-quality accommodation units with a splendid view over the Tamar River were opened in September 2003.

♥♥♥♥♡ **Gewurztraminer 2004** Rose petal and spice varietal fruit; good length and balance. **RATING** 90 **DRINK** 2008 $ 20

♥♥♥♥ **Sauvignon Blanc 2004** Undoubtedly varietal but does have some sweaty reduction on the bouquet; pleasant gooseberry/kiwifruit with balanced acidity. **RATING** 89 **DRINK** Now $ 20
Pinot Noir 2003 Good colour; ripe, dark plum fruit; solid rather than graceful; should develop. Screwcap. **RATING** 88 **DRINK** 2007 $ 28
Unwooded Chardonnay 2004 Faint reduction; tangy citrus/grapefruit/stone fruit flavours; light to medium-bodied, good length. Screwcap. **RATING** 87 **DRINK** 2007 $ 24

♥♥♥♡ **Riesling 2004** **RATING** 86 **DRINK** 2009 $ 20
Notley Gorge Pinot Noir 2004 **RATING** 86 **DRINK** 2008 $ 21
Merlot 2003 **RATING** 84 **DRINK** 2008

Rosily Vineyard ★★★★

Yelveton Road, Wilyabrup, WA 6284 **REGION** Margaret River
T (08) 9755 6336 **F** (08) 9221 3309 **WEB** www.rosily.com.au **OPEN** By appointment
WINEMAKER Mike Lemmes, Dan Pannell (Consultant) **EST.** 1994 **CASES** 7000
summary The partnership of Mike and Barb Scott and Ken and Dot Allan acquired the Rosily Vineyard site in 1994. Under the direction of consultant Dan Pannell (of the Pannell family), 12 ha of vineyard were planted over the next 3 years: first up sauvignon blanc, semillon, chardonnay and cabernet sauvignon, and thereafter merlot, shiraz and a little grenache and cabernet franc. The first crops were sold to other makers in the region, but in 1999 Rosily built a winery with a 120-tonne capacity; it is now moving to fully utilise that capacity.

♥♥♥♥♡ **Shiraz 2002** Elegant, medium-bodied; fragrant cherry, raspberry and blackberry mix; fine tannins, subtle oak. **RATING** 91 **DRINK** 2012 $ 23
Sauvignon Blanc 2004 Spotlessly clean and fresh; vibrant and crunchy lemon, mineral, spice and gooseberry; good balance and finish. **RATING** 90 **DRINK** 2007 $ 18
Semillon Sauvignon Blanc 2004 Bright, light colour; added complexity through a hint of oak on both bouquet and palate, sweetening up the fruit profile; nice wine. **RATING** 90 **DRINK** 2010 $ 19
Chardonnay 2003 Nicely balanced stone fruit, melon and cashew flavours; good acid balance; stylish. **RATING** 90 **DRINK** 2009

♥♥♥♥ **Cabernet Sauvignon 2002** Lively, fresh redcurrant and blackcurrant fruit; slightly light overall. **RATING** 87 **DRINK** 2007 $ 23

Rosnay Organic Wines ★★☆

Rivers Road, Canowindra, NSW 2804 **REGION** Cowra
T (02) 6344 3215 **F** (02) 6344 3229 **WEB** www.organicfarms.com.au **OPEN** By appointment
WINEMAKER Various contract **EST.** 2002 **CASES** 3000
summary Rosnay Organic Wines is, to put it mildly, an interesting business venture, with the Statham and Gardner families at its centre. There are 36 ha of vineyard on the 140-ha property, part of which has been divided into 12 blocks ranging from 8 to 10 ha, along with ten housing blocks, each of 5000m², with all the requisite building approvals and services provided. The viticulture is organic, and the management company provides active growers or absentee investors with a range of specialist organic farming machinery and contract management. Winemaking is split between John Cassegrain of Cassegrain Wines, Kevin Karstrom of Botobolar and Rodney Hooper of Windowrie, each one of whom has expertise in organic grapegrowing and organic winemaking.

Ross Estate Wines

★★★★☆

Barossa Valley Way, Lyndoch, SA 5351 **REGION** Barossa Valley
T (08) 8524 4033 **F** (08) 8524 4533 **WEB** www.rossestate.com.au **OPEN** Mon–Sat 10–5, Sun 1–5
WINEMAKER Rod Chapman, Angela Hercock **EST.** 1999 **CASES** 20 000
SUMMARY Darius and Pauline Ross laid the foundation for Ross Estate Wines when they purchased
43 ha of vines which included two blocks of 75 and 90-year-old grenache. Also included were blocks
of 30-year-old riesling and semillon, and 13-year-old merlot. Chardonnay, sauvignon blanc, cabernet
sauvignon, cabernet franc and shiraz, were planted 8 years ago. A winery was built in time for the
1998 vintage, and a tasting room was opened in 1999. The immensely experienced Rod Chapman,
with many vintages under his belt, including 18 years as red winemaker with Southcorp/Penfolds, is
in charge of winemaking. Exports to the US, Europe and Asia.

ŸŸŸŸŸ **Estate Shiraz 2002** Supple, rich blackberry, dark chocolate and vanilla aromas and
flavours; soft tannins and well-handled oak; good length. **RATING** 94 **DRINK** 2017 $ 25

ŸŸŸŸŸ **Reserve Barossa Valley Shiraz 2003** Dense colour; full-bodied; very powerful,
concentrated, ripe blackberry fruit, but restrained alcohol (14.5°). Suspect cork. **RATING** 92
DRINK 2015 $ 38

Estate Barossa Cabernet Sauvignon 2002 Supple texture and mouthfeel; black
fruits/blackcurrant supported by sweet oak and savoury, ripe tannins. **RATING** 91
DRINK 2012 $ 25

Estate Barossa Valley Shiraz 2003 Smooth, rich, soft blackberry, plum and vanilla;
balanced oak and tannins. Indifferent cork. **RATING** 90 **DRINK** 2013 $ 26

Northridge Shiraz 2002 Firm but not harsh mouthfeel; mix of blackberry, plum and
blackcurrant; fine tannins, good length. Value. **RATING** 90 **DRINK** 2010 $ 18

Lynedoch Estate 2003 A complex and substantial wine; blackcurrant and mulberry;
smooth, round, ripe tannins; good oak. Cabernet Sauvignon/Franc/Merlot. Quality cork.
RATING 90 **DRINK** 2013 $ 25

ŸŸŸŸ **Estate Barossa Cabernet Sauvignon 2003** Full-bodied; very ripe blackcurrant and
blackberry fruit; persistent but ripe tannins. Good cork. **RATING** 89 **DRINK** 2013 $ 25

Estate Barossa Old Vine Grenache 2003 Sweet, juicy, jammy varietal fruit; light to
medium-bodied; very typical Barossa Grenache style. Suspect cork. **RATING** 88 **DRINK** 207
$ 19

Lynedoch Estate 2002 Savoury olive and earth aromas; mid-palate red fruit, reverting to
a savoury finish. Food style. Cabernet blend. **RATING** 88 **DRINK** 2010 $ 25

Northridge Cabernet Merlot 2002 Earth, olive, savoury aromas; more red and black
fruits on the palate; fine tannins, subtle oak. **RATING** 87 **DRINK** 2008 $ 18

ŸŸŸŸ **Estate Barossa Old Vine Grenache 2002** **RATING** 86 **DRINK** Now $ 20
Estate Barossa TG NV **RATING** 84 **DRINK** 2010 $ 19

Ross Hill Vineyard

★★★★

62 Griffin Road, via Ammerdown, Orange, NSW 2800 **REGION** Orange
T (02) 6360 0175 **F** (02) 6363 1674 **WEB** www.rosshillwines.com.au **OPEN** By appointment
WINEMAKER David Lowe, Stephen Doyle (Contract) **EST.** 1994 **CASES** 3000
SUMMARY Peter and Terri Robson began planting 12 ha of vines in 1994. Chardonnay, sauvignon
blanc, merlot, cabernet sauvignon, shiraz and cabernet franc have been established on north-facing,
gentle slopes at an elevation of 800m. No insecticides are used in the vineyard, the grapes are hand-
picked and the vines are hand-pruned. Ross Hill also has an olive grove with Italian and Spanish
varieties and a free-range organic snail production business. Exports to the UK.

ŸŸŸŸŸ **Jack's Lot Cabernet Franc 2003** Good colour; vibrant, spicy berry aromas; light to
medium-bodied bright fruit; crisp finish. **RATING** 90 **DRINK** 2013 $ 24

ŸŸŸŸ **Mick's Lot Shiraz 2003** Solid, ripe, blackberry fruit; fine, savoury tannins. Twin Top.
RATING 88 **DRINK** 2009 $ 24

Mick's Lot Merlot 2003 Light to medium-bodied; clean; supple mouthfeel; gently ripe
red and black fruits, fine tannins. Very nice wine. Cork. **RATING** 88 **DRINK** 2012 $ 24

Isabelle Cabernet Shiraz 2003 Good colour; bright, fresh, juicy red fruit style; not
forced, good length. Cork. **RATING** 88 **DRINK** 2012 $ 16

Rothbury Ridge

NR

Talga Road, Rothbury, NSW 2320 **REGION** Lower Hunter Valley
T (02) 4930 7122 **F** (02) 4930 7198 **OPEN** Mon–Sat 9–5, Sun 10–5
WINEMAKER Peter Jorgensen **EST.** 1998 **CASES** 10 000
SUMMARY Rothbury Ridge has an extraordinarily eclectic choice of varieties planted, with between 1.2 ha and 2.4 ha each of chardonnay, semillon, verdelho, chambourcin, durif, shiraz and cabernet sauvignon. It is owned by a public company (not listed on the Stock Exchange) with an imposing array of directors, and actively markets its wines through a wine club.

Rothvale Vineyard

★★★☆

Deasy's Road, Pokolbin, NSW 2321 **REGION** Lower Hunter Valley
T (02) 4998 7290 **F** (02) 4998 7926 **WEB** www.rothvale.com.au **OPEN** 7 days 10–5
WINEMAKER Max Patton, Luke Patton **EST.** 1978 **CASES** 8000
SUMMARY Owned and operated by the Patton family, headed by Max Patton, who has the fascinating academic qualifications of BVSc, MSc London, BA Hons Canterbury – the scientific part has no doubt come in useful for his winemaking. The wines are sold only through the cellar door and direct to an imposing list of restaurants in the Hunter Valley and Sydney. Rothvale also has four vineyard cottages available for B&B accommodation. The wines have already accumulated an impressive array of medals, and are of commendably consistent style and quality. Exports to China.

ŸŸŸŸ **Vat 8 Semillon 2003** Fragrant herb and lemongrass aromas; quite full in the mouth; soft finish. **RATING** 88 **DRINK** 2007 $ 18
Luke's Shiraz 2002 Light to medium-bodied; regional earthy overtones; fine, savoury tannins and subtle oak. **RATING** 88 **DRINK** 2009 $ 25
Barrel-Fermented Semillon 2003 Complex; oak a major part of the structure and flavour; catching slightly on the finish, but a good alternative style of Semillon. **RATING** 87 **DRINK** 2008 $ 18
Late Picked Traminer Muscat 2003 Moderately sweet, clean, grapey fruit flavours; not complex, but well balanced. **RATING** 87 **DRINK** Now $ 15

ŸŸŸŸ **Unwooded Chardonnay 2003 RATING** 86 **DRINK** 2007 $ 14
Lightly Oaked Chardonnay 2003 RATING 84 **DRINK** Now $ 17

ŸŸŸ **Reserve Chardonnay F 2003 RATING** 83 $ 32
Reserve Chardonnay A 2003 RATING 82 $ 25

Roundstone Winery & Vineyard

★★★★

54 Willow Bend Drive, Yarra Glen, Vic 3775 **REGION** Yarra Valley
T (03) 9730 1181 **F** (03) 9730 1151 **WEB** www.yarravalleywine.com/network **OPEN** Thurs–Sun & public hols 10–5, or by appointment
WINEMAKER John Derwin, Rob Dolan, Kate Goodman (Consultants) **EST.** 1998 **CASES** 2000
SUMMARY John and Lynne Derwin have moved quickly since establishing Roundstone, planting 8 ha of vineyard (half to pinot noir with a mix of the best clones), building a small winery and opening a cellar door and restaurant on the side of a dam. The Derwins tend the vineyard, enlist the aid of friends to pick the grapes; John makes the wine with advice from Rob Dolan and Kate Goodman; Lynne is the chef and sommelier. Her pride and joy is a shearer's stove which was used at the Yarra Glen Grand Hotel for 100 years before being abandoned, and which is now at the centre of the kitchen. The restaurant opened in December 2001, and has established itself as one of the best winery restaurants in the valley.

ŸŸŸŸŸ **Rubies Pinot Noir 2003** Good balance and length; nicely judged touch of oak; fine tannins. Cork. **RATING** 90 **DRINK** 2010 $ 30

ŸŸŸŸ **Merlot 2003** Fresh colour; equally fresh and fragrant posy of red fruits; light to medium-bodied; not much structure, but delicious flavours. Quality cork. **RATING** 89 **DRINK** 2008 $ 22
Gamay 2004 Good colour; aromatic morello cherry; good flavour length, though unsurprisingly, not much structure. Nonetheless, fairly impressive. Screwcap. **RATING** 88 **DRINK** 2007 $ 20

Pinot Noir 2003 Light to medium-bodied; fresh, elegant, spicy, savoury stemmy style; good balance and length. Quality cork. **RATING** 88 **DRINK** 2009 $ 20

Roses 2004 Rich, light, crisp and clean strawberry and cherry; dry finish; attractive Rose. Screwcap. **RATING** 87 **DRINK** Now $ 16

ŸŸŸŸ **Shiraz Viognier 2003** **RATING** 86 **DRINK** 2007 $ 25

Rumbalara   NR

Fletcher Road, Fletcher, Qld 4381 **REGION** Granite Belt
T (07) 4684 1206 **F** (07) 4684 1299 **OPEN** 7 days 9–5
WINEMAKER Wayne Beecham (Contract) **EST.** 1974 **CASES** 1500
SUMMARY Has produced some of the Granite Belt's finest honeyed Semillon and silky, red berry Cabernet Sauvignon, but quality does vary. The winery incorporates a spacious restaurant, and there are also barbecue and picnic facilities. No recent tastings, but the change of owners in 2003 will hopefully see more activity.

Rumball Sparkling Wines   NR

55 Charles Street, Norwood, SA 5067 **REGION** Adelaide Zone
T (08) 8332 2761 **F** (08) 8364 0188 **WEB** www.rumball.com.au **OPEN** Mon–Fri 9–5
WINEMAKER Peter Rumball **EST.** 1988 **CASES** 10 000
SUMMARY Peter Rumball has been making and selling sparkling wine for as long as I can remember, but has led a somewhat peripatetic life, starting in the Clare Valley but now operating one of the 12 Methode Champenoise lines in Australia. The grapes are purchased and the wines made under the supervision of Peter Rumball. His specialty has always been Sparkling Shiraz, and was so long before it became 'flavour of the month'. National retail distribution; exports to the UK, the US and Japan.

Rusden Wines   NR

Magnolia Road, Tanunda, SA 5352 (postal) **REGION** Barossa Valley
T (08) 8563 2976 **F** (08) 8563 0885 **WEB** www.rusdenwines.com.au **OPEN** Not
WINEMAKER Christian Canute **EST.** 1998 **CASES** 2250
SUMMARY The Canute family (Dennis, Christine and Christian) have been long-term grapegrowers with 14 ha of sauvignon blanc, chenin blanc, grenache, cabernet sauvignon, merlot, shiraz, mourvedre and zinfandel. While only part of the production is vinified under the Rusden label, exports have been established to all major markets.

Russet Ridge   ★★★

Cnr Caves Road/Riddoch Highway, Naracoorte, SA 5271 **REGION** Wrattonbully
T (08) 8762 0114 **F** (08) 8762 0341 **OPEN** Thurs–Mon 11–4.30
WINEMAKER Philip Laffer, Sam Kurtz **EST.** 2000 **CASES** 35 000
SUMMARY This is the former Heathfield Ridge winery, built in 1998 as a contract crush and winemaking facility for multiple clients, but purchased by Orlando in 2000. It is the only winery in the large Wrattonbully region, and also receives Orlando's Coonawarra and Padthaway grapes, and other Limestone Coast fruit.

ŸŸŸŸ **Coonawarra Cabernet Shiraz Merlot 2002** A mix of juicy and more minty notes; light to medium-bodied; sweetened by vanilla oak. **RATING** 87 **DRINK** 2007 $ 17.99

Rutherglen Estates   ★★★☆

Cnr Great Northern Road/Murray Valley Highway, Rutherglen, Vic 3685 **REGION** Rutherglen
T (02) 6032 7999 **F** (02) 6032 7998 **OPEN** 7 days 10–4, Tuileries Building, Drummond St, Rutherglen
WINEMAKER Nicole Esdaile **EST.** 2000 **CASES** 45 000
SUMMARY The Rutherglen Estates brand is an offshoot of a far larger contract crush and make business, with a winery capacity of 4000 tonnes (roughly equivalent to 280 000 cases). Rutherglen is

in a declared phylloxera region, which means all the grapes grown within that region have to be vinified within it, itself a guarantee of business for ventures such as Rutherglen Estates. It also means that some of the best available material can be allocated for the brand, with an interesting mix of varieties. A new entry-level range priced at $10 a bottle was introduced in 2005. Exports to the UK, the US, Canada, New Zealand and Brazil.

ΨΨΨΨ **Viognier 2004** Lively and fresh; has more elegance and delicacy than most Viogniers; apricot and a touch of musk varietal fruit. **RATING** 90 **DRINK** 2007 $ 19.95

ΨΨΨΨ **Alliance Marsanne Viognier 2004** The blend of 70% Marsanne and 30% Viognier works well; nice honeysuckle, almond and apricot flavours; crisp finish. **RATING** 88 **DRINK** 2007 $ 15

ΨΨΨΨ **Marsanne 2004** Clean, fresh, mineral/talc aromas; very light palate; a hint of citrus; well balanced, needs time. **RATING** 86 **DRINK** 2010 $ 17.95

Ryland River   NR

RMB 8945, Main Creek Road, Main Ridge, Vic 3928 **REGION** Mornington Peninsula
T (03) 5989 6098 **F** (03) 9899 0184 **OPEN** Weekends & public hols 10–5, or by appointment
WINEMAKER John W Bray **EST.** 1986 **CASES** 2000
SUMMARY John Bray has been operating Ryland River for a number of years, but not without a degree of controversy over the distinction between Ryland River wines from Mornington Peninsula grapes and those from grapes purchased from other regions. A large lake with catch-your-own trout and a cheese house are general tourist attractions.

Rymill Coonawarra

The Riddoch Run Vineyards, Riddoch Highway, Coonawarra, SA 5263 **REGION** Coonawarra
T (08) 8736 5001 **F** (08) 8736 5040 **WEB** www.rymill.com.au **OPEN** 7 days 10–5
WINEMAKER John Innes, Clemence Haselgrove **EST.** 1970 **CASES** 50 000
SUMMARY The Rymills are descendants of John Riddoch and have long owned some of the finest Coonawarra soil, upon which they have grown grapes since 1970; present plantings are 170 ha. Peter Rymill made a small amount of Cabernet Sauvignon in 1987 but has long since plunged headlong into commercial production, with winemaker John Innes presiding over the striking winery portrayed on the label. Australian distribution is through Negociants Australia; exports to all major markets.

ΨΨΨΨ **Cabernet Sauvignon 2001** Medium-bodied; classic structure and texture; a savoury, long flow of interwoven blackberry, earth and tannins. **RATING** 89 **DRINK** 2011 $ 28.50
Shiraz 2001 Pleasant, relatively light-bodied, gaining interest with a spicy, savoury finish. **RATING** 87 **DRINK** 2008 $ 23

ΨΨΨΨ **Sauvignon Blanc 2004 RATING** 86 **DRINK** 2007 $ 15
The Bees Knees Sparkling Red NV RATING 86 **DRINK** 2007 $ 22

Sabella Vineyards   NR

PO Box 229, McLaren Vale, SA 5171 **REGION** McLaren Vale
T 0416 361 369 **F** (08) 8323 8270 **OPEN** Not
WINEMAKER Michael Petrucci **EST.** 1999 **CASES** 450
SUMMARY Giuseppe (Joe) Petrucci was born at Castellino in Campobasso, in the Molise region of Italy, where his family were farmers. His father migrated to Australia in 1960, the rest of the family following him in 1966. In 1976 Joe and wife Rosa (and their children) moved to McLaren Vale, where they purchased their first vineyard, in McMurtrie Road. Over the years their vineyards have increased from 10 ha to 44 ha, and their grapes are sold to Wirra Wirra, Kreglinger, Beringer Blass, Rosemount, Middlebrook Estate and RockBare Estate. In 1999 they decided to keep some grapes back for release under the Sabella label; the word comes from a pseudonym given to the Petrucci name six generations ago. Son Michael just happens to be the winemaker at Middlebrook, which completes the circle. The wines are distributed by Unique Wines, Athol Park, SA.

Saddlers Creek   NR

Marrowbone Road, Pokolbin, NSW 2320 **REGION** Lower Hunter Valley
T(02) 4991 1770 **F**(02) 4991 2482 **WEB** www.saddlerscreekwines.com.au **OPEN** 7 days 9–5
WINEMAKER John Johnstone **EST.** 1989 **CASES** 20 000
SUMMARY Made an impressive entrance to the district with consistently full-flavoured and rich wines,
and has continued on in much the same vein, with good wines across the spectrum. Limited retail
distribution in NSW, Queensland and Victoria. Exports to Canada, New Zealand and Mauritius.

St Aidan   ★★★☆

RMB 205, Ferguson Road, Dardanup, WA 6236 **REGION** Geographe
T(08) 9728 3007 **F**(08) 9728 3006 **WEB** www.saintaidan.com **OPEN** Weekends & public hols 10–5,
or by appointment
WINEMAKER Mark Messenger (Contract) **EST.** 1996 **CASES** 1000
SUMMARY Phil and Mary Smith purchased their property at Dardanup in 1991; it is 20 minutes' drive
from the Bunbury hospitals for which Phil Smith works. They first ventured into Red Globe table
grapes, planting 1 ha in 1994–5, followed by 1 ha of mandarins and oranges. With this experience,
and with Mary completing a TAFE viticulture course, they extended their horizons by planting 1 ha
each of cabernet sauvignon and chardonnay in 1997. A little muscat followed in 2001. Each vintage
since the first in 2000 has been rewarded with medals, chiefly at the Qantas West Australian Wine
Show.

YYYY **K Rose 2004** Substantial rose; bright fuchsia; lots of sweet mid-palate fruit and a
(deliberately) sweet finish. **RATING** 89 **DRINK** Now $14

St Anne's Vineyards   ★★☆

Cnr Perricoota Road/24 Lane, Moama, NSW 2731 **REGION** Perricoota
T(03) 5480 0099 **F**(03) 5480 0077 **OPEN** 7 days 9–5, also at Garrards Lane, Myrniong
WINEMAKER Richard McLean **EST.** 1972 **CASES** 18 000
SUMMARY St Anne's is by far the most active member of the newly registered Perricoota region.
Richard McLean has established 80 ha of estate vineyards, with another 120 ha of grower vineyards
to draw upon. Shiraz, cabernet sauvignon, grenache and mourvedre account for over 75% of the
plantings, but there is a spread of the usual white wines and few red exotics. The wines are all
competently made. Most of the St Anne's wines are sold through the two cellar door operations, in
particular the Myrniong cellar door, which is surrounded by a somewhat scrappy vineyard, but which
attracts considerable passing trade and wedding receptions.

Saint Derycke's Wood Winery   NR

Cnr Greenhills Road/Joadja Road, Berrima, NSW 2576 **REGION** Southern Highlands
T(02) 4878 5439 **F**(02) 4878 5133 **WEB** www.saintderyckeswood.com.au **OPEN** Weekends & public
hols 10–5, or by appointment
WINEMAKER Sean O'Regan **EST.** 1995 **CASES** NA
SUMMARY Sue and John Rappell own the intriguingly-named winery, one of the many newcomers to
the Southern Highlands region. He has planted 6.5 ha to riesling, chardonnay, marsanne, pinot noir,
cabernet sauvignon, merlot, shiraz and cabernet franc and the wines are made onsite – except, one
would imagine, the fortified wines. The wines are sold by mail order and through the cellar door
(when open); many local restaurants also list the wines.

St Gregory's   NR

Bringalbert South Road, Bringalbert South via Apsley, Vic 3319 **REGION** Henty
T(03) 5586 5225 **OPEN** By appointment
WINEMAKER Gregory Flynn **EST.** 1983 **CASES** NFP
SUMMARY Unique Port-only operation selling its limited production direct to enthusiasts (by
mailing list).

St Hallett ★★★★☆

St Hallett's Road, Tanunda, SA 5352 **REGION** Barossa Valley
T (08) 8563 7000 **F** (08) 8563 7001 **WEB** www.sthallett.com.au **OPEN** 7 days 10–5
WINEMAKER Stuart Blackwell, Di Ferguson, Matt Gant **EST.** 1944 **CASES** 100 000
SUMMARY Nothing succeeds like success. St Hallett merged with Tatachilla to form Banksia Wines, which was then acquired by New Zealand's thirsty Lion Nathan. St Hallett understandably continues to ride the Shiraz fashion wave, but all its wines are honest and well priced. Exports to the UK, the US, Canada, Hong Kong and Japan.

♥♥♥♥♡ **Blackwell Shiraz 2002** Medium-bodied; excellent mouthfeel and structure; bright red fruit; fine, ripe tannins; sheer pleasure. **RATING** 93 **DRINK** 2017 $ 29.95
Eden Valley Riesling 2004 Classic Eden Valley lime juice aromas; plenty of flavour, again archetypal Eden Valley; just needed a touch more drive through the finish for top points. **RATING** 92 **DRINK** 2014 $ 19
Blackwell Shiraz 2003 Rich, luscious and supple but avoids jamminess/split fruit characters; blackberry and plum; ripe tannins, good oak; 14.5° alcohol. **RATING** 92 **DRINK** 2015 $ 29.50
Old Block Shiraz 2001 A clean, fresh mix of red and black fruits plus subtle oak. Good mouthfeel and overall elegance. **RATING** 92 **DRINK** 2016
Faith Shiraz 2003 Attractive juicy plum, raspberry and blackberry aromas and flavours; subtle oak. **RATING** 90 **DRINK** 2010 $ 21.50

♥♥♥♥ **Barossa Semillon 2002** Glowing yellow-gold; quite powerful flavours; ripe citrus and lemon zest, a hint of spice, but no oak. Lower alcohol would be better still. **RATING** 89 **DRINK** 2007 $ 24
Barossa GST 2003 A rich and aromatic array of red fruits; medium-bodied, fruit-driven; fine tannins. **RATING** 89 **DRINK** 2010 $ 19.50
Gamekeeper's Reserve 2004 Light to medium-bodied; fresh, bright red cherry and raspberry fruit; soft tannins and mouthfeel; well made; good value. Shiraz/Grenache. Screwcap. **RATING** 87 **DRINK** 2007 $ 13.95

♥♥♥♡ **Gamekeeper's Reserve 2003 RATING** 86 **DRINK** 2007 $ 13.95
Poacher's Blend 2004 RATING 85 **DRINK** Now $ 13.95

St Huberts ★★★★

Maroondah Highway, Coldstream, Vic 3770 **REGION** Yarra Valley
T (03) 9739 1118 **F** (03) 9739 1096 **WEB** www.sthuberts.com.au **OPEN** Mon–Fri 9–5, weekends 10.30–5.30
WINEMAKER Matt Steel (former) **EST.** 1966 **CASES** 15 000
SUMMARY A once famous winery (in the context of the Yarra Valley) which seems to have lost its focus since the merger of Mildara with Blass, and now part of Beringer Blass. However, the wines are very reliable, and the cellar door – if somewhat humble – is well situated.

♥♥♥♥♡ **Chardonnay 2003** Quite rich peach and melon fruit; round in the mouth; restrained barrel ferment/malolactic inputs. **RATING** 93 **DRINK** 2009 $ 25
Roussanne 2003 Pear, apple and spice aromas; crisp palate; nice touch of minerality; good length. **RATING** 92 **DRINK** 2010 $ 28
Pinot Noir 2003 Solid, strong dark plum fruit with savoury undertones. Will improve. **RATING** 90 **DRINK** 2010 $ 28

♥♥♥♡ **Cabernet Sauvignon 2002 RATING** 86 **DRINK** 2007 $ 28

St Ignatius Vineyard ★★★★

Sunraysia Highway, Avoca, Vic 3467 **REGION** Pyrenees
T (03) 5465 3542 **F** (03) 5465 3542 **WEB** www.stignatiusvineyard.com.au **OPEN** 7 days 10–5
WINEMAKER Enrique Diaz **EST.** 1992 **CASES** 1000
SUMMARY Silvia and husband Enrique Diaz began establishing their vineyard, winery and restaurant complex in 1992. They have planted 8 ha of shiraz, chardonnay, cabernet sauvignon, sauvignon blanc, merlot and sangiovese. The vineyard has already received three primary production awards; all the wine is made onsite by Enrique Diaz. Exports to the UK.

❡❡❡❡❡ **Hangmans Gully Shiraz 2002** Intense licorice, spice and black fruits; long travel and finish. Cork. RATING 91 DRINK 2015 $25

❡❡❡❡ **Hangmans Gully Cabernet Sauvignon 2002** Savoury, earthy, briary style; black fruits on the mid-palate; has good length. Cork. RATING 89 DRINK 2012 $25

❡❡❡❡ **Hangmans Gully Chardonnay 2003** RATING 85 DRINK 2008 $25

St Leonards ★★★☆

St Leonards Road, Wahgunyah, Vic 3687 **REGION** Rutherglen
T(02) 6033 1004 **F**(02) 6033 3636 **WEB** www.stleonardswine.com.au **OPEN** 7 days 10–5
WINEMAKER Peter Brown, Dan Crane **EST.** 1860 **CASES** NFP
SUMMARY An old favourite, relaunched in late 1997 with a range of three premium wines cleverly marketed through a singularly attractive cellar door and bistro at the historic winery on the banks of the Murray. All Saints and St Leonards are now wholly owned by Peter Brown; the vast majority of the wines are sold through the cellar door and by mailing list.

❡❡❡❡ **Cabernet Franc 2003** Bright colour; very fresh, clean, positive raspberry and redcurrant fruit; all in all, a surprise packet. RATING 89 DRINK 2007 $19.50
Shiraz Viognier 2002 An aromatic mix of spice, earth, blackberry, leather and vanilla; soft and supple. Viognier 6%. RATING 88 DRINK 2012 $25
Rose 2004 A fresh and lively mix of strawberry and cherry; balanced acidity and dry finish. RATING 87 DRINK Now $15.50
Dry Orange Muscat 2004 Lively, fresh, crisp and grapey; as the name suggests, quite dry. A table, not fortified, wine. RATING 87 DRINK Now $16.50

❡❡❡❡ **Wahgunyah Sparkling Shiraz NV** RATING 86 DRINK Now $27.50

St Mary's ★★★☆

V & A Lane, via Coonawarra, SA 5277 **REGION** Penola
T(08) 8736 6070 **F**(08) 8736 6045 **OPEN** 7 days 10–4
WINEMAKER Barry Mulligan **EST.** 1986 **CASES** 4000
SUMMARY The Mulligan family has lived in the Penola/Coonawarra region since 1909. In 1937 a 250-ha property 15 km to the west of Penola, including an 80-ha ridge of terra rossa over limestone, was purchased for grazing. The ridge was cleared; the remainder of the property was untouched and is now a private wildlife sanctuary. In 1986 Barry and Glenys Mulligan planted shiraz and cabernet sauvignon on the ridge, followed by merlot in the early 1990s. Exports to the UK, the US, Canada, Singapore, Belgium and Switzerland.

❡❡❡❡ **Limestone Coast Shiraz 2001** Good colour; quite powerful structure; blackberry fruit; persistent, fine tannins; ageing potential. Cork. RATING 89 DRINK 2011 $25
House Block Limestone Coast Cabernet Sauvignon 2001 Good colour; ripe blackcurrant/cassis fruit; medium-bodied and just carries the tannins. Cork. RATING 89 DRINK 2009 $25
Penola Petit Verdot 2003 Powerful dark fruits; distinctly savoury, slight bitter aloe characters; has attitude. Cork. RATING 88 DRINK 2013 $27
Penola Merlot 2003 A clean bouquet; abundant cassis/raspberry red fruits in a light to medium-bodied frame; light tannins. Cork. RATING 87 DRINK 2008 $25

❡❡❡ **Limestone Coast Riesling 1998** RATING 83 $15

St Matthias ★★★

113 Rosevears Drive, Rosevears, Tas 7277 **REGION** Northern Tasmania
T(03) 6330 1700 **F**(03) 6330 1975 **WEB** www.moorilla.com.au **OPEN** 7 days 10–5
WINEMAKER Michael Glover **EST.** 1983 **CASES** 16 000
SUMMARY After an uncomfortable period in the wilderness following the sale of the vineyard to Moorilla Estate, and the disposal of the wine made by the previous owners under the St Matthias label, Moorilla has re-introduced the label, and markets a full range of competitively priced wines which are in fact made at Moorilla Estate.

❡❡❡ **Chardonnay 2003** RATING 83 $22.50

St Michael's Vineyard ★★★★

503 Pook Road, Toolleen, Vic 3521 **REGION** Heathcote
T (03) 5433 2580 **F** (03) 5433 2612 **OPEN** By appointment
WINEMAKER Mick Cann **EST.** 1994 **CASES** 300
SUMMARY Owner/winemaker Mick Cann has established 5 ha of vines on the famous deep red Cambrian clay loam on the east face of the Mt Camel Range. Planting began in 1994, continued in 1995, with a further extension in 2000. Shiraz (3 ha), merlot (1.5 ha) and petit verdot (0.25 ha) are the main varieties, with a smattering of cabernet sauvignon and semillon. Part of the production is sold to David Anderson of Wild Duck Creek, the remainder made by Mick Cann, using open fermentation, hand-plunging of skins and a basket press, a low-technology but highly effective way of making high-quality red wine.

ŸŸŸŸŸ **Personal Reserve Heathcote Shiraz 2003** A complex fusion of black fruits and spicy French oak; abundant total flavour of sweet fruit; not alcoholic or tannic. One hogshead made. Very stained cork. **RATING** 93 **DRINK** 2013
Estate Grown Heathcote Shiraz 2003 Full-bodied; powerful blackberry/cherry sweet fruit entry; drought year dip on the mid-palate; controlled tannins, good oak. Stained cork. **RATING** 91 **DRINK** 2010
Bin 6040 Heathcote Shiraz Merlot 2003 Medium-bodied; dominant red and black fruits ex Shiraz; lower alcohol (13.7°) evident. Shiraz and Merlot co-fermented. Cork. **RATING** 90 **DRINK** 2010

ŸŸŸŸ **Personal Reserve Heathcote Cabernet Sauvignon 2003** Good colour and concentration; again shows the drought stripping the mid-palate of vinosity; impressive, yet slightly empty. Cork. **RATING** 89 **DRINK** 2012
French Oak Heathcote Merlot 2002 Very concentrated, full-bodied, powerful black fruits; tannins and extraction over the top; 14° alcohol. **RATING** 87 **DRINK** 2011

St Petrox NR

352 Luskintyre Road, Luskintyre, NSW 2321 **REGION** Lower Hunter Valley
T (02) 4930 6120 **F** (02) 4930 6070 **OPEN** Not
WINEMAKER Peter Jorgensen **EST.** 2000 **CASES** 3000
SUMMARY Peter Jorgensen has established 4 ha of vines, choosing to plant two varieties ignored by all others in the Hunter Valley: mondeuse and durif. If recognised at all, most people will associate mondeuse with Brown Brothers and northeast Victoria, but it is a rarely propagated yet interesting red varietal.

🐝 St Regis ★★★☆

35 Princes Highway, Waurn Ponds, Vic 3216 **REGION** Geelong
T (03) 5241 8406 **F** (03) 5241 8946 **OPEN** 7 days 11–6
WINEMAKER Peter Nicol **EST.** 1997 **CASES** 600
SUMMARY St Regis is a family-run boutique winery focusing on estate-grown Shiraz, Chardonnay and Pinot Noir. Each year the harvest is hand-picked by 40 people (members of the family and friends), with Peter Nicole (assisted by wife Viv) the executive, onsite winemaker.

ŸŸŸŸ **Geelong Chardonnay 2004** Light-bodied; light, fresh honeydew melon and nectarine; very subtle oak inputs; well balanced. Screwcap. **RATING** 88 **DRINK** 2009 $ 18
Geelong Shiraz 2003 Lively red fruit flavours; tight structure and acidity; should develop well. **RATING** 88 **DRINK** 2013 $ 20

Salem Bridge Wines NR

Salem Bridge Road, Lower Hermitage, SA 5131 **REGION** Adelaide Hills
T (08) 8380 5240 **F** (08) 8380 5240 **OPEN** Not
WINEMAKER Barry Miller **EST.** 1989 **CASES** 300
SUMMARY Barry Miller acquired the 45-ha Salem Bridge property in 1988. A little under 2 ha of cabernet franc were planted in 1989, and Cabernet Franc was the only commercial release prior to 1999. However, a further 14 ha have been planted to cabernet sauvignon, shiraz and merlot, with a

Shiraz and Cabernet Sauvignon release in the pipeline. The core business is contract growing, with only 10% of the production vinified for Salem Bridge.

Salena Estate   NR

Bookpurnong Road, Loxton, SA 5333 **REGION** Riverland
T (08) 8584 1333 **F** (08) 8584 1388 **WEB** www.salenaestate.com.au **OPEN** Mon–Fri 8.30–4.30
WINEMAKER Robert Patynowski **EST.** 1998 **CASES** 480 000
SUMMARY This business, established in 1998, encapsulates the hectic rate of growth across the entire Australian wine industry. Its 1998 crush was 300 tonnes, and by 2001 it was processing 7000 tonnes. This was in part produced from over 200 ha of estate vineyards, supplemented by grapes purchased from other growers. It is the venture of Bob and Sylvia Franchitto, the estate being named after their daughter Salena. Exports to the US, the UK, Malaysia, The Philippines, Hong Kong and Singapore; the export market will take the lion's share.

Salitage   ★★★★☆

Vasse Highway, Pemberton, WA 6260 **REGION** Pemberton
T (08) 9776 1771 **F** (08) 9776 1772 **WEB** www.salitage.com.au **OPEN** 7 days 10–4
WINEMAKER Patrick Coutts, Greg Kelly **EST.** 1989 **CASES** 20 000
SUMMARY Salitage is the showpiece of Pemberton. If it had failed to live up to expectations, it is a fair bet the same fate would have befallen the whole of the Pemberton region. The quality and style of Salitage did vary substantially, presumably in response to vintage conditions and yields, but since 1999 seems to have found its way, with a succession of attractive wines. Key retail distribution in all states, and exports to the UK, the US and other major markets.

▼▼▼▼▼ **Chardonnay 2003** Medium straw-gold; clean, fragrant melon, stone fruit and citrus aromas; bright and fresh fruit-driven palate; subtle oak, good acidity. **RATING** 94 **DRINK** 2008 $ 33

▼▼▼▼▽ **Pinot Noir 2003** Exotic spices and dried forest leaves on the bouquet; spicy red cherry and plum fruit; good length. Twin Top. **RATING** 90 **DRINK** 2008 $ 35

▼▼▼▼ **Sauvignon Blanc 2004** Grass, herb and nettle; herbaceous, crisp palate. Screwcap. **RATING** 89 **DRINK** 2007 $ 20
Treehouse Sauvignon Blanc 2004 Light, crisp; mineral and grass aromas and flavours; clean finish. Screwcap. **RATING** 87 **DRINK** Now $ 17
Treehouse Pinot Noir 2003 Developed colour; savoury/stemmy/woodsy style; fair length and balance. **RATING** 87 **DRINK** 2007 $ 20

▼▼▼▽ **Treehouse Chardonnay Verdelho 2004 RATING** 86 **DRINK** 2007 $ 17
Unwooded Chardonnay 2004 RATING 85 **DRINK** Now $ 18
Treehouse Cabernet Sauvignon Merlot 2002 RATING 84 **DRINK** 2007 $ 20

Salomon Estate   ★★★★☆

PO Box 621, McLaren Vale, SA 5171 **REGION** Currency Creek
T 0419 864 155 **F** (08) 8323 7726 **OPEN** Not
WINEMAKER Bert Salomon, Mike Farmilo **EST.** 1997 **CASES** NA
SUMMARY Bert Salomon is an Austrian winemaker with a long-established family winery in the Kremstal region, not far from Vienna. He became acquainted with Australia during his time with import company Schlumberger in Vienna; he was the first to import Australian wines (Penfolds) into Austria in the mid-1980s, and later became head of the Austrian Wine Bureau. He was so taken by Adelaide that he moved his family there for the first few months each year, sending his young children to school and setting in place an Australian red winemaking venture. He has now retired from the Bureau, and is a full-time travelling winemaker, running the family winery in the northern hemisphere vintage, and overseeing the making of the Salomon Estates wines at Boar's Rock in the first half of the year. The circle closes as Mike Farmilo, former Penfolds chief red winemaker, now makes Salomon Estate wines.

▼▼▼▼▼ **Finniss River Shiraz 2002** Elegant, medium-bodied; excellent texture and structure; perfect fruit ripeness ranging through blackberry, spice and bitter chocolate. Tannins perfect. High-quality cork. **RATING** 94 **DRINK** 2015 $ 30

ŢŢŢŢŶ Norwood Shiraz Cabernet Merlot 2003 Medium-bodied; good savoury structure based on persistent tannins; needs a little more flesh on the bones. Good cork. **RATING** 90 **DRINK** 2012 $ 20

Finniss River Cabernet Merlot 2002 Light to medium-bodied; red berry, mint and leaf off-set by nice, sweet oak; fine tannins, good length. High-quality cork. **RATING** 90 **DRINK** 2012 $ 30

Altus Red 2001 Smooth, medium-bodied; very ripe fruit components; prune, blackberry and jam; ripe tannins; oak in support. Cork. **RATING** 90 **DRINK** 2011 $ 50

ŢŢŢŢ Bin 4 Baan Homage to Asia Shiraz Petit Verdot 2003 An array of dark berry and plum fruit; the tannins nicely rounded, the oak subtle; cleverly put together. Quality cork. **RATING** 89 **DRINK** 2010 $ 18

Saltram ★★★★☆

Salters Gully, Nuriootpa, SA 5355 **REGION** Barossa Valley
T (08) 8564 3355 **F** (08) 8564 2209 **WEB** www.saltramwines.com.au **OPEN** 7 days 10–5
WINEMAKER Nigel Dolan **EST.** 1859 **CASES** NFP
SUMMARY There is no doubt that Saltram has taken giant strides towards regaining the reputation it held 30 or so years ago. Under Nigel Dolan's stewardship, grape sourcing has come back to the Barossa Valley for the flagship wines, a fact of which he is rightly proud. The red wines, in particular, have enjoyed great show success over the past few years, with No. 1 Shiraz, Mamre Brook and Metala leading the charge.

ŢŢŢŢŢ No. 1 Reserve Shiraz 2001 Another great wine in an under-recognised brand; red and black fruits, oak and tannins all perfectly balanced and integrated; supple and silky. **RATING** 95 **DRINK** 2012 $ 68

ŢŢŢŢŶ Mamre Brook Shiraz 2002 Built in heroic style, with blackberry, blackcurrant, tannins and oak folding together. Patience demanded. **RATING** 93 **DRINK** 2022 $ 22.99

Pepperjack Grenache Rose 2004 Fragrant and abundant juicy red berry fruits; dry finish; very good food style. **RATING** 92 **DRINK** Now $ 24

Pepperjack Barossa Shiraz 2002 Rich, warm blackberry, plum and chocolate; soft, ripe tannins; positive oak. **RATING** 92 **DRINK** 2015 $ 24

Metala Black Label Shiraz 2001 Very attractive, medium-bodied wine; clear blackberry/raspberry mix; fine tannins and oak; long finish. **RATING** 92 **DRINK** 2016 $ 45

Mamre Brook Barossa Riesling 2004 Clean lime and ripe apple; light to medium-bodied; mineral, slate and spice; pleasing, dry finish. Screwcap. **RATING** 90 **DRINK** 2009 $ 24

Pepperjack Viognier 2004 A complex and interesting wine, fruit and oak interwoven, yet retaining freshness thanks to spicy acidity. Subtle barrel fermentation a plus. **RATING** 90 **DRINK** 2007 $ 23

Metala Shiraz Cabernet 2002 Medium to full-bodied; generous mid-palate fruit; good structure and length. **RATING** 90 **DRINK** 2012 $ 18

Pepperjack Barossa Cabernet Sauvignon 2003 Good colour; medium to full-bodied; sweet, supple, smooth blackcurrant and a touch of cassis; fine, ripe tannins; nice cedary oak. Quality cork. **RATING** 90 **DRINK** 2011 $ 23

ŢŢŢŢ Pepperjack Barossa Shiraz 2003 Medium-bodied; mainstream Barossa style; supple blackberry fruit and vanilla all merge. Cork. **RATING** 89 **DRINK** 2010 $ 23

Mamre Brook Cabernet Sauvignon 2002 Abundant blackcurrant and blackberry fruit, and even more abundant tannins. Needs a decade or more. **RATING** 89 **DRINK** 2015 $ 27

Next Chapter Semillon Sauvignon Blanc 2004 Rich, mouthfilling style; ripe tropical, gooseberry fruit; no oak. **RATING** 88 **DRINK** 2007 $ 16.50

Barossa Semillon Sauvignon Blanc 2004 Solid wine; clean, ripe fruit; well balanced; lacks aromaticity. **RATING** 87 **DRINK** Now $ 17

Mamre Brook Chardonnay 2003 Well made; nicely balanced fruit and oak inputs; soft peachy fruit; slightly short. **RATING** 87 **DRINK** Now $ 22

Pepperjack Barossa Grenache Shiraz Mourvedre 2003 Quite firm given the blend; savoury flavours; brisk acidity. **RATING** 87 **DRINK** 2008 $ 24

Next Chapter Barossa Cabernet Merlot 2002 Elegant, light to medium-bodied, red fruits; fine tannins run through the finish. **RATING** 87 **DRINK** 2007 $ 17

ŢŢŢŶ Maker's Table Chardonnay 2004 More focus and flavour than the Maker's Table Sauvignon Blanc; sweet melon fruit and some nectarine; imperceptible oak. **RATING** 86 **DRINK** 2008 $ 11

Next Chapter Barossa Shiraz 2002 RATING 86 DRINK 2009 $16.50
Maker's Table Sauvignon Blanc 2004 RATING 84 DRINK Now $11
Pepperjack Chardonnay 2004 RATING 84 DRINK 2007

ＹＹＹ Maker's Table Shiraz 2003 RATING 83 $11

Sam Miranda of King Valley ★★★★

Cnr Snow Road/Whitfield Road, Oxley, Vic 3678 REGION King Valley
T (03) 5727 3888 F (03) 5727 3851 OPEN 7 days 10–5
WINEMAKER Sam Miranda EST. 2004 CASES 5000
SUMMARY Sam Miranda, grandson of Francesco Miranda, joined the family business in 1991, striking out on his own in 2004 after Miranda Wines was purchased by McGuigan Simeon. The High Plains Vineyard is in the Myrrhee district of the Upper King Valley at an altitude of 450m; 13 ha of vines are supplemented by some purchased grapes.

ＹＹＹＹＹ High Plains King Valley Chardonnay 2004 Elegant, fresh and stylish; light to medium-bodied; gentle barrel ferment/malolactic inputs; very good mouthfeel. RATING 91 DRINK 2008 $18.50
High Plains King Valley Sauvignon Blanc 2004 Aromatic passionfruit, citrus and gooseberry fruit; lingering, lemony acidity; excellent value. Screwcap. RATING 90 DRINK Now $16

ＹＹＹＹ High Plains King Valley Riesling 2004 Spice and apple florals; not particularly intense, but clean and crisp. Screwcap. RATING 87 DRINK 2008 $16
High Plains King Valley Bianco 2004 Lively, fresh, tangy and crisp; a mix of mineral and juicy fruit. Sauvignon Blanc/Chardonnay. Screwcap. RATING 87 DRINK Now $16

ＹＹＹＹ High Plains King Valley Rose 2004 RATING 86 DRINK Now $17

Samson Hill Estate ★★★★

360 Eltham–Yarra Glen Road, Kangaroo Ground, Vic 3097 REGION Yarra Valley
T (03) 9712 0715 F (03) 9712 0815 OPEN 7 days 10–6
WINEMAKER Steven Sampson, Pago Sampson EST. 1997 CASES 3000
SUMMARY In a region noted for its spectacular scenery, Samson Hill Estate has been established by Steven and Pago Sampson on one of the most spectacular sites of all. At the very top of Kangaroo Ground, it looks to the city of Melbourne (with the buildings clearly visible), thence to King Lake and the Dandenongs, and then all the way to Mt Macedon. They have planted 3 ha of pinot noir, 2 ha of verdelho and 0.5 ha of shiraz, the verdelho firmly aimed at the cellar door market. The cellar door offers casual dining and catering for all functions.

ＹＹＹＹＹ Lucky Bastard Yarra Valley Shiraz Reserve 2003 Dense purple-red; concentrated and rich; oozing black plum and berry fruit; ripe tannins, subtle oak. Terrible cork. RATING 91 DRINK 2013 $35
Lucky Bastard Yarra Valley Pinot Noir Reserve 2003 Deep colour; very rich, concentrated and powerful; extract on the edge of going over the top; needs patience, but the cork is distressingly pitted and stained. RATING 90 DRINK 2013 $28

ＹＹＹＹ Yarra Valley Pinot Noir 2001 Light red-purple; light-bodied, but has developed well; spicy plum fruit; satin-smooth texture and tannins. Quality cork. RATING 89 DRINK 2007 $12
Yarra Valley Verdelho 2004 Yes, it is indeed sweet, but it has very good length and persistence, and the acidity to counterbalance the sweetness. Cork. RATING 87 DRINK Now $19

ＹＹＹＹ Fresh Palate Yarra Valley Rose 2004 RATING 86 DRINK Now $10

Sandalford ★★★★☆

West Swan Road, Caversham, WA 6055 REGION Margaret River/Swan Valley
T (08) 9374 9374 F (08) 9274 2154 WEB www.sandalford.com OPEN 7 days 10–5
WINEMAKER Paul Boulden EST. 1840 CASES 100 000

SUMMARY Some years ago the upgrading of the winery and the appointment of Paul Boulden as chief winemaker resulted in far greater consistency in quality, and the proper utilisation of the excellent vineyard resources of Sandalford in Margaret River and Mount Barker. Things have continued on an even keel since. Exports to the UK, the US and other major markets.

ᵀᵀᵀᵀᵀ **Margaret River Cabernet Sauvignon 2003** Medium to medium-full bodied; classic cabernet mix of cassis, blackcurrant and earth; fine, long, savoury tannins; subtle oak. **RATING** 94 **DRINK** 2017 $ 28.95

ᵀᵀᵀᵀᵀ **Margaret River Semillon Sauvignon Blanc 2004** A crisp and lively mix of gooseberry, tropical and passionfruit; limey acidity, long finish. **RATING** 93 **DRINK** 2007 $ 19.95
Margaret River Shiraz 2003 Abundant blackberry/black cherry/chocolate and spice mix; medium-bodied; good tannin structure and controlled American oak. No reduction. Screwcap. **RATING** 93 **DRINK** 2016 $ 33.95
Margaret River Riesling 2004 Fresh and clean; good focus and vivacity; light grapefruit and apple flavours. **RATING** 90 **DRINK** 2009 $ 19.95

ᵀᵀᵀᵀ **Margaret River Chardonnay 2003** Slightly reduced characters still linger; melon, stone fruit and cashew with well-integrated oak. Cork. **RATING** 88 **DRINK** 2009 $ 33.95
Element Cabernet Sauvignon 2003 Fresh, clean, fruit-driven; light to medium-bodied mix of cassis, raspberry and blackcurrant. **RATING** 88 **DRINK** Now $ 12.99
Element Shiraz 2003 Attractive, early-drinking style; plenty of soft, ripe plum and black fruits; minimal tannins, a flick of American oak. Screwcap. **RATING** 87 **DRINK** 2007 $ 12.95
Element Late Harvest 2004 Clean; highly aromatic lemony aromas; not much off-dry; will develop; nice style. Screwcap. **RATING** 87 **DRINK** 2010 $ 12.95

ᵀᵀᵀᵀ **Element Chardonnay 2004** **RATING** 86 **DRINK** Now $ 12.99
Margaret River Verdelho 2004 **RATING** 86 **DRINK** Now $ 19.95
Element Classic White 2004 **RATING** 86 **DRINK** Now $ 12.99
Element Shiraz Cabernet 2003 **RATING** 86 **DRINK** 2007 $ 12.99
Element Merlot 2004 **RATING** 86 **DRINK** 2008 $ 12.95

Sandalyn Wilderness Estate NR

162 Wilderness Road, Rothbury, NSW 2321 **REGION** Lower Hunter Valley
T (02) 4930 7611 **F** (02) 4930 7611 **WEB** www.huntervalleyboutiques.com.au **OPEN** 7 days 10–5
WINEMAKER Lindsay Whaling **EST.** 1988 **CASES** 6000
SUMMARY Sandra and Lindsay Whaling preside over the picturesque cellar door building of Sandalyn on the evocatively named Wilderness Road, where you will find a one-hole golf range and views to the Wattagan, Brokenback and Molly Morgan ranges. The estate has 9 ha of vineyards planted to chardonnay, pinot noir, verdelho and semillon. Exports to Ireland.

Sand Hills Vineyard NR

Sandhills Road, Forbes, NSW 2871 **REGION** Western Plains Zone
T (02) 6852 1437 **F** (02) 6852 4401 **OPEN** Mon–Sat 9–5, Sun 12–5
WINEMAKER John Saleh, Jill Lindsay (Contract) **EST.** 1920 **CASES** 400
SUMMARY Having purchased Sand Hills from long-term owner Jacques Genet, the Saleh family has replanted the vineyard to appropriate varieties, with over 6 ha of premium varieties having been established.

Sandhurst Ridge ★★★★

156 Forest Drive, Marong, Vic 3515 **REGION** Bendigo
T (03) 5435 2534 **F** (03) 5435 2548 **WEB** www.sandhurstridge.com.au **OPEN** Wed–Mon 11–5, or by appointment
WINEMAKER Paul Greblo, George Greblo **EST.** 1990 **CASES** 2500
SUMMARY The Greblo brothers (Paul and George), with combined experience in business, agriculture, science and construction and development began the establishment of Sandhurst Ridge in 1990 with the planting of the first 2 ha of shiraz and cabernet sauvignon. Plantings have now been increased to over 7 ha, principally cabernet and shiraz, but also a little merlot, sauvignon blanc and nebbiolo. The fully equipped winery was completed in 1996 with a cellar capacity of 400 barriques. The winery rating is given for its red wines. Exports to the US, Canada and Hong Kong.

ŸŸŸŸ♀ Reserve Shiraz 2003 Deep colour, good hue; full-bodied, powerful, rich blackberry and plum; ripe but not aggressive tannin and extract; 14.5° alcohol. Diam. **RATING** 93 **DRINK** 2018 $ 36

Fringe Shiraz 2003 Medium red-purple; solid, sweet plummy fruit; medium-bodied; soft tannins, well-handled extract. Diam. **RATING** 91 **DRINK** 2013 $ 26

Shiraz 2003 Strongly savoury aspects to the fruit; firm tannins; shows the impact of drought on the mid-palate; may resolve with time. Diam. **RATING** 90 **DRINK** 2013 $ 32

Fringe Cabernet Sauvignon 2003 Polar opposite to Fringe Shiraz; massively ripe black fruits and strong tannins; again shows drought structure; 14.4° alcohol. Diam. **RATING** 90 **DRINK** 2013 $ 26

ŸŸŸŸ Cabernet Sauvignon 2003 Savoury, slightly herbal; touches of mint to red fruit and cassis; light to medium-bodied; restrained oak. Diam. **RATING** 88 **DRINK** 2009 $ 32

🐢 Sandow's End ★★★★

Sandow Road, Verdun, SA 5245 **REGION** Adelaide Hills
T (08) 8388 7008 **F** (08) 8388 7100 **WEB** www.sandowsend.com.au **OPEN** By appointment
WINEMAKER Matt Wenk (Contract) **EST.** 2001 **CASES** 1000
SUMMARY Kati and Andrew Wenk purchased the former Pibbin Vineyard in 2001, acquiring 20-year-old vines which, with some refurbishment, are producing grapes of very high quality. Both a varietal and Reserve Pinot Noir are made from the 2.8-ha vineyard. The wines are made by Andrew Wenk's brother Matt, and are being sold through the website, and through restaurants in Adelaide Hills, Mt Hotham and Falls Creek, the link being, according to Kati Wenk, altitude.

ŸŸŸŸ♀ Adelaide Hills Reserve Pinot Noir 2002 Complex; intense spicy/savoury/stemmy overtones to a core of dark plum fruit; long, lingering finish. **RATING** 93 **DRINK** 2010 $ 55

ŸŸŸŸ Adelaide Hills Pinot Noir 2002 Light colour; spicy, savoury, light-bodied; varietal character not in doubt, but the alcohol heats the finish. **RATING** 87 **DRINK** Now $ 28

Sandstone ★★★☆

Cnr Johnson Road/Caves Road, Wilyabrup, WA 6280 **REGION** Margaret River
T (08) 9755 6271 **F** (08) 9755 6292 **OPEN** 7 days 11–4
WINEMAKER Mike Davies, Jan Davies **EST.** 1988 **CASES** 4000
SUMMARY The family operation of consultant winemakers Mike and Jan Davies, who also operate very successful mobile bottling plants. It will eventually be estate-based following the planting of 9 ha (semillon and cabernet sauvignon).

Sandy Farm Vineyard NR

RMB 3734, Sandy Farm Road, Denver via Daylesford, Vic 3641 **REGION** Macedon Ranges
T (03) 5348 7610 **WEB** www.sandyfarm.primetap.com **OPEN** Weekends 10–5, or by appointment
WINEMAKER Peter Comisel **EST.** 1988 **CASES** 800
SUMMARY Peter Comisel and Dot Hollow have acquired Sandy Farm from founder Peter Covell. There are 1.5 ha of cabernet sauvignon, cabernet franc and merlot and 0.5 ha of pinot noir, with a small, basic winery in which they make preservative-free Cabernet Sauvignon, Merlot and Pinot Noir, attracting a loyal local following.

Sanguine Estate ★★★★

77 Shurans Lane, Heathcote, Vic 3523 (postal) **REGION** Heathcote
T (03) 9646 6661 **F** (03) 9646 1746 **WEB** www.sanguine-estate.com.au **OPEN** Not
WINEMAKER Mark Hunter, Peter Dredge (Contract) **EST.** 1997 **CASES** 450
SUMMARY The Hunter family, with parents Linda and Tony at the head, and their 2 children, Mark and Jodi, with their respective partners Melissa and Brett, began establishing the vineyard in 1997. From a starting base of 4 ha of shiraz planted that year, it has now grown to 13.4 ha of shiraz, and 2 ha of 8 different varieties, including chardonnay, viognier, merlot, tempranillo, zinfandel, petit verdot, cabernet sauvignon, merlot and cabernet franc. Yet another planting (in the spring of 2002) added another 7.3 ha of shiraz. Low-yielding vines and the magic of the Heathcote region have produced Shiraz of exceptional intensity, which has received rave reviews in the US, and led to the 'sold out'

sign being posted almost immediately upon release. With the ever-expanding vineyard, Mark Hunter has become full-time vigneron, and Jodi Marsh part-time marketer and business developer. For the foreseeable future the wines will continue to be contract-made. Exports to the US.

ŸŸŸŸŸ Heathcote Shiraz 2003 Fresh, clean blackberry, spice and plum aromas; very ripe, sweet fruit shows its 14.5° alcohol; ripe tannins. Cork. **RATING** 91 **DRINK** 2003 **$** 35.99

Saracen Estates ★★★★

731 Caves Road, Wilyabrup, WA 6280 **REGION** Margaret River
T (08) 9221 4955 **F** (08) 9221 4966 **WEB** www.saracenestates.com.au **OPEN** By appointment
WINEMAKER Bill Crappsley **EST.** 1998 **CASES** 40 000
SUMMARY The Cazzolli and Saraceni families have established 40 ha of vines on their 80-ha property, with a striking restaurant and cellar door opened in 2005. The name not only echoes one of the founding families, but also pays tribute to the Saracens, one of the most advanced races in cultural and social terms at the time of the Crusades. Exports to the UK, Singapore, Malaysia, Hong Kong, India and Denmark.

ŸŸŸŸŸ Margaret River Sauvignon Blanc 2004 Bright green-yellow; attractive mix of herbaceous, grassy notes with riper gooseberry, kiwifruit and citrus; long finish. Quality cork. **RATING** 92 **DRINK** 2007 **$** 20
Margaret River Semillon Sauvignon Blanc 2003 Similar fruit characters and structure to the Sauvignon Blanc, though tightened slightly by the minerally, clean finish of the Semillon; should evolve well. Quality cork. **RATING** 91 **DRINK** 2008 **$** 15
Margaret River Chardonnay 2004 Light to medium-bodied; sophisticated winemaking; ripe stone fruit, melon and fig interplay with malolactic/barrel ferment characters; good mouthfeel. Poor cork. **RATING** 90 **DRINK** 2009 **$** 20

ŸŸŸŸ Margaret River Cabernet Merlot 2003 Youthful purple-red; light to medium-bodied; clean, fresh redcurrant and blackcurrant fruit; very fine tannins, subtle oak. Elegant. Cork. **RATING** 89 **DRINK** 2012 **$** 15

Sarsfield Estate ★★★☆

345 Duncan Road, Sarsfield, Vic 3875 **REGION** Gippsland
T (03) 5156 8962 **F** (03) 5156 8970 **OPEN** By appointment
WINEMAKER Dr Suzanne Rutschmann **EST.** 1995 **CASES** 1000
SUMMARY The property is owned by Suzanne Rutschmann, who has a PhD in Chemistry, a Diploma in Horticulture and and a BSc (Wine Science) from Charles Sturt University, and Swiss-born Peter Albrecht, a civil and structural engineer who has also undertaken various courses in agriculture and viticulture. For a part-time occupation, these are exceptionally impressive credentials. Their 2-ha vineyard was planted between 1991 and 1998; the first vintage made at the winery was 1998, the grapes being sold to others in previous years. High-quality packaging is a plus.

ŸŸŸŸ Cabernets Shiraz Merlot 2003 Light to medium-bodied; fresh and vibrant in the estate style; a cascade of red and black fruits; minimal oak and tannin input. Poor cork. **RATING** 89 **DRINK** 2011 **$** 18.50
East Gippsland Pinot Noir 2003 Fresh and vibrant cherry and strawberry fruit; light, direct, unforced; slightly simple but correct. Cork. **RATING** 88 **DRINK** 2007 **$** 22
Rose 2004 Vibrant fuchsia; the odd blend of Mourvedre/Shiraz/Pinot gives more structure than usual; has length and freshness; well made. Cork. **RATING** 87 **DRINK** Now **$** 17.50

Savaterre NR

PO Box 337, Beechworth, Vic 3747 **REGION** Beechworth
T (03) 5727 0551 **F** (03) 5727 0551 **WEB** www.savaterre.com **OPEN** Not
WINEMAKER Keppell Smith **EST.** 1996 **CASES** NA
SUMMARY Keppell Smith embarked on a career in wine in 1996, studying winemaking at Charles Sturt University and (at a practical level) with Phillip Jones at Bass Phillip. He purchased the 40-ha property on which Savaterre has been established, and has close planted (7500 vines per ha) 1 ha each of chardonnay and pinot noir at an elevation of 440m. Organic principles govern the viticulture, and the winemaking techniques look to the old world rather than the new. Smith's stated aim is to produce outstanding, individualistic wines far removed from the mainstream. Details of restaurants offering Savaterre are on the website.

Sawtooth Ridge

NR

Lot 295 Waggon Road, Victor Harbor, SA 5211 **REGION** Southern Fleurieu
T (08) 8552 8450 **F** (08) 8552 8450 **WEB** www.sawtoothridge.com.au **OPEN** 7 days 9–5
WINEMAKER Harry Duerden **EST.** 1996 **CASES** NA
SUMMARY The former Duerden's Wines was purchased by Andrea Sutherland and Frank Falco in
November 2003, and renamed Sawtooth Ridge. The unique overhead sawtooth trellis (a traditional
structure in parts of Italy) remains unchanged, and the panoply of conventional wines, liqueurs
(including quandong), syrups, honeys, jelly and vinegar remain available.

Scarborough

179 Gillards Road, Pokolbin, NSW 2320 **REGION** Lower Hunter Valley
T (02) 4998 7563 **F** (02) 4998 7786 **WEB** www.scarboroughwine.com.au **OPEN** 7 days 9–5
WINEMAKER Ian Scarborough, Jerome Scarborough **EST.** 1985 **CASES** 15 000
SUMMARY Ian Scarborough honed his white winemaking skills during his years as a consultant, and
has brought all those skills to his own label. He makes two radically different styles of Chardonnay:
the Blue Silver Label in a light, elegant, Chablis style for the export market and a much richer,
strongly barrel-fermented wine (with a mustard/gold label) for the Australian market. However, the
real excitement lies with the portion of the old Lindemans Sunshine Vineyard which he has
purchased (after it lay fallow for 30 years) and planted with semillon and (quixotically) pinot noir.
The first vintage from the legendary Sunshine Vineyard was made in 2004; in the meantime, Ian has
kept his hand in with contract-grown semillon. Exports to the UK and the US.

⟡⟡⟡⟡⟡ **Traditional Chardonnay 2003** Clean, gently sweet melon and stone fruit; perfectly
ripened; good mouthfeel and balance. Screwcap. **RATING** 91 **DRINK** 2008 **$** 23

⟡⟡⟡⟡ **Semillon 2004** Light to medium-bodied; clean, fresh lemon, herb and lanolin; 12° alcohol
a fraction high, softening the focus and finish. Screwcap. **RATING** 89 **DRINK** 2009
Pinot Noir 2003 Interesting wine; has some varietal character in a sappy, earthy
spectrum, but also with cherry fruit and spice; moderate ageing potential. Screwcap.
RATING 87 **DRINK** 2008 **$** 21

⟡⟡⟡⟡ **Pinot Noir NV RATING** 85 **DRINK** Now **$** 21

Scarpantoni Estate

Scarpantoni Drive, McLaren Flat, SA 5171 **REGION** McLaren Vale
T (08) 8383 0186 **F** (08) 8383 0490 **WEB** www.scarpantoni-wines.com.au **OPEN** Mon–Fri 9–5,
weekends & public hols 11–5
WINEMAKER Michael Scarpantoni, Filippo Scarpantoni **EST.** 1979 **CASES** 30 000
SUMMARY With 20 ha of shiraz, 11 ha of cabernet sauvignon, 3 ha each of chardonnay and sauvignon
blanc, 1 ha each of merlot and gamay, and 0.5 ha of petit verdot, Scarpantoni has come a long way
since Domenico Scarpantoni purchased his first property of 5.6 ha in 1958. At that time he was
working for Thomas Hardy at its Tintara winery; he subsequently became vineyard manager for
Seaview Wines, responsible for the contoured vineyards which were leading edge viticulture in the
1960s. In 1979 his two sons, Michael and Filippo, built the winery, which has now been extended to
enable all the grapes from the estate plantings to be used to make wine under the Scarpantoni label.
As the vines have matured, quality has improved. Distribution in all states; exports to the US, the
UK, Switzerland, The Netherlands, Germany and New Zealand.

⟡⟡⟡⟡⟡ **Sauvignon Blanc 2004** A clean mix of lemon, tropical and passionfruit aromas and
flavours; well balanced; good finish. **RATING** 90 **DRINK** 2007 **$** 18
Ceres Rose 2004 Abundant cherry and strawberry fruit; good balance and length; not
sugary. Blue Gold Sydney International Winemakers Competition 2005 **RATING** 90
DRINK Now **$** 14
Block 3 Shiraz 2003 Rich wine, with lots of dark chocolate and dark berry fruit; moderate
tannins; still coming together. **RATING** 90 **DRINK** 2013 **$** 22

⟡⟡⟡⟡ **Black Tempest NV** Clean, fresh and firm; lively berry, black fruit and chocolate flavours; a
relatively dry finish; impressive. **RATING** 89 **DRINK** 2014 **$** 28
Unwooded Chardonnay 2004 Shows the tangy, citrussy overlay to nectarine fruit from
the cool 2004 vintage; almost into Sauvignon Blanc. **RATING** 87 **DRINK** Now **$** 14

Scarp Valley Vineyard

NR

6 Robertson Road, Gooseberry Hill, WA 6076 **REGION** Perth Hills
T (08) 9454 5748 **OPEN** By appointment
WINEMAKER Contract **EST.** 1978 **CASES** 25
SUMMARY Owner Robert Duncan presides over what has to be one of the smallest producers in Australia, with 0.1 ha (quarter of an acre) of shiraz and 30 cabernet sauvignon vines producing a single cask of wine each year if the birds do not get the grapes first.

Schild Estate Wines

Cnr Barossa Valley Way/Lyndoch Valley Road, Lyndoch, SA 5351 **REGION** Barossa Valley
T (08) 8524 5560 **F** (08) 8524 4333 **WEB** www.schildestate.com.au **OPEN** 7 days 10–5
WINEMAKER Daniel Eggleton **EST.** 1998 **CASES** 20 000
SUMMARY Ed Schild is a Barossa Valley grapegrower who first planted a small vineyard at Rowland Flat in 1952, steadily increasing his vineyard holdings over the past 50 years to their present 157 ha. Currently 12% of the production from these vineyards (now managed by son Michael Schild) is used to produce Schild Estate Wines, but the plans are to increase this percentage. The flagship wine is made from 154-year-old shiraz vines on the Moorooroo Block. The cellar door is in what was the ANZ Bank at Lyndoch, and provides the sort of ambience which can only be found in the Barossa Valley. Exports to the UK, the US and Canada.

ᵀᵀᵀᵀᵀ **Ben Schild Reserve Barossa Shiraz 2003** Deep purple-red; rich, complex, powerful, concentrated blackberry and prune fruit; has soaked up 18 months in new oak; high-alcohol style. Diam. **RATING** 93 **DRINK** 2018 $ 24
Limited Release Shiraz 2003 Full red-purple; rich, dark fruits, blackberry and chocolate; nice spicy notes; particularly good tannins; controlled oak. Diam. **RATING** 90 **DRINK** 2015 $ 24
GMS Barossa Grenache Shiraz Mourvedre 2004 Light to medium-bodied; fresh but polished red and black fruits; nicely ripened ultra-fine tannins; hides 15° alcohol very successfully. Screwcap. **RATING** 90 **DRINK** 2011 $ 19

ᵀᵀᵀᵀ **Alma Schild Reserve Barossa Chardonnay 2003** Medium-bodied; sweet peach and melon fruit; solid oak backdrop; lacks finesse. Diam. **RATING** 87 **DRINK** 2008 $ 23
Barossa Cabernet Sauvignon 2003 Some development; very ripe, with slight confection characters to berry fruit; dusty tannins. Diam. **RATING** 87 **DRINK** 2010 $ 24

ᵀᵀᵀᵀ **Frontignac 2004** **RATING** 86 **DRINK** Now $ 14
Reserve Shiraz 2003 **RATING** 86 **DRINK** 2015 $ 40
Barossa Merlot 2003 **RATING** 86 **DRINK** 2010 $ 24
Barossa Valley Riesling 2004 **RATING** 84 **DRINK** 2007 $ 15

Schindler Northway Downs

★★★★

437 Stumpy Gully Road, Balnarring, Vic 3926 **REGION** Mornington Peninsula
T (03) 5983 1945 **F** (03) 9580 4262 **OPEN** First weekend each month
WINEMAKER Tammy Schindler-Hands **EST.** 1996 **CASES** 250
SUMMARY The Schindler family began this vineyard by planting the first 2 ha of pinot noir and chardonnay in 1996. A further 4 ha of pinot noir were planted on an ideal north-facing slope in 1999, and the first vintage followed in 2000. The cellar door was then established; it is open on the first weekend of each month, and offers Austrian food and live Austrian music on the Sunday.

ᵀᵀᵀᵀᵀ **Chardonnay 2003** Light to medium-bodied; elegant, delicate stone fruit and citrus; lingering, crisp, clean finish. Cork. **RATING** 90 **DRINK** 2008 $ 20

ᵀᵀᵀᵀ **Pinot Noir 2003** Complex, savoury, foresty, stemmy style; has length, though not overmuch richness. Cork. **RATING** 89 **DRINK** 2008 $ 24

Schubert Estate

★★★★★

Roennfeldt Road, Marananga, SA 5355 **REGION** Barossa Valley
T (08) 8562 3375 **F** (08) 8562 4338 **WEB** www.schubertestate.com.au **OPEN** By appointment
WINEMAKER Steve Schubert, Cecilia Schubert **EST.** 2000 **CASES** 100

SUMMARY Steve and Cecilia Schubert are primarily grapegrowers, with 14 ha of shiraz and little over 1 ha of semillon, and almost all the production is sold to Torbreck. They purchased the 25-ha property from a relative in 1986, when it was in such a derelict state that there was no point trying to save the old vines. Moreover, both were working in other areas, so it was some years before they began replanting, at a little under 2 ha per year. In 2000 they decided to keep enough grapes to make a barrique of wine for their own (and friends') consumption. They were sufficiently encouraged by the outcome to obtain the necessary licence and venture into the dizzy heights of two hogsheads a year. The wine is made onsite, with wild yeast, open fermentation, basket pressing and bottling without filtration. Exports to the US, Denmark and Japan.

ŶŶŶŶŶ **Goose Yard Block Shiraz 2003** Deep colour; dense, deep blackberry and plum fruit; ripe but not overly so; good extract and tannins; subtle oak. Good cork. **RATING** 94 **DRINK** 2018 $ 55

Scorpo Wines ★★★★

23 Old Bittern–Dromana Road, Merricks North, Vic 3926 **REGION** Mornington Peninsula
T (03) 5989 7697 **F** (03) 9813 3371 **WEB** www.scorpowines.com.au **OPEN** By appointment
WINEMAKER Paul Scorpo, Sandro Mosele (Contract) **EST.** 1997 **CASES** 2600
SUMMARY Paul Scorpo has a 27-year background as a horticulturist and landscape architect, and has worked in major projects ranging from private gardens to golf courses in Australia, Europe and South-East Asia. His family has a love of food, wine and gardens, all of which led to them buying a derelict apple and cherry orchard on gentle rolling hills halfway between Port Phillip and Westernport Bay. It is part of a ridge system which climbs up to Red Hill, and offers north and northeast-facing slopes on red-brown, clay loam soils. Here they have established 4.5 ha of pinot noir, chardonnay, pinot gris and shiraz. The wines are made by Paul Scorpo and Sandro Mosele at Kooyong, and were first released in 2002. A cellar door, forming part of the original house on the property, is planned; it will have extensive ocean views from each side.

ŶŶŶŶŶ **Chardonnay 2003** Fresh citrus and melon fruit; a nice touch of toasty oak; squeaky acidity on a fresh finish. Quality cork. **RATING** 91 **DRINK** 2009 $ 32
Pinot Noir 2003 Medium purple-red; full-bodied Pinot style with lots of plum fruit; also considerable, albeit fine, tannins; spicy notes add character. Cork. **RATING** 91 **DRINK** 2009 $ 36
Pinot Gris 2004 Very elegant and fresh, pear and citrus; no heat at all from 14° alcohol; good length and finish. Diam. **RATING** 90 **DRINK** 2007 $ 28

ŶŶŶŶ **Shiraz 2003** Light to medium-bodied; strongly spicy savoury notes; possibly reduced in flavour from leaky cork. **RATING** 88 **DRINK** 2010 $ 38

ŶŶŶŶ **Rose 2004 RATING** 86 **DRINK** Now $ 22
Rose 2003 RATING 86 **DRINK** Now $ 23

Scotchmans Hill ★★★★★

190 Scotchmans Road, Drysdale, Vic 3222 **REGION** Geelong
T (03) 5251 3176 **F** (03) 5253 1743 **WEB** www.scotchmanshill.com.au **OPEN** 7 days 10.30–5.30
WINEMAKER Robin Brockett **EST.** 1982 **CASES** 70 000
SUMMARY Situated on the Bellarine Peninsula, southeast of Geelong, with a well-equipped winery and first-class vineyards. It is a consistent performer with its Pinot Noir and has a strong following in Melbourne and Sydney for its astutely priced, competently made wines. A doubling in production has seen the establishment of export markets in the UK, Holland, Switzerland, Hong Kong and Singapore. The second label, Swan Bay, has been joined at the other end of the spectrum with top-end individual vineyard wines.

ŶŶŶŶŶ **Sutton Vineyard Chardonnay 2002** Bright yellow-green; intense, tightly focused grapefruit and melon; long and lingering; the finish lasts forever. High-quality cork. **RATING** 95 **DRINK** 2010 $ 75
Shiraz 2003 Attractive medium-bodied; very well balanced and structured; ripe, small black fruits; good tannin and oak management. **RATING** 94 **DRINK** 2013 $ 29

ŶŶŶŶ **Pinot Noir 2003** Fine, elegant red cherry with hints of forest ex the savoury tannins; well balanced and long. **RATING** 93 **DRINK** 2008 $ 29
Chardonnay 2003 Light straw-green; fresh, lively and well balanced; attractive melon, fig and stone fruit mix; restrained oak. **RATING** 92 **DRINK** 2010 $ 27

▼▼▼▼ **Swan Bay Sauvignon Blanc Semillon 2004** Good flavour intensity; ripe tropical fruit; off-setting acidity. **RATING** 89 **DRINK** Now $17.50
Swan Bay Chardonnay 2004 Attractive nectarine and white peach fruit; quite intense and long; subtle oak, clean finish. Screwcap. **RATING** 89 **DRINK** 2008 $17.50
Swan Bay Pinot Noir 2004 Attractive plummy bouquet; clear varietal character throughout; firm, slightly linear palate; needs to soften. Screwcap. **RATING** 89 **DRINK** 2010 $17.50
Norfolk Vineyard Pinot Noir 2002 Bright but light colour; elegant, savoury woodsy; lacks the expected concentration of fruit from 2002. Stained cork. **RATING** 89 **DRINK** 2008 $75
Cabernet Sauvignon 2003 Medium-bodied; red and blackcurrant fruit, slightly dusty tannins; balanced oak. Screwcap. **RATING** 89 **DRINK** 2013 $29
Sauvignon Blanc 2004 Some floral notes to the bouquet; nicely balanced, but diminished varietal fruit. **RATING** 88 **DRINK** Now $22.50
Swan Bay Pinot Grigio 2004 Lively, crisp, tingling lemon drop acidity; excellent seafood/Chinese style. **RATING** 87 **DRINK** Now $17.50

▼▼▼▽ **Swan Bay Shiraz 2003 RATING** 86 **DRINK** 2007 $17.50
Swan Bay Rose 2004 RATING 85 **DRINK** Now $17.50

Scotts Brook

Scotts Brook Road, Boyup Brook, WA 6244 **REGION** Blackwood Valley
T (08) 9765 3014 **F** (08) 9765 3015 **OPEN** Weekends, school hols 10–5, or by appointment
WINEMAKER Contract **EST.** 1987 **CASES** 1000
SUMMARY The Scotts Brook winery at Boyup Brook (equidistant between the Margaret River and Great Southern regions) has been developed by local schoolteachers Brian Walker and wife Kerry – hence the opening hours. There are 17 ha of vineyards, but the majority of the production is sold to other winemakers.

▼▼▼▼ **Sauvignon Blanc 2004** Clean, quite intense, lemon citrus, touch of passionfruit.
RATING 88 **DRINK** Now

Scotts Hill Vineyard NR

280 Lillicur Road, Amherst, Vic 3371 (postal) **REGION** Pyrenees
T (03) 5463 2468 **OPEN** Not
WINEMAKER Lester Scott, Pamela Scott **EST.** 2000 **CASES** NA
SUMMARY Lester and Pamela Scott have established 3 ha of pinot noir, cabernet sauvignon, merlot, shiraz, cabernet franc and petit verdot at Amherst. They make the wine onsite, but are yet to establish a distribution system.

Scrubby Creek Wines NR

566 Crystal Creek Road, Alexandra, Vic 3714 **REGION** Upper Goulburn
T (03) 5772 2191 **F** (03) 5772 1048 **WEB** www.scrubbycreek.com **OPEN** 7 days 9–5
WINEMAKER MasterWineMakers (Contract) **EST.** 1995 **CASES** 400
SUMMARY The Stastra and Napier families are next-door neighbours who have jointly planted 3.5 ha of chardonnay. As well as the cellar door and mail order sales route, the wines are exported to the UK and the US.

Seashell Wines NR

Ammon Road, Balingup, WA 6253 (postal) **REGION** Blackwood Valley
T (08) 9307 1469 **F** (08) 9307 1469 **WEB** www.seashellwines.com.au **OPEN** Not
WINEMAKER Stephen Bullied (Contract) **EST.** 1994 **CASES** 1500
SUMMARY Dr Barry Wilson is a biologist and specialist on Australian marine shells and marine ecology, and a director of the Australian Wildlife Conservancy. He and his family planted the first 4 ha of semillon and shiraz in 1993, subsequently extending the plantings to 6 ha. Part of the proceeds of the sale of the wines is donated to various wildlife conservation activities, particularly the restoration of endangered species.

Sea Winds Vineyard

NR

PO Box 511, Dromana, Vic 3936 **REGION** Mornington Peninsula
T (03) 5989 6204 **F** (03) 5989 6204 **OPEN** Not
WINEMAKER Kevin McCarthy (Contract) **EST.** 1990 **CASES** NA
SUMMARY Douglas Schwebel has established 3 ha of sauvignon blanc, chardonnay and pinot noir; the wines are sold by mail order.

Secret Garden Wines

251 Henry Lawson Drive, Mudgee, NSW 2850 **REGION** Mudgee
T (02) 6373 3874 **F** (02) 6373 3854 **OPEN** Fri–Sun & public hols 9–5
WINEMAKER Ian MacRae **EST.** 2000 **CASES** NA
SUMMARY Secret Garden Wines is owned by Ian and Carol MacRae, and is a sister operation to their main business, Miramar Wines. Estate plantings consist of 10 ha of shiraz and about 2 ha each of cabernet sauvignon and chardonnay. The wines are made at Miramar; the cellar door is at Secret Garden. The property is only 5 km from Mudgee, and also fronts Craigmoor Road, giving it a prime position in the so-called 'golden triangle'.

     Eljamar Shiraz 2003 Vivid purple-red; powerful, ripe concentrated blackberry fruit; good tannin and oak extract. **RATING** 94 **DRINK** 2018 $ 22

     Chardonnay 2001 Quite complex and rich stone fruit/peach plus a hint of cashew; long finish, good acidity. **RATING** 90 **DRINK** 2009 $ 22

     Rose 2003 Clean and dry cherry and strawberry aromas and flavours; does shorten off a little. **RATING** 87 **DRINK** Now $ 12
     Shiraz 2002 Bright colour; medium-bodied; a mix of blackberry, earth and leather; quite regional, and a nice touch of chocolate. **RATING** 87 **DRINK** 2009 $ 22
     Cabernet Sauvignon 2002 Medium-bodied; a mix of blackcurrant and sweet vanilla oak; low tannins. **RATING** 87 **DRINK** 2010 $ 22

Seppelt

1 Seppeltsfield Road, Seppeltsfield via Nuriootpa, SA 5355 **REGION** Barossa Valley
T (08) 8568 6217 **F** (08) 8562 8333 **WEB** www.seppelt.com.au **OPEN** Mon–Fri 10–5, weekends & public hols 11–5
WINEMAKER James Godfrey **EST.** 1851 **CASES** NFP
SUMMARY A multi-million dollar expansion and renovation program has seen the historic Seppeltsfield winery become the production centre for the Seppelt fortified and SA table wines, adding another dimension to what was already the most historic and beautiful major winery in Australia. It is now home to some of the world's great fortified wines, nurtured and protected by the passionate James Godfrey. Exports to all major markets.

     Vintage Port 1998 Lovely complex oriental spice and smoke aromas; fine spirit, very good balance and length in classic drier style; approachable even now. **RATING** 94 **DRINK** 2015
     Vintage Fortified Barossa Valley Touriga 1987 Radically different from traditional Australian Vintage Ports; spicy, lemony, savoury fruit; clean spirit; 6 gold medals and 1 trophy between 2000 and 2002. The beginning of its maturity. **RATING** 94 **DRINK** 2010 $ 41.50

Seppelt Great Western

Moyston Road, Great Western via Ararat, Vic 3377 **REGION** Grampians
T (03) 5361 2222 **F** (03) 5361 2200 **WEB** www.seppelt.com.au **OPEN** 7 days 10–5
WINEMAKER Arthur O'Connor, James Godfrey **EST.** 1865 **CASES** NFP
SUMMARY Australia's best-known producer of sparkling wine, always immaculate in its given price range but also producing excellent Great Western-sourced table wines, especially long-lived Shiraz and Australia's best Sparkling Shirazs. The glitzy labels have rightly been consigned to the rubbish bin, and the product range has been significantly rationalised.

     Drumborg Riesling 2004 Intense, fragrant and flowery aromas announce a brilliantly poised and focused wine with long citrus and mineral flavours. Shines like a diamond. Exceptional value. **RATING** 96 **DRINK** 2019 $ 23.99

St Peters Shiraz 2002 Very good colour; aromatic spice and blackberry; has a degree of finesse not always found in St Peters; immaculate judgment of oak and fruit. Quality cork. **RATING** 96 **DRINK** 2025 $45.90

St Peters Shiraz 2001 Strong purple-red; marries power with grace, intensity with elegance; black fruits, and ripe, slightly spicy/savoury tannins; 14° alcohol and sheer class. **RATING** 96 **DRINK** 2021 $45.90

St Peters Shiraz 2000 Deep colour; another dimension of weight and intensity; great depth of blackberry and licorice fruit; perfect integration of French oak. **RATING** 96 **DRINK** 2020 $45

Jaluka Drumborg Vineyard Chardonnay 2003 Glowing green-yellow; fragrant, classic melon and citrus cool-grown chardonnay; despite subtle barrel ferment inputs, fruit-driven, with a very long palate. Top stuff. **RATING** 95 **DRINK** 2013 $24.99

Chalambar Bendigo Grampians Shiraz 2001 Rich, concentrated blackberry and dark chocolate fruits; velvety tannins; very good oak handling; 6 gold medals, 1 trophy. **RATING** 95 **DRINK** 2016 $19

Show Sparkling Shiraz 1994 A complex array of spicy, savoury, blackberry and licorice aromas and flavours; best balanced and driest for some time; will continue to develop in bottle. Crown seal underwrites the future. **RATING** 95 **DRINK** 2014 $65

Coborra Drumborg Vineyard Pinot Gris 2004 The very cool Henty region can provide real challenges, but this spicy, flinty, floral wine has exceptional length and intensity, and could only come from such a climate. Simply outstanding. **RATING** 94 **DRINK** 2007 $19.99

Chalambar Bendigo Grampians Shiraz 2003 Abundant, lush plum, blackberry, licorice and spice; round and mouthfilling, but not at all overripe; fine tannins, good balance. Screwcap. **RATING** 94 **DRINK** 2018 $21.90

Chalambar Bendigo Grampians Shiraz 2000 A beguiling mix of black fruits, spice and leather; complex, supple, silky tannins and texture. Grampians/Bendigo/Strathbogie Ranges. **RATING** 94 **DRINK** 2015 $21.99

ＹＹＹＹＹ **Jaluka Drumborg Vineyard Chardonnay 2004** Super-elegant, restrained style; nectarine, melon and citrus fruit in a near-invisible web of French oak; will evolve over many years. Screwcap. **RATING** 93 **DRINK** 2012 $22.50

Salinger 2001 Complex bready/yeasty autolysis characters help impart very good mouthfeel, the finish tightened and lengthened by good acidity. **RATING** 93 **DRINK** Now $25.06

Victoria Riesling 2004 Floral, flowery lime and spice aromas; fine, long and intense; very pure, good crisp acidity to close. In fact 100% Drumborg grapes. A bargain. **RATING** 92 **DRINK** 2014 $16.50

Bellfield Marsanne Roussanne 2004 A complex and quite floral bouquet; intense, lively, long citrus-accented mid-palate; crunchy, crisp acidity. From the Pyrenees Glen Lofty Vineyard. **RATING** 92 **DRINK** 2009 $23.99

Original Sparkling Shiraz 2002 Full of flavour; vibrant spicy shiraz black fruits and spice; good balance and length. **RATING** 91 **DRINK** 2010 $17.61

Chalambar Bendigo Grampians Shiraz 2002 Medium-bodied; fine black fruits, silky tannins, subtle oak. A bit more expected. **RATING** 90 **DRINK** 2012 $19.99

ＹＹＹＹ **Victoria Chardonnay 2004** Lively, fresh, tangy melon and citrus; slippery mouthfeel and acidity; subtle oak. Cool-climate Victoria. **RATING** 89 **DRINK** 2008 $16.50

Fleur de Lys Pinot Noir Chardonnay 2001 Fresh, lively citrus, melon and spice; long, clean, crisp finish. **RATING** 88 **DRINK** Now $16.95

Victoria Cabernet Sauvignon Merlot 2003 Brightly coloured; elegant, light to medium-bodied; sweet red and black fruits; subtle oak and tannins; good length. **RATING** 87 **DRINK** 2008 $16.99

Fleur de Lys Chardonnay Pinot NV Plenty of nectarine, citrus and apple fruit; good balance of acidity and sweetness. **RATING** 87 **DRINK** Now $12

ＹＹＹＹ **Victoria Shiraz 2003** **RATING** 86 **DRINK** 2009 $16.50

Victorian Premium Reserve Shiraz 2003 Light to medium-bodied; cedary, spicy overtones; fine tannins but a little weak on the finish; good value. **RATING** 86 **DRINK** 2007 $12.95

Great Western Brut Reserve NV **RATING** 86 **DRINK** Now $7.50

ＹＹＹ **Minchinbury Brut NV** **RATING** 83 $6.40

Matthew Lang Brut Cuvee NV **RATING** 82 $5

Serafino Wines ★★★☆

McLarens on the Lake, Kangarilla Road, McLaren Vale, SA 5171 **REGION** McLaren Vale
T (08) 8323 0157 **F** (08) 8323 0158 **OPEN** Mon–Fri 10–5, weekends & public hols 10–4.30
WINEMAKER Scott Rawlinson **EST.** 2000 **CASES** 17 000
SUMMARY In wake of the sale of Maglieri Wines to Beringer Blass in 1998, Maglieri founder Steve
Maglieri acquired the McLarens on the Lake complex originally established by Andrew Garrett. The
accommodation has been upgraded and a larger winery was commissioned prior to the 2002 vintage.
The operation draws upon 40 ha each of shiraz and cabernet sauvignon, 7 ha of chardonnay, 2 ha
each of merlot, semillon, barbera, nebbiolo and sangiovese, and 1 ha of grenache. Part of the grape
production is sold to others; the remainder goes to wines under the Serafino and McLarens on the
Lake labels. Exports to the UK, the US, Asia, Italy and New Zealand.

TTTTT **Shiraz 2002** Delicious plum and raspberry fruit; as with other commercial wines these
days, sweetness is the moot point. **RATING** 90 **DRINK** 2009

TTTT **McLaren Vale Barrel-Fermented Chardonnay 2003** **RATING** 86 **DRINK** Now

Serenella NR

Lot 300 Hermitage Road, Pokolbin, NSW 2325 **REGION** Lower Hunter Valley
T (02) 4998 7992 **F** (02) 4998 7993 **WEB** www.serenella.com.au **OPEN** 7 days 9.30–5
WINEMAKER Letitia Cecchini **EST.** 1971 **CASES** 5000
SUMMARY The establishment date of 1971 is that of the original incarnation of Serenella, which is now
James Estate. It was in that year that Giancarlo and Maria Cecchini, who had immigrated from Italy
21 years earlier, established their first vineyard in the Upper Hunter. In 1997 they sold the assets (but
not the name) of Serenella Estate, with a view to re-establishing the business in the Lower Hunter
Valley. The following year they were able to buy a 43-ha block on Hermitage Road, and lost no time
in building a state-of-the-art winery, a restaurant (Arlecchino Trattoria), and a cellar door sales and
small function area, and planting 2.5 ha of sangiovese. Daughter Tish Cecchini continues the senior
winemaking role. The Serenella Estate range is produced from Hunter Valley grapes; the cheaper
Arlecchino range is sourced from the Hunter Valley and Mudgee.

Serventy Organic Wines ★★★★

Rocky Road, Forest Grove, WA 6286 **REGION** Margaret River
T (08) 9757 7534 **F** (08) 9757 7272 **OPEN** Fri–Sun, hols 10–5
WINEMAKER Frank Kittler **EST.** 1984 **CASES** 1500
SUMMARY In 2003 a small group of wine enthusiasts from Perth acquired the business from the
famous naturalist Serventy family (one of the early movers in organic viticulture and winemaking).
Substantial investments have been made to both vineyard and winery, and the house on the property
has been restored for short-term holiday stays. The quality of the wines has improved significantly,
without losing the original identity. Exports to the UK.

TTTTT **Purely Organic Shiraz 2004** Medium to full-bodied; abundant spicy blackberry aromas;
follows through on a long palate, with fine tannins and gentle oak; 175 cases made. Quality
cork. **RATING** 92 **$** 29
Purely Organic Chardonnay 2004 Clean; light to medium-bodied; gently ripe fig, melon
and cashew; subtle touch of oak; 100 cases made. Cork. **RATING** 90 **DRINK** 2007 **$** 24

Setanta Wines ★★★★★

RSD 43, Williamstown Road, Forreston, SA 5233 (postal) **REGION** Adelaide Hills
T (08) 8380 5516 **F** (08) 8380 5516 **WEB** www.setantawines.com.au **OPEN** Not
WINEMAKER Rod Chapman, Rebecca Wilson **EST.** 1997 **CASES** 2500
SUMMARY Setanta is a family-owned operation involving Sheilagh Sullivan, her husband Tony and
brother Bernard; the latter is the viticulturist, while Tony and Sheilagh manage marketing,
administration and so forth. Of Irish parentage (they are first-generation Australians), they chose
Setanta, Ireland's most famous mythological hero, as the brand name. The beautiful and striking
labels tell the individual stories which give rise to the names of the wines, immediately prompting
questions about how much of *Lord of the Rings* was inspired by Celtic myth. The wines are
distributed by Aria Wine Co. into selected wine retailers in Adelaide and the eastern states capital

cities. They are well worth tracking down, for both the outstanding quality of the wine and those marvellous labels. Superb, hand-sorted corks of the highest quality. Exports to Ireland, of course; also to the UK, the US, Canada, Singapore and Hong Kong.

▼▼▼▼▼ **Cuchulain Shiraz 2003** Highly scented, spicy black fruit aromas; medium-bodied; elegant, intense and long; exemplary oak handling. RATING 94 DRINK 2012 $22
Black Sanglain Cabernet Sauvignon 2003 Ripe blackcurrant fruit, gently sweet; supple, medium-bodied; good length. Trophy Adelaide Hills Wine Show 2003. RATING 94 DRINK 2013 $22

▼▼▼▼▽ **Emer Chardonnay 2003** Fine, elegant and long; citrus, apple and stone fruit mix; good oak handling and length. RATING 93 DRINK 2008 $21
Speckled House Adelaide Hills Riesling 2003 Pale straw-green; floral apple blossom aromas; intense and fresh apple, slate and lime flavours. RATING 92 DRINK 2008 $19

Settlers Ridge Organic Wines ★★★

54b Bussell Highway, Cowaramup, WA 6284 REGION Margaret River
T (08) 9755 5883 F (08) 9755 5883 WEB www.settlersridge.com.au OPEN 7 days 10–5
WINEMAKER Wayne Nobbs EST. 1994 CASES 3500
SUMMARY Wayne and Kaye Nobbs have established what they say is the only vineyard in Western Australia with organic certification and the only producer in Australia with dual classification from NASAA (National Association for Sustainable Agriculture Australia) and OVAA (Organic Vignerons Association of Australia Inc.). They have 7.5 ha of vineyard, including shiraz, cabernet sauvignon, merlot, sangiovese, malbec, chenin blanc and sauvignon blanc. Exports to Germany.

▼▼▼▼ **Margaret River Cabernet Sauvignon 2002** Light to medium-bodied; clean blackcurrant, earth and spice; fresh mouthfeel; good acidity, subtle oak. Said to be vegetarian-friendly. RATING 89 DRINK 2010 $33

Settlers Rise Montville ★★★

249 Western Avenue, Montville, Qld 4560 REGION Queensland Coastal
T (07) 5478 5558 F (07) 5478 5655 WEB www.settlersrise.com.au OPEN 7 days 10–5
WINEMAKER Peter Scudamore-Smith MW (Contract) EST. 1998 CASES 3000
SUMMARY Settlers Rise is located in the beautiful highlands of the Blackall Range, 75 minutes' drive north of Brisbane and 20 minutes from the Sunshine Coast. A little over 1 ha of chardonnay, verdelho, shiraz and cabernet sauvignon have been planted at an elevation of 450m on the deep basalt soils of the property. First settled in 1887, Montville has gradually become a tourist destination, with a substantial local arts and crafts industry and a flourishing B&B and lodge accommodation infrastructure.

▼▼▼▽ **Tawny Port NV** RATING 86 DRINK Now $20
▼▼▼ **Razorback Red 2004** RATING 83 $16

7 Acres Winery NR

374 Mons Road, Forest Glen, Buderim, Qld 4556 REGION Queensland Coastal
T (07) 5445 1198 F (07) 5445 1799 WEB www.sunshinecoastwine.com.au/7acres_winery.htm
OPEN Mon–Fri 10–4, weekends 10–5
WINEMAKER Tom Weidmann EST. 1985 CASES 3000
SUMMARY When Swiss-trained winemaker Tom Weidmann bought the former Moonshine Valley Winery, which had originally been established to produce fruit wines, he changed both the name and the focus of the business. The 2005 vintage was Tom Weidmann's 24th, and he seeks to make wines from single-vineyard sources, showing the grower and the place of the vineyard on the label. At the other extreme, there is also a range of ports and liqueurs for the general tourist, and the first sparkling wine from the Sunshine Coast, named Rose of Buderim.

Sevenhill Cellars ★★★★☆

College Road, Sevenhill, SA 5453 REGION Clare Valley
T (08) 8843 4222 F (08) 8843 4382 WEB www.sevenhillcellars.com.au OPEN Mon–Fri 9–5, weekends 10–5

WINEMAKER Brother John May, Tim Eniel **EST.** 1851 **CASES** 35 000
SUMMARY One of the historical treasures of Australia; the oft-photographed stone wine cellars are the oldest in the Clare Valley, and winemaking is still carried out under the direction of the Jesuitical Manresa Society, and in particular Brother John May. Quality is very good, particularly of the powerful Shiraz; all the wines reflect the estate-grown grapes from old vines. Extensive retail distribution throughout all states; exports to New Zealand, Switzerland and the UK.

ҶҶҶҶҶ **Riesling 2004** Classic Clare style; restrained but tightly focused; precise, interwoven citrus and mineral; long finish. **RATING** 94 **DRINK** 2014 $19

ҶҶҶҶҶ **Shiraz 2002** Rich, voluptuous blackberry and spice fruit; gentle but ripe tannins; sensitive oak handling. **RATING** 92 **DRINK** 2010 $19
Shiraz 2001 Medium-bodied; a wine with length and elegance; black fruits, a touch of spice, and fine tannins. **RATING** 92 **DRINK** 2016 $20

ҶҶҶҶ **Verdelho 2004** **RATING** 85 **DRINK** Now $19

Seven Mile Vineyard NR

84 Coolangatta Road, Shoalhaven Heads, NSW 2535 **REGION** Shoalhaven Coast
T (02) 4448 5466 **F** (02) 9357 3141 **WEB** www.sevenmilevineyard.com.au **OPEN** Wed–Sun 10–6 (summer), Thurs–Sun 10–5 (winter)
WINEMAKER Eric Swarbrick **EST.** 1998 **CASES** 1500
SUMMARY The 1.8-ha Seven Mile Vineyard was established by Joan and Eric Swarbrick in 1997, east of the town of Berry, and within the sound of the surf on the Seven Mile Beach. The vineyard overlooks Coomonderry Swamp, one of the largest coastal wetlands in NSW.

Sevenoaks Wines ★★★☆

304 Doyles Creek Road, Jerrys Plains, NSW 2330 **REGION** Upper Hunter Valley
T (02) 6576 4285 **F** (02) 9586 3685 **WEB** www.sevenoakswines.com.au **OPEN** By appointment
WINEMAKER John Hordern (Contract) **EST.** 1997 **CASES** 1800
SUMMARY Robert and Deborah Sharp established Sevenoaks Wines in 1997, with the intention of selling the grapes to other winemakers. With only 2 ha of shiraz, 1.5 ha of sangiovese and 0.5 ha of petit verdot, it was inevitable that the wine from their grapes would be blended with many others, so in 2000 the Sharps changed course, retaining John Hordern as winemaker. The vineyard is part of a 68-ha property which abuts the Wollemi National Park at the bottom of the slopes that rises to be Mt Woodlands. Exports to Singapore, Malaysia and China.

ҶҶҶҶ **Rows 1 to 26 Shiraz 2003** Quite sweet plum and berry fruit on entry and mid-palate, then grippy tannins on the finish. **RATING** 87 **DRINK** 2010

ҶҶҶҶ **Rows 36 to 44 Sangiovese 2003** **RATING** 85 **DRINK** 2010

Severn Brae Estate ★★☆

Lot 2, Back Creek Road (Mt Tully Road), Severnlea, Qld 4352 **REGION** Granite Belt
T (07) 4683 5292 **F** (07) 3391 3821 **OPEN** Mon–Fri 12–3, weekends 10–5, or by appointment
WINEMAKER Bruce Humphery-Smith **EST.** 1987 **CASES** 1400
SUMMARY Patrick and Bruce Humphery-Smith have established 5.5 ha of chardonnay with relatively close spacing, and trained on a high two-tier trellis. Two-thirds of the production is sold, one-third used for the Severn Brae label.

ҶҶҶ **Reserve Verdelho 2004** **RATING** 83
Merlot 2002 **RATING** 83

Seville Estate

65 Linwood Road, Seville, Vic 3139 **REGION** Yarra Valley
T (03) 5964 2622 **F** (03) 5964 2633 **WEB** www.sevilleestate.com.au **OPEN** By appointment
WINEMAKER Dylan McMahon **EST.** 1970 **CASES** 4000
SUMMARY First planted in 1972 by Dr Peter McMahon and wife Margaret. Seville Estate was one of the first vineyards in the Yarra Valley in the modern era. In 1997 Brokenwood Wines took

control of it. In 2003 Rob Hawkings and his wife bought Brokenwood's direct shares, but the other partners retained their ownership. In 2004 Seville Estate re-established its position as one of the leading Yarra Valley wineries, focused on estate-grown and produced wines. Dylan McMahon is the grandson of Peter and Margaret McMahon. Exports to the UK, the US, Malaysia and Singapore.

ŦŦŦŦŦ **Old Vine Reserve Shiraz 2003** Superb colour; very pure yet powerful evocation of cool-climate Shiraz; intensely interwoven spicy black fruits and quality French oak. **RATING** 95 **DRINK** 2018 **$** 66
The Barber Chardonnay 2004 Intense, elegant and very, very long; grapefruit and melon with perfectly integrated oak; Yarra Valley at its best. **RATING** 94 **DRINK** 2014 **$** 19
Reserve Chardonnay 2003 Intense but fine; citrus, melon and stone fruit has absorbed 100% barrel ferment oak; very classy wine. **RATING** 94 **DRINK** 2013 **$** 40

ŦŦŦŦŸ **Reserve Pinot Noir 2003** Very complex array of dark cherry/plum fruit, spice, French oak and tannins; the same alcohol as the unfiltered Pinot, but more depth. **RATING** 93 **DRINK** 2013
Shiraz 2003 Vigorous spice, licorice and blackberry aromas and flavours; long palate; fine tannins, subtle oak. **RATING** 92 **DRINK** 2013 **$** 27
Unfiltered Pinot Noir 2003 Spicy, vibrant and stylish; complex, ripe plum flavours, but does show some heat (14.5° alcohol) on the finish. **RATING** 91 **DRINK** 2010 **$** 27
Pinot Noir 2002 Highly aromatic spice and herb aromas; an elegant, relatively light-bodied palate with nice touches of red cherry. **RATING** 91 **DRINK** 2007 **$** 29.95
Beechworth Pinot Gris 2004 Highly perfumed and aromatic; spice, apricot and musk; good depth and length; carries its 14.5° alcohol. **RATING** 90 **DRINK** 2007 **$** 19

ŦŦŦŦ **Pinot Noir 2003** Deep colour; strong, powerful, plummy fruit; stem and oak thereafter; slight bite to finish. **RATING** 88 **DRINK** 2010 **$** 27
Chardonnay 2003 Complex wine with lots of barrel ferment and other winemaker inputs allied with ripe fruit, and a twisted finish. **RATING** 87 **DRINK** 2009 **$** 27
Rose 2004 Full-on rose style; strong red fruit flavours; good length, not sweet. **RATING** 87 **DRINK** Now **$** 16

Seville Hill ★★★☆

8 Paynes Road, Seville, Vic 3139 **REGION** Yarra Valley
T (03) 5964 3284 **F** (03) 5964 2142 **WEB** www.sevillehill.com.au **OPEN** 7 days 10–6
WINEMAKER Dom Bucci, John D'Aloisio **EST.** 1991 **CASES** 3000
SUMMARY John and Josie D'Aloisio have had a long-term involvement in the agricultural industry, which ultimately led to the establishment of the Seville Hill vineyard in 1991. There they have 2.4 ha of cabernet sauvignon and 1.3 ha each of merlot, shiraz and chardonnay. John D'Aloisio makes the wines with Dominic Bucci, a long-time Yarra resident and winemaker.

ŦŦŦŦ **Yarra Valley Sauvignon Blanc 2004** Tight herb, mineral, asparagus and green pea fruit; fresh, bright finish. Cork. **RATING** 88 **DRINK** 2007 **$** 19
Yarra Valley Chardonnay 2004 Light to medium-bodied; slightly funky barrel ferment notes; mineral and citrus fruit; not concentrated. Cork. **RATING** 87 **DRINK** 2008 **$** 22

ŦŦŦŸ **Yarra Valley Merlot Cabernet 2003** **RATING** 86 **DRINK** 2008 **$** 22
Yarra Valley Rose 2004 **RATING** 84 **DRINK** Now **$** 15

Sewards ★★☆

Lot 2, Wildwood Road, Yallingup, WA 6282 **REGION** Margaret River
T 0413 567 693 **F** (08) 6267 8009 **OPEN** Not
WINEMAKER Michael Kelly (Contract) **EST.** 1995 **CASES** 625
SUMMARY The 10-ha vineyard was established by Dr John McCarthy Seward in 1995, and is now run by family members. Most of the grapes are sold to Fermoy Estate, where the wines are contract-made. Sales are by mail order only, but a cellar door may be opened down the track.

ŦŦŦŸ **Shiraz 2003** **RATING** 85 **DRINK** 2007

Shadowfax ★★★★★

K Road, Werribee, Vic 3030 **REGION** Geelong
T (03) 9731 4420 **F** (03) 9731 4421 **WEB** www.shadowfax.com.au **OPEN** 7 days 11–5
WINEMAKER Matt Harrop **EST.** 2000 **CASES** 15 000
SUMMARY Shadowfax is part of an awesome development at Werribee Park, a mere 20 minutes from Melbourne. The truly striking winery, designed by Wood Marsh architects, erected in time for the 2000 vintage crush, is adjacent to the extraordinary 60-room private home built in the 1880s by the Chirnside family and known as The Mansion. It was then the centrepiece of a 40 000-ha pastoral empire, and the appropriately magnificent gardens were part of the reason why the property was acquired by Parks Victoria in the early 1970s. The Mansion is now The Mansion Hotel, with 92 rooms and suites, with the emphasis on conference bookings during the week and general tourism on the weekend. The striking packaging of the wines, and the quality of the first releases, all underline the thoroughly serious nature of this quite amazing venture. Exports to the UK, Japan, New Zealand and Singapore.

ΨΨΨΨΨ **Chardonnay 2003** Bright, light green-yellow; beautifully constructed wine, a seamless fusion of multi-regional fruit and oak; great balance and finish. Geelong/Beechworth/Yarra Valley/Adelaide Hills. **RATING** 95 **DRINK** 2010 $ 30
One Eye Heathcote Shiraz 2002 Very potent, powerful and focused; full-bodied; silky, slippery tannins on a long finish. Single-vineyard. **RATING** 94 **DRINK** 2022 $ 70
Pink Cliffs Heathcote Shiraz 2002 Rich, deep structure; multi-faceted black fruits; full-bodied; ripe tannins, subtle oak influence. **RATING** 94 **DRINK** 2027 $ 70

ΨΨΨΨΨ **Pinot Noir 2003** Clean, fresh and fragrant; light to medium-bodied; long and fine red and black cherry; a hint of spice; transparent tannins. Geelong/Gippsland/Yarra Valley. **RATING** 93 **DRINK** 2009 $ 32
Geelong Pinot Noir 2003 Funky, feral and quite oaky, but with abundant spicy fruit and length. **RATING** 92 **DRINK** 2012 $ 30
Werribee Shiraz 2003 Funky, feral and quite oaky, but with abundant plum, blackberry and currant fruit and length. **RATING** 92 **DRINK** 2015 $ 30

ΨΨΨΨ **K Road Sangiovese Merlot Shiraz 2002** Spicy, savoury aromas; elegant, light to medium-bodied palate; spicy cherry fruit; 45/35/20 blend. Screwcap. **RATING** 89 **DRINK** 2007 $ 24

Shantell ★★★★☆

1974 Melba Highway, Dixons Creek, Vic 3775 **REGION** Yarra Valley
T (03) 5965 2155 **F** (03) 5965 2331 **WEB** www.shantellvineyard.com.au **OPEN** 7 days 10.30–5
WINEMAKER Shan Shanmugam, Turid Shanmugam **EST.** 1980 **CASES** 2500
SUMMARY The substantial and now fully mature Shantell vineyards provide the winery with a high-quality fruit source; part is sold to other Yarra Valley makers, the remainder vinified at Shantell. In January 1998 Shantell opened a new cellar door at 1974 Melba Highway, 50m along a service road from the highway proper. Chardonnay, Semillon and Cabernet Sauvignon are its benchmark wines, sturdily reliable, sometimes outstanding. The restaurant is open Thurs–Mon. Domestic and international distribution through Australian Prestige Wines.

ΨΨΨΨΨ **Chardonnay 2002** Intense melon, citrus and nectarine; shows all the concentration of the vintage. Cork. **RATING** 92 **DRINK** 2010 $ 28
Pinot Noir 2002 Light to medium-bodied; elegant, spicy style; has considerable length; silky tannins. Cork. **RATING** 92 **DRINK** 2009 $ 35
Semillon 2004 Intense and rich, but not the least phenolic; grass, apple and citrus; from 25-year-old vines. Twin Top. **RATING** 91 **DRINK** 2009 $ 20
Cabernet Sauvignon 2001 Earthy blackberry fruit; touches of bottle-developed cedar; rich and round; good tannins. High-quality cork. **RATING** 91 **DRINK** 2012 $ 28
Shiraz 2001 Medium-bodied; smooth and supple; sweet blackberry fruit and balanced vanilla oak; ripe tannins. Cork. **RATING** 90 **DRINK** 2010 $ 28

Sharmans ★★★☆

Glenbothy, 175 Glenwood Road, Relbia, Tas 7258 **REGION** Northern Tasmania
T (03) 6343 0773 **F** (03) 6343 0773 **OPEN** Thurs–Sun 10–5, closed during winter
WINEMAKER Andrew Pirie, Rosevears Estate (Contract) **EST.** 1987 **CASES** 1000

SUMMARY Mike Sharman pioneered one of the more interesting wine regions of Tasmania, not far south of Launceston but with a distinctly warmer climate than (say) Pipers Brook. Ideal north-facing slopes are home to a vineyard now approaching 4 ha, most now in bearing.

 TTTT **Sauvignon Blanc 2004** Good depth to moderately ripe apple and gooseberry fruit; good balance and length. **RATING** 89 **DRINK** Now $ 18
Chardonnay 2003 Elegant and controlled, almost to the point of simplicity; clean and fresh; will develop. **RATING** 88 **DRINK** 2010 $ 18
Noble Late Harvest 2004 Good balance, but lacks the fruit flavour complexity for higher points. **RATING** 87 **DRINK** 2008

TTTY **Pinot Noir 2003** **RATING** 85 **DRINK** 2009 $ 23

Sharpe Wines of Orange ★★★★

Stagecoach Road, Emu Swamp, Orange, NSW 2800 **REGION** Orange
T (02) 6361 9046 **F** (02) 6361 1645 **WEB** www.sharpewinesoforange.com.au **OPEN** First weekend of the month, or by appointment
WINEMAKER Margot Sharpe, Rob Black **EST.** 1998 **CASES** 1200
SUMMARY When Margot and Tony Sharpe began planting their 3-ha vineyard, predominantly to cabernet sauvignon, with lesser amounts of merlot and cabernet franc, the wheel turned in a somewhat wayward full circle. Sharpe Bros Cordials was established in 1868 by strict Methodists to give the working man something to drink other than the demon alcohol. Says Margot Sharpe, 'I do believe there might be some serious grave turning over the product.' The Rose and Single Barrel Cabernet Sauvignon were made by the Sharpes in a tiny winery established in small stables at the back of their house; the Jack Demmery Cabernet Sauvignon was named in honour of Margot Sharpe's late father, who died just as planting of the vineyard was completed.

TTTTY **Chardonnay 2002** Powerful grapefruit and stone fruit aromas; long and intense palate; ageing slowly; well priced. **RATING** 91 **DRINK** 2008 $ 18
Merlot 2003 Shows the undoubted synergy between variety and region; ripe but not jammy small berry fruits and a nice twist of olive. Well made. **RATING** 91 **DRINK** 2010 $ 18

TTTT **The Jack Demmery Cabernet Sauvignon 2003** Medium-bodied; good mouthfeel, ripe and supple; blackcurrant and spice; good tannins and extract. **RATING** 89 **DRINK** 2011 $ 20
Gentleman's Claret 2003 A range of red berry, mint, leaf and stem; light to medium-bodied and quite fresh. A foot-stamped blend of Cabernet Sauvignon/Merlot/Cabernet Franc. **RATING** 87 **DRINK** 2008 $ 16

TTTY **The Jack Demmery Cabernet Sauvignon 2002** **RATING** 86 **DRINK** 2007 $ 25
The Foot Trod Cabernet Sauvignon 2003 **RATING** 85 **DRINK** 2007 $ 15

TTT **The Rose 2004** **RATING** 83 $ 14

Shaw & Smith ★★★★★

Lot 4 Jones Road, Balhannah, SA 5242 **REGION** Adelaide Hills
T (08) 8398 0500 **F** (08) 8398 0600 **WEB** www.shawandsmith.com **OPEN** Weekends 11–4
WINEMAKER Martin Shaw **EST.** 1989 **CASES** 35 000
SUMMARY Has progressively moved from a contract grape-grown base to estate production with the development of a 40-ha vineyard at Balhannah, followed by the erection prior to the 2000 vintage of a state-of-the-art, beautifully designed and executed winery, ending the long period of tenancy at Petaluma. Exports to the UK, the US, Canada, Hong Kong, Japan and Singapore.

TTTTT **M3 Vineyard Chardonnay 2003** Complex, intense and tight aromas and flavours of stone fruit, melon and fig interlaced with cashew and spicy oak in the background; a fine example of winemaking. **RATING** 95 **DRINK** 2009 $ 35
Riesling 2004 A strongly structured minerally frame; pear, apple and citrus; long finish. **RATING** 94 **DRINK** 2014 $ 25

TTTTY **Sauvignon Blanc 2004** Spotlessly clean; no reduction ex ferment or screwcap; some mid-palate gooseberry fruit; very good balance and length. Better than the vast majority from this vintage. **RATING** 93 **DRINK** Now $ 25

TTTT **Shiraz 2003** Fragrant and fresh aromas; light to medium-bodied, with juicy red fruits and touches of spice. **RATING** 89 **DRINK** 2008 $ 35

Shaw Vineyard Estate

NR

Isabelle Drive, Murrumbateman, NSW 2582 **REGION** Canberra District
T 0412 633 542 **F** (02) 6227 5865 **OPEN** Not
WINEMAKER Bill Calabria, Ken Helm (Contract) **EST.** 1999 **CASES** NA
SUMMARY Graeme and Michael Shaw have established a little over 30 ha of vineyard, planted to
semillon, riesling, shiraz, merlot and cabernet sauvignon. Most of the production is sold to Hardys.
A winery, cellar door and restaurant opened in 2005.

Shawwood Estate

★★★

Cnr Craigmoor Road/Henry Lawson Drive, Mudgee, NSW 2850 **REGION** Mudgee
T (02) 6372 0237 **F** (02) 6372 0238 **WEB** www.shawwood.com.au **OPEN** Weekends & public hols
10–4
WINEMAKER Craig Bishop **EST.** 1998 **CASES** 2500
SUMMARY Shawwood Estate has been established a mere 2.5 km from the Mudgee GPO, on a slight
rise on the northern side of Mudgee overlooking the township. A group of investors, including
Charles Tym, Alison Bishop and Craig Bishop, have planted 3.3 ha each of shiraz and cabernet
sauvignon, and 1.7 ha each of chardonnay and verdelho. The wines are made onsite by Craig Bishop,
who is also responsible for the vineyard.

Sheep's Back

★★★★☆

PO Box 441, South Melbourne, Vic 3205 **REGION** Barossa Valley
T (03) 9696 7018 **F** (03) 9686 4015 **OPEN** Not
WINEMAKER Dean Hewitson **EST.** 2001 **CASES** 3000
SUMMARY Sheep's Back is a joint venture between Neil Empson (with 30 years' experience as an
exporter to Australia and elsewhere of Italian wines) and Dean Hewitson. They decided to produce a
single estate-grown shiraz after an extensive search found a 6-ha vineyard of 75-year-old vines.
Australian distribution by Trembath & Taylor; exports to the US and Canada.

ŢŢŢŢ♀ **Old Vine Barossa Valley Shiraz 2002** Generous, not over-ripe blackberry and plum
fruit; ripe, supple tannins; subtle French oak. Cork. **RATING** 91 **DRINK** 2015 $ 25.80

Shelmerdine Vineyards

★★★★★

Merindoc Vineyard, Lancefield Road, Tooborac, Vic 3522 **REGION** Heathcote and Yarra Valley
T (03) 5433 5188 **F** (03) 5433 5118 **WEB** www.shelmerdine.com.au **OPEN** Mon–Fri 11–3, weekends
11–5
WINEMAKER Kate Goodman (Contract) **EST.** 1989 **CASES** NA
SUMMARY Stephen Shelmerdine has been a major figure in the wine industry for well over 20 years,
like his family before him (who founded Mitchelton Winery), and has been honoured for his many
services to the industry. The venture has 130 ha of vineyards spread over three sites: Lusatia Park in
the Yarra Valley and Merindoc Vineyard and Willoughby Bridge in the Heathcote region. Substantial
quantities of the grapes produced are sold to others; a small amount of high-quality wine is contract-
made at the Punt Road Winery. The cellar door is at the Merindoc Vineyard.

ŢŢŢŢŢ **Heathcote Shiraz 2003** Medium-bodied; supple red and black fruits; fine, silky tannins;
more elegant than most thanks to 13.5° alcohol. Screwcap. **RATING** 94 **DRINK** 2017 $ 28
Heathcote Cabernet Sauvignon 2002 Deep colour; supple, rich blackcurrant fruit;
excellent mouthfeel and length; fine tannins, integrated oak. **RATING** 94 **DRINK** 2015 $ 26

ŢŢŢŢ♀ **Yarra Valley Chardonnay 2003** Fragrant melon, stone fruit and citrus; long, fine
structure and finish; subtle oak. **RATING** 93 **DRINK** 2013 $ 25
Heathcote Cabernet Sauvignon 2003 Youthful purple; flooded with cassis and
blackcurrant fruit; ripe tannins; elegance with flavour (13° alcohol). Screwcap. **RATING** 93
DRINK 2016 $ 28
Yarra Valley Sauvignon Blanc 2004 Clean and fresh; good varietal gooseberry fruit, then
firm lemony acidity through to the finish. **RATING** 90 **DRINK** 2007 $ 20
Yarra Valley Pinot Noir 2003 Lots of plum and black cherry; plenty of mid-palate flavour
and structure; shortens marginally. **RATING** 90 **DRINK** 2008 $ 25

ΥΥΥΥ **Merlot 2003** Very savoury minty/leafy/spicy aromas; light to medium-bodied; has length rather than weight. **RATING** 87 **DRINK** 2008 $ 20

ΥΥΥ **Heathcote Viognier 2004** **RATING** 86 **DRINK** 2008 $ 25

🐚 Shepherd's Hut

PO Box 194, Darlington, WA 6070 **REGION** Porongurup
T (08) 9299 6700 **F** (08) 9299 6703 **OPEN** Not
WINEMAKER Rob Diletti **EST.** 1996 **CASES** 1300
SUMMARY The shepherd's hut which appears on the wine label was one of four stone huts used in the 1850s to house shepherds tending large flocks of sheep. When WA pathologist Dr Michael Wishart (and family) purchased the property in 1996, the hut was in a state of extreme disrepair. It has since been entirely restored, still featuring the honey-coloured Mt Barker stone. A total of 18 ha of riesling, chardonnay, sauvignon blanc, shiraz and cabernet sauvignon have been established; the daily running of the vineyard is the responsibility of son Philip, who also runs a large farm of mainly cattle; the other son, William, helps with marketing and sales. Most of the grapes are sold to other makers in the region. The wine is sold by mail order and direct to restaurants.

ΥΥΥΥ **Porongurup Shiraz 2003** Fragrant, spicy, plummy aromas and flavours; light to medium-bodied with fine tannins and appropriately frugal oak. **RATING** 89 **DRINK** 2008 $ 18
Porongurup Cabernet Sauvignon 2003 Light to medium-bodied; fine, silky mouthfeel; quite delicate cassis and blackcurrant; unforced. **RATING** 87 **DRINK** 2009 $ 18

ΥΥΥ **Porongurup Shiraz 2002** Big, bold, slightly over-ripe and tarry style. **RATING** 86 **DRINK** 2010 $ 20

Shepherd's Moon ★★★☆

Barwang Ridge, 1 Barwang Road, via Young, NSW 2594 **REGION** Hilltops
T (02) 6382 6363 **F** (02) 6382 6363 **OPEN** Sat–Mon 10–5, or by appointment
WINEMAKER Contract **EST.** 1979 **CASES** 2000
SUMMARY Rick and Julie Hobba purchased the Hansen Hilltops property in December 2002. They have since engaged in an extensive rehabilitation program in the vineyard, with minimal crops in the meantime; the yield is expected to reach its full potential in 2006.

ΥΥΥΥ **Unwooded Chardonnay 2004** Has well-above average intensity of flavour and structure; melon and stone fruit; good length. May improve. **RATING** 88 **DRINK** 2009

Sherwood Estate NR

1187 Gowings Hill Road, Sherwood, NSW 2440 **REGION** Hastings River
T (02) 6581 4900 **F** (02) 6581 4728 **WEB** www.sherwoodestatewines.com.au **OPEN** Fri–Sun & public hols 11–4, or by appointment
WINEMAKER Karen Legget **EST.** 1998 **CASES** 750
SUMMARY John and Helen Ross began planting the Sherwood Estate vineyard in 1998, with 2 ha of chambourcin. Subsequently, verdelho, chardonnay, cabernet franc, semillon and (most recently) sangiovese have been planted, with 10 ha now under vine. The vineyard is in the Macleay Valley, 15 minutes west of Kempsey on the NSW North Coast. The property has a total of 43 ha of undulating fertile soils, rich in limestone. The wines are also available from the Sherwood Wine Embassy, Pacific Highway, Port Macquarie (open 7 days).

Shingleback ★★★★

1 Main Road, McLaren Vale, SA 5171 **REGION** McLaren Vale
T (08) 8370 3299 **F** (08) 8370 0088 **WEB** www.shingleback.com.au **OPEN** 7 days 9–5
WINEMAKER John Davey, Don Hill **EST.** 1995 **CASES** 50 000
SUMMARY Shingleback has 80 ha of vineyards in McLaren Vale, with part of the grape production vinified under the Shingleback label. It is a specialist export business, with sales to Germany, Switzerland and the US, but the wines are also available by mail order locally. The excellent 2002 vintage wines, in particular, have characters one more readily associates with cool climates; it will be

interesting to see whether this was a vintage effect, or due to vineyard site and aspect, or the winery. Exports to the US.

ΥΥΥΥΥ **White Knot McLaren Vale Chardonnay 2004** Generous stone fruit flavours, with far more depth than many from the 2004 vintage. **RATING** 90 **DRINK** 2008 $17

ΥΥΥΥ **Chardonnay 2004** Quiet, slightly subdued bouquet; comes alive on a long palate with cashew and lemony/minerally acidity. Screwcap. **RATING** 89 **DRINK** 2008 $25
Red Knot McLaren Vale Cabernet Sauvignon 2003 Light to medium-bodied; supple and sweet blackcurrant fruit with touches of regional chocolate; soft tannins. Zork. **RATING** 87 **DRINK** 2008 $17

ΥΥΥΥ **Red Knot McLaren Vale Shiraz 2003** **RATING** 84 **DRINK** 2009 $17

Shiralee Wines   NR

PO Box 260, Nuriootpa, SA 5355 **REGION** Barossa Valley
T (08) 8564 2799 **F** (08) 8564 2799 **OPEN** Not
WINEMAKER Bob Mitchell **EST.** 2001 **CASES** NA
SUMMARY Shiralee Wines is the venture of Graeme Ruwoldt and Bob Mitchell, with access to 25 ha of chardonnay and shiraz in the Barossa Valley. Only part of the output is vinified for the Shiralee brand; the major market is the US.

Shirvington   NR

PO Box 222, McLaren Vale, SA 5171 **REGION** McLaren Vale
T (08) 8383 0554 **F** (08) 8383 0556 **WEB** www.shirvington.com **OPEN** Not
WINEMAKER Sarah Marquis, Sparky Marquis **EST.** 1996 **CASES** 2000
SUMMARY The Shirvington family began the development of their McLaren Vale vineyards in 1996 under the direction of viticulturist Peter Bolte, and now have 35 ha under vine, the majority to shiraz and cabernet sauvignon, and with small additional plantings of merlot, cabernet franc and verdelho. A substantial part of the production is sold as grapes; the best is reserved for the Shirvington wines. Exports to New Zealand and the US.

Shottesbrooke   ★★★★

Bagshaws Road, McLaren Flat, SA 5171 **REGION** McLaren Vale
T (08) 8383 0002 **F** (08) 8383 0222 **WEB** www.shottesbrooke.com.au **OPEN** Mon–Fri 10–4.30, weekends & public hols 11–5
WINEMAKER Nick Holmes, Hamish Maguire **EST.** 1984 **CASES** 12 000
SUMMARY For many years now the full-time business of former Ryecroft winemaker Nick Holmes (now with stepson Hamish Maguire), drawing primarily on estate-grown grapes at his Myoponga vineyard. He has always stood out for the finesse and elegance of his wines compared with the dambuster, high-alcohol reds for which McLaren Vale has become famous (or infamous, depending on one's point of view). Now the wheel has started to turn full circle, and finesse and elegance are much more appreciated. Exports to the UK, the US and Europe; distribution through all Australian states.

ΥΥΥΥΥ **Shiraz 2003** In typical Shottesbrooke style, super-elegant with lovely spicy/silky mouthfeel. **RATING** 93 **DRINK** 2013 $18

ΥΥΥΥ **Fleurieu Adelaide Hills Sauvignon Blanc 2004** **RATING** 86 **DRINK** Now $15
Merlette Free Run Merlot Rose 2004 **RATING** 85 **DRINK** Now $14
Merlot 2003 **RATING** 85 **DRINK** 2007 $17

Sienna Estate   ★★★☆

Canal Rocks Road, Yallingup, WA 6282 **REGION** Margaret River
T (08) 9755 2028 **F** (08) 9755 2028 **WEB** www.siennaestate.com.au **OPEN** Weekends & hols 10–5
WINEMAKER David Hunt **EST.** 1978 **CASES** 1200
SUMMARY The 3.7-ha vineyard, planted to semillon, sauvignon blanc, riesling and cabernet sauvignon, was established by David Hunt in 1978. It has now passed into the ownership of the Rusilas family, but winemaking remains in the hands of David Hunt. The strikingly-labelled wines are sold only through the cellar door and onsite restaurant and accommodation; all are 100% estate-grown.

ȲȲȲȲ **Momentum Semillon 2004** Light-bodied; clean, fresh and lively; attractive spicy touches run through to the back palate. Screwcap. **RATING** 89 **DRINK** 2010 $14
Momentum Cabernet 2002 Light to medium-bodied; softly sweet cassis and blackcurrant; super-fine tannins; subtle oak. Screwcap. **RATING** 88 **DRINK** 2010 $22
Momentum Riesling 2004 Clean; sweet apple, pear and citrus; loses focus on the finish. Screwcap. **RATING** 87 **DRINK** 2008 $14

ȲȲȲȲ **Momentum Semillon Sauvignon Blanc 2004** **RATING** 85 **DRINK** 2007 $16

Silk Hill ★★★

324 Motor Road, Deviot, Tas 7275 **REGION** Northern Tasmania
T (03) 6394 7385 **F** (03) 6394 7392 **OPEN** By appointment
WINEMAKER Gavin Scott **EST.** 1990 **CASES** 500
SUMMARY Pharmacist Gavin Scott has been a weekend and holiday viticulturist for many years, having established the Glengarry Vineyard, which he sold, and then establishing the 1.5-ha Silk Hill (formerly Silkwood Vineyard) in 1989, planted exclusively to pinot noir. Growing and making Pinot Noir and fishing will keep him occupied when he sells his pharmacy business.

ȲȲȲȲ **Pinot Noir 2003** Powerful wine; high tannin extract on ripe, plummy fruit. **RATING** 87 **DRINK** 2010 $25

ȲȲȲȲ **Pinots Rose 2004** **RATING** 86 **DRINK** Now
The Supply Pinot Noir 2003 **RATING** 86 **DRINK** 2009 $33

Silkwood Wines ★★★

Lot 5204 Channybearup Road, Pemberton, WA 6260 **REGION** Pemberton
T (08) 9776 1584 **F** (08) 9776 0019 **WEB** www.silkwoodwines.com.au **OPEN** 7 days 11–4
WINEMAKER Contract **EST.** 1998 **CASES** 800
SUMMARY Third-generation farmers Pam and John Allen returned from a short break running small businesses in Adelaide and Perth to purchase Silkwood in 1998. Plantings began with 5 ha of shiraz and sauvignon blanc in 1999, followed by a further 5.5 ha of riesling, pinot noir, merlot and cabernet sauvignon in 2000. The vineyard is patrolled by a large flock of guinea fowl, eliminating most insect pests, and reducing the use of chemicals. The wines are sold through the cellar door and website.

ȲȲȲȲ **Sauvignon Blanc 2004** Clean and fresh but very light fruit; does have length thanks to lemony acidity. Twin Top. **RATING** 86 **DRINK** Now $17
Shiraz 2003 **RATING** 85 **DRINK** 2008 $19

Silver Wings Winemaking ★★★★☆

Paramoor Farm, 439 Three Chain Road, Carlsruhe, Vic 3442 **REGION** Central Victoria Zone
T (03) 5429 2444 **F** (03) 5429 2442 **OPEN** By appointment
WINEMAKER Keith Brien **EST.** 2003 **CASES** 1000
SUMMARY This is the new venture of Keith Brien, formerly of Cleveland. After a brief shared occupation with Goona Warra Winery in Sunbury, he has moved Silver Wings to a little winery at Carlsruhe, near Lancefield. Here he offers contract winemaking and export consulting, as well as making the Silver Wings wines from 4 ha of contract-grown grapes (3 ha of mourvedre, 1 ha of shiraz) coming from 50-year-old vines.

ȲȲȲȲȲ **Grand Reserve Macedon Ranges Brut XO 2003** Elegant and fine; still very fresh; subtle complexity; long and lingering. Ten years on lees; liqueured with XO Cognac. **RATING** 94 **DRINK** 2010

ȲȲȲȲȲ **Macedon Ranges Brut NV** #97. Bright, fresh, crisp and lively citrussy/minerally notes; amazingly fresh still; very good balance and length; 70% 1997 vintage, 30% aged reserve component. Chardonnay/Pinot Noir. **RATING** 92 **DRINK** 2007 $25

ȲȲȲȲ **Macedon Ranges Chardonnay 2001** Soft, bottle-developed nutty, cashew, melon entry through subtle bottle ferment characters; dips slightly on the back palate, but good finish. **RATING** 88 **DRINK** 2007 $20

Silverwood Wines

Bittern–Dromana Road, Balnarring, Vic 3926 **REGION** Mornington Peninsula
T 0419 890 317 **F** (03) 9888 5303 **WEB** www.silverwoodwines.com.au **OPEN** Not
WINEMAKER Paul Dennis, Phillip Kittle **EST.** 1997 **CASES** 350
SUMMARY Paul and Denise Dennis were inspired to establish Silverwood by living in France for a
year. They, with members of their family, did much of the establishment work on the vineyard, which
is meticulously maintained. Most of the grapes are sold to other Mornington Peninsula wineries, but
a small amount of attractive wine is made under the Silverwood label.

ΥΥΥΥΥ **Chardonnay 2003** Light to medium-bodied; clean, bright and nicely focused style;
grapefruit and melon; long finish. Cork. **RATING** 90 **DRINK** 2008 $24

ΥΥΥΥ **Rose 2004** Very intense strawberry and cherry flavours; a touch of sweetness to charm
cellar door visitors. **RATING** 87 **DRINK** Now $15.95

Simon Gilbert Wines

1220 Sydney Road, Mudgee, NSW 2850 **REGION** Mudgee
T (02) 9958 1322 **F** (02) 8920 1333 **WEB** www.simongilbertwines.com.au **OPEN** 7 days 9–5
WINEMAKER Andrew Ewart, Simon Gilbert (Consultant) **EST.** 1993 **CASES** 35 000
SUMMARY The arrival of high-profile, ex-Southcorp senior executives David Coombe as chairman and
Paul Pacino as chief executive has seen a complete restructuring of this $20 million, 5000-tonne
winery. The wines, with new products being introduced, continue to be sourced from the Central
Ranges regions of NSW, including Orange, Mudgee and Cowra.

ΥΥΥΥ **Card Series Central Ranges Cabernet Sauvignon 2003** Well made; blackcurrant fruit
interwoven with tannins; good structure, swelling on the mid to back palate. **RATING** 89
DRINK 2012 $15
Card Series Central Ranges Chardonnay 2003 No frills, but has good balance, length
and flavour; gently ripe peachy fruit; delicate touch of oak. **RATING** 88 **DRINK** 2007 $15
Card Series Central Ranges Cabernet Merlot 2003 Well-balanced and integrated sweet
red and black fruits and oak; tannins a fraction grippy, but should soften. **RATING** 88
DRINK 2010 $15
Card Series Central Ranges Shiraz 2003 Medium-bodied; clean, fresh black cherry,
plum and blackberry fruit; fine, soft tannins; minimal oak. **RATING** 87 **DRINK** 2010 $15

ΥΥΥΥ **Card Series Central Ranges Semillon Sauvignon Blanc 2004** **RATING** 85 **DRINK** Now $15
Card Series Central Ranges Verdelho 2004 **RATING** 85 **DRINK** 2007 $15

Simon Hackett

Budgens Road, McLaren Vale, SA 5171 **REGION** McLaren Vale
T (08) 8323 7712 **F** (08) 8323 7713 **OPEN** Wed–Sun 11–5
WINEMAKER Simon Hackett **EST.** 1981 **CASES** 20 000
SUMMARY In 1998 Simon Hackett acquired the former Taranga winery in McLaren Vale, which has
made his winemaking life a great deal easier. He has 8 ha of estate vines, and has contract growers in
McLaren Vale and the Barossa Valley, with another 32 ha of vines.

ΥΥΥΥΥ **Anthony's Reserve McLaren Vale Shiraz 2001** Ripe, blackberry, prune, plum and
vanilla; medium-bodied; good balance and extract; 14° alcohol a relief. Twin Top.
RATING 90 **DRINK** 2011 $25

ΥΥΥΥ **McLaren Vale Shiraz 2002** Soft black and red fruits; spice and vanilla aromas and
flavours; quite supple; carries 15° alcohol. Stained cork. **RATING** 89 **DRINK** 2012 $18
Foggo Road McLaren Vale Cabernet Sauvignon 2001 Good colour; nicely ripened
blackcurrant, spice and earth fruit expression; restrained oak; good structure. **RATING** 89
DRINK 2012 $35
Brightview Barossa Valley Chardonnay 2004 Light to medium-bodied; nicely balanced
vanilla oak and gently peachy fruit; has no pretensions. **RATING** 87 **DRINK** 2007 $15

ΥΥΥΥ **McLaren Vale Riesling 2003** **RATING** 86 **DRINK** 2007 $15
Brightview Barossa Valley Semillon 2004 **RATING** 85 **DRINK** 2007 $15
Old Vine McLaren Vale Grenache 2002 **RATING** 85 **DRINK** 2007 $15

Sinclair Wines

Graphite Road, Glenoran, WA 6258 **REGION** Manjimup
T(08) 9335 6318 **F**(08) 9433 5489 **WEB** www.sinclairwines.com.au **OPEN** By appointment
WINEMAKER Brenden Smith (Contract) **EST.** 1994 **CASES** 2800
SUMMARY Sinclair Wines is the child of Darelle Sinclair, a science teacher, wine educator and graduate viticulturist from Charles Sturt University, and John Healy, a lawyer, trad jazz musician and graduate wine marketing student of Adelaide University, Roseworthy campus. The 5 ha of estate plantings underpin high-quality wines at mouthwatering prices. Exports to the UK, The Netherlands and Japan.

ΨΨΨΨΨ Giovanni Manjimup Cabernet Sauvignon 2003 Remarkably rich, supple and fleshy for the region; abundance of blackcurrant and cassis fruit; ripe tannins, good oak. Quality cork. **RATING** 94 **DRINK** 2015 $20

ΨΨΨΨΨ Swallow Hill Manjimup Sauvignon Blanc 2004 Clean; minerally/spicy aromas, latent gooseberry coming through strongly on the palate; good total flavour and acidity. Screwcap. **RATING** 92 **DRINK** 2007 $18

ΨΨΨΨ Manjimup Chardonnay 2003 Elegant, restrained style; citrus and stone fruit have absorbed the French oak; good length and finish. Cork. **RATING** 89 **DRINK** 2010 $18

ΨΨΨΨ The Nikstar Manjimup Unwooded Chardonnay 2004 **RATING** 86 **DRINK** 2008 $18
The Nikstar Manjimup Unwooded Chardonnay 2003 **RATING** 85 **DRINK** 2007 $18

🐌 Sir Paz Estate

384 George Street, Fitzroy, Vic 3065 (postal) **REGION** Yarra Valley
T(03) 9417 9337 **F**(03) 9417 3981 **WEB** www.sirpaz.com **OPEN** Not
WINEMAKER Scott McCarthy, John Zapris **EST.** 1997 **CASES** 4600
SUMMARY The Zapris family established Sir Paz Estate in 1997, planting just under 11 ha of shiraz; the first release of 2001 scored an emphatic gold medal at the Victorian Wines Show 2003 as the highest scored entry. Subsequent vintages have not disappointed, and the success led to the planting of an additional 7 ha of merlot (even though the original intention was to simply make one wine). A cellar door is due to be established in 2006; till then the wines are available through the website.

ΨΨΨΨΨ Shiraz 2003 Very attractive, medium-bodied, spicy style; nice twist of red fruits; long finish, fine tannins. **RATING** 90 **DRINK** 2012 $35

Sirromet Wines

850–938 Mount Cotton Road, Mount Cotton, Qld 4165 **REGION** Queensland Coastal
T(07) 3206 2999 **F**(07) 3206 0900 **WEB** www.sirromet.com **OPEN** 7 days 10–5
WINEMAKER Adam Chapman, Craig Stevenson, Lindon Smallwood **EST.** 1998 **CASES** 66 500
SUMMARY This is an unambiguously ambitious venture, with the professed aim of creating Queensland's premier winery. The Morris family, founders of Sirromet Wines, which owns Mount Cotton Estate, retained a leading architect to design the striking state-of-the-art winery with an 80 000-case production capacity; the State's foremost viticultural consultant to plant the four major vineyards which total over 100 ha; and the most skilled winemaker practising in Queensland, Adam Chapman, to make the wine. It has a 200-seat restaurant, a wine club offering all sorts of benefits to its members, and is firmly aimed at the domestic and international tourist market, taking advantage of its situation, halfway between Brisbane and the Gold Coast. The intention is to move to a predominantly estate-based operation as quickly as the vineyards (planted to 14 varieties) come into production. Both the consistency and quality of the wines released so far and their modest pricing bode well for the future. Exports to the UK, the US and The Netherlands.

ΨΨΨΨ Seven Scenes Shiraz 2002 Generous, concentrated blackberry and plum; substantial but velvety tannins; positive oak. **RATING** 91 **DRINK** 2012 $22
Vineyard Selection Cabernet Merlot 2003 Solid wine; medium to full-bodied, with dark fruits and a tannin structure needing to soften. **RATING** 90 **DRINK** 2012 $16
Special Release Mick Doohan Cabernet Sauvignon 2002 Medium-bodied; attractive blackcurrant fruit with touches of earth; good texture and mouthfeel; fine, ripe tannins; 6% Merlot. **RATING** 90 **DRINK** 2010 $36

Vineyard Selection Petit Verdot 2003 Good varietal character and structure; black fruits and black olive; finely balanced tannins, nice touch of French oak; good varietal example. **RATING** 90 **DRINK** 2011 $ 16

ŢŢŢŢ **Seven Scenes Shiraz Viognier 2003** Clear colour; elegant, light to medium-bodied; bright, fresh cherry and plum; apricot touches ex Viognier; minimal tannins and oak. Cork. **RATING** 89 **DRINK** 2008 $ 22

Vineyard Selection Pinot Gris 2004 Lively, fresh, clean and crisp in summer seafood style; fresh aftertaste. **RATING** 88 **DRINK** 2007 $ 16

Vineyard Selection Shiraz 2003 Good colour; medium to full-bodied; powerful black fruits and savoury tannins; should age well. Screwcap. **RATING** 88 **DRINK** 2012 $ 16

Vineyard Selection Verdelho 2004 Better balanced than most; spiced apple and fruit salad; a touch of residual sugar flanked by acidity. **RATING** 87 **DRINK** Now $ 16

Vineyard Selection Marsanne Viognier 2004 Bright colour; positive pastille, apricot and peach ex Viognier; substrate of chalky minerality ex Marsanne. Interesting. Screwcap. **RATING** 87 **DRINK** Now $ 16

ŢŢŢ▽ **Perfect Day Beginnings 2004** **RATING** 86 **DRINK** Now $ 10.99
Vineyard Selection Chardonnay 2002 **RATING** 85 **DRINK** Now $ 16
Perfect Day Father Davadi Rose 2004 **RATING** 85 **DRINK** Now $ 12
Perfect Day Unwooded Chardonnay 2004 **RATING** 84 **DRINK** Now $ 12

ŢŢŢ **Perfect Day Burnbelt Syrah Cabernet Sauvignon Merlot 2002** **RATING** 83 $ 12

Sittella Wines ★★★★

100 Barrett Road, Herne Hill, WA 6056 **REGION** Swan Valley
T (08) 9296 2600 **F** (08) 9296 2600 **WEB** www.sittella.com.au **OPEN** Tues–Sun & public hols 11–4
WINEMAKER John Griffiths, Matthew Bourness **EST.** 1998 **CASES** 5000
SUMMARY Perth couple Simon and Maaike Berns acquired a 7-ha block (with 5 ha of vines) at Herne Hill, making the first wine in February 1998 and opening a most attractive cellar door facility later in the year. They also own the 10-ha Wildberry Springs Estate vineyard in the Margaret River region.

ŢŢŢŢ▽ **Margaret River Cabernet Sauvignon 2003** Light to medium-bodied; smooth, supple blackcurrant and cassis flavours; fine tannins; good length. Cork. **RATING** 90 **DRINK** 2010 $ 21.95

ŢŢŢŢ **Shiraz 2003** Medium to full-bodied; abundant ripe blackberry fruit; controlled tannins and oak; good length. Cork. **RATING** 89 **DRINK** 2010 $ 15.95

Verdelho 2004 Clean, fresh, light to medium-bodied; tropical fruit and a twist of lemon. Screwcap. **RATING** 87 **DRINK** 2007 $ 17.95

ŢŢŢ▽ **Unwooded Chardonnay 2004** Well above average, particularly for the Swan Valley; tangy, citrus-tinged; fair length. Screwcap. **RATING** 86 **DRINK** 2007 $ 15.95

ŢŢŢ **Chenin Blanc 2004** **RATING** 83 $ 14.20
Silk 2004 **RATING** 83 $ 14.95

S Kidman Wines ★★★

Riddoch Highway, Coonawarra, SA 5263 **REGION** Coonawarra
T (08) 8736 5071 **F** (08) 8736 5070 **WEB** www.kidmanwines.com.au **OPEN** 7 days 9–5
WINEMAKER John Innes (Contract) **EST.** 1984 **CASES** 8000
SUMMARY One of the district pioneers, with a 16-ha estate vineyard which is now fully mature. Limited retail distribution in Melbourne and Adelaide; exports through Australian Prestige Wines.

ŢŢŢŢ **Coonawarra Shiraz 2002** medium-bodied; pleasant black fruits on the mid-palate; fractionally dry finish. **RATING** 87 **DRINK** 2009 $ 18

ŢŢŢ▽ **Coonawarra Cabernet Sauvignon 2002** **RATING** 84 **DRINK** 2008 $ 20

Skillogalee ★★★★

Off Hughes Park Road, Sevenhill via Clare, SA 5453 **REGION** Clare Valley
T (08) 8843 4311 **F** (08) 8843 4343 **WEB** www.skillogalee.com.au **OPEN** 7 days 10–5
WINEMAKER Dave Palmer, Daniel Palmer **EST.** 1970 **CASES** 10 000

SUMMARY David and Diana Palmer purchased the small hillside stone winery from the George family at the end of the 1980s and have capitalised to the full on the exceptional fruit quality of the Skillogalee vineyards. The winery also has a well-patronised lunchtime restaurant. All the wines are generous and full flavoured, particularly the reds. In July 2002 the Palmers purchased next-door neighbour Waninga Vineyards, with 30 ha of 30-year-old vines, allowing a substantial increase in production without any change in quality or style. Exports to the UK, Switzerland, the US, Malaysia and Hong Kong.

ՇՇՇՇՇ **Clare Valley Shiraz 2003** Powerful, rich, concentrated blackberry, bitter chocolate and spice; good oak and tannins; no heat ex 14.5° alcohol. Screwcap. **RATING** 91 **DRINK** 2013 $ 25.50

ՇՇՇՇ **Clare Valley Riesling 2004** Glowing yellow-green; aromatic, rich, soft tropical, pineapple and lime; ready now. Screwcap. **RATING** 89 **DRINK** 2007 $ 19
Clare Valley Gewurztraminer 2004 Big, high-flavoured lychee and spice; full and soft; some alcohol heat. Screwcap. **RATING** 89 **DRINK** 2007 $ 20
Clare Valley Shiraz 2002 Still coming together, with fruit, oak and tannin in compartments; be patient. **RATING** 88 **DRINK** 2017 $ 27.50

Small Gully Wines ★★★

Roenfeldt Road, Greenock, SA 5355 (postal) **REGION** Barossa Valley
T 0411 690 047 **F** (08) 8376 4276 **OPEN** Not
WINEMAKER Stephen Black **EST.** 2000 **CASES** 2000
SUMMARY Stephen Black is producing a carefully positioned range of wines, from Barossa Valley Semillon and Gawler River Shiraz in cleanskin form progressing upwards to the Ringbark Red Shiraz Cabernet and the flagship, Small Gully Shiraz.

ՇՇՇՇ **Ringbark White Semillon Chardonnay 2002 RATING** 84 **DRINK** 2009

🐛 Smidge Wines ★★★★

62 Austral Terrace, Malvern, SA 5061 (postal) **REGION** Southeast Australia
T (08) 8272 0369 **F** (08) 8272 0369 **WEB** www.smidgewines.com **OPEN** Not
WINEMAKER Matt Wenk **EST.** 2004 **CASES** 900
SUMMARY Matt Wenk and Trish Callaghan have many things in common: their joint ownership of Smidge Wines, their marriage, and their real day jobs. Matt has a distinguished record as Flying Winemaker and, in Australia, with Tim Knappstein and then Peter Leske at Nepenthe Wines. These days he is the winemaker for Two Hands Winery (and Sandow's End). Trish holds a senior position in one of the world's largest IT services companies, and in 2003 was a finalist in the Australian Young Business Woman of the Year. The elegantly labelled wines are Le Grenouille (The Frog) Adelaide Hills Merlot, from a small vineyard in Verdun, and The Tardy Langhorne Creek Zinfandel which (and I quote) 'is named The Tardy in honour of Matt's reputation for timekeeping (or lack thereof)'. It is the first in what is planned to be a regional Zinfandel series.

ՇՇՇՇՇ **The Cellar Pod Adelaide Hills Viognier 2004** Light to medium-bodied; gently ripe citrus/pastille fruit; good balance and length; unusual elegance for the variety. **RATING** 90 **DRINK** 2007 $ 22.50

ՇՇՇՇ **De Grenouille Adelaide Hills Merlot 2003** Fresh, lively redcurrant, raspberry and mint aromas and flavours; light tannins; nice twist of French oak to the finish. **RATING** 89 **DRINK** 2008 $ 22.50
The Tardy Langhorne Creek Zinfandel 2003 Light colour; almost extravagant red fruit juice aromas typical of ripe zinfandel; light-bodied palate lets it down somewhat. **RATING** 87 **DRINK** Now $ 45

ՇՇՇ **The Tardy Langhorne Creek Zinfandel 2002 RATING** 82 $ 45

Smithbrook ★★★★☆

Smith Brook Road, Pemberton, WA 6260 **REGION** Pemberton
T (08) 9772 3557 **F** (08) 9772 3579 **WEB** www.smithbrook.com.au **OPEN** By appointment
WINEMAKER Michael Symons, Jonathan Farrington **EST.** 1988 **CASES** 15 000

SUMMARY Smithbrook is a major player in the Pemberton region, with 60 ha of vines in production. Owned by Petaluma/Lion Nathan, but continues its role as a contract grower for other companies, as well as supplying Petaluma's needs and making relatively small amounts of wine under its own label. Perhaps the most significant change has been the removal of Pinot Noir from the current range of products, and the introduction of Merlot. National distribution, and exports to the UK and Japan.

ŸŸŸŸŸ **Pemberton Sauvignon Blanc 2004** Fragrant, tropical passionfruit and gooseberry aromas; light-bodied, but long palate. **RATING** 91 **DRINK** Now $19.50

Naked Grape Sauvignon Blanc Semillon 2004 Aromatic, clean and fresh; an attractive array of gooseberry and passionfruit ex 75% Sauvignon Blanc, and lemon and mineral from the Semillon; good length and structure. Screwcap. **RATING** 91 **DRINK** 2008 $15

Yilgarn Blanc 2004 Barrel fermentation of sauvignon blanc in new French oak works well; gooseberry and herb fruit woven through oak; good structure and length; 160 cases made. Cork. **RATING** 90 **DRINK** 2010 $28

Pemberton Merlot 2002 Light to medium-bodied; elegant, clear-cut black olive and blackcurrant varietal fruit; fine tannins and oak. High-quality cork. **RATING** 90 **DRINK** 2010 $24

SmithLeigh Vineyard ★★★

53 Osborne Road, Lane Cove, NSW 2066 **REGION** Lower Hunter Valley
T 0418 484 565 **F** (02) 9420 2014 **OPEN** Not
WINEMAKER Andrew Margan (Contract) **EST.** 1997 **CASES** 3000
SUMMARY As the name suggests, a partnership between Rod and Ivija Smith and John and Jan Leigh, which purchased part of the long-established Lindeman Cobcroft Road vineyard from Southcorp in 1996. A lot of work in the vineyard, and skilled winemaking, has produced the right outcomes.

Smiths Vineyard NR

27 Groom Lane, Beechworth, Vic 3747 **REGION** Beechworth
T 0412 475 328 **F** (03) 5728 1603 **WEB** www.smithsvineyard.com.au **OPEN** Weekends & public hols 10–5 , or by appointment
WINEMAKER Jeanette Henderson, Will Flamsteed **EST.** 1978 **CASES** 600
SUMMARY Pete Smith established the first vineyard in Beechworth in 1978, with the encouragement of John Brown Jnr of Brown Brothers. Most of the production of the Smiths' 2.5 ha of chardonnay, cabernet sauvignon and merlot is sold to Shadowfax; the remainder is being made and sold under the Smiths Vineyard label; Flamsteed is one of the label brands.

Snobs Creek Wines ★★★

486 Goulburn Valley Highway, via Alexandra, Vic 3714 **REGION** Upper Goulburn
T (03) 5774 2017 **F** (03) 5774 2017 **WEB** www.snobscreekvineyard.com.au **OPEN** Weekends 11–5, closed in winter
WINEMAKER MasterWineMakers (Contract) **EST.** 1997 **CASES** 3500
SUMMARY The vineyard is situated where Snobs Creek joins the Goulburn River, 5 km below the Lake Eildon wall. A little over 8 ha were planted in 1996 by the Gillon family on a mix of river flats and harder hillsides. The varieties grown (and wines made) are shiraz, chardonnay, pinot noir, dolcetto, and a little roussanne. Winemaking is split between MasterWineMakers and an onsite winery. In addition to cellar door, mail order and website ordering, there is limited Melbourne distribution.

ŸŸŸŸ **Reserve Chardonnay 2003** Clean and understated; some cashew and gentle melon fruit; good length and balance; subtle oak. **RATING** 88 **DRINK** Now $25

ŸŸŸŸ **Shiraz 2003** **RATING** 85 **DRINK** 2009 $18

Snowy River Winery NR

Rockwell Road, Berridale, NSW 2628 **REGION** Southern New South Wales Zone
T (02) 6456 5041 **F** (02) 6456 5005 **OPEN** Wed–Sun, 7 days during school hols
WINEMAKER Manfred Plumecke **EST.** 1984 **CASES** 2500

SUMMARY An operation which relies entirely on the substantial tourist trade passing through or near Berridale on the way to the Snowy Mountains. The product range is, to put it mildly, eclectic; all the wines are said to be made onsite, and the grapes for all the white varietals are estate-grown.

Somerbury Estate ★★★☆

133 Jones Road, Somerville, Vic 3912 (postal) **REGION** Mornington Peninsula
T (03) 5977 7795 **F** (03) 5977 9695 **OPEN** Not
WINEMAKER Travis Bush (Contract) **EST.** 1998 **CASES** 5000
SUMMARY It's a long story, but after establishing a very large and very successful herb-producing business in the UK, Rob Frewer and family migrated to Australia in 1997. By another circuitous route they ended up with a property on the Mornington Peninsula, promptly planting pinot noir and chardonnay, then pinot gris, sauvignon blanc and merlot; they have since leased another vineyard, at Mt Eliza. Production is set to increase significantly from its already substantial level. Distribution by contract winemaker Dominion Wines; exports to the UK.

TTTT **Jones Road Cabernet Merlot 2003** Strong colour; very ripe cassis blackcurrant fruit; full entry; tapers off slightly. **RATING** 88 **DRINK** 2009 $ 32
Jones Road Chardonnay 2003 Strong, slightly feral oak/barrel ferment inputs; fruit struggles to keep up with the overlay; time may help. **RATING** 87 **DRINK** 2007 $ 28
Jones Road Pinot Gris 2004 Minerally, but, not unusually, without particular fruit definition; does have good length and overall mouthfeel. **RATING** 87 **DRINK** Now $ 28
Jones Road Pinot Noir 2003 Spicy savoury fruit; light to medium-bodied; oak tending towards vanilla. **RATING** 87 **DRINK** Now $ 32

TTTY **Jones Road Pinot Gris 2003** **RATING** 86 **DRINK** Now $ 28
Jones Road Unwooded Chardonnay 2004 **RATING** 85 **DRINK** Now

Somerset Hill Wines ★★★★☆

891 McLeod Road, Denmark, WA 6333 **REGION** Denmark
T (08) 9840 9388 **F** (08) 9840 9394 **WEB** www.somersethillwines.com.au **OPEN** 7 days 11–5 summer, winter 11–4
WINEMAKER James Kellie (Contract) **EST.** 1995 **CASES** 3000
SUMMARY Graham Upson commenced planting 11 ha of pinot noir, chardonnay, semillon, merlot and sauvignon blanc in 1995, and then opened a limestone cellar door sales area with sweeping views out over the ocean. Limited retail distribution in Melbourne and Sydney; exports to the UK, Denmark, Greenland and Poland.

TTTTT **Semillon 2004** Crisp and clean; unusual power and intensity on the palate; lime/tropical flavours almost akin to Riesling; not phenolic. Screwcap. **RATING** 94 **DRINK** 2012 $ 21

TTTTY **Sauvignon Blanc 2004** Clean; intense passionfruit and gooseberry aromas and flavours; nice mineral notes on the finish. Screwcap. **RATING** 93 **DRINK** 2007 $ 21

TTTT **Harmony Classic White 2004** Crisp, citrus, herb and a touch of nectarine; a synergistic blend in this cool climate. Semillon/Sauvignon Blanc/Chardonnay. Screwcap. **RATING** 88 **DRINK** 2007 $ 19.50
Pinot Noir 2002 Savoury, foresty, stemmy; austere style, but does have some varietal character; needs food. Cork. **RATING** 87 **DRINK** 2008 $ 30

TTTY **Unwooded Chardonnay 2004** **RATING** 86 **DRINK** 2007 $ 22

Sorrenberg ★★★☆

Alma Road, Beechworth, Vic 3747 **REGION** Beechworth
T (03) 5728 2278 **F** (03) 5728 2278 **WEB** www.sorrenberg.com **OPEN** Mon–Fri by appointment, most weekends 1–5 (by appointment)
WINEMAKER Barry Morey **EST.** 1986 **CASES** 1200
SUMMARY Barry and Jan Morey keep a low profile, but the wines from their 2.5-ha vineyard at Beechworth have a cult following not far removed from that of Giaconda; chardonnay, sauvignon blanc, cabernet sauvignon and gamay are the principal varieties planted on the north-facing, granitic slopes. Gamay and Chardonnay are two of the winery specialties.

▼▼▼▼ **Cabernet Sauvignon Cabernet Franc Malbec 2001** Slightly opaque colour; savoury earth, olive and black fruit mix; fine, savoury tannins. **RATING** 89 **DRINK** 2010 $ 30

Southern Dreams ★★★

10293 Deeside Coast Road, Northcliffe, WA 6262 **REGION** Pemberton
T (08) 9775 1027 **F** (08) 9389 9242 **OPEN** By appointment
WINEMAKER John Wade (Contract) **EST.** 1997 **CASES** NA
SUMMARY John Akehurst and family have planted 12 ha of sauvignon blanc, chardonnay, merlot, shiraz and cabernet sauvignon. Giant Karri, Marri and Jarrah trees surround the property, which has the Shannon National Park on one side. The adjacent 10-ha dam is home to a family of black swans, ducks and visiting pelicans. The vineyard is managed by Brian Roche and the wines are made by the highly credentialled John Wade. So far, the wines are sold through the website, by mail order and, to a lesser degree, through the cellar door.

▼▼▼▽ **Shiraz 2002 RATING** 84 **DRINK** 2007

Southern Highland Wines ★★★

Oldbury Road, Sutton Forest, NSW 2577 **REGION** Southern Highlands
T (02) 4868 2300 **F** (02) 4868 1808 **WEB** www.southernhighlandwines.com **OPEN** 7 days 10–5
WINEMAKER Eddy Rossi **EST.** 2003 **CASES** 10 000
SUMMARY The venture is owned by its five directors, who together have 50 years of experience in the wine industry and in commerce. John Gilbertson ran Ericsson in New Zealand and then China between 1983 and 2000. Darren Corradi and Eddy Rossi, respectively in charge of viticulture and winemaking, both have lengthy careers in various Griffith wineries, also the training ground for production director Frank Colloridi. New Zealand-born Simon Gilbertson graduated from Lincoln University with a degree in agriculture, and after 13 years in corporate life, purchased 3 vineyards in Hawke's Bay, NZ; he is de facto general manager and sales director. There are 41 ha of vines, a veritable fruit salad of pinot gris, riesling, gewurztraminer, sauvignon blanc, chardonnay, viognier, nebbiolo, sangiovese, pinot noir, shiraz and cabernet sauvignon.

▼▼▼▼ **Pinot Noir 2003** Black cherry, plum and some spice; light-bodied, but has elegance and balance. **RATING** 87 **DRINK** 2007
▼▼▼▽ **Golden Vale Botrytis 2003 RATING** 85 **DRINK** Now $ 35

🍇 Splitters Swamp Vineyards ★★★

Rose Valley, Bolivia via Tenterfield, NSW 2372 **REGION** Northern Slopes Zone
T (02) 6737 3640 **F** (02) 6737 3640 **OPEN** By appointment
WINEMAKER Mark Ravenscroft (Contract) **EST.** 1997 **CASES** 550
SUMMARY Ken Hutchison and Mandy Sharpe have made a cautious entry, planting a 1-ha vineyard equally to shiraz, cabernet sauvignon and merlot. As knowledge of the region grows, and as their experience as vignerons increases, they intend to increase the size of the vineyard and plant additional varieties. In the meantime they are producing Shiraz, Cabernet Merlot and Merlot, made by the skilled Mark Ravenscroft, and have already won several bronze medals for their wines.

▼▼▼▽ **Lloyd's Block Merlot 2002 RATING** 86 **DRINK** 2010 $ 18

Spoehr Creek Wines ★★★★

Greenhill Road, Balhannah, SA 5242 **REGION** Adelaide Hills
T (08) 8398 0884 **F** (08) 8398 0885 **OPEN** Weekends 11–5, or by appointment
WINEMAKER Stephen Black **EST.** 2001 **CASES** 2000
SUMMARY Philip Reid and Margie Ringwood purchased the previous Pibbin vineyard and winery (excluding the brand name and stock) in March 2001. It is one of a handful of onsite wineries in the Adelaide Hills; very few licences have been issued due to the desire to protect the quality of the ground water, which is an important source of Adelaide's water supply. The 6-ha vineyard is planted to merlot, pinot noir, sauvignon blanc and viognier, and the grape intake is supplemented by purchases from Adelaide Hills growers, and from the Riverland and Adelaide Plains for the rose and shiraz (at lower price points). A much expanded range of wines will take the production to around 5000 cases.

ΨΨΨΨ? **Adelaide Hills Pinot Noir 2002** Light to medium-bodied; pleasingly complex spice, bramble and plum mix; good mouthfeel, balance and length. RATING 91 DRINK 2008 $17.25

ΨΨΨΨ **Adelaide Hills Chardonnay 2003** Fragrant peach blossom aromas; medium-bodied; stone fruit and melon; good balance and length; subtle oak. RATING 89 DRINK 2007 $14.50

Adelaide Hills Viognier 2003 A mix of fresh, dried and pastille fruit flavours; nicely balanced. RATING 87 DRINK Now $16.50

Adelaide Hills Merlot 2002 Strongly varietal savoury/olive, but not green, aromas and flavours; light to medium-bodied; fine tannins, clean finish. RATING 87 DRINK 2008 $14.75

ΨΨΨ? **Adelaide Hills Sauvignon Blanc 2004** RATING 86 DRINK Now $14.50

Adelaide Hills Sparkling Merlot 2001 RATING 86 DRINK 2007 $20

ΨΨΨ **Riverland Shiraz 2002** RATING 83 $10

Springbrook Mountain Vineyard   NR

2824 Springbrook Road, Springbrook, Qld 4213 REGION Queensland Coastal
T (07) 5533 5300 F (07) 5533 5212 WEB www.springbrookvineyard.com OPEN 7 days 10–4
WINEMAKER Bruce Humphery-Smith (Contract) EST. 2000 CASES 2000
SUMMARY The 6-ha Springbrook Mountain Vineyard has been established on a 32-ha property surrounded by rainforest on the Springbrook Plateau, part of the volcanic rim of Mt Warning. It is also in the heart of a tourist wonderland, 45 minutes from Surfers Paradise and just north of the NSW border. A 100-tonne onsite winery is to be constructed, plus a church for weddings, 9 chalets and 10 permanent tents, all over the next 5 years. The attention of Bruce Humphery-Smith as winemaker suggests it's not all tourism, however.

SpringLane   ★★★★☆

PO Box 390, Yarra Glen, Vic 3775 REGION Yarra Valley
T (03) 9730 1107 F (03) 9739 0135 OPEN Not
WINEMAKER Tom Carson (Contract) EST. 1998 CASES 1800
SUMMARY SpringLane is the separately owned wine business of Graeme Rathbone, brother of Doug Rathbone, who is the (corporate) owner of Yering Station. The wines are made at Yering Station from grapes grown on the SpringLane Vineyard, which was established some years ago. There are 14 ha planted to merlot, pinot noir, shiraz, cabernet sauvignon, viognier and cabernet franc. Part of the production is sold to Yering Station, part used for the SpringLane label. They are sold by mail order and through specialty retail and restaurant outlets.

ΨΨΨΨΨ **Yarra Valley Shiraz Viognier 2003** Very good colour; highly aromatic and vibrant juicy berry fruit with the hallmark Viognier lift (7% Viognier); silky, supple and graceful medium-bodied wine. Cork. RATING 94 DRINK 2013

ΨΨΨΨ? **Yarra Valley Pinot Noir 2003** Medium-bodied; supple, smooth, black cherry, plum and spice; fine, ripe tannins; subtle oak. Cork. RATING 91 DRINK 2009

Yarra Valley Chardonnay 2003 Spotlessly clean; light-bodied; fresh, crisp citrus, stone fruit and mineral have absorbed the French oak fermentation and maturation; Chablis-like. Screwcap. RATING 90 DRINK 2009

Yarra Valley Viognier 2003 Light to medium-bodied; an attractive mix of pastille, stone fruit and a hint of apricot; texture ex 100% barrel fermentation in used French oak easily carries 14.6° alcohol; indeed, quite elegant overall. Cork. RATING 90 DRINK 2008

ΨΨΨΨ **Yarra Valley Cabernet Franc 2003** Light to medium-bodied; fair varietal character, but not a lot of sparkle; gently savoury tobacco; fine tannins, and has some redeeming length. Screwcap. RATING 88 DRINK 2009

Spring Ridge Wines   NR

880 Darbys Falls Road, Cowra, NSW 2794 REGION Cowra
T (02) 6341 3820 F (02) 6341 3820 OPEN By appointment
WINEMAKER Contract EST. 1997 CASES NA

SUMMARY Peter and Anne Jeffery have established 12.5 ha of shiraz, chardonnay, semillon, cabernet sauvignon and of merlot. They sell by far the greatest part of the grape production, having only a small amount made under the Spring Ridge Wines label.

Springton Cellars

NR

14 Miller Street, Springton, SA 5235 **REGION** Southern Flinders Ranges
T 0429 709 081 **F** (08) 8346 9533 **WEB** www.agale.com.au/winery **OPEN** 7 days 10–5
WINEMAKER Chris Thomas, Colin Forbes **EST.** 1999 **CASES** NA
SUMMARY Dr Allen E. Gale has a CV of extraordinary length, specialising in allergy. Together with Chris Thomas he has established 1 ha of vines at Wilmington, a very promising new area. The cabernet sauvignon and shiraz are made offsite by Chris Thomas, and are sold at the adjoining Café C Restaurant, by mail order, and at hotels and restaurants throughout the mid and far north.

Spring Vale Vineyards

130 Spring Vale Road, Cranbrook, Tas 7190 **REGION** East Coast Tasmania
T (03) 6257 8208 **F** (03) 6257 8598 **WEB** www.springvalewines.com **OPEN** Mon–Fri 10–5, or by appointment
WINEMAKER Kristen Cush, David Cush **EST.** 1986 **CASES** 5000
SUMMARY Rodney Lyne progressively established 1.5 ha each of pinot noir and chardonnay and then added 0.5 ha each of gewurztraminer and pinot gris; the latter produced a first crop in 1998. Frost has caused havoc from time to time; this is financially destructive and frustrating, for Spring Vale can, and does, produce first-class wines when the frost stays away. Exports to the UK.

🍷🍷🍷🍷🍷 **Gewurztraminer 2004** Plenty of fruit weight and power; more to lime juice than spice, but has real presence. **RATING** 91 **DRINK** 2009 $23
Chardonnay 2003 Excellent colour; medium-bodied and elegant; balanced and integrated oak with nectarine fruit; considerable length and high-profile Tasmanian acidity to close. **RATING** 90 **DRINK** 2008 $21
Pinot Noir 2003 Intense spicy/savoury backdrop to a mix of black cherry and plum fruit; frugal oak; good length. **RATING** 90 **DRINK** 2009 $35

🍷🍷🍷🍷 **Pinot Gris 2004** Potent and powerful pear, musk and spice; has length. **RATING** 87 **DRINK** 2008 $23

🍷🍷🍷🍷 **Pinot Noir Pinot Meunier 2004 RATING** 86 **DRINK** Now $18

🍷🍷🍷 **Chardonnay 2004 RATING** 83 $21

Springviews Wine

★★★

Woodlands Road, Porongurup, WA 6324 **REGION** Porongurup
T (08) 9853 2088 **F** (08) 9853 2098 **OPEN** 7 days 10–5
WINEMAKER Harewood Estate (Contract) **EST.** 1994 **CASES** 400
SUMMARY Andy and Alice Colquhoun planted their 5-ha vineyard (chardonnay, cabernet sauvignon and riesling) in 1994. The wine is sold through the cellar door and by mailing list.

🍷🍷🍷 **Cabernet Sauvignon 2003 RATING** 83 $20

Stanley Brothers

 ★★★

Barossa Valley Way, Tanunda, SA 5352 **REGION** Barossa Valley
T (08) 8563 3375 **F** (08) 8563 3758 **WEB** www.stanleybrothers.com.au **OPEN** 7 days 9–5
WINEMAKER Lindsay Stanley **EST.** 1994 **CASES** 15 000
SUMMARY Former Anglesey winemaker and industry veteran Lindsay Stanley established his own business in the Barossa Valley when he purchased (and renamed) the former Kroemer Estate in late 1994. As one would expect, the wines are competently made, although usually very light-bodied. The 21 ha of estate plantings have provided virtually all the grapes for the business. Exports to Switzerland, France, Luxembourg, Japan, Hong Kong, Malaysia and the US.

Stanton & Killeen Wines ★★★★★

Jacks Road, Murray Valley Highway, Rutherglen, Vic 3685 **REGION** Rutherglen
T (02) 6032 9457 **F** (02) 6032 8018 **WEB** www.stantonandkilleenwines.com.au **OPEN** Mon–Sat 9–5, Sun 10–5
WINEMAKER Chris Killeen **EST.** 1875 **CASES** 15 000
SUMMARY Chris Killeen has skilfully expanded the portfolio of Stanton & Killeen but without in any way compromising its reputation as a traditional maker of smooth, rich reds, some of Australia's best Vintage Ports, and attractive, fruity Muscats and Tokays. All in all, deserves far greater recognition. Exports to the UK, the US and New Zealand.

🍷🍷🍷🍷🍷 **Rare Rutherglen Muscat NV** Deep brown, olive-rimmed; has fantastic flair and style; in the mouth, there is still a core of fresh muscat fruit encased in a complex web of nutty, raisin-accented rancio, with spirit the hidden scalpel. **RATING** 96 **DRINK** Now **$** 100
Durif 2002 Deep, royal purple; dark, dense but not extractive black fruits and chocolate; carefully hewn and molded tannins; top example. Cork. **RATING** 94 **DRINK** 2022 **$** 30
Vintage Port 2000 Totally stylish; a complex, spicy mix of three Portuguese varieties (80% of total blend); harmonious, dry palate. **RATING** 94 **DRINK** 2017 **$** 27
Grand Rutherglen Muscat NV Full olive-brown; clear-cut rancio aligns with clean spirit and spicy/grapey fruit; excellent balance and structure, the tannins subliminal, but giving another dimension to the flavour; very long, fine finish. **RATING** 94 **DRINK** Now **$** 75

🍷🍷🍷🍷½ **Classic Rutherglen Tokay NV** Light to medium golden-brown; great clarity and freshness, with honey and tea leaf aromas; lively and vibrant, with similar finesse and harmony to the Campbell wines. Finishes with excellent acidity and a clean, crisp aftertaste. **RATING** 92 **DRINK** Now **$** 25
Classic Rutherglen Muscat NV Has a great display of grapey varietal fruit, skilfully combining younger and older material. Fine tannins give the wine extra structure and intensity. **RATING** 92 **DRINK** Now **$** 25

🍷🍷🍷🍷 **Cabernet Merlot 2003** Ripe blackcurrant and blackberry fruit, neither jammy nor over-extracted; ripe tannins. Cork. **RATING** 89 **DRINK** 2012 **$** 22
Rutherglen Muscat NV Bright tawny, with a faint crimson blush; high-toned spirit on the bouquet lifts rather than obscures the fruit; intense, raisiny yet fresh. **RATING** 89 **DRINK** Now **$** 16.50

Stanton Estate ★★★

135 North Isis Road, Childers, Qld 4660 **REGION** Queensland Zone
T (07) 4126 1255 **F** (07) 4126 1823 **OPEN** Weekends 10–5, or by appointment
WINEMAKER Symphony Hill (Contract) **EST.** 2000 **CASES** 500
SUMMARY Keith and Joy Stanton have established 2 ha of verdelho, marsanne, cabernet sauvignon and merlot using organic growing methods, and are seeking organic certification, making Stanton Estate the only organically grown wine in Queensland. The wines are also made to BFA standards, which permit the use of some SO_2, but within strictly controlled limits. The wines sell out rapidly through the cellar door and Woodgate Restaurant.

🍷🍷🍷½ **Verdelho 2004** **RATING** 86 **DRINK** Now

🍷🍷🍷 **Cabernet Merlot Reserve 2004** **RATING** 80

Star Lane NR

RMB 1167, Star Lane, Beechworth, Vic 3747 **REGION** Beechworth
T (03) 5728 7268 **OPEN** By appointment
WINEMAKER Keppell Smith (Contract) **EST.** 1996 **CASES** NA
SUMMARY Liz and Brett Barnes have established 4 ha of shiraz and merlot (planted in 1996) with further plantings of riesling and chardonnay planned. When Liz Barnes completed her winemaking course, she will take responsibility for winemaking from Keppell Smith (of Savaterre), but even then, they will continue to sell 70% of their grape production.

Statford Park NR

Farmgate at Statford Park, Pearson's Lane, Wildes Meadow, NSW 2577 **REGION** Southern Highlands
T (02) 4885 1101 **F** (02) 4885 1035 **WEB** www.statford.com.au **OPEN** 7 days 10–5
WINEMAKER Contract **EST.** 2000 **CASES** 1000
SUMMARY Statford Park is situated in the triangle bounded by Robertson 5 km east, Burrawang 5 km to the northwest and Wildes Meadow, some 6 km southwest. The Wildes Meadow Creek rises in the northeastern end of the valley, runs east–west through to Lake Fitzroy a few kilometres further west. In 1997/8, 6500 vines were planted; the first wine release was in June 2001. The cellar door has an exotic array of lavender and other products.

Station Creek NR

Edi Road, Cheshunt, Vic 3678 **REGION** King Valley
T (03) 5729 8265 **F** (03) 5729 8056 **OPEN** 7 days
WINEMAKER Warren Proft (Contract) **EST.** 1999 **CASES** 2000
SUMMARY David and Sharon Steer have established 5 ha of vineyards at Cheshunt, planted to sauvignon blanc, cabernet sauvignon, merlot and shiraz. Sales are by mail order and through the cellar door, which offers light meals, crafts, a gallery and local produce.

Staughton Vale Vineyard ★★★

20 Staughton Vale Road, Anakie, Vic 3221 **REGION** Geelong
T (03) 5284 1477 **F** (03) 5284 1229 **OPEN** Fri–Mon & public hols 10–5, or by appointment
WINEMAKER Paul Chambers **EST.** 1986 **CASES** 2000
SUMMARY Paul Chambers has 6 ha of closely planted vines, with the accent on the classic Bordeaux mix of cabernet sauvignon, merlot, cabernet franc and petit verdot, although chardonnay and pinot noir are also planted. Weekend lunches are available at the Staughton Cottage Restaurant.

 Reserve Cabernet Sauvignon 2001 Clean; nice blackcurrant/cassis fruit, but oak is overly intrusive. **RATING** 87 **DRINK** 2008

Steels Creek Estate ★★★★☆

1 Sewell Road, Steels Creek, Vic 3775 **REGION** Yarra Valley
T (03) 5965 2448 **F** (03) 5965 2448 **WEB** www.steelsckestate.com.au **OPEN** Weekends & public hols 10–6, or by appointment
WINEMAKER Simon Peirce **EST.** 1981 **CASES** 400
SUMMARY A 1.7-ha vineyard, family-operated since establishment in 1981, located in the picturesque Steels Creek Valley with views towards to the Kinglake NP. Red wines are made onsite, white wines with the assistance of consultants. Production is predominantly sold through the cellar door, where visitors can also view the winemaking operations.

 Yarra Valley Chardonnay 2003 Glowing yellow-green; elegant stone fruit and melon drive the wine with background support from quality French oak. Screwcap. **RATING** 93 **DRINK** 2010 $18
Yarra Valley Shiraz 2002 Very unusual lantana notes within a bouquet of black fruits and pepper; very concentrated, powerful and potent, reflecting the tiny crop; savoury tannins; some question about possible bacterial activity. Pro Cork. **RATING** 91 **DRINK** 2015 $22
 Yarra Valley Cabernet Sauvignon 2002 Mint, berry, leaf, spice and dust; brisk acidity; arms and legs. Pro Cork. **RATING** 88 **DRINK** 2009 $20

🐿 Stefani Estate ★★★★

Lot 3, Rochester Road, Heathcote, Vic 3523 **REGION** Yarra Valley/Heathcote
T (03) 9579 1193 **F** (03) 9579 1532 **OPEN** By appointment
WINEMAKER Mario Marson **EST.** 2002 **CASES** 1100
SUMMARY Stefano Stefani came to Australia in 1985. Business success has allowed him and his wife Rina to follow in the footsteps of Stefano's grandfather, who had a vineyard and was an avid wine collector. The first property they acquired was at Long Gully Road in the Yarra Valley, with pinot

grigi, cabernet sauvignon, chardonnay and pinot noir. The next acquisition was in Heathcote, where he acquired a property adjoining that of Mario Marson, and both built a winery and established 8.5 ha of vineyard, planted predominantly to shiraz, then cabernet sauvignon and merlot and a mixed block of cabernet franc, malbec and petit verdot. In 2003 a second Yarra Valley property was purchased where Dijon clones of chardonnay and pinot noir have been planted. Mario Marson (ex Mount Mary) oversees the operation of all the vineyards and is also the winemaker. He is also able to use the winery to make his own brand wines, completing the business link.

♥♥♥♥♡ **Heathcote Shiraz 2002** A rich and sensuous array of red and black fruits; medium-bodied, and not over the top; gently ripe tannins. RATING 93 DRINK 2012 $ 35

♥♥♥♡ **Yarra Valley Pinot Grigio 2003** Pale pink; minerally earthy flavours, the fruit downplayed; lingering acidity adds to the length. RATING 86 DRINK 2007 $ 20

Stefano Lubiana ★★★★★

60 Rowbottoms Road, Granton, Tas 7030 REGION Southern Tasmania
T (03) 6263 7457 F (03) 6263 7430 WEB www.slw.com.au OPEN Sun–Thurs 11–3 (closed some public hols)
WINEMAKER Steve Lubiana EST. 1990 CASES 10 000
SUMMARY The charming, self-effacing Steve Lubiana has moved from one extreme to the other, having run Lubiana Wines at Moorook in the SA Riverland for many years before moving to Granton to set up a substantial winery. The estate-produced Stefano Lubiana wines come from 18 ha of beautifully located vineyards sloping down to the Derwent River. All the Lubiana wines are immaculately crafted. Exports to Denmark and Japan.

♥♥♥♥♥ **Estate Pinot Noir 2002** Holding colour very well; rich and complex dark fruit aromas; delicious, complex texture, structure and flavour, again with dark plum and spice fruit. RATING 95 DRINK 2010 $ 49
Merlot 2003 Good colour; perfectly expressed varietal character in a medium-bodied frame; small red fruits, fine, silky tannins. Trophy winner 2005 Tasmanian Wines Show. RATING 94 DRINK 2010 $ 25

♥♥♥♥♡ **Vintage Brut 1998** Complex, yet very refined and elegant; long but precise; crystal bright finish. RATING 93 DRINK 2008 $ 47
Sur Lie Chardonnay 2002 Touches of biscuit and toast aromas ex lees; relatively soft stone fruit and peach flavours; good acidity to balance. RATING 90 DRINK 2007 $ 24.99
Primavera Pinot Noir 2003 Medium purple-red; clean, dark plum and spice aromas joined by a hint of mocha on the palate; firm acidity; deserves time. RATING 90 DRINK 2013 $ 24.99

♥♥♥♥ **Pinot Grigio 2004** Delicate, crisp, clean, minerally style; some nashi pear. RATING 87 DRINK 2008 $ 24

♥♥♥♡ **Primavera Chardonnay 2003** RATING 85 DRINK 2007 $ 24

Steler Estate Wines NR

26 Belvedere Close, Pakenham Upper, Vic 3810 REGION Gippsland
T (03) 9796 5766 F (03) 9796 5695 WEB www.stelerestatewines.com.au OPEN By appointment
WINEMAKER Tomo Steller EST. 1996 CASES 460
SUMMARY Croatian-born Tomo Steler had a tough upbringing as an orphan in his native country, but he overcame many obstacles to obtain a degree in forestry before migrating to Australia in 1970. Shortly thereafter he met wife Suzanna, and together they established a successful UV coating and spray-painting business. They planted the first vines in 1996, intending simply to make wine for their own consumption, but further plantings in 1997 have resulted in a little less than a hectare of shiraz and merlot.

Stellar Ridge Estate ★★★

Clews Road, Cowaramup, WA 6284 REGION Margaret River
T (08) 9755 5635 F (08) 9755 5636 WEB www.stellar-ridge.com OPEN 7 days 10–5
WINEMAKER Mark Lane EST. 1994 CASES 2000

SUMMARY Colin and Helene Hellier acquired a 49-ha grazing property at Cowaramup in 1993; it included 2.5 ha of chardonnay and sauvignon blanc planted in 1987. A large dam was constructed in 1994, and the following year 11 ha of new vineyards and 4 ha of olive trees were planted; 1.6 ha of zinfandel followed in 1996, bringing total plantings to 15.1 ha. The majority of the 100 tonne grape production is sold to other local wineries; 14 to 15 tonnes are retained for the Stellar Ridge label. The wines are sold exclusively through the cellar door and by mailing list.

Stephen John Wines ★★★★

Government Road, Watervale, SA 5452 **REGION** Clare Valley
T (08) 8843 0105 **F** (08) 8843 0105 **OPEN** 7 days 11–5
WINEMAKER Stephen John **EST.** 1994 **CASES** 10 000
SUMMARY The John family is one of the best-known in the Barossa Valley, with branches running Australia's best cooperage (AP John & Sons) and providing the chief winemaker of Lindemans (Philip John) and the former chief winemaker of Quelltaler (Stephen John). Stephen and Rita John have now formed their own family business in the Clare Valley, based on a 6-ha vineyard overlooking the town of Watervale, and supplemented by modest intake from a few local growers. The cellar door sales area is an 80-year-old stable which has been renovated and is full of rustic charm. The significantly increased production and good quality of the current releases has led to the appointment of distributors in the eastern states; exports to the UK, the US, Malaysia and Singapore.

Step Road Winery ★★★☆

Davidson Road, Langhorne Creek, SA 5255 (postal) **REGION** Langhorne Creek
T (08) 8537 3342 **F** (08) 8537 3357 **WEB** www.steprd.com **OPEN** Not
WINEMAKER Rob Dundon **EST.** 1998 **CASES** 70 000
SUMMARY Step Road has 96 ha of vineyard in Langhorne Creek, and 40 ha in the Adelaide Hills, supplementing the production from those vineyards with cabernet sauvignon and shiraz purchased from McLaren Vale. It is an autonomous business, but operationally part of the Beresford Wines group. National distribution; exports to the UK, the US, Denmark, Hong Kong and New Zealand.

 Langhorne Creek Sangiovese 2002 Attractive, light to medium-bodied wine; quite strongly varietal sour cherries and spice; good balance. Value. Cork. **RATING** 88 **DRINK** 2009 $18
Adelaide Hills Sauvignon Blanc 2004 Light-bodied, clean and fresh; passionfruit/tropical aromas and flavours; good value. Screwcap. **RATING** 87 **DRINK** Now $15
Langhorne Creek Shiraz 2002 Light to medium-bodied; smooth, supple red fruits; slightly simple. **RATING** 87 **DRINK** 2010 $20

 Langhorne Creek Cabernet Sauvignon 2002 RATING 85 **DRINK** 2009 $20

Sterling Heights NR

PO Box 115, Launceston, Tas 7250 **REGION** Northern Tasmania
T (03) 6376 1419 **OPEN** Not
WINEMAKER Moorilla Estate (Contract) **EST.** 1988 **CASES** 400
SUMMARY Geoff and Jenny Wells have sold their 2-ha vineyard at Winkleigh, which was the source for the Sterling Heights wines. They have retained the Sterling Heights brand, and will continue to sell the packaged wine they have in stock. A new planting at St Helens is being contemplated.

Stevens Brook Estate ★★★

620 High Street, Echuca, Vic 3564 **REGION** Perricoota
T (03) 5480 1916 **F** (03) 5480 2004 **OPEN** 7 days 10–5
WINEMAKER Mal Stewart, David Cowburn **EST.** 1995 **CASES** 8000
SUMMARY The Stevens Brook Estate vineyard was established in 1996, with the first commercial production in 1999. Initially the grapes were sold; they are now being used for the Stevens Brook Estate label. The yield is restricted to 3–4 tonnes per acre, roughly half the regional average. The 1500-tonne winery was built in 1999 on a separate 40 ha property on the Echuca side of the Murray River, which will be fully planted. Just to complicate the picture a little further, Bill Stevens has

established the cellar door operation in the Port of Echuca district, the philosophy being to take the cellar door to the customer, rather than try to draw the customer to the vineyard.

ŦŦŦŦ **Verdelho 2004** Fresh, lively citrussy overtones to fruit salad; length and life. Twin Top. Second bottle tasted; first bottle had extreme TCA taint. **RATING** 87 **DRINK** 2008 $ 20

ŦŦŦ **Bacchus Liqueur Verdelho NV RATING** 83 $ 15
Selene Liqueur Sangiovese NV RATING 83 $ 15

Sticks ★★★★☆

Glenview Road, Yarra Glen, Vic 3775 **REGION** Yarra Valley
T (03) 9739 0666 **F** (03) 9739 0633 **WEB** www.sticks.com.au **OPEN** 7 days 10–5
WINEMAKER Rob Dolan **EST.** 2000 **CASES** 25 000
SUMMARY In February 2005 the former Yarra Ridge winery, with a 3000-tonne capacity, and 24 ha of vineyards planted mainly in 1983, was acquired by a partnership headed by Rob 'Sticks' Dolan. He will make all the Sticks wines here, and also provide contract making facilities for wineries throughout the Yarra Valley.

ŦŦŦŦ℗ **Chardonnay 2004** Very attractive sweet white peach/stone fruit aromas and flavours; length and intensity; a subtle flick of oak. Screwcap. **RATING** 93 **DRINK** 2010 $ 14.99
Shiraz 2003 Abundant weight and supple mouthfeel; hints of spice to a basket of ripe, red fruits; fine tannins and good oak. **RATING** 92 **DRINK** 2013 $ 18
Cabernet Sauvignon 2003 Good colour; plenty of weight and depth; sweet cassis and blackcurrant neatly tempered on the finish by fine tannins and good oak. **RATING** 90 **DRINK** 2013 $ 18

ŦŦŦŦ **Sauvignon Blanc 2004** Clean, firm and minerally aromas; no reduction; lemon and herb fruit run through the length of the palate; above average, and good value. **RATING** 89 **DRINK** 2007 $ 16
Merlot 2003 Fresh, vibrant and bright fruits; minimal oak; slightly one-dimensional; similar to Punt Road. **RATING** 87 **DRINK** 2010 $ 18

🍂 Stirling Wines ★★★☆

PO Box 12, Lochinvar, NSW 2321 **REGION** Lower Hunter Valley
T (02) 4930 6189 **F** (02) 4930 6186 **OPEN** Not
WINEMAKER David Hook (Contract) **EST.** 2000 **CASES** 3000
SUMMARY The Stirling Wines vineyard is adjacent to the original Hunter Valley vineyard of WC Wentworth, one of the leading pioneers of NSW, who established his Windermere Vineyard in the 1830s. There are 1.5 ha each of semillon and verdelho and 0.25 ha of shiraz planted; the wines are sold direct to Hunter Valley and Sydney restaurants and selected retailers, but are also available by mail order. Small exports to Hong Kong.

Stone Bridge Estate NR

RMB 189, Holleys Road, Manjimup, WA 6258 **REGION** Manjimup
T (08) 9773 1371 **F** (08) 9773 1309 **OPEN** By appointment
WINEMAKER Syd Hooker, Kate Hooker **EST.** 1991 **CASES** 3000
SUMMARY Syd and Sue Hooker purchased the property on which Stone Bridge Estate is established in 1990, and planted the first vines that year. A subsequent planting in 1996 has increased the vineyard size to 8 ha, with shiraz, pinot noir and chardonnay, cabernet sauvignon, merlot, caberent franc, semillon, sauvignon blanc and sangiovese. The pinot noir and chardonnay go to provide the Methode Champenoise, made (onsite, like all the other wines) by daughter Kate, a graduate winemaker and viticulturist from the Lycee Viticole d'Avize in Champagne.

🍂 Stonebrook Estate ★★★

RSM 361, Busselton, WA 6280 (postal) **REGION** Margaret River
T (08) 9755 1104 **F** (08) 9755 1001 **WEB** www.stonebrookestate.com **OPEN** Not
WINEMAKER Mark Lane (Contract) **EST.** 1997 **CASES** 750

SUMMARY Perth lawyer Jonathan Meyer decided on a sea change in 1992, moving with his family to their beach house at Dunsborough. From the outset, the intention was to establish a vineyard, and a property was selected in 1996; planting of 7.8 ha of chardonnay, cabernet sauvignon and merlot began in 1997. Most of the production is sold; part is made under the Stonebrook Estate label, and a small amount under the second label, Station Gully.

 TTTT **The Small Block Chardonnay 2003** Light to medium-bodied, but quite complex; nicely balanced and integrated French oak; nutty characters to the fruit. Produced from a mere 336 vines. RATING 89 DRINK 2010

TTTY **Station Gully Cabernet Merlot 2003** RATING 86 DRINK 2008 $ 14
Margaret River Cabernet Sauvignon 2002 RATING 86 DRINK 2007 $ 23.50
Margaret River Chardonnay 2003 RATING 85 DRINK 2008 $ 24

Stone Chimney Creek   NR

PO Box 401, Angaston, SA 5353 REGION Barossa Valley
T (08) 8565 3339 F (08) 8565 3339 OPEN Not
WINEMAKER Chris Ringland EST. 1989 CASES 70
SUMMARY Another tiny production wine produced by ringmaster Chris Ringland, and effectively sold only in the US through The Grateful Palate: 2 ha of old-vine shiraz produce between 60 and 100 cases per year of wine at a breathtaking price. Chris Ringland politely explains that due to the tiny production, he cannot routinely provide bottles for evaluation.

Stone Coast Wines

18 North Terrace, Adelaide, SA 5000 (postal) REGION Wrattonbully
T (08) 8239 4949 F (08) 8239 4959 WEB www.stonecoastwines.com OPEN Not
WINEMAKER Steve Maglieri, Scott Rawlinson EST. 1997 CASES 900
SUMMARY The development of the 33 ha of cabernet sauvignon and 11 ha of shiraz which constitutes the vineyard was exceptionally difficult. It is situated on a terra rossa ridge top, but had unusually thick limestone slabs running through it, which had caused others to bypass the property. A 95-tonne bulldozer was hired to deep rip the limestone, but was unequal to the task, and ultimately explosives had to be used to create sufficient inroads to allow planting. Only 15% of the production from the vineyard is used by the immensely experienced Steve Maglieri to make the wines.

TTTTT **Cabernet Sauvignon 2002** Medium-bodied; nicely balanced blackberry and chocolate fruit; fine tannin finish. Has improved out of sight since first tasted. RATING 94 DRINK 2012 $ 20

TTTTY **Limestone Coast Shiraz 2002** Excellent depth of blackberry and dark plum fruit; overall medium-bodied, with ripe tannins and subtle oak. RATING 90 DRINK 2012 $ 20

Stonehaven   ★★★★★

Riddoch Highway, Padthaway, SA 5271 REGION Padthaway
T (08) 8765 6166 F (08) 8765 6177 WEB www.stonehavenvineyards.com.au OPEN 7 days 10–4
WINEMAKER Susanne Bell, Gary Stokes EST. 1998 CASES 200 000
SUMMARY It is, to say the least, strange that it should have taken 30 years for a substantial winery to be built at Padthaway. However, when Hardys took the decision, it was no half measure: $20 million has been invested in what is the largest greenfields winery built in Australia for more than 20 years. Exports to the US, Canada and the UK.

TTTTT **Limited Vineyard Release Padthaway Chardonnay 2000** Beautifully focused and structured; lingering nectarine and citrus fruit melded with very good barrel ferment oak. RATING 95 DRINK 2010 $ 28
Limited Release Coonawarra/Padthaway Cabernet Sauvignon 2000 Excellent texture and mouthfeel from both barrel and bottle age; supple, silky black fruits and tannins; distinguished wine. RATING 95 DRINK 2014
Limited Release Padthaway Shiraz 2001 Still has strong colour; tight blackberry fruit and lingering but not abrasive tannins run through a particularly long finish. RATING 94 DRINK 2014

ŶŶŶŶ **Limestone Coast Cabernet Sauvignon 2000** A smooth and supple mix of blackcurrant and redcurrant fruit; fine tannins and oak. **RATING** 89 **DRINK** 2008 $19
Stepping Stone Padthaway Chardonnay 2004 Bright colour; light to medium-bodied; classic grapefruit, melon and tropical fruit mix; easy flow; fruit-driven. Screwcap. **RATING** 88 **DRINK** 2009
Limestone Coast Shiraz 2002 Generous black fruits and ripe tannins; good balance, although on the oaky side. **RATING** 88 **DRINK** 2012

ŶŶŶŶ **Winemaker's Release Gewurztraminer 2004** **RATING** 86 **DRINK** 2008 $18
Limestone Coast Viognier 2004 **RATING** 86 **DRINK** 2007
Winemaker's Release Sangiovese 2003 **RATING** 86 **DRINK** 2007 $20
Limestone Coast Chardonnay 2003 **RATING** 85 **DRINK** Now
Stepping Stone Padthaway Shiraz 2002 **RATING** 85 **DRINK** 2009 $12.99

Stonehurst Cedar Creek ★★★

Wollombi Road, Cedar Creek, NSW 2325 **REGION** Lower Hunter Valley
T (02) 4998 1576 **F** (02) 4998 0008 **WEB** www.cedarcreekcottages.com.au **OPEN** 7 days 10–5
WINEMAKER Contract **EST.** 1995 **CASES** 3500
SUMMARY Stonehurst (subtitled Cedar Creek) has been established by Daryl and Phillipa Heslop on a historic 220-ha property in the Wollombi Valley, underneath the Pokolbin Range. They have 6.5 ha of vineyards, planted to chambourcin, semillon, chardonnay and shiraz; the wines are made at Monarch Winemaking Services. A substantial part of the business, however, is the 6 self-contained cottages on the property, which can be seen on their website.

ŶŶŶŶ **Hunter Valley Semillon 1999** Developed colour; curious wine; appropriately developed, but little happening on the palate; crisp finish. Cork. **RATING** 87 **DRINK** Now $17

ŶŶŶŶ **Hunter Valley Chambourcin Shiraz 2003** **RATING** 86 **DRINK** 2008 $19.50

Stonemont ★★★

421 Rochford Road, Rochford, Vic 3442 **REGION** Macedon Ranges
T (03) 5429 1540 **F** (03) 5429 1878 **OPEN** By appointment
WINEMAKER Contract **EST.** 1997 **CASES** 500
SUMMARY Ray and Gail Hicks began the establishment of their vineyard in 1993, extending plantings to a total of 1.5 ha each of chardonnay and pinot noir in 1996. The tiny production of Chardonnay, Pinot Noir and Sparkling Macedon is contract-made by various Macedon Ranges winemakers, and the wines are sold by mail order and (by appointment) through the cellar door, which is situated in a heritage stone barn in the vineyard.

ŶŶŶŶ **Macedon Brut 2000** Citrussy/lemony acidity; clean, but somewhat singular; needs time. **RATING** 88 **DRINK** 2008

ŶŶŶŶ **Chardonnay 2003** **RATING** 86 **DRINK** 2008
Chardonnay 2002 **RATING** 86 **DRINK** 2007

ŶŶŶ **Pinot Noir 2002** **RATING** 82

Stone Ridge NR

35 Limberlost Road, Glen Aplin, Qld 4381 **REGION** Granite Belt
T (07) 4683 4211 **F** (07) 4683 4211 **OPEN** 7 days 10–5
WINEMAKER Jim Lawrie, Anne Kennedy **EST.** 1981 **CASES** 2100
SUMMARY Jim Lawrie and Anne Kennedy were among the new arrivals at the start of the expansion of the Granite Belt region. They have progressed from a tiny make of Shiraz in a microscopic winery to a very much larger business, with some particularly interesting varietal wines.

Stoney Rise ★★★★

Hendersons Lane, Gravelly Beach, Tas 7276 **REGION** Northern Tasmania
T 0419 540 770 **F** (03) 6344 3684 **OPEN** 7 days 10–4
WINEMAKER Joe Holyman **EST.** 2000 **CASES** 2000

SUMMARY Changes came fast at Stoney Rise in 2004. Surf and sun-loving Joe Holyman has gone back to his native Tasmania, having purchased one of the State's most distinguished vineyard sites, Rotherhythe. Though small, this Tamar Valley vineyard has produced magnificent Pinot Noir and Cabernet Sauvignon (the latter to be replaced by Chardonnay) in the past. The three SA wines in the Stoney Rise portfolio, Sauvignon Blanc, Shiraz and Hey Hey Rose, are still being produced; 2005 was the first vintage from the Tamar Valley. Exports to the US.

ŸŸŸŸŸ **Limestone Coast Sauvignon Blanc 2004** Spotlessly clean; strong herb, grass, gooseberry and mineral aromas and flavours; clean, crisp, dry finish; good length. Screwcap. **RATING** 92 **DRINK** 2007 $ 20

ŸŸŸŸ **Holyman Pinot Noir 2003** Medium-bodied; ripe plum fruit; quite supple; good line. **RATING** 89 **DRINK** 2009 $ 25

ŸŸŸŸ **Holyman Chardonnay 2003** **RATING** 86 **DRINK** 2008 $ 25
Holyman Chardonnay 2004 **RATING** 85 **DRINK** 2007 $ 25
Hey Hey Mclaren Vale Rose 2004 **RATING** 85 **DRINK** Now $ 18

Stonier Wines ★★★★★

362 Frankston–Flinders Road, Merricks, Vic 3916 **REGION** Mornington Peninsula
T (03) 5989 8300 **F** (03) 5989 8709 **WEB** www.stoniers.com.au **OPEN** 7 days 11–5
WINEMAKER Geraldine McFaul **EST.** 1978 **CASES** 25 000
SUMMARY One of the most senior wineries on the Mornington Peninsula, now part of the Petaluma group, which is in turn owned by Lion Nathan of New Zealand. Wine quality is assured, as is the elegant, restrained style of the majority of the wines. Exports to all major markets.

ŸŸŸŸŸ **Reserve Pinot Noir 2003** Expressive and voluminous aromas of cherry blossom and plum; elegant, long palate; very good tannins. **RATING** 95 **DRINK** 2009 $ 45
Reserve Chardonnay 2003 Strong malolactic overlay in traditional Mornington Peninsula style, yet retains good acidity and fruit expression; melon, stone fruit and a touch of citrus. **RATING** 94 **DRINK** 2009 $ 40

Stratherne Vale Estate NR

Campbell Street, Caballing, WA 6312 **REGION** Central Western Australia Zone
T (08) 9881 2148 **F** (08) 9881 3129 **OPEN** Not
WINEMAKER Contract **EST.** 1980 **CASES** 600
SUMMARY Stratherne Vale Estate stretches the viticultural map of Australia yet further. It is near Narrogin, which is north of the Great Southern region and south of the most generous extension of the Darling Ranges. The closest viticultural area of note is at Wandering, to the northeast.

Strathewen Hills ★★★★

1090 Strathewen Road, Strathewen, Vic 3099 **REGION** Yarra Valley
T (03) 9714 8464 **F** (03) 9714 8464 **OPEN** By appointment
WINEMAKER William Christophersen **EST.** 1991 **CASES** NA
SUMMARY Joan and William (whom I have always called Bill) Christophersen began the slow process of establishing Strathewen Hills in 1991. The vineyard was established with ultra-close spacing, with 3 ha planted predominantly in pinot noir, chardonnay, shiraz, merlot and small amounts of cabernet sauvignon, cabernet franc and a few bits and pieces, but frost caused persistent losses until protective sprinklers were installed. Since then a series of high-quality small-volume wines have been made.

Strathkellar NR

Murray Valley Highway, Cobram, Vic 3644 **REGION** Goulburn Valley
T (03) 5873 5274 **F** (03) 5873 5270 **OPEN** 7 days 10–5
WINEMAKER Tahbilk (Contract) **EST.** 1990 **CASES** 2000
SUMMARY Dick Parkes planted his 6-ha vineyard to chardonnay, shiraz and chenin blanc in 1990, and has the wine contract-made at Tahbilk by Alister Purbrick. This guarantees quality, and the prices are modest.

Strath Valley Vineyard   NR

Strath Valley Road, Strath Creek, Vic 3658 **REGION** Upper Goulburn
T (03) 5784 9229 **F** (03) 5784 9381 **OPEN** Weekends 10–5, or by appointment
WINEMAKER Contract **EST.** 1994 **CASES** 1300
SUMMARY Chris and Robyn Steen have established 12.5 ha of chardonnay, sauvignon blanc, cabernet sauvignon and shiraz. By far the largest part of the production is sold as grapes; the Strath Valley Vineyard Sauvignon Blanc and Shiraz are sold through the cellar door.

Straws Lane   ★★★★☆

1282 Mount Macedon Road, Hesket, Vic 3442 **REGION** Macedon Ranges
T (03) 9654 9380 **F** (03) 9663 6300 **OPEN** Weekends & public hols 10–4, or by appointment
WINEMAKER Stuart Anderson, John Ellis (Contract) **EST.** 1987 **CASES** 1800
SUMMARY The Straws Lane vineyard was planted in 1987, but the Straws Lane label is a relatively new arrival on the scene; after a highly successful 1995 vintage, adverse weather in 1996 and 1997 meant that little or no wine was made in those years, but the pace picked up again with later vintages. Stuart Anderson guides the making of the Pinot Noir, Hanging Rock Winery handles the Gewurztraminer and the sparkling wine base. It's good to have co-operative neighbours.

❦❦❦❦❦ **Gewurztraminer 2004** Excellent varietal character, with flowery rose petal aromas and lychee flavours. **RATING** 94 **DRINK** 2008 $ 30

❦❦❦❦❦ **Shiraz 2003** Vivid purple-red hue; clean, fresh and vibrant; light to medium-bodied; pure black cherry and plum fruit, with nice touches of spice; super-fine tannins; 13.9° alcohol. High-quality cork. **RATING** 91 **DRINK** 2013 $ 30
Pinot Noir 2003 Strong colour; an abundance of rich, spiced plums; complex and layered; there may be a hint of brett, but it doesn't detract; good mouthfeel and balance. High-quality cork. **RATING** 90 **DRINK** 2008 $ 28

❦❦❦❦ **Blanc de Noir 1997** Spice, yeast, nutmeg aromas; incredibly fine, tight and crisp palate; zero dosage style; will it ever age? **RATING** 88 **DRINK** 2010 $ 35

Stringybark   NR

2060 Chittering Road, Chittering, WA 6084 **REGION** Perth Hills
T (08) 9571 8069 **F** (08) 9561 6547 **OPEN** Thurs–Sun 12–5
WINEMAKER Stephen Murfitt (Contract) **EST.** 1985 **CASES** NA
SUMMARY Bruce and Mary Cussen have a vineyard dating back to 1985, but the cellar door and restaurant complex is far more recent. They have 2 ha of verdelho, chardonnay and cabernet sauvignon at Chittering, and have the wines contract-made by Stephen Murfitt at Lilac Hill Estate. Their cellar door and country-style restaurant is open from 12–5pm Thursday to Sunday; prices will not unduly hurt the pocket.

Stringy Brae of Sevenhill   ★★★★★

Sawmill Road, Sevenhill, SA 5453 **REGION** Clare Valley
T (08) 8843 4313 **F** (08) 8843 4319 **WEB** www.stringybrae.com.au **OPEN** Weekends & public hols 11–5, Mon–Fri refer to sign
WINEMAKER O'Leary Walker (Contract) **EST.** 1991 **CASES** 3500
SUMMARY Donald and Sally Willson began planting their 10-ha vineyard in 1991, having purchased the property 8 years earlier. In 2004 daughter Hannah Rantanen took over day-to-day management from father Donald. Retail distribution in Adelaide, Melbourne and Sydney; exports to the UK.

❦❦❦❦❦ **Clare Valley Riesling 2004** Intense flowery/floral citrus blossom aromas; flavoursome lemon/lime fruit; long, focused and well structured. **RATING** 95 **DRINK** 2014 $ 23
Clare Valley Cabernet Shiraz 2002 Dense colour; luscious blackberry/currant/dark chocolate mix; ripe tannins. **RATING** 94 **DRINK** 2017 $ 18

Stuart Range ★★★

67 William Street, Kingaroy, Qld 4610 **REGION** South Burnett
T (07) 4162 3711 **F** (07) 4162 4811 **WEB** www.stuartrange.com.au **OPEN** 7 days 9–5
WINEMAKER Graham Helmhold **EST.** 1997 **CASES** 5000
SUMMARY Stuart Range is a prime example of the extent and pace of change in the Queensland wine industry, coming from nowhere in 1997 to crushing just under 120 tonnes of grapes in its inaugural vintage in 1998. The grapes are supplied by up to seven growers in the South Burnett Valley; 52 ha had been planted by 1996. A state-of-the-art winery has been established in an old butter factory building. Production continues unchanged in the wake of a change of ownership in early 2005.

ŸŸŸŸ **Goodger Chardonnay 2003** Attractive stone fruit and peach flavours; falls away slightly on the finish, but does have good mid-palate fruit. **RATING** 89 **DRINK** 2007 $16

ŸŸŸŸ **Goodger Verdelho 2004** **RATING** 85 **DRINK** Now $16

ŸŸŸ **Semillon 2004** **RATING** 83
Verdelho 2004 **RATING** 83
Goodger Cabernet Sauvignon Shiraz Merlot 2003 **RATING** 81 $16

Stuart Wines ★★★★

93A Killara Road, Gruyere, Vic 3770 (postal) **REGION** Yarra Valley
T (03) 5964 9000 **F** (03) 5964 9313 **OPEN** Not
WINEMAKER Peter Wilson **EST.** 1999 **CASES** 2000
SUMMARY The Indonesian Widjaja family have major palm oil plantations in Java, with downstream refining. Under the direction of Hendra Widjaja it has decided to diversify into the Australian wine business, establishing two very significant vineyards, one in the Yarra Valley planted to no less than 12 varieties, and an even larger one in Heathcote, with 7 varieties – shiraz, nebbiolo, tempranillo, merlot, cabernet sauvignon, viognier and chardonnay. Between them the 2 vineyards cover 128 ha. Since 2004 all the wines have been made at a new $7 million winery at Heathcote. While the major part of the production will be exported to Asia and the US, there are also direct sales in Australia. Wines are released under the Cahillton and White Box labels.

ŸŸŸŸ **White Box Heathcote Shiraz 2003** Ripe, rich array of sweet black fruits; dashes of chocolate and spice; soft, ripe tannins. **RATING** 90 **DRINK** 2009 $18

Studley Park Vineyard ★★★★

5 Garden Terrace, Kew, Vic 3101 (postal) **REGION** Port Phillip Zone
T (03) 9254 2777 **F** (03) 9853 4901 **WEB** www.studleypark.com **OPEN** Not
WINEMAKER Llew Knight (Contract) **EST.** 1994 **CASES** 250
SUMMARY Geoff Pryor's Studley Park Vineyard is one of Melbourne's best-kept secrets. It is on a bend of the Yarra River barely 4 km from the Melbourne CBD, on a 0.5-ha block once planted to vines, but for a century used for market gardening, then replanted with cabernet sauvignon. A spectacular aerial photograph shows that immediately across the river, and looking directly to the CBD, is the epicentre of Melbourne's light industrial development, while on the northern and eastern boundaries are suburban residential blocks. Most sales are direct from the website.

ŸŸŸŸ **Cabernet Sauvignon 2001** Medium-bodied; spice, earth, olive cabernet varietal aromas; a core of gently sweet fruit, then fine, ripe tannins. Subtle oak. **RATING** 91 **DRINK** 2013 $25

Stumpy Gully ★★★★

1247 Stumpy Gully Road, Moorooduc, Vic 3933 **REGION** Mornington Peninsula
T (03) 5978 8429 **F** (03) 5978 8419 **WEB** www.stumpygully.com.au **OPEN** Weekends 11–5
WINEMAKER Wendy Zantvoort, Maitena Zantvoort, Ewan Campbell **EST.** 1988 **CASES** 9000
SUMMARY When Frank and Wendy Zantvoort began planting their first vineyard in 1989 there were no winemakers in the family; now there are three, plus two viticulturists. Mother Wendy was first to obtain her degree from Charles Sturt University. She was followed by daughter Maitena, who then married Ewan Campbell, another winemaker. Father Frank and son Michael look after the vineyards. The original vineyard has 9 ha of vines, but in establishing the new 20-ha Moorooduc vineyard (first harvest 2001) the Zantvoorts have deliberately gone against prevailing thinking, planting it solely to

red varieties, predominately cabernet sauvignon, merlot and shiraz. They believe they have one of the warmest sites on the Peninsula, and that ripening will in fact present no problems. In all they now have 10 varieties planted, producing a dozen different wines. Exports to the UK and Holland.

ΥΥΥΥΥ **Pinot Noir 2003** Light to medium-bodied; fresh spice, plum and blackberry; fine, faintly savoury tannins; elegant. Screwcap. **RATING** 92 **DRINK** 2010 $ 20
Riesling 2004 Fresh, bright, clean and crisp; driven by lemony/minerally acidity on the finish. Screwcap. **RATING** 90 **DRINK** 2010 $ 22
Chardonnay 2004 Bright green-yellow; elegant, light to medium-bodied; stone fruit, harmonious mouthfeel and subtle oak. Screwcap. **RATING** 90 **DRINK** 2009 $ 18

ΥΥΥΥ **Sauvignon Blanc 2004** Crisp mineral stone, slate and herb aromas; a light touch of grass and gooseberry on the palate. Screwcap. **RATING** 88 **DRINK** 2007 $ 18

ΥΥΥΥ **Sangiovese 2004** **RATING** 86 **DRINK** 2007 $ 22

ΥΥΥ **Marsanne 2004** **RATING** 83 $ 16

Suckfizzle & Stella Bella ★★★★★

PO Box 536, Margaret River, WA 6285 **REGION** Margaret River
T (08) 9757 6377 **F** (08) 9757 6022 **WEB** www.stellabella.com.au **OPEN** Not
WINEMAKER Janice McDonald **EST.** 1997 **CASES** 50 000
SUMMARY First things first. The back label explains: 'the name Suckfizzle has been snaffled from the 14th century monk and medico-turned-writer Rabelais and his infamous character the great Lord Suckfizzle'. Suckfizzle is the joint venture of two well-known Margaret River winemakers who, in deference to their employers, do not identify themselves on any of the background material or the striking front and back labels of the wines. Production has increased dramatically in the wake of deserved market success, with exports to the UK, the US and other major markets.

ΥΥΥΥΥ **Suckfizzle Cabernet Sauvignon 2002** Potent but pure, beautifully enunciated, Margaret River Cabernet; sweet blackcurrant/cassis fruit; ripe, flowing tannins; perfect oak integration. Cork. **RATING** 96 **DRINK** 2022 $ 41
Stella Bella Semillon Sauvignon Blanc 2004 Bright, brisk, fresh stony/minerally aromas; long, lively palate and finish; fresh and dry; great seafood style. **RATING** 94 **DRINK** Now $ 20

ΥΥΥΥΥ **Stella Bella Chardonnay 2003** Light, smoky barrel ferment aromas, grapefruit and melon on a long palate and lingering finish. **RATING** 91 **DRINK** 2008 $ 25
Stella Bella Shiraz 2003 Blackberry, plum and licorice; abundant but soft and ripe tannins; well-integrated oak. **RATING** 91 **DRINK** 2010 $ 23
Stella Bella Cabernet Sauvignon Merlot 2002 Powerful but supple array of cassis, blackcurrant and spice fruit; ripe, fine tannins; subtle oak. Cork. **RATING** 91 **DRINK** 2012 $ 25
Suckfizzle Sauvignon Blanc Semillon 2003 Strong toasty oak barrel ferment characters dominant; fruit still needing to develop and fight back, but may do so. Food style. Cork. **RATING** 90 **DRINK** 2010 $ 41
Stella Bella Sangiovese Cabernet Sauvignon 2003 Interesting blend: an element of Italianate austerity to the structure and tannins, but plenty of sweet black fruits as well. Cork. **RATING** 90 **DRINK** 2015 $ 27

ΥΥΥΥ **Stella Bella Sauvignon Blanc 2004** Curiously subdued bouquet; varietal fruit likewise locked up, though the structure and balance are good. **RATING** 89 **DRINK** 2007 $ 19.50
Stella Bella Tempranillo 2003 Fragrant; exotic savoury, lemony mix, then persistent, lingering tannins; as much climate and winemaking as inherent varietal character. Screwcap. **RATING** 89 **DRINK** 2013 $ 27
Skuttlebutt Sauvignon Blanc Semillon Chardonnay 2004 Very fresh and aromatic; delicate palate, dry finish. **RATING** 87 **DRINK** Now $ 17
Skuttlebutt Cabernet Shiraz Merlot 2003 Juicy, lively, brisk and bright red fruits; not overmuch structure or depth. **RATING** 87 **DRINK** Now $ 17

☙ Sugarloaf Creek Vineyard ★★★★

20 Zwars Road, Broadford, Vic 3658 **REGION** Goulburn Valley
T (03) 5784 1291 **F** (03) 5784 1291 **WEB** www.sugarloafcreek.com **OPEN** By appointment
WINEMAKER Adrian Munari **EST.** 1998 **CASES** 500

SUMMARY The 2-ha vineyard, planted exclusively to shiraz, was established by the Blyth and Hunter families in the 1990s, the first vintage in 2001. While situated in the Goulburn Valley, it is in fact near the boundary of the Upper Goulburn, Goulburn Valley and Macedon Ranges regions, and the climate is significantly cooler than that of the major part of the Goulburn Valley. Adding the skilled winemaking by Adrian Munari, it became immediately apparent that this is a distinguished site: the 2001 vintage (the first) won silver medals at the Victorian Wines Show and Cowra Wine Show, the 2002 won the trophy at the Winewise Small Vignerons Awards for Best Shiraz, and there have been gold medals at three other wine shows. With this sort of pedigree, and with such limited production, distribution is limited to a few fine wine outlets in Sydney, the ACT and Melbourne, and through the website.

ŶŶŶŶŶ **Central Victoria Shiraz 2002** Medium-bodied; clean, ripe red and black fruits and a touch of chocolate; smooth mouthfeel, supple tannins, balanced oak. RATING 90 DRINK 2012 $ 34

ŶŶŶŶ **Shiraz 2003** Deep colour; very ripe plum and prune fruit; soft tannins. RATING 87 DRINK 2010 $ 34

Sugarloaf Ridge ★★★

Kentigern Vineyard, 336 Sugarloaf Road, Carlton River, Tas 7173 (postal) REGION Southern Tasmania
T (03) 6265 7175 F (03) 6266 7275 WEB www.sugarloafridge.com OPEN Not
WINEMAKER Julian Alcorso (Contract) EST. 1999 CASES NA
SUMMARY Dr Simon and wife Isobel Stanley are both microbiologists, but with thoroughly unlikely specialties: he in low-temperature microbiology, taking him to the Antarctic, and she in a worldwide environmental geosciences company. It is an extended family business, with daughter Kristen and husband Julian Colvile partners. Since 1999, multiple clones of pinot noir, sauvignon blanc, pinot gris, viognier and lagrein have been planted. And 1580 native trees, 210 olive trees and 270 cherry trees have helped transform the property from bare, sheep grazing pasture. A cellar door will open in late 2005/early 2006.

ŶŶŶŶ **Pinot Noir 2003** RATING 86 DRINK 2007

Summerfield ★★★★★

5967 Stawell–Avoca Road, Moonambel, Vic 3478 REGION Pyrenees
T (03) 5467 2264 F (03) 5467 2380 WEB www.summerfieldwines.com OPEN 7 days 9–5.30
WINEMAKER Mark Summerfield EST. 1979 CASES 8000
SUMMARY A specialist red wine producer, the particular forte of which is Shiraz. The red wines are consistently excellent: luscious and full-bodied and fruit-driven, but with a slice of vanillin oak to top them off. Exports to the US and the UK.

ŶŶŶŶŶ **Reserve Shiraz 2002** Typically dense colour; ultra-complex and dense flavours, texture and structure; luscious plum and dark berry; good finish. Cork. RATING 95 DRINK 2017 $ 50
Reserve Shiraz 2003 Very good colour; rich, opulent blackberry fruit floods the mouth; soft tannins; excellent balance. Quality cork. RATING 94 DRINK 2023 $ 43

ŶŶŶŶŶ **Reserve Cabernet Shiraz 2003** Very aromatic and ripe, bordering essency, bouquet; luscious, rich blackberry, blackcurrant, plum, chocolate and prune; vanilla oak; controlled tannins; a success for the vintage. Quality cork. RATING 93 DRINK 2018 $ 43
Merlot 2003 Very sweet cassis berry fruit; soft and round, with some spice; balanced tannins; another success. Quality cork. RATING 91 DRINK 2013

ŶŶŶŶ **Sauvignon Blanc 2004** Light to medium-bodied; attractive gooseberry and passionfruit varietal flavours; squeaky acidity; cool vintage a plus. Screwcap. RATING 89 DRINK 2007 $ 15
Tradition 2003 Medium-bodied; gently savoury, spicy, earthy edges to soft red fruits. Cabernet Sauvignon/Shiraz/Merlot. How on earth did it win a double gold at the Sydney International Winemakers Competition? Cork. RATING 88 DRINK 2009 $ 23

ŶŶŶŶ **Trebbiano 2004** RATING 85 DRINK Now $ 15
Rose 2004 RATING 84 DRINK Now $ 15

Summerhill Wines   NR

64–65 Dandenong–Hastings Road, Somerville, Vic 3912 **REGION** Mornington Peninsula
T 0413 784 317 **OPEN** By appointment
WINEMAKER Robert Zagar **EST.** 1998 **CASES** NA
SUMMARY Robert Zagar has established 4 ha of pinot noir and shiraz, and (apparently with material from elsewhere) makes both table and fortified wines under the Summerhill, Coat of Arms, Brockville and Pattersons Estate labels. Wines available by mail order; exports to Malaysia.

Summit Estate   ★★★★

291 Granite Belt Drive, Thulimbah, Qld 4377 **REGION** Granite Belt
T (07) 4683 2011 **F** (07) 4683 2600 **WEB** www.summitestate.com.au **OPEN** 7 days 9–5
WINEMAKER Paola Cabezas Rhymer **EST.** 1997 **CASES** 4500
SUMMARY Summit Estate is the public face of the Stanthorpe Wine Co., owned by a syndicate of 10 professionals who work in Brisbane, and share a love of wine. They operate the Stanthorpe Wine Centre, which offers wine education as well as selling wines from other makers in the region (and, of course, from Summit Estate). The 17-ha vineyard is planted to chardonnay, marsanne, pinot noir, shiraz, merlot, tempranillo, petit verdot and cabernet sauvignon, and they have set up a small, specialised winemaking facility.

ΤΤΤΤΤ **Cabernet Merlot 2002** Powerful; medium to full-bodied; dark fruits and a touch of chocolate; good balance and structure. **RATING** 94 **DRINK** 2012

ΤΤΤΤ **Reserve Cabernet Merlot 2003** Very savoury and fairly lean, but does have considerable length; fine tannins. **RATING** 88 **DRINK** 2010 $ 24
Marsanne 2004 Clean, fresh, with honeysuckle varietal fruit expression; hints of spice; well balanced. **RATING** 87 **DRINK** 2008 $ 19
Emily Rose 2003 Fresh, strawberry-tinged; good balance and acidity. **RATING** 87 **DRINK** Now $ 12

ΤΤΤΥ **Shiraz Pinot 2003** **RATING** 84 **DRINK** 2007 $ 19

ΤΤΤ **Cabernet Merlot 2003** **RATING** 83
Chardonnay 2004 **RATING** 82 $ 19

ΤΤΥ **Verdelho 2004** **RATING** 79 $ 24

🕸 Sunnyhurst Winery   ★★★

Lot 16 Doust Street, Bridgetown, WA 6255 **REGION** Blackwood Valley
T (08) 9761 4525 **F** (08) 9761 4525 **WEB** www.sunnyhurst.com.au **OPEN** 7 days 10–6
WINEMAKER Ashley Lewkowski, Mark Staniford **EST.** 2000 **CASES** 700
SUMMARY Mark and Lainie Staniford purchased a 108-year-old stone house surrounded by extensive gardens on the outskirts of Bridgetown in 2000. It gave Mark Staniford the opportunity to realise a lifelong dream of making wine (he opened WA's first specialist wine shop, in North Fremantle in 1965). He has established 0.25 ha each of semillon, sauvignon blanc, cabernet sauvignon and merlot, the original intention being to make the equivalents of white and red Bordeaux respectively. However, son-in-law and winemaker Ashley Lewkowski acquired a property planted to 0.5 ha each of shiraz and chardonnay in 1990, which has led to a slightly different path. Both red and white wines are pressed in hand-operated basket presses; the whites are barrel-fermented, the reds mainly open-fermented.

ΤΤΤΤ **Basket Press Shiraz 2003** Quite elegant, medium-bodied, spicy, savoury style; cool climate. **RATING** 87 **DRINK** 2008 $ 15
Cabernet Sauvignon 2003 Light to medium-bodied; savoury/earthy overtones to blackcurrant fruit; moderate length. **RATING** 87 **DRINK** 2008 $ 14

ΤΤΤΥ **Classic Chardonnay 2003** **RATING** 84 **DRINK** Now $ 15

🕸 Sunset Winery   NR

Main Penneshaw–Kingscote Road, Penneshaw, SA 5222 **REGION** Kangaroo Island
T (08) 8553 1378 **F** (08) 8553 1379 **WEB** www.sunset-wines.com.au **OPEN** 7 days 11–5
WINEMAKER Colin Hopkins **EST.** 2003 **CASES** 1500

SUMMARY This boutique winery is owned and run by friends and business partners Colin Hopkins and Athalie and David Martin. Construction of the winery and cellar door, with elevated sea views overlooking Eastern Cove and beyond, was completed in April 2003. It is otherwise surrounded by 14 ha of native bushland, with a profusion of wildlife. Sunset Winery was the first dedicated cellar door on Kangaroo Island, and offers a range of products to accompany the Chardonnay, Cabernet Sauvignon, Shiraz and Sparkling Shiraz produced at the winery.

Surveyor's Hill Winery NR

215 Brooklands Road, Wallaroo, NSW 2618 **REGION** Canberra District
T (02) 6230 2046 **F** (02) 6230 2048 **OPEN** Weekends & public hols, or by appointment
WINEMAKER Contract **EST.** 1986 **CASES** 1000
SUMMARY Surveyor's Hill has 10 ha of vineyard, but most of the grapes are sold to Hardys Kamberra, which vinifies the remainder for Surveyor's Hill; this should guarantee the quality of the wines. Also offers B&B accommodation.

Susannah Brook Wines NR

43 Beryl Avenue, Millendon, WA 6056 **REGION** Swan District
T (08) 9296 4129 **OPEN** By appointment
WINEMAKER John Daniel **EST.** 1984 **CASES** NA
SUMMARY Susannah Brook is a small but long-established Swan Valley business, where John Daniel has 2 ha of chenin blanc, chardonnay, verdelho, cabernet sauvignon, merlot, malbec, shiraz and muscat, and makes the range of table and fortified wines onsite. The small production is largely sold by mail order.

Sutherland Estate ★★★★☆

2010 Melba Highway, Dixons Creek, Vic 3775 **REGION** Yarra Valley
T 0402 052 287 **F** (03) 9762 1122 **OPEN** 7 days 10–5 summer, or Thurs–Sun & public hols
WINEMAKER Alex White (Contract) **EST.** 2000 **CASES** 2000
SUMMARY The Phelan family (father Ron, mother Sheila, daughter Catherine and partner Angus Ridley) established Sutherland Estate in 2000, when they acquired a mature 2-ha vineyard on the Melba Highway at Dixons Creek. Later that year they planted another 3.2 ha, including a small amount of tempranillo. Both Catherine and Angus are in their sixth and final year of the part-time viticulture and oenology course at Charles Sturt University; when a planned onsite winery is completed in 2007, they will take over winemaking. In the meantime, Angus is gaining further experience as a full-time winemaker at Coldstream Hills. A cellar door complex, designed and built by Ron Phelan, is already open. The DHV range is estate-grown on Daniel's Hill Vineyard.

DHV Shiraz 2003 Medium-bodied; very good balance, texture and structure; black fruits, mocha and sweet, ripe tannins; overall, supple and round; good length. **RATING** 93 **DRINK** 2015 $30

DHV Cabernet Sauvignon 2003 Medium-bodied; elegant, very pure cabernet fruit expression; cassis and blackcurrant; fine tannins, good oak. Cork. **RATING** 92 **DRINK** 2013 $30

DHV Pinot Noir 2002 Fine, elegant and focused; light to medium-bodied; plum, spice and touches of stem/forest; lingering finish. **RATING** 91 **DRINK** 2007 $30

DHV Chardonnay 2002 Glowing yellow-green; intense citrus, melon and nectarine; concentration of the vintage almost into honey; well-controlled oak. High-quality cork. **RATING** 90 **DRINK** 2008 $30

DHV Pinot Noir 2003 Soft, round, plummy fruit; good texture and mouthfeel; moderate length. **RATING** 89 **DRINK** 2007 $33

Shiraz 2001 Spicy oaky style; nice texture and mouthfeel; black fruits, but less oak would have been better. Young vine/purchased fruit. **RATING** 89 **DRINK** 2011 $24

Sutherland Smith Wines NR

Cnr Falkners Road/Murray Valley Highway, Rutherglen, Vic 3685 **REGION** Rutherglen
T (02) 6032 8177 **F** (02) 6032 8177 **OPEN** Weekends, public & Victorian school hols 10–5, other Fridays 11–5

WINEMAKER George Sutherland-Smith **EST.** 1993 **CASES** 1000
SUMMARY George Sutherland-Smith, for decades managing director and winemaker at All Saints, has opened up his own small business at Rutherglen, making wine in the refurbished Emu Plains winery, originally constructed in the 1850s. He draws upon fruit grown in a leased vineyard at Glenrowan and also from grapes grown in the King Valley.

Sutton Grange Winery ★★★★

PO Box 181, East Kew, Vic 3102 **REGION** Bendigo
T (03) 5474 8277 **F** (03) 9859 5655 **WEB** www.suttongrangewines.com **OPEN** By appointment
WINEMAKER Gilles Lapalus **EST.** 1998 **CASES** 2200
SUMMARY The 400-ha Sutton Grange property is a thoroughbred stud acquired in 1996 by Peter Sidwell, a Melbourne-based businessman with horse racing and breeding among his activities. A lunch visit to the property by long-term friends Alec Epis and Stuart Anderson led to the decision to plant 12 ha of syrah, merlot, cabernet sauvignon, viognier and sangiovese, and to the recruitment of French winemaker Gilles Lapalus, who just happens to be the partner of Stuart Anderson's daughter. The onsite winery, built from West Australian limestone, was completed in time for the 2001 vintage. Exports to the UK and Switzerland.

ㅸㅸㅸㅸㅸ **Fairbank Syrah 2002** Redcurrant, raspberry, plum, mint and herb aromas and flavours; far more delicate than the 14.1° alcohol suggests. Nice twist of herb on the finish. **RATING** 90 **DRINK** 2012 $ 22

ㅸㅸㅸㅸ **Fairbank Viognier 2004** Spotlessly clean; subdued varietal character but still a quite imposing wine with both intensity and length; may develop further. **RATING** 89 **DRINK** 2008 $ 21
Fairbank Syrah 2003 Light to medium-bodied; cool-grown, fresh red fruits, gentle spice; fine tannins and unforced. **RATING** 89 **DRINK** 2008 $ 26
Fairbank Cabernet Sauvignon 2003 Medium-bodied; ripe blackcurrant and blackberry mix; earthy tannins need to soften a touch. **RATING** 88 **DRINK** 2013 $ 25
Fairbank Rose 2004 Fresh, light to medium-bodied; some small red fruits; nicely balanced, dry finish. Shiraz/Cabernet Saignee. **RATING** 87 **DRINK** Now

ㅸㅸㅸㅸ **Fairbank Cabernet Sauvignon 2002** **RATING** 86 **DRINK** 2009 $ 22

Swallows Welcome

Wallis Road, East Witchcliffe, WA 6286 **REGION** Margaret River
T (08) 9757 6312 **F** (08) 9757 6312 **OPEN** 7 days by appointment
WINEMAKER Tim Negus **EST.** 1994 **CASES** 700
SUMMARY Tim Negus has planted a 3-ha vineyard to cabernet sauvignon, merlot and cabernet franc, and makes the wine onsite. The wine is sold by mail order and through the cellar door, which offers barbecue and garden facilities for the visitor (by appointment).

ㅸㅸㅸ **Cabernet Sauvignon 2003** **RATING** 83 $ 10

Swanbrook Estate Wines ★★★☆

38 Swan Street, Henley Brook, WA 6055 **REGION** Swan Valley
T (08) 9296 3100 **F** (08) 9296 3099 **OPEN** 7 days 10–5
WINEMAKER Rob Marshall **EST.** 1998 **CASES** 10 000
SUMMARY This is the reincarnation of Evans & Tate's Gnangara Winery. It secures most of its grapes from contract growers in the Perth Hills and Swan Valley, but also has a 60-year-old block of shiraz around the winery. A little under 40% of the annual crush is for the Swanbrook label; the remainder is sold to others. Owner John Andreou (a Perth restaurateur) has invested $2 million in upgrading and expanding the facilities, and former Evans & Tate winemaker Rob Marshall provides valuable continuity.

Swan Valley Wines ★★★

261 Haddrill Road, Baskerville, WA 6065 **REGION** Swan Valley
T (08) 9296 1501 **F** (08) 9296 1733 **WEB** www.swanvalleywines.com.au **OPEN** Fri–Sun & public hols 10–5
WINEMAKER Julie White (Consultant) **EST.** 1999 **CASES** 6600

SUMMARY Peter and Paula Hoffman, with sons Paul and Thomas, acquired their 6-ha property in 1989. It had a long history of grapegrowing, and the prior owner had registered the name Swan Valley Wines back in 1983. In 1999 the family built a new winery to handle the grapes from 5.5 ha of chenin blanc, grenache, semillon, malbec, cabernet sauvignon and shiraz. Exports to Japan.

ŶŶŶŶ **Semillon 2004** Clean, fresh, lemony aromas and flavours; 12.7° alcohol but still quite bright and clean; modern style, unsullied by oak. Screwcap. **RATING** 88 **DRINK** 2009 **$** 14
Amphisbaena Tawny Port 2004 Aged, complex toffee and raisin aromas and flavours; more to sweet white than Tawny Port in style; terrible cork. **RATING** 87 **DRINK** Now **$** 20

ŶŶŶŶ **The Roadbull 2004** Fresh fruit; the disjointed tannins need to integrate, but should do so by the time of release in 2006. Made using a high proportion of whole-bunch fermentation and minimalist handling. Cabernet Sauvignon/Shiraz/Barbera. Screwcap.
RATING 86 **DRINK** 2012 **$** 25
Shiraz 2004 **RATING** 85 **DRINK** 2008 **$** 16.50
Chenin Blanc 2004 **RATING** 84 **DRINK** 2007 **$** 15

Sweet Water Hill Wines

NR

17 Roberts Road, Anderleigh, Qld 4570 **REGION** Queensland Zone
T (07) 5485 7007 **F** (07) 5485 7007 **OPEN** 7 days 10–5
WINEMAKER Tony Totivan **EST.** 1999 **CASES** NA
SUMMARY Tony Totivan has established 5 ha of semillon, chardonnay, cabernet sauvignon, shiraz, muscat hamburg and white muscat, and makes the wine onsite. A range of table and fortified wines are available. The cellar door offers light meals and picnic and barbecue facilities.

🦗 Swings & Roundabouts

PO Box 1520, Margaret River, WA 6285 **REGION** Margaret River
T (08) 9322 2502 **F** (08) 9286 1933 **WEB** www.swings.com.au **OPEN** Not
WINEMAKER Mark Lane **EST.** 2004 **CASES** NA
SUMMARY The winemaking skills of Mark Lane and the marketing skills of Ian Latchford have come together to create three ranges: the super-premium Swings & Roundabouts (Chardonnay, Semillon Sauvignon Blanc, Shiraz and Cabernet Merlot); the varietal Laneway series of The Italian, Tempranillo and Shiraz, targeted at on-premise sales, and with exceptionally striking labels; and the premium Kiss Chasey range of Premium White, Premium Red and Rose.

ŶŶŶŶŶ **Margaret River Shiraz 2003** Light to medium-bodied; good mouthfeel from ripe but fine tannins running throughout; a nice mix of ripe and more savoury fruit. **RATING** 90
DRINK 2011 **$** 20

ŶŶŶŶ **Margaret River Semillon Sauvignon Blanc 2004** Spotlessly clean; light-bodied; grass, herb and lemon flavours; some length. **RATING** 87 **DRINK** Now **$** 17
Pemberton Chardonnay 2003 The citrus overtones to the melon aromas are more akin to sauvignon blanc, but there is more weight on the palate from the 14° alcohol; no evidence of oak. **RATING** 87 **DRINK** 2007 **$** 20

Sylvan Springs

RSD 405, Blythmans Road, McLaren Flat, SA 5171 (postal) **REGION** McLaren Vale
T (08) 8383 0500 **F** (08) 8383 0499 **WEB** www.sylvansprings.com.au **OPEN** Not
WINEMAKER Brian Light (Consultant) **EST.** 1974 **CASES** 2200
SUMMARY The Pridmore family has been involved in grapegrowing and winemaking in McLaren Vale for four generations, spanning over 100 years. The pioneer was Cyril Pridmore, who established The Wattles Winery in 1896, and purchased Sylvan Park, one of the original homesteads in the area, in 1901. The original family land in the township of McLaren Vale was sold in 1978, but not before third-generation Digby Pridmore had established new vineyards (in 1974) near Blewitt Springs. When he retired in 1990, his son David purchased the 45-ha vineyard (planted to 11 different varieties) and, with sister Sally, began winemaking in 1996. Exports to the US.

ŶŶŶŶŶ **Cabernet Sauvignon 2002** Rich, ripe, plush mix of blackcurrant and dark chocolate; soft, ripe tannins; long finish. **RATING** 92 **DRINK** 2012 **$** 19.90

▼▼▼▼ **Shiraz 2002** Medium-bodied; gentle dark fruits with touches of chocolate and vanilla; fine ripe tannins. **RATING** 88 **DRINK** 2009 $ 19.90

▼▼▼▽ **Ram's Revenge Shiraz 2003** **RATING** 85 **DRINK** 2007 $ 13.50

Symphonia Wines   ★★★★

1699 Boggy Creek Road, Myrrhee, Vic 3732 **REGION** King Valley
T (03) 5729 7519 **F** (03) 5729 7519 **OPEN** By appointment
WINEMAKER Peter Read **EST.** 1998 **CASES** 2000
SUMMARY Peter Read and his family are veterans of the King Valley, commencing the development of their vineyard in 1981 to supply Brown Brothers. As a result of extensive trips to both Western and Eastern Europe, Peter Read embarked on an ambitious project to trial a series of grape varieties little known in this country. The process of evaluation and experimentation continues; Symphonia released the first small quantities of wines in mid-1998. A number of the wines have great interest and no less merit.

▼▼▼▼▽ **Las Triadas Winemakers Reserve Tempranillo 2004** Complex aromas and flavours; plum, tobacco and spice; good texture and richness; impressive. Cork. **RATING** 90 **DRINK** 2014 $ 20
La Solista Tempranillo 2004 Bright purple-red; fresh dark fruits, licorice and spice; vibrant licorice and anise; a particular quality to the tannins and aftertaste. Screwcap. **RATING** 90 **DRINK** 2009 $ 17.50

▼▼▼▼ **King Valley Viognier Petit Manseng 2004** Good mouthfeel and weight; peach and apricot off-set by quite fine, minerally acidity. Quality cork. **RATING** 89 **DRINK** 2008 $ 20
King Valley Cabernet Sauvignon 2003 Light to medium-bodied; spicy black fruits; sweet, ripe tannins; good mouthfeel and flow, controlled oak. Cork. **RATING** 89 **DRINK** 2010 $ 17.50
Tannat 2004 Spicy and earthy; the structure profile is the reverse of the Saperavi, with the typical powerful tannins driving the back palate and finish. Cork. **RATING** 89 **DRINK** 2014 $ 25
Saperavi 2004 As it should be, densely coloured; the wine has a powerful entry with lots of flavour, but is like a Chambourcin on steroids, falling away on the finish and aftertaste. Cork. **RATING** 89 **DRINK** 2008 $ 22.50
King Valley Blanc de Blanc 1999 Fine straw-green; lively, fresh, citrussy minerally palate; very dry, crisp finish. **RATING** 89 **DRINK** 2008 $ 20

▼▼▼▽ **King Valley Pinot Grigio 2004** **RATING** 86 **DRINK** 2008 $ 17.50
King Valley Blanc de Blanc 2001 **RATING** 86 **DRINK** 2009 $ 20

Symphony Hill Wines   ★★★★☆

2017 Eukey Road, Ballandean, Qld 4382 **REGION** Granite Belt
T (07) 4684 1388 **F** (07) 4684 1399 **WEB** www.symphonyhill.com.au **OPEN** 7 days 10–4
WINEMAKER Blair Duncan **EST.** 1999 **CASES** 2000
SUMMARY Ewen and Elissa Macpherson purchased an old table grape and orchard property in 1996. In partnership with Ewen's parents, Bob and Jill Macpherson, they have developed 4 ha of vineyards, and Ewen completed his Bachelor of Applied Science (Viticulture) in 2003. They have also secured the services of Blair Duncan as winemaker. He has had a long career with Penfolds, then Arrowfield Wines, and now in Queensland. The vineyard has been established using state-of-the-art technology; vineyard manager, Mike Hayes, has a degree in viticulture and is a third-generation viticulturist in the Granite Belt region. He and Ewen have planted a trial block of 50 varieties, including such rarely encountered varieties as picpoul, tannat and mondeuse. The wines are also available by mail order and through the website.

▼▼▼▼▽ **Reserve Shiraz 2003** Medium to full-bodied; rich, ripe, spicy blackberry fruit with good sweetness and no green tannins; controlled oak. **RATING** 93 **DRINK** 2012 $ 45
Reserve Ballandean Cabernet Sauvignon 2002 Medium-bodied and elegant; good varietal expression; cedary, earthy blackcurrant; fine tannins, nice oak. Cork. **RATING** 91 **DRINK** 2012 $ 35
Reserve Ballandean Sauvignon Blanc 2004 Clean, fresh, spicy, apple, herb and asparagus aromas and flavours; particularly good example from Ballandean. Screwcap. **RATING** 90 **DRINK** Now $ 18

Family Reserve Ballandean Shiraz 2002 Clean; medium-bodied; supple, round red fruits; gentle tannins and oak; nice wine, but very expensive. Cork. **RATING** 90 **DRINK** 2010 $ 65

Estate Cabernet Sauvignon 2003 Medium-bodied; quite elegant and long, though fractionally green fruit catches on the aftertaste. **RATING** 89 **DRINK** 2010 $ 25

Reserve Ballandean Verdelho 2004 Light to medium-bodied; fair balance and length; a neat flick of residual sugar. **RATING** 87 **DRINK** Now $ 22

Reserve Ballandean Pinot Noir 2003 Medium-bodied red wine; dark plum and blackberry; moderate tannins. Suppressed varietal character hardly surprising. Screwcap. **RATING** 87 **DRINK** 2009 $ 65

Tahbilk ★★★★★

Goulburn Valley Highway, Tabilk, Vic 3608 **REGION** Nagambie Lakes
T (03) 5794 2555 **F** (03) 5794 2360 **WEB** www.tahbilk.com.au **OPEN** Mon–Sat 9–5, Sun 11–5
WINEMAKER Alister Purbrick, Neil Larson, Alan George **EST.** 1860 **CASES** 120 000
SUMMARY A winery steeped in tradition (with high National Trust classification), which should be visited at least once by every wine-conscious Australian, and which makes wines – particularly red wines – utterly in keeping with that tradition. The essence of that heritage comes in the form of the tiny quantities of Shiraz made entirely from vines planted in 1860. As well as national distribution, Tahbilk has agents in every principal wine market, including the UK and the US.

Reserve Shiraz 1999 Tight and restrained; intense, but long and deceptively powerful; very good black fruits and fine, ripe tannins; lingering finish; best under this label to date. **RATING** 95 **DRINK** 2019 $ 69.95

Reserve Cabernet Sauvignon 1999 Medium-bodied; ripe blackcurrant; smooth, supple and cedary; none of the ferocious tannins; history proves longevity. **RATING** 94 **DRINK** 2015 $ 69.95

1860 Vines Shiraz 1999 Polished by time in oak and bottle; understated dark fruits, the fine tannins largely absorbed. Will go on forever; 300 cases made. **RATING** 91 **DRINK** 2019 $ 119.95

Viognier 2004 Highly aromatic; the wine is laden with peach pastille mid-palate fruit, the finish clear and uncluttered. **RATING** 90 **DRINK** Now $ 19

Chardonnay 2002 Nice peachy stone fruit flavours; good length and balance; holding up well. **RATING** 89 **DRINK** 2007 $ 16.45

Marsanne 2004 Bright yellow-green; balanced honey/honeysuckle; needs a gram more acid. **RATING** 88 **DRINK** 2009 $ 13.50

Shiraz 2001 Typical no-frills style; medium-bodied; blackberry and plum fruit; lingering tannins, minimal oak. **RATING** 88 **DRINK** 2010 $ 14.35

Cabernet Sauvignon 2001 Medium-bodied; red berry fruits in a savoury mix of persistent, but quite fine, tannins. **RATING** 88 **DRINK** 2011 $ 20.80

Riesling 2004 Generous tropical/lime/pineapple aromas and flavours; good balance. **RATING** 87 **DRINK** 2009 $ 15.80

Tait Wines ★★★☆

Yaldara Drive, Lyndoch, SA 5351 **REGION** Barossa Valley
T (08) 8524 5000 **F** (08) 8524 5220 **WEB** www.taitwines.com.au **OPEN** Weekends & public hols 11–5, or by appointment
WINEMAKER Bruno Tait **EST.** 1994 **CASES** 2000
SUMMARY The Tait family has been involved in the wine industry in the Barossa for over 100 years, making not wine but barrels. Their more recent venture into winemaking was immediately successful; retail distribution through single outlets in Melbourne, Adelaide and Sydney; exports to the US, Germany, Malaysia and Singapore.

Talijancich NR

26 Hyem Road, Herne Hill, WA 6056 **REGION** Swan Valley
T (08) 9296 4289 **F** (08) 9296 1762 **OPEN** Sun–Fri 11–5
WINEMAKER James Talijancich **EST.** 1932 **CASES** 10 000

SUMMARY A former fortified wine specialist (with old Liqueur Tokay) now making a select range of table wines, with particular emphasis on Verdelho – on the third Saturday of August each year there is a tasting of fine 3-year-old Verdelho table wines from both Australia and overseas. Also runs an active wine club and exports to China, Japan and Hong Kong. Won the Wine Press Club Trophy at the 2003 Qantas Wine Show of Western Australia for most successful under 250-tonne producer.

Taliondal   NR

270 Old North Road, Pokolbin, NSW 2320 **REGION** Lower Hunter Valley
T (02) 9427 6812 **F** (02) 9427 6812 **OPEN** By appointment
WINEMAKER Frank Brady **EST.** 1974 **CASES** 240
SUMMARY The Brady Bunch, headed by Frank Brady, acquired Taliondal in 1974 as a family hideaway. Says Frank Brady, 'When in the Hunter, do as the Hunter does', so 1 ha of cabernet sauvignon was planted in 1974, and 1.5 ha of traminer the following year. For many years the family was content to sell the grapes to local vignerons; they now take a small portion of the production and make wine on the property. The Cabernet Sauvignon has been a consistent medal winner at Hunter shows.

Tallarook   ★★★★

2 Delaney's Road, Warranwood, Vic 3134 **REGION** Upper Goulburn
T (03) 9876 7022 **F** (03) 9876 7044 **WEB** www.tallarook.com **OPEN** Not
WINEMAKER MasterWineMakers (Contract) **EST.** 1987 **CASES** 11 000
SUMMARY Tallarook has been established on a property between Broadford and Seymour at an elevation of 200–300m. Since 1987, 14 ha of vines have been planted, mainly to chardonnay, shiraz and pinot noir. The retaining of Martin Williams as winemaker in the 1998 vintage brought a substantial change in emphasis, and the subsequent release of an impressive Chardonnay. The wines are mainly sold by mail order; also, retail distribution in Melbourne and exports to the UK and Europe.

🍷🍷🍷🍷🍷 **Terra Felix Marsanne Roussanne 2004** Very attractive cascade of light, fresh fruits; apricot to peach to lemon; subtle barrel ferment; clean finish. Screwcap. **RATING** 92 **DRINK** 2008 $14.95
Terra Felix Shiraz Viognier 2004 Bright, fresh, lively, scented red fruits and a touch of apricot ex the Viognier; delicious, fresh wine style. Screwcap. **RATING** 90 **DRINK** 2007 $14.95

🍷🍷🍷🍷 **Terra Felix Chardonnay 2004** Rather light; some touches of sweetness to fill out stone fruit and grapefruit flavours. Screwcap. **RATING** 86 **DRINK** 2007 $14.95
Rose 2004 RATING 86 **DRINK** Now $18.95
Terra Felix Mourvedre 2004 RATING 85 **DRINK** 2007 $14.95

Tallavera Grove Vineyard & Winery   NR

Mount View Road, Mount View via Cessnock, NSW 2325 **REGION** Lower Hunter Valley
T (02) 4990 7535 **F** (02) 4990 5232 **OPEN** Thurs–Mon 10–5
WINEMAKER Chris Cameron **EST.** 2000 **CASES** 1800
SUMMARY Tallavera Grove is one of the many wine interests of John Davis and family. The family is a 50% owner of Briar Ridge; a 12-ha vineyard in Coonawarra; a 100-ha vineyard at Wrattonbully (the Stonefields Vineyard); and a 36-ha vineyard at Orange (Jokers Peak). The Mount View winery will eventually be equipped to handle between 200 and 300 tonnes of fruit.

Tallis Wine   ★★★

PO Box 10, Dookie, Vic 3646 **REGION** Central Victoria Zone
T (03) 5823 5383 **F** (03) 5828 6532 **WEB** www.talliswine.com.au **OPEN** Not
WINEMAKER Richard Tallis, Gary Baldwin (Consultant) **EST.** 2000 **CASES** 750
SUMMARY Richard, Mark and Alice Tallis have a substantial vineyard, with 16 ha of shiraz, 5 ha of cabernet sauvignon, 2 ha of viognier and 1 ha of merlot. While most of the grapes are sold, they have embarked on winemaking with the aid of Gary Baldwin of Wine Net, and have had considerable success. The philosophy of their viticulture and winemaking is to create a low-input and sustainable system; all environmentally harmful sprays are eliminated.

ΥΥΥΥ **Dookie Hills Cabernet Sauvignon 2003** Light to medium-bodied; pleasant red and blackcurrant fruit; fine tannins, minimal oak. **RATING** 87 **DRINK** 2008 $ 19

ΥΥΥΥ **Dookie Hills Viognier 2004** **RATING** 86 **DRINK** 2008 $ 19

Tall Poppy Wines   ★★☆

PO Box 4147, Mildura, Vic 3502 **REGION** Murray Darling
T (03) 5022 7255 **F** (03) 5022 7250 **WEB** www.tallpoppywines.com **OPEN** 7 days 8.30–5
WINEMAKER Barossa Vintners (Contract) **EST.** 1997 **CASES** 20 000
SUMMARY Tall Poppy Wines is in its infancy as a wine brand, but has lofty ambitions. It owns 4.5 ha each of shiraz and viognier, but is able to draw upon grapes sourced from 170 ha of vineyards owned by its directors, with a volume potential of 300 000 to 400 000 cases aimed at the export market (the UK, Vietnam, Malaysia, Singapore, New Zealand and The Philippines.)

Taltarni   ★★★★☆

339 Taltarni Road, Moonambel, Vic 3478 **REGION** Pyrenees
T (03) 5459 7918 **F** (03) 5467 2306 **WEB** www.taltarni.com.au **OPEN** 7 days 10–5
WINEMAKER Leigh Clarnette, Loic Le Calvez, Louella McPhan **EST.** 1972 **CASES** 80 000
SUMMARY After a hiatus of 2 years or so following the departure of long-serving winemaker and chief executive Dominique Portet, Taltarni gathered new momentum and inspiration, with a new winemaking team. Major changes in the approach to the vineyards; major upgrading of winery equipment and investment in new oak barrels; a long-term contract for the purchase of grapes from the Heathcote region; and the release of the flagship wine, Cephas, are the visible signs of the repositioning of the business. The Red Earth Café is open daily 10–5. Exports to all major markets.

ΥΥΥΥΥ **Cephas 2002** Rich, luscious, ripe and potent cascade of red and black fruits; ripe tannins and quality oak in support. Quality cork. **RATING** 94 **DRINK** 2017 $ 49.70

ΥΥΥΥΥ **Brut Tache 2003** Vibrant pink; explosively fragrant berry and cassis; flavour-packed, but not heavy; very good acidity and length. **RATING** 93 **DRINK** 2008 $ 22.35
Sauvignon Blanc 2004 Crisp, lively, zesty lemon and gooseberry aromas and flavours; good finish. Victoria/Tasmania blend. **RATING** 92 **DRINK** Now $ 19.50
Pyrenees Cabernet Sauvignon 2001 Powerful wine, one foot in the old Taltarni style, one in the new; precise cabernet varietal fruit with savoury tannins on the finish. **RATING** 91 **DRINK** 2016 $ 30.60
Heathcote Shiraz 2003 Powerful, focused wine; a range of red and black fruits, spice and lingering tannins; needs time. **RATING** 90 **DRINK** 2015 $ 42.20
Brut 2002 A blend of Chardonnay and Pinot Noir from the Pyrenees, Yarra Valley and Tasmania (ex Clover Hill). The latter two regions give the wine its freshness and vivacity, expressed in the citrus and pear fruit, and its clean, lingering, brisk, finish. **RATING** 90 **DRINK** Now $ 21.50

ΥΥΥΥ **Rose 2004** Bright red-purple; plenty of mid-palate red fruit; dry finish, balanced acidity. **RATING** 89 **DRINK** Now $ 19.50
Brut Tache 2002 Bright pink, with no salmon hues; plenty of flavour, with the auto-suggestion of strawberry; a dry but balanced finish. **RATING** 89 **DRINK** Now $ 21.50
Pyrenees Shiraz 2002 Clean, elegant, light to medium-bodied style; savoury, spicy edges to black fruits, though less concentration than expected from '02; does have length. Cork. **RATING** 88 **DRINK** 2010 $ 32.30
Three Monks Cabernet Merlot 2002 Fresh, bright, red fruit and blackcurrant; light to medium-bodied, easily approachable. **RATING** 88 **DRINK** 2007 $ 21.20
Fiddleback Semillon Sauvignon Blanc 2004 Pleasant wine; gentle tropical aromas and flavours; good finish. **RATING** 87 **DRINK** Now $ 15.70
Lalla Gully Chardonnay 2002 Barrel ferment oak inputs tend to dominate, but the wine has good overall flavour. **RATING** 87 **DRINK** 2008 $ 27.30

ΥΥΥΥ **Fiddleback Shiraz 2003** **RATING** 86 **DRINK** 2008 $ 15.70

ΥΥΥ **Lalla Gully Riesling 2004** **RATING** 81 $ 22

Talunga   NR

Adelaide to Mannum Road, Gumeracha, SA 5233 **REGION** Adelaide Hills
T (08) 8389 1222 **F** (08) 8389 1233 **OPEN** Wed–Sun & public hols 10.30–5
WINEMAKER Vince Scaffidi **EST.** 1994 **CASES** 6000
SUMMARY Talunga owners Vince and Tina Scaffidi have a one-third share of the 62-ha Gumeracha Vineyards, and it is from these vineyards that the Talunga wines are sourced. In November 2002 the 2001 Sangiovese won the trophy for Best Red Wine of Show at the Australian Alternative Varieties Wine Show.

Tamar Ridge

Auburn Road, Kayena, Tas 7270 **REGION** Northern Tasmania
T (03) 6394 1111 **F** (03) 6394 1126 **WEB** www.tamarridgewines.com.au **OPEN** 7 days 10–5
WINEMAKER Michael Fogarty, Matt Lowe **EST.** 1994 **CASES** 40 000
SUMMARY In April 2003 Gunns Limited, a large, publicly listed Tasmanian forestry and agribusiness entity, purchased Tamar Ridge. With the retention of Dr Richard Smart as viticultural advisor, the largest expansion of Tasmanian plantings is now underway, with 219 ha of wines, 72.5 in bearing, in the vicinity of the winery. A further development at Waterhouse, in the far northeastern corner of the State, is also planned. Exports to the UK, the US and other major markets.

🍷🍷🍷🍷🍷 **Chardonnay 2002** Very attractive stone fruit and citrus; elegant, intense and long. **RATING** 94 **DRINK** 2013 $ 21

🍷🍷🍷🍷🍷 **Pinot Noir 2003** Medium purple-red; intense plum and spice fruit runs through a long palate; lingering finish and aftertaste. **RATING** 93 **DRINK** 2010 $ 26
Sauvignon Blanc 2004 A mix of gooseberry and mineral; clean, firm, long palate; lemony acidity. **RATING** 90 **DRINK** 2008 $ 19.99

🍷🍷🍷🍷 **Chardonnay 2003** Big, rich, ripe stone fruit and melon; some creamy malolactic fermentation notes. **RATING** 89 **DRINK** 2009 $ 21
Reserve Pinot Noir 2002 Medium-bodied; quite stylish and spicy; good length. **RATING** 89 **DRINK** 2007 $ 25
Riesling 2004 Aromas and flavours of talc, mineral and slate; fearsome acidity needs to soften and integrate. **RATING** 87 **DRINK** 2014 $ 19

🍷🍷🍷🍷 **Devils Corner Riesling 2004** **RATING** 86 **DRINK** 2008 $ 14
Gewurztraminer 2004 **RATING** 86 **DRINK** 2008 $ 19
Pinot Gris 2004 **RATING** 86 **DRINK** 2008 $ 21
Devils Corner Pinot Noir 2004 **RATING** 86 **DRINK** 2007 $ 18
Devils Corner Rose 2004 **RATING** 85 **DRINK** Now $ 14

Tamborine Estate Wines   ★★★

32 Hartley Road, North Tamborine, Qld 4272 **REGION** Queensland Coastal
T (07) 5545 1711 **F** (07) 5545 3522 **WEB** www.tamborineestate.com.au **OPEN** 7 days 10–4
WINEMAKER John Cassegrain **EST.** 1990 **CASES** 4000
SUMMARY Tamborine Estate is a joint venture between the well-known John Cassegrain (of Cassegrain Wines at Port Macquarie) and French-born entrepeneur Bernard Forey (owner of the large Richfield Vineyard at Tenterfield in northern NSW). They have acquired the former Mount Tamborine Winery and its 2.5 ha of merlot, cabernet franc and malbec, planted adjacent to the winery. Exports to Switzerland, Singapore and Thailand.

🍷🍷🍷🍷 **Reserve Chardonnay 2003** Very well made; good grapefruit and melon varietal aromas and flavours; sensitive barrel ferment oak inputs; good length. **RATING** 90 **DRINK** 2008 $ 28

🍷🍷🍷🍷 **Shiraz Cabernet 2000** Medium-bodied; well balanced; good line; simply a little light and straightforward. **RATING** 88 **DRINK** 2009 $ 22
Unwooded Chardonnay 2004 Light to medium-bodied; stone fruit; some elegance, but nippy acid adjustment. **RATING** 87 **DRINK** Now $ 16

🍷🍷🍷 **Chardonnay 2003** **RATING** 85 **DRINK** Now $ 22
Sauvignon Blanc 2004 **RATING** 84 **DRINK** Now $ 22
Hinterland Botrytis Semillon Chardonnay NV **RATING** 84 **DRINK** 2007 $ 19

Rosso Dolce NV RATING 84 DRINK Now $15
Hinterland Tawny NV RATING 84 DRINK Now $17
Hinterland Mist 2003 RATING 84 DRINK Now $17

ΥΥΥ Verdelho 2003 RATING 83 $19
Rose 2004 RATING 83 $15
Cabernet Merlot 2003 RATING 83 $17
Sparkling Cuvee NV RATING 83 $17
Sparkling Shiraz NV RATING 83 $19
Verdelho Semillon 2002 RATING 82 $19
Bianco Dolce NV RATING 82 $15
Reserve Black Shiraz 2001 RATING 81 $29

Tamburlaine

358 McDonalds Road, Pokolbin, NSW 2321 REGION Lower Hunter Valley
T (02) 4998 7570 F (02) 4998 7763 WEB www.mywinery.com OPEN 7 days 9.30–5
WINEMAKER Mark Davidson, Jeremy Gordon EST. 1966 CASES 50 000
SUMMARY A thriving business which, notwithstanding the fact that it has doubled its already substantial production in recent years, sells over 90% of its wine through the cellar door and by mailing list (with an active tasting club members' cellar program offering wines which are held and matured at Tamburlaine). The maturing of the estate-owned Orange vineyard has led to a dramatic rise in quality across the range. Exports to Europe, the US and Japan.

ΥΥΥΥΥ Hunter Valley Semillon 2004 Attractive, well balanced; lots of flavour and character, ranging through citrus to near-tropical; clean, crisp finish. Screwcap. RATING 93
DRINK 2014 $22
Members Orange Vineyard Syrah 2003 Scented, spicy red and black cherry; medium-bodied; fine, silky tannins; delicious, fluid line and mouthfeel. Screwcap. RATING 93
DRINK 2013 $32
Members Orange Vineyard Chardonnay 2003 Elegant, light to medium-bodied; citrus and melon; a subtle touch of spicy oak; good length. Screwcap. RATING 90 DRINK 2008 $28
Members Orange Vineyard Cabernet Sauvignon 2003 Light to medium-bodied; fresh, vibrant red and black fruits; silky smooth; laser-precise vineyard and regional style; elegant. Screwcap. RATING 90 DRINK 2013 $32

ΥΥΥΥ Members Orange Vineyard Riesling 2003 Clean; gentle passionfruit/tropical aromas; high flavour, slightly blurred finish. Screwcap. RATING 89 DRINK 2008 $22
Hunter Valley Syrah 2003 Medium-bodied; quite fresh red and black fruits; vanilla oak, fine tannins. Screwcap. RATING 89 DRINK 2013 $32
Members Orange Vineyard Merlot 2003 Strongly varietal in olive/earth/red fruit spectrum; medium-bodied, with firmish tannins; needs time. Screwcap. RATING 89
DRINK 2010 $32
Hunter Valley Cabernet Merlot 2003 Solid, ripe black fruits/blackcurrant/plum; plenty of depth; good balance. Screwcap. RATING 89 DRINK 2013 $28
Hunter Valley Chardonnay 2004 Medium-bodied; nicely balanced nectarine, peach and spicy oak; crisp finish. Screwcap. RATING 88 DRINK 2009 $28
Hunter Valley Chambourcin 2003 Fine, soft, ripe plum and spice entry; wanders away on the finish. Screwcap. RATING 87 DRINK Now $28

ΥΥΥΥ Hunter Valley Verdelho 2004 RATING 86 DRINK 2007 $22

Taminick Cellars

Booth Road, Taminick, Vic 3675 REGION Glenrowan
T (03) 5766 2282 F (03) 5766 2151 OPEN Mon–Sat 9–5, Sun 10–5
WINEMAKER Peter Booth EST. 1904 CASES 4000
SUMMARY Traditional producer of massively flavoured and very long-lived red wines, most sold to long-term customers and through the cellar door.

ΥΥΥΥ Cliff Booth Shiraz 2002 Deep colour; potent, concentrated, ripe prune and plum; slight heat on the finish, but impressive. RATING 89 DRINK 2015
Liqueur Muscat NV Christmas cake, raisin, sweet multi-spices; some rancio; good length.
RATING 89 DRINK Now

Tandou Wines ★★★

Nixon Road, Monash, SA 5342 **REGION** Riverland
T (08) 8583 6500 **F** (08) 8583 6599 **WEB** www.tandou.com.au **OPEN** Mon–Fri 10–4
WINEMAKER Stuart Auld, John Lempens **EST.** 2001 **CASES** 30 000
SUMMARY Tandou is a subsidiary of a diversified public company which has 17 000 ha of land 142 km southeast of Broken Hill and 50 km from Mildura. At its Millewa vineyard, 450 ha of vines have been planted to chardonnay, verdelho, cabernet sauvignon, merlot, shiraz and sangiovese. A winery with a 21 000-tonne capacity has been built, and produces a range of wine sold in bulk, as cleanskin bottles and under the proprietary Broken Earth and Wontanella brands (the latter is a cheaper, second label). The wines are well made and competitively priced.

▼▼▼▼ **Broken Earth Viognier 2003** Clean, rich; medium to full-bodied; ripe pastille and apricot fruit nicely balanced by acidity. Screwcap. **RATING** 87 **DRINK** Now $ 14.50
Broken Earth Shiraz 2003 Some structure and above-average flavour for the region; blackberry and fine tannins. Screwcap. **RATING** 87 **DRINK** Now $ 14.50
Wontanella Cabernet Merlot 2003 Punches above its weight; lots of blackcurrant fruit; minimal tannins and oak. Screwcap. **RATING** 87 **DRINK** 2008 $ 10.95
Broken Earth Petit Verdot 2003 Plenty of good colour, body and dark berry fruits; ripe, not aggressive, tannins. Cork. **RATING** 87 **DRINK** 2007 $ 14.50

▼▼▼▽ **Wontanella Colombard Viognier 2003** Vigour ex the Colombard; quite tangy and long; good overall flavour and balance. Screwcap. **RATING** 86 **DRINK** Now $ 10.95
Wontanella Shiraz 2003 **RATING** 86 **DRINK** Now $ 10.95
Broken Earth Sangiovese 2003 Light to medium-bodied; good mouthfeel; fair varietal typicity; cherry and spice; thins off on the finish. Cork. **RATING** 86 **DRINK** Now $ 14.50
Wontanella Chardonnay 2003 **RATING** 85 **DRINK** Now $ 10.95
Broken Earth Chardonnay 2003 **RATING** 85 **DRINK** Now $ 14
Broken Earth Cabernet Sauvignon 2003 **RATING** 85 **DRINK** 2007 $ 14.50
Wontanella Tempranillo 2003 **RATING** 84 **DRINK** Now $ 10.95

▼▼▼ **Broken Earth Verdelho 2003** **RATING** 83 $ 14
Wontanella Sangiovese Petit Verdot 2003 **RATING** 83 $ 10.95

Tangaratta Estate NR

RMB 637, Old Winton Road, Tamworth, NSW 2340 **REGION** Northern Slopes Zone
T (02) 6761 5660 **F** (02) 6766 5383 **OPEN** Sun–Fri 10–5
WINEMAKER John Hordern (Contract) **EST.** 1999 **CASES** 23 000
SUMMARY Another recent entry into the Northern Slopes Zone, with a 29-ha vineyard planted to verdelho, cabernet sauvignon, merlot and shiraz. The wines are exported to Canada, Japan, Malaysia, Singapore and the US, and are also available by mail order and through the cellar door, which has light meals and barbecue facilities when open.

Tanglewood Downs NR

Bulldog Creek Road, Merricks North, Vic 3926 **REGION** Mornington Peninsula
T (03) 5974 3325 **F** (03) 5974 4170 **OPEN** Sun–Mon 12–5
WINEMAKER Ken Bilham, Wendy Bilham **EST.** 1984 **CASES** 1200
SUMMARY One of the smaller and lower-profile wineries on the Mornington Peninsula, with Ken Bilham quietly doing his own thing on 2.5 ha of estate plantings. Lunch and dinner are available by arrangement.

Tanglewood Vines NR

RMB 383, Bridgetown, WA 6255 (postal) **REGION** Blackwood Valley
T (08) 9764 4051 **OPEN** Not
WINEMAKER Contract **EST.** 1999 **CASES** NA
SUMMARY Tanglewood Vines has established 2.4 ha of cabernet sauvignon and 2 ha of merlot, with a planting of viognier in 2002.

Tanjil Wines ★★★★

11 Brigantine Court, Patterson Lakes, Vic 3197 (postal) **REGION** Gippsland
T (03) 9773 0378 **F** (03) 9773 0378 **OPEN** Not
WINEMAKER Robert Hewet, Olga Garot **EST.** 2001 **CASES** 1200
SUMMARY Robert Hewet and Olga Garot planted 3 ha of pinot noir and 1 ha of pinot grigio on a
north-facing slope at an altitude of 200m between the Latrobe and Tanjil valleys. The red-brown
loam over clay has good water retention, and the vines have not been nor will be irrigated; the
expected yield is 5 tonnes per hectare. The 2002 vintage wines were made from purchased fruit;
2003 was the first estate-grown production of pinot noir.

 Gippsland Pinot Grigio 2004 Highly aromatic and floral; fresh and lively, with hints of
spice and musk; excellent length and balance. **RATING** 90 **DRINK** Now **$** 17
Gippsland Pinot Noir 2004 Slightly cloudy, unfiltered; complex, tangy, spicy, foresty
edges to black cherry and plum fruit; good length and acidity. Screwcap. **RATING** 90
DRINK 2009

Tannery Lane Vineyard ★★★

174 Tannery Lane, Mandurang, Vic 3551 **REGION** Bendigo
T (03) 5439 3227 **F** (03) 5439 4003 **OPEN** By appointment
WINEMAKER Lindsay Ross (Contract) **EST.** 1990 **CASES** 250
SUMMARY In 1990 planting of the present total of 2 ha of shiraz, cabernet sauvignon, cabernet franc,
sangiovese, merlot and nebbiolo began. Their sangiovese was one of the first plantings of the variety
in the Bendigo region. The micro-production is sold through the cellar door while stocks last, which
typically is not for very long. Now owned by the Williams family.

Tantemaggie NR

Mullineaux Road, Pemberton, WA 6260 **REGION** Pemberton
T (08) 9776 1164 **F** (08) 9776 1810 **OPEN** By appointment
WINEMAKER Contract **EST.** 1987 **CASES** 300
SUMMARY Tantemaggie was established by the Pottinger family with the help of a bequest from a
deceased aunt named Maggie. It is part of a mixed farming operation, and by far the greatest part of
the 28 ha is under long-term contract to Houghton. The bulk of the plantings are cabernet
sauvignon, verdelho, chardonnay and sauvignon blanc, the former producing the light-bodied style
favoured by the Pottingers.

Tapanappa NR

PO Box 174, Crafers, SA 5152 **REGION** Wrattonbully
T 0418 818 223 **F** (08) 8370 8374 **OPEN** Not
WINEMAKER Brian Croser **EST.** 2003 **CASES** NA
SUMMARY Arguably the most interesting of all new wineries to be announced in Australia over the
past few years. Its partners are Brian Croser of Petaluma, Jean-Michel Cazes of Chateau Lynch-
Bages in Pauillac and Societe Jacques Bollinger, the parent company of Champagne Bollinger. The
core of the business is the Koppamurra vineyard acquired from Koppamurra Wines prior to the
2003 vintage; the 2003 Cabernet Sauvignon Merlot and Cabernet Franc were released under the
Tapanappa brand in 2005.

Tapestry ★★★★

Olivers Road, McLaren Vale, SA 5171 **REGION** McLaren Vale
T (08) 8323 9196 **F** (08) 8323 9746 **WEB** www.tapestrywines.com.au **OPEN** 7 days 11–5
WINEMAKER Jon Ketley **EST.** 1971 **CASES** 15 000
SUMMARY After a relatively brief period of ownership by Brian Light, the former Merrivale Winery
was acquired by the Gerard family, previously owners of Chapel Hill, in 1997. It has 40 ha of 30-year-
old vineyards, 6.5 ha in McLaren Vale and 33.5 ha in Bakers Gully. Less than half the grapes are used
for the Tapestry label. Exports to the UK, the US, Singapore, Hong Kong and New Zealand.

Tarcoola Estate

NR

60 Spiller Road, Lethbridge, Vic 3332 **REGION** Geelong
T (03) 5281 9337 **F** (03) 5281 9311 **OPEN** Weekends 10–5, or by appointment
WINEMAKER Keith Wood **EST.** 1972 **CASES** 3250
SUMMARY The establishment date is both accurate and misleading. The 7.2-ha vineyard was planted between 1972 and 1974. When Keith Wood, who provided engineering services to Seppelt at Great Western, purchased the property in 1990, the winery and the vineyard needed rehabilitation. He decided to gain experience working weekends at other vineyards in 1990 and 1991; during that time he met wife-to-be Annelies, who took over the resurrection of the vineyards. Between 1991 and 1996 the grapes were sold; from 1997 to 1999 wine was made in bulk, but also sold; and it was not until the 2000 vintage that Keith Wood made the wine for sale by Tarcoola Estate (Muller Thurgau, Riesling, Chardonnay, Shiraz, Cabernet Shiraz and Cabernet Sauvignon). Very significant wine show success has followed, and Tarcoola Estate is already buying grapes from other growers in the region, and making the wine for another local producer.

Tarrangower Estate

★★☆

17 Baldry Street, Malmsbury, Vic 3446 **REGION** Macedon Ranges
T (03) 5423 2088 **F** (03) 5423 2088 **WEB** www.macedonranges.com/tarrangowerestate
OPEN Weekends 10–5, or by appointment
WINEMAKER Tom Gyorffy **EST.** 1993 **CASES** 200
SUMMARY Tarrangower Estate is on the northeastern edge of the township of Malmsbury, at the western end of the Macedon Ranges. It has an altitude of 470m, it is one of the warmest sites in the region. The varieties planted are chardonnay, shiraz, cabernet sauvignon and merlot. Tom Gyorffy is a Melbourne lawyer, but as a mature-age student he graduated with an associate degree in applied science (winegrowing) from Charles Sturt University in 1997. His philosophy is to make 'natural wines' and to deliberately oxidise the chardonnay (hyper-oxidation).

♈♈♈ **The Revolutionary's Chardonnay 2002 RATING** 79

Tarrawarra Estate

★★★★★

Healesville Road, Yarra Glen, Vic 3775 **REGION** Yarra Valley
T (03) 5962 3311 **F** (03) 5962 3887 **WEB** www.tarrawarra.com.au **OPEN** 7 days 11–5
WINEMAKER Clare Halloran, Bruce Walker **EST.** 1983 **CASES** 4000
SUMMARY Slowly developing Chardonnay of great structure and complexity is the winery specialty; robust Pinot Noir also needs time and evolves impressively if given it. The opening of the large onsite art gallery (and its attendant café/restaurant) in early 2004 adds another dimension to the tourism tapestry of the Yarra Valley. For the time being, the gallery is only open Wed–Sun, but as the Michelin Guide says, it is definitely worth a detour. National retail distribution; exports to the UK, Switzerland, Belgium, Singapore, Italy and the US.

♈♈♈♈♈ **Chardonnay 2002** Complex barrel ferment characters interwoven through tightly framed nectarine and melon fruit; good acidity; stylish. **RATING** 94 **DRINK** 2010 $ 40
Pinot Noir 2002 Very clear-cut varietal aromas and fruit flavours; relatively light-bodied, but elegant; spicy cherry fruit and fine tannins. **RATING** 94 **DRINK** 2009 $ 50

Tarrington Vineyards

★★★★☆

Hamilton Highway, Tarrington, Vic 3301 **REGION** Henty
T (03) 5572 4509 **F** (03) 5572 4509 **OPEN** By appointment
WINEMAKER Tamara Irish, Dianne Nagorcka **EST.** 1993 **CASES** 300
SUMMARY The grapegrowing and winemaking practices of Burgundy permeate every aspect of Tarrington Vineyards. While its establishment began in 1993, there has been no hurry to bring the vineyard into production. Two varieties only have been planted: pinot noir and chardonnay, with a planting density varying between 3333 and 8170 vines per hectare. There are 9 clones in the 2 ha of pinot noir, and 4 clones in the 0.5 ha of chardonnay. The approach to making the Pinot Noir is common in Burgundy; the unoaked Chardonnay is kept in tank on fine lees for 9 months, the traditional method of making Chablis. Everything about the operation, including the packaging and

the background material, speaks of a labour of love. The exemplary wines are to be found on a thoroughly impressive collection of Victoria's top restaurant wine lists. Exports to the UK.

ŢŢŢŢŢ **Chardonnay 2003** Intense, lemony, minerally acidity provides the core around which the wine is woven; flowery, fresh-cut stone fruit; long finish; no oak intrusion. Quality cork. **RATING** 94 **DRINK** 2010 $47

ŢŢŢŢ **Pinot Noir 2003** Light to medium-bodied; bright cherry/forest fruit aromas; unusual flavours for the vineyard; not showing its 13.5° alcohol; lemony acidity to close. Well off the normal pace, but may improve. **RATING** 89 **DRINK** 2009 $45

Tarwin Ridge

NR

Wintles Road, Leongatha South, Vic 3953 **REGION** Gippsland
T (03) 5664 3211 **F** (03) 5664 3211 **OPEN** Weekends & hols 10–5
WINEMAKER Brian Anstee **EST.** 1983 **CASES** 700
SUMMARY For the time being Brian Anstee is making his wines at Nicholson River, under the gaze of fellow social worker Ken Eckersley; the wines come from 2 ha of estate pinot and 0.5 ha each of cabernet and sauvignon blanc.

Tassell Park Wines

Treeton Road, Cowaramup, WA 6284 **REGION** Margaret River
T (08) 9755 5440 **F** (08) 9755 5442 **WEB** www.tassellparkwines.com **OPEN** 7 days 10–5
WINEMAKER Peter Stanlake (Consultant) **EST.** 2001 **CASES** 1500
SUMMARY One of the light brigade of newcomers to the Margaret River region. Ian and Tricia Tassell have 7 ha of sauvignon blanc, chenin blanc, semillon, cabernet sauvignon, merlot, shiraz and petit verdot. From the 2004 vintage, winemaking moved onsite under the direction of Peter Stanlake. The wines are sold through the website, by mail order and through the cellar door (which offers light meals to take away).

ŢŢŢŢ **Margaret River Shiraz 2003** Light to medium-bodied; an array of predominantly red and black fruits; raspberry, black cherry and plum; ripe, supple mouthfeel; minimal tannins and oak. **RATING** 89 **DRINK** 2010 $22
Margaret River Cabernet Sauvignon 2003 As with all the red wines from Tassell Park, light to medium-bodied; sweet redcurrant fruit; minimal tannin structure. Cork. **RATING** 89 **DRINK** 2009 $22
Margaret River Cabernet Sauvignon Merlot 2003 Light to medium-bodied; quite sweet, juicy berry, blackcurrant and cassis fruit; fine, lingering tannins. Cork. **RATING** 88 **DRINK** 2010 $20
Margaret River Sauvignon Blanc Semillon 2004 Spotlessly clean; delicate, seamless fusion of varietals; light-bodied, but has length. Screwcap. **RATING** 87 **DRINK** 2007 $17

ŢŢŢŢ **Margaret River Chenin Blanc 2004** **RATING** 85 **DRINK** Now $17

Tatachilla

★★★★☆

151 Main Road, McLaren Vale, SA 5171 **REGION** McLaren Vale
T (08) 8323 8656 **F** (08) 8323 9096 **WEB** www.tatachillawinery.com.au **OPEN** Mon–Sat 10–5, Sunday & public hols 11–5
WINEMAKER Michael Fragos, Justin McNamee **EST.** 1901 **CASES** 250 000
SUMMARY Tatachilla was reborn in 1995 but has had an at-times tumultuous history going back to 1901. For most of the time between 1901 and 1961 the winery was owned by Penfolds. It was closed in that year and reopened in 1965 as the Southern Vales Co-operative. In the late 1980s it was purchased and renamed The Vales but did not flourish; in 1993 it was purchased by local grower Vic Zerella and former Kaiser Stuhl chief executive Keith Smith. After extensive renovations, the winery was officially reopened in 1995 and won a number of tourist awards and accolades. The star turns are Keystone (Grenache Shiraz) and Foundation Shiraz, bursting with vibrant fruit. Became part of Banksia Wines in 2001, in turn acquired by Lion Nathan in 2002. Exports to the UK, the US and New Zealand.

ɣɣɣɣɣ **1901 McLaren Vale Cabernet Sauvignon 2001** Strong regional bitter chocolate overlay; medium to full-bodied; supple and smooth; ripe tannins, long finish. **RATING** 94 **DRINK** 2016 $ 42

ɣɣɣɣɣ **McLaren Vale Chardonnay 2003** Attractive grapefruit and melon aromas and flavours; refined style; subtle oak. **RATING** 90 **DRINK** 2007 $ 16.50
Partners Cabernet Sauvignon Shiraz 2003 Typically powerful wine; black fruits with substantial, but balanced tannins; a little rustic, but honest. **RATING** 90 **DRINK** 2010 $ 14.90

ɣɣɣɣ **Growers 2004 RATING** 86 **DRINK** Now $ 14.90

Tatehams Wines ★★★

Main North Road, Auburn, SA 5451 **REGION** Clare Valley
T (08) 8849 2030 **F** (08) 8849 2260 **OPEN** Wed–Sun 10–5
WINEMAKER Mike Jeandupeux **EST.** 1998 **CASES** 500
SUMMARY Mike and Isabel Jeandupeux left the French-speaking part of Switzerland in September 1997 to begin a new life in Australia. They now operate a restaurant and guesthouse at Auburn, in the southern end of the Clare Valley. The 1863 stone building, which originally operated as a general store and stables, has been completely refurbished, with several buildings offering a variety of upmarket accommodation. The winemaking side of the business is effectively an add-on; most of the wine is sold through the restaurant and cellar door, and by a mailing list. Limited distribution in Adelaide.

ɣɣɣɣ **Sangiovese 2003** Clear varietal character; light to medium-bodied; red cherry, tea and spice; fine tannins, not forced. **RATING** 87 **DRINK** 2008 $ 24

ɣɣɣɣ **Clare Valley Merlot 2003 RATING** 84 **DRINK** 2010 $ 24

Tatler Wines ★★★★☆

477 Lovedale Road, Lovedale, NSW 2321 **REGION** Lower Hunter Valley
T (02) 4930 9139 **F** (02) 4930 9145 **WEB** www.tatlerwines.com **OPEN** 7 days 9.30–5.30
WINEMAKER Jim Chatto, Ross Pearson, Alasdair Sutherland, Jenny Bright (Contract) **EST.** 1998
CASES 2000
SUMMARY Tatler Wines is a family-owned company headed by Theo and Spiro Isakidis, Sydney hoteliers. The name comes via the Tatler Hotel on George Street, Sydney, where the Isakidis family met Tony Brown and wife Deborah; the latter two now run the Hunter vineyard and cellar door. It is a substantial one, with 21 ha of estate vineyards planted to chardonnay, shiraz, semillon, pinot gris, cabernet franc and sangiovese.

ɣɣɣɣɣ **Nigel's Hunter Valley Semillon 2004** Feather-light, crisp and lively lemongrass and lemon zest; excellent finish. Screwcap. **RATING** 94 **DRINK** 2014 $ 19

ɣɣɣɣɣ **Whispers Semillon Sauvignon Blanc 2004** The blend works very well, the structure ex Semillon, and abundant passionfruit and gooseberry flavour ex Sauvignon Blanc. Screwcap. **RATING** 93 **DRINK** 2008 $ 19
Archie's Paddock Hunter Valley Shiraz 2003 Fresh, firm, vibrant black fruits; long, moderately brisk finish; fine tannins. Cork. **RATING** 90 **DRINK** 2013 $ 22

ɣɣɣɣ **Dimitri's Paddock Hunter Valley Chardonnay 2004** Fresh, medium-bodied; sweet melon, fig and stone fruit; substantial flavour; oak just a little heavy. Screwcap. **RATING** 89 **DRINK** 2008 $ 20
Archie's Paddock Hunter Valley Shiraz 2002 Firm style; slightly hard edges to red and black fruits; has absorbed 17 months in oak; possibly too much acid adjustment. Cork. **RATING** 87 **DRINK** 2012 $ 22

Tawonga Vineyard ★★★

2 Drummond Street, Tawonga, Vic 3697 **REGION** Alpine Valleys
T (03) 5754 4945 **F** (03) 5754 4925 **WEB** www.tawongavineyard.com **OPEN** By appointment
WINEMAKER John Adams **EST.** 1994 **CASES** 490

SUMMARY Diz and John Adams' vineyard is at the head of the Kiewa Valley, looking out onto the four main mountains of the area: Mt Bogong, Mt Emu, Mt York and Mt Tawonga. It is on a northeast slope with a mixture of deep, red loam/clay and shallow red loam over ancient river stone soils, at an altitude of 1200 ft. Over the years, the Shiraz has won many wine show medals.

ΤΤΤ�ﾖ **Merlot 2001 RATING** 86 **DRINK** 2007 **$** 12.95

Taylors   ★★★★★

Taylors Road, Auburn, SA 5451 **REGION** Clare Valley
T (08) 8849 2008 **F** (08) 8849 2240 **WEB** www.taylorswines.com.au **OPEN** Mon–Fri 9–5, Sat & public hols 10–5, Sun 10–4
WINEMAKER Adam Eggins, Helen McCarthy **EST.** 1969 **CASES** 400 000
SUMMARY The family-founded and owned Taylors continues to flourish and expand; its vineyards now total over 500 ha, by far the largest holding in Clare Valley. There have also been substantial changes both in terms of the winemaking team and in terms of the wine style and quality, particularly through the outstanding St Andrews range. Exports to the UK, the US and other major markets.

ΤΤΤΤΤ **St Andrews Riesling 2000** Glowing yellow-green; an intense mix of lime and toast aromas; very intense, very long lime juice flavours with outstanding drive. **RATING** 95 **DRINK** 2009 **$** 35
Jaraman Clare Valley McLaren Vale Shiraz 2002 Very good colour; an exercise in controlled generosity; long, intense, lingering black fruit flavours; good control of extract. Two gold and two silver medals. **RATING** 94 **DRINK** 2017 **$** 29.50
St Andrews Cabernet Sauvignon 1999 A mix of blackcurrant, blackberry, earth and mocha/vanilla aromas and flavours; fine, lingering, ripe tannins add length. Multiple trophy and gold medal winner. **RATING** 94 **DRINK** 2017 **$** 59.95

ΤΤΤΤﾖ **St Andrews Shiraz 2001** Big, dense chocolate, blackberry and plum fruit; well-integrated oak and ripe tannins. **RATING** 93 **DRINK** 2021 **$** 55
Jaraman Clare Valley Coonawarra Cabernet Sauvignon 2002 Very complex wine; multiple layers of flavours and black fruits, with hints of Coonawarra earth; long, savoury tannins to close. **RATING** 92 **DRINK** 2017 **$** 29.50
Jaraman Riesling 2004 Very pale straw-green; spotlessly clean; aromatic lime, spice and mineral; fine, elegant and harmonious mouthfeel. Clare Valley/Eden Valley. **RATING** 91 **DRINK** 2010 **$** 24.50
St Andrews Shiraz 2000 A potent, long palate; savoury/earthy overtones to black fruits; good oak and tannin management; long finish. **RATING** 90 **DRINK** 2010 **$** 60
Clare Valley Merlot 2004 Positive varietal fruit in riper mode; good balance and mouthfeel from blackcurrant and redcurrant fruit; ripe tannins, subtle oak. **RATING** 90 **DRINK** 2012 **$** 17
St Andrews Merlot 2002 Not for the only time, shows surprising varietal character; fine structure; earth, olive and blackcurrant fruits; controlled oak. Screwcap. **RATING** 90 **DRINK** 2010 **$** 55

ΤΤΤΤ **Clare Valley Riesling 2004** Clean lime-accented aromas; good balance and mouthfeel; shortens slightly on the finish. **RATING** 89 **DRINK** 2010 **$** 17
Clare Valley Shiraz 2004 While not reduced, the bouquet was shut down soon after bottling; potent juicy blackberry fruit; minimal oak impact; lots of potential to improve. **RATING** 89 **DRINK** 2014 **$** 17
Adelaide Hills Sauvignon Blanc 2004 Sweet tropical fruit; light to medium-bodied; balanced acidity. **RATING** 88 **DRINK** Now **$** 18
Clare Valley Shiraz 2003 Medium-bodied; black fruits with fine, savoury tannins; subtle oak. **RATING** 88 **DRINK** 2010 **$** 18
Promised Land Semillon Sauvignon Blanc 2004 Well put together; citrus and more tropical fruit; good acidity, subliminal sweetness. **RATING** 87 **DRINK** Now **$** 13.95
Jaraman Chardonnay 2003 Light to medium-bodied peachy fruit, soft oak; easy, early-drinking style. Clare Valley/Adelaide Hills. **RATING** 87 **DRINK** Now **$** 24.50
Clare Valley Cabernet Sauvignon 2003 Fresh cassis and redcurrant; light to medium-bodied, but does have fine tannins to close, and may grow in bottle. **RATING** 87 **DRINK** 2009 **$** 17
Clare Valley Cabernet Sauvignon 2002 Strongly savoury/earthy in austere mode; black fruits and a touch of bitter chocolate. **RATING** 87 **DRINK** 2010 **$** 19

ΨΨΨΨ **Clare Valley Pinot Noir 2003** RATING 86 DRINK 2009 $17
Promised Land Shiraz Cabernet 2002 RATING 86 DRINK 2007 $13.95
Promised Land Cabernet Merlot 2003 RATING 84 DRINK Now $12

ΨΨΨ **Promised Land Unwooded Chardonnay 2004** RATING 83 $13.95
Clare Valley Chardonnay 2004 RATING 83 $17
Promised Land Crouchen Chardonnay 2004 RATING 83 $13

Teakles Hill Wines   NR

PO Box 251, Woodside, SA 5244 **REGION** Adelaide Hills
T (08) 8389 9375 **F** (08) 8389 9375 **OPEN** Not
WINEMAKER Contract **EST.** 2001 **CASES** 1000
SUMMARY William Borchardt and James Bidstrup have established 4 ha of vineyard, planted to pinot
noir, cabernet sauvignon and shiraz. A small amount is made for sale under the Teakles Hill brand,
sold by mail order.

Temple Bruer

Milang Road, Strathalbyn, SA 5255 **REGION** Langhorne Creek
T (08) 8537 0203 **F** (08) 8537 0131 **WEB** www.templebruer.com.au **OPEN** Mon–Fri 9.30–4.30
WINEMAKER David Bruer **EST.** 1980 **CASES** 14 000
SUMMARY Always known for its eclectic range of wines, Temple Bruer (which also carries on a
substantial business as a vine propagation nursery) has seen a sharp lift in wine quality. Clean,
modern redesigned labels add to the appeal of a stimulatingly different range of red wines. Part of the
production from the 24 ha of estate vineyards is sold to others, the remainder being made under the
Temple Bruer label. The vineyard is now certified organic. Exports to the US and Japan.

ΨΨΨΨΨ **Reserve Organically Grown Cabernet Sauvignon Petit Verdot 2001** Very powerful, very
intense black fruits and cigar box; despite the power, has great line and flow; Petit Verdot
(19%) contribution obvious; very good tannins. High-quality cork. **RATING** 94 **DRINK** 2016
$25.50

ΨΨΨΨΨ **Reserve Organically Grown Merlot 1999** Impressive structure, mouthfeel and flavour;
has developed very well; spice, olive and dark fruits; fine, ripe, soft tannins; good French
oak. **RATING** 93 **DRINK** 2009 $25.50
Shiraz Malbec 2001 Medium-bodied; clean, sweet red and black fruits, the Malbec
making a positive contribution; supple and soft mouthfeel; fine, ripe tannins; exceptional
value. **RATING** 92 **DRINK** 2011 $18

ΨΨΨΨ **Cabernet Merlot 2001** Powerful, savoury and tightly structured black fruits, olive and
bramble; pleasing austerity, though not the usual soft and supple regional mouthfeel.
RATING 89 **DRINK** 2010 $18
Reserve Botrytis Semillon (500 ml) 1999 Golden brown; a complex and rich honey and
raisin mix on a layered palate. Drink soon. **RATING** 89 **DRINK** 2007 $25.50
Langhorne Creek Grenache Shiraz Viognier 2002 Fresh, vibrant, juicy wine; 10%
Viognier; synergistic, but obvious apricot edge to raspberry flavours. **RATING** 87
DRINK 2007 $18

ΨΨΨΨ **Riesling 2004** RATING 85 DRINK 2007 $15.50
Chenin Blanc 2004 RATING 85 DRINK Now $15.50

Templer's Mill   NR

The University of Sydney, Leeds Parade, Orange, NSW 2800 **REGION** Orange
T (02) 6360 5570 **F** (02) 6362 7625 **WEB** www.orange.usyd.edu.au/ **OPEN** 7 days 11–4
WINEMAKER Reynolds Wines **EST.** 1997 **CASES** 1300
SUMMARY Templer's Mill was one of Australia's first flour mills, providing flour for early goldfields at
Ophir near Orange. this historic mill is now a ruin on Narrambla, a property adjacent to the
University of Sydney's Orange campus farm, and the birthplace of AB (Banjo) Paterson. The 19.4-ha
vineyard is planted to cabernet sauvignon, chardonnay, shiraz, sauvignon blanc and merlot (in
descending order of magnitude); part of the production is made under the Temper's Mill label, part
sold as grapes, the operation overseen by viticulture lecturer Peter Hedberg.

Tempus Two Wines ★★★☆

Broke Road, Pokolbin, NSW 2321 REGION Lower Hunter Valley
T (02) 4993 3999 F (02) 4993 3988 WEB www.tempustwo.com.au OPEN 7 days 9–5
WINEMAKER Sarah-Kate Dineen EST. 1997 CASES 50 000
SUMMARY Tempus Two is the name for what was once Hermitage Road Wines. It is a mix of Latin (Tempus means time) and English; the change was forced on the winery by the EU Wine Agreement and the prohibition of the use of the word 'hermitage' on Australian wine labels. Some very attractive wines have appeared so far, and will do so in the future, no doubt, particularly given the arrival of Sarah-Kate Dineen as winemaker in the striking new winery on Broke Road. Exports to the UK.

ŶŶŶŶ **Mayday Hill Sangiovese 2003** Fragrant spice, tobacco leaf, lemon and red berry aromas and flavours; attractive slippery tannins. Beechworth. RATING 89 DRINK 2007 $ 35

ŶŶŶ **Pewter Vine Vale Barossa Shiraz 2003** RATING 83

Ten Minutes by Tractor Wine Co. ★★★★★

111 Roberts Road, Main Ridge, Vic 3928 REGION Mornington Peninsula
T (03) 5989 6455 F (03) 5989 6433 WEB www.tenminutesbytractor.com.au OPEN Weekends & hols 11–5, 7 days in Jan
WINEMAKER Richard McIntyre, Alex White (Contract) EST. 1999 CASES 3500
SUMMARY Ten Minutes by Tractor was sold to Martin Spedding in early 2004, but the same three families (Judd, McCutcheon and Wallis), with their vineyards 10 minutes by tractor from each other, continue to supply the fruit, and the contract winemaking continues. There are now three wine ranges: Individual Vineyard at the top; Reserve in the middle; and 10 x Tractor, with its striking label graphics, the base range. There are strong elements of the Da Vinci Code in the new labels for the Reserve and Individual Vineyard, but I suppose a $60 bottle of Pinot is not an impulse buy.

ŶŶŶŶŶ **10 x Tractor Chardonnay 2002** Bright green-yellow; very lively, very intense nectarine and citrus has soaked up the oak; long finish. Cork. RATING 94 DRINK 2009 $ 28
Wallis Vineyard Pinot Noir 2003 Good colour; very considerable depth to the dark fruit flavours; good oak and tannins; long travel. Demands time. Cork. RATING 94 DRINK 2008 $ 60

ŶŶŶŶŶ **Reserve Chardonnay 2003** Complex aromas, probably ex wild yeast; tightly focused stone fruit, mineral and citrus palate; subtle French oak. Cork. RATING 93 DRINK 2010 $ 39
10 x Tractor Pinot Noir 2002 Complex, intense spicy/savoury elements from the cool vintage; very long palate and finish. Better balanced and fresher fruit than the '03 Reserve. Cork. RATING 93 DRINK 2009 $ 32
Reserve Pinot Noir 2003 Fragrant strawberry, red cherry and plum fruit; a fine, elegant, long palate; lingering finish. Cork. RATING 92 DRINK 2010 $ 45
Reserve Pinot Noir 2002 Powerful; distinctly riper and richer than the 10 x Tractor; dark plummy flavours with some dislocation/dead fruit characters. RATING 92 DRINK 2009 $ 45
10 x Tractor Sauvignon Blanc 2004 Attractive, ripe apple and passionfruit, then dries appropriately on a long finish. RATING 90 DRINK Now $ 23
10 x Tractor Pinot Noir 2003 Rich, ripe, sweetly opulent red fruits; ripe tannins, good structure. Screwcap. RATING 90 DRINK 2009 $ 32

ŶŶŶŶ **10 x Tractor Chardonnay 2003** Elegant white peach, melon and nectarine; good texture and length; downplayed style still developing. Screwcap. RATING 89 DRINK 2009 $ 28
10 x Tractor Pinot Gris 2003 Powerful wine in a high-alcohol, fleshy style; plenty of presence. RATING 89 DRINK Now $ 30
Rose 2004 Pale salmon-pink; light-bodied rose petal and strawberry fruit; moderately sweet cellar door style. RATING 87 DRINK Now $ 20

ŶŶŶŶ **10 x Tractor Tempranillo 2003** RATING 85 DRINK 2007 $ 30

Terrace Vale NR

Deasey's Lane, Pokolbin, NSW 2321 REGION Lower Hunter Valley
T (02) 4998 7517 F (02) 4998 7814 WEB www.terracevale.com.au OPEN 7 days 10–4
WINEMAKER Alain Leprince EST. 1971 CASES 9000

SUMMARY In April 2001, the Batchelor family (headed by former AMP chief executive Paul Batchelor) acquired Terrace Vale. in late 2004 Terrace Vale (and its various second labels and brands) were merged with Cheviot Bridge, of which Paul Batchelor is now non-executive chairman. Future marketing of the brands in Australia and overseas will be undertaken by Cheviot Bridge.

Terrel Estate Wines   NR

Whitton Stock Route, Yenda, NSW 2681 **REGION** Riverina
T (02) 6968 1110 **F** (02) 6968 1120 **OPEN** By appointment
WINEMAKER Robert Guadagnini **EST.** 1994 **CASES** NA
SUMMARY Gonzalo Terrel Sr heads a very large operation, little known in the domestic market, but with 250 ha of all the major varietals and a few out of left field, such as tempranillo. It is primarily a bulk processing facility, with much of the wine sold in bulk to other winemakers; part is vinified under the Terrel Estate, Morning Mist, Pebblestone and Majestic brands.

🐛 Teusner   ★★★★☆

29 Jane Place, Tanunda, SA 5352 **REGION** Barossa Valley
T (08) 8563 0898 **F** (08) 8562 1177 **WEB** www.teusner.com.au **OPEN** Not
WINEMAKER Kym Teusner **EST.** 2001 **CASES** 3000
SUMMARY Teusner is a partnership between former Torbreck, and now Rolf Binder winemaker Kym Teusner and brother-in-law Michael Page, and is typical of the new wave of winemakers determined to protect very old, low-yielding, dry-grown Barossa vines. The winery approach is based on lees ageing, little racking, no fining or filtration, and no new American oak. The very reasonably priced wines, made either from 100% shiraz or from Southern Rhône blends, are stocked by the best specialist retailers and in top restaurants in Adelaide, Melbourne, Sydney, Perth and Brisbane. Limited distribution to the US, Canada and the UK quickly mops up the remainder of the available wines.

ȲȲȲȲȲ **Albert Shiraz 2003** Medium-bodied; gently sweet blackberry, cherry and raspberry fruit; silky, soft tannins and mouthfeel; exemplary oak handling, restrained alcohol. **RATING** 94 **DRINK** 2018

ȲȲȲȲȲ **Avatar Grenache Mataro Shiraz 2003** Complex, spicy, savoury but fresh fruit aromas; flavours of raspberry, berry and plum; oak adds more to texture than flavour; perfect tannin management. Quality cork. **RATING** 93 **DRINK** 2015 $ 29.80

Joshua Grenache Mataro Shiraz 2004 Delicious, silky, supple, fruit-forward array of raspberry, mulberry and blackberry fruits; fine tannins; unoaked. Quality cork. **RATING** 90 **DRINK** 2010 $ 26

T'Gallant   ★★★★

1385 Mornington–Flinders Road, Main Ridge, Vic 3928 **REGION** Mornington Peninsula
T (03) 5989 6565 **F** (03) 5989 6577 **WEB** www.tgallant.com.au **OPEN** 7 days 10–5
WINEMAKER Kathleen Quealy, Kevin McCarthy **EST.** 1990 **CASES** 30 000
SUMMARY Husband and wife consultant winemakers Kathleen Quealy and Kevin McCarthy carved out such an important niche market for the T'Gallant label that in April 2003, after protracted negotiations, it was acquired by Beringer Blass. The acquisition of a 15-ha property, and the planting of 10 ha of pinot gris gives the business a firm geographic base, as well as providing increased resources for its signature wine. The yearly parade of new (usually beautiful and striking, it is true) labels designed by Ken Cato do not make my life at all easy. No sooner is the database built up than it is discarded for next year's rash of labels. La Baracca Trattoria is open 7 days for lunch and for specially booked evening events. Exports to the UK and the US.

ȲȲȲȲȲ **Unwooded Chardonnay 2003** Gentle floral aromas; fine and elegant, entirely driven by melon and fig fruit. **RATING** 92 **DRINK** 2009 $ 23

ȲȲȲȲ **Juliet Pinot Grigio 2004** Medium-bodied; very good balance and line to citrus and musk fruit; good finish; good value. Very clever use of barrel fermentation and malolactic fermentation. **RATING** 89 **DRINK** Now $ 15

Tribute Pinot Gris 2003 More weight to the mouthfeel ex alcohol; touches of blossom and mineral. **RATING** 89 **DRINK** Now $ 30

Pinot Grigio 2004 Spotlessly clean; crisp, minerally; nicely balanced, but neutral fruit. **RATING** 87 **DRINK** Now $ 22

Imogen Pinot Gris 2003 Clean; nicely balanced, and good mouthfeel; little flavour distinction. **RATING** 87 **DRINK** Now $22

Juliet Pinot Noir 2004 Light-bodied; fresh, direct strawberry and cherry fruit; one jump up from Rose, but attractive and fresh. Screwcap. **RATING** 87 **DRINK** Now $15.50

Cape Schanck Pinot Noir 2003 Clean, fresh; light to medium-bodied mix of savoury and cherry fruit flavours. **RATING** 87 **DRINK** Now $18

ᵧᵧᵧᵧ **Moscato 2004 RATING** 86 **DRINK** Now $20

Thalgara Estate

NR

De Beyers Road, Pokolbin, NSW 2321 **REGION** Lower Hunter Valley
T (02) 4998 7717 **F** (02) 4998 7774 **OPEN** 7 days 10–5
WINEMAKER Steve Lamb **EST.** 1985 **CASES** 3000
SUMMARY A low-profile winery which had its moment of glory at the 1997 Hunter Valley Wine Show, when it won the Doug Seabrook Memorial Trophy for Best Dry Red of Show with its 1995 Show Reserve Shiraz.

The Blok Estate

NR

Riddoch Highway, Coonawarra, SA 5263 **REGION** Coonawarra
T (08) 8737 2734 **F** (08) 8737 2994 **OPEN** 7 days 10–4
WINEMAKER Contract **EST.** 1999 **CASES** 600
SUMMARY Di and John Blok have owned a tiny vineyard planted to cabernet sauvignon for the past 5 years. They are now taking the production from this and from contract-grown grapes elsewhere in Coonawarra for release under their own label. The cellar door is in an old stone home; it has recently been renovated, and is surrounded by newly landscaped gardens.

The Carriages Vineyard

549 Kotta Road, Echuca, Vic 3564 **REGION** Goulburn Valley
T (03) 5483 7767 **F** (03) 5483 7767 **OPEN** By appointment
WINEMAKER Plunkett Wines (Contract) **EST.** 1996 **CASES** 600
SUMMARY David and Lyndall Johnson began the development of The Carriages in 1996, planting 2.5 ha of merlot and 3.5 ha of cabernet sauvignon. The wines are made at Plunkett, where David Johnson was previously employed. The name and the extremely innovative packaging stems from the four old railway carriages which the Johnsons have painstakingly rehabilitated, and now live in. Each bottle is identified with a cardboard rail ticket which is strikingly similar to the tickets of bygone years. Vertically bisected, with brown on the left side and yellow on the right side, the ticket manages to show the brand name, the vintage, the variety, the number of standard drinks, the alcohol and the bottle number (which is in fact the ticket number, or vice versa). The ticket is fixed to the label with fine twine, so it can be removed either as a memento or for further orders.

🍇 The Cups Estate

269 Browns Road, Fingal, Vic 3939 **REGION** Mornington Peninsula
T 1300 131 741 **F** (03) 9886 1254 **WEB** www.thecupsestate.com **OPEN** 7 days 10–4
WINEMAKER Dr Richard McIntyre **EST.** 1999 **CASES** 2000
SUMMARY Joe Fisicaro has returned to his roots after a career as a financial executive, establishing The Cups Estate on Browns Road near Rye. The name comes from the rolling dune region of the Peninsula known as 'the cups country'; the soils are light, with relatively low fertility, but drainage is excellent. Wind and frost have both been problems, but the 4 ha of pinot noir and 0.8 ha each of shiraz and merlot are now coming through with interesting wines, no doubt also thanks to the skills of winemaker Rick McIntyre.

ᵧᵧᵧᵧᵧ **Raimondo Reserve Pinot Noir 2003** Light to medium-bodied; complex spice, stem and plum fruit; long, lingering, spicy finish. **RATING** 91 **DRINK** 2008 $32

ᵧᵧᵧᵧ **Shiraz 2003** Elegant, medium-bodied; sweet berry fruit; nice oak and tannins; some volatile lift. **RATING** 88 **DRINK** 2010 $29.95

▼▼▼⛉ **Pinot Noir 2003** RATING 86 DRINK 2008 $ 25
Mornington Peninsula Merlot 2003 RATING 85 DRINK 2007 $ 20

The Deanery Vineyards

PO Box 1172, Balhannah, SA 5242 **REGION** Adelaide Hills
T (08) 8390 1948 **F** (08) 8390 0321 **OPEN** Not
WINEMAKER Duncan Dean (Sangiovese), Contract **EST.** 1995 **CASES** 500
SUMMARY The Dean family – Pat and Henry, and sons Duncan, Nick and Alan – purchased a 30-ha dairy farm at Balhannah in late 1994, and planted 6.5 ha of chardonnay, sauvignon blanc and semillon in the spring of 1995, subsequently adding 0.67 ha of shiraz. Pinot noir and a tiny block of sangiovese were also planted at a property at Piccadilly. A further 8 ha are now being developed on a third property, adjacent to the original Balhannah holding. Alan Dean, a Charles Sturt University-trained viticulturist and former Petaluma vineyard manager, is in charge of the vineyards, working alongside brother Duncan, and with part-time help from the third generation. The primary aim of the business is contract grapegrowing, the purchasers including Petaluma, Tower Estate and Jeffrey Grosset.

The Duke Vineyard

★★★

38 Paringa Road, Red Hill South, Vic 3937 **REGION** Mornington Peninsula
T (03) 5989 2407 **F** (03) 5989 2407 **OPEN** Weekends & public hols (summer) 12–5
WINEMAKER Geoff Duke **EST.** 1989 **CASES** 600
SUMMARY Geoff and Sue Duke run a tiny, low-key winery with a 1.6-ha vineyard equally divided between chardonnay and pinot noir. Its establishment goes back to 1989; 1994 marked the first commercial Chardonnay and 1997 the first Pinot Noir. The wines are made in an onsite micro-winery and back vintages are available; none of the wines are sold until they are 2 years old.

▼▼▼▼ **Chardonnay 2002** Very developed colour; powerful wine; very ripe peach, shows 14.5° alcohol. Good cork. **RATING** 88 **DRINK** Now $ 25

▼▼▼ **Pinot Noir 2002** RATING 83 $ 25

The Falls Vineyard

RMB 2750, Longwood–Gobur Road, Longwood East, Vic 3665 **REGION** Strathbogie Ranges
T (03) 5798 5291 **F** (03) 5798 5437 **WEB** www.cameronsbythefalls.com.au **OPEN** Weekends & public hols 10–5, or by appointment
WINEMAKER Andrew Cameron **EST.** 1969 **CASES** 1000
SUMMARY The Falls Vineyard was planted by Andrew and Elly Cameron way back in 1969, as a minor diversification for their pastoral company. There are 2 ha of shiraz, originally established on a wide T-trellis, but now converted to vertical spur positioning, that provide both the Longwood Shiraz and the Longwood Reserve Shiraz. The wines are basically sold by word of mouth. B&B accommodation is available.

▼▼▼▼⛉ **Longwood Old Vineyard Reserve Shiraz 2003** Good colour; a trace of mint, but far greater fruit ripeness than in earlier years; black cherry, gentle spice and good mouthfeel; 14° alcohol. Cork. **RATING** 90 **DRINK** 2010 $ 20

▼▼▼▼ **Lemon Grove Shiraz 2000** Elegant, light to medium-bodied; bright cherry fruit, fine tannins, subtle oak and good acidity; 13° alcohol. Cork. **RATING** 88 **DRINK** 2007 $ 16

The Fleurieu

Main Road, McLaren Vale, SA 5171 **REGION** McLaren Vale
T (08) 8323 8999 **F** (08) 8323 9332 **OPEN** 7 days 9–5
WINEMAKER Mike Farmilo **EST.** 1994 **CASES** 3500
SUMMARY A specialist Shiraz producer, with 6.5 ha of estate vineyards and contract winemaking by former long-serving Seaview/Edwards & Chaffey winemaker Mike Farmilo. Exports to the UK, the US, Singapore, Hong Kong, Japan, The Philippines and Canada.

The Gap Vineyard ★★★

Pomonal Road, Halls Gap, Vic 3381 **REGION** Grampians
T (03) 5356 4252 **F** (03) 5356 4645 **OPEN** Wed–Sun 10–5, 7 days school & public hols
WINEMAKER Trevor Mast, Dan Buckle **EST.** 1969 **CASES** 1500
SUMMARY The Gap is the reincarnation of Boroka, a spectacularly situated vineyard 5 km east of
Halls Gap, with the slopes of the Mt William Range forming a backdrop. The vineyard was planted in
1969 but following its acquisition by Mount Langi Ghiran has been rehabilitated (including
transplanting the riesling vines); extensive renovations have been made to the cellar door sales area
which offers estate-grown wines. Exports to Germany.

ΨΨΨΨ **Billi Billi Sauvignon Blanc Semillon 2004** **RATING** 86 **DRINK** 2008 $16

The Garden Vineyard NR

174 Graydens Road, Moorooduc, Vic 3933 **REGION** Mornington Peninsula
T (03) 5978 8336 **F** (03) 5978 8343 **WEB** www.thegardenvineyard.websyte.com.au **OPEN** Weekends
Nov–Apr, or by appointment
WINEMAKER Dr Richard McIntyre (Contract) **EST.** 1995 **CASES** 130
SUMMARY This captures the delights of the Mornington Peninsula in so many ways. As the name
suggests, it is as much a garden as it is a vineyard; Di and Doug Johnson began establishing a walled
garden 7 years ago, at much the same time that they decided to increase the existing 0.5 ha of pinot
noir (planted in 1989) by an additional 1 ha of pinot noir and 0.5 ha of pinot gris. The entrance fee to
the garden is $5.

The Grove Vineyard NR

Cnr Metricup Road/Carter Road, Wilyabrup, WA 6284 **REGION** Margaret River
T (08) 9755 7458 **F** (08) 9755 7458 **WEB** www.thegrovevineyard.com.au **OPEN** 7 days 9–4
WINEMAKER Steven Hughes **EST.** 1995 **CASES** 1500
SUMMARY Steve and Val Hughes gave their vineyard its name to acknowledge their former residence
in a street called The Grove; it was part of an olive grove planted by the monks from the New Norcia
monastery north of Perth. They have planted a fruit salad vineyard, the major varieties being
sauvignon blanc (2.65 ha), chardonnay (1.5 ha), cabernet sauvignon (1.88 ha), with lesser but not
insignificant plantings of semillon, pinot noir, shiraz, merlot, verdelho, tempranillo and graciano.
They run a restaurant, provide accommodation, feature coffee roasting, sales and tastings, a gourmet
delicatessen, olive oil and, of course, cellar door sales with a wide range of wines reflecting the
plantings.

The Gurdies NR

St Helier Road, The Gurdies, Vic 3984 **REGION** Gippsland
T (03) 5997 6208 **F** (03) 5997 6511 **OPEN** 7 days 10–5, or by appointment
WINEMAKER Peter Kozik **EST.** 1991 **CASES** 1500
SUMMARY The only winery in the southwest Gippsland region, established on the slopes of The
Gurdies hills overlooking Westernport Bay and French Island. Plantings of the 3.5-ha vineyard
commenced in 1981, but no fruit was harvested until 1991, owing to bird attack. A winery has been
completed, and it is intended to increase the vineyards to 8 ha and ultimately build a restaurant
onsite.

The Islander Estate Vineyards ★★★★☆

PO Box 621, McLaren Vale, SA 5171 **REGION** Kangaroo Island
T (08) 8553 9008 **F** (08) 8323 7726 **WEB** www.islanderestatevineyards.com.au **OPEN** Not
WINEMAKER Jacques Lurton **EST.** NA **CASES** 4000
SUMMARY Established by one of the most famous Flying Winemakers in the world, Bordeaux-born,
trained and part-time resident Jacques Lurton, who has established 10 ha of close-planted vineyard.
The principal varieties are sangiovese and cabernet franc; then lesser amounts of semillon, viognier,
grenache, malbec and merlot. The wines are made and bottled at the onsite winery, in true estate
style. The ultimate flagship wine will be an esoteric blend of Sangiovese, Cabernet Franc and Malbec.

Production of this wine will be limited to 2000 cases, with another 2000 cases of the Bark Hut Road label. Tastings from barrel in late 2004 leave no doubt that some outstandingly different wines will come from this venture.

ŦŦŦŦ **Bark Hut Road 2003** Aromatic black fruits, licorice and spice coming from both the Shiraz and Viognier components, with some dark chocolate makings its appearance in the background; medium to medium-full bodied; soft, plush tannins. Cabernet Sauvignon/Shiraz/Viognier. **RATING** 91 **DRINK** 2010 $42
Pink Penguin 2004 Light but bright pink colour; aromatic and perfumed; good balance and length; 3 g per litre residual sugar gives a tactile feel, but not sweetness. Grenache/Sangiovese/Cabernet Franc/Malbec. **RATING** 90 **DRINK** Now $19.95

The Lane   ★★★★☆

Ravenswood Lane, Hahndorf, SA 5245 **REGION** Adelaide Hills
T(08) 8388 1250 **F**(08) 8388 7233 **WEB** www.thelane.com.au **OPEN** 7 days 10–4.30 from October 2005
WINEMAKER Robert Mann, John Edwards **EST.** 1993 **CASES** 35 000
SUMMARY With their sales and marketing background, John and Helen Edwards opted for a major lifestyle change when they began establishing the first of the present 28.1 ha of vineyards in 1993. Initially, part of the production was sold to Hardys, but now some of the wine is made for release under The Lane label (until 2003, Ravenswood Lane). A joint venture with Hardys has been terminated, which will result in the reintroduction of the Starvedog Lane brand; also, John Edwards has applied to build a 500-tonne onsite winery, and plans to open a cellar door and café. Exports to the UK.

ŦŦŦŦŦ **Adelaide Hills Chardonnay 2002** Elegant; excellent structure and texture; malolactic and barrel ferment inputs seamlessly woven with melon and stone fruit; flow and line; good lemony acidity. High-quality cork. **RATING** 94 **DRINK** 2012

ŦŦŦŦ **Starvedog Lane Chardonnay Pinot Noir 2000** Smooth, silky stone fruit with some creamy/yeasty notes; lots of overall flavour; good length. **RATING** 91 **DRINK** 2007 $28
Starvedog Lane Shiraz 2001 Appealing blackberry and dark chocolate fruit; ripe tannins and good oak. **RATING** 90 **DRINK** 2011

ŦŦŦŦ **Starvedog Lane Sauvignon Blanc 2004** Clean, light to medium-bodied; moderate varietal character; balanced tropical/gooseberry fruit. **RATING** 89 **DRINK** Now $20
Starvedog Lane Shiraz Viognier 2003 Medium-bodied; lively, fresh, spicy/savoury black fruits; the Viognier less assertive than often in such blends; good length. Screwcap. **RATING** 89 **DRINK** 2010 $24
Starvedog Lane Cabernet Merlot 2003 Fresh red and black fruits; light to medium-bodied; direct line, easy style. **RATING** 88 **DRINK** 2007 $29
Starvedog Lane No Oak Chardonnay 2003 Gentle nectarine and melon with some creamy malolactic and lees notes added to lift it from the boring ruck. Screwcap. **RATING** 87 **DRINK** 2008 $24

ŦŦŦŦ **Starvedog Lane No Oak Chardonnay 2004** **RATING** 85 **DRINK** 2007

The Lily Stirling Range   NR

Lot 3004 Chester Pass Road, Stirling Range via Borden, WA 6338 **REGION** Porongurup
T(08) 9827 9205 **F**(08) 9827 9206 **WEB** www.thelily.com.au **OPEN** 7 days 10–5
WINEMAKER Pleun Hitzert **EST.** 1990 **CASES** NA
SUMMARY An interesting, indeed exotic tourism complex owned and run by two Dutch families, Hennie and Pleun Hitzert and Ron and Sue Terwijn. It features The Lily Railway Station restaurant, on the reconstructed 1924 Gnowangerup Railway Station, and a windmill. This was completed in August 2003 with the help of a group of millwrights from Schiedam in The Netherlands; a 3-tonne heavy grinding stone now produces flour: it is available from The Lily now and soon from outlets around Western Australia. Less exotic, perhaps, is the 3-ha vineyard planted to chenin blanc, chardonnay, grenache, cabernet sauvignon and cabernet franc; the wines are sold through the cellar door, by mail order and in the restaurant.

The Little Wine Company ★★★☆

824 Milbrodale Road, Broke, NSW 2330 **REGION** Lower Hunter Valley
T (02) 6579 1111 **F** (02) 6579 1440 **WEB** www.thelittlewinecompany.com.au **OPEN** At the Small Winemakers Centre, McDonalds Road, Pokolbin
WINEMAKER Ian Little, Suzanne Little **EST.** 2000 **CASES** 13 000
SUMMARY Having sold their previous winery (and Little's brand name), Ian and Susan Little moved in stages to their new winery at Broke. The Little Wine Company is part-owner of the 50-acre Lochleven Vineyard in Pokolbin, and contracts 3 vineyards in the Broke–Fordwich area. It also has access to the Talga Vineyard in the Gundaroo Valley near Canberra.

ⵣⵣⵣ **Olivine Hunter Valley Sangiovese 2003** Improbably, does well in both varietal and structural terms; savoury and spicy, but not green, and little flashes of cherry and plum. Screwcap. **RATING** 89 **DRINK** 2008 **$** 18
Olivine Hunter Valley Shiraz Viognier 2002 Lifted, tangy, savoury style; light to medium-bodied; minimal tannins and oak. Cork. **RATING** 87 **DRINK** 2007 **$** 18
Talga Canberra District Shiraz 2001 Very ripe fruit aromas and flavour, higher than the 13.5° alcohol would suggest; prune, blackberry and a hint of jam. Cork. **RATING** 87 **DRINK** 2008 **$** 23

The Mews NR

84 Gibson Street, Kings Meadows, Tas 7249 **REGION** Northern Tasmania
T (03) 6344 2780 **F** (03) 6343 2076 **OPEN** Not
WINEMAKER Graham Wiltshire **EST.** 1984 **CASES** 300
SUMMARY Robin and Anne Holyman have established 0.4 ha of pinot noir and 9.2 ha of chardonnay at Kings Meadows, only 4 km from the centre of Launceston. Most of the grapes are sold; industry veteran Graham Wiltshire acts as winemaker for the remainder, and the wines are sold by direct contact with the Holymans.

The Minya Winery ★★★☆

Minya Lane, Connewarre, Vic 3227 **REGION** Geelong
T (03) 5264 1397 **F** (03) 5264 1097 **OPEN** Public hols, or by appointment
WINEMAKER Susan Dans **EST.** 1974 **CASES** 1400
SUMMARY Geoff Dans first planted vines in 1974 on his family's dairy farm; he planted more in 1982 and 1988, lifting the total to 4 ha. The concerts staged in summer sound appealing. Grenache is a highly unusual variety for this neck of the woods.

ⵣⵣⵣ **Grenache 2003** Nice wine; soft, plush red fruits; not jammy and well balanced. **RATING** 88
DRINK Now

The Natural Wine Company

217 Copley Road, Upper Swan, WA 6069 **REGION** Swan Valley
T (08) 9296 1436 **F** (08) 9296 1436 **OPEN** Wed–Sun & public hols 10–5
WINEMAKER Colin Evans **EST.** 1998 **CASES** 1500
SUMMARY Owners Colin and Sandra Evans say the name of the business is intended to emphasise that no herbicides or systemic pesticides are used in the vineyard, which is on the western slopes of the Darling Range; weed control is achieved through mulching. Sandra does the vineyard work and helps with the night shift during vintage. She was also responsible for the koala emerging from the barrel on the label. The vineyard is within a short walk of Bells Rapids and close to the Walunga National Park.

The Oaks Vineyard & Winery

31 Melba Highway, Yering, Vic 3770 **REGION** Yarra Valley
T (03) 9739 0070 **F** (03) 9739 0577 **OPEN** Weekends 10.30–5, or by appointment
WINEMAKER Karen Coulston (Contract) **EST.** 2000 **CASES** 500
SUMMARY The Oaks has been established in what was originally a Presbyterian Manse, the change in use coming after a long period of neglect, and thus not incurring the wrath of the previous occupants. Owner Pauline Charlton spent 12 months restoring the Victorian homestead to its former glory prior

to the opening. An onsite gallery features photographs by Pauline Charlton's daughter, Mackenzie, and fellow students of the Photography Studies College. The vineyard is close-planted, and the wine competently made.

🍷🍷🍷 **Chardonnay for Terri 2004** Harmonious melon and stone fruit aromas and flavours; light to medium-bodied; good length and balance. Cork. **RATING** 89 **DRINK** 2007 $ 20

🍷🍷🍷🍷 **Deschamps White 2004** **RATING** 86 **DRINK** 2007 $ 15

The Rothbury Estate ★★★

Broke Road, Pokolbin, NSW 2321 **REGION** Lower Hunter Valley
T (02) 4998 7363 **F** (02) 4993 3559 **OPEN** 7 days 9.30–4.30
WINEMAKER Mike de Garis **EST.** 1968 **CASES** 82 500
SUMMARY Rothbury celebrated its 30th birthday in 1998, albeit not quite in the fashion that founder and previous chief executive Len Evans would have wished. After a protracted and at times bitter takeover battle, it became part of the Beringer Blass empire. The style and quality of the wines is unashamedly commercial these days; by rights they should be better.

🍷🍷🍷🍷 **Neil McGuigan Series Hunter Valley Shiraz 2002** Clean red and black fruits; medium-bodied, savoury notes, and will become more regional with age. **RATING** 87 **DRINK** 2008 $ 17

🍷🍷🍷🍷 **Neil McGuigan Series Mudgee Chardonnay 2003** **RATING** 85 **DRINK** Now
Hunter Valley Verdelho 2004 **RATING** 85 **DRINK** Now $ 13
Neil McGuigan Series Hunter Valley Merlot 2002 **RATING** 85 **DRINK** 2007 $ 17
Neil McGuigan Series Mudgee Cabernet Sauvignon 2002 **RATING** 85 $ 20
Orange Sauvignon Blanc 2004 **RATING** 84 **DRINK** Now $ 13

The Settlement Wine Co. ★★★☆

Cnr Olivers Road/Chalk Hill Road, McLaren Vale, SA 5171 **REGION** McLaren Vale
T (08) 8323 7344 **F** (08) 8323 7355 **WEB** www.thesettlementwineco.com.au **OPEN** 7 days 10–5
WINEMAKER Vincenzo Berlingieri **EST.** 1992 **CASES** 3500
SUMMARY Vincenzo Berlingieri, one of the great characters of the wine industry, arrived in Sydney with beard flowing and arms waving in the 1970s, and gained considerable publicity for his then McLaren Vale winery. Fortune did not follow marketing success for this research scientist, who had arrived to work in plant genetics at Melbourne University's Botany Department in 1964, armed with a doctorate in agricultural science from Perugia University, Italy. However, after various moves he is in business again with his children, Jason, John and Annika, sourcing most of the grapes from Langhorne Creek and McLaren Vale.

🍷🍷🍷🍷🍷 **Black Pedro Ximinez NV** Obvious age; dark colour, olive rim; extremely luscious raisin fruit; authentic Pedro Ximinez style. **RATING** 90 **DRINK** Now $ 30

🍷🍷🍷🍷 **Verdelho Liqueur NV** Correct pale orange-brown colour and Christmas cake flavours; gently biscuity finish. **RATING** 88 **DRINK** Now $ 25
Cabernet Franc 2000 Savoury, cedary, tobacco leaf varietal character; clean, light to medium-bodied; fair length; nice bottle development. **RATING** 87 **DRINK** Now $ 20
White White Pedro NV Sweet raisin and biscuit mix cleansed by fortifying spirit; some age; Pedro Ximinez/Palomino. **RATING** 87 **DRINK** 2007 $ 30

🍷🍷🍷🍷 **Langhorne Creek Tinta Negra 1997** **RATING** 86 **DRINK** Now $ 30
Arneis 2004 **RATING** 85 **DRINK** Now $ 15

🍷🍷🍷 **Cabernet Rose 2004** **RATING** 83 $ 15

The Silos Estate NR

Princes Highway, Jaspers Brush, NSW 2535 **REGION** Shoalhaven Coast
T (02) 4448 6082 **F** (02) 4448 6246 **WEB** www.thesilos.com **OPEN** 7 days 10–5
WINEMAKER Bevan Wilson **EST.** 1985 **CASES** 1000
SUMMARY Since 1995, Gaynor Sims and Kate Khoury, together with viticulturist Jovica Zecevic, have worked hard to improve the quality of the wine, both in the 5 ha of estate vineyards and in the winery. The winery continues to rely on the tourist trade; the wines do not appear in normal retail outlets.

The Vineyards Estate ★★☆

555 Hermitage Road, Pokolbin, NSW 2320 **REGION** Lower Hunter Valley
T (02) 4998 7822 **F** (02) 6574 7276 **WEB** www.thevineyardsestate.com.au **OPEN** 7 days 10–5, Splash Restaurant Wed–Sun from 6.30
WINEMAKER Greg Silkman (Contract) **EST.** 1993 **CASES** 500
SUMMARY The major investment and principal business of The Vineyards Estate is the 8-suite guesthouse sitting among the 5 ha of vines. There is also a high-quality restaurant (Splash): all-inclusive gourmet weekends are around $695 per couple. The estate wines are sold through the restaurant and guesthouse; other local wines are also available in the restaurant.

The Warren Vineyard ★★★☆

Conte Road, Pemberton, WA 6260 **REGION** Pemberton
T (08) 9776 1115 **F** (08) 9776 1115 **WEB** www.warrenvineyard.com.au **OPEN** 7 days 11–5
WINEMAKER Phillip Wilkinson **EST.** 1985 **CASES** 700
SUMMARY The 1.5-ha vineyard was established in 1985 and is one of the smallest in the Pemberton region, coming to public notice when its 1991 Cabernet Sauvignon won the award for the Best Red Table Wine from the Pemberton Region at the 1992 SGIO Western Australia Winemakers Exhibition. It is owned and run by Anne Wandless and husband Arthur Hawke. An extensive range of back-vintage wines (to 1997) is available at the cellar door.

ᵧᵧᵧᵧ **Pemberton Cabernet Merlot 2000** Medium-bodied; good intensity and focus; savoury, earthy, olive notes around black fruits; fine, ripe tannins. Stained cork. **RATING** 89 **DRINK** 2008 $ 25
Pemberton Cabernet Merlot 1997 Fragrant, earthy, leafy, spicy; light to medium-bodied, with a nice mix of blackcurrant and fine, sweet tannins. Good cork. **RATING** 89 **DRINK** 2008 $ 30
Pemberton Cabernet Merlot 1998 Holding hue well; light to medium-bodied; slightly lighter than the '00, but more savoury structure, particularly tannins; a fine skein of red fruits. Cork. **RATING** 88 **DRINK** 2008 $ 30

ᵧᵧᵧᵧ **Pemberton Merlot 1999** **RATING** 86 **DRINK** 2007 $ 25
Pemberton Cabernet Sauvignon 1999 **RATING** 86 **DRINK** 209 $ 20

The Willows Vineyard ★★★★☆

Light Pass Road, Light Pass, Barossa Valley, SA 5355 **REGION** Barossa Valley
T (08) 8562 1080 **F** (08) 8562 3447 **WEB** www.thewillowsvineyard.com.au **OPEN** Wed–Mon 10.30–4.30, Tues by appointment
WINEMAKER Peter Scholz, Michael Scholz **EST.** 1989 **CASES** 6000
SUMMARY The Scholz family have been grapegrowers for generations and have almost 40 ha of vineyards, selling part and retaining part of the crop. Current generation winemakers Peter and Michael Scholz make smooth, well-balanced and flavoursome wines under their own label. These are all marketed with some years' bottle age. Exports to the UK, the US and Singapore.

ᵧᵧᵧᵧᵧ **Barossa Valley Riesling 2004** Nettle, spice and apple aromas; crisp, clean, firm and long palate; good acidity; impressive for vintage. Screwcap. **RATING** 92 **DRINK** 2014 $ 13
Barossa Valley Shiraz 2002 Medium to full-bodied; focused blackberry and bitter chocolate fruit; firm but ripe tannins; restrained power and oak usage. Quality cork. **RATING** 92 **DRINK** 2017 $ 23

ᵧᵧᵧᵧ **Barossa Valley Semillon 2002** Generously flavoured buttered toast, honey and lemon; easy access; 66-year-old vines; part French barrel ferment. Cork. **RATING** 88 **DRINK** 2007 $ 14

Thistle Hill ★★★

McDonalds Road, Mudgee, NSW 2850 **REGION** Mudgee
T (02) 6373 3546 **F** (02) 6373 3540 **WEB** www.thistlehill.com.au **OPEN** Mon–Sat 9.30–5, Sun & public hols 9.30–4
WINEMAKER Lesley Robertson, Robert Paul (Consultant) **EST.** 1976 **CASES** 4000

SUMMARY The Robertson family has put the sudden death of husband and father Dave behind it. The estate-grown wines are made onsite with the help of Robert Paul. Whatever additional assistance is needed is happily provided by the remaining wine community of Mudgee. The vineyard, incidentally, is registered by the National Association for Sustainable Agriculture Australia (NASAA), which means no weedicides, insecticides or synthetic fertilisers – the full organic system.

Thomas Wines ★★★★☆

c/- The Small Winemakers Centre, McDonalds Road, Pokolbin, NSW 2321 REGION Lower Hunter Valley
T (02) 6574 7371 F (02) 6574 7371 WEB www.thomaswines.com.au OPEN 7 days 10–5
WINEMAKER Andrew Thomas EST. 1997 CASES 2000
SUMMARY Andrew Thomas came to the Hunter Valley from McLaren Vale, to join the winemaking team at Tyrrell's. After 13 years with Tyrrell's, he left to undertake contract work and to continue the development of his own winery label, a family affair run by himself and his wife Jo. The Semillon is sourced from a single vineyard owned by local grower Ken Bray, renowned for its quality; the Shiraz is a blend of Hunter Valley and McLaren Vale. The wines are available only at the Small Winemakers Centre, and in some restaurants in Sydney.

ŸŸŸŸŸ **Shiraz 2002** A Hunter Valley/McLaren Vale blend with classic antecedents; medium-bodied; excellent texture and structure; blackberry, spice, chocolate; polished tannins; good oak. RATING 93 DRINK 2017 $ 27
Braemore Semillon 2004 Above-average weight, but does not lose clear focus or brightness; lemon blossom/lemon zest, with some minerally spritz on the finish. RATING 92 DRINK 2014 $ 24
Semillon Sauvignon Blanc 2004 Aromatic, ripe citrus and passionfruit; considerable depth of flavour; 40% Sauvignon Blanc (Adelaide Hills) contributing most. Screwcap. RATING 90 DRINK 2008 $ 20

Thompson Estate ★★★★

Harmans Road South, Wilyabrup, WA 6280 REGION Margaret River
T (08) 9386 1751 F (08) 9386 1708 WEB www.thompsonestate.com OPEN Fri–Sun 11–4
WINEMAKER Michael Peterkin, Mark Messenger, Flying Fish Cove, Harold Osborne (Contract)
EST. 1998 CASES 3000
SUMMARY Cardiologist Peter Thompson began the establishment of Thompson Estate in 1994, when the first vines were planted. He was inspired by his and his family's shareholdings in the Pierro and Fire Gully vineyards, and by visits to many of the world's premium wine regions. A total of 12 ha has since been established, 4.8 ha to cabernet sauvignon, cabernet franc and merlot, the remainder more or less equally divided between chardonnay and pinot noir. The plantings came into full production in 2004, with an ultimate maximum production of 5800 cases. The Thompsons have split the winemaking between specialist winemakers: Chardonnay by Mike Peterkin of Pierro, Cabernet Merlot by Mark Messenger of Juniper Estate and previously of Cape Mentelle, Pinot Noir by Flying Fish Cove, and Pinot Chardonnay by Harold Osborne of Cloudy Bay.

ŸŸŸŸŸ **Semillon Sauvignon Blanc 2004** Crisp, firm and tight, the 60% Semillon at work; lemon rind, asparagus and gooseberry flavours; minerally acidity, small percentage barrel-fermented. Screwcap. RATING 91 DRINK 2008 $ 22
Chardonnay 2003 Complex funky/oaky bouquet; melon, fig, nuts and cream on the palate, with lots happening; slightly elevated alcohol. RATING 90 DRINK 2010 $ 33

ŸŸŸŸ **Pinot Noir 2003** Light to medium red-purple; getting close in varietal terms, and may evolve with time; fair structure. RATING 86 DRINK 2008 $ 25

Thomson Brook Wines NR

Lot 1, Thomson Road, Donnybrook, WA 6239 REGION Geographe
T (08) 9731 0590 F (08) 9731 0590 OPEN Wed–Sun & public hols
WINEMAKER Terry Foster EST. 1993 CASES NA
SUMMARY Pam and Terry Foster have established 6 ha of riesling, sauvignon blanc, semillon, chardonnay, verdelho, pinot noir, shiraz, merlot, cabernet sauvignon and barbera, and make the wine onsite. The principal sales outlet is through the cellar door, supplemented by mail order; the cellar door offers barbecue facilities and local produce.

Thomson Vintners NR

5 O'Loughlin Street, Waikerie, SA 5330 **REGION** Riverland
T(08) 8541 2168 **F**(08) 8541 3369 **WEB** www.woolpunda.com.au **OPEN** Mon–Fri 9–5
WINEMAKER Colin Glaetzer, Ben Glaetzer **EST.** 1996 **CASES** 50 000
SUMMARY Although the year of establishment is shown as 1996, Thomson Vintners had been grapegrowers in the Riverland since 1961, among the first to plant cabernet sauvignon, and also (much later on) among the first to introduce regulated deficit irrigation (to reduce yield and improve quality). Most of the 7000–8000 tonnes of grapes produced from the 480 ha of vineyards are sold to major wine companies; the long-term plan is to lift the amount used for the Thomson's Woolpunda label from its present level of approximately 8–9% to 20%. With the experienced winemaking team of Colin and Ben Glaetzer in charge, the under $10 price point for the wines is obviously attractive, and the wines are now distributed in most states, with exports to the UK, Canada, Germany, Denmark, China, Norway and Singapore.

Thornborough Estate NR

PO Box 678, Virginia, SA 5120 **REGION** Adelaide Plains
T(08) 8235 0419 **OPEN** Not
WINEMAKER George Girgolas **EST.** 2000 **CASES** 2000
SUMMARY George Girgolas has been a long-term grapegrower near Virginia in the Adelaide Plains region, with 116 ha of 38-year-old vines, the grapes all previously contract-sold to Yalumba; he was Yalumba's Grower of the Year in 2000. Three years ago he and his family acquired the Thornborough property (5 km from the vineyard) which includes a 2-storey stone house built in 1827, and straddles the Gawler River. The plans are to convert Thornborough into a guesthouse.

Thorn-Clarke Wines ★★★★

Milton Park, Gawler Park Road, Angaston, SA 5353 **REGION** Barossa Valley
T(08) 8564 3036 **F**(08) 8564 3255 **WEB** www.thornclarkewines.com **OPEN** Mon–Fri 9–5
WINEMAKER Derek Fitzgerald, Jim Irvine (Consultant) **EST.** 1997 **CASES** 50 000
SUMMARY Established by David and Cheryl Clarke (née Thorn), and son Sam. Thorn-Clarke is one of the largest Barossa grapegrowers, with 264 ha across 4 vineyard sites. Shiraz (136 ha), cabernet sauvignon (59 ha) and merlot (28 ha) are the principal plantings, with lesser amounts of petit verdot, cabernet franc, chardonnay, riesling and pinot gris. As with many such growers, most of the grape production is sold, but the best is retained for the Thorn-Clarke label. Thorn-Clarke's stated aim is to over-deliver on quality at each price point, and it succeeds in so doing. Exports the the US, Europe and New Zealand.

Shotfire Ridge Barossa Valley Shiraz 2003 Deep colour; richly robed blackberry fruit and vanilla oak; medium to full-bodied; soft, ripe tannins. **RATING** 91 **DRINK** 2010 $23

SandPiper Eden Valley Riesling 2004 Mineral, apple, apple blossom aromas and flavours; good length and balance; very good value. **RATING** 89 **DRINK** 2009 $15
Shotfire Ridge Barossa Valley Quartage 2003 Savoury minty berry aromas and flavours, and touches of dark chocolate; fine, savoury tannins. Cabernet Sauvignon/Shiraz Cabernet Franc/Merlot. **RATING** 89 **DRINK** 2013 $23
SandPiper Barossa Cabernet Sauvignon 2003 Attractive medium-bodied wine; nice cassis/redcurrant/blackcurrant fruit and a touch of chocolate; subtle oak; good value. **RATING** 88 **DRINK** 2010 $15
Sandpiper Eden Valley Pinot Gris 2004 Fragrant spice, pear and wild flower aromas; ripe, rich, big-impact style in the mouth. **RATING** 87 **DRINK** 2007 $15

Sandpiper Brut Reserve Pinot Noir Chardonnay NV **RATING** 84 **DRINK** Now $15

Sorriso Barossa Rose 2004 **RATING** 83 $15

Thornhill/The Berry Farm ★★★

Bessell Road, Margaret River, WA 6285 **REGION** Margaret River
T(08) 9757 5054 **F**(08) 9757 5116 **WEB** www.berryfarm.com.au **OPEN** 7 days 10–4.30
WINEMAKER Eion Lindsay **EST.** 1990 **CASES** 3500

SUMMARY The fruit wines under The Berry Farm label are extraordinarily good. The sparkling strawberry wine has intense strawberry flavour; the plum port likewise, carrying its 16° alcohol with remarkable ease.

3 Drops ★★★☆

5 Blount Close, Winthrop, WA 6150 (postal) **REGION** Mount Barker
T (08) 9310 7198 **F** (08) 9310 7264 **WEB** www.3drops.com **OPEN** Not
WINEMAKER Robert Diletti (Contract), John Wade (Consultant) **EST.** 1998 **CASES** 4000
SUMMARY The 3 Drops are not the three owners (John Bradbury, Joanne Bradbury and Nichole Wallich), but wine, olive oil and water, all of which come from the property, a substantial vineyard at Mt Barker. The 16 ha are planted to riesling, sauvignon blanc, semillon, chardonnay, cabernet sauvignon, merlot, shiraz and cabernet franc. Australian Prestige Wines is the national distributor, and the wines are also available by mail order.

YYYYY **Shiraz 2003** Clean, delicious, spicy black cherry and blackberry mix; long, fine palate; balanced tannins. Screwcap. **RATING** 92 **DRINK** 2013 $ 23

YYYY **Sauvignon Blanc 2004** Light, crisp, lemony/minerally aromas and flavours; not overmuch fruit intensity. Screwcap. **RATING** 88 **DRINK** 2007 $ 18.50

YYYY **Cabernets 2003** **RATING** 86 **DRINK** 2008 $ 18

Three Wise Men ★★★★★

95 Hayseys Road, Narre Warren East, Vic 3804 (Woongarra Winery) **REGION** Port Phillip Zone
T (03) 9796 8886 **F** (03) 9796 8580 **WEB** www.threewisemen.com.au **OPEN** Thurs–Sun 9–5 by appointment
WINEMAKER Graeme Leith **EST.** 1994 **CASES** 800
SUMMARY The Three Wise Men are (or were) Graeme Leith (of Passing Clouds fame), Dr Bruce Jones (Woongarra vineyard owner and grapegrower) and Dr Graham Ellender (a semi-retired dentist-turned-winemaker). It came about after a trial batch was made in 1998 by Bruce Jones' consultant, Andrew Clarke. The 1999 and 2000 vintages were made at Graham Ellender's winery, but he thereafter retired from the venture as his own production grew. There are now two wise men: Graham Leith as winemaker and Bruce Jones as grapegrower. Each takes half of the resulting wine; it is sold through their respective wineries, Passing Clouds and Woongarra.

YYYYY **Pinot Noir 2003** Powerful, focused and foresty aromas; an intense palate, almost uncomfortably so, but very long and ultimately stylish. **RATING** 94 **DRINK** 2010 $ 20

Thumm Estate Wines NR

87 Kriedeman Road, Upper Coomera, Qld 4209 **REGION** Queensland Coastal
T (07) 5573 6990 **F** (07) 5573 4099 **WEB** www.thummestate.com **OPEN** 7 days 9.30–5
WINEMAKER Robert Thumm **EST.** 2000 **CASES** 3000
SUMMARY Robert Thumm, born in 1950 (eldest son of Hermann Thumm, founder of Chateau Yaldara in the Barossa Valley), gained his degree in oenology from the University of Geisenheim, Germany. In 1999, when the family business was sold, he and wife Janet decided to move to Queensland, establishing the new winery in a valley below the Tamborine Mountain Tourist Centre. Here they have planted cabernet sauvignon and petit verdot; they also have 1.5 ha of riesling and 1.2 ha of sauvignon blanc in production in the Adelaide Hills. The venture, and its associated wine club, is firmly aimed at the general tourist market; this part of Australia relies heavily on tourism, and offers a great deal to tourists.

Tibooburra Wines ★★★★

Stringybark Lane, off Beenak Road, Yellingbo, Vic 3139 (postal) **REGION** Yarra Valley
T 0418 367 319 **F** (03) 5964 8577 **WEB** www.tibooburra.com **OPEN** Not
WINEMAKER Paul Evans (Contract) **EST.** 1996 **CASES** 1000
SUMMARY The Kerr family has done much with Tibooburra since they began assembling their 1000-ha property in 1967. They have established a champion Angus herd, planted a 33-ha vineyard in 1996 on elevated northern and northwest slopes, established a truffliere in 2001 to supply

Japanese and northern hemisphere restaurants with black truffles, and launched the Tibooburra Wine label in 2002. Four generations have been and are now involved in the business, which is, by any standards, a substantial one. Most of the grapes are sold under long-term contract to Oakridge. Plantings (in descending order of magnitude) are pinot noir, chardonnay, shiraz, sauvignon blanc, merlot and cabernet sauvignon, and the quality of the early releases is all one could possibly ask for.

ᵀᵀᵀᵀ♡ **Yarra Valley Merlot 2002** Good colour; olive, herb and spice a powerful expression of varietal fruit; long, intense palate. **RATING** 92 **DRINK** 2014 $ 24
Yarra Valley Shiraz 2003 Medium-bodied; lively blackberry, spice and licorice; considerable intensity; subtle oak. **RATING** 91 **DRINK** 2003 $ 24
Yarra Valley Chardonnay 2002 Light to medium-bodied; quite intense, elegant and focused melon and grapefuit; subtle oak inputs. **RATING** 90 **DRINK** 2009 $ 19.95

ᵀᵀᵀᵀ **Yarra Valley Chardonnay 2003** Light to medium-bodied; elegant melon and stone fruit flavours; good balance and length; unforced, frugal oak. **RATING** 88 **DRINK** 2007 $ 19.95
Yarra Valley Pinot Noir 2002 Strong colour; very ripe plummy fruit in an intense, concentrated style and line; subtle oak. **RATING** 88 **DRINK** 2007 $ 19.95
Yarra Valley Pinot Noir 2003 Light to medium-bodied; a well-balanced mix of strawberry, cherry and plum; subtle oak and tannins; radically different from the '02 in style. **RATING** 87 **DRINK** 2007 $ 24

ᵀᵀᵀ♡ **Yarra Valley Sauvignon Blanc 2004** Clean, crisp and correct; well made, but simply lacking the varietal intensity for higher points. **RATING** 86 **DRINK** Now $ 17.50

Tilba Valley   NR

Lake Corunna Estate, 947 Old Highway, Narooma, NSW 2546 **REGION** South Coast Zone
T (02) 4473 7308 **F** (02) 4473 7484 **WEB** www.tilbavalleywines.com **OPEN** Oct–April 7 days 10–5, May–Sept Wed–Sun 11–4 (closed August)
WINEMAKER Bevan Wilson **EST.** 1978 **CASES** 600
SUMMARY A strongly tourist-oriented operation, serving a ploughman's lunch daily from 12–2. Has 8 ha of estate vineyards.

🍃 Tilbrook   NR

17/1 Adelaide–Lobethal Road, Lobethal, SA 5241 **REGION** Adelaide Hills
T (08) 8389 5315 **F** (08) 8389 5318 **OPEN** Sat 11–5, Sun 12–5, or by appointment
WINEMAKER James Tilbrook **EST.** 2001 **CASES** 1000
SUMMARY James and Annabelle Tilbrook have 4.4 ha of multi-clone chardonnay and pinot noir, and 0.4 ha of sauvignon blanc, planted in 1999 at Lenswood. The winery and cellar door are in the old Onkaparinga Woollen Mills building in Lobethal; this not only provides an atmospheric home, but also helps meet the very strict environmental requirements of the Adelaide Hills region in dealing with winery waste water. English-born James Tilbrook came to Australia in 1986, aged 22; a car accident led to his return to England. Working for Oddbins for 7 years, and passing the WSET diploma (with a scholarship) set his future course. A working holiday back in Australia in 1995, with vintage experience in the Barossa Valley, resulted in meeting and marrying Australian wife Annabelle. Further work at Mountadam in the Adelaide Hills coincided with the purchase of the vineyard property and the 1999 plantings. Plantings are continuing, and for the moment most of the chardonnay and pinot noir is sold to Beringer Blass. Over time, more will be retained for self-use. Exports to the UK.

Tim Adams   ★★★★☆

Warenda Road, Clare, SA 5453 **REGION** Clare Valley
T (08) 8842 2429 **F** (08) 8842 3550 **WEB** www.timadamswines.com.au **OPEN** Mon–Fri 10.30–5, weekends 11–5
WINEMAKER Tim Adams **EST.** 1986 **CASES** 35 000
SUMMARY After almost 20 years slowly and carefully building the business, based on 11 ha of the Clare Valley classic varieties of riesling, semillon, grenache, shiraz and cabernet sauvignon, Tim and Pat Adams have decided to more than double their venture. Like their move to a total reliance on screwcaps, there is nothing unexpected in that. However, the makeup of the new plantings is anything but usual: they will give Tim Adams more than 10 ha of tempranillo and pinot gris, and

about 3.5 ha of viognier, in each case with a very clear idea about the style of wine to be produced. Exports to the UK, Sweden, The Netherlands, the US and Canada.

♥♥♥♥♀ **Riesling 2004** Flowery and aromatic; lively, fresh passionfruit, citrus and mineral; fine and elegant. **RATING** 93 **DRINK** 2012 $ 22

Cabernet 2002 Strong, ripe, focused blackcurrant fruit; excellent length and structure; iron fist, velvet glove style. **RATING** 93 **DRINK** 2017 $ 25

The Aberfeldy Shiraz 2002 An exotically ripe mix of blackberry, licorice, raspberry and mulberry, plus vanilla smoothie oak. **RATING** 92 **DRINK** 2017 $ 50

Shiraz 2003 Rich and ripe; masses of dark fruits, plums and prunes; some spicy elements; soft tannins. **RATING** 91 **DRINK** 2013 $ 25

♥♥♥♥ **Pinot Gris 2004** Definite musk varietal aromas; a tangy, lively palate; good acidity and just the faintest hint of sweetness. Altogether, a surprise packet. **RATING** 89 **DRINK** Now $ 18

The Fergus 2003 Finely boned and structured wine; red fruits, then fine, slightly sandy tannins. Grenache/Cabernet Franc. Screwcap. **RATING** 89 **DRINK** 2010 $ 25

Tim Gramp ★★★★

Mintaro/Leasingham Road, Watervale, SA 5452 **REGION** Clare Valley
T (08) 8344 4079 **F** (08) 8342 1379 **OPEN** Weekends & hols 10.30–4.30
WINEMAKER Tim Gramp **EST.** 1990 **CASES** 6000
SUMMARY Tim Gramp has quietly built up a very successful business with a limited product range, and by keeping overheads to a minimum, provides good wines at modest prices. The operation is supported by 2 ha of cabernet sauvignon around the cellar door. Exports to the UK, the US, Malaysia and New Zealand.

♥♥♥♥♀ **Clare Valley Riesling 2004** Herb, nettle and slate aromas; solidly structured; powerful, minerally palate; good acidity. Screwcap. **RATING** 90 **DRINK** 2010 $ 19.80

Timmins Wines ★★★★

PO Box 1481, Lane Cove, NSW 1595 **REGION** Southeast Australia
T (02) 9480 4722 **F** (02) 9472 4733 **WEB** www.timminswines.com.au **OPEN** Not
WINEMAKER John Timmins **EST.** 2001 **CASES** 400
SUMMARY Unusually, this is a micro-wine operation without its own vineyard. Pharmacist John Timmins completed his Bachelor of Applied Science (Wine Science) degree in 2003, and is using his qualifications to make wines in small volumes from grapes grown in the Hunter Valley and Orange regions. Exports to Singapore.

♥♥♥♥♀ **Hunter Valley Shiraz 2002** Medium to full-bodied; smooth, supple, blackberry, plum and black cherry; fine tannins; 12.5° alcohol. Cork. **RATING** 90 **DRINK** 2010 $ 25

♥♥♥♥ **Orange District Cabernet Sauvignon 2001** Medium-bodied; savoury, spice, leaf and lemon aspects to blackcurrant fruit; lively, tangy finish. Quality cork. **RATING** 89 **DRINK** 2009 $ 25

Hunter Valley Shiraz 2003 Full-bodied; big, brawny, muscular wine; earthy edge to the aromas; robust finish; 13.5° alcohol. Indifferent cork. **RATING** 88 **DRINK** 2013 $ 25

Tim Smith Wines ★★★★☆

PO Box 446, Tanunda, SA 5352 **REGION** Barossa Valley
T (08) 8563 0939 **F** (08) 8563 0939 **WEB** www.timsmithwines.com.au **OPEN** Not
WINEMAKER Tim Smith **EST.** 2001 **CASES** 1000
SUMMARY Tim Smith aspires to make wines in the mould of the great producers of Cote Rotie and Chateauneuf du Pape, but using a New World approach. It is a business in its infancy, with only two wines, a Shiraz and a Grenache/Shiraz/Mourvedre blend. Exports to the UK and the US.

♥♥♥♥♀ **Barossa Valley Shiraz 2003** Complex black fruit, spice; hints of licorice and game; rich, intense and powerful. **RATING** 93 **DRINK** 2018 $ 33

Grenache Mataro Shiraz 2003 Silky, supple, slurpy mouthfeel; juicy berry red fruits; fine tannins, neat oak. **RATING** 93 **DRINK** 2015 $ 27

Tin Cows

★★★★☆

Tarrawarra Estate, Healesville Road, Yarra Glen, Vic 3775 **REGION** Yarra Valley
T (03) 5962 3311 **F** (03) 5962 3887 **WEB** www.tarrawarra.com.au **OPEN** 7 days 11–5
WINEMAKER Clare Halloran, Bruce Walker **EST.** 1983 **CASES** 15 000
SUMMARY Tin Cows (formerly Tunnel Hill) is regarded by Tarrawarra as a separate business, drawing most of its grapes from the 21-ha Tin Cows Vineyard next to the Maroondah Highway. The wines are intended to be more accessible when young, and are significantly cheaper than Tarrawarra wines.

ᵀᵀᵀᵀ♔ **Yarra Valley Chardonnay 2003** Elegant but complex wine; medium-bodied; melon, stone fruit, barrel ferment and malolactic ferment inputs all coalesce. Screwcap. **RATING** 91 **DRINK** 2008 $19.99
Yarra Valley Heathcote Shiraz 2002 The rich, luscious blood/satsuma plum Heathcote component provides the dominant flavour; elegant Yarra the structure. Screwcap. **RATING** 91 **DRINK** 2012 $18.99
Yarra Valley Sauvignon Blanc 2004 Spotlessly clean; herb, grass and mineral aromas and flavours; bright acidity, clean finish; has length. Screwcap. **RATING** 90 **DRINK** 2007 $17.99
Yarra Valley Pinot Noir 2003 Ripe, rich plum and spice aromas and flavours; plenty of tannins in support; will evolve further. Good value. Screwcap. **RATING** 90 **DRINK** 2010 $19.99
Yarra Valley Pinot Noir 2002 Good varietal character and length; a mix of savoury herb and red fruit flavours; ultra-fine tannins. **RATING** 90 **DRINK** 2008 $19.99

ᵀᵀᵀᵀ **Yarra Valley Chardonnay 2002** Fine, tight and restrained style; melon fruit dominant, with touches of cashew. **RATING** 88 **DRINK** 2007 $19.99
Yarra Valley Rose 2004 Uncompromisingly fresh, crisp and bone-dry; winemaker's style; for food or even as an aperitif. Screwcap. **RATING** 87 **DRINK** Now $17.99

Tinderbox Vineyard

★★★☆

Tinderbox, Tas 7054 **REGION** Southern Tasmania
T (03) 6229 2994 **F** (03) 6229 2994 **OPEN** By appointment
WINEMAKER Andrew Hood (Contract) **EST.** 1994 **CASES** 185
SUMMARY Liz McGown is a Hobart nurse who has established her vineyard on the slope beneath her house, overlooking the entrance to the Derwent River and the D'Entrecasteaux Channel, doubling the size from 1 to 2 ha in 2003. The attractive label was designed by Barry Tucker, who was so charmed by Liz McGown's request that he waived his usual (substantial) fee.

ᵀᵀᵀᵀ **Chardonnay 2003** Light-bodied; typically very shy, restrained, minerally style; some citrus fruit; beyond Chablis. Screwcap. **RATING** 87 **DRINK** 2009 $30
Pinot Noir 2003 Light red; light-bodied; clean and fresh strawberry, here veering to Beaujolais; consistent house style. Cork. **RATING** 87 **DRINK** 2007 $30

Tingle-Wood

★★★☆

Glenrowan Road, Denmark, WA 6333 **REGION** Denmark
T (08) 9840 9218 **F** (08) 9840 9218 **WEB** www.tinglewoodwines.com.au **OPEN** Thurs–Mon 9–5, 7 days during hols
WINEMAKER Brenden Smith (Contract) **EST.** 1976 **CASES** 1000
SUMMARY An intermittent producer of Riesling of extraordinary quality, although birds and other disasters do intervene and prevent production in some years. The rating is given for the Riesling, which remains a sentimental favourite of mine. Exports to the UK.

ᵀᵀᵀᵀ **Red Tingle Shiraz Cabernet 2001** Spicy, savoury notes; blackberry, blackcurrant and plum; some sweet oak. Cork. **RATING** 87 **DRINK** 2008 $16
Yellow Tingle Late Harvest Riesling 2004 Delicate, fine lime/lemon juice; just off-dry; will reward 5 years' patience. Screwcap. **RATING** 87 **DRINK** 2012 $13

Tinklers Vineyard

★★★★

Pokolbin Mountains Road, Pokolbin, NSW 2330 **REGION** Lower Hunter Valley
T (02) 4998 7435 **F** (02) 4998 7529 **OPEN** 7 days 10–4
WINEMAKER Usher John Tinkler **EST.** 1997 **CASES** 1000

SUMMARY Three generations of the Tinkler family have been involved with the property since 1942. Originally a beef and dairy farm, vines have been both pulled out and replanted at various stages along the way, and part of the adjoining old Ben Ean Vineyard acquired, the net result being a little over 41 ha of vines. The major part of the production is sold as grapes, but when Usher John Tinkler returned from Charles Sturt University in 2001, he turned the tractor shed into a winery, and since then the wines have been made onsite. Four wines are made each year (Semillon, Verdelho, Chardonnay and Shiraz); they have had significant show success.

TTTTY **U&I Hunter Valley Shiraz 2002** Impressively ripe and concentrated for the vintage; luscious black fruits and a strong dash of dark chocolate; ripe tannins. Cork. **RATING** 92 **DRINK** 2014 $ 20

School Block Hunter Valley Semillon 2004 Mineral, flint and herb aromas; tight, fresh and lively; delicate but balanced and focused finish. Cork. **RATING** 91 **DRINK** 2010 $ 15

TTTT **Poppy's Hunter Valley Chardonnay 2004** Well made; a fusion of stone fruit and gentle French oak; light to medium-bodied, and glides across the tongue. Cork. **RATING** 89 **DRINK** 2007 $ 20

Lucerne Paddock Hunter Valley Verdelho 2004 Above-average fruit salad varietal character; nicely balanced acidity. Screwcap. **RATING** 87 **DRINK** 2008 $ 15

Tinlins
NR

Kangarilla Road, McLaren Flat, SA 5171 **REGION** McLaren Vale
T (08) 8323 8649 **F** (08) 8323 9747 **OPEN** 7 days 9–5
WINEMAKER Warren Randall **EST.** 1977 **CASES** 30 000
SUMMARY A very interesting operation run by former Seppelt sparkling winemaker Warren Randall, drawing upon 100 ha of estate vineyards, and specialising in bulk-wine sales to major Australian wine companies. A small proportion of the production is sold direct through the cellar door at mouthwateringly low prices to customers who provide their own containers and purchase by the litre. McLaren Vale's only bulk-wine specialist.

Tinonee Vineyard
NR

Milbrodale Road, Broke, NSW 2330 **REGION** Lower Hunter Valley
T (02) 6579 1308 **F** (02) 9719 1833 **WEB** www.tinoneewines.com.au **OPEN** Weekends & public hols 11–4
WINEMAKER Andrew Margan, Ray Merger (Contract) **EST.** 1997 **CASES** 384
SUMMARY Ian Craig has established 14 ha of vineyards on a mix of red volcanic and river flat soils at Broke. Part are in production, the remainder are coming into bearing; ultimately, production of 5000 cases of wine per year will be possible.

Tin Shed Wines
NR

PO Box 504, Tanunda, SA 5352 **REGION** Eden Valley
T (08) 8563 3669 **F** (08) 8563 3669 **WEB** www.tinshedwines.com **OPEN** Not
WINEMAKER Andrew Wardlaw, Peter Clarke **EST.** 1998 **CASES** 3000
SUMMARY Tin Shed proprietors Andrew Wardlaw and Peter Clarke weave all sorts of mystique in producing and marketing the Tin Shed wines. They say, 'our wines are hand-made so we can only produce small volumes; this means we can take more care at each step of the winemaking process . . . most bizarre of all we use our nose, palette (sic) and commonsense as opposed to the safe and reliable formula preached by our Uni's and peers'. The Tin Shed newsletter continues with lots of gee-whizz, hayseed jollity, making one fear the worst, when the reality is that the wines (even the Wild Bunch Riesling, wild-fermented without chemicals) are very good indeed. Exports to the UK, the US, New Zealand and Japan.

Tintagel Wines
★★★★

Sebbes Road, Forest Grove, WA 6286 **REGION** Margaret River
T (08) 9386 2420 **F** (08) 9386 2420 **WEB** www.tintagelwines.com.au **OPEN** By appointment
WINEMAKER Mark Messenger (Contract) **EST.** 1993 **CASES** 1000

SUMMARY The Westphal family began establishing their 8-ha vineyard in 1993; there are now 2 ha each of chardonnay, shiraz and cabernet sauvignon, and 1 ha each of semillon and merlot. It is just south of the township of Margaret River, rubbing shoulders with names such as Leeuwin Estate and Devil's Lair. Part of the crop is sold to other makers. Exports to Malaysia.

ŢŢŢŢŢ **Semillon Sauvignon Blanc 2004** Complex and powerful, the semillon subsumed by sauvignon blanc; ripe gooseberry/kiwi/passionfruit mix. Clean. Screwcap. RATING 90 DRINK 2007 $18

Tintilla Wines ★★★★

725 Hermitage Road, Pokolbin, NSW 2320 REGION Lower Hunter Valley
T (02) 6574 7093 F (02) 9767 6894 WEB www.tintilla.com OPEN 7 days 10.30–6
WINEMAKER James Lusby, Jim Chatto (Contract) EST. 1993 CASES 4500
SUMMARY The Lusby family has established a 25-ha vineyard (including 1 ha of sangiovese) on a northeast-facing vineyard with red clay and limestone soil. They have also planted an olive grove producing four different types of olives, which are cured and sold on the estate.

ŢŢŢŢŢ **Reserve Hunter Semillon 2004** Herb and wet wool/lanolin aromas; very bright, crisp and tight palate; imposing length. Screwcap. RATING 93 DRINK 2014
Reserve Hunter Valley Shiraz 2002 Elegant savoury/earthy/spice overtones; light to medium-bodied; gently ripe fruits; well balanced. RATING 93 DRINK 2014 $25.60

ŢŢŢŢ **Reserve Hunter Valley Shiraz 2003** Distinctly regional, savoury, earthy aromas; brisk acidity needs to soften. RATING 87 DRINK 2010 $25.60
Justine Merlot 2002 Firm blackcurrant/redcurrant fruit; brisk acidity; needs time. RATING 87 DRINK 2009 $25.60

ŢŢŢŢ **Hunter Semillon 2003** RATING 86 DRINK 2009 $18
4 Marys Pinot Noir 2004 RATING 84 DRINK 2007
Justine Merlot 2003 RATING 84 DRINK 2007 $25.60
Catherine de'M Sangiovese Merlot 2003 RATING 84 DRINK 2007 $25.60
Saphira Sangiovese 2002 RATING 84 DRINK 2008 $22.50
Esmerillon Celeste Merlot 2003 RATING 84 DRINK 2007 $35

৯ Tipperary Estate ★★★☆

167 Tipperary Road, Moffatdale via Murgon, Qld 4605 REGION South Burnett
T (07) 4168 4802 F (07) 4168 4839 WEB www.tipperaryestate.com.au OPEN 7 days 10–4
WINEMAKER Stuart Pierce (Contract) EST. 2002 CASES 900
SUMMARY The 2.5-ha vineyard of Tipperary Estate, planted to shiraz, verdelho and chardonnay, has been established high on the northern slopes overlooking the Barambah Valley. Additional grapes are purchased from other growers in the South Burnett region. Tipperary Estate is open 7 days for lunch, and for dinner on Saturday evenings (bookings essential), and has a fully self-contained B&B cottage; an additional attraction is the adjacent Bjelke-Petersen Dam.

ŢŢŢŢ **Chardonnay 2002** Light to medium-bodied; an elegant style, with a touch of oak complexity, but needs a touch more intensity. RATING 89 DRINK 2007 $16
Verdelho 2004 Has fruit integrity, length and balance, supported by the clever use of residual sugar. RATING 87 DRINK Now $16

Tipperary Hill Estate NR

Alma–Bowendale Road, Alma via Maryborough, Vic 3465 REGION Bendigo
T (03) 5461 3312 F (03) 5461 3312 OPEN Weekends 10–5, or by appointment
WINEMAKER Paul Flowers EST. 1986 CASES 500
SUMMARY All the wine is sold through the cellar door and onsite restaurant (open on Sundays). Paul Flowers says production depends 'on the frost, wind and birds', which perhaps explains why this is very much a part-time venture. Situated 7 km west of the city of Maryborough, Tipperary Hill Estate is the only winery operating in the Central Goldfields Shire. Paul built the rough-cut pine winery and the bluestone residential cottage next door with the help of friends.

Tizzana Winery ★★★

518 Tizzana Road, Ebenezer, NSW 2756 **REGION** Sydney Basin
T (02) 4579 1150 **F** (02) 4579 1216 **WEB** www.tizzana.com.au **OPEN** Weekends, hols 12–6, or by appointment
WINEMAKER Peter Auld **EST.** 1887 **CASES** 500
SUMMARY Tizzana has been a weekend and holiday occupation for Peter Auld for many years now. It operates in one of the great historic wineries built (in 1887) by Australia's true renaissance man, Dr Thomas Fiaschi. The wines may not be great, but the ambience is. Moreover, the cabernet sauvignon and shiraz have been replanted on the same vineyard as that first planted by Fiaschi in 1885. Peter Auld has also developed Tizzana as a wine education centre.

ȲȲȲȲ **Fortified Shiraz 2004** Light colour; has some elegance; light, spicy fruit and clean spirit; medium-term development. Estate-grown. **RATING** 86 **DRINK** 2009 $ 18
Clarissa 2003 **RATING** 85 **DRINK** 2007 $ 22

TK Wines ★★★★☆

c/- Kilikanoon Wines, Penna Lane, Penwortham, SA 5453 **REGION** Adelaide Hills
T (08) 8389 8111 **F** (08) 8389 8555 **WEB** www.tkwines.com.au **OPEN** Not
WINEMAKER Tim Knappstein **EST.** 1991 **CASES** 10 000
SUMMARY Yet another name change for the wine business of Tim and Annie Knappstein, although on this occasion doing no more than reflecting the difficulty of using the Lenswood Vineyards name, thanks to the Geographic Indication legislation. The label will be used for all the wines, regardless of whether they come entirely from the Lenswood Vineyard, and hence Lenswood GI. Exports to all major markets.

ȲȲȲȲȲ **The Palatine 2001** Aromatic, cedary, spicy; cassis and blackcurrant; medium-bodied; long, well structured, with fine, ripe tannins; lovely finish and aftertaste. Cork. **RATING** 94 **DRINK** 2015 $ 40

ȲȲȲȲ **Sauvignon Blanc 2004** Clean and firm; good mouthfeel and varietal character; ripe gooseberry fruit, then lingering, but not mouth-puckering, acidity. Backbone from the Knappstein Lenswood Vineyard. **RATING** 93 **DRINK** 2008 $ 20
Knappstein Lenswood Vineyards Chardonnay 2003 Elegant, refined style; subtle malolactic and barrel ferment inputs with a nice hint of funk; excellent length and finish. Screwcap. **RATING** 93 **DRINK** 2009 $ 24
Tim Knappstein Riesling 2004 Intense, focused lime/lemon aromas; crisp mineral, lime and slate flavours; good length. **RATING** 91 **DRINK** 2014 $ 22

ȲȲȲȲ **Gewurztraminer 2004** Gentle spice, rose petal, apple blossom aromas and flavours; altogether delicate, but nicely balanced. **RATING** 87 **DRINK** 2009 $ 20

Tobias Wines NR

PO Box 296, Angaston, SA 5353 **REGION** Eden Valley
T (08) 8565 3395 **F** (08) 8565 3379 **OPEN** Not
WINEMAKER Toby Hueppauff **EST.** 2000 **CASES** 2000
SUMMARY When Toby and Treena Hueppauff sold their well-known Kaesler Wines property at Nuriootpa they wasted no time in purchasing another vineyard, with a little under 6 ha of vines. They intend to export most of the wine, and to make Riesling, Shiraz, Merlot and Pinot Noir.

Tobin Wines NR

34 Ricca Road, Ballandean, Qld 4382 **REGION** Granite Belt
T (07) 4684 1235 **F** (07) 4684 1235 **OPEN** By appointment
WINEMAKER Adrian Tobin, David Gianini, Mark Ravenscroft (Contract) **EST.** 1964 **CASES** 1000
SUMMARY In the early 1900s the Ricca family planted table grapes; they planted shiraz and semillon in 1964/5 – these are said to be the oldest vinifera vines in the Granite Belt region. The Tobin family (headed by Adrian and Frances Tobin) purchased the vineyard in 2000 and have substantially increased plantings. There are now nearly 10 ha planted to semillon, verdelho, chardonnay, sauvignon blanc, shiraz, merlot, cabernet sauvignon and tempranillo, with some remaining rows of

table grapes. However, one thing has not changed: bulk wine made in traditional Italian style and sold in 15–20 litre drums at enticingly low prices.

Tokar Estate ★★★★☆

6 Maddens Lane, Coldstream, Vic 3770 **REGION** Yarra Valley
T(03) 5964 9585 **F**(03) 5964 9587 **WEB** www.tokarestate.com.au **OPEN** 7 days 10–5
WINEMAKER Paul Evans (Contract) **EST.** 1996 **CASES** 5000
SUMMARY Leon Tokar is one of the new arrivals on Maddens Lane; he has established 12 ha of pinot noir, shiraz, cabernet sauvignon and tempranillo. Part of the grape production is sold to Southcorp. The cellar door, barrel room and restaurant, opened in late 2002, are now open 7 days, reflecting the significantly increased production.

▼▼▼▼▼ **The Reserve Pinot Noir 2003** Fragrant, spicy black cherry and plum; intense and powerful, but keeps line, balance and, above all, length. Excellent tannins. Diam. **RATING** 94 **DRINK** 2011

▼▼▼▼▽ **Tempranillo 2003** Deep red-purple; rich, supple and smooth red and black fruits; minimal tannins. Gold medal Victorian Wines Show 2004. **RATING** 93 **DRINK** 2012 $ 26

▼▼▼▼ **Cabernet Sauvignon 2003** Dense blackberry and prune fruit; vanilla oak; a faint suggestion of some bacterial or similar activity. Diam. **RATING** 89 **DRINK** 2013 $ 30

Tollana ★★★★☆

Tanunda Road, Nuriootpa, SA 5355 **REGION** Eden Valley
T(08) 8568 9389 **F**(08) 8568 9489 **WEB** www.australianwines.com.au/tollana **OPEN** Not
WINEMAKER Andrew Baldwin **EST.** 1888 **CASES** NFP
SUMMARY As the Southcorp wine group moves to establish regional identity for its wines, Tollana is emphasising its Eden Valley base. Seemingly as a by-product of Penfolds' development of Yattarna and related wines, the Tollana Chardonnay style has become more elegant, and now stands comfortably alongside the flavoursome Riesling and Shiraz.

▼▼▼▼▼ **Viognier 2004** Strong and exemplary varietal character throughout the bouquet and palate; rich, voluptuous honeysuckle, musk and pear. **RATING** 94 **DRINK** 2008 $ 18.99

▼▼▼▼▽ **Bin TR16 Shiraz 2003** An old favourite returns; medium to full-bodied; savoury dark berry fruits; classy fine tannins and oak. Not all Eden Valley; South Australian appellation. **RATING** 91 **DRINK** 2013 $ 18.99

🍇 Tomboy Hill ★★★★★

204 Sim Street, Ballarat, Vic 3350 (postal) **REGION** Ballarat
T(03) 5331 3785 **OPEN** Not
WINEMAKER Scott Ireland (Contract) **EST.** 1984 **CASES** 1550
SUMMARY Former schoolteacher Ian Watson seems to be following the same path as Lindsay McCall of Paringa Estate (also a former schoolteacher) in extracting greater quality and style than any other winemaker in his region, in this case Ballarat. Since 1984 Watson has slowly and patiently built up a patchwork quilt of small plantings (most from 0.33 ha to 2 ha), all clustered around the town of Ballarat. In the better years, the Single Vineyard wines of Chardonnay and/or Pinot Noir are released; Rebellion Chardonnay and Pinot Noir are multi-vineyard blends, but all 100% Ballarat. This is the most exciting new winery in this year's *Companion*. There are 6 vineyards contributing to the wines up to 2003, with a total area of 7.5 ha.

▼▼▼▼▼ **Nintinbool Vineyard Pinot Noir 2002** Deep colour; powerful, intense and long; savoury, foresty overtones to black cherry, plum and spice fruit; very stylish, great length; 100 cases made; 14° alcohol. Quality cork. **RATING** 95 **DRINK** 2012 $ 36

Rebellion Pinot Noir 2002 Powerful, classy and intense; spicy, savoury bouquet; sweeter pinot fruit on the palate, bordering luscious, but still fine and long; 13.7° alcohol. Cork. **RATING** 94 **DRINK** 2015 $ 30

Rebellion Chardonnay 2002 Intense, complex and stylish; nectarine and grapefruit; perfectly balanced and integrated oak; long finish. Quality cork. **RATING** 94 **DRINK** 2009 $ 27

TTTTY Rokewood Junction Pinot Noir 2002 Powerful, savoury, foresty, spicy bouquet; rich, ripe and mouthfilling spiced black plums; fine tannins on the finish; 13.8° alcohol. Cork. **RATING** 93 **DRINK** 2013 $ 32
The Tomboy Chardonnay 2003 More complexity and weight than the Rebellion; cashew, softer fruit line; good oak handling; 13.5° alcohol; 80 dozen made. **RATING** 92 **DRINK** 2008 $ 33
Rebellion Chardonnay 2003 Fresh, lively grapefruit and melon; excellent balance and ripeness; likewise harmonious oak handling; 13.5° alcohol. Screwcap. **RATING** 92 **DRINK** 2009 $ 27
The Tomboy Pinot Noir 2003 Light to medium-bodied; has both aromatic and flavour complexity; smoky, spicy, plummy fruit; hallmark acidity. Screwcap. **RATING** 92 **DRINK** 2010 $ 38
Pinot Noir 2002 Intensely spicy aromas and flavours; red cherry fruit and a hint of lemon zest; lively, fine, savoury tannins; 13.7° alcohol. Cork. **RATING** 92 **DRINK** 2012 $ 38
Rebellion Pinot Noir 2003 Clean spice, plum and black cherry; clear-cut varietal character; light to medium-bodied; good structure and length, particularly natural acidity; 13.5° alcohol. Screwcap. **RATING** 91 **DRINK** 2009 $ 30
Ballarat Goldfields Chardonnay 2002 Elegant, lively, citrus and melon; long, but not deep, palate; fresh finish; balanced acidity; 13° alcohol. Quality cork. **RATING** 90 **DRINK** 2008 $ 33

TTTT Rokewood Ballarat Goldfields Pinot Noir 2003 Light-bodied; clean, fresh, bright strawberry, cherry and plum fruit; good balance and natural acidity. Minimal French oak. **RATING** 89 **DRINK** 2007 $ 32
Nintinbool Vineyard Pinot Noir 2003 Light red-purple; light-bodied, clean, fresh, red cherry, strawberry and plum fruit; not complex, but balanced; 13.5° alcohol; 150 cases made. Screwcap. **RATING** 89 **DRINK** 2007 $ 36

Tombstone Estate   NR

5R Basalt Road, Dubbo, NSW 2830 **REGION** Western Plains Zone
T (02) 6882 6624 **F** (02) 6882 6624 **OPEN** Fri–Mon & school hols 10–5, or by appointment
WINEMAKER Ian Robertson **EST.** 1997 **CASES** 600
SUMMARY The ominously named Tombstone Estate has been established by Rod and Patty Tilling, who have planted 5 ha of chardonnay, pinot noir, shiraz, cabernet sauvignon, sangiovese, barbera and muscat. The wine is made onsite, with sales through local outlets, mail order and cellar door, the last with barbecue and picnic facilities.

Toms Cap Vineyard   NR

322 Lays Road, Carrajung Lower, Vic 3844 **REGION** Gippsland
T (03) 5194 2215 **F** (03) 5194 2369 **WEB** www.tomscap.com.au **OPEN** Weekends by appointment
WINEMAKER Owen Schmidt (Contract) **EST.** 1994 **CASES** NA
SUMMARY Graham Morris began developing the vineyard on his 40-ha property in 1992 surrounded by the forests of the Strzelecki Ranges, the 90-mile beach at Woodside, and the Tarra Bulga NP, one of the four major areas of cool temperate rainforest in Victoria. The vineyard has 2.4 ha of cabernet sauvignon, chardonnay, sauvignon blanc and riesling. The property also has a 3-bedroom family cottage, and two 2-bedroom spa cottages. The wines are made at nearby Lyre Bird Hill winery.

Tom's Waterhole Wines   NR

Felton, Longs Corner Road, Canowindra, NSW 2804 **REGION** Cowra
T (02) 6344 1819 **F** (02) 6344 2172 **WEB** www.tomswaterhole.com.au **OPEN** Weekends & public hols 10–4, or by appointment
WINEMAKER Graham Kerr **EST.** 1997 **CASES** 1500
SUMMARY Graham Timms and Graham Kerr started the development of Tom's Waterhole Wines in 1997, progressively establishing 6 ha of shiraz, cabernet sauvignon, semillon and merlot. The planting program was completed in 2001. They have decided to bypass the use of irrigation, so the yields will be low.

Toolangi Vineyards ★★★★★

2 Merriwee Crescent, Toorak, Vic 3142 (postal) REGION Yarra Valley
T (03) 9822 9488 F (03) 9804 3365 WEB www.toolangi.com OPEN Not
WINEMAKER Contract EST. 1995 CASES 3500
SUMMARY Garry and Julie Hounsell acquired their property in the Dixons Creek subregion of the
Yarra Valley, adjoining the bottom edge of the Toolangi State Forest, in 1995. Plantings have taken
place progressively since then, with 13 ha now in the ground. The primary accent is on pinot noir,
chardonnay and cabernet, accounting for all but 1 ha, which is predominantly shiraz, and a few rows
of merlot. As only half the vineyards are in bearing, production is supplemented by chardonnay and
pinot noir from the Coldstream subregion, cropped at 2 tonnes per acre. Winemaking is by Tom
Carson of Yering Station, Rick Kinzbrunner of Giaconda and Trevor Mast of Mount Langi Ghiran, as
impressive a trio of winemakers as one could wish for. Exports to the UK.

▼▼▼▼▼ **Estate Chardonnay 2003** Light green-yellow; very elegant and graceful; skilful marriage
of barrel ferment and creamy malolactic inputs to melon and nectarine fruit; very good
length; 13° alcohol. Made at Yering Station. RATING 95 DRINK 2010 $ 37
Reserve Chardonnay 2003 Light to medium green-yellow; textured, complex and
powerful, showing its 14° alcohol; ripe fig, hazelnut and peach fruit; balanced acidity.
Made at Giaconda. RATING 94 DRINK 2009 $ 62

▼▼▼▼▽ **Pinot Noir 2002** Light but bright colour; fresh, clean, lively cherry and strawberry fruit;
subtle oak, super-fine tannins. Made at Yering Station. RATING 93 DRINK 2009 $ 37
Chardonnay 2003 Elegant nectarine and melon fruit with a hint of citrus; fine structure;
balanced oak. RATING 90 DRINK 2007 $ 19.50

Toolleen Vineyard NR

2004 Gibb Road, Toolleen, Vic 3551 (postal) REGION Heathcote
T (03) 5433 6397 F (03) 5433 6397 OPEN Not
WINEMAKER Dominque Portet (Contract) EST. 1996 CASES 1000
SUMMARY Owned by Mr KC Huang and family, Toolleen's 14.7 ha of shiraz, cabernet sauvignon,
merlot, cabernet franc and durif are planted on the western slope of Mt Camel, 18 km north of
Heathcote. The lower Cambrian red soils are now well recognised for their suitability for making full-
bodied and strongly structured red wines. Most of the wine (80%) is exported to Taiwan, Malaysia,
Singapore, Hong Kong and the US.

Toomah Wines NR

'Seven Oaks', 635 Toomuc Valley Road, Pakenham, Vic 3810 REGION Port Phillip Zone
T (03) 5942 7583 F (03) 5942 7583 OPEN Weekends 11–6, or by appointment
WINEMAKER Matt Robinson EST. 1996 CASES 2000
SUMMARY Toomah Wines is owned and managed by Matt and Michelle Robinson; the 6.5 ha of
vineyards have been planted on Matt's parents' historically important 226-ha grazing property. Once
owned by the Kitchen family (of Lever & Kitchen fame), the property boasted the largest orchard in
the southern hemisphere in its 1930s heyday. Matt Robinson has a Bachelor of Agricultural Science
from Melbourne University, and is completing his Bachelor of Applied Science (Wine Science)
degree (by correspondence) through Charles Sturt University. Various historic buildings on the
property are being restored: one serves as the winery, the other as cellar door.

Toorak Estate ★★★

Toorak Road, Leeton, NSW 2705 REGION Riverina
T (02) 6953 2333 F (02) 6953 4454 WEB www.toorakwines.com.au OPEN Mon–Sat 10–5
WINEMAKER Robert Bruno EST. 1965 CASES 400 000
SUMMARY A traditional, long-established Riverina producer with a strong Italian-based clientele
around Australia. Production has been increasing significantly, utilising 150 ha of estate plantings
and grapes purchased from other growers. The prices are low, only the Botrytis Semillon more than
$15 a bottle. Significant taint problems with Twin Top cork closures.

ŸŸŸŸŸ **Willandra Estate Langhorne Creek Shiraz 2004** Dense purple-red; abundant blackberry and satsuma plum fruit; good structure, fine tannins; entirely fruit-driven. **RATING** 90 **DRINK** 2014 $12

ŸŸŸŸŸ **Willandra Premium Chardonnay 2004 RATING** 85 **DRINK** Now $12
Willandra Leeton Selection Cabernet Merlot 2004 RATING 85 **DRINK** 2007 $8
Willandra Leeton Selection Shiraz Cabernet 2004 RATING 84 **DRINK** Now $8

ŸŸŸ **Willandra Leeton Selection Semillon Chardonnay 2004 RATING** 83 $8
Willandra Leeton Selection Unwooded Chardonnay 2004 RATING 82 $8

🐌 Toowoomba Hills Estate   NR

5 Berrys Road, Vale View, Qld 4352 **REGION** Queensland Zone
T (07) 4696 2459 **F** (07) 4696 2459 **OPEN** Weekends & hols 9–6, or by appointment
WINEMAKER Matthew Chersini, Irene Wilson **EST.** 1995 **CASES** 600
SUMMARY The 2.5-ha vineyard (cabernet sauvignon, shiraz, chardonnay, semillon, cabernet franc and malbec) was planted in the late 1980s and early 1990s by Matthew Chersini and family. Irene Wilson (then working in New Zealand wineries) and Matthew met at Charles Sturt University during their wine science degree course; they now have 3 children, and together run the vineyard, winery, wine garden and cellar door on the outskirts of Toowoomba. The winery produces small quantities of Chardonnay, Semillon, Shiraz, Cabernet Sauvignon, Shiraz Cabernet Malbec, plus sweet and fortified wines.

Torbreck Vintners   ★★★★★

Roennfeldt Road, Marananga, SA 5352 **REGION** Barossa Valley
T (08) 8562 4155 **F** (08) 8562 4195 **WEB** www.torbreck.com **OPEN** 7 days 10–6
WINEMAKER David Powell, Dan Standish **EST.** 1994 **CASES** 45 000
SUMMARY Of all the Barossa Valley wineries to grab the headlines in the US, with demand pulling prices up to undreamt of levels, Torbreck stands supreme. David Powell has not let success go to his head, or subvert the individuality and sheer quality of his wines, all created around very old, dry-grown, bush-pruned vineyards. The top trio are led by The RunRig (Shiraz/Viognier), then The Factor (Shiraz) and The Descendant (Shiraz/Viognier); next The Struie (Shiraz) and The Steading (Grenache/Shiraz). Notwithstanding the depth and richness of the wines, they have a remarkable degree of finesse.

ŸŸŸŸŸ **The Descendant 2003** Deep colour; full-bodied; very complex, high-toned spicy aromas with the apricot influence of Viognier obvious, but not overdone; excellent texture and structure. High-quality cork. **RATING** 96 **DRINK** 2023 $145
The Factor 2002 Fragrant, luscious fruit aromas; gorgeous texture and structure; a complex array of both red and black fruits drive the wine, oak merely a vehicle; fine, filigreed tannins. **RATING** 96 **DRINK** 2015 $140
The Struie 2003 Complex licorice, spice and sweet earth overtones to blackberry, plum, dark chocolate and licorice; medium to full-bodied; marvellous tannin management. Barossa/Eden Valley. High-quality cork. **RATING** 95 **DRINK** 2018 $55
The RunRig 2002 Medium-bodied; fragrant, elegant style with lifted aromatics and a finely drawn, structured and balanced palate; smoky blackberry fruit with just a hint of apricot; fine, long tannins. High-quality cork. **RATING** 95 **DRINK** 2015 $225

ŸŸŸŸŸ **Les Amis Grenache 2002** Richly perfumed and spiced; far more density and flavour than most Barossa Valley examples; sultry, smoky berry fruit; very good structure. Grenache. **RATING** 93 **DRINK** 2012
The Steading 2002 Complex texture, structure and flavour; a melange of sweet tobacco, spice and fruits; sophisticated medium-bodied wine; fine, savoury tannins. **RATING** 93 **DRINK** 2010 $40
Woodcutter's Shiraz 2003 Attractive wine; an array of spice and red fruits, sweet but not jammy; soft, supple tannins. **RATING** 90 **DRINK** 2007 $20

ŸŸŸŸ **Woodcutter's Semillon 2003** Rich, full and flavoursome; generous, early-drinking style. **RATING** 87 **DRINK** Now $17

ŸŸŸŸ **The Juveniles 2003 RATING** 86 **DRINK** Now $27
The Bothie Shiraz 2003 RATING 85 **DRINK** Now $18.50

Totino Wines

NR

982 Port Road, Albert Park, SA 5014 (postal) **REGION** Adelaide Hills
T (08) 8268 8066 **F** (08) 8268 3597 **OPEN** Not
WINEMAKER Scott Rawlinson **EST.** 1992 **CASES** 15 000
SUMMARY Don Totino migrated from Italy in 1968, and at the age of 18 became the youngest barber in Australia. He soon moved on, establishing a pizza bar with the challenging name of Lick a Chic before moving into general food and importing and distribution. Festival City, as the business is known, has been highly successful, recognised by a recent significant award from the Italian government. In 1998 he purchased a run-down vineyard at Paracombe in the Adelaide Hills, since extending the plantings to 29 ha of chardonnay, pinot grigio, sauvignon blanc, sangiovese, shiraz and cabernet sauvignon. The wines have retail distribution throughout Australia, with various members of his family, including daughter Linda, involved in the business.

Touchwood Wines

★★★

PO Box 91, Battery Point, Tas 7004 **REGION** Southern Tasmania
T (03) 6223 3996 **F** (03) 6223 2384 **OPEN** Not
WINEMAKER Moorilla Estate (Contract) **EST.** 1992 **CASES** 1500
SUMMARY Peter and Tina Sexton planted 5 ha of vineyard in the early 1990s; pinot noir and chardonnay are the principal varieties, with a small amount of cabernet sauvignon and merlot. While on a north-facing hill, with heavy black soil over a calcareous lime base, it has never been an easy site; frost has claimed some vintages, and lack of heat others.

ŸŸŸŸ Pinot Noir 2003 RATING 86 **DRINK** 2007

Tower Estate

★★★★★

Cnr Broke Road/Hall Road, Pokolbin, NSW 2320 **REGION** Lower Hunter Valley
T (02) 4998 7989 **F** (02) 4998 7919 **WEB** www.towerestatewines.com.au **OPEN** 7 days 10–5
WINEMAKER Dan Dineen **EST.** 1999 **CASES** 10 000
SUMMARY Tower Estate is a joint venture headed by Len Evans, featuring a luxury conference centre and accommodation. It draws upon varieties and regions which have a particular synergy, coupled with the enormous knowledge of Len Evans and the winemaking skills of Dan Dineen. Exports to the UK, Denmark, Singapore, Canada and Japan.

ŸŸŸŸŸ **Hunter Valley Semillon 2004** Spotlessly clean and fragrant; herb, lemon, spice and mineral; fruit, not sugar, sweetness. **RATING** 94 **DRINK** 2010 $ 26
Hunter Valley Chardonnay 2003 Generous fruit aromas and flavours, but not the least overblown; white peach and good oak handling. **RATING** 94 **DRINK** 2007 $ 28
Adelaide Hills Chardonnay 2003 Complex, attractive, slightly funky barrel ferment aromas; clean citrus and stone fruit flavours with excellent balance and length; developing slowly. **RATING** 94 **DRINK** 2009 $ 28
Yarra Valley Pinot Noir 2003 Clean, fragrant and correct; elegant cherry and plum fruit, touches of spice; silky mouthfeel; belies its 14.5° alcohol. **RATING** 94 **DRINK** 2010 $ 38
Hunter Valley Shiraz 2003 Abundant black fruits, layered and deep; tannins like built-in cupboards; absolutely shows the great vintage. **RATING** 94 **DRINK** 2018 $ 38

ŸŸŸŸŸ Adelaide Hills Sauvignon Blanc 2004 Pale straw-green; clean, fresh and lively; nice fruit expression, and attractive squeaky acidity. **RATING** 93 **DRINK** Now $ 32
Orange Merlot 2003 Herb and olive aromas; medium-bodied; much sweeter blackcurrant fruit on the palate; ripe tannins. **RATING** 92 **DRINK** 2013 $ 32
Clare Valley Riesling 2004 Clean but subdued bouquet; lively fresh apple, lime and mineral flavours; moderate intensity. **RATING** 90 **DRINK** 2012 $ 26

Towerhill Estate

★★★☆

Albany Highway, Mount Barker, WA 6324 **REGION** Mount Barker
T (08) 9851 1488 **F** (08) 9851 2982 **OPEN** Fri–Sun 10–5 (7 days during school hols)
WINEMAKER James Kellie (Contract) **EST.** 1993 **CASES** 750
SUMMARY The Williams family, headed by Alan and Diane, began the establishment of Towerhill Estate in 1993, planting 6.5 ha of chardonnay, cabernet sauvignon, riesling and merlot. Initally the

grapes were sold to other producers, but since 1999 limited quantities have been made for Towerhill. These wines have had consistent show success at the Qantas Wine Show of Western Australia, and sell out quickly through the cellar door and local outlets.

Trafford Hill Vineyard

Lot 1 Bower Road, Normanville, SA 5204 **REGION** Southern Fleurieu
T (08) 8558 3595 **WEB** www.traffordhillwines.com.au **OPEN** Thurs–Mon & hols 10.30–5
WINEMAKER John Sanderson **EST.** 1996 **CASES** 650
SUMMARY Irene and John Sanderson have established 2 ha of vineyard on the coast of the Fleurieu Peninsula, near to its southern extremity. Irene carries out all the viticulture, and John makes the wine with help from district veteran Allan Dyson. Distribution is through local restaurants, the remainder through mail order and the cellar door.

ȲȲȲȲ **Monique Family Reserve Red 2002** A curious blend, but comes together well, with ample dark fruit flavours, soft and round. Shiraz/Cabernet Sauvignon/Grenache. Cork. **RATING** 89 **DRINK** 2012 $ 20
Premium Master Liam Riesling 2004 Very concentrated and powerful citrussy fruit; some reduction; questionable cork. **RATING** 87 **DRINK** Now $ 15

Train Trak ★★★★

957 Healesville–Yarra Glen Road, Yarra Glen, Vic 3775 **REGION** Yarra Valley
T (03) 9429 4744 **F** (03) 9427 1510 **WEB** www.traintrak.com.au **OPEN** By appointment
WINEMAKER MasterWineMakers (Contract) **EST.** 1995 **CASES** 6000
SUMMARY The unusual name comes from the Yarra Glen to Healesville railroad, which was built in 1889 and abandoned in 1980 – part of it passes by the Train Trak vineyard. A total of 16.4 ha of vines have been planted, the oldest dating back to 1995; all are now in bearing.

ȲȲȲȲȲ **Yarra Valley Shiraz 2003** Medium-bodied; supple, rich, rounded black fruits and gentle spice; well-handled oak. **RATING** 92 **DRINK** 2013 $ 26.50
Yarra Valley Cabernet Sauvignon 2003 Good colour; sweet, ripe blackcurrant fruit; medium-bodied; good tannins and oak. **RATING** 91 **DRINK** 2014 $ 25
Yarra Valley Pinot Noir 2003 Strong colour; clean, ripe plummy fruit; concentrated, powerful, and needs time to soften and grow complexity. **RATING** 90 **DRINK** 2009 $ 25

ȲȲȲȲ **Yarra Valley Pinot Rose 2004** Fragrant strawberry aromas; very light, but resisted the temptation to sweeten it up; fresh and crisp. **RATING** 87 **DRINK** Now $ 20

Tranquil Vale

325 Pywells Road, Luskintyre, NSW 2321 **REGION** Lower Hunter Valley
T (02) 4930 6100 **F** (02) 4930 6105 **WEB** www.tranquilvalewines.com.au **OPEN** Thurs–Mon 10–4, or by appointment
WINEMAKER Andrew Margan, David Hook, Phil Griffiths (Contract) **EST.** 1996 **CASES** 2000
SUMMARY Phil and Lucy Griffiths purchased the property sight unseen from a description in an old copy of the *Australian Weekend* found in the High Commission Office in London. The vineyard they established is on the banks of the Hunter River, opposite Wyndham Estate, on relatively fertile, sandy, clay loam. Irrigation has been installed, and what is known as VSP trellising. Within the blink of an eye they have found themselves 'in the amusing position that people ask us our opinion!' There are 3 luxury self-contained cottages onsite (with a swimming pool, tennis court, gymnasium, etc), they sleep a family or two couples each. Competent winemaking has resulted in good wines, some of which have already had show success.

ȲȲȲȲ **Hunter Valley Semillon 2004** Clean, crisp and focused; tight, minerally, lemony acidity; needs time. Screwcap. **RATING** 89 **DRINK** 2010 $ 17
Hunter Valley Chardonnay 2003 Obvious barrel ferment oak inputs on peach and nectarine fruit; plenty of overall flavour; good balance. Screwcap. **RATING** 88 **DRINK** 2007 $ 19
Old Luskie NV Nicely balanced honey, lemon and acid; good length. Cork. **RATING** 87 **DRINK** Now $ 17

ȲȲȲȲ **Hunter Valley Chardonnay 2004** **RATING** 86 **DRINK** 2007 $ 19
Hunter Valley Shiraz Cabernet 2003 **RATING** 85 **DRINK** 2008 $ 18

Transylvania Winery   NR

Monaro Highway, Cooma, NSW 2630 **REGION** Southern New South Wales Zone
T (02) 6452 4374 **F** (02) 6452 6281 **OPEN** 7 days 9–5, restaurant 11–11 by appointment
WINEMAKER Peter Culici **EST.** 1989 **CASES** NA
SUMMARY Peter Culici operates the vineyard and winery, drawing in part on a 2.4-ha vineyard of
sauvignon blanc, gewurztraminer, chardonnay, pinot noir, cabernet sauvignon, merlot and
muscadelle. Table and fortified wines are sold through the cellar door and onsite restaurant, which is
14 km north of Cooma.

🐌 Traolach/Xabregas

Cnr Spencer Road/Hay River Road, Narrikup, WA 6326 **REGION** Mount Barker
T (08) 9321 2366 **F** (08) 9327 9393 **WEB** www.traolach.com.au **OPEN** By appointment
WINEMAKER Diane Miller, Mike Garland, James Kelly (Contract) **EST.** 1996 **CASES** 8500
SUMMARY In 1996 stockbrokers Terry Hogan and Eve Broadley, the major participants in the Spencer
Wine Joint Venture, commenced a viticulture business which has now grown into 3 vineyards totalling
120 ha on sites 10 km south of Mount Barker. The varieties planted are riesling, chardonnay, sauvignon
blanc, cabernet sauvignon, cabernet franc, merlot and shiraz. As well as being contracted growers to
Houghtons, Howard Park and Forest Hill and acting as contract managers to surrounding vineyards,
they have developed two labels: Traolach (premium range), which is Gaelic for Terry, and Xabregas (line
range), which is an old family company name. The wines are modestly priced; I devoutly hope the joint
venture does not intend to export to the US, where the names would cause phonetic meltdown. They are
distributed by John Burke Winecraft in WA and Vitarelli Fine Wines in Victoria.

🍷🍷🍷🍷 **Traolach Mount Barker Riesling 2003** Clean and crisp; light-bodied apple, spice and
mineral; balanced acidity; in transition phase. Screwcap. **RATING** 89 **DRINK** 2010 $15.99
Traolach Mount Barker Noble Riesling 2003 Yellow-gold; moderately rich botrytis; lime
juice varietal character still present; long and lingering finish. Screwcap. **RATING** 89
DRINK 2008 $21.95
Xabregas Mount Barker Shiraz 2002 Cedary, multi-spice, pepper, black fruits; light to
medium-bodied; gentle oak. Diam. **RATING** 87 **DRINK** 2009 $13.95

🍷🍷🍷🍸 **Xabregas Great Southern Unwooded Chardonnay 2004** **RATING** 86 **DRINK** 2007
$13.95
Xabregas Mount Barker Merlot 2002 **RATING** 85 **DRINK** 2008 $13.95
Xabregas Mount Barker Cabernet Merlot 2003 **RATING** 85 **DRINK** 2008 $10.95
Xabregas Mount Barker Cabernet Sauvignon 2003 **RATING** 85 **DRINK** 2007 $17.95

Trappers Gully

Lot 6 Boyup Road, Mount Barker, WA 6324 **REGION** Mount Barker
T (08) 9851 2565 **F** (08) 9851 3565 **OPEN** By appointment
WINEMAKER Clea Candy, James Kelly (Consultant) **EST.** 1998 **CASES** 1000
SUMMARY The Lester and Candy families began the development of Trappers Gully in 1998. Clea
Candy has the most directly relevant CV, as a qualified viticulturist and practised winemaker, and,
according to the official history, 'mother, daughter and wife, and pretty much the instigator of all
heated discussions'. The families have progressively planted 1.2 ha each of chenin blanc, sauvignon
blanc, cabernet sauvignon and shiraz, and slightly less than 1 ha of cabernet sauvignon. Trappers
Gully plans to erect an onsite winery.

🍷🍷🍷🍷 **Mount Barker Sauvignon Blanc 2004** Crisp, lively, zesty mineral, herb and lemon mix.
Indifferent cork. **RATING** 88 **DRINK** 2007 $17
Mount Barker Shiraz 2003 Light to medium-bodied; spicy, savoury edges to blackberry
fruit. Well balanced. **RATING** 87 **DRINK** 2010 $19

🍷🍷🍷🍸 **Mount Barker Chenin Blanc 2004** **RATING** 86 **DRINK** 2008 $17

Treen Ridge Estate   NR

Packer Road, Pemberton, WA 6260 **REGION** Pemberton
T (08) 9776 1131 **F** (08) 9776 0442 **WEB** www.wn.com.au/treenridgeestat **OPEN** Wed–Fri 11–5,
weekends 10–5

WINEMAKER Andrew Mountford (Contract) **EST.** 1992 **CASES** 600
SUMMARY The 1.7-ha Treen Ridge vineyard and 3-room accommodation is set between the Treen Brook State Forest and The Warren National Park and is operated by Mollie and Barry Scotman.

Treeton Estate   NR

North Treeton Road, Cowaramup, WA 6284 **REGION** Margaret River
T (08) 9755 5481 **F** (08) 9755 5051 **OPEN** 7 days 10–6
WINEMAKER David McGowan **EST.** 1984 **CASES** 3000
SUMMARY In 1982 David McGowan and wife Corinne purchased the 30-ha property upon which Treeton Estate is established, beginning to plant the vines 2 years later. David has done just about everything in his life, and in the early years was working in Perth, which led to various setbacks for the vineyard. The wines are light and fresh, sometimes rather too much so.

Trentham Estate   ★★★★

Sturt Highway, Trentham Cliffs, NSW 2738 **REGION** Murray Darling
T (03) 5024 8888 **F** (03) 5024 8800 **WEB** www.trenthamestate.com.au **OPEN** 7 days 9.30–5
WINEMAKER Anthony Murphy, Shane Kerr **EST.** 1988 **CASES** 65 000
SUMMARY Remarkably consistent tasting notes across all wine styles from all vintages since 1989 attest to the expertise of ex-Mildara winemaker Tony Murphy, now making the Trentham wines from his family vineyards. All the wines offer great value for money. The winery restaurant is also recommended. National retail distribution; exports to the US, the UK, Belgium and New Zealand.

 Shiraz 2001 Red and black fruits; medium-bodied, with excellent mouthfeel, texture and structure, the hallmark of all the Trentham wines; good length and acidity. **RATING** 90 **DRINK** 2010 $15
Merlot 2002 Medium red-purple; typically good mouthfeel and texture; a nice mix of savoury and darker fruits; very good finish. **RATING** 90 **DRINK** 2010 $14.50

♇♇♇♇ **Sauvignon Blanc 2004** Clearly articulated varietal character; lemon, asparagus and passionfruit; medium-bodied, with good structure. Great value. **RATING** 89 **DRINK** 2007 $12.50
Cabernet Sauvignon Merlot 2002 Medium to full red-purple; fine, supple and ripe tannins; black fruits, mocha and earth interplay. **RATING** 89 **DRINK** 2010 $14.50
Pinot Noir 2003 Works the same magic as Joe Grilli does with colombard; light to medium-bodied; good savoury texture and structure, with legitimate varietal expression. **RATING** 87 **DRINK** 2008 $12.50
Cabernet Sauvignon Merlot 2003 Good colour; clean, fresh cassis/blackcurrant aromas; good tannin structure on the finish; misses a beat on the mid-palate. Screwcap. **RATING** 87 **DRINK** 2009 $14.50

♇♇♇♈ **Chardonnay 2004** **RATING** 86 **DRINK** 2007 $14.50
Brut 2003 **RATING** 86 **DRINK** 2007 $18
Murphy's Lore Shiraz Cabernet 2002 **RATING** 85 **DRINK** 2007 $10
Ruby Sparkling Red 2002 **RATING** 84 **DRINK** 2007 $18
Murphy's Lore Spatlese Lexia 2004 **RATING** 84 **DRINK** Now $10

♇♇♇ **Murphy's Lore Autumn Red 2004** **RATING** 83 $10
Murphy's Lore Chardonnay 2004 **RATING** 82 $10

Trevelen Farm

Weir Road, Cranbrook, WA 6321 **REGION** Great Southern
T (08) 9826 1052 **F** (08) 9826 1209 **WEB** www.trevelenfarmwines.com.au **OPEN** Thurs–Mon 10–4.30, or by appointment
WINEMAKER James Kellie (Harewood Estate) **EST.** 1993 **CASES** 3000
SUMMARY John and Katie Sprigg, together with their family, operate a 1300-ha wool, meat and grain-producing farm, run on environmental principles with sustainable agriculture at its heart. As a minor, but highly successful, diversification they established 5 ha of sauvignon blanc, riesling, chardonnay, cabernet sauvignon and merlot in 1993, adding 1.5 ha of shiraz in 2000. Vines, it seems, are in the genes, for John Sprigg's great-great-grandparents established 20 ha of vines at Happy Valley, SA, in the 1870s. The quality of the wines is as consistent as the prices are modest, and visitors

to the cellar door have the added attraction of both garden and forest walks, the latter among 130 ha of remnant bush which harbours many different orchids which flower from May to December. Exports to the UK, Hong Kong, Malaysia and Japan.

ŶŶŶŶŶ **Riesling 2004** Pale straw-green; herb and lime aromas; intense, tightly focused lime juice palate, long and balanced; sweet fruit finish. Screwcap. **RATING** 94 **DRINK** 2014 $ 18

ŶŶŶŶŶ **Sauvignon Blanc 2004** Clean and intense aromas of cut grass; hints of passionfruit and gooseberry; long, minerally finish. Screwcap. **RATING** 93 **DRINK** 2007 $ 16
Cabernet Merlot 2003 Good colour; medium-bodied; supple, smooth black fruits and a touch of spice; balanced and integrated French oak; fine tannins. Cork. **RATING** 91 **DRINK** 2013 $ 18

ŶŶŶŶ **Unwooded Chardonnay 2004 RATING** 85 **DRINK** 2007 $ 16

Tuart Ridge   NR

344 Stakehill Road, Baldivis, WA 6171 **REGION** Peel
T (08) 9524 3333 **F** (08) 9524 2168 **WEB** www.tuartridgewines.com **OPEN** Weekends 10–4
WINEMAKER Phil Franzone **EST.** 1996 **CASES** 2000
SUMMARY Phil Franzone has established 5 ha of chardonnay, verdelho, shiraz, cabernet sauvignon, grenache and merlot on the coastal tuart soils. The first vintage was 2001, and production will peak at around 3000 cases. Phil Franzone also acts as contract winemaker for several of the many new ventures springing up in the Peel region.

Tuck's Ridge   ★★★★

37 Shoreham Road, Red Hill South, Vic 3937 **REGION** Mornington Peninsula
T (03) 5989 8660 **F** (03) 5989 8579 **WEB** www.tucksridge.com.au **OPEN** 7 days 11–5
WINEMAKER Contract **EST.** 1988 **CASES** 7000
SUMMARY Tuck's Ridge has changed focus significantly since selling its large Red Hill vineyard. Estate plantings are now an eclectic mix of pint noir (3 ha), 1 ha each of chardonnay and albarino; it has reduced its contract grape purchases. Quality, not quantity, is the key. Exports to the US.

ŶŶŶŶŶ **Chardonnay 2003** Intense grapefruit, melon and citrus; controlled barrel ferment oak inputs; focused and long, lingering finish. Cork. **RATING** 93 **DRINK** 2010 $ 27
Pinot Noir 2002 Complex, savoury, spicy/stemmy style; good length and structure. **RATING** 90 **DRINK** 2008 $ 27

ŶŶŶŶ **Pinot Gris 2004** Tangy, lively pear, lemon, spice and mineral mix; has length and attitude. Screwcap. **RATING** 89 **DRINK** 2008 $ 27

Tulloch   ★★★★

'Glen Elgin', 638 De Beyers Road, Pokolbin, NSW 2321 **REGION** Lower Hunter Valley
T (02) 4998 7580 **F** (02) 4998 7226 **OPEN** 7 days 10–5
WINEMAKER Jay Tulloch **EST.** 1895 **CASES** 30 000
SUMMARY The revival of the near-death Tulloch brand continues apace. Angove's, the national distributors for the brand, have invested in the business, the first time the Angove family has taken a strategic holding in any business other than its own. Inglewood Vineyard (aka Two Rivers) also has a shareholding in the new venture, and will be the primary source of grapes for the brand. A lavish new cellar door and function facility has been built and opened, and Jay Tulloch is in overall control, with his own label, JYT Wines, also available at the cellar door.

ŶŶŶŶŶ **Hunter Valley Chardonnay 2004** Light-bodied; excellent balance of melon, stone fruit, a hint of citrus and a subtle flick of oak; may have been lucky to score its gold medal at the '05 Sydney Wine Show, but is a good wine and great value. Screwcap. **RATING** 90 **DRINK** 2008 $ 14.99

ŶŶŶŶ **Hunter Valley Semillon 2003** Classic fresh, young Semillon; sweet lemon/lemon rind; good balance and soft acidity. **RATING** 89 **DRINK** 2008 $ 15
Hunter Valley Cabernet Sauvignon 2003 Surprising wine; nice medium-bodied weight; clean blackcurrant fruit; fine tannins and minimal oak. Good value. **RATING** 87 **DRINK** 2009 $ 15

ΤΤΤ♀ **Hunter Valley Verdelho 2004** Archetypal Verdelho; just enough to sustain the interest in the tension between acidity and sweetness on the finish. **RATING** 86 **DRINK** Now $15
Hector Shiraz 1999 RATING 86 **DRINK** 2008 $35

Tumbarumba Wine Estates ★★★☆

Glenroy Hills Road, Tumbarumba, NSW 2653 **REGION** Tumbarumba
T (02) 6948 8326 **F** (02) 6948 8326 **OPEN** 7 days
WINEMAKER Monarch Winemaking Services (Contract) **EST.** 1989 **CASES** 2000
SUMMARY Within sight of the Snowy Mountains, Tumbarumba Wine Estates' Mannus Vineyard was established by a group of Sydney businessmen, all wine enthusiasts, with the aim of producing high-quality cool-climate wines. The vineyard is currently undergoing some refinement, with some cabernet sauvignon being grafted to more suited varieties (sauvignon blanc and chardonnay). The major part of the production from the 21 ha of vineyard (principally chardonnay and sauvignon blanc) is sold to other producers.

ΤΤΤΤ♀ **Mannus Sauvignon Blanc 2002** Very pale straw-green; the clean, crisp and minerally bouquet also has some blossom aromas, characters which flow through into the light, bright and fresh palate with its mix of lemon and apple blossom; good mouthfeel; spotlessly clean. **RATING** 90 **DRINK** Now $19

ΤΤΤ♀ **Mannus Shiraz 2003** Vibrant spicy cherry fruit has a skein of lemony acidity running throughout; fruit-driven, minimal oak/tannins. Screwcap. **RATING** 86 **DRINK** 2008 $19

Tumbarumba Wine Growers NR

Sunnyside, Albury Close, Tumbarumba, NSW 2653 **REGION** Tumbarumba
T (02) 6948 3055 **F** (02) 6948 3055 **OPEN** Weekends & public hols, or by appointment
WINEMAKER (Contract) **EST.** 1996 **CASES** 600
SUMMARY Tumbarumba Wine Growers has taken over the former George Martins Winery (established in 1990) to provide an outlet for wines made from Tumbarumba region grapes. It is essentially a co-operative venture, involving local growers and businessmen, and with modest aspirations to growth.

Turkey Flat ★★★★★

Bethany Road, Tanunda, SA 5352 **REGION** Barossa Valley
T (08) 8563 2851 **F** (08) 8563 3610 **WEB** www.turkeyflat.com.au **OPEN** 7 days 11–5
WINEMAKER Peter Schell **EST.** 1990 **CASES** 16 000
SUMMARY The establishment date of Turkey Flat is given as 1990 but it might equally well have been 1870 (or thereabouts), when the Schulz family purchased the Turkey Flat vineyard, or 1847, when the vineyard was first planted to the very shiraz which still grows there today. In addition there are 8 ha of very old grenache and 8 ha of much younger semillon and cabernet sauvignon, together with a total of 7.3 ha of mourvedre, dolcetto and (a recent arrival) marsanne. An onsite winery completed in 2001 gives Turkey Flat complete control over its wine production. Retail distribution in Adelaide, Melbourne and Sydney; exports to the US, Canada, the UK, Germany, Switzerland and New Zealand.

ΤΤΤΤΤ **Shiraz 2002** An intense and concentrated fruit bowl of blackberry, licorice and spice; outstanding balance and length; great style and quality. **RATING** 96 **DRINK** 2022 $45
The Last Straw Marsanne 2002 Golden yellow-green; a beautifully balanced late-harvest style (partially dried, hence the name); a likely 30-year life span. **RATING** 95 **DRINK** 2027 $40
Cabernet Sauvignon 2002 Perfectly focused and balanced; pristine cabernet varietal character; blackcurrant with a touch of olive; very good tannin and oak management. **RATING** 95 **DRINK** 2017 $40
Cabernet Sauvignon 2001 Ripe, luscious blackcurrant and blackberry; nice touches of French oak and supple tannins. Deserves its trophies. **RATING** 94 **DRINK** 2016 $40

ΤΤΤΤ♀ **Semillon Marsanne 2003** Glowing yellow-green; complex, some toasty notes; the blend and partial barrel ferment work very well. **RATING** 93 **DRINK** 2007 $22
Rose 2004 Vividly coloured and fragrant; fresh red and black cherry, raspberry and strawberry fruit; clean, long finish. **RATING** 93 **DRINK** Now $19

The Turk 2002 A lush basket of black fruit flavours within a finely crafted frame; gentle tannins. Shiraz/Grenache/Cabernet Sauvignon/Mourvedre. **RATING** 90 **DRINK** 2010 $ 17
Grenache 2002 Excellent purple; raspberry and redcurrant fruit, then a fine web of tannins for structure. **RATING** 90 **DRINK** 2010 $ 25

Turner's Flat Vineyard

NR

PO Box 104, Inglewood, Qld 4387 **REGION** Granite Belt
T (07) 4652 1179 **F** (07) 4652 1179 **OPEN** Not
WINEMAKER Contract **EST.** 1999 **CASES** NA
SUMMARY Bruce and Lynette Babington have established their vineyard at the far western outskirts of the Granite Belt, where they have planted 16 ha of semillon, chardonnay, cabernet sauvignon, shiraz and ruby cabernet. The wines are sold only by mail order.

Turner's Vineyard

NR

Mitchell Highway, Orange, NSW 2800 **REGION** Orange
T (02) 6369 1045 **F** (02) 6369 1046 **WEB** www.turnersvineyard.com.au **OPEN** 7 days 10–5
WINEMAKER Contract **EST.** 1996 **CASES** 8000
SUMMARY Turner's Vineyard is one of the larger developments in the Orange region, and includes a substantial motel with 30 suites, and 12 luxury 1 and 2-bedroom spa villa units.

Turramurra Estate

RMB 4327, Wallaces Road, Dromana Vic 3926 **REGION** Mornington Peninsula
T (03) 5987 1146 **F** (03) 5987 1286 **WEB** www.turramurraestate.com.au **OPEN** Wed–Sun 12–5, or by appointment
WINEMAKER Dr David Leslie **EST.** 1989 **CASES** 6000
SUMMARY Dr David Leslie gave up his job as a medical practitioner after completing the Bachelor of Applied Science (Wine Science) at Charles Sturt University, to concentrate on developing the family's 10-ha estate at Dromana; wife Paula is the viticulturist. It has also established what is described as the first purpose-built cooking school in an Australian vineyard (details on the website). Limited retail distribution in Melbourne and Sydney; exports to the UK, the US and Hong Kong.

▼▼▼▼▼ **Shiraz 2000** Colour still deep, predominantly purple; medium to medium-full bodied in a fully ripe, cool-climate style; excellent spicy aspects to the fruit and tannins, and appealing brightness to the edges of the fruit; almost 2 years in barriques. **RATING** 94 **DRINK** 2015 $ 40

▼▼▼▼ **Pinot Rose 2004** Highly aromatic strawberries and rose petals; fresh, lively and quite dry; good style. **RATING** 88 **DRINK** Now

Twelve Acres

★★★

Nagambie–Rushworth Road, Bailieston, Vic 3608 **REGION** Goulburn Valley
T (03) 5794 2020 **F** (03) 5794 2020 **WEB** http://users.mcmedia.com.au/~12acres **OPEN** Thurs–Mon 10.30–5.30, July weekends only
WINEMAKER Peter Prygodicz, Jana Prygodicz **EST.** 1994 **CASES** 600
SUMMARY The charmingly named Twelve Acres is a red wine specialist, with Peter and Jana Prygodicz making the wines onsite in a tiny winery. The wines could benefit from renewal of the oak in which they are matured; the underlying fruit is good.

Twelve Staves Wine Company

NR

Box 620, McLaren Vale, SA 5171 **REGION** McLaren Vale
T (08) 8178 0900 **F** (08) 8178 0900 **OPEN** Not
WINEMAKER Peter Dennis, Brian Light (Consultant) **EST.** 1997 **CASES** 600
SUMMARY Twelve Staves has a single vineyard block of a little under 5 ha of 70-year-old, bush-pruned grenache vines. The highly experienced team of Peter Dennis and Brian Light (in a consulting role) produce an appealing Grenache in a lighter mode and a monumental Shiraz. An eclectic range of retail outlets on the east coast, and limited exports to the US, Canada and the UK.

Twin Bays

NR

Lot 1 Martin Road, Yankalilla, SA 5203 **REGION** Southern Fleurieu
T(08) 8267 2844 **F**(08) 8239 0877 **WEB** www.twinbays.net **OPEN** Weekends & hols
WINEMAKER Dr Bruno Giorgio **EST.** 1989 **CASES** 2700
SUMMARY Adelaide doctor and specialist Dr Bruno Giorgio, together with wife Ginny, began planting their vineyard back in 1989, but have opted to keep it small (and beautiful). The principal plantings are of cabernet sauvignon, with lesser amounts of shiraz and riesling, taking the total plantings to 2 ha. It was the first vineyard to be established in the Yankalilla district of the Fleurieu Peninsula, and has spectacular views from the vineyard, on the slopes above Normanville, taking in hills, valleys, the coastal plains, and the rugged Rapid Bay and more tranquil Lady Bay. The cellar door features the ocean views; the wines on sale are complemented by red and white wine vinegar, Fleurieu olive oil and other local souvenirs.

Twin Oaks

NR

146 Windsor Street, Woodford, Qld 4514 **REGION** Queensland Coastal
T(07) 5496 1368 **F**(07) 5496 1076 **WEB** www.twinoaks.com.au **OPEN** 7 days 10–5
WINEMAKER Trevor Phillips **EST.** 1998 **CASES** NA
SUMMARY The Twin Oaks property was purchased by Trevor and Carlin Phillips in 1980, but it was not until 1998 that the first plantings of verdelho, chardonnay and cabernet sauvignon took place. The first vintage followed 2 years later, and the winery and restaurant were opened in December 2002. The restaurant is open 7 days for lunch and for dinner Fri–Sat; other nights by arrangement. Twin Oaks caters for small and large functions, including weddings.

Two Hands Wines

★★★★★

Neldner Road, Marananga, SA 5355 **REGION** Southeast Australia
T(08) 8562 4566 **F**(08) 8562 4744 **WEB** www.twohandswines.com **OPEN** Wed–Fri 11–5, weekends & public hols 10–5
WINEMAKER Matthew Wenk **EST.** 2000 **CASES** 20 000
SUMMARY The 'Hands' in question are those of SA businessmen Michael Twelftree and Richard Mintz, Twelftree in particular having extensive experience in marketing Australian wine in the US (for other producers) and now turning that experience to his and Mintz's account. On the principle that if big is good, bigger is better, and biggest is best, the style of the wines has been aimed fairly and squarely at the palate of Robert Parker Jnr and the *Wine Spectator*'s Harvey Steiman. Each of the wines is made in microscopic quantities (down to 50 dozen) and exported to the US, Canada and the UK, the policy being (one assumes) to keep demand well in excess of supply in any given market.

ΥΥΥΥΥ **Lily's Garden Shiraz 2003** Potent but smooth, velvety black fruits and dark chocolate; excellent tannins and length. **RATING** 95 **DRINK** 2018 $ 55
Ares Barossa Valley Shiraz 2002 Gently voluptuous, supple and smooth; concentrated black fruits and a hint of chocolate; ultra-fine tannins. Very good oak. **RATING** 95 **DRINK** 2022 $ 120
Harry & Edward's Garden Langhorne Creek Shiraz 2003 Quite juicy, fruit-forward style; particularly good length and balancing acidity; overall elegance. **RATING** 94 **DRINK** 2015 $ 55
Brave Faces Barossa Valley Shiraz Grenache 2003 A complex array of fruit, spice and attractive oak; delicious fruit profile on the palate; easy access, but will live. **RATING** 94 **DRINK** 2013 $ 32.50

ΥΥΥΥϙ **Bella's Garden Shiraz 2003** Very ripe dark fruits; generous mouthfeel; good tannin structure. **RATING** 93 **DRINK** 2013 $ 55
Bad Impersonator Barossa Valley Shiraz 2003 Complex array of black fruits, spice, licorice and game; silky tannins, medium-bodied; nice French oak. **RATING** 93 **DRINK** 2013 $ 45
Sophie's Garden Shiraz 2003 Spicy, cedary, earthy aromas and flavours; a lingering, tangy, almost lemony, finish. **RATING** 92 **DRINK** 2013 $ 55
Max's Garden Heathcote Shiraz 2003 Luscious red and black plum fruit; medium to full-bodied; soft tannins, but doesn't carry the line quite as well as the others. **RATING** 91 **DRINK** 2013 $ 55

Angel's Share McLaren Vale Shiraz 2003 A generous but not heavy bundle of red and black fruits; appealing licorice twist on the finish. RATING 90 DRINK 2010 $ 25

ŦŦŦŦ Tyre Kickers Shiraz Cabernet 2002 Deep colour; very ripe, slightly stewy, juicy berry fruit; lots of presence and flavour. RATING 89 DRINK 2010 $ 18
The Wolf Clare Valley Riesling 2004 Somewhat closed; a ghost of reduction; generous palate; quite soft lime and passionfruit; slightly short. Screwcap. RATING 88 DRINK 2010 $ 25
Shovel Blanc Merlot Cabernet Franc 2003 Complex herb, spice and mint aromas; lively but slightly sharp tannins detract; may settle down. RATING 88 DRINK 2013 $ 32.50
Brilliant Disguise Moscato 2004 Intense, lively, lemony-accented fruit salad; sweetness just balanced by acidity. RATING 87 DRINK Now $ 13.50

Two People's Bay Wines ★★★★

RMB 8700, Nanarup Road, Lower Kalgan, WA 6331 REGION Albany
T (08) 9846 4346 F (08) 9846 4346 OPEN 7 days 12–4, 11–5 in peak season
WINEMAKER Diane Miller (Contract) EST. 1998 CASES 2700
SUMMARY The Saunders family (Phil and Wendy Saunders, with sons Warren and Mark) began the establishment of their 10-ha vineyard, planted to sauvignon blanc, riesling, semillon, shiraz, cabernet sauvignon, cabernet franc and pinot noir, in 1998, continuing the plantings in 1999. The name comes from the Two People's Bay Nature Reserve, which can be seen from the vineyard to the east; it also has spectacular views to the Porongorups and Sterling Ranges 60 km north.

ŦŦŦŦŸ 2 Albany Great Southern Riesling 2002 Spotlessly clean; fine, tight minerally backbone; lively lemony acidity through to the finish. Screwcap. RATING 91 DRINK 2009

ŦŦŦŸ 2 Albany Great Southern Cabernet Sauvignon 2002 RATING 86 DRINK 2009

Two Rivers ★★★☆

2 Yarrawa Road, Denman, NSW 2328 (postal) REGION Upper Hunter Valley
T (02) 6547 2556 F (02) 6547 2546 WEB www.tworiverswines.com.au OPEN Not
WINEMAKER Greg Silkman (Contract) EST. 1988 CASES 20 000
SUMMARY A significant part of the viticultural scene in the Upper Hunter Valley, with almost 170 ha of vineyards established, involving a total investment of around $7 million. Part of the fruit is sold under long-term contracts, and part is made for the expanding winemaking and marketing operations of Two Rivers, the chief brand of Inglewood Vineyards. The emphasis is on Chardonnay and Semillon, and the wines have been medal winners on the wine show circuit. It is also a partner in the Tulloch business, together with the Tulloch and Angove families.

ŦŦŦŦŸ Stone's Throw Semillon 2004 Light green-yellow; light to medium-bodied; clean, fresh, tangy, sweet citrus; good flow and feel. Screwcap. RATING 90 DRINK 2010 $ 13

ŦŦŦŦ Reserve Chardonnay 2003 Again, well made, with restrained inputs providing complexity without submerging the nectarine fruit; good length and balance. Dodgy cork. RATING 89 DRINK 2008 $ 18
Lightning Strike Chardonnay 2004 Fresh, clean nectarine and peach; light to medium-bodied; nicely balanced and well made; faint whisk of oak. Screwcap. RATING 88 DRINK 2007 $ 13
Reserve Semillon 2003 More to medium-bodied, but with less definition; possibly also entering its transition phase. Cork. RATING 87 DRINK 2009 $ 18
Reserve Shiraz 2003 Light to medium-bodied; savoury, earthy, leathery regional notes to blackberry fruit; balanced tannins, could evolve well over the short term. Screwcap. RATING 87 DRINK 2010 $ 24

ŦŦŦŸ Hidden Hive Verdelho 2004 RATING 85 DRINK Now $ 13
Rocky Crossing Cabernet Sauvignon 2003 RATING 84 DRINK 2007 $ 15

Two Tails Wines NR

963 Orara Way, Nana Glen, NSW 2450 REGION Northern Rivers Zone
T (02) 6654 3633 F (02) 6654 3633 OPEN 7 days 10–5
WINEMAKER Jeff Maher EST. 1998 CASES NA

SUMMARY Four members of the Maher family have established Two Tails Wines, with an exotic mix of gewurztraminer, semillon, chardonnay, verdelho, pinot noir, shiraz, chambourcin, ruby cabernet and villard blanc on their 2-ha vineyard. The wines are made onsite, and are sold by mail order and through the cellar door, which also has crafts, and barbecue and picnic facilities.

Tyrrell's ★★★★★

Broke Road, Pokolbin, NSW 2321 **REGION** Lower Hunter Valley
T (02) 4993 7000 **F** (02) 4998 7723 **WEB** www.tyrrells.com.au **OPEN** Mon–Sat 8–5
WINEMAKER Andrew Spinaze, Mark Richardson **EST.** 1858 **CASES** 500 000
SUMMARY One of the most successful family wineries, a humble operation for the first 110 years of its life which grew out of all recognition over the past 35 years. In 2003 it cleared the decks by selling its Long Flat range of wines for an 8-figure sum, allowing it to focus on its premium, super-premium and ultra-premium wines: Vat 1 Semillon is one of the most dominant wines in the Australian show system, and Vat 47 Chardonnay is one of the pace-setters for this variety. It has an awesome portfolio of single-vineyard Semillons released when 5–6 years old. Exports to the US, Canada and the UK.

ΨΨΨΨΨ **Stevens Reserve Semillon 2000** Elegant but intense lemon/acacia aromas lead into a similarly fine, intense and long palate; still with a decade, cork permitting. **RATING** 94 **DRINK** 2015 $20
Belford Semillon 1998 Still evolving; tight, crisp and long; fresh, bright aftertaste. **RATING** 94 **DRINK** 2013 $30

ΨΨΨΨΨ **Vat 8 Shiraz Cabernet 2002** Powerful wine from start to finish; blackcurrant and blackberry; medium to full-bodied; persistent tannins. **RATING** 93 **DRINK** 2017 $40
Vat 47 Chardonnay 2002 Stone fruit, some fig and subtle spicy oak aromas; an elegant light to medium-bodied wine veering more to melon and stone fruit; fresh acidity. **RATING** 92 **DRINK** 2007 $40
Stevens Reserve Shiraz 2000 A mix of red and black fruits and regional savoury characters; could well develop into a classic; top vintage. **RATING** 91 **DRINK** 2015 $23
Rufus Stone McLaren Vale Shiraz 2002 Attractive, medium-bodied fruit-driven wine; smooth and supple; carries 14.5° alcohol easily. **RATING** 90 **DRINK** 2012 $24

ΨΨΨΨ **Old Winery Semillon 2004** Stylish lemon and herb flavours, a brisk, light-bodied palate, and lively, crunchy acidity to lengthen the finish and aftertaste. **RATING** 89 **DRINK** 2012 $13
Rufus Stone Cabernet Sauvignon Malbec 2002 The fruit-sweetening effect of Malbec very obvious, partly off-set by tannins on the finish; plenty of flavour. **RATING** 89 **DRINK** 2015 $27
Rufus Stone Heathcote Shiraz 2003 Massive black fruits, dark chocolate, prune and plum; some dead fruit characters. **RATING** 88 **DRINK** 2010
Lost Block Semillon 2004 Clean, crisp lemon rind flavours on the lively palate; distracting levels of spritz. **RATING** 87 **DRINK** 2010 $14.50
Old Winery Shiraz 2003 Some minty edges to the fruit, but is firm and has some length. **RATING** 87 **DRINK** 2009 $12
Lost Block Cabernet Sauvignon 2003 Attractive, easy-drinking style; the focus is on sweet blackcurrant/cassis fruit. Multi-region blend. **RATING** 87 **DRINK** 2008 $14.50

ΨΨΨΨ **Quintus Chardonnay 2004 RATING** 86 **DRINK** 2008
Lost Block Merlot 2003 RATING 86 **DRINK** Now $14.50
Brokenback Shiraz 2002 RATING 85 **DRINK** 2007 $21

ΨΨΨ **Lost Block Unwooded Chardonnay 2004 RATING** 83 $14.50

Uleybury Wines ★★★★☆

Uley Road, Uleybury, SA 5114 **REGION** Adelaide Zone
T (08) 8280 7335 **F** (08) 8280 7925 **WEB** www.uleybury.com **OPEN** 7 days 10–4
WINEMAKER Tony Pipicella **EST.** 1995 **CASES** 10 000
SUMMARY The Pipicella family – headed by Italian-born Tony – has established nearly 45 ha of vineyard near the township of One Tree Hill in the Mt Lofty Ranges; 10 varieties have been planted, with more planned. Daughter Natalie Pipicella, who has completed the wine marketing course at the University of South Australia, was responsible for overseeing the design of labels, the promotion and advertising, and the creation of the website. A cellar door opened in June 2002; an onsite winery followed in 2003.

ᵀᵀᵀᵀᵧ **Basket Press Petit Verdot 2003** Deep, dark colour; a robust wine; lashings of black fruits and dark chocolate, but not over-extractive. Top T-bone steak match. Cork. **RATING** 91 **DRINK** 2017 $19.50

Uley Chapel Shiraz 2003 Rich, plush, sweet plum, black cherry and blackberry; sweetness in part reflecting its 14.5° alcohol; soft tannins; fruit-driven. Good cork. **RATING** 90 **DRINK** 2013 $23

ᵀᵀᵀᵀ **Basket Press Cabernet Sauvignon 2003** Rich, ripe, lush blackcurrant fruit to open, then powerful tannins attack; needs faith and patience. Cork. **RATING** 89 **DRINK** 2016 $23

Ulithorne   NR

PO Box 487, McLaren Vale, SA 5171 **REGION** McLaren Vale
T (08) 8382 5528 **F** (08) 8382 5528 **OPEN** Not
WINEMAKER Brian Light (Contract) **EST.** 1971 **CASES** 800
SUMMARY If ever a wine had an accidental, not to say off-putting, birth, Ulithorne is it. The vineyard was planted in 1971 to absorb the effluent from the piggery which Frank Harrison (father/father-in-law of the now-owners) wished to establish. The council was not persuaded, the piggery did not go ahead, and the vineyard was neglected. In 1997 abstract painter Sam Harrison and marketing consultant partner Rose Kentish purchased the vineyard, becoming full-time vignerons and resurrecting it from its near-derelict state. They extended the plantings with 8 ha of cabernet sauvignon, 3 ha of merlot and an additional 3 ha of shiraz. Exports to the UK, France, The Netherlands, the US and New Zealand.

Undercliff   NR

Yango Creek Road, Wollombi, NSW 2325 **REGION** Lower Hunter Valley
T (02) 4998 3322 **F** (02) 4998 3322 **WEB** www.undercliff.com.au **OPEN** 7 days 10–5, or by appointment
WINEMAKER David Carrick **EST.** 1990 **CASES** 1600
SUMMARY Peter and Jane Hamshere are the new owners of Undercliff; it continues to function as both winery cellar door and art gallery. The wines, produced from 2.5 ha of estate vineyards, have won a number of awards in recent years at the Hunter Valley Wine Show and the Hunter Valley Small Winemakers Show. All the wine is sold through the cellar door.

Upper Murray Estate   ★★★

Murray River Road, Walwa, Vic 3709 **REGION** North East Victoria Zone
T (02) 6037 1456 **F** (03) 6037 1457 **OPEN** 7 days 10–6
WINEMAKER Steve Thomson (Contract) **EST.** 1998 **CASES** 4000
SUMMARY The Upper Murray Estate vineyard has been established at an elevation of 400m roughly equidistant between Tumbarumba and Corryong. It is on the banks of the Murray River, which here is fast-flowing as it descends from the mountains. The estate is part of a business offering the largest tourism and convention facilities in northeast Victoria, based on 16 single and double-storey cottages and 4 motel-type rooms. There are approximately 17 ha of vineyard, planted to cabernet sauvignon, merlot, shiraz, chardonnay, pinot noir and riesling. The first two vintages, 2000 and 2001, were, to put it mildly, interesting. It will be fascinating to see what emerges as the vines mature and weather patterns (presumably) cease to be so extreme.

ᵀᵀᵀᵀ **Naretha Vineyard Merlot 2002** Medium-bodied; olive, earth, blackcurrant and briar; has the length and intensity not found in the '03 red wines. Cork. **RATING** 88 **DRINK** 2010 $13.50

Naretha Vineyard Riesling 2003 Light, delicate flowery; hints of blossom and lime; crisp finish. Quality cork. **RATING** 87 **DRINK** 2008 $13.50

ᵀᵀᵀᵧ **Naretha Vineyard Shiraz 2003** **RATING** 86 **DRINK** Now $13.50
Naretha Vineyard Merlot 2003 **RATING** 86 **DRINK** 2008 $13.50
Naretha Vineyard Cabernet Sauvignon 2002 **RATING** 86 **DRINK** 2008 $13.50
Naretha Vineyard Cabernet Merlot 2003 **RATING** 85 **DRINK** 2007 $13.50
Naretha Vineyard Riesling 2004 **RATING** 84 **DRINK** 2008 $13.50
Naretha Vineyard Cabernet Sauvignon 2003 **RATING** 84 **DRINK** 2007 $13.50

▼▼▼ **Naretha Vineyard Unwooded Chardonnay 2004** RATING 83 $13.50
Naretha Vineyard Unwooded Chardonnay 2003 RATING 80 $13.50

Upper Reach Vineyard ★★★

77 Memorial Avenue, Baskerville, WA 6056 REGION Swan Valley
T (08) 9296 0078 F (08) 9296 0278 WEB www.upperreach.com.au OPEN Thurs–Mon 11–5
WINEMAKER Derek Pearse, John Griffiths EST. 1996 CASES 5000
SUMMARY This 10-ha property on the banks of the upper reaches of the Swan River was purchased by
Laura Rowe and Derek Pearse in 1996. The original vineyard was 4 ha of 12-year-old chardonnay; it
has been expanded by 1.5 ha of shiraz and 1 ha of cabernet sauvignon, and there are plans for trials of
merlot, zinfandel and barbera. The partners also own 4 ha of vineyard in the Margaret River region,
planted to shiraz, cabernet sauvignon, merlot and semillon, but the releases so far have been drawn
from the Swan Valley vineyards. The fish on the label, incidentally, is black bream, which can be
found in the pools of the Swan River during the summer months. Exports to the UK.

▼▼▼▼ **Reserve Chardonnay 2003** Bright peachy fruit and spicy oak still to fully integrate.
RATING 87 DRINK Now $20.35

Vale Wines ★★★★

2914 Frankston–Flinders Road, Balnarring, Vic 3926 REGION Mornington Peninsula
T (03) 5983 1521 F (03) 5983 1942 WEB www.valewines.com.au OPEN By appointment
WINEMAKER John Vale EST. 1991 CASES 1000
SUMMARY After a lifetime in the retail liquor industry, John and Susan Vale took a busman's
retirement by purchasing a grazing property at Balnarring in 1991. They planted a little under 0.5 ha
of cabernet sauvignon, and John Vale undertook what he describes as 'formal winemaking training';
he then built a 20-tonne winery, in 1997, from stone and recycled materials. In 2000 they extended
the plantings with 1.4 ha of tempranillo, riesling and durif. Verduzzo and Arneis have been made
from grapes grown nearby, and will be sold exclusively through a local restaurant. In the meantime
the range has been extended by the purchase of chardonnay and pinot grigio from local growers.

▼▼▼▼▽ **Riesling 2004** Quiet opening on the bouquet; builds progressively through the palate and
aftertaste; a mix of mineral and citrus. RATING 90 DRINK 2008 $18

▼▼▼▼ **Chardonnay 2003** Ripe stone fruit flavours and integrated French oak; some alcohol
sweetening/heat on the finish. RATING 88 DRINK 2007 $25

▼▼▼▽ **Durif 2003** RATING 86 DRINK 2007 $25
Pinot Grigio 2003 RATING 85 DRINK Now $18

🐚 Valley View Vineyard ★★★☆

21 Boundary Road, Coldstream, Vic 3770 (postal) REGION Yarra Valley
T (03) 9739 1692 F (03) 9739 0430 OPEN Not
WINEMAKER Contract EST. 2000 CASES 200
SUMMARY Judy and John Thompson purchased their property in 1998, and with the unanimous
advice of various contacts in the wine industry they planted 2.2 ha of pinot noir on a north and
northwest-facing rocky slope. The wines are distributed in Melbourne by Full Bottle Pty Ltd.

▼▼▼▼ **Yarra Valley Pinot Noir 2003** Clean, fresh and correct; light cherry and plum fruit; some
spice. Appropriately restrained. RATING 89 DRINK 2008 $15

Valley Wines NR

352 Lennard Street, Herne Hill, WA 6056 REGION Swan District
T (08) 9296 4416 F (08) 9296 4754 OPEN Wed–Sun
WINEMAKER Charlie Zannino EST. 1973 CASES NA
SUMMARY Valley Wines is a long-established, traditional Swan Valley winery owned by Charlie
Zannino. Primarily a grapegrower, he has 16 ha of chenin blanc, semillon, chardonnay, grenache,
shiraz and pedro ximenez, and makes table and fortified wines from a small portion of the annual
production. Sales through the cellar door.

Varrenti Wines

NR

'Glenheather', Blackwood Road, Dunkeld, Vic 3294 **REGION** Grampians
T (03) 5577 2368 **F** (03) 5577 2367 **OPEN** 7 days 12–5
WINEMAKER Ettore Varrenti **EST.** 1999 **CASES** 500
SUMMARY Ettore Varrenti has established 4 ha of pinot noir, shiraz, sangiovese and cabernet sauvignon at the extreme southern end of the Grampians NP. It is remote from any other winery, and appears to be on the edge of the Grampians region.

Vasse Felix

★★★★★

Cnr Caves Road/Harmans Road South, Wilyabrup, WA 6284 **REGION** Margaret River
T (08) 9756 5000 **F** (08) 9755 5425 **WEB** www.vassefelix.com.au **OPEN** 7 days 10–5
WINEMAKER Clive Otto, David Dowden **EST.** 1967 **CASES** 200 000
SUMMARY In 1999 the production of Vasse Felix wines moved to a new 2000-tonne winery; the old winery is now dedicated entirely to the restaurant and tasting rooms. A relatively new 140-ha vineyard at Jindong in the north of the Margaret River region supplies a large part of the increased fruit intake. National Australian distribution; exports to all major markets.

ΤΤΤΤΤ **Heytesbury 2002** Powerful and concentrated as befits this icon; beautifully ripened cassis/blackcurrant fruit; impeccable texture and structure; long finish. High-quality cork. **RATING** 96 **DRINK** 2022 $ 65
Margaret River Semillon 2004 Excellent varietal character has soaked up the barrel ferment oak, leaving just a hint of lanolin; excellent balance and mouthfeel. **RATING** 95 **DRINK** 2014 $ 22.50
Heytesbury Chardonnay 2003 Very fresh, spotlessly clean; silky mouthfeel; long and lingering melon and citrus; lemony acidity; subtle oak. Screwcap. **RATING** 94 **DRINK** 2013 $ 35

ΤΤΤΤΥ **Chardonnay 2004** Spotlessly clean; fine melon and stone fruit; discreet oak; good finish and length. Screwcap. **RATING** 92 **DRINK** 2010 $ 22.50
Margaret River Cabernet Sauvignon 2003 Medium-bodied; focused and refined blackcurrant and earth cabernet fruit; very good tannin structure; harmonious oak. **RATING** 92 **DRINK** 2013 $ 29
Margaret River Cabernet Sauvignon 2002 Medium-bodied, long and relatively tight palate; hints of mint and leaf with blackcurrant and fine tannins. **RATING** 91 **DRINK** 2010 $ 30
Classic Dry White 2004 Clean and fresh; zesty lemony/herby fruit; good length and balance. **RATING** 90 **DRINK** Now $ 19
Margaret River Shiraz 2003 Strong colour; rich, full-bodied marriage of black fruits, licorice and oak; soft but ample tannins. **RATING** 90 **DRINK** 2015 $ 38

ΤΤΤΤ **Margaret River Cabernet Merlot 2003** Savoury/earthy/cedary/spicy overtones to a mix of red and black fruits; medium-bodied; not forced. Dodgy cork. **RATING** 89 **DRINK** 2010 $ 22.50
Cane Cut Semillon 2004 Apricot, cumquat and peach; good balance between residual sugar and acidity; not complex. Screwcap. **RATING** 88 **DRINK** 2009 $ 19

ΤΤΤΥ **Classic Dry Red 2002** **RATING** 86 **DRINK** 2007 $ 19
Margaret River Cabernet Merlot 2002 **RATING** 86 **DRINK** 2009 $ 22.50

Vasse River Wines

★★★★

Bussell Highway, Carbunup, WA 6280 **REGION** Margaret River
T (08) 9755 1011 **F** (08) 9755 1011 **OPEN** 7 days 10–5
WINEMAKER Robert Credaro, Bernie Stanlake, Frank Kittler **EST.** 1993 **CASES** 5000
SUMMARY This is a major and rapidly growing business owned by the Credaro Family; 90 ha of chardonnay, semillon, verdelho, sauvignon blanc, cabernet sauvignon, merlot and shiraz have been planted on the typical gravelly red loam soils of the region. The wines are released under two labels: Vasse River for the premium, and Carbunup Estate for the lower-priced varietals.

ΤΤΤΤΥ **Margaret River Semillon Sauvignon Blanc 2004** Clean and aromatic; fresh, bright grass and kiwifruit flavours; crunchy acidity and a long finish. **RATING** 90 **DRINK** Now $ 18

Veritas ★★★★

Cnr Seppeltsfield Road/Stelzer Road, Tanunda, SA 5352 **REGION** Barossa Valley
T (08) 8562 3300 **F** (08) 8562 1177 **WEB** www.veritaswinery.com **OPEN** Mon–Fri 10–4.30, weekends 11–4
WINEMAKER Rolf Binder, Christa Deans **EST.** 1955 **CASES** 25 000
SUMMARY The Hungarian influence is obvious in the naming of some of the wines, but Australian technology is paramount in shaping the generally very good quality. Veritas has 28 ha of estate vineyards to draw on. A near-doubling of production has coincided with the establishment of export markets to the UK, Germany, Belgium, Austria, Asia, Canada and the US. The occasional tasting here and there fully justifies the rating.

Verona Vineyard NR

Small Winemakers Centre, McDonalds Road, Pokolbin, NSW 2321 **REGION** Lower Hunter Valley
T (02) 4998 7668 **F** (02) 4998 7430 **OPEN** 7 days 10–5
WINEMAKER Greg Silkman, Gary Reed (Contract) **EST.** 1972 **CASES** NA
SUMMARY Verona has had a chequered history, and is still a significant business, acting as a sales point for a number of other Hunter Valley winemakers from its premises, which are directly opposite Brokenwood. The wines come from 22 ha at Muswellbrook and 5 ha surrounding the winery.

Vicarys NR

Northern Road, Luddenham, NSW 2745 **REGION** Sydney Basin
T (02) 4773 4161 **F** (02) 4773 4411 **WEB** www.vicaryswinery.com.au **OPEN** Tues–Fri 9–5, weekends 10–5
WINEMAKER Chris Niccol **EST.** 1923 **CASES** 3000
SUMMARY Vicarys justifiably claims to be the Sydney region's oldest continuously operating winery, having been established in a large and very attractive stone shearing shed built about 1890. Most of the wines come from other parts of Australia, but the winery does draw upon 1 ha of estate traminer and 3 ha of chardonnay for those wines, and has produced some good wines of all styles over the years.

Vico NR

Farm 1687 Beelbangera Road, Griffith, NSW 2680 **REGION** Riverina
T (02) 6962 2849 **OPEN** Mon–Fri 9–5
WINEMAKER Ray Vico **EST.** 1973 **CASES** 1200
SUMMARY Ray Vico has been growing grapes for many years with his 9 ha of vines; more recently he has decided to bottle and sell part of the production under the Vico label. On last advice, the prices were positively mouthwatering. Be aware, however, that the message on the answer phone is in Italian.

Victor Harbor Winery NR

Cnr Mont Rosa Road/Adelaide Road, Hindmarsh Valley, SA 5211 **REGION** Southern Fleurieu
T (08) 8554 6504 **F** (08) 8554 6504 **WEB** www.victorharborwinery.com.au **OPEN** Wed–Sun & public hols 10–5
WINEMAKER Alan Dyson (Contract) **EST.** 1999 **CASES** 500
SUMMARY The business is based on 4 ha of sauvignon blanc, semillon, pinot noir, cabernet sauvignon and shiraz. Sales also through the onsite Monta Rosa Restaurant, the website and by mail order.

Viking Wines

RSD 108, Seppeltsfield Road, Marananga, SA 5355 **REGION** Barossa Valley
T (08) 8562 3842 **F** (08) 8562 4266 **WEB** www.vikingwines.com **OPEN** 7 days 11–5
WINEMAKER Steve Black (Contract) **EST.** 1995 **CASES** 1200
SUMMARY Based upon 50-year-old, dry-grown and near-organic vineyards with a yield of only 1–1.5 tonnes per acre, Viking Wines has been 'discovered' by Robert Parker with inevitable consequences for the price of its top Shiraz. There are 5 ha of shiraz and 3 ha of cabernet sauvignon. The Odin's Honour wines (made by sister company Todd-Viking Wines) also come from old (20 to 100 years) dry-grown vines around Marananga and Greenoch. Exports to the US, the UK and France.

YYYYY **Odin's Honour Reserve Shiraz 2002** Rich, mouthfilling blackberry, plum fruit, the oak absorbed and the tannins soft and integrated; carries its 15° alcohol with grace. **RATING** 94 **DRINK** 2012 $40

YYYY **Grand Shiraz Cabernet 2003** Rich, ripe, concentrated black fruits, prune and plum jam; vanilla/mocha oak; milky tannins. Stained cork. **RATING** 89 **DRINK** 2011 $40

YYY **Grand Shiraz 2003 RATING** 83 $45

🍇 Villa Caterina Wines ★★★☆

4 Wattletree Road, Drumcondra, Geelong, Vic 3215 (postal) **REGION** Geelong
T (03) 5278 2847 **F** (03) 5278 4884 **OPEN** Not
WINEMAKER Ernesto Vellucci **EST.** 2001 **CASES** 400
SUMMARY Ernesto Vellucci was born in Italy. His parents owned a vineyard, so he was brought up in the traditional and cultural way of Italian winemaking, a legacy he has not forgotten. On the other hand, he has qualified as an industrial chemist, and has worked with laboratory equipment and techniques for years. He offers the only wine laboratory services in Geelong with microbiological testing facilities and gas chromotography, directed to the detection of brettanomyces/dekkera yeasts. His small production is made from purchased grapes.

YYYYY **Shiraz 2003** Big, rich, dense blackberry and Christmas cake flavours; solidly structured, but not over the top. **RATING** 90 **DRINK** 2015 $22

YYYY **Pinot Noir 2003 RATING** 86 **DRINK** 2007 $16

Villacoola Vineyard & Winery NR

Carnarvon Highway, Surat, Qld 4417 **REGION** Queensland Zone
T (07) 4626 5103 **F** (07) 4626 5516 **OPEN** 7 days 10–5
WINEMAKER Contract **EST.** 1992 **CASES** NA
SUMMARY Ron Ritchie has ventured far to the west to establish Villacoola Vineyard and Winery – its nearest neighbour is Romavilla (at Roma), 78 km to the north. The 2.5-ha vineyard is planted to sauvignon blanc, semillon, chardonnay, merlot, shiraz and muscat; the muscats provide the fortified wines for which Romavilla has been famous for 140 years. The cellar door offers light meals.

Villa d'Esta Vineyard NR

2884 Wallambah Road, Dyers Crossing, NSW 2429 **REGION** Northern Rivers Zone
T (02) 6550 2236 **F** (02) 6550 2236 **OPEN** 7 days 10–5
WINEMAKER Zoltan Toth **EST.** 1997 **CASES** NA
SUMMARY Zolton Toth and Maria Brizuela have 2.25 ha of chardonnay, verdelho, chasselas dore, pinot noir, cabernet sauvignon, merlot, shiraz, muscat, hamburg and chambourcin. They make the wines onsite, and sell by mail order and through the cellar door.

Villa Primavera NR

Mornington–Flinders Road, Red Hill, Vic 3937 **REGION** Mornington Peninsula
T (03) 5989 2129 **F** (03) 5931 0045 **OPEN** Weekends, public hols 10–5, 7 days from Dec 26 to end Jan
WINEMAKER Gennaro Mazzella **EST.** 1984 **CASES** 300
SUMMARY A most unusual operation: in reality, a family Italian-style restaurant at which the wine is sold and served, and which offers something totally different on the Mornington Peninsula. A consistent winner of tourism and food awards, it is praised by all who go there.

Villa Terlato NR

1200 Bass Highway, The Gurdies, Vic 3984 **REGION** Gippsland
T (03) 5997 6381 **OPEN** 7 days
WINEMAKER John Terlato **EST.** 1988 **CASES** NA
SUMMARY John and Francis Terlato have planted 2 ha of riesling, chardonnay, pinot noir and cabernet sauvignon, and make the wine onsite. The cellar door offers barbecue and picnic facilities.

🦎 Villa Tinto ★★★

Krondorf Road, Tanunda, SA 5352 **REGION** Barossa Valley
T (08) 8563 3044 **F** (08) 8563 0460 **OPEN** 7 days by appointment
WINEMAKER Albert Di Palma **EST.** 2001 **CASES** 700
SUMMARY Albert and Dianne Di Palma began the development of their business in 1987, planting a little under 2 ha of cabernet sauvignon and 0.7 ha of shiraz. Until 1999 they were content to sell their grapes, but they are now making an increasing amount of wine at their small onsite winery. The wines are also available at the Barossa Small Winemakers Centre at Chateau Tanunda, Birdwood Wine and Cheese, and Edinburgh Cellars in Adelaide.

ΥΥΥΥ **Barossa Valley Shiraz 2003** Medium-bodied; spicy, savoury edges to a core of black fruits; fine tannins; carries its 14.5° alcohol well. **RATING** 89 **DRINK** 2010 $20

ΥΥΥΥ **Barossa Valley Cabernet Shiraz 2002** **RATING** 84 **DRINK** 2009 $18

ΥΥΥ **Barossa Valley Cabernet Semillon Shiraz 2002** **RATING** 83 $16

Vinden Estate ★★★

17 Gillards Road, Pokolbin, NSW 2320 **REGION** Lower Hunter Valley
T (02) 4998 7410 **F** (02) 4998 7421 **WEB** www.vindenestate.com.au **OPEN** 7 days 10–5
WINEMAKER Guy Vinden, John Baruzzi (Consultant) **EST.** 1998 **CASES** 3000
SUMMARY Sandra and Guy Vinden have bought their dream home, with landscaped gardens in the foreground, and 9 ha of vineyard, and the Brokenback mountain range in the distance. Much of the winemaking is now done onsite, and increasingly from the estate vineyards. The wines are available through the cellar door and also via a wine club. The restaurant, Thai on Gillards Road, is open weekends and public holidays 10.30–4.

ΥΥΥΥ **Semillon 2004** Gentle lemon, lanolin and wet wool; very soft finish; 11° alcohol. Screwcap. **RATING** 87 **DRINK** 2008 $19.50
Chardonnay 2003 Bright green-yellow; gentle yellow peach and rockmelon fruit; wisp of oak. Twin Top. **RATING** 87 **DRINK** Now $21
Basket Press Shiraz 2003 Light to medium-bodied; savoury, earthy, regional edges to black fruits; balanced tannins, minimal oak. Twin Top. **RATING** 87 **DRINK** 2009 $22

ΥΥΥΥ **Merlot 2003** **RATING** 85 **DRINK** 2007 $28
Unwooded Chardonnay 2004 **RATING** 84 **DRINK** Now $20

ΥΥΥ **Alicante Bouschet Rose 2004** **RATING** 83 $22

Vinecrest ★★★

Cnr Barossa Valley Way/Vine Vale Road, Tanunda, SA 5352 **REGION** Barossa Valley
T (08) 8563 0111 **F** (08) 8563 0444 **WEB** www.vinecrest.com.au **OPEN** 7 days 11–4
WINEMAKER Mos Kaesler **EST.** 1999 **CASES** 5000
SUMMARY The Mader family has a long connection with the Barossa Valley. Ian Mader is a fifth-generation descendant of Gottfried and Maria Mader, who immigrated to the Barossa Valley in the 1840s, and his wife Suzanne is the daughter of a former long-serving vineyard manager for Penfolds. In 1969 Ian and Suzanne established their 12-ha Sandy Ridge Vineyard, and more recently a further 12 ha on the Turrung Vineyard, a few minutes from the township of Tanunda. Having been grapegrowers for 30 years, in 1999 they established Vinecrest, using a small portion of the production from their vineyards. Their cellar door is at the Turrung Vineyard, next to the tall gum trees of Kroemer's Reserve.

ΥΥΥΥΥ **A Capital C Cabernet Sauvignon 2002** Strong colour; packed with cassis, redcurrant and blackcurrant fruit; soft tannins. **RATING** 90 **DRINK** 2015 $21

ΥΥΥΥ **One Colour White Semillon 2004** **RATING** 85 **DRINK** Now $16

ΥΥΥ **Two Colours White Semillon Sauvignon Blanc 2004** **RATING** 81 $16

Vinifera Wines ★★★☆

194 Henry Lawson Drive, Mudgee, NSW 2850 **REGION** Mudgee
T (02) 6372 2461 **F** (02) 6372 6731 **WEB** www.viniferawines.com.au **OPEN** 7 days 10–5.30

WINEMAKER Phillip van Gent, Tony McKendry **EST.** 1997 **CASES** 2500

SUMMARY Having lived in Mudgee for 15 years, Tony McKendry (a regional medical superintendent) and wife Debbie succumbed to the lure; they planted their small (1.5-ha) vineyard in 1995. In Debbie's words, 'Tony, in his spare two minutes per day, also decided to start Wine Science at Charles Sturt University in 1992.' She continues, 'His trying to live 27 hours per day (plus our four kids!) fell to pieces when he was involved in a severe car smash in 1997. Two months in hospital stopped full-time medical work, and the winery dreams became inevitable.' Financial compensation finally came through and the small winery was built. The vineyard is now 11 ha, including 2 ha of tempranillo and 1 ha of graciano.

▼▼▼▼ **Cabernet Sauvignon 2003** Clear, bright colour; light to medium-bodied; fresh cassis and blackcurrant fruit; fine, ripe tannins. Twin Top. **RATING** 87 **DRINK** 2009 $22

▼▼▼▼ **Easter Semillon 2003** **RATING** 85 **DRINK** 2007 $19

▼▼▼ **Tempranillo 2003** **RATING** 83 $25

Vino Italia   NR

81 Campersic Road, Middle Swan, WA 6056 **REGION** Swan District
T (08) 9396 4336 **F** (08) 9296 4924 **OPEN** 7 days 10–5
WINEMAKER Eugenio Valenti, Allesandro Calabrese **EST.** 1954 **CASES** NA
SUMMARY Surprising though it may seem to some, the Italian winemaking community in the Swan Valley is significantly smaller than that from Dalmatia. Nonetheless, this business is well named, for Eugenio Valenti and Alessandro Calabrese have 34 ha of chenin blanc, semillon, grenache, shiraz and muscadelle. They make both table and fortified wines; sales by mail order and through the cellar door.

Virgin Block Vineyard   NR

Caves Road, Yallingup, WA 6282 **REGION** Margaret River
T (08) 9755 2394 **F** (08) 9755 2357 **WEB** www.virginblock.com **OPEN** 7 days 10–5
WINEMAKER Bruce Dukes, Anne-Coralie Fleury (Contract) **EST.** 1995 **CASES** 3000
SUMMARY Virgin Block has been established on a 30-ha property that is 3 km from the Indian Ocean, and surrounded by large Jarrah and Marri trees. The substantial, indeed ornate, buildings onsite include a cellar door and café emporium (opened in 2004).

Virgin Hills   NR

Salisbury Road, Lauriston West via Kyneton, Vic 3444 **REGION** Macedon Ranges
T (03) 5422 7444 **F** (03) 5422 7400 **OPEN** By appointment
WINEMAKER Josh Steele **EST.** 1968 **CASES** 2500
SUMMARY Virgin Hills has passed through several ownership changes in a short period. It is now owned by Michael Hope, who presides over the Hope Estate in the Hunter Valley. The absence of tastings over the past two years has forced the removal of the previous 5-star rating. Exports to the UK and the US.

Voyager Estate   ★★★★★

Lot 1 Stevens Road, Margaret River, WA 6285 **REGION** Margaret River
T (08) 9757 6354 **F** (08) 9757 6494 **WEB** www.voyagerestate.com.au **OPEN** 7 days 10–5
WINEMAKER Cliff Royle **EST.** 1978 **CASES** 30 000
SUMMARY Voyager Estate has come a long way since it was acquired by Michael Wright (of the mining family) in May 1991. It now has a high-quality 103-ha vineyard which means it can select only the best parcels of fruit for its own label, and supply surplus (but high-quality) wine to others. The Cape Dutch-style tasting room and vast rose garden are a major tourist attraction. Exports to the UK, Holland, Switzerland, China, Malaysia, Singapore, Japan, New Zealand, Canada and the US.

▼▼▼▼▼ **Chardonnay 2003** An elegantly constructed and perfectly balanced wine; the fruit has soaked up all the new French oak in which the wine was fermented, driving through on the long, lingering finish. **RATING** 96 **DRINK** 2013 $38
Reserve Semillon Sauvignon Blanc 2001 Bright, glowing yellow-green; complex and balanced, oak perfectly integrated; developing very well indeed. **RATING** 94 **DRINK** 2007 $38

ΥΥΥΥΥ **Shiraz 2003** Medium-bodied; cool-climate flavour and structure; spicy red fruits and a crisp finish. **RATING** 93 **DRINK** 2010 $ 29.50
Sauvignon Blanc Semillon 2004 Light straw-green; no reduction; neatly balanced and composed with a mix of gooseberry, lemon and herb, then crisp acidity. **RATING** 92 $ 22

Wadjekanup River Estate
NR

Flatrocks Road, Broomehill, WA 6318 **REGION** Central Western Australia Zone
T (08) 9825 3080 **F** (08) 9825 3007 **OPEN** By appointment
WINEMAKER Michael Staniford (Alkoomi) **EST.** 1995 **CASES** 400
SUMMARY The Witham family (Scott and Sue, Jim and Ann) began the development of Wadjekanup River Estate in 1995 as a minor diversification for a 3000-ha wool, prime lamb, beef and cereal cropping enterprise worked by the family. They began with 1.2 ha of shiraz and sauvignon blanc, since extended to 8 ha, including a 1-ha block of merlot (first production in 2001). The aims for the future include a purpose-built cellar for storage and sales, with a possibility of farm-stay accommodation. The present wine range of Sauvignon Blanc and Shiraz will be extended with a varietal Merlot, and perhaps a Semillon or other white.

🍃 Wagga Wagga Winery
NR

RMB 427, Oura Road, Wagga Wagga, NSW 2650 **REGION** Riverina
T (02) 6922 1221 **F** (02) 6922 1101 **OPEN** 7 days 11 until late
WINEMAKER Peter Fitzpatrick **EST.** 1987 **CASES** 1805
SUMMARY Planting of the 4-ha vineyard, 200m from the Murrumbidgee River, began in 1987; there were further plantings in 1990, 1995, 2000 and 2001. Chardonnay, riesling, shiraz, cabernet sauvignon, cabernet franc and touriga have been established. Situated just 15 minutes from Wagga Wagga, the tasting room and restaurant offer a full food and wine menu.

🍃 Walla Wines
NR

RMB 201, Walla Walla, NSW 2659 **REGION** Big Rivers Zone
T (02) 6029 2128 **F** (02) 6029 2508 **WEB** www.wallawines.com.au **OPEN** Weekends & public hols 10–5, or by appointment
WINEMAKER Paul Robey **EST.** 1998 **CASES** NA
SUMMARY Paul and Chris Robey moved to Walla Walla in 1981 after working in Papua New Guinea, the Northern Territory and at Puckapunyal in Victoria. Paul is an agriculturist and teacher; Chris is a registered nurse. After making wine as a hobby for some years, they planted the vineyard to semillon, shiraz, taminga and tarrango. Paul has completed a graduate diploma in viticulture at Charles Sturt University, and has also completed short courses in winemaking at the Dookie campus of Melbourne University. The pair do all the vineyard and winemaking operations except bottling.

Walsh Family Winery
NR

90 Walnut Road, Bickley, WA 6076 **REGION** Perth Hills
T (08) 9291 7341 **F** (08) 9291 7341 **OPEN** Weekends 11–5
WINEMAKER Rob Marshall (Contract) **EST.** 1995 **CASES** 200
SUMMARY Walsh Family Winery is aptly named: it is a partnership of the Walshes and their 8 children. One of those children has established 11 ha of vines near Bridgetown in the Great Southern; the grapes from those vines form part of the Walsh Family winery intake.

Wandana Estate
★★★

113 Oakey Creek Road, Hall, NSW 2618 **REGION** Canberra District
T (02) 6230 2140 **F** (02) 6230 2151 **OPEN** By appointment
WINEMAKER Various contract **EST.** 1997 **CASES** 300
SUMMARY The small Wandana Estate is managed by Colin Bates; it has 4.25 ha of cabernet sauvignon, merlot and shiraz. The wines are sold by mail order and through the cellar door.

ΥΥΥΥ **Shiraz 2003** Well made; ripe, spicy blackberry fruit; well-integrated oak, ripe tannins. **RATING** 89 **DRINK** 2010 $ 18

ȚȚȚȚ **Cabernet Merlot 2003** RATING 86 DRINK 2008 $18
Cabernet Sauvignon 2001 RATING 86 DRINK 2008 $25
Shiraz 2002 RATING 84 DRINK 2007 $20

Wandering Brook Estate   NR

North Wandering Road, Wandering, WA 6308 **REGION** Peel
T (08) 9884 1084 **F** (08) 9884 1064 **OPEN** Weekends 9.30–6
WINEMAKER Steve Radojkovich (Jadran) **EST.** 1989 **CASES** 1400
SUMMARY Laurie and Margaret White have planted 10 ha of vines on their 130-year-old family
property in a move to diversify. Until 1994 the winery was known as Red Hill Estate. Over half the
annual production of grapes is sold.

Wandin Valley Estate

Wilderness Road, Lovedale, NSW 2320 **REGION** Lower Hunter Valley
T (02) 4930 7317 **F** (02) 4930 7814 **WEB** www.wandinvalley.com.au **OPEN** 7 days 10–5
WINEMAKER Matthew Burton, Dan Dineen (Contract) **EST.** 1973 **CASES** 10 000
SUMMARY After 15 years in the wine and hospitality business, owners Phillipa and James Davern
decided to offer the property as a going concern, with vineyard, winery, accommodation, function
centre, cricket ground and restaurant in the package, aiming to keep its skilled staff as part of the
business, and ensure that all existing contracts are ongoing. The Café Crocodile is open Wed–Sun for
lunch, and dinner Fri–Sat. Ironically, being offered for sale just as the overall quality has increased.
Exports to the UK, the US and other major markets.

ȚȚȚȚȚ **Reserve Hunter Valley Chardonnay 2004** Elegant but intense; a lovely balance of
nectarine and melon fruit, and subtle French oak; good length and finish. Cork. RATING 92
DRINK 2008 $22
Hunter Valley Semillon 2004 Delicate but fresh and quite intense lemon blossom
aromas; a touch of fruit, not sugar, sweetness. High-quality cork. RATING 91 DRINK 2009
$18
Sauvignon Blanc Semillon 2004 Light but appealing juicy, citrussy flavours;
harmonious; good length and balance. Orange sauvignon blanc/Mudgee semillon.
RATING 90 DRINK 2009 $17
Hunter Valley Orange Shiraz 2003 Delicious, elegant, light to medium-bodied, fruit-
driven style; spice, plum, black cherry and pepper; minimal oak and tannins. Cork.
RATING 90 DRINK 2010 $18

ȚȚȚȚ **Pavilion Rose 2004** Lively, fresh, juicy red fruits/redcurrant; good length and balance.
RATING 88 DRINK Now $17

ȚȚȚȚ **Hunter Valley Verdelho 2004** RATING 85 DRINK Now $17

Wandoo Farm

'Glencraig', Duranillin, WA 6393 **REGION** Central Western Australia Zone
T (08) 9863 1066 **F** (08) 9863 1067 **OPEN** By appointment
WINEMAKER Camilla Vote **EST.** 1997 **CASES** 1750
SUMMARY Wandoo Farm lies outside all the existing wine regions; it is due east of the Blackwood
Valley, its nearest regional neighbour. Donald Cochrane owns a 650-ha sheep, cattle and grain farm
near Duranillin, with a 23-inch rainfall and abundant underground water. His maternal grandfather
came to Australia from Kaiser Stuhl in Germany, later settling near Kojonup, where he planted a
vineyard and made the community wine. Donald Cochrane has one of his original vines (malbec)
growing in the Wandoo Farm vineyard. There are also 7 ha of cabernet sauvignon, shiraz, zinfandel,
verdelho, viognier and marsanne. When he planted the vineyard, he says he had no intention of ever
having any wine made. Now he says he does not intend to build a winery, but acknowledges that
intentions change.

ȚȚȚȚ **Shiraz 2002** Attractive, warm mouthful of sweet black cherry and plum fruit; not over-
extracted. RATING 87 DRINK 2009

Wangolina Station ★★★☆

Cnr Southern Ports Highway/Limestone Coast Road, Kingston SE, SA 5275 **REGION** Mount Benson
T (08) 8768 6187 **F** (08) 8768 6149 **WEB** www.wangolinastation.com.au **OPEN** 7 days 10–5
WINEMAKER Anita Goode **EST.** 2001 **CASES** 3000
SUMMARY Four generations of the Goode family have been graziers at Wangolina Station, renowned for its shorthorn cattle stud. The family now has two connections with the wine industry: it sold the land to Kreglinger for its Norfolk Rise Vineyard and winery, and also sold land to Ralph Fowler. The second connection is even more direct: fifth-generation Anita Goode has become a vigneron, with 3.2 ha of shiraz and 1.6 ha each of cabernet sauvignon, sauvignon blanc and semillon established on the family property.

ΨΨΨΨΨ **Sauvignon Blanc 2004** Light to medium-bodied, with gooseberry, capsicum and mineral flavours; nice mouthfeel and good balance; plenty of varietal character. **RATING** 90 **DRINK** 2007 $ 15

ΨΨΨΨ **Semillon 2004** Very dry, crisp and minerally; well balanced; has length and is well made; simply needs time. **RATING** 87 **DRINK** 2014 $ 15

ΨΨΨΨ **Semillon 2003** **RATING** 86 **DRINK** 2011 $ 15

ΨΨΨ **Shiraz 2003** **RATING** 82 $ 20

Wansbrough Wines NR

Richards Road, Ferguson, WA 6236 **REGION** Geographe
T (08) 9728 3091 **F** (08) 9728 3091 **OPEN** Weekends 10–5
WINEMAKER Willespie Wines (Contract) **EST.** 1986 **CASES** 250
SUMMARY Situated east of Dardanup in the picturesque Ferguson Valley, Wansbrough enjoys views of the distant Geographe Bay and the nearer State forest, and has the Bibblemun Track running along the vineyard's northern and eastern borders. To taste the wine you need to either order by mail or visit the Wansbrough restaurant on weekends.

Wantirna Estate NR

Bushy Park Lane, Wantirna South, Vic 3152 **REGION** Yarra Valley
T (03) 9801 2367 **F** (03) 9887 0225 **OPEN** Not
WINEMAKER Maryann Egan, Reg Egan **EST.** 1963 **CASES** 800
SUMMARY Situated well within the boundaries of the Melbourne metropolitan area, Wantirna Estate is an outpost of the Yarra Valley. It was one of the first established in the rebirth of the valley. In deference to Reg Egan's very firmly held views on the subject, neither the winery nor the wines are rated.

NR **Isabella Chardonnay 2003** Gently complex fig, melon and cashew; good balance and length. Cork. **DRINK** 2009 $ 45

Lily Pinot Noir 2003 Attractive red cherry and plum fruit; supple, gently sweet mouthfeel; long finish. Cork. **DRINK** 2010 $ 50

Amelia Cabernet Sauvignon Merlot 2002 Savoury/earth cool vintage characters; minty berry fruit; fine tannins. Cork. **DRINK** 2010 $ 50

Waratah Vineyard ★★★☆

11852 Gladstone Road, Mungungo via Monto, Qld 4630 **REGION** Queensland Zone
T (07) 4166 5100 **F** (07) 4166 5200 **WEB** www.waratahvineyard.com.au **OPEN** Tues–Sun & public hols 10–5
WINEMAKER Peter Scudamore-Smith MW (Consultant) **EST.** 1998 **CASES** 900
SUMMARY David Bray is one of the doyens of wine journalism in Brisbane, and, indeed, Australia. After decades of writing about wine he and wife Pamela have joined Max Lindsay (Pamela's brother) and partner Lynne Tucker in establishing the Waratah Vineyard at Mungungo, near Monto, at the top of the Burnett Valley. The wines are principally sourced from the 4-ha Waratah Vineyard, with 3.2 ha of vineyard planted to chardonnay, verdelho, semillon, marsanne, viognier, shiraz, merlot and petit verdot, an exotic mix if ever there was one, but supplemented by grapes grown at Inglewood and Murgon.

▼▼▼▼ **Monal Creek Shiraz 2003** Light to medium-bodied; complex spicy fruit, with a touch of green leaf. **RATING** 89 **DRINK** 2009 $25
Monal Creek Verdelho 2004 Quite lively; tropical/citrus mix; good length. **RATING** 87 **DRINK** Now $18

Warrabilla ★★★★★

Murray Valley Highway, Rutherglen, Vic 3685 **REGION** Rutherglen
T (02) 6035 7242 **F** (02) 6035 7298 **WEB** www.warrabillawines.com.au **OPEN** 7 days 10–5
WINEMAKER Andrew Sutherland Smith **EST.** 1990 **CASES** 10 000
SUMMARY Andrew Sutherland Smith and wife Carol have built a formidable reputation for their wines, headed by the reserve trio of Durif, Cabernet Sauvignon and Shiraz, quintessential examples of Rutherglen red wine at its best. Their 18.5-ha vineyard has been extended with the planting of some riesling and zinfandel. Andrew spent 15 years with All Saints, McWilliam's, Yellowglen, Fairfield and Chambers before setting up Warrabilla, and his accumulated experience shines through in the wines.

▼▼▼▼▼ **Parola's Limited Release Shiraz 2004** Brooding black fruits; licorice, blackberry, prune and dark chocolate have eaten the vanilla oak; ripe tannins; 16° alcohol. Quality cork. **RATING** 95 **DRINK** 2024 $30
Parola's Limited Release Durif 2004 Impenetrable purple colour stains the glass; a massive palate, way beyond the normal dimensions of full-bodied red; the 17.5° alcohol gives sweetness rather than heat to the luscious black fruits, chocolate and licorice; 10 months in American oak has disappeared. Quality cork. **RATING** 95 **DRINK** 2029

▼▼▼▼▽ **Parola's Limited Release Cabernet Sauvignon 2004** Opaque purple-red; inward-looking, but you sense it is all there; cassis to burn; not too jammy or extractive; oak well done; juicy fruit, soft tannins; 16.1° alcohol. Cork. **RATING** 93 **DRINK** 2014 $30
Reserve Durif 2003 Inky dense colour; massively concentrated and dense, almost viscous, yet not extractive or coarse. **RATING** 93 **DRINK** 2023 $22
Reserve Cabernet Sauvignon 2004 Deep, dense colour; more tightly structured than Parola's, and (relatively) more elegance; just that slight mid-palate hole affecting many Cabernets; 15.5° alcohol. Cork. **RATING** 92 **DRINK** 2013 $22
Reserve Cabernet Sauvignon 2003 A ripe, rich mix of bitter chocolate, cassis and blackcurrant; smooth, ripe tannins; subtle oak. **RATING** 92 **DRINK** 2013 $22
Reserve Shiraz 2004 Opaque purple-red; dense black fruits; lots of fruit impact, though the structure isn't as strong as it might be; needs to loosen up; 16° alcohol. Cork. **RATING** 91 **DRINK** 2016 $22
Reserve Shiraz 2003 Dense colour; licorice, blackberry and spice; potent and concentrated; abundant but soft tannins. Excellent development potential. **RATING** 91 **DRINK** 2013 $22
Reserve Durif 2004 Completely opaque; lashings of black chocolate, spice and licorice; dense, yet not particularly vinous. **RATING** 91 **DRINK** 2013 $22

Warramate ★★★★

27 Maddens Lane, Gruyere, Vic 3770 **REGION** Yarra Valley
T (03) 5964 9219 **F** (03) 5964 9219 **WEB** www.warramatewines.com.au **OPEN** 7 days 10–6
WINEMAKER David Church **EST.** 1970 **CASES** 900
SUMMARY A long-established and perfectly situated winery is reaping the full benefits of its 35-year-old vines; recent plantings will increase production. All the wines are well made, the Shiraz providing further proof (if such be needed) of the suitability of the variety to the region.

Warraroong Estate ★★★★

247 Wilderness Road, Lovedale, NSW 2321 **REGION** Lower Hunter Valley
T (02) 4930 7594 **F** (02) 4930 7199 **WEB** www.warraroongestate.com **OPEN** Thurs–Mon 10–5
WINEMAKER Andrew Thomas, Adam Rees **EST.** 1978 **CASES** 2500
SUMMARY Warraroong Estate was formerly Fraser Vineyard, and adopted its new name after it changed hands in 1997. The name 'Warraroong' is an Aboriginal word for hillside, reflecting the southwesterly aspect of the property, which looks back towards the Brokenback Range and Watagan

Mountains. The label design is from a painting by Aboriginal artist Kia Kiro who, while coming from the Northern Territory, is now living and working in the Hunter Valley. The mature vineyard plantings were extended in 2004 with a little over 1 ha of verdelho.

ŸŸŸŸŸ **Hunter Valley Sauvignon Blanc 2004** Utterly remarkable varietal character for the Hunter Valley; very well made; crisp herb, grass and lime; very good mouthfeel and balance. Screwcap. **RATING** 90 **DRINK** 2007 $ 14

ŸŸŸŸ **Hunter Valley Shiraz 2003** High-toned, ripe, juicy blackberry and blackcurrant fruit; tails off slightly on the finish. Quality cork. **RATING** 88 **DRINK** 2012 $ 20
Hunter Valley Malbec 2003 Soft, slurpy blackberry jam on entry and mid-palate; light to medium-bodied, the tannins slight. High-quality cork. **RATING** 87 **DRINK** 2010 $ 17

Warrego Wines ★★☆

9 Seminary Road, Marburg, Qld 4306 **REGION** Queensland Coastal
T (07) 5464 4400 **F** (07) 5464 4800 **WEB** www.warregowines.com.au **OPEN** 7 days 10–4
WINEMAKER Kevin Watson **EST.** 2000 **CASES** 27 000
SUMMARY Kevin Watson has completed his wine science degree at Charles Sturt University, and the primary purpose of his business is custom winemaking for the many small growers in the region, including all the clients of Peter Scudamore-Smith MW. In 2001, the Marburg Custom Crush company, developed a state-of-the-art winery (as the cliché goes), cellar door and restaurant. $500 000 in government funding, local business investment and significant investment from China provided the funds, and the complex opened in April 2002. Since then, the business has expanded further with a public shareholder raising. (In 2004 Warrego crushed over 400 tonnes, 95% of which was contract winemaking for others.) The 3000-case own-brand Warrego wines come from 0.5 ha of estate chambourcin, plus grapes purchased in various regions. Exports to the US and China.

ŸŸŸ **The Ranges Red NV** **RATING** 83 $ 11.95

Warrenmang Vineyard & Resort ★★★★☆

Mountain Creek Road, Moonambel, Vic 3478 **REGION** Pyrenees
T (03) 5467 2233 **F** (03) 5467 2309 **WEB** www.bazzani.com.au **OPEN** 7 days 10–5
WINEMAKER Luigi Bazzani, Chris Collier **EST.** 1974 **CASES** 8000
SUMMARY The proposed merger of Warrenmang with other wine interests in 2004 failed to eventuate, through no fault of Luigi and Athalie Bazzani, who, as at February 2005, had resumed full control of the business, securing a number of large export orders to the US and Singapore. After 28 years at the helm, retirement is nonetheless on their minds, and discussions with other potential purchasers may lead to a change of ownership sometime soon.

ŸŸŸŸŸ **Black Puma Pyrenees Shiraz 2002** Deep colour; medium to full-bodied; ultra-ripe prune, plum and blackberry fruit running through to the mid-palate, then abrupt tannins needing to soften. Cork. **RATING** 92 **DRINK** 2017 $ 80
Grand Pyrenees 2001 Fine, elegant earthy/savoury/spicy aromas, with ripe black fruits at the core; very good texture from fine-grained tannins. Cabernet Franc/Shiraz/Merlot/Cabernet Sauvignon. Terrible cork. **RATING** 92 **DRINK** 2012 $ 35
Pyrenees Cabernet Sauvignon 2001 Full-bodied; abundant blackcurrant, chocolate and earth flavours; good balance and mouthfeel; ripe tannins, good oak. Cork. **RATING** 91 **DRINK** 2011 $ 33
Estate Shiraz 2002 Medium-bodied; similar sweet fruit characters to Black Puma, but less obvious, even though the alcohol is higher (15°); spicy, savoury notes, good balance. Cork. **RATING** 90 **DRINK** 2012 $ 60

ŸŸŸŸ **Estate Chardonnay 2002** Medium-bodied; nicely balanced ripe peach and fig fruit with French oak; solid line. Cork. **RATING** 88 **DRINK** 2008 $ 25

ŸŸŸŸ **Pyrenees Sauvignon Blanc 2003** **RATING** 84 **DRINK** Now $ 25

Warrina Wines NR

Back Road, Kootingal, NSW 2352 **REGION** Northern Slopes Zone
T (02) 6760 3985 **F** (02) 6765 5746 **OPEN** Weekends 10–4
WINEMAKER David Nicholls **EST.** 1989 **CASES** 100

SUMMARY David and Susan Nicholls began the establishment of their 2.5-ha vineyard back in 1989, and for some years were content to sell the grapes to other producers and make occasional forays into winemaking. In 2001 they decided to commence winemaking on a commercial basis.

Watchbox Wines ★★★

Indigo Creek Road, Barnawartha, Vic 3688 **REGION** Rutherglen
T (03) 6026 9299 **F** (03) 6026 9299 **OPEN** Fri–Sun & public hols 10–5
WINEMAKER Alan Clark **EST.** 2001 **CASES** NA
SUMMARY Alan and Lisa Clark have established a 5-ha vineyard in the Indigo Valley, planted to riesling, sauvignon blanc, chardonnay, cabernet sauvignon, merlot, shiraz, durif and muscat. They make the wine onsite and sell it by mail order and through the cellar door (which offers light meals and barbecue and picnic facilities).

Watershed Wines

Cnr Bussell Highway/Darch Road, Margaret River, WA 6285 **REGION** Margaret River
T (08) 9758 8633 **F** (08) 9757 3999 **WEB** www.watershedwines.com.au **OPEN** 7 days 10–5
WINEMAKER Cathy Spratt **EST.** 1999 **CASES** 76 000
SUMMARY Watershed Wines has been set up by a syndicate of investors, and no expense has been spared in establishing the vineyard and building a striking cellar door sales area, with a 200-seat café and restaurant recently completed. Situated towards the southern end of the Margaret River region, its neighbours include Voyager Estate and Leeuwin Estate. Exports to the UK, the US and other major markets.

ㅜㅜㅜㅜ**Shiraz 2003** Very fragrant and scented; an attractive mix of red cherry, plum and blackberry; gently assertive, fine tannins. Cork. **RATING** 92 **DRINK** 2010 $ 26.95
Shades 2003 Aromatic and sweet array of red and black fruits; medium-bodied, smooth palate; long, fruit-driven finish. Cabernet/Shiraz/Merlot/Cabernet Franc. Cork. **RATING** 91 **DRINK** 2012 $ 17.95
Viognier 2004 Aromatic fruit pastille/apricot; a hint of smoky oak works well on the palate; good length and structure. Screwcap. **RATING** 90 **DRINK** 2008 $ 17.95

ㅜㅜㅜㅜ**Margaret River Sauvignon Blanc Semillon 2004** Very rich and powerful palate; mouthfilling, ripe fruit; cloys slightly on the finish. **RATING** 88 **DRINK** Now $ 17.95

ㅜㅜㅜ**Unoaked Chardonnay 2004** **RATING** 80 $ 17.95

Water Wheel ★★★★

Bridgewater-on-Loddon, Bridgewater, Vic 3516 **REGION** Bendigo
T (03) 5437 3060 **F** (03) 5437 3082 **WEB** www.waterwheelwine.com **OPEN** Oct–Apr 7 days 11–5,
May–Sept Mon–Fri 11–5, weekends & public hols 1–4
WINEMAKER Peter Cumming, Bill Trevaskis **EST.** 1972 **CASES** 35 000
SUMMARY Peter Cumming, with two decades of winemaking under his belt, has quietly built on the reputation of Water Wheel year by year. The winery is owned by the Cumming family, which has farmed in the Bendigo region for 50 years, with horticulture and viticulture special areas of interest. The wines are of remarkably consistent quality and modest price. National distribution; exports to New Zealand, The Philippines, the UK, Switzerland, Belgium, the US and Canada.

ㅜㅜㅜㅜ**Bendigo Shiraz 2003** Concentrated, powerful blackberry fruit; good texture and structure; oak a backdrop as ever. Great value. **RATING** 90 **DRINK** 2013 $ 18
Memsie Shiraz Cabernet Malbec 2003 A quite powerful array of dark, black fruits; firm structure and tannins around a core of sweetness. Screwcap. **RATING** 90 **DRINK** 2008 $ 12

ㅜㅜㅜㅜ**Bendigo Sauvignon Blanc 2004** Very pleasant wine; nicely balanced; plenty of mid-palate varietal fruit. **RATING** 88 **DRINK** Now $ 15
Bendigo Chardonnay 2004 Melon, fig fruit; minimal oak; some length, but painfully shy. Screwcap. **RATING** 87 **DRINK** Now $ 15
Bendigo Cabernet Sauvignon 2002 Powerful, savoury briary style; black fruits are there within overall austerity. **RATING** 87 **DRINK** 2012 $ 18

ㅜㅜㅜ**Memsie Sauvignon Blanc Semillon Roussanne 2004** **RATING** 84 **DRINK** Now $ 12

Wattagan Estate Winery

NR

'Wattagan', Oxley Highway, Coonabarabran, NSW 2357 **REGION** Western Plains Zone
T (02) 6842 2456 **F** (02) 6842 2656 **OPEN** 7 days 10–5
WINEMAKER Contract **EST.** 1996 **CASES** NFP
SUMMARY Coonabarabran is known for its sheep grazing, but most emphatically not for viticulture. As far north of Sydney as Port Macquarie, it is 440 km west of that town, with the striking Warrumbungle Range on one side and the national park on the other. The modest production is sold through three outlets in Coonabarabran, and 'exported' to Gunnedah and Boggabri.

Wattlebrook Vineyard

★★★★

Fordwich Road, Broke, NSW 2330 **REGION** Lower Hunter Valley
T (02) 9929 5668 **F** (02) 9929 5668 **WEB** www.wattlebrook.com **OPEN** By appointment
WINEMAKER Andrew Margan (Contract) **EST.** 1994 **CASES** 1000
SUMMARY Wattlebrook Vineyard was founded by NSW Supreme Court Justice Peter McClellan and family in 1994; the substantial vineyard lies between the Wollemi NP and Wollombi Brook. The family planted another major vineyard, in 1998, on Henry Lawson Drive at Mudgee, to shiraz, merlot and cabernet sauvignon. The Wollombi Vineyard is planted to chardonnay, semillon, verdelho, cabernet sauvignon and shiraz. The wines have been consistent medal winners at New South Wales and Hunter Valley Wine Shows.

 Bird's Keep Wollemi Reserve Shiraz 2003 Good colour; good depth and concentration of blackberry fruit; smooth, supple tannins. Top vintage. **RATING** 91 **DRINK** 2018 $ 22
Chardonnay 2003 Ripe, smooth melon and peach fruit; good balance and mouthfeel; clearly shows the advantage of the screwcap. **RATING** 90 **DRINK** 2008 $ 17

Chardonnay 2002 Developed colour; advanced, toasty melon and peach sustained by good acidity; a suspicion of random bottle oxidation. **RATING** 87 **DRINK** Now $ 17

Verdelho 2004 RATING 86 **DRINK** 2007 $ 14.50

Wattle Mist Wines

NR

Taste Mount Barker Wine Café, 26 Langton Road, Mount Barker, WA 6324 **REGION** Mount Barker
T (08) 9851 **F** (08) 9851 2569 **OPEN** 7 days 10.30–5 winter, weekends 10.30–5 summer
WINEMAKER Mike Garland (Contract) **EST.** 1992 **CASES** 800
SUMMARY Wattle Mist Wines is the retirement vehicle for Ray Burring and Joan Bath. With a desire for a relaxed country lifestyle, Ray and Joan purchased their 100-acre property in Mount Barker in 1992 and have developed the vineyard slowly. The wines are made in an early-drinking style, and are available through the Taste Mount Barker Wine Café (also owned by Ray and Joan), which stocks around 50 local wines and offers light lunches and local produce.

Wattle Ridge Vineyard

★★★★

Lot 11950, Boyup–Greenbushes Road, Greenbushes, WA 6254 **REGION** Blackwood Valley
T (08) 9764 3594 **F** (08) 9764 3594 **OPEN** 7 days 10–5
WINEMAKER Contract **EST.** 1997 **CASES** 1000
SUMMARY James and Vicky Henderson have established 6.5 ha of vines at their Nelson vineyard, planted to riesling, verdelho, merlot and cabernet sauvignon. The wines are sold by mail order and through the cellar door, which offers light meals, crafts and local produce.

 Two Tinsmith Greenbushes Cabernet Sauvignon 2003 Good colour; excellent, lively cassis redcurrant fruit; balanced oak; stylish wine. **RATING** 93 **DRINK** 2013

Waverley Estate

★★★

Waverley-Honour, Palmers Lane, Pokolbin, NSW 2320 **REGION** Lower Hunter Valley
T (02) 4998 7953 **F** (02) 4998 7952 **WEB** www.wineloverslane.com.au **OPEN** 7 days 10–5
WINEMAKER Gary Reed (Contract) **EST.** 1989 **CASES** 4500
SUMMARY Waverley Estate Aged Wines (to give it its full name) is the new name for the Maling Family Estate; as its name suggests, it specialises in offering a range of fully mature wines. Vintages

stretching back more than 10 years are available for most of the wines at the cellar door. The wines are chiefly made from the 21.5 ha of estate plantings (shiraz, semillon, chardonnay, cabernet sauvignon).

Waybourne

NR

60 Lemins Road, Waurn Ponds, Vic 3221 **REGION** Geelong
T (03) 5241 8477 **F** (03) 5241 8477 **OPEN** By appointment
WINEMAKER David Cowburn (Contract) **EST.** 1980 **CASES** 730
SUMMARY Owned by Tony and Kay Volpato, who have relied upon external consultants to assist with the winemaking.

Wayne Thomas Wines

★★★

26 Kangarilla Road, McLaren Vale, SA 5171 **REGION** McLaren Vale
T (08) 8323 9737 **F** (08) 8323 9737 **OPEN** Not
WINEMAKER Wayne Thomas, Tim Geddes **EST.** 1994 **CASES** 5000
SUMMARY Wayne Thomas is a McLaren Vale veteran, having started his winemaking career in 1961, working for Stonyfell, Ryecroft and Saltram before establishing Fern Hill with his late wife Pat in 1975. When they sold Fern Hill in April 1994 they started again, launching the Wayne Thomas Wines label, and using grapes sourced from 10 growers throughout McLaren Vale. Exports to the US; limited retail distribution through all Australian States except WA.

Wedgetail Estate

40 Hildebrand Road, Cottles Bridge, Vic 3099 **REGION** Yarra Valley
T (03) 9714 8661 **F** (03) 9714 8676 **WEB** www.wedgetailestate.com.au **OPEN** Weekends & public hols 12–5, or by appointment, closed from 25 Dec, reopens Australia Day weekend
WINEMAKER Guy Lamothe **EST.** 1994 **CASES** 1500
SUMMARY Canadian-born photographer Guy Lamothe and partner Dena Ashbolt started making wine in the basement of their Carlton home in the 1980s. The idea of their own vineyard started to take hold, and the search for a property began. Then, in their words, 'one Sunday, when we were 'just out for a drive", we drove past our current home. The slopes are amazing, true goat terrain, and it is on these steep slopes that in 1994 we planted our first block of pinot noir.' While the vines were growing – they now have 5.5 ha in total – Lamothe enrolled in the wine-growing course at Charles Sturt University, having already gained practical experience working in the Yarra Valley (Tarrawarra), the Mornington Peninsula and Meursault. The net result is truly excellent wine. Exports to the UK, China and Singapore.

▼▼▼▼▼ **Yarra Valley Pinot Noir 2003** Medium-bodied; sweet damson plum and spice; silky texture and considerable length; has finesse. Quality cork. **RATING** 93 **DRINK** 2010 $ 38
Single Vineyard Yarra Valley Shiraz 2003 Aromatic spicy, peppery, lemony cherry fruit; light to medium-bodied, clean and lively; fine, lingering tannins. Stained cork. **RATING** 91 **DRINK** 2010 $ 38
Par 3 Yarra Valley Sauvignon Blanc 2004 Clean, aromatic passionfruit bouquet; delicate but quite intense palate; 10% barrel ferment adds texture and doesn't diminish the fruit. Screwcap. **RATING** 90 **DRINK** 2007 $ 22
Yarra Valley Chardonnay 2003 Developed yellow; super-rich, ripe and concentrated; sweet yellow peach has absorbed the oak. Rapid development. Cork. **RATING** 90 **DRINK** 2008 $ 33
Yarra Valley Cabernet Merlot 2002 Sweet minty/spicy red berry fruit; super-fine tannins; long finish, elegant. Quality cork. **RATING** 90 **DRINK** 2012 $ 32

▼▼▼▼ **Par 3 Yarra Valley Pinot Noir 2003** Elegant, fresh, light to medium-bodied; red and black cherry with touches of spice; not forced. Screwcap. **RATING** 89 **DRINK** 2009 $ 22

Wedgetail Ridge Estate

NR

656 Kingsthorpe–Haden Road, Kingsthorpe, Qld 4400 **REGION** Darling Downs
T (07) 4699 3029 **F** (07) 4699 3371 **OPEN** 7 days 10–4
WINEMAKER Ross Whiteford **EST.** 1999 **CASES** NA

SUMMARY Suzanne Nation has established an 8-ha vineyard 30 km northeast of Toowoomba. It is planted to chardonnay, viognier, merlot, shiraz, cabernet sauvignon and durif, and the wine is made on the premises. Light meals are available at the café, but the primary purpose of the business is as a contract winemaking facility.

Wehl's Mount Benson Vineyards ★★★★

Wrights Bay Road, Mount Benson, SA 5275 REGION Mount Benson
T (08) 8768 6251 F (08) 8678 6251 OPEN 7 days 10–4
WINEMAKER Contract EST. 1989 CASES 1800
SUMMARY Peter and Leah Wehl were the first to plant vines in the Mount Benson area, beginning the establishment of their 24-ha vineyard, two-thirds shiraz and one-third cabernet sauvignon, in 1989. While primarily grapegrowers, they have moved into winemaking via contract makers, and plan to increase the range of wines available by grafting 1 ha of merlot and 1.5 ha of sauvignon blanc onto part of the existing plantings.

TTTTY **Cabernet Sauvignon 2003** Medium-bodied; attractive blackcurrant and cassis fruit; soft tannins; restrained oak. Screwcap. RATING 90 DRINK 2013 $ 26

TTTT **Rose 2004** Highly aromatic and flowery red fruits/strawberries; nicely balanced palate; fresh, fruity, dry finish. Screwcap. RATING 88 DRINK Now $ 18

TTTY **Shiraz 2003** RATING 85 DRINK 2008 $ 26

Wellington Vale Wines ★★★★

'Wellington Vale', Deepwater, NSW 2371 (postal) REGION Northern Slopes Zone
T (02) 6734 5226 F (02) 6734 5226 OPEN Not
WINEMAKER Contract EST. 1997 CASES 200
SUMMARY David and Dierdri Robertson-Cuninghame trace their ancestry (via David) back to the Duke of Wellington, with Cuninghame Senior being the ADC to the Duke, and his son, Arthur Wellesley-Robertson, the godson. Arthur Wellesley migrated to Australia and took up the land upon which Wellington Vale is situated in 1839. Planting began in 1997 with 0.7 ha of semillon, and continued with 1 ha of pinot noir and 0.3 ha of riesling. The first vintage was in 2000, and the subsequent vintages have won bronze medals at the highly competitive Australian Small Winemakers Show.

TTTTY **Deepwater Red Pinot Noir 2003** Bell-clear black cherry varietal fruit aromas and flavours; good texture, weight and balance; long finish; major surprise. RATING 90 DRINK 2009 $ 15

TTTT **Semillon 2002** Fresh herb and grass aromatics; good balance and length; well made. RATING 87 DRINK 2009 $ 12

TTTY **Semillon 2003** Clean, classic semillon varietal aromas, but shortens fractionally on the palate. RATING 86 DRINK 2008 $ 12

TTT **Louisa's Sweet Semillon 2003** RATING 80 $ 8

Wells Parish Wines NR

Benerin Estate, Sydney Road, Kandos, NSW 2848 REGION Mudgee
T (02) 6379 4168 F (02) 6379 4996 OPEN By appointment
WINEMAKER Philip Van Gent EST. 1995 CASES 1000
SUMMARY Richard and Rachel Trounson, with help from father Barry Trounson, have established 18 ha of vineyards at Benerin Estate since 1995. Most of the grapes are sold to Southcorp, but small quantities of wine are made for the Wells Parish label. The vineyards are at the eastern extremity of the Mudgee region, near Rylstone, and both the soils and climate are distinctly different from those of the traditional Mudgee area.

Welshmans Reef Vineyard NR

Maldon–Newstead Road, Welshmans Reef, Vic 3462 REGION Bendigo
T (03) 5476 2733 F (03) 5476 2537 WEB www.welshmansreef.com OPEN Weekends & public hols 10–5
WINEMAKER Ronald Snep EST. 1994 CASES 1200

SUMMARY The Snep family (Ronald, Jackson and Alexandra) began developing Welshmans Reef Vineyard in 1986, planting cabernet sauvignon, shiraz and semillon. Chardonnay and merlot were added in the early 1990s, with sauvignon blanc and tempranillo later. For some years the grapes were sold to other wineries, but in the early 1990s the Sneps decided to share winemaking facilities established in the Old Newstead Co-operative Butter Factory with several other small vineyards. When the Butter Factory facility was closed down, the Sneps built a winery and mudbrick tasting room onsite: 6 km north of Newstead, just before the hamlet which gave the vineyard its name. An Italian-style domed pizza oven has been completed, and the winery stages concerts ranging from Baroque to jazz.

Welwyn Meadows

NR

PO Box 62, Legana, Tas 7277 **REGION** Northern Tasmania
T (03) 6330 1467 **F** (03) 6330 3005 **WEB** www.questhinterland.com **OPEN** Not
WINEMAKER Corey Baker (Contract) **EST.** 1998 **CASES** NA
SUMMARY Judith and Keith Starkey planted 1 ha each of chardonnay and pinot noir in 1998, doing it themselves with the benefit of a TAFE viticulture course, and followed up with a small winery commissioned for the 2005 vintage. A cellar door is due to open in late 2005; meanwhile, the wines are available through the website and by mail order.

Wendouree

★★★★★

Wendouree Road, Clare, SA 5453 **REGION** Clare Valley
T (08) 8842 2896 **OPEN** By appointment
WINEMAKER Tony Brady **EST.** 1895 **CASES** 2000
SUMMARY The iron fist in a velvet glove best describes these extraordinary wines. They are fashioned with passion and precision from the very old vineyard with its unique terroir by Tony and Lita Brady, who rightly see themselves as custodians of a priceless treasure. The 100-year-old stone winery is virtually unchanged from the day it was built; this is in every sense a treasure beyond price. For two reasons, neither Tony Brady nor I see any point in providing tasting notes for the most recently released vintage. First, the wines will have sold out (and there is no room for newcomers on the mailing list for the next release). Second, all I will ever be able to say is wait for 20 years before drinking the wine.

We're Wines

★★★★

Cnr Wildberry Road/Johnson Road, Wilyabrup, WA 6280 **REGION** Margaret River
T (08) 9755 6273 **F** (08) 9389 9166 **WEB** www.werewines.com.au **OPEN** Wed–Sun & public hols 10.30–5
WINEMAKER Jan Davies (Contract) **EST.** 1998 **CASES** 4000
SUMMARY Owners Diane and Gordon Davies say, 'We are different. We're original, we're bold, we're innovative and we want to be.' This is all reflected in the design of the front labels; the even more unusual back labels, incorporating pictures of the innumerable pairs of braces which real estate agent Gordon Davies wears on his Perth job; in the early move to screwcaps for both white and red wines; and, for that matter, in the underground trickle irrigation system in their Margaret River vineyard which can be controlled from Perth. Exports to the US, The Philippines and Singapore.

ᵀᵀᵀᵀᵀ Wooded Semillon 2004 Pleasantly funky barrel ferment aromas; semillon fruit drives the palate, well-handled oak in second place. **RATING** 90 **DRINK** 2009 $ 22

ᵀᵀᵀᵀ Margaret River Semillon Sauvignon Blanc 2004 Bold style; slightly funky aromas, then bursting ripe, tropical flavours on the palate. Screwcap. **RATING** 88 **DRINK** 200 $ 15
Cabernet Sauvignon 2002 Direct, fruit-driven, medium-bodied; blackberry and blackcurrant flavours; clean finish. **RATING** 87 **DRINK** 2009 $ 25

ᵀᵀᵀᵀ Shiraz 2002 RATING 86 **DRINK** 2008 $ 19.99
Sauvignon Blanc Semillon 2003 RATING 85 **DRINK** 2007 $ 16

West Cape Howe Wines

★★★★☆

Lot 42 South Coast Highway, Denmark, WA 6333 **REGION** Denmark
T (08) 9848 2959 **F** (08) 9848 2903 **OPEN** 7 days 10–5
WINEMAKER Gavin Berry, Dave Cleary, Coby Ladwig **EST.** 1997 **CASES** 53 000

SUMMARY After a highly successful 7 years, West Cape Howe founders Brenden and Kylie Smith have moved on, selling the business to a partnership including Gavin Berry (until May 2004, senior winemaker at Plantagenet) and viticulturist Rob Quenby. As well as existing fruit sources, West Cape Howe now has the 80-ha Lansdale Vineyard, planted in 1989, as its primary fruit source. The focus now will be less on contract winemaking, and more on building the very strong West Cape Howe brand. Exports to the US, Hong Kong, Singapore, Japan, Denmark and The Netherlands.

ΨΨΨΨΨ **Chardonnay 2004** Medium-bodied; complex barrel ferment aromas; an equally complex and intense palate with grapefruit and stone fruit; excellent length. Possible wild yeast. Screwcap. **RATING** 94 **DRINK** 2010 $ 24

ΨΨΨΨ **Chardonnay 2003** A rich and complex marriage of ripe stone fruit and barrel ferment inputs; good balance; ready now. **RATING** 93 **DRINK** 2007 $ 24
Semillon Sauvignon Blanc 2004 Spotlessly clean; lively multi-fruit flavours, and a long, lemony finish. Very attractive. **RATING** 92 **DRINK** 2010 $ 17
Riesling 2004 Spotlessly clean and fresh; delicate grapefruit and apple flavours; good balance and length. **RATING** 91 **DRINK** 2012 $ 19
Shiraz 2003 Medium-bodied; fragrant, spicy, peppery overtones to black cherry/blackberry fruit; fine tannins. **RATING** 90 **DRINK** 2010 $ 19

ΨΨΨΨ **Unwooded Chardonnay 2004** Clever winemaking with some complexity to the aromatics; plenty of stone fruit and citrus flavour, but not phenolic. **RATING** 89 **DRINK** 2008 $ 19
Cabernet Sauvignon 2003 Distinctly savoury/earthy overtones to blackcurrant fruit; fairly fine tannins and oak. **RATING** 89 **DRINK** 2012 $ 24
Sauvignon Blanc 2004 Fresh, clean, flowery aromas; stone and mineral elements on the palate; balanced finish and good length. Screwcap. **RATING** 87 **DRINK** Now $ 16
Rose 2004 Tangy and lively; distinctly herbal and lingering acidity; clearly shows the Cabernet Franc varietal background. Screwcap. **RATING** 87 **DRINK** Now $ 16

ΨΨΨ **Viognier 2004** **RATING** 86 **DRINK** 2007 $ 24
Cabernet Merlot 2003 **RATING** 85 **DRINK** 2007 $ 17

Westend Estate Wines ★★★

1283 Brayne Road, Griffith, NSW 2680 **REGION** Riverina
T (02) 6964 1506 **F** (02) 6962 1673 **WEB** www.westendestate.com **OPEN** Mon–Fri 8.30–5, weekends 10–4
WINEMAKER William Calabria, Bryan Currie **EST.** 1945 **CASES** 100 000
SUMMARY Along with a number of Riverina producers, Westend Estate is making a concerted move to lift both the quality and the packaging of its wines. Its leading 3 Bridges range, which has an impressive array of gold medals to its credit since being first released in 1997, is anchored in part on 20 ha of estate vineyards. Exports to the UK, Germany, Finland, Switzerland, New Zealand, Korea, Hong Kong, China, Taiwan and Malaysia.

ΨΨΨΨ **Cabernet Sauvignon Shiraz 2003** Good colour; dark fruit flavours and overall balance. **RATING** 87 **DRINK** 2009

ΨΨΨ **Old Vine Shiraz 2003** **RATING** 86 **DRINK** 2008
3 Bridges Shiraz 2002 **RATING** 86 **DRINK** 2007 $ 19.95

Western Range Wines ★★★★

1995 Chittering Road, Lower Chittering, WA 6084 **REGION** Perth Hills
T (08) 9571 8800 **F** (08) 9571 8844 **WEB** www.westernrangewines.com.au **OPEN** Wed–Sun 10–5
WINEMAKER Ryan Sudano, John Griffiths (Consultant) **EST.** 2001 **CASES** 40 000
SUMMARY Between the mid-1990s and 2001, several prominent West Australians, including Marilyn Corderory, Malcolm McCusker, Terry and Kevin Prindiville and Tony Rechner, have established approximately 125 ha of vines (under separate ownerships) in the Perth Hills, with a kaleidoscopic range of varietals. The next step was to join forces to build a substantial winery. This is a separate venture, but takes the grapes from the individual vineyards and markets the wine under the Western Range brand. In 2004 the releases were rebranded and regrouped at four levels: Lot 88 ($13.50), Goyamin Pool ($16), Julimar ($22) and Julimar Organic ($22). The label designs are clear and attractive. Distribution through all mainland states, primarily by Australian Liquor Merchants. Exports to the UK, the US and other major markets.

ŸŸŸŸ♀ **Julimar Shiraz Viognier 2003** Voluptuous sweet apricot, blackberry and black cherry fruit; supple mouthfeel; good oak and tannins. Quality cork. **RATING** 91 **DRINK** 2012 $ 22
Julimar Organic Shiraz 2003 Medium-bodied; blackberry, black fruit, spice and pepper; positive oak handling; silky, ripe tannins. Quality cork. **RATING** 90 **DRINK** 2009 $ 22
Julimar Carnelian Shiraz 2003 Light to medium-bodied; bright, fresh juicy plum and licorice fruit; a fine web of tannins and oak; interesting, with the rare grape carnelian a major component. Screwcap. **RATING** 90 **DRINK** 2008 $ 22
Goyamin Pool Shiraz 2003 Clean, fresh, bright and supple red and black fruits; minimal oak, fine, ripe tannins. Very well made. Screwcap. **RATING** 90 **DRINK** 2010 $ 16

ŸŸŸŸ **Goyamin Pool Chardonnay Viognier 2004** A very elegant and improbably harmonious blend of sweet melon, stone fruit and a hint of apricot. Screwcap. **RATING** 89 **DRINK** 2008 $ 16
Julimar Viognier 2003 A quite lively array of fruit flavours and aromas; apricot, citrus and incipient honey; balanced acidity. **RATING** 89 **DRINK** 2007 $ 20
Lot 88 Shiraz Grenache 2003 Medium-bodied; good structure and tight tannins ex the Shiraz; a nice touch of sweet berry fruit ex Grenache. Top value. Screwcap. **RATING** 89 **DRINK** 2007 $ 13.50
Julimar Viognier 2004 Light to medium-bodied; spice, apricot, ripe/dried peach aromas and flavours; soft fruit, good acidity. Screwcap. **RATING** 88 **DRINK** 2007 $ 22
Julimar Carnelian Shiraz 2002 Light to medium-bodied; elegant, spicy, savoury aromas and flavours; fine, but lingering, tannins. Cork. **RATING** 88 **DRINK** Now $ 22
 2003 Light to medium-bodied; smooth, supple juicy raspberry and mulberry Grenache fruit; fine tannins. Screwcap. **RATING** 88 **DRINK** 2007 $ 16
Goyamin Pool Verdelho 2003 Light-bodied; spotlessly clean; lively, fresh fruit salad with nice touches of lemony acidity. Screwcap. **RATING** 87 **DRINK** Now $ 16
Lot 88 Chenin Verdelho 2004 Well made with lots of fruit salad; nice balance, and not too sweet. Screwcap. **RATING** 87 **DRINK** Now $ 13.50

Westgate Vineyard ★★★★★

180 Westgate Road, Armstrong, Vic 3377 **REGION** Grampians
T (03) 5356 2394 **F** (03) 5356 2594 **WEB** www.westgatevineyard.com.au **OPEN** At Garden Gully
WINEMAKER Bruce Dalkin **EST.** 1997 **CASES** 400
SUMMARY Westgate has been in the Dalkin family ownership since the 1860s, the present owners Bruce and Robyn Dalkin being the sixth generation owners of the property, which today focuses on grape production, a small winery, four and a half star accommodation, and wool production. There are now 14 ha of vineyards, progressively established since 1969, including a key holding of 10 ha of shiraz; most of the grapes are sold to Mount Langi Ghiran and Seppelt Great Western, but a vigneron's licence was obtained in 1999 and a small amount of wine is made under the Westgate Vineyard label. It has had considerable show success: both the 2002 and the 2003 Shiraz were gold medal winners at the Ballarat Wine Show.

ŸŸŸŸŸ **Endurance Shiraz Viognier 2003** Typical vivid hue; spotlessly clean and fragrant aromas; beautiful texture, structure and mouthfeel; silky, elegant and intense. Screwcap. **RATING** 96 **DRINK** 2015 $ 44
Endurance Shiraz 2002 Of pristine clarity; lovely expression of cool-grown shiraz; silky black cherry and blackberry fruit; subtle oak. Three trophies Ballarat Wine Show 2004. Cork. **RATING** 95 **DRINK** 2015 $ 44

Whale Coast Wines ★★★★

65 Ocean Street, Victor Harbor, SA 5211 **REGION** Southern Fleurieu
T (08) 8552 1444 **F** (08) 8552 2611 **OPEN** By appointment
WINEMAKER Duncan Fergusson, Susanna Fernandez, Tim Knappstein (Contract) **EST.** 1994 **CASES** 2000
SUMMARY This is the venture of obstetrician and general practitioner David Batt, partner Chris and their 5 children; it is no longer a hobby, as one of the daughters is completing oenology studies at Adelaide University. Since purchasing the 64-ha farm in 1994, 25 ha of vineyard has been planted, to shiraz, cabernet sauvignon, riesling, sauvignon blanc, viognier, tempranillo, merlot and petit verdot. The house on the Whale Coast Wines vineyard (built in 1852) is being gradually restored. Most of the grapes have been sold to Cascabel, where Duncan Fergusson and Susanna Fernandez also make

limited quantities of Crow's Nest Shiraz, Kondole Cabernet and Balaena Cabernet Shiraz for Whale Coast. The first white wine, a 2004 Crockery Bay Sauvignon Blanc, was made by Tim Knappstein. Sales by mail order and through the cellar door; distribution by Jonathon Hyams Global Fine Wines in NSW; exports to the US and the UK.

▼▼▼▼▽ **The Crows Nest Shiraz 2001** Similar weight and style to the '02, perhaps a fraction riper, but still elegant and holding fruit very well. **RATING** 91 **DRINK** 2009 $ 22

The Crows Nest Shiraz 2002 Spicy, leafy, savoury, cedary aromas; light to medium-bodied; cool-climate style, with some sweet fruits; long palate and finish. **RATING** 90 **DRINK** 2010 $ 22

▼▼▼▼ **Kondole Cabernet Sauvignon 2002** Herb, spice and mint aromas; blackcurrant, mint and herbal tannins; long finish; faintly reduced. Screwcap. **RATING** 89 **DRINK** 2012 $ 22

Balaena Cabernet Shiraz 2003 Youthful; cedary, earthy tinges to red and black fruits; lingering, fine tannins; medium-bodied. **RATING** 89 **DRINK** 2012 $ 17

Crockery Bay Sauvignon Blanc 2004 Clearly articulated varietal character from start to finish; tropical, kiwifruit mould; fractionally sweet, and better not so. **RATING** 88 **DRINK** Now $ 17

Kondole Cabernet Sauvignon 2001 Medium-bodied; black fruits and savoury edges; very persistent tannins, slightly out of balance. **RATING** 88 **DRINK** 2010 $ 22

Wharncliffe ★★★

Summerleas Road, Kingston, Tas 7050 **REGION** Southern Tasmania
T (03) 6229 7147 **F** (03) 6229 2298 **OPEN** Weekends by appointment, ph: 0438 297 147
WINEMAKER Andrew Hood (Contract) **EST.** 1990 **CASES** 125
SUMMARY With total plantings of 0.75 ha, Wharncliffe could not exist without the type of contract-winemaking service offered by Andrew Hood, which would be a pity, because the vineyard is beautifully situated on the doorstep of Mt Wellington, the Huon Valley and the Channel regions of southern Tasmania.

Whiskey Gully Wines ★★★

Beverley Road, Severnlea, Qld 4352 **REGION** Granite Belt
T (07) 4683 5100 **F** (07) 4683 5155 **WEB** www.whiskeygullywines.com.au **OPEN** 7 days 9–5
WINEMAKER Philippa Hambleton, Rod MacPherson (Contract) **EST.** 1997 **CASES** 500
SUMMARY Close inspection of the winery letterhead discloses that The Media Mill Pty Ltd trades as Whiskey Gully Wines. It is no surprise, then, to find proprietor John Arlidge saying, 'Wine and politics are a heady mix; I have already registered the 2000 Republic Red as a voter in 26 marginal electorates and we are considering nominating it for Liberal Party pre-selection in Bennelong.' Wit to one side, John Arlidge has big plans for Whiskey Gully Wines: to establish 40 ha of vineyards, extending the varietal range with petit verdot, malbec, merlot, semillon and sauvignon blanc. At present the wines are made offsite, but if production and sales increase significantly, onsite winemaking will be introduced.

▼▼▼▼ **Upper House Cabernet Sauvignon 2002** Light to medium-bodied; savoury, earthy, minty, leafy fruit is off-set by sweet vanilla oak. **RATING** 87 **DRINK** 2008 $ 26

Republic Red Cabernet Shiraz 2002 Medium-bodied; fractionally over-oaked, but has some nice mid-palate fruit; a touch of green leaf on the finish. **RATING** 87 **DRINK** 2009 $ 17

▼▼▼▽ **Nectar 2004** **RATING** 85 **DRINK** 2007 $ 35

▼▼▼ **Beverley Chardonnay 2002** **RATING** 83 $ 19

Zing 2004 **RATING** 82 $ 15

Whispering Brook ★★★☆

Hill Street, Broke, NSW 2330 **REGION** Lower Hunter Valley
T (02) 9818 4126 **F** (02) 9818 4156 **WEB** www.whispering-brook.com **OPEN** By appointment
WINEMAKER Jim Chatto (Shiraz), Susan Frazier, Steve Langham (Merlot) **EST.** 2000 **CASES** 900
SUMMARY Susan Frazier and Adam Bell say the choice of Whispering Brook was a result a of a 5-year search to find the ideal viticultural site (while studying for wine science degrees at Charles Sturt University). Some may wonder whether the Broke subregion of the Hunter Valley needed such

persistent effort to locate, but the property does in fact have a combination of terra rossa loam soils on which the reds are planted, and sandy flats for the white wines. The partners have also established an olive grove and accommodation for 6–14 guests in the large house set in the vineyard. Exports to the UK and South-East Asia.

ŸŸŸŸ **Shiraz 2003** Savoury, earthy, strongly regional aromas; opens up to red and black fruits on the palate; good length. Cork. **RATING** 89 **DRINK** 2010 $ 24

Merlot 2004 Positive varietal character through the bouquet and palate; appealing, light to medium-bodied mix of sweet berry fruits and olive. Cork. **RATING** 89 **DRINK** 2010 $ 22

Whispering Hills   ★★★★

580 Warburton Highway, Seville, Vic 3139 **REGION** Yarra Valley
T (03) 5964 2822 **F** (03) 5964 2064 **WEB** www.whisperinghills.com.au **OPEN** 7 days 10–6
WINEMAKER Murray Lyons, MasterWineMakers (Contract) **EST.** 1985 **CASES** 1200
SUMMARY The minuscule production of Whispering Hills from its 3.5-ha vineyard is limited to four wines, which are sold through the cellar door and website. The Lyons family (Murray, Marie and Audrey) own and operate both the vineyard and the cellar door. Murray (with a degree in viticulture and oenology from Charles Sturt University) concentrates on the vineyard and winemaking, Marie (with a background in sales and marketing) and Audrey take care of the cellar door and distribution of the wines. The vineyard was established in 1985 (riesling, chardonnay and cabernet sauvignon), with further plantings in 1996, and some grafting in 2003. The cellar door was opened in January 2004, and a new winery is under construction.

ŸŸŸŸ♈ **Yarra Valley Cabernet Sauvignon 2003** Ripe cassis and blackcurrant fruit; smooth, supple mouthfeel; controlled oak and length. Cork. **RATING** 91 **DRINK** 2013 $ 25

Yarra Valley Chardonnay 2002 Medium green-yellow; light to medium-bodied; gentle melon, cashew and hazelnut mix; good mouthfeel and balance. Quality cork. **RATING** 90 **DRINK** 2008 $ 25

ŸŸŸŸ **Yarra Valley Pinot Noir 2003** Light-bodied; fresh red cherry and strawberry fruit off-set by savoury, spice nuances. Screwcap. **RATING** 88 **DRINK** 2008 $ 25

Yarra Valley Riesling 2004 Very pale; slightly muffled bouquet; apple, slate and mineral flavours bring the wine to life. Screwcap. **RATING** 87 **DRINK** 2009 $ 20

Whisson Lake   ★★★★☆

Lot 2, Gully Road, Carey Gully, SA 5144 **REGION** Adelaide Hills
T (08) 8390 1303 **F** (08) 8390 3822 **WEB** www.whissonlake.com **OPEN** By appointment
WINEMAKER Mark Whisson **EST.** 1985 **CASES** 400
SUMMARY Mark Whisson (a plant biochemist) is primarily a grapegrower, with 5 ha of close-planted, steep-sloped north-facing vineyard on Mt Carey in the Piccadilly Valley. Over the years small portions of the grape production have been vinified under the Whisson Lake label, initially by Roman Bratasiuk, then Dave Powell of Torbreck, but since 2002 by Mark Whisson. The wine has a consistent style, distinctly savoury, and ages well. His partners in the venture are Bruce Lake (a Perth-based engineer) and Bill Bisset, who has helped broaden the the business base to include Pinot Gaz (an early-drinking Pinot), Shiraz from the Adelaide Hills, and Grenache from Blewitt Springs. Tiny quantities are exported to the US and the UK.

ŸŸŸŸŸ **Piccadilly Valley Pinot Noir 2002** Good hue; fragrant and spicy aroma; intense and long palate; lovely plum and spice fruit; fine, ripe tannins; by far the best to date from Whisson Lake. Cork. **RATING** 94 **DRINK** 2010 $ 35

ŸŸŸŸ **Pinot Gaz 2001** Very savoury, spicy, foresty style; a whisk of game; lemony finish. Very confusing message from the label design and name. Cork. **RATING** 87 **DRINK** Now $ 24

Whistler Wines   ★★★★

Seppeltsfield Road, Marananga, SA 5355 **REGION** Barossa Valley
T (08) 8562 4942 **F** (08) 8562 4943 **WEB** www.whistlerwines.com **OPEN** 7 days 10.30–5
WINEMAKER Troy Kalleske, Christa Deans (Contract) **EST.** 1999 **CASES** 3500
SUMMARY Whistler Wines had a dream start at the 2000 Barossa Valley Wine Show, when its 2000 Semillon won trophies for the Best Dry White and for the Most Outstanding Barossa White Table

Wine. Add to that the distinguished US importer Weygandt-Metzler, and it is no surprise to find the sold out sign going up on the extremely attractive (modern) galvanised iron cellar door building. The operation is presently based on 5 ha of shiraz, 2 ha each of semillon and merlot and 1 ha of cabernet sauvignon, with an additional 4 ha of grenache, mourvedre and riesling planted in 2001. The hope is to gradually increase production to match existing demand. Exports to the US and Canada.

Whistle Stop Wines ★★★

8 Elk Street, Nanango, Qld 4615 **REGION** South Burnett
T (07) 4163 2222 **F** (07) 4163 2288 **WEB** www.whistlestop.com.au **OPEN** Thurs–Mon 10–5
WINEMAKER Blair Duncan (Symphony Hill) **EST.** 1998 **CASES** 400
SUMMARY Terry and Margaret Walsh are the fourth generation to have carried on farming on the property settled by their ancestor John Walsh in 1861. The location of the cellar door, a renovated 1937 cottage in the town of Nanango, gave rise to the name, as it is next to a railway line which operated between 1911 and 1964. The wines are made from 1.5 ha of cabernet sauvignon (and 0.5 ha of recently grafted verdelho) and from purchased grapes. They are available through the cellar door, and at the Whistle Stop Bottle Shop in the Sheraton Hotel, Brisbane.

♥♥♥♥ **Verdelho 2004** Clean, crisp and tangy; no phenolics; good length and balance; thoroughly impressive. **RATING** 88 **DRINK** 2007 $ 16

♥♥♥♡ **Cabernet Sauvignon 2002 RATING** 85 **DRINK** Now $ 15.50

Whitehorse Wines NR

4 Reid Park Road, Mt Clear, Vic 3350 **REGION** Ballarat
T (03) 5330 1719 **F** (03) 5330 1288 **OPEN** Weekends 11–5
WINEMAKER Noel Myers **EST.** 1981 **CASES** 900
SUMMARY The Myers family has moved from grapegrowing to winemaking, using the attractive site on its sloping hillside south of Ballarat. There are 4 ha of vines in production, with pinot noir and chardonnay the principal varieties.

Whitsend Estate ★★★

52 Boundary Road, Coldstream, Vic 3770 **REGION** Yarra Valley
T (03) 9739 1917 **F** (03) 9739 0217 **WEB** www.whitsend.com.au **OPEN** By appointment
WINEMAKER Paul Evans **EST.** 1998 **CASES** 500
SUMMARY The Baldwin family, headed by Ross and Simone, but with Trish, Tim and Jenny all involved in one way or another, have planted a 13-ha vineyard to pinot noir, shiraz, merlot and cabernet sauvignon. Most of the production is sold to local wineries; a small amount is retained for the Baldwins. Exports to the US and Canada.

♥♥♥♥ **Merlot 2003** Strongly varietal olive, fern and briar with a background touch of mint; persistent palate and length. Diam. **RATING** 88 **DRINK** 2010 $ 25

♥♥♥♡ **Chardonnay 2004 RATING** 85 **DRINK** Now $ 24
Cabernet Sauvignon 2003 RATING 84 $ 25

Wignalls Wines ★★★★

Chester Pass Road (Highway 1), Albany, WA 6330 **REGION** Albany
T (08) 9841 2848 **F** (08) 9842 9003 **OPEN** 7 days 11–4
WINEMAKER Rob Wignall **EST.** 1982 **CASES** 6000
SUMMARY A noted producer of Pinot Noir which has extended the map for the variety in Australia. The Pinots have shown style and flair, but do age fairly quickly. The white wines are elegant, and show the cool climate to good advantage. A winery was constructed and opened for the 1998 vintage, using the production from the 16 ha of estate plantings. Exports to the UK, the US, Japan, Singapore and Indonesia.

♥♥♥♥♡ **Sauvignon Blanc 2004** Fresh and expressive varietal character throughout; sweet kiwifruit and passionfruit; good acidity. **RATING** 91 **DRINK** Now $ 16

♥♥♥♡ **Unwooded Chardonnay 2004 RATING** 86 **DRINK** 2007 $ 16

Wildcroft Estate   NR

98 Stanleys Road, Red Hill South, Vic 3937 **REGION** Mornington Peninsula
T (03) 5989 2646 **F** (03) 9783 9469 **OPEN** 7 days 10–5
WINEMAKER Phillip Jones (Bass Phillip) **EST.** 1988 **CASES** 650
SUMMARY Wildcroft Estate is the brainchild of Devendra Singh, best known as the owner of one of
Victoria's oldest Indian restaurants. In 1988 he purchased the land upon which 4 ha of pinot noir,
chardonnay, shiraz and cabernet sauvignon have been established, with the management and much
of the physical work carried out by Devendra's wife Shashi Singh, who is currently undertaking a
viticulture course. The vineyard is one of the few unirrigated vineyards on the Peninsula. The
mudbrick cellar door also has a restaurant – Café 98 – allowing Devendra Singh to explore the
matching of Indian food with wine. Chef Lindsey Perry serves modern cuisine with Indian and
Middle Eastern influences, using local produce wherever possible.

Wild Dog   NR

South Road, Warragul, Vic 3820 **REGION** Gippsland
T (03) 5623 1117 **F** (03) 5623 6402 **WEB** www.winesofgippsland.com **OPEN** 7 days 9–5
WINEMAKER John Farrington **EST.** 1982 **CASES** 3500
SUMMARY An aptly named winery which produces somewhat rustic wines from the 12 ha of estate
vineyards; even the Farringtons say that the Shiraz comes 'with a bite', but they also point out that
there is minimal handling, fining and filtration.

Wild Duck Creek Estate   NR

Spring Flat Road, Heathcote, Vic 3523 **REGION** Heathcote
T (03) 5433 3133 **F** (03) 5433 3133 **OPEN** By appointment
WINEMAKER David Anderson **EST.** 1980 **CASES** 4000
SUMMARY The first release of Wild Duck Creek Estate from the 1991 vintage marked the end of
12 years of effort by David and Diana Anderson. They began planting the 4.5-ha vineyard in 1980,
made their first tiny quantities of wine in 1986, the first commercial quantities of wine in 1991, and
built their winery and cellar door facility in 1993. Exports to the US (where Duck Muck has become a
cult wine), Canada, the UK, Singapore, Belgium and New Zealand.

Wild Soul   ★★★

Horans Gorge Road, Glen Aplin, Qld 4381 **REGION** Granite Belt
T (07) 4683 4201 **F** (07) 4683 4201 **WEB** www.wildsoul.netfirms.com **OPEN** Weekends & public
hols 10–4
WINEMAKER Andy Boullier **EST.** 1995 **CASES** 200
SUMMARY Andy and Beth Boullier have been on the land their whole lives, in various capacities,
before buying their small property at Glen Aplin. They have established a little over 1 ha of vines,
more or less equally split between cabernet sauvignon and shiraz, with a little merlot. They use
organic principles in growing the fruit; which is a challenge for themselves, compounded by birds,
drought, kangaroos and bushfires. Andy Boullier makes the wine onsite.

Wildwood   ★★★★

St John's Lane, Wildwood, Bulla, Vic 3428 **REGION** Sunbury
T (03) 9307 1118 **F** (03) 9331 1590 **WEB** www.wildwoodvineyards.com.au **OPEN** 7 days 10–6
WINEMAKER Dr Wayne Stott, Kirk Macdonald **EST.** 1983 **CASES** 800
SUMMARY Wildwood is just 4 km past Melbourne airport, at an altitude of 130m in the Oaklands
Valley, which provides unexpected views back to Port Phillip Bay and the Melbourne skyline. Plastic
surgeon Dr Wayne Stott has taken what is very much a part-time activity rather more seriously than
most by undertaking (and completing) the wine science degree at Charles Sturt University. Four
years of drought has cut production and forced the early release of the red wines.

 Shiraz 2002 Aromatic spicy, peppery, sweet raspberry and blackberry fruit; elegant,
medium-bodied, with fine, silky tannins and balanced oak. Cork. **RATING** 93 **DRINK** 2012
$ 25

Chardonnay 2004 Super-fine, elegant citrus and stone fruit; subtle hint of French oak; good length. Screwcap. **RATING** 92 **DRINK** 2010 $ 20

Pinot Noir 2003 Very ripe, sweet, rounded plummy fruit; while it shows 14.6° alcohol, is not jammy, simply crammed with flavour. Screwcap. **RATING** 91 **DRINK** 2009 $ 25

ŸŸŸ **Cabernet Sauvignon 2002 RATING** 81 $ 25

Wildwood of Yallingup ★★★★

Caves Road, Yallingup, WA 6282 **REGION** Margaret River
T (08) 9755 2066 **F** (08) 9754 1389 **OPEN** 7 days 10–5
WINEMAKER James Pennington **EST.** 1984 **CASES** 3000
SUMMARY In the wake of the demise of the Hotham Valley wine group, and its subsequent restructuring and renaming, James Pennington acquired the 5.5-ha Wildwood vineyard, planted in the mid-1980s, having been first cleared in the late 1940s. The vineyard was established without irrigation and remains dry-grown. All the future releases will be under the Wildwood of Yallingup label or Pennington.

ŸŸŸŸŸ **Margaret River Shiraz 2002** Spicy, fresh red and black cherry and plum; light to medium-bodied; supple and smooth; nice tannins. Diam. **RATING** 90 **DRINK** 2012 $ 18

ŸŸŸŸ **Margaret River Unwooded Chardonnay 2004** Bright colour; fragrant citrus and melon; tangy, long and fresh; the exception proves the rule. Screwcap. **RATING** 89 **DRINK** 2007 $ 16

Margaret River Semillon Sauvignon Blanc 2004 Rounded, gently tropical fruit; Sauvignon Blanc-driven; soft, ready now. Screwcap. **RATING** 87 **DRINK** Now $ 16

Wilkie Estate NR

Lot 1, Heaslip Road, Penfield, SA 5121 **REGION** Adelaide Plains
T (08) 8284 7655 **F** (08) 8284 7618 **OPEN** 7 days 10–5
WINEMAKER Trevor Spurr **EST.** 1990 **CASES** NA
SUMMARY Trevor and Bill Spurr have 17.5 ha of organic-certified vineyards planted to verdelho, cabernet sauvignon, merlot and ruby cabernet. They make the wine onsite, and, in addition to cellar door sales and mail order, have established exports to England and Japan.

Willespie ★★★☆

Harmans Mill Road, Wilyabrup via Cowaramup, WA 6284 **REGION** Margaret River
T (08) 9755 6248 **F** (08) 9755 6210 **WEB** www.willespie.com.au **OPEN** 7 days 10.30–5
WINEMAKER Kevin Squance **EST.** 1976 **CASES** 10 000
SUMMARY Willespie has produced many attractive white wines over the years, typically in brisk, herbaceous Margaret River style. All are fruit rather than oak-driven; the newer Merlot also shows promise. The wines have had such success that the Squance family (which founded and owns Willespie) has substantially increased winery capacity, drawing upon an additional 26 ha of estate vineyards now in bearing. Exports to the UK, the US, Brazil, Hong Kong and Singapore.

ŸŸŸŸŸ **Winery Block Reserve Cabernet Sauvignon 1997** Pleasant, largely mature wine; savoury/earthy overtones to black fruits; fine tannin structure. Museum release. **RATING** 90 **DRINK** 2007 $ 50

ŸŸŸŸ **Verdelho 2001 RATING** 85 **DRINK** Now $ 1750

William Downie Wines ★★★★

PO Box 1024, Healesville, Vic 3777 **REGION** Yarra Valley
T 0400 654 512 **F** (03) 5962 6630 **OPEN** Not
WINEMAKER William Downie **EST.** 2003 **CASES** 300
SUMMARY William Downie spends 6 months each year making wine in Burgundy, the other 6 based in the Yarra Valley with De Bortoli. He uses purchased grapes from older vines to make the wines, avoiding the use of pumps, filtration and fining. The striking label, designed by artist Reg Mombassa, has helped obtain listings at The Prince Wine Store, Europa Cellars, The Healesville Hotel, Grossi Florentino, Pearl and Cecconi's, all icon Melbourne and local establishments.

ℙℙℙℙ℘ **Yarra Valley Pinot Noir 2003** Attractive light to medium-bodied Pinot; spice, plum and black cherry mix; moderately sweet fruit overall; fine ripe tannins, good oak. Stained cork. **RATING** 91 **DRINK** 2008

Williams Springs Road

NR

76 Dauncey Street, Kingscote, Kangaroo Island, SA 5223 **REGION** Kangaroo Island
T (08) 8553 2053 **F** (08) 8553 3042 **OPEN** By appointment
WINEMAKER Contract **EST.** 1995 **CASES** 500
SUMMARY Roger and Kate Williams have established 11 ha of chardonnay, cabernet sauvignon, shiraz and petit verdot. Most of the grapes are sold to Kangaroo Island Trading Co.; a small amount of Chardonnay and Shiraz are made under the Williams Springs Road label.

Willow Bridge Estate

Gardin Court Drive, Dardanup, WA 6236 **REGION** Geographe
T (08) 9728 0055 **F** (08) 9728 0066 **WEB** www.willowbridgeestate.com **OPEN** 7 days 11–5
WINEMAKER David Crawford **EST.** 1997 **CASES** 40 000
SUMMARY The Dewar family has followed a fast track in developing Willow Bridge Estate since acquiring the spectacular 180-ha hillside property in the Ferguson Valley in 1996: 70 ha of chardonnay, semillon, sauvignon blanc, shiraz and cabernet sauvignon were planted, with tempranillo added in 2000. The winery is capable of handling the 1200 to 1500 tonnes from the estate plantings. Exports to the UK, France, Germany, the US, Canada, New Zealand, Japan and Hong Kong.

ℙℙℙℙℙ **Reserve Sauvignon Blanc 2004** Elegant, but intense and long; kiwifruit, gooseberry and passionfruit; lemony acidity, fresh finish. Cork. **RATING** 94 **DRINK** 2007 $ 20

ℙℙℙℙ℘ **Sauvignon Blanc Semillon 2004** A tight and fresh minerally backbone to gently ripe gooseberry and lime juice fruit; good finish. Screwcap. **RATING** 93 **DRINK** 2008 $ 14.50
The Black Dog Shiraz 2003 Complex, spicy, savoury, tangy cool-grown flavours; medium-bodied; integrated oak. Stained cork. **RATING** 91 **DRINK** 2015 $ 60
Reserve Shiraz 2003 Licorice, spice, black pepper, black cherry and plum aromas; medium-bodied; gently smooth, supple and sweet fruit palate; positive, fine tannins; hides 15.5° alcohol. Cork. **RATING** 91 **DRINK** 2012 $ 28

ℙℙℙℙ **Chardonnay 2004** Sweet stone fruit and melon aromas and flavours; clever winemaking with a hint of residual sugar masking the absence of oak. Screwcap. **RATING** 89 **DRINK** 2007 $ 14.50
Shiraz 2003 Medium-bodied; elegant spicy, savoury notes to gentle black fruits; light tannins. Cork. **RATING** 89 **DRINK** 2009 $ 15
Cabernet Sauvignon Rose 2004 Elegant, fine style; strawberry and cherry; crisp finish, good acidity. Screwcap. **RATING** 88 **DRINK** 2007 $ 17

ℙℙℙ℘ **Cabernet Sauvignon Merlot 2003** **RATING** 86 **DRINK** 2008 $ 15

Willow Creek

166 Balnarring Road, Merricks North, Vic 3926 **REGION** Mornington Peninsula
T (03) 5989 7448 **F** (03) 5989 7584 **WEB** www.willow-creek.com.au **OPEN** 7 days 10–5
WINEMAKER Phil Kerney **EST.** 1989 **CASES** 8000
SUMMARY Yet another significant player in the Mornington Peninsula area, with 12 ha of vines planted to cabernet sauvignon, chardonnay, pinot noir and sauvignon blanc. Expansion of the cellar door was completed in 1998, and the winery was constructed for the 1998 vintage. The restaurant is open for lunch 7 days and for dinner Fri–Sat. Wines are released under the Willow Creek and Tulum labels; exports to the US.

ℙℙℙℙℙ **Tulum Chardonnay 2003** Bright, light green-yellow; elegant and restrained, silky smooth, fine, melon and stone fruit; nuances of malolactic and barrel ferment do little more than support the fruit. Screwcap. **RATING** 95 **DRINK** 2010 $ 35
Tulum Chardonnay 2002 Pale straw-green; very intense, tight and powerful palate; nectarine and grapefruit have eaten the oak, and also the malolactic influence; very long future, in part thanks to screwcap. **RATING** 94 **DRINK** 2012 $ 35

Tulum Pinot Noir 2003 Light red-purple; intensely fragrant, spicy, tangy varietal fruit; delicate yet intense fruit floats across the tongue; excellent acidity. Screwcap. **RATING** 94 **DRINK** 2010 $ 35

Tulum Pinot Noir 2002 Light to medium red-purple; complex, savoury, spicy aromas; poised, focused and powerful spiced plum; long travel; very different style from the '03. Screwcap. **RATING** 94 **DRINK** 2010 $ 35

TTTTY **Sauvignon Blanc 2004** Clean, delicate, fresh and crisp touches of passionfruit caress the mouth; long finish. Screwcap. **RATING** 93 **DRINK** 2007 $ 25

TTTT **Chardonnay 2004** Fresh and lively citrussy stone fruit; unoaked, but has length and personality. Screwcap. **RATING** 88 **DRINK** 2007 $ 20

Pinot Saignee 2004 Light rose-pink; has length and mid-palate fruit grip; good acidity. **RATING** 88 **DRINK** Now $ 20

Willowvale Wines

NR

Black Swamp Road, Tenterfield, NSW 2372 **REGION** Northern Slopes Zone
T (02) 6736 3589 **F** (02) 6736 3753 **WEB** www.willowvalewines.com.au **OPEN** 7 days 9–5
WINEMAKER John Morley **EST.** 1994 **CASES** 1200
SUMMARY John and Lyn Morley began establishing 1.8 ha of vineyard, with equal portions of chardonnay, merlot and cabernet sauvignon, in 1994; there were further planting in 1999 and 2000. The vineyard is at an altitude of 940m, and was the first in the Tenterfield region. Advanced vineyard climatic monitoring systems have been installed, and a new winery building was constructed and equipped in 2000.

Wills Domain Vineyard

★★★★

35 Ash Grove, Duncraig, WA 6023 (postal) **REGION** Margaret River
T (08) 9755 2172 **F** (08) 9755 2172 **OPEN** Not
WINEMAKER Bruce Dukes (Contract) **EST.** 2000 **CASES** 5200
SUMMARY Another newcomer to the Margaret River, with a little over 10 ha of semillon, chardonnay, viognier, cabernet sauvignon, merlot, malbec, shiraz, cabernet franc and petit verdot under the control of Darren Haunold. The wines are sold by mail order and through a few retail outlets.

TTTTY **Semillon 2003** Live, tangy and aromatic; sweet fruit edges, but finishes dry; lots of character and complexity. **RATING** 91 **DRINK** 2007 $ 19

Will Taylor Wines

★★★★☆

1B Victoria Avenue, Unley Park, SA 5061 **REGION** Southeast Australia
T (08) 8271 6122 **F** (08) 8271 6122 **OPEN** By appointment
WINEMAKER Various contract **EST.** 1997 **CASES** 1500
SUMMARY Will Taylor is a partner in the leading Adelaide law firm Finlaysons, and specialises in wine law. He and Suzanne Taylor have established a classic negociant wine business, having wines contract-made to their specifications. Moreover, they choose what they consider the best regions for each variety. Most of the wine is sold to restaurants, with small volumes sold to a select group of fine wine stores and by mail order. Exports to the US.

TTTTY **Coonawarra Cabernet Sauvignon 2003** Aromatic and stylish; nicely ripened blackcurrant and earth in a varietal/region expression; good tannin, fruit and oak balance and very good mouthfeel. Quality cork. **RATING** 93 **DRINK** 2017 $ 40

Yarra Valley Geelong Pinot Noir 2003 Deep colour; strong, rich plum and oriental spice fruit; considerable depth; needs a few years. Good cork. **RATING** 92 **DRINK** 2009 $ 40

Hunter Valley Semillon 2004 Herb, spice, grass and lemon aromas; light to medium-bodied; well balanced; moderately early development in prospect. Screwcap. **RATING** 90 **DRINK** 2010 $ 21

TTTT **Clare Valley Riesling 2004** Like many '04 Clare Rieslings, not particularly intense; some early shutdown, too; light apple fruit and mineral backbone. May well emerge with more time. Screwcap. **RATING** 88 **DRINK** 2010 $ 21

🐌 Willy Bay ★★★☆

19 Third Avenue, Mt Lawley, WA 6050 (postal) **REGION** Geographe
T (08) 9271 9890 **F** (08) 9271 7771 **WEB** www.willybay.com.au **OPEN** Not
WINEMAKER Peter Stanlake **EST.** 2003 **CASES** 1000
SUMMARY Willy Bay Wines is jointly owned and run by the Siciliano and Edwards families. They have established 6.5 ha of shiraz, 2.8 ha of cabernet sauvignon and 1.7 ha of chardonnay. The wine styles are unusual – the Last Fling Cane Cut Cabernet Sauvignon, for example. One suspects that young vine influences are at work.

ꔷꔷꔷꔷ **Middle Stump Shiraz 2003** Very elegant style; savoury, spicy; light to medium-bodied, but balanced; long finish. **RATING** 88 **DRINK** 2009 $ 35
Pink Fling Rose 2004 Pale but bright pink; good balance of red fruits; pleasingly dry finish. **RATING** 87 **DRINK** Now $ 18

ꔷꔷꔷꔷ **Last Fling Cane Cut Cabernet Sauvignon 2004** **RATING** 86 **DRINK** Now $ 25

Wilmot Hills Vineyard NR

407 Back Road, Wilmot, Tas 7310 **REGION** Northern Tasmania
T (03) 6492 1193 **F** (03) 6492 1193 **WEB** www.wilmothills.tascom.net **OPEN** 7 days 9–7
WINEMAKER John Cole, Ruth Cole **EST.** 1991 **CASES** NA
SUMMARY The beautiful Wilmot Hills Vineyard is on the western side of Lake Barrington, not far from the Cradle Mountain road, with marvellous views to Mt Roland and the adjacent peaks. It is very much a family affair, and produces both wine and cider. John Cole spent 18 years in Melbourne in engineering design and some graphic art, and Ruth worked in the hospitality industry for 10 years and making fruit wines for 20 years. The neat onsite winery was designed and built by the Coles, as was much of the wine and cider-making equipment.

Wilson's Legana Vineyard ★★★

24 Vale Street, Prospect Vale, Tas 7250 **REGION** Northern Tasmania
T (03) 6344 8030 **F** (03) 6343 2937 **OPEN** By appointment
WINEMAKER Michael Wilson **EST.** 1966 **CASES** 150
SUMMARY After several changes in ownership, what was the original Legana Vineyard of Heemskerk is now owned by Michael and Mary Wilson, who have appended their name to the brand. Michael Wilson, with a viticulture course under his belt and a little home winemaking experience, has now taken on full responsibility for all aspects of the business.

ꔷꔷꔷꔷ **Unwooded Chardonnay 2004** Pleasing grapefruit flavours; good balance; vintage acidity controlled. **RATING** 88 **DRINK** 2007

ꔷꔷꔷꔷ **Cabernet 2002** **RATING** 85 **DRINK** 2007
Cabernet Sauvignon 2003 **RATING** 84 **DRINK** 2008

ꔷꔷꔷ **Pinot Noir 2002** **RATING** 83

Wilson Vineyard ★★★★★

Polish Hill River, Sevenhill via Clare, SA 5453 **REGION** Clare Valley
T (08) 8843 4310 **WEB** www.wilsonvineyard.com.au **OPEN** Weekends 10–4
WINEMAKER Dr John Wilson, Daniel Wilson **EST.** 1974 **CASES** 4000
SUMMARY Dr John Wilson is a tireless ambassador for the Clare Valley and for wine (and its beneficial effect on health) in general. His wines were made using techniques and philosophies garnered early in his wine career; they can occasionally be idiosyncratic, but in recent years have been most impressive. The wines are sold through the cellar door and an email mailing list, and retail in Sydney, Melbourne, Brisbane and Adelaide. Exports to the US.

ꔷꔷꔷꔷꔷ **Polish Hill River Riesling 2004** Bell-clear notes of spice, lime and mineral on the bouquet; the palate is very long, as is the lingering aftertaste. As with all these rieslings, bottle age will invest the wine with great complexity and texture. **RATING** 95 **DRINK** 2014 $ 22
DJW Riesling 2004 Glowing yellow-green; abundant lime juice and tropical aromas and flavours; a long, linear palate and finish. **RATING** 94 **DRINK** 2014 $ 22

ŶŶŶŶ **Polish Hill River Merlot 2001** RATING 85 DRINK Now $16
Leaucothea NV RATING 85 DRINK 2007 $21

Wily Trout

Marakei–Nanima Road, via Hall, NSW 2618 **REGION** Canberra District
T (02) 6230 2487 **F** (02) 6230 2211 **WEB** www.wilytrout.com.au **OPEN** 7 days 10–5
WINEMAKER Dr Roger Harris, Andrew McEwen (Contract) **EST.** 1998 **CASES** 2750
SUMMARY The 20-ha Wily Trout vineyard shares its home with the Poachers Pantry, a renowned
gourmet smokehouse. Thus the Smokehouse Café doubles as a tasting room and a cellar door. The
quality of the wines is very good, and a testament to the skills of the contract winemakers. The
northeast-facing slopes, at an elevation of 720m, provide some air drainage and hence protection
against spring frosts.

ŶŶŶŶ **Canberra District Sauvignon Blanc 2004** Clean, fresh, crisp and correct; a mix of herb
and grass and more tropical counter-notes; good length. Screwcap. **RATING** 89 **DRINK** 2007
$25.20
Canberra District Cabernet Sauvignon Merlot 2003 Fresh, fruit-driven style; light-
bodied; blackcurrant and cassis; minimal tannin/oak contribution. Screwcap. **RATING** 87
DRINK 2009

ŶŶŶŶ **Canberra District Merlot 2003** RATING 86 DRINK 2008 $30.60
Canberra District Chardonnay 2004 RATING 85 DRINK 2007 $20.70
Canberra District Shiraz 2003 RATING 85 DRINK 2007 $30.60

Wimbaliri Wines

Barton Highway, Murrumbateman, NSW 2582 **REGION** Canberra District
T (02) 6227 5921 **F** (02) 6227 5921 **OPEN** 7 days 10–5
WINEMAKER John Andersen **EST.** 1988 **CASES** 700
SUMMARY John and Margaret Andersen moved to the Canberra district in 1987 and began establishing
their vineyard at Murrumbateman in 1988; the property borders highly regarded Canberra
producers Doonkuna and Clonakilla. The vineyard is close-planted with a vertical trellis system, with
a total of 2.2 ha planted to chardonnay, pinot noir, shiraz, cabernet sauvignon and merlot (plus a few
vines of cabernet franc).

ŶŶŶŶ **Gravel Block Shiraz 2003** Powerful black fruits; savoury/earthy elements add to the
structure; fine, firm tannins. Seriously stained cork. **RATING** 88 **DRINK** 2010 $24
Chardonnay 2003 Glowing yellow-gold; complex and developed; sweet butterscotch
overtones to yellow peach. Cork. **RATING** 87 **DRINK** Now $20

ŶŶŶŶ **Pinot Noir 2003** Strong structure, tending towards dry red; savoury foresty black fruits.
RATING 86 **DRINK** 2008 $24

Winbirra Vineyard

★★★

173 Point Leo Road, Red Hill South, Vic 3937 **REGION** Mornington Peninsula
T (03) 5989 2109 **F** (03) 5989 2109 **WEB** www.winbirravineyards.com.au **OPEN** 1st weekend each
month & public hols 10.30–5.30, or by appointment
WINEMAKER Sandro Mosele (Contract) **EST.** 1990 **CASES** 800
SUMMARY Winbirra is a small, family-owned and run vineyard which has been producing grapes
since 1990, between then and 1997 selling the grapes to local winemakers. Since 1997 the wine has
been made and sold under the Winbirra label. There is 1.5 ha of pinot noir (with three clones) at
Merricks and 1.5 ha on a second site at Merricks South.

ŶŶŶŶ **Southern Basalt Pinot Melange 2003** Deep colour; powerful, spicy, briary, woodsy;
some plum; slightly extractive finish. Cork. **RATING** 87 **DRINK** 2008 $15.50

ŶŶŶ **Pinot Rose 2004** RATING 83 $13

Winbourne Wines

Bunnan Road, Scone, NSW 2337 **REGION** Upper Hunter Valley
T 0417 650 0834 **F** (02) 6545 1636 **WEB** www.winbournewines.com **OPEN** By appointment
WINEMAKER John Hordern, Stephen Hagan, Michael De Iuliis **EST.** 1996 **CASES** 3000
SUMMARY A legal contemporary of mine, whom I have known for 40 years, is one of the faces behind
Winbourne Wines. He still practises law at his law firm in Muswellbrook, but has also established a
little under 50 ha of vineyards planted to semillon, chardonnay, verdelho, shiraz, merlot and cabernet
sauvignon. Most of the production is sold as grapes, a little made into wine. Says David White, 'it
could well be wondered why we are doing – have done – this'. I guess it simply proves that old lawyers
are not necessarily wise lawyers.

Winburndale

116 Saint Anthony's Creek Road, Bathurst, NSW 2795 **REGION** Central Ranges Zone
T (02) 6337 3134 **F** (02) 6337 3134 **WEB** www.winburndalewines.com.au **OPEN** By appointment
WINEMAKER Mark Renzaglia, David Lowe (Consultant) **EST.** 1998 **CASES** 2500
SUMMARY Michael Burleigh and family acquired the 200-ha Winburndale property in September
1998: 160 ha is forest, to be kept as a nature reserve; three separate vineyards, each with its own site
characteristics, have been planted under the direction of viticulturist Mark Renzaglia. The winery
paddock has 2.5 ha of shiraz facing due west at an altitude of 800–820m; the south paddock, with
north and northwest aspects, varying from 790–810m, has chardonnay (1.2 ha), shiraz (1 ha) and
cabernet sauvignon (3.5 ha). The home paddock is the most level, with a slight north aspect, and with
1.2 ha each of merlot and cabernet franc. The name, incidentally, derives from Lachlan Macquarie's
exploration of the Blue Mountains in 1815. Exports to the US and Denmark.

ŸŸŸŸŸ **Solitary Shiraz 2003** Vibrant, fresh, spicy, tangy cool-climate style; balanced and
integrated oak; fine, silky tannins; 13.8° alcohol. Impressive. **RATING** 90 **DRINK** 2013 $30

ŸŸŸŸ **Alluvial Chardonnay 2004** Melon fruit; appreciable sweetness on the finish, but skilfully
handled. Screwcap. **RATING** 86 **DRINK** Now $25
Lost & Found Shiraz Cabernet 2003 RATING 85 **DRINK** 2007 $15

Windance Wines

★★★★

Lot 12, Loc 589, Caves Road, Yallingup, WA 6282 **REGION** Margaret River
T (08) 9755 2293 **F** (08) 9755 2293 **WEB** www.windance.com.au **OPEN** 7 days 10–5
WINEMAKER Janice McDonald **EST.** 1998 **CASES** 3400
SUMMARY Drew and Rosemary Brent-White own this family business, situated 5 km south of
Yallingup. A little over 6.5 ha of sauvignon blanc, shiraz, merlot and cabernet sauvignon have been
established, incorporating sustainable land management and organic farming practices where
possible. The wines are exclusively estate-grown, and are sold through the cellar door and Perth CBD
outlets serviced directly from the winery.

ŸŸŸŸŸ **Cabernet Merlot 2003** Powerful, concentrated blackcurrant and blackberry; medium to
full-bodied; persistent tannins, long future. Screwcap. **RATING** 92 **DRINK** 2018 $16
Shiraz 2003 Elegant, medium-bodied spicy blackberry mix; fine tannins, controlled oak.
Screwcap. **RATING** 90 **DRINK** 2012 $20

ŸŸŸŸ **Sauvignon Blanc 2004 RATING** 84 **DRINK** Now $15

Windarra

NR

De Beyers Road, Pokolbin, NSW 2321 **REGION** Lower Hunter Valley
T (02) 4998 7648 **F** (02) 4998 7648 **OPEN** Tues–Sun 10–5
WINEMAKER Tom Andresen-Jung **EST.** 1985 **CASES** 2500
SUMMARY The Andresen family has 6 ha of semillon, chardonnay and shiraz. The exotic array of
fortified wines are likely to come from further afield; they are aimed at the tourist market.

Windermere Wines   NR

Lot 3, Watters Road, Ballandean, Qld 4382 **REGION** Granite Belt
T (07) 4684 1353 **F** (07) 4684 1353 **OPEN** 7 days 9.30–5
WINEMAKER Wayne Beecham, Kate Beecham **EST.** 1995 **CASES** 500
SUMMARY After spending 3 years travelling in Europe (1983–86), Wayne Beecham returned to
Australia to take up a position with what was then Thomas Hardy Wines, specifically to establish
the RhineCastle wine distribution in Queensland. He studied wine marketing at Roseworthy while
working for Hardys, but in 1993 he, wife Julie and daughter Kate decided to move to the Granite
Belt to establish Windermere Wines from the ground up. His long service with Hardys stood him in
good stead, landing him a cellar position at Hardys Tintara in the 1994 vintage, working with
winemaker David O'Leary. In typical Australian fashion, Wayne Beecham says they decided on the
Granite Belt because, 'if we were to succeed, we might as well do it in the toughest new region in the
industry'.

Windowrie Estate

Windowrie, Canowindra, NSW 2804 **REGION** Cowra
T (02) 6344 3234 **F** (02) 6344 3227 **WEB** www.windowrie.com.au **OPEN** At the Mill, Vaux Street, Cowra
WINEMAKER John Holmes **EST.** 1988 **CASES** 70 000
SUMMARY Windowrie Estate was established in 1988 on a substantial grazing property at
Canowindra, 30 km north of Cowra and in the same viticultural region. A portion of the grapes from
the 116-ha vineyard are sold to other makers, but increasing quantities are being made for the
Windowrie Estate and The Mill labels; the Chardonnays have enjoyed show success. The cellar door
is in a flour mill built in 1861 from local granite. It ceased operations in 1905 and lay unoccupied for
91 years until restored by the O'Dea family. The quality of recent releases has seen production double
to 70 000 cases. Exports to the UK, the US and other major markets.

** TTTTY Family Reserve Shiraz 2002** Excellent varietal character and fruit concentration; ripe
plum and blackberry; no dead fruit or over-extraction. Cork. **RATING** 90 **DRINK** 2012 **$** 26
Family Reserve Cabernet Sauvignon 2002 Pure varietal cassis and blackcurrant fruit;
medium-bodied; long and balanced palate. **RATING** 90 **DRINK** 2012 **$** 26

TTTT The Mill Cabernet Merlot 2003 Good structure and texture; positive, not aggressive
tannins; overall savoury, but enough black fruits. Cork. **RATING** 87 **DRINK** 2008 **$** 14
The Mill Cowra Petit Verdot 2003 Clean, sweet, raspberry, redcurrant and blackcurrant
on entry; strong tannins to close. **RATING** 87 **DRINK** 2008 **$** 14

TTTY The Mill Cowra Sangiovese 2003 Light to medium-bodied; sweet fruit, then a slight
break in line; savoury, spicy tannins. **RATING** 86 **DRINK** 2007 **$** 14
The Mill Cowra Verdelho 2004 RATING 85 **DRINK** Now **$** 14
The Mill Shiraz 2003 RATING 84 **DRINK** 2007 **$** 14

Windsors Edge   NR

McDonalds Road, Pokolbin, NSW 2320 **REGION** Lower Hunter Valley
T (02) 4998 7737 **F** (02) 4998 7341 **WEB** www.windsorsedge.com.au **OPEN** Fri–Mon 10–5, or by
appointment
WINEMAKER Tim Windsor, Jessie Windsor **EST.** 1996 **CASES** 1500
SUMMARY In 1995 Tim Windsor (a Charles Sturt winemaking graduate) and wife Jessie (an industrial
chemist) purchased the old Black Creek picnic racetrack at the northern end of McDonalds Road in
Pokolbin. The first vines were planted in 1996, and planting has continued: to date, 17 ha of shiraz,
semillon, chardonnay, tempranillo, tinta cao and touriga are in the ground. Three luxury cottages
have been built, followed by a restaurant and cellar door, and a small winery.

Windy Creek Estate   NR

27 Stock Road, Herne Hill, WA 6056 **REGION** Swan Valley
T (08) 9296 4210 **OPEN** Tues–Sun 11–5
WINEMAKER Tony Cobanov, Tony Roe **EST.** 1960 **CASES** 10 000
SUMMARY A substantial family-owned operation (previously known as Cobanov Wines) producing a
mix of bulk and bottled wine from 21 ha of estate grapes. Part of the annual production is sold as

grapes to other producers, including Houghton; part is sold in bulk; part is sold in 2-litre flagons, and the remainder in modestly priced bottles.

Windy Ridge Vineyard ★★★★

Foster–Fish Creek Road, Foster, Vic 3960 **REGION** Gippsland
T (03) 5682 2035 **WEB** www.windyridgewinery.com.au **OPEN** Holiday weekends 10–5
WINEMAKER Graeme Wilson **EST.** 1978 **CASES** 300
SUMMARY The 2.8-ha Windy Ridge Vineyard was planted between 1978 and 1986, with the first vintage not taking place until 1988. Winemaker Graeme Wilson favours prolonged maturation, part in stainless steel and part in oak, before bottling his wines, typically giving the Pinot Noir 3 years and the Cabernet 2 years.

TTTT **Pinot Noir 2001** Light to medium-bodied; elegant, savoury, spicy style; restrained plum fruit, but neither green nor stemmy. Gold Winewise Small Winemakers '04. Cork.
RATING 90 **DRINK** 2007 **$** 35

Wine & Truffle Company NR

PO Box 611, Mt Hawthorn, WA 6915 **REGION** Pemberton
T (08) 9228 0328 **WEB** www.wineandtruffle.com.au **OPEN** Not
WINEMAKER Mark Aitken **EST.** 1996 **CASES** NA
SUMMARY The name precisely describes this unusual venture. It is owned by a group of investors from various parts of Australia who share the common vision of producing fine wines and black truffles. The winemaking side is under the care of Mark Aitken, who, having graduated as dux of his class in applied science at Curtin University in 2000, joined Chestnut Grove as assistant winemaker in February 2002. He now is contract maker for the Wine & Truffle Company, as well as working for Chestnut Grove. The truffle side of the business is under the care of former CSIRO scientist Dr Nicholas Malajcsuk. He has overseen the planting of 13,000 truffle-inoculated hazelnut and oak trees on the property. As a sign of faith, he is actively involved in the day-to-day monitoring of the trees as well as the management of the dog training and truffle hunting program.

wine by brad ★★★☆

PO Box 475, Margaret River, WA 6285 **REGION** Margaret River
T (08) 9757 2957 **F** (08) 9757 3701 **WEB** www.winebybrad.com.au **OPEN** Not
WINEMAKER Various (Contract) **EST.** 2003 **CASES** 1100
SUMMARY Brad Wehr says that wine by brad, 'is the result of a couple of influential winemakers and shadowy ruffians deciding that there was something to be gained by putting together some pretty neat parcels of wine from the region, creating their own label, releasing it with minimal fuss, and then remaining anonymous for fear of reprisals'. This, therefore, is another version of the virtual winery, with sales by email and through the website.

TTTT **Margaret River Semillon Sauvignon Blanc 2004** Clean, intense and focused; gooseberry, passionfruit, asparagus and lemon; crisp, lively finish. The wine appeals more than the label. Screwcap. **RATING** 92 **DRINK** 2008 **$** 16.95

TTTT **Margaret River Semillon Sauvignon Blanc 2003** **RATING** 86 **DRINK** Now **$** 16.95
Cabernet Merlot 2001 **RATING** 86 **DRINK** 2008 **$** 16.95

Wine Trust Estates ★★★☆

PO Box 541, Balgowlah, NSW 2093 **REGION** Southeast Australia
T (02) 9949 9250 **F** (02) 9907 8179 **WEB** www.winetrustestates.com **OPEN** Not
WINEMAKER Various Contract **EST.** 1999 **CASES** 5000
SUMMARY Mark Arnold is the man behind Wine Trust Estates; he draws on a lifetime of experience in wine marketing. It is a virtual winery operation, using grapes from various parts of Australia, and contract winemakers according to the grapes. The top-of-the-range red wines come from the Limestone Coast. The wines are available through a number of outlets in Sydney, and are also exported.

▼▼▼▼ Picarus Mount Benson Cabernet Sauvignon 2002 Extremely ripe fruit; concentrated; a hint of what seems to have been a long time held in stainless steel. **RATING** 89 **DRINK** 2014
Picarus Wrattonbully Shiraz 2002 Rich, juicy berry style; nice up-front and mid-palate flavour; trails away on the finish. **RATING** 88 **DRINK** 2009
Ocean Grove Shiraz 2002 Plenty of substance and extract; red and black fruits; good tannins and length; gold medal Australian Inland Wine Show 2004. **RATING** 87 **DRINK** 2008 $ 12

▼▼▼▽ Ocean Grove Semillon Sauvignon Blanc 2004 RATING 85 **DRINK** Now $ 12

Winewood

NR

Sundown Road, Ballandean, Qld 4382 **REGION** Granite Belt
T (07) 4684 1187 **F** (07) 4684 1187 **OPEN** Weekends & public hols 9–5
WINEMAKER Ian Davis **EST.** 1984 **CASES** 1000
SUMMARY A weekend and holiday activity for schoolteacher Ian Davis and town-planner wife Jeanette; the tiny winery is a model of neatness and precision planning. The use of marsanne with chardonnay and semillon shows an interesting change in direction. Has 4.5 ha of estate plantings, having added shiraz and viognier. All wine is sold through the cellar door; tutored tastings available.

Winstead

★★★★☆

75 Winstead Road, Bagdad, Tas 7030 **REGION** Southern Tasmania
T (03) 6268 6417 **F** (03) 6268 6417 **OPEN** By appointment
WINEMAKER Neil Snare **EST.** 1989 **CASES** 350
SUMMARY The good news about Winstead is the outstanding quality of its extremely generous and rich Pinot Noirs, rivalling those of Freycinet for the abundance of their fruit flavour without any sacrifice of varietal character. The bad news is that production is so limited, with only 0.8 ha of pinot noir and 0.4 ha riesling being tended by fly-fishing devotee Neil Snare and wife Julieanne. Retail distribution in Melbourne.

▼▼▼▼▼ Reserve Pinot Noir 2002 Deep colour; complex, rich, intense black plums, forest and spice; very good balance and length. **RATING** 95 **DRINK** 2010
Pinot Noir 2002 Dense, powerful, complex and potent; Leroy (Burgundy) style; masses of flavour and length. Still developing. **RATING** 94 **DRINK** 2013

▼▼▼▼▽ Pinot Noir 2003 Full-on ripe style; plenty of plush, plummy fruit; good length and balance. **RATING** 92 **DRINK** 2010
Ensnared Riesling 2004 Interesting wine, with slightly left of centre spicy notes; very intense and long. **RATING** 91 **DRINK** 2009

▼▼▽ Riesling 2004 RATING 79

Winya Wines

NR

145 Sandy Creek Road, Kilcoy, Qld 4515 (postal) **REGION** Queensland Zone
T (07) 5497 1504 **F** (07) 5497 1504 **WEB** www.winyawines.com.au **OPEN** Not
WINEMAKER Craig Robinson (Contract) **EST.** 1997 **CASES** 350
SUMMARY Gary and Susanne Pratten have established 2 ha of merlot and malbec in the Somerset Valley area. The wines are made using contract-grown grapes until the estate vineyards come into production. Semillon, Chardonnay, Chardonnay Semillon, Shiraz, Merlot and Malbec are the dry table wines, with Winya White and Winya Red sweet alternatives. Until a cellar door opens in January 2006 the wines are available through most of the nearby hotels.

Wirilda Creek

★★★

RSD 91, McMurtrie Road, McLaren Vale, SA 5171 **REGION** McLaren Vale
T (08) 8323 9688 **F** (08) 8323 9260 **OPEN** 7 days 10–5
WINEMAKER Kerry Flanagan **EST.** 1993 **CASES** 1500
SUMMARY Wirilda Creek may be one of the newer arrivals in McLaren Vale but it offers the lot: wine, lunch every day (Pickers Platters reflecting local produce) and accommodation (four rooms opening onto a private garden courtyard). Co-owner Kerry Flanagan (with partner Karen Shertock) has had

great experience in the wine and hospitality industries: a Roseworthy graduate (1980), he has inter alia worked at Penfolds, Coriole and Wirra Wirra and also owned the famous Old Salopian Inn for a period. A little under 4 ha of McLaren Vale estate vineyards have now been joined by a little over 3 ha of vineyards at Antechamber Bay, Kangaroo Island. Limited retail distribution in NSW and SA; exports to the US, Canada and Germany.

Wirra Wirra ★★★★★

McMurtie Road, McLaren Vale, SA 5171 **REGION** McLaren Vale
T (08) 8323 8414 **F** (08) 8323 8596 **WEB** www.wirrawirra.com **OPEN** Mon–Sat 10–5, Sun 11–5
WINEMAKER Samantha Connew, Paul Carpenter **EST.** 1969 **CASES** 110 000
SUMMARY Long respected for the consistency of its white wines, Wirra Wirra has now established an equally formidable reputation for its reds. Right across the board, the wines are of exemplary character, quality and style, The Angelus Cabernet Sauvignon and RSW Shiraz battling with each other for supremacy. Long may the battle continue under the direction of the highly respected Tim James, lured from his senior position at Hardys late in 2000. The wines are exported to the US, the UK, Europe and Asia.

ŸŸŸŸŸ **RSW Shiraz 2002** Dense but delicious black fruits and dark chocolate have a fine veneer of high quality, perfectly balanced and integrated oak. A wine with all the power of the 2002 vintage, but held in a 14.5°-velvet glove. **RATING** 97 **DRINK** 2017 **$** 48
McLaren Vale Shiraz 2002 Deep colour; complex, spicy overtones to the bouquet; a resounding palate, with a cascade of blackberry, plum and dark chocolate. **RATING** 95 **DRINK** 2015 **$** 30
The Angelus Cabernet Sauvignon 2002 Very complex but seamless marriage of McLaren Vale and Coonawarra components, each a perfect foil for the other. Blackberry, cassis, bitter chocolate, ripe tannins and quality oak all coalesce. High-quality cork. **RATING** 95 **DRINK** 2017

ŸŸŸŸŸ **Hand Picked Riesling 2004** Classic mineral and lime aromas and palate; more structure and length than many '04s. Adelaide Hills/Fleurieu/Clare Valley. Screwcap. **RATING** 93 **DRINK** 2012
Adelaide Hills Chardonnay 2003 Light straw-green; fine, relatively restrained but highly focused; light to medium-bodied; nectarine fruit, gentle oak. **RATING** 93 **DRINK** 2008 **$** 28
Mrs Wigley Rose 2004 Bright colour; highly aromatic; joyous red fruits and perfect lemony acidity; length, too. **RATING** 93 **DRINK** Now **$** 17
Scrubby Rise Red 2002 Good colour; a strong and robust wine with a mix of dark fruits, bitter chocolate and earth. Obvious development potential. **RATING** 90 **DRINK** 2012 **$** 16
Church Block 2003 Elegant, fresh, medium-bodied; black and redcurrant fruit; fine, ripe, spicy tannins. Cabernet Sauvignon/Shiraz/Merlot. **RATING** 90 **DRINK** 2010

ŸŸŸŸ **Adelaide Hills Sauvignon Blanc 2004** Clean, crisp and fresh; subdued varietal fruit, but nice minerally texture; may develop. **RATING** 89 **DRINK** 2007 **$** 22
Sexton's Acre Unwooded Chardonnay 2004 Fragrant and citrussy; cleverly made, with hints of sweetness off-set by good acidity. **RATING** 89 **DRINK** 2008
Scrubby Rise Red 2003 Clean, focused array of red and black fruits; nicely balanced oak; fine, ripe tannins. Screwcap. **RATING** 89 **DRINK** 2013
McLaren Vale Grenache 2003 Has the power and structure often absent in the Barossa Valley; sweet, dark fruit and touches of spice; fine tannins, minimal oak interplay. Cork. **RATING** 88 **DRINK** 2012

ŸŸŸŸ **Scrubby Rise 2004 RATING** 86 **DRINK** Now **$** 16

Wise Wine ★★★★★

Lot 4 Eagle Bay Road, Dunsborough, WA 6281 **REGION** Margaret River
T (08) 9756 8627 **F** (08) 9756 8770 **OPEN** 7 days 10–5
WINEMAKER Amanda Kramer, Bruce Dukes (Consultant) **EST.** 1986 **CASES** 40 000
SUMMARY Wise Vineyards, headed by Perth entrepreneur Ron Wise, is going from strength to strength, with 18 ha at the Meelup Vineyard in Margaret River, 10 ha at the Donnybrook Vineyard in Geographe, and leases over the Bramley and Bunkers Bay vineyards, with a total of almost 40 ha. Wine quality, too, has taken a leap forward, with a number of excellent wines.

ŸŸŸŸŸ **Single Vineyard Pemberton Reserve Chardonnay 2003** Medium yellow-green; beautifully made; relatively light sweet nectarine fruit has not been submerged in oak; fresh finish and aftertaste. **RATING** 95 **DRINK** 2010 $ 35
Single Vineyard Donnybrook Valley Chardonnay 2003 Beautiful colour; complex barrel ferment inputs, but the nectarine and stone fruit more than cope; long and stylish. **RATING** 94 **DRINK** 2010
Single Vineyard Donnybrook Valley Chardonnay 2002 Ripe stone fruit and a nice touch of spicy nutmeg oak; perfect malolactic creamy complexity. **RATING** 94 **DRINK** 2012 $ 28

ŸŸŸŸŸ **Single Vineyard Verdelho 2004** As with the prior vintage, more drive and interest than most; citrus blossom; nice acidity and length. **RATING** 90 **DRINK** 2008 $ 24

ŸŸŸŸ **Unwooded Chardonnay 2004** Above-average fruit weight; peachy stone fruit flavours; inevitably, slightly simple. **RATING** 89 **DRINK** 2007

ŸŸŸŸ **Classic White 2004 RATING** 86 **DRINK** Now $ 16

ŸŸŸ **Eagle Bay Shiraz 2002 RATING** 83 $ 35

Witchmount Estate

557 Leakes Road, Rockbank, Vic 3335 **REGION** Sunbury
T (03) 9747 1188 **F** (03) 9747 1066 **WEB** www.witchmount.com.au **OPEN** Wed–Sun 10–5
WINEMAKER Tony Ramunno, Steve Goodwin **EST.** 1991 **CASES** 10 000
SUMMARY Gaye and Matt Ramunno operate Witchmount Estate in conjunction with its onsite Italian restaurant and function rooms, which are open Wed–Sun for lunch and dinner. Over 20 ha of vines have been established since 1991: varieties include nebbiolo, barbera, tempranillo and the rare northern Italian white grape picolit. The quality of the wines is consistently good, the prices very modest. Exports to Canada.

ŸŸŸŸŸ **Shiraz 2002** Highly fragrant red fruits and spice aromas; cherry, raspberry and plum fruit; long, fine palate. **RATING** 93 **DRINK** 2017 $ 25
Olivia's Paddock Chardonnay 2003 Complex, with nicely controlled barrel ferment inputs on grapefruit and melon; good length and intensity. **RATING** 91 **DRINK** 2008 $ 20

ŸŸŸŸ **Kleenskin Cabernet Shiraz 2002** Medium-bodied; attractive black fruits; some spicy tannins provide structure. Twin Top. **RATING** 88 **DRINK** 2009 $ 15
Kleenskin Chardonnay 2004 Light-bodied; fresh melon and peach fruit; direct unwooded, but flavoursome, style. Twin Top. **RATING** 87 **DRINK** Now $ 15

ŸŸŸŸ **Pinot Gris 2004 RATING** 86 **DRINK** Now $ 18

WJ Walker Wines ★★★★★

Burns Road, Lake Grace, WA 6353 **REGION** Central Western Australia Zone
T (08) 9865 1969 **OPEN** 7 days 10–4
WINEMAKER Porongurup Winery (Contract) **EST.** NA **CASES** 1000
SUMMARY Lake Grace is 300 km due east of Bunbury, one of those isolated viticultural outposts which are appearing in many parts of Australia these days. There are 1.5 ha of shiraz and 0.5 ha of chardonnay, and the wines are sold through local outlets.

ŸŸŸŸŸ **Lake Grace Shiraz 2003** Excellent colour; rich plum and cherry fruit; good balance and structure; integrated oak. Gold medal winner Qantas Western Australian Wines Show. **RATING** 94 **DRINK** 2013 $ 15

Wolf Blass

Bilyara Vineyards, Sturt Highway, Nuriootpa, SA 5355 **REGION** Barossa Valley
T (08) 8562 1955 **F** (08) 8562 2156 **WEB** www.wolfblass.com.au **OPEN** Mon–Fri 9.15–4.30, weekends 10–4.30
WINEMAKER Chris Hatcher (Chief), Caroline Dunn (Red), Kirsten Glaetzer (White) **EST.** 1966
CASES NFP
SUMMARY Although merged with Mildara and now under the giant umbrella of Beringer Blass, the brands (as expected) have been left largely intact. The white wines are particularly impressive, none

more so than the Gold Label Riesling. After a short pause, the red wines have improved out of all recognition thanks to the sure touch (and top palate) of Caroline Dunn. All of this has occurred under the leadership of Chris Hatcher, who has harnessed the talents of the team and encouraged the changes in style. Exports to all major markets.

TTTTT **Platinum Label Barossa Shiraz 2002** Deep colour; supple, round and fleshy, but retains grace and elegance; a spicy array of black and red fruits caress the mouth; beautifully integrated oak; 14.5° alcohol. Screwcap. **RATING** 96 **DRINK** 2017 $ 165

Black Label Shiraz Cabernet 2001 Complex, seamless integration of spicy black fruits and oak; supple, round, silk and velvet mouthfeel; an evolving classic. Quality cork. **RATING** 95 **DRINK** 2015 $ 130

Gold Label Adelaide Hills Shiraz Viognier 2003 As always, sensitively crafted and balanced; fragrant red and black fruits, spice and apricot; fine tannins; subtle, but positive, oak. Screwcap. **RATING** 94 **DRINK** 2015

Grey Label Shiraz 2003 Powerful, intense, archetypal blackberry and bitter chocolate; neat touch of barrel ferment; supple, round and velvety; not over the top; near invisible 15° alcohol. Screwcap. **RATING** 94 **DRINK** 2015 $ 39

Gold Label Barossa Shiraz 2002 Very elegant and fine style; red and black fruits, long palate and silky tannins. **RATING** 94 **DRINK** 2012 $ 24

Grey Label Cabernet Sauvignon 2003 Complex, fragrant berry fruit and spicy oak aromas; excellent balance and structure; cassis, blackcurrant and mulberry; soft, fine tannins. Quality cork. **RATING** 94 **DRINK** 2013 $ 39

TTTTY **Gold Label Riesling 2004** Clean, aromatic lime and apple blossom aromas; delicate and crisp, but with considerable length. Eden/Clare Valley blend. **RATING** 93 **DRINK** 2014 $ 24

Shadowood Eden Valley Shiraz 2002 Immaculately made and moulded wine; bright, fresh red and black fruits (no reduction via screwcap); fine tannins, minimal oak. **RATING** 91 **DRINK** 2012

Shadowood Eden Valley Riesling 2004 Elegant, floral passionfruit and lime aromas; light-bodied, but has length and balance; will fill out. **RATING** 90 **DRINK** 2012

Gold Label Mount Gambier Sauvignon Blanc 2004 Delicate, crisp, clean; lively and fresh passionfruit and gooseberry; fine acidity, good varietal character. A region with lots of potential. Screwcap. **RATING** 90 **DRINK** 2007 $ 22

Shadowood Eden Valley Chardonnay 2003 Bright green-yellow; attractive melon fruit interwoven with subtle barrel ferment aromas and flavours; the bright fruit flavours seem lighter than 13.5°. **RATING** 90 **DRINK** 2010

Shadowood Eden Valley Cabernet Sauvignon 2002 Good colour; elegant and medium-bodied; supple blackcurrant fruit; fine tannins, long, even finish. **RATING** 90 **DRINK** 2012

Gold Label Adelaide Hills Cabernet Sauvignon Cabernet Franc 2003 Medium-bodied; aromatic and elegant; restrained spice, berry and leaf flavours; gentle French oak; fine, savoury tannins. Screwcap. **RATING** 90 **DRINK** 2009

TTTT **Yellow Label Riesling 2004** Generous lime, passionfruit and tropical fruit flavours balanced by clean acidity. **RATING** 89 **DRINK** 2010 $ 13.50

Gold Label Coonawarra Cabernet Sauvignon 2002 Big, chunky blackberry fruit, with persistent tannins leading to a rather austere finish. Should soften and come together with age. **RATING** 89 **DRINK** 2012 $ 22

Gold Label Pinot Chardonnay 2001 Lively, fresh, lemony/citrussy flavours; long finish, brisk and clear. **RATING** 89 **DRINK** Now $ 11

Eaglehawk Riesling 2004 Honest wine, with plenty of tropical/lime fruit, especially for the vintage. **RATING** 87 **DRINK** 2010 $ 11

Yellow Label Chardonnay 2004 Nicely balanced sweet stone fruit and oak. **RATING** 87 **DRINK** Now $ 18

Eaglehawk Rose 2004 Fragrant red fruits and blossom aromas; the palate with delicate fruit and appreciable, but acceptable, sweetness on the finish. **RATING** 87 **DRINK** Now $ 11

TTTY **Yellow Label Sauvignon Blanc 2004** **RATING** 86 **DRINK** 2007 $ 13.50

Red Label Chardonnay Pinot Noir NV **RATING** 85 **DRINK** Now

Red Label Semillon Sauvignon Blanc 2004 **RATING** 84 **DRINK** Now $ 15

Gold Label Adelaide Hills Chardonnay 2004 **RATING** 84 **DRINK** Now

TTT **Eaglehawk Semillon Chardonnay 2004** **RATING** 83 $ 11

Eaglehawk Cuvee Brut NV **RATING** 83 $ 9

🍇 Wolseley Wines ★★★★

1790 Hendy Main Road, Moriac, Geelong, Vic 3240 **REGION** Geelong
T 0412 990 638 **OPEN** Weekends & public hols 11–6
WINEMAKER Will Wolseley **EST.** 1992 **CASES** 2500
SUMMARY Will Wolseley grew up in Somerset, England, and from an early age started making blackberry wine at home. He came to Australia in 1986 and enrolled in wine science at Charles Sturt University, gathering vintage experience at various wineries over the next 5 years. A 2-year search for an ideal vineyard site resulted in the acquisition of property on the gently sloping hills of Paraparap, just off the Great Ocean Road, inland from Bells Beach, Torquay. Here he established 6.5 ha of vineyard planted to pinot noir, cabernet sauvignon, chardonnay, shiraz, cabernet franc and semillon. Hail storms, frost and drought delayed the first commercial vintage until 1998, but the winery is now in full production. Uniquely, the winery runs on solar power, with solar power cabins also planned. The wines are sold through the cellar door and by mail order.

🍷🍷🍷🍷 **Geelong Cabernet Sauvignon 2001** A sweet mix of blackcurrant, mocha and spice; fine, ripe tannins. **RATING** 91 **DRINK** 2010 $ 25
Geelong Botrytis Semillon 2003 Deep gold, already advanced; an exceptionally rich and luscious wine well into the Tokaji Essencia spectrum. Incredibly, picking started on 6 May, with one pass per week for the next 2 months. Just as well the labour comes free. **RATING** 90 **DRINK** 2007 $ 30

🍷🍷🍷🍷 **Geelong Shiraz 2001** Light to medium-bodied structure, but with quite ripe plum and cherry fruit; subtle oak; fine tannins. **RATING** 89 **DRINK** 2011 $ 30
Geelong Pinot Noir 2003 A mix of savoury/bramble and sweeter components; light to medium-bodied; good length. **RATING** 87 **DRINK** Now $ 30
Geelong Pinot Noir 2000 Slightly overripe juicy/jammy plum fruit and sundry spices. **RATING** 87 **DRINK** Now $ 20

🍷🍷🍷🍷 **Geelong Chardonnay 2003 RATING** 84 **DRINK** Now $ 20

🍇 Wombat Forest ★★★

RMB 4060, Denver via Daylesford, Vic 3461 (postal) **REGION** Macedon Ranges
T (03) 5423 9331 **OPEN** Not
WINEMAKER Brendon Lawlor **EST.** 1997 **CASES** 300
SUMMARY Wombat Forest is jointly owned and operated by two local couples: Brendon and Deidre Lawlor and David and Elizabeth Nikcevich. They personally planted the 1.2 ha of cabernet sauvignon and pinot noir between 1997 and 1999, and are ready to plant out the next stage. Pinot Noir, Cabernet Sauvignon and Sparkling (Pinot Noir) are the three wines; they are sold through local bottle shops and hotels, and by mail order.

🍷🍷🍷🍷 **Cabernet Sauvignon 2002** Elegant and fine; struggles for fruit ripeness, but avoids green tannins. **RATING** 86 **DRINK** 2008 $ 20

Wonbah Estate NR

302 Wonbah Road, Wonbah via Gin Gin, Qld 4671 **REGION** Queensland Coastal
T (07) 4156 3029 **F** (07) 4156 3035 **WEB** www.wonbahwinery.com **OPEN** 7 days 9.30–4
WINEMAKER Bruce Humphery-Smith **EST.** 1997 **CASES** 1500
SUMMARY The 5-ha vineyard, planted to shiraz, chardonnay, cabernet sauvignon, ruby cabernet, muscat and verdelho, is near Mt Perry, an hour's drive west of Bundaberg at the extreme northern end of the Burnett Valley, extending the viticultural map of Queensland yet further. The 100-tonne onsite winery is under the direction of the omnipresent Bruce Humphery-Smith, and the tasting room is in a restored slab hut dating from the turn of the 20th century. There are numerous tourist attractions around Mt Perry, not the least being the Boolboonda Tunnel, the largest self-supporting tunnel in the southern hemisphere, hand-hewn, and home to a colony of fairy bats.

🍇 Wonga Estate ★★★★★

201 Jumping Creek Road, Wonga Park, Vic 3115 **REGION** Yarra Valley
T (03) 9722 2122 **F** (03) 9722 1715 **WEB** www.wongaestate.com.au **OPEN** Mon–Sat 9–5, Sun 10–5 by appointment

WINEMAKER Sergio Carlei (Consultant), Greg Roberts **EST.** 1997 **CASES** 450
SUMMARY Greg (formerly Grollo's national construction manager) and Jady Roberts began the development of their 1.8-ha vineyard in 1997, with a minor expansion in 2002. The clones of pinot noir and chardonnay were selected with the advice of Sandro Mosele (of Mornington Peninsula's Kooyong Estate) with continuing viticultural advice from Bill Christophersen (ex Coldstream Hills). The wines are made at the onsite micro-winery by Greg Roberts with the direction and assistance of Carlei. Since 2002 the range has been expanded with Shiraz grown in the Colbinabbin area of Heathcote, open-fermented and basket-pressed. Foot-treading of whole bunches of pinot has also been successfully employed. The limited production has not stopped the listing of the winery at an impressive range of Melbourne and Yarra Valley restaurants, plus specialist Melbourne retailers.

🍷🍷🍷🍷🍷 **Heathcote Shiraz 2002** Brilliant colour; intense but supple black fruits and touches of spice; fine, ripe tannins; very stylish indeed; 13° alcohol. Innovative packaging. Cork. **RATING** 95 **DRINK** 2015 **$** 33

Yarra Valley Chardonnay 2002 Light yellow-green; intense, focused and long; citrus and melon fruit the driver; barrel ferment oak second. Diam. **RATING** 94 **DRINK** 2012 **$** 22

🍷🍷🍷🍷½ **Yarra Valley Chardonnay 2003** Considerable fruit weight and concentration; ripe melon and fig; well-controlled malolactic and barrel ferment inputs. Diam. **RATING** 93 **DRINK** 2010 **$** 22

Heathcote Shiraz 2003 Vibrant, fresh plum, black cherry and blackberry fruit; silky tannins, minimal oak. Admirable 13° alcohol. Diam. **RATING** 93 **DRINK** 2015 **$** 33

Yarra Valley Pinot Noir 2002 Good colour; rich and concentrated plum and spice fruit; excellent mouthfeel and texture. Diam. **RATING** 91 **DRINK** 2010 **$** 22

Yarra Valley Pinot Noir 2001 Hue good, though not deep; spicy and vibrant cherry, plum and strawberry; considerable length. Cork. **RATING** 90 **DRINK** 2008 **$** 22

🍷🍷🍷🍷 **Yarra Valley Pinot Noir 2003** Some tangy/foresty/stemmy characters ex whole bunch; plum and cherry; brisk acid. Very poor cork. **RATING** 87 **DRINK** 2008 **$** 22

🍷🍷🍷½ **Yarra Valley Pinot Noir 2004** Light to medium-bodied; fresh cherry fruit; crisp and direct; high acid, low pH style. Quality cork. **RATING** 86 **DRINK** 2010 **$** 22

Woodlands ★★★★★

Cnr Caves Road/Metricup Road, Wilyabrup via Cowaramup, WA 6284 **REGION** Margaret River
T (08) 9755 6226 **F** (08) 9755 6236 **WEB** www.woodlands-wines.com **OPEN** 7 days 10.30–5
WINEMAKER Stuart Watson, David Watson **EST.** 1973 **CASES** 5000
SUMMARY The quality of the grapes, with a priceless core of 6.8 ha of 30+-year-old cabernet sauvignon, more recently joined by merlot, malbec, cabernet franc, pinot noir and chardonnay, has never been in doubt. Whatever the shortcomings of the 1990s, these days Woodlands is producing some spectacular wines in small quantities. The super-luxury, super-expensive Chateau corks have extensive wine seepage along the sides, suggesting either that the bore of the bottle is too large for the cork, or that the bottles have been laid down too quickly after being corked and/or exposed to heat. I have assumed that the innate quality of the cork will prevail. Exports to Singapore, Hong Kong and Indonesia.

🍷🍷🍷🍷🍷 **Margaret Cabernet Merlot 2003** Wonderfully rich yet not over-ripe wine; plush array of black fruits; ripe tannins, good oak. Lovely wine. **RATING** 95 **DRINK** 2018 **$** 35

Chloe Chardonnay 2003 Fresh, delicate, fine and elegant; gentle citrus and stone fruit with subtle malolactic and barrel ferment inputs; long, clean finish; evolving slowly; 54mm French Chateau cork. **RATING** 94 **DRINK** 2012 **$** 40

Reserve du Cave Cabernet Franc Merlot 2003 Intensely elegant and savoury; none of the desiccated fruit of the 'Margaret' Cabernet Malbec Merlot; strong Bordeaux similarities; needs years for full potential. Stained 54mm Chateau cork. **RATING** 94 **DRINK** 2023 **$** 60

Reserve du Cave Cabernet Franc 2003 Clean, vibrant, fresh and luscious; only Margaret River can produce such excellent stand-alone Cabernet Franc; redcurrant, fine tannins. Stained 54mm Chateau cork. **RATING** 94 **DRINK** 2018 **$** 60

🍷🍷🍷🍷½ **Chardonnay 2004** Pale straw-green; fresh, fragrant grapefruit and stone fruit; very good acidity and fine French oak. Screwcap. **RATING** 93 **DRINK** 2010

Emily Special Reserve 2003 Very good purple-red; a luscious array of blackcurrant, cassis and mulberry; tannins as much on the mid-palate as the finish; now or later. Unspecified blend. Quality cork. **RATING** 93 **DRINK** 2013

Reserve du Cave Malbec 2003 Much better fruit flavour and profile than the McDonagh; supple jammy, juicy black fruits; 54mm Chateau cork. **RATING** 91 **DRINK** 2013 $60
Unwooded Chardonnay 2003 Creamy, nutty malolactic influences on a nicely balanced melon and fig palate; medium-bodied, and not too sweet. **RATING** 90 **DRINK** 2009 $15

▼▼▼▼ **McDonagh Malbec 2003** Excessively jammy dead fruit varietal character; a caricature of the variety. **RATING** 87 **DRINK** 2012 $20

▼▼▼ **Pinot Noir 2003 RATING** 80

Woodonga Hill

NR

Cowra Road, Young, NSW 2594 **REGION** Hilltops
T (02) 6382 2972 **F** (02) 6382 2972 **OPEN** 7 days 9–5
WINEMAKER Jill Lindsay **EST.** 1986 **CASES** 4000
SUMMARY Early problems with white wine quality appear to have been surmounted. The wines have won bronze or silver medals at regional wine shows in NSW and Canberra, and Jill Lindsay is also a contract-winemaker for other small producers.

Wood Park

★★★☆

263 Kneebone Gap Road, Markwood, Vic 3678 **REGION** King Valley
T (03) 5727 3367 **F** (03) 5727 3682 **WEB** www.woodparkwines.com.au **OPEN** At Milawa Cheese Factory
WINEMAKER John Stokes **EST.** 1989 **CASES** 4000
SUMMARY John Stokes planted the first vines at Wood Park in 1989 as part of a diversification program for his property at Bobinawarrah, in the hills of the Lower King Valley, east of Milawa. The bulk of the 16-ha production is sold to Brown Brothers. In an unusual twist, Stokes acquires his chardonnay from cousin John Leviny, one of the King Valley pioneers, who has his vineyard at Meadow Creek. Exports to the US and Europe.

Woodside Valley Estate

NR

PO Box 332, Greenwood, WA 6924 **REGION** Margaret River
T (08) 9345 4065 **F** (08) 9345 4541 **WEB** www.woodsidevalleyestate.com.au **OPEN** Not
WINEMAKER Kevin McKay **EST.** 1998 **CASES** 500
SUMMARY Woodside Valley has been developed by a small syndicate of investors headed by Peter Woods. In 1998 they acquired 67 ha of land at Yallingup, and have now established 19 ha of chardonnay, sauvignon blanc, cabernet sauvignon, shiraz, malbec and merlot. The experienced Albert Haak is consultant viticulturist, and together with Peter Woods, took the unusual step of planting south-facing in preference to north-facing slopes. In doing so they indirectly followed in the footsteps of the French explorer Thomas Nicholas Baudin, who mounted a major scientific expedition to Australia on his ship *The Geographe*, and defied established views and tradition of the time in (incorrectly) asserting that the best passage for sailing ships travelling between Cape Leeuwin and Bass Strait was from west to east. It's a long bow, but it's a story for a winery which managed to produce some excellent wines from very young vines. Exports to the US and Japan.

WoodSmoke Estate

NR

Lot 2 Kemp Road, Pemberton, WA 6260 **REGION** Pemberton
T (08) 9776 0225 **F** (08) 9776 0225 **OPEN** By appointment
WINEMAKER Julie White **EST.** 1992 **CASES** 1500
SUMMARY The former Jimlee Estate was acquired by the Liebeck family in 1998 and renamed WoodSmoke Estate. The original 2 ha of semillon, sauvignon blanc, cabernet franc and cabernet sauvignon were expanded with 2.5 ha of cabernet franc and merlot in 2000.

Woodstock

★★★★☆

Douglas Gully Road, McLaren Flat, SA 5171 **REGION** McLaren Vale
T (08) 8383 0156 **F** (08) 8383 0437 **WEB** www.woodstockwine.com.au **OPEN** Mon–Fri 9–5,
weekends, hols 12–5
WINEMAKER Scott Collett **EST.** 1974 **CASES** 20 000

SUMMARY One of the stalwarts of McLaren Vale, producing archetypal and invariably reliable full-bodied red wines, and spectacular botrytis sweet whites and high-quality (14-year-old) Tawny Port. Also offers a totally charming reception-cum-restaurant, which does a roaring trade with wedding receptions. Has supplemented its 22 ha of McLaren Vale vineyards with 10 ha at its Wirrega Vineyard, in the Limestone Coast Zone. Exports to the UK, Switzerland, Denmark, Canada, Hong Kong, China, Malaysia and Singapore.

ΥΥΥΥΥ **The Stocks McLaren Vale Shiraz 2002** Has all the opulence and generosity typical of the vintage; blackberry fruit and spice; ripe, fine tannins; good oak. High-quality cork. **RATING** 94 **DRINK** 2012 $ 40

ΥΥΥΥΥ **Botrytis 2003** Glowing yellow-green; complex and tangy; very good balance of sweetness and acidity; the full gamut of tropical flavours. Long practice has made perfect. **RATING** 92 **DRINK** 2007 $ 17
McLaren Vale Limestone Coast Chardonnay 1999 Complex bottle-developed characters with tangy grapefruit, lemon and citrus. Cork; random bottle oxidation a problem with this wine. **RATING** 90 **DRINK** 2007 $ 20

ΥΥΥΥ **McLaren Vale Semillon Sauvignon Blanc 2004** Light to medium-bodied; clean, fresh and fruity passionfruit and herbaceous mix; early-developing style. Screwcap. **RATING** 88 **DRINK** 2007 $ 14
Five Feet White 2004 A varietal witches' brew (Viognier/Semillon/Riesling); somewhat unexpectedly, Viognier makes the running; apricot/musk/pastille fruit sweetness, then a dry finish. Screwcap. **RATING** 88 **DRINK** 2007 $ 16
McLaren Vale Riesling 2003 Largely typical of the region, with not much happening until the finish, where mineral and citrus come together with brisk acidity. Screwcap. **RATING** 87 **DRINK** 2008 $ 14
The Stocks McLaren Vale Shiraz 2000 Medium-bodied; pleasant red and black fruits, but a slight break in the palate line. **RATING** 87 **DRINK** 2009 $ 45
McLaren Vale Cabernet Sauvignon 2001 Solid, traditional style; blackcurrant and chocolate; no-frills, honest flavour. **RATING** 87 **DRINK** 2011 $ 20
Five Feet Red 2001 Light to medium-bodied; ripe, and shows the varietal fruit interplay (Cabernet/Shiraz/Malbec), particularly spicy/juicy Malbec. **RATING** 87 **DRINK** 2011 $ 16

ΥΥΥΥ **Rose 2004** **RATING** 85 **DRINK** Now $ 15
Shiraz 2001 **RATING** 85 **DRINK** 2008 $ 20

ΥΥΥ **McLaren Vale Grenache 2002** **RATING** 83 $ 20

Woody Nook ★★★★

Metricup Road, Wilyabrup, WA 6280 **REGION** Margaret River
T (08) 9755 7547 **F** (08) 9755 7007 **WEB** www.woodynook.com.au **OPEN** 7 days 10–4.30
WINEMAKER Neil Gallagher **EST.** 1982 **CASES** 5000
SUMMARY This improbably named and not terribly fashionable winery has produced some truly excellent wines over the years, featuring in such diverse competitions as Winewise, the Sheraton Wine Awards and the Qantas West Australian Wines Show. Cabernet Sauvignon has always been its strong point, but it has a habit of also bobbing up with excellent white wines in various guises. Since 2000 owned by Peter and Jane Bailey; Neil Gallagher continues as viticulturist, winemaker and minority shareholder. Exports to the UK, the US, Brazil, Hong Kong and Singapore.

ΥΥΥΥΥ **Gallagher's Choice Cabernet Sauvignon 2002** Fresh cassis, blackcurrant and mulberry; medium-bodied; smooth and silky; fine tannins, subtle oak. Quality cork. **RATING** 93 **DRINK** 2012 $ 29.95

Woolshed Wines ★★★

380 Horseflat Lane, Mullamuddy via Mudgee, NSW 2850 **REGION** Mudgee
T (02) 6373 1299 **F** (02) 6373 1299 **OPEN** 7 days 10–5
WINEMAKER David Lowe (Contract) **EST.** 1999 **CASES** NA
SUMMARY Kay and Mick Burgoyne own and run the 8-ha vineyard formerly known as Valley View Estates, planted to chardonnay, cabernet, merlot, shiraz and muscat hamburg. The wines are primarily sold through the cellar door and by mail order; the cellar door offers barbecues in a garden setting, and can cater for functions, concerts or festivals by arrangement.

Woongarra Estate

95 Hayseys Road, Narre Warren East, Vic 3804 **REGION** Port Phillip Zone
T (03) 9796 8886 **F** (03) 9796 8580 **WEB** www.woongarrawinery.com.au **OPEN** Thurs–Sun 9–5 by appointment
WINEMAKER Graeme Leith, Greg Dedman, Bruce Jones **EST.** 1992 **CASES** 2000
SUMMARY Dr Bruce Jones, and wife Mary, purchased their 16-ha property many years ago; it falls within the Yarra Ranges Shire Council's jurisdiction and is zoned 'Landscape', but because nearby Cardinia Creek does not flow into the Yarra River, it is not within the Yarra Valley wine region. In 1992 they planted 1 ha of sauvignon blanc, a small patch of shiraz and a few rows of semillon. Over 1 ha of sauvignon blanc and pinot noir followed in 1996 (mostly MV6, some French clone 114 and 115) with yet more 114 and 115 pinot noir in 2000, lifting total plantings to 3.2 ha of pinot noir, 1.4 ha of sauvignon blanc and a splash of the other two varieties. The white grapes have had various purchasers and contract makers; spectacular success has come with the Three Wise Men Pinot Noir, (a joint venture between Woongarra and Passing Clouds).

ᵧᵧᵧᵧᵧ Sauvignon Blanc 2004 Pale straw-green; fresh, clean and bright; lovely juicy, sweet citrus fruit flavour and feel; a touch of passionfruit; elegant. Screwcap. **RATING** 93 **DRINK** 2007 **$** 15
Shiraz 2003 Clean, firm, fresh red and black fruits; subtle oak and fine, ripe tannins; no drought stress; clean finish and aftertaste. Diam. **RATING** 91 **DRINK** 2010 **$** 15

Woongooroo Estate NR

35 Doyles Road, Mt Archer, Kilcoy, Qld 4515 (postal) **REGION** Queensland Coastal
T (07) 5496 3529 **F** (07) 5496 3529 **WEB** www.westatewine.com **OPEN** Not
WINEMAKER Sam Costanzo, Ray Costanzo (Golden Grove Estate) **EST.** 1997 **CASES** NFP
SUMMARY Woongooroo Estate was established by primary school teachers Phil and Gail Close, who planted a little over 3 ha of chardonnay, semillon, shiraz, cabernet franc, merlot and verdelho, together with a commercial olive grove. It is part of the new Queensland wine region known as the Somerset Valleys Grape and Wine Producers Association, falling within the Queensland Coastal Hinterland. A cellar door/vineyard café is planned.

Word of Mouth Wines

Campbell's Corner, Pinnacle Road, Orange, NSW 2800 **REGION** Orange
T (02) 6362 3509 **F** (02) 6365 3517 **WEB** www.wordofmouthwines.com.au **OPEN** Fri–Sun & public hols 11–5
WINEMAKER David Lowe, Jane Wilson (Contract) **EST.** 1991 **CASES** 1500
SUMMARY Word of Mouth Wines acquired the former Donnington Vineyard in 2003, with its 10 ha of mature vineyards, planted (in descending order of size) to sauvignon blanc, chardonnay, merlot, cabernet sauvignon, pinot noir, riesling and pinot gris between 1991 and 1996. Word of Mouth Wines Pty Limited has four shareholders, two based in Sydney and two in Orange. The vineyard and cellar door, at an altitude of over 950m, has panoramic views over the surrounding countryside.

ᵧᵧᵧᵧᵧ Orange Pinot Gris 2004 Clean, crisp and fresh; attractive pear, lemon and citrus; supple, fine and long; clean finish. Screwcap. **RATING** 92 **DRINK** 2007 **$** 22
Orange Sauvignon Blanc 2004 Wild herb and wild flower aromas; lemony notes; squeaky acidity, long finish. Screwcap. **RATING** 90 **DRINK** 2007 **$** 20

ᵧᵧᵧᵧ Orange Pinot Gris 2003 Clean and crisp floral apple aromas; fresh, lively and balanced; dry. **RATING** 89 **DRINK** Now **$** 22
Reserve Orange Cabernet Sauvignon 2003 Bright, clear colour; light to medium-bodied; minty, leafy, spicy red and black fruit mix; quite supple but not much texture (only 12° alcohol). Screwcap. **RATING** 88 **DRINK** 2009 **$** 30

ᵧᵧᵧᵧ Orange Rose 2004 RATING 85 **DRINK** Now **$** 15

Wordsworth Wines

Cnr South Western Highway/Thompson Road, Harvey, WA 6220 **REGION** Geographe
T (08) 9733 4576 **F** (08) 9733 4269 **WEB** www.wordsworthwines.com.au **OPEN** 7 days 10–5
WINEMAKER Tim Mortimer **EST.** 1997 **CASES** 5000

SUMMARY David Wordsworth has established a substantial business in a relatively short space of time: 27 ha of vines have been planted, with cabernet sauvignon (10 ha) and shiraz (5 ha) predominant, and lesser amounts of zinfandel, petit verdot, chardonnay, chenin blanc and verdelho. The winery features massive jarrah beams, wrought iron and antique furniture, and the tasting room seats 80 people. The wines have already had show success. Exports to the UK, the US and Singapore.

ＹＹＹＹ **Verdelho 2003** Gentle tropical fruit; good length and balance; nice acidity. **RATING** 88 **DRINK** 2007 $ 22
Shiraz 2002 A mix of ripe and more minty/leafy berry fruit; light to medium-bodied; overall spicy flavours. **RATING** 87 **DRINK** 2009 $ 25
Cabernet Sauvignon 2002 Light to medium-bodied; supple, smooth cassis and blackcurrant; slightly simple structurally. **RATING** 88 **DRINK** 2010 $ 25

ＹＹＹＹ **Chardonnay 2003** **RATING** 86 **DRINK** Now $ 24
Chardonnay 2002 **RATING** 86 **DRINK** Now $ 24

ＹＹＹ **Chenin Blanc 2002** **RATING** 83 $ 20

Wright Family Wines ★★★☆

'Misty Glen', 293 Deasey Road, Pokolbin, NSW 2320 **REGION** Lower Hunter Valley
T (02) 4998 7781 **F** (02) 4998 7768 **WEB** www.mistyglen.com.au **OPEN** 7 days 10–4
WINEMAKER Contract **EST.** 1985 **CASES** 800
SUMMARY Jim and Carol Wright purchased the property on which they live in 1985, with a small existing vineyard in need of tender loving care. This was duly given, and the semillon, chardonnay and cabernet sauvignon revived. In 2000, 1.5 ha of shiraz was planted; 1.5 ha of chambourcin was added in 2002, lifting total plantings to 7.5 ha. Carol has been involved in the wine industry since the early 1970s, and is now helped by husband Jim (he retired from the coal mines in 2002), and by children and grandchildren.

ＹＹＹＹＹ **Misty Glen Semillon 2004** Bright green-yellow; lemon zest, lemon oil and sweet herb aromas and flavours; an interesting wine of contrasts (10° alcohol); 100 cases made. Screwcap. **RATING** 90 **DRINK** 2009 $ 18.50

ＹＹＹＹ **Misty Glen Chardonnay 2004** Light to medium-bodied; soft, gentle peach and melon fruit; matching vanillin oak. Screwcap. **RATING** 88 **DRINK** 2007 $ 20
Misty Glen Shiraz 2003 Spicy, earthy, savoury; light to medium-bodied; very regional, early-drinking style; 12.6° alcohol. Cork. **RATING** 87 **DRINK** 2008 $ 25

ＹＹＹＹ **Misty Glen Semillon 2003** **RATING** 84 **DRINK** 2008 $ 15
Misty Glen Cabernet Sauvignon 2003 **RATING** 84 **DRINK** 2007 $ 20

Wright Robertson of Glencoe ★★☆

'Waratah Ridge', New England Highway, Glencoe, NSW 2365 **REGION** Northern Slopes Zone
T (02) 6733 3255 **F** (02) 6733 3220 **WEB** www.wrightwine.com **OPEN** Mon–Fri 9–5, Sat 10–4
WINEMAKER Scott Wright **EST.** 1999 **CASES** 3000
SUMMARY Scott and Julie Wright began establishing their 4-ha vineyard (pinot noir, pinot gris, riesling, shiraz and cabernet sauvignon) in 1999, and now operate an onsite winery making both their own wines and wines for three other producers. They also purchase grapes from other growers; an estate-grown Organic Syrah is the flagship wine. The wines are available in local restaurants and hotels.

ＹＹＹＹ **Waratah Ridge Chardonnay 2003** **RATING** 84 **DRINK** 2007 $ 15

Wroxton Wines ★★★★

Flaxman's Valley Road, Angaston, SA 5353 **REGION** Eden Valley
T (08) 8565 3227 **F** (08) 8565 3312 **WEB** www.wroxton.com.au **OPEN** By appointment
WINEMAKER Contract **EST.** 1995 **CASES** 60
SUMMARY Ian and Jo Zander are third-generation grapegrowers on the 200-ha Wroxton Grange property, which was established and named in 1845. The Zander family purchased the property in 1920, and planted their first vines; since 1973 an extensive planting program has seen the progressive establishment of riesling (15.4 ha), shiraz (10.5 ha), chardonnay (6.9 ha), semillon (2.5 ha) and

traminer (2 ha). The vast majority of the grapes are sold; limited amounts are contract-made, primarily for consumption by guests at the B&B cottage or the self-contained suite in the large bluestone homestead (built around 1890). The two wines produced are Riesling and Shiraz.

ŸŸŸŸŸ Single Vineyard Eden Valley Riesling 2001 Complex, rich, full lime juice; very regional; developing beautifully, emerging from transition. Cork. **RATING** 92 **DRINK** 2008 $15

ŸŸŸŸ Eden Valley Shiraz 2000 Light to medium-bodied; soft spice, earth, leaf and berry; fine tannins, a touch of vanilla oak. Quality cork. **RATING** 87 **DRINK** 2008 $18

Wyanga Park ★★☆

Baades Road, Lakes Entrance, Vic 3909 **REGION** Gippsland
T (03) 5155 1508 **F** (03) 5155 1443 **OPEN** 7 days 9–5
WINEMAKER Damien Twigg **EST.** 1970 **CASES** 3000
SUMMARY Offers a broad range of wines of diverse provenance directed at the tourist trade; one of the Chardonnays and the Cabernet Sauvignon are estate-grown. Winery cruises up the north arm of the Gippsland Lake to Wyanga Park are scheduled 4 days a week all year.

Wyndham Estate

700 Dalwood Road, Dalwood, NSW 2335 **REGION** Lower Hunter Valley
T (02) 4938 3444 **F** (02) 4938 3555 **WEB** www.wyndhamestate.com.au **OPEN** 7 days 10–4.30
WINEMAKER Brett McKinnon **EST.** 1828 **CASES** 1 million
SUMMARY This historic property is now merely a shopfront for the Wyndham Estate label. Winemaking was transferred from the Hunter to Mudgee (Poet's Corner) many years ago; it, too has been closed down, and winemaking has reverted to South Australia. The Bin wines often surprise with their quality, representing excellent value; the Show Reserve wines, likewise, can be very good.

ŸŸŸŸŸ Show Reserve Cabernet Merlot 1998 Medium to full-bodied; rich, moderately ripe style, developing slowly but surely; blackcurrant, touches of cedar and spice; good balance, ripe tannins. Quality cork. **RATING** 92 **DRINK** 2013

ŸŸŸŸ Show Reserve Chardonnay 2003 Tangy grapefruit and nectarine neatly balanced by oak; good length. **RATING** 89 **DRINK** Now $19
Show Reserve Shiraz 1999 Complex; rich and ripe licorice, blackberry and earth; good length and tannins. **RATING** 89 **DRINK** 2009
Bin 777 Semillon Sauvignon Blanc 2004 Crisp, clean and lively; delicate lemony fruit; minerally acidity. **RATING** 87 **DRINK** Now $13.99

ŸŸŸŸ Bin 999 Merlot 2003 RATING 86 **DRINK** 2007
Bin 444 Cabernet Sauvignon 2002 RATING 86 **DRINK** 2007 $13.99
Bin 333 Pinot Noir 2003 RATING 85 **DRINK** Now $13.99
Bin 555 Shiraz 2002 RATING 85 **DRINK** 2008 $13.99
Bin 222 Sparkling Chardonnay NV RATING 85 **DRINK** Now $13.99
Bin 555 Sparkling Shiraz NV RATING 85 **DRINK** 2008
Bin 888 Cabernet Merlot 2001 RATING 84 **DRINK** Now $13.99

ŸŸŸ Bin 111 Verdelho 2004 RATING 82 $13.99
Show Reserve Shiraz 2000 RATING 80

Wynns Coonawarra Estate

Memorial Drive, Coonawarra, SA 5263 **REGION** Coonawarra
T (08) 8736 2225 **F** (08) 8736 2228 **WEB** www.wynns.com.au **OPEN** 7 days 10–5
WINEMAKER Sue Hodder, Sarah Pidgeon **EST.** 1891 **CASES** NFP
SUMMARY The large-scale production has not prevented Wynns from producing excellent wines covering the full price spectrum, from the bargain basement Riesling and Shiraz through to the deluxe John Riddoch Cabernet Sauvignon and Michael Shiraz. Even with steady price increases, Wynns offers extraordinary value for money. Good though that may be, there is even greater promise for the future; the vineyards are being rejuvenated by new trellising or replanting, and a regime directed to quality rather than quantity has been introduced, all under the direction of Allen Jenkins. He is receiving enthusiastic support from the winemaking team headed by Sue Hodder.

ŢŢŢŢŢ **Michael Shiraz 2003** Rich, luscious, rounded and velvety; ripe but not over the top; blackberry plum fruit; restrained oak and tannins. Quality cork. **RATING** 95 **DRINK** 2018

ŢŢŢŢŢ **J Block Shiraz 2003** Aromatic, clean and vibrant red fruit aromas; supple, smooth and silky palate; very good integration of tannins and oak. Quality cork. **RATING** 93 **DRINK** 2015
Black Label Cabernet Sauvignon 2002 Deep purple-red; blackberry, blackcurrant and earth; shows the cool '02 vintage character; firm, faintly austere, but with a long, even fruit structure. Slow-developing style. **RATING** 91 **DRINK** 2014
Harold Vineyard Cabernet Sauvignon 2001 Plenty of earthy dark berry/dark chocolate fruit; typical Coonawarra profile, particularly with fine tannins; integrated oak. Planted 1971; dry-grown. High-quality cork. **RATING** 91 **DRINK** 2016 $ 35
Riesling 2004 Clean apple, lime and passionfruit; light but focused; nice minerally acidity. **RATING** 90 **DRINK** 2009 $ 15.95
Shiraz 2002 Quite intense and firm structure; black fruits; good oak, fine tannins and long carry. Will improve. **RATING** 90 **DRINK** 2010 $ 18.95

ŢŢŢŢ **Cabernet Shiraz Merlot 2002** Fine and medium-bodied; a mix of spice and savoury black fruits. **RATING** 88 **DRINK** 2012 $ 20

ŢŢŢŢ **Chardonnay 2003** **RATING** 84 **DRINK** Now $ 14.90

Xanadu Wines ★★★★

Boodjidup Road, Margaret River, WA 6285 **REGION** Margaret River
T (08) 9757 2581 **F** (08) 9757 3389 **WEB** www.xanadunormans.com **OPEN** 7 days 10–5
WINEMAKER Jurg Muggli, Glenn Goodall, Jodie Opie **EST.** 1977 **CASES** 150 000
SUMMARY Xanadu, once a small and somewhat quirky family winery, has reinvented itself with the arrival of substantial outside capital and the acquisition of the key brands of Normans Wines of South Australia. The 130 ha of vineyard estate and much expanded winemaking facilities have been complemented by a large, open courtyard, a bar area, a new cellar door and a café-style restaurant. Wine quality, led by outstanding Merlot, has also risen. Exports to all major markets.

ŢŢŢŢŢ **Margaret River Merlot 2002** Stylish wine; considerable depth and structure without sacrificing varietal character; dark fruits and a twist of briar. **RATING** 93 **DRINK** 2012 $ 24.99
Frankland/Margaret River Shiraz 2001 Elegant and lively cherry and raspberry fruits with spicy edges; light to medium-bodied; fine tannins. **RATING** 90 **DRINK** 2011 $ 24.99

ŢŢŢŢ **Secession Semillon Sauvignon Blanc 2004** Crisp, clean semillon dominant, but with some sweeter gooseberry notes. **RATING** 89 **DRINK** 2007 $ 14.99
Secession Merlot 2003 A mix of red and more savoury fruits; persistent but fine tannins. **RATING** 87 **DRINK** 2007 $ 14.99

Yabby Lake Vineyard ★★★★★

112 Tuerong Road, Tuerong, Vic 3933 (postal) **REGION** Mornington Peninsula
T (03) 5974 3729 **F** (03) 5974 3111 **WEB** www.yabbylake.com **OPEN** Not
WINEMAKER Tod Dexter, Larry McKenna **EST.** 1998 **CASES** NA
SUMMARY This high-profile wine business is owned by Robert and Mem Kirby (of Village Roadshow) who have been landowners in the Mornington Peninsula for decades. In 1998 they established Yabby Lake Vineyard, under the direction of vineyard manager Keith Harris; the vineyard is on a north-facing slope, capturing maximum sunshine while also receiving sea breezes. The main focus is the 21 ha of pinot noir, 10 ha of chardonnay and 5 ha of pinot gris; the 2 ha each of shiraz and merlot take a back seat. Tod Dexter (former long-term winemaker at Stonier) and Larry McKenna (ex Martinborough Vineyards and now the Escarpment in New Zealand) both have great experience. Retail distribution through Red+White.

ŢŢŢŢŢ **Mornington Peninsula Chardonnay 2002** Intense fruit and oak marriage; balance and integration impeccable in a complex, multilayered and rich palate; persistent and deep finish and aftertaste. **RATING** 95 **DRINK** 2010 $ 35
Mornington Peninsula Pinot Noir 2003 Silky smooth; long and impeccable balance and structure; black plums, hints of forest and spice; not stemmy. Quality cork. **RATING** 95 **DRINK** 2011 $ 55

Mornington Peninsula Chardonnay 2003 Layer-upon-layer of texture and complexity; stone fruit, melon and creamy cashew interwoven with oak; good acidity. High-quality cork. **RATING** 94 **DRINK** 2009 $ 38.50

Mornington Peninsula Pinot Noir 2002 Slightly opaque, unfiltered, deep colour; complex, powerful and intense dark fruits; considerable length; will become more savoury as the finish softens. **RATING** 94 **DRINK** 2012 $ 50

Yaldara Wines ★★★★☆

Gomersal Road, Lyndoch, SA 5351 **REGION** Barossa Valley
T (08) 8524 4200 **F** (08) 8524 4678 **WEB** www.yaldara.com.au **OPEN** 7 days 9–5
WINEMAKER Matt Tydeman **EST.** 1947 **CASES** 500 000
SUMMARY At the very end of 1999 Yaldara became part of the publicly listed Simeon Wines, the intention being that it (Yaldara) should become the quality flagship of the group. Despite much expenditure and the (short-lived) stay of at least one well-known winemaker, the plan failed to deliver the expected benefits. In February 2002 McGuigan Wines made a reverse takeover of Simeon; the various McGuigan brands will (presumably) fill the role intended for Yaldara.

YYYYY **The Farms Barossa Valley Shiraz 2002** A big wine; plenty of depth to the plum and dark chocolate fruit; good tannins and oak. **RATING** 94 **DRINK** 2017 $ 120

YYYY **Earth's Portrait Shiraz 2003** Light to medium-bodied; clean, slightly lean style, with clear fruit and crisp acidity. **RATING** 89 **DRINK** 2010

YYYY **The Farms Barossa Valley Shiraz 2003** **RATING** 85 **DRINK** 2008

Yalumba ★★★★☆

Eden Valley Road, Angaston, SA 5353 **REGION** Barossa Valley
T (08) 8561 3200 **F** (08) 8561 3393 **WEB** www.yalumba.com **OPEN** Mon–Fri 8.30–5, Sat 10–5, Sun 12–5
WINEMAKER Brian Walsh, Alan Hoey, Louisa Rose, Peter Gambetta, Kevin Glastonbury, Natalie Fryar, Philip Lehmann **EST.** 1849 **CASES** 900 000
SUMMARY Family-owned and run by Robert Hill Smith; much of its prosperity in the late 1980s and early 1990s turned on the great success of Angas Brut in export markets, but the company has always had a commitment to quality and shown great vision in its selection of vineyard sites, new varieties and brands. It has always been a serious player at the top end of full-bodied (and full-blooded) Australian reds, and was the pioneer in the use of screwcaps (for Pewsey Vale Riesling). While its 940 ha of estate vineyards are largely planted to mainstream varieties, it has taken marketing ownership of Viognier. Exports to all major markets.

YYYYY **Eden Valley Viognier 2003** Bright green-yellow; abundant fruit flavours ranging through citrus, apricot and honeysuckle; carries its alcohol with ease. **RATING** 93 **DRINK** 2007 $ 22.95

Barossa Valley Hand-Picked Shiraz Viognier 2002 Ultra-complex, fragrant and vibrant aromas and flavours, clearly driven by the Viognier; super-elegant, the Viognier just a fraction over the top. **RATING** 93 **DRINK** 2060 $ 28.95

Y Series Viognier 2004 Bright, light green-yellow; clear apricot and incipient honey varietal fruit; good balance, mouthfeel and aftertaste. **RATING** 91 **DRINK** 2007 $ 11.95

Eden Valley Semillon Sauvignon Blanc 2004 Spotlessly clean; vibrant lemon blossom/lemon rind characters; plenty of flavour, not phenolic. **RATING** 90 **DRINK** Now $ 16.95

Barossa Growers Shiraz 2002 A lively mix of red and black fruits supported by sweet vanilla oak; ripe tannins. **RATING** 90 **DRINK** 2010 $ 16.95

D 1998 Still has the complex array of earthy/stalky/spicy aromas it had when first tasted in October 2001; now with well over 3 years on lees, and prolonged bottle maturation, it represents excellent value. **RATING** 90 **DRINK** Now $ 30

YYYY **Oxford Landing Sauvignon Blanc 2004** Highly aromatic and distinct varietal gooseberry and passionfruit aromas; similar flavours on the palate, though not quite as intense; nonetheless, a great bargain. **RATING** 89 **DRINK** 2007 $ 8

Adelaide Hills Single Spur Chardonnay 2003 Intense, tangy citrus aromas, with the faintest touch of reduction; intense and long, with an ever so slightly grippy finish. Screwcap. **RATING** 89 **DRINK** 2008 $ 23.95

Antipodean Sangiovese Rose 2004 Cherry and a hint of spice aroma; good acidity and length. **RATING** 89 **DRINK** Now $14.95

Barossa Cabernet Shiraz 2001 Fresh blackberry/blackcurrant fruit; savoury tannins, subtle oak. **RATING** 89 **DRINK** 2007 $16.95

ㅜㅜㅜ♀ **Y Series Riesling 2004 RATING** 86 **DRINK** 2008 $12.95
Oxford Landing Chardonnay 2004 RATING 86 **DRINK** 2007 $8
Ringbolt Cabernet Sauvignon 2002 RATING 86 **DRINK** 2007 $22.95
Barossa MGS Mourvedre Grenache Shiraz 2003 RATING 86 **DRINK** Now $28.95
Bush Vine Grenache 2003 RATING 85 **DRINK** 2008 $16.95

ㅜㅜㅜ **Oxford Landing Merlot 2003 RATING** 83 $8

Yalumba The Menzies (Coonawarra) ★★★★☆

Riddoch Highway, Coonawarra, SA 5263 **REGION** Coonawarra
T (08) 8737 3603 **F** (08) 8737 3604 **WEB** www.yalumba.com **OPEN** 7 days 10–4.30
WINEMAKER Louisa Rose, Peter Gambetta **EST.** 2002 **CASES** 5000
SUMMARY Like many SA companies, Yalumba had been buying grapes from Coonawarra and elsewhere in the Limestone Coast Zone long before it became a landowner there. In 1993 it purchased the 20-ha vineyard which had provided the grapes previously purchased, and a year later added a nearby 16-ha block. Together, these vineyards now have 22 ha of cabernet sauvignon and 4 ha each of merlot and shiraz. The next step was the establishment of 82 ha of vineyard in the Wrattonbully region, led by 34 ha of cabernet sauvignon, the remainder equally split between shiraz and merlot. The third step was to build The Menzies Wine Room and Vineyard on the first property acquired – named Menzies Vineyard – and to offer the full range of Limestone Coast wines through this striking rammed-earth tasting and function centre.

ㅜㅜㅜㅜㅜ **Smith & Hooper Wrattonbully Cabernet Sauvignon Merlot 2002** A mix of red and black berries and spice; medium-bodied, but has excellent structure and length; fine, sweet tannins. **RATING** 94 **DRINK** 2009 $16.95

ㅜㅜㅜㅜ♀ **The Menzies Coonawarra Shiraz 2002** Generous, ripe black fruits; good oak and tannins; lovely texture. **RATING** 93 **DRINK** 2015 $16.95
Mawsons 2002 Clear-cut and focused; bright red and black fruit flavours; savoury tannins and positive oak. **RATING** 93 **DRINK** 2012 $12.95

ㅜㅜㅜㅜ **The Menzies Cabernet Sauvignon 2002** Powerful, potent and intense; tannins just a fraction grippy. **RATING** 88 **DRINK** 2012 $42.95

ㅜㅜㅜ♀ **Smith & Hooper Merlot 2002 RATING** 86 **DRINK** 2009 $36.95

Yandoit Hill Vineyard NR

Nevens Road, Yandoit Creek, Vic 3461 **REGION** Bendigo
T (03) 9379 1763 **F** (03) 9379 1763 **OPEN** By appointment (special open days for mailing list customers)
WINEMAKER Colin Mitchell **EST.** 1988 **CASES** 300
SUMMARY Colin and Rosa Mitchell began the development of Yandoit Hill with the first plantings in 1988; they now have merlot, a little under 1 ha each of cabernet franc and cabernet sauvignon, 0.5 ha each of arneis (the first planting in Australia) and nebbiolo. The vineyard is 20 km north of Daylesford, roughly halfway between Ballarat and Bendigo; although it is on the north-facing slope of Yandoit Hill, it is in an uncompromisingly cool climate.

Yangarra Estate ★★★★

Kangarilla Road, McLaren Vale, SA 5171 **REGION** McLaren Vale
T (08) 8383 7459 **F** (08) 8383 7518 **WEB** www.yangarra.com **OPEN** By appointment
WINEMAKER Peter Fraser **EST.** 2000 **CASES** 10 000
SUMMARY This is the Australian operation of Kendall-Jackson, one of the leading premium wine producers in California. In December 2000 Kendall-Jackson acquired the 172-ha Eringa Park vineyard from Normans Wines; 97 ha are under vine, the oldest dating back to 1923. The renamed Yangarra Park is the estate base for the operation, and from the 2003 vintage, the wines will be virtually 100% estate-grown. Exports to the US, the UK and Europe.

ŶŶŶŶ⍦ **Shiraz 2003** A fresh mix of blackberry, plum, spice and dark chocolate; carries 15° alcohol with a certain amount of grace. Screwcap. **RATING** 91 **DRINK** 2013 $ 28

ŶŶŶŶ **Old Vine Grenache 2003** Good hue; sweet, juicy berry varietal character, sweetness in part from 15.8° alcohol. **RATING** 89 **DRINK** 2010 $ 28
Cadenzia 2003 Nice spicy juicy fruits; attractive ripe but fine tannins; very different from the varietal blend of the same wines (Grenache/Shiraz/Mourvedre). **RATING** 89 **DRINK** 2009 $ 28
Grenache Shiraz Mourvedre 2003 Light to medium-bodied; a sweet array of fruits; modest tannins and overall structure. **RATING** 87 **DRINK** 2008 $ 28

Yanmah Ridge   NR

Yanmah Road, Manjimup, WA 6258 **REGION** Manjimup
T (08) 9772 1301 **F** (08) 9772 1501 **WEB** www.yanmahridge.com.au **OPEN** By appointment
WINEMAKER Peter Nicholas, John Wade (Consultant) **EST.** 1987 **CASES** 3500
SUMMARY Peter and Sallyann Nicholas have established 26 ha of vineyards on elevated, north-facing slopes, with semillon, sauvignon blanc, chardonnay, pinot noir, sangiovese, merlot, cabernet franc and cabernet sauvignon. The property was identified by Peter Nicholas in 1986 as 'the perfect location' after a study of grapegrowing regions in Western Australia. The project was the last requirement for Nicholas to complete his winemaking degree at Roseworthy Agricultural College. Their viticulture is environmentally friendly, with no residual herbicides or chemical pesticides. A new winery was built onsite in time for the 2001 vintage, but the majority of the annual production is still sold (as grapes or wine) to other producers. Wholesale distribution through Working Wine (Victoria); Lionel Samson (Western Australia); and Simsed Agencies (NSW and Queensland). Exports to England, Canada and Hong Kong.

Yarrabank   ★★★★★

38 Melba Highway, Yarra Glen, Vic 3775 **REGION** Yarra Valley
T (03) 9730 0100 **F** (03) 9739 0135 **WEB** www.yering.com **OPEN** 7 days 10–5
WINEMAKER Michel Parisot, Tom Carson, Darren Rathbone **EST.** 1993 **CASES** 5000
SUMMARY The 1997 vintage saw the opening of the majestic new winery, established as part of a joint venture between the French Champagne house Devaux and Yering Station. Until 1997 the Yarrabank Cuvee Brut was made under Claude Thibaut's direction at Domaine Chandon, but thereafter the entire operation has been conducted at Yarrabank. There are now 4 ha of dedicated 'estate' vineyards at Yering Station; the balance of the intake comes from other growers in the Yarra Valley and southern Victoria. Wine quality has been quite outstanding, the wines having a delicacy unmatched by any other Australian sparkling wines. Exports to all major markets.

ŶŶŶŶŶ **Cuvee 2002** In typical style; extremely youthful, fresh and delicate, but with very good length and balance; citrussy, but not green; still to grow. **RATING** 95 **DRINK** 2010 $ 35

ŶŶŶŶ⍦ **Creme de Cuvee NV** Pale salmon; full-on dosage in answer to Domaine Chandon Cuvee Riche; a blend of Pinot Noir and Chardonnay with 3 years on lees and high dosage. **RATING** 92 **DRINK** Now $ 30

Yarra Brook Estate   ★★★★

Yarraview Road, Yarra Glen, Vic 3775 **REGION** Yarra Valley
T (03) 9763 7066 **F** (03) 9763 8757 **WEB** www.yarrabrook.com.au **OPEN** By appointment
WINEMAKER Timo Mayer, Charlie Brydon (Contract) **EST.** 1997 **CASES** 1000
SUMMARY Beginning in 1997, Chris Dhar has established 26 ha of vines: pinot noir (10.4 ha) and chardonnay (6.8 ha), and the remainder equally shared by sauvignon blanc, merlot, shiraz and cabernet sauvignon. Most of the grapes are sold, but part of the production is contract-made. The prices ex the mail list are very reasonable, thanks to the exemption from WET for small wineries selling direct. Exports to Sri Lanka and India.

ŶŶŶŶ⍦ **Yarra Valley Shiraz 2004** Supple, rich, ripe satsuma plum flavour; fruit-driven, but has weight and very good mouthfeel. Twin Top. **RATING** 91 **DRINK** 2014 $ 13.75
Yarra Valley Sauvignon Blanc 2004 A clean and intense palate; mineral, stone, herbs, spice and lime; even flow and line. Screwcap. **RATING** 90 **DRINK** 2007 $ 13.75

ΨΨΨΨ **Yarra Valley Pinot Noir 2003** Good colour; abundant dark cherry/plum fruit with ripe but persistent tannins. **RATING** 89 **DRINK** 2010 $13.75
Yarra Valley Chardonnay 2003 Elegant and well balanced; light to medium-bodied; melon and a touch of creamy cashew. **RATING** 87 **DRINK** 2007 $13.75
Yarra Valley Shiraz Merlot 2004 Light to medium-bodied; the fruit-driven blend more or less works; early-drinking style. Twin Top. **RATING** 87 **DRINK** 2008 $13.75

ΨΨΨΨ **Yarra Valley Chardonnay 2004** **RATING** 86 **DRINK** 2008 $13.75

Yarra Burn ★★★★

Settlement Road, Yarra Junction, Vic 3797 **REGION** Yarra Valley
T (03) 5967 1428 **F** (03) 5967 1146 **WEB** www.hardywines.com.au/brands/yarra.html **OPEN** 7 days 10–5
WINEMAKER Ed Carr, Tom Newton, Mark O'Cllaghan **EST.** 1975 **CASES** 15 000
SUMMARY Acquired by Hardys in 1995 and, for the time being, the headquarters of Hardys' very substantial Yarra Valley operations, the latter centring on the large production from its Hoddles Creek vineyards. The new brand direction has largely taken shape. Care needs to be taken in reading the back labels of the wines other than the Bastard Hill duo, for the majority are regional blends, albeit with a substantial Yarra Valley component. Exports to the UK and the US.

ΨΨΨΨ **Pinot Noir Chardonnay 2001** Abundant fruit flavour through the length of the palate, ranging through apple, citrus and nectarine; long, dry finish. **RATING** 91 **DRINK** 2007 $25
Chardonnay 2002 Quite intense and long grapefruit and nectarine; immaculate balance. **RATING** 90 **DRINK** 2007 $20

Yarra Edge ★★★☆

PO Box 390, Yarra Glen, Vic 3775 **REGION** Yarra Valley
T (03) 9730 0100 **F** (03) 9739 0135 **WEB** www.yering.com **OPEN** At Yering Station
WINEMAKER Tom Carson, Darren Rathbone **EST.** 1984 **CASES** 2000
SUMMARY Now leased to Yering Station, which makes the wines but continues to use the Yarra Edge brand for grapes from this estate. Tom Carson, Yering Station winemaker, was briefly winemaker/manager at Yarra Edge and knows the property intimately, so the rich style can be expected to continue. Exports to Hong Kong.

Yarraman Estate ★★★★

Yarraman Road, Wybong, NSW 2333 **REGION** Upper Hunter Valley
T (02) 6547 8118 **F** (02) 6547 8039 **WEB** www.yarramanestate.com **OPEN** 7 days 10–5
WINEMAKER Chris Mennie **EST.** 1958 **CASES** 55 000
SUMMARY This is the oldest winery and vineyard in the Upper Hunter, established in 1958 as Penfolds Wybong Estate; it was acquired by Rosemount in 1974, and retained until 1994. During 1999–2001 a new winery and storage area was built; after hitting financial turbulence it was acquired by a small group of Sydney businessmen. Board changes and subsequent strengthening of the management and winemaking team has seen a surge in exports to all major markets.

ΨΨΨΨ **Aged Release Classic Hunter Semillon 2000** Light-bodied; still largely in primary phase; minerally, flinty; light herb and citrus nuances. Cork. **RATING** 92 **DRINK** 2010
Classic Hunter Merlot 2002 Surprisingly pure varietal character; medium-bodied black and redcurrant and olive; good length and balance; fine tannins. Good cork. **RATING** 90 **DRINK** 2010

ΨΨΨΨ **Black Cypress Hunter Valley Shiraz 2003** Good colour; medium-bodied; nicely balanced black cherry and blackberry fruit, oak and tannins. Poor-quality cork. **RATING** 89 **DRINK** 2010
Reserve Hunter Valley Gewurztraminer 2000 Clean, still and quite fresh; well-balanced mouthfeel; long finish. Little or no varietal character, however. Screwcap. **RATING** 87 **DRINK** Now
Classic Hunter Shiraz 2002 Sweet, juicy berry fruit and mouthfeel; positive use of vanillin oak. Cork. **RATING** 87 **DRINK** 2009

 TTTY Black Cypress Hunter Valley GWT 2004 RATING 85 DRINK 2007
Black Cypress Hunter Valley Rose 2004 RATING 85 DRINK Now
Black Cypress Hunter Valley Chambourcin 2004 RATING 85 DRINK Now
Classic Hunter Chardonnay 2004 RATING 84 DRINK Now

TTY Black Cypress Hunter Valley Chardonnay 2004 RATING 83
Black Cypress Hunter Valley Verdelho 2004 RATING 83

Yarrambat Estate

45 Laurie Street, Yarrambat, Vic 3091 (postal) REGION Yarra Valley
T (03) 9717 3710 F (03) 9717 3712 WEB www.yarrambatestate.com OPEN Not
WINEMAKER John Ellis (Contract) EST. 1995 CASES 1500
SUMMARY Ivan McQuilkin has a little over 2.6 ha of chardonnay, pinot noir, cabernet sauvignon and
merlot on his vineyard in the northwestern corner of the Yarra Valley, not far from the Plenty River,
which joins the Yarra River near Melbourne. He and Hayden Gregson run the vineyard (Ivan is
responsible for the commercial aspects of the vineyard, Hayden for viticulture and wine production).
It is very much an alternative occupation for McQuilkin, whose principal activity is as an
international taxation consultant to expatriate employees. While the decision to make the wine was
at least in part triggered by falling grape prices, hindsight proves it to have been a good one, because
some of the wines have impressed. There are no cellar door sales; the conditions of the licence are
that wine sales can only take place by mail order or over the internet.

TTTT Pinot Noir 2002 Fresh, bright and lively early-picked style; needs a bit more flesh on the
bones. Cork. RATING 87 DRINK 2008 $ 30

TTTY Chardonnay 2003 Gentle melon fruit; minimal oak inputs; slightly fuzzy, fractionally
sweet finish. Cork. RATING 86 DRINK 2007 $ 25

Yarra Ridge

c/- Beringer Blass, GPO Box 753F, Melbourne, Vic 3001 REGION Yarra Valley
T (03) 8626 3300 WEB www.yarraridge.com.au OPEN Not
WINEMAKER Matt Steel (former) EST. 1983 CASES 45 000
SUMMARY Now simply a brand owned by Beringer Blass, the winery having been sold to a partnership
including Rob 'Sticks' Dolan. For the time being, Yarra Ridge wines will be made at Sticks, but they
will presumably migrate to South Australia in due course.

TTTTY Rose 2004 Aromatic strawberry and cherry fruit; plenty of life; crisp, dry finish.
RATING 90 DRINK Now $ 24

TTTY Eye Spy Sauvignon Blanc Semillon 2004 RATING 85 DRINK Now $ 15
Eye Spy Cabernet Merlot 2003 RATING 85 DRINK 2007 $ 15
Eye Spy Pinot Chardonnay NV RATING 84 DRINK Now $ 15

Yarra Track Wines

518 Old Healesville Road, Yarra Glen, Vic 3775 REGION Yarra Valley
T (03) 9730 1349 F (03) 9730 1910 OPEN 7 days 10–5.30
WINEMAKER MasterWineMakers (Contract) EST. 1989 CASES 800
SUMMARY Jim and Diana Viggers began establishing their vineyard back in 1989; it now has 3.1 ha of
chardonnay and 3.4 ha of pinot noir. The Viggers intend to increase wine production progressively,
and sell part of the grape production in the meantime. The wine is sold only through the cellar door
and local restaurants.

TTTT Viggers Reserve Pinot Noir 2003 Deep colour; potent, very complex and very powerful
wine typical of the vineyard; tannins take it over the top; a pity. A decade may tell.
Screwcap. RATING 89 DRINK 2018 $ 50

Yarra Vale

NR

Paynes Road, Seville, Vic 3139 REGION Yarra Valley
T (03) 9735 1819 F (03) 9737 6565 OPEN Not
WINEMAKER Domenic Bucci EST. 1982 CASES 1500

SUMMARY This is the first stage of Rochford (formerly Eyton-on-Yarra), and second time around for Domenic Bucci, who built the first stage of Eyton-on-Yarra before being compelled to sell the business in the hard times of the early 1990s. He has established 2 ha of cabernet sauvignon and 0.5 ha of merlot, supplemented by chardonnay which is supplied in return for his winemaking services to the grower. Retail distribution in Melbourne through Sullivan Wine Agencies; exports via Rubins Productions.

Yarra Valley Gateway Estate ★★★★

669 Maroondah Highway, Coldstream, Vic 3770 **REGION** Yarra Valley
T (03) 9739 0568 **F** (03) 9739 0568 **OPEN** 7 days 9–5
WINEMAKER Matt Aldridge (Contract) **EST.** 1993 **CASES** 2600
SUMMARY Rod Spurling extended his successful hydroponic tomato-growing business by planting 5 ha of sauvignon blanc, chardonnay and pinot noir in 1993. This is part of the grouping of so-called Micro Masters in the Yarra Valley.

🍷🍷🍷🍷 **Semillon Sauvignon Blanc 2004** Spotlessly clean; very long and intense mix of tropical gooseberry and herb; lemony acidity. Screwcap. **RATING** 92 **DRINK** 2010 $ 22

🍷🍷🍷🍷 **Spurling Hill Vineyard Chardonnay 2004** Good wine; nectarine and melon fruit; subtle barrel ferment oak inputs; good length. **RATING** 89 **DRINK** 2008 $ 20

🍷🍷🍷 **Spurling Hill Vineyard Sauvignon Blanc 2004 RATING** 83 $ 17

Yarra Valley Vineyards NR

159 Lilydale–Monbulk Road, Silvan, Vic 3795 **REGION** Yarra Valley
T (03) 9737 9630 **F** (03) 9737 9634 **OPEN** By appointment
WINEMAKER Gary Mills (Simpatico Wine Services) **EST.** 1993 **CASES** 3000
SUMMARY Don Smarelli has an 8-ha vineyard at Silvan, one of the cooler parts of the Yarra Valley, with red volcanic soils. The wines are released under the Playing Card and Segreto (Italian for secret) labels, and are available through the Twisted Vine Restaurant.

Yarrawa Estate ★★★

PO Box 6018, Kangaroo Valley, NSW 2577 **REGION** Shoalhaven Coast
T (02) 4465 1165 **WEB** www.yarrawaestate.com **OPEN** Not
WINEMAKER Bevan Wilson **EST.** 1998 **CASES** 500
SUMMARY Susan and Mark Francis Foster established Yarrawa Estate in 1998, planting a wide variety of trees, table grapes and 2.5 ha of verdelho, chardonnay, chambourcin, merlot and cabernet sauvignon. The hillside vineyard has views across the Kangaroo Valley, with the Kangaroo River directly below. Finger board directions up the hill point the way for the first-time visitor. At the 2005 South Coast Wine Show Yarrawa Estate had the top-pointed Chambourcin (2004), following the success of the 2003.

🍷🍷🍷🍷 **Chambourcin 2003** Light to medium-bodied, but with slightly more fruit density than the '04; plum and black cherry; as always, structure lacking, the limitation of the variety, not the winemaking. Quality cork. **RATING** 86 **DRINK** 2007 $ 18.50
Chambourcin 2004 RATING 84 $ 19

Yarrawalla Wines NR

Maddens Lane, Coldstream, Vic 3770 **REGION** Yarra Valley
T (03) 5964 9363 **F** (03) 5964 9363 **WEB** www.yarrawallavineyards.com.au **OPEN** By appointment
WINEMAKER Dominique Portet (Contract) **EST.** 1994 **CASES** NA
SUMMARY A very prominent vineyard on Maddens Lane, with 24 ha of chardonnay, 12.7 ha of pinot noir and 6.5 ha of sauvignon blanc. Significant amounts of the grapes have gone to Coldstream Hills over the years. With the arrival of Dominique Portet (also on Maddens Lane), Yarrawalla has ventured into winemaking under its own label, although the major part of the production continues to be sold as grapes.

Yarra Yarra ★★★★★

239 Hunts Lane, Steels Creek, Vic 3775 **REGION** Yarra Valley
T (03) 5965 2380 **F** (03) 5965 2086 **OPEN** By appointment
WINEMAKER Ian Maclean **EST.** 1979 **CASES** NFP
SUMMARY Despite its small production, the wines of Yarra Yarra found their way onto a veritable who's who of Melbourne's best restaurants, encouraging Ian Maclean to increase the estate plantings from 2 ha to over 7 ha in 1996 and 1997. Demand for the beautifully crafted wines continued to exceed supply, so the Macleans have planted yet more vines and increased winery capacity. Exports to the UK and Singapore.

▼▼▼▼▼ **The Yarra Yarra 2002** Significantly deeper colour than the Cabernets; velvety, rich and profound blackcurrant, earth, cedar and spice; built-in ripe tannins; classic wine. Stained cork a worry. **RATING** 96 **DRINK** 2015 **$** 60
The Yarra Yarra 2001 As ever, an exceptional wine with great texture and structure; abundance of blackcurrant and cassis fruit perfectly framed by silky, round tannins and immaculate oak. **RATING** 96 **DRINK** 2021 **$** 60
Cabernets 2002 A fragrant, fine and stylish mix of spicy black fruits and cedary oak; supple, feline grace. Very stained cork. **RATING** 95 **DRINK** 2012 **$** 45
Syrah Viognier 2003 Intense anise, spice and apricot overlay to blackberry and plum fruit; medium to full-bodied; rich and round; fine tannins, quality oak. Good cork.
RATING 94 **DRINK** 2018 **$** 40
Syrah Viognier 2002 Ultra-fragrant Viognier lift; refined, elegant and smooth; sotto voce style. **RATING** 94 **DRINK** 2012 **$** 40

▼▼▼▼▽ **Sauvignon Blanc Semillon 2002** Complex, powerful and rich, in typical white Bordeaux style; ripe fruits, nuts and spice all in a firm framework; oak welded in. Diam. **RATING** 93 **DRINK** 2010 **$** 35

▼▼▼▼ **Sauvignon Blanc Semillon 2001** Powerful, complex wine into the secondary phase of development; nutty edges but uncompromising acidity. **RATING** 89 **DRINK** Now **$** 35

Yarra Yering ★★★★★

Briarty Road, Coldstream, Vic 3770 (postal) **REGION** Yarra Valley
T (03) 5964 9267 **F** (03) 5964 9239 **OPEN** Usually first Saturday in May
WINEMAKER Dr Bailey Carrodus, Mark Haisma **EST.** 1969 **CASES** NA
SUMMARY Dr Bailey Carrodus makes extremely powerful, occasionally idiosyncratic, wines from his 35-year-old, low-yielding unirrigated vineyards. Both red and white wines have an exceptional depth of flavour and richness, although my preference for what I believe to be his great red wines is well known. As he has expanded the size of his vineyards, so has the range of wines become ever more eclectic; it now includes the only Vintage Port being produced in the Yarra Valley. Exports to the UK, the US, Switzerland, Germany, Hong Kong, Japan, Malaysia and Singapore.

Yass Valley Wines ★★★

5 Crisps Lane, Murrumbateman, NSW 2582 **REGION** Canberra District
T (02) 6227 5592 **F** (02) 6227 5592 **OPEN** Wed–Sun & public hols 10–5, or by appointment
WINEMAKER Michael Withers **EST.** 1978 **CASES** 1000
SUMMARY Michael Withers and Anne Hillier purchased Yass Valley in January 1991; they have since rehabilitated the run-down vineyards and extended the plantings. Mick Withers is a chemist by profession and has completed a wine science degree at Charles Sturt University; Anne is a registered psychologist and has completed a Viticulture diploma at Charles Sturt. Crisps Lane Café is open weekends and public holidays 10–5; it focuses on local produce.

▼▼▼▼ **Barbera 2004** Very good purple-red colour; sweet, fruit-driven raspberry and blueberry flavours; clean finish; no oak or tannin intrusion; 13% Shiraz. Screwcap. **RATING** 87 **DRINK** 2008 **$** 18

▼▼▼ **Chardonnay Semillon 2003** **RATING** 83 **$** 16

Yaxley Estate   NR

31 Dransfield Road, Copping, Tas 7174 **REGION** Southern Tasmania
T (03) 6253 5222 **F** (03) 6253 5222 **OPEN** 7 days 10–6.30
WINEMAKER Andrew Hood (Contract) **EST.** 1991 **CASES** 500
SUMMARY While Yaxley Estate was established back in 1991, it was not until 1998 that it offered each
of the four wines from its vineyard plantings, which total just under 2 ha. Once again, it is the small
batch handling skills (and patience) of Andrew Hood that have made the venture possible.

Yellowglen   ★★★☆

Whites Road, Smythesdale, Vic 3351 **REGION** Ballarat
T (03) 5342 8617 **F** (03) 5333 7102 **WEB** www.yellowglen.com.au **OPEN** Mon–Fri 10–5, weekends
11–5
WINEMAKER Charles Hargrave **EST.** 1975 **CASES** 420 000
SUMMARY Just as the overall quality of Australian sparkling wine has improved out of all recognition
over the past 15 years, so has that of Yellowglen. Initially the quality lift was apparent at the top end of
the range; it now extends to the non-vintage commercial releases. The winemaking facility is being
closed down in 2005.

ŸŸŸŸŸ **Aged Release 2000** Elegant; biscuity/brioche flavours layered on apple and stone fruit;
fine, elegant finish; good dosage; 3 years on lees. **RATING** 92 **DRINK** Now $ 25

ŸŸŸŸ **Vintage Pinot Chardonnay 2003** Good mousse; very fresh, lively and bright apple/stone
fruit flavours; not particularly complex. **RATING** 87 **DRINK** Now

ŸŸŸŸ **Cremant 2003 RATING** 85 **DRINK** Now $ 22
Red NV RATING 85 **DRINK** 2007 $ 12

ŸŸŸ **Yellow NV RATING** 83 **DRINK** Now
Pink NV RATING 82

Yellymong   ★★★

Moulamein Road, Swan Hill, Vic 3585 **REGION** Swan Hill
T (03) 5032 2160 **F** (03) 5032 2160 **OPEN** By appointment
WINEMAKER Allan Cooper **EST.** 2000 **CASES** 500
SUMMARY Gary and Jo Jeans have a tiny 0.4 ha of pinot gris, supplemented by purchases of other
varieties from local growers, all of which are hand-picked. The Pinot Gris can be remarkably good
given the (theoretically) unsuitable (too warm) climate.

Yengari Wine Company   ★★★★

Dookie–Nalinga Road, Dookie, Vic 3646 **REGION** Beechworth
T (03) 5833 9295 **F** (03) 5833 9205 **WEB** www.yengari.com **OPEN** By appointment
WINEMAKER Tony Lacy **EST.** 1990 **CASES** 1000
SUMMARY Tony Lacy and partner Trish Flores run an interesting grape and olive produce business,
with wines from the 2.4 ha of shiraz, 1.2 ha of chardonnay and 0.5 ha of viognier forming just part of
the range of products. Painted candles coloured with wine lees, stationery tinted using the same
colour bases, wine soap (shiraz, chardonnay and cabernet sauvignon) and water colour paints (shiraz
from 100% sun-dried wine lees and chardonnay from sun-dried wine lees plus traces of natural water
colour) are all produced and sold.

ŸŸŸŸŸ **Reserve Shiraz Viognier 2002** Complex, aromatic and powerful apricot, cedar and spice
lift to the bouquet; again, silky tannins. Cork. **RATING** 91 **DRINK** 2013 $ 24
Granite Beechworth Shiraz 2002 Spicy, peppery aromas; medium-bodied; blackberry,
licorice and spice; fine, silky, ripe tannins; good finish. Creased, stained cork. **RATING** 90
DRINK 2011 $ 26

ŸŸŸŸ **Reserve Cabernet Sauvignon 2002** Much better colour than Barrique 42; blackberry,
earth and spice; medium-bodied; balanced tannins, subtle oak; has length. Cork.
RATING 89 **DRINK** 2012 $ 32

ŸŸŸŸ **Barrique 42 Cabernet Sauvignon 2002 RATING** 85 **DRINK** 2007 $ 22

Yeringberg ★★★★★

Maroondah Highway, Coldstream, Vic 3770 **REGION** Yarra Valley
T (03) 9739 1453 **F** (03) 9739 0048 **OPEN** By appointment
WINEMAKER Guill de Pury **EST.** 1863 **CASES** 1100
SUMMARY Makes wines for the new millennium from the low-yielding vines re-established on the heart of what was one of the most famous (and infinitely larger) vineyards of the 19th century. In the riper years, the red wines have a velvety generosity of flavour which is rarely encountered, yet never lose varietal character, while the Yeringberg White takes students of history back to Yeringberg's fame in the 19th century. Exports to the UK, the US, Canada, Switzerland, Malaysia and Hong Kong.

Yering Farm ★★★★☆

St Huberts Road, Yering, Vic 3770 **REGION** Yarra Valley
T (03) 9739 0461 **F** (03) 9739 0467 **WEB** www.yeringfarm.com.au **OPEN** 7 days 10–5
WINEMAKER Alan Johns **EST.** 1988 **CASES** 7000
SUMMARY Former East Doncaster orchardist Alan Johns acquired the 40-ha Yeringa Vineyard property in 1980; the property had originally been planted by the Deschamps family in the mid-19th century, and known as Yeringa Cellars. The plantings now extend to 12 ha, and the first wines were made in 1992. Since then all the wines have been made onsite; they have enjoyed consistent show success over the years.

ŸŸŸŸŸ Chardonnay 2003 Fine, elegant; gentle cashew; quite creamy; good balance and length.
RATING 94 **DRINK** 2012 $ 28

Yering Range Vineyard NR

14 McIntyre Lane, Coldstream, Vic 3770 **REGION** Yarra Valley
T (03) 9739 1172 **F** (03) 9739 1172 **OPEN** By appointment
WINEMAKER John Ellis (Hanging Rock Winery) **EST.** 1989 **CASES** 200
SUMMARY Yering Range has 2 ha of cabernet sauvignon under vine; part is sold and part is made under the Yering Range label. The tiny production is sold through a mailing list.

Yering Station ★★★★★

38 Melba Highway, Yarra Glen, Vic 3775 **REGION** Yarra Valley
T (03) 9730 0100 **F** (03) 9739 0135 **WEB** www.yering.com **OPEN** 7 days 10–5
WINEMAKER Tom Carson, Darren Rathbone, Caroline Mooney **EST.** 1988 **CASES** 50 000
SUMMARY The historic Yering Station (or at least the portion of the property on which the cellar door sales and vineyard are established) was purchased by the Rathbone family in January 1996 and is now the site of a joint venture with the French Champagne house Devaux. A spectacular and very large winery has been erected; it handles the Yarrabank sparkling wines and the Yering Station and Yarra Edge table wines. It has immediately become one of the focal points of the Yarra Valley, particularly as the historic Chateau Yering, where luxury accommodation and fine dining are available, is next door. Yering Station's own restaurant is open every day for lunch, providing the best cuisine in the Valley. Since 2002, a sister company of Mount Langi Ghiran, now also owned by the Rathbone family. In 2004 Yering Station, via Tom Carson, was named International Winemaker of the Year by the International Wine & Spirit Competition in London. Exports to all major markets.

ŸŸŸŸŸ Pinot Noir ED Rose 2004 Spicy, savoury aromas; excellent length and structure; spice and strawberry flavours; serious style. **RATING** 95 **DRINK** Now $ 17.50
Reserve Yarra Valley Pinot Noir 2003 Rich, deep, profound black fruits and spice; another dimension above the varietal version; velvety mouthfeel and balance. High-quality cork. **RATING** 95 **DRINK** 2012 $ 58
Reserve Yarra Valley Shiraz Viognier 2003 Deep colour; highly aromatic; smooth and supple plum and black fruits; integrated oak; balanced tannins. **RATING** 95 **DRINK** 2018 $ 58
Yarra Valley Shiraz Viognier 2002 The very cool vintage required the skilled viticulture and winemaking evident in this fragrant, ultra-complex mix of spice, licorice and black fruits, with fine, silky tannins and equally fine French oak. Fantastic value. **RATING** 95 **DRINK** 2012 $ 23

ŸŸŸŸŸ **Yarra Valley Pinot Noir 2003** Powerful, ripe plum, black cherry and spice; supple and smooth; immaculate oak and tannin management. Screwcap. **RATING** 93 **DRINK** 2010 $ 23
Yarra Valley Pinot Gris 2004 Bright, pale straw-green; floral spice and apple blossom aromas; crisp, pear, apple and citrus. Only 12.5° alcohol, yet all the flavour you could wish for. Very good example. Screwcap. **RATING** 92 **DRINK** 2008 $ 17.50
Muir Yarra Valley Sangiovese 2003 Excellent palate structure; cherry, spice and tobacco; fine ripe tannins; overall fruit sweetness. **RATING** 92 **DRINK** 2009 $ 23
Yarra Valley Sauvignon Blanc 2004 Fresh, delicate mineral, herb and gooseberry mix; bright acidity on the finish. **RATING** 91 **DRINK** Now $ 17.50
Yarra Valley Chardonnay 2003 Light to medium-bodied; stone fruit and melon aromas and flavours; subtle malolactic and barrel ferment notes; a hint of sweetness somewhere. Screwcap. **RATING** 90 **DRINK** 2008 $ 20.50
Yarra Valley Shiraz Viognier 2003 Medium-bodied; typically fragrant, with sweet red and black fruits; nicely balanced tannins. **RATING** 90 **DRINK** 2013 $ 23

ŸŸŸŸ **MVR 2004** Pale straw; overall nicely balanced, but young vines show in lack of intensity. May surprise with development in bottle. **RATING** 89 **DRINK** 2010 $ 23

Yerong Creek Estate   NR

'Barwon', Yerong Creek, NSW 2642 **REGION** Riverina
T (02) 6920 3569 **F** (02) 6920 3503 **OPEN** 7 days 10–5
WINEMAKER Damien Cofield (Contract) **EST.** 1996 **CASES** NA
SUMMARY Robert and Julie Yates have 5 ha planted to chardonnay and shiraz. The wines are chiefly sold by mail order and through the cellar door.

Yilgarnia   ★★★★☆

6634 Redmond West Road, Redmond, WA 6327 **REGION** Denmark
T (08) 9845 3031 **F** (08) 9845 3031 **WEB** www.yilgarnia.com.au **OPEN** Not
WINEMAKER Contract **EST.** 1997 **CASES** 2000
SUMMARY Melbourne-educated Peter Buxton travelled across the Nullarbor and settled on a bush block of 405 acres on the Hay River, 6 km north of Wilson Inlet. That was 40 years ago, and for the first 10 years Buxton worked for the WA Department of Agriculture in Albany. While there, he surveyed several of the early vineyards in Western Australia, and recognised the potential of his family's property. Today there are 10 ha of vines in bearing, with another 6 ha planted in 2002 and 2003. All the vineyard plantings (eight varieties in all) are on north-facing blocks, the geological history of which stretches back 2 billion years.

ŸŸŸŸŸ **Denmark Sauvignon Blanc 2004** Intense cut-grass, herb, mineral and citrus aromas; the powerful palate is a replay; has attitude. Screwcap. **RATING** 92 **DRINK** 2007 $ 15.95
Denmark Classic White 2004 Highly aromatic, lively, citrussy bouquet; the palate kicks on in similar fashion; an exceptionally good example of Chardonnay/Sauvignon Blanc/Semillon. Screwcap. **RATING** 92 **DRINK** 2008 $ 14.95
Denmark Unwooded Chardonnay 2003 Attractive, pure nectarine fruit flavours; good length and balance; excellent unwooded style. **RATING** 91 **DRINK** 2007 $ 16.50
Denmark Sauvignon Blanc 2003 Light-bodied, but has good length, finish and aftertaste; asparagus, gooseberry and grass flavours, no tropical components. **RATING** 90 **DRINK** Now $ 15.95
Denmark Merlot 2003 Light to medium-bodied; good varietal character from a core of redcurrant/blackcurrant fruit; sweet, spicy, savoury tannins. **RATING** 90 **DRINK** 2010 $ 20.95

ŸŸŸŸ **Denmark Shiraz 2003** Plush, ripe plum and blackberry fruit with a hint of spice in the background. Nice oak. **RATING** 88 **DRINK** 2010 $ 20.95
Denmark Cabernet Sauvignon 2002 Good colour; a powerful though fractionally reduced bouquet; strong, youthful cabernet fruit needs time to soften and sort itself out. **RATING** 88 **DRINK** 2012 $ 20.95
Denmark Unwooded Chardonnay 2004 Attractive stone fruit/grapefruit flavours; crisp, dry finish. **RATING** 87 **DRINK** Now $ 16.50
Denmark Shiraz 2002 Light to medium-bodied; fresh and bright appealing red fruits; fine tannins. **RATING** 87 **DRINK** 2009 $ 20.95

Yokain Vineyard Estate ★★★

Worsley Back Road, Allanson, WA 6225 (postal) **REGION** Geographe
T (08) 9725 3397 **F** (08) 9725 3397 **WEB** www.yokain.com.au **OPEN** Not
WINEMAKER Siobhan Lynch **EST.** 1998 **CASES** 1000
SUMMARY David and Julie Gardiner began the establishment of their 17-ha vineyard in 1998, with all but 2 ha planted in that year. Verdelho, chardonnay, semillon, shiraz, cabernet sauvignon, merlot and cabernet franc are in production; the 2000 plantings of riesling and zinfandel produced their first grapes in 2003. The wine is sold through the website and by mail order.

ΨΨΨΨ **Reserve Merlot 2003** Ripe red and blackcurrant fruit; hints of olive; tannins dominate on the finish, but there is scope for development. **RATING** 87 **DRINK** 2010 $ 15

ΨΨΨΨ **Riesling 2003 RATING** 86 **DRINK** 2004 $ 8
Zinfandel 2003 RATING 86 **DRINK** 2008 $ 12
Shiraz 2002 RATING 85 **DRINK** 2007 $ 8

Yrsa's Vineyard ★★★★

105 Tucks Road, Main Ridge, Vic 3928 **REGION** Mornington Peninsula
T (03) 5989 6500 **F** (03) 5989 6501 **WEB** www.yrsasvineyard.com **OPEN** By appointment
WINEMAKER Craig McLeod, Judy Gifford (Contract) **EST.** 1994 **CASES** 1500
SUMMARY Yrsa's Vineyard is named after the lady from whom Steven and Marianne Stern acquired the property. She, in turn, was named after Queen Yrsa of Sweden, born in 565AD, whose story is told in the Norse sagas. Well-known patent and trademark attorney Steven Stern (whose particular area of expertise is in the wine and liquor business) and wife Marianne have established around 2.5 ha each of pinot noir and chardonnay, and initially marketed the wines only in the UK. A wine tasting studio available for small wine tastings (up to 10 people) is available by arrangement.

ΨΨΨΨΨ **Ursa Major Mornington Peninsula Chardonnay 2003** Complex bouquet with a nice touch of funk; stone fruit, grapefruit and citrus; particularly long, squeaky acidity on the finish. Really nice wine. Cork. **RATING** 92 **DRINK** 2009 $ 28

ΨΨΨΨ **Ursa Major Mornington Peninsula Pinot Noir 2003** Slightly hazy/cloudy; gamey spicy aromas; a mix of stem and red fruits; possible low-level microbial activity. **RATING** 89 **DRINK** 2008 $ 28

Zanella Estate NR

Burnets Road, Traralgon, Vic 3844 **REGION** Gippsland
T (03) 5174 0557 **F** (03) 5174 0557 **OPEN** 7 days
WINEMAKER Ettore Zanella **EST.** 1996 **CASES** NA
SUMMARY Ettorre Zanella has established 1.5 ha of chardonnay, cabernet sauvignon, merlot and shiraz and makes the wine onsite. They are sold through the cellar door.

Zappacosta Estate Wines ★★☆

301 Kidman Way, Hanwood, NSW 2680 **REGION** Riverina
T (02) 6963 0278 **F** (02) 6963 0278 **OPEN** 7 days 10–5 by appointment
WINEMAKER Dino Zappacosta **EST.** 1956 **CASES** 70 000
SUMMARY Zappacosta Estate, briefly known as Hanwood Village Wines, is primarily a bulk winemaker and supplier to others. Small amounts of Shiraz under the Zappacosta Estate label are made from time to time.

ΨΨΨΨ **Reserve Shiraz 2002 RATING** 84 **DRINK** 2007 $ 11.50

Zarephath Wines ★★★★

Moorialup Road, East Porongurup, WA 6324 **REGION** Porongurup
T (08) 9853 1152 **F** (08) 9853 1152 **WEB** www.zarephathwines.com **OPEN** Mon–Sat 10–5, Sun 12–4
WINEMAKER Robert Diletti (Contract) **EST.** 1994 **CASES** 3000

SUMMARY The 9-ha Zarephath vineyard is owned and operated by Brothers and Sisters of The Christ Circle, a Benedictine community. They say the most outstanding feature of the location is the feeling of peace and tranquility which permeates the site, something I can well believe on the basis of numerous visits to the Porongurups. Exports to the UK and New Zealand.

🍷🍷🍷🍷🍷 **Chardonnay 2003** Very intense; a complex hint of funk on the bouquet; long grapefruit and melon; sweet, spicy oak. Screwcap. **RATING** 93 **DRINK** 2013 $ 23

🍷🍷🍷🍷 **Little Brother Unwooded Chardonnay 2004** Aromatic and flavoursome though faintly reduced. Strong citrus, grapefruit and stone fruit; shows how good unwooded Chardonnay can be. Screwcap. **RATING** 89 **DRINK** 2008 $ 16
Little Brother Shiraz Cabernet Sauvignon 2003 Spotlessly clean; medium-bodied; supple, silky and fresh mouthfeel; red fruit-driven; minimal tannins and oak. Screwcap. **RATING** 89 **DRINK** 2007 $ 16
Pinot Noir 2003 Oaky/stemmy aromas and flavours; slightly minty, but has good mouthfeel and length. **RATING** 87 **DRINK** 2007 $ 25

🍷🍷🍷🍷 **Riesling 2004** **RATING** 85 **DRINK** 2008 $ 19

Zema Estate

Riddoch Highway, Coonawarra, SA 5263 **REGION** Coonawarra
T (08) 8736 3219 **F** (08) 8736 3280 **WEB** www.zema.com.au **OPEN** 7 days 9–5
WINEMAKER Tom Simons **EST.** 1982 **CASES** 20 000
SUMMARY Zema is one of the last outposts of hand-pruning in Coonawarra, with members of the Zema family tending a 60-ha vineyard progressively planted since 1982 in the heart of Coonawarra's terra rossa soil. Winemaking practices are straightforward; if ever there was an example of great wines being made in the vineyard, this is it. Exports to the UK, France, Germany, Malaysia, Thailand, Hong Kong and New Zealand.

🍷🍷🍷🍷 **Cabernet Sauvignon 2002** Strong, tight blackcurrant fruit, well focused; savoury tannins add to length. Will evolve. **RATING** 90 **DRINK** 2012 $ 25.95
Family Selection Cabernet Sauvignon 2002 Well made; medium-bodied and well balanced, though not particularly intense; good tannins and length. **RATING** 90 **DRINK** 2012 $ 40

🍷🍷🍷🍷 **Shiraz 2002** Elegant, fresh, light to medium-bodied; spicy raspberry and blackberry fruit drives the palate; no fault, but dwarfed by the best of the vintage. **RATING** 89 **DRINK** 2009 $ 25.95
Family Selection Shiraz 2002 Medium-bodied; blackberry and blackcurrant fruit; some touches of spice; on the elegant side. **RATING** 88 **DRINK** 2012 $ 40
Cluny 2002 Clean, light to medium-bodied and well balanced; spicy, leafy berry flavours; simply didn't attain desired ripeness. **RATING** 87 **DRINK** 2007 $ 25.95

Ziebarth Wines

Foleys Road, Goodger, Qld 4610 **REGION** South Burnett
T (07) 4162 3089 **F** (07) 4162 3084 **WEB** www.ziebarthwines.com.au **OPEN** Thurs–Sun & public hols 10–5, or by appointment
WINEMAKER John Crane (Contract) **EST.** 1998 **CASES** 650
SUMMARY The 4-ha vineyard (with 1 ha each of semillon, cabernet sauvignon, merlot and chardonnay, and 0.25 ha of chambourcin) is a minor diversification on a beef cattle property set on the edge of the Stuart Range (and which enjoys superb views). It is a small family operation which aims to provide a wine experience for visitors.

🍷🍷🍷🍷 **Reserve Shiraz 2000** Ripe plum and blackcurrant; smooth and supple; long finish. **RATING** 89 **DRINK** 2010 $ 26

Zig Zag Road

NR

201 Zig Zag Road, Drummond, Vic 3461 **REGION** Macedon Ranges
T (03) 5423 9390 **F** (03) 5423 9390 **OPEN** Weekends & public hols 10–6, or by appointment
WINEMAKER Alan Stevens, Eric Bellchambers **EST.** 1972 **CASES** 300

SUMMARY Alan Stevens and Deb Orton purchased the vineyard in 1988; it was then 16 years old, having been established by Roger Aldridge. The dry-grown vines produce relatively low yields, and until 1996 the grapes were sold to Hanging Rock Winery. In 1996 the decision was taken to manage the property on a full-time basis, and to make the wine onsite, using 0.25 ha each of riesling, merlot and pinot noir, and 1 ha each of shiraz and cabernet sauvignon.

Zilzie Wines ★★★☆

Lot 66 Kulkyne Way, Karadoc via Red Cliffs, Vic 3496 **REGION** Murray Darling
T (03) 5025 8100 **F** (03) 5025 8116 **WEB** www.zilziewines.com **OPEN** Not
WINEMAKER Bob Shields, Leigh Sparrow **EST.** 1999 **CASES** NFP
SUMMARY The Forbes family has been farming Zilzie Estate since 1911; it is currently run by Ian and Ros Forbes, and their sons Steven and Andrew. A diverse range of farming activities now include grapegrowing – there are 250 ha of vineyards. Having established a position as a dominant supplier of grapes to Southcorp, Zilzie formed a wine company in 1999 and built a winery in 2000. It has a capacity of 16 000 tonnes now, but is so designed that modules can be added to take it to 50 000 tonnes. The winery business includes contract storage, contract processing, contract winemaking, bulk wine production and bottled and branded wines. National distribution through Rutherglen Wine & Spirit Company Limited; exports to the UK, the US, Canada, New Zealand, Singapore and Thailand.

ΨΨΨΨΨ **Buloke Reserve Chardonnay 2004** Excellent green-yellow colour; lively, fresh melon and nectarine fruit; particularly good crisp finish. Subliminal oak. **RATING** 90 **DRINK** Now $9.99

ΨΨΨΨ **Pinot Gris 2004** Surprising grip and length; nashi pear flavours; lots of expression. **RATING** 88 **DRINK** Now $16
Estate Viognier 2004 Clean, solid; some varietal fleshy/pastille characters. Well made. **RATING** 87 **DRINK** Now
Buloke Reserve Classic Dry White 2004 Clean, fresh tropical fruit salad; balanced acidity and a hint of sweetness; impressive at the price. **RATING** 87 **DRINK** Now $9.99

ΨΨΨΨ **Rose 2004** **RATING** 86 **DRINK** Now $16
Shiraz 2002 **RATING** 86 **DRINK** 2010 $16.99
Estate Chardonnay 2004 **RATING** 85 **DRINK** Now $16
Sangiovese 2003 **RATING** 85 **DRINK** Now $13
Buloke Reserve Sauvignon Blanc 2004 **RATING** 84 **DRINK** Now $9.99

ΨΨΨ **Unwooded Chardonnay 2004** **RATING** 83 $16

Zonte's Footstep ★★★★

Wellington Road/PO Box 53, Langhorne Creek, SA 5255 **REGION** Langhorne Creek
T (08) 8537 3334 **F** (08) 8537 3231 **WEB** www.zontesfootstep.com.au **OPEN** Not
WINEMAKER Ben Riggs (Contract) **EST.** 1997 **CASES** 50 000
SUMMARY The 215-ha vineyard of Zonte's Footstep dates back to 1997, when a group of old school mates banded together to purchase the land and established the vineyard under the direction of viticulturist Geoff Hardy and vigneron John Pargeter. Obviously enough, a large percentage of the grapes are sold to others; the remainders are skilfully made by Ben Riggs. While it is not clear who Zonte was, the footprint on the label is that of a Diprotodon or giant wombat, these inhabited the southeastern corner of South Australia for more than 20 million years, becoming extinct 10–20,000 years ago. The wine quality is as good as the prices are modest.

ΨΨΨΨΨ **Langhorne Creek Shiraz Viognier 2004** Deeply coloured; succulent, rich, round plum jam, blackberry, spice and licorice; soft tannins. Felicitous marriage. Good value. Screwcap. **RATING** 91 **DRINK** 2004 $18
Langhorne Creek Shiraz Viognier 2003 Luscious, soft, velvety blackberry, spice and blackcurrant fruit; soft regional tannins; stylish wine. **RATING** 91 **DRINK** 2010 $17.50

ΨΨΨΨ **Langhorne Creek Cabernet Malbec 2004** Dense purple-red; full-bodied; exceedingly powerful, dense, concentrated and luscious black fruits on the mid-palate, marred by excessive dry tannins on the finish. Patience may cure. Screwcap. **RATING** 89 **DRINK** 2024 $15

Langhorne Creek Viognier 2003 Quite rich, ripe tropical fruit flavours with hints of honey. Screwcap. **RATING** 87 **DRINK** Now $ 17.50

▼▼▼♀ **Langhorne Creek Cabernet Petit Verdot Rose 2004** Good colour; sweet red fruits in a bizarre rose blend which very nearly works. Rose, incidentally, does not appear on the front label. Screwcap. **RATING** 86 **DRINK** Now $ 15

Langhorne Creek Verdelho 2004 **RATING** 85 **DRINK** Now $ 15

Langhorne Creek Viognier 2004 **RATING** 85 **DRINK** Now $ 18

Acknowledgments

The Australian wine industry continues to grow apace, not without some growing pains in 2005, likely to continue into 2006. It is a major export earner, and a serendipitous source of taxation for the Federal Government. There is the purpose-built Wine Equalisation Tax of 26 per cent (WET) unique to the industry, there is GST, and income tax on the earnings of the tens of thousands of people directly or indirectly deriving all or part of their income from grapegrowing, winemaking, teaching, publishing, researching, writing about and/or selling wine.

Amongst those thousands are a few who have made this book possible. In no particular order there is the team working for HarperCollins, particularly Sarah Shrubb (proofreader), Graeme Jones (typesetter) and Ali Orman (senior editor), who work to tight deadlines with the maximum of understanding. My PA Paula Grey achieves astonishing feats at all times of day and night with the database, and Beth Anthony works from the second she arrives to the second she leaves each day, often on humdrum tasks such as following up the hundreds of wineries which forget to give us the prices of their wines.

The logistics of organising the tastings throughout the year are ever more frightening. Over the past 12 months over 8000 bottles of wine have arrived, most through the admirably efficient and economic Australia Post wine delivery service. The local newsagency doubles up as a sub-post office and bank, and at peak periods is engulfed with wine parcels of every shape and size imaginable. My thanks to the team there, headed by Vernice and Ron.

Finally, there are my stewards Marcus Hutson and Kate Fleming, who unpack, enter the wines onto sheets on the way through to the database, re-sort by variety once entered, open the bottles, pour the wines, re-sort the tasting sheets, then top up and recork the bottles for all at Coldstream Hills to taste at their leisure some time later.

Index

Adelaide Hills (SA)

Aldgate Ridge 60
Annvers Wines 70
Arranmore Vineyard 73
Ashton Hills 75
Balhannah Vineyards 81
Barratt 88
Basket Range Wines 91
Battunga Vineyards 93
Bird in Hand 105
Birdwood Estate 106
Cawdor Wines 151
Chain of Ponds 154
Christmas Hill 164
Cobb's Hill 172
FUSE 238
Galah 239
Geoff Hardy Wines 244
Geoff Weaver 245
Griffin Wines 263
Grove Hill 264
Hahndorf Hill Winery 265
Harris Estate 273
Johnston Oakbank 311
Jupiter Creek Winery 313
Leabrook Estate 345
Leland Estate 347
Llangibby Estate 356
Longview Vineyard 359
Malcolm Creek Vineyard 370
Mawson Ridge 377
Maximilian's Vineyard 377
Millers Samphire 385
Morialta Vineyard 397
Mt Lofty Ranges Vineyard 407
Mount Torrens Vineyards 410
Murdoch Hill 415
Nepenthe Vineyards 420
New Era Vineyard 421
Next Generation Wines 422

Adelaide Hills (SA) (*continued*)

Normans 424
Paracombe Wines 438
Parish Hill Wines 440
Perrini Estate 453
Petaluma 454
Pfitzner 458
Piccadilly Fields 460
Pike & Joyce 462
Salem Bridge Wines 509
Sandow's End 514
Setanta Wines 522
Shaw & Smith 527
Spoehr Creek Wines 538
Talunga 561
Teakles Hill Wines 569
The Deanery Vineyards 573
The Lane 575
Tilbrook 582
TK Wines 587
Totino Wines 592
Whisson Lake 622

Adelaide Plains (SA)

Ceravolo Wines 153
Diloreto Wines 198
Dominic Versace Wines 203
Farosa Estate 223
Gawler River Grove 242
Hazyblur Wines 276
Primo Estate 473
Thornborough Estate 580
Wilkie Estate 625

Adelaide Zone (SA)

Patritti Wines 443
Penfolds Magill Estate 449
Rumball Sparkling Wines 504
Uleybury Wines 601

Albany (WA)

Jinnunger Vineyard 310
Montgomery's Hill 391
Oranje Tractor Wine/Lincoln & Gomm 432
Phillips Brook Estate 459
Two People's Bay Wines 600
Wignalls Wines 623

Alpine Valleys (Vic)

Annapurna Wines 70
Bogong Estate 112
Boynton's 115
Ceccanti Kiewa Valley Wines 151
Gapsted Wines 240
Kancoona Valley Wines 315
Michelini Wines 383
Park Wines 440
Tawonga Vineyard 567

Ballarat (Vic)

Captains Creek Organic Wines 143
Chepstowe Vineyard 162
Dulcinea 209
Eastern Peake 211
Mount Beckworth 401
Mount Buninyong Winery 402
Mount Coghill Vineyard 403
Tomboy Hill 588
Whitehorse Wines 623
Yellowglen 652

Barossa Valley (SA)

Balthazar of the Barossa 83
Barossa Ridge Wine Estate 87
Barossa Settlers 87
Barossa Valley Estate 87
Basedow 91
Beer Brothers 97
Bethany Wines 101
Burge Family Winemakers 131
Cellarmasters 151
Charles Cimicky 158
Charles Melton 158
Chateau Dorrien 160
Chateau Tanunda 161
Craneford 180
Domain Day 201
Dutschke Wines 210
Elderton 213
Gibson 247
Glaetzer Wines 249
Glen Eldon Wines 251
Gnadenfrei Estate 253

Barossa Valley (SA) (*continued*)

Gomersal Wines 254
Gordon Sunter Wines 255
Grant Burge 260
Greenock Creek Wines 262
Haan Wines 265
Hamilton's Ewell Vineyards 267
Harbord Wines 269
Hare's Chase 271
Heritage Wines 282
Jenke Vineyards 307
John Duval Wines 310
Kabminye Wines 314
Kaesler Wines 314
Kalleske 315
Kassebaum Wines 318
Kellermeister/Trevor Jones 320
Kies Family Wines 322
Kurtz Family Vineyards 335
Langmeil Winery 342
Leo Buring 348
Liebich Wein 349
Limb Vineyards 352
Linfield Road Wines 354
McLean's Farm Wines 365
Magpie Estate 369
Marschall Groom Cellars 375
Massena Vineyards 376
Mengler View Wines 379
Murray Street Vineyard 417
Orlando 433
Paulmara Estate 444
Penfolds 448
Peter Lehmann 455
Richmond Grove 487
Rockford 496
Rocland Wines 497
Roehr 497
Rosenvale Wines 500
Ross Estate Wines 502
Rusden Wines 504
St Hallett 507
Saltram 511
Schild Estate Wines 517
Schubert Estate 517
Seppelt 520
Sheep's Back 528
Shiralee Wines 530
Small Gully Wines 535
Stanley Brothers 540
Stone Chimney Creek 546
Tait Wines 558
Teusner 571
The Willows Vineyard 578
Thorn-Clarke Wines 580

Barossa Valley (SA) (*continued*)
Tim Smith Wines 583
Torbreck Vintners 591
Turkey Flat 597
Veritas 605
Viking Wines 605
Villa Tinto 607
Vinecrest 607
Whistler Wines 622
Wolf Blass 635
Yaldara Wines 645
Yalumba 645

Beechworth (Vic)

Amulet Vineyard 66
battely wines 92
Castagna Vineyard 148
Cow Hill 179
Fighting Gully Road 227
Giaconda 246
Golden Ball 253
Pennyweight Winery 451
Savaterre 515
Smiths Vineyard 536
Sorrenberg 537
Star Lane 541
Yengari Wine Company 652

Bendigo (Vic)

Avonmore Estate 78
Balgownie Estate 81
Bendigo Wine Estate 99
Big Hill Vineyard 103
BlackJack Vineyards 107
Blanche Barkly Wines 107
Bress 118
Charlotte Plains 159
Chateau Dore 160
Chateau Leamon 160
Connor Park Winery 175
Cooperage Estate 176
Glenalbyn 250
Harcourt Valley Vineyards 269
Kangderaar Vineyard 316
Karee Estate 317
Laanecoorie 336
Langanook Wines 341
Mandurang Valley Wines 371
Minto Wines 387
Mount Moliagul 408
Nuggetty Vineyard 426
Old Loddon Wines 429
Passing Clouds 441
Pondalowie Vineyards 468

Bendigo (Vic) (*continued*)
Sandhurst Ridge 513
Sutton Grange Winery 555
Tannery Lane Vineyard 564
Tipperary Hill Estate 586
Water Wheel 614
Welshmans Reef Vineyard 617
Yandoit Hill Vineyard 646

Big Rivers Zone (NSW)

Charles Sturt University Winery 159
Walla Wines 609

Blackwood Valley (WA)

Blackwood Crest Wines 107
Blackwood Wines 107
Hillbillé 286
Lauren Brook 344
Scotts Brook 519
Seashell Wines 519
Sunnyhurst Winery 553
Tanglewood Vines 563
Wattle Ridge Vineyard 615

Canberra District (ACT/NSW)

Affleck (NSW) 59
Brindabella Hills (ACT) 120
Clonakilla (NSW) 169
Dionysus Winery (NSW) 199
Doonkuna Estate (NSW) 204
England's Creek (NSW) 218
Four Winds Vineyard (NSW) 233
Gallagher Wines (NSW) 239
Gidgee Estate Wines (NSW) 247
Helm (NSW) 279
Hillbrook (NSW) 286
Jeir Creek (NSW) 307
Kamberra (ACT) 315
Kyeema Estate (ACT) 335
Lake George Winery (NSW) 339
Lambert Vineyards (NSW) 340
Lark Hill (NSW) 342
Lerida Estate (NSW) 348
Little Bridge (NSW) 355
McKellar Ridge Wines 365
Madew Wines (NSW) 369
Milimani Estate (NSW) 384
Mount Majura Vineyard (ACT) 407
Mundoonen (NSW) 414
Murrumbateman Winery (NSW) 417
Pankhurst (NSW) 437
Pialligo Estate (ACT) 460
Ravensworth (ACT) 480

Canberra District (ACT/NSW) (*continued*)

Shaw Vineyard Estate (NSW) 528
Surveyor's Hill Winery (NSW) 554
Wandana Estate (NSW) 609
Wily Trout (NSW) 629
Wimbaliri Wines (NSW) 629
Yass Valley Wines (NSW) 651

Central Ranges Zone (NSW)

Bell River Estate 98
Bunnamagoo Estate 130
Chateau Champsaur 159
Hermes Morrison Wines 282
Monument Vineyard 392
Mount Panorama Winery 408
Winburndale 630

Central Victoria Zone

Gentle Annie 244
Green Ant Wines 261
New Mediterranean Winery 422
Pretty Sally Estate 472
Silver Wings Winemaking 531
Tallis Wine 559

Central Western Australia Zone

Across the Lake 58
Avonbrook Wines 78
Chapman Valley Wines 157
Rex Vineyard 486
Stratherne Vale Estate 548
Wadjekanup River Estate 609
Wandoo Farm 610
WJ Walker Wines 635

Clare Valley (SA)

Adelina Wines 58
Annie's Lane 70
Australian Domaine Wines 77
Brian Barry Wines 119
Cardinham Estate 144
Claymore Wines 167
Clos Clare 169
Crabtree of Watervale 179
Eldredge 213
Eyre Creek 221
Fireblock 227
FUSE 238
Grosset 263
Inchiquin Wines 299
Inghams Skilly Ridge Wines 300

Clare Valley (SA) (*continued*)

Jeanneret Wines 307
Jim Barry Wines 308
Kilikanoon 323
Kirrihill Estates 329
Knappstein Wines 330
Leasingham 345
Little Brampton Wines 355
Mintaro Wines 386
Mitchell 388
Mount Horrocks 405
Mt Surmon Wines 410
Neagles Rock Vineyards 419
O'Leary Walker Wines 430
Olssens of Watervale 431
Paulett 444
Pearson Vineyards 445
Penna Lane Wines 450
Pikes 462
Pycnantha Hill Estate 476
Reilly's Wines 485
Sevenhill Cellars 523
Skillogalee 534
Stephen John Wines 544
Stringy Brae of Sevenhill 549
Tatehams Wines 567
Taylors 568
Tim Adams 582
Tim Gramp 583
Wendouree 618
Wilson Vineyard 628

Coonawarra (SA)

Balnaves of Coonawarra 82
Banks Thargo Wines 84
Bowen Estate 114
Brand's of Coonawarra 116
DiGiorgio Family Wines 197
Ey Estate 221
Flint's of Coonawarra 230
Highbank 285
Hollick 289
Jamiesons Run 304
Katnook Estate 319
Koonara 332
Ladbroke Grove 337
Lawrence Victor Estate 344
Leconfield 346
Lindemans (Coonawarra) 352
Majella 370
Murdock 415
Parker Coonawarra Estate 440
Patrick T Wines 442
Penley Estate 449

Coonawarra (SA) (*continued*)

Punters Corner 475
Redman 483
Reschke Wines 485
Rymill Coonawarra 505
S Kidman Wines 534
The Blok Estate 572
Wynns Coonawarra Estate 643
Yalumba The Menzies (Coonawarra) 646
Zema Estate 656

Cowra (NSW)

Bindaree Estate 105
Catherine's Ridge 150
Chiverton 164
Cowra Estate 179
Danbury Estate 187
Falls Wines 223
Hamiltons Bluff 267
Kalari Wines 315
McGlashan Wines 364
Mulligan Wongara Vineyard 413
Mulyan 414
Nassau Estate 419
River Park 492
Rosnay Organic Wines 501
Spring Ridge Wines 539
Tom's Waterhole Wines 589
Windowrie Estate 631

Currency Creek (SA)

Ballast Stone Estate Wines 82
Currency Creek Estate 184
Middleton Wines 384
Salomon Estate 510

Darling Downs (Qld)

Gowrie Mountain Estate 257
Lilyvale Wines 351
Rangemore Estate 480
Rimfire Vineyards 489
Wedgetail Ridge Estate 616

Denmark (WA)

Due South 209
Harewood Estate 272
Howard Park (Denmark) 293
John Wade Wines 311
Karriview 318
Mariners Rest 373
Matilda's Estate 376

Denmark (WA) (*continued*)

Moombaki Wines 392
Nelson Touch 420
Rickety Gate 488
Somerset Hill Wines 537
Tingle-Wood 584
West Cape Howe Wines 618
Yilgarnia 654

East Coast Tasmania

Apsley Gorge Vineyard 71
Coombend Estate 176
Craigie Knowe 179
Freycinet 236
Spring Vale Vineyards 540

Eden Valley (SA)

Barossa Cottage Wines 87
Eden Hall 211
Eden Springs 212
Glen Eldon Wines 251
Hartz Barn Wines 273
Heathvale 278
Heggies Vineyard 278
Henschke 280
Hill Smith Estate 287
Hutton Vale Vineyard 298
Irvine 302
Karl Seppelt 318
Mountadam 400
Pewsey Vale 457
Robert Johnson Vineyards 493
Tin Shed Wines 585
Tobias Wines 587
Tollana 588
Wroxton Wines 642

Fleurieu Zone (SA)

Marquis Phillips 374
see also Southern Fleurieu (SA)

Frankland River (WA)

Alkoomi 61
Ferngrove Vineyards 226
Frankland Estate 235
Old Kent River 429

Geelong (Vic)

Amietta Vineyard 65
Austin's Barrabool 76
Banks Road 83

Geelong (Vic) (*continued*)

Bannockburn Vineyards 84
Barrgowan Vineyard 88
Barwon Plains 91
Bellarine Estate 98
Brown Magpie Wines 127
by Farr 133
Clyde Park Vineyard 170
Curlewis Winery 183
del Rios 195
Farr Rising 224
Gralaine Vineyard 258
Grassy Point/Coatsworth Wines 261
Heytesbury Ridge 284
Innisfail Vineyards 301
Jindalee Estate 309
Kilgour Estate 323
Kurabana 334
Le 'Mins Winery 347
Lethbridge Wines 348
Leura Park Estate 349
Longboard Wines 358
McGlashan's Wallington Estate 364
Mermerus Vineyard 380
Moranghurk Vineyard 395
Mount Anakie Wines 400
Mount Duneed 404
Otway Estate 435
Pettavel 457
Prince Albert 473
Provenance Wines 475
St Regis 509
Scotchmans Hill 518
Shadowfax 526
Staughton Vale Vineyard 542
Tarcoola Estate 565
The Minya Winery 576
Villa Caterina Wines 606
Waybourne 616
Wolseley Wines 637

Geographe (WA)

Barrecas 88
Brookhampton Estate 124
Byramgou Park 133
Capel Vale 141
Donnybrook Estate 204
Ferguson Falls Estate 225
Ferguson Hart Estate 225
Hackersley 265
Harvey River Bridge Estate 273
Henty Brook Estate 281
Kingtree Wines 328
Kotai Estate 333

Geographe (WA) (*continued*)

Lone Crow Wines 358
Mandalay Estate 371
St Aidan 506
Thomson Brook Wines 579
Wansbrough Wines 611
Willow Bridge Estate 626
Willy Bay 628
Wordsworth Wines 641
Yokain Vineyard Estate 655

Gippsland (Vic)

Ada River 58
Bass Phillip 92
Bass Valley Estate Wines 92
Bellvale Wines 99
Briagolong Estate 119
Caledonia Australis 134
Cannibal Creek Vineyard 137
Chestnut Hill Vineyard 163
Coalville Vineyard 171
Dargo Valley Winery 188
Djinta Djinta Winery 200
Drummonds Corrina Vineyard 208
Ensay Winery 218
Holley Hill 289
Jinks Creek Winery 309
Kongwak Hills Winery 332
Kouark Vineyard 333
Lochmoore 357
Lyre Bird Hill 362
Moondarra 393
Mount Markey 408
Narkoojee 418
Nicholson River 422
Paradise Enough 439
Phillip Island Vineyard 459
Ramsay's Vin Rose 479
Sarsfield Estate 515
Steler Estate Wines 543
Tanjil Wines 564
Tarwin Ridge 566
The Gurdies 574
Toms Cap Vineyard 589
Villa Terlato 606
Wild Dog 624
Windy Ridge Vineyard 632
Wyanga Park 643
Zanella Estate 655

Glenrowan (Vic)

Auldstone 76
Baileys of Glenrowan 80
Goorambath 255

Glenrowan (Vic) (*continued*)
Judds Warby Range Estate 312
Taminick Cellars 562

Goulburn Valley (Vic)

Avenel Park/Hart Wines 78
Beckingham Wines 96
Beechwood Wines 96
Brave Goose Vineyard 117
Cape Horn Vineyard 139
Fyffe Field 239
Goulburn Terrace 256
Goulburn Valley Estate Wines 256
Hankin Estate 268
Hayward's Whitehead Creek 276
Heritage Farm Wines 282
Monichino Wines 390
Murchison Wines 415
New Glory 421
Strathkellar 548
Sugarloaf Creek Vineyard 551
The Carriages Vineyard 572
Twelve Acres 598
see also Upper Goulburn (Vic)

Grampians (Vic)

Armstrong Vineyards 73
Best's Wines 101
Cathcart Ridge Estate 149
Clayfield Wines 167
Donovan Wines 204
Fratin Brothers Vineyard 235
Garden Gully Vineyards 241
Grampians Estate 258
Kimbarra Wines 325
Michael Unwin Wines 383
Montara 391
Mount Langi Ghiran Vineyards 406
Seppelt Great Western 520
The Gap Vineyard 574
Varrenti Wines 604
Westgate Vineyard 620

Granite Belt (Qld)

Aventine Wines 78
Bald Mountain 80
Ballandean Estate 82
Boireann 112
Bungawarra 130
Casley Mount Hutton Winery 148
Castle Glen Vineyard 149
Catspaw Farm 150

Granite Belt (Qld) (*continued*)
Cody's 172
Emerald Hill Winery 217
Felsberg Winery 224
Golden Grove Estate 254
Granite Ridge Wines 259
Harrington Glen Estate 272
Heritage Estate 281
Hidden Creek 284
Jester Hill Wines 308
Kominos Wines 331
Lucas Estate 361
Mary Byrnes Wine 375
Mountview Wines 411
Old Caves Winery 429
Preston Peak 472
Pyramids Road Wines 477
Ravens Croft Wines 480
Robert Channon Wines 492
Robinsons Family Vineyards 494
Rumbalara 504
Severn Brae Estate 524
Stone Ridge 547
Summit Estate 553
Symphony Hill Wines 557
Tobin Wines 587
Turner's Flat Vineyard 598
Whiskey Gully Wines 621
Wild Soul 624
Windermere Wines 631
Winewood 633

Great Southern (WA)

Trevelen Farm 595

Greater Perth (WA)

Coorinja 176
Paul Conti Wines 443

Gundagai (NSW)

Bidgeebong Wines 103
Borambola Wines 113
Paterson's Gundagai Vineyard 442

Hastings River (NSW)

Bago Vineyards 79
Cassegrain 148
Inneslake Vineyards 301
Long Point Vineyard 358
Sherwood Estate 529

Heathcote (Vic)

Baptista 85
Barfold Estate 86
Barnadown Run 86
Burke & Wills Winery 132
Coliban Valley Wines 174
Dead Horse Hill 190
Domaines Tatiarra 202
Downing Estate Vineyard 206
Eppalock Ridge 218
Grace Devlin Wines 258
Heathcote Estate 277
Heathcote Winery 277
Huntleigh Vineyards 298
Jasper Hill 306
Knots Wines 330
Lake Cooper Estate 338
McIvor Creek 364
McIvor Estate 364
Milvine Estate Wines 386
Mount Burrumboot Estate 402
Mount Ida 405
Munari Wines 414
Occam's Razor 428
Paul Osicka 444
Red Edge 482
Redesdale Estate Wines 482
St Michael's Vineyard 509
Sanguine Estate 514
Shelmerdine Vineyards 528
Stefani Estate 542
Toolleen Vineyard 590
Wild Duck Creek Estate 624

Henty (Vic)

Barretts Wines 88
Bochara Wines 111
Crawford River Wines 181
Hochkirch Wines 288
Kelso 322
St Gregory's 506
Tarrington Vineyards 565

Hilltops (NSW)

Barwang Vineyard 89
Chalkers Crossing 155
Demondrille Vineyards 196
Freeman Vineyards 236
Grove Estate 263
Shepherd's Moon 529
Woodonga Hill 639

Hunter Valley (NSW)

see Lower Hunter Valley (NSW);
    Upper Hunter Valley (NSW)

Kangaroo Island (SA)

Agincourt Partners 59
Bay of Shoals 94
Cape d'Estaing 139
Dudley Partners 208
Kangaroo Island Vines 316
Lashmar 343
Sunset Winery 553
The Islander Estate Vineyards 574
Williams Springs Road 626

King Valley (Vic)

Avalon Vineyard 77
Bettio Wines 102
Boggy Creek Vineyards 111
Brown Brothers 125
Chrismont Wines 164
Ciavarella 165
Dal Zotto Estate 186
Darling Estate 188
Henderson Hardie 279
John Gehrig Wines 310
King River Estate 326
La Cantina King Valley 336
Markwood Estate 374
Pizzini 464
Politini Wines 468
Reads 481
Sam Miranda of King Valley 512
Station Creek 542
Symphonia Wines 557
Wood Park 639

Langhorne Creek (SA)

Angas Plains Estate 68
Angas Vineyards 68
Ben Potts Wines 100
Bleasdale Vineyards 108
Bremerton Wines 118
Brothers in Arms 125
Casa Freschi 146
Cleggett Wines 168
Lake Breeze Wines 338
Lindrum 354
Marandoo Estate 372
Oddfellows Wines 428
Raydon Estate 481
Step Road Winery 544
Temple Bruer 569
Zonte's Footstep 657

Limestone Coast Zone (SA)

Frog Island 237
Governor Robe Selection 257
Heartland Wines 277
Heathfield Ridge Wines 278
Marquis Phillips 374

Lower Hunter Valley (NSW)

Allandale 62
Apthorpe Estate 71
Audrey Wilkinson Vineyard 76
Bainton Family Wines 80
Ballabourneen Wines 82
Beaumont Estate 95
Belgenny Vineyard 97
Ben's Run 100
Beyond Broke Vineyard 102
Bimbadgen Estate 104
Bishop Grove Wines 106
Blueberry Hill Vineyard 109
Bluebush Estate 109
Boatshed Vineyard 111
Braydon Estate 117
Briar Ridge 119
Broke Estate/Ryan Family Wines 122
Brokenwood 123
Broke's Promise Wines 124
Brown's Farm Winery 127
Brush Box Vineyard 128
Calais Estate 134
Capercaillie 142
Carindale Wines 145
Catherine Vale Vineyard 150
Chateau Francois 160
Chateau Pâto 161
Chatto Wines 162
Cockfighter's Ghost 172
Colvin Wines 174
Constable & Hershon 175
Cooper Wines 176
Crisford Winery 181
De Bortoli (Hunter Valley) 192
De Iuliis 194
Drayton's Family Wines 206
Drews Creek Wines 206
Elsmore's Caprera Grove 216
Elysium Vineyard 217
Emma's Cottage Vineyard 217
Ernest Hill Wines 218
Evans Family Wines 221
Fairview Wines 222
Farrell's Limestone Creek 224
First Creek Wines 228
Foate's Ridge 231

Lower Hunter Valley (NSW) (continued)

Gabriel's Paddocks Vineyard 239
Gartelmann Hunter Estate 242
Glenguin 252
Golden Grape Estate 253
Hanging Tree Wines 268
Heartland Vineyard 276
Hillside Estate Wines 287
Hollyclare 290
Honeytree Estate 290
Hope Estate 291
House of Certain Views 293
Hudson's Peak Wines 295
Hungerford Hill 296
Idlewild 299
Iron Gate Estate 301
Ivanhoe Wines 303
Jackson's Hill Vineyard 303
Keith Tulloch Wine 320
Kelman Vineyards 321
Kevin Sobels Wines 322
Krinklewood 334
Kulkunbulla 334
Lake's Folly 339
Latara 343
Lindemans (Hunter Valley) 353
Littles 355
Louis-Laval Wines 360
Lucy's Run 362
Mabrook Estate 363
McGuigan Wines 364
McLeish Estate 366
Macquariedale Estate 367
McWilliam's Mount Pleasant 368
Madigan Vineyard 369
Margan Family 372
Marsh Estate 375
Meerea Park 378
Millbrook Estate 384
Millfield 385
Mistletoe Wines 387
Molly Morgan Vineyard 389
Monahan Estate 389
Montvalley 391
Moorebank Vineyard 393
Mount Broke Wines 402
Mount Eyre Vineyards 404
Mount View Estate 410
Mt Vincent Estate 412
Nightingale Wines 422
Oakvale 427
Outram Estate 435
Palmers Wines 437
Peacock Hill Vineyard 445
Pendarves Estate 447

Lower Hunter Valley (NSW) (*continued*)

Pepper Tree Wines 452

Peschar's 454

Peterson Champagne House 456

Petersons 456

Piggs Peake 461

Pokolbin Estate 467

Poole's Rock 469

Pothana 471

Racecourse Lane Wines 478

Reg Drayton Wines 485

Roche Wines 494

Rocklea Vineyard 497

Rosebrook Estate 499

Rothbury Ridge 503

Rothvale Vineyard 503

Saddlers Creek 506

St Petrox 509

Sandalyn Wilderness Estate 513

Scarborough 516

Serenella 522

SmithLeigh Vineyard 536

Stirling Wines 545

Stonehurst Cedar Creek 547

Taliondal 559

Tallavera Grove Vineyard & Winery 559

Tamburlaine 562

Tatler Wines 567

Tempus Two Wines 570

Terrace Vale 570

Thalgara Estate 572

The Little Wine Company 576

The Rothbury Estate 577

The Vineyards Estate 578

Thomas Wines 579

Tinklers Vineyard 584

Tinonee Vineyard 585

Tintilla Wines 586

Tower Estate 592

Tranquil Vale 593

Tulloch 596

Tyrrell's 601

Undercliff 602

Verona Vineyard 605

Vinden Estate 607

Wandin Valley Estate 610

Warraroong Estate 612

Wattlebrook Vineyard 615

Waverley Estate 615

Whispering Brook 621

Windarra 630

Windsors Edge 631

Wright Family Wines 642

Wyndham Estate 643

Macedon Ranges (Vic)

big shed wines 104

Bindi Wine Growers 105

Blackgum Estate 106

Braewattie 115

Candlebark Hill 137

Chanters Ridge 156

Cleveland 169

Cobaw Ridge 171

Cope-Williams 177

Curly Flat 183

Domaine Epis 202

Ellender Estate 215

Farrawell Wines 223

Gisborne Peak 249

Glen Erin Vineyard Retreat 251

Granite Hills 259

Hanging Rock Winery 268

Kyneton Ridge Estate 336

Lancefield Winery 340

Lane's End Vineyard 341

Langleyvale Vineyard 342

Loxley Vineyard 361

Metcalfe Valley 381

Midhill Vineyard 384

MorganField 396

Mount Charlie Winery 403

Mount Gisborne Wines 405

Mount Macedon Winery 407

Mount William Winery 412

O'Shea & Murphy Rosebery Hill Vineyard 434

Patrick's Vineyard 442

Pegeric Vineyard 447

Portree 470

Riddells Creek Winery 488

Rock House 497

Sandy Farm Vineyard 514

Stonemont 547

Straws Lane 549

Tarrangower Estate 565

Virgin Hills 608

Wombat Forest 637

Zig Zag Road 656

McLaren Vale (SA)

Aldinga Bay Winery 61

Andrew Garrett 67

Arakoon 72

Aramis Vineyards 72

Battle of Bosworth 93

Bent Creek Vineyards 100

Beresford Wines 101

Blown Away 108

McLaren Vale (SA) (*continued*)
Brick Kiln 120
Brini Estate Wines 121
Cape Barren Wines 138
Cascabel 147
Chalk Hill 155
Chapel Hill 157
Clarence Hill 166
Clarendon Hills 166
Classic McLaren Wines 167
Coriole 177
d'Arenberg 187
Dennis 196
DogRidge Vineyard 200
Dowie Doole 205
Dyson Wines 210
Fern Hill Estate 227
Five Geese/Hillgrove Wines 229
Foggo Wines 231
Fox Creek Wines 234
Gemtree Vineyards 243
Geoff Merrill Wines 244
Gilligan 248
Grancari Estate Wines 259
Halifax Wines 266
Hardys 270
Hardys Tintara 271
Haselgrove 274
Hastwell & Lightfoot 274
Hawkers Gate 275
Hills View Vineyards 288
Hoffmann's 289
Horndale 292
Hugh Hamilton 295
Hugo 295
Ingoldby 300
Kangarilla Road Vineyard 316
Kay Bros Amery 319
Kimber Wines 325
Koltz 331
La Curio 337
McLaren Vale III Associates 365
Maglieri of McLaren Vale 369
Marienberg 372
Marius Wines 373
Maxwell Wines 377
Middlebrook Estate 383
Mitolo Wines 388
Morgan Simpson 396
Mr Riggs Wine Company 412
Needham Estate Wines 420
Neighbours Vineyards 420
Nick Haselgrove/Blackbilly 422
Noon Winery 423
Oliverhill 430

McLaren Vale (SA) (*continued*)
Olivers Taranga Vineyards 430
Paxton Wines 445
Penny's Hill 451
Pertaringa 453
Pirramimma 464
Possums Vineyard 471
Potters Clay Vineyards 472
Richard Hamilton 486
RockBare Wines 495
Rogues Gallery 497
Rosemount Estate (McLaren Vale) 500
Sabella Vineyards 505
Scarpantoni Estate 516
Serafino Wines 522
Shingleback 529
Shirvington 530
Shottesbrooke 530
Simon Hackett 532
Sylvan Springs 556
Tapestry 564
Tatachilla 566
The Fleurieu 573
The Settlement Wine Co. 577
Tinlins 585
Twelve Staves Wine Company 598
Ulithorne 602
Wayne Thomas Wines 616
Wirilda Creek 633
Wirra Wirra 634
Woodstock 639
Yangarra Estate 646

Manjimup (WA)

Batista 92
Black George 106
Chestnut Grove 162
Fonty's Pool Vineyards 232
Middlesex 31 383
Peos Estate 452
Piano Gully 460
Sinclair Wines 533
Stone Bridge Estate 545
Yanmah Ridge 647

Margaret River (WA)

AbbeyVale 57
Adinfern 59
Alexandra Bridge Wines 61
Allison Valley Wines 62
Amarok Estate 64
Amberley Estate 64
Arlewood Estate 73
Artamus 74

Margaret River (WA) (*continued*)
Ashbrook Estate 75
Bare Rooted 85
Barwick Wines 90
Beckett's Flat 95
Bettenay's 102
Bramley Wood 116
Briarose Estate 119
Brookland Valley 124
Brookwood Estate 125
Broomstick Estate 125
Brown Hill Estate 126
Calem Blue/Shelton Wines 135
Cape Grace 139
Cape Lavender 140
Cape Mentelle 142
Carbunup Crest Vineyard 144
Casas Wines 147
Cavalier Crest 150
Chalice Bridge Estate 154
Chapman's Creek Vineyard 157
Churchview Estate 165
Clairault 165
Cullen Wines 182
Deep Woods Estate 193
Devil's Lair 197
Driftwood Estate 206
Eagle Vale 210
Edwards Vineyard 212
Etain 219
Evans & Tate 220
Fermoy Estate 226
Fire Gully 228
Flinders Bay 230
Flying Fish Cove 231
Forester Estate 233
Frazer Woods Wines 236
Frog Choir Wines 237
Gralyn Estate 258
Green Valley Vineyard 262
Hamelin Bay 266
Happs 269
Harmans Ridge Estate 272
Hay Shed Hill Wines 275
Heron Lake Estate 282
Hesperos Wines 283
Higher Plane Wines 285
Howard Park (Margaret River) 294
Hunt's Foxhaven Estate 298
Injidup Point 300
Island Brook Estate 303
Jarvis Estate 306
Juniper Estate 313
Karri Grove Estate 318
Killerby 324

Margaret River (WA) (*continued*)
Laurance of Margaret River 343
Leeuwin Estate 346
Lenton Brae Wines 348
Maiolo Wines 370
Marri Wood Park 374
Marybrook Vineyards 375
Maslin Old Dunsborough Wines 376
Merops Wines 380
Minot Vineyard 386
Mongrel Creek Vineyard 390
Moss Brothers 399
Moss Wood 399
Olsen 431
Palandri Wines 436
Palmer Wines 437
Peacetree Estate 445
Pierro 461
Preveli Wines 473
Random Valley Organic Wines 480
Redgate 483
Rivendell 490
Rockfield Estate 496
Rosabrook Estate 498
Rosily Vineyard 501
Sandalford 512
Sandstone 514
Saracen Estates 515
Serventy Organic Wines 522
Settlers Ridge Organic Wines 523
Sewards 525
Sienna Estate 530
Stellar Ridge Estate 543
Stonebrook Estate 545
Suckfizzle & Stella Bella 551
Swallows Welcome 555
Swings & Roundabouts 556
Tassell Park Wines 566
The Grove Vineyard 574
Thompson Estate 579
Thornhill/The Berry Farm 580
Tintagel Wines 585
Treeton Estate 595
Vasse Felix 604
Vasse River Wines 604
Virgin Block Vineyard 608
Voyager Estate 608
Watershed Wines 614
We're Wines 618
Wildwood of Yallingup 625
Willespie 625
Wills Domain Vineyard 627
Windance Wines 630
wine by brad 632
Wise Wine 634

Margaret River (WA) (*continued*)
Woodlands 638
Woodside Valley Estate 639
Woody Nook 640
Xanadu Wines 644

Mornington Peninsula (Vic)

Barak Estate 85
Barrymore Estate 89
Bayview Estate 94
B'darra Estate 94
Beckingham Wines 96
Boneo Plains 112
Box Stallion 114
Bristol Farm 121
Charlotte's Vineyard 159
Craig Avon Vineyard 179
Crittenden at Dromana 181
Darling Park 188
Dromana Estate 207
Dromana Valley Wines 208
Elan Vineyard 212
Eldridge Estate 213
Elgee Park 214
Ermes Estate 218
Five Sons Estate 229
Foxeys Hangout 234
Frogspond 238
Hickinbotham of Dromana 284
HPR Wines 294
Hurley Vineyard 298
Karina Vineyard 317
Kooyong 332
Lindenderry at Red Hill 353
Little Valley 356
McCrae Mist Wines 363
Main Ridge Estate 369
Mantons Creek Vineyard 371
Marinda Park Vineyard 373
Maritime Estate 373
Massoni 376
Merli 380
Merricks Creek Wines 381
Merricks Estate 381
Miceli 382
Montalto Vineyards 390
Moorooduc Estate 394
Morning Star Estate 397
Morning Sun Vineyard 397
Mount Eliza Estate 404
Myrtaceae 418
Nazaaray 419
Osborns 434
Paradigm Hill 439

Mornington Peninsula (Vic) (*continued*)
Paringa Estate 439
Phaedrus Estate 459
Pier 10 461
Poplar Bend 470
Port Phillip Estate 470
Principia 474
Rahona Valley Vineyard 479
Red Hill Estate 483
Rigel Wines 489
Ryland River 505
Schindler Northway Downs 517
Scorpo Wines 518
Sea Winds Vineyard 520
Silverwood Wines 532
Somerbury Estate 537
Stonier Wines 548
Stumpy Gully 550
Summerhill Wines 553
Tanglewood Downs 563
Ten Minutes by Tractor Wine Co. 570
T'Gallant 571
The Cups Estate 572
The Duke Vineyard 573
The Garden Vineyard 574
Tuck's Ridge 596
Turramurra Estate 598
Vale Wines 603
Villa Primavera 606
Wildcroft Estate 624
Willow Creek 626
Winbirra Vineyard 629
Yabby Lake Vineyard 644
Yrsa's Vineyard 655

Mount Barker (WA)

Chatsfield 161
Deep Water Estate 193
Forest Hill Vineyard 233
Galafrey 239
Garlands 241
Gilberts 247
Goundrey 256
Hay River Wines 275
Marribrook 374
Merrebee Estate 380
Pattersons 443
Plantagenet 465
Poacher's Ridge Vineyard 466
3 Drops 581
Towerhill Estate 592
Traolach/Xabregas 594
Trappers Gully 594
Wattle Mist Wines 615

Mount Benson (SA)

Baudin Rock Wines 93
Cape Jaffa Wines 140
Dawson Estate 190
Guichen Bay Vineyards 264
Karatta Wine 317
M. Chapoutier Australia 378
Murdup Wines 416
Norfolk Rise Vineyard 424
Ralph Fowler Wines 479
Wangolina Station 611
Wehl's Mount Benson Vineyards 617

Mount Gambier (SA)

Benarra Vineyards 99
Haig 266

Mount Lofty Ranges Zone (SA)

Macaw Creek Wines 363

Mudgee (NSW)

Abercorn 57
Andrew Harris Vineyards 67
Blue Wren 110
Botobolar 114
Burnbrae 132
Burrundulla Vineyards 132
Clearview Estate Mudgee 168
Cooyal Grove 176
County View Vineyard/Moothi Mud 178
Creeks Edge Wines 181
di Lusso Wines 198
Elliot Rocke Estate 215
Farmer's Daughter Wines 223
5 Corners Wines 228
Frog Rock Wines 238
High Valley Wines 286
Huntington Estate 297
Knights Vines 330
Knowland Estate 331
Lawson Hill Estate 344
Louee 360
Lowe Family Wines 361
Mansfield Wines 371
Martins Hill Wines 375
Miramar 387
Mountilford 406
Mudgee Growers 412
Mudgee Wines 413
Pieter van Gent 461
Poet's Corner 466
Red Clay Estate 481
Robert Stein Vineyard 493

Mudgee (NSW) (continued)

Secret Garden Wines 520
Shawwood Estate 528
Simon Gilbert Wines 532
Thistle Hill 578
Vinifera Wines 607
Wells Parish Wines 617
Woolshed Wines 640

Murray Darling (NSW/SA/Vic)

Abbey Rock (SA) 57
Brockville Wines (Vic) 122
Callipari Wine (Vic) 135
Capogreco Winery Estate (Vic) 143
Carn Estate (Vic) 146
Currans Family Wines (Vic) 184
Deakin Estate (Vic) 190
Evans & Tate Salisbury (Vic) 220
Irymple Estate Winery (Vic) 302
Lindemans (Karadoc) (Vic) 353
Mulcra Estate Wines (Vic) 413
Murray Darling Collection (NSW) 416
Murray Estate (Vic) 416
Nursery Ridge Estate (Vic) 426
Pasut Family Wines (Vic) 441
Purple Patch Wines (Vic) 476
Ribarits Estate Wines (NSW) 486
Roberts Estate (Vic) 493
Robinvale (Vic) 494
Tall Poppy Wines (Vic) 560
Trentham Estate (NSW) 595
Zilzie Wines (Vic) 657

Nagambie Lakes (Vic)

Burramurra 132
Dalfarras 185
David Traeger 189
Kirwan's Bridge Wines 329
McGee Wines 363
McPherson Wines 366
Mitchelton 388
Tahbilk 558

North East Victoria Zone

Upper Murray Estate 602

Northern Rivers Zone (NSW)

Divers Luck Wines 199
Great Lakes Wines 261
Ilnam Estate 299
Port Stephens Winery 471
Raleigh Winery 479

Northern Rivers Zone (NSW) (continued)

Red Tail Wines 484
Two Tails Wines 600
Villa d'Esta Vineyard 606

Northern Slopes Zone (NSW)

Dumaresq Valley Vineyard 209
Gilgai Winery 248
Kurrajong Downs 335
New England Estate 421
Reedy Creek Vineyard 484
Richfield Estate 487
Splitters Swamp Vineyards 538
Tangaratta Estate 563
Warrina Wines 613
Wellington Vale Wines 617
Willowvale Wines 627
Wright Robertson of Glencoe 642

Northern Tasmania

Andrew Pirie 67
Barringwood Park 89
Bass Fine Wines 91
Bay of Fires 93
Brook Eden Vineyard 124
Bundaleera Vineyard 130
Chartley Estate 159
Cliff House 169
Clover Hill 170
Dalrymple 185
Delamere 194
East Arm Vineyard 211
Elmslie 216
Ghost Rock Vineyard 245
Golders Vineyard 254
Grey Sands 262
Hawley Vineyard 275
Hillwood Vineyard 288
Holm Oak 290
Humbug Reach Vineyard 296
Iron Pot Bay Wines 301
Jansz 305
Jinglers Creek Vineyard 309
Kelly's Creek 321
Lake Barrington Estate 337
Leven Valley Vineyard 349
Moores Hill Estate 393
Motton Terraces 400
Pipers Brook Vineyard 463
Providence Vineyards 475
Rosevears Estate 500
St Matthias 508
Sharmans 526
Silk Hill 531

Northern Tasmania (continued)

Sterling Heights 544
Stoney Rise 547
Tamar Ridge 561
The Mews 576
Welwyn Meadows 618
Wilmot Hills Vineyard 628
Wilson's Legana Vineyard 628

Orange (NSW)

Angullong Wines 69
Belgravia Vineyards 97
Belubula Valley Vineyards 99
Bloodwood 108
Borrodell on the Mount 113
Brangayne of Orange 116
Burke & Hills 131
Bush Piper Vineyard 133
Canobolas-Smith 137
Cargo Road Wines 145
Cumulus Wines 183
Dindima Wines 198
Faisan Estate 222
Gold Dust Wines 253
Golden Gully Wines 254
Highland Heritage Estate 285
Ibis Wines 298
Indigo Ridge 300
Jarretts of Orange 305
Logan Wines 357
Mortimers of Orange 398
Nashdale Wines 419
Orange Country Wines 431
Orange Mountain Wines 431
Orchard Road 432
Pinnacle Wines 463
Prince of Orange 474
Printhie Wines 474
Ross Hill Vineyard 502
Sharpe Wines of Orange 527
Templer's Mill 569
Turner's Vineyard 598
Word of Mouth Wines 641

Padthaway (SA)

Browns of Padthaway 127
Henry's Drive 280
Lindemans (Padthaway) 353
Morambro Creek Wines 395
Padthaway Estate 436
Stonehaven 546

Peel (WA)

Amarillo Vines 64
Cape Bouvard 139
Drakesbrook Wines 206
Peel Estate 446
Tuart Ridge 596
Wandering Brook Estate 610

Pemberton (WA)

Bellarmine Wines 98
Channybearup Vineyard 156
Donnelly River Wines 204
Gloucester Ridge Vineyard 253
Hidden River Estate 285
Hillbrook Wines 286
Lillian 350
Lost Lake 359
Merum 381
Mountford 404
Phillips Estate 460
Picardy 460
Salitage 510
Silkwood Wines 531
Smithbrook 535
Southern Dreams 538
Tantemaggie 564
The Warren Vineyard 578
Treen Ridge Estate 594
Wine & Truffle Company 632
WoodSmoke Estate 639

Peninsulas Zone (SA)

Gregory's Wines 262

Penola (SA)

St Mary's 508

Perricoota (NSW/Vic)

Morrisons Riverview Winery (NSW) 398
St Anne's Vineyards (NSW) 506
Stevens Brook Estate (Vic) 544

Perth Hills (WA)

Ashley Estate 75
Avalon Wines 77
Briery Estate 120
Brookside Vineyard 125
Carosa 146
Chidlow's Well Estate 164
Chittering Valley Winery/
     Nesci Estate Wines 164
Cosham 178

Perth Hills (WA) (continued)

Darlington Estate 189
Deep Dene Vineyard 193
Francois Jacquard 235
Glen Isla Estate 252
Hainault 266
Halina Brook Estate 266
Hartley Estate 273
Jadran 303
Jarrah Ridge Winery 305
Jylland Vineyard 313
Kyotmunga Estate 336
Lake Charlotte Wines 338
Millbrook Winery 385
Piesse Brook 461
Scarp Valley Vineyard 517
Stringybark 549
Walsh Family Winery 609
Western Range Wines 619

Porongurup (WA)

Abbey Creek Vineyard 57
Castle Rock Estate 149
Duke's Vineyard 209
Fernbrook Estate Wines 226
Gibraltar Rock 246
Ironwood Estate 302
Jingalla 309
Millinup Estate 385
Mount Trio Vineyard 410
Shepherd's Hut 529
Springviews Wine 540
The Lily Stirling Range 575
Zarephath Wines 655

Port Phillip Zone (Vic)

Brunswick Hill Wines 128
Limbic 352
Patterson Lakes Estate 443
Rojo Wines 498
Studley Park Vineyard 550
Three Wise Men 581
Toomah Wines 590
Woongarra Estate 641

Pyrenees (Vic)

Amherst Winery 65
Berrys Bridge 101
Blue Pyrenees Estate 109
Dalwhinnie 186
Eurabbie Estate 219
Horvat Estate 292
Hundred Tree Hill 296

Pyrenees (Vic) (*continued*)
Kara Kara Vineyard 316
Landsborough Valley Estate 340
Massoni 376
Moonbark Estate Vineyard 392
Mount Avoca Winery 401
Peerick Vineyard 446
Polleters 468
Pyrenees Ridge Vineyard 478
Redbank Winery 481
St Ignatius Vineyard 507
Scotts Hill Vineyard 519
Summerfield 552
Taltarni 560
Warrenmang Vineyard & Resort 613

Queensland Coastal

Albert River Wines 60
Archer Falls Vineyard & Winery 72
Big Barrel Vineyard and Winery 103
Blind Man's Bluff Vineyard 108
Brischetto Wines 121
Canungra Valley Vineyards 138
Cedar Creek Estate 151
Delaney's Creek Winery 194
Dingo Creek Vineyard 198
Eumundi Winery 219
Gecko Valley 242
Gin Gin Wines 248
Glastonbury Estate Wines 249
Glengariff Estate Winery 252
Ironbark Ridge Vineyard 301
Kenilworth Bluff Wines 322
Maroochy Springs 374
Mount Appallan Vineyards 400
Nirvana Estate 423
Noosa Valley Winery 423
Norse Wines 425
O'Regan Creek Vineyard and Winery 432
Settlers Rise Montville 523
7 Acres Winery 523
Sirromet Wines 533
Springbrook Mountain Vineyard 539
Tamborine Estate Wines 561
Thumm Estate Wines 581
Twin Oaks 599
Warrego Wines 613
Wonbah Estate 637
Woongooroo Estate 641

Queensland Zone

Governor's Choice Winery 257
Jimbour Wines 308
Kooroomba Vineyards 332

Queensland Zone (*continued*)
Normanby Wines 424
Riversands Vineyards 492
Romavilla 498
Stanton Estate 541
Sweet Water Hill Wines 556
Toowoomba Hills Estate 591
Villacoola Vineyard & Winery 606
Waratah Vineyard 611
Winya Wines 633

Riverina (NSW)

Australian Old Vine Wine 77
Baratto's 85
Beelgara Estate 96
Casella Wines 147
Clancy's of Conargo 166
De Bortoli 191
Lillypilly Estate 351
McWilliam's 367
Melange Wines 379
Miranda Wines 387
Murrin Bridge Wines 417
Nugan Estate 425
Piromit Wines 464
Riverina Estate 491
Terrel Estate Wines 571
Toorak Estate 590
Vico 605
Wagga Wagga Winery 609
Westend Estate Wines 619
Yerong Creek Estate 654
Zappacosta Estate Wines 655

Riverland (SA)

Angove's 68
Banrock Station 84
Bonneyview 113
Cockatoo Ridge 172
Golden Mile Wines 254
Loch Luna 357
O'Donohoe's Find 428
Organic Vignerons Australia 433
Pennyfield Wines 451
Red Mud 484
Salena Estate 510
Tandou Wines 563
Thomson Vintners 580

Rutherglen (Vic)

All Saints Estate 62
Anderson 66
Bullers Calliope 129

Rutherglen (Vic) (*continued*)

Campbells 136
Chambers Rosewood 156
Cofield Wines 173
drinkmoor wines 207
Gehrig Estate 243
Jones Winery & Vineyard 312
Lake Moodemere Vineyard 339
Lilliput Wines 351
Morris 398
Mount Prior Vineyard 409
Pfeiffer 458
Rutherglen Estates 504
St Leonards 508
Stanton & Killeen Wines 541
Sutherland Smith Wines 554
Warrabilla 612
Watchbox Wines 614

Shoalhaven Coast (NSW)

Cambewarra Estate 135
Coolangatta Estate 175
Crooked River Wines 182
Fern Gully Winery 227
Jasper Valley 306
Kladis Estate 329
Nowra Hill Vineyard 425
Seven Mile Vineyard 524
The Silos Estate 577
Yarrawa Estate 650

South Australia

Edwards & Chaffey 212

South Burnett (Qld)

Barambah Ridge 85
Bridgeman Downs 120
Captain's Paddock 143
Clovely Estate 170
Copper Country 177
Crane Winery 180
Dusty Hill Estate 210
Hunting Lodge Estate 297
Kingsley Grove 326
Rodericks 497
Stuart Range 550
Tipperary Estate 586
Whistle Stop Wines 623
Ziebarth Wines 656

South Coast Zone (NSW)

Cobbitty Wines 172
Grevillea Estate 262

South Coast Zone (NSW) (*continued*)

Lyrebird Ridge Organic Winery 362
Remo & Son's Vineyard 485
Tilba Valley 582

Southeast Australia (NSW/SA/Vic)

Angus the Bull (NSW) 69
Broken Gate Wines (Vic) 122
Burton Premium Wines (NSW) 133
Byrne & Smith Wines (SA) 134
Calyla Vines Estate (SA) 135
Celtic Farm (Vic) 152
Feet First Wines (SA) 224
Hewitson (SA) 283
Journeys End Vineyards (SA) 312
Kingston Estate (SA) 327
Lengs & Cooter (SA) 347
Paperbark Vines (SA) 438
Pepperton Estate (NSW) 452
Peter Howland Wines (NSW) 455
Queen Adelaide (Vic) 478
Smidge Wines (SA) 535
Timmins Wines (NSW) 583
Two Hands Wines (SA) 599
Will Taylor Wines (SA) 627
Wine Trust Estates (NSW) 632

Southern Eyre Peninsula (SA)

Boston Bay Wines 114
Delacolline Estate 194

Southern Fleurieu (SA)

Allusion Wines 63
Angus Wines 69
Minko Wines 386
Mt Billy 401
Mt Jagged Wines 406
Parri Estate 441
Sawtooth Ridge 516
Trafford Hill Vineyard 593
Twin Bays 599
Victor Harbor Winery 605
Whale Coast Wines 620

Southern Flinders Ranges (SA)

Bartagunyah Estate 89
Bundaleer Wines 130
Springton Cellars 540

Southern Highlands (NSW)

Blue Metal Vineyard 109
Centennial Vineyards 153

Southern Highlands (WA) (*continued*)
Cuttaway Hill Estate 184
Howards Lane Vineyard 294
Joadja Vineyards 310
Kells Creek Vineyards 320
McVitty Grove 367
Mundrakoona Estate 415
Saint Derycke's Wood Winery 506
Southern Highland Wines 538
Statford Park 542

Southern New South Wales Zone

Eling Forest Winery 214
Snowy River Winery 536
Transylvania Winery 594

Southern Tasmania

Bamajura 83
Bracken Hill 115
Bream Creek 117
Broadview Estate 122
Charles Reuben Estate 158
Clemens Hill 168
Coal Valley Vineyard 171
Colmaur 174
Craigow 180
Cross Rivulet 182
Crosswinds Vineyard 182
Darlington Vineyard 189
Derwent Estate 196
Domaine A 201
Elsewhere Vineyard 216
ese Vineyards 219
572 Richmond Road 229
Fluted Cape Vineyard 230
Frogmore Creek 237
Geebin Wines 242
GlenAyr 250
Grandview Vineyard 259
Hartzview Wine Centre 273
Herons Rise Vineyard 283
Home Hill 290
Hood Wines/Wellington 291
Jollymont 311
Kelvedon 322
Kinvarra Estate 328
Kraanwood 333
Laurel Bank 344
Meadowbank Estate 378
Meure's Wines 382
Milford Vineyard 384
Moorilla Estate 394
Morningside Wines 397
Nandroya Estate 418

Southern Tasmania (*continued*)
No Regrets Vineyard 424
Observatory Hill Vineyard 428
Orani Vineyard 432
Oyster Cove Vineyard 436
Palmara 437
Panorama 438
Pembroke 447
Pontville Station 469
Pooley Wines 469
Puddleduck Vineyard 475
Richmond Park Vineyard 488
Stefano Lubiana 543
Sugarloaf Ridge 552
Tinderbox Vineyard 584
Touchwood Wines 592
Wharncliffe 621
Winstead 633
Yaxley Estate 652

Strathbogie Ranges (Vic)

Antcliff's Chase 71
Baarrooka Vineyard 78
Bogie Man Wines 111
Dominion Wines 203
Elgo Estate 214
Kithbrook Estate 329
Maygars Hill Winery 377
Plunkett Wines 466
The Falls Vineyard 573

Sunbury (Vic)

Andraos Bros 66
Arundel 74
Bacchanalia Estate 79
Bacchus Hill 79
Craiglee 180
Diggers Rest 197
Fenton Views Winery 225
Galli Estate 240
Goona Warra Vineyard 255
Kennedys Keilor Valley 322
Ray-Monde 481
Wildwood 624
Witchmount Estate 635

Swan District (WA)

Carabooda Estate 144
Faranda Wines 223
Gilead Estate 248
Platypus Lane Wines 465
Riseborough Estate 490

Swan District (WA) (*continued*)

Susannah Brook Wines 554
Valley Wines 603
Vino Italia 608

Swan Hill (Vic)

Andrew Peace Wines 67
Brumby Wines 128
Bulga Wine Estates 128
Bullers Beverford 129
Carpinteri Vineyards 146
Dos Rios 205
Oak Dale Wines 426
Renewan Murray Gold Wines 485
Yellymong 652

Swan Valley (WA)

Ambrook Wines 65
Baxter Stokes Wines 93
Carilley Estate 145
Faber Vineyard 222
Garbin Estate 241
Henley Park Wines 280
Highway Wines 286
Houghton 292
Jane Brook Estate 304
John Kosovich Wines 311
Lamont's 340
LedaSwan 346
Lilac Hill Estate 350
Little River Wines 355
Mann 371
Moondah Brook 393
Oakover Estate 427
Olive Farm 430
Pinelli 463
RiverBank Estate 491
Sandalford 512
Sittella Wines 534
Swanbrook Estate Wines 555
Swan Valley Wines 555
Talijancich 558
The Natural Wine Company 576
Upper Reach Vineyard 603
Windy Creek Estate 631

Sydney Basin (NSW)

Camden Estate Vineyards 136
Gledswood Homestead & Winery 250
Kirkham Estate 328
Richmond Estate 487
Tizzana Winery 587
Vicarys 605

Tasmania

see East Coast Tasmania; Northern Tasmania;
   Southern Tasmania

Tumbarumba (NSW)

Excelsior Peak 221
Glenburnie Vineyard 250
Lighthouse Peak 350
Tumbarumba Wine Estates 597
Tumbarumba Wine Growers 597

Upper Goulburn (Vic)

Barwite Vineyards 90
Beattie Wines 95
Cathedral Lane Wines 150
Cheviot Bridge/Long Flat 163
Delatite 195
Glen Creek Wines 250
Growlers Gully 264
Henke 280
Kinloch Wines 328
Little River Estate 355
Lost Valley Winery 360
Melaleuca Grove 379
Mount Cathedral Vineyards 403
Mt Samaria Vineyard 409
Murrindindi 417
Nillahcootie Estate 423
Penbro Estate 447
Peppin Ridge 453
Rees Miller Estate 484
Scrubby Creek Wines 519
Snobs Creek Wines 536
Strath Valley Vineyard 549
Tallarook 559

Upper Hunter Valley (NSW)

Allyn River Wines 63
Arrowfield 73
Bell's Lane Wines 99
Birnam Wood Wines 106
Camyr Allyn Wines 137
Cruickshank Callatoota Estate 182
Glendonbrook 251
Horseshoe Vineyard 292
Hunter Park 297
James Estate 304
London Lodge Estate 357
Penmara 450
Polin & Polin Wines 468
Pyramid Hill Wines 477
Rosemount Estate (Hunter Valley) 499
Sevenoaks Wines 524

Upper Hunter Valley (NSW) (*continued*)
Two Rivers 600
Winbourne Wines 630
Yarraman Estate 648

Warehouse (SA/Vic)

Ainsworth & Snelson 59
Barokes Wines 86
Heath Wines 278
JAG Wine 303

Western Australia South East Coastal Zone

Dalyup River Estate 186

Western Plains Zone (NSW)

Boora Estate 113
Canonbah Bridge 138
Glenfinlass 251
Hoppers Hill Vineyards 292
Lazy River Estate 344
Red Earth Estate Vineyard 482
Sand Hills Vineyard 513
Tombstone Estate 589
Wattagan Estate Winery 615

Western Victoria Zone

Empress Vineyard 217
Norton Estate 425
Red Rock Winery 484

Wrattonbully (SA)

Kopparossa Wines 332
Russet Ridge 504
Stone Coast Wines 546
Tapanappa 564

Yarra Valley (Vic)

Acacia Ridge 58
Ainsworth Estate 60
Allinda 62
Arthurs Creek Estate 74
Badger's Brook 79
Balgownie Estate (Yarra Valley) 81
Bianchet 102
Boat O'Craigo 110
Brahams Creek Winery 116
Britannia Creek Wines 121
Bulong Estate 129
Burgi Hill Vineyard 131
Carlei Estate & Green Vineyards 145

Yarra Valley (Vic) (*continued*)
Coldstream Hills 173
Coombe Farm Vineyard 175
Copper Bull Wines 177
Dawson's Patch 190
De Bortoli (Victoria) 192
Diamond Valley Vineyards 197
Di Stasio 199
Dixons Run 199
Domaine Chandon 201
Dominique Portet 204
Elmswood Estate 216
Eltham Vineyards 217
Evelyn County Estate 221
Fergusson 225
Five Oaks Vineyard 229
Gembrook Hill 243
Giant Steps 246
Gracedale Hills Estate 257
Hanson-Tarrahill Vineyard 268
Healesville Wine Co. 276
Helen's Hill Estate 279
Henkell Wines 280
Hillcrest Vineyard 287
Hills of Plenty 287
Hoddles Creek Estate 288
Immerse 299
International Vintners Australia 301
Kellybrook 320
Killara Park Estate 324
Kiltynane Estate 325
Kings of Kangaroo Ground 326
Labyrinth 336
Langbrook Estate Vineyard 341
Lillydale Estate 351
Lirralirra Estate 354
Long Gully Estate 358
Lovegrove Vineyard and Winery 361
Metier Wines 382
Monbulk Winery 389
Morgan Vineyards 396
Mount Delancey Winery 403
Mount Mary 408
Naked Range Wines 418
Oakridge 427
Outlook Hill 435
Panton Hill Winery 438
Paternoster 442
Punt Road 476
Ridgeback Wines 488
Ridgeline 489
RiverStone Wines 492
Rochford Wines 495
Roundstone Winery & Vineyard 503
St Huberts 507

Yarra Valley (Vic) (*continued*)
Samson Hill Estate 512
Seville Estate 524
Seville Hill 525
Shantell 526
Shelmerdine Vineyards 528
Sir Paz Estate 533
SpringLane 539
Steels Creek Estate 542
Stefani Estate 542
Sticks 545
Strathewen Hills 548
Stuart Wines 550
Sutherland Estate 554
Tarrawarra Estate 565
The Oaks Vineyard & Winery 576
Tibooburra Wines 581
Tin Cows 584
Tokar Estate 588
Toolangi Vineyards 590
Train Trak 593
Valley View Vineyard 603
Wantirna Estate 611
Warramate 612

Yarra Valley (Vic) (*continued*)
Wedgetail Estate 616
Whispering Hills 622
Whitsend Estate 623
William Downie Wines 625
Wonga Estate 637
Yarrabank 647
Yarra Brook Estate 647
Yarra Burn 648
Yarra Edge 648
Yarrambat Estate 649
Yarra Ridge 649
Yarra Track Wines 649
Yarra Vale 649
Yarra Valley Gateway Estate 650
Yarra Valley Vineyards 650
Yarrawalla Wines 650
Yarra Yarra 651
Yarra Yering 651
Yeringberg 653
Yering Farm 653
Yering Range Vineyard 653
Yering Station 653